THE INTERACTIVE CASEBOOK SERIES™

ADMINISTRATIVE LAW

A Contemporary Approach

SECOND EDITION

By

Andrew F. Popper

PROFESSOR OF LAW
AMERICAN UNIVERSITY WASHINGTON COLLEGE OF LAW

Gwendolyn M. McKee

LAW CLERK TO THE HONORABLE JUDGE DOLORES K. SLOVITER
UNITED STATES COURT OF APPEALS FOR THE THIRD CIRCUIT

Anthony E. Varona

PROFESSOR OF LAW AND ASSOCIATE DEAN FOR ACADEMIC AFFAIRS
AMERICAN UNIVERSITY WASHINGTON COLLEGE OF LAW

and

Philip J. Harter

EARL F. NELSON PROFESSOR OF LAW
UNIVERSITY OF MISSOURI–COLUMBIA

WEST®

A Thomson Reuters business

Mat #40920112

Interactive Casebook Series is a trademark registered in the U.S. Patent and Trademark Office.

© 2009 Thomson Reuters
© 2010 Thomson Reuters
        610 Opperman Drive
        St. Paul, MN 55123
        1–800–313–9378

Printed in the United States of America

ISBN: 978–0–314–25557–0

For Diane, Jeffrey, Brian, and Katie – A.F.P.

For Anna – G.M.M.

For John – A.E.V.

For Nancy, Alexa, and Reinaldo – P.J.H.

Preface

This is a casebook – and the first interactive text – in the field of administrative law. Our goal is to provide students and faculty a logical presentation of traditional and familiar cases including those essential decisions (followed by commentary, updating materials, and questions) taught in every administrative law course. However, what distinguishes these materials is that in addition to the carefully edited judicial opinions and notes, linked to the on-line version of this book are hundreds of cases, underlying administrative agency decisions, and other unique supplementary material that illuminate the doctrines, arguments, and principles in the field.

Taken in the aggregate, administrative law covers a broad array of topics: rulemaking, adjudication, constitutional imperatives affecting agency action, the Administrative Procedure Act, distinctions between state and federal administrative law, separation of powers, federalism, judicial review of agency action, deregulation, reregulation, privatization, cost-benefit analysis, and of course questions related to the success or effectiveness of administrative action in particular fields.

We wrote this casebook with the understanding that there is no broad agreement on the order in which topics should be covered or the emphasis to be given to any particular subject area. While we believe the materials in this book flow organically from beginning to end, we recognize that the order of presentation is very much an individual choice – and almost any order will work. Accordingly, the book is prepared to facilitate faculty who have evolved their own order of presentation, allowing one to move selectively between and among the cases, notes, and linked materials. The notes following each case are, for the most part, a unit of material connected with that case. They were prepared with the idea that one could assign any primary case in any order desired and the notes and linked documents would serve to illuminate the main case without requiring (for the most part) references to immediately adjacent material. We have linked electronically material between and among cases, providing a pedagogical opportunity to move at will throughout the casebook, rather than a pedagogical obligation to proceed in any one particular order.

The fact that this course can be taught using any coherent organization of case material is in part a reflection of the nature of the regulatory state. At different times in our history, separate aspects or subfields within the administrative domain have been dominant. For example, some years ago, the focus in Congress, the courts, and the legal academy shifted to efficiency – or the lack thereof – of the regulatory process. At other times, the intensity of judicial review, the role of the president, the economics of regulation, citizen participation, and many other areas became – at least for a time – dominant. Each of those periods in our regulatory history has a sustaining influence. Each can still be the focus of a course – each survives at present, at varying levels of importance.

We have shied away from declaring, by word or emphasis, the defining theme in administrative law at the end of the first decade of the 21st Century. It seems to us that legitimate study of the field is not just possible but extremely workable regardless of the central theme or focus of a course.

———————

Editorial notes:

1. We recommend strongly reference to the original scholarship and full text of all cases and articles to get a complete sense of the material. Since all major cases and most of the secondary source materials we use are available in full through the on-line version of this text with a keystroke or two, we took the liberty of consolidating language and editing aggressively all opinions and articles. We relied on ellipses and square brackets to denote omitted materials instead of using asterisks.

2. We dropped many concurring and dissenting opinions and omitted most footnotes, references, and citations we saw as non-essential. Where they added or clarified important points, non-majority opinions survived the editorial scalpel.

3. We cut multiple case references within opinions to streamline the presentation and allow students to focus on the core material in this book: the primary cases. We did so in part because all such references are readily available on-line and because we wanted to limit the distracting effect of multiple case citations where a single cite would get you to the source on which a court relied. For example, we edited out many "case cites within case cites" leaving only those references we believe have pedagogical value.

4. Every effort has been made to identify all sources from which this material is drawn. We place great faith in the interactive nature of these materials. Every quote or reference can be secured in its original form with ease. In compiling and

editing thousands of documents (including cases and scholarship) it is possible to make errors. We have made effort to quote all original sources and note all edits – but mistakes can happen for which we are, in the end, responsible.

We wish you great success in your study of this exciting field.

A.F.P.
G.M.M.
Washington, D.C. 2008

Preface to the Second Edition

It has been just over a year since the publication of the first edition of ADMIN-ISTRATIVE LAW: A CONTEMPORARY APPROACH. Since that time, three events prompted us to prepare a second edition to this text.

First, we are thrilled to announce the addition of two new and distinguished co-authors, Professor Anthony E. Varona, American University, Washington College of Law, and Professor Philip J. Harter, the Earl F. Nelson Professor of Law, University of Missouri School of Law. They bring to this exciting project a wealth of experience – both are wonderful teachers and legal scholars – and both have years of experience in practice of administrative law.

Second, we felt it imperative to provide materials to facilitate coverage of the substantive changes in the field driven by the presidential election.

Third, we have added six new Supreme Court cases – three decided in recent months and three decided decades ago but allow for a better understanding of executive power, particularly during a time of transition.

Our new cases include *Wyeth*, *Fox*, and *Summers*, as well as fully developed notes and questions for each case. In addition, we added a more fully elaborated section on presidential powers, including as main cases *Myers*, *Humphrey's Executor*, and *Wiener*.

As a consequence of the election of a new president, we have added more than 30 items such as Executive Orders and Executive Declarations, some in full-text but most hot-linked to the on-line version of this text, reflecting the changes that have taken place since January 2009 that affect the regulatory state.

Beyond the substance of the text, there are a number of new developments we wanted to call to your attention:

  (a) We added 130 new highlighted text boxes including 50 boxes under a new category, "Good Question!";

(b) Of great importance to the second edition, we added 25 new and challenging practice hypotheticals covering many areas in the field; and,

(c) Although the text is fully searchable, we have added a new index at the back of the book.

As with the 1st edition, cases and supporting materials were edited and organized in a manner compatible with many pedagogical approaches to teaching administrative law, and with an eye towards facilitating self-contained, efficient, and engaging reading assignments for individual class sessions. For the most part, each case is a self-contained teaching unit, allowing one to reorganize the materials in any manner that fits the goals and objectives of a particular course.

We will continue to add materials to the interactive casebook web site to keep you up to date on developments in the field. We will also make available any additional substantive or teaching materials, beyond the manual and statutory supplement. If you would like to suggest materials (we will of course give full attribution) to be posted on the site, please contact us.

We look forward to hearing from you and wish you the very best in your study of administrative law.

A.F.P.
G.M.M.
A.E.V.
P.J.H.

Washington, DC
March 2010

Acknowledgments

Great thanks are due Dean Claudio Grossman for his generous support, counsel, and assistance. We wish also to thank our senior research assistants, Alexia M. Emmermann, Suriya Jayanti, Clara Lyons, Dianna K. Muth, and Kimberly Nguyen for their dedication and hard work on this project as well as the following American University Washington College of Law students: Emily Alves Burlis, Kaitlyn P. Coogan, Mariano Corcilli, Jacklyn DeMar, Pietro DeVolpi, Maria Dorn-Lopez, J. Eric Elder, Andrew Guhr, Elizabeth McInturff, Lucia D. Rich, Brian Stanford, Emily Strunk, Mary Underwood, Jasmine Watson, Colin Winkler, and Julie Yeagle.

We want to thank the fine professional staff of the American University Washington College of Law for their unconditional support. In particular, we wish to express our deep appreciation to Frankie Winchester for her insight, academic and technical assistance, and commitment.

Finally, we wish to thank our colleagues, families, and friends who provided support and understanding throughout this process.

Table of Contents

Chapter 7 *Judicial Review of Facts, Law, and Agency Policy in Adjudication*

Hypotheticals and Questions
for Class Discussion

Table of Cases

The principal cases are in bold type. Cases cited or discussed in the text are in roman type. References are to pages. Cases cited in principal cases and within other quoted materials are not included.

Table of Scholarship, Statutes, and Other Authorities

Authorities

Anthony, Robert A., *Which Agency Interpretations Should Bind Citizens and the Courts?*, 7 YALE J. ON REG. 1 (1990), 685

Appleman, Laura I., *Retributive Justice and Hidden Sentencing*, 68 OHIO ST. L.J. 1307 (2006), 937

Araiza, William D., *Judicial and Legislative Checks on Ex Parte OMB Influence Over Rulemaking*, 54 ADMIN. L. REV. 611 (2002), 3

Arcila, Jr., Fabio, *In the Trenches: Searches and the Misunderstood Common-Law History of Suspicion and Probable Cause*, 10 U. PA. J. CONST. L. 1 (2007), 975

Argetsinger, Cameron, Note, *Procedural Bungling in Disciplinary Actions Against Federal Employees: Harmless Error or Due Process Violation?*, 15 FED. CIR. B. J. 445 (2005/2006), 591

Arnon, Harel, *Legal Reasoning: Justifying Tolerance in the U.S. Supreme Court*, 2 N.Y.U. J.L. & LIBERTY 262 (2007), 380

Ashcroft, John, Attorney General, to Heads of all Federal Departments and Agencies (Oct. 12, 2001), 1007

Ashmore, Anne, Library of Congress, *Dates of Supreme Court Decisions and Arguments, United States Reports, Volumes 2-107 (1791-1882)*, 329

Asimow & Sullivan, *Due Process in Local Land Use Decision Making: Is the Imperfect Way of Doing Business Good Enough or Should We Radically Reform It?*, 29 ZONING & PLAN. L. REP. 1 (2006), 19, 775, 967

Auerbach, Carl A., *Informal Rule Making: A Proposed Relationship Between Administrative Procedures and Judicial Review*, 72 NW. U.L. REV. 15 (1977), 140

Bach, Jason J., *Students Have Rights, Too: The Drafting of Student Conduct Codes*, 2003 BYU EDUC. & L. J. 1, 916

Bagley, Nicholas & Revesz, Richard L., *Centralized Oversight of the Regulatory State*, 106 COLUM. L. REV. 1260 (2006), 382

Baker, C. Edwin, *The Ideology of the Economic Analysis of Law*, 5 PHIL. & PUB. AFF. 3 (1975), 458

Bales, Richard A., *A Constitutional Defense of Qui Tam*, 2001 WIS. L. REV. 381, 337

Ball, Carlos A. & Reynolds, Laurie, *Exactions and Burden Distribution in Takings Law*, 47 WM. & MARY L. REV. 1513, 1531 (2006), 614

Bandes, Susan, *Reinventing Bivens: the Self-Executing Constitution*, 68 S. Cal. L. Rev. 289, 345-50 (1995), 659

Bandes, Susan, *The Negative Constitution: A Critique*, 88 MICH. L. REV. 2271 (1990), 901

Barkow, Rachel E., *The Ascent of the Administrative State and the Demise of Mercy*, 121 HARV. L. REV. 1332, 1334-35 (2008), 2

Barksdale, Yvette M., *The Presidency and Administrative Value Selection*, 42 AM. U.L. REV. 273, 290-92 (1993), 48

Barnes, Mario L. & Bowman, F. Greg, *The Uses and Abuses of Executive Power: Entering Unprecedented Terrain: Charting a Method To Reduce Madness in Post-9/11 Power and Rights Conflicts*, 62 U. MIAMI L. REV. 365 (2008), 887

Barrett, Amy Coney, *Stare Decisis and Due Process*, 74 U. COLO. L. REV. 1011 (2003), 706

Barron, David J. & Lederman, Martin S., *The Commander-in-Chief at the Lowest Ebb - A Constitutional History*, 121 HARV. L. REV. 941 (2008), 583

Bloom, Scott, *Spare the Rod, Spoil the Child? A Legal Framework for Recent Corporal Punishment Proposals*, 25 GOLDEN GATE U.L. REV. 361 (1995), 928

Blumenauer, Kerri R., *Note, Privileged or Not? How the Current Application of the Government Attorney-Client Privilege Leaves the Government Feeling Unprivileged*, 75 FORDHAM L. REV. 75 (2006), 1051

Blumoff, Theodore Y., *Illusions of Constitutional Decisionmaking: Politics and the Tenure Powers in the Court*, 73 IOWA L. REV. 1079, n. 613 (1988), 41, 49

Boyle, Katherine, *Dems Say Johnson Is a Puppet for White House*, 10 ENV'T & ENERGY DAILY, 9 (2008), 403

Breger, Marshall J. & Edles, Gary J., *Established By Practice: The Theory and Operation of Independent Federal Agencies*, 52 ADMIN. L. REV.1111 (2000), 41

Breker-Cooper, Steven, *The Appointments Clause and the Removal Power: Theory and Séance*, 60 TENN. L. REV. 841, 868-69 (1993), 41

Bremner, Faith, *Tester Takes on War Contracting*, GREAT FALLS TRIB., Feb. 28, 2008 available at http://tester.senate.gov/Newsroom/02282008_tribune_contracting.cfm, 449

Bressman, Lisa S., *Judicial Review of Agency Inaction: An Arbitrariness Approach*, 79 N.Y.U. L. REV. 1657, 1668 (2004), 382

Bressman, Lisa Schultz, *How Mead Has Muddled Judicial Review of Agency Action*, 58 VAND. L. REV. 1443, 1459 (2005), 233

Bressman, Lisa Schultz, *Procedures as Politics in Administrative Law*, 107 COLUM. L. REV. 1749 (2007), 69

Briffault, Richard, *The Item Veto in State Courts*, 66 TEMP. L. REV. 1171, 1175 (1993), 494

Brooks, Heath A., *American Trucking Associations v. EPA: The D.C. Circuit's Missed Opportunity to Unambiguously Discard the Hard Look Doctrine*, 27 HARV. ENVTL. L. REV. 259 (2003), 481

Brown, Richard D., THE STRENGTH OF A PEOPLE: THE IDEA OF AN INFORMED CITIZENRY IN AMERICA, 1650-1870 xv (1996), 1026

Burk, Dan L., *The Milk Free Zone: Federal and Local Interests in Regulating Recombinant bST*, 22 COLUM. J. ENVTL. L. 227 (1997), 247

Burkoff, John M., *Appointment and Removal Under the Federal Constitution: The Impact of Buckley v. Valeo*, 22 WAYNE L. REV. 1335 (1976), 41

Bush, George W., REMARKS AT THE AMERICA'S SMALL BUSINESS SUMMIT, PUB. PAPERS OF THE PRESIDENTS (Apr. 21, 2008), 13

Bush, George W., Remarks on the War on Terror, 42 WEEKLY COMP. PRES. DOC. 1569, 1571, 1573 (SEPT. 11, 2006), 582

Bush, Jeff & Wiitala Knutson, Kristal, *The Building and Maintenance of "Ethics Walls" in Administrative Adjudicatory Proceedings*, 24 J. NAALJ 2 (2004), 731

Buss, Emily, *Constitutional Fidelity Through Children's Rights*, 2004 SUP. CT. REV. 355, 916

Calabresi, Guido, *The Pointlessness of Pareto: Carrying Coase Further*, 100 YALE L.J. 1211, 1212, 1218-19 (1991), 458

Calabresi, Steven G., *Some Normative Arguments for the Unitary Executive*, 48 ARK. L. REV. 23 (1995), 3

Rossi, Jim, *Redeeming Judicial Review: The Hard Look Doctrine and the Federal Regulatory Efforts to Restructure the Electric Utility Industry,* 1994 Wis. L. Rev. 763, 506

Rossi, Jim, *Respecting Deference: Conceptualizing Skidmore Within the Architecture of Chevron,* 42 Wm. & Mary L. Rev. 1105 (2001), 192

Ruhl et al., J.B., *Symposium: The Coevolution of Administrative Law with Everything Else,* 28 Fla. St. U.L. Rev. 1 (2000), 3

S. Comm. on the Judiciary, S. Doc. No. 248, *reprinted in* The Administrative Procedure Act : Legislative history (1946), 60

Sabel, Charles F. & Simon, William H., *Destabilization Rights: How Public Law Litigation Succeeds,* 117 Harv. L. Rev. 1016 (2004), 337

Salkin, Patricia E., *Intersection Between Environmental Justice and Land Use Planning,* 58 Plan. & Envt'l 5 (2006), 967

Salkin, Patricia E., *Judging Ethics for Administrative Law Judges: Adoption of a Uniform Code of conduct for the Administrative Judiciary* (2008), 740

Sargentich, Thomas O., *Bowsher v. Synar: The Contemporary Debate About Legislative-Executive Separation of Powers,* 72 Cornell L. Rev. 430, 463-64 (1987), 49

Savage, Charles, *Introduction Symposium, The Last Word: The Constitutional Implications of Presidential Signing Statements,* 16 Wm. & Mary Bill of Rts. J. 1 (2007), 834

Sax, Joanna K., *The States "Race" with the Federal Government for Stem Cell Research,* 15 Ann. Health L. 1 (2006), 374

Scalia, Antonin, *Judicial Deference to Administrative Interpretations of Law* 1989 Duke L.J. 514, 172,

Schuck, Peter H. and Elliott, E. Donald, *To the Chevron Station: An Empirical Study of Federal Administrative Law,* 1990 Duke L.J. 984, 172

Schuck, Peter H., *Taking Immigration Federalism Seriously,* 2007 U. Chi. Legal F. 57, 891, 961

Scordato, Marin R., *Federal Preemption of State Tort Claims,* 35 U.C. Davis L. Rev. 1, 3 (2001), 476

Seidenfeld, Mark, *The Psychology of Accountability and Political Review of Agency Rules,* 51 Duke L.J. 1059 (2001), 3

Seidenfeld, Mark, *Why Agencies Act: A Reassessment of the Ossification Critique of Judicial Review,* 70 Ohio State L. J. 251 (2009), 70

Seidman, Louis Michael, *The Secret Life of the Political Question Doctrine,* 37 J. Marshall L. Rev. 441, 460 (2004), 329

Select Bipartisan Comm. To Investigate the Preparation and Response To Hurricane Katrina, 109th Cong., A Failure of Initiative (2006), 10

Selmi, Daniel P., *Jurisdiction to Review Agency Inaction Under Federal Environmental Law,* 72 Ind. L.J. 65 (1996), 381

Selmi, Daniel P., *The Promise and Limits of Negotiated Rulemaking: Evaluating the Negotiation of a Regional Air Quality Rule,* 35 Envtl. L. 415 (2005), 522

Selmi, Michael, *The Supreme Court's 2006-2007 Term Employment Law Cases: A Quiet But Revealing Term,* 11 Empl. Rts. & Employ. Pol'y 219 (2007), 225

Statutes

5 U.S.C.A.App.--Government Organization and Employees

7 U.S.C.A.--Agriculture

8 U.S.C.A.--Aliens and Nationality

10 U.S.C.A.--Armed Forces

Copyright Permission for Select Scholarship and Other Materials

We very much appreciate the generosity of authors and publishers who granted permission to use excerpts of their valuable and eloquent scholarship. Copyright permission was received for the following excerpted scholarship and materials:

Bressman, Lisa. *Procedures as Politics in Administrative Law,* 107 COLUM. L. REV. 1749 (2007). Copyright © 2007, by Columbia Law Review. Reprinted with permission of publisher.

Burk, Dan. *The Milk Free Zone: Federal and Local Interests in Regulating RecombinantbST,* 22 COLUM J. ENVTL. L. 227 (1997). Copyright © 1997, by Columbia Journal of Environmental Law and the author. Reprinted with permission of the author and publisher.

Coglianese, Cary. *Assessing the Advocacy of Negotiated Rulemaking: A Response to Philip Harter,* 9 N.Y.U. ENVTL. L. J. 386 (2001). Copyright © 2001, by the author. Reprinted with permission.

Custos, Dominque. *The Rulemaking Power of Independent Regulatory Agencies,* 54 AM. J. COMP. L. 615 (2006). Copyright © 2006, by American Journal of Comparative Law and the author. Reprinted with permission.

Flatt, Victor. *Notice and Comment for Nonprofit Organizations.* Originally published in 55 RUTGERS L. REV. 65 (2002). Copyright © 2002, by Rutgers Law Review. Reprinted with permission of the publisher.

Freeman, Jody. *Public Value in the Era of Privatization: Extending Public Law Norms through Privatization,* 116 HARV. L. REV. 1285, 1302-1306 (2003). Copyright © 2003, the President and Fellows of Harvard College and the Harvard Law Review. Reprinted with permission.

Funk, William. *Bargaining Toward the New Millennium: Regulatory Negotiation and the Subversion of the Public Interest,* 46 Duke L. J. 1351, 1374-1375 (1997). Copyright © 1997, by the author. Reprinted with permission.

CHAPTER 1

An Introduction to Administrative Law

I. Overview

Administrative law is the study of governance. While Congress creates authority, the President enforces that authority, and courts confine or discipline the exercise of that authority, it is agencies that govern. That said, the starting point for many administrative law cases is an act of Congress that allows the agency to function. "It is axiomatic that administrative agencies may issue regulations only pursuant to authority delegated to them by Congress." *Am. Library Ass'n v. FCC*, 406 F.3d 689, 691 (D.C. Cir. 2005).

Bottom Line

Federal, state, and local administrative agencies are the vital, hands-on forces of government in the United States.

The starting point for judicial review of and, where appropriate, deference to agency action is an assessment of the "congressional delegation of administrative authority." *Adams Fruit Co. v. Barrett*, 494 U.S. 638, 649 (1990). Courts assessing agency action are obliged first to determine "whether the will of Congress has been obeyed." *Skinner v. Mid-America Pipeline Co.*, 490 U.S. 212, 218 (1989) (citing *Yakus v. United States*, 321 U.S. 414, 426 (1944)). If you are wondering why we did not start with better known cases pertaining to delegation, fear not – they lie ahead in this text. We refer you to the above cases not because they are unique or precedent setting but because they reflect the common denominator in this field – agencies are the active "governors," but only of the power given them by the legislature.

On a day-to-day basis, it is the agencies that have the capacity and authority to reach out and touch us all. It is the Internal Revenue Service, not Congress, that reaches into the pockets of private citizens and businesses. It is the Occupational Safety and Health Administration, not a congressional oversight committee, that assesses workplace safety. It is the Food and Drug Administration that approves and sets standards for all pharmaceuticals. It is the Nuclear Regulatory Commission that has comprehensive licensing authority for the operation of nuclear power plants – and on and on. From the outset of the modern administrative state, this exercise of power came with acknowledged risks. Regarding the advent of modern administrative agency power, Roscoe Pound noted that "the revival of executive justice" can be seen as a "partial reversion[] to justice without law. . . ." ROSCOE POUND, 2 JURISPRUDENCE 425, *cited in* Michael Lassiter, <u>Comparative Readings of Roscoe Pound's Jurisprudence</u>, 50 AM. J. COMP. L. 719, 745 (2002).

Unelected administrative officials can announce standards that interpret statutes and shift significantly interests and entitlements, and courts reviewing such standards may be required to defer to that agency pronouncement – or at least respect the decision of the agency – even if a court determines the standards are far from ideal. Does that strike you as "justice without law?" For some different perspectives on this, see Eric Biber & Frank B. Cross, <u>Two Sides of the Same Coin: Judicial Review of Administrative Agency Action and Inaction</u>, 26 VA. ENVTL. L.J. 461 (2008); Frank B. Cross, <u>Pragmatic Pathologies of Judicial Review of Administrative Rulemaking</u>, 78 N.C.L. REV. 1013 (2000); Anuradha Vaitheswaran & Thomas A. Mayes, <u>The Role of Deference in Judicial Review of Agency Action: A Comparison of Federal Law, Uniform State Acts, and the Iowa APA</u>, 27 J. NAT'L ASS'N L. JUD. 402 (2007), and Rachel E. Barkow, <u>The Ascent of the Administrative State and the Demise of Mercy</u>, 121 HARV. L. REV. 1332, 1334-35 (2008). Professor Barkow notes that "the rise of the administrative state has made unchecked discretion an anomaly in the law, and a phenomenon to be viewed with suspicion. The expansion of the administrative state has showcased the dangers associated with the exercise of discretion. . . . With the rise of administrative law, our legal culture has come to view unreviewable discretion to decide individual cases as the very definition of lawlessness."

Key Concept

Regardless of the field in which one practices, administrative agency action is likely to play a central role. This is true in criminal law, where much of the parole and post-conviction practice is administrative. It is also true in corporate law, where agency actors play a decisive role on issues such as taxes, employment, and securities regulation. Environmental law, international law, healthcare law, energy regulation, telecommunications, public interest practice, and virtually all other specializations require an understanding of the way administrative agencies function.

Not only are federal, state, and local agencies involved in regulating, guiding, or limiting behavior, they are also the focal point for much of the practice of law. "Administrative law, properly understood, is of paramount importance. Its enterprise bears considerable credit or blame for the very structure, operation, and even the ultimate efficacy of governance." Christopher Edley, Jr., <u>The Government Crisis, Legal Theory, and Political Ideology</u>, 41 DUKE L.J. 561, 562 (1991). Professor Edley notes further that "those . . . dissatisfied with the evolutionary direction of administrative law must recognize that doctrinal change is part of a larger ideological and theoretical whole." As noted above, this is about both the practice of law and governance. *See* J.B. Ruhl et al., Symposium, <u>The Coevolution of Administrative Law with Everything Else, 28 FLA. ST. U.L. REV. 1 (2000)</u>; Nathan Block & Robin Smith Houston, <u>*Toward a Responsible System of Regulating Practice at Administrative Agencies: Administrative Agencies and the Changing Definition of the Practice of Law*, 2 TEX. TECH ADMIN. L.J. 251 (2001)</u>.

Bottom Line

Notwithstanding the dominant role agencies can play, judicial review by courts provides the primary means by which administrative law is studied. Furthermore, it is judicial decisions that shape the contours of the administrative state. For that reason, heavy emphasis is placed on conventional case analysis both in this casebook and in the field.

From the outset, you should be aware that while the powers of government might be separated into three branches, nothing happens in isolation. For a review of the relationship between the executive, legislative, judicial branches and the agencies, see William D. Araiza, <u>*Judicial and Legislative Checks on Ex Parte OMB Influence Over Rulemaking*, 54 ADMIN. L. REV. 611 (2002)</u>; Steven Croley, <u>*White House Review of Agency Rulemaking: An Empirical Investigation*, 70 U. CHI. L. REV. 821 (2003)</u>; Jonathan R. Macey, <u>*Organizational Design and the Political Control of Administrative Agencies*, 8 J.L. ECON. & ORG. 93 (1992)</u>; Mark Seidenfeld, <u>*The Psychology of Accountability and Political Review of Agency Rules*, 51 DUKE L.J. 1059 (2001)</u>.

The primary focus of the vast majority of law school courses in administrative law, of necessity, is procedural. *See* Kristin Booth Glen, <u>*Thinking Out of the Bar Exam Box: A Proposal to "MacCrate" Entry to the Profession*, 23 PACE L. REV. 343, 362 (2003)</u> (urging – wisely we believe – that law schools require administrative law). As lawyers, we need to understand how agencies function, what rules they follow, and what power they possess in relation to subsequent judicial action. These inquiries require an assessment of how agency action is affected by constitutional constraints, how agencies maintain order in proceedings involving numerous conflicting interests, how agencies formulate rules and regulations, and how they exercise their power to search and investigate. *See* Robert L. Rabin, <u>*Federal Regulation in Historical Perspective*, 38 STAN. L. REV. 1189 (1986)</u> (setting out the historical context of the field), and on the role the executive plays in shaping the agency state; Elena Kagan, <u>*Presidential Administration*, 114 HARV. L. REV. 2245 (2001)</u>; Martin S. Flaherty, <u>*The Most Dangerous Branch*, 105 YALE L.J. 1725 (1996)</u>; Abner S. Greene, <u>*Checks and Balances in an Era of Presidential Lawmaking*, 61 U. CHI. L. REV. 123 (1994)</u>; and Steven G. Calabresi, <u>*Some Normative Arguments for the Unitary Executive*, 48 ARK. L. REV. 23 (1995)</u>.

This predominant focus on process comes at a price; most administrative law courses can devote only limited time to delve into the dynamics of whether and why activities and behaviors should be regulated. Study of these compelling and essential political options, bounded by public need, economic imperative, public acceptability, and market realities, is relegated to other courses. However, as you start the study of this field, we thought it useful to set out in broad strokes some of the traditional arguments underlying the choice to regulate.

Every major political campaign of the last quarter-century has focused in part on the question of deregulation, an ideology with considerable political appeal – and strident support from some quarters. "There is a dearth of arresting hypotheses to set off against the Coase Theorem, the Hand Formula, the efficiency theory of the common law, . . . the economics of property rights versus liability rules, the activity-level theory of strict liability, . . . and the myriad of other concepts, many counterintuitive, that have made economic analysis of law intellectually exciting." Richard Posner, *The Sociology of the Sociology of Law: A View from Economics*, 2 EUR. J.L. & ECON. 265, 273 (1995).

Food for Thought

Our political leaders, regardless of party, understand that there is inherent resistance to command and control regulation. Politicians are in safe territory when they announce that they will make efforts to "get the government off the people's backs," and that they believe deeply in allowing free markets to function. Candidates who run on a platform of "more invasive regulation" are doomed.

While there is undeniable resistance to the concept of regulation, the demand for regulatory services is high. When the air we breathe and water we drink make us sick, when security is threatened, food products are contaminated, telecommunication systems fail, energy prices escalate beyond the reach of the average consumer, pharmaceutical products cause unexpected catastrophic consequences, when traffic snarls and schools fail, it is not hard to find loud and powerful voices asking why the government failed to "do something about it." There is of course a good deal of literature with a decidedly open-market perspective – rejecting the public interest model of regulation. *See, e.g.*, Michael E. Levine & Jennifer L. Forrence, *Regulatory Capture, Public Interest, and the Public Agenda: Toward a Synthesis*, 6 J.L. ECON. & ORG. 167, 168-69 (1990); John S. Moot, *Economic Theories of Regulation and Electricity Restructuring*, 25 ENERGY L.J. 273 (2004) (the public interest theory of regulation lacks any disciplined sense of economic imperative). However, we leave to you to decide whether "governmental failure" is an atypical response to the above mentioned health, safety, welfare, and economic problems. *See* Andrew P. Morriss et al., *Choosing How to Regulate*, 29 HARV. ENVTL. L. REV. 179 (2005); Steven P. Croley, *Theories of Regulation: Incorporating the Administrative Process*, 98 COLUM. L. REV. 1 (1998); Reza Dibadj, *Regulatory Givings and the*

Anticommons, 64 Ohio St. L.J. 1041 (2003); and for a fascinating perspective of one of the most "active" regulatory periods in U.S. history, see Thomas W. Merrill, *Capture Theory and the Courts: 1967-1983*, 72 Chi.-Kent L. Rev. 1039, 1048-50 (1997).

Often the discussion of why we regulate through the administrative state is sidetracked by discussions about *who* should regulate: If the Constitution mandates that Congress formulate basic public policy (and we read Article I to say just that), then why permit unelected, "unaccountable" agency actors (with arguably unbridled discretion) to govern? *See* Jack Beermann, *Congressional Administration*, 43 San Diego L. Rev. 61 (2006) (check out the second half of the article for a wonderful discussion on the capacity and propriety of congressional control over administrative action); Jonathan G. Pray, Comment, *Congressional Reporting Requirements: Testing the Limits of the Oversight Power*, 76 U. Col. L. Rev. 297 (2005).

Beyond the fact that Congress has neither the technical skills nor the personnel to undertake the regulatory missions set forth in the legislation it enacts, the likelihood of delay, political abuse, and conflicts of interest suggest that Congress is not the best entity to accomplish the day-to-day regulation that legislation requires. *See* Harold J. Krent, *Turning Congress into an Agency: The Propriety of Requiring Legislative Findings*, 46 Case W. Res. L. Rev. 731 (1996); David E. Engdahl, *Intrinsic Limits of Congress' Power Regarding the Judicial Branch*, 1 BYU L. Rev. 75 (1999). Similarly, the President and those who work with the President have neither the skills nor the staff to engage in regulation. Accordingly, the basic tasks of regulation fall to administrative agencies, referred to occasionally as the "fourth branch" of government. *See* Terry M. Moe & William G. Howell, *The Presidential Power of Unilateral Action*, 15 J.L. Econ. & Org. 132, 155 (1999); Kevin M. Stack, *The Statutory President*, 90 Iowa L. Rev. 539, 551 (2005) (exploring the direct lawmaking power of presidential proclamation).

The use of this term can be traced back at least a half-century, when the Supreme Court found that agencies "have become a veritable fourth branch of the Government, which has

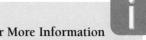

For More Information

To those troubled by the fourth branch reference, we express our apologies and leave the debate to others. *See* Strauss, *The Place of Agencies in Government: Separation of Powers and the Fourth Branch*, 84 Colum. L. Rev. 573 (1984); Sidney A. Shapiro & Richard E. Levy, *Heightened Scrutiny of the Fourth Branch: Separation of Powers and the Requirement of Adequate Reasons for Agency Decisions*, 1987 Duke L.J. 387; Joshua W. Abbott, Note, *Checks and Balances on the Fifth Branch of Government: Colorado Environmental Coalition v. Wenker and the Justiciability of the Federal Advisory Committee Act*, 2005 BYU L. Rev. 1047 (counting Federal Advisory Committees as a fifth branch).

deranged our three-branch legal theories much as the concept of a fourth dimension unsettles our three-dimensional thinking." *FTC v. Ruberoid*, 343 U.S. 470, 487 (1952).

While we do not take sides on the branch issue, in this text, we refer to agencies primarily as executive, even though agencies are created by Congress, directed and organized by the President, and subject to judicial review by the courts. The executive can both appoint and remove critical actors within certain agencies, subject to constraints discussed at length in the materials that follow. *See* Saikrishna Prakash, *Regulating Presidential Powers*, 91 CORNELL L. REV. 215 (2005). Of equal or greater importance, the executive establishes enforcement priorities and can control the level of vigor with which an agency proceeds. A newly elected President can not govern through the Congress or the courts, but can through the agencies.

Others argue that agencies are a creature of the legislative branch. They are created by legislative action, subject to legislative oversight, funded by legislative appropriations and are capable of being "closed down" by legislative determination. While we will use the term executive agency, this book does not focus on that discussion. From our perspective your time is better spent wondering how and why we regulate rather than how we label regulatory agencies.

To guide the exploration of "why we regulate" we set out in the simplest form possible some of the classical arguments for regulation as well as some of the classical arguments against it.

> **Food for Thought**
>
> Keep in mind that one way to assess the nature and potential of administrative agencies is by comparing them with the characteristics of the judicial, executive, and legislative branches. What can agencies do well that the other branches of government do poorly – or not at all?

II. Traditional Arguments Favoring Agency Governance

a. <u>Continuity</u>. In order to have an effective regulatory program, there must be some level of reliability for those who must conform to various administrative mandates. Because of our electoral system, neither the President nor Congress can provide this continuity – but agencies can. Further strengthening this continuity, in *Motor Vehicle Manufacturers Association v. State Farm Mutual*, the Court made clear that the public has a right to rely on regulations as written, and while an agency may change regulations, when doing so the agency must, at a minimum, explain the basis and purpose for such revisions.

There is an obvious value in continuity for those regulated: Government becomes reliable. Regulation that provides constancy allows for long-term planning and justifies costly improvements in the production of goods and services. "Establishing independent administrative agencies . . . promotes continuity of policy from administration to administration, since independent agencies are bound to perform their statutory functions in good faith even if the statutory standards set by Congress become politically unpalatable to the current administration." Evan J. Criddle, *Fiduciary Foundations of Administrative Law*, 54 UCLA L. REV. 117, 170 (2006). Seen in this light, a trust or fiduciary relationship is possible between an agency and those subject to its regulation.

As will become apparent, continuity in regulatory administration – a foundational justification for the administrative state – is at odds with other notions of responsive government. At the most basic level, when a new President is elected, one would expect changes consistent with the promises made in the course of the presidential campaign; one would expect that after the election, the agencies will align with the new administration. However, political transition and regulatory transition do not happen simultaneously.

Anxious to force regulatory transition that matched a change in ideology following the defeat of President Jimmy Carter, President Ronald Reagan executed Executive Order No. 12,291

> requiring cost-benefit evaluation of major regulatory proposals. Only regulations having a net benefit – and the greatest possible net benefit for the regulatory goal – would get the President's stamp of approval. The President's Office of Management and Budget (OMB) was given power to review . . . cost-benefit evaluations and . . . quash unsatisfactory regulations. [From Abner J. Mikva, *Deregulating Through the Back Door: The Hard Way to Fight a Revolution*, 57 U. CHI. L. REV. 521, 529-30 (1990).]

When the federal agencies did not respond at a pace consistent with President Reagan's expectations by the end of his first term, he signed Executive Order 12,498 directing agencies to implement only those regulations and programs that were "consistent with the goals of the agency and the Administration." Exec. Order No. 12,498 § 1(b), 50 F.R. 1036.

Comprehending the inevitability of the struggle between continuity and the political necessity of the President

Take Note

Presumably, the point of an election is to allow the public to express its will – and if the agencies do not go along with the policies of the elected candidate (under the banner of continuity), conflict is inevitable. During the Reagan Administration, by "1986, one-third of all federal regulatory proposals reportedly were vetoed or held up by OMB, including over half of the Environmental Protection Agency (EPA) proposals in one three year period. . . ." Mikva, at 530.

to implement the policies on which they were elected is one of the best ways to understand this field. Every President faces this task, some with more success than others.

> This "continuity" once prompted a frustrated President Kennedy to respond to a request for his assistance by saying, "I can do it, but I don't know if the government can." A Carter Administration official [commented]: "It's like steering a supertanker. You may put the wheel over hard, but it's not going to turn on a dime." [From Mikva, at 530-31.]

b. Flexibility. In theory, agencies can proceed with speed and flexibility. They are not encumbered by the necessity of securing majority votes, cloture, or a presidential signature. They can and do respond to market changes, notwithstanding the criticism that agency procedures have become unduly brittle or ossified. Thomas O. McGarity, *Some Thoughts on Deossifying the Rulemaking Process*, 41 DUKE L.J. 1385 (1992). Agencies also respond to political change, which is one of the driving forces in *Chevron v. NRDC*, *infra* Chapter 3, a case that demonstrates the importance of allowing agencies to adapt to new challenges and the limits on judicial interference with such changes.

The importance of an agency reviewing policy and making changes – the importance of flexibility – evokes a basic debate in administrative law: On whom does the responsibility for change lie? As you will see, this question is at the heart of the seminal *Chevron* decision where the Court held, *inter alia*, that the primary responsibility rests with the agency – although over the last decade, the Court has come back to this issue over and over again.

Food for Thought

How should a court respond if, when reviewing an agency determination, the changes the agency seeks to implement seem inappropriate to the court?

In some legislation, Congress makes clear the expanse of the agency's discretion (range of flexibility). In other legislation, while Congress establishes basic policy, there are substantial gaps to be filled in by the agency. In the land management area for example, the range of regulatory flexibility is substantial. *See* 16 U.S.C. § 583j-2 (1990) (giving the Forest Service authority for "any and all acts necessary and proper" to carry out the legislative purpose); 16 U.S.C. § 3703 (1984) (giving the National Fish and Wildlife Foundation authority for "any and all acts necessary and proper"); 20 U.S.C. § 5509 (giving the National Environmental Education and Training Foundation power to perform "any and all acts necessary and proper"); 43 U.S.C. § 373 (1902) (giving the Secretary of the Interior the power to undertake "any and all acts" to implement a reclamation and irrigation program). Legislation of this type prompts a basic delegation question central to the study of administrative law: Does this type of broad power without clear limitations constitute a congressional abdication of the responsibility to make public policy?

c. <u>Specialization and Expertise</u>. Every federal, state, and local agency makes use of both staff and non-staff technical experts. Whether the field is electrical power, nuclear energy, telecommunications, or finance, agencies retain a permanent staff of experts so that the agency can be both aware of developments in the field and able to respond to technical changes as they occur. That cannot be said of the President, Congress, or the courts. *Commodity Futures Trading Commission v. Schor*, *infra* Chapter 10, explores, *inter alia*, whether the expertise of the CFTC permits that agency to serve as an adjudicatory forum for disputes normally heard in Article III tribunals.

This rationale was a foundational premise of New Deal regulation. "During the New Deal era, a key feature of the organization of law and order was the commitment to centralized, institutional decision-making authorities relying on professional, official expertise: 'The New Deal believed in experts. Those who rationalized its regulatory initiatives regarded expertise and specialization as the particular strengths of the administrative process.'" Orly Lobel, *The Renew Deal: The Fall of Regulation and the Rise of Governance in Contemporary Legal Thought*, 89 Minn. L. Rev. 342 (2004), *citing* James O. Freedman, Crisis and Legitimacy: The Administrative Process and American Government 44 (1978); *see also* James M. Landis, The Administrative Process 23-24 (1938).

Key Concept

The ideas underlying the specialization rationale have not changed – there is, however, a forceful counter argument that a governmental agency will never be as wise or prescient as the open market.

Specialization and expertise are central to the doctrine of primary jurisdiction – a rarely asserted prudential jurisdictional filter that can delay access to an Article III court when an agency has not concluded its process, has statutory responsibility, and an evident need for continuity and technical expertise. *See, e.g.*, <u>Nader v. Allegheny Airlines Inc., 426 U.S. 290, 304 (1976)</u>; Paula K. Knippa <u>Note, *Primary Jurisdiction Doctrine and the Circumforaneous Litigant*, 85 Tex. L. Rev. 1289 (2007)</u>.

d. <u>Essential Values</u>. Agencies are often required and uniquely positioned to implement unpopular and controversial legislative (or constitutional) imperatives regarding equal protection and fairness. Unencumbered by the necessity of reelection, agencies are capable of protecting non-majoritarian interests, a phenomenon that can be almost impossible in a politically-charged environment such as Congress. We believe this is an obvious virtue – market driven effects are often the result of popular balloting on goods and services. There is a place in the legal system for certain core values to be represented and asserted regardless of the popularity of those values at a particular moment in time.

e. <u>Emergencies</u>. One of the classical arguments regarding the administrative state is that it is capable of functioning quickly and aggressively in an emergency. While there is little doubt that agencies can function more rapidly than Congress, the courts, or the President, there are glaring examples of agency ineptitude where inaction has also led to catastrophic consequences. *See, e.g.*, David Gottlieb, *Katrina Consequences: What Has the Government Learned: Introduction and Background*, 53 LOYOLA L. REV. 1113 (2006); SELECT BIPARTISAN COMM. TO INVESTIGATE THE PREPARATION AND RESPONSE TO HURRICANE KATRINA, 109TH CONG., A FAILURE OF INITIATIVE (2006), *available at* http://a257.g.akamaitech.net/7/257/2422/15feb20061230/www. gpoaccess.gov/katrinareport/mainreport.pdf (last visited July 4, 2008).

f. <u>Volume</u>. Administrative agencies, using simplified decision-making systems, can process millions of claims on an annual basis. While there are backlogs in agencies at different times, it is inconceivable that courts could handle a similar volume of cases. This efficiency is a result of the rules governing agency functions or actions. <u>*Richardson v. Perales*</u>, *infra* Chapter 9, uses the capacity to handle a large volume of cases as one explanation for permitting the use of nothing but hearsay as the exclusive evidentiary basis for an order at the conclusion of an adjudication.

Make the Connection

For the most part, the rules of evidence are "relaxed" in administrative adjudicatory proceedings and hearsay is generally admissible.

g. <u>Ongoing Supervision</u>. The vast majority of cases that proceed through Article III courts come to an end when a judgment is reached. While there may be injunctions, courts rarely engage in any form of long-term continuing supervision after a case has been decided. In contrast, agencies often devote themselves to ongoing supervision for years. <u>*Donovan v. Dewey*</u>, *infra* Chapter 11, explains that pervasive regulation is vital in certain industries and that on-going supervision of a trade or business may require certain compromises, e.g., warrantless searches.

h. <u>Economic Justification</u>. Agencies play a role in creating a "level playing field" in various markets. Agencies can address unfair business practices that could lead to distorted market power, including monopoly power, suppression of innovation, or creation of artificial barriers to market entry. As noted earlier, there are strong deregulatory sentiments in counterpoise to this justification.

i. <u>Public Safety</u>. Agencies can use regulatory force to mandate increased levels of safety and efficiency in goods and services. <u>*North American Cold Storage v. City*</u>

of Chicago, *infra* Chapter 6, establishes that protection of public safety is of such consequence that it may trump a due process claim to a hearing in advance of adverse government action. This does not deny the reality of market-force in achieving the same objectives; it simply recognizes that the marketplace may respond more slowly than public safety demands.

Take Note

Consumer safety regarding various goods and services depends on a reliable flow of information and internally disciplined action by every consumer. Since uniformly reliable market information and internal discipline exist only in an idealized world, protection of health and safety becomes one of the dominant roles for the regulatory state.

j. <u>Dissemination of Information</u>. Agencies are the primary vehicle for implementing the <u>Freedom of Information Act</u> (FOIA), as well as compiling and distributing an amazing array of data, studies, and information of every conceivable type. FOIA is the topic of Chapter 12 of this text. For now, *see, e.g.*, DEP'T OF JUST., ATTORNEY GENERAL'S REPORT TO THE PRESIDENT ON EXECUTIVE ORDER 13,392, "IMPROVING DISCLOSURE OF AGENCY INFORMATION" (2007), *available at* http://www.usdoj.gov/oip/foiapost/2008foiapost19.htm (last visited July 11, 2008); GOV'T ACCOUNTABILITY OFFICE, GAO REPORT 01-428, INFORMATION MANAGEMENT; ELECTRONIC DISSEMINATION OF GOVERNMENT INFORMATION (2001) (on the topic of electronic disclosure and distribution of information).

III. Traditional Arguments Disfavoring Agency Governance

a. <u>Incompetence</u>. The lack of competence is a standing criticism of virtually every local, state, and federal agency. If the assumption is that those who are most competent will work in areas where compensation is maximized, then the assumption may be correct. However, this is an area where reasonable minds most assuredly differ. There are many (including your authors) who contend that agencies are repositories of genuine competence, staffed by those motivated by factors beyond compensation. Rather than argue the point, suffice it to say that there are advocates for both points of view.

Textual Note

The question of assessing competence extends to the administrative judiciary. The topic of the competence and objectivity of the administrative judiciary is the focus of Chapter 11 of the text.

b. <u>Favoritism</u>. There is little question that political and economic power play a role in regulation. Regulatory agencies are vulnerable. Annual budget reviews, appointment power vested in the executive, and legislative oversight all play a role in creating pressures by which agency decisions can be compromised.

c. <u>Capture</u>. Extended exposure to a regulated industry brings those who regulate in constant contact with those who are regulated. Over time, objectivity can be lost as the regulator and the regulated become aligned. For a broad range of reasons, those charged with the responsibility of regulation may become too identified with those they regulate and in that moment they are said to be "captured." *See, e.g.*, Christine H. Kim, *The Case for Preemption of Prescription Drug Failure-To-Warn Claims, 62 FOOD & DRUG L.J. 399, 401 (2007)* (discussing charges of capture at the FDA); Ernesto Dal Bo, *Regulatory Capture: A Review*, 22 OXFORD REV. ECON. POL'Y 203, 214 (2006); Mathew D. Zinn, *Policing Environmental Regulatory Enforcement: Cooperation, Capture, and Citizen Suits, 21 STAN. ENVTL. L.J. 81(2002)*; Thomas W. Merrill, *Capture Theory and the Courts: 1967-1983, 72 CHI.-KENT L. REV. 1039, 1064-67 (1997)*; Michael E. Levine & Jennifer L. Forrence, *Regulatory Capture, Public Interest, and the Public Agenda: Toward a Synthesis*, 6 J.L. ECON. & ORG. 167 (1990); John Shepard Wiley, Jr., *A Capture Theory of Antitrust Federalism, 99 HARV. L. REV. 713 (1986)*; William H. Page, *Capture, Clear Articulation, and Legitimacy: A Reply to Professor Wiley, 61 S. CAL. L. REV. 1343 (1988)*.

d. <u>Loss of Market Forces</u>. A properly functioning market will achieve greater measures of success, including safety and efficiency, than a marketplace that is controlled by non-participants performing a regulatory role. Of course, the notion of a "properly functioning market" is one subject to considerable debate. Nonetheless, aggressive regulation is seen as a counter-force to the free market. These theories are expressed perfectly in GEORGE J. STIGLER, MEMOIRS OF AN UNREGULATED ECONOMIST (1988). *See generally* FRANK H. EASTERBROOK & DANIEL R. FISCHEL, THE ECONOMIC STRUCTURE OF CORPORATE LAW (1991); and Frank H. Easterbrook, *The State of Madison's Vision of the State: A Public Choice Perspective, 107 HARV. L. REV. 1328 (1994)*.

Key Concept

Unquestionably, one of the primary criticisms of regulation is that it displaces market forces.

e. <u>Compromised Privacy</u>. An administrative decisionmaker will function most effectively when there is optimal access to comprehensive information about all aspects of the problem. That said, the goal of securing information can be in conflict with the goal of protecting privacy. Agencies are not encumbered by the general requirement of "probable cause" when they secure information. So long as the agency has a reasonable basis for the information it seeks, the chances are the agency will get what it is after. The cost is obvious: Privacy is compromised when the government has unbridled discretion to secure information. *See Wyman v. James*, *infra* Chapter 11.

IV. Beyond the Pros and Cons: Privatization and Re-regulation

a. Perhaps because of the inherently political nature of administrative law, debate regarding the efficacy of the administrative state is relentless and difficult to pin down. For example, in his 1996 State of the Union Address, then-President William J. Clinton made the bold announcement that "[t]he era of big government is over." ADDRESS BEFORE A JOINT SESSION OF THE CONGRESS ON THE STATE OF THE UNION, 1 PUB. PAPERS 79, 79 (Jan. 23, 1996). Interestingly, in that same speech, President Clinton announced a substantial number of new regulatory initiatives. Moreover, since 1996, numerous "deregulated" programs have either been re-regulated or privatized.

b. <u>Re-regulation</u>. Re-regulation of various markets seems almost inevitable. The Spring 2008 sub-prime mortgage debacle produced regulatory initiatives that will fundamentally change the landscape of mortgage financing, with the encouragement of anti-regulatory President George W. Bush. REMARKS AT THE AMERICA'S SMALL BUSINESS SUMMIT, PUB. PAPERS OF THE PRESIDENTS (Apr. 21, 2008).

With the U.S. airline industry faltering – in one 45 day period, Alaska Airlines, Aloha Airlines, ATA, Frontier Airlines, and Skybus Airlines all declared bankruptcy – many are asking the re-regulation question directly. *See, e.g.*, Tom Farrell, Op-Ed., *Electricity Re-Regulation: New Model Provides Direction Virginia Requires*, RICH. TIMES-DISPATCH, Feb. 4, 2007 (advocating for re-regulation); Michael E. Levine, <u>*Why Weren't the Airlines Reregulated?*, 23 YALE J. ON REG. 269 (2006)</u>; Andrew E.G. Jonas & Gavin Bridge, *Governing Nature: The Re-Regulation of Resources, Land Use Planning, and Nature Conservation*, 84 SOC. SCI. Q. 958 (2003); Timothy M. Ravich, <u>*Re-Regulation and Airline Passengers' Rights*, 67 J. AIR L. & COM. 935, 942-46 (2002)</u>; SIMON DEAKIN & FRANK WILKINSON, THE ECONOMICS OF EMPLOYMENT RIGHTS 34 (1991) (stating there is scant evidence that deregulation generates the open-market forces needed to achieve clearly defined public goals).

c. <u>Privatization.</u> Privatization is a bit more difficult to assess – and far more prevalent – than direct re-regulation. While there are roughly two million full-time federal civilian government employees, there are about six times that number working in the private sector in positions funded by the federal government. Paul R. Verkuil, <u>*Public Law Limitations on Privatization of Government Functions*, 84 N.C. L. REV. 397, n.1-2 (2006)</u>. What happens when functions considered governmental in nature are contracted to the private sector? Circular A-76 issued by the Office of Management and Budget (OMB) requires governmental agencies to undertake activities that are "inherently government functions." OFFICE OF MGMT. & BUDGET, EXECUTIVE OFFICE OF THE PRESIDENT, OMB CIRCULAR A-76, PERFORMANCE OF COMMERCIAL ACTIVITIES, <u>68 Fed. Reg. 32,134 (2003)</u>, *available at* <u>http://www.white-</u>

house.gov/omb/circulars/a076/a76 rev2003.pdf. In the event a seemingly governmental function is contracted out privately, the agency involved must undertake a market study to identify the best means to achieve the statutory objective and use a competitive bidding procedure on any activities that are commercial in nature.

Bottom Line

Basic protections should not easily be contracted away, especially in settings where private companies have government contracts to provide primary and secondary education, run prison systems, administer public assistance programs, manage immigration documentation, and even perform national defense activities.

Assuming that the mandates of Circular A-76 are met, what due process protections apply? To avoid disappointment down the road, we'll let you know right now that this question cannot be answered by a simplistic "under color of law" analysis. *See* David H. Rosenbloom & Suzanne J. Piotrowski, *Reinventing Public Administration While "De-Inventing" Administrative Law: Is it Time for an "APA" for Regulating Outsourced Government Work?*, 33 SYRACUSE J. INT'L L. & COM. 175 (2005).

The literature in the field is substantial – and growing. *See* Alexander Volokh, *Privatization and the Law and Economics of Political Advocacy*, 60 STAN. L. REV. 1197 (2008); David A. Super, *Privatization, Policy Paralysis, and the Poor*, 96 CAL. L. REV. 393 (2008); Benjamin A. Templin, *The Public Trust in Private Hands: Social Security and the Politics of Government Investment*, 96 KY. L.J. 369 (2007/2008); Paul R. Verkuil, *Privatizing Due Process*, 57 ADMIN. L. REV. 963, 987 (2005); Paul R. Verkuil, *Public Law Limitations on Privatization of Government Functions*, 84 N.C. L. REV. 397 (2006); Michael P. Vandenbergh, *The Private Life of Public Law*, 105 COLUM. L. REV. 2029 (2005); *Symposium, New Forms of Governance: Ceding Public Power to Private Actors*, 49 UCLA L. REV. 1687 (2002); Jody Freeman, *The Private Role in Public Governance*, 75 NYU L. REV. 543 (2000).

Those anxious about public accountability and fairness when seemingly public functions are privatized have every reason to be concerned. Although privatization has generated its own theoretical cause of action, (termed a "wrongful privatization"), in *Sugar v. West*, 1998 U.S. Dist. LEXIS 15132 (E.D.N.C. 1998), the plaintiffs "brought a 'wrongful privatization' claim under the Administrative Procedure Act . . ., 5 U.S.C. § 702," prompting the court to hold that a "contracting-out decision pursuant to OMB Circular A-76 is an internal management directive of the Executive Branch that creates no enforceable rights in third parties and provides no law to be applied."

Assuming legislative authorization, when a decision is made to have private enti-

For More Information

Privatization of governmental functions continues to be tested regularly in the courts. See *Nat'l Air Traffic Controllers Ass'n v. DOT*, No. 06-3466, 2007 WL 2141941 (6th Cir. 2007), one of a number of decisions issued during a thirteen year saga exploring standing and related judicial review issues pertaining to air traffic controllers.

ties undertake various tasks that are funded federally, frequently the mechanism for the transfer of resources and authority is a contract. To see a recent executive order regarding government contracting and the economy, click HERE.

V. The Process of Regulation – The Introductory Cases

For most of the 19th Century, with the exception of the Post Office, patents and copyrights, limited public safety and some nearly invisible regulation of agriculture, the country functioned in a deregulated state. By the end of the 19th Century, many of the major industries were dominated by cartels or monopolies. Steel, oil, lumber and many food products were controlled by market forces unlikely to produce healthy competition much less optimal efficiency and public good. The unregulated 19th Century saw the rise of heavy industry – and the creation of deadly, nightmarish workplaces. It was apparent that some additional level of governance was required. Slowly, government agencies evolved and, by the middle of the 20th Century, the regulatory state was firmly established.

Every case that follows allows you to think through the grand substantive question of administrative law: Should this field be regulated? We invite you to consider that inquiry as a regular part of your study. Your primary mission, however, involves the process of regulation – how regulation takes place and what rights and responsibilities parties have as they encounter the administrative state.

With these concepts in mind, we come to our first case and perhaps the most basic inquiry: When can a governmental entity proceed by announcing rules or policies and when is it required, instead, to conduct a hearing prior to taking action?

LONDONER V. CITY AND COUNTY OF DENVER

<u>210 U.S. 373 (1908)</u>

[JUSTICE MOODY] The plaintiffs in error began this proceeding in a state court of Colorado to relieve lands owned by them from an assessment of a tax for the cost of paving a street upon which the lands abutted. The relief sought was granted by the trial court, but its action was reversed by the Supreme Court of the State . . . . The Supreme Court held that the tax was assessed in conformity with the constitution and laws of the State, and its decision on that question is conclusive. . . .

The tax complained of was assessed under the provisions of the charter of the city of Denver, which confers upon the city the power to make local improvements and to assess the cost upon property specially benefited. . . .

It appears from the charter that, in the execution of the power to make local improvements and assess the cost upon the property specially benefited, the main steps to be taken by the city authorities are plainly marked and separated:

> 1. The board of public works must transmit to the city council a resolution ordering the work to be done and [a proposed] ordinance authorizing it and creating an assessment district. This it can do only upon certain conditions, one of which is that there shall first be filed a petition asking for the improvement, signed by the owners of the majority of the frontage to be assessed.

> 2. The passage of that ordinance by the city council, which is given authority to determine conclusively whether the action of the board was duly taken.

> 3. The assessment of the cost upon the landowners after due notice and opportunity for hearing.

In the case before us the board took the first step by transmitting to the council the resolution to do the work and [a proposed] ordinance authorizing it. It is contended, however, that there was wanting an essential condition . . ., namely, . . . a petition from the owners . . . . The trial court found [however, that the city council found] ". . . that in their action and proceedings in relation to said Eighth Avenue Paving District Number One the said board of public works has fully complied with the requirements of the city charter relating thereto." The state Supreme Court held that the determination of the city council was conclusive that a proper petition was filed. . . .

The [first] question for this court is whether the charter provision authorizing such a finding, without notice to the landowners, denies to them due process of law. We think it does not. The proceedings, from the beginning up to and including the passage of the ordinance authorizing the work did not include any assessment or necessitate any assessment, although they laid the foundation for an assessment, which might or might not subsequently be made. Clearly all this might validly be done without hearing to the landowners, provided a hearing upon the assessment itself is afforded. . . . This disposes of the first assignment of error, which is overruled. . . .

The fifth assignment . . . raises . . . the question whether the assessment was made without notice and opportunity for hearing to those affected by it, thereby denying to them due process of law. The trial court found as a fact that no opportunity for hearing was afforded, and the Supreme Court did not disturb this finding. The record discloses what was actually done, and there seems to be no dispute about it. After the improvement was completed the board of public works, in compliance with § 29 of the charter, certified to the city clerk a statement of the cost, and an apportionment of it to the lots of land to be assessed. Thereupon the city clerk, in compliance with § 30, published a notice stating, *inter alia*, that the written complaints or objections of the owners, if filed within thirty days, would be "heard and determined by the city council before the passage of any ordinance assessing the cost."

Those interested, therefore, were informed that if they reduced their complaints and objections to writing, and filed them within thirty days, those complaints and objections would be heard, and would be heard before any assessment was made. . . . Resting upon the assurance that they would be heard, the plaintiffs in error filed within the thirty days the following paper:

> To the Honorable Board of Public Works, . . . Mayor and City Council . . .
>
> The undersigned . . . strenuously protest . . . the passage of the contemplated . . . ordinance against the property in Eighth Avenue Paving District No. 1 . . . for . . . the following reasons . . . .
>
> . . . 3d. That [the] property in [question] is not benefited by said pretended improvement . . . to the extent of the assessment; that the individual pieces of property . . . are not benefited . . . that the assessment is [arbitrary] and property assessed in an equal amount is not benefited equally. . . .
>
> Wherefore . . . the undersigned object and protest against the passage of the said proposed assessing ordinance.

. . . Instead of affording the plaintiffs in error an opportunity to be heard upon its allegations, the city council, without notice to them, met as a board of equalization, not in a stated but in a specially called session, and, without any hearing, adopted the following resolution:

> Whereas, complaints have been filed by the various persons and firms . . . against the proposed assessments on said property for the *cost of said paving* . . . and
>
> Whereas, no complaint or objection has been filed or made against the apportionment . . ., but the complaints and objections filed deny wholly the right of the city to assess any district or portion of the assessable property of the city of Denver; therefore, be it
>
> Resolved . . . that the apportionments of said assessment made by said board of public works be, and the same are . . . approved.

[W]ithout further notice or hearing, the city council enacted the ordinance of assessment whose validity is to be determined in this case . . . .

From beginning to end of the proceedings the landowners, although allowed to formulate and file complaints and objections, were not afforded an opportunity to be heard upon them. Upon these facts was there a denial by the State of the due process of law guaranteed by the Fourteenth Amendment to the Constitution of the United States?

In the assessment, apportionment and collection of taxes upon property within their jurisdiction the Constitution of the United States imposes few restrictions upon the States . . . . But where the legislature of a State, instead of fixing the tax itself, commits to some subordinate body the duty of determining whether, in what amount, and upon whom it shall be levied, and of making its assessment and apportionment, due process of law requires that at some stage of the proceedings before the tax becomes irrevocably fixed, the taxpayer shall have an opportunity to be heard, of which he must have notice, either personal, by publication, or by a law fixing the time and place of the hearing. It must be remembered that the law of Colorado denies the landowner the right to object in the courts to the assessment, upon the ground that the objections are cognizable only by the board of equalization.

[W]e think that something more than [an opportunity to submit objections in writing], even in proceedings for taxation, is required by due process of law. Many requirements essential in strictly judicial proceedings may be dispensed with in proceedings of this nature. But even here a hearing in its very essence demands that he who is entitled to it shall have the right to support his allegations by argument however brief, and, if need[ed], by [oral presentation of] proof, however informal. It is apparent that such a hearing was denied to the plaintiffs in error. The denial was by the city council, which, while acting as a board of equalization, represents the State. The assessment was therefore void . . . .

> ## Underlying Case Documents
>
> The case referenced:
> <u>The Denver Charter of 1893</u>
> <u>The Petition to pave the street</u>
> <u>The notice to the residents including the laws passed establishing the paving district</u>

1. *Londoner* is the starting point for the study of agency adjudication and prompted governmental entities (at the local, state, and federal level) to rethink decision-making modalities. What criteria should be used to determine when decisions of local zoning boards, or by federal agencies, are legislative? Can you use the same criteria to determine if the action of an agency is adjudicatory? If a zoning decision fits the *Londoner* model and affects an individual or a defined and uniquely configured small group, do conventional notions of procedural due process, applicable in courts of general jurisdiction (which are referred to in this text as Article III courts), apply? Should they – particularly in land use cases? *See* Asimow & Sullivan, *Due Process in Local Land Use Decision Making: Is the Imperfect Way of Doing Business Good Enough or Should We Radically Reform It?*, 29 ZONING & PLAN. L. REP. 1 (2006).

2. Are governmental decisions to be weighed based on the interest affected – or the number of individuals and interests affected? What about a general building moratorium that has an explicitly negative affect on one parcel of property? *See* <u>75 Acres, LLC v. Miami-Dade County, 338 F.3d 1288, 1293-94 (11th Cir. 2003)</u>:

> [I]f government action is viewed as legislative in nature, property owners generally are not entitled to procedural due process. Or, as one set of commentators has summarized, "When the legislature passes a law which affects a general class of persons, those persons have all received procedural due process – the legislative process. The challenges to such laws must be based on their substantive compatibility with constitutional guarantees." RONALD E. ROTUNDA & JOHN E. NOWAK, <u>TREATISE ON CONSTITUTIONAL LAW § 17.8 (3d ed. 1999)</u>.

3. Does the type of factual question in play determine the nature of a hearing? In <u>In re Asbestos Litigation, 829 F.2d 1233, 1250 (3d Cir. 1987)</u>, a product liability case, the court interpreted *Londoner* to mean that "a legislative fact is not an individualized fact [and] the Constitution does not mandate that [legislative facts] be found through a process of individualized fact-finding. . . ." The Third Circuit explained that "[a]djudicative facts are simply the facts of the particular case. Legislative facts, on the other hand, are those which have relevance to legal rea-

soning and the lawmaking process, whether in the formulation of a legal principle or ruling by a judge or court or in the enactment of a legislative body."

If an administrative determination – in an individual case – requires application of a novel legal interpretation to specific facts (pertaining to identifiable parties), would that mandate an evidentiary hearing? In *FCC v. WJR, The Goodwill Station, Inc.*, 337 U.S. 265, 274-75 (1949), the Court made clear that there was no set rule – but that a *Londoner* oral/evidentiary hearing was not the default position:

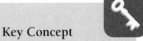

Key Concept

How does the difference between legislative and adjudicatory facts affect the right to a hearing? The distinction was famously described by Professor Kenneth Culp Davis, in his article, *Judicial Notice*, 55 COLUM. L. REV. 945, 952 (1955), and KENNETH CULP DAVIS, ADMINISTRATIVE LAW TREATISE §12.3 (2nd ed., 1979), and adopted in the Advisory Committee Note to Federal Rules of Evidence, 201(a), 56 F.R.D. 183, 201-04 (1972). The Advisory Committee stated that "[adjudicative facts are] simply the facts of the particular case [while legislative facts] are those which have relevance to legal reasoning and the lawmaking process . . . ."

> Taken at its literal and explicit import, the [lower court's] broad constitutional ruling [mandating a hearing] cannot be sustained. So taken, it would require oral argument upon every question of law, apart from the excluded interlocutory matters, arising in administrative proceedings of every sort. This would be regardless of whether the legal question were substantial or insubstantial; of the substantive nature of the asserted right or interest involved; of whether Congress had provided a procedure, relating to the particular interest, requiring oral argument or allowing it to be dispensed with; and regardless of the fact that full opportunity for judicial review may be available.

> We do not stop to consider the effects of such a ruling, if accepted, upon the work of the vast and varied administrative as well as judicial tribunals of the federal system and the equally numerous and diversified interests affected by their functioning; or indeed upon the many and different types of administrative and judicial procedures which Congress has provided for dealing adjudicatively with such interests. It is enough to say that due process of law . . . has never been cast in so rigid and all-inclusive confinement.

> On the contrary, due process of law has never been a term of fixed and invariable content.

Why not make a "fair hearing" a fixed rule in any case where a constitutionally cognizable interest is affected adversely by governmental action? Isn't the promise of due process the commitment to provide an evidentiary hearing before the government takes action?

4. There is also an additional lens through which adjudicative and legislative

facts can be distinguished. Typical of this perspective is <u>Greenwood Manor v. Iowa Department of Public Health, 641 N.W.2d 823 (Iowa 2002)</u>:

> Generally, a person has a constitutional due process right to an evidentiary hearing in accordance with contested case procedures if the underlying proceeding involves adjudicative facts. . . . Conversely, if the agency decision rests on legislative facts, the parties are not constitutionally entitled to an evidentiary hearing. . . . Thus, whether due process demands an agency to provide affected persons in certificate of need proceedings an evidentiary hearing depends upon whether the proceedings involve adjudicative or legislative facts.
>
> Adjudicative facts relate to the specific parties and their particular circumstances. . . . They involve individualized facts peculiar to the parties, and ordinarily answer the questions of who did what, where, when, how, why, with what motive or intent . . . . Legislative facts, on the other hand, do not pertain to the specific parties. Instead, legislative facts are generalized factual propositions, often consisting of demographical data and statistics compiled from surveys and studies, which aid the decisionmaker in determining questions of policy and discretion. . . . [Internal citations and quotations omitted. *See* K. DAVIS, ADMINISTRATIVE LAW TREATISE § 7.02 (1970).]

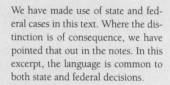

Textual Note

We have made use of state and federal cases in this text. Where the distinction is of consequence, we have pointed that out in the notes. In this excerpt, the language is common to both state and federal decisions.

Good Question!

The more elaborate the rights received by those affected by agency action, the more time-consuming and expensive the process is for the government. If the rights are nominal — meaning a less elaborate process — will the public have faith in the decisions of the agencies or will the agencies be perceived as authoritarian, inquisitorial entities?

5. Assuming due process protections apply based on *Londoner*, what does that mean? Was the Court envisioning full trials that included discovery, prehearing motions, testimony by direct and cross examination, and decisions supported by the manifest weight of the evidence, all set forth in a written record? Alternatively, was the Court contemplating an individual hearing with only the right to appear before an agency official who then had summary power to render a decision?

The basic premise in *Londoner* should seem both familiar and part of the current conventional due process discourse. In <u>Corey v. Department of Land Conservation & Development, 152 P.3d 933, 934-35 (Or. Ct. App. 2007)</u>, the complainants alleged that without permitting a fair hearing, the government affected adversely their property through both a taking of the property (in this instance a diminution in land value) and a forced remedy (a waiver of certain regulations) instead of direct compensation. Citing *Londoner*, the court found:

> Before a governmental entity applies pre-existing legislative or quasi-legislative standards in such a way as to deprive a person (or small group of persons) of an interest in property, the Due Process Clause of the Fourteenth Amendment requires the government to provide notice and a meaningful opportunity to be heard.

The *Corey* court also acknowledged that the fair hearing outcome was not necessarily mandated by the Supreme Court. Interpreting "the teaching" of <u>American Manufacturers Mutual Insurance Co. v. Sullivan, 526 U.S. 40, 60-61 (1999)</u>, the court found "that a person obtains a protected property interest in a benefit only when the person has *actually proven that he or she is fully entitled to it*; only at that point must denial be accompanied by due process." [Emphasis added.]

How can that be? If one does not have a hearing, how would they marshal evidence to show they are "fully entitled" to a hearing? This cart-before-the-horse phenomenon is troubling – and a regular part of this field. Consider the problem from the perspective of the government: Should absolutely anyone who has a complaint about something the government has allegedly done to them be entitled to a hearing? What threshold of proof is required to establish that one has a right worthy of protection? We will return to this question in <u>Roth</u>, *infra* Chapter 6.

Good Question!

Occasionally in this casebook we will urge you to personalize administrative law, using your law school as a model. This is one such moment. What type of hearing entitlements exist at your school for student misconduct cases? For faculty retention or dismissal? Do those procedures conform with general principles of due process? Later in the text, we provide a series of educational fair hearing cases – for now, you might look at the seminal article in the field, Curtis J. Berger & Vivian Berger, <u>Academic Discipline: A Guide to Fair Process for the University Student</u>, 99 COLUM. L. REV. 289 (1999).

6. The exercise of power in question in *Londoner* was based on the Denver Home Rule City Charter that implemented Article XX, Section 6 of the Colorado Constitution. Article XX allowed any city with two thousand or more residents to assess any "property in such city or town for municipal taxation and the levy and collection of taxes thereon for municipal purposes and special assessments for local improvements . . . ." <u>COLO. CONST. art. XX, § 6(g)</u>.

Denver Mayor Robert Speer and other political leaders in the city saw the Charter and the Constitution as a license to secure tax revenue without the time, expense, and inconvenience of individual hearings. Speer once said:

> Red tape and restricting laws will not make a crooked politician straight but will make a straight politician useless. Personally, I believe in the concentration of all administrative powers in the hands of one official. It fixes the responsibility for good or bad government. [From http://www.denvergov.org/aboutdenver/history_narrative_6.asp (last visited May 11, 2008).]

Speer and his colleagues saw taxation determinations as legislative acts for which individual hearings were simply unnecessary. Their perspective continues to be shared by many governmental entities. In <u>*South Gwinnett Venture v. Puitt*, 482 F.2d 389 (5th Cir. 1973)</u>, the court struggled with the distinction between legislative and adjudicatory actions. Citing *Londoner*, the Eighth Circuit held that "a legislative plan for the entire community must be distinguished from the treatment which a specific tract of land receives when its owner petitions for reclassification under that plan. . . . [Reclassification of a tract is] an *exercise of legislative power in a case-by-case adjudicative setting*." [Emphasis added.]

7. While *Londoner* did not address the details of the hearing to be provided, it did find those affected by the proposed action of the city had a right to present their position orally. Nearly a half-century later, in *F.C.C. v. WJR, The Goodwill Station* (note 3 above), the Court held that the "right of oral argument as a matter of procedural due process varies from case to case in accordance with differing circumstances, as do other procedural regulations. . . ." <u>337 U.S. at 276</u>. Later courts have interpreted <u>*F.C.C. v. WJR, The Goodwill Station*</u> to mean that there is "no general constitutional right to oral arguments before an administrative agency." <u>*First Bank & Trust Co. v. Bd. of Governors of Fed. Reserve Sys.*, 605 F. Supp. 555 (D. Ky. 1984)</u>.

The case did establish one bedrock principle: The Constitution is in play when governmental entities make determinations that are inherently adjudicatory and affect constitutionally cognizable interests. Just what rights are in play and how they are to be protected is the basis of much of the second half of this text.

Good Question!

What circumstances demand oral presentation of information? How is fact finding enhanced by "in person" presentations as opposed to written, sworn statements? With the modern regulatory state about to emerge, *Londoner* raised far more questions than it answered.

Bi-Metallic Investment Company v. State Board of Equalization of Colorado

<u>239 U.S. 441 (1915)</u>

[Justice Holmes] This is a suit to enjoin . . . an order of the boards increasing the valuation of all taxable property in Denver forty per cent. The order was sustained and the suit directed to be dismissed by the Supreme Court of the State. The plaintiff is the owner of real estate in Denver and brings the case here on the ground that it was given no opportunity to be heard and that therefore its property will be taken without due process of law, contrary to the Fourteenth Amendment of the Constitution of the United States. That is the only question with which we have to deal. . . .

For the purposes of decision we assume that the constitutional question is presented in the baldest way – that neither the plaintiff nor the assessor of Denver, who presents a brief on the plaintiff's side, nor any representative of the city and county, was given an opportunity to be heard, other than such as they may have had by reason of the fact that the time of meeting of the boards is fixed by law. On this assumption it is obvious that injustice may be suffered if some property in the county already has been valued at its full worth. But if certain property has been valued at a rate different from that generally prevailing in the county the owner has had his opportunity to protest and appeal as usual in our system of taxation so that it must be assumed that the property owners in the county all stand alike. The question then is whether all individuals have a constitutional right to be heard before a matter can be decided in which all are equally concerned – here, for instance, before a superior board decides that the local taxing officers have adopted a system of undervaluation throughout a county, as notoriously often has been the case. The answer of this court in the *State Railroad Tax Cases* at least as to any further notice, was that it was hard to believe that the proposition was seriously made.

Where a rule of conduct applies to more than a few people it is impracticable that every one should have a direct voice in its adoption. The Constitution does not require all public acts to be done in town meeting or an assembly of the whole. General statutes within the state power are passed that affect the person or property of individuals, sometimes to the point of ruin, without giving them a chance to be heard. Their rights are protected in the only way that they can be in a complex society, by their power, immediate or remote, over those who make the rule. If the result in this case had been reached as it might have been by the State's doubling the rate of taxation, no one would suggest that the Fourteenth Amendment was violated unless every person affected had been allowed an opportunity to raise his voice against it before the body entrusted by the state constitution with the power. In considering this case in this court we must assume that the proper state machinery has been used, and the question is whether, if the state constitution had declared that Denver had been undervalued as compared with the rest of the State and had decreed that for the current year the valuation should be forty per cent. higher, the objection now urged could prevail. It appears to us that to put the question is to answer it. There must be a limit to individual argument in such matters if government is to go on. In *Londoner v. Denver* a local board had to determine "whether, in what amount, and upon whom" a tax for paving a street should be levied for special benefits. A relatively small number of persons was concerned, who were exceptionally affected, in each case upon individual grounds, and it was held that they had a right to a hearing. But that decision is far from reaching a general determination dealing only with the principle upon which all the assessments in a county had been laid.

Underlying Case Documents

The case referenced:

The letter to the County Assessor increasing the tax rate in Denver

The letter to the Clerk of the City and County of Denver informing him of the tax increase

---

1. *Bi-Metallic* is the starting point for the study of rulemaking. Unlike *Londoner*, which imposed limits on governmental action, *Bi-Metallic* expanded the range and nature of actions a governmental entity could undertake. Even if interests of a clearly cognizable constitutional nature were affected, such as real or personal property, the local, state, and federal administrative agencies now had a basis to act by legislative pronouncement without the burden of providing an individual hearing to every person affected adversely. So long as the action contemplated was designed to address a class or group of similarly situated individuals, and was otherwise legislative in character, the action of the agency could be defended based on the principles set forth in *Bi-Metallic*.

2. The constraints on the ability of executive entities to make legislative decisions, including the specific procedural requirements to which gov-

Key Concept

Bi-Metallic involves neither the type of agency you will typically encounter in this course nor the types of rulemaking you will typically see. The principle is what is important: Large groups of similarly situated people may well not have a right to an individual hearing even if their property is affected adversely.

ernmental entities must adhere and judicial review of agency judgments (reflected in rules, policy statements, interpretations, and similar issuances), are the focus of much of the rulemaking materials that follow in this text. *Bi-Metallic* establishes a decent historical platform for what was to become modern rulemaking but provides little meaningful detail regarding the process.

3. In *Harris v. County of Riverside*, 904 F.2d 497, 501-02 (9th Cir. 1990), the court found "little guidance in formalistic distinctions." In the notes following *Londoner*, we raised the possibility that procedural entitlements might be determined based on an assessment of whether legislative or adjudicative facts were in issue. The Ninth Circuit rejected the distinction as facile:

> As the Supreme Court . . . recognized in *Bi-Metallic*, the character of the action, rather than its label, determines whether those affected by it are entitled to constitutional due process.

If the Ninth Circuit is correct and the "character of the action" is used to determine process, does that include the nature of the individual rights affected by the proposed action of the government? Does the "character of the action" include the nature of the governmental objectives and interests in play, e.g., improvements in efficiency, public safety, environmental quality, education, or transportation that underlie the government's position? How are such interests balanced? *See Mathews*, Chapter 6.

4. One approach is to think about governmental action in its most primitive terms: Acquisition of information followed by a decision based on that information. Seen in that light, the nature of individual interests do not fit readily into the equation – and yet we know from rudimentary constitutional law that exclusion of individual interests is problematic. Nonetheless, there is a school of thought suggesting that as the challenge set forth in *Londoner* and *Bi-Metallic* involves deciding on process – choosing between some form of rulemaking or some form of adjudication – the key is analyzing the data gathering needs of the government required for a reasoned decision. This process might lead you back to the "legislative" and "adjudicative facts" distinction discussed in the notes following *Londoner* – but a better way to look at this might be to ask: What facts are to be found? If little or no fact-finding is required, if witness credibility and veracity are not in play, a legislative process (read – rulemaking) is the likely outcome.

5. Perhaps the most important and least debatable factor in *Bi-Metallic* involves numbers. How many are affected by the proposed governmental action? In *Minnesota State Board for Community Colleges v. Knight*, 465 U.S. 271 (1984), the Court found that efficient government would "grind to a halt" if all affected voices had to be heard before formulating policy through administrative action. This perspective relies on JUSTICE HOLMES' assurances in *Bi-Metallic*. JUSTICE HOLMES under-

Good Question!

To test your understanding of Justice Holmes' reasoning, assume that
without notice, your tuition is raised
40% in one year. You are understandably outraged. Would you be
content with the knowledge that one
day, those who raised your tuition
might be replaced? The increase in
Bi-Metallic was 40%.

stood that if too many people need
individual process, efficient decisionmaking would cease. He asserted that
the public would be protected by the
electoral process and by the fact that
specific applications of generic rules
could always be contested.

6. If the number affected is the key factor in making the distinction between
rulemaking and adjudication, how
many people are included in Justice
Holmes characterization of "a rela-
tively small number of persons?" For example, in *Anaconda Co. v. Ruckelshaus, 482
F.2d 1301 (10th Cir. 1973)*, a rule issued for sulfur dioxide that appeared only
to address the Anaconda Company – yet the court found that no adjudicatory
proceeding was needed because the rule had a potential impact on many others. A similar outcome occurred in *Air Line Pilots Association v. Quesada, 276 F.2d
892 (2d Cir. 1960)*, *cert. denied*, 366 U.S. 962 (1961), when the Federal Aviation
Administration (FAA) issued a rule that, in effect, imposed a mandatory retirement on commercial pilots over age 60. The Association argued – unsuccessfully
– that the rule was invalid since this was an individual decision and required a
hearing for each pilot.

7. The number affected, in the end, seems to be part of the baseline for deciding
between rulemaking and adjudication. It is clear that the cost and efficiency of
agency action are relevant if the number affected is the decisive factor in determining the level of individual process. What is not clear is how those affected
profoundly by action that affects a large group are protected. Does *Bi-Metallic*
allow those who regulate to govern by ex cathedra pronouncement?

8. *Bi-Metallic* raises – but, like *Londoner*, does not resolve – the most basic questions: Who, beyond the administrative or governmental entity itself, can participate when unelected governmental officials issue regulations that have the force of
law? To what notice, if any, are members of the public entitled when binding rules
are promulgated by anyone other than elected representatives? If, as the Court
finds, certain decision-making tasks must be relegated to non-elected officials,
including members of the executive branch (the agencies), what is the proper role
for courts reviewing such action?

9. Keep in mind that while courts can and do review legislation, the review of
enacted statutes is generally limited to questions of constitutional propriety.
Should that limitation also apply to judicial review of rules issued by agencies,

given that rulemaking is, in most instances, a legislative act? If courts were to engage in that form of review, how would that affect the notion of separation of powers?

10. The note cases that follow provide a quick look at recent cases that still fall back on the criteria and principles in *Londoner* and *Bi-Metallic*. Should zoning cases be considered legislative or adjudicative? Such cases usually involve a single landowner affected by the action of a zoning board or, in the *Coniston* case below, a single Board of Trustees. Nevertheless, communities often use legislative-type rules to achieve zoning objectives. What are the pros and cons – and propriety – of this method of decision-making? As you read the note cases below, ask yourself if the principles set forth in *Londoner* and *Bi-Metallic* are being followed.

Food for Thought

If judicial review of agency action involves tests generally applied in civil cases and goes beyond a check for constitutional sufficiency, could that result in a court rewriting agency rules or regulation based on what the court perceives to be the rule a "reasonable person" would have written?

a. *Coniston v. Village of Hoffman Estates*, 844 F.2d 461 (7th Cir. 1988):

> The plaintiffs own a tract of several hundred acres of land, originally undeveloped, in the Village of Hoffman Estates, Illinois. Their complaint . . . charges that in turning down the site plan for a 17-acre parcel in the tract, the Village Board of Trustees and its members violated the Constitution. . . .
>
> The plaintiffs complain . . . about the Board of Trustees' action in going into executive session [to make its decision]. . . . These complaints might have considerable force if the zoning decision had been adjudicative in nature, but it was not. The . . . Board's decision to approve or disapprove a site plan is a legislative rather than adjudicative decision. The difference is critical. . . . The Constitution does not require legislatures to use adjudicative-type procedures, to give reasons for their enactments, or to act "reasonably" in the sense in which courts are required to do . . . legislatures can base their actions on considerations – such as the desire of a special-interest group for redistributive legislation in its favor – that would be thought improper in judicial decision-making. . . .
>
> It is not labels that determine whether action is legislative or adjudicative. A legislature is not allowed to circumvent the due process clause by the facile expedient of announcing that the state's courts and administrative agencies are henceforth to be deemed legislative bodies even though nothing in their powers and procedures has changed. But neither is the legislature required to judicialize zoning, and perhaps it would not be well advised to do so. . . . The decision to make a judgment legislative is perforce a decision not to use judicial procedures, since they are geared to the making of more circumscribed, more "reasoned" judgments. . . .

The Board of Trustees is the Village's legislature . . . and it has reserved to itself the final decision in zoning matters. Naturally it has not sought to tie its hands with criteria for approval of site plans or with a requirement that it give reasons for its action and always act in a fishbowl. The check on its behavior is purely electoral . . . in a democratic polity this method of checking official action cannot be dismissed as inadequate per se. . . .

A reason . . . why legislatures are not required to follow trial-type procedures is the across-the-board character of legislation. A statute, unlike a judicial decision, applies directly to a whole class of people, and it is this attribute that makes democratic checking feasible, though it is far from perfect. The smaller the class affected by a nominally legislative act, the weaker the democratic check; in the limit, where the class has only one member, we have the bill of attainder, which Congress and state legislatures are forbidden to enact. . . . The class here is small. This might support an argument that some type of individualized hearing was required. *See Londoner v. City & County of Denver*, 210 U.S. 373, 385-86 (1908). [However, the governmental entities involved as well as the Supreme Court in *City of Eastlake v. Forest City Enters., Inc.*, 426 U.S. 668 (1976), have already decided it is acceptable] to submit a single landowner's zoning application to a referendum, [cutting] the other way.

b. *Pro-Eco v. Board of Commissioners, 57 F.3d 505 (7th Cir. 1995)*:

Pro-Eco seeks damages against the Jay County Board of Commissioners ("the Board") that allegedly stem from an illegal landfill moratorium ordinance . . . which the Board passed in 1989 to prevent Pro-Eco from building a landfill in Jay County. . . . Pro-Eco . . . alleges . . . that, in enacting the ordinance barring landfills . . . the Board . . . violated Pro-Eco's constitutional right to due process. . . .

The Board is an elected body that acted legislatively in enacting the moratorium. It . . . enacted a generally applicable ordinance. Governing bodies may enact generally applicable laws, that is, they may legislate, without affording affected parties so much as notice and an opportunity to be heard. *Bi-Metallic*. "The fact that a statute (or statute-like regulation) applies across the board provides a substitute safeguard. . . ." It is likely, as Pro-Eco asserts, that the Board acted specifically because it saw Pro-Eco's landfill coming, and we have noted that "more [process] may be required . . . where the legislation affects only a tiny class of people – maybe a class with only one member. . . ." The Supreme Court, however, has held that even the functional equivalent of a petition for a variance may be put to a referendum. *City of Eastlake v. Forest City Enters., Inc., 426 U.S. 668 (1976)*. We do not believe that generally applicable prophylactic legislation provoked by the fear of one particular actor converts an elected body's legislative act into a quasi-judicial or administrative act that would require more process. *See Anaconda Co. v. Ruckelshaus, 482 F.2d 1301, 1306 (10th Cir. 1973)* . . . .

[However, i]f an ordinance professed general applicability, but it were so specific in describing the prohibited acts that only one actor could ever come within its purview, the ordinance might amount to a bill of attainder and no manner of process would be sufficient. U.S. CONST. art. I § 10. . . .

c. The more a decision looks genuinely legislative, the less likely the protections articulated in *Londoner* will be applicable. The next case involves the activity of a state legislature. Can you conceive of a situation where a legislature could be construed as acting in an adjudicative manner? As the note case above suggests, the constitutional prohibition against Bills of Attainder generally prevent such bodies from acting as adjudicatory entities – yet there are still some adjudicatory proceedings in our legislatures. U.S. CONST. art. II, § 4.

Common Cause of Pennsylvania v. Commonwealth of Pennsylvania, 447 F. Supp. 2d 415 (D. Pa. 2006):

> The Complaint is an aggressive indictment of state government in Pennsylvania, containing shocking accusations that the House and Senate leadership, the Governor, and the Chief Justice of the Supreme Court of Pennsylvania acted in concert to pass, sign, and validate, ill-conceived legislation, in a manner that foreclosed public debate and independent judicial review, all in violation of Plaintiffs' rights to free speech, due process, and equal protection.
>
> [T]he Amended Complaint advances 13 counts . . . including . . . a claim that the "truncated legislative process" that was allegedly employed in enacting Act 44 represented "a continuing pattern of illegal statutory enactment" that violated Plaintiffs' rights to due process and equal protection; [and] a claim that Plaintiffs' First Amendment right to free speech was violated because they were allegedly prevented from lobbying their elected state representatives prior to passage of Act 44 . . . .
>
> Even were one or more Plaintiffs able to modify their claims to allege individualized harm, they must state a cognizable constitutional claim that would entitle them to relief. No Plaintiff has done so here. In reaching this conclusion, the Court again notes that the mere fact that Plaintiffs have alleged constitutional deprivation does not automatically entitle Plaintiffs to present those claims in federal court; rather, it is the specific nature of the rights asserted that determines whether Plaintiffs have stated a recognized constitutional claim. . . .
>
> Plaintiffs . . . appear to be suggesting that they were entitled to receive notice and procedural safeguards before Act 44 was even enacted. As Defendants aptly note, such a claim reflects a misunderstanding of our representative form of government. Plaintiffs are constructively noticed and present for every legislative act of government through their elected representatives. When their representatives are misguided, unresponsive, or ineffectual, they are directly answerable to the people. Absent an actionable claim for institutional exclusions or specific and particular claims of individual harm, as in the narrow circumstances discussed above, Plaintiffs resort is to the ballot box, not the courts.

Hypothetical

Most of the 310 homeowners in the Town of Pleasanton are dog lovers and have at least one family dog. Many of these residents have enclosed large portions of their properties with tall stockade (wood panel) fences in order to allow their pets to romp securely in their yards untethered. Concerned that the proliferation of prominent stockade fencing would damage the town's aesthetic appeal and lower property values across the board, the Pleasanton Town Council, in consultation with the town's Board of Planning and Zoning, voted unanimously at a public legislative hearing to restrict stockade fencing to back yard areas not visible from the street, and to prohibit such fencing entirely from front and side yards abutting sidewalks. The 14 owners of homes on corner lots in the town are concerned that the new ordinance effectively prohibits them from building any panel fencing on their lots, since their properties do not have back yards but only front and side yards abutting sidewalks. Were these corner lot owners due notice and a hearing in advance of the town's decision to restrict the stockade fencing?

VI. Independent or Executive?

Up to this point, we have been using the term "government agency" without differentiating between the different types of entities that fall within that classification. Broadly speaking, at the federal level there are two types of agencies – independent and executive. In addition to independent and executive agencies, there are advisory committees, boards, panels, review committees, and numerous other entities that function under the Administrative Procedure Act and are subject to the <u>Freedom of Information Act</u>, the <u>Sunshine Act</u> and other requirements.

Executive agencies are those under the most direct control of the President. They are cabinet-level agencies such as the Department of Commerce, the Department of Transportation, the Department of Defense, the Justice Department, the Department of Homeland Security, the Department of Agriculture, and the Department of the Interior. These agencies share a number of characteristics. The agency head (Secretary) is appointed by and serves at the pleasure of the President. These are single-administrator agencies, as opposed to collegial bodies. The heads of these agencies serve in a special advisory role to the President and are part of the line of presidential succession, in the event that the President can no longer serve in office.

Executive agencies are complex institutions that house sub-agencies. For example, the Surface Transportation Board and the Federal Aviation Administration are within the Department of Transportation and the National Park Service is within the Department of the Interior.

While the standard administrative law model applies to decision-making in these agencies – i.e., adjudicatory decisions must be based on substantial evidence, and rules must be supported by a record and not be arbitrary or capricious – as discussed throughout this text, the agencies have a distinctly executive quality. Before regulations issue, the Office of Information and Regulatory Affairs (OIRA) has the opportunity to examine regulations from all executive agencies to determine if the rules are consistent with the policies of the President and if the rules presented provide more benefits than costs.

Take Note

Based on Executive Order No. 13422, issued in January 2007, major rules could not go forward unless they were approved by a political appointee within the agency and were in response to a "market failure." That Order was repealed in January 2009.

In contrast to the executive agencies, at least structurally, are the independent agencies. These are entities such as the Nuclear Regulatory Commission, the Securities Exchange Commission, the Federal Communications Commission and the Consumer Product Safety Commission. Unlike the executive agencies, these are "collegial" decision-making bodies, meaning that decisions are made after deliberation and a vote by the commissioners. Commissioners serve for a period of years rather than at the pleasure of the President. While they are appointed initially by a President, often a Commissioner's term of office will extend beyond a President's term. Further, in a number of independent agencies, there is a requirement that the Commissioners are politically diverse, i.e., that the agency is not dominated by one political party.

For More Information

See Mathew D. McCubbins, Roger G. Noll & Barry R. Weingast, writing under the nom de plume McNollgast, *The Political Origins of the Administrative Procedure Act*, 15 J.L. ECON. & ORG. 180 (1999); George B. Shepherd, *Fierce Compromise: The Administrative Procedure Act Emerges from New Deal Politics*, 90 Nw. U.L. REV. 1557 (1996).

While the President appoints Commissioners (who, like Secretaries, must be approved by the advice and consent of the Senate), the President cannot remove Commissioners except for "good cause." These regulatory bodies are focused on specific areas of commerce and, like executive agencies, function pursuant to the Administrative Procedure Act found at 5 U.S.C. §§ 551 et. seq. Because there are a number of Commissioners in each agency, decision-making takes on a very different quality. At the conclusion of an agency proceeding, Commissioners vote, occasionally issuing opinions similar to those issued by judges in Article III courts.

MYERS V. UNITED STATES

272 U.S. 52 (1926)

[CHIEF JUSTICE TAFT]

This case presents the question whether under the Constitution the President has the exclusive power of removing executive officers of the United States whom he has appointed by and with the advice and consent of the Senate.

Myers, appellant's intestate, was on July 21, 1917, appointed by the President, by and with the advice and consent of the Senate, to be a postmaster of the first class at Portland, Oregon, for a term of four years. On January 20, 1920, Myers' resignation was demanded. He refused the demand. On February 2, 1920, he was removed from office by order of the Postmaster General, acting by direction of the President. February 10th, Myers sent a petition to the President and another to the Senate Committee on Post Offices, asking to be heard, if any charges were filed. He protested to the Department against his removal, and continued to do so until the end of his term. He pursued no other occupation and drew compensation for no other service during the interval. On April 21, 1921, he brought this suit in the Court of Claims for his salary from the date of his removal, which, as claimed by supplemental petition filed after July 21, 1921, the end of his term, amounted to $ 8,838.71. In August, 1920, the President made a recess appointment of one Jones, who took office September 19, 1920.

The Court of Claims gave judgment against Myers, and this is an appeal from that judgment. . . .

[Based on] Article II of the Constitution [the government argued that] the President's power of removal of executive officers appointed by him with the advice and consent of the Senate is full and complete without consent of the Senate. If this view is sound, the removal of Myers by the President without the Senate's consent was legal and the judgment of the Court of Claims against the appellant was correct and must be affirmed. . . . .

The relevant parts of Article II of the Constitution are as follows:

"Section 1. The executive Power shall be vested in a President of the United States of America . . . .

"Section 2. The President shall . . . appoint Ambassadors, other public Ministers and Consuls, Judges of the Supreme Court, and all other Officers of the United States whose Appointments are not herein otherwise provided for, and which shall be established by Law: but the Congress may be Law vest the Appointment of such inferior Officers, as they think proper, in the President alone, in the Courts of Law, or in the Heads of Departments. . . .

"Section 4. The President, Vice President and all civil Officers of the United States, shall be removed from Office on Impeachment for, and Conviction of, Treason, Bribery, or other High Crimes and Misdemeanors."

The question where the power of removal of executive officers appointed by the President by and with the advice and consent of the Senate was vested, was presented early in the first session of the First Congress. There is no express provision respecting removals in the Constitution, except as Section 4 of Article II, above quoted, provides for removal from office by impeachment. . . .

[This lack of apparent clarity regarding removal became an issue in 1789 when the House of Representatives voted on] whether it should recognize and declare the power of the President under the constitution to remove the Secretary of Foreign Affairs without the advice and consent of the Senate. . . .[T]here is not the slightest doubt, after an examination of the record, that the vote was, and was intended to be, a legislative declaration that the power to remove officers appointed by the President and the Senate vested in the President alone, and until the Johnson Impeachment trial in 1868, its meaning was not doubted even by those who questioned its soundness.

The vesting of the executive power in the President was essentially a grant of the power to execute the laws. But the President alone and unaided could not execute the laws. He must execute them by the assistance of subordinates. . . . As he is charged specifically to take care that they be faithfully executed, the reasonable implication, even in the absence of express words, was that as part of his executive power he should select those who were to act for him [and] in the absence of any express limitation respecting removals, [remove] those for whom he can not continue to be responsible. . . . If such appointments and removals were not an exercise of the executive power, what were they? They certainly were not the exercise of legislative or judicial power in government as usually understood. . . . .

. . . . When a nomination is made, it may be presumed that the Senate is, or may become, as well advised as to the fitness of the nominee as the President, but in the nature of things the defects in ability or intelligence or loyalty in the administration of the laws of one who has served as an officer under the President, are facts as to which the President, or his trusted subordinates, must be better informed than the Senate, and the power to remove him may, therefore, be regarded as confined, for very sound and practical reasons, to the governmental authority which has administrative control. The power of removal is incident to the power of appointment, not to the power of advising and consenting to appointment, and when the grant of the executive power is enforced by the express mandate to take care that the laws be faithfully executed, it emphasizes the necessity for including within the executive power as conferred the exclusive power of removal. . . .

It is reasonable to suppose also that, had it been intended to give to Congress power to regulate or control removals in the manner suggested, it would have been included among the specifically enumerated legislative powers in Article I, or in the specified limitations on the executive power in Article II. . . . .The fact that the executive power is given in general terms strengthened by specific terms where emphasis is appropriate, and limited by direct expressions where limitation is needed and that no express limit is placed on the power of removal by the executive, is a convincing indication that none was intended.

Made responsible under the Constitution for the effective enforcement of the law, the President needs as an indispensable aid to meet it the disciplinary influence upon those who act under him of a reserve power of removal. But it is contended that executive officers appointed by the President with the consent of the Senate are bound by the statutory law and are not his servants to do his will, and that his obligation to care for the faithful execution of the laws does not authorize him to treat them as such. The degree of guidance in the discharge of their duties that the President may exercise over executive officers varies with the character of their service as prescribed in the law under which they act. The highest and most important duties which his subordinates perform are those in which they act for him. In such cases they are exercising not their own but his discretion. This field is a very large one. It is sometimes described as political. Each head of a department is and must be the President's alter ego in the matters of that department where the President is required by law to exercise authority. . . .

In all such cases, the discretion to be exercised is that of the President in determining the national public interest and in directing the action to be taken by his executive subordinates to protect it. In this field his cabinet officers must do his will. He must place in each member of his official family, and his chief executive subordinates, implicit faith. The moment that he loses confidence in the intelligence, ability, judgment or loyalty of any one of them he must have the power to remove him without delay. To require him to file charges and submit them to the consideration of the Senate might make impossible that unity and coordination in executive administration essential to effective action.

The duties of the heads of departments and bureaus in which the discretion of the President is exercised and which we have described, are the most important in the whole field of executive action of the Government. There is nothing in the Constitution which permits a distinction between the removal of the head of a department or a bureau, when he discharges a political duty of the President or exercises his discretion, and the removal of executive officers engaged in the discharge of their other normal duties. The imperative reasons requiring an unrestricted power to remove the most important of his subordinates in their most important duties must, therefore, control the interpretation of the Constitution as to all appointed by him. . . .

We come now to consider an argument advanced and strongly pressed on behalf of the complainant, that this case concerns only the removal of a postmaster; that a postmaster is an inferior officer; that such an office was not included within the legislative decision of 1789, which related only to superior officers to be appointed by the President by and with the advice and consent of the Senate. . . .

The power to remove inferior executive officers, like that to remove superior executive officers, is an incident of the power to appoint them, and is in its nature an executive power. The authority of Congress given by the excepting clause to vest the appointment of such inferior officers in the heads of departments carries with it authority incidentally to invest the heads of departments with power to remove. It has been the practice of Congress to do so and this Court has recognized that power. The Court also has recognized . . . that Congress, in committing the appointment of such inferior officers to the heads of departments, may prescribe incidental regulations controlling and restricting the latter in the exercise of the power of removal. But the Court never has held, nor reasonably could hold, although it is argued to the contrary on behalf of the appellant, that the excepting clause enables Congress to draw to itself, or to either branch of it, the power to remove or the right to participate in the exercise of that power. To do this would be to go beyond the words and implications of that clause and to infringe the constitutional principle of the separation of governmental powers.

Assuming then the power of Congress to regulate removals as incidental to the exercise of its constitutional power to vest appointments of inferior officers in the heads of departments, certainly so long as Congress does not exercise that power, the power of removal must remain where the Constitution places it, with the President, as part of the executive power, in accordance with the legislative decision of 1789 which we have been considering. . . .

Our conclusion . . . is that Article II grants to the President the executive power of the Government, i.e., the general administrative control of those executing the laws, including the power of appointment and removal of executive officers -- a conclusion confirmed by his obligation to take care that the laws be faithfully executed; that Article II excludes the exercise of legislative power by Congress to provide for appointments and removals, except only as granted therein to Congress in the matter of inferior offices; that Congress is only given power to provide for appointments and removals of inferior officers after it has vested, and on condition that it does vest, their appointment in other authority than the President with the Senate's consent; that the provisions of the second section of Article II, which blend action by the legislative branch, or by part of it, in the work of the executive, are limitations to be strictly construed and not to be extended by implication; that the President's power of removal is further established as an incident to his specifically enumerated function of appointment by and with the advice of the Senate, but that such incident does not by implication extend to removals the Senate's power of checking appointments; and finally that to hold otherwise would make it impossible for the President, in case of political or other differences with the Senate or Congress, to take care that the laws be faithfully executed. . . .

An argument *ab inconvenienti* has been made against our conclusion in favor of the executive power of removal by the President, without the consent of the Senate -- that it will open the door to a reintroduction of the spoils system. The evil of the spoils system aimed at in the civil service law and its amendments is in respect of inferior offices. It has never been attempted to extend that law beyond them. Indeed, Congress forbids its extension to appointments confirmed by the Senate, except with the consent of the Senate. . . . The independent power of removal by the President alone, under present conditions, works no practical interference with the merit system. Political appointments of inferior officers are still maintained in one important class, that of the first, second and third class postmasters, collectors of internal revenue, marshals, collectors of customs and other officers of that kind, distributed through the country. They are appointed by the President with the consent of the Senate. It is the intervention of the Senate in their appointment, and not in their removal, which prevents their classification into the merit system. If such appointments were vested in the heads of departments to which they belong, they could be entirely removed from politics, and that is what a number of Presidents have recommended. . . .

For the reasons given, we must therefore hold that the provision of the law of 1876, by which the unrestricted power of removal of first class postmasters is denied to the President, is in violation of the Constitution, and invalid. . . .

Judgment affirmed.

MR. JUSTICE HOLMES, dissenting

. . . .

The arguments drawn from the executive power of the President, and from his duty to appoint officers of the United States (when Congress does not vest the appointment elsewhere), to take care that the laws be faithfully executed, and to commission all officers of the United States, seem to me spider's webs inadequate to control the dominant facts

We have to deal with an office that owes its existence to Congress and that Congress may abolish tomorrow. Its duration and the pay attached to it while it lasts depend on Congress alone. Congress alone confers on the President the power to appoint to it and at any time may transfer the power to other hands. With such power over its own creation, I have no more trouble in believing that Congress has power to prescribe a term of life for it free from any interference than I have in accepting the undoubted power of Congress to decree its end. I have equally little trouble in accepting its power to prolong the tenure of an incumbent until Congress or the Senate shall have assented to his removal. The duty of the President to see that the laws be executed is a duty that does not go beyond the laws or require him to achieve more than Congress sees fit to leave within his power.

The separate opinion of MR. JUSTICE McREYNOLDS.

. . . . .

Nothing short of language clear beyond serious disputation should be held to clothe the President with authority wholly beyond congressional control arbitrarily to dismiss every officer whom he appoints except a few judges. There are no such words in the Constitution, and the asserted inference conflicts with the heretofore accepted theory that this government is one of carefully enumerated powers under an intelligible charter. . .

If the phrase "executive power" infolds the one now claimed, many others heretofore totally unsuspected may lie there awaiting future supposed necessity; and no human intelligence can define the field of the President's permissible activities. "A masked battery of constructive powers would complete the destruction of liberty."

. . . . The legislature is charged with the duty of making laws for orderly administration obligatory upon all. It possesses supreme power over national affairs and may wreck as well as speed them. It holds the purse; every branch of the government functions under statutes which embody its will; it may impeach and expel all civil officers. The duty is upon it "to make all laws which shall be necessary and proper for carrying into execution" all powers of the federal government. We have no such thing as three totally distinct and independent departments; the others must look to the legislative for direction and support. "In republican government the legislative authority necessarily predominates." Perhaps the chief duty of the President is to carry into effect the will of Congress through such instrumentalities as it has chosen to provide. Arguments, therefore, upon the assumption that Congress may willfully impede executive action are not important.

. . . . Generally, the actual ouster of an officer is executive action; but to prescribe the conditions under which this may be done is legislative. The act of hanging a criminal is executive; but to say when and where and how he shall be hanged is clearly legislative. . . .

. . . . It is well to emphasize that our present concern is with the removal of an "inferior officer," within Art. II, Sec. 2, of the Constitution, which the statute positively prohibits without consent of the Senate. This is no case of mere suspension. The demand is for salary and not for restoration to the service. We are not dealing with an ambassador, public minister, consul, judge or "superior officer." Nor is the situation the one which arises when the statute creates an office without a specified term, authorizes appointment and says nothing of removal. In the latter event, under long-continued practice and supposed early legislative construction, it is now accepted doctrine that the President may remove at pleasure. This is entirely consistent with implied legislative assent; power to remove is commonly incident to the right to appoint when not forbidden by law. . . .

MR. JUSTICE BRANDEIS, dissenting.

. . . .

The contention that Congress is powerless to make consent of the Senate a condition of removal by the President from an executive office rests mainly upon the clause in § 1 of Article II which declares that "The executive Power shall be vested in a President." The argument is that appointment and removal of officials are executive prerogatives. . . . The simple answer to the argument is this: The ability to remove a subordinate executive officer, being an essential of effective government, will, in the absence of express constitutional provision to the contrary, be deemed to have been vested in some person or body. . . . But it is not a power inherent in a chief executive. The President's power of removal from statutory civil inferior offices, like the power of appointment to them, comes immediately from Congress. . . . [T]he Constitution has confessedly granted to Congress the legislative power to create offices, and to prescribe the tenure thereof; and it has not in terms denied to Congress the power to control removals. . . .

It is also argued that the clauses in Article II, § 3, of the Constitution, which declare that the President "shall take Care that the Laws be faithfully executed, and shall Commission all the Officers of the United States" imply a grant to the

President of the alleged uncontrollable power of removal. I do not find in either cause anything which supports this claim. . . . There is no express grant to the President of incidental powers resembling those conferred upon Congress by clause 18 of Article I, § 8. A power implied on the ground that it is inherent in the executive, must, according to established principles of constitutional construction, be limited to "the least possible power adequate to the end proposed." . . . The end to which the President's efforts are to be directed is not the most efficient civil service conceivable, but the faithful execution of the laws consistent with the provisions therefore made by Congress. . . . Power to remove, as well as to suspend, a high political officer, might conceivably be deemed indispensable to democratic government and, hence, inherent in the President. But power to remove an inferior administrative officer appointed for a fixed term cannot conceivably be deemed an essential of government.

To imply a grant to the President of the uncontrollable power of removal from statutory inferior executive offices involves an unnecessary and indefensible limitation upon the constitutional power of Congress to fix the tenure of inferior statutory offices. . . .Checks and balances were established in order that this should be "a government of laws and not of men." [A]n uncontrollable power of removal in the Chief Executive "is a doctrine not to be learned in American governments." . . . The doctrine of the separation of powers was adopted by the Convention of 1787, not to promote efficiency but to preclude the exercise of arbitrary power. . . . In order to prevent arbitrary executive action, the Constitution provided in terms that presidential appointments be made with the consent of the Senate, unless Congress should otherwise provide. . . .

———————

1. Flip the arguments in the case: Can *Myers* be read as a reflection of Chief Justice Taft's unease with congressional patronage and the spoils system? Presidential power to remove administrative officials, unconditionally, eliminated a role that seemingly provided political opportunity to members of Congress. Take a quick look at the full opinion (an admittedly difficult task since it covers over 200 pages in the U.S. REPORTS) and you will notice that the Court addresses the political issue as if it had never surfaced before, perhaps to give room for Taft's expansive opinion. The Chief Justice journeys through the FEDERALIST PAPERS and other sources to support his conclusion that removal is clearly an executive function, a conclusion that just might be based on Taft's prior role – as President of the United States. Taft was determined to implement the agenda of the Progressives but his inclination was to do so by executive (administrative) action, not by cajoling or relying on Congress.

Although *Myers* involved an executive officer appointed with the advice and consent of the Senate, Chief Justice Taft's reasoning appears to support a much broader reading. In particular, his insistence that Congress may leave itself no role in the removal process strongly suggests that the President must be able to remove all officers he appointed with the advice and consent of the Senate. Given that the President must appoint all superior officers, and that Chief Justice Taft was not prepared to allow Congress to have any role in the removal of such officers, it follows that if the President cannot remove them, then no one can.

Steven Breker-Cooper, *The Appointments Clause and the Removal Power: Theory and Séance*, 60 Tenn. L. Rev. 841, 868-69 (1993).

2. The removal question deserves the attention it has received over the last century. Most agree that the matter cannot be resolved unequivocally by the text of the Constitution. "The problem inherent in determining removal authority, implicating as it did the larger question of who was to control the government – Congress or the President, could not have been solved by the founding fathers; thus they left the issue to future political decisionmaking, not judicial determination." Theodore Y. Blumoff, *Illusions of Constitutional Decisionmaking: Politics and the Tenure Powers in the Court*, 73 Iowa L. Rev. 1079, 1085 (1988). Cases before *Myers* provided little clarity. *See Parsons v. United States*, 167 U.S. 324 (1897) (removal required implied consent by the Senate); *McAllister v. United States*, 141 U.S. 174 (1891) (for quasi-judicial appointments, senatorial participation is a required component of removal). For Taft, such notions were deeply problematic. From his perspective, the executive must be free of coercive influence from the other branches of government. Only those who reflect the perspective of the President should be in positions of power – and those who do not share that perspective must be removed unless there is clear legislation to the contrary.

3. How much was actually at stake in *Myers*? Do you think the postmaster of Portland was a major player in national politics? Should it matter? If your answer is that, with all due deference to Oregonians, the officer in question was not likely to affect national policy, was this really about nothing but patronage? Alternatively, was the majority opinion driven by the realization that Congress was quite

For More Information

For more reading on *Myers*, take a look at: Richard H. Pildes, *Separation of Powers, Independent Agencies, and Financial Regulation: The Case of the Sarbanes-Oxley Act*, 5 N.Y.U. J. L. & Bus. 485 (2009); *Note, Congressional Restrictions on the President's Appointment Power and the Role of Longstanding Practice in Constitutional Interpretation*, 120 Harv. L. Rev. 1914, 1916 (2007); Marshall J. Breger & Gary J. Edles, *Established By Practice: The Theory and Operation of Independent Federal Agencies*, 52 Admin. L. Rev. 1111 (2000); and, *Appointment and Removal Under the Federal Constitution: The Impact of Buckley v. Valeo*, 22 Wayne L. Rev. 1335 (1976).

capable of expediting or destroying White House initiatives and executive power had to be asserted? This interpretation is somewhat consistent with Holmes' dissent which reflects basic republicanism – in the end, Congress is the dominant branch and should not be excluded from engagement in decisions that might be the result of executive fiat. However you see the case, our real concern is in appreciating the tension between Congress and the Presidency. For background reading, see, Elizabeth Magill, *The Real Separation in Separation of Powers Law*, 86 Va. L. Rev. 1127 (2000); Neal Devins, *Political Will and the Unitary Executive: What Makes an Independent Agency Independent?*, 15 CARDOZO L. REV. 273 (1993); Lawrence Lessig & Cass R. Sunstein, *The President and the Administration*, 94 COLUM. L. REV. 1 (1994); and Peter L. Strauss, *The Place of Agencies in Government: Separation of Powers and the Fourth Branch*, 84 COLUM. L. REV. 573, (1984).

4. Does *Myers* suggest an executive/independent agency distinction regarding removal of officials? It is an older case – but not older than the Interstate Commerce Commission (1887) and the Federal Trade Commission (1914). Independence, *i.e.*, freedom from political meddling, was central to those independent agencies, something Chief Justice Taft knew intimately. Why, then, the somewhat overreaching assertion of executive power in *Myers*? During the 1970s and 1980s, the issue resurfaced in a very different way and boiled down to a question of the role of the President as a direct participant in central matters pertaining to the administrative state. See Peter P. Swire, Note, *Incorporation of Independent Agencies into the Executive Branch*, 94 YALE L.J. (1985); Strauss, *The Place of Agencies in Government: Separation of Powers and the Fourth Branch*, 84 COLUM. L. REV. 573 (1984); Bernstein, *The Presidential Role in Administrative Rulemaking: Improving Policy Directives: One Vote for Not Tying the President's Hands*, 57 TUL. L. REV. 818 (1982); and Cutler & Johnson, *Regulation and the Political Process*, 84 YALE L.J. 1395 (1975). The question of presidential power is, once again, central to the administrative law discourse. Removal is but one vista to understand the tension in the field. Consider the language of Executive Orders 12896 (3 C.F.R. 638 (1994)), reprinted at 5 U.S.C. § 601 (2000), and 13422 (Exec. Order No. 13,422, 72 Fed. Reg. 2763 issued Jan. 18, 2007), the dominant regulatory directives of the last two decades. Both demand allegiance to White House policy – and both raise questions of agency independence.

———

Hypothetical

At most state law schools, employment contracts for faculty are the result of a negotiation between the dean (the executive) and the prospective faculty member. However, there is an essential "advice and consent" process whereby those seeking fulltime, tenure-track positions are reviewed by a faculty hiring committee and often the full faculty (the legislature). In the absence of approval through the committee and faculty, offers cannot be made by the dean. Assume a new dean takes office and wants to hire faculty who will carry forward the dean's pedagogical and scholarly agenda. There are no open faculty lines or "slots" to be filled on the faculty – and none are expected for some years to come. Can the new dean "free up slots" by firing current faculty who write and teach in fields the new dean does not value? Putting aside academic freedom issues, solely as a matter of administration, can you imagine a scenario where a new dean would have that power? How would your answer vary in the absence of tenure? What if a school does not have formalized tenure and academic freedom is "protected" by having faculty appointments for a term of years (*e.g.*, seven-year terminable or renewable contracts). Can a new dean remove faculty in their third or fourth year if they write and teach in fields the new dean does not value?

HUMPHREY'S EXECUTOR v. UNITED STATES

295 U.S. 602 (1935)

[JUSTICE SUTHERLAND]

. . . .

William E. Humphrey, the decedent, on December 10, 1931, was nominated by President Hoover to succeed himself as a member of the Federal Trade Commission, and was confirmed by the United States Senate. He was duly commissioned for a term of seven years expiring September 25, 1938; and, after taking the required oath of office, entered upon his duties. On July 25, 1933, President Roosevelt addressed a letter to the commissioner asking for his resignation, on the ground "that the aims and purposes of the Administration with respect to the work of the Commission can be carried out most effectively with personnel of my own selection," but disclaiming any reflection upon the commissioner personally or upon his services. The commissioner replied, asking time to consult his friends. After some further correspondence upon the subject, the President on August 31, 1933, wrote the commissioner expressing the hope that the resignation would be forthcoming and saying:

"You will, I know, realize that I do not feel that your mind and my mind go along together on either the policies or the administering of the Federal Trade Commission, and, frankly, I think it is best for the people of this country that I should have a full confidence."

The commissioner declined to resign; and on October 7, 1933, the President wrote him:

"Effective as of this date you are hereby removed from the office of Commissioner of the Federal Trade Commission."

Humphrey never acquiesced in this action, but continued thereafter to insist that he was still a member of the commission, entitled to perform its duties and receive the compensation provided by law at the rate of $10,000 per annum. . . .

The Federal Trade Commission Act creates a commission of five members to be appointed by the President by and with the advice and consent of the Senate, and § 1 provides: ". . . Any commissioner may be removed by the President for inefficiency, neglect of duty, or malfeasance in office. . . ."

. . . . The statute fixes a term of office, in accordance with many precedents. The first commissioners appointed are to continue in office for terms of three, four, five, six, and seven years, respectively; and their successors are to be appointed for terms of seven years -- any commissioner being subject to removal by the President for inefficiency, neglect of duty, or malfeasance in office. The words of the act are definite and unambiguous.

The government says the phrase "continue in office" is of no legal significance and, moreover, applies only to the first commissioners. We think it has significance. It may be that literally, its application is restricted as suggested; but it, nevertheless, lends support to a view contrary to that of the government as to the meaning of the entire requirement in respect of tenure; for it is not easy to suppose that Congress intended to secure the first commissioners against removal except for the causes specified and deny like security to their successors. Putting this phrase aside, however, the fixing of a definite term subject to removal for cause, unless there be some countervailing provision or circumstance indicating the contrary, which here we are unable to find, is enough to establish the legislative intent that the term is not to be curtailed in the absence of such cause. . . .

The commission is to be non-partisan; and it must, from the very nature of its duties, act with entire impartiality. It is charged with the enforcement of no policy except the policy of the law. Its duties are neither political nor executive, but predominantly quasi-judicial and quasi-legislative. Like the Interstate Commerce Commission, its members are called upon to exercise the trained judgment of a body of experts "appointed by law and informed by experience."

The legislative reports in both houses of Congress clearly reflect the view that a fixed term was necessary to the effective and fair administration of the law. . . .

[From the legislative history:] "The work of this commission will be of a most exacting and difficult character demanding persons who have experience in the problems to be met -- that is, a proper knowledge of both the public requirements and the practical affairs of industry. It is manifestly desirable that the terms of the commissioners shall be long enough to give them an opportunity to acquire the expertness in dealing with these special questions concerning industry that comes from experience."

The report declares that one advantage which the commission possessed over the Bureau of Corporations (an executive subdivision in the Department of Commerce which was abolished by the act) lay in the fact of its independence, and that it was essential that the commission should not be open to the suspicion of partisan direction. The report quotes a statement to the committee by Senator Newlands, who reported the bill, that the tribunal should be of high character and "independent of any department of the government.... a board or commission of dignity, permanence, and ability, independent of executive authority, except in its selection, and independent in character."

The debates in both houses demonstrate that the prevailing view was that the commission was not to be "subject to anybody in the government but... only to the people of the United States"; free from "political domination or control" or the "probability or possibility of such a thing"; to be "separate and apart from any existing department of the government -- not subject to the orders of the President."

More to the same effect appears in the debates, which were long and thorough and contain nothing to the contrary. . . .

Thus, the language of the act the legislative reports, and the general purposes of the legislation as reflected by the debates, all combine demonstrate the Congressional intent to create a body of experts who shall gain experience by length of service -- a body which shall be independent of executive authority, except in its selection, and free to exercise its judgment without the leave or hindrance of any other official or any department of the government. To the accomplishment of these purposes, it is clear that Congress was of opinion that length and certainty of tenure would vitally contribute. And to hold that, nevertheless, the members of the commission continue in office at the mere will of the President, might be to thwart, in large measure, the very ends which Congress sought to realize by definitely fixing the term of office.

We conclude that the intent of the act is to limit the executive power of removal to the causes enumerated, the existence of none of which is claimed here. . . .

To support its contention that the removal provision of § 1, as we have just construed it, is an unconstitutional interference with the executive power of the President, the government's chief reliance is *Myers v. United States*. That case has been so recently decided, and the prevailing and dissenting opinions so fully review the general subject of the power of executive removal, that further discussion would add little of value to the wealth of material there collected. . . . Nevertheless, the narrow point actually decided was only that the President had power to remove a postmaster of the first class, without the advice and consent of the Senate as required by act of Congress. In the course of the opinion of the court, expressions occur which tend to sustain the government's contention, but these are beyond the point involved and, therefore, do not come within the rule of *stare decisis*. In so far as they are out of harmony with the views here set forth, these expressions are disapproved. . . .

The office of a postmaster is so essentially unlike the office now involved that the decision in the *Myers* case cannot be accepted as controlling our decision here. A postmaster is an executive officer restricted to the performance of executive functions. He is charged with no duty at all related to either the legislative or judicial power. The actual decision in the Myers case finds support in the theory that such an officer is merely one of the units in the executive department and, hence, inherently subject to the exclusive and illimitable power of removal by the Chief Executive, whose subordinate and aid he is. Putting aside dicta, which may be followed if sufficiently persuasive but which are not controlling, the necessary reach of the decision goes far enough to include all purely executive officers. It goes no farther; -- much less does it include an officer who occupies no place in the executive department and who exercises no part of the executive power vested by the Constitution in the President.

The Federal Trade Commission is an administrative body created by Congress to carry into effect legislative policies embodied in the statute in accordance with the legislative standard therein prescribed, and to perform other specified duties as a legislative or as a judicial aid. Such a body cannot in any proper sense be characterized as an arm or an eye of the executive. Its duties are performed without executive leave and, in the contemplation of the statute, must be free from executive control. In administering the provisions of the statute in respect of "unfair methods of competition" -- that is to say in filling in and administering the details embodied by that general standard -- the commission acts in part quasi-legislatively and in part quasi-judicially. In making investigations and reports thereon for the information of Congress under § 6, in aid of the legislative power, it acts as a legislative agency. Under § 7, which authorizes the commission to act as a master in chancery under rules prescribed by the court, it acts as an agency of the judiciary. To the extent that it exercises any executive function -- as distinguished from executive power in the constitutional sense -- it does so in the discharge and effectuation of its quasi-legislative or quasi-judicial powers, or as an agency of the legislative or judicial departments of the government.

If Congress is without authority to prescribe causes for removal of members of the trade commission and limit executive power of removal accordingly, that power at once becomes practically all-inclusive in respect of civil officers with the exception of the judiciary provided for by the Constitution. The Solicitor General, at the bar, apparently recognizing this to be true, with commendable candor, agreed that his view in respect of the removability of members of the Federal Trade Commission necessitated a like view in respect of the Interstate Commerce Commission and the Court of Claims. We are thus confronted with the serious question whether not only the members of these quasi-legislative and quasi-judicial bodies, but the judges of the legislative Court of Claims, exercising judicial power continue in office only at the pleasure of the President.

We think it plain under the Constitution that illimitable power of removal is not possessed by the President in respect of officers of the character of those just named. The authority of Congress, in creating quasi-legislative or quasi-judicial agencies, to require them to act in discharge of their duties independently of executive control cannot well be doubted; and that authority includes, as an appropriate incident, power to fix the period during which they shall continue in office, and to forbid their removal except for cause in   the meantime. For it is quite evident that one who holds his office only during the pleasure of another, cannot be depended upon to maintain an attitude of independence against the latter's will.

The fundamental necessity of maintaining each of the three general departments of government entirely free from the control or coercive influence, direct or indirect, of either of the others, has often been stressed and is hardly open to serious question. . . .

The power of removal here claimed for the President falls within this principle, since its coercive influence threatens the independence of a commission, which is not only wholly disconnected from the executive department, but which, as already fully appears, was created by Congress as a means of carrying into operation legislative and judicial powers, and as an agency of the legislative and judicial departments.

. . . .The result of what we now have said is this: Whether the power of the President to remove an officer shall prevail over the authority of Congress to condition the power by fixing a definite term and precluding a removal except for cause, will depend upon the character of the office; the *Myers* decision, affirming the power of the President alone to make the removal, is confined to purely executive officers; and as to officers of the kind here under consideration, we hold that no removal can be made during the prescribed term for which the officer is appointed, except for one or more of the causes named in the applicable statute.

To the extent that, between the decision in the *Myers* case, which sustains the unrestrictable power of the President to remove purely executive officers, and our present decision that such power does not extend to an office such as that here involved, there shall remain a field of doubt, we leave such cases as may fall within it for future consideration and determination as they may arise.

———————————

1. How much of *Myers* remains after *Humphrey's*? Do you agree with the following assessment?

> [L]ess than a decade after *Myers*, the Supreme Court in *Humphrey's Executor* set forth a significantly narrower vision of presidential power in which the President's Article II managerial authority does not include supervisory power over congressionally delegated administrative authority. In *Myers*, the Court used language to suggest that the authority delegated to the executive branch inheres to the President. The Supreme Court in *Humphrey's Executor*, however, appeared to view administrative agencies as constitutionally independent from the Executive or perhaps even as arms or extensions of Congress. Agencies might be arms of Congress, according to the Court, at least in their exercise of what the Court termed the "quasi-legislative" or "quasi-judicial" administrative authority of the modern regulatory agency.

Yvette M. Barksdale, *The Presidency and Administrative Value Selection*, 42 AM. U.L. REV. 273, 290-92 (1993).

Assuming the above characterization, are independent agencies legislative? How can that be if the President retains the power of appointment, the power to set an agency agenda, and, by executive order, the power to determine what rules the agency may or may not issue?

2. Was *Humphrey's Executor* driven by the necessity of complete political indepen-dence of decisionmakers, other than those in "executive" agencies?

> *Myers* temporarily established that the President could remove executive officers even when he could not direct their decisions. . . . It was *Myers'* short-lived dogma concerning presidential removal that the Court overcame in *Humphrey's Executor* when it recognized that an officer subject to presidential removal without cause cannot be expected to exercise independent judgment. By the time of the decision in *Wiener* [the next case in this text], the notion that an officer subject to presidential removal would be completely free from presidential direction was rejected. In *Wiener*, Justice Frankfurter described the need for an officer to be free from removal in order to be completely independent from direction on particular decisions as "*a fortiori*" in its certainty.

Charles Tiefer, *The Constitutionality of Independent Officers as Checks on Abuses of Executive Power*, 63 B.U.L. REV. 59, 96-97 (1983).

A similar perspective is found in David M. Driesen, *Toward a Duty-Based Theory of Executive Power*, 78 FORDHAM L. REV. 71, 119 (2009): "In *Humphrey's Executor v. United States* and *Wiener v. United States*, the Supreme Court distinguished and to some extent repudiated *Myers's* unitary *dicta*, in order to uphold the practice of insulating independent agencies exercising quasi-judicial and quasi-legislative powers."

3. How much of your comparison translates into a "formalism vs. functional-ism" discussion? Is *Humphrey's* simply a functionalist approach to the tasks of governance? Compare:

> a. Theodore Y. Blumoff, *Illusions of Constitutional Decisionmaking: Politics and the Tenure Powers in the Court*, 73 IOWA L. REV. 1079, n. 613 (1988): "The Taftian taxonomy is unworkable. One cannot operate a government based upon rigidly defined conceptions of governing functions."

> b. Thomas O. Sargentich, *BOWSHER V. SYNAR: The Contemporary Debate About Legislative-Executive Separation of Powers*, 72 CORNELL L. REV. 430, 463-64 (1987):

>> While moving away from *Myers'* institutional formalism, *Humphrey's* Executor does not abandon the theory [of formalism] completely. The very idea of "quasi-legislative" power, for instance, depends on the concept of a "legislative" role. The qualifier cannot obscure reliance on underlying categories that are themselves called into question by the qualification. *Humphrey's Executor* ultimately retained the supposition that governmental entities have substantive essences which depend on their role in the creation and implementation of law. To this extent, the formalist conception retains a lingering hold on the doctrine.

> c. Peter P. Swire, Note, *Incorporation of Independent Agencies into the Executive Branch*, 94 YALE L.J. 1766, 1768 (1985): "The decision of *Humphrey's Executor* was part of

a major shift to functionalism after 1935. The Supreme Court relaxed the *Myers* rule that all governmental actions had to fit into one of the three formal boxes of legislative, executive, or judicial action."

4. *Humphrey's* seemingly deprives the plenary power of the President to remove officials who are "out of step" with the administration. What if an official is both "out of step" and somewhat ineffective? Takes an unusually long time to make decisions? Misunderstands the holdings of important Supreme Court cases? A term of years can provide protection from undue political influence and aid in independent thinking – but can it also shield incompetence? There is a "good cause" exception that allows the President

> to remove [administrative officials] in certain circumstances. . . . [T]he words good cause and inefficiency, neglect of duty, or malfeasance in office seem best read to grant the President at least something in the way of supervisory and removal power – allowing him, for example, to discharge, as inefficient or neglectful of duty, those commissioners who show lack of diligence, ignorance, incompetence, or lack of commitment to their legal duties.

Lawrence Lessig and Cass R. Sunstein, *The President and The Administration*, 94 COLUM. L. REV. 1, 111(1994).

Hypothetical

Assume that both houses of Congress are controlled by a party different from that of the President, and that the leadership of the House of Representatives and of the Senate have lost confidence in the Secretary of State. They arrange to pass a resolution in both the House and the Senate directing the President to remove the incumbent "in light of the irreconcilably deteriorated relationship between the Secretary and this Congress." Is the President required to abide by such a bicameral resolution? If not, by what other means could Congress take action against the Secretary of State? Note: Skip ahead and take a sneak peek at *Chadha*. We, your authors, do not think *Chadha* resolves this problem.

---

5. In 2009 Professor Sunstein (co-author of the article excerpted above) was named Administrator of the Office of Information and Regulatory Affairs, the primary "voice" of regulatory policy of a presidential administration. Professor Sunstein notes in that 1994 article that "[t]he statutory words [good cause] might even allow discharge of commissioners who have frequently or on important occasions acted in ways inconsistent with the President's wishes with respect to what is required by sound policy." *Id*. Doesn't that perspective cut at the core

values of *Humphrey's*? The protection *Humphrey's* anticipated is illusory if one can be fired for making a decision consistent with a statute but not consistent with the "President's wishes."

6. If there was much doubt about the position of the Court regarding the necessity for those in quasi-adjudicatory roles to be free from a White House pressures expressed in terms of job-security, at least at independent agencies, that doubt was resolved in *Wiener v. United States*.

WIENER v. UNITED STATES

357 U.S. 349 (1957)

[JUSTICE FRANKFURTER]

This is a suit for back pay, based on petitioner's alleged illegal removal as a member of the War Claims Commission. The facts are not in dispute. By the War Claims Act of 1948, Congress established that Commission with "jurisdiction to receive and adjudicate according to law," § 3, claims for compensating internees, prisoners of war, and religious organizations, §§ 5, 6 and 7, who suffered personal injury or property damage at the hands of the enemy in connection with World War II. The Commission was to be composed of three persons, at least two of whom were to be members of the bar, to be appointed by the President, by and with the advice and consent of the Senate. The Commission was to wind up its affairs not later than three years after the expiration of the time for filing claims. . . .

Having been duly nominated by President Truman, the petitioner was confirmed on June 2, 1950, and took office on June 8, following. On his refusal to heed a request for his resignation, he was, on December 10, 1953, removed by President Eisenhower. . . .The following day, the President made recess appointments to the Commission, including petitioner's post. . . .Thereupon, petitioner brought this proceeding in the Court of Claims for recovery of his salary as a War Claims Commissioner. . . .We brought the case here, because it presents a variant of the constitutional issue decided in Humphrey's Executor v. United States, 295 U.S. 602 [and Myers].

[In Myers, the Court] announced that the President had inherent constitutional power of removal also of officials who have "duties of a quasi-judicial character . . . whose decisions after hearing affect interests of individuals, the discharge of which the President can not in a particular case properly influence or control." . . .

The assumption was short-lived that the Myers case recognized the President's inherent constitutional power to remove officials, no matter what the relation of the executive to the discharge of their duties and no matter what restrictions Congress may have imposed regarding the nature of their tenure. . . . Within less than ten years a unanimous Court, in Humphrey's Executor v. United States, narrowly confined the scope of the Myers decision to include only "all purely executive officers." The Court explicitly "disapproved" the expressions in Myers supporting the President's inherent constitutional power to remove members of quasi-judicial bodies. . . . In the present case, Congress provided for a tenure defined by the relatively short period of time during which the War Claims Commission was to operate -- that is, it was to wind up not later than three years after the expiration of the time for filing of claims. But nothing was said in the Act about removal.

     . . . . We start with one certainty. The problem of the President's power to remove members of agencies entrusted with duties of the kind with which the War Claims Commission was charged was within the lively knowledge of Congress. . . . Humphrey's case was a cause celebre -- and not least in the halls of Congress. And what is the essence of the decision in Humphrey's case? It drew a sharp line of cleavage between officials who were part of the Executive establishment and were thus removable by virtue of the President's constitutional powers, and those who are members of a body "to exercise its judgment without the leave or hindrance of any other official or any department of the government," as to whom a power of removal exists only if Congress may fairly be said to have conferred it. This sharp differentiation derives from the difference in functions between those who are part of the Executive establishment and those whose tasks require absolute freedom from Executive interference. "For it is quite evident," again to quote Humphrey's Executor, "that one who holds his office only during the pleasure of another, cannot be depended upon to maintain an attitude of independence against the latter's will."

Thus, the most reliable factor for drawing an inference regarding the President's power of removal in our case is the nature of the function that Congress vested in the War Claims Commission. What were the duties that Congress confided to this Commission? And can the inference fairly be drawn from the failure of Congress to provide for removal that these Commissioners were to remain in office at the will of the President? For such is the assertion of power on which petitioner's removal must rest. The ground of President Eisenhower's removal of petitioner was precisely the same as President Roosevelt's removal of Humphrey. Both Presidents desired to have Commissioners, one on the Federal Trade Commission, the other on the War Claims Commission, "of my own selection." They wanted these Commissioners to be their men. The terms of removal in the two cases are identical and express the assumption that the agencies of which the two Commissioners were members were subject in the discharge of their duties to the control of the Executive. An analysis of the Federal Trade Commission Act left this Court in no doubt that such was not the conception of Congress in creating the Federal Trade Commission. The terms of the War Claims Act of 1948 leave no doubt that such was not the conception of Congress regarding the War Claims Commission.

. . . . Congress could, of course, have given jurisdiction over these claims to the District Courts or to the Court of Claims. The fact that it chose to establish a Commission to "adjudicate according to law" the classes of claims defined in the statute did not alter the intrinsic judicial character of the task with which the Commission was charged. The claims were to be "adjudicated according to law," that is, on the merits of each claim, supported by evidence and governing legal considerations, by a body that was "entirely free from the control or coercive influence, direct or indirect," *Humphrey's Executor v. United States,* either the Executive or the Congress. If, as one must take for granted, the War Claims Act precluded the President from influencing the Commission in passing on a particular claim, a fortiori must it be inferred that Congress did not wish to have hang over the Commission the Damocles' sword of removal by the President for no reason other than that he preferred to have on that Commission men of his own choosing.

. . . . Judging the matter in all the nakedness in which it is presented, namely, the claim that the President could remove a member of an adjudicatory body like the War Claims Commission merely because he wanted his own appointees on such a Commission, we are compelled to conclude that no such power is given to the President directly by the Constitution, and none is impliedly conferred upon him by statute simply because Congress said nothing about it. The philosophy of Humphrey's Executor, in its explicit language as well as its implications, precludes such a claim.

––––––––––

1. *Wiener* could not be more clear: decisionmakers in independent agencies must be free from the "Sword of Damocles" of presidential removal. The position seems perfectly logical and just – after all, we want our decisionmakers to act objectively, free from political pressure or fear. And yet, what is the point of electing a president every four years if changes in personnel are limited? With this backdrop, consider the 2006 remarks of President Bush who explained that decisions of consequence must be made by the President. Said President Bush, "I'm the decider." Ed Henry & Barbara Starr, Bush: "I'm the Decider" on Rumsfeld, CNN.com, Apr. 18, 2006, http://www.cnn.com/2006/POLITICS/04/18/rumsfeld/ (last visited November 29, 2009). The Bush perspective has deep roots. *See* 1 Op. Att'y Gen. 624, 625 (1823) (suggesting that Department Heads were forbidden from acting in a manner at odds with the "will of the President).

a. Do *Humphrey's Executor* and *Wiener* frustrate the ability of a new presidential administration to pursue a path consistent with "the will of the President?" For example, can a newly elected president, on taking office, replace the heads of independent agencies? Consider the following question: can a newly elected President appoint a new Chair at the Consumer Product Safety Commission if the term of the Chair in office (recall that these appointments are for a period of years) has not expired?

b. The original Consumer Product Safety Act provided that the Chair "shall act as Chairman until the expiration of his term of office as a Commissioner." The 1978 amendments (P.L. 95-631, 92 Stat. 3742) raised issues about the exercise of that power. In 2001, the Justice Department's Office of the Legal Counsel issued a memo (*PRESIDENT'S AUTHORITY TO REMOVE THE CHAIRMAN OF THE CONSUMER PRODUCT SAFETY COMMISSION, JULY 31, 2001* authored by John Yoo, then Deputy Assistant Attorney General) on that point proclaiming the presence of an executive power to remove the Chair and appoint a new person to that position. The memo involves, *inter alia, Humphrey's Executor and Wiener.* An excerpted version of the OLC Opinion follows.

> . . . . As head of the executive branch, the President . . . must be able to supervise subordinate officials and to coordinate executive branch policies and positions. *See generally* <u>Myers v. United States, 272 U.S. 52 (1926)</u> [*supra* in this text]. The power to remove is the power to control. . . . As reflected in the great debate over removal in the very first Congress, the Framers rejected a legislative role in removal in favor of plenary presidential power over officers appointed by the President with the advice and consent of the Senate. . . .

> To be sure, the Court has refused to invalidate all limitations on presidential authority over all executive branch officials. In *Humphrey's Executor v. United States*, 295 U.S. 602 (1935) [*supra* in this text] the Court upheld a for-cause removal provision over members of the Federal Trade Commission due to the Commission's "quasi-legislative or quasi-judicial" functions. <u>Id. at 628.</u> In <u>*Wiener v. United States*, 357 U.S. 349 (1958)</u>, [*supra* in this text] the Court inferred the existence of a for-cause limitation on removal, but again because the official in question, a member of the War Claims Commission, performed a quasi-judicial function. . . .In light of these cases, it is clear that the Constitution generally reserves to the President alone the power to remove officials. . . . [T]he statute establishing the CPSC does not include any limitation on the President's power to remove the Chairman. . . .

> . . . . As originally enacted in 1972, [Pub. L. No. 92-573, § 4(a), 86 Stat. 1207, 1210 (1972)] the Consumer Product Safety Act had stated that [the CPSC will have five ccommissioners]: "[O]*ne of whom shall be designated by the President as Chairman. The Chairman, when so designated shall act as Chairman until the expiration of his term of office as Commissioner.* Any member of the Commission may be removed by the President for neglect of duty or malfeasance in office but for no other cause. . . ."(emphasis added)

In amending the statute in 1978 [Pub. L. No. 95-631, § 2(a), 92 Stat. 3742, 3742 (1978)], Congress clarified the CPSC removal provisions. . . . The statutory language was changed to: *"The Chairman shall be appointed by the President, by and with the advice and consent of the Senate, from among the Members of the Commission. An individual may be appointed as a member of the Commission and as Chairman at the same time.* Any member of the Commission may be removed by the President for neglect of duty or malfeasance in office but for no other cause. (emphasis added).

. . . . In its report on the 1978 Act, the Senate Commerce Committee . . . made clear that the "chairman of the agency shall serve at the pleasure of the President." Consumer Product Safety Act Authorization Act of 1978, Sen. Rep. No. 95-889, 95th Cong., 2d Sess.at 10 (1978). . . . We conclude that the President has the authority to remove the Chairman of the CPSC for *any reason.* . . . [emphasis added]

c. Do you read *Humphrey's Executor* and *Wiener* – or the CPSA language – to permit the removal of the Chair of an independent agency for "any reason?"

2. Presidential power, whether expressed through the removal of agency officials, presidential proclamation, executive orders, or "signing statements," (Michael T. Crabb, *Comment,"The Executive Branch Shall Construe": The Canon of Constitutional Avoidance and the Presidential Signing Statement,* 56 KAN. L. REV. 711 (2008); Chad M. Eggspuehler, *Note, The S-Words Mightier than the Pen: Signing Statements as Express Advocacy of Unlawful Action,* 43 GONZ. L. REV. 461 (2007/2008)) is a matter of great interest in the field. How much change is permissible after an election results in a new president? How does one balance the limits on presidential action in *Wiener* with the constitutional import of a national election?

3. Just how much a president can be a "decider" varies greatly based on the agency involved and also on the goals of the agency officials involved. Consider the following regarding the Food and Drug Administration:

The law permits the President to appoint a Secretary of Health and Human Services. . . . The President also has the power, subject to confirmation by the Senate, to select FDA Commissioners. . . . However, the Commissioners who have been appointed . . . since the Bush Administration arrived in 2001 have held the office for an average tenure of about one year after confirmation. The appointees tend to pursue these jobs only in furtherance of their future careers, gaining appointment with the help of White House insiders who, in turn, seek those candidates most likely to implement the President's policies.

James T. O'Reilly, *Symposium, Losing Deference in the FDA's Second Century: Judicial Review, Politics, and a Diminished Legacy of Expertise,* 93 CORNELL L. REV. 939, 959-60 (2008).

4. Does *Wiener* permit the removal of a U.S. Attorney if the basis for that action is non-conformity with White House priorities? David C. Weiss, Note, *Nothing Improper? Examining Constitutional Limits, Congressional Action, Partisan Motivation,*

and Pretextual Justification in the U.S. Attorney Removals, 107 MICH. L. REV. 317 (2008). Does non-conformity with White House priorities constitute anything close to "good cause"? In *Mistretta v. United States*, 488 U.S. 361 (1989) (*infra* in this text), the Court characterized the power to remove for good cause as a "limited power." Echoing *Humphrey's Executor*, misuse of this power could become a "coercive influence" – language repeated by the Court in *Wiener* (357 U.S. at 355).

Hypothetical

Frustrated by what some Members of Congress have characterized as the White House's profligate disbursement of Federal Emergency Management Agency (FEMA) disaster relief funds, a majority of Congress is considering passing a bill that would grant the Comptroller General (the head of the U.S. Government Accountability Office) the authority to reject any FEMA expenditures. Would such a bill be constitutional?

5. The excerpted article below reflects a current view of the difference between independent and executive agencies from a comparative law perspective. The distinction has been blurred over the last quarter-century. Presidential influence over both types of agencies has been powerful. Nevertheless, as the article excerpt makes clear, the distinction is still of consequence.

Dominique Custos, *The Rulemaking Power of Independent Regulatory Agencies*, 54 AM. J. OF COMP. L. 615 (2006):

I. Definition and Characteristics of Independent Regulatory Agencies (IRAs)

Similar to some European constitutions, the U.S. constitutional text has no provision dealing with independent regulatory agencies. Its "necessary and proper clause" merely confers the authority to create the government on Congress. Apart from a constitutional reference to the cabinet departments, the design of the U.S. federal government is Congress's responsibility. Therefore, the establishment of the category of independent regulatory agencies, at the American federal level, as in European countries, results from legislation.

The definition and characteristics of American independent agencies must be articulated against the backdrop of the structure of the U.S. government. Beside the presidency, the study of the structure of the U.S. government stresses a main distinction between executive regulatory agencies and independent regulatory agencies. The distinction is based primarily on their respective location in the administrative architecture and secondarily on their distinct type of leadership.

The executive agencies are cabinet agencies directly located within one department in the Executive Branch whereas the independent agencies are placed outside such presidential realm. As multi-member agencies, the independent agencies are headed by a college of Commissioners and are otherwise referred to as "commissions". Comparatively, the executive agencies are under the leadership of a single administrator.

The rules governing the appointment and the removal of the Commissioners guarantee their independence. Commissioners are nominated by the President and confirmed by Congress. Bipartisanship, staggered dates and fixed term of appointment, are designed to prevent a perfect political consonance between the President and a given independent agency. Removal of Commissioners is confined to a non political cause, thus making it, at least in principle, impossible for the President to censor or sanction political disagreement.

In light of the two aforementioned criteria, the independent agency is defined as a form of administrative government that is placed outside any cabinet department and under the leadership of a college of Commissioners independent of the President. Such a definition in structural and relational terms must be completed by an inquiry into the functions of the independent agency. Thus amended, the definition becomes: a form of administrative government that is responsible to regulate human activities and is placed outside any cabinet department and under the leadership of a college of Commissioners independent of the President. The significance of the functional dimension of the independent agency must be properly assessed. Historically, it was both an element of definition and, along with location and its oversight implications, a fundamental feature of distinction from the executive agency. Nowadays, it still has a definitional value but it is no more a source of differentiation from the executive agency.

Originally, the independent agency symbolized the vesting in idealized experts of regulatory powers over the economy, that challenged the common law notions of property and contractual freedom, in the name of the public interest. It contrasted with the executive agency which theoretically was confined to managerial tasks and could not venture into decision making as far-reaching and encompassing as congressional action. Accordingly, it was termed the independent regulatory agency. The regulatory mission was translated into "the model of combined-function agency" which makes the rules, investigates, prosecutes, and adjudicates. Nevertheless, de facto, this functional distinction proved not to be fully operational. First, executive agencies carry out regulatory functions also. Second, some independent agencies simultaneously devote a substantial part of their action to non regulatory functions. In other words, it has now become clear that the two institutional categories both carry out regulatory and executive missions and enjoy intermingled powers. Therefore, if as a matter of definition, the independent agency is regulatory, as a matter of differentiation it is not exclusively such.

The original value of the functional criterion as a way to differentiate the then new independent agency from its existing executive counterpart mirrored one of the current criteria of distinction among executive and regulatory agencies in Europe either at the national level or at the European Union level. The difference of historical stratification of the development of independent administrative structures in the U.S. and Europe certainly explains the discrepancy between the American and the

European conceptions. The question raised by this comparative historical perspective is whether Europe will experience another age in the study of regulation whereby the diffusion of the regulatory function across the administrative government will be fully recognized.

Although it reflects the main feature of the American administrative architecture the dual account of the American governmental structure is not quite faithful to the diversity of its forms. Mid-way between the main two categories, exist the independent executive agencies which was pioneered in the 1970s with respect to environmental protection. In other words, beside the independent regulatory agency, there is a second type of independent agency. In both cases, the independent characteristic is based on the lack of location in a cabinet department. But in this second type, the independence is reduced for two reasons. First, the independent executive agency is still part of the Executive branch despite its non incorporation into a department. Second, the independent executive agency is headed by an administrator who can be discharged at will by the President.

For additional caselaw in the field, you might take a look at: *Freytag v. Comm'r*, 501 U.S. 868 (1991); *AFGE v. Gates*, 486 F.3d 1316 (D.C. Cir. 2007); *Nat'l Treasury Employees Union v. Chertoff*, 452 F.3d 839 (D.C. Cir. 2006); *Consumer Energy Council v. FERC*, 673 F.2d 425 (D.C. Cir. 1982). For additional scholarship in the field, you might take a look at: Michael Hertz, *United States v. United States: When Can the Government Sue Itself?*, 32 WM. & MARY L. REV. 893 (1991); Peter L. Strauss, *The Place of Agencies in Government: Separation of Powers and the Fourth Branch*, 84 COLUM. L. REV. 573, 581-96 (1984); Nathaniel Nathanson, *Separation of Powers and Administrative Law: Delegation, the Legislative Veto, and the "Independent" Agencies*, 75 NW. U. L. REV. 1064, 1078 n.55 (1981).

VII. The APA: A Brief Historical Perspective

a. The study of administrative law is, for the most part, a study of process. While the omni-presence of cost-benefit analysis and non-stop political rhetoric regarding deregulation might suggest that the burning questions for lawyers ought to involve the substance – or even the existence – of the regulatory state, most private sector, public interest, trade association, corporate, and government lawyers do not spend their time analyzing why and whether various components of the social order ought to be subjected to agency oversight, sanction, or benefit.

Take Note

The focus of lawyers in this field is on how to represent clients, interests, entities, and the government itself, and therefore on the rules and strategies that must be understood to secure a public or private client's just and best interest. The starting point for the study of administrative process is the Administrative Procedure Act, 5 U.S.C. §§551 et. seq., referred to in this text – and throughout the profession – as the APA.

b. The importance of the APA is not a matter of debate. Some law faculty organize the course in administrative law around sections of the APA. Others use an approach that weaves in and out of the APA – but *all* courses in this field require a basic understanding of the APA. Judges likewise rely on this relatively simple legislation in one way or another in most administrative law cases.

Food for Thought

In a concurring opinion in <u>Bowen v. Georgetown University Hospital</u>, 488 U.S. 204, 216 (1988), JUSTICE SCALIA wrote: "I write separately because I find it incomplete to discuss general principles of administrative law without reference to the basic structural legislation which is the embodiment of those principles, the Administrative Procedure Act (APA), <u>5 U.S.C. §§ 551</u> et. seq. . . . ."

The APA both provides a basic (and in some ways gossamer) structure for agency action as well as setting forth fundamental precepts regarding judicial review of agency action. In <u>Lincoln v. Vigil</u>, 508 U.S. 182, 191 (1993), the Supreme Court summarized the basic APA entitlement to judicial review thusly: "The APA provides that '[a] person suffering legal wrong because of agency action, or adversely affected or aggrieved by agency action within the meaning of a relevant statute, is entitled to judicial review thereof,' <u>5 U.S.C. § 702</u>, and we have read the APA as embodying a 'basic presumption of judicial review,' *Abbott Laboratories v. Gardner*, 387 U.S. 136, 140 (1967). This is 'just' a presumption, however . . . agency action is not subject to judicial review 'to the extent that' such action 'is committed to agency discretion by law.' [Section 701(a) provides:] 'This chapter [relating to judicial review] applies . . . except to the extent that – (1) statutes preclude judicial review; or (2) agency action is committed to agency discretion by law.' . . . ."

c. There are literally thousands of cases in which courts ponder the question of the role, function, and availability of judicial review. In some areas, e.g., immigration, veteran's rights, and public assistance, the pronounced unavailability of judicial review creates controversy and can lead to charges of agency (executive) authoritarianism. In other areas where judicial review is available, courts, again in countless cases, ponder the grand and inevitable separation of powers questions that exist when a judicial decision expresses, clarifies, or articulates for the first time important public policy. After all, Article I of the Constitution does state that Congress is the representative of the people – and presumably the source for policy.

Regardless of the issues such cases discuss, it is a safe assumption that a court is not involved in a matter pertaining to administrative law unless an agency has done something – and what agencies do is almost always affected by the APA (unless Congress has, for its own reason, decided that some other process ought to apply).

d. As with any area of study where a statute plays a central role, it makes sense to explore the circumstances that led to the enactment of the legislation. Fortunately, there a great deal of history available on the APA. First, there is a comprehensive legislative history: S. COMM. ON THE JUDICIARY, S. Doc. No. 248, *reprinted in* THE ADMINISTRATIVE PROCEDURE ACT: LEGISLATIVE HISTORY (1946). In addition, we have provided two excerpts from law review articles that provide some historical context for the APA. The first was written by Professor Walter Gellhorn, one of the scholars who played a lead role in drafting the APA. The second, by Professor George Shepherd, sets out the fascinating political environment in which the APA was formed. We have excised very substantial portions and omitted the footnotes from the articles below. This scholarship is most assuredly best understood and appreciated by careful study of the original text.

e. Walter Gellhorn, *The Administrative Procedure Act: The Beginnings*, 72 VA. L. REV. 219 (1986):

> The story begins in May 1933, when the American Bar Association created a Special Committee on Administrative Law. . . . Within four months, scarcely enough time to allow the committee's membership to do more than contemplate their own navels, the committee was reportedly convinced that the "judicial function" then lodged in administrators' hands should be transferred to an independent tribunal or, alternatively, that officials' decisions should be completely reviewable on the facts as well as on the law by a tribunal marked by judicial independence.
>
> The Special Committee's first formal report and proposal of legislation came in 1934. It was aimed at coping with "the evils notoriously prevalent" among administrative tribunals, which the committee thought would be achieved by creating a federal administrative court with branches and an appellate division, or, failing that, "an appropriate number of independent tribunals" unencumbered by "legislative and executive functions."
>
> Thus began a continuing practice of prescribing a cure-all for the shortcomings, real or imagined, of administrative agencies. That shortcomings did exist is incontrovertible, and some of them were amenable to statutory correction. . . . The Committee seemingly preferred, however, to avoid specifics and instead to generalize in ringingly oratorical terms. The "independent" tribunal proposal was supported by shadowy references to the unwholesome combination of judicial, executive, and legislative powers and by the stated belief that "the judicial branch of the federal government is being rapidly and seriously undermined and, if the tendencies are permitted to develop unchecked, is in danger of meeting a measure of the fate of the Merovingian Kings. . . ."
>
> In 1938 Roscoe Pound became the Committee's chairman. The decibel count rose markedly. This was the heyday of Congressman Martin Dies and the House Committee on Un-American Activities. . . . Consideration of administrative law moved perceptibly to the level of "the good guys against the bad guys." Scholarly critics of past proposals were challenged not on the merits of their criticisms, but by characterizations, as in the following passage from the 1938 report:

Much of the case for administrative absolutism, a doctrine which has made great headway especially in American institutions of learning, with which therefore, the legal profession must sooner or later contend, rests upon a use of "administrative law" in a sense quite repugnant to what "law" had been supposed to be. . . . Hence administrative law would be the actual course of the administrative process whatever it is. . . .Those who would turn the administration of justice over to administrative absolutism regard this meaning as illusory. . . . This is a Marxian idea. . . .

In early 1939 President Roosevelt requested Attorney General Murphy to appoint a Committee to undertake a more particularized examination of administrative functioning. The Committee was to investigate "the need for procedural reform" and to make a "thorough and comprehensive study" of then "existing practices and procedures, with a view to detecting any existing deficiencies and pointing the way to improvements." . . . .

Then began the first intensive and extensive inquiry into the methods of the federal agencies, whose rules and regulations or whose adjudications of rights bore substantially upon persons outside the Government. . . .

The Final Report of the Attorney General's Committee on Administrative Procedure and the investigations that preceded it set the stage for the federal Administrative Procedure Act of 1946 even though most of the committee's members had not favored so embracive a legislative approach. . . .

At times the Administrative Procedure Act has been used as a pretext for intrusion into administrative processes, as happened in the realm of administrative rulemaking until the Supreme Court sought to stem the practice. . . . [A]s JUSTICE FRANKFURTER remarked, "Congress expressed a mood" when it adopted the Administrative Procedure Act and the statutes it influenced.

f. George B. Shepherd, *Fierce Compromise: The Administrative Procedure Act Emerges from New Deal Politics*, 90 Nw. U.L. Rev. 1557 (1996):

I. Introduction

The landmark Administrative Procedure Act (APA) was the bill of rights for the new regulatory state. Enacted in 1946, the APA established the fundamental relationship between regulatory agencies and those whom they regulate – between government, on the one hand, and private citizens, business, and the economy, on the other hand. The balance that the APA struck between promoting individuals' rights and maintaining agencies' policy-making flexibility has continued in force, with only minor modifications, until the present. The APA's impact has been large. It has provided agencies with broad freedom, limited only by relatively weak procedural requirements and judicial review, to create and implement policies in the many areas that agencies touch: from aviation to the environment, from labor relations to the securities markets. The APA permitted the growth of the modern regulatory state.

The APA and its history are central to the United States' economic and political development. In the 1930s and 1940s when the APA was debated, much in the

United States was uncertain. Many believed that communism was a real possibility, as were fascism and dictatorship. Many supporters of the New Deal favored a form of government in which expert bureaucrats would influence even the details of the economy, with little recourse for the people and businesses that felt the impacts of the bureaucrats' commands. To New Dealers, this was efficiency. To the New Deal's opponents, this was dictatorial central planning. The battle over the APA helped to resolve the conflict between bureaucratic efficiency and the rule of law, and permitted the continued growth of government regulation. The APA expressed the nation's decision to permit extensive government, but to avoid dictatorship and central planning. The decision has shaped the nation for fifty years.

Since the time of the APA's adoption, and even before, some commentators have suggested that the APA was universally beloved legislation. They have argued that, although various factions initially disagreed about the APA's virtues, the factions unanimously approved the bill once they discovered its excellence. They suggest that the bill was so carefully and scientifically drafted that to know it was to admire it. . . . Likewise, even before the bill's passage, commentators attempted to cover the bill's contentious history with a pretty veneer. They suggested that, because all finally understood the bill, all now adored it. For example, shortly before Congress passed the APA, the president of the American Bar Association asserted: "Contrary to the impression which some people seem to have, the proposed Administrative Procedure Act is not a compromise. . . . It was a simple matter of good citizenship and good statesmanship to seek the best and fairest provisions for each subject. . . ."

This widely held perception of the APA's history is inaccurate. The APA's development was not primarily a search for administrative truth and efficiency. Nor was it a theoretically centered debate on appropriate roles for government and governed. Instead, the fight over the APA was a pitched political battle for the life of the New Deal. . . . Every legislator, both Roosevelt Democrats and conservatives, recognized that a central purpose of the proponents of administrative reform was to constrain liberal New Deal agencies. . . . They understood . . . that the shape of the administrative law statute that emerged would determine the shape of the policies that the New Deal administrative agencies would implement.

The APA that finally emerged in 1946 did not represent a unanimous social consensus about the proper balance between individual rights and agency powers. The APA was a hard-fought compromise that left many legislators and interest groups far from completely satisfied. Congressional support for the bill was unanimous only because many legislators recognized that, although the bill was imperfect, it was better than no bill. The APA passed only with much grumbling.

Nor was the APA an obvious triumph of truth over ignorance, as some commentators now contend. Instead [the] APA was a cease-fire armistice agreement that ended the New Deal war on terms that favored New Deal proponents. . . . Reprinted by special permission of Northwestern University School of Law, Northwestern University Law Review.

g. For related caselaw in the field, you might take a look at: *Freytag v. Comm'r*, 501 U.S. 868 (1991); *AFGE v. Gates*, 486 F.3d 1316 (D.C. Cir. 2007); *National Treasury Employees Union v. Chertoff*, 452 F.3d 839 (D.C. Cir. 2006); *Consumer Energy Council v. FERC*, 673 F.2d 425 (D.C. Cir. 1982).

h. For a sense of the fundamental scholarship in the field, you might take a look at: Michael Hertz, *United States v. United States: When Can the Government Sue Itself?*, 32 Wm. & Mary L. Rev. 893 (1991); Peter L. Strauss, *The Place of Agencies in Government: Separation of Powers and the Fourth Branch*, 84 Colum. L. Rev. 573, 581-96 (1984); Nathaniel Nathanson, *Separation of Powers and Administrative Law: Delegation, the Legislative Veto, and the "Independent' Agencies*, 75 Nw. U. L. Rev. 1064, 1078 n.55 (1981).

i. One of the best original sources used to understand the APA is the Attorney General's Manual on the Administrative Procedure Act (1947), written under the direction of Attorney General (and later Supreme Court Justice) Tom C. Clark. It is referred to in hundreds of cases where the meaning of the APA is in play – most recently in *Benzman v. Whitman*, 523 F.3d 119, 130 (2d Cir. 2008), a case involving claims against the EPA stemming from injuries sustained by workers on the World Trade Center site after the catastrophic events of September 11, 2001. The workers claimed they were misled by characterizations made by EPA Administrator Whitman regarding allegedly toxic airborne dust particles. At issue, *inter alia*, is the meaning of section 706 of the APA, and the matter of agency inaction, for which the court turned to the Manual to guide interpretation.

For More Information

The Manual is available at a variety of web sites; we recommend the site maintained by the U.S. Department of Labor, Office of Administrative Law Judges: U.S. Dep't of Justice, Attorney General's Manual on the Administrative Procedure Act (1947), http://www.oalj.dol.gov/PUBLIC/ APA/REFERENCES/REFERENCE WORKS/AGTC.HTM (last visited July 14, 2008).

CHAPTER 2

Rulemaking at the Agency

I. The Need for Rules

a. Uncertainty or indeterminacy in our legal system is not only the bane of law students, it is the basis for endless criticism of government. For obvious reasons, those subject to regulation need to know the content of the rules and policies with which they must comply, as well as the consequences of noncompliance.

> **Major Theme**
>
> When federal, state, or local governments proceed without notice, initiating enforcement without first providing clarity regarding the rules and standards to be implemented, criticism is both harsh and justified. As basic as this point may sound, it is the foundation for a good deal of administrative law.

b. Neither Congress nor state legislatures are in a position to articulate with great detail or precision all the standards with which the public must comply. Furthermore, as technology evolves and resources shift, rules and legal standards must adapt to accommodate these changes. While the legislative process is not designed to address these demands, administrative agencies are. The primary method agencies use for the promulgation of standards, that is, for articulating legal requirements, is rulemaking.

c. The idea that an administrative agency, primarily an executive body empowered by the legislature, can enact substantive, binding standards that have the force of law raises immediate questions regarding accountability. Fundamental to our constitutional system is the notion that those who make law and public policy are evaluated on a regular basis by the electorate and, if those laws and policies are unacceptable, removed from public office. This measure of protection does not exist for the most part when dealing with the administrative state. Thus, there is both an undeniable need for agencies to formulate rules and regulations as well as an inherent resistance to regulations being formed – to substantive law making – by a bureaucracy that lacks direct political accountability. This dynamic produces a healthy tension in our legal system.

II. The Nature and Substance of Rules

a. There are three distinctly different types of agency rulemaking: Formal rulemaking (a trial-like process), informal rulemaking (a participatory process predicated on providing the public notice of proposed rules and an opportunity to comment on those proposed rules before final rules issue), and rulemaking exempt from process (a non-participatory system by which agencies issues interpretative rules, policy statements, guidelines, or other standards that do not have the force of law). There are also variations on each of these that are referred to as hybridized rulemaking.

Rules affect classes of individuals and are prospective in nature. Rules promulgated by formal rulemaking or notice and comment rulemaking are binding and have the force of law. These rules are sometimes called legislative rules to reinforce their binding nature. They change, enhance, establish, or limit rights and obligations; amend existing rules; and articulate enforceable norms. Their existence makes it easier to achieve the goals of uniformity, continuity and clarity. In addition, both formal rulemaking and notice and comment rulemaking provide the public with participatory rights as well as the opportunity to challenge those rules in court. Furthermore, while the issuance of rules can be seen as an exercise of executive power, the presence of rules also provides a constraint on governmental action, limiting the range of activities or behaviors an agency might address, and can been seen as one way to check the exercise of "unbridled" discretion by administrative agencies.

b. The power to issue legislative, substantive rules must come initially from Congress or, at the state level, from the legislature. In most instances, that power is explicit, although some courts have been relatively liberal in interpreting the power to enact rules, even declaring in one instance that an agency had the right to issue substantive rules when, for nearly a half-century, the agency took the position that it did not posses that legal authority. *See Nat'l Petroleum Refiners Ass'n v. FTC*, 482 F.2d 672 (D.C. Cir. 1073).

c. The starting point for understanding rulemaking is the APA. Excerpts from the three articles below provide a solid introductory perspective to the APA and rulemaking. As will become clear, rulemaking is a legislative act.

d. Stare decisis, the judicial obligation to adhere to authoritative decisions within a circuit or state (*see Vasquez v. Hillery*, 474 U.S. 254, 265 (1986)),

Bottom Line

Regardless of the level of formality an agency is required – or decides – to use, there is a bottom line: Rulemaking produces norms that either have the actual force of law or serve to inform the public of the agency's position on a specific topic. It is arguable that everything an agency does has a lawmaking consequence.

is generally inapplicable in administrative law. That said, those affected by the actions of an agency are well advised to be aware of all action an agency takes – formal or informal, rulemaking or adjudicatory – because (a) that action reflects the agency's current approach, and (b) the chances are good that the agency will follow a similar position in the future. For that reason, agencies are patently, transparently, and appropriately political institutions of government.

e. Rulemaking on the 50th anniversary of the APA: Richard J. Pierce, Jr., *The Fiftieth Anniversary of the Administrative Procedure Act: Past and Prologue: Rulemaking and the Administrative Procedure Act*, 32 Tulsa L.J. 185 (1996):

> Government agencies have been issuing rules since the earliest days of the Republic. Congress instructed the President to issue rules to provide pensions for disabled veterans of the Revolutionary War in an Act of September 29, 1789. The tremendous increase in the size and scope of the federal government during the twentieth century has increased dramatically the number of rules issued by federal agencies. The Code of Federal Regulations now occupies many feet of library shelf space, and it contains only the most important agency rules. Every major agency has a file room full of interpretative rules, characterized variously as staff manuals, design criteria, advisories, policy statements, enforcement guides, etc.
>
> [T]he history of rules and rulemaking in the U.S. legal system is characterized by powerful ambivalence rooted in two conflicting characteristics of our political and social culture. We place a high value on efficiency, fairness, and accountability. Rules and rulemaking further those values. Yet, we harbor a deep distrust of government and government officials. That distrust induced the Framers to create a government that consists of three independent branches, each with enough power to serve as an effective check on the exercise of the powers conferred on the other two branches. Our distrust is particularly apparent in the procedures required to enact a statute. A bill can become law only by navigating a tortuous course through both Houses of Congress and the President. It should come as no great surprise that our distrust of government also manifests itself in the context of agency rules and rulemaking. The most important category of agency rules, legislative rules, have effects that are functionally indistinguishable from those of statutes.
>
> The history of rulemaking reflects the tension between the cultural values that lead us to place a high value on rules and the cultural values that cause us to distrust the individuals and institutions that are the source of rules. . . . In truth, at all times there exist powerful social forces that are simultaneously pulling the legal system toward polar extremes: maximizing the issuance of rules to enhance efficiency, fairness, and accountability, and minimizing the issuance of rules to guard against the risks of tyranny. There is no reason to expect the future of rules and rulemaking to differ materially from its history in this respect. Requests "full attribution."

f. Rulemaking in its historical context: Peter L. Strauss, *The Rulemaking Continuum*, 41 Duke L.J. 1463 (1992):

> The place to start is with a brief outline of the spectrum of activities identified as rulemaking for APA purposes. Although commonly we speak of "rulemaking"

as synonymous with the notice and comment procedures of informal legislative rulemaking under section 553, careful attention to the APA reveals four different species of activity that can produce an outcome that fits the definition of "rule" given in section 551(4): "the whole or a part of an agency statement of general or particular applicability and future effect designed to implement, interpret, or prescribe law or policy. . . ."

First, what is usually called "formal rulemaking" under section 553 consists of procedures by which rules are "made on the record after opportunity for an agency hearing [following the procedures of] sections 556 and 557 of this title. . . ." Such procedures are commonly employed for the setting of particular rates, but otherwise it is widely known that they are disfavored, and will be found mandatory only when a specific statute so requires in unmistakable terms.

Second, what is usually called "informal rulemaking" requires, in the section's explicit terms, a brief and rather unspecific notice warning of "either the terms or substance of the proposed rule or a description of the subjects and issues involved," followed by the affording to interested persons of "an opportunity to participate in the rule making through the submission of written data, views, or arguments" and concluded by an instrument of adoption that includes "a concise general statement of [the adopted rule's] basis and purpose." An agency following this procedure can create a legal instrument that, if substantively valid, has the force and effect of a statute on all those who are subject to it. It binds the agency, private parties, and the courts, and may preempt state statutes. If a statute so authorizes, its violation may form the basis for penal consequences. In formal contemplation, a valid legislative rule may be modified only by adoption of an amending rule or overruling statute. . . .

Third, what I have elsewhere styled "publication rulemaking" is typically effected by agency staff without participation at the agency's head. For these rules, the parameters are set not by section 553, which excepts them, but by sections 552(a)(1) and (2). The latter provisions require certain agency documents either to be published in the Federal Register before a person can "in any manner be required to resort to, or be adversely affected by" them, or to be indexed and made available for inspection and copying or purchase before the documents "may be relied on, used, or cited as precedent by an agency against a party other than an agency" to "affect[] a member of the public." "Actual and timely notice" suffices to defend the rules' application in either case, however. Section 552(a) is explicit in identifying the documents being referred to as including "statements of general policy or interpretations of general applicability formulated and adopted by the agency," which may or may not be published in the Federal Register as the agency chooses, and "administrative staff manuals and instructions to staff that affect a member of the public," which are to be indexed and made available. Note that the rather elaborate language of section 552(a) contemplates that if the agency does follow the stated publication requirements it will be able to require people to resort to these instruments, and will be able to rely on them in proceedings in ways that "adversely affect" members of the public; yet more strikingly, it also strongly suggests that even if these steps are not taken, such materials may be "relied on, used, or cited as precedent" against the agency although they do not serve to bind the public.

Fourth, and finally, comes the body of materials that fit the APA definition of "rule" and are in some respects the product of agency process, but that meet none of the procedural specifications of the preceding three classes. Here we encounter guidance documents that might be "publication rules" if appropriately made available or if timely and actual notice were given, and also other materials of lesser dignity – press releases and the like. The public cannot be adversely affected by such rules; but, to repeat, there is at least the implication that the agency may be so affected.

g. The current rulemaking environment: Lisa Schultz Bressman, *Procedures as Politics in Administrative Law*, 107 Colum. L. Rev. 1749 (2007):

C. The Current Period

By the 1980s, administrative law theory and doctrine had transitioned to presidential control of agency decisionmaking as a principal mechanism for legitimating such decisionmaking. The "presidential control" model displays a strikingly similar disregard for administrative procedures as the expertise model, but for a different reason. The model comes with its own procedures – presidentially-generated procedures – set forth in executive orders rather than statutes. Those procedures, together with other tools, enable the White House to monitor and influence agency action as it unfolds.

The centerpiece is Executive Order 12,291 and its successors. Executive Order 12,291 required agencies to consider cost-benefit analysis "to the extent permitted by law" and to submit their proposed major rules, along with a "Regulatory Impact Analysis" of the rule, for centralized White House review by the Office of Management and Budget (OMB). Within OMB, the Office of Information and Regulatory Activities (OIRA) now performs the review function. President Reagan issued this executive order to improve the efficiency and coordination of agency rulemaking. All subsequent Presidents have maintained it, and two have expanded it. President Clinton issued Executive Order 12,866, which enlarged the focus of White House regulatory review by instructing agencies to consider not only the cost-effectiveness of their proposals but their distributional effects as well. President George W. Bush instituted a more dramatic change. He issued Executive Order 13,422, amending Executive Order 12,866 and enlarging the scope of regulatory review to include not only rulemaking proposals but also guidance documents. In addition, Executive Order 13,422 requires a presidential political appointee in each agency to oversee the development of regulatory policy, including guidance documents.

The presidential control model has enjoyed widespread support. In addition to bipartisan political appeal, it has broad scholarly appeal. Formalists or originalists contend that it brings agencies within the four corners – or rather the three Articles – of the Constitution. Because agency decision-making occurs under the direction of the Chief Executive, it is no longer constitutionally suspect. More instrumentalist scholars argue that the strong President model subjects agencies to the direction of an elected official who may best ensure their accountability and efficacy. The President is elected by the entire nation and therefore best represents popular preferences. The President is uniquely visible and therefore can be held responsible for his actions. The President, a single actor, has the capacity to coordinate and manage the executive branch through tools such as centralized review of agency proposals under principles of cost-benefit analysis.

Administrative law reflects the presidential control model by increasing judicial deference to agency decisions. The most prominent example is <u>*Chevron U.S.A. Inc. v. Natural Resources Defense Council, Inc.*</u> In that case, the Court held that agencies are entitled to judicial deference for interpretations of ambiguous statutory provisions in large part because they are subject to presidential control:

> An agency to which Congress has delegated policymaking responsibilities may, within the limits of that delegation, properly rely upon the incumbent administration's views of wise policy to inform its judgments. While agencies are not directly accountable to the people, the Chief Executive is, and it is entirely appropriate for this political branch of the Government to make such policy choices – resolving the competing interests which Congress itself either inadvertently did not resolve, or intentionally left to be resolved by the agency charged with the administration of the statute in light of everyday realities.

<u>*Chevron*</u>, more than any other case, is responsible for anchoring the presidential control model. It recognized that politics is a permissible basis for agency policymaking.

Despite the strength of the presidential control model, the Court has departed from it in significant ways, again shifting its focus back to traditional administrative procedures. The classic example is <u>*Motor Vehicle Manufacturers Ass'n v. State Farm Mutual Automobile Insurance Co.*</u>, in which the Court refused to uphold a rule rescission that the Reagan administration supported absent a more reasoned explanation for the action. Another is <u>*United States v. Mead Corp.*</u> There the Court held that an agency is entitled to Chevron deference for reasonable interpretations of ambiguities in the statutes that they administer only if they select a procedural format that Congress anticipates will "carry[] the force of law."

In sum, the evolution of administrative law has been generally characterized by vacillation between procedures, which serve due process or rule-of-law values, and politics, which appeal to the values of accountability and efficiency (and, previously, expertise). This vacillation, according to legal scholars, has produced rules that reflect contradictory procedural and political impulses. Administrative law therefore sends conflicting signals to agencies regarding choice of administrative procedures, intensity of judicial review, and availability of judicial review.

h. For a recent critique of the federal regulatory environment, see Mark Seidenfeld, *Why Agencies Act: A Reassessment of the Ossification Critique of Judicial Review*, 70 OHIO STATE L. J. 251 (2009). For insight into the workings of OIRA, see <u>http://whitehouse.gov/omb/regulatory_affairs/default/</u>

III. The Primary Sections of the APA Pertaining to Rulemaking

a. <u>5 U.S.C. § 551</u>. Definitions

. . . .

(4) "rule" means the whole or a part of an agency statement of general or particular applicability and future effect designed to implement, interpret, or prescribe law or policy or describing the organization, procedure, or practice requirements of an agency and includes the approval or prescription for the future of rates, wages, corporate or financial structures or reorganizations thereof, prices, facilities, appliances, services or allowances therefor[e] or of valuations, costs, or accounting, or practices bearing on any of the foregoing;

(5) "rule making" means agency process for formulating, amending, or repealing a rule;

§ 553. Rule making

(a) This section applies, according to the provisions thereof, except to the extent that there is involved –

(1) a military or foreign affairs function of the United States; or

(2) a matter relating to agency management or personnel or to public property, loans, grants, benefits, or contracts.

(b) General notice of proposed rule making shall be published in the Federal Register, unless persons subject thereto are named and either personally served or otherwise have actual notice thereof in accordance with law. The notice shall include –

(1) a statement of the time, place, and nature of public rule making proceedings;

(2) reference to the legal authority under which the rule is proposed; and

(3) either the terms or substance of the proposed rule or a description of the subjects and issues involved.

Except –

(A) to interpretative rules, general statements of policy, or rules of agency organization, procedure, or practice; or

(B) when the agency for good cause finds (and incorporates the finding and a brief statement of reasons therefor[e] in the rules issued) that notice and public procedure thereon are impracticable, unnecessary, or contrary to the public interest.

(c) After notice required by this section, the agency shall give interested persons an opportunity to participate in the rule making through submission of written data, views, or arguments with or without opportunity for oral presentation. After consideration of the relevant matter presented, the agency shall incorporate in the rules adopted a concise general statement of their basis and purpose. When rules are required by statute to be made on the record after opportunity for an agency hearing, sections 556 and 557 of this title [5 U.S.C.S §§ 556 and 557] apply instead of this subsection.

(d) The required publication or service of a substantive rule shall be made not less than 30 days before its effective date, except –

> (1) a substantive rule which grants or recognizes an exemption or relieves a restriction;

> (2) interpretative rules and statements of policy; or

> (3) as otherwise provided by the agency for good cause found and published with the rule.

(e) Each agency shall give an interested person the right to petition for the issuance, amendment, or repeal of a rule.

§ 555.   Ancillary matters

(e) Prompt notice shall be given of the denial in whole or in part of a written application, petition, or other request of an interested person made in connection with any agency proceeding. Except in affirming a prior denial or when the denial is self-explanatory, the notice shall be accompanied by a brief statement of the grounds for denial.

§ 701.   Application; definitions

(a) This chapter applies, according to the provisions thereof, except to the extent that –

> (1) statutes preclude judicial review; or

> (2) agency action is committed to agency discretion by law.

§ 702.   Right of review

A person suffering legal wrong because of agency action, or adversely affected or aggrieved by agency action within the meaning of a relevant statute, is entitled to judicial review thereof. An action in a court of the United States seeking relief other than money damages and stating a claim that an agency or an officer or employee thereof acted or failed to act in an official capacity or under color of legal authority shall not be dismissed nor relief therein be denied on the ground that it is against the United States or that the United States is an indispensable party.

§ 704.   Actions reviewable

Agency action made reviewable by statute and final agency action for which there is no other adequate remedy in a court are subject to judicial review. A preliminary, procedural, or intermediate agency action or ruling not directly reviewable is subject to review on the review of the final agency action.

§ 706.   Scope of review

(2) hold unlawful and set aside agency action, findings, and conclusions found to be –

(A) arbitrary, capricious, an abuse of discretion, or otherwise not in accordance with law;

(B) contrary to constitutional right, power, privilege, or immunity;

(C) in excess of statutory jurisdiction, authority, or limitations, or short of statutory right;

(D) without observance of procedure required by law;

(E) unsupported by substantial evidence in a case subject to sections 556 and 557 of this title or otherwise reviewed on the record of an agency hearing provided by statute; or

(F) unwarranted by the facts to the extent that the facts are subject to trial de novo by the reviewing court.

b. The Administrative Procedure Act – as well as many courses in administrative law – is divided into two sections – rulemaking and adjudication. This text, for the most part, is similarly organized. As you study this field, you will begin to see that the separation is somewhat artificial. For example, one of the principle cases you will probably study, *Vermont Yankee*, *infra* Chapter 3, involved a licensing proceeding (licensing is inherently adjudicatory) *and* a rulemaking that took place during the pendency of the adjudicatory hearing. Similarly, if you represent a client in a zoning case, you will find there are often rules that issue affecting the piece of property in question as well as individual determinations that are adjudicatory in nature. With that said, however, it is important to be able to distinguish which category of procedure an agency is currently undertaking, which is why we have chosen to organize the book in this way.

c. Consider the structure of the APA as it pertains to the distinction between rulemaking and adjudication. Section 553(c) of the APA establishes rules for informal rulemaking – a field you will cover in some depth. Section 554 sets out basic standards for adjudication, the focus of the second half of this text. Sections 556 and 557 deal with formal (trial-like) processes applicable to both formal rulemaking and formal adjudication. Accordingly, looking at formal processes entails both rulemaking and adjudication.

Parenthetically, there isn't much in the APA addressing informal adjudication. This is not an oversight; given that there is an almost infinite range and variety of informal adjudicatory actions agencies can and do take, from writing opinion letters to more conventional (but informal) adversary processes, there is no one set of rules or procedures that can be applied uniformly. Informal adjudication covers everything from initial responses on special use permits, *see, e.g.*, *Everett v. United States*, 158 F.3d 1364, 1368 (D.C. Cir. 1998), to an initial Freedom of Information Act (FOIA) response, *see, e.g.*, *Daisy Mfg. Co. v. Consumer Prods. Safety Comm'n*, 133 F.3d 1081, 1083 (D.C. Cir. 1998).

Make the Connection

As you study the first topic, formal rulemaking – limited in frequency though it may be – the rights, entitlements, established procedures, arguments and issues translate with little effort into formal adjudication. After all, they involve the same sections of the APA and many of the same strategic considerations.

d. In *Pension Benefit Guarantee Corp. v. LTV Corp.*, 496 U.S. 633, 655 (1990), the Court set out the basic requirements for formal processes ("that parties be given notice of 'the matters of fact and law asserted,' § 554(b)(3), an opportunity for 'the submission and consideration of facts [and] arguments,' § 554(c)(1), and an opportunity to submit 'proposed findings and conclusions' or 'exceptions,' § 557(c)(1), (2)"). The Court noted that for informal adjudication, one could gain some guidance from 5 U.S.C. § 555 but cautioned that this provides only "minimal requirements." You might also look to sections 551(7) (for a definition of adjudication) and section 706 (for judicial review standards).

Disputes regarding the necessity of both formal rulemaking and formal adjudication often focus on the same interpretive issues: Was formality intended by Congress? When Congress directs "a public hearing" as a predicate to agency action, does it envision a formal hearing with witnesses, cross-examination, and a decision based substantially on a record consisting of testimony and authenticated data proffered by parties presented in a trial like setting – or does it envision something far less formal? *See Sierra Club v. Davies, 955 F.2d 1188 (8th Cir. 1992); Ass'n of Nat'l Advertisers, Inc. v. FTC, 627 F.2d 1151 (D.C. Cir. 1980)* (holding that the same evidentiary test – substantial evidence – applies to formal rulemaking and formal adjudication).

Hypothetical

Without first providing notice and an opportunity for comment, the Federal Trade Commission promulgated a regulation requiring that all written submissions to the agency, including documents associated with notice and comment rulemaking and formal adjudication proceedings, be submitted in hard copy triplicate as well as via upload on the new "FTC E-filings" website. Citizens for Green Government (CGG) objects to the new requirement as a waste of paper and wishes to challenge the agency's failure to provide notice and an opportunity for comment before promulgating the new regulation. What would be their strongest argument(s)? What would be the agency's strongest argument(s)?

IV. Formal Rulemaking

Providing parties (1) notice; (2) an opportunity to be heard, cross-examine, confront and challenge evidence; and (3) a fair and impartial decisionmaker is a solid recipe for satisfying the historical mandate of due process. It might seem logical, then, to use a trial-like model to promulgate rules. Sections 554 to 557 of the APA set out a workable set of rules for agencies conducting trial-like proceedings. As it turns out, trial-like rulemaking (formal rulemaking) is an extraordinarily expensive, time-consuming, and cumbersome process.

On the plus side, formal rulemaking not only permits extensive public participation but also requires complete transparency in agency decision-making. Like any trial, all evidence proffered in support of or in opposition to the proposed rule is subject to scrutiny. All witnesses are subject to cross-examination by any and all parties who opt to participate in the proceeding. While the rules of evidence are relaxed in administrative practice, in a formal rulemaking, far more attention is given to the nature and quality of the information placed in the record. Finally, any rule that issues from a formal rulemaking must be supported by "substantial evidence" in a public record.

As appealing as the virtues of a formal or trial-like rulemaking are to those who believe that fairness mandates the protections of an Article III court – or, quite simply, distrust government – the process cannot be implemented efficiently in regulatory proceedings where there might be hundreds or even thousands of interested parties. At the most basic level, try to imagine an agency hearing in which each and every witness is subject to cross-examination by hundreds of different lawyers representing all the different parties potentially affected by the rule.

In addition to the absurdity of nearly infinite cross-examination is the fact that trial-like rulemaking can negate agency expertise, one of the foundational premises for the existence of administrative agencies. If all of the information on which the agency is permitted to rely comes only from direct testimony presented by sworn witnesses in a hearing, the accumulated knowledge of an agency in a particular field will either have to be reduced to a parade of agency witnesses and experts or will be lost because of the procedural requirements inherent in formal rulemaking.

There are two instances where formal hearings must be held. First, there are some areas where congressional mandate compels unambiguously a trial-like process prior to the issuance of rules. The Federal Trade Commission, Federal Communications Commission, Department of Interior, Environmental Protection Administration and the Drug Enforcement Administration all have formal rulemaking requirements in certain areas within their jurisdiction. *See, e.g.*, 42 U.S.C. § 7410(a)(1). Second, there are areas where Congress has delegated the power to an agency to issue rules only after conducting a proceeding "on the record after an opportunity for a hearing." The phrase "on the record" has been at the center of a number of cases focused on the nature of the process an agency follows. Note the language of the Sixth Circuit: "The Supreme Court has . . . implied that formal adjudication procedures are only necessary when a statute uses the magic words 'on the record.'" *Cf. United States v. Fla. E. Coast Ry.*, 410 U.S. 224, 237-38 (1973) (holding that formal rulemaking procedures . . . are required only when a statute mandates that rules be made "on the record"); *Crestview Parke Care Ctr. v. Thompson*, 373 F.3d 743, 748 (6th Cir. 2004).

Food for Thought

Despite the "magic" quality of the "on the record" language, formal rulemakings are relatively rare.

The cases that follow are focused on the issues raised in the formal rulemaking process.

UNITED STATES V. FLORIDA EAST COAST RAILWAY COMPANY

410 U.S. 224 (1973)

[JUSTICE REHNQUIST] Appellees, two railroad companies, brought this action . . . to set aside the incentive per diem rates established by appellant Interstate Commerce Commission in a rulemaking proceeding. . . . The District Court held that . . . the Commission's determination to receive submissions from the appellees only in written form was a violation of [§ 1(14)(a) of the Interstate Commerce Act n.1] because the appellees were "prejudiced" by that determination within the meaning of that section.

> n.1 Section 1(14)(a) provides:
>
>> The Commission may, after hearing . . . establish reasonable rules [for] railroad[s] subject to this chapter, including the compensation to be paid . . . for the use of any . . . car . . . not owned by the carrier using it . . . .

. . . We here decide that the Commission's proceeding was governed only by 5 U.S.C.A. § 553 of [the APA], and that appellees received the "hearing" required by § 1(14)(a) . . . .

I. BACKGROUND OF CHRONIC FREIGHT CAR SHORTAGES

"[F]or a number of years portions of the nation have been plagued with seasonal shortages of freight cars in which to ship goods." . . . . Congressional concern for the problem was manifested in the enactment in 1966 of an amendment to § 1(14)(a) of the Interstate Commerce Act, enlarging the Commission's authority to prescribe per diem charges for the use by one railroad of freight cars owned by another. The Senate Committee on Commerce stated in its report accompanying this legislation:

> Car shortages, which once were confined to the Midwest during harvest seasons, have become increasingly more frequent, more severe, and nationwide in scope as the national freight car supply has plummeted.

> . . . .

In December 1967, the Commission initiated the rulemaking procedure giving rise to the order that appellees here challenged. It . . . directed . . . railroads to compile and report detailed information with respect to freight-car demand and supply . . . . Some of the affected railroads voiced [concerns]. In response

. . ., the Commission staff held an informal conference in April 1968, at which the objections and proposed modifications were discussed. Twenty railroads . . . were represented at this conference . . . . The conference adjourned on a note that undoubtedly left the impression that hearings would be held at some future date. A detailed report of the conference was sent to all parties to the proceeding before the Commission. . . .

The Commission . . . issued in December 1969 an interim report announcing its tentative decision . . . that so-called "incentive" per diem charges should be paid by any railroad using . . . a standard boxcar owned by another railroad. Before the enactment of the 1966 amendment to the Interstate Commerce Act, it was generally thought that the Commission's authority to fix per diem payments for freight car use was limited to setting an amount that reflected fair return on investment for the owning railroad . . . . The Commission concluded, however, that in view of the 1966 amendment it could impose additional "incentive" per diem charges to spur prompt return of existing cars and to make acquisition of new cars financially attractive to the railroads. . . . Embodied in the report was . . . a notice to the railroads to file statements of position within 60 days . . . . Both appellee railroads filed statements objecting to the Commission's proposal and requesting an oral hearing, as did numerous other railroads. In April 1970, the Commission, without having held further "hearings," . . . overrul[ed] in toto the requests of appellees. The District Court held that in so doing the Commission violated § 556(d) of the Administrative Procedure Act . . . .

II. APPLICABILITY OF ADMINISTRATIVE PROCEDURE ACT

In *United States v. Allegheny-Ludlum Steel Corp.*, we held that the language of § 1(14)(a) of the Interstate Commerce Act authorizing the Commission to act "after hearing" was not the equivalent of a requirement that a rule be made "on the record after opportunity for an agency hearing" as the latter term is used in § 553(c) of the Administrative Procedure Act. . . . We recognized in *Allegheny-Ludlum* that the actual words "on the record" and "after . . . hearing" used in § 553 were not words of art, and that other statutory language having the same meaning could trigger the provisions of §§ 556 and 557 in rulemaking proceedings. But we adhere to our conclusion, expressed in that case, that the phrase "after hearing" in § 1(14)(a) of the Interstate Commerce Act does not have such an effect.

III. "HEARING" REQUIREMENT OF § 1(14)(a) OF THE INTERSTATE COMMERCE ACT

. . . Appellees, both here and in the court below, contend that the Commission procedure here fell short of that mandated by the "hearing" requirement of § 1(14)(a), even though it may have satisfied § 553 of the Administrative Procedure Act. The Administrative Procedure Act states that none of its provisions "limit or repeal additional requirements imposed by statute or otherwise recognized by law." Thus, even though the Commission was not required to comply with §§ 556 and 557 of that Act, it was required to accord the "hearing" specified in § 1(14)(a) of the Interstate Commerce Act. Though the District Court did not pass on this contention, it is so closely related to the claim based on the Administrative Procedure Act that we proceed to decide it now.

. . . The term "hearing" in its legal context undoubtedly has a host of meanings. . . . It is by no means apparent what the drafters of the Esch Car Service Act of 1917, which became the first part of § 1(14)(a) of the Interstate Commerce Act, meant by the term [and] none of the parties refer to any legislative history that would shed light on the intended meaning of the words "after hearing." [Nor is it clear what was meant when the 1966 amendment was passed.] What is apparent, though, is that the term was used in granting authority to the Commission to make rules and regulations of a prospective nature. . . .

Under these circumstances, confronted with a grant of substantive authority made after the Administrative Procedure Act was enacted, we think that reference to that Act, in which Congress devoted itself exclusively to questions such as the nature and scope of hearings, is a satisfactory basis for determining what is meant by the term "hearing" used in another statute. . . . Section 553 excepts from its requirements rulemaking devoted to "interpretative rules, general statements of policy, or rules of agency organization, procedure, or practice" . . . . This exception does not apply, however, "when notice or hearing is required by statute" . . . . But since [the § 553] requirements themselves do not mandate any oral presentation it cannot be doubted that a statute that requires a "hearing" prior to rulemaking may in some circumstances be satisfied by procedures that meet only the standards of § 553. . . .

Similarly, even where the statute requires that the rulemaking procedure take place "on the record after opportunity for an agency hearing," thus triggering the applicability of § 556, subsection (d) provides that the agency may proceed by the submission of all or part of the evidence in written form if a party will not be "prejudiced thereby." . . . . Here, the Commission promulgated a tentative draft of an order, and accorded all interested parties 60 days in which to file statements of position, submissions of evidence, and other relevant observations. The parties had fair notice of exactly what the Commission proposed to do . . . . The final order of the Commission indicates that it gave consideration to the statements of the two appellees here. Given the "open-ended" nature of the proceedings, and the Commission's announced willingness to consider proposals for modification after operating experience had been acquired, we think the hearing requirement of § 1(14)(a) of the Act was met. . . .

. . . .

. . . *FCC v. WJR* established that there was no across-the-board constitutional right to oral argument in every administrative proceeding regardless of its nature . . . . The Commission's procedure satisfied both the provisions of § 1(14)(a) of the Interstate Commerce Act and of the Administrative Procedure Act, and were not inconsistent with prior decisions of this Court. We, therefore, reverse the judgment of the District Court, and remand the case so that it may consider those contentions of the parties that are not disposed of by this opinion. . . .

Underlying Case Documents

The case referenced:
The Interstate Commerce Act
The 1966 Amendments to the Act
The 1967 Proposed Rule
The 1969 Interim Decision
The Esch Car Service Act of 1917

1. As you might guess, the frequency of formal rulemakings declined radically after the above decision. With almost no exceptions, agencies and courts have followed the unequivocal preference for informal rulemaking evident in *Florida East Coast Railway*, outside of congressional directives to proceed by formal rule-making – and with good reason.

2. First, both in *Florida East Coast Railway* and a year earlier in *United States v. Allegheny-Ludlum Steel, 406 U.S. 742 (1972)*, the Court limited dramatically the circumstances in which formality in the rulemaking process was required.

3. Second, cases decided at about the same time reflected the frustrations inherent in the formal rulemaking model. In *National Nutritional Foods Association v. FDA, 504 F.2d 761 (2d Cir. 1974)*, a case involving vitamins and related food supplements, the Food and Drug Administration (FDA) was prevented from issuing a

rule because of a limitation of cross-examination of a witness, notwithstanding an elaborate process that had covered nearly two years and aired all relevant positions of the parties. In an earlier case, <u>Corn Products v. FDA, 427 F.2d 511 (3d Cir. 1970)</u>, the agency was compelled to permit seemingly endless cross-examination of witnesses on the exact percentile content of peanuts in peanut butter.

4. Formal rulemaking has survived, though only in limited circumstances, i.e., because of a statutory directive or an "on the record" statutory mandate. *See* <u>Farmers Union Central Exch. v. FERC, 734 F.2d 1486 (D.C. Cir. 1984)</u>.

5. As the next case discusses, when legislation requires a "public hearing" with a decision based "on the record," there is an assumption that a formal process should occur before a decision is reached. That language, however, is not the norm. In cases involving the asserted necessity of formal rulemaking – and in cases involving the asserted necessity of formal adjudication – the procedural battle-lines are defined by legislative text. These disputes are framed around arguments regarding the canons of statutory construction, textualism, originalism, plain meaning, and the relevance and suitability of legislative history and related secondary sources (e.g., committee testimony and records of floor debate).

6. So that there is no misunderstanding at this early stage, there is a general rule regarding choice of process in administrative law: To the extent legislation permits, the choice of process is left to the agency.

7. Finally, while "on the record" phraseology or a direct statutory command can compel formality, how do prior agency practices affect the formality of a proceeding? The next case explores that topic in the context of a Nuclear Regulatory Commission proceeding.

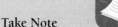

> **Take Note**
>
> Courts defer to the agency's decision on process if the question is unresolved by statute – for the most part. If the choice of the government agency is arbitrary, at odds with the statute, or on its face unconstitutional (as was the case in <u>*Londoner*</u>), it is the role of the courts to correct the problem.

CITY OF WEST CHICAGO, ILLINOIS v. UNITED STATES NUCLEAR REGULATORY COMMISSION

<u>701 F.2d 632 (7th Cir. 1983)</u>

[CHIEF JUDGE CUMMINGS] Petitioner . . . challenges a Nuclear Regulatory Commission (NRC) order of February 11, 1982, granting Kerr-McGee Corporation (KM) a license amendment (Amendment No. 3) authorizing demolition of certain buildings at KM's West Chicago facility, and acceptance for on site storage of contaminated soil from offsite locations. . . . We uphold the NRC order . . . .

I. *Facts*

KM operated a milling facility in West Chicago for the production of thorium and thorium compounds from 1967 to 1973. Although the plant closed in 1973, there is presently on site approximately 5 million cubic feet of contaminated waste material consisting of building rubble, contaminated soil, and tailings from the milling of thorium ore. . . . The current NRC license for the West Chicago site is a "source material" license . . . authorizing KM to possess and store thorium ores. . . . Amendment No. 3 [to KM's license], which is the focus of the City's suit challenging the NRC order, was issued in September 1981 and allowed demolition of six . . . buildings on site in a non-emergency situation. Amendment No. 3 also authorized receipt and storage on site of contaminated material that was formerly taken from the site for use as landfill.

On October 14, 1981, the City brought suit challenging the issuance of Amendment No. 3 . . . . JUDGE MCGARR temporarily enjoined KM's activities under the amendment and ordered the NRC to give notice to the City and consider any request for hearing that the City might make. NRC did so, and on February 11, 1982, issued its order denying the City's request for a formal, trial-type hearing, addressing the contentions raised by the City in the written materials it submitted, and issuing Amendment No. 3. Meanwhile, the City filed a preliminary injunction motion raising the same claims in the district court. On April 5 the district court dismissed the City's motion . . . . [The city then appealed this dismissal.]

The City challenges the NRC order . . . on both procedural and substantive grounds, contending first, that the NRC violated its own regulations, the Atomic Energy Act, due process, and the National Environmental Policy Act (NEPA) in issuing Amendment No. 3, and second, that the order must be set aside because it is both unsupported by substantial evidence in the record and arbitrary and capricious. We address the political issues first.

The Atomic Energy Act of 1954 (AEA), § 189(a), clearly requires NRC to grant a "hearing" if requested "in any proceeding under this chapter, for the granting, suspending, revoking, or amending of any license or construction permit . . . ." The parties in this case are arguing about the kind of "hearing" the NRC is required to conduct when issuing an amendment to a source materials license. The City argues that NRC must hold a formal, adversarial, trial-type hearing as provided by NRC regulations . . . . NRC and intervenor KM argue that the NRC may hold an informal hearing in which it requests and considers written materials without providing for traditional trial-type procedures such as oral testimony and cross-examination. . . . In the circumstances of this case, we find that an informal hearing suffices. . . .

. . . NRC agrees that a party who requests a hearing pursuant to the notice of opportunity for a hearing issued under [10 C.F.R. §] 2.105 is entitled to a notice of hearing under Section 2.104 and a formal hearing will be convened. However, Section 2.105 by its own terms requires issuance of a notice of proposed action only in limited circumstances . . . . [n.5] The City argues that Amendment No. 3 effectively licenses KM to receive offsite thorium for commercial disposal under Section 2.105(a)(2). By its terms Section 2.105(a)(2) requires notice of proposed action as to (1) commercial disposal, which this is not, since KM is only a temporary storage site and is apparently not being reimbursed or otherwise compensated for its actions, (2) by a waste disposal licensee, such as those licensed at Hanford, Washington, or Barnwell, South Carolina. KM, to the contrary, operates under a source materials license, rather than under a license for a commercial waste disposal site, and had no intention of changing its status . . . .

> n.5 § 2.105 Notice of proposed action.
>
> (a) If a hearing is not required by the Act or this chapter, and if the Commission has not found that a hearing is in the public interest, it will, prior to acting thereon, cause to be published in the FEDERAL REGISTER a notice of proposed action with respect to an application for:
>
> > (1) A license for a facility;
> >
> > (2) A license for receipt of waste radioactive material from other persons for the purpose of commercial disposal by the waste disposal licensee; or
> >
> > (3) An amendment of a license specified in paragraph (a)(1) or (2) of this section and which involves a significant hazards consideration;
> >
> > . . . .
> >
> > (6) Any other license or amendment as to which the Commission determines that an opportunity for a public hearing should be afforded.

Finally, the City argues that NRC should have found that the "public interest" required a formal hearing. We note that the determination of whether the public interest requires a hearing is left to NRC's discretion, and find that in this case, NRC had ample cause to reject the City's argument.

. . . .

The City claims that a materials licensing hearing under Section 189(a) of the AEA must be in accordance with Section 5 of the Administrative Procedure Act (APA), 5 U.S.C. § 554. Section 554 does not by its terms dictate the type of hearing to which a party is entitled; rather it triggers the formal hearing provisions of

Section 556 and 557 of the APA if the adjudication in question is required by the agency's governing statute to be "determined on the record after opportunity for an agency hearing . . . ." The City argues that Section 189(a) of the AEA triggers the formal hearing provisions of the APA because it provides that the "Commission shall grant a hearing upon the request of any person whose interest may be affected by the proceeding, and shall admit any such person as a party to such proceeding."

[The] three magic words ["on the record"] need not appear for a court to determine that formal hearings are required. *See, e.g.*, *Seacoast Anti-Pollution League v. Costle*. However, even the City agrees that in the absence of these magic words, Congress must clearly indicate its intent to trigger the formal, on-the-record hearing provisions of the APA. [*Florida East Coast.*] We find no such clear intention in the legislative history of the AEA, and therefore conclude that formal hearings are not statutorily required for amendments to materials licenses.

. . . .

In adopting rules to carry out the AEA . . . the Atomic Energy Commission (AEC) . . . provide[d] by regulation for formal hearings on request in all licensing cases. . . . In 1957, the Act was amended to add the second sentence of Section 189(a), mandating a hearing on certain applications for construction permits even when uncontested. . . . After the 1957 amendment took effect, there was a significant amount of criticism of the AEC for overformalizing the licensing process. The staff of the Joint Committee on Atomic Energy published a report criticizing the AEC for going "further in some respects than the law required, particularly in regard to the number of hearings required and the formality of procedures." With respect to materials licenses, the Joint Committee staff suggested registration rather than licensing of materials, though it did recommend hearings before a hearing examiner in contested materials licensing cases. The Joint Committee then held hearings to explore legislative improvements to the AEC regulatory process. . . . [T]he Committee concentrated mainly on reactor licensing, . . . and dispensed with the mandatory hearing requirement in uncontested operating license, but not construction permit, proceedings.

The AEC continued to hold formal hearings in all contested reactor cases, as well as in materials licensing cases. However, based on the threadbare legislative history concerning materials licenses, we are unable to conclude that the AEC's procedures were mandated by statute. Even if the legislative history indicates that formal procedures are required by statute in reactor licensing cases . . . we do not accept the City's argument that this by necessity indicates that all hearings under the first sentence must be formal as well. . . .

. . . .

The City argues that under the APA, agency action is classified either as rule-making or adjudication, and since licensing is adjudication, NRC is obliged to provide a formal hearing in this case. The "on the record" requirement of APA Section 554, according to the City has been relevant primarily in cases involving rulemaking, not adjudication, *United States v. Florida East Coast Ry*; in adjudication, the City claims the absence of the "on the record" requirement is not decisive. For example, Section 402 of the Federal Water Pollution Control Act (FWPCA), which provides for a "public hearing," has been held by three courts including this one to require a formal hearing pursuant to Section 554. *Seacoast*. . . . [In *Seacoast*, the] First Circuit relied principally on the adjudicative nature of the decision at issue – issuance of a permit to allow discharge of a pollutant – finding that primarily the rights of the particular applicant would be affected, and that resolution of the issues required specific factual findings by the EPA Administrator. *Seacoast*. The court also mentioned the judicial review provision of Section 509 of the FWPCA, which provides for review of a determination required under the FWPCA to be made "on the record." . . . . [However, unlike] the "on the record" requirement of Section 509 of the FWPCA, there is no indication even in the judicial review Section of the AEA, the governing statute, that Congress intended to require formal hearings under the APA.

Thus even in adjudication, the "on the record" requirement is significant at least as an indication of congressional intent. We agree with the courts and commentators who recognize that adjudication may be either informal or formal. Formal adjudications are those required by statute to be conducted through on-the-record proceedings. Informal adjudications constitute a residual category including "all agency actions that are not rulemaking and that need not be conducted through 'on the record' hearings."

Despite the fact that licensing is adjudication under the APA, there is no evidence that Congress intended to require formal hearings for all Section 189(a) activities. In light of the above analysis, we conclude that NRC did not violate the AEA when it denied the City's request for a formal hearing. . . .

Underlying Case Documents

The case referenced:
NRC's February 11, 1982 order
The Atomic Energy Act
The report prepared for the Joint Committee on Atomic Energy includ-

ing comments from those previously solicited by the committee.

West Chicago had reason to be concerned. Thorium processing generated four superfund sites in the West Chicago area. Read about them HERE. One important lesson of this case is not to accept free fill dirt from a nuclear processing facility. A current update on the situation is available HERE.

Karen Silkwood, a 28-year-old employee of the Kerr-McGee plutonium processing plant, was killed in a car accident while on her way to deliver important documents to a newspaper reporter. Those interested in conspiracy theories might check out the following book discussing the case available HERE, or the following song discussing nuclear accidents that mentions her by name available HERE.

1. This case embodies a "presumption of informality" in the absence of an explicit legislative command for a more formal process. While there is little question that the NRC process went forward with greater speed, did you pick up on the argument that this was a change in procedure *and* a substantive environmental decision? Was it genuinely in the interest of the affected public to be forced to proceed on both matters with a silent "paper hearing"? In the absence of any oral presentations, cross-examination or other common methods to challenge the veracity and accuracy of the information on which the government relied, what was lost? Do the efficiency gains in this model off-set the loss of information, public confidence, and accountability? Moreover, the precedent the case set is noteworthy. Relying on *City of West Chicago*, the Eastern District of Virginia held that "[i]nformal adjudications constitute a residual category including 'all agency actions that are not rulemaking and that need not be conducted through on the record hearings.'" *Blaustein & Reich, Inc. v. Buckles, 220 F. Supp. 2d 535 (E.D. Va. 2002)*. Are informal adjudications the proper default process for decisions that both determine rights and make policy?

2. It is easy to overlook the fact that *City of West Chicago* included a change in process. The court, however, did not question "the authority of the NRC to change its procedures on a case-by-case basis with timely notice to the parties involved," although it did "question the wisdom of [changing the rules of procedure] without the benefit of published regulations." How would publication change the process? For a recent critique of the case, see Professor Melissa M. Berry, *Beyond Chevron's*

Domain: Agency Interpretations of Statutory Procedural Provisions, 30 Seattle U.L. Rev. 541, 553-55 (2007).

3. What is a "Public Hearing?" *Environmental Defense Fund v. Costle,* 631 F.2d 922 (D.C. Cir. 1980), involved, *inter alia,* a procedural dispute regarding the type of hearing required before the Environmental Protection Agency (EPA) could deny registration to a specified pesticide under the Federal Insecticide, Fungicide and Rodenticide Act (FIFRA), 7 U.S.C.S. § 136d(b), and particularly section 16(b) of that Act. FIFRA required a "public hearing" but didn't give any further meaningful guidance. The court found as follows:

> Section 16(b) has been litigated rarely, and no decision has defined precisely the term "public hearing" as it is used in that section. In *Louisiana v. Train,* 392 F. Supp. 564 (W.D.La.) *aff'd mem.,* 514 F.2d 1070 (5th Cir. 1975), [the] district court . . . addressed the question of appellate court jurisdiction under section 16(b). The EPA hearing that was the focus of the case had consisted of the presentation of 93 witnesses . . . and 1080 pages of exhibits over a period of five days. The proceeding was an informal public hearing, rather than a formal adjudicatory hearing within the meaning of section 554 of the APA. [Note that § 554 is adjudicatory.] The district court recognized that section 6(d) of FIFRA contemplated formal public hearings for cases of cancellation, suspension, or refusal to register a pesticide. In addition, however, the court noted that section 21(b) allows the Administrator to solicit the views of interested persons concerning actions taken under the Act. [Note: this is the comment process, common to rulemaking.] This solicitation, the court concluded, would involve informal, rather than formal, public hearings. Because these FIFRA provisions indicated that Congress had contemplated that both formal and informal proceedings were "public hearings," and because legislative history did not suggest that Congress intended "public hearing" to mean only a formal public hearing, the district court concluded that an EPA order following an informal public hearing was sufficient. . . . The Fifth Circuit affirmed without opinion. . . .
>
> Absent a definition or conclusive indications of the meaning of "public hearing" in FIFRA and interpretive case law, it . . . appears that the term "hearing" does not always require formal proceedings, or even oral presentations.

4. History and Magic. The statute in *City of West Chicago* did not mandate an "on the record" hearing. Should statutory text that is overtly ambiguous be used in such a dispositive manner? To be sure, Congress did not use the magic words "public hearing to be held on the record" – but does it make sense to require Congress to be that precise? It would be one thing if the court found that the expertise of the agency and its wealth of experience would be best put to use with a less formal process – but that was not the case in *Costle.* An example of a holding where it did happen is *Chemical Waste Management v. EPA,* 873 F.2d 1477 (D.C. Cir. 1989), where the expertise of the agency was the basis for the procedural choice. In *City of West Chicago,* the language that is absent in the statute takes on a talismatic quality: "[I]n the absence of the[] magic words ["on the record"], Congress must clearly indicate its intent to trigger the formal, on-the-record hear-

ing provisions of the APA." On the other hand, the court did take a look at the legislative history of the Atomic Energy Act and prior agency action as part of the decision not to compel a more formal process.

5. *Hemp Industries Association v. Drug Enforcement Administration*, 357 F.3d 1012 (9th Cir. 2004):

> Appellants' business activities include importing and distributing sterilized hemp seed and oil and cake derived from hemp seed, and manufacturing and selling food and cosmetic products made from hemp seed and oil. On October 9, 2001, the DEA . . . proposed two rules that subsequently became final on . . . March 21, 2003. . . . DEA-205F amends the DEA's regulations at 21 C.F.R. § 1308.11(d)(27) so that the listing of THC in Schedule I includes natural as well as synthetic THC. . . . We stayed enforcement of the Final Rules pending disposition of this appeal.
>
> The non-psychoactive hemp used in Appellants' products is derived from industrial hemp plants . . . which contain only a trace amount of the THC contained in marijuana varieties grown for psychoactive use. The hemp seed used in food products is . . . either hulled for direct consumption or crushed for oil. It "contains 20 percent high-quality, digestible protein, which can be consumed by humans." U.S. Dept. of Agriculture, INDUSTRIAL HEMP IN THE UNITED STATES: STATUS AND MARKET POTENTIAL 15 (Jan. 2000). Hemp seed oil "has a better profile of key nutrients, such as essential fatty acids and gamma-linolenic acid, than other oils . . . ." Appellants list a wide range of current and planned commercial products that use hemp oil or seed, including roasted hulled seed, nutrition bars, tortilla chips, pretzels, beer, candy bars, margarine, sauces, dressings, and non-dairy versions of milk and cheese. . . .
>
> The DEA concedes that it did not use the . . . procedures spelled out in the CSA to adopt the Final Rules[, which] calls for formal rulemaking procedures, as described in 5 U.S.C. §§ 556 and 557. . . . The DEA has no authority to regulate drugs that are not scheduled, and it has not followed procedures required to schedule a substance. . . . The amendments to 21 C.F.R. § 1308.11(d)(27) that make THC applicable to all parts of the *Cannabis* plant are therefore void. We grant Appellants' petition and permanently enjoin enforcement of the Final Rules with respect to non-psychoactive hemp or products containing it.

6. The formal/informal rulemaking dichotomy is quite workable for a survey course in administrative law but a bit oversimplified. Three other terms deserve mention:

a. First, following *Florida East Coast Railway*, Congress, the agencies, and courts began to explore various forms of "hybrid" rulemaking that borrow different procedural components from the informal and formal rulemaking model. *See, e.g.*, *Vt. Yankee Nuclear Power Corp. v. NRDC*, 435 U.S. 519 (1978); *AFL-CIO v. Marshall*, 617 F.2d 636 (D.C. Cir 1979); *Neighborhood Toxic Cleanup Emergency v. Reilly*, 716 F. Supp. 828 (D.N.J. 1989).

b. Second, during the last decade, the many and varied options and alternatives created by the Internet have given rise to "e-rulemaking." For more information on e-rulemaking, we suggest the following: Ethan J. Leib, *Can Direct Democracy Be Made Deliberative?*, 54 BUFFALO L. REV. 903 (2006); Stuart Minor Benjamin, *The Role of the Internet in Agency Decision-Making: Evaluating E-Rulemaking: Public Participation and Political Institutions*, 55 DUKE L.J. 893 (2006); Cary Coglianese, *Citizen Participation in Rulemaking: Past, Present, and Future*, 55 DUKE L.J. 943 (2006); Cary Coglianese, *E-Rulemaking: Information Technology and the Regulatory Process*, 56 ADMIN. L. REV. 353 (2004); Beth Simone Noveck, *The Electronic Revolution in Rulemaking*, 53 EMORY L.J. 433 (2004).

c. Finally, by the mid-1970s, alternative dispute resolution became a fixed and important stage in decision-making in all areas of law – including rulemaking. The idea is straightforward: A rule emerging from a negotiation between those affected by the rule and the government entities involved will have a higher likelihood of compliance and, concomitantly, lower enforcement costs. The embodiment of this idea came with the passage of the Negotiated Rulemaking Act in 1990, 5 U.S.C. §§ 561-570. Over the last 15 years, a process for "regulatory negotiation" has emerged, discussed in this text *infra* Chapter 5. Credit for this creative approach belongs to Professor Philip J. Harter, who introduced the concept in *Negotiating Regulations: A Cure for Malaise*, 71 GEO. L.J. 1 (1982).

Of the different modalities for developing and publishing regulations over the last 30 years, the centerpiece has been notice and comment rulemaking pursuant to 553(c) of the APA.

V. Notice and Comment Rulemaking

The material that follows is focused on notice and comment rulemaking. As you might expect, formal rulemaking is not the preferred mode of the agency, and far more rules are produced through informal or notice and comment rulemaking than formal rulemaking. Rules issued at the conclusion of a notice and comment process are statements of "general or partial applicability and future effect designed to implement, interpret, or prescribe law or policy." 5 U.S.C. § 551(4) (APA).

a. Informal Rules Are Anything But Informal

While notice and comment rulemaking is officially referred to as "informal rulemaking," it bears noting from the outset that this process has few of the attributes one normally associates with the term "informal." Section 553 of the APA provides a procedural structure for the timing, content, and other requirements for the publication of the notice of a proposed rule and also sets forth requirements for the issuance of the final rule. The specific substantive statutes promulgated for many different agencies enhance and modify these procedures. Section 706 of the APA makes clear that parties aggrieved by agency action can seek relief through judicial review, and while the substance of rules is often vested to the discretion of the agency issuing the rule, it is fair to say that as many as one in three rules are reviewed in court. Finally, Congress has the power, either through the passage of law or through a rarely used procedure called direct review, to set aside rules that agencies have issued.

Food for Thought

Given the detailed procedures informal rulemaking requires and the omnipresence of judicial review and political intervention, notice and comment rulemaking has proven less efficient than was hoped when the Administrative Procedure Act was first adopted. This has led some commentators to conclude that the process, once thought to be simple and efficient, is today "ossified."

Given the complexity of informal rulemaking, other forms of rulemaking have emerged, such as negotiated rulemaking (discussed at the end of the rulemaking section of this text). Furthermore, some agencies, unwilling to expend the time and resources notice and comment requires, rely heavily on "exempt" processes, issuing policy statements, guidance documents, official letters, and even press releases as one of their primary means of informing the public of the goals and standards the agency will implement. These regulatory issuances do not require public participation through notice and comment and are not easily reviewable in court; thus, they have the speed and efficiency that was the promise of notice and comment rulemaking – but they raise serious problems of accountability and are attacked as lacking essential procedural fairness.

Notwithstanding the challenges notice and comment (informal) rulemaking presents, it is still the most fundamental form of law making power in the administrative state.

b. The Notice and Comment Process

A rule begins with the agency determining there is a need for either clarification or articulation of the standards the agency will implement. Once that need is defined, the agency issues a "notice of proposed rule making" (NOPR) that is published in the Federal Register.

Publication in the Federal Register of the NOPR initiates a comment period during which any member of the public may submit in writing their perspective on the proposed rule. In order for the public to provide meaningful commentary, the agency must set forth the substance of the proposed rule itself or, alternatively, the subjects that the rule will address. In most instances, an agency does not need to provide the exact text of the rule it plans to issue, although there are substantive statutes that do require, from time to time, that the rule in the NOPR be stated with specificity and that the final rule not deviate from the proposed rule.

While there is no right to discover the documents on which an agency relies prior to the issuance of the rule, parties who have an interest in or will be affected by the proposed rule may use the <u>Freedom of Information Act</u> to secure data to determine what information the agency will rely on. Furthermore, courts have occasionally required an agency to disclose or make available the general data on which the agency relies when the absence of that information would make it impossible for members of the public to provide meaningful commentary.

Food for Thought

The notice of proposed rulemaking must also contain the legal authority for the issuance of the rule, the time and place for the submission of comments, and any additional information reasonably necessary for the public to provide meaningful commentary.

For the most part, comments are filed in writing, although in some instances agencies are required to have more elaborate oral hearings. In addition, a number of agencies permit comments to be filed electronically.

c. Final Rule

At the conclusion of the notice and comment period the agency has the opportunity to evaluate the comments received, evaluate all other information relevant to the proposed rule, and then make a decision regarding the content of the "final rule" it will issue. Section 553(c) requires an agency to provide a "concise and general statement of basis and purpose," when it issues the final rule. That statement becomes the basis for analyzing all aspects of the rule, and subsequently, when requested, for judicial review of the rule. The statement must demonstrate how the rule fits into the existing regulatory structure and aligns with the legal authority underlying the rule. Furthermore, the statement must explain the process used and the basis on which the agency relied for its final rule.

Key Concept

According to section 706 of the APA, neither the content of the rule nor the process used to adopt the rule may be arbitrary, capricious, or an abuse of discretion. The rule must be "a logical outgrowth" of the NOPR. In other words, the notice must have adequately predicted or foreshadowed the final rule.

As you might guess, those affected by a rule have come to see the statement of basis and purpose as an invitation to challenge the rule in court. In some cases, questions are raised regarding whether the rule was consistent with the initial NOPR. In other cases, parties will argue that the rule is invalid because it is outside of the delegated authority of the agency. Furthermore, a rule can be challenged on the premise that the record on which the agency relied is insufficient to support the rule.

The fact is that command and control regulation by informal rulemaking seems to produce, in some members of the public, an immediate negative knee-jerk reaction. Perhaps it is nothing more complicated than the fact that people do not like to be told what to do, particularly by those who are seemingly unaccountable from a political perspective.

The cases and material that follow explore some of the issues and options involved with informal rulemaking.

CHOCOLATE MANUFACTURERS ASSOCIATION OF THE UNITED STATES V. BLOCK

755 F.2d 1098 (4th Cir. 1985)

[JUDGE SPROUSE] Chocolate Manufacturers Association (CMA) [protests] a rule promulgated by the . . . United States Department of Agriculture (USDA or Department) . . . that prohibits the use of chocolate flavored milk in the federally funded Special Supplemental Food Program for Women, Infants and Children (WIC Program). Holding that the Department's proposed rulemaking did not provide adequate notice that the elimination of flavored milk would be considered in

the rulemaking procedure, we reverse.

. . . .

In 1975 Congress . . ., for the first time, defined the "supplemental foods" which the program was established to provide. The term

> shall mean those foods containing nutrients known to be lacking in the diets of populations at nutritional risk and, in particular, those foods and food products containing high-quality protein, iron, calcium, vitamin A, and vitamin C . . . . The contents of the food package shall be made available in such a manner as to provide flexibility, taking into account medical and nutritional objectives and cultural eating patterns.

Pursuant to this statutory definition, the Department promulgated new regulations specifying the contents of WIC Program food packages. These regulations specified that flavored milk was an acceptable substitute for fluid whole milk in the food packages for women and children, but not infants. This regulation formalized the Department's practice of permitting the substitution of flavored milk, a practice observed in the WIC Program since its inception in 1973 as well as in several of the other food programs administered by the Department.

In 1978 Congress [added this qualifier:] "[t]o the degree possible, the Secretary shall assure that the fat, sugar, and salt content of the . . . foods is appropriate." . . . . [After a number of] public hearings [including] many interested and informed parties . . . the Department . . . published for comment the proposed rule at issue in this case. 44 Fed. Reg. 69254 (1979). Along with the proposed rule, the Department published a preamble . . . . Discussing the issue of sugar at length, it noted, for example, that continued inclusion of high sugar cereals may be "contrary to nutrition education principles and may lead to unsound eating practices." It also noted that high sugar foods are more expensive than foods with lower sugar content, and that allowing them would be "inconsistent with the goal of teaching participants economical food buying patterns."

The rule proposed a maximum sugar content . . . for . . . cereals. The preamble also contained a discussion of the sugar content in juice, but the Department did not propose to reduce the allowable amount of sugar in juice because of technical problems involved in any reduction. Neither the rule nor the preamble discussed sugar in relation to flavoring in milk. Under the proposed rule, the food packages for women and children without special dietary needs included milk that could be "flavored or unflavored."

The notice allowed sixty days for comment and specifically invited comment . . .: "The public is invited to submit written comments in favor of or in objection to the proposed regulations or to make recommendations for alternatives not considered in the proposed regulations." Over 1,000 comments were received . . . . Seventy-eight commenters, mostly local WIC administrators, recommended that the agency delete flavored milk from the list of approved supplemental foods.

In promulgating the final rule, the Department . . . deleted flavored milk from the list, explaining:

> In the previous regulations, women and children were allowed to receive flavored or unflavored milk. No change in this provision was proposed by the Department. However, 78 commenters requested the deletion of flavored milk from the food packages since flavored milk has a higher sugar content than unflavored milk. They indicated that providing flavored milk contradicts nutrition education and the Department's proposal to limit sugar in the food packages. Furthermore, flavored milk is more expensive than unflavored milk. The Department agrees with these concerns. . . . Therefore, to reinforce nutrition education, for consistency with the Department's philosophy about sugar in the food packages . . . the Department is deleting flavored milk from the food packages for women and children. . . .

After the final rule was issued, CMA petitioned the Department to reopen the rulemaking to allow it to comment, maintaining that it had been misled into believing that the deletion of flavored milk would not be considered. [The department] declined to reopen the rulemaking procedure.

. . . .

The requirement of notice and a fair opportunity to be heard is basic to administrative law. Our single chore is to determine . . . whether inclusion of flavored milk in the allowable food packages under the proposed rule should have alerted interested persons that the Department might reverse its position and exclude flavored milk if adverse comments recommended its deletion from the program.

Section 4 of the Administrative Procedure Act (APA) requires that the notice in the Federal Register of a proposed rulemaking contain "either the terms or substance of the proposed rule [or] a description of the subjects and issues involved." 5 U.S.C. § 553(b)(3) (1982). . . . The notice and comment procedure encourages public participation in the administrative process and educates the agency, thereby helping to ensure informed agency decisionmaking.

The Department's published notice [discussed] the negative effect of high sugar content in general and specifically in relation to some foods such as cereals and juices, but it did not mention high sugar content in flavored milk. The proposed rule eliminated certain foods with high sugar content but specifically authorized flavored milk as part of the permissible diet. In a discussion characterized by pointed identification of foods with high sugar content, flavored milk was [conspicuous] by its exclusion. If after comments the agency had adopted without change the proposed rule as its final rule, there could have been no possible objection to the adequacy of notice. The public was fully notified as to what the Department considered to be a healthy and adequate diet for its target group. The final rule, however, dramatically altered the proposed rule . . . by deleting flavored milk. . . .

This presents then not the simple question of whether the notice of a proposed rule adequately informs the public of its intent, but rather the question of how to judge the adequacy of the notice when the proposal it describes is replaced by a final rule which reaches a conclusion exactly opposite to that proposed, on the basis of comments received from parties representing only a single view of a controversy. . . .

There is no question that an agency may promulgate a final rule that differs in some particulars from its proposal. Otherwise the agency "can learn from the comments on its proposals only at the peril of starting a new procedural round of commentary." . . . . [H]owever . . . [a]n interested party must have been alerted by the notice to the possibility of the changes eventually adopted from the comments.

[The basic question is whether those challenging a modified rule have] "a fair opportunity to present their views." . . . . [N]otice is adequate if the changes in the original plan "are in character with the original scheme," and the final rule is a "logical outgrowth" of the notice and comments already given. . . . Stated differently, if the final rule materially alters the issues involved in the rulemaking or . . . if the final rule "substantially departs from the terms or substance of the proposed rule," the notice is inadequate.

There can be no doubt that the final rule in the instant case was the "outgrowth" of the original rule proposed by the agency, but the question of whether the change in it was in character with the original scheme and whether it was a "*logical* outgrowth" is not easy to answer. . . . [I]n the final analysis each case "must turn on how well the notice that the agency gave serves the policies underlying the notice requirement." . . . . [W]e do not feel that CMA was fairly treated or that the administrative rulemaking process was well served by the drastic alteration of the rule without an opportunity for CMA to be heard.

. . . .

At the time the proposed rulemaking was published, neither CMA nor the public in general could have had any indication from the history of either the WIC Program or any other food distribution programs that flavored milk was not part of the acceptable diet for women and children without special dietary needs. The discussion in the preamble to the proposed rule was very detailed and identified specific foods which the agency was examining for excess sugar. This specificity, together with total silence concerning any suggestion of eliminating flavored milk, strongly indicated that flavored milk was not at issue. The proposed rule positively and unqualifiedly approved the continued use of flavored milk. Under the specific circumstances of this case, it cannot be said that the ultimate changes in the proposed rule were in character with the original scheme or a logical outgrowth of the notice. We can well accept that, in general, an approval of a practice in a proposed rule may properly alert interested parties that the practice may be disapproved in the final rule in the event of adverse comments. The total effect of the history of the use of flavored milk, the preamble discussion, and the proposed rule, however, could have led interested persons only to conclude that a change in flavored milk would not be considered. Although ultimately their comments may well have been futile, CMA and other interested persons at least should have had the opportunity to make them. We believe that there was insufficient notice that the deletion of flavored milk from the WIC Program would be considered if adverse comments were received, and, therefore, that affected parties did not receive a fair opportunity to contribute to the administrative rulemaking process. . . .

The judgment of the district court is therefore reversed, and the case is remanded to the administrative agency with instructions to reopen the comment period and thereby afford interested parties a fair opportunity to comment on the proposed changes in the rule.

Underlying Case Documents

The case referenced:
The <u>original statute</u> defining supplemental food
The <u>regulations</u> based on this definition
The <u>congressional redefinition</u> of supplemental food
The <u>proposed rule</u> that did not limit flavored milk
The <u>final rule</u> that did limit flavored milk

On the remand following this decision, the agency was ordered to reinstate the regulations allowing flavored milk. It did so, but noted repeatedly that state officials implementing the WIC program should abide by state nutritional standards, which might be higher than federal standards by, for instance, prohibiting flavored milk. The Federal Register entry is available <u>HERE</u>.

1. Neither regulatory process nor substantive decisions regarding chocolate were resolved in the opinion above. As this text goes to press, regulatory battles regarding chocolate continue. Michael S. Rosenwald, *Chocolate Purists Alarmed by Proposal To Fudge Standards; Lines Drawn Over Cocoa Butter*, WASH. POST, Apr. 27, 2007, at A1:

> Rarely do documents making their way through federal agencies cause chocolate lovers to totally melt down. . . . [T]he current FDA standard for chocolate says it must contain cacao fat – a.k.a. cocoa butter – [the new] proposal would make it possible to call something chocolate even if it had vegetable oil instead of that defining ingredient. Whoppers malted milk balls, for instance, do not have cocoa butter.

> Chocolate purists, of which there are apparently many, have undertaken a grassroots letter-writing campaign to the FDA to inform the agency that such a change to the standards is just not okay with them . . . because chocolate isn't just food . . . for its lovers, it borders on religion. . . .

2. *Emily's List v. Federal Election Commission*, 362 F. Supp. 2d 43 (D.D.C. 2005):

> Presently before the Court is a Motion for Preliminary Injunction filed against the Federal Election Commission ("FEC") by Plaintiff EMILY's List, an organization that recruits and funds pro-choice women candidates for political office. Plaintiff is challenging regulations promulgated by the Federal Election Commission to implement the provisions of the [Bipartisan Campaign Reform Act of 2002 (BCRA)]. . . . BCRA was intended to stem the tide of nonfederal funds being improperly used to influence federal elections. . . .

> On March 11, 2004, the FEC published its official Notice of Proposed Rulemaking ("NPRM") . . . . The FEC [took comments] until April 9, 200[4], . . . and held a hearing on April 14 and 15, 2004. EMILY's List's representatives did not submit any comments and did not testify at the hearing, although over 100,000 comments were filed by other parties on a variety of issues raised by the rulemaking. On August 12, 2004, the General Counsel to the FEC submitted draft final rules . . . . On August 17, 2004, EMILY's List wrote a letter to the FEC noting that "the new proposed rules . . . provide for substantially different allocation rules for separate segregated funds and non-connected committees," and requested that the FEC publish the draft final rules for new comment. However, the FEC did not provide a new comment period. . . .

> Although EMILY's List claims that the FEC failed to provide adequate notice of the rules it eventually promulgated, . . . [i]t is abundantly clear that Plaintiff had sufficient notice of the proposed revisions to the FEC's allocation regulations. . . . In the NPRM, under the heading "Minimum Federal percentage," the FEC wrote that "the proposal would add a minimum Federal percentage to the 'funds expended' allocation method" . . . . The NPRM specifically asked "should the Commission adopt a fixed minimum Federal percentage," and proposed that nonconnected committees that conduct activities "in 10 or more States would face a minimum Federal percentage of 50 percent." In light of the language included in the NPRM, it is simply implausible that EMILY's List was not on notice that a fixed 50 percent federal funds minimum requirement might be incorporated into the final rules. . . .

3. *Emily's List*, like the *Chocolate Manufacturers Association* case, reveals some of the basic problems and advantages of notice and comment rulemaking. Admittedly, the process is cumbersome — some would say both ossifying and stultifying — and time-consuming and expensive. It has, however, the potential of genuinely democratic governance. It is law-making open to all.

Key Concept

There are no standing or ripeness requirements in a rulemaking, see *Chapter 4, infra.* Anyone can comment and, at least in theory, the agency responsible for issuing the rule will consider those comments before issuing the final rule.

4. The nature of notice and comment rulemaking is such that it can be considered for rulemaking in the international context. *See* Richard B. Stewart, *U.S. Administrative Law: A Model for Global Administrative Law?*, 68 LAW & CONTEMP. PROB. 63 (2005). As the excerpt below suggests, it can also be adapted to formulate rules for non-governmental organizations, including non-profits.

Hypothetical

Concerned that the flammability of uncontained liquid propane fumes presents a significant consumer safety hazard, the U.S. Consumer Product Safety Commission (CPSC) issued a Notice of Proposed Rule-making seeking comments on a new proposed rule pertaining to all those involved in production and distribution of liquid propane-fueled equipment - including barbecues, portable stoves and furnaces. The rule would require producers to incorporate into their product designs a new in-tank containment valve mechanism that prevents the release of fumes during installation, removal, refilling and at other times when the escape of propane fumes is likely. The comments of the trade associations for some of the retailers, wholesalers, and designers urged the agency to consider much less expensive and more effective solutions. Among these options, the producers suggested that modest changes in the proportions and physical properties of liquid propane fuel alone will inhibit the conversion of propane from the liquid to gas states, thereby adequately reducing the risk of accidental release of propane fumes. The CPSC issued a final rule abandoning the containment valve mechanism idea and adopting the proposal for changes in the chemical and physical composition of the liquid propane fuel only. The liquid propane producers and their trade association did not file comments in response to the NPRM. Having read the final rule and concluded that the proposed change to the composition of liquid propane would be more expensive and complicated than the CPSC assumed, could the propane providers succeed at challenging the validity of the final rule? How? Would they likely prevail?

5. Based on the cases above and the article below, can you envision a notice and comment process as the dominant vehicle to make rules and regulations in your university?

Victor B. Flatt, *Notice and Comment for Nonprofit Organizations*, 55 RUTGERS L. REV. 65 (2002):

> IV. What is the Notice and Comment System and How Does it Relate to Nonprofit Management?
>
> The so-called "Notice and Comment" system [requires that] agencies publish notices of proposed actions and allow a certain time for "interested parties" to comment on those actions. . . .
>
> The basic procedure of Notice and Comment rulemaking is as follows:

(1). An agency that seeks to create a general rule . . . publishes the notice of this proposed rule in a document called the Federal Register. (2). The notice must contain reference to the claimed legal authority to undertake the rulemaking, the text or substance of the proposed rule, a "summary" or "description" of the rule, and notice of where and when public hearings will take place. (3). Interested persons (usually any member of the general public) can then participate in the process by submission of data, arguments, or opinions. (4). The agency must then consider all relevant comments before reaching its decision on a final rule.

Theoretically, this process . . . informs the public of issues which may affect them in the future, educates the public and other agencies of government, allows the public to bring up information which the agency may not have considered, renders the agency's decision making process transparent to the public, and requires a certain minimal amount of deliberation with respect to the agency's exercise of its discretion.

The APA Notice and Comment procedure also helps preserve the participation rights of individuals in government action that may affect them. . . . The predictable sharing of information, increased transparency of decision-making, and ability for input from a wide variety of sources are positive outcomes that could be utilized to address many of the problems in nonprofit governance that are identified above.

In the nonprofit sector, the executive director and the staff members would replace the government agency. . . . [While it not difficult to see the downside of this model s]uch simple procedures actually synergistically solve a whole host of problems that exist in nonprofits and also existed for agencies prior to the enactment of the APA. . . .

First and foremost, the Notice and Comment model . . . limits inefficiency. . . . [D]onors and beneficiaries of the nonprofit are less likely to challenge the result or say that they did not get a voice. . . .

Notice and Comment procedures should allow less argument over whether staff actions are taken improperly. . . . The Notice and Comment model not only helps the efficiency in the oversight function of the Board, but also the efficiency of the work of the staff themselves. They can act in accordance with a specific, tailored set of actions to take for particular situations. Just as the agency personnel know what procedures they must follow, so too will the staff of the nonprofit. . . .

With a new "set" model of required procedures and consultations, the organization staff only has to answer to one set of rules – not twenty sets of individual Board expectations.

In addition to reducing oversight times by harmonizing expectations between Board and staff, a specific set of requirements can allow for the efficiency of finality. . . .

Nonprofits routinely face the challenge of having decisions revisited again and again. One of the largest problems that exists in nonprofits is repose. . . . Under the Notice and Comment model . . . Board member would have only a certain period of time to lodge such comments. After that, the staff can proceed with a clear mandate. . . .

The Notice and Comment approach also increases the transparency of nonprofit staff actions and decisions to the Board. If major decisions are to be justified, it forces discipline by pushing the staff making those decisions to justify them. This, in turn, limits the possibilities of fraud and questionable practices. . . .

[A] formal consultation processes can actually give new and better information to those who make decisions. . . . This approach also insulates the dedicated staff from unfair criticism. Taking occasional potshots at staff decisions is easy if one is not required to offer a solution. . . .

Board members presumably will gain a greater appreciation of the challenges and complexities that face the staff and be more willing to provide resources where truly needed. Or conversely, this may allow Board members to view and correct any deficiencies of the staff in a clearer light, which is also important for increasing the efficiency of the organization. . . . "originally appeared at 55 Rutgers L. Rev. 65 (2002)."

VI. Notice and Comment Process Derived from Other Statutes

When is the action of an agency a "rule" mandating a particular process? In the next case consider this question in a setting where the APA is not the dominant procedural measure.

TRIPOLI ROCKETRY ASSOCIATION, INC. V. UNITED STATES BUREAU OF ALCOHOL, TOBACCO AND FIREARMS

2002 WL 33253171 (D.D.C. 2002)

[JUDGE WALTON] Tripoli Rocketry Association, Inc. ("Tripoli") [and another plaintiff] are dedicated to the advancement and operation of non-professional high-powered rocketry . . . . The hobby of high-powered sport rocketry involves the design, construction, launch, and recovery of aero-vehicles that ascend into the air using rocket motor engines generally containing more than 62.5 grams of ammonium [perchlorate] composite propellant ("APCP") as the fuel source. . . .

On April 20, 1994, . . . the United States Bureau of Alcohol, Tobacco & Firearms ("ATF"), wrote a letter to Aerotech, Inc. ("Aerotech"), one of the manufacturers of APCP, stating that APCP was an "explosive" . . . . ATF wrote this letter in response to a letter from Aerotech requesting clarification regarding how Aerotech's business would be regulated under the "Federal Firearms and explosives laws." . . . . Further, ATF told Aerotech in [a] second letter that any rocket motor having a propellant weight greater than 62.5 grams would be subject to regulation under the ECA [Explosives Control Act].

On February 4, 1999, plaintiffs' representatives met with ATF employees

. . . . At that meeting, ATF maintained its positions . . . . On October 15, 1999, plaintiffs' representatives again met with ATF employees . . . . [Finally, after more meetings and letters,] on December 22, 2000, ATF wrote a letter to plaintiffs' counsel reiterating its position that:

(i) ATF had properly classified APCP as an explosive;

. . .

(iii) . . . sport[] rocket[] motors are not exempt from ATF regulation; and

(iv) ATF properly decided to exempt sport[] rocket motors containing 62.5 grams (or less) of propellant.

. . . .

[P]laintiffs allege that ATF's civil regulation of individuals who purchase and store rocket motors that use more than 62.5 grams of APCP as a fuel source violates the ECA . . . and the APA, 5 U.S.C. § 553(b)-(c), because ATF failed to provide notice and . . . comment when it decided to regulate such rocket motors. . . . Direction from the ECA itself is the starting point from which the Court launches its analysis. The notice and opportunity for comment provisions of the ECA, 18 U.S.C. § 847, provides:

> The Secretary may [prescribe] such rules and regulations as he deems reasonably necessary to carry out the provisions of this chapter. The Secretary shall give reasonable public notice, and afford to interested parties opportunity for hearing, prior to [prescribing] such rules and regulations.

[T]his provision [therefore] requires that notice and . . . comment be afforded before the Secretary adopts rules and regulations . . . . The question as to whether ATF's . . . announcements . . . had to be preceded by notice and . . . comment turns on whether [the] announcement[s] constituted a rule or regulation.

. . . .

Chapter 40 of Title 18 is devoid of a definition of the term "rule." Guidance, however, is found in the APA, which defines the terms "rule" and "rulemaking" . . . as follows:

> (4) "rule" means the whole or a part of an agency statement of general or particular applicability and future effect designed to implement, interpret, or prescribe law or policy . . .; (5) "rulemaking" means agency process for formulating, amending, or repealing a rule . . .

However, as the Supreme Court has recognized, "whether an agency's statement is what the APA calls a 'rule' can be a difficult exercise." "Rulemaking can be described in terms of three key indicators: generalized nature, policy orientation, and a prospective applicability." According to the Attorney General's Manual on the Administrative Procedure Act (1947):

> [t]he object of the rulemaking proceeding is the implementation of prescription of law or policy for the future, rather than the evaluation of a respondent's past conduct. Typically, the issues relate not to the evidentiary facts, as to which the veracity and demeanor of witnesses would often be important, but rather to the policy-making conclusions to draw from the facts . . . .

Whether an agency characterizes its own actions as rulemaking is not determinative. Rather, "it is the substance of what the agency has purported to do and has done which is decisive."

Here, according to the amended complaint, ATF, in several letters written to a manufacturer of APCP in 1994, for the first time indicated that only sport rocket motors that use 62.5 grams or less of APCP as a propellant were exempt from regulation under the ECA. . . . This position was again reiterated by ATF in a letter written to plaintiffs on December 22, 2000.

It is the Court's conclusion that ATF's pronouncements concerning the non-exempt status of sport rocket motors that use more than 62.5 grams of APCP amounted to rulemaking under § 847. Although contained in letters and oral statements, they were official pronouncements made on behalf of ATF . . . . As a first time announcement that was devoid of any retroactive implications, ATF's initial 1994 statement, and its subsequent statements, clearly had only future effect from the date of that first announcement. And, the statements were designed to convey a final pronouncement of ATF's legal position or policy . . . . The presence of these three ingredients fall squarely into the recipe of what constitutes a rule. Because § 847 does not exempt certain types of rules from its notice and comment command, these unqualified procedural prerequisites had to be employed before the rule was adopted. There being no claim that notice and opportunity for comment were afforded, ATF's motion to dismiss . . . must be denied.

Underlying Case Documents

The case referenced:
The notice and comment provision of the <u>Explosives Control Act</u>.
To see final *Tripoli Rocketry* order in this case, click <u>HERE</u>.

1. Up to this point, the APA has been the primary source for procedural obligations and entitlements. There are, however, a number of areas where Congress has determined that the APA should be overridden or supplanted. This process was contemplated – and included expressly – in the APA. Supplanting the APA requires an explicit statutory directive. Section 559 states that a "[s]ubsequent statute may not be held to supersede or modify [the APA] . . . except to the extent that it does so expressly." However, this is hardly an impossible task, as Professor William Allen once noted that "Congress can simply bypass the APA in prescribing agency procedures, and it has done so often." William Allen, *The Durability of the Administrative Procedure Act*, 72 VA. L. REV. 235, 251 (1986).

2. The Supreme Court first addressed congressional override of the APA in *Marcello v. Bonds, 349 U.S. 302, 310 (1955)* (stating that "[e]xemptions from the terms of the Administrative Procedure Act are not lightly to be presumed in view of the statement in [section 559] that modifications must be express," in reference to *Shaughnessy v. Pedreiro, 349 U.S. 48, (1955)*). The notion that the APA can be supplanted implicitly has been outright rejected. *See, e.g., Ninilchik Traditional Council v. United States, 227 F.3d 1186, 1193 (9th Cir. 2000)* ("[C]hallenges to agency actions are subject to the APA . . . unless Congress specifies a contrary intent. . . ."); *Yale-New Haven Hosp. v. Leavitt, 470 F.3d 71 (2d Cir. 2006)*.

3. The question posed in *Tripoli* is both common and of real consequence to client interests. An agency does not speak with a singular voice. From technical staff and support personnel to the Administrator or Commissioners, all those acting under the imprimatur of the agency have the power to educate, inform, and influence the public.

Food for Thought

It is hard to imagine that the APA – or any statute – was designed to silence agency actors or impose inordinate costs on governmental speech. Yet public process – like notice and comment – is expensive and time-consuming. Balancing the need for this public input against the need for agency actors at every level to speak, to inform, and to set forth parameters and priorities, is no small task.

4. This question prompts an even broader inquiry: Should agency actors serve primarily as assessors of public opinion and then give the dominant perspective voice, or are they responsible for implementing the goals and objectives of the executive? If it is not the latter, how is the voice of elected officials expressed? Presidents, governors, and mayors are elected because of their policies, not because they seem likely to hold fair, impartial, and balanced hearings. That said, authoritarian governments are characterized by their practice of ignoring all opinions and perspectives except those of the ruling elite.

SUGAR CANE GROWERS COOPERATIVE OF FLORIDA v. VENEMAN

289 F.3d 89 (D.C. Cir. 2002)

[JUDGE SILBERMAN] In the United States, sugar production, which the government supports through a variety of programs, is about evenly divided between sugar cane and sugar beet production. . . . The Food Security Act gives the Department authority to implement a payment-in-kind (PIK) program for sugar, which it did for sugar beet farmers in August 2000. For the 2000 PIK program, sugar beet farmers submitted bids to the Department offering to destroy (or "divert") a certain amount of their crops in return for sugar from USDA storage. A farmer's bid is his asking price for that amount of destruction; the price is expressed in terms of a percentage of the three-year average value of the crop yield for the acreage diverted. Thus, a farmer bidding 80 percent would receive eight dollars [worth of sugar] for every acre destroyed if an average acre of their farm produced ten dollars worth of sugar. [Farmers can bid less than they would have made because they save the labor costs of harvesting.] In fact, the average bid was approximately 84 percent and resulted in the distribution of about 277,000 tons of government sugar and the diversion of approximately 102,000 acres. Participants were prohibited from participating in future PIK programs if they increased their acreage planted with sugar beets over 2000 levels. The Agency did not proceed by notice and comment, but no party challenged that decision or the program itself.

Appellants claim the 2000 PIK program unfairly provided participants with below-harvest-cost government sugar which gave them a competitive advantage over appellants. And they claim that the program depressed sugar prices. . . .

In January 2001, the Department met with interested persons (including representatives of appellants) and indicated that while it was considering a PIK program for the 2001 sugar crop, it would not do so without notice and comment. . . . The Department announced by an August 31, 2001 press release, however, that it was implementing a PIK program for the 2001 sugar crop without using APA rulemaking. The Agency followed that announcement a week later with a "Notice of Program Implementation" in the . . . Federal Register. For the 2001 PIK program, the Department set a 200,000 ton limit in order to encourage more competitive bidding and made both beet and cane sugar producers eligible. But a statutory restriction limiting payments to $ 20,000 per producer effectively eliminated appellants' opportunity to participate because of their size. . . .

Appellants filed suit shortly after the press release appeared, seeking injunctive and declaratory relief. They argued that the Department did not comply with the APA because it promulgated a rule without notice and comment rulemaking. . . . The APA sets forth several steps an agency must take when engaged in rulemaking: it must publish a general notice of proposed rulemaking in the Federal Register; give an opportunity for interested persons to participate in the rulemaking through submission of written data, views, or arguments; and issue publication of a concise general statement of the rule's basis and purpose. 5 U.S.C. § 553(b), (c). The government defends the Department's failure to engage in notice and comment rulemaking by asserting the PIK announcement was not really a rule and, even if it were, the failure to engage in rulemaking was a harmless error. . . . [T]he government argues that because the announcement of the 2001 PIK program was an "isolated agency act" that did not propose to affect subsequent Department acts and had "no future effect on any other party before the agency" it was not a rule. The government would have us see its announcement of the PIK program as analogous to an agency's award of a contract pursuant to an invitation of bids or an agency's decision to approve an application or a proposal – in administrative law terms an informal adjudication . . . .

We have little difficulty – as did the district court – in rejecting this argument. The . . . press release . . . and most notably the . . . Notice of Program Implementation set forth the bid submission procedures which all applicants must follow, the payment limitations of the program, and the sanctions that will be imposed on participants if they plant more in *future* years than in 2001. It is simply absurd to call this anything but a rule "by any other name."

[T]he government alternatively claims harmless error [arguing] that appellants cannot identify any additional arguments they would have made in a notice and comment procedure that they did not make to the Department in the several informal sessions. . . . It is true that we have recognized certain technical APA errors as harmless. . . . [A]n utter failure to comply with notice and comment cannot be considered harmless if there is any uncertainty at all as to the effect of that failure. . . .

Here the government would have us virtually repeal section 553's requirements: if the government could skip those procedures, engage in informal consultation, and then be protected from judicial review unless a petitioner could show a new argument – not presented informally – section 553 obviously would be eviscerated. The government could avoid the necessity of publishing a notice of a proposed rule and perhaps, most important, would not be obliged to set forth a statement of the basis and purpose of the rule, which needs to take account of the major comments – and often is a major focus of judicial review. . . . [The court rejected this as unsupported by precedent and at odds with the prevailing perception of administrative governance.]

. . . .

[W]e reverse the district court's grant of summary judgment and remand to that court to in turn remand to the Department.

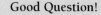

Underlying Case Documents

The case referenced:
The Food Security Act
Notice of Program Implementation from the Federal Register

1. One of the more curious arguments in the *Sugar Cane Growers* case involves the apparent assertion by the government that providing the complainants an opportunity to comment was, in effect, a hollow gesture since the government had already decided on its course of action. Such assertions are not likely to win over many judges. If there is any justification for the argument, it would involve the "harmless error" rule.

Good Question!

When is denial of process to which one has an entitlement harmless?

2. The D.C. Circuit recently held: "A plaintiff asserting procedural injury 'never has to prove that if he had received the procedure the substantive result would have been altered.'" *City of Dania Beach v. FAA*, 485 F.3d 1181, 1185 (D.C. Cir. 2007). A few years earlier, however, that same court drew the following distinction relevant specifically to rulemaking: "In contrast to an informal adjudication or a mere policy statement, which 'lacks the firmness of a [prescribed] standard,' an agency's imposition of requirements that 'affect subsequent [agency] acts' and have a 'future effect' on a party before the agency triggers the APA notice requirement." *Sprint Corp. v. FCC*, 315 F.3d 369 (D.C. Cir. 2003).

3. *Sugar Cane Growers* and these cases raise an interesting problem: It cannot be that a party challenging agency action in a rulemaking has to prove that the rule the agency seeks to issue would have been different had they been given the chance to comment – but what is required?

Good Question!

Can the failure to provide an opportunity for comment, or similar procedural infirmity, constitute harmless error?

4. Professor Kristin E. Hickman addressed the harmless error problem recently in *Coloring Outside the Lines: Examining Treasury's (Lack of) Compliance with Administrative Procedure Act Rulemaking Requirements*, 82 NOTRE DAME L. REV. 1727, 1791-92 (2007):

> The APA offers one more provision that might operate to excuse at least some of Treasury's failures to adhere to the procedural requirements of APA section 553. Recognizing that "no administrative agency is perfect," APA section 706 instructs courts reviewing agency action to take "due account . . . of the rule of prejudicial error." The courts occasionally employ this "harmless error" rule to excuse deviations from APA rulemaking requirements.

> Absent good cause or some other APA section 553(b) exception, the harmless error rule will not save the regulations from those projects in which Treasury skips notice and comment altogether. The notice and comment requirements are the very heart of APA section 553. Thus, several circuits hold an agency's "failure to provide notice and comment [to be] harmless only where the agency's mistake clearly had no bearing on the procedure used or the substance of decision reached." The D.C. Circuit follows a rule that "an utter failure to comply with notice and comment cannot be considered harmless if there is any uncertainty at all as to the effect of that failure." Under such circumstances, the degree of uncertainty required to defeat an agency's harmless error claim is not great. It is simply too difficult to prove that pursuing the notice and comment process would have made absolutely no difference. Even where agencies can demonstrate that interested parties have been given the opportunity to present their concerns in other ways, the courts generally have been reluctant to excuse agencies from APA notice and comment. Reprinted with permission (c) by NOTRE DAME LAW REVIEW, University of Notre Dame. [The publisher bears responsibility for errors in the use of the above excerpted piece.]

5. Finally, in a recent district court opinion, JUDGE WALTON stated what is probably the majority position in the field: "The 'plaintiff who alleges a deprivation of a procedural protection to which [it] is entitled never has to prove that if [it] had received the procedure the substantive result would have been altered. All that is necessary is to show that the procedural step was connected to the substantive

Good Question!

How would you prove that a denial of process was "connected to the substantive result" in a rulemaking case? Does "connection with the result" imply an obligation to establish that the denial of process had substantive impact?

result.'" *United States Women's Chamber of Commerce v. United States SBA*, 2005 WL 3244182 (D.D.C.), *citing* *Nat'l Parks Conservation Ass'n. v. Manson*, 414 F.3d 1, 5 (D.C. Cir. 2005) (quoting *Sugar Cane Growers*, 289 F.3d at 94-95).

6. In the case that follows, the question shifts to a more fundamental problem: What happens when, rather than failing to follow optimal process, as occurred in *Sugar Cane Growers*, the agency issues no standards at all? The statute in question

in *Morton v. Ruiz*, <u>The Snyder Act, 25 U.S.C. § 13 et. seq.</u>, gave the Secretary of Interior and her or his officers in the Bureau of Indian Affairs, considerable power:

> The Bureau of Indian Affairs, under the supervision of the Secretary of the Interior, shall direct, supervise, and expend such moneys as Congress may from time to time appropriate, for the benefit, care, and assistance of the Indians throughout the United States for the following purposes: General support and civilization, including education; For relief of distress and conservation of health; . . . [a]nd for general and incidental expenses in connection with the administration of Indian affairs.

Given the power to "expend such moneys as Congress may . . . appropriate," is there really a need for additional published rules?

MORTON V. RUIZ ET UX.

<u>415 U.S. 199 (1974)</u>

[JUSTICE BLACKMUN] The pertinent facts are agreed upon . . . . The respondents, Ramon Ruiz and his wife, Anita, are Papago Indians and United States citizens. In 1940 they left the Papago Reservation in Arizona to seek employment 15 miles away at the Phelps-Dodge copper mines at Ajo. Mr. Ruiz found work there, and they settled in a community at Ajo called the "Indian Village" and populated almost entirely by Papagos. . . . [M]ost of the homes in the Village are owned or rented by Phelps-Dodge. The Ruizes have lived in Ajo continuously since 1940 . . . . A minor daughter lives with them. They speak and understand the Papago language but only limited English. Apart from Mr. Ruiz' employment with Phelps-Dodge, they have not been assimilated into the dominant culture, and they appear to have maintained a close tie with the nearby reservation.

In July 1967, 27 years after the Ruizes moved to Ajo, the mine where he worked was shut down by a strike. It remained closed until the following March. While the strike was in progress, Mr. Ruiz' sole income was a $15 per week striker's benefit paid by the union. . . . [In] December . . . Mr. Ruiz applied for general assistance benefits from the Bureau of Indian Affairs (BIA). He was immediately notified by letter that he was ineligible for general assistance because of the provision . . . in 66 Indian Affairs Manual 3.1.4 . . . that eligibility is limited to Indians living "on reservations" . . . . n.6 . . . . The sole ground for the denial of general assistance benefits was that the Ruizes resided outside the boundaries of the Papago Reservation.

n.6 The [Bureau of Indian Affairs manual states], in pertinent part: . . . .

4 Eligibility Conditions.

A. Residence. Eligibility for general assistance is limited to Indians living on reservations . . . .

The respondents then instituted the present purported class action against the Secretary, claiming, as a matter of statutory interpretation, entitlement to the general assistance for which they had applied . . . .

. . . .

The appropriation legislation [directs the] Department of Interior, Bureau of Indian Affairs, [to allocate funds] "[f]or expenses necessary to provide education and welfare services for Indians, either directly or in cooperation with States and other organizations, including payment (in advance or from date of admission), of care, tuition . . . grants and other assistance to needy Indians . . . ."

This wording . . . is identical to that employed in similar legislation for prior fiscal years and, indeed, for subsequent ones . . . . [N]either the language of the Snyder Act nor that of the Appropriations Act imposes any geographical limitation on the availability of general assistance benefits and does not prescribe eligibility requirements or the details of any program. Instead, the Snyder Act states that the BIA (under the supervision of the Secretary) "shall direct, supervise, and expend . . . for the benefit, care, and assistance of the Indians throughout the United States" for the stated purposes including, as the two purposes first described, "general support" and "relief of distress. . . ."

. . . .

V.

[We believe] that the congressional appropriation was intended to cover welfare services at least to those Indians residing "on or near" the reservation, [however,] it does not necessarily follow that the Secretary is without power to create reasonable classifications and eligibility requirements in order to allocate the limited funds available to him for this purpose. Thus, if there were only enough funds appropriated to provide meaningfully for 10,000 needy Indian beneficiaries and the entire class of eligible beneficiaries numbered 20,000, it would be incumbent upon the BIA to develop an eligibility standard to deal with this problem, and the standard, if rational and proper, might leave some of the class otherwise encompassed by the appropriation without benefits. But in such a case the agency must, at a minimum, let the standard be generally known so as to assure that it is being applied consistently and so as to avoid both the reality and the appearance of arbitrary denial of benefits to potential beneficiaries.

Assuming, arguendo, that the Secretary rationally could limit the "on or near" appropriation to include only the smaller class of Indians who lived directly "on" the reservation . . ., the question that remains is whether this has been validly accomplished. The power of an administrative agency to administer a congressionally created and funded program necessarily requires the formulation of policy and the making of rules to fill any gap left, implicitly or explicitly, by Congress. In the area of Indian affairs, the Executive has long been empowered to promulgate rules and policies, and the power has been given explicitly to the Secretary and his delegates at the BIA. This agency power to make rules that affect substantial individual rights and obligations carries with it the responsibility not only to remain consistent with the governing legislation, but also to employ procedures that conform to the law. No matter how rational or consistent with congressional intent a particular decision might be, the determination of eligibility cannot be made on an ad hoc basis by the dispenser of the funds.

The Administrative Procedure Act was adopted to provide, *inter alia*, that administrative policies affecting individual rights and obligations be promulgated pursuant to certain stated procedures so as to avoid the inherently arbitrary nature of unpublished ad hoc determinations. That Act states in pertinent part:

> Each Agency shall . . . publish in the Federal Register for the guidance of the public
> . . . .
>
> (D) substantive rules of general applicability adopted as authorized by law, and statements of general policy or interpretations of general applicability formulated and adopted by the agency.

The sanction added in 1967 . . . provides:

> Except to the extent that a person has actual and timely notice of the terms thereof, a person may not in any manner be required to resort to, or be adversely affected by, a matter required to be published in the Federal Register and not so published.

In the instant case the BIA itself has recognized the necessity of formally publishing its substantive policies . . . . The 1968 introduction to the Manual reads:

> . . . Directives which relate to the public, including Indians, are published in the Federal Register and codified in 25 Code of Federal Regulations. These directives inform the public of privileges and benefits available; eligibility qualifications, requirements and procedures; and of appeal rights and procedures. They are published in accordance with . . . the Administrative Procedure Act . . . .

Bureau of Indian Affairs Manual: Policies, procedures, and instructions which do not relate to the public but are required to govern the operations of the Bureau are published in the Bureau of Indian Affairs Manual.

Unlike numerous other [BIA] programs . . ., the BIA has chosen not to publish its eligibility requirements for general assistance in the Federal Register or in the CFR. . . . The only official manifestation of this alleged policy . . . is . . . in the Manual which is, by BIA's own admission, solely an internal-operations brochure intended to cover policies that "do not relate to the public." Indeed, at oral argument the Government conceded that for this to be a "real legislative rule," itself endowed with the force of law, it should be published in the Federal Register.

Where the rights of individuals are affected, it is incumbent upon agencies to follow their own procedures. This is so even where the internal procedures are possibly more rigorous than otherwise would be required. The BIA, by its Manual, has declared that all directives that "inform the public of privileges and benefits available" and of "eligibility requirements" are among those to be published. The requirement that, in order to receive general assistance, an Indian must reside directly "on" a reservation is clearly an important substantive policy that fits within this class of directives. Before the BIA may extinguish the entitlement of these otherwise eligible beneficiaries, it must comply, at a minimum, with its own internal procedures. . . .

The overriding duty of our Federal Government to deal fairly with Indians wherever located has been recognized by this Court on many occasions. Particularly here, where the BIA has continually represented to Congress, when seeking funds, that Indians living near reservations are within the service area, it is essential that the legitimate expectation of these needy Indians not be extinguished by what amounts to an unpublished ad hoc determination of the agency that was not promulgated in accordance with its own procedures, to say nothing of those of the Administrative Procedure Act. The denial of benefits to these respondents under such circumstances is inconsistent with "the distinctive obligation of trust incumbent upon the Government in its dealings with these dependent and sometimes exploited people." Before benefits may be denied to these otherwise entitled Indians, the BIA must first promulgate eligibility requirements according to established procedures. . . .

We emphasize that our holding does not . . . make general assistance available to all Indians "throughout the country." Even respondents do not claim this much. The appropriation, as we see it, was for Indians "on or near" the reservation. This is broad enough, we hold, to include the Ruizes who live . . . in an Indian community only a few miles from their reservation, who maintain their close economic and social ties with that reservation, and who are unassimilated. The parameter of their class will be determined, to the extent necessary, by the District Court on remand of the case. Whether other persons qualify for general assistance will be left to cases that arise in the future. . . .

The judgment of the Court of Appeals is affirmed and the case is remanded for further proceedings consistent with this opinion. . . .

Underlying Case Documents

The case referenced:

The Snyder Act

The Indian Affairs Manual

1. Post-*Morton* case law is limited as is the scholarship pertaining to the case – and understandably so. There is no single convincing interpretation of the case. One reading of *Morton* suggests that the Court, in a misguided judicial moment, found that an agency cannot function at all in the absence of clearly articulated comprehensive rules promulgated in notice and comment procedures – a proposition that is clearly not correct. That reading of *Morton* would produce a bureaucracy bound by rules and regulations to the point of suffocation. Listed below are other readings of the case that are less strained:

> i. Agencies must conform with statutory obligations in their enabling legislation.

> ii. Eligibility determinations made on an unpredictable and ad hoc basis are arbitrary.

> iii. Guidelines for eligibility ought to be published, particularly when there is a legislative directive to do so.

> iv. Agencies have not only the authority to "fill in the gaps" in legislation, they have an obligation to do so.

> v. Agencies can use the adjudicatory process to develop standards – and also use the rulemaking process to formulate standards – but in any case agencies ought to follow their own procedures, even "where the internal procedures are more rigorous than otherwise would be required."

> vi. Finally, substantively, the federal trust responsibility to Native Americans goes beyond reservation boundaries.

2. Look back through the case. Which of the above notions is supported by the opinion? Assuming there is a basis for each, what is it about this case that caused a fairly negative reaction? *See generally* Kenneth Culp Davis, *Administrative Law Surprises in the Ruiz Case*, 75 COLUM. L. REV. 823 (1975).

Put simply, those who are inclined to limit judicial intervention and maximize the options available to agencies are troubled by the idea that an agency ought to publish rules establishing parameters before taking action in a specific case. On the other side of the aisle, those who believe good government requires notice before adverse action is taken find *Morton* of value. Either way, the case stakes out two positions: properly promulgated rules enhance fairness, and a fixation on rules stifles government and prevents agencies from filling in gaps left by Congress.

These two positions are not as incompatible as they might appear. Fairness is advanced when the public is informed of the standards by which the government will allocate benefits – and it is impossible to produce rules for every variable. Whether the failure to publish rules or standards in a particular setting is error – or is even reviewable – is a source of controversy. Based on *Sugar Cane* and the notes thereafter, is any failure of process reviewable with the exception of those that constitute "harmless error?"

3. In <u>*Port of Jacksonville Maritime Ad Hoc Committee v. United States Coast Guard,*</u> <u>788 F.2d 705 (11th Cir. 1986)</u>, the court noted that the review trigger was not substantial prejudice:

> One commentator has faulted *Morton v. Ruiz* for departing from <u>*American Farm Lines*</u> <u>[*v. Black Ball Freight,* 397 U.S. 532 (1970),]</u> by failing to require a showing of substantial prejudice. *See* Davis, Administrative Law Surprises in the Ruiz Case, [supra, n.2]. We read *Morton v. Ruiz* differently. The internal guideline at issue there "declared that all directives that 'inform the public of privileges and benefits available' and of 'eligibility requirements'" be published. *Morton v. Ruiz,* 415 U.S. at 235. The guideline clearly was intended to confer a procedural benefit and therefore . . . no inquiry into substantial prejudice was necessary.

Take Note

In *American Farm Lines v. Black Ball Freight,* 397 U.S. 532 (1970), the Court cited with favor *NLRB v. Monsanto Chemical,* 205 F.2d 763, 764 (8th Cir. 1953). In that case, the Eighth Circuit found as follows: "It is always within the discretion of a court or an administrative agency to relax or modify its procedural rules adopted for the orderly transaction of business before it when in a given case the ends of justice require it. The action of either in such a case is not reviewable except upon a showing of substantial prejudice to the complaining party." While the substantial prejudice rule seems logical, it has been used only a few times in the first decade of the 21st Century. *See Wilson v. Comm'r of Soc. Sec.,* 378 F.3d 541, 547 (6th Cir. 2004)

4. Twenty years after the decision, the Supreme Court returned to *Morton* in <u>*Lincoln*</u> <u>*v. Vigil*</u>, 508 U.S. 182 (1993), and, much like the decision in *Port of Jacksonville*, focused on publication responsibilities. *Lincoln*, a case involving the discontinuance of a program designed to benefit Native American children, is seen by some as a limitation on *Morton* since the agency decision – which was upheld – was made without a rule issued through notice and comment.

First, the agency decision in *Lincoln* was found to be within "§ 553(b)(A)[, which] exempts 'rules of agency organization' from notice and comment requirements. . . . Moreover, § 553(b)(A) also exempts 'general statements of policy. . . .'" Second, the Court focused on the specific publication responsibilities in *Morton*. "[The] provisions . . . at issue in *Ruiz*, . . . contained in a Bureau of Indian Affairs manual, . . . restricted eligibility for Indian assistance. . . . [T]he Bureau's own regulations required it to publish the provision in the Federal Register. . . . We held that the Bureau's failure to abide by its own procedures rendered the provision invalid . . . ."

Good Question!

What if the final exam you are given in administrative law requires an analysis of issues and principles significantly different from what you studied over the course of the semester – and you learn of this change on the day of the exam. Would that be unfair – a denial of notice regarding important standards that should have been published in advance – or would it be a defensible exercise of professional judgment and an expression of essential academic freedom?

5. *Lewis v. Weinberger*, 415 F. Supp. 652 (D.N.M. 1976):

> According to the [Health, Education and Welfare] regulations, a person is within the scope of the Indian health and medical service program if: (1) he is of Indian descent; and (2) he belongs to the Indian community served by the local [Indian Health Services (IHS)] facilities and program. . . .
>
> Arthur Lewis is a full-blood, enrolled member of the Choctaw Tribe . . . . Gwendolyn Lewis, his wife, is a full-blood, enrolled member of the Wichita Tribe . . . . [I]t has been stipulated that they are fully eligible under the <u>Snyder Act</u> . . . to receive health care from the IHS . . . . Gwendolyn Lewis began to suffer internal hemorrhaging from the uterus [in] 1973. She was admitted to the [local] IHS hospital . . . where she received direct medical care for three weeks. At the end of three weeks, plaintiff's condition had seriously deteriorated, and her IHS attending physician rushed her to . . . a non-IHS facility, for emergency surgery necessary to save her life. . . . After surgery . . . she was informed that she would have to pay the cost. Neither Gwendolyn nor Arthur Lewis can afford to pay the still outstanding balance of the hospital's bill.
>
> The denial of contract care to Mr. and Mrs. Lewis results from a relatively recent change in IHS policy . . . . [T]he IHS, in effect, defines two classes of Indians . . . . [R]eservation Indians [are] eligible to receive both direct care and contract care. . . . [O]ff-reservation Indians [are] eligible to receive direct care only. [This policy does not appear] in the relevant statutes, the applicable regulations, or in the Indian Health Manual. The only . . . official statement of present IHS contract care policy is [in a] memorandum, available at IHS offices, . . . sent from the IHS Director . . . .
>
> It is the Court's conclusion that the IHS policy . . . is ineffective for lack of publication in the Federal Register . . . . In this case, publication of the contested IHS policy is necessary not only to avoid the "reality and appearance of arbitrary denial of benefits" but also to guide the legitimate expectations of that segment of the Indian public whose substantive rights are affected. . . . [A]dministrative actions taken pursuant

to this unpublished policy are void with respect to persons adversely affected thereby. . . . Therefore, defendants are responsible for paying the outstanding balance of Mrs. Lewis' health care bill . . . and they will be enjoined from refusing to consider Indians for participation in the IHS contract care program on the sole ground that they are classifiable as off-reservation pursuant to their unpublished policy.

6. The failure of an agency to follow the proper procedures for promulgating rules does not necessarily mean the agency can use the lack of publication as a defense, as the following note points out.

Cutlip v. Commissioner of Social Security Administration, 1999 U.S. Dist. LEXIS 23497 (D. W. Va. 1999):

> Title 42, U.S.C. § 423(d)(2)(C) provides: "An individual shall not be considered to be disabled for purposes of this title if alcoholism or drug addiction would . . . be a contributing factor material to the Commissioner's determination that the individual is disabled." In addition to other mental impairments, plaintiff has a long history of alcoholism and the ALJ found that her alcohol use is a material factor in her disability, preventing him from awarding SSI benefits to her. The magistrate judge, however, relying on an August 30, 1996 memorandum to various departments within the Social Security Administration ("SSA"), found that SSA policy mandated a finding that plaintiff's alcoholism was not material. The memorandum states: "When it is not possible to separate the mental restrictions and limitations imposed by [drug and alcohol abuse] and the various other mental disorders shown by the evidence, a finding of 'not material' would be appropriate." . . . .
>
> [The government] objects to this conclusion arguing that the . . . memorandum . . . was not binding and, therefore, the magistrate judge erred by relying solely upon that memorandum to reverse the Commissioner's decision. . . . This Court finds defendant's argument unpersuasive. . . . [The memorandum is] the only "official manifestation" of the SSA's policy toward interpreting "material" in section 432(d)(2)(C) that has been brought to this Court's attention . . . . Also, like the manual in *Morton*, the memorandum announces a "binding norm" that affects entitlement to federal benefits. . . . Specifically, the memorandum directs [Administrative Law Judges] ALJs to find the addiction "not material" in [certain] circumstances. As a result of such a finding, an applicant would be entitled to benefits assuming the criteria for eligibility are met. Thus, the memorandum constitutes more than an announcement of general intention; instead, it is intended to have a "present-day binding effect." As such, this Court finds that the agency was not free to ignore its own pronouncement. Accordingly, [the] decision denying plaintiff SSI benefits should be reversed. . . .

7. Direct Final Rules. In <u>*Sierra Club v. United States EPA*, 99 F.3d 1551, 1554, n.4 (10th Cir. 1996)</u>, EPA issued a direct final rule to exempt Salt Lake and Davis Counties, Utah from the Clean Air Act's "nonattainment area" without initially designating and assessing the region an "attainment area," arguably a precondition based on <u>42 U.S.C. § 7407(d)(3)(E)(i)-(v) (1994)</u>. Sierra Club challenged the direct final rule after it was "noticed" in the Federal Register. Under EPA rules, when a challenge is made to a direct final rule, the agency must withdraw the rule

and allow for public comment. The court characterized the process thusly:

> A direct final rule becomes effective without further administrative action, unless adverse comments are received within the time limit specified in the proposed rule. If adverse comments are received, the Environmental Protection Agency withdraws its direct final rule and issues a final rule that addresses those comments. In this case, the Environmental Protection Agency received comments from the Sierra Club and one other commenter. The Environmental Protection Agency therefore withdrew its direct final rule. . . .

Direct final rules, then, are a way to shortcut the conventional notice and comment process, but only when no comments are received after the initial publication of the rule. Assuming the absence of comments in opposition to a direct final rule, the rule can have the same binding effect as a rule issued at the conclusion of a notice and comment process. In the case of the EPA, once the agency publishes a direct final rule, a 30 day time period begins during which comments can be filed. *See, e.g.*, Clean Air Act Promulgation of Reclassification of Ozone Nonattainment Areas in Virginia, and Attainment Determinations, 40 C.F.R. Part 81, 60 Fed. Reg. 3349 (January 17, 1995). Other agencies do it differently. The FDA, for instance, will issue a proposed rule simultaneously with a direct final rule so that if comments are received the direct final rule is withdrawn, but no time has been lost in the process. *See, e.g.*, Current Good Manufacturing Practice and Investigational New Drugs Intended for Use in Clinical Trials, 73 Fed. Reg. 40453 (July 15, 2008) (to be codified at 21 C.F.R. Part 210) (discussing the issuance of a final rule that had previously been issued as a direct final rule and withdrawn after adverse comments were received).

The APA does not address with specificity direct final rules. *See* Administrative Conference of the United States, Recommendation 95-4, Procedures for Noncontroversial and Expedited Rulemaking, 60 Fed. Reg. 43,108, 43,110-13 (Aug. 18, 1995). For further study on the use and frequency of direct final rules, see Anne Joseph O'Connell, *Political Cycles of Rulemaking: An Empirical Portrait of the Modern Administrative State*, 94 VA. L. REV. 889 (2008) (commenting on the hypothesis that direct final rules tend to be used for more technical matters); Jacob E. Gersen & Anne Joseph O'Connell, *Deadlines in Administrative Law*, 156 U. PA. L. REV. 923 (2008) (discussing the timing variables for rulemaking); Ronald M. Levin, *Direct Final Rulemaking*, 64 GEO. WASH. L. REV. 1 (1995) (providing a summary of the field of direct final rulemaking).

Take Note

Like direct final rules, interim final rules are not addressed in the APA. A comparison of these unconventional processes follows:

> In promulgating a direct final rule, an agency does not request comments; in promulgating an interim final rule, an agency asks for comments and leaves open the possibility that it may modify the interim final rule into a final rule at a later date. Another important distinction between interim final rules and direct final rules is the predicate for their issuance: direct final rules are rules for which the agency has found public comment to be unnecessary (rules in which the agency infers the public will have little interest), whereas interim final rules are ones with respect to which the agency has determined that public comment is impractical (usually because of some type of emergency).

Stuart Shapiro, *Presidents and Process: A Comparison of the Regulatory Process Under the Clinton and Bush (43) Administrations*, 23 J.L. & Politics 393, 403 (2007).

VII. Rulemaking, Records, and Review

To what extent must an agency set forth support for the decisions it makes? When an agency makes a decision based primarily on political considerations, must it justify its action to a court? Does your answer depend on whether the political decision of the agency is based on central beliefs and values of a newly elected President?

Major Theme

It is one thing for a court to remand if the agency fails to undertake specific tasks its enabling legislation requires, or fails to assess factors Congress has declared are a predicate to agency action. It is quite another thing for a court to interject its opinion and judgment for that of an agency.

In the following case, the Supreme Court confronted some of the most fundamental questions in administrative law: While we all agree that "reasoned decisions" are best, what evidence of reasoning do we demand from agencies? What evidence of reasoning do we demand from the political appointees who have been appointed by the President to carry out the policies of the administration?

Good Question!

If the President directs a cabinet officer to undertake an action clearly within the statutory authority of that officer's agency, can it really be that the President – or that cabinet officer – is required to support their actions with a reasoned decision based on a record the agency compiles?

As you read the *State Farm* decision, below, ask if the opinion crosses into "wisdom substitution" by the Court or whether the opinion reveals the more accepted "hard look" judicial review.

MOTOR VEHICLE MANUFACTURERS ASSOCIATION OF THE UNITED STATES, INC. V. STATE FARM MUTUAL AUTOMOBILE INSURANCE COMPANY

463 U.S. 29 (1983)

[handwritten margin notes: reading statute; legis; background]

[JUSTICE WHITE] Since 1929, motor vehicles have been the leading cause of accidental deaths and injuries in the United States. . . . In 1966, Congress decided that at least part of the answer lies in improving the design and safety features of the vehicle itself. But much of the technology for building safer cars was undeveloped or untested. . . . Congress responded by enacting the National Traffic and Motor Vehicle Safety Act of 1966 (Act). The Act . . . directs the Secretary of Transportation . . . to issue motor vehicle safety standards [after considering] "relevant available motor vehicle safety data," whether the proposed standard "is reasonable, practicable and appropriate" for the particular type of motor vehicle, and the "extent to which such standards will contribute to carrying out the purposes" of the Act.

[handwritten margin note: issue]

[W]e review today whether NHTSA [the National Highway Traffic Safety Administration] acted arbitrarily and capriciously in revoking the requirement in Motor Vehicle Safety Standard 208 that new motor vehicles produced after September 1982 be equipped with passive restraints . . . . Briefly summarized, we hold that the agency failed to present an adequate basis and explanation for rescinding the passive restraint requirement and that the agency must either consider the matter further or adhere to or amend Standard 208 along lines which its analysis supports.

I

The regulation whose rescission is at issue bears a complex and convoluted history. . . . As originally issued by the Department of Transportation in 1967, Standard 208 simply required the installation of seatbelts in all automobiles. It soon became apparent that the level of seatbelt use was too low to reduce traffic injuries to an acceptable level. The Department therefore began consideration of "passive occupant restraint systems" – devices that do not depend for their effectiveness upon any action taken by the occupant except that necessary to operate the vehicle. Two types of automatic crash protection emerged: automatic seatbelts and airbags. . . . [I]t was estimated by NHTSA that passive restraints could prevent approximately 12,000 deaths and over 100,000 serious injuries annually.

[handwritten margin note: regulation]

In 1969, the Department formally proposed a standard requiring the installation of passive restraints . . . . [I]n 1972, the agency amended the Standard to require full passive protection for all front seat occupants of vehicles manufactured after August 15, 1975. In the interim, vehicles . . . were to carry either passive restraints or lap and shoulder belts coupled with an "ignition interlock" that would prevent starting the vehicle if the belts were not connected. . . . In preparing for the upcoming model year, most car makers chose the "ignition interlock" option, a decision which was highly unpopular, and led Congress to amend the Act to prohibit a motor vehicle safety standard from requiring or permitting compliance by means of an ignition interlock or a continuous buzzer designed to indicate that safety belts were not in use. . . .

[I]n June 1976, Secretary of Transportation William T. Coleman, Jr., initiated a new rulemaking on the issue. After hearing testimony and reviewing written comments, Coleman . . . suspended the passive restraint requirement. Although he found passive restraints technologically and economically feasible, the Secretary [believed] there would be widespread public resistance to the new systems. He instead proposed a demonstration project involving up to 500,000 cars . . . .

Coleman's successor as Secretary of Transportation disagreed. Within months of assuming office, Secretary Brock Adams decided that the demonstration project was unnecessary. He issued a new . . . regulation, known as Modified Standard 208. The Modified Standard mandated the phasing in of passive restraints beginning with large cars in model year 1982 and extending to all cars by model year 1984. The two principal systems that would satisfy the Standard were airbags and passive belts; the choice of which system to install was left to the manufacturers. . . .

Over the next several years, the automobile industry geared up to comply with Modified Standard 208. . . . In February 1981, however, Secretary of Transportation Andrew Lewis reopened the rulemaking due to . . . the difficulties of the automobile industry. . . . After receiving written comments and holding public hearings, NHTSA issued a final rule . . . that rescinded . . . Modified Standard 208.

II

In a statement explaining the rescission, NHTSA maintained that it was no longer able to find, as it had in 1977, that the automatic restraint requirement would produce significant safety benefits. . . . By 1981 it became apparent that automobile manufacturers planned to install the automatic seatbelts in approximately 99% of the new cars [and] the overwhelming majority of passive belts planned to be installed by manufacturers could be detached easily and left that way permanently. Passive belts, once detached, then required "the same type of affirmative action that is the stumbling block to obtaining high usage levels of manual belts." For this reason, the agency concluded that there was no longer a basis for reliably predicting that the Standard would lead to any significant increased usage of restraints at all.

In view of the possibly minimal safety benefits, the automatic restraint requirement no longer was reasonable or practicable in the agency's view. The requirement would require approximately $ 1 billion to implement and the agency did not believe it would be reasonable to impose such substantial costs on manufacturers and consumers without more adequate assurance that sufficient safety benefits would accrue. In addition, NHTSA concluded that automatic restraints might have an adverse effect on the public's attitude toward safety. Given the high expense and limited benefits of detachable belts, NHTSA feared that many consumers would regard the Standard as an instance of ineffective regulation . . . "poisoning . . . popular sentiment toward efforts to improve occupant restraint systems in the future." . . . .

III

. . . Both the [Act] and the 1974 Amendments concerning occupant crash protection standards indicate that motor vehicle safety standards are to be promulgated under the informal rulemaking procedures of the Administrative Procedure Act. 5 U.S.C. § 553. The agency's action in promulgating such standards therefore may be set aside if found to be "arbitrary, capricious, an abuse of discretion, or otherwise not in accordance with law." 5 U.S.C. § 706(2)(A); *Citizens to Preserve Overton Park v. Volpe*. We believe that the rescission or modification of an occupant-protection standard is subject to the same test. Section 103(b) of the [Act] suggests no difference in the scope of judicial review depending upon the nature of the agency's action.

Petitioner . . . disagrees, contending that the rescission of an agency rule should be judged by the same standard [as] an agency's refusal to promulgate a rule in the first place – a standard . . . considerably narrower than the traditional arbitrary-and-capricious test. We reject this view. The Act expressly equates orders "revoking" and "establishing" safety standards; neither that Act nor the APA suggests that revocations are to be treated as refusals to promulgate standards. . . . Moreover, the revocation of an extant regulation is substantially different than a failure to act. Revocation constitutes a reversal of the agency's former views as to the proper course. . . . Accordingly, an agency . . . rescinding a rule is obligated to supply a reasoned analysis for the change beyond that which may be required when an agency does not act in the first instance. In so holding, we fully recognize that "[regulatory] agencies do not establish rules of conduct to last forever," *American Trucking Assns., Inc. v. Atchison, T. & S. F. R. Co.*, 387 U.S. 397, 416 (1967), and that an agency must be given ample latitude to "adapt their rules and policies to the demands of changing circumstances." *Permian Basin Area Rate Cases*, 390 U.S. 747, 784 (1968). But the forces of change do not always or necessarily point in the direction of deregulation. In the abstract, there is no more reason to presume that changing circumstances require the rescission of prior action, instead of a revision in or even the extension of current regulation. If Congress established a presumption from which judicial review should start, that presumption – contrary to petitioners' views – is not *against* safety regulation, but *against* changes in current policy that are not justified by the rulemaking record. While the removal of a regulation may not entail the monetary expenditures and other costs of enacting a new standard, and, accordingly, it may be easier for an agency to justify a deregulatory action, the direction in which an agency chooses to move does not alter the standard of judicial review established by law. . . .

The Department of Transportation accepts the applicability of the "arbitrary and capricious" standard. It argues that under this standard, a reviewing court may not set aside an agency rule that is rational, based on consideration of the relevant factors, and within the scope of the authority delegated to the agency by the statute. We do not disagree with this formulation. The scope of review under the "arbitrary and capricious" standard is narrow and a court is not to substitute its judgment for that of the agency. Nevertheless, the agency must examine the relevant data and articulate a satisfactory explanation for its action including a "rational connection between the facts found and the choice made." . . . . Normally, an agency rule would be arbitrary and capricious if the agency has relied on factors which Congress has not intended it to consider, entirely failed to consider an important aspect of the problem, offered an explanation for its decision that runs counter to the evidence before the agency, or is so implausible that it could not be ascribed to a difference in view or the product of agency expertise. The reviewing court . . . may not supply a reasoned basis for the agency's action that the agency itself has not given. <u>SEC v. Chenery Corp.</u> We will, however, "uphold a decision of less than ideal clarity if the agency's path may reasonably be discerned." For purposes of these cases, it is also relevant that Congress required a record of the rulemaking proceedings to be compiled and submitted to a reviewing court, and intended that agency findings under the Act would be supported by "substantial evidence on the record considered as a whole." . . . .

V.

. . . We conclude, as did the Court of Appeals, that [the revision of Standard 208 was arbitrary and capricious].

A.

The first and most obvious reason for finding the rescission arbitrary and capricious is that NHTSA apparently gave no consideration whatever to modifying the Standard to require that airbag technology be utilized. . . . [T]he agency's original proposed Standard contemplated the installation of inflatable restraints in all cars. Automatic belts were added as a means of complying with the Standard because they were believed to be as effective as airbags in achieving the goal of occupant crash protection. At that time, the passive belt approved by the agency could not be detached. Only later, at a manufacturer's behest, did the agency approve of the detach-ability feature – and only after assurances that the feature would not compromise the safety benefits of the restraint. Although it was then foreseen that 60% of the new cars would contain airbags and 40% would have automatic seatbelts, the ratio between the two was not significant as long as the passive belt would also assure greater passenger safety.

The agency has now determined that the detachable automatic belts will not attain anticipated safety benefits because so many individuals will detach the mechanism. Even if this conclusion were acceptable in its entirety, standing alone it would not justify any more than an amendment of Standard 208 to [require only airbags]. . . . At the very least this alternative way of achieving the objectives of the Act should have been addressed . . . . But the agency not only did not require compliance through airbags, it also did not even consider the possibility in its 1981 rulemaking. Not one sentence of its rulemaking statement discusses the airbags-only option. . . .

The automobile industry has opted for the passive belt over the airbag, but surely it is not enough that the regulated industry has eschewed a given safety device. . . . Indeed, the [Act] was necessary because the industry was not sufficiently responsive to safety concerns. . . . [P]etitioners recite a number of difficulties that they believe would be posed by a mandatory airbag standard. . . . But these are not the agency's reasons for rejecting [such a] standard. Not having discussed the possibility, the agency submitted no reasons at all. The short – and sufficient – answer to petitioners' submission is that the courts may not accept . . . counsel's post hoc rationalizations for agency action. It is well established that an agency's action must be upheld, if at all, on the basis articulated by the agency itself.

Petitioners also invoke our decision in *Vermont Yankee Nuclear Power Corp. v. Natural Resources Defense Council, Inc.* [to say] that to require an agency to consider an airbags-only alternative is, in essence, to dictate to the agency the procedures it is to follow. Petitioners both misread *Vermont Yankee* and misconstrue the nature of the remand that is in order. In *Vermont Yankee*, we held that a court may not impose additional procedural requirements upon an agency. We do not require today any specific procedures which NHTSA must follow. Nor do we broadly require an agency to consider all policy alternatives in reaching decision. It is true that rulemaking "cannot be found wanting simply because the agency failed to include every alternative device and thought conceivable by the mind of man . . . regardless of how uncommon or unknown that alternative may have been . . . ." But the airbag is more than a policy alternative to the passive restraint Standard; it is a technological alternative within the ambit of the existing Standard. We hold only that given the judgment made in 1977 that airbags are an effective and cost-beneficial life-saving technology, the mandatory passive restraint rule may not be abandoned without any consideration whatsoever of an airbags-only requirement.

B.

Although the issue is closer, we also find that the agency was too quick to dismiss the safety benefits of automatic seatbelts. NHTSA's critical finding was that, in light of the industry's plans to install readily detachable passive belts, it could not reliably predict "even a 5 percentage point increase [in] the minimum level of expected usage . . . ." The Court of Appeals rejected this finding because there is "not one iota" of evidence that Modified Standard 208 will fail to increase nationwide seatbelt use by at least 13 percentage points, the level of increased usage necessary for the Standard to justify its cost. Given the lack of probative evidence, the court held that "only a well justified refusal to seek more evidence could render rescission non-arbitrary."

Petitioners object to this conclusion. . . . We agree with petitioners that . . . an agency may . . . revoke a standard on the basis of serious uncertainties if supported by the record and reasonably explained. . . . It is not infrequent that the available data do not settle a regulatory issue, and the agency must then exercise its judgment in moving from the facts . . . on the record to a policy conclusion. . . . [H]owever, [this] does not imply that it is sufficient for an agency to merely recite the terms "substantial uncertainty" as a justification for its actions. . . . Generally, one aspect of [the required] explanation would be a justification for rescinding the regulation before engaging in a search for further evidence.

In th[is] case[], the agency's explanation for rescission of the passive restraint requirement is *not* sufficient to enable us to conclude that the rescission was the product of reasoned decisionmaking. . . . [T]he agency's view of the field tests on passive restraints indicates only that there is no reliable real-world experience that usage rates will substantially increase. . . . [But this takes] no account of the critical difference between detachable automatic belts and current manual belts. A detached passive belt does require an affirmative act to reconnect it, but – unlike a manual seatbelt – the passive belt, once reattached, will continue to function automatically unless again disconnected. Thus, inertia – a factor which the agency's own studies have found significant in explaining the current low usage rates for seatbelts – works in *favor* of, not *against*, use of the protective device. . . . [T]here would [thus] seem to be grounds to believe that seatbelt use by occasional users will be substantially increased by the detachable passive belts. Whether this is in fact the case is a matter for the agency to decide, but it must bring its expertise to bear on the question. . . .

The agency also failed to articulate a basis for not requiring nondetachable belts under Standard 208. . . . In 1978, when General Motors obtained the agency's approval to install a continuous passive belt, it assured the agency that nondetachable belts with spool releases were as safe as detachable belts with buckle releases. NHTSA was satisfied that this belt design assured easy extricability . . . . While the agency is entitled to change its view on the acceptability of continuous passive belts, it is obligated to explain its reasons for doing so. . . .

VI.

"An agency's view of what is in the public interest may change, either with or without a change in circumstances. But an agency changing its course must supply a reasoned analysis . . . ." We do not accept all of the reasoning of the Court of Appeals but we do conclude that the agency has failed to supply the requisite "reasoned analysis" in this case. Accordingly, we vacate the judgment of the Court of Appeals and remand the cases to that court with directions to remand the matter to the NHTSA for further consideration consistent with this opinion. . . .

[JUSTICE REHNQUIST, concurring in part.]

I do not believe . . . that NHTSA's view of detachable automatic seatbelts was arbitrary and capricious. . . . It seems to me that the agency's explanation, while by no means a model, is adequate. The agency acknowledged that there would probably be some increase in belt usage, but concluded that the increase would be small and not worth the cost of mandatory detachable automatic belts. . . .

The agency's changed view of the standard seems to be related to the election of a new President of a different political party. . . . A change in administration brought about by the people casting their votes is a perfectly reasonable basis for an executive agency's reappraisal of the costs and benefits of its programs and regulations. As long as the agency remains within the bounds established by Congress, it is entitled to assess administrative records and evaluate priorities in light of the philosophy of the administration.

———

Underlying Case Documents

The case referenced:

<u>The National Traffic and Motor Vehicle Safety Act of 1966</u>
The Original Version of <u>Standard 208</u>
<u>The 1969 Proposed Standard</u>
The <u>1971 Reconsideration</u> adding automatic seat belts as a permissible passive restraint system
<u>The 1972 Amended Standard</u>
<u>The Motor Vehicle and Schoolbus Safety Amendments of 1974</u>
<u>The 1976 Rulemaking</u>
<u>The 1978 Amendment</u> allowing carmakers to use alternative methods of release for automatic seatbelts
<u>The Modified Standard</u>
<u>The 1981 Rulemaking</u>
<u>The Final Rule Rescinding Standard 208</u>

Learn more about the history of the airbag <u>HERE.</u>
For NHTSA's assessment on the value of seatbelts click <u>HERE.</u>

1. The *State Farm* decision articulates a basis to decide when a decision is arbitrary and capricious: "[Reliance on] factors . . . Congress had not intended, [failing] to consider an important aspect of the problem, [a] decision . . . counter to the evidence, or [a decision] so implausible that it could not be ascribed to a difference in view or the product of agency expertise." Look closely at these criteria. These are the easy cases – they involve outright, patent failures to assess criteria in the relevant statute. The more difficult cases involve a questionable connection or correlation between the "facts found and the conclusions made." *See, e.g.,* <u>*W. Watersheds Project v. Kraayenbrink*, 2007 WL 1667618 (D. Idaho June 8, 2007)</u>; <u>*NRDC v. Kempthorne*, 506 F. Supp. 2d 322, 371 (E.D. Cal. 2007)</u>; <u>*Utah Envt'l. Cong. v. Zieroth*, 190 F. Supp. 2d 1265 (D. Utah 2002)</u>.

2. In <u>*Oceana, Inc. v. Evans*, 384 F. Supp. 2d 203 (D.D.C. 2005)</u>, as clarified by <u>*Oceana, Inc. v. Evans*, 389 F. Supp. 2d 4 (D.D.C. 2005)</u>, the district court sought to evaluate a "jeopardy analysis [regarding] the current and future impacts of the scallop fishery on turtle population trends. . . ." The court also reviewed the merits of the technical model the agency used. Based on *State Farm*, the court sought to determine whether there was a "rational connection between the facts found and the choice made," and whether the agency had failed "to respond to comments submitted by the EPA." Are district court judges qualified to make these kinds of

judgments? Is this the kind of review *State Farm* contemplated?

3. Having read *State Farm*, can you tell how hard a court should look – or even if a hard look is mandatory? In a recent article, Dean and Professor Paul R. Verkuil noted: "State Farm is really two opinions: the unanimous opinion that condemned the [agency's] failure to consider the airbags-only alternative; and the five-to-four opinion that invigorated a hard-look version of the arbitrary-and-capricious clause." Paul R. Verkuil, <u>*Reply: The Wait Is Over: Chevron as the Stealth* Vermont Yankee II, 75 GEO. WASH. L. REV. 921, 923 (2007)</u>. The narrow majority on hard look is reflected in the case law. Notwithstanding the many, many cases interpreting *State Farm*, "Supreme Court and lower court jurisprudence . . . provides little guidance in determining how searching a court's review of an agency's justification for a revision or rescission of a regulation must be." David H. Becker, *Changing Direction in Administrative Agency Rulemaking: "Reasoned Analysis," the Roadless Rule Repeal, and the 2006 National Park Service Management Policies*, 30 ENVIRONS ENVTL. L. & POL'Y J. 65 (2006).

4. After the *State Farm* case was decided, the DOT issued a revised rule regarding airbags. DOT, Federal Motor Vehicle Safety Standard; Occupant Crash Protection, <u>49 C.F.R. Part 571 (1986)</u>, <u>49 Fed. Reg. 28962 (July 17, 1984)</u>. Portions of that revised rule follow:

> After a thorough review of the issue of automobile occupant protection, including the long regulatory history of the matter; the comments on the notice of Proposed Rulemaking (NPRM) and the Supplemental Notice of Proposed Rulemaking (SNPRM); and extensive studies, analyses, and data on the subject; and the court decisions that have resulted from law suits over the different rulemaking actions, the Department of Transportation has reached a final decision that it believes will offer the best method of fulfilling the objectives and purpose of the governing statute, the National Traffic and Motor Vehicle Safety Act. As part of this decision, the Department has reached three basic conclusions:

> Effectively enforced state mandatory seatbelt use laws (MULs) will provide the greatest safety benefits most quickly of any of the alternatives, with almost no additional cost.

> Automatic occupant restraints provide demonstrable safety benefits, and, unless a sufficient number of MULs are enacted, they must be required for the most frequently used seats in passenger automobiles.

> Automatic occupant protection systems that do not totally rely upon belts, such as airbags or passive interiors, offer significant additional potential for preventing fatalities and injuries, at least in part because the American public is likely to find them less intrusive; their development and availability should be encouraged through appropriate incentives.

> As a result of these conclusions, the Department has decided to require automatic

occupant protection in all passenger automobiles based on a phased-in schedule beginning on September 1, 1986, with full implementation being required by September 1, 1989, unless, before April 1, 1989, two-thirds of the population of the United States are covered by MULs meeting specified conditions. More specifically, the rule would require the following:

Passenger cars manufactured for sale in the United States after September 1, 1986, will have to have automatic occupant restraints based on the following phase-in schedule:

• Ten percent of all automobiles manufactured after September 1, 1986.

• Twenty-five percent of all automobiles manufactured after September 1, 1987.

• Forty-percent of all automobiles manufactured after September 1, 1988.

• One-hundred percent of all automobiles manufactured after September 1, 1989.

• The requirement for automatic occupant restraints will be rescinded if MULs meeting specified conditions are passed by a sufficient number of states before April 1, 1989 to cover two-thirds of the population of the United States

• During the phase-in period, each passenger automobile that is manufactured with a system that provides automatic protection to the driver without automatic belts will be given an extra credit equal to one-half of an automobile toward meeting the percentage requirement.

• The front center seat of passenger cars will be exempt from the requirement for automatic occupant protection.

• Rear seats are not covered by the requirements for automatic protection.

After the rule issued, the industry again brought suit. The rule was upheld in *State Farm Mutual Automotive Insurance Co. v. Dole*, 802 F.2d 474 (D.C. Cir. 1986). JUDGE MIKVA, concurring in part and dissenting in part, wrote that, "the agency has [again] failed to make the requisite rational connection between the facts in evidence and its judgment . . . . [Therefore, the rule fails] arbitrary-and-capricious [review]."

6. While the current topic is rulemaking, consider briefly the controversy regarding presidential signing statements. Between 2001 and 2008, President George W. Bush authored more than 150 signing statements expressing his perspective on more than 750 bills passed by Congress. For a list of statements, see http://www.coherentbabble.com/signingstatements/TOCindex.htm (last visited May 17, 2008). The criticism of this practice has been vocal, prompting the American Bar Association to empanel a special task force to examine the practice. http://www.abanet.org/op/signingstatements/aba_final_signing_statements_recommendation-report_7-24-06.pdf (last visited July 13, 2008). The Task Force report

begins:

> Resolved, That the American Bar Association opposes, as contrary to the rule of law and our constitutional system of separation of powers, the issuance of presidential signing statements that claim the authority or state the intention to disregard or decline to enforce all or part of a law the President has signed, or to interpret such a law in a manner inconsistent with the clear intent of Congress. . . . That the American Bar Association urges the President to confine any signing statements to his views regarding the meaning, purpose and significance of bills presented by Congress, and if he believes that all or part of a bill is unconstitutional, to veto the bill in accordance with Article I, § 7 of the Constitution of the United States, which directs him to approve or disapprove each bill in its entirety. . . .

Could it be that it is inappropriate for the President to express his or her reasoning regarding an executive decision – at least this appears to be the import of the ABA Task Force report – while an agency must express it reasons, demonstrate the legitimacy of its reasoning, and show (according to the following case) "a rational basis between the facts found and the choices made." Why is the President crossing the line into legislative activity vested to Congress, while an agency rulemaking decision (which certainly has a legislative quality) is treated so differently?

7. *State Farm* reflects a distinct perspective in administrative law. At the time of the decision, the notion that courts reviewing agency action must take a "hard look" at the decisions agencies make was generally accepted – but what does "hard look" entail? Is it sufficient to look closely at the processes the agency followed or should courts delve into the substance of the record? This question divided two of the great jurists on the D.C. Circuit, JUDGES BAZELON (who favored review of process) and LEVENTHAL (who favored review of the substance of agency decisions). Jonathan T. Molot, *Ambivalence About Formalism*, 93 VA. L. REV. 1 (2007); Ronald J. Krotoszynski, Jr., *History Belongs to the Winners: The Bazelon-Leventhal Debate and the Continuing Relevance of the Process/Substance Dichotomy in Judicial Review of Agency Action*, 58 ADMIN. L. REV. 995 (2006); Bazelon, *Coping with Technology Through the Legal Process*, 62 COR-NELL L. REV. 817 (1977); *International Harvester Co. v. Ruckelshaus*, 478 F.2d 615, 647, 652 (D.C. Cir. 1973) (CHIEF JUDGE BAZELON, concurring). The question was decided in both *Vermont Yankee Nuclear Power Corp. v. Natural Res. Def. Council, Inc.*, 435 U.S. 519,

For More Information

For interesting critiques of "hard look" see Michael Herz, *The Rehnquist Court and Administrative Law*, 99 Nw. U.L. REV. 297 (2004); Sidney A. Shapiro & Richard E. Levy, *Heightened Scrutiny of the Fourth Branch: Separation of Powers and the Requirement of Adequate Reasons for Agency Decisions*, 1987 DUKE L.J. 387; Jonathan Masur, *A Hard Look or a Blind Eye: Administrative Law and Military Deference*, 56 HASTINGS L.J. 441 (2005); Patrick M. Garry, *The Unannounced Revolution: How the Court Has Indirectly Effected a Shift in the Separation of Powers*, 57 ALA. L. REV. 689 (2006).

524 (1978), which limited review of procedure, and *Chevron v. Natural Resource Defense Council, Inc.*, 467 U.S. 837 (1984), which limited review of substance.

8. Even with limitations on judicial review, it is inevitable that the appellate process will include courts second-guessing agencies at one level or another. When that happens, is the judiciary making decisions that should be made by the executive, thereby violating separation of powers norms? On the other hand, if courts provide only a superficial review of agency action, the right of an "aggrieved party" to judicial review becomes little more than a formality.

9. One other point on *State Farm*: Those who are subject to rules that have the force of law often argue that the obligations inherent in the rule are sufficient to preempt state tort liability. As you read the above rule, does it establish a basis for express or implied preemption? *See Geier v. Am. Honda Motor Co., 529 U.S. 861 (2000).*

10. *Northwest Environmental Defense Center v. Bonneville Power Administration, 477 F.3d 668 (9th Cir. 2007)*:

> In response to declining salmon and steelhead runs [on the Columbia River], Congress passed the Northwest Power Planning and Conservation Act of 1980. The Act created the Northwest Power and Conservation Council, an interstate compact agency, and directs the Council to prepare programs to protect and enhance the fish and wildlife . . . . The Act also instructs the Bonneville Power Administration [BPA], the federal agency that operates the dams on the Columbia River, to use its authority in a manner consistent with the programs developed by the Council.
>
> In 1982, the Council called for the creation of what would eventually become the Fish Passage Center [FPC]. . . . Since 1987, the Bonneville Power Administration [BPA] has funded the Fish Passage Center, and the Fish Passage Center has gathered, analyzed, and publicly-disseminated data regarding fish passage. . . . In light of language in two 2005 congressional committee reports, however, the [BPA] decided to transfer the functions performed by the Fish Passage Center to [two separate groups]. . . .
>
> BPA argues that, even if language in the congressional committee reports did not provide a rational basis for its action transferring the functions of the FPC, its decision can be upheld as a reasonable application of the Act's requirement that it exercise its authority in a manner consistent with the Council's Fish and Wildlife Program. BPA contends that it carefully considered the issues before it and therefore we should let stand its decision to transfer the functions of the FPC. . . .
>
> In this case, BPA departed from its long-standing practice of funding a unitary Fish Passage Center and transferred the FPC's functions to two separate entities. An agency is entitled to change its course when its view of what is in the public's interest changes. However, "an agency changing its course must supply a reasoned analysis indicating that prior policies and standards are being deliberately changed, not casually ignored . . . ." . . . As the Supreme Court has explained, we "may not accept appellate counsel's post hoc rationalizations for agency action," and we "may not supply a reasoned basis

for the agency's action that the agency itself has not given. . . ." . . . .

BPA has not cogently explained its decision to transfer the functions of the FPC, and the record does not indicate that that decision was the output of a rational decision-making process. Instead, BPA departed from its two-decade-old precedent without supplying a reasoned analysis for its change of course. BPA's decision to transfer the functions of the FPC was arbitrary and capricious. . . .

11. *International Ladies' Garment Workers' Union v. Donovan*, 722 F.2d 795 (D.C. Cir. 1983):

[An agency report in the 1940s] led the Administrator [of the Wage and Hour Division of the U.S. Department of Labor] to conclude that "[i]ndustrial homework furnishes a ready means of circumventing or evading the minimum wage . . . ." The Administrator soon prohibited homework in the seven industries studied, unless homeworkers came within certain narrow exceptions. . . .

On December 5, 1980, the Division published a notice of hearings to obtain information on . . . the extent [industrial homework might affect] "the Secretary's statutory responsibility to prevent the . . . evasion of . . . the minimum wage rate . . . ." At the hearings, opposition to the restrictions on homework came almost entirely from homeknitters (and their representatives) from Vermont, and government officials from Vermont.

Following receipt and consideration of more than 10,000 comments, the Secretary "decided to remove the restrictions on the employment of homeworkers in the knitted outerwear industry . . . ." This decision was based primarily on the finding that "substantial curtailment of employment opportunities and earning power will result from a continuation of the restrictions on industrial homework in the knitted outerwear industry. . . ."

Both parties agree that the rescission was informal, notice and comment, rulemaking . . . and as such is to be found unlawful if it is "arbitrary, capricious, an abuse of discretion, or otherwise not in accordance with the law." . . . .

We find [*State Farm's*] reasoning particularly compelling as applied to the case at hand, since this case involves review of an agency's rescission of a longstanding policy. The Division's decision in 1942 to restrict homework was an outgrowth of many years of unsuccessful attempts by state and Federal officials to regulate homework. . . . The Division's comprehensive review . . . led it to conclude that restricting homework was the only effective way to enforce the minimum wage in the knitted outerwear industry, and this position was adhered to by the Division for almost forty years.

[Therefore,] the Secretary's expression of a willingness to modify the rescission if new information suggests that this is appropriate, hardly counsels any alteration in the standard of review. Agencies remain free to react to new information as part of their standard regulatory procedure, but their expressed willingness to do so certainly cannot insulate their decisions from meaningful judicial review. . . . Second, if the Secretary believed that significant uncertainties existed, he was obligated to identify these uncertainties and to explain why this justified rescission *prior* to "engaging in a search for further evidence."

12. *State Farm* obligates agencies to disclose the basis for their reasoning when they rescind or repudiate a rule. For the issuance of a rule, as opposed to rescission, section 553(c) of the APA requires an agency to publish a "concise and general" statement of basis and purpose. The APA does not provide a template for such a statement.

Good Question!

Presumably, the agency should disclose the information on which it relied to come to its final decision to issue the rule – but what this would mean in practice can be tricky. Large numbers of staff, technical and legal, are likely to work on a rulemaking. Must all of them disclose the contents of their files?

In the *Nova Scotia* case that follows, the question before the court was the nature of the information the agency must disclose. How much information should be required? At what point must the "record" (whatever that means) be disclosed? How thorough must the disclosure be to satisfy the requirements of the APA?

If an agency holds back information during the course of a rulemaking, disclosing it only after the rule has issued or contemporaneously with the issuance of the rule, the effect on those who are commenting on the proposed rule is obvious: If one does not know the basis on which the agency plans to rely, it is not possible to provide intelligent commentary to the agency regarding the suitability, scientific worth, relevance, or authenticity of the information. Moreover, if the information is not disclosed, the public is denied the opportunity to asses whether the information is potentially compromised, e.g., derived from a source that has a direct interest in the content of the proposed rule.

UNITED STATES OF AMERICA V. NOVA SCOTIA FOOD PRODUCTS CORPORATION

<u>568 F.2d 240 (2d Cir. 1977)</u>

[JUDGE GURFEIN] This appeal involving a regulation of the Food and Drug Administration is not here upon a direct review of agency action. It is an appeal from a judgment of the District Court for the Eastern District of New York . . . enjoining the appellants, after a hearing, from processing hot smoked whitefish except in accordance with time-temperature-salinity (T-T-S) regulations contained in 21 C.F.R. Part 122 (1977). . . . The injunction was sought and granted on the ground that smoked whitefish which has been processed in violation of the T-T-S regulation is "adulterated."

Appellant Nova Scotia receives frozen or iced whitefish in interstate commerce which it processes by brining, smoking and cooking. The fish are then sold as smoked whitefish. The regulations cited above require that hot-process smoked fish be heated by a controlled heat process that provides a monitoring system positioned in as many strategic locations in the oven as necessary to assure a continuous temperature through each fish of not less than 180° F. for a minimum of 30 minutes for fish which have been brined to contain 3.5% water phase salt or at 150° F. for a minimum of 30 minutes if the salinity was at 5% water phase. Since *each* fish must meet these requirements, it is necessary to heat an entire batch of fish to even higher temperatures so that the lowest temperature for *any* fish will meet the minimum requirements.

Government inspection of appellants' plant established without question that the minimum T-T-S requirements were not being met. There is no substantial claim that the plant was processing whitefish under "insanitary conditions" in any other material respect. . . . The hazard which the FDA sought to minimize was the outgrowth and toxin formation of Clostridium botulinum Type E spores . . . . These bacteria can . . . invade fish in their natural habitat and can be further disseminated in the course of evisceration and preparation of the fish for cooking. A failure to destroy such spores through an adequate brining, thermal, and refrigeration process was found to be dangerous to public health.

The Commissioner of Food and Drugs ("Commissioner"), employing informal "notice and comment" procedures under 21 U.S.C. § 371(a), issued a proposal for the control of C. botulinum bacteria Type E in fish. For his statutory authority to promulgate the regulations, the Commissioner specifically relied only upon § 342(a)(4) of the Act which provides:

> A food shall be deemed to be adulterated –
>
> (4) if it has been prepared, packed, or held under insanitary conditions whereby it may have become contaminated with filth, or whereby it may have been rendered injurious to health;

Similar guidelines for smoking fish had been suggested by the FDA several years earlier, and were generally made known to people in the industry. At that stage, however, they were merely guidelines without substantive effect as law. Responding to the Commissioner's invitation in the notice of proposed rulemaking, members of the industry, including appellants and the intervenor-appellant, submitted comments on the proposed regulation. . . .

The intervenor [National Fisheries Institute, Inc.] suggested that "specific parameters" be established. This referred to particular processing parameters for different species of fish on a "species by species" basis. Such "species by species" determination was proposed not only by the intervenor but also by the Bureau of Commercial Fisheries of the Department of the Interior. That Bureau objected to the general application of the T-T-S requirement proposed by the FDA on the ground that application of the regulation to all species of fish being smoked was not commercially feasible, and that the regulation should therefore specify time-temperature-salinity requirements, as developed by research and study, on a species-by-species basis. The Bureau suggested that "wholesomeness considerations could be more practically and adequately realized by reducing processing temperature and using suitable concentrations of nitrite and salt." The Commissioner took cognizance of the suggestion, but decided, nevertheless, to impose the T-T-S requirement on *all* species of fish (except chub, which were [separately] regulated . . .).

[The Commissioner acknowledged] in his "basis and purpose" statement . . . that "adequate times, temperatures and salt concentrations have not been demonstrated for each individual species of fish presently smoked". The Commissioner concluded, nevertheless, that "the processing requirements of the proposed regulations are the safest now known to prevent the outgrowth and toxin formation of *C. botulinum* Type E". He determined that "the conditions of current good manufacturing practice for this industry should be established without further delay."

The Commissioner did not answer the suggestion by the Bureau of Fisheries that nitrite and salt as additives could safely lower the high temperature otherwise required, a solution which the FDA had accepted in the case of chub. Nor did the Commissioner respond to the claim of Nova Scotia through its trade association, the Association of Smoked Fish Processors, Inc., Technical Center that "the proposed process requirements suggested by the FDA for hot processed smoked fish are neither commercially feasible nor based on sound scientific evidence obtained with the variety of smoked fish products to be included under this regulation." Nova Scotia, in its own comment, wrote to the Commissioner that "the heating of certain types of fish to high temperatures will completely destroy the product". It suggested, as an alternative, that "specific processing procedures could be established for each species after adequate work and [experimentation] has been done – but not before." . . . .

When, after several inspections and warnings, Nova Scotia failed to comply with the regulation, an action by the United States Attorney for injunctive relief . . . resulted in the judgment here on appeal. . . . The key issues were (1) whether, in the light of the rather scant history of botulism in whitefish, that species should have been considered separately rather than included in a general regulation which failed to distinguish species from species; (2) whether the application of the proposed T-T-S requirements to smoked whitefish made the whitefish commercially unsaleable; and (3) whether the agency recognized that prospect, but nevertheless decided that the public health needs should prevail even if that meant commercial death for the whitefish industry. The procedural issues were whether, in the light of these key questions, the agency procedure was inadequate because (i) it failed to disclose to interested parties the scientific data and the methodology upon which it relied; and (ii) because it failed utterly to address itself to the pertinent question of commercial feasibility.

1. *The History of Botulism in Whitefish*

The history of botulism occurrence in whitefish, as established in the trial record, which we must assume was available to the FDA in 1970, is as follows. Between 1899 and 1964 there were only eight cases of botulism reported as attributable to hot-smoked whitefish. In all eight instances, vacuum-packed whitefish was involved. . . . The industry has abandoned vacuum-packing, and there has not been a single case of botulism associated with commercially prepared white-fish since 1963, though 2,750,000 pounds of whitefish are processed annually. Thus, in the seven-year period from 1964 through 1970, 17.25 million pounds of whitefish have been commercially processed in the United States without a single reported case of botulism. The evidence also disclosed that defendant Nova Scotia has been in business some 56 years, and that there has never been a case of botulism illness from the whitefish processed by it.

2. *The Scientific Data*

Interested parties were not informed of the scientific data, or at least of a selection of such data deemed important by the agency, so that comments could be addressed to the data. Appellants argue that unless the scientific data relied upon by the agency are spread upon the public records, criticism of the methodology used or the meaning to be inferred from the data is rendered impossible.

We agree with appellants in this case, for although we recognize that an agency may resort to its own expertise outside the record in an informal rulemaking procedure, we do not believe that when the pertinent research material is readily available and the agency has no special expertise on the precise parameters involved, there is any reason to conceal the scientific data relied upon from the interested parties. . . . This is not a case where the agency methodology was based on material supplied by the interested parties themselves. Here all the scientific research was collected by the agency, and none of it was disclosed to interested parties as the material upon which the proposed rule would be fashioned. Nor was an articulate effort made to connect the scientific requirements to available technology that would make commercial survival possible, though the burden of proof was on the agency. This required it to "bear a burden of adducing a reasoned presentation supporting the reliability of its methodology." . . . .

If the failure to notify interested persons of the scientific research upon which the agency was relying actually prevented the presentation of relevant comment, the agency may be held not to have considered all "the relevant factors." We can think of no sound reasons for secrecy or reluctance to expose to public view (with an exception for trade secrets or national security) the ingredients of the deliberative process. Indeed, the FDA's own regulations now specifically require that every notice of proposed rulemaking contain "references to all data and information on which the Commissioner relies for the proposal . . . ." And this is, undoubtedly, the trend.

We think that the scientific data should have been disclosed to focus on the proper interpretation of "insanitary conditions." . . . . One cannot ask for comment on a scientific paper without allowing the participants to read the paper. Scientific research is sometimes rejected for diverse inadequacies of methodology; and statistical results are sometimes rebutted because of a lack of adequate gathering technique or of supportable extrapolation. Such is the stuff of scientific debate. To suppress meaningful comment by failure to disclose the basic data relied upon is akin to rejecting comment altogether. . . . [W]e conclude that the failure to disclose to interested persons the scientific data upon which the FDA relied was procedurally erroneous. Moreover, the burden was upon the agency to articulate rationally why the rule should apply to a large and diverse class, with the same T-T-S parameters made applicable to *all* species.

Appellants additionally attack the "concise general statement" required by APA, 5 U.S.C. § 553, as inadequate. We think that, in the circumstances, it was less than adequate. It is not in keeping with the rational process to leave vital questions, raised by comments which are of cogent materiality, completely unanswered. The agencies certainly have a good deal of discretion in expressing the basis of a rule, but the agencies do not have quite the prerogative of obscurantism reserved to legislatures. . . . The test of adequacy of the "concise general statement" was expressed by JUDGE MCGOWAN in the following terms: "[T]he 'concise general statement of . . . basis and purpose' . . . will enable us to see what major issues of policy were ventilated by the informal proceedings and why the agency reacted to them as it did."

. . . .

The Secretary was squarely faced with the question whether it was necessary to formulate a rule with specific parameters that applied to all species of fish, and particularly whether lower temperatures with the addition of nitrite and salt would not be sufficient. Though this alternative was suggested by an agency of the federal government, its suggestion, though acknowledged, was never answered.

Moreover, the comment that to apply the proposed T-T-S requirements to whitefish would destroy the commercial product was neither discussed nor answered. We think that to sanction silence in the face of such vital questions would be to make the statutory requirement of a "concise general statement" less than an adequate safeguard against arbitrary decision-making. . . . One may recognize that even commercial unfeasibility cannot stand in the way of an overwhelming public interest. Yet the administrative process should disclose, at least, whether the proposed regulation is considered to be commercially feasible, or whether other considerations prevail even if commercial infeasibility is acknowledged. This kind of forthright disclosure and basic statement was lacking . . . . It is easy enough for an administrator to ban everything. In the regulation of food processing, the worldwide need for food also must be taken into account in formulating measures taken for the protection of health. . . .

. . . When the District Court held the regulation to be valid, it properly exercised its discretion to grant the injunction. In view of our conclusion to the contrary, we must reverse the grant of the injunction and direct that the complaint be dismissed.

————————

Underlying Case Documents

The case referenced:
21 U.S.C. § 342(a)(4)
The Proposed Rule
The Final Rule
Comments submitted by the National Fisheries Institute
Comments submitted by the Fish and Wildlife Service
Comments submitted by the Association of Smoked Fish Processors
A history of prior botulism outbreaks

1. The policy in this case was neatly summarized by the Eleventh Circuit: "When a proposed rule is based on scientific data, the agency should identify the data and methodology used to obtain it." *Lloyd Noland Hosp. & Clinic v. Heckler*, 762 F.2d 1561 (11th Cir. 1985). All the data? Who decides?

2. Any interested person is free to petition an agency for the disclosure of information to try to avoid the problem of the agency issuing substantive rules that

carry the force of law without sufficient information. Results of such petitions are mixed at best. Interested persons may also file claims under the Freedom of Information Act (FOIA), 5 U.S.C. § 552, but again, results are mixed. Thus, access to information issues are as potent today as when the *Nova Scotia* opinion issued, notwithstanding a statutory response time of 20 days and new legislation designed to facilitate access to information. *See* Honest Leadership and Open Government Act of 2007, Pub. L. No. 110-81, 121 Stat. 735 (2007), *available at* http://frwebgate.access.gpo.gov/cgi-bin/getdoc.cgi?dbname=110_cong_public_laws&docid=f:publ081.110 (last visited July 16, 2008).

Hypothetical

The Environmental Protection Agency determined that certain consumer-grade air purifiers containing ionizing coils designed to trap pollens, odors and other pollutants may emit dangerously high levels of ozone. Consequently, it issued a Notice of Proposed Rulemaking inviting comments on a proposed rule restricting ozone emissions from such ionizing air purifiers. In response, four medical, consumer and air quality associations filed comments insisting that the state of the applicable technology, and uncontrollable variables having to do with ventilation conditions in individual home environments, would make it impossible for manufacturers of air purifiers to calibrate their ionizing equipment in such as a way as to ensure that ozone emissions would be within any limits prescribed by the EPA. In its final rule, the EPA set the level of "acceptable ozone emission" at an imperceptible level, even in the smallest of rooms, and about 95% lower than the average emission rate of the leading models on the market today. The new limit nullifies any of the air purifying qualities of the ionizing feature in the household air cleaners. The manufacturers wish to challenge the final rule as violative of APA Section 553. What are their strongest arguments? And what is the EPA's strongest defense?

3. JUDGE LEVENTHAL, the proponent of "hard look" review of the substance of an agency record, made clear the disclosure rationale for rulemaking: "It is not consonant with the purpose of a rulemaking proceeding to promulgate rules on the basis of inadequate data, or on data . . . known only to the agency." *Portland Cement Ass'n v. Ruckelshaus*, 486 F.2d 375, 393 (D.C. Cir. 1973). Naturally, if the information is known to and provided by parties to the proceeding, attacking a rulemaking based on non-disclosure will not be successful. *Int'l Harvester Co. v. Ruckelshaus*, 478 F.2d 615, 632 (D.C. Cir. 1973).

Hypothetical

Assume that the Food and Drug Administration (FDA) decides on its own initiative to impose an in-person, oral hearing component to all of its notice and comment (APA § 553) rulemaking proceedings addressing safety standards for prescription and over-the-counter pharmaceutical products. Arguing that the major drug companies and other special interests have "captured" the FDA, the Consumers Advocacy League (CAL) urges the FDA to incorporate, in addition, an evidentiary record requirement in all of its notice and comment rulemakings. Under such a requirement, the agency would be limited to making rulemaking decisions on the basis of a formal record comprised of public hearing transcripts, written testimony and comments, and other documentary evidence filed in the proceeding. The FDA refused to accede to CAL's demands. CAL, in a related case, requests that the reviewing court impose this additional evidentiary record requirement upon FDA rulemakings. Could the court legally impose such a requirement? And is the FDA's decision to incorporate in-person, oral hearings in its pharmaceutical safety rulemakings itself legal?

4. The less accessible and more controversial the data on which the agency relies, the less trouble courts have in remanding and directing disclosure. _Endangered Species Committee of the Bldg. Indus. Ass'n v. Babbitt_, 852 F. Supp. 32 (D.D.C. 1994). Of course the question is: How would one know if the data on which the agency relied is controversial if it is not disclosed?

Disclosure cases in rulemakings are not all that common. Further, the apparent entitlements in *Nova Scotia* do not open the door to challenging agency action on the premise that the agency failed to consider all possible options based on all available information. _Simms v. Nat'l Highway Traffic Safety Admin._, 45 F.3d 999 (6th Cir. 1995).

5. Some agencies have established systems designed to facilitate requests for disclosure, including most recently the Environmental Protection Agency (EPA). *See* Integrated Risk Info. Sys. (IRIS); Announcement of Availability of Literature Searches for IRIS Assessments, 73 Fed. Reg. 22366, 22366-67 (April 25, 2008).

It is worth asking if there is anything special about the nature of the information in the *Nova Scotia* case. Does it matter that it was scientific in nature? Does the case establish precedent for disclosure of social science data as well? How about internal white papers?

Practice Pointer

Naturally, it makes sense to secure information as early as possible in the rulemaking process. Because non-disclosure cases require standing and finality, the likelihood is that by the time a court hears such a case, positions will have hardened and a great deal of time and energy will have already been spent on generating – and thereafter defending – the rule in question. One way to address this is to file a petition with the agency early in the process to secure information regarding the data on which the agency is likely to rely. *See, e.g.*, Petition to U.S. Dep't of Agric., Dep't of Food Safety and Inspection Serv., Ctr. for Sci. in the Pub. Interest, Petition, A Petition for Rulemaking to Require Disclosure of Major Food Allergens, Submitted by the Center for Science and the Public Interest (Feb. 1, 2005), available at http://www.cspinet.org/foodsafety/usdapetition.html.

6. Finally, while accountability and transparency seem to dictate disclosure, *Nova Scotia* did not open agency files to the public any more than FOIA did. What are the limits on access to information? Take a look at the nine exceptions to FOIA (5 U.S.C. § 552(b)). Do those exceptions apply to the disclosure obligations referred to in *Nova Scotia*?

VIII. A Concise General Statement of Basis and Purpose

A great deal of information is available to an agency during the course of an informal 553(c) rulemaking, with some generated by the notice and comment process and other data supplied (or in existence) within the agency itself. The goal is to provide the agency the best information available so that when it exercises the power to issue a legislative (substantive) rule that has the force of law, it has made an informed and balanced judgment. As we have just learned, there is good reason for the agency to disclose the data on which it relies – after all, in the absence of the information, how would a court determine if the agency acted arbitrarily or in a manner at odds with the substantive data in the record?

While lawyers tend to think of a record as the official repository of evidence generated in the course of a legal proceeding through the submission of admissible evidence, that is not a correct understanding of the "record" in a rulemaking case. Further, a traditional understanding of the adversarial process requires that a decision is supported by a "manifest weight of the evidence"; "a preponderance of the

Take Note

Comments filed in a rulemaking by an interested member of the public do form an important body of information. They do not, however, constitute the whole of the record because they may not include other information on which the agency relies. This both reduces the control that non-agency lawyers have over the record and increases the difficulty of the task of a reviewing court.

evidence"; or, in formal administrative proceedings, "substantial evidence," based on the evidence in the record that has been proffered and admitted (therefore meeting the standard for administrative agencies as being reliable, substantive, and probative). Again, these concepts do not apply directly to 553(c) rulemakings.

How can a court decide if a rule resulting from a 553(3) process is arbitrary, capricious, or an abuse of discretion (the review standard from the APA, 5 U.S.C. § 706(2)(A)) if the court does not know the data on which the agency relied?

The APA anticipated this problem, and required the agency to issue a "concise general statement of basis and purpose" at the conclusion of the rulemaking. Ideally, such a statement should provide the public and a reviewing court sufficient information to assess the propriety of the action of the agency. The statement should set forth clearly and thoroughly the information and data on which the agency relied, the statutory authority that allows the agency to issue the particular rule, and the place the rule fits in the existing regulatory structure of the agency. Such a statement ought to describe the external demand(s) or circumstance(s) that necessitated the rule, the regulatory history that surrounds the rule, and the purpose or goal of the rule.

As you read the case below, ask if the information the agency provided is sufficient to inform the public of the basis and purpose of the agency's action. Does the court's concern boil down to the fact that the statement was overly informal?

Good Question!

Given the "component part list" above for a "concise general statement of basis and purpose," you may be wondering how a statement can both provide that information and be concise – and further, how a statement can be both "concise" and "general." You would not be the first to raise that question. *See, e.g.,* Carl A. Auerbach, *Informal Rule Making: A Proposed Relationship Between Administrative Procedures and Judicial Review,* 72 Nw. U.L. Rev. 15 (1977).

CALIFORNIA HOTEL AND MOTEL ASSOCIATION v. INDUSTRIAL WELFARE COMMISSION

599 P.2d 31 (Cal. 1979)

[BY THE COURT] The California Hotel and Motel Association . . . appeal[s] from a judgment denying the association's petition . . . to invalidate Order 5-76 of the . . . Industrial Welfare Commission . . . . Order 5-76 fixes wages, hours, and conditions of employment in the public housekeeping industry, which provides meals, lodging, and maintenance services to the public. . . . [We find] that . . .

Order 5-76 is invalid because the commission did not include an adequate statement of basis to support the order . . . .

       . . . .

   Section 1177 [of the California Labor Code] provides in relevant part: "Each order of the commission shall include a statement as to the basis upon which the order is predicated and shall be concurred in by a majority of the Commissioners." . . . . An effective statement of basis fulfills several functions. First, the statement satisfies the legislative mandate of section 1177. Second, the statement facilitates meaningful judicial review of agency action. . . . Third, the exposition requirement subjects the agency, its decision-making processes, and its decisions to more informed scrutiny by the Legislature, the regulated public, lobbying and public interest groups, the media, and the citizenry at large. Fourth, requiring an administrative agency to articulate publicly its reasons for adopting a particular order, rule, regulation, or policy induces agency action that is reasonable . . . . Fifth, by publicizing the policies, considerations and facts that the agency finds significant, the agency introduces an element of predictability into the administrative process. This enables the regulated public to anticipate agency action and to shape its conduct accordingly. Sixth, requiring an agency to publicly justify its [actions] stimulates public confidence in agency action by promoting both the reality and the appearance of rational decision making in government. . . .

   . . . A statement of basis will necessarily vary depending on the material supporting an order and the terms of the order. The statement should reflect the factual, legal, and policy foundations for the action taken. The statement of basis must show that the order adopted is reasonably supported by the material gathered by or presented to the commission – through its own investigations, the wage board proceedings, and the public hearings – and is reasonably related to the purposes of the enabling statute.

   The statement of basis is not the equivalent of the findings of fact that a court may be required to make. A statement of basis is an explanation of how and why the commission did what it did. If terms of the order turn on factual issues, the statement must demonstrate reasonable support in the administrative record for the factual determinations. If, on the other hand, the terms of the order turn on policy choices, an assessment of risks or alternatives, or predictions of economic or social consequences, the statement of basis must show how the commission resolved conflicting interests and how that resolution led to the order chosen. If an order differentiates among classes of industries . . . the statement of basis must show that the distinctions drawn are reasonably supported by the administrative record and are reasonably related to the purposes of the enabling statute. A statement meeting these standards will facilitate review . . . by presenting a reasoned response to or resolution of the salient comments, criticisms, issues, and alternatives developed during the commission's proceedings.

The "To Whom It May Concern" provision of Order 5-76 does not satisfy this standard. The provision is simply a recitation of the commission's authority and of the procedures outlined in sections 1171 through 1204. This purported statement of basis does not fulfill any of the functions of an effective statement outlined above. The commission argues that even if the "To Whom It May Concern" provision does not satisfy the statement of basis requirement of section 1177, the document entitled "Statement of Findings" included in the administrative record does satisfy section 1177. The commission adopted the Statement of Findings and Order 5-76 at the same meeting. The Statement of Findings does not satisfy the statement of basis requirement for several reasons.

First, section 1177 states that each order shall include a statement of basis. Sections 1182 and 1183 require that an order be published and mailed to employers. Order 5-76 does not include or even mention the Statement of Findings, and the statement was not published or mailed to employers. The statement simply remained in the administrative record. . . .

Second, the Statement of Findings does not address salient comments and alternatives presented during the public hearings on proposed Order 5-76. For example, the commission exempted a number of industries from its regulations covering hours and days of work, because the commission concluded that collective bargaining agreements "adequately" protected employees in those industries. However, the commission did not exempt the public housekeeping industry from coverage, even though the association presented evidence that collective bargaining in the industry was "adequate" rather than "weak." . . . . Similarly, the commission reduced the workweek in the public housekeeping industry from 48 to 40 hours, without responding to the association's argument that the industry practice of having a longer workweek benefitted both employers and employees because of the peak-load demand for employment peculiar to the industry. The Statement of Findings thus does not satisfy the standard of an adequate statement of basis . . . .

In conclusion, the commission failed to include an adequate statement of basis in Order 5-76 . . . . Order 5-76 is therefore invalid as promulgated. However, the order has been in effect since 1976. The minimum wage order is of critical importance to significant numbers of employees. Those employees bear no responsibility for the deficiencies of Order 5-76. This court has inherent power to make an order appropriate to preserve the status quo pending correction of deficiencies. Order 5-76 is to remain operative pending further proceedings to be taken promptly by the commission. . . .

[JUDGE NEWMAN, dissenting.]

I dissent. I believe that experienced observers of how government agencies work will be astonished to learn that, when a statute requires a statement "as to the basis" on which rules are predicated, administrative rulemaking in California is now to be encumbered [by all the requirements in the majority opinion. The majority provides a] much-too-detailed set of instructions [and more than the APA requires]. *See* Att'y Gen. Manual on the APA 32 (1947):

> Except as required by statutes providing for "formal" rule making procedure, findings of fact and conclusions of law are not necessary. Nor is there required an elaborate analysis of the rules or of the considerations upon which the rules were issued. Rather, the statement is intended to advise the public of the general basis and purpose of the rules.

[Furthermore,] the California statute that governs here does not require a "statement of . . . basis and purpose." It does not even require a "statement of basis" (though that phrase appears more than 25 times in the majority opinion here). . . . By no means is the To-Whom-It-May-Concern provision of Order 5-76 a model or prototype statement. It hardly merits inclusion in any formbook. In my view, though, its arguable defects have not caused prejudicial error. . . .

Underlying Case Documents

The case referenced:
California Labor Code §§ 1177, 1182, 1183

1. Courts have worked on this problem for decades. At a bare minimum, a court must be able to tell "what major issues of policy were ventilated . . . and why the agency reacted to them as it did." *Auto. Parts & Accessories Ass'n v. Boyd*, 407 F.2d 330, 338 (D.C. Cir. 1968). Can you tell what issues were ventilated in the above case and why the agency reacted as it did?

2. The end product of a rulemaking has to allow a court to determine if the agency failed to give appropriate consideration to a factor the agency was obligated (by statute or its own rules) to assess, *see Scenic Hudson Pres. Conf. v. FPC*, 354 F.2d 608 (2d Cir. 1968), or if the agency glossed over mandatory criteria, making unsupported assumptions. *See Nat'l Tire Dealers & Retreaders v. Brinegar*, 491 F.2d 31, 40 (D.C. Cir. 1974); *Telocater Network of Am. v. FCC*, 691 F.2d 525 (D.C. Cir. 1982). Looking to the above case, does the record, including the "to whom it may

concern" letter, meet the criteria from *Scenic Hudson*?

3. The above criteria are both rational and troubling. An agency that has to write in detail about all policy issues ventilated and all data considered is engaged in a task unlikely to be concise or general. In <u>Pension Benefit Guarantee Corp. v. LTV</u>, 496 U.S. 633 (1990), and <u>Mobile Oil Exploration & Producing, Southeast v. United Distributing, 498 U.S. 211 (1991)</u>, the Supreme Court cautioned that excessive findings or record requirements for informal processes (both adjudicatory and rulemaking) would have an undesirable limiting effect on an agency's capacity or willingness to use the these mechanisms. The Court found, *inter alia*, that an agency did not have to consider all related problems that might be relevant to the rule or decision the agency makes. Looking at the excerpt from JUDGE NEWMAN's dissenting opinion, is the dissent's perspective more consistent with the APA – and with the *LTV* opinion?

4. Limitations on the content of the record and the statement of basis and purpose also extend to an agency's assessment of the comments filed. <u>Reytblatt v. U.S. Nuclear Reg. Comm'n, 105 F.3d 715, 722 (D.C. Cir. 1997)</u> ("An agency need not address every comment, but it must respond in a reasoned manner to those that raise significant problems."). Agency findings will be upheld even if there is contradictory information in the record, so long as the decision is not arbitrary and capricious. *See, e.g.*, <u>Ashley County Med. Ctr. v. Thompson</u>, 205 F. Supp. 2d 1026 <u>(E.D. Ark. 2002)</u>. Given these standards, was the agency decision in <u>California Motel</u> arbitrary?

5. <u>United Mine Workers of America v. Dole, 870 F.2d 662 (D.C. Cir. 1989)</u>:

> In this case we review new regulations on roof support in underground coal mines. Roof cave-ins due to a lack of adequate support are the leading cause of fatalities and injuries in underground mining . . . .
>
> In 1988 the Secretary of Labor ("Secretary"), acting through the Mine Safety and Health Administration ("MSHA"), promulgated new standards . . . . Under the <u>Mine Safety and Health Act of 1977</u> ("Mine Act") . . . the Secretary is authorized to replace existing mandatory health and safety standards only if the new standards provide at least the same level of protection to miners as the old ones (the "no-less protection rule"). . . .
>
> [T]he United Mine Workers of America ("Union") . . . challenges the new roof bolt . . . standards on the ground that they do not satisfy the no-less protection rule. . . . [T]he Secretary was required to ensure that the new regulations did not reduce miner protection. . . .
>
> The Secretary's statement of basis and purpose, however, is virtually silent on this issue. While she did discuss the general safety features of the new regulations, she did not discuss how protective the old regulations were nor how the new regulations

maintain or improve upon this level of protection. Indeed, the complete absence of any discussion of the no-less protection rule and the Secretary's hazy post hoc arguments to the court attempting to belatedly supply the necessary justification leave us no alternative but to conclude that the Secretary simply failed to take account of this statutory limitation on her authority. The statement of basis and purpose is therefore patently inadequate and the rulemaking was arbitrary and capricious with respect to the roof bolt and support removal standards.

Hypothetical

In response to several requests by individuals and organizations with expertise in passenger safety, the Department of Transportation's Federal Railroad Administration issues a Notice of Proposed Rulemaking seeking comment on a proposed new rule requiring that all passenger railroads including AMTRAK and commuter train services install passenger restraints (*i.e.*, safety belts like those worn on airplanes) in all passenger cars on railroad lines that exceed 30 miles per hour at any time in their routes. The proposed rule exempts subway systems, monorails and other passenger train services in which most passengers are unseated. Of the 455 comments received by the agency, 400 were supportive. Twelve comments, however, were filed by passenger safety experts and organizations presenting research concluding that the use of safety belts in trains would have no cognizable effect on passenger safety in the event of collisions and derailments and, to the contrary, may result in the slowing of emergency evacuations and even physical harm to improperly restrained children and small adults. In its final published rule requiring safety belts on passenger trains, the FRA noted that "not all commentators agreed that the implementation of the new passenger rail safety belt requirements would have an overall positive net effect on safety." It did not provide details from, nor otherwise discuss, any of those commentators' concerns. Several of the twelve commentators opposing the new safety belt regulation seek to challenge it. If they retained you as their lawyer, what arguments would you make in challenging the new rule?

Good Questions!

What agency decision-making mode – formal rulemaking, informal (notice and comment) rulemaking, formal adjudication or informal adjudication – would be most appropriate for:

a. The Federal Communications Commission's revocation of the broadcasting license held by Seattle, WA radio station KXYZ-FM for failure to comply with multiple regulations concerning content and technical engineering (radiofrequency transmission) standards?

b. The Food and Drug Administration's issuance of new truth-in-labeling standards for organic foods, establishing guidelines for organic food production, processing and labeling?

c. The Occupational Safety and Health Administration's identification of safe exposure level for a set of newly discovered carcinogens found in office carpeting and fabric wallcoverings?

d. The Federal Elections Commission's assessment of major fines against five political action committees (PACs) for violations of Federal campaign finance laws?

e. The Social Security Administration's decision to increase the benefits calculation formula for all claimants deemed eligible for disability insurance benefits?

f. The Social Security Administration's determination that a particular beneficiary is no longer eligible for disability benefits because she no longer suffers from an impairment that prevents her from working at substantial gainful employment?

g. The U.S. Customs Service's issuance of a tariff classification ruling (one of approximately 10,000 issued every year by 46 different Customs Service offices) that Mead Corporation "day planners" are subject to an import tariff as "Diaries…, bound?"

IX. Ex Parte Communication in Rulemaking

In the next case, *Sierra Club*, the court addresses ex parte communications in informal rulemaking. As a general rule, the prohibitions against ex parte communications that are in place for Article III courts do not apply in rulemaking pursuant to section 553(c). In fact, there is an expectation that such contacts will take place. As you read through the case, see if you can determine the rationale for giving insiders a special advantage or opportunity to have an effect on administrative decisionmakers. What benefits are derived from such contacts – and at what cost?

SIERRA CLUB V. COSTLE

657 F.2d 298 (D.C. Cir. 1981)

rev'd sub nom RUCKELSHAUS V. SIERRA CLUB, 463 U.S. 680 (1983)

[JUDGE WALD] In June of 1979 EPA revised the regulations . . . governing emission control by coal burning power plants. . . . For the reasons stated below, we hold that EPA did not exceed its statutory authority under the Clean Air Act in promulgating the [regulations], and we decline to set aside the standards. . . .

2. Meetings Held With Individuals Outside EPA

. . . Oral face-to-face discussions are not prohibited anywhere, anytime, in the Act. . . . Where agency action resembles judicial action, where it involves formal rulemaking [or] adjudication . . . the insulation of the decisionmaker from ex parte contacts is justified by basic notions of due process to the parties involved. But where agency action involves informal rulemaking . . . the concept of ex parte contacts is of more questionable utility.

Under our system of government, the very legitimacy of general policymaking . . . depends in no small part upon the openness, accessibility, and amenability of [unelected administrators] to the . . . public from whom their ultimate authority derives, and upon whom their commands must fall. As judges . . . we must refrain from the easy temptation to look askance at all face-to-face lobbying efforts . . . merely because we see them as inappropriate in the judicial context. Furthermore, the importance to effective regulation of . . . contact with . . . the public cannot be underestimated. Informal contacts may enable the agency to win needed support for its program, reduce future enforcement requirements by helping those regulated to anticipate and shape their plans for the future, and spur the provision of information which the agency needs. . . . [However, although t]he statute does not require the docketing of all post-comment period . . . meetings, . . . we believe that . . . in some instances such docketing may be needed . . . . This is so because unless oral communications of central relevance to the rulemaking are also docketed . . ., information central to the justification of the rule could be obtained without ever appearing on the docket, simply by communicating it by voice rather than by pen. . . .

EDF is understandably wary of a rule which permits the agency to decide for itself when oral communications are of such central relevance that a docket entry for them is required. Yet the statute itself vests EPA with discretion to decide whether "documents" are of central relevance and therefore must be placed in the docket; surely EPA can be given no less discretion in docketing oral communications, concerning which the statute has no explicit requirements whatsoever. . . .

A judicially imposed blanket requirement that all post-comment period oral communications be docketed would . . . contravene our limited powers of review . . . and is unnecessary . . . to enable reviewing courts to fully evaluate the stated justification given by the agency for its final rule.

Turning to the particular oral communications in this case, [t]he agency has maintained that, as to the . . . meeting where Senate staff . . . were briefed . . ., its failure to place a summary of the briefing in the docket was an oversight. We find no evidence that this oversight was anything but an honest inadvertence; furthermore, a briefing . . . is not the type of oral communication which would require a docket entry under the statute.

The other undocketed meeting [was] attended by the President [and] other high ranking members of the Executive Branch . . . . We note initially that section 307 makes specific provision for including in the rulemaking docket the "written comments" of other executive agencies along with accompanying documents on any proposed draft rules circulated in advance of the rulemaking proceeding. . . . This specific requirement does not . . . refer to oral comments of any sort. Yet it is hard to believe Congress was unaware that intra-executive meetings . . . would occur throughout the rulemaking process. . . .

[T]he President . . . and his White House advisers surely must be briefed fully and frequently about rules in the making . . . . The executive power under our Constitution, after all, is not shared . . . . The idea of a "plural executive" . . . was considered and rejected by the Constitutional Convention. Instead the Founders chose to risk the potential for tyranny inherent in placing power in one person, in order to gain the advantages of accountability fixed on a single source. . . . Regulations such as those involved here demand a careful weighing of cost, environmental, and energy considerations. They also have broad implications for national economic policy. Our form of government simply could not function effectively or rationally if key executive policymakers were isolated from each other and from the Chief Executive. Single mission agencies do not always have the answers to complex regulatory problems. [They] need[] to know the arguments and ideas of policymakers in other agencies [and] the White House.

We recognize, however, that there may be instances where the docketing of conversations between the President or his staff and other Executive Branch officers . . . may be necessary [such as] where a statute like this one specifically requires that essential "information or data" . . . be docketed. But in the absence of any further Congressional requirements, we hold that it was not unlawful . . . for EPA not to docket a face-to-face policy session involving the President . . ., since EPA makes no effort to base the rule on any "information or data" arising from that meeting. Where the President himself is directly involved in oral communications with Executive Branch officials, Article II considerations combined with the strictures of <u>*Vermont Yankee*</u> require that courts tread with extraordinary caution in mandating disclosure beyond that already required by statute.

[F]ull-record review . . . do[es] not require that courts know the details of every White House contact . . . . After all, any rule issued . . . must have the requisite factual support in the rulemaking record . . . . Of course, it is always possible that undisclosed Presidential prodding may direct an outcome that is factually based on the record, but different from the outcome that would have obtained in the absence of Presidential involvement. . . . But we do not believe that Congress intended that the courts convert informal rulemaking into a rarified technocratic process, unaffected by political considerations or the presence of Presidential power. In sum, we find . . . the failure to docket [the] meeting involving the President . . . violated neither the procedures mandated by the Clean Air Act nor due process.

(b) Meetings Involving Alleged Congressional Pressure

Finally, EDF challenges the rulemaking on the basis of alleged Congressional pressure . . . . But among the cases EDF cites . . ., only *D. C. Federation of Civil Associations v. Volpe* seems relevant to the facts here.

In *D. C. Federation* the Secretary of Transportation . . . made certain safety and environmental findings in designating a proposed bridge as part of the interstate highway system. Civic associations sought to have these determinations set aside . . . because of possible . . . improper Congressional influensce. Such influence chiefly included public statements by the Chairman of the House Subcommittee on the District of Columbia, Representative Natcher, indicating in no uncertain terms that money earmarked for the . . . District of Columbia's subway system would be withheld unless the Secretary approved the bridge. While a majority of this court could not decide whether [this] pressure had in fact influenced the Secretary's decision, a majority did agree . . . "that the decision (of the Secretary) would be invalid if based in whole or in part on the pressures emanating from Representative Natcher." In remanding to the Secretary for new determinations concerning the bridge, however, the court went out of its way to "emphasize that we have not found [any] suggestion of impropriety or illegality in the actions of Representative Natcher . . . ." The court remanded simply so that the Secretary could make this decision strictly and solely on the basis of considerations made relevant by Congress in the applicable statute.

D. C. Federation thus requires that two conditions be met before an administrative rulemaking may be overturned simply on the grounds of Congressional pressure. First, the content of the pressure upon the Secretary is designed to force

him to decide upon factors not made relevant by Congress in the applicable statute. Representative Natcher's threats were of precisely that character, since deciding to approve the bridge in order to free the "hostage" mass transit appropriation
was not among the decision making factors Congress had in mind when it enacted
the [statute]. . . . Second, the Secretary's determination must be affected by those
extraneous considerations.

In the case before us, there is no persuasive evidence that either criterion is
satisfied. Senator Byrd requested a meeting . . . to express "strongly" his already
well-known views that the SO_2 standards' impact on coal reserves was a matter of
concern to him. . . . [There is no] allegation that EPA made any commitments to
Senator Byrd. . . . We believe it entirely proper for Congressional representatives
vigorously to represent the interests of their constituents before administrative
agencies engaged in informal . . . rulemaking . . . . Where Congressmen keep
their comments focused on the substance of the proposed rule and we have no
substantial evidence to cause us to believe Senator Byrd did not do so here, n.539
administrative agencies are expected to balance Congressional pressure with the
pressures emanating from all other sources. To hold otherwise would deprive the
agencies of legitimate sources of information and call into question the validity of
nearly every controversial rulemaking.

> n.539 The only hint we are provided that extraneous "threats" were made comes from
> a newspaper article which states, in part,
>
>> The . . . decision came after two weeks of what one Senate source called
>> "hard-ball arm-twisting" by Byrd and other coal state Senators. Byrd . . .
>> strongly hint[ed] that the Administration needs his support on strategic
>> arms limitation treaty (SALT) and the windfall profits tax . . . .
>
> The Washington Post, May 5, 1979, at A-1. We do not believe that a single newspaper
> account of strong "hint(s)" [is] enough to warrant a finding of unlawful congressional
> interference.

In sum, we conclude that EPA's adoption of the [regulations] was free from
procedural error. . . .

---

1. At the state administrative level, ex parte contacts in administrative rulemaking
proceedings are also treated liberally. Pamela M. Giblin & Jason D. Nichols, *Ex
parte Contacts in Administrative Proceedings: What the Statute Really Means and What
It Should Mean*, 57 BAYLOR L. REV. 23 (2005).

2. The permissive approach mentioned above would not be applicable if a non-
disclosed ex parte communication ends up being the underlying basis for a rule,
thereby frustrating meaningful judicial review. However, in the *Sierra Club* case,

there was a very substantial record (beyond the ex parte dialogue in question) to support the decision. In _Ruckelshaus v. Sierra Club_, 463 U.S. 680, 697-98 (1983), which dealt with a claim for attorney's fees emanating from the *Sierra Club* litigation, the Court provided the following summary:

> In formulating the regulation, EPA had prepared 120 studies, collected 400 items of reference literature, received almost 1,400 comments, written 650 letters and 200 interagency memoranda, held over 50 meetings and substantive telephone conversations with the public, and conducted four days of public hearings. The statement accompanying the regulation took up to 43 pages with triple columns and single-spaced type. Approximately 700 pages of briefs were submitted to this court on the merits of the case. The joint appendix contained 5,620 pages, bound in 12 volumes. The certified index to the record listed over 2,520 submissions. _Sierra Club v. Gorsuch_, 672 F.2d 33, 40 (1982) [_referencing_ Patricia M.] Wald, _Making "Informed" Decisions on the District of Columbia Circuit_, 50 GEO. WASH. L. REV. 135, 145 (1982).

3. As noted above, one explanation for this case might be that beyond the ex parte opinions discussed above, the agency invested enormous resources and collected vast amounts of information before coming to its decision. Thus, even if one were to excise any information derived from the ex parte communications in issue, there remained an extensive record.

4. _Ammex, Inc. v. United States_, 62 F. Supp. 2d 1148 (Ct. Int'l Trade 1999), is a fairly typical application of the *Sierra Club* doctrine:

> Plaintiff's challenge . . . Customs Headquarters Ruling 227385[,] which found that the activities of duty-free stores should not be extended to cover unidentifiable fungible goods, such as gasoline, when sold on a retail basis. . . . [Plaintiffs allege that the Customs office engaged in various discussions, ex parte, and failed to memorialize such communications in the record.]

> Even assuming that this evidence did provide a reasonable basis to believe that such contact took place . . . Plaintiff has failed to demonstrate that such ex parte contact is improper or that, as a result of such contact, there is a strong reason to believe that Customs' decisionmakers weighed improper considerations in deciding HQ 227385. By all appearances, HQ 227385 constitutes an exercise of "informal" rulemaking under the Administrative Procedure Act and, as such, is not subject to the prohibition on ex parte communications set forth in 5 U.S.C. § 557(d)(1) (1994). . . ."

Food for Thought

The *Ammex* court held both that the agency had not "weighed improper considerations" and that informal rulemaking is not subject to the prohibition on ex parte communication. What are the circumstances in which an ex parte communication could contaminate an informal rulemaking?

5. If a proceeding is construed as formal rulemaking or quasi-adjudicatory, differ-

ent standards apply. *Portland Audubon Society v. Oregon Lands Coalition*, 984 F.2d 1534 (9th Cir. 1993):

> [P]etitioners Portland Audubon Society et al. (collectively "the environmental groups") challenge the decision of the statutorily-created Endangered Species Committee ("the Committee"), known popularly as "The God Squad", to grant an exemption from the requirements of the Endangered Species Act. . . . [T]he environmental groups . . . argue . . . that ex parte communications between the White House and its members are [im]permissible under applicable law. . . .
>
> We agree with the environmental groups that ex parte communications between the White House and the God Squad are contrary to law. We further hold that a record that does not include all matters on which the Committee relied does not constitute the "whole record" required for judicial review and that the failure to include all materials in the record violates the Administrative Procedure Act . . . .
>
> The public's right to . . . participate . . . would be effectively nullified if the Committee were permitted to base its decisions on the private conversations and secret talking points and arguments to which the public and the participating parties have no access. . . .

Why are the standards so different for adjudication?

6. Congressional Communication. *Sierra Club* permitted ex parte communication with members of Congress in rulemakings, finding such dialogue with "administrative agencies [to be] expected to balance Congressional pressure with the pressures emanating from all other sources. To hold otherwise would deprive the agencies of legitimate sources of information. . . ." The court articulated limits, finding that if the communication "forced" consideration of factors not relevant to the statute in question and affected outcome, the communication would be prohibited. How likely is it that such communications are actually disclosed?

Hypothetical

The Communications Act of 1934 authorizes the Federal Communications Commission (FCC) to regulate American broadcasters "in furtherance of the public interest, convenience and necessity." Concerned about the effect of television advertising on children, the FCC initiated a notice and comment rulemaking proceeding (under APA § 553) addressing the use of familiar children's cartoon characters in commercial advertising spots. After three public hearings and its review of 250 public comments (235 of which were supportive of the proposed rules), the FCC issued a final rule limiting the use of cartoon characters in commercial spots during programs drawing an audience predominated by children under thirteen years of age. Standard Mills, Inc. (SMI), the nation's second largest manufacturer of breakfast cereals and a major broadcast advertiser that utilizes cartoon characters in its advertising, recommended in its comments that the FCC allow for a "safe harbor" for such advertising to air, without restrictions or risk of penalties, between 9:00 pm and 7:00 am. Although the FCC's order promulgating the new rule addressed and rejected 8 other proposed alternatives, it did not address nor incorporate SMI's proposal. SMI wishes to appeal the FCC's rule.

a. What are the strongest arguments available to SMI? To the FCC?

b. Assume the same facts as in (a), except as follows:

Three years after the FCC promulgated its regulation restricting the airing of commercial advertising featuring cartoon characters, and without prior notice, its new chairman issues the following public statement via press release and a posting on the FCC website's home page:

In light of the changed circumstances in the media marketplace and valid First Amendment concerns raised by broadcasters, a majority of the Commission today voted in favor of eliminating the regulation restricting the use of cartoon characters in commercial advertising effective January 1. We will revisit this decision, and will reinstitute any appropriate limitation, should the performance of broadcasters or advertisers merit such reinstatement.

Several child welfare organizations and public interest media advocacy groups seek to challenge this decision. What are its best arguments?

c. Assume the same facts as in (a), except as follows: Two years after the FCC promulgated its regulation restricting the airing of commercial advertising featuring cartoon characters, the FCC in a formal adjudication of a complaint against WXYZ-TV, Channel 6 (New York City), makes the following decision in an Order:

The regulation restricting animated or "cartoon" caricatures in broadcast advertising is hereby interpreted to encompass computer-manipulated photographic, claymation or robotic depictions of animals or human beings, as presented in the WXYZ-TV children's program, "Real Life Critters," and its associated advertising.

If this order were challenged in court, what standard of review should the reviewing court apply?

7. Non-disclosure problems in Washington led to the passage of the Government in the Sunshine Act found in the APA at 5 U.S.C. § 552(b) and 557(d). In *Electric Power Supply Association v. FERC*, 391 F.3d 1255 (D.C. Cir. 2004), the court discussed the relationship between the goals of the Sunshine Act and the ex parte communication rules:

> Section 557(d) of the Administrative Procedure Act, enacted as part of the Government in the Sunshine Act, . . . prohibits "ex parte communications relevant to the merits of [a prescribed] proceeding" between an "interested person outside the agency" and an agency decisionmaker. 5 U.S.C. § 557(d)(1)(A), (B) (2000). . . . Electric Power Supply Association . . . challenges two FERC orders purporting to amend Rule 2201 to exempt communications between private "market monitors" and FERC decisional employees from the Sunshine Act's ban on ex parte communications. . . .
>
> On the merits, the Commission argues that the proposed exemption does not violate the Sunshine Act, because it effects a reasonable balance between the need for enhanced monitoring of national energy markets through timely reporting of market information with the need for fairness and openness in Commission proceedings. We reject all of FERC's arguments. . . . FERC's orders violate the clear mandate of the Sunshine Act. An agency may lawfully adopt regulations that faithfully implement the requirements of § 557(d). But no federal agency . . . subject to the Sunshine Act is authorized to modify, abrogate, or otherwise violate the statutory ban on ex parte communications.

Good Question!

Are policies of openness and transparency impossible to achieve if ex parte communication is permitted? Do you believe that disclosure after the communication is a sufficient remedy?

8. Rulemaking is both a critical sub-part in the study of administrative law and a field unto itself. Often, the study of rulemaking relies heavily on cases and law review articles in the field. For those who want to understand fully the rulemaking process and its broader relationship to lawmaking in the United States, we strongly recommend Dr. Cornelius M. Kerwin's RULEMAKING: HOW GOVERNMENT AGENCIES WRITE LAW AND MAKE POLICY, 3d Ed. (CQ Press 2003). There is no better comprehensive source providing both legal and critical social science perspectives in the field. In addition to the Kerwin treatise, we also highly recommend a publication of the American Bar Association, Section of Administrative Law and Regulatory Practice, Jeffrey S. Lubbers' A GUIDE TO FEDERAL AGENCY RULEMAKING, 4th Ed. (2006).

Good Question!

Does it make sense that the prohibitions against ex parte communication in Article III courts are so clear – and the consequences so serious – when there are extremely liberal rules for identical communications in rulemaking proceedings that could end up determining the rights and entitlements of large segments of the population?

CHAPTER 3

Judicial Review of Legislative Rulemaking: Deference to Agency Action

I. The Basic Limitation on Judicial Review

Judicial review of rulemaking is at the heart of much of administrative law. This is a complicated field that begins with an easily stated question: What is the role of courts when reviewing properly promulgated rules? Article I of the Constitution places the power to legislate in Congress, and (non-delegation arguments notwithstanding), that power can be delegated to administrative agencies, and finally, rulemaking is a consequence of that assignment of congressional power. More often than not, rules reflect policy – and policy is the province of Congress (in this instance hopefully delegated with clarity to an agency) and the executive – not necessarily the province of the courts.

Naturally, if an agency proceeds in a manner that violates due process or the very limited demands of the APA, if the agency exceeds statutory authority, or if the action of the agency is simply wrong (e.g., a clearly erroneous reading of a statute), the role of a court is not complex. The agency action has to be set aside. These, of course, are the easy cases. They do not involve the more important administrative and constitutional question: Under what circumstances can a court overturn the procedurally correct action of an agency, where the agency has promulgated a rule that expresses the policy of the agency – and therefore presumably means the policy of the executive and Congress? This raises the omnipresent separation of power issue inherent in judicial review.

When the problem is posed simplistically, most federal courts parrot the two-step test from *Chevron U.S.A., Inc. v. Natural Resources Defense Council, Inc.*, 467 U.S. 837, 842-44 (1984), *infra* Chapter 4. *Chevron* holds that if a statute is clear, both court and agency must follow the unambiguously expressed will of the legislature. If the statute is silent or ambiguous, courts are obligated to defer to the agency's

Take Note

Chevron, for all its importance in the field, was by no means the first time the Supreme Court tried to nudge appellate courts away from the business of rulemaking – and since the case was decided, the Supreme Court has tried at least a dozen different times to refine, qualify, and elaborate on its meaning.

interpretation if it is a "permissible" construction of the law in question.

Forty years before *Chevron*, the Court held that "an appellate court cannot intrude upon the domain which Congress has exclusively entrusted to an administrative agency." *SEC v. Chenery Corp. [I]*, 318 U.S. 80, 88 (1943). The First Circuit stated the principle directly: "[W]here Congress has entrusted rulemaking and administrative authority to an agency, courts normally accord the agency particular deference in respect to the interpretation of regulations promulgated under that authority." *South Shore Hosp., Inc. v. Thompson*, 308 F.3d 91, 97 (1st Cir. 2002).

The case that follows, decided six years before *Chevron*, articulated basic principles limiting the parameters of judicial review of agency rulemaking. As you read *Vermont Yankee Nuclear Power Corporations v. Natural Resources Defense Council*, ask yourself if it differs from the basic principle in *South Shore*, above.

VERMONT YANKEE NUCLEAR POWER CORPORATION V. NATURAL RESOURCES DEFENSE COUNCIL, INC.

435 U.S. 519 (1978)

[Justice Rehnquist] [G]enerally speaking . . . the [Administrative Procedure Act] established the maximum procedural requirements which Congress was willing to have the courts impose upon agencies in conducting rulemaking proceedings. This is not to say necessarily that there are no circumstances which would ever justify a court in overturning agency action because of a failure to employ procedures beyond those required by the statute. But such circumstances, if they exist, are extremely rare.

Even apart from the [APA,] this Court has for more than four decades emphasized that the formulation of procedures was basically to be left within the discretion of the agenc[y].

I

A

Under the Atomic Energy Act of 1954 the Atomic Energy Commission was given broad regulatory authority over the development of nuclear energy. . . . [A] utility seeking to construct and operate a nuclear power plant must obtain a separate permit or license at both the construction and the operation stage of the project. In order to obtain the construction permit, the utility must file [many documents including] an environmental report . . . . This application then undergoes exhaustive review by the Commission's staff and by the Advisory Committee on Reactor Safeguards (ACRS) . . . . Thereupon a three-member Atomic Safety and Licensing Board conducts a public adjudicatory hearing, and reaches a decision which can be appealed [within the agency]. The final agency decision may be appealed to the courts of appeals. The same sort of process occurs when the utility applies for a license to operate the plant, except that a hearing need only be held in contested cases and may be limited to the matters in controversy.

. . . .

B

In December 1967, after the mandatory . . . review, the Commission granted petitioner Vermont Yankee a permit to build a nuclear power plant in Vernon, Vt. Thereafter, Vermont Yankee applied for an operating license. Respondent Natural Resources Defense Council (NRDC) objected[, triggering the] hearing [requirement]. Excluded from consideration at the hearings, over NRDC's objection, was the issue of the environmental effects of operations to reprocess fuel or dispose of wastes resulting from the reprocessing operations. This ruling was affirmed by the Appeal Board in June 1972.

In November 1972, however, the Commission, making specific reference to the Appeal Board's decision . . ., instituted rulemaking proceedings "that would specifically deal with the question of consideration of environmental effects associated with the uranium fuel cycle . . . ." The notice of proposed rulemaking offered two alternatives, both predicated on a report prepared by the Commission's staff entitled Environmental Survey of the Nuclear Fuel Cycle. The first would have required no quantitative evaluation of the environmental hazards of fuel reprocessing or disposal because the Environmental Survey had found them to be slight. The second would have specified numerical values for the environmental impact of this part of the fuel cycle, which values would then be incorporated into a table, along with the other relevant factors, to determine the overall cost-benefit balance for each operating license.

Much of the controversy in this case revolves around the procedures used in the rulemaking hearing[, in] which . . . the Commission indicated that while discovery or cross-examination would not be utilized, the Environmental Survey would be available to the public before the hearing along with the extensive background documents cited therein. All participants would be given a reasonable opportunity to present their position . . . . Written and, time permitting, oral statements would be received and incorporated into the record. All persons giving oral statements would be subject to questioning by the Commission. At the conclusion of the hearing, a transcript would be made available to the public and the record would remain open for 30 days to allow the filing of supplemental written statements. . . . The hearing was held on February 1 and 2, with participation by a number of groups . . . . After the hearing, the Commission's staff filed a supplemental document for the purpose of clarifying and revising the Environmental Survey. . . .

In April 1974, the Commission issued a rule which adopted the second of the two proposed alternatives described above. The Commission also approved the procedures used at the hearing, and indicated that the record, including the Environmental Survey, provided an "adequate data base for the regulation adopted." Finally, the Commission ruled that to the extent the rule differed from the Appeal Board decisions in Vermont Yankee . . . since "the environmental effects of the uranium fuel cycle have been shown to be relatively insignificant . . . it is unnecessary to [reconsider the decision under the new rule]." Respondents appealed from both the Commission's adoption of the rule and its decision to grant Vermont Yankee's license . . . .

D

[D]espite the fact that it appeared that the agency employed all the procedures required by 5 U.S.C. § 553 and more, the court determined the proceedings to be inadequate and overturned the rule. Accordingly, the Commission's determination with respect to Vermont Yankee's license was also remanded for further proceedings. . . .

II

A

[The Commission can consider] the environmental impact of the fuel processes when licensing nuclear reactors. . . . Vermont Yankee will produce annually well over 100 pounds of radioactive wastes, some of which . . . must be isolated for . . . hundreds of thousands of years. It is hard to argue that these wastes do not constitute "adverse environmental effects which cannot be avoided should the proposal be implemented," or that by operating nuclear power plants we are not making "irreversible and irretrievable commitments of resources." . . . .

B

. . . Absent constitutional constraints or extremely compelling circumstances the "administrative agencies 'should be free to fashion their own rules of procedure . . . .'" Congress intended that the discretion of the *agencies* and not that of the courts be exercised in determining when extra procedural devices should be employed.

There are compelling reasons for [this distinction]. In the first place, if courts . . . determine whether the agency employed procedures which were, in the court's opinion, perfectly tailored to reach what the court perceives to be the "best" or "correct" result, . . . agencies . . . would undoubtedly adopt full adjudicatory procedures in every instance. Not only would this totally disrupt the statutory scheme, through which Congress enacted "a formula upon which opposing social and political forces have come to rest" but all the inherent advantages of informal rulemaking would be totally lost.

Secondly, it is obvious that the court in these cases reviewed the agency's choice of procedures on the basis of the record actually produced at the hearing and not on the basis of the information available to the agency when it made the decision to structure the proceedings in a certain way. This sort of Monday morning quarterbacking not only encourages but almost compels the agency to conduct all rulemaking proceedings with the full panoply of procedural devices normally associated only with adjudicatory hearings.

Finally, and perhaps most importantly, [judicial review of] informal rulemaking need not be based solely on the transcript of a hearing held before an agency. Indeed, the agency need not even hold a formal hearing. Thus, the adequacy of the "record" in this type of proceeding . . . turns on whether the agency has followed the statutory mandate of the Administrative Procedure Act or other relevant statutes. . . .

. . . In short, nothing in the APA, NEPA, the circumstances of this case, the nature of the issues being considered, past agency practice, or the statutory mandate under which the Commission operates permitted the court to review and overturn the rulemaking proceeding on the basis of the procedural devices employed (or not employed) by the Commission so long as the Commission employed at least the statutory minima, a matter about which there is no doubt in this case.

There remains, of course, the question of whether the challenged rule finds sufficient justification in the administrative proceedings that it should be upheld by the reviewing court. . . . We accordingly remand so that the Court of Appeals may review the rule as the Administrative Procedure Act provides. . . .

III

A

[We now] make one further observation of some relevance to this case. To say that the Court of Appeals' final reason for remanding is insubstantial at best is a gross understatement. Consumers Power first applied in 1969 for a construction permit . . . . The proposed plant underwent an incredibly extensive review. The reports filed and reviewed literally fill books. . . . Nuclear energy may some day be a cheap, safe source of power or it may not. But Congress has made a choice to at least try nuclear energy, establishing a reasonable review process in which courts are to play only a limited role. The fundamental policy questions appropriately resolved in Congress and in the state legislatures are *not* subject to reexamination in the federal courts under the guise of judicial review of agency action. Time may prove wrong the decision to develop nuclear energy, but it is Congress or the States within their appropriate agencies which must eventually make that judgment. In the meantime courts should perform their appointed function. . . . Administrative decisions should be set aside in this context, as in every other, only for substantial procedural or substantive reasons as mandated by statute not simply because the court is unhappy with the result reached. . . .

Underlying Case Documents

The case referenced:
The Atomic Energy Act of 1954

You can access the original order granting the permit HERE.

Five years after this order issued, the Commission institute a rulemaking and mentioning a future hearing, 37 Fed. Reg. 24191 (Nov. 15, 1972).

That hearing was announced at 38 Fed. Reg. 49 (January 3, 1973).

---

1. Do the limitations on judicial review imposed in *Vermont Yankee* prevent judges from sharing their wisdom and experience in one area where courts have genuine expertise: The legal process?

2. The *Vermont Yankee* decision seems to draw a line in the sand, limiting judicial intervention with agency action: "Absent constitutional constraints or extremely compelling circumstances the 'administrative agencies should be free to fashion their own rules of procedure and methods of inquiry permitting them to discharge their multitudinous duties.'" What would constitute an "extremely compelling circumstance?" *See, e.g., Alaska Prof'l Hunters Ass'n v. FAA, 177 F.3d 1030, 1030-31 (D.C. Cir. 1999)* (analyzed in

Good Question!

It is one thing to base a decision on the fact that most judges do not have specialized expertise, particularly in highly technical areas like atomic energy. It is quite another to limit the role of the judiciary in questions pertaining to the submission of evidence or the nature of pre- and post-hearing processes, an area where there is a long history of judicial activity. Why exclude judges from evaluating procedures that affect the right of the public to participate in agency hearings?

Ryan DeMotte, Note, *Interpretive Rulemaking and the Alaska Hunters Doctrine: A Necessary Limit on Agency Discretion*, 66 U. PITT. L. REV. 357 (2004); <u>Nat'l Wildlife Fed'n v. Marsh, 721 F.2d 767, 784-86 (11th Cir. 1983)</u>).

3. Professor John Duffy noted that "Vermont Yankee . . . deference is not unlimited, and agency procedural choices . . . may be overturned in 'extremely compelling circumstances' or where the agency makes 'a totally unjustified departure from well-settled agency procedures of long standing.' True, federal courts have not frequently explored the possibilities left open by these exceptions: Decisions overturning agency procedural discretion are rare. . . ." John F. Duffy, <u>Administrative Common Law in Judicial Review, 77 TEX. L. REV. 113 (1998)</u>. Does the failure of an agency to act when there is the apparent power to regulate a field constitute an extremely compelling circumstance? *See* <u>Massachusetts v. EPA</u>, *infra* Chapter 4.

4. Is there any latitude for judicial action outside of the Supreme Court's admonition in *Vermont Yankee*? The D.C. Circuit's position is unequivocal: "'[A]bsent constitutional constraints or extremely compelling circumstances' courts are *never* free to impose on the NRC (or any other agency) a procedural requirement not provided for by Congress." <u>Union of Concerned Scientists v. NRC, 920 F.2d 50, 53 (D.C. Cir. 1990)</u>.

5. <u>Bowles v. Seminole Rock & Sand Co., 325 U.S. 410, 414 (1945)</u>, is a basic case in this field that, in the view of the authors of this casebook, is on the brink of being rediscovered. It provides understandable guidelines for judicial review of agency action and may, like *Skidmore* (<u>infra at Chapter 3</u>), become a primary measure for the more nuanced questions regarding judicial review of agency rulemaking. *See* Kristin E. Hickman & Matthew

Food for Thought

Not all courts are quite as extreme in their recitation of the *Vermont Yankee* principle. *See, e.g., Fleming Cos. v. USDA*, 322 F. Supp. 2d 744 (D. Tex. 2004): "Although administrative agencies may add additional procedures to the rulemaking process, 'reviewing courts are generally not free to impose them.'" There is a meaningful difference between the words "never" and "generally not free." Which seems correct?

D. Krueger, <u>In Search of the Modern Skidmore Standard, 107 COLUM. L. REV. 1235 (2007)</u>; Thomas W. Merrill, <u>The D.C. Circuit Review July 2004-2005, Recent Decisions of the United States Court of Appeals of the District of Columbia, 74 GEO. WASH. L. REV. 569 (2006)</u>.

6. At every level, the "hands off" principle is given voice. In a recent military tribunal proceeding, the dissent noted that "[t]he Court should leave the rulemaking function where it belongs – to the executive and legislative branches." <u>United States v. Moreno, 63 M.J. 129 (2006)</u>. Whether dealing with the APA or special-

ized legislation, the statement of policy appears uniform. In <u>*Citizens Awareness Network, Inc. v. United States*, 391 F.3d 338 (1st Cir. 2004)</u>, the court held that "the action at issue here – a rulemaking – would appear to fall outside the scope of review provided by the Hobbs Act." If an agency's interpretation of the statute "reflects a plausible construction of the plain language of the statute and does not otherwise conflict with Congress' expressed intent," a court must defer to the action of that agency. <u>*Rust v. Sullivan*, 500 U.S. 173, 184 (1991)</u>.

7. Though decided 30 years ago, *Vermont Yankee* is still of consequence when courts are asked to examine agency practices that are on the border of the APA "statutory minimum" that forms the rather fuzzy dividing line between appropriate and inappropriate judicial review. <u>*Senville v. Capka*, 2008 WL 783530 (D. Vt., Mar. 21, 2008)</u>; <u>*High Sierra Hikers Ass'n v. U.S. Forest Serv.*, 436 F. Supp. 2d 1117 (E.D. Cal. 2006)</u>.

8. *Vermont Yankee* was more than a technical legal dispute about the APA. It was major litigation regarding the powerful and unanswered questions pertaining to fuel reprocessing as well as a fight over nuclear power as a source for generating electricity. The case brought together some of the most prominent industry and public interest lawyers, including Anthony Roisman, one of the better known and effective public interest advocates in the field.

The various proceedings covered more than a decade, culminating in the 1978 decision one year before the <u>Three Mile Island</u> disaster that signaled the end of new nuclear power plants for the next three decades.

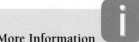

For More Information

For further information on Three Mile Island and nuclear power in the 21st Century, see *President's Commission on the Accident at Three Mile Island, The Need for Change: The Legacy of TMI* (1979) (The Kemeny Commission Report); J. Samuel Walker, THREE MILE ISLAND: A NUCLEAR CRISIS IN HISTORICAL PERSPECTIVE (2004); *Speaking of Power*, 151 POWER MAGAZINE, no. 9, at 4, September 2007 (suggesting that 17 new nuclear power plants are under consideration as of Fall 2007).

9. <u>*Baltimore Gas & Electric Co. v. Natural Resources Defense Council, Inc.*, 462 U.S. 87 (1983)</u>, continues the litigation from *Vermont Yankee*.

> At the heart of each rule is Table S-3, a numerical compilation of the estimated resources used and effluents released by . . . a year's operation of a typical light-water reactor. . . . [The Commission] declared that . . . for individual licensing proceedings the environmental costs of the fuel cycle "shall be as set forth" in Table S-3 and that "[no] further discussion of such environmental effects shall be required." The original Table S-3 contained no numerical entry for the long-term environmental effects of storing . . . wastes, because the Commission staff believed that technology would be developed to isolate the wastes from the environment. . . . [This is] the "zero-release"

assumption: the reasonableness of this assumption is at the core of the present controversy.

It is clear that the Commission, in making this determination, has made the careful consideration and disclosure required by NEPA. . . . As *Vermont Yankee* made clear, NEPA does not require agencies to adopt any particular internal decisionmaking structure. Here, the . . . generic method chosen by the agency is clearly an appropriate method of conducting the "hard look" required by NEPA. The environmental effects of much of the fuel cycle are not plant specific, for any plant, regardless of its particular attributes, will create additional wastes that must be stored in a common long-term repository. Administrative efficiency and consistency of decision are both furthered by a generic determination of these effects without needless repetition of the litigation in individual proceedings, which are subject to review by the Commission in any event.

Second, the Commission emphasized that the zero-release assumption is but a single figure in an entire Table, which the Commission expressly designed as a risk-averse estimate . . . . It noted that Table S-3 assumed that the fuel storage canisters and the fuel rod cladding would be corroded before a repository is closed and that all volatile materials in the fuel would escape to the environment. Given that assumption, and the improbability that materials would escape after sealing, the Commission determined that the overall Table represented a conservative (i.e., inflated) statement of environmental impacts. It is not unreasonable for the Commission to counteract the uncertainties in postsealing releases by balancing them with an overestimate of presealing releases. A reviewing court should not magnify a single line item beyond its significance as only part of a larger Table.

Third, a reviewing court must remember that the Commission is making predictions, within its area of special expertise, at the frontiers of science. When examining this kind of scientific determination, as opposed to simple findings of fact, a reviewing court must generally be at its most deferential. With these three guides in mind, we find the Commission's zero-release assumption to be within the bounds of reasoned decisionmaking required by the APA. . . .

10. *City of Alexandria v. Slater*, 198 F.3d 862 (D.C. Cir. 1999):

The Woodrow Wilson Memorial Bridge is a microcosm of the Washington, D.C. metropolitan area's traffic . . . problems. . . . [T]he configuration of an eight-lane Beltway feeding into a six-lane bridge . . . has produced one of the worst rush-hour "bottlenecks" in the region. . . . Efforts to replace the Bridge began over ten years ago. . . . Each of the alternatives in the draft proposed expanding the river crossing from six to twelve lanes, and included a similar expansion of the [surrounding] Beltway corridor . . . .

Reaction to the draft was less than enthusiastic; the Administration was criticized for assessing inadequately the environmental and cultural impacts of its proposal . . . . In response the Administration organized a "Coordination Committee" . . . . The Committee revisited the entire process . . . ultimately soliciting and considering over 350 proposals . . . . In the meantime, pursuant to its obligations under . . . the National Historic Preservation Act and section 4(f) of the Department of Transportation Act, the Administration continued to assess the project's potential impacts on historic, archaeological, and cultural resources in the area. . . . Among the eight options [made available for comment] the Administration designated a "Preferred Alternative" that would replace the Bridge with two parallel six-lane drawbridges . . . . After a brief comment period the Administration approved the Preferred Alternative . . . and submitted, as is required by . . . the National Historic Preservation Act, a Memorandum of Agreement evidencing the Administration's cooperation with state historic preservation officers in identifying historic sites that might be impacted. . . . The City of Alexandria filed an action in the district court challenging the Administration's approval of the project . . . .

Appellees . . . argue . . . that the Administration violated section 4(f)(2)'s requirement that the agency engage in "all possible planning" to minimize harm to 4(f) properties, but this argument is . . . unpersuasive. . . . [A]ppellees do not question the Administration's express findings that . . . the preferred alternative "results in the least overall impact to section 4(f) resources." [Further,] the Administration made several significant project modifications to avoid or minimize impacts to section 4(f) properties, including altering an interchange design to avoid impacting a schoolground and eliminating the construction of a temporary Beltway overpass to minimize the risk of harm to Freedman's Cemetery. Where the Administration could identify no feasible and prudent plan for avoiding impact to a 4(f) site, it offered plans to mitigate that impact . . . .

During the course of our consideration of this case, appellees have attempted to bolster their position by pointing to the opposition of prominent legislators to the project, and by noting the hurdles to ultimate congressional approval that still lie in the Administration's path. These political impediments are irrelevant to us but they indicate where appellees should concentrate their efforts. We have been admonished by the Supreme Court with respect to the very statute that is at the heart of this case to avoid using its requirements as a vehicle to impose our own judgment. *Vermont Yankee*. Our obligation is not to further our *beau ideal* of a bridge design, but merely to ensure that the procedures mandated by these statutes have been complied with. We hold that the Administration has satisfied the requirements of NEPA, the National Historic Preservation Act, and the Department of Transportation Act, and reverse.

11. Change in Content from NPRM to Final Rule: While there is more to come with this case, this is the most recent iteration: *Nutraceutical Corp. v. Eschenbach*, 477 F. Supp. 2d 1161 (Utah 2007):

In 2004, the Food and Drug Administration promulgated a rule that banned ephedrine-alkaloid dietary supplements ("EDS") at any dosage level from the United States market. Before the effective date of this rule . . . Nutraceutical . . . marketed EDS in the United States. . . . Nutraceutical seeks to enjoin the FDA from enforcing this rule [claiming that the FDA failed to give adequate notice and an opportunity for comment on the final rule, basing their argument in part on the premise that the final rule that issued deviated from the initial proposed rule.]

After the agency provides the requisite notice, it must provide an opportunity for comment . . . . The APA requires only limited opportunity to participate – no more. To impose on the FDA more stringent procedural requirements than called for in § 553 would violate the Supreme Court's direction that agencies must have discretion to formulate their own procedures. *Vermont Yankee*. . . . [I]t is not unusual for an agency's final rule to differ from its proposed rule. Change is often a natural result of the notice and comment procedure:

> That an agency changes its approach to the difficult problems it must address does not signify the failure of the administrative process. Instead, an agency's change of course, so long as generally consistent with the tenor of its original proposals, indicates that the agency treats the notice and comment process seriously . . . . "To hold otherwise would 'lead to the absurdity that in rule making under the APA the agency can learn from the comments on its proposals only at the peril of starting a new procedural round of commentary.'" Generally, if the final rule is a "logical outgrowth" of the proposed rule, the notice of proposed rulemaking will be sufficient to forecast the final rule.

Nutraceutical's own participation in the rulemaking process belies its claims that the FDA provided statutorily inadequate notice or failed to comply with comment requirements. . . . That the FDA was unpersuaded by Nutraceutical's [comments] does not call into question the sufficiency of the FDA's notice and comment procedures.

II. Deference and Judicial Review

While no case has had more notoriety on the topic of judicial review of administrative action in the last quarter-century than *Chevron*, the ideas and standards were not new. The task the court faced began with *Marbury v. Madison*: Balancing the need for judicial review with the need for the executive (in the guise of the agency) to govern and express the will of the electorate. Are judges who demand excellence from those charged with running an agency intrusive? Is it a violation of separation of powers to push an agency to make decisions that best protect the public interest? On the other hand, should judges, many of whom lack technical expertise, have the last word on complex scientific matters? Thomas W. Merrill, *Marbury v. Madison as the First Great Administrative Law Decision*, 37 J. MARSHALL L. REV. 481 (2004).

Activist judges are often condemned by "strict constructionists" for transgressing the proper range of their authority. Nonetheless, there is little question that courts are required to take a careful look at agency decisions. *Chevron* is an attempt to strike this balance.

CHEVRON, U.S.A., INC. V. NATURAL RESOURCES DEFENSE COUNCIL

467 U.S. 837 (1984)

[JUSTICE STEVENS] In the Clean Air Act Amendments of 1977, Congress enacted certain requirements applicable to States that had not achieved the national air quality standards established by the Environmental Protection Agency (EPA) pursuant to earlier legislation. The amended Clean Air Act required these "nonattainment" States to establish a permit program regulating "new or modified major stationary sources" of air pollution. Generally, a permit may not be issued for a new or modified major stationary source unless several stringent conditions are met. The EPA regulation promulgated to implement this permit requirement allows a State to adopt a plantwide definition of the term "stationary source." Under this definition, an existing plant that contains several pollution-emitting devices may install or modify one piece of equipment without meeting the permit conditions if the alteration will not increase the total emissions from the plant. The question presented by these cases is whether EPA's decision to allow States to treat all of the pollution-emitting devices within the same industrial grouping as though they were encased within a single "bubble" is based on a reasonable construction of the statutory term "stationary source."

I.

The EPA regulations containing the plantwide definition of the term stationary source were promulgated on October 14, 1981. Respondents filed a timely petition for review in the United States Court of Appeals for the District of Columbia Circuit pursuant to 42 U.S.C. § 7607(b)(1). The Court of Appeals set aside the regulations.

The court observed that the relevant part of the amended Clean Air Act "does not explicitly define what Congress envisioned as a 'stationary source,' to which the permit program . . . should apply," and further stated that the precise issue was not "squarely addressed in the legislative history." In light of its conclusion that the legislative history bearing on the question was "at best contradictory," it reasoned that "the purposes of the non-attainment program should guide our decision here." Based on two of its precedents concerning the applicability of the bubble concept to certain Clean Air Act programs, the court stated that the bubble concept was "mandatory" in programs designed merely to maintain existing air quality, but held that it was "inappropriate" in programs enacted to improve air quality. Since the purpose of the permit program . . . was to improve air quality, the court held that the bubble concept was inapplicable in these cases under its prior precedents. It therefore set aside the regulations embodying the bubble concept as contrary to law. We . . . now reverse. . . .

II.

When a court reviews an agency's construction of the statute which it administers, it is confronted with two questions. First, always, is the question whether Congress has directly spoken to the precise question at issue. If the intent of Congress is clear, that is the end of the matter; for the court, as well as the agency, must give effect to the unambiguously expressed intent of Congress. n.9 If, however, the court determines Congress has not directly addressed the precise question at issue, the court does not simply impose its own construction on the statute, as would be necessary in the absence of an administrative interpretation. Rather, if the statute is silent or ambiguous with respect to the specific issue, the question for the court is whether the agency's answer is based on a permissible construction of the statute. n.11

> n.9 The judiciary is the final authority on issues of statutory construction and must reject administrative constructions which are contrary to clear congressional intent. If a court, employing traditional tools of statutory construction, ascertains that Congress had an intention on the precise question at issue, that intention is the law and must be given effect.

> n.11 The court need not conclude that the agency construction was the only one it permissibly could have adopted to uphold the construction, or even the reading the court would have reached if the question initially had arisen in a judicial proceeding.

"The power of an administrative agency to administer a congressionally created . . . program necessarily requires the formulation of policy and the making of rules to fill any gap left, implicitly or explicitly, by Congress." *Morton v. Ruiz*. If Congress has explicitly left a gap for the agency to fill, there is an express delegation of authority to the agency to elucidate a specific provision of the statute by regulation. Such legislative regulations are given controlling weight unless they are arbitrary, capricious, or manifestly contrary to the statute. Sometimes the legislative delegation to an agency on a particular question is implicit rather than explicit. In such a case, a court may not substitute its own construction of a statutory provision for a reasonable interpretation made by the administrator of an agency. . . .

In light of these well-settled principles it is clear that the Court of Appeals misconceived the nature of its role in reviewing the regulations at issue. Once it determined, after its own examination of the legislation, that Congress did not actually have an intent regarding the applicability of the bubble concept to the permit program, the question before it was not whether in its view the concept is "inappropriate" in the general context of a program designed to improve air quality, but whether the Administrator's view that it is appropriate in the context of this particular program is a reasonable one. Based on the examination of the legislation and its history which follows, we agree with the Court of Appeals that Congress did not have a specific intention on the applicability of the bubble concept in these cases, and conclude that the EPA's use of that concept here is a reasonable policy choice for the agency to make.

III.

[Congress enacted the 1970 Clean Air Amendments directing the EPA to issue new source performance standards for each major new source of pollution. The EPA did so, saying that in the nonferrous smelting industry modifications to major smelting equipment could be offset by reductions in other parts of the same plant. Although this finding was later overturned by a lower court, it was the standard in place when Congress enacted the 1977 Clean Air Act Amendments.]

IV.

The Clean Air Act Amendments of 1977 are a lengthy, detailed, technical, complex, and comprehensive response to a major social issue. A small portion of the statute . . . expressly deals with nonattainment areas. The focal point of this controversy is one phrase in that portion of the Amendments.

The 1977 Amendments contain no specific reference to the "bubble concept." Nor do they contain a specific definition of the term "stationary source" . . . . Section 302(j), however, defines the term "major stationary source" as follows:

> (j) Except as otherwise expressly provided, the terms "major stationary source" and "major emitting facility" mean any stationary facility or source of air pollutants which directly emits, or has the potential to emit, one hundred tons per year or more of any air pollutant . . . .

V.

The legislative history of the portion of the 1977 Amendments dealing with nonattainment areas does not contain any specific comment on the "bubble concept" or the question whether a plantwide definition of a stationary source is permissible under the permit program. . . .

VI.

As previously noted, prior to the 1977 Amendments, the EPA had adhered to a plantwide definition of the term "source" under a NSPS program. . . . In August 1980, however, the EPA adopted a regulation that . . . took particular note of the two then-recent Court of Appeals decisions, which had created the bright-line rule that the "bubble concept" should be employed in a program designed to maintain air quality but not in one designed to enhance air quality. Relying heavily on those cases, EPA adopted a dual definition of "source" for nonattainment areas that required a permit whenever a change in either the entire plant, or one of its components, would result in a significant increase in emissions even if the increase was completely offset by reductions elsewhere in the plant. . . .

In 1981 a new administration took office and initiated a "Government-wide re-examination of regulatory burdens and complexities." In the context of that review, the EPA re-evaluated the various arguments that had been advanced in connection with the proper definition of the term "source" and concluded that the term should be given the same definition in both nonattainment areas and PSD areas.

In explaining its conclusion, the EPA first noted that the definitional issue was not squarely addressed in either the statute or its legislative history and therefore that the issue involved an agency "judgment as how to best carry out the Act." It then set forth several reasons for concluding that the plantwide definition was more appropriate. It pointed out that the dual definition "can act as a disincentive to new investment and modernization by discouraging modifications to existing facilities" and "can actually retard progress in air pollution control by discouraging replacement of older, dirtier processes or pieces of equipment with new, cleaner ones." Moreover, the new definition "would simplify EPA's rules by using the same definition of 'source' for PSD, nonattainment new source review and the construction moratorium. This reduces confusion and inconsistency." Finally, the agency explained that additional requirements that remained in place would accomplish the fundamental purposes of achieving attainment with NAAQS's as expeditiously as possible. These conclusions were expressed in a proposed rulemaking in August 1981 that was formally promulgated in October.

VII.

. . . Respondents . . . contend that the text of the Act requires the EPA to use a dual definition – if either a component of a plant, or the plant as a whole, emits over 100 tons of pollutant, it is a major stationary source. They thus contend that the EPA rules adopted in 1980, insofar as they apply to the maintenance of the quality of clean air, as well as the 1981 rules which apply to nonattainment areas, violate the statute.

Statutory Language

. . . We are not persuaded that parsing of general terms in the text of the statute will reveal an actual intent of Congress. . . . To the extent any congressional "intent" can be discerned from this language, it would appear that the listing of overlapping, illustrative terms was intended to enlarge, rather than to confine, the scope of the agency's power to regulate particular sources in order to effectuate the policies of the Act.

Legislative History

. . . Based on our examination of the legislative history, we agree with the

Court of Appeals that it is unilluminating. . . . [T]he legislative history as a whole is silent on the precise issue before us. It is, however, consistent with the view that the EPA should have broad discretion in implementing the policies of the 1977 Amendments.

More importantly, that history plainly identifies the policy concerns that motivated the enactment; the plantwide definition is fully consistent with one of those concerns – the allowance of reasonable economic growth – and, whether or not we believe it most effectively implements the other, we must recognize that the EPA has advanced a reasonable explanation for its conclusion that the regulations serve the environmental objectives as well. Indeed, its reasoning is supported by the public record developed in the rulemaking process, as well as by certain private studies. n.37

> n.37. "Economists have proposed that economic incentives be substituted for the cumbersome administrative-legal framework. The objective is to make the profit and cost incentives that work so well in the marketplace work for pollution control. . . . [The 'bubble' or 'netting' concept] is a first attempt in this direction. By giving a plant manager flexibility to find the places and processes within a plant that control emissions most cheaply, pollution control can be achieved more quickly and cheaply." L. LAVE & G. OMENN, CLEANING THE AIR: REFORMING THE CLEAN AIR ACT 28 (1981).

Our review of the EPA's varying interpretations of the word "source" – both before and after the 1977 Amendments – convinces us that the agency primarily responsible for administering this important legislation has consistently interpreted it flexibly – not in a sterile textual vacuum, but in the context of implementing policy decisions in a technical and complex arena. The fact that the agency has from time to time changed its interpretation of the term "source" does not, as respondents argue, lead us to conclude that no deference should be accorded the agency's interpretation of the statute. An initial agency interpretation is not instantly carved in stone. On the contrary, the agency, to engage in informed rulemaking, must consider varying interpretations and the wisdom of its policy on a continuing basis. Moreover, the fact that the agency has adopted different definitions in different contexts adds force to the argument that the definition itself is flexible, particularly since Congress has never indicated any disapproval of a flexible reading of the statute.

Significantly, it was not the agency in 1980, but rather the Court of Appeals that read the statute inflexibly to command a plantwide definition for programs designed to maintain clean air and to forbid such a definition for programs designed to improve air quality. The distinction the court drew may well be a sensible one, but our labored review of the problem has surely disclosed that it is not a distinction that Congress ever articulated itself, or one that the EPA found in the statute before the courts began to review the legislative work product. We conclude that it was the Court of Appeals, rather than Congress or any of the decisionmakers who are authorized by Congress to administer this legislation, that was primarily responsible for the 1980 position taken by the agency.

Policy.

The arguments over policy that are advanced in the parties' briefs create the impression that respondents are now waging in a judicial forum a specific policy battle which they ultimately lost in the agency and in the 32 jurisdictions opting for the "bubble concept," but one which was never waged in the Congress. Such policy arguments are more properly addressed to legislators or administrators, not to judges.

[T]he Administrator's interpretation represents a reasonable accommodation of manifestly competing interests and is entitled to deference: the regulatory scheme is technical and complex, the agency considered the matter in a detailed and reasoned fashion, and the decision involves reconciling conflicting policies. Congress intended to accommodate both interests, but did not do so itself on the level of specificity presented by these cases. Perhaps that body consciously desired the Administrator to strike the balance at this level, thinking that those with great expertise and charged with responsibility for administering the provision would be in a better position to do so; perhaps it simply did not consider the question at this level; and perhaps Congress was unable to forge a coalition on either side of the question, and those on each side decided to take their chances with the scheme devised by the agency. For judicial purposes, it matters not which of these things occurred.

Judges are not experts in the field, and are not part of either political branch of the Government. Courts must, in some cases, reconcile competing political interests, but not on the basis of the judges' personal policy preferences. In contrast, an agency to which Congress has delegated policymaking responsibilities may, within the limits of that delegation, properly rely upon the incumbent administration's views of wise policy to inform its judgments. While agencies are not directly accountable to the people, the Chief Executive is, and it is entirely appropriate for this political branch of the Government to make such policy choices – resolving the competing interests which Congress itself either inadvertently did not resolve, or intentionally left to be resolved by the agency charged with the administration of the statute in light of everyday realities.

When a challenge to an agency construction of a statutory provision, fairly conceptualized, really centers on the wisdom of the agency's policy, rather than whether it is a reasonable choice within a gap left open by Congress, the challenge must fail. In such a case, federal judges – who have no constituency – have a duty to respect legitimate policy choices made by those who do. The responsibilities for assessing the wisdom of such policy choices and resolving the struggle between competing views of the public interest are not judicial ones: "Our Constitution vests such responsibilities in the political branches."

We hold that the EPA's definition of the term "source" is a permissible construction of the statute which seeks to accommodate progress in reducing air pollution with economic growth. . . .

Underlying Case Documents

The case referenced:

The Clean Air Act Amendments of 1977

The rules EPA promulgated under the Clear Air Act Amendments of 1977

The "unilluminating" legislative history

1. Few cases in administrative law have generated more scholarship and case law than *Chevron*. After all, it is not often that the Court gives definition and new boundaries to the relationship between the three branches of government. At a primitive level, the case creates a methodology – a step-by-step plan for judicial review of agency action. It also can be seen as asserting the basic political position – and arguable constitutional precept: It is not the task of federal courts to re-write the policy preferences of the legislative or executive branches of government.

Take Note

Chevron has been cited at least 4000 times in federal cases and countless times in law reviews. The impact of the case was predicted within a few years of the decision. *See* Richard J. Pierce, Jr., *Chevron and its Aftermath: Judicial Review of Agency Interpretations of Statutory Provisions*, 41 VAND. L. REV. 301 (1988); Antonin Scalia, *Judicial Deference to Administrative Interpretations of Law*, 1989 DUKE L.J. 514; Cass R. Sunstein, *Law and Administration After Chevron*, 90 COLUM. L. REV. 2071 (1990); Peter H. Schuck and E. Donald Elliott, *To the Chevron Station: An Empirical Study of Federal Administrative Law*, 1990 DUKE L.J. 984; Michael Herz, *Deference Running Riot: Separating Interpretation and Lawmaking Under Chevron*, 6 ADMIN L.J. 187 (1992).

2. Step Zero. While the *Chevron* two-step process has validity, the deference question – even the ambiguity question – does not get asked unless the agency is act-

ing within its statutory authority. In *Gonzales v. Oregon*, 546 U.S. 243 (2006), *infra* Chapter 3, the Court explained: "To begin with, the rule must be promulgated pursuant to authority Congress has delegated to the official. . . ." This notion, referred to as "step zero" is discussed by Professor Cass R. Sunstein in *Chevron Step Zero*, 92 VA. L. REV. 187, 191 (2006).

When an agency is simply wrong, *Chevron* issues melt away. *General Dynamics Land Sys. v. Cline*, 540 U.S. 581 (2004). However, deciding that an agency has interpreted a statute incorrectly involves judgment – and one is well advised to recognize that such decisions can be quite subjective.

3. Step One. In *Eurodif S.A. v. United States*, 423 F.3d 1275 (Fed. Cir. 2005) the court held:

> At step one we determine "whether the statute's plain terms directly address the precise question at" issue. If we determine that the statute is ambiguous on the precise question at issue, we defer at step two to the agency's interpretation so long as the construction is a reasonable policy choice for the agency to make. On the other hand, if we determine that the statute is unambiguous on the precise question at issue, we do not defer to the agency's interpretation, regardless of whether that interpretation is grounded in a reasonable policy choice. [Internal quotations omitted.]

a. Often, there are a number of different ways to interpret a statute and, accordingly, a number of different ways to assess whether the interpretation an agency adopts is completely off the mark. The step one doctrine pre-supposes the capacity of a court to discern the unambiguous meaning of a statute and then decide if the action of the agency is consistent with that meaning. In *AFL-CIO v. FEC*, 333 F.3d 168 (D.C. Cir. 2003), the majority determined there was at least one reading of the agency action that was arguably consistent with one (of the several possible) interpretations of the relevant statute, moving the analysis to step two. In a concurring opinion, JUDGE HENDERSON took the position that there really was but one fair reading of the action of the agency – and based on that reading, the agency improperly applied an unambiguous statute, meaning that no deference was due.

This becomes a problem of statutory construction, which is, generally speaking, an obligation of courts. For an example of the application of conventional canons of statutory construction, see generally *Edward J. DeBartolo Corp. v. Florida Gulf Coast Building & Construction Trades Council*, 485 U.S. 568 (1988); *National Credit Union Administration v. First National Bank*, 522 U.S. 479 (1998).

b. In *Fink v. Chao*, 395 F. Supp. 2d 625 (N.D. Ohio 2005), the court held: "Federal courts, not administrative agencies, are the 'final authority on issues of statutory construction.' Thus, a federal court reviews de novo an agency's determination of whether a law is clear or ambiguous." See *Cajun Elec. Power Coop., Inc. v. FERC*, 924 F.2d 1132, 1136 (D.C. Cir. 1991) ("We have always seen the first step [of the *Chevron* doctrine] as one conducted under [a] de novo standard. An agency is given no deference at all on the question [of] whether the statute is ambiguous . . .").

4. While the task of interpreting legislation may be judicial, there is a powerful argument that the hard business of determining congressional intention in a particular field requires a very careful assessment of the agency's reading of the statute in question. Consider this excerpt from Professor Cass R. Sunstein's *Law and Administration After Chevron*, 90 COLUM. L. REV. 2071, 2085-87 (1990):

> Frequently, however, Congress does not speak in explicit terms on the question of deference. When this is so, the court's task is to make the best reconstruction that it can of congressional instructions. And if Congress has not made a clear decision one way or the other, the choice among the alternatives will call for an assessment of which strategy is the most sensible one to attribute to Congress under the circumstances. This assessment is not a mechanical exercise of uncovering an actual legislative decision. It calls for a frankly value-laden judgment about comparative competence, undertaken in light of the regulatory structure and applicable constitutional considerations.
>
> If all this is so, the *Chevron* approach might well be defended on the ground that the resolution of ambiguities in statutes is sometimes a question of policy as much as it is one of law, narrowly understood, and that agencies are uniquely well situated to make the relevant policy decisions. In some cases, there is simply no answer to the interpretive question if it is posed as an inquiry into some real or unitary instruction of the legislature. Sometimes congressional views cannot plausibly be aggregated in a way that reflects a clear resolution of regulatory problems, many of them barely foreseen or indeed unforeseeable. In these circumstances, legal competence, as narrowly understood, is insufficient for decision. The resolution of the ambiguity calls for an inquiry into something other than the instructions of the enacting legislature. And in examining those other considerations, the institution entrusted with the decision must make reference to considerations of both fact and policy.
>
> *Chevron* nicely illustrates the point. The decision about whether to adopt a plantwide definition of "source" required distinctly administrative competence because it called for a complex inquiry, not foreseen by Congress, into the environmental and economic consequences of the various possibilities. If regulatory decisions in the face of ambiguities amount in large part to choices of policy, and if Congress has delegated basic implementing authority to the agency, the *Chevron* approach might reflect a belief, attributable to Congress in the absence of a clear contrary legislative statement, in the comparative advantages of the agency in making those choices.
>
> All this suggests that *Chevron* reflects not merely a particular view about who ought to interpret ambiguous statutes, but also, and perhaps more interestingly, a distinctive theory of interpretation. In the last generation it has frequently been suggested that the process of interpretation is often not merely a mechanical reconstruction of legislative desires. Instead that process sometimes calls for an inquiry into questions of both policy and principle. Thus, for example, it has been said that statutory ambiguities should or must be sorted out on the basis of an assessment of which interpretation is "reasonable," or makes the statute "the best piece of statesmanship it can be," or takes

account of appropriate background norms dealing with the functions and failures of the regulatory state.

At least as a general rule, these suggestions argue powerfully in favor of administrative rather than judicial resolution of hard statutory questions. The fact-finding capacity and electoral accountability of the administrators are far greater than those of courts. *Chevron* is best understood and defended as a frank recognition that sometimes interpretation is not simply a matter of uncovering legislative will, but also involves extratextual considerations of various kinds, including judgments about how a statute is best or most sensibly implemented. *Chevron* reflects a salutary understanding that these judgments of policy and principle should be made by administrators rather than judges.

5. Step Two. If there is no clearly discernible congressional intent, the inquiry shifts to determining the reasonability of the agency's action — i.e., whether the decision of the agency is a "permissible construction" of the statute.

a. Professor Michael Herz recently addressed step two review in, Symposium, _The Rehnquist Court and Administrative Law_, 99 Nw. U.L. Rev. 297, 315-17 (2004):

> Under step two, the court considers whether an agency's "interpretation" of a vague statute is "reasonable" or "permissible." Courts take two different approaches to this inquiry. One asks whether the agency reading is "permissible" under the statute. Courts often characterize this as part of the step two inquiry, but it actually is better understood as an aspect of step one, since it looks to statutory boundaries. This version of "step two" has nothing to do with arbitrary and capricious review. The other version of

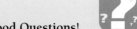

Good Questions!

As any first- year student can attest, once an inquiry shifts to "reasonability," the probability of subjective assessment escalates dramatically. Furthermore, there is some question about the very consist of this inquiry. Should the reviewing court assess reasonability based on an "arbitrary and capricious" test? How is a reasonability critique different from the review standards in _State Farm_, *supra* Chapter 2? To what extent does agency expertise play a role in this assessment? *See*, Note, _The Two Faces of Chevron_, 120 Harv. L. Rev. 1562 (2007).

step two, in contrast, is essentially indistinguishable from review under the arbitrary and capricious standard. Courts consider, for example, the sufficiency of the agency's explanation or the rationality of its conclusions. Perhaps this is where hard look review has fled?

Not so. Since *Chevron* was decided, the Court has set aside an agency decision under step two of *Chevron* only twice. And each of those cases was an instance of the statutory interpretation version rather than the arbitrary and capricious version of step two. On the other hand, it has repeatedly sided with the agency under step two. Indeed, the fact that _State Farm_ is universally seen as a rigorous test and step two as a toothless one has led at least one commentator to argue that step two and the arbitrary and capricious test are not the same. . . . In short, the Court is undeniably engaged in arbitrary and capricious review within *Chevron*, but hard look review has not migrated to step two. . . .

The rate of D.C. Circuit rejection of agency actions on hard look grounds focused on faulty reasoning or lack of a factual basis now often approaches fifty percent. . . . Agency regulatory actions have slowed down as the APA's required "concise general statement" has been transmogrified by intrusive judicial review. Agencies anticipating rigorous judicial review now accompany issuance of new regulations with Federal Register explanations of regulatory choices that frequently cover hundreds of pages.

6. Rules and Orders. *Chevron* is used both in rulemaking and in adjudicatory proceedings that involve interpretations of statutes. It does not apply when reviewing agency fact-finding. In *Emokah v. Mukasey*, 523 F.3d 110 (2d Cir. 2008), a case applying the Immigration and Naturalization Act, the Second Circuit explained the distinction as follows: "Pursuant to *Chevron U.S.A. Inc. v. NRDC* we defer to the agency's interpretations of ambiguous provisions of the Immigration and Naturalization Act, unless those interpretations are "arbitrary, capricious, or manifestly contrary to the statute." *See, e.g.,* *Singh v. Gonzales*, 468 F.3d 135, 138-39 (2d Cir. 2006). We review an agency's factual findings under the substantial evidence standard, treating them as "conclusive unless any reasonable adjudicator would be compelled to conclude to the contrary." 8 U.S.C. § 1252(b)(4)(B). *See, e.g.,* *Corovic v. Mukasey*, 519 F.3d 90, 95 (2d Cir. 2008).

7. Revenue Rulings and *Chevron*. One of the more pressing – and unresolved – questions from the *Chevron* case involves the applicability of the doctrine to revenue rulings. Are courts obligated to defer to such rulings – and if so, do they carry the force of law? While much has been written on the question, it is not easily resolved. A perfect starting point is Professor Linda Galler's article, *Judicial Deference to Revenue Rulings: Reconciling Divergent Standards*, 56 OHIO ST. L.J. 1037 (1995), which sets out the issues and arguments eloquently. A decade later, two articles appeared suggesting that such rulings (and certainly treasury regulations) are entitled to deference. Ryan C. Morris, Comment, *Substantially Deferring to Revenue Rulings After Mead*, 2005 BYU L. REV. 999, and Professor Kristin E. Hickman's *The Need for Mead: Rejecting Tax Exceptionalism in Judicial Deference*, 90 MINN. L. REV. 1537 (2006).

Professor Hickman's position is clear: "Whether *Chevron* deference applies to Treasury regulations depends upon whether Congress and the agency intended for them to carry the force and effect of law. . . . [Recent actions in Congress and at the agency] strongly support a conclusion that Congress intends for all Treasury [regulations to] carry the force and effect of law."

a. The matter is of great consequence – Treasury issues thousands of rulings affecting an enormous range of economic activity. A number of courts have gotten close to deciding the question but then backed off. For example, in *National*

Railroad Passenger Corp. v. United States, 431 F.3d 374, 379 (D.C. Cir. 2005), the court addressed the issue as follows: "[A]lthough the parties discuss whether we should defer to [a revenue ruling] we need not resolve that question. Even were we to afford *Chevron* deference . . . we could not let stand an agency decision that deviates from the statute's unambiguous meaning." This reasoning is relatively common. *See Reese Bros., Inc. v. United States*, 447 F.3d 229 (3d Cir. 2006).

b. A recent bankruptcy court opinion, however, confronted the matter head on. In *In re Worldcom, Inc., Reorganized Debtors*, 371 B.R. 19 (Bankr. S.D.N.Y. 2007), the Chapter 11 Bankruptcy Court found: "In light of the Supreme Court's holding in *Mead*, and the conclusions of the circuit courts that have considered the issue, the Court concludes that the Revenue Rulings are not entitled to *Chevron* deference. Accordingly, the Court will defer to those revenue rulings insofar as they are persuasive, 'the thoroughness evident in [their] consideration, the validity of [their] reasoning, [their] consistency with earlier and later pronouncements, and all those facts which give [them] power to persuade.'"

8. The Basic Doctrine. One of the best summaries of the *Chevron* doctrine and the broad questions the case evokes is in Professor Kathryn A. Watts' *Adapting to Administrative Law's* Erie *Doctrine*, 101 Nw. U.L. Rev. 997 (2007):

> At one side, *Chevron* operates as a mandatory deference doctrine that allocates primary interpretive authority to the relevant agency rather than the courts. When operating under *Chevron's* "deferential model," . . . courts frame the inquiry in terms of whether the relevant agency has selected a "reasonable" interpretation from various plausible readings. . . . [If so] *Chevron* compels the courts to accept the agency's reading, even if the court would declare a different meaning if left to its own devices.
>
> In *Chevron* itself, the Court explained the mandatory rule of deference by referring to notions of congressional intent: "[If] Congress has explicitly left a gap for the agency to fill, there is an express delegation of authority to the agency to elucidate a specific provision of the statute by regulation." The Court, however, also relied upon principles of accountability, concluding that politically accountable agencies are better suited than courts to choose between competing policies when filling statutory gaps. . . .
>
> [Based on current doctrine] Congress must have given the relevant agency the power to act with the "force of law" — meaning that Congress must have given the agency the power to bind those outside the agency, including the courts. Second, the agency must have invoked its delegated authority in rendering the interpretation at issue. . . . [Thus] Chevron will apply to the fruits of notice and comment rulemaking and formal adjudication but generally will not reach more informal agency views, such as those expressed in policy statements, agency manuals, and enforcement guidelines." Reprinted by special permission of Northwestern University School of Law, Northwestern University Law Review.

9. One reaction to diluting *Chevron*. Even though the principles in *Chevron* have

been the subject of re-interpretation in numerous subsequent Supreme Court decisions, many, including JUSTICE SCALIA, still find the opinion a compelling vehicle to determine the extent to which a court should defer to the decision of an agency. In *Smith v. City of Jackson*, 544 U.S. 228 (2005), involving pre-existing EEOC and Department of Labor standards in an age discrimination/disparate impact case, JUSTICE SCALIA concurred, writing: "Even under the unduly constrained standards of agency deference recited in *United States v. Mead Corp.*, 533 U.S. 218 (2001), the EEOC's reasonable view that the ADEA authorizes disparate-impact claims is deserving of deference. *A fortiori*, it is entitled to deference under the pre-*Mead* formulation of *Chevron*, to which I continue to adhere."

10. The legal standard is straightforward: if the statute the agency interprets is one that requires clarification, i.e., it is ambiguous, courts ought to defer to the agency on the interpretation. If the statute is unambiguous, the agency – and a reviewing court – must give the statute its overt and clear meaning. The trick, of course, is in determining when a statute is ambiguous.

Arnett v. Commissioner of Internal Revenue, 473 F.3d 790 (7th Cir. 2007).

> Petitioner Dave Arnett was . . . stationed in Antarctica for the calendar year 2001. When he filed his tax return for that year, he claimed an exclusion for income earned in a foreign country under 26 U.S.C. § 911 ("section 911") for the income he earned while working in Antarctica. The Internal Revenue Service ("IRS") assessed a deficiency for this exclusion based on its view that Antarctica is not a "foreign country" for purposes of section 911. Mr. Arnett challenged that deficiency . . . .
>
> We must first determine whether the term "foreign country" is unambiguous. The term has been defined in other contexts by the Supreme Court. In *Smith v. United States*, the Court had to determine whether Antarctica was a foreign country for purposes of the Federal Tort Claims Act ("FTCA"). . . . [I]n order to arrive at a definition of "country" for purposes of the FTCA, the Court examined the rest of the FTCA. . . . The Court reasoned that, if Antarctica were not a foreign country under the statute, the FTCA would waive the United States' sovereign immunity in Antarctica and, at the same time, direct the district "courts to look to the law of a place that has no law in order to determine the liability of the United States," a result the Court found "bizarre" [and] incompatible with the presumption that "Congress does not in general intend to create venue gaps." . . . .
>
> In short, in order to give meaning to the term "foreign country" in the FTCA, the Supreme Court focused in *Smith* on the purpose and operation of the FTCA. The Court's resort to the statute's context in order to give meaning to the term undercuts Mr. Arnett's claim that the term "foreign country" unambiguously includes Antarctica. n.2 *Smith* demonstrates that the term "foreign country" has meaning only when that term is interpreted in the particular statutory context in which it appears.
>
>> n.2 [Later caselaw] also makes clear that we cannot rely directly on [*Smith*] to give meaning to the term "foreign country." . . . . [A] prior judicial interpretation of a statutory term will foreclose *Chevron* deference only if

the "judicial precedent hold that the statute unambiguously forecloses the agency's interpretation, and therefore contains no gap for the agency to fill." *Nat'l Cable & Telecomms. Ass'n v. Brand X Internet Servs.*

The conclusion that the term "foreign country" is inherently ambiguous is certainly validated by an examination of the text of section 911. . . .

11. *Global Crossing Telecommunications, Inc. v. Metrophones Telecommunications, Inc.*, 550 U.S. 45 (2007):

In 1990, Congress enacted special legislation requiring payphone operators to allow a payphone user to obtain "free" access to the carrier of his or her choice, i.e., access from the payphone without depositing coins. At the same time, Congress recognized that the "free" call would impose a cost upon the payphone operator; and it consequently required the FCC to "prescribe regulations that . . . establish a per call compensation plan to ensure that all payphone service providers are fairly compensated for each and every completed intrastate and interstate call."

Using traditional ratemaking methods, [the FCC] found that the . . . costs of a "free" call . . . warranted reimbursement of (at the time relevant to this litigation) $ 0.24 per call. The FCC ordered carriers to reimburse the payphone operators in this amount unless a carrier and an operator agreed upon a different amount. . . . The FCC subsequently determined that a carrier's refusal to pay the compensation ordered amounts to an "unreasonable practice" within the terms of § 201(b).

In our view the FCC's § 201(b) "unreasonable practice" determination is a reasonable one; hence it is lawful. *See Chevron.* The determination easily fits within the language of the statutory phrase. That is to say, in ordinary English, one can call a refusal to pay Commission-ordered compensation despite having received a benefit from the payphone operator a "practice . . . in connection with [furnishing a] communication service . . . that is . . . unreasonable." The service that the payphone operator provides constitutes an integral part of the total long-distance service the payphone operator and the long-distance carrier together provide to the caller, with respect to the carriage of his or her particular call. The carrier's refusal to divide the revenues it receives from the caller with its collaborator, the payphone operator, despite the FCC's regulation requiring it to do so, can reasonably be called a "practice" "in connection with" the provision of that service that is "unreasonable."

Good Questions!

Having concluded that the term "foreign country" is ambiguous, the *Arnett* court deferred to the IRS interpretation because it found the interpretation not unreasonable. This raises two rather basic questions: (1) Is the term "foreign country" actually ambiguous? (2) Is it reasonable to conclude that Antarctica is not a foreign country?

To what extent should a court give deference to an agency's interpretation of its own regulations?

AUER V. ROBBINS

519 U.S. 452 (1997)

[JUSTICE SCALIA] The Fair Labor Standards Act of 1938 (FLSA) exempts "bona fide executive, administrative, or professional" employees from overtime pay requirements. This case presents the question whether the Secretary of Labor's "salary-basis" test for determining an employee's exempt status reflects a permissible reading of the statute as it applies to public-sector employees. . . .

I

Petitioners are sergeants and a lieutenant employed by the St. Louis Police Department. They brought suit in 1988 against respondents, members of the St. Louis Board of Police Commissioners, seeking payment of overtime pay that they claimed was owed under § 7(a)(1) of the FLSA, 29 U.S.C. § 207(a)(1). Respondents argued that petitioners were not entitled to such pay because they came within the exemption provided by § 213(a)(1) for "bona fide executive, administrative, or professional" employees.

Under regulations promulgated by the Secretary, one requirement for exempt status under § 213(a)(1) is that the employee will earn a specified minimum amount on a "salary basis." 29 C.F.R. §§ 541.1(f), 541.2(e), 541.3(e) (1996). According to the regulations, "[a]n employee will be considered to be paid 'on a salary basis' . . . if under his employment agreement he regularly receives . . . a predetermined amount . . . which . . . is not subject to reduction because of variations in the quality or quantity of the work performed." § 541.118(a). Petitioners contended that the salary-basis test was not met in their case because, under the terms of the St. Louis Metropolitan Police Department Manual, their compensation could be reduced for a variety of disciplinary infractions related to the "quality or quantity" of work performed. . . .

Because Congress has not "directly spoken to the precise question at issue," we must sustain the Secretary's approach so long as it is "based on a permissible construction of the statute." While respondents' objections would perhaps support a different application of the salary-basis test for public employees, we cannot conclude that they compel it. The Secretary's view that public employers are not *so* differently situated with regard to disciplining their employees as to require wholesale revision of his time-tested rule simply cannot be said to be unreasonable. . . .

The Secretary of Labor, in an amicus brief filed at the request of the Court, interprets the salary-basis test to deny exempt status when employees are covered by a policy that permits disciplinary or other deductions in pay "as a practical matter." That standard is met, the Secretary says, if there is either an actual practice of making such deductions or an employment policy that creates a "significant likelihood" of such deductions. The Secretary's approach rejects a wooden requirement of actual deductions, but in their absence it requires a clear and particularized policy – one which "effectively communicates" that deductions will be made in specified circumstances. This avoids the imposition of massive and unanticipated overtime liability . . . in situations in which a vague or broadly worded policy is nominally applicable to a whole range of personnel but is not "significantly likely" to be invoked against salaried employees.

Because the salary-basis test is a creature of the Secretary's own regulations, his interpretation of it is, under our jurisprudence, controlling unless "plainly erroneous or inconsistent with the regulation." . . . .

. . . Petitioners complain that the Secretary's interpretation comes to us in the form of a legal brief; but that does not, in the circumstances of this case, make it unworthy of deference. The Secretary's position is in no sense a "post hoc rationalization" advanced by an agency seeking to defend past agency action against attack. There is simply no reason to suspect that the interpretation does not reflect the agency's fair and considered judgment on the matter in question. . . . [T]he Secretary [has the] power to resolve ambiguities in his own regulations. A rule requiring the Secretary to construe his own regulations narrowly would make little sense, since he is free to write the regulations as broadly as he wishes, subject only to the limits imposed by the statute. . . .

> ## Underlying Case Documents
>
> The case referenced:
> The Fair Labor Standards Act of 1938
> The following portions of the C.F.R. § to analyze the term "salary basis"
> 29 C.F.R. § 541.1(f)
> 29 C.F.R. § 541.2(e)
> 29 C.F.R. § 541.3(e)
> 29 C.F.R. § 541.602(a)
>
> The salary basis regulations were first published at 19 Fed. Reg. 440.

1. Limits on *Auer* Deference. Would it be sufficient for an agency to support a new interpretation of its own regulations by doing nothing more than quoting or paraphrasing the statute it interprets to secure *Auer* deference? Does *Auer* require a

reasoned, documented opinion at the agency level? After all, the *Auer* Court found that unless the interpretation itself (as opposed to the record supporting the interpretation) was clearly erroneous, deference was due. The "clearly erroneous" standard is expansive – and more forgiving than *Chevron's* "permissible interpretation" test.

In *Gonzales v. Oregon, 546 U.S. 243 (2006)*, the Court held that mere recitation of statutory language is insufficient to secure *Auer* deference. The concern is straightforward: If taken to the extreme, *Auer* could become a shield against meaningful judicial review.

2. In theory, an agency could conduct a notice and comment process pursuant to § 553(c), issue an expansive general rule, and then issue interpretations of that rule that create obligations and the possibility of sanctions without any further process (policy statements and interpretive rules do not require a notice and comment process). Under *Auer*, the agency could claim deference using the "clearly erroneous" standard and impose sanctions on entities that both did not have an opportunity to comment on the regulations and very well had no idea the interpretations had issued.

The above scenario is affected by a second limitation in *Auer*: If an agency uses a process (or the lack thereof) that prevents those who are regulated from having reasonable notice of activity that could be subject to sanction, the lack of notice will trump an agency claim of deference under the *Auer* standard. *Fabi Constr. Co. v. Sec'y of Labor, 508 F.3d 1077 (D.C. Cir. 2008)*.

3. Current application of *Auer*. *Federal Express Corp. v. Holowecki, 552 U.S. 389 (2008)* ("Just as we defer to an agency's reasonable interpretations of the statute when it issues regulations in the first instance, the agency is entitled to further deference when it adopts a reasonable interpretation of regulations it has put in force . . . . Under Auer, we accept the agency's position unless it is "plainly erroneous or inconsistent with the regulation. . . ."); *Silvas v. E*Trade Mortg. Corp., 514 F.3d 1001 (9th Cir. 2008)* ("[A]n agency's interpretation of its own regulation is "controlling" under Auer."); *L.A. Closeout, Inc. v. Dep't of Homeland Sec., 513 F.3d 940 (9th Cir. 2008)* ("[W]e defer to the agency's interpretation of its regulation unless an alternative reading is compelled by the regulation's plain language or by other indications of the [agency's] intent at the time of the regulation's promulgation. . . ."); *O'Hara v. GMC, 508 F.3d 753 (5th Cir. 2007)* ("Federal agency statements interpreting specific agency regulations are given substantial deference."). For an excellent synopsis of *Auer*, see Kristin E. Hickman and Matthew D. Krueger, *In Search of the Modern Skidmore Standard*, 107 Colum. L. Rev. 1235 (2007).

4. Retroactivity. In <u>*Motorola, Inc. v. United States*, 436 F.3d 1357, 1366 (Fed. Cir. 2006)</u>, the court held that "[s]o long as an agency's interpretation of a statute is not a post hoc rationalization . . . seeking to defend past agency action against attack . . . or wholly unsupported by regulations, rulings or administrative practice . . . *Chevron* [and *Auer*] deference is due even if the adoption of the agency's interpretation postdates the events to which the interpretation is applied." Does this permit an agency to publish an interpretation of a rule that condemns a behavior and sanction that behavior, even if no regulation existed at the time the behavior took place? What is the difference between agency action of this type and a Bill of Attainder?

5. *Auer* Concerns. Securing *Auer* deference means blocking substantive judicial review of the content of agency interpretations. These concerns are evident in Professor Stephen M. Johnson's <u>*Bringing Deference Back (But for How Long?): Justice Alito,* Chevron, Auer, *and* Chenery *in the Supreme Court's 2006 Term*, 57 CATH. U.L. REV. 1 (2007)</u>:

> Just as the Court appeared to accord greater deference to agencies in their interpretations of statutes in the 2006 Term, the Court appeared to revitalize *Auer* deference to agencies' interpretations of their own regulations. In 1997, in *Auer v. Robbins*, the Supreme Court held that an agency's interpretation of its own regulations is "controlling unless plainly erroneous or inconsistent with the regulation." This standard, which is even more deferential than *Chevron* deference, was initially set forth by the Court in 1945 in *Bowles v. Seminole Rock & Sand Co.* Courts have accorded deference to agency interpretations of their own regulations under *Auer* even when the agencies have initially advanced those interpretations in the course of litigation. . . .
>
> Most commentators have agreed, though, that the continuing vitality of *Auer* after <u>*Mead*</u> creates an incentive for agencies to avoid diminished <u>*Skidmore*</u> deference by adopting broad, ambiguous legislative rules. . . .
>
> [I]n <u>*Long Island Care at Home*</u>, *infra* Chapter 3 [the Court] accorded *Auer* deference to an agency's interpretation of a rule that it had labeled merely an "interpretation" and that the challenger asserted was an interpretive rule. The Court accorded *Auer* deference . . . even though the agency's interpretation of the rule had changed over time and even though the new interpretation was adopted in an advisory memorandum to internal agency personnel as part of the litigation.
>
> Later in the Term, the Supreme Court decided <u>*National Ass'n of Home Builders*</u>. On review, the Court accorded *Auer* deference to the agency's new interpretation of the requirement of its own act even though the new interpretation was adopted in a different administrative proceeding after the agency's action in the case before the Court, and even though the new interpretation conflicted with the interpretation that the agency adopted in forty-four proceedings. . . .

6. <u>*Newton v. Federal Aviation Administration*, 457 F.3d 1133 (10th Cir. 2006)</u>:

> [Robert] Newton became an air traffic controller in 1968, when the Federal Aviation

Administration (FAA) issued his first ATCS certificate. . . . On December 7, 2003, the Utah [Air National Guard] suspended Mr. Newton's ATCS certificate and restricted him from performing air-traffic-control duties because "[i]t has been determined that [he is] a hazard to aviation safety for repeated failure in performing the duties of an Air Traffic Control Supervisor." His ATCS certificate was [thereafter] permanently withdrawn . . . . Newton appealed the withdrawal of the ATCS certificate to the [National Transportation Safety Board] . . . .

On June 14, 2004, an NTSB Administrative Law Judge (ALJ) issued an "Order . . . Terminating Proceeding for Lack of Jurisdiction." The ALJ observed that the NTSB's statutory jurisdiction to review certificate actions encompasses only orders of the FAA respecting certificates issued under 49 U.S.C. chapter 447. The ALJ decided that the ATCS certificate was not such a certificate. . . . Mr. Newton appealed the ALJ's decision to the Board. Rejecting Mr. Newton's arguments relying on [a handbook called] FAA Order 7220.1A, . . . the NTSB affirmed . . . the ALJ and denied the appeal.

[We must determine the standard of review for] (2) FAA regulations governing airman certificates; and (3) the FAA handbook, FAA Order 7220.1A, which establishes ATCS certificates and contrasts them with airman certificates. . . . As for the FAA's regulations, they are clearly entitled to *Chevron* deference. The FAA handbook, in contrast, was not issued as a regulation. Nevertheless, insofar as the handbook is interpreting the provisions of the Federal Aviation Act governing air traffic controllers, it is entitled to deference to the extent that it is persuasive; and it is entitled to great deference insofar as it is interpreting the agency's own regulations, *Auer v. Robbins*. Should we encounter an inconsistency between the interpretation of the NTSB and that of the FAA, we would likely give greater deference to the FAA as the primary agency overseeing the certification provisions of the Federal Aviation Act. . . . [The court then reviewed the NTSB decision and found it entitled to deference.]

7. *Chevron* and *Auer* in a Criminal Case. *United States v. Ward,* 2001 WL 1160168 (D. Penn. Sep. 5, 2001):

The PSM Regulation, the regulation that ["Chip"] Ward is said to have violated, governs the process safety management of highly hazardous chemicals. . . . The Government contends that, because CSI's process involved a highly hazardous chemical, hydroxylamine, at its highest commercially available concentration . . . , CSI was required under the Act to comply with . . . the PSM Regulation. The Government further contends that Ward was aware of these standards and that he willfully violated them, causing the deaths of four . . . CSI employees and one additional individual.

Only 11 of the 136 chemicals listed in Appendix A have a requisite concentration level . . . . The Government concedes that the PSM Regulation does not, on its face, apply to [CSI's] hydroxylamine . . . , but urges this Court to defer to OSHA's interpretations of the PSM Regulation, which the Government contends cover hydroxylamine at its highest commercially available concentration, i.e., in a 50% aqueous solution. . . .

We have found only a few cases in the criminal context that have deferred to an agency's interpretation of an ambiguous regulation[, none of which] involved criminal sanctions. . . . Drawing from the void-for-vagueness doctrine, it is our opinion that, if a regulation is aimed at a class of people with specialized knowledge of what is being regulated, due process is satisfied if, in light of the common understanding of the group, the meaning of the statute is sufficiently ascertainable to enable the individuals being regulated . . . to correctly apply the law. . . .

It is clear that the PSM Regulation is ambiguous with respect to . . . whether it applies to liquid hydroxylamine at a concentration level substantially less than pure . . . . As a result . . ., Ward could not reasonably have known whether CSI's hydroxylamine production process was covered by the PSM Regulation. Ward, therefore, cannot be guilty of willfully violating OSHA's Regulation.

Although [this] strict standard . . . may not have survived the Supreme Court's holding in *Chevron* in the civil context, we do not hesitate to find that strict construction of promulgated rules and regulations is required when implicated in a criminal case.

> **Make the Connection**
>
> *Auer* is a strong expression of the separation of power ideal embodied in *Chevron. Auer* values agency expertise in decisionmaking and limits the impact of courts seeking to give a "hard look" to the content of agency action. *Christensen*, the case that follows, was not written explicitly as a reaction to *Auer* – but it signals the beginning of a scaling back of the hands-off model of agency decisionmaking for all but rules promulgated through formal rulemaking, notice and comment rulemaking, and formal adjudication.

8. In many ways, *Auer* marks the highwater point for deference. While it is not hard to see why an agency's interpretation of its own rules is entitled to deference (assuming the interpretation is consistent with the actual regulation), the power to create standards that have the capacity to affect behavior without notice and comment and without judicial review was not lost on the Court. An *Auer* interpretation might not have the formal "force of law" required – but, de facto, may well have major consequences for those subject to the interpretation.

————————

CHRISTENSEN V. HARRIS COUNTY

529 U.S. 576 (2000)

[JUSTICE THOMAS] Under the Fair Labor Standards Act of 1938 (FLSA), States and their political subdivisions may compensate their employees for overtime by granting them compensatory time or "comp time," which entitles them to take time off work with full pay. If the employees do not use their accumulated compensatory time, the employer is obligated to pay cash compensation under certain circumstances. . . .

Petitioners are 127 deputy sheriffs employed by respondents Harris County,

Texas . . . . As petitioners accumulated compensatory time, Harris County became concerned that it lacked the resources to pay monetary compensation to employees who worked overtime after reaching the statutory cap on compensatory time accrual and to employees who left their jobs with sizable reserves of accrued time. As a result, the county began looking for a way to reduce accumulated compensatory time. It wrote to the United States Department of Labor's Wage and Hour Division, asking "whether the Sheriff may schedule non-exempt employees to use or take compensatory time." The Acting Administrator of the Division replied:

> It is our position that a public employer may schedule its nonexempt employees to use their accrued FLSA compensatory time as directed if the prior agreement specifically provides such a provision . . . .

> Absent such an agreement, it is our position that neither the statute nor the regulations permit an employer to require an employee to use accrued compensatory time.

After receiving the letter[, and in contradiction to it], Harris County implemented a policy under which the employees' supervisor sets a maximum number of compensatory hours that may be accumulated. When an employee's stock of hours approaches that maximum, the employee is advised of the maximum and is asked to take steps to reduce accumulated compensatory time. If the employee does not do so voluntarily, a supervisor may order the employee to use his compensatory time at specified times.

Petitioners sued, claiming that the county's policy violates the FLSA because § 207(o)(5) – which requires that an employer reasonably accommodate employee requests to use compensatory time – provides the exclusive means of utilizing accrued time in the absence of an agreement or understanding permitting some other method. The District Court agreed . . . . The Court of Appeals for the Fifth Circuit reversed, holding that the FLSA did not speak to the issue and thus did not prohibit the county from implementing its compensatory time policy. . . .

In an attempt to avoid the conclusion that the FLSA does not prohibit compelled use of compensatory time, petitioners and the United States contend that we should defer to the Department of Labor's opinion letter, which takes the position that an employer may compel the use of compensatory time only if the employee has agreed in advance to such a practice. Specifically, they argue that the agency opinion letter is entitled to deference under . . . *Chevron* . . . . Here, however, we confront an interpretation contained in an opinion letter, not one arrived at after, for example, a formal adjudication or notice and comment rulemaking. Interpretations such as those in opinion letters – like interpretations contained in policy statements, agency manuals, and enforcement guidelines, all of which lack the force of law – do not warrant *Chevron*-style deference. . . .

Of course, the framework of deference set forth in <u>Chevron</u> does apply to an agency interpretation contained in a regulation. But in this case the Department of Labor's regulation does not address the issue of compelled compensatory time. The regulation provides only that "the agreement or understanding [between the employer and employee] may include other provisions governing the preservation, use, or cashing out of compensatory time so long as these provisions are consistent with [§ 207(o)]." Nothing in the regulation even arguably requires that an employer's compelled use policy must be included in an agreement. The text of the regulation itself indicates that its command is permissive, not mandatory.

Seeking to overcome the regulation's obvious meaning, the United States asserts that the agency's opinion letter interpreting the regulation should be given deference under our decision in *Auer v. Robbins*. In *Auer*, we held that an agency's interpretation of its own regulation is entitled to deference. But *Auer* deference is warranted only when the language of the regulation is ambiguous. The regulation in this case, however, is not ambiguous – it is plainly permissive. To defer to the agency's position would be to permit the agency, under the guise of interpreting a regulation, to create de facto a new regulation. Because the regulation is not ambiguous on the issue of compelled compensatory time, *Auer* deference is unwarranted. . . . The judgment of the Court of Appeals is affirmed.

[JUSTICE SCALIA, concurring in part.]

<u>Skidmore</u> deference to authoritative agency views is an anachronism, dating from an era in which we declined to give agency interpretations (including interpretive regulations, as opposed to "legislative rules") authoritative effect. . . . . <u>Chevron</u> . . . established the principle that "a court may not substitute its own construction of a statutory provision for a reasonable interpretation made by the administrator of an agency." While *Chevron* in fact involved an interpretive regulation, the rationale of the case was not limited to that context . . . Quite appropriately, therefore, we have accorded *Chevron* deference not only to agency regulations, but to authoritative agency positions set forth in a variety of other formats.

In my view, therefore, the position that the county's action in this case was unlawful unless permitted by the terms of an agreement with the sheriff's department employees warrants <u>Chevron</u> deference if it represents the authoritative view of the Department of Labor. The fact that it appears in a single opinion letter signed by the Acting Administrator of the Wage and Hour Division might not alone persuade me that it occupies that status. But the Solicitor General of the United States, appearing as an *amicus* in this action, has filed a brief, cosigned by the Solicitor of Labor, which represents the position set forth in the opinion letter to be the position of the Secretary of Labor. That alone, even without existence of the opinion letter, would in my view entitle the position to *Chevron* deference.

Underlying Case Documents

The case referenced:
The Fair Labor Standards Act of 1938
The opinion letter from the Wage and Hour Division of the United States Department of Labor
29 U.S.C. § 207

---

1. In case you missed it, the critical sentence reads: "Interpretations such as those in opinion letters – like interpretations contained in policy statements, agency manuals, and enforcement guidelines, all of which lack the force of law – do not warrant *Chevron*-style deference. . . ." With this determination, the *Christensen* decision fundamentally changed the administrative law landscape. Having declared that deference was not due for interpretive rules, policy statements, guidelines, opinion letters and more, the court resurrected the notion of Skidmore (the case that follows) "respect."

Henceforth, an agency would have to demonstrate that standards issued without notice and comment or other formalized process bounded by §§ 556 and 557 of the APA were entitled to a court's respect. Those that can be shown to be valid (consonant with the statutory text and existing rules that carry the force of law), presented in a persuasive manner, and the result of a thorough and searching process, will be respected on review. Those issuances that do live up to these standards are not entitled to any special preference and can be set aside by a reviewing court.

2. In a strongly worded concurring opinion, JUSTICE SCALIA opined that *Auer* devalued the carefully considered decisions of the agency, potentially putting courts in a policy making role:

> The Secretary's position is in no sense a "post hoc rationalizatio[n]" advanced by an agency seeking to defend past agency action . . . . There is simply no reason to suspect that the interpretation does not reflect the agency's fair and considered judgment on the matter in question.

3. JUSTICE BREYER also wrote separately in *Christensen*. He focused on congressional intention and the "specialized experience" or expertise of an agency. His opinion suggests that expertise can be a basis for a court to give respect to agency action.

More importantly, he asserted that a court ought to look at the statutory scheme to see if "Congress had delegated to the agency the legal authority to make those determinations." If so, then permitting judicial reconfiguration of agency action is at odds with legislative intent and, presumably, efficient administrative governance. Assuming a primary mission of every agency is to implement its statute, is JUSTICE BREYER right? Should a court accept on good faith an agency judgment solely because Congress declared the specific area to be within the agency's jurisdiction?

Good Questions!

The problem JUSTICE SCALIA raises is quite real. If the head of an agency makes a policy decision, is that decision easily rejected (no respect, no deference) if the decision is not accompanied by a thorough and persuasive report, white paper, brief, or other text? Shouldn't the Secretary of a cabinet level office be able to make policy decisions without writing a "term paper" (the academic phrase) to support her or his action?

4. *Christensen* is in part the basis for the decision by the Third Circuit to declare preempted state tort claims brought by families on behalf of relatives who committed suicide after taking certain antidepressants. The preemption argument was predicated on an FDA publication produced without a rulemaking or formal adjudicatory process. The court held as follows: "[A]n agency's position concerning preemption need not be contained in a formal regulation in order to be considered, and . . . such a position is subject to a level of deference approximating that set forth in *Skidmore* and *Christensen*. . . . The fair measure of deference to an agency administering its own statute has been understood to vary with circumstances, and courts have looked to the degree of the agency's care, its consistency, formality, and relative expertness, and to the persuasiveness of the agency's position." *Colacicco v. Apotex, Inc.*, 521 F.3d 253 (3d Cir. 2008).

5. While *Christensen* appears to create a "bright line" distinction, limiting *Chevron* to rulemakings and formal processes, the line has hazed over considerably. In *Gonzales v. Department of Homeland Security*, 508 F.3d 1227 (D.C. Cir. 2007), an interpretation that seemed destined for *Christensen* "respect" at best instead ended up with *Chevron* deference.

For More Information

For an excellent discussion of *Christensen* and the cases that follow, see Kristin E. Hickman and Matthew D. Krueger, *In Search of the Modern Skidmore Standard*, 107 COLUM. L. REV. 1235 (2007).

III. Deference or Respect?

Four decades before *Chevron*, the Supreme Court decided *Skidmore*. As you read this case, you might ask yourself: Was *Chevron* really necessary? Are the principles in *Skidmore* markedly different from those in *Chevron*?

SKIDMORE v. SWIFT & CO.

323 U.S. 134 (1944)

[JUSTICE JACKSON] Seven employees of the Swift and Company packing plant at Fort Worth, Texas, brought an action under the Fair Labor Standards Act to recover overtime, liquidated damages, and attorneys' fees, totalling approximately $ 77,000. . . . It is not denied that the daytime employment of these persons was working time within the Act. . . .

Under their oral agreement of employment, however, petitioners [also] undertook to stay in the fire hall on the Company premises, or within hailing distance, three and a half to four nights a week. This involved no task except to answer alarms, either because of fire or because the sprinkler was set off for some other reason. No fires occurred during the period in issue, the alarms were rare, and the time required for their answer rarely exceeded an hour. For each alarm answered the employees were paid in addition to their fixed compensation an agreed amount, fifty cents at first, and later sixty-four cents. The Company provided a brick fire hall equipped with steam heat and air-conditioned rooms. It provided sleeping quarters, a pool table, a domino table, and a radio. The men used their time in sleep or amusement as they saw fit, except that they were required to stay in or close by the fire hall and be ready to respond to alarms. . . . The trial court . . . made no findings of fact . . . as to whether under the arrangement of the parties and the circumstances of this case . . . the fire-hall duty or any part thereof constituted working time. It said, however, as a "conclusion of law" that "the time plaintiffs spent in the fire hall subject to call to answer fire alarms does not constitute hours worked, for which overtime compensation is due them under the Fair Labor Standards Act . . .," and in its opinion observed, "of course we know pursuing such pleasurable occupations or performing such personal chores, does not constitute work." The . . . Court of Appeals affirmed.

[W]e hold that no principle of law found either in the statute or in Court decisions precludes waiting time from also being working time. We have not attempted to, and we cannot, lay down a legal formula to resolve cases so varied in their facts as are the many situations in which employment involves waiting time. Whether in a concrete case such time falls within or without the Act is a question of fact to be resolved by appropriate findings of the trial court. This involves scrutiny and construction of the agreements between the particular parties, appraisal of their practical construction of the working agreement by conduct, consideration of the nature of the service, and its relation to the waiting time, and all of the surrounding circumstances. . . . The law does not impose an arrangement upon the parties. It imposes upon the courts the task of finding what the arrangement was.

. . . .

Congress did not utilize the services of an administrative agency to find facts and to determine in the first instance whether particular cases fall within or without the Act. Instead, it put this responsibility on the courts. But it did create the office of Administrator, impose upon him a variety of duties, endow him with powers to inform himself of conditions in industries and employments subject to the Act, and put on him the duties of bringing injunction actions to restrain violations. Pursuit of his duties has accumulated a considerable experience in the problems of ascertaining working time in employments involving periods of inactivity and a knowledge of the customs prevailing in reference to their solution. From these he is obliged to reach conclusions as to conduct without the law, so that he should seek injunctions to stop it, and that within the law, so that he has no call to interfere. He has set forth his views of the application of the Act under different circumstances in an interpretative bulletin and in informal rulings. They provide a practical guide to employers and employees as to how the office representing the public interest in its enforcement will seek to apply it. . . .

There is no statutory provision as to what, if any, deference courts should pay to the Administrator's conclusions. . . . The rulings of this Administrator are not reached as a result of hearing adversary proceedings . . . . They are not, of course, conclusive, even in the cases with which they directly deal, much less in those to which they apply only by analogy. They do not constitute an interpretation of the Act . . . which binds a district court's processes, as an authoritative pronouncement of a higher court might do. But the Administrator's policies are made in pursuance of official duty, based upon more specialized experience and broader investigations and information than is likely to come to a judge in a particular case. . . . Good administration of the Act and good judicial administration alike require that the standards of public enforcement and those for determining private rights shall be at variance only where justified by very good reasons. The fact that the Administrator's policies and standards are not reached by trial in adversary form does not mean that they are not entitled to respect. This Court has long given considerable and in some cases decisive weight to Treasury Decisions and to interpretative regulations of the Treasury and of other bodies that were not of adversary origin.

We consider that the rulings, interpretations and opinions of the Administrator under this Act, while not controlling upon the courts by reason of their authority, do constitute a body of experience and informed judgment to which courts and litigants may properly resort for guidance. The weight of such a judgment in a particular case will depend upon the thoroughness evident in its consideration, the validity of its reasoning, its consistency with earlier and later pronouncements, and all those factors which give it power to persuade, if lacking power to control.

. . . Each case must stand on its own facts. But in this case, although the District Court referred to the Administrator's Bulletin, its evaluation and inquiry were apparently restricted by its notion that waiting time may not be work, an understanding of the law which we hold to be erroneous. Accordingly, the judgment is reversed and the cause remanded for further proceedings consistent herewith.

———

Underlying Case Documents

The case referenced:
The Fair Labor Standards Act of 1938
Interpretive Bulletin No. 13
Letter from the Deputy Administrator

For the relevant statutory provisions click Here. Do not forget the dispute in the case does not revolve around these provisions.

1. Professor Jim Rossi's *Respecting Deference: Conceptualizing Skidmore Within the Architecture of* Chevron, 42 WM. & MARY L. REV. 1105 (2001), provides a succinct summary of the case:

> *Skidmore* deference is sometimes referred to as "weak deference," in contrast to the strong deference that has evolved post-*Chevron*. It is deference nevertheless, as JUSTICE JACKSON recognized in providing normative reasons for the Court's approach. As *Skidmore* explained, an agency administrator's rulings are entitled to some respect because they are "made in pursuance of official duty, based upon more specialized experience and broader investigations and information than is likely to come to a judge in a particular case." Agencies determine policy on behalf of government and provide guidance for the enforcement of statutes. By giving weight to agency interpretations, courts avoid resorting to legislative history as a means of discerning statutory meaning. Moreover . . . judicial respect for agency interpretation of law under *Skidmore* allows for enhanced consistency in the application of statutes. Without a doubt, however, *Skidmore* affords less deference than *Chevron*. . . .

[Professor Rossi then provides this insight into *Skidmore*, using three opinions from <u>Christensen</u> as a comparative vehicle, beginning with JUSTICE THOMAS' majority opinion.]

The *Christensen* majority's application of *Skidmore* deference goes something like this: A court makes its own interpretation of the statute, comparing it to the interpretation of the litigants. In so doing, the court determines whether it is persuaded that the agency's interpretation is "better," without affording the agency's interpretation any presumption of validity. If the agency's interpretation is "unpersuasive," no deference is due under *Skidmore*. Only after determining which reading of the statute it believes best does the majority decide what level of deference to afford the agency interpretation.

JUSTICE STEVENS relies on at least two of the *Skidmore* factors – thoroughness of the agency's consideration and consistency of the agency's position – in deciding whether the agency's interpretation was persuasive and warrants respect.

JUSTICE BREYER . . . focuses on two of the *Skidmore* factors – thoroughness of consideration and consistency – JUSTICE BREYER also addresses Skidmore's third factor. "[P]articularly in a rather technical case such as this one," JUSTICE BREYER writes, "an agency's views . . . 'meri[t] respect.'"

2. *Skidmore* Applied. In <u>Wilton Indus. v. United States, 493 F. Supp. 2d 1294 (U.S. Ct. of Trade 2007)</u>, a case involving "festive" items, notably "cake toppers, . . . wedding cake figurine/topper bases, separator plates, pillars, columns, plate legs, and plate pegs" the Court of International Trade was asked to determine if a trade publication was entitled to Skidmore respect: "[The] Government . . . asserts that Customs' position is entitled to the full measure of *Skidmore* deference. . . . According to the Government, *Skidmore* deference is due because "Customs' classification decisions in this case are consistent with its position regarding the classification of cake decorations as set forth in several Headquarters Ruling Letters ('HQ') . . . and its interpretation of the tariff term 'festive articles' set forth in the informed compliance publication entitled 'What Every Member of the Trade Community Should Know About Classification of Festive Articles as a result of the *Midwest of Cannon Falls* Court Case (1997).'" But Customs has no colorable claim to deference under the circumstances of this case.

First . . . not only was Customs' position in this matter not the product of a deliberative notice and comment process, it was not even embodied in a ruling letter specific to the merchandise at issue in this action. Nor does the Government suggest that any of the other Customs ruling letters to which it alludes were subject to notice and comment.

Further, the "position" for which the Government seeks deference is entirely unclear. The Government's brief . . . asserts broadly that Customs' classification decisions in this case are "consistent with [the agency's] position. . . . However, nowhere in its briefs does the Government identify the specific Customs ruling letters to which it is there referring. And nowhere in its briefs does the Government explain how those

> unspecified Customs ruling letters concerning cake decorations are consistent with Customs' actions in this case. . . .
>
> In addition . . . the Government also asserts that Customs' determination in this matter is consistent with the agency's position on the classification of "festive articles" as set forth in the Customs publication, "What Every Member of the Trade Community Should Know About Classification of Festive Articles. . . ." However, that publication has been so thoroughly discredited that Customs has now withdrawn it. . . .
>
> For all these reasons, Customs' position lacks "power to persuade," and thus merits no deference in this action. *See Skidmore.*

3. While one might take issue with the idea that only decisions that are thorough will be given respect by a reviewing court, the concept is at least understandable – and quite subjective. A lack of thoroughness is fairly obvious. *See, e.g.,* <u>Hass v. Nicholson, Sec'y of Veterans Affairs, 20 Vet. App. 257, 275 (2006)</u>. It is not a difficult requirement to meet, putting aside disingenuous "padding" of a record that is at least a possibility.

Persuasiveness is likewise highly subjective and potentially controversial. First, do you believe that a cabinet level secretary (e.g., the Secretary of Commerce, Transportation, Defense, or Homeland Security) has a responsibility to persuade a federal district court judge of the efficacy of major policy decisions in order to avoid having that judge second-guess the actions of the Secretary? Second, if Congress gives an agency the power to issue rules, what more should be required to secure "respect" from a reviewing court? As you will see, a distinction exists between those actions where congressional authority is explicit (generally today, <u>Chevron</u> deference applies) and those where the authority is implicit (generally, *Skidmore* applies).

4. In the end, any interpretive statement, opinion letter, guidance, or similar issuance must reflect an acceptable application of the statute authorizing the action of the agency. Law school courses and treatises are devoted to the complexity of statutory construction. NORMAN J. SINGER, STATUTES AND STATUTORY CONSTRUCTION (6th ed. 2000); KENT GREENAWALT, LEGISLATION – STATUTORY INTERPRETATION: 20 QUESTIONS (1999).

The Ninth Circuit recently provided a quick summary of some of the themes in the field. In <u>Wilderness Society v. United States, 353 F.3d 1051 (9th Cir. 2003)</u>, the court found as follows:

> Canons of statutory construction help give meaning to a statute's words. We begin with the language of the statute. . . . Another fundamental canon of construction provides that "unless otherwise defined, words will be interpreted as taking their ordinary, contemporary, common meaning." It is also "a fundamental canon that the words of a statute must be read in their context and with a view to their place in the

overall statutory scheme." <u>FDA v. Brown & Williamson Tobacco Corp., 529 U.S. 120</u> <u>(2001)</u>. If necessary to discern Congress' intent, we may read statutory terms in light of the purpose of the statute. Thus, the structure and purpose of a statute may also provide guidance in determining the plain meaning of its provisions.

United States v. Mead Corporation

533 U.S. 218 (2001)

[Justice Souter] The question is whether a tariff classification ruling by the United States Customs Service deserves judicial deference. The Federal Circuit rejected Customs's invocation of *Chevron* in support of such a ruling, to which it gave no deference. We agree that a tariff classification has no claim to judicial deference under *Chevron*, . . . but we hold that under *Skidmore* the ruling is eligible to claim respect according to its persuasiveness.

A.

Imports are taxed under the Harmonized Tariff Schedule of the United States (HTSUS). . . . The Secretary provides for tariff rulings . . . by regulations authorizing "ruling letters" setting tariff classifications for particular imports. A ruling letter represents the official position of the Customs Service with respect to the particular transaction or issue described therein and is binding on all Customs Service personnel in accordance with the provisions of this section until modified or revoked. In the absence of a change of practice or other modification or revocation which affects the principle of the ruling set forth in the ruling letter, that principle may be cited as authority . . . .

After the transaction that gives it birth, a ruling letter is to "be applied only with respect to transactions involving articles . . . whose description is identical to the description set forth in the ruling letter." As a general matter, such a letter is "subject to modification or revocation without notice to any person, except the person to whom the letter was addressed," and the regulations consequently provide that "no other person should rely on the ruling letter or assume that the principles of that ruling will be applied in connection with any transaction other than the one described in the letter." Since ruling letters respond to transactions of the moment, they are not subject to notice and comment before being issued [and] may be published but need only be made "available for public inspection" . . . .

Any of the 46 port-of-entry Customs offices may issue ruling letters, and so may the Customs Headquarters Office. . . . Most ruling letters contain little or no reasoning, but simply describe goods and state the appropriate category and tariff. A few letters, like the Headquarters ruling at issue here, set out a rationale in some detail.

B.

Respondent, the Mead Corporation, imports "day planners," three-ring binders with pages having room for notes of daily schedules and phone numbers and addresses, together with a calendar and suchlike. The tariff schedule on point falls under the HTSUS heading for "registers, account books, notebooks, order books, receipt books, letter pads, memorandum pads, diaries and similar articles," which comprises two subcategories. Items in the first, "diaries, notebooks and address books, bound; memorandum pads, letter pads and similar articles," were subject to a tariff of 4.0% at the time in controversy. Objects in the second, covering "other" items, were free of duty.

Between 1989 and 1993, Customs repeatedly treated day planners under the "other" HTSUS subheading. In January 1993, however, Customs changed its position, and issued a Headquarters ruling letter classifying Mead's day planners as "Diaries . . . bound" subject to tariff . . . . That letter was short on explanation, but after Mead's protest, Customs Headquarters issued a new letter, carefully reasoned but never published, reaching the same conclusion. This letter considered two definitions of "diary" from the Oxford English Dictionary, the first covering a daily journal of the past day's events, the second a book including "printed dates for daily memoranda and jottings; also . . . calendars . . . ." Customs concluded that "diary" was not confined to the first, in part because the broader definition reflects commercial usage . . . . As for the definition of "bound," Customs concluded that HTSUS was not referring to "bookbinding," but to a less exact sort of fastening described in the Harmonized Commodity Description and Coding System Explanatory Notes . . . which spoke of binding by "reinforcements or fittings of metal, plastics, etc."

Customs rejected Mead's further protest of the second Headquarters ruling letter, and Mead filed suit in the Court of International Trade (CIT). The CIT granted the Government's motion for summary judgment, adopting Customs's reasoning without saying anything about deference.

Mead then went to the United States Court of Appeals for the Federal Circuit. . . . The Federal Circuit . . . thought classification rulings had a weaker *Chevron* claim even than Internal Revenue Service interpretive rulings, to which that court gives no deference; unlike rulings by the IRS, Customs rulings issue from many locations and need not be published. The Court of Appeals accordingly gave no deference . . . and rejected the agency's reasoning as to both "diary" and "bound." It thought that planners were not diaries because they had no space for "relatively extensive notations about events, observations, feelings, or thoughts" in the past. And it concluded that diaries "bound" . . . presupposed "unbound" diaries, such that treating ring-fastened diaries as "bound" would leave the "unbound diary" an empty category.

. . . We hold that administrative implementation of a particular statutory provision qualifies for *Chevron* deference when it appears that Congress delegated authority to the agency generally to make rules carrying the force of law, and that the agency interpretation claiming deference was promulgated in the exercise of that authority. . . . The Customs ruling at issue here fails to qualify, although the possibility that it deserves some deference under *Skidmore* leads us to vacate and remand.

II.

A.

When Congress has "explicitly left a gap for an agency to fill, there is an express delegation of authority to the agency to elucidate a specific provision of the statute by regulation," *Chevron*, and any ensuing regulation is binding in the courts unless procedurally defective, arbitrary or capricious in substance, or manifestly contrary to the statute. But . . . agencies charged with applying a statute necessarily make all sorts of interpretive choices, and while not all of those choices bind judges to follow them, they certainly may influence courts facing questions the agencies have already answered. "The well-reasoned views of the agencies implementing a statute 'constitute a body of experience and informed judgment to which courts and litigants may properly resort for guidance.'" . . . . [This] has produced a spectrum of judicial responses, from great respect at one end to near indifference at the other. JUSTICE JACKSON summed things up in *Skidmore*:

> The weight [accorded to an administrative] judgment in a particular case will depend upon the thoroughness evident in its consideration, the validity of its reasoning, its consistency with earlier and later pronouncements, and all those factors which give it power to persuade, if lacking power to control. . . .

We have recognized a very good indicator of delegation meriting *Chevron* treatment in express congressional authorizations to [produce] regulations or rulings for which deference is claimed. It is fair to assume generally that Congress contemplates administrative action with the effect of law when it provides for a relatively formal administrative procedure tending to foster the fairness and deliberation that should underlie a pronouncement of such force. Thus, the overwhelming number of our cases applying *Chevron* deference have reviewed the fruits of notice and comment rulemaking or formal adjudication. That said, and as significant as notice and comment is in pointing to *Chevron* authority, the want of that procedure here does not decide the case, for we have sometimes found reasons for *Chevron* deference even when no such administrative formality was required and none was afforded. The fact that the tariff classification here was not a product of such formal process does not alone, therefore, bar the application of *Chevron*.

There are, nonetheless, ample reasons to deny <u>*Chevron*</u> deference here. The authorization for classification rulings, and Customs's practice in making them, present a case far removed not only from notice and comment process, but from any other circumstances reasonably suggesting that Congress ever thought of classification rulings as deserving the deference claimed for them here.

No matter which angle we choose for viewing the Customs ruling letter in this case, it fails to qualify under <u>*Chevron*</u>. On the face of the statute, to begin with, the terms of the congressional delegation give no indication that Congress meant to delegate authority to Customs to issue classification rulings with the force of law. We are not, of course, here making any global statement about Customs's authority, for it is true that the general rulemaking power conferred on Customs authorizes some regulation with the force of law . . . . It is true as well that Congress had classification rulings in mind when it explicitly authorized, in a parenthetical, the issuance of "regulations establishing procedures for the issuance of binding rulings prior to the entry of the merchandise concerned." The reference to binding classifications does not, however, bespeak the legislative type of activity that would naturally bind more than the parties to the ruling, once the goods classified are admitted into this country. And though the statute's direction to disseminate "information" necessary to "secure" uniformity seems to assume that a ruling may be precedent in later transactions, precedential value alone does not add up to *Chevron* entitlement . . . . In any event, any precedential claim of a classification ruling is counterbalanced by the provision for independent review of Customs classifications by the CIT . . . .

It is difficult, in fact, to see in the agency practice itself any indication that Customs ever set out with a lawmaking pretense in mind when it undertook to make classifications like these. . . . Customs has regarded a classification as conclusive only as between itself and the importer to whom it was issued and even then only until Customs has given advance notice of intended change. Other importers are in fact warned against assuming any right of detrimental reliance.

Indeed, to claim that classifications have legal force is to ignore the reality that 46 different Customs offices issue 10,000 to 15,000 of them each year. Any suggestion that rulings intended to have the force of law are being churned out at a rate of 10,000 a year at an agency's 46 scattered offices is simply self-refuting. Although the circumstances are less startling here, with a Headquarters letter in issue, none of the relevant statutes recognizes this category of rulings as separate or different from others. . . . In sum, classification rulings are best treated like "interpretations contained in policy statements, agency manuals, and enforcement guidelines." *Christensen*. They are beyond the *Chevron* pale.

To agree with the Court of Appeals that Customs ruling letters do not fall within *Chevron* is not, however, to place them outside the pale of any deference whatever. *Chevron* did nothing to eliminate *Skidmore's* holding that an agency's interpretation may merit some deference whatever its form, given the "specialized experience and broader investigations and information" available to the agency and given the value of uniformity in its administrative and judicial understandings of what a national law requires.

There is room at least to raise a *Skidmore* claim here, where the regulatory scheme is highly detailed, and Customs can bring the benefit of specialized experience to bear on the subtle questions in this case: whether the daily planner with room for brief daily entries falls under "diaries," when diaries are grouped with "notebooks and address books, bound; memorandum pads, letter pads and similar articles," and whether a planner with a ring binding should qualify as "bound," when a binding may be typified by a book, but also may have "reinforcements or fittings of metal, plastics, etc." Such a ruling may surely claim the merit of its writer's thoroughness, logic and expertness, its fit with prior interpretations, and any other sources of weight.

Underlying the position we take here, like the position expressed by JUSTICE SCALIA in dissent, is a choice about the best way to deal with an inescapable feature of the body of congressional legislation authorizing administrative action. That feature is the great variety of ways in which the laws invest the Government's administrative arms with discretion, and with procedures for exercising it . . . . Although we all accept the position that the Judiciary should defer to at least some . . . administrative action, we have to decide how to take account of the great range of its variety. . . . JUSTICE SCALIA's first priority over the years has been to limit and simplify. The Court's choice has been to tailor deference to variety. This acceptance of the range of statutory variation has led the Court to recognize more than one variety of judicial deference, just as the Court has recognized a variety of indicators that Congress would expect *Chevron* deference.

Our respective choices are repeated today. JUSTICE SCALIA would pose the question of deference as an either-or choice . . . when courts owe any deference it is *Chevron* deference that they owe. . . . The Court, on the other hand, said nothing in *Chevron* to eliminate *Skidmore's* recognition of various justifications for deference depending on statutory circumstances and agency action . . . . Without being at odds with congressional intent much of the time, we believe that judicial responses to administrative action must continue to differentiate between *Chevron* and *Skidmore*, and that continued recognition of *Skidmore* is necessary for just the reasons JUSTICE JACKSON gave when that case was decided.

Since the *Skidmore* assessment called for here ought to be made in the first instance by the Court of Appeals for the Federal Circuit or the Court of International Trade, we go no further than to vacate the judgment and remand the case for further proceedings consistent with this opinion. . . .

[JUSTICE SCALIA, dissenting.]

The Court has largely replaced <u>*Chevron*</u> . . . with that test most beloved by a court unwilling to be held to rules (and most feared by litigants who want to know what to expect): th' ol' "totality of the circumstances" test. The Court's new doctrine is neither sound in principle nor sustainable in practice. . . . As for the practical effects of the new rule:

> (1) The principal effect will be protracted confusion. . . . [T]he one test for <u>*Chevron*</u> deference that the Court enunciates is wonderfully imprecise: whether "Congress delegated authority to the agency generally to make rules carrying the force of law, . . . as by . . . adjudication[,] notice and comment rulemaking, or . . . some other [procedure] indicating comparable congressional intent." . . . .

> (2) Another practical effect of today's opinion will be an artificially induced increase in informal rulemaking. Buy stock in the GPO. . . . [I]nformal rulemaking – which the Court was once careful to make voluntary unless required by statute, *see* <u>*Bell Aerospace*</u> and <u>*Chenery*</u>, will now become a virtual necessity. . . .

> (3) Worst of all, the majority's approach will lead to the ossification of large portions of our statutory law. . . . For the indeterminately large number of statutes taken out of <u>*Chevron*</u> by today's decision, however, ambiguity (and hence flexibility) will cease with the first judicial resolution. <u>*Skidmore*</u> deference gives the agency's current position some vague and uncertain amount of respect, but it does not, like *Chevron*, leave the matter within the control of the Executive Branch for the future. Once the court has

Take Note

"The term 'ossification' refers to the inefficiencies that plague regulatory programs because of analytic hurdles that agencies must clear in order to adopt new rules."

Mark Seidenfeld, *Demystifying Deossification: Rethinking Recent Proposals to Modify Judicial Review of Notice and Comment Rulemaking*, 75 TEXAS L. REV. 483 (1997).

spoken, it becomes *unlawful* for the agency to take a contradictory position; the statute now *says* what the court has prescribed.

(4) And finally, the majority's approach compounds the confusion it creates by breathing new life into the anachronism of *Skidmore* . . . . [T]he rule of *Skidmore* deference is an empty truism and a trifling statement of the obvious: A judge should take into account the well-considered views of expert observers.

———

Underlying Case Documents

The case referenced:
The Harmonized Tariff Schedule of the United States
The regulations on ruling letters
    Describing ruling letters
    Authorizing the Secretary to issue ruling letters
The opinion letter from Customs

1. Lest there be any question of the meaning of this case, read the summary provided in the majority opinion:

> We hold that administrative implementation of a particular statutory provision qualifies for Chevron deference when it appears that Congress delegated authority to the agency generally to make rules carrying the force of law, and that the agency interpretation claiming deference was promulgated in the exercise of that authority. Delegation of such authority may be shown in a variety of ways, as by an agency's power to engage in adjudication or notice and comment rulemaking, or by some other indication of a comparable congressional intent. 533 U.S. at 227.

It seems simple enough: The "bright line" of *Christensen* is now dimmed considerably. Formal rulemaking, notice and comment rulemaking, and formal adjudication aside, *Chevron* deference *is* available (not just *Skidmore* respect) when Congress has given the agency the authority to make rules that carry the force of law and the rule or interpretation that issues is in furtherance of that authority. Where the action of the agency is required and responsive to a statute, designed to be relied upon by the public, not likely to change any time soon, and persuasive, valid, and thorough, deference (or something resembling it) may well be available.

2. Professor Adrian Vermeules' *Recent Decision of the United States Court of Appeals of the District of Columbia – Introduction: Mead in the Trenches*, 71 GEO. WASH. L. REV.

347, 349 (2003), notes that:

> *Mead* creates a complex, finely reticulated structure of analysis that courts must apply at the preliminary stage of deciding what deference is due, before deciding the ultimate merits of the interpretive question at hand. In the trenches of the D.C. Circuit, however, *Mead's* ambitious recasting of deference law has gone badly awry, for reasons that expose deficiencies in the decision itself. Important cases purporting to apply *Mead* have devolved into extensive, and likely inefficient, litigation over threshold questions; have taken *Mead*, quite mistakenly, to license an all-things-considered de novo judicial determination of whether an agency's interpretation is correct or incorrect.

3. The apparent détente between courts and agencies wrought by <u>Chevron</u> came to a close, if not in <u>Christensen</u>, then certainly in *Mead*. In some ways, *Mead* puts courts back in the business of second-guessing agencies. To be sure, if an agency has the authority, resources, time, and inclination, it can avoid "judicial intrusion" by cloaking its issuances in notice and comment rulemaking. As you have learned, however, 553(c) rulemaking is by no means a "free pass." Beyond the time and expense, there are avenues of review even assuming deference – and there is the inordinate and inevitable delay inherent in that process. Accordingly, since *Mead*, thousands of "temporary final rules" have issued and the number of guidance documents issued (without notice and comment) has increased. Do you believe that these developments signal a return to "hard look" review?

4. JUSTICE SCALIA's dissent in <u>National Cable & Telecommications Association v. Brand X Internet Services</u>, 545 U.S. 967, 1015 (2005), *infra* Chapter 3, recites a stinging critique of *Mead*, characterizing the post-*Mead* period as an

> *administrative-law improvisation project* . . . . To the extent it set forth a comprehensible rule, *Mead* drastically limited the categories of agency action that would qualify for deference under *Chevron*. . . . For example, the position taken by an agency before the Supreme Court, with full approval of the agency head, would not qualify. Rather, some unspecified degree of formal process was required – or was at least the only safe harbor. [Emphasis added.]

> This meant that many more issues appropriate for agency determination would reach the courts without benefit of an agency position entitled to *Chevron* deference, requiring the courts to rule on these issues de novo. As I pointed out in dissent, this in turn meant (under the law as it was understood until today) that many statutory ambiguities that might be resolved in varying fashions by successive agency administrations would be resolved finally, conclusively, and forever, by federal judges – producing an "ossification of large portions of our statutory law. . . ."

> It is indeed a wonderful new world that the Court creates, one full of promise for administrative-law professors in need of tenure articles and, of course, for litigators.

We will return to this characterization several times. Has JUSTICE SCALIA hit the nail on the head? Are we mid-stream in an administrative law improvisation project?

If so, is that necessarily unexpected? Would one not expect the evolution of complex doctrine to entail a less than perfectly linear path?

5. In the customs and taxation area, rulings similar to the letter in this case are common. They are also published and highly informative – and issued based on the expertise of the agency. What is the best argument for requiring courts to defer to agencies issuing such documents?

> **Good Question!**
>
> Were you counsel to the Customs Office, what would you advise – can you think of a way to reconfigure the process that was used in *Mead* to increase the likelihood that a court would not undo the decisions of your office?

6. *United States v. W.R. Grace & Co.*, 429 F.3d 1224 (9th Cir. 2005):

> The situation confronting the EPA in Libby is truly extraordinary. This cleanup site is not a remote, abandoned mine. Rather, the population of Libby and nearby communities, which the EPA estimates at about 12,000, faces ongoing, pervasive exposure to asbestos particles being released through documented exposure pathways. We cannot escape the fact that people are sick and dying as a result of this continuing exposure. Confronted with this information, the EPA determined on the basis of its professional judgment, and in accord with its administrative interpretation of the scope of removal actions, that the situation warranted an immediate, aggressive response to abate the public health threat. . . .
>
> The EPA's ability to recover the costs of its cleanup in Libby hinges on whether its response is properly characterized as a removal action, as argued by the EPA and found by the district court, or a remedial action, as argued by Grace. . . . [U]nder modified deference or full *Chevron* deference, the result would be the same: The EPA's cleanup activities in Libby are properly categorized as a removal action.

DE LA MOTA V. UNITED STATES DEPARTMENT OF EDUCATION

412 F.3d 71 (2d Cir. 2005)

[JUDGE PARKER] Title IV of the HEA [Higher Education Act] directs the Secretary of the Department of Education to implement . . . federal student financial aid programs [including the] Perkins Loan Program . . . . Under the program, the DOE provides federal monies to participating institutions. . . . In other words, Perkins Loans are "campus-based": The schools independently determine eligibility, advance funds, collect payments and make decisions concerning loan forgiveness. . . .

In 1985 . . . Congress amended the statute to encourage graduates to work in various areas of public service, such as teaching and the Peace Corps. This encouragement took the form of partial or total Perkins Loan cancellation. . . . The section of the statute pivotal to this appeal . . . provides that "loans shall be canceled . . . for service": "(I) as a full-time employee of a public or private nonprofit child or family service agency who is providing, or supervising the provision of, services to high-risk children who are from low-income communities and the families of such children." . . . . [For loan cancellation, the] borrower applies to the lending school, which, rather than the DOE, bears the responsibility for determining the applicant's eligibility for loan cancellation.

[Since 1992 DOE has given] participating institutions guidance about eligibility for loan cancellation for child or family service. The extent to which we are required to defer to these efforts is the critical issue on this appeal. In 1995, the DOE enacted a regulation purportedly implementing the child or family service cancellation provision. In doing so, the DOE [simply] incorporated verbatim the statute into its own regulation. . . . In addition . . ., each year the Federal Student Aid Office of the DOE issues a Student Financial Aid Handbook to participating institutions to assist them in responding to loan cancellation requests. The Handbooks introduced a new qualification . . . not found in the statute, requiring that the services be extended "only" to high-risk children . . . . Along with these sources of assistance, participating institutions may obtain guidance on loan cancellation requests by contacting the Policy Development Division of the DOE's Office of Post-secondary Education. . . .

De La Mota

De La Mota applied for loan cancellation in 2000 through three academic institutions: City University of New York ("CUNY") and Manhattanville College where she did her undergraduate work, and New York Law School ("NYLS"). In the ACS Child Support Litigation Unit, she litigates paternity actions and prosecutes child support cases. For two years her loans were forgiven, but in the third year . . . NYLS, rejected her application and demanded back payment for the previous two years. CUNY and Manhattanville continued to forgive her loans.

The DOE advised NYLS not to cancel her loans, because the services she provided to children were neither "direct" nor "only to high-risk children." The word "only" originated in the Handbooks, not the . . . statute or . . . regulation. The requirement of "direct" services . . . first appeared in an April 12, 2001 informal e-mail from a DOE Program Specialist to NYLS: "The borrower must be providing services directly to the high-risk children. In this case, the borrower is providing services to the City of New York as an attorney, she is not providing services directly to high-risk children." . . . . Upon advice from the Program Specialist that De La Mota's services and supervision of the provision of services were not "directly" nor "only" targeted to low-income, high-risk children, NYLS rejected her application . . . .

As an initial matter, we note that the Appellants appear comfortably to meet the statute's textual qualifications for loan forgiveness. They are "full-time employee of a public . . . nonprofit child or family service agency" who are "providing . . . services to high-risk children who are from low-income communities and the families of such children." . . . . Congress thought cancellation subsidies were necessary because, traditionally, child and family service work tended to be low-paying, and the subsidies would encourage qualified graduates to enter the field.

II.

Notwithstanding the text of the statute and its intended purposes, . . . the DOE inserted "only" as a qualification in the 1996-1997 and 2001-2002 Handbooks . . . . On the basis of this qualification, the DOE recommended denial of loan forgiveness if an applicant performed any service, however sporadic or minimal, for anyone not at high-risk and not from a low-income community. Later, a DOE Program Specialist concluded and informally opined that loan cancellation was available only to applicants who provided services "directly" and "exclusively" to high-risk children and their families. This requirement effectively disqualified any public interest attorney litigating on behalf of poor, high-risk children; according to the DOE, an ACS attorney's client is New York City and an attorney provides services directly only to her client. . . . Significantly, the DOE did not use its regulation to interpret the statute, as the regulation simply repeated the text of the statute verbatim, without . . . any perceived ambiguity in the meaning of "providing services." . . . .

Chevron deference is clearly inapplicable to the DOE's interpretation . . . . Here the "directly" and "exclusively" qualifications did not emerge from any formal rule-making procedures. As far as we can determine, they are ad hoc, previously unwritten rules, supplied by a DOE staff employee when determining appellants' eligibility. The requirement of "only" serving high-risk children, which first surfaced in the Handbook, fares no better, as its provenance is equally informal. *Christensen v. Harris County* made clear that "interpretations contained in policy statements, agency manuals and enforcement guidelines, all of which lack the force of law – do not warrant *Chevron* style deference."

. . . The DOE urges deference under *Skidmore*, because when denying loan cancellation, it contends that it "bring[s] the benefit of specialized experience to bear." *Mead*. We disagree. The DOE's critical narrowing requirements – "exclusively" and "directly" – hardly rise to the level of an *agency* interpretation since, as we have seen, they were pronounced initially by a DOE staff member. By contrast, the official narrowing of the statute with the addition of the qualification "only" originated in two DOE Handbooks; therefore the weight we accord the DOE's interpretation of this statute is determined through *Skidmore* analysis.

III.

Skidmore respect . . . depends on [the interpretation's] "thoroughness," "validity," "consistency," and "power to persuade."

A. Thoroughness

The DOE's . . . Handbooks interpret the eligibility requirement as applicable to those "providing services only to high risk children." In application, the DOE Program Specialist did not rely solely on "only," but grafted on "exclusively" and "directly." These latter requirements are neither synonymous with "only" nor equivalent in their narrowing force. For us to find "thoroughness evident in its consideration," the DOE would have had, at minimum, to adhere in practice to its own Handbook language and meaning. Furthermore, thoroughness is impossible for an agency staff member to demonstrate when the staff member does not report to the Secretary, bears no law-making authority, and is unconstrained by political accountability. . . .

B. Validity

The "validity" element of *Skidmore* analysis draws our attention to whether an agency pronouncement is well-reasoned, substantiated, and logical. The DOE contends that, in practice, it needs to narrow § 1087ee(a)(2)(I) in order to distinguish, for instance, between the support staff (administrative assistants, janitors, fund-raisers) at a child or family service agency and those properly deserving loan cancellation. However, the addition of "only" does not help to reach this end.

The "directly" requirement, when interpreted to exclude public interest attorneys because the government is their "client," further erodes § 1087ee(a)(2)(I). All qualifying [employees] serve multiple beneficiaries – the children at risk, the community, the government, the employing agency, the donors and trustees of the employing agency, to name the most obvious. The mere fact that a public interest attorney represents a client does not necessarily make that client the exclusive beneficiary of their work.

The DOE also requires provision of services "exclusively" to high-risk and low-income children. . . . The statute does not require that the children be low-income, but simply that they be from low-income *communities*. . . .

C. Power to Persuade

Perhaps most importantly, . . . the DOE conceded that it "does not make the determination of whether a borrower qualifies for a cancellation but *upon request provides guidance* to institutions that make the decisions." (emphasis added). We are especially disinclined to defer to an agency when it does not purport to speak authoritatively. . . .

In sum, the DOE's interpretation – the addition of "only" in the Handbooks, coupled with the use of "directly" and "exclusively" in an advisory role – lacks the power to persuade, and the DOE fails to show thoroughness in its consideration or validity in its reasoning. Thus, even assuming arguendo that the agency offered consistent guidance, we are not bound to defer to its construction of the statute. . . . [Therefore appellants] qualify for cancellation of their Perkins Loan obligations.

Underlying Case Documents

The case referenced:
The Higher Education Act
The 1995 DOE regulation
A handbook from before the time the "only" requirement was added
A handbook with the "only" requirement

After the case was decided the Department of Education revised the regulations to add the directly and exclusively requirement. For the Federal Register publication of these final rules click HERE.

1. *De La Mota* involves the application of *Skidmore* respect to less-than-formal guidelines, standards, manuals, and letters. The reasoning in *De La Mota* was recently applied by the Second Circuit in *Boykin v. Keycorp, 521 F.3d 202 (2d Cir. 2008)*. In *Boykin*, the government issued a "final letter" that rejected a claim made under the Fair Housing Act. The letter included a description of HUD's practices that justified dismissal of the complaint. On appeal, the question became the deference – or respect – due the theretofore unpublished practices.

> We consider the informal, unpublished "practice" described in the HUD Letter under the framework for a more limited standard of deference described in *Skidmore* and *Christensen v. Harris County* (holding that agency interpretations "in opinion letters[,] policy statements, agency manuals, and enforcement guidelines, all of which lack the force of law" are entitled only to *Skidmore* deference). Under *Skidmore*, the weight we accord an agency interpretation depends upon "the thoroughness evident in

its consideration, the validity of its reasoning, its consistency with earlier and later pronouncements, and all those factors which give it power to persuade."

How is an unpublished practice a rule under the APA?

Hypothetical

The Social Security Act provides for the payment of disability insurance benefits to eligible disabled individuals. At Section 423(d)(1)(A), the Act defines "disability" as the "[i]nability to engage in any substantial gainful activity by reason of any medically determinable physical or mental impairment which can be expected to result in death or which has lasted or can be expected to last for a continuous period of not less than 12 months." In implementing this definition, the Social Security Administration (SSA) generally requires claimants to demonstrate an inability to engage in gainful work for 12 months. A claimant, whose inability to engage in gainful employment lasted only 11 months, filed for benefits for that period of disability and was denied by the SSA for failure to demonstrate an inability to engage in gainful employment lasting at least 12 months. He appealed, arguing that the statute's 12-month requirement only modifies "impairment" and not "inability," and that because his impairment *could have* lasted for 12 months or longer, he was entitled to benefits. In response, the SSA argued that it reasonably interpreted the "inability" requirement as inextricably linked to the 12-month duration requirement, and that the "expected to last" term is applicable only to those cases where the inability to work was still in effect and had not yet reached the 12-month duration on the date the claim was filed. Should a reviewing court defer to the SSA's interpretation or reverse its decision? *See* Barnhart v. Walton, 535 U.S. 212 (2002).

---

2. Who decides counts. The *De La Mota* text makes clear that the role the decisionmaker plays in the agency that issues the letter, manual, or guideline in question is of consequence. "Thoroughness is impossible for an agency staff member to demonstrate when the staff member does not report to the Secretary, bears no lawmaking authority, and is unconstrained by political accountability. Thorough consideration requires a macro perspective that a staff member, acting alone, lacks." Can an agency secure <u>*Skidmore*</u> respect by having a more senior officer sign off on a letter? Avoid judicial review (on a ripeness or finality basis) by making sure a more senior official does *not* sign off on the issuance?

Hypothetical

(a) The Patent Act delegates to the U.S. Patent and Trademark Office
(PTO) the authority to promulgate regulations administering the American patent regime. Section 102(a) of the Patent Act provides that a patent must be denied if "the invention was known or used by others in this
country, or patented or described in a printed publication in this or a foreign country, before the invention thereof by the applicant for patent…."
Assume that in a notice and comment rulemaking, the PTO interpreted
"printed publication" to include Internet web pages. Assume also that
the Patent Act's text and its legislative history are silent on the definition
of "printed publication" but that its contextual use in the statutory text,
legislative history, and agency regulations in all circumstances refers to
tangible, bound printed material (*e.g.*, books, magazines, scholarly journals, etc.). Your client has just been denied a US patent on her invention
on the grounds that it had been described in an Internet webpage three
years before she filed her patent application. She wants to challenge the
PTO's interpretation of "printed publication" as encompassing Internet
materials. What standard of review should a court apply, and to what
likely effect?

(b) Assume the same facts as in (a), except that the PTO interpreted
"printed publication" as encompassing Internet web pages by means of
a denial letter (known as an "Office Action") from the patent examiner
assigned a review of the client's patent application. What standard of review
should a court apply to such an agency action, and to what likely effect?

---

3. Would notice and comment help?
In *Shikles v. Sprint/United Mgmt. Co.,*
426 F.3d 1304, 1316 (10th Cir. 2005),
the court dealt with the *De La Mota*
thoroughness standard. In that case,
the evidence of thoroughness came
primarily from the brief the agency
filed. The court found: "The EEOC's
brief provides no indication of whether
the agency has been thorough in its
consideration of the issue, and it
appears that the agency's position has
not been subjected to any sort of public scrutiny." Does this mean that an
expedited notice and comment pro-

For More Information

Presumably, the *De La Mota* case is
of personal interest to some law students. It was mentioned in 11 CITY
LAW 112, September/October 2005,
*Policies and Benefits: Loan Forgive-
ness: ACS Attorneys Win Student Loan
Benefits.* Otherwise, little has been
written on the decision. There are,
however, a number of fine articles
on law student loan forgiveness including Kenneth M. Rosen, *Lessons
on Lawyers, Democracy, and Professional Responsibility,* 19 GEO. J. LEGAL
ETHICS 155 (2006); and Howard M.
Erichson, *Doing Good, Doing Well,* 57
VAND. L. REV. 2087 (2004).

cess would shield the agency and insure deference? <u>*Gonzales v. Oregon*</u> suggests the answer may be yes. Further, how is a brief anything other than a post hoc rationalization? Is a post hoc rationalization acceptable when dealing with interpretive rules, guidelines, policy statements, letters, and similar issuances?

Hypothetical

The Freedom of Information Act (FOIA) requires Federal agencies, when requested, to make "promptly" available to "any person" any written information in their possession unless the information is encompassed with one or more of nine exemptions. Assume that by means of a notice and comment rulemaking, the Federal Communications Commission interpreted the term "record" to exclude the video and sound recordings taken by Commissioners and other senior staff members on government-issued recording units (including the video and sound recording applications on their cell phones and other personal communication devices). Assume also that FOIA's provisions and legislative history do not speak directly to whether "record" in fact excludes such recordings. Upon the FCC's refusal to release such recordings, your client, the Center for Ethics in Government, wishes to challenge the agency's interpretation of FOIA in court. What standard of review would the reviewing court apply and why?

IV. Improving or Maturing Deference?

Between 2005 and 2007 the Supreme Court decided three cases that have deepened the complexity – and confusion – generated by <u>*Christensen*</u> and <u>*Mead*</u>. In what Justice Scalia has called the court's attempt at "improvisation" of administrative law, these opinions raise jurisprudential and political questions that go well beyond the initial separation of powers issues that were the driving force behind Justice Stevens' opinion in <u>*Chevron*</u>.

In *National Cable & Telecommunications Association v. Brand X Internet Services*, the court appears to redefine the relationship between federal courts and federal agencies, holding, according to one reading of the case, that federal agencies have the power to overturn federal court decisions. If *Christensen* and <u>*Mead*</u> represent a departure from <u>*Chevron*</u>'s preference for agency decisionmaking, *Brand X* seems to move back to *Chevron*, and decisively so.

In <u>*Gonzales v. Oregon*</u>, the Court moves in an entirely different direction, finding that an agency decision is entitled to no deference, despite the fact that it constitutes an interpretation of both the agency's own regulations and an existing statute. Criticizing the agency for "parroting" existing rules and laws, the Court voids the action of the agency. How does that square with *Auer*?

Food for Thought

As you read through these cases, if you get the sense that these decisions do not line up, either ideologically or jurisprudentially, you would not be alone. Perhaps JUSTICE SCALIA is correct: the Court is engaged in some type of experiment begun with the *Christensen* and *Mead* decisions, and the results are not yet conclusive.

Finally, in *Long Island Care at Home*, the Court assessed an agency determination that appeared highly problematic and somewhat at odds with congressional intent. Nevertheless, in part because the agency chose to use an expedited notice and comment process, the Court found the agency action not just somewhat reasonable and arguably coherent, but almost magically entitled to something resembling deference.

NATIONAL CABLE & TELECOMMUNICATIONS ASSOCIATION V. BRAND X INTERNET SERVICES

545 U.S. 967 (2005)

[JUSTICE THOMAS] Congress has delegated to the [Federal Communications] Commission the authority to "execute and enforce" the Communications Act and to "prescribe such rules and regulations as may be necessary in the public interest to carry out the provisions" of the Act. These provisions give the Commission the authority to promulgate binding legal rules; the Commission issued the order under review in the exercise of that authority; and no one questions that the order is within the Commission's jurisdiction. Hence . . . we apply the *Chevron* framework to the Commission's interpretation of the Communications Act. . . .

B.

The Court of Appeals declined to apply *Chevron* because it thought the Commission's interpretation of the Communications Act foreclosed by the conflicting construction of the Act it had adopted in *Portland*. It based that holding on the assumption that *Portland's* construction overrode the Commission's, regardless of whether *Portland* had held the statute to be unambiguous. That reasoning was incorrect.

A court's prior judicial construction of a statute trumps an agency construction otherwise entitled to *Chevron* deference only if the prior court decision holds that its construction follows from the unambiguous terms of the statute and thus leaves no room for agency discretion. This principle follows from *Chevron* itself. *Chevron* established a "presumption that Congress, when it left ambiguity in a statute meant for implementation by an agency, understood that the ambiguity would be resolved, first and foremost, by the agency, and desired the agency (rather than the courts) to possess whatever degree of discretion the ambiguity allows." Yet allowing a judicial precedent to foreclose an agency from interpreting an ambiguous statute, as the Court of Appeals assumed it could, would allow a court's interpretation to override an agency's. *Chevron's* premise is that it is for agencies, not courts, to fill statutory gaps. The better rule is to hold judicial interpretations contained in precedents to the same demanding *Chevron* step one standard that applies if the court is reviewing the agency's construction on a blank slate: Only a judicial precedent holding that the statute unambiguously forecloses the agency's interpretation, and therefore contains no gap for the agency to fill, displaces a conflicting agency construction.

A contrary rule would produce anomalous results. It would mean that whether an agency's interpretation of an ambiguous statute is entitled to <u>*Chevron*</u> deference would turn on the order in which the interpretations issue: If the court's construction came first, its construction would prevail, whereas if the agency's came first, the agency's construction would command *Chevron* deference. Yet whether Congress has delegated to an agency the authority to interpret a statute does not depend on the order in which the judicial and administrative constructions occur. The Court of Appeals' rule, moreover, would "lead to the ossification of large portions of our statutory law" by precluding agencies from revising unwise judicial constructions of ambiguous statutes. Neither *Chevron* nor the doctrine of stare decisis requires these haphazard results.

The dissent answers that allowing an agency to override what a court believes to be the best interpretation of a statute makes "judicial decisions subject to reversal by Executive officers." It does not. Since <u>*Chevron*</u> teaches that a court's opinion as to the best reading of an ambiguous statute an agency is charged with administering is not authoritative, the agency's decision to construe that statute differently from a court does not say that the court's holding was legally wrong. Instead, the agency may, consistent with the court's holding, choose a different construction, since the agency remains the authoritative interpreter (within the limits of reason) of such statutes. . . .

IV.

We next address whether the Commission's construction of the definition of "telecommunications service" is a permissible reading of the Communications Act under the <u>*Chevron*</u> framework. . . .

A.

. . . The issue before the Commission was whether cable companies providing cable modem service are providing a "telecommunications service" in addition to an "information service." The Commission first concluded that cable modem service is an "information service," a conclusion unchallenged here. . . .

At the same time, the Commission concluded that cable modem service was not "telecommunications service." . . . . "Telecommunications" . . . is defined as "the transmission, between or among points specified by the user, of information of the user's choosing, without change in the form or content of the information as sent and received." The Commission conceded that, like all information-service providers, cable companies use "telecommunications" to provide consumers with Internet service; cable companies provide such service via the high-speed wire that transmits signals to and from an end user's computer. For the Commission, however, the question whether cable broadband Internet providers "offer" telecommunications involved more than whether telecommunications was one necessary component of cable modem service. Instead, whether that service also includes a telecommunications "offering" "tur[ned] on the nature of the functions the *end user* is offered," for the statutory definition of "telecommunications service" does not "res[t] on the particular types of facilities used."

Seen from the consumer's point of view, the Commission concluded, cable modem service is not a telecommunications offering because the consumer uses the high-speed wire always in connection with the information-processing capabilities provided by Internet access, and because the transmission is a necessary component of Internet access . . . .

B.

This construction passes *Chevron's* first step. . . . The word "offering" as used in § 153(46) . . . can reasonably be read to mean a "stand-alone" offering of telecommunications, i.e., an offered service that, from the user's perspective, transmits messages unadulterated by computer processing. That conclusion follows not only from the ordinary meaning of the word "offering," but also from the regulatory history of the Communications Act.

1.

. . . It is common usage to describe what a company "offers" to a consumer as what the consumer perceives to be the integrated finished product, even to the exclusion of discrete components that compose the product, as the dissent concedes. One might well say that a car dealership "offers" cars, but does not "offer" the integrated major inputs that make purchasing the car valuable, such as the engine or the chassis. . . . Even if it is linguistically permissible to say that the car dealership "offers" engines when it offers cars, that shows, at most, that the term "offer," when applied to a commercial transaction, is ambiguous . . . .

. . . The entire question is whether the products here are functionally integrated (like the components of a car) or functionally separate (like pets and leashes). That question turns not on the language of the Act, but on the factual particulars of how Internet technology works and how it is provided, questions *Chevron* leaves to the Commission to resolve in the first instance. . . . [The relevant law should] be set by the Commission, not by warring analogies.

[T]he Commission reasonably concluded, a consumer cannot purchase Internet service without also purchasing a connection to the Internet and the transmission always occurs in connection with information processing. . . .

2.

The Commission's traditional distinction between basic and enhanced service also supports the conclusion that the Communications Act is ambiguous about whether cable companies "offer" telecommunications with cable modem service. Congress passed the definitions in the Communications Act against the background of this regulatory history, and we may assume that the parallel terms "telecommunications service" and "information service" substantially incorporated their meaning, as the Commission has held. . . .

C.

We also conclude that the Commission's construction was "a reasonable policy choice for the [Commission] to make" at *Chevron's* second step.

Respondents argue that the Commission's construction is unreasonable because it allows any communications provider to "evade" common-carrier regulation by the expedient of bundling information service with telecommunications. Respondents argue that under the Commission's construction a telephone company could, for example, offer an information service like voice mail together with telephone service, thereby avoiding common-carrier regulation of its telephone service.

We need not decide whether a construction that resulted in these consequences would be unreasonable because we do not believe that these results follow from the construction the Commission adopted. As we understand the Declaratory Ruling, the Commission did not say that any telecommunications service that is priced or bundled with an information service is automatically unregulated under Title II. The Commission said that a telecommunications input used to provide an information service that is not "separable from the data-processing capabilities of the service" and is instead ". . . integral to [the information service's] other capabilities" is not a telecommunications offering. . . .

V.

Respondent MCI, Inc., urges that the Commission's treatment of cable modem service is inconsistent with its treatment of DSL service and therefore is an arbitrary and capricious deviation from agency policy. MCI points out that when local telephone companies began to offer Internet access through DSL technology in addition to telephone service, the Commission applied its *Computer II* facilities-based classification to them and required them to make the telephone lines used to transmit DSL service available to competing ISPs on nondiscriminatory, common-carrier terms. MCI claims that the Commission's decision not to regulate cable companies similarly under Title II is inconsistent with its DSL policy.

We conclude, however, that the Commission provided a reasoned explanation for treating cable modem service differently from DSL service. As we have already noted, the Commission is free within the limits of reasoned interpretation to change course if it adequately justifies the change. It has done so here. The traditional reason for its *Computer II* common-carrier treatment of facilities-based carriers (including DSL carriers), as the Commission explained, was "that the *telephone network* [is] the primary, if not exclusive, means through which information service providers can gain access to their customers." The Commission applied the same treatment to DSL service based on that history, rather than on an analysis of contemporaneous market conditions.

The Commission in the order under review, by contrast, concluded that changed market conditions warrant different treatment of facilities-based cable companies providing Internet access. Unlike at the time of *Computer II*, substitute forms of Internet transmission exist today: "[R]esidential high-speed access to the Internet is evolving over multiple electronic platforms, including wireline, cable, terrestrial wireless and satellite." The Commission concluded that "broadband services should exist in a minimal regulatory environment that promotes investment and innovation in a competitive market." This, the Commission reasoned, warranted treating cable companies unlike the facilities-based enhanced-service providers of the past. We find nothing arbitrary about the Commission's providing a fresh analysis of the problem as applied to the cable industry, which it has never subjected to these rules. This is adequate rational justification for the Commission's conclusions. . . .

[JUSTICE SCALIA with JUSTICE GINSBURG, dissenting.]

The [FCC] has once again attempted to concoct "a whole new regime of regulation (or of free-market competition)" under the guise of statutory construction. Actually, in these cases, it might be more accurate to say the Commission has attempted to establish a whole new regime of *non*-regulation, which will make for more or less free-market competition, depending upon whose experts are believed. The important fact, however, is that the Commission has chosen to achieve this through an implausible reading of the statute, and has thus exceeded the authority given it by Congress.

I.

The first sentence of the FCC ruling under review reads as follows: "Cable modem service provides high-speed access to the Internet, *as well as* many applications or functions that can be used with that access, over cable system facilities." Does this mean that cable companies "offer" high-speed access to the Internet? Surprisingly not, if the Commission and the Court are to be believed.

It happens that cable-modem service is popular precisely because of the high-speed access it provides, and that, once connected with the Internet, cable-modem subscribers often use Internet applications and functions from providers other than the cable company. Nevertheless, for purposes of classifying what the cable company does, the Commission (with the Court's approval) puts all the emphasis on the rest of the package (the additional "applications or functions"). It does so by claiming that the cable company does not "offe[r]" its customers high-speed Internet access because it offers that access only in conjunction with particular applications and functions, rather than "separate[ly]," as a "stand-alone offering." . . . .

After all is said and done, after all the regulatory cant has been translated, and the smoke of agency expertise blown away, it remains perfectly clear that someone who sells cable-modem service is "offering" telecommunications. For that simple reason set forth in the statute, I would affirm the Court of Appeals.

II.

In Part III-B of its opinion, the Court continues the administrative-law improvisation project it began four years ago in <u>United States v. Mead Corp</u>. To the extent it set forth a comprehensible rule, *Mead* drastically limited the categories of agency action that would qualify for deference under *Chevron*. For example, the position taken by an agency before the Supreme Court, with full approval of the agency head, would not qualify. Rather, some unspecified degree of formal process was required – or was at least the only safe harbor.

This meant that many more issues appropriate for agency determination would reach the courts without benefit of an agency position entitled to *Chevron* deference, requiring the courts to rule on these issues de novo. As I pointed out in dissent, this in turn meant (under the law as it was understood until today) that many statutory ambiguities that might be resolved in varying fashions by successive agency administrations, would be resolved finally, conclusively, and forever, by federal judges – producing an "ossification of large portions of our statutory law." The Court today moves to solve this problem of its own creation by inventing yet another breathtaking novelty: judicial decisions subject to reversal by Executive officers.

Imagine the following sequence of events: FCC action is challenged as ultra vires under the governing statute; the litigation reaches all the way to the Supreme Court of the United States. The Solicitor General sets forth the FCC's official position (approved by the Commission) regarding interpretation of the statute. Applying *Mead*, however, the Court denies the agency position *Chevron* deference, finds that the *best* interpretation of the statute contradicts the agency's position, and holds the challenged agency action unlawful. The agency promptly conducts a rulemaking, and adopts a rule that comports with its earlier position – in effect disagreeing with the Supreme Court concerning the best interpretation of the statute. According to today's opinion, the agency is thereupon free to take the action that the Supreme Court found unlawful.

This is not only bizarre. It is probably unconstitutional. As we held [previously], Article III courts do not sit to render decisions that can be reversed or ignored by Executive officers. . . .

I respectfully dissent.

Underlying Case Documents

The case referenced:
The Communications Act
§ 153(46)

---

1. Is this a fair statement: A federal agency is not bound to prior federal court precedent unless the precedent involves an interpretation of an unambiguous statute? Putting aside the subjective nature of determinations of ambiguity or the lack thereof, this seems straightforward enough – and controversial. Is it possible that a federal agency has the authority to ignore clearly articulated precedent handed down by a United States Federal Court of Appeals? Putting aside Supreme Court cases, does this case abolish the remnants of the "rule of the circuit"?

2. In <u>Zuni Public School District 89 v. Department of Education, 127 S. Ct. 1534 (2007)</u>, a case involving fiscal support for local school districts, the Court focused on the agency interpretation of a federal statute JUSTICE BREYER considered to be a "highly technical, specialized interstitial matter . . . ." Both the lower court opinions and the Supreme Court majority involve a fairly extensive critique of the statute and the ultimate conclusion that the analysis of the relevant provisions was sufficiently permissible to justify <u>Chevron</u> deference. In his dissent, JUSTICE SCALIA blistered the majority for engaging in judicial legislative analysis of a statute that, on its face, had a "plain meaning." He characterized the majority opinion as an example of "judge supposed legislative intent over clear statutory text . . . ." JUSTICE SCALIA goes on to note that opinions of this type constitute an "exemplar of judicial disregard of crystal-clear text. We must interpret the law as Congress has written it, not as we would wish it to be."

JUSTICE STEVENS, in a concurring opinion, took on JUSTICE SCALIA directly, writing that SCALIA's dissent "rests on the incorrect premise that every policy-driven interpretation implements a judge's personal view . . . rather than a faithful attempt to carry out the will of the legislature. Quite the contrary is true of the work of judges with whom I have worked for many years. If we presume that our judges are intellectually honest – and I do – there is no reason to fear 'policy-driven interpretation' of Acts of Congress." JUSTICE STEVENS goes on to say that the statutory language in this case was "sufficiently ambiguous to justify the court's exegesis . . . ." Having decided that the statute is unclear, STEVENS asserts that the proper role for the court is to review that which the agency has done and to look at the legislative history that, in this case, he declared to be "pellucidly clear."

3. Should the executive have the dominant role in interpreting legislation – or does that responsibility rest with the judiciary? The vast majority of state supreme court judges would probably answer that question with little difficulty: They would tell you that it is the role of judges to interpret the law. They, however, are not bound by <u>Chevron</u> and its progeny.

4. <u>State Farm</u> and §§ 701 through 706 of the APA suggest that courts have a clear responsibility to review the decisions of federal agencies and to take a hard look to ensure that the decisions are, at a minimum, permissible interpretations and acceptable exercises of agency power. Does *Brand X* render "hard look" impossible? What is the point of engaging in a rigorous review of the action of an agency if the agency is free to ignore the precedent established by those decisions (outside of unambiguous statutes)? A recent law review article reconceptualizes judicial review as a process by which courts learn "something about the agency's willingness to invest resources into providing the kind of detailed record and lawyerly analysis that courts consider," which the author characterizes as signaling. Matthew Stephenson, <u>A Costly Signaling Theory of "Hard Look" Judicial Review, 58 ADMIN. L. REV. 753 (2006)</u>.

5. *Brand X* is part of a substantial number of Supreme Court cases in which the focus on statutory construction becomes the dominant modality for decisionmaking. *See, e.g.,* Rapanos v. United States, 547 U.S. 715 (2006); IBP, Inc. v. Alvarez, 546 U.S. 21 (2005); Envtl. Defense v. Duke Energy, 127 S. Ct. 1423 (2007); Massachusetts v. EPA, 549 U.S. 497 (2007); General Dynamics Land Sys. v. Cline, 540 U.S. 581 (2004); S.D. Warren Co. v. Maine Bd. of Envtl. Protection, 547 U.S. 370 (2006); Gonzales v. Oregon, 546 U.S. 243 (2006).

6. *Brand X*, among many other things, is a battle over stare decisis. The general rule is simple to state: Agencies are not bound internally by their own precedent. Circumstances change, technology evolves – that which was unfair 20 years ago may today be perfectly acceptable. Since one premise for the very existence of the regulatory state is flexibility and responsiveness, it would be somewhat odd to have agencies bound by prior decisions. Some agencies, by declaration, agree to adhere to their own precedent in order to allow those subject to regulation to adjust their behavior accordingly – although such declarations are riddled with exceptions.

The stare decisis problem in *Brand X* is not of the intra-agency variety but rather the relationship between courts and agencies. The clarity of this problem in *Brand X* is undeniable. In Brand X Internet Services v. FCC, 345 F.3d 1120 (9th Cir. 2003) – the Ninth Circuit decision under review in the Supreme Court – there was no question about the stare decisis problem. JUDGE O'SCANNLAIN understood the tension between the *Portland* decision and the emerging, but as yet unclear, FCC policy. In a concurring opinion, JUDGE O'SCANNLAIN wrote: "Our *Portland* decision, in essence, beat the FCC to the punch, leading to the strange result that we are compelled to reach today: three judges telling an agency acting within the area of its expertise that its interpretation of the statute it is charged with administering cannot stand – and that our interpreta-tion of how the act should be applied to a 'quicksilver technological environ-ment. . . .' is correct, indeed the only interpretation. . . ." *Brand X* raises then not only the question of stare decisis, but the question of who gets to define the meaning of a statute; the agency or the court. *See* Douglas Geyser, Note, Courts Still "Say What the Law Is": Explaining the Functions of the Judiciary and Agencies after Brand X, 106 COLUM. L. REV. 2129 (2006).

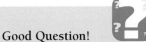

Good Question!

Take a step back from the holding in *Brand X*: Why was this case not resolved based on *Auer* deference? After all, the agency interpretation in question derived from an in-depth assessment of FCC regulations. Given the "clearly erroneous" test for *Auer* deference, would the result have been the same?

7. Do you agree with the factual premise relied on by the FCC? Do you think

broadband is a service separate from and unrelated to the regulated aspects of telecommunications? If one assumes the technologies are interdependent or "braided," was the decision of the FCC to exclude regulation of broadband an example of deregulatory excess? An abdication of statutory responsibility?

Marguerite Reardon, News.com, *What is* Brand X *Really About?* Posted on ZDNet News: June 27, 2005 2:54:00 PM, http://news.zdnet.com/2100-6005_22-5764187.html:

> In a 6-3 decision led by Justice Clarence Thomas, the court overturned a federal court decision that would force cable companies to share their infrastructure with Internet service providers such as Brand X and EarthLink.
>
> The case[, which] pit the FCC and the cable industry against a small California-based Internet service provider called Brand X, revolved around a highly technical legal definition of cable Internet.
>
> The FCC defines cable broadband services in a way that exempts cable providers from many of the regulations that phone companies must follow. As a result, cable companies can refuse to share their networks with competing ISPs. Brand X and other Net service providers argued that cable networks should be like telephone lines, on which any ISP can offer services. . . .
>
> Specifically, the court focused on the question of whether a cable company provides "telecommunications services" or "information services." According to the Telecommunications Act, providers of information services are subject to much less stringent regulations than companies that provide telecommunications services.
>
> At stake is whether cable broadband providers must share their lines with rivals – as happens in the phone industry – or whether they should be exempt from such rules. Though seemingly arcane, the issue could influence how quickly high-speed Internet services come online across the country, what features they will have and how much they will cost . . . .
>
> If cable companies are not required to share their networks, Brand X argued, consumers will pay higher prices and have fewer choices. Brand X and its supporters said this is especially true in areas of the country where cable is the only broadband service available.
>
> The FCC argued that rules that have applied to the phone industry have led to higher prices and slower broadband growth. Keeping cable companies exempt from line-sharing rules will spur investment, and benefit consumers more in the long run. This is why the FCC classified cable broadband as an information service.
>
> DSL – the technology that allows high-speed Internet access over copper phone lines – is classified as a telecommunications service. The Bell phone companies, which have built the vast majority of DSL networks in the United States, are required to share that infrastructure with ISPs such as Brand X, EarthLink and America Online. Competitive local exchange carriers that have built their own DSL networks, such as Covad Communications, are also required to share their networks with competitors. . . .

> Some . . . argue that the real solution would be to recognize that there is not much
> difference between cable and telephone services, which would require a complete
> overhaul of the 1996 Telecommunications Act.

8. What if instead of a prior circuit court decision (*Portland*), the FCC had been faced with a prior Supreme Court decision – would the "*Chevron* premise" that underlies *Brand X* have come out differently? If it is true that in the absolutist model of the majority, the agency task of filling in the gaps is sacrosanct (unless the agency is misinterpreting an unambiguous statute), would that apply when the gap filled is at odds with an older Supreme Court case?

9. For a very recent application by the U.S. Supreme Court of *Chevron*, *Mead*, and *Brand X*, you might take a look at *United States v. Eurodif*.

Long Island Care At Home, Ltd. v. Coke

551 U.S. 158 (2007)

[Justice Breyer] A provision of the Fair Labor Standards Act exempts from the statute's minimum wage and maximum hours rules "any employee employed in domestic service employment to provide companionship services for individuals who . . . are unable to care for themselves . . . ." A Department of Labor regulation (labeled an "interpretation") says that this statutory exemption includes those "companionship" workers who "are employed by an employer or agency other than the family or household using their services." The question before us is whether . . . the Department's regulation is valid and binding.

I.

A.

In 1974, Congress amended the Fair Labor Standards Act of 1938 (FLSA or Act), to include many "domestic service" employees not previously subject to its minimum wage and maximum hour requirements. When doing so, Congress simultaneously created an exemption that excluded from FLSA coverage certain subsets of employees "employed in domestic service employment," including babysitters "employed on a casual basis" and the companionship workers described above.

The Department of Labor (Department or DOL) then promulgated a set of regulations that included two regulations at issue here. The first defines the statutory term "domestic service employment" as "services of a household nature performed by an employee in or about a private home . . . of the person by whom he or she is employed . . . such as cooks, . . . housekeepers, caretakers, [and] babysitters employed on other than a casual basis." The second, set forth in a later subsection entitled "Interpretations," says that exempt companionship workers include those "who are employed by an employer or agency other than the family or household using their services . . . . This latter regulation (which we shall call the "third party regulation") has proved controversial in recent years.

In April 2002, Evelyn Coke (respondent), a domestic worker who provides "companionship services" to elderly and infirm men and women, brought this lawsuit against her former employer, Long Island Care at Home, Ltd., and its owner, Maryann Osborne. She alleged that the petitioners failed to pay her the minimum wages and overtime wages to which she was entitled under the FLSA. . . . All parties assume . . . the FLSA entitles Coke to the payments [if] the statutory exemption for "companionship services" does not apply to companionship workers paid by third-party agencies such as Long Island Care. The District Court found the Department's third-party regulation valid and controlling, and it consequently dismissed Coke's lawsuit. On appeal, the Second Circuit found the Department's third-party regulation "unenforceable" and set aside the District Court's judgment.

II.

. . . When an agency fills [a statutory] "gap" reasonably, and in accordance with other applicable (e.g., procedural) requirements, the courts accept the result as legally binding. *Chevron*; *Mead*. In this case, the FLSA explicitly leaves gaps . . . as to the scope and definition of "domestic service employment" and "companionship services." [T]he Department of Labor [has] the power to fill these gaps through rules and regulations. The subject matter of the regulation in question concerns a matter in which the agency is expert [and] which Congress entrusted the agency to work out. . . . The resulting regulation says that employees who provide "companionship services" fall within the terms of the statutory exemption irrespective of who pays them. Since on its face the regulation fill[s] a statutory gap, one might ask what . . . is it about the regulation that [is allegedly] unlawful?

Respondent claims that the regulation falls outside the scope of Congress' delegation; that it is inconsistent with another, legally governing regulation; [and] that it is an "interpretive" regulation not warranting judicial deference . . . . Respondent . . . claims that the words "domestic service employment" limit the provision's scope to those workers employed by persons who themselves receive the services (or are part of that person's household) and exclude those who are employed by "third parties." . . . . Respondent bolster[s] this argument by pointing to statements made by some Members of Congress during floor debates over the 1974 Amendments. And she also points to a different statute, the Social Security statute, which defines "domestic service employment" as domestic work performed in "a private home of the employer."

We do not find these arguments convincing. The statutory language refers broadly to "domestic service employment" and to "companionship services." It expressly instructs the agency to work out the details of those broad definitions. And whether to include workers paid by third parties within the scope of the definitions is one of those details. . . .

Respondent also argues that, even if the third-party regulation is within the scope of the statute's delegation, is perfectly reasonable, and otherwise complies with the law, courts still should not treat the regulation as legally binding. Her reason is a special one. She says that the regulation is an "interpretive" regulation, a kind of regulation that may be used, not to fill a statutory "gap," but simply to describe an agency's view of what a statute means. That kind of regulation may "persuade" a reviewing court, _Skidmore_, but will not necessarily "bind" a reviewing court. *Cf.* _Mead_ ("interpretive rules . . . enjoy no *Chevron* status as a class").

These reasons do not convince us that the Department [did not intend] the third-party regulation [to be] a binding application of its rulemaking authority. The regulation directly governs the conduct of members of the public, "affecting individual rights and obligations." *Chrysler Corp. v. Brown*, 441 U.S. 281 (1979). When promulgating the rule, the agency used full public notice and comment procedures, which under the Administrative Procedure Act an agency need not use when producing an "interpretive" rule. 5 U.S.C. § 553(b)(A) (exempting "interpretative rules, general statements of policy, or rules of agency organization, procedure, or practice" from notice and comment procedures). Each time the Department has considered amending the rule, it has similarly used full notice and comment rulemaking procedures. And for the past 30 years . . . the Department has treated the third-party regulation . . . as a legally binding exercise of its rulemaking authority.

Finally, the ultimate question is whether Congress would have intended, and expected, courts to treat an agency's rule, regulation, application of a statute, or other agency action as within, or outside, its delegation to the agency of "gap-filling" authority. Where an agency rule sets forth important individual rights and duties, where the agency focuses fully and directly upon the issue, where the agency uses full notice and comment procedures to promulgate a rule, where the resulting rule falls within the statutory grant of authority, and where the rule itself is reasonable, then a court ordinarily assumes that Congress intended it to defer to the agency's determination. *See* _Mead_.

For these reasons the Court of Appeals' judgment is reversed, and we remand the case for further proceedings consistent with this opinion.

———————————————

1. *Long Island Care at Home* is typical of the deference cases decided during the jurisprudentially turbulent first decade of the 21st Century. In some respects, after *Mead*, all bets were off – and while deference or *Skidmore* respect may have ceased to be fully predictable, in that uncertainty there has been a renaissance of creative reading of Supreme Court cases. This decision is no exception.

a. Fair and Considered Views are Due Deference? In *Alcoa, Inc. v. United States, 509 F.3d 173 (3d Cir. 2007)*, the Third Circuit found that *Long Island Care at Home* meant "that an 'Advisory Memorandum' of the Department of Labor, issued only to Department personnel and written in response to the litigation, should be afforded deference because it reflected the Department's fair and considered views developed over many years and did not appear to be a 'post hoc rationalization' of past agency action. . . ."

b. Interpretive Regulations, Once Properly Labeled are Due Deference? In *Estate of Gerson v. Comm'r, 507 F.3d 435 (6th Cir. 2007)*, the Sixth Circuit found *Long Island Care at Home* to hold that an "interpretive regulation that 'governs the conduct of members of the public' [is] entitled to Chevron deference where the agency used notice and comment procedures. . . ."

c. All about *Auer*? In *Cement Kiln Recycling Coalition v. EPA, 493 F.3d 207 (D.C. Cir. 2007)*, the D.C. Circuit found this meaning in *Long Island Care at Home*: "Since this is EPA's interpretation of its own regulation, it "is 'controlling' unless 'plainly erroneous or inconsistent with' the regulation[]. . . ."

d. Notice and Comment as a Cure-All. In *Taylor v. Progress Energy, Inc., 493 F.3d 454 (4th Cir. 2007)*, the Fourth Circuit found *Long Island Care at Home* as holding that "as long as interpretive changes create no unfair surprise – and the Department's recourse to notice and comment rulemaking in an attempt to codify its new interpretation makes any such surprise unlikely here – the change in interpretation alone presents no separate ground for disregarding the Department's present interpretation."

2. The authors of this casebook are of the opinion that JUSTICE STEVENS probably did not anticipate that his opinion in *Chevron* would be cited in at least 4000 subsequent judicial opinions and define an entire regime in administrative law. However, there is little doubt that he understood precisely the holding of that case. Similarly, JUSTICE BREYER, a preeminent scholar in administrative law, provided two very conventional bases for his decision in *Long Island Care at Home*.

a. Generally speaking, a rule or regulation that emerges after a notice and comment process is not flawed merely because it deviates from the text of the original notice, so long as the final pronouncement is a "logical outgrowth" of the initial statement. From the opinion:

Respondent's . . . claim is that the 1974 agency notice and comment procedure, leading to the promulgation of the third-party regulation, was legally "defective" because notice was inadequate and the Department's explanation also inadequate. We do not agree.

The Administrative Procedure Act requires an agency conducting notice and comment rulemaking to publish in its notice of proposed rulemaking "either the terms or substance of the proposed rule or a description of the subjects and issues involved. The Courts of Appeals have generally interpreted this to mean that the final rule the agency adopts must be "a 'logical outgrowth' of the rule proposed."

Initially the Department proposed a rule of the kind that respondent seeks. . . . As it turned out, the Department did withdraw the proposal for special treatment of employees of "covered enterprises." The result was a determination that exempted all third-party-employed companionship workers from the Act. We do not understand why such a possibility was not reasonably foreseeable. . . .

b. Congress intended the agency to fill in the gaps in the operant statute. From the opinion:

> Finally, the ultimate question is whether Congress would have intended, and expected, courts to treat an agency's rule, regulation, application of a statute, or other agency action as within, or outside, its delegation to the agency of "gap-filling" authority. Where an agency rule sets forth important individual rights and duties, where the agency focuses fully and directly upon the issue, where the agency uses full notice and comment procedures to promulgate a rule, where the resulting rule falls within the statutory grant of authority, and where the rule itself is reasonable, then a court ordinarily assumes that Congress intended it to defer to the agency's determination. . . .

3. Regulations vs. Interpretations: In *English v. Ecolab, Inc.*, 2008 WL 878456 (S.D.N.Y. Mar. 28, 2008), the Southern District of New York determined that *Long Island Care at Home* was about "the distinction between regulations and interpretations, and the corresponding deference to which they are entitled. . . . Using *Chevron*-style deference, the court upheld the regulation." Do you believe that there is a meaningful distinction between these terms – or does the difference in *Long Island Care at Home* boil down to the fact that there was a notice and comment process prior to the issuance of the standard in question?

4. Professor Michael Selmi's discussion of the case, in *The Supreme Court's 2006-2007 Term Employment Law Cases: A Quiet But Revealing Term*, 11 EMPL. RTS. & EMPLOY. POL'Y J. 219 (2007), is most helpful – and takes an entirely different approach.

> [W]hen the question is . . . whether courts should defer to the agency interpretation . . . the question is not so much whether the interpretation is correct but whether it is defensible. . . . JUSTICE BREYER, writing for a unanimous Court, found that the regulation was, in fact, defensible primarily because there was no strong reason to conclude otherwise. . . .

The Supreme Court does not always apply its _Chevron_-deference with great consistency or fidelity to the underlying principles, and one might reasonably ask why the Court chose to be so deferential in the case. . . . [The] liberal wing of the Court may have taken an opportunity to shore up the Court's deference doctrine with an eye towards the shifting political sands. Those Justices who were thinking strategically might have decided that in the long run more good would result for employees if the Court is constrained by its *Chevron* doctrine, and the liberal Justices might have seen this case as providing a fruitful opportunity to cabin other potentially wayward Justices. It may also be that politics did not play a significant role in the decision – maybe the Court simply thought that this was an appropriate case for deference regardless of the result.

[G]iven the statutory delegation, and the ambiguity regarding how far the exemption should extend, it seemed fair to conclude that the exemption was subject to several different interpretations, and if that is the case, *Chevron* deference will almost always ensure that the regulation is upheld. . . .

5. In _Levy v. Sterling Holding Company_, 475 F. Supp. 2d 463 (D. Del. 2007), a complex derivative shareholder action challenging alleged "insider speculative short-swing trading" a question arose whether the SEC had exempted the transaction at issue in the case. The SEC interpretations of Section 16(b) had been the subject of a prior Third Circuit decision. One question was whether the Third Circuit's decision on 16(b) was dispositive or whether Chevron analysis – and deference – was due:

Here . . . Congress explicitly afforded the SEC the authority to exempt transactions from the reach of section 16(b). Therefore, section 16(b) does not unambiguously foreclose the SEC's interpretation but, rather, requires the SEC to interpret which transactions are exempt from its application. In other words, Congress did not speak to the precise question at issue, but explicitly left a gap for the SEC to fill. The SEC filled this gap by promulgating rules exempting certain transactions. As the Third Circuit noted in *Levy*, however, "the SEC [rules did] not set forth [the SEC's] interpretation [of section 16(b)] clearly." Thus, the court endeavored to determine the proper interpretation of those rules. Noteworthy, however, is the fact that the Third Circuit did not hold that its interpretation of the SEC Rules was derived from the unambiguous language of either section 16(b) or Rules 16b-3 and 16b-7. In response to the Third Circuit's criticism of its lack of clarity in the interpretation of section 16(b), the SEC released the Amendments to "resolve any doubt as to the meaning and interpretation of these rules [Rules 16b-3 and 16b-7]." Accordingly, because the Third Circuit did not conclude that section 16(b) unambiguously foreclosed the SEC's interpretation as set forth in the Amendments, its ruling in the *Levy* case does not displace that interpretation. The court, therefore, must apply the second prong of the _Chevron_ analysis to determine whether the Amendments are based on a permissible construction of section 16(b).

V. Interpretative Rules, Guidances, and Beyond

Informal (notice and comment) rulemaking requires a substantial commitment of time and resources – and is subject to judicial review. The far-less used formal rulemaking has multiple procedural requirements and is reviewed in a

manner similar to adjudicatory hearings
conducted pursuant to Section 554 of
the APA. In contrast, interpretive rules
have few procedural requirements and
are less likely to be reviewed. Accordingly, agencies use interpretive rules,
guidances, and advisories, regulatory
guides, bulletins, manuals, information
sheets, and other vehicles that require
little or no public process for many
situations – generating the predictable

Take Note

The next few cases explore interpretive rules and statements of policy,
referred to in some instances as
guidance documents. These agency
issuances are most easily understood
in relation to or comparison with
legislative or substantive rules.

complaint that the agency has by-passed required procedures and negated public
input into the decisionmaking process.

Well before *Mead* and *Christensen* made inroads into *Chevron* and signaled
the rebirth of *Skidmore* "respect," courts not only adhered to the APA distinctions
between legislative or substantive rules that carry the force of law and interpretive
rules and policy statements that do not, they also understood that judicial review
of interpretive rules (unlike substantive/legislative rules) could be penetrating and
comprehensive. Simply put, judicial review of interpretive rules is not uniformly
bound by notions of obligatory *Chevron* deference.

The APA distinction is overt: Section 553(b)(A) exempts from notice and
comment requirements "interpretative rules, general statements of policy, or rules
of agency organization, procedure, or practice." In the absence of any public
process, the potential for arbitrariness, authoritarianism, and abuse of executive
power increases. Accordingly, courts do not have the kinds of restrictions in taking a "hard look" at agency action that limit review for rules issued through notice
and comment or other formalized processes.

PACIFIC GAS & ELECTRIC COMPANY V. FEDERAL POWER COMMISSION

506 F.2d 33 (D.C. Cir. 1974)

[JUDGE MACKINNON] This country appears to be experiencing a natural gas
shortage which necessitates the curtailment of supplies to certain customers during peak demand periods. The problem confronting many pipeline companies
is whether to curtail on the basis of existing contractual commitments or on
the basis of the most efficient end use of the gas. In some instances the pipeline
companies are concerned that withholding gas due under existing contracts may
subject them to civil liability.

. . . .

Sensing a need for guidance and uniformity in the curtailment area, on January 8, 1973 the Commission promulgated Order No. 467 . . . . Entitled "Statement of Policy," Order No. 467 was issued without prior notice or opportunity for comment. The statement . . . expresses the Commission's policy that the national interest would be best served by assigning curtailment priorities on the basis of end use rather than on the basis of prior contractual commitments. Order No. 467 further states the Commission's intent to follow this priority schedule unless a particular pipeline company demonstrates that a different curtailment plan is more in the public interest. . . . The Commission immediately received numerous petitions for rehearing, reconsideration, modification or clarification of Orders Nos. 467 and 467-A, and several parties requested permission to intervene.

II. STATEMENTS OF POLICY

A. General Principles

The APA requires that before an agency adopts a substantive rule, it must publish a notice of the proposed rule and provide interested persons an opportunity to comment. 5 U.S.C. § 553. The FPC did not utilize this rulemaking procedure in adopting Order No. 467. However, section 553(b)(A) of the APA provides an exception to the general rulemaking requirements:

> Except when notice or hearing is required by statute, this subsection does not apply –
>
> > (A) to interpretative rules, general statements of policy, or rules of agency organization, procedure, or practice . . . .

The Commission maintains that Order No. 467 was exempt from the rulemaking requirements because it is a "general statement of policy" within the meaning of section 553(b)(A).

. . . .

Professor Davis has described the distinction between substantive rules and general statements of policy as a "fuzzy product." Unfortunately the issues in this case compel us to attempt to define the fuzzy perimeters of a general statement of policy. An administrative agency has available two methods for formulating policy that will have the force of law. An agency may establish binding policy through rulemaking procedures by which it promulgates substantive rules, or through adjudications which constitute binding precedents. A general statement of policy is the outcome of neither a rulemaking nor an adjudication; it is neither a [substantive] rule nor a precedent[al opinion] but is merely an announcement to the public of the policy which the agency hopes to implement in future rulemakings or adjudications. A general statement of policy, like a press release, presages an upcoming rulemaking or announces the course which the agency intends to follow in future adjudications.

As an informational device, the general statement of policy serves several beneficial functions. By providing a formal method by which an agency can express its views, the general statement of policy encourages public dissemination of the agency's policies prior to their actual application in particular situations. Thus the agency's initial views do not remain secret but are disclosed well in advance of their actual application. Additionally, the publication of a general statement of policy facilitates long range planning within the regulated industry and promotes uniformity in areas of national concern.

The critical distinction between a substantive rule and a general statement of policy is the different practical effect that these two types of pronouncements have in subsequent administrative proceedings. . . . A properly adopted substantive rule establishes a standard of conduct which has the force of law. In subsequent administrative proceedings involving a substantive rule, the issues are whether the adjudicated facts conform to the rule and whether the rule should be waived or applied in that particular instance. The underlying policy embodied in the rule is not generally subject to challenge before the agency.

A general statement of policy, on the other hand, does not establish a "binding norm." It is not finally determinative of the issues or rights to which it is addressed. The agency cannot apply or rely upon a general statement of policy as law because a general statement of policy only announces what the agency seeks to establish as policy. A policy statement announces the agency's tentative intentions for the future. When the agency applies the policy in a particular situation, it must be prepared to support the policy just as if the policy statement had never been issued. An agency cannot escape its responsibility to present evidence and reasoning supporting its substantive rules by announcing binding precedent in the form of a general statement of policy.

Often the agency's own characterization of a particular order provides some indication of the nature of the announcement. The agency's express purpose may be to establish a binding rule of law not subject to challenge in particular cases. On the other hand the agency may intend merely to publish a policy guideline that is subject to complete attack before it is finally applied in future cases. When the agency states that in subsequent proceedings it will thoroughly consider not only the policy's applicability to the facts of a given case but also the underlying validity of the policy itself, then the agency intends to treat the order as a general statement of policy.

. . . The tentative effect of a general statement of policy has ramifications in subsequent judicial review proceedings as well as in administrative proceedings. Because a general statement of policy is adopted without public participation, the scope of review may be broader than the scope of review for a substantive rule. The rulemaking process prescribed by the APA insures a thorough exploration of the relevant issues. The public is notified of the proposed rule and interested parties submit arguments supporting their positions. The rulemaking process culminates in the agency applying its experience and expertise to the issues. A court reviewing a rule that was adopted pursuant to this extensive rulemaking process will defer to the agency's judgment if the rule satisfies the minimal criterion of reasonableness.

But when an agency promulgates a general statement of policy, the agency does not have the benefit of public exploration of the issues. Judicial review may be the first stage at which the policy is subjected to full criticism by interested parties. Consequently a policy judgment expressed as a general statement of policy is entitled to less deference than a decision expressed as a [substantive] rule or an adjudicative order. Although the agency's expertise and experience cannot be ignored, the reviewing court has some leeway to assess the underlying wisdom of the policy and need not affirm a general statement of policy that merely satisfies the test of reasonableness. . . .

. . . In the absence of [Order No. 467], the Commission could have proceeded on an ad hoc basis and tentatively approved curtailment plans filed under section 4 of the Act which the Commission found to be just and reasonable. In following such a course the only difference from the present situation would be that the Commission would be acting under a secret policy rather than under the publicized guidelines of Order No. 467. The argument that an agency must follow rulemaking procedures when it elects to formulate policy by a substantive rule has no application in this case. Order No. 467 does not establish a substantive rule. Although the Commission is free to initiate a rulemaking proceeding to establish a binding substantive rule, the Commission apparently intends to establish its curtailment policies by proceeding through individual adjudications. Order No. 467 merely announces the general policy which the Commission hopes to establish in subsequent proceedings. . . .

Petitioners contend that Order No. 467 has an immediate and significant practical effect by shifting the burden of proof in curtailment cases from the pipeline companies to their customers because the order "established a presumption that the curtailment rules prescribed are consistent with the Natural Gas Act . . . ." Under section 4 of the Natural Gas Act a pipeline company filing a new curtailment plan has the burden of proving that its plan is reasonable and fair. . . . Petitioners maintain that by stating that tariffs which conform to the proposed plan will be permitted to become effective, Order No. 467 relieves the pipeline companies of their burden of justifying their plans. However, the language of Order No. 467 is as follows:

> Proposed tariff sheets which conform to the policies expressed in [Order No. 467] will be accepted for filing, and permitted to become effective, *subject to the rights of intervenors to hearing and adjudication of any claim of preference, discrimination, unjustness or unreasonableness* of the provisions contained in the proposed tariff sheets, and subject to the further right of anyone adversely affected to seek individualized special relief because of extraordinary circumstances.

We interpret the italicized proviso to mean that in appropriate cases the Commission will conduct a section 4 proceeding to consider a challenge to the underlying validity of a curtailment plan, even though the plan conforms to Order No. 467. Section 4 renders unlawful curtailment plans which are preferential, discriminatory, unreasonable or unfair and provides for a hearing concerning the lawfulness of newly filed curtailment plans. The Commission has processed curtailment plans under section 4 in the past, and the Supreme Court recently emphasized that section 4 is by far the most appropriate mechanism for evaluating such plans. We expect the Commission generally to continue processing curtailment plans in section 4 proceedings, in which the pipeline company has the burden of proof, and to refrain from treating Order No. 467 as anything more than a general statement of policy.

While Petitioners broadly allege the impropriety of the order of priorities . . ., their concern appears to be directed more to their position on the priority scale than urging the impropriety of the priorities themselves. . . . Accordingly, the need to initiate a Section 4 hearing to determine the lawfulness of the priorities per se[] has not been demonstrated. . . . We conclude that Order No. 467 is a general statement of policy and that it was therefore unnecessary for the Commission to conduct rulemaking proceedings under the Administrative Procedure Act.

Underlying Case Documents

The case referenced:
Section 4 of the Natural Gas Act
Order No. 467
Order No. 467-A

1. Having read *Pacific Gas*, can you be certain of the difference between a legislative or substantive rule and an interpretive rule or policy statement? Interpretive rules and policy statements do not require a notice and comment process, at least from the perspective of the APA – or do they? "[W]hen an agency possesses legislative rulemaking authority and has followed legislative rulemaking procedures, then a distinction between an interpretation expressed in a "regulation" and in an "interpretive guideline" is anachronistic, once the delegation of interpretive authority has been recognized." Barbara Hoffman, *Reports of Its Death Were Greatly Exaggerated: The EEOC Regulations that Define "Disability" Under the ADA After* Sutton v. United Air Lines, 9 TEMP. POL. & CIV. RTS. L. REV. 253, 259 (2000); *Stinson v. United States*, 508 U.S. 36, 45-47 (1993).

2. The Federal Circuit attempted a simple distinction between these modalities in *National Organization of Veterans' Advocates v. Secretary of Veterans Affairs*, 260 F.3d 1365 (Fed. Cir. 2001):

> [The] distinction between substantive and interpretive rules [is] as follows: "Substantive rules" [are] those that effect a change in existing law or policy or which affect individual rights and obligations. *Interpretative rules*, on the other hand, clarify or explain existing law or regulation and are exempt from notice and comment under section 553(b)(A) . . . . An *interpretative statement* simply indicates an agency's reading of a statute or a rule. It does not intend to create new rights or duties, but only reminds affected parties of existing duties." An "interpretive rule," in other words, merely "represents the agency's reading of statutes and rules rather than an attempt to make new law or modify existing law."

These distinctions are nuanced – and in this instance, the nuances have consequences. In Professor Stephen M. Johnson's *Good Guidance, Good Grief!*, 72 MO. L. REV. 695, 699-700, 711 (2007), the differences are set out as follows:

> Interpretive rules and policy statements, referred to in the introduction as "guidance documents," are more traditionally known as "nonlegislative rules." There are several important differences between legislative rules, the rules issued by agencies pursuant to a delegation of rulemaking authority from Congress, and nonlegislative rules. First, nonlegislative rules are subject to fewer procedural requirements than legislative rules. Interpretive rules and general statements of policy are exempt from the notice and comment rulemaking procedures of the APA. Instead, the APA merely requires that agencies publish and make available some, but not all, nonlegislative rules. Accordingly, agencies generally use very few procedures to develop nonlegislative rules.
>
> Another major difference between legislative rules and nonlegislative rules is that legislative rules have the force of law and bind agencies and the public, while nonlegislative rules do not bind agencies or the public. Similarly, reviewing courts generally accord greater deference to agencies' legislative rules than they accord to nonlegislative rules. Finally, while judicial challenges to legislative rules are quite common, it is often very difficult to challenge nonlegislative rules in court, either because the rules are not "final agency action" or because challenges to the rules

are not ripe. These differences between legislative and nonlegislative rules have played a significant role in influencing the current trend in agencies towards making policy decisions through nonlegislative rules, rather than through legislative rules or adjudication. . . .

A rule has the "force of law" or "legally binding effect" when (1) in the absence of the rule, there would not be an adequate legislative basis for enforcement action; (2) the agency has explicitly invoked its general legislative authority; or (3) the rule effectively amends a prior legislative rule. If the court determines that the rule has the "force of law," it will usually find that the rule is a legislative rule and the court will invalidate the rule if it was not adopted through notice and comment rulemaking. . . .

Professor Lisa Schultz Bressman suggests that there is a split among the lower courts regarding whether *Chevron* deference applies to nonlegislative rules and policies, with some courts focusing on whether the agency's interpretation has a binding effect (the *Mead* focus) and others focusing on whether the agency's interpretation reflects careful consideration and involves issues associated with agency expertise. . . . [*citing* Lisa Schultz Bressman, *How* **Mead** *Has Muddled Judicial Review of Agency Action*, 58 VAND. L. REV. 1443, 1459 (2005).]

3. Presumably, the announcement of policy alone is not an activating event for purposes of judicial review. Policy statements that merely clarify existing rules, remind parties of obligations, or organize statutory requirements fall outside the notice and comment requirement. This gets tricky when the policy binds the agency and the public and appears to be the final word from the agency on the topic. *See Am. Mining Cong. v. Mine Safety & Health Admin.*, 995 F.2d 1106 (D.C. Cir. 1993); *Community Nutrition Inst. v. Young*, 818 F.2d 943, 946 (D.C. Cir. 1987); and *Texas Savings and Community Bankers Ass'n v. Federal Housing Finance Bd.*, 201 F.3d 551, 556 (5th Cir. 2000).

4. That an agency designates something a policy statement may, in the end, not be dispositive. If the policy statement produces a meaning quite different from current agency rules, or irreconcilable with the approach of current agency rules and practices, a court might well determine that a statement is in fact a legislative rule necessitating notice and comment procedures and allowing for judicial review. Should the court in *Pacific Gas* have given any weight to the agency's designation of the standard in question? *See* William Funk, *Legislating for Nonlegislative Rules*, 56 ADMIN. L. REV. 1023, 1032-35 (2004).

5. While it has been argued for years that an interpretive statement becomes a substantive rule if it produces a "substantial impact" on an individual or entity, courts (arguably with the exception of the Fifth Circuit) have generally rejected the substantial impact test. This is discussed in the *Dismas* case below and in *Prof'ls & Patients for Customized Care v. Shalala*, 56 F.3d 592, 596-601 (5th Cir. 1995); *U.S. Tel. Ass'n v. FCC*, 28 F.3d 1232, 1234-35 (D.C. Cir. 1994); *Animal Legal Defense League v. Quigg*, 710 F. Supp. 728 (N.D. Cal 1989); *Cabais v. Egger*, 690

F 2d 234, 237-38 (D.C. Cir. 1982); and *American Postal Workers Union v. United States Postal Service*, 707 F 2d 548, 560 (D.C. Cir. 1983). That said, discerning what is interpretive is a challenge that calls into play the cases in this section as well as *Chevron* and its progeny. Should courts *defer* to an agency declaration that its actions are mere clarifications?

6. The policy statement in *Pacific Gas* included a process for seeking an exception to the use/contract priority. Exceptions to rules are not unusual – indeed, they are the hope of many clients or interests you may represent. Exceptions to policy are a bit more scarce. Does the fact that the agency created a structure for seeking an exception invalidate the claim that the stand the agency issued was solely interpretive?

7. In *Sentara Hampton General Hospital v. Sullivan*, 799 F. Supp. 128 (D.D.C. 1991), the court found: "[I]nterpretative rule[s] 'unlike legislative rules, [are] nonbinding policy statements [that] carry no more weight on judicial review than their inherent 'persuasiveness commands.'" *Batterton v. Marshall*, 648 F.2d 694, 702 (D.C. Cir. 1980). "To determine the [respect they] deserve, the court must consider the thoroughness evident in its consideration, the validity of its reasoning, its consistency with earlier and later pronouncements and all those factors which give it power to persuade, if lacking power to control." *Pfizer, Inc. v. Heckler*, 735 F.2d 1502, 1510 (D.C. Cir. 1984).

These differences are not lost on agencies. Part of a government lawyer's responsibility prior to the issuance of a statement defining agency policies or standards is consideration of the form the issuance should take. As Professor Kristin E. Hickman notes, "[t]he Internal Revenue Manual maintains that 'most' Treasury regulations are interpretative rules exempt from the APA's public notice and comment requirements, even though Treasury 'usually publishes its NPRMs in the Federal Register and solicits public comments.'" Kristin E. Hickman, *Coloring Outside the Lines: Examining Treasury's (Lack of) Complaince with Administrative Procedure Act Rulemaking Requirements*, 82 NOTRE DAME L. REV. 1727 (2007).

8. There are also policy statements that are binding and final (and arguably reviewable) and those that are not (and therefore arguably non-reviewable). Professor Charles H. Koch's *Policymaking by the Administrative Judiciary*, 56 ALA. L. REV. 693, 713-20 (2005), provides a comprehensive and valuable taxonomy for these differences.

> [P]olicy pronouncements are distinct from policy statements which do not purport to be made from delegated authority and consequently do not carry the force of law. . . . [These are] "nonlegislative" rules. Nonlegislative rules are a categorically different type of pronouncement from legislative rules, and this difference should be reflected in the weight given by an agency's adjudicators. . . . They are intended to disclose the agency's views and offer guidance regarding agency law. . . .

For years, courts have been bound by "*Skidmore* deference" when reviewing the
application [as opposed to the announcement] of nonlegislative rules. This dictates
that a court, while not bound to the rule, may find that the nonlegislative rule has the
"power to persuade. . .".

However, in both interpretation and application, a judge should be mindful of the effect
policy pronouncements have on the public. Regardless of the policy pronouncement's
formal effect, a member of the public to which the policy applies would be ill-advised
to ignore it; hence the pronouncement creates a variety of agency law.

9. Reviewability of interpretive rules is an entire subset of administrative law.
These rules are often characterized by agencies as advisory, for guidance, as
opposed to admonitory, leading to the argument that rules cannot be reviewed
because they are neither final dispositions of a matter before the agency nor are
they ripe for resolution in court. There are many different schools of thought on
this point although Professor Matthew C. Stephenson cautions that: "This concern
should not be overstated, however, given that most courts will treat an agency
interpretation as final and ripe if it is likely to have a significant practical impact
on regulated parties." Matthew C. Stephenson, *The Strategic Substitution Effect:
Textual Plausibility, Procedural Formality, and Judicial Review of Agency Statutory
Interpretations,* 120 HARV. L. REV. 528 (2000). For further discussion, see Robert A.
Anthony, *Interpretive Rules, Policy Statements, Guidances, Manuals, and the Like –
Should Federal Agencies Use Them To Bind the Public?,* 41 DUKE L.J. 1311, 1318
(1992), and Peter L. Strauss, *Publication Rules in the Rulemaking Spectrum: Assuring
Proper Respect for an Essential Element,* 53 ADMIN. L. REV. 803, 817-22 (2001).

10. The ripeness problem with interpretive rules has perplexed courts for
decades.

Ripeness cases often revolve around
the question of the binding effect of
the rule, the probability and impact of
enforcement, and whether additional
facts are need to allow for meaningful
review. *See, e.g., Tennessee Gas Pipeline
Co. v. FERC,* 736 F.2d 747, 751 (D.C.
Cir. 1984)* ("Were we to entertain
anticipatory challenges [to an interpretative rule] pressed by parties facing

For More Information

*See General Motors Corp. v. Ruck-
elshaus,* 724 F.2d 979 (D.C. Cir.
1983); *FCC v. WNCN Listeners Guild,*
450 U.S. 582, 585-86 (1981); *Babbitt v. United Farm Workers Nat'l
Union,* 442 U.S. 289, 301-03 (1979);
*Duke Power Co. v. Carolina Envtl.
Study Group, Inc.,* 438 U.S. 59, 81-
82 (1978); and *Nat'l Wildlife Fed. v.
Snow,* 561 F.2d 227, 236-37 (D.C.
Cir. 1976).

no imminent threat of adverse agency action, no hard choice between compliance
certain to be disadvantageous and a high probability of strong sanctions . . . we
would venture away from the domain of judicial review into a realm more accurately described as judicial preview.").

Ripeness is still bounded by the principles in *Abbott Laboratories v. Gardner*, 387 U.S. 136 (1967), and its companion case, *Toilet Goods Ass'n, Inc. v. Gardner*, 387 U.S. 158 (1967). These cases establish that it is possible to review an interpretive rule – but there are obstacles to be overcome. In *Florida Power & Light Co. v. EPA, 145 F.3d 1414, 1420-21 (D.C. Cir. 1998)*, the court found that the "ripeness doctrine represents a prudential attempt to balance the interests of the court and the agency in delaying review against the petitioner's interest in prompt consideration of allegedly unlawful agency action. . . . When a challenged decision is not 'fit' for review, the petitioner must show 'hardship' in order to overcome a claim of lack of ripeness. . . . Under the fitness prong, we inquire into whether the disputed claims raise purely legal, as opposed to factual, questions and whether the court or the agency would benefit from postponing review until the policy in question has sufficiently 'crystallized.'"

AMERICAN HOSPITAL ASSOCIATION V. BOWEN

834 F.2d 1037 (D.C. Cir. 1987)

[JUDGE WALD] We face here the issue of whether the Department of Health and Human Services ("HHS"), in implementing the system of "peer review" of Medicare outlays called for by Congress in its 1982 amendments to the Medicare Act, erred in not first undertaking the notice and comment rulemaking generally prescribed by the Administrative Procedure Act ("APA"), 5 U.S.C. § 553. . . .

I

. . . In 1982, Congress amended the Medicare Act to provide for a new method of reviewing the quality and appropriateness of the health care provided by these medical providers to Medicare beneficiaries. It did so by passing the Peer Review Improvement Act of 1982, which called for HHS to contract with "peer review organizations," or PROs, private organizations of doctors that would monitor "some or all of the professional activities" of the provider of Medicare services in their areas. . . .

. . . The principal function of a PRO, once having been designated by HHS and having entered into agreements with hospitals in its jurisdiction, is to review for conformance with the substantive standards of the Medicare Act the professional activities of physicians, hospitals, and other providers of health care. The standard of review is whether the services and items provided by the doctor or hospital "are or were reasonable and medically necessary," and thus whether these activities satisfy the standards for federal government reimbursement under Medicare. The PRO's determination on whether Medicare should pay for the services in question is generally conclusive. . . .

Beyond those relatively skeletal requirements, Congress left much of the spe-
cifics of the hospital-PRO relationship to the inventiveness of HHS, empowering it
to promulgate regulations governing PROs in order to implement the peer review
program. . . . Congress apparently expected HHS to design and put into place the
numerous procedures necessary to administer the PRO program.

The initial flurry of regulations promulgated by HHS filled in a variety of
these details regarding PRO procedures. . . . [T]hese regulations were promulgated in conformance with the Administrative Procedure Act, 5 U.S.C. § 553, and
thus they are not under challenge here. In addition to these regulations, HHS
issued a series of directives and transmittals governing the PRO program that are
the subject of this lawsuit. . . . HHS concedes that neither the [directives nor]
transmittals . . . were issued pursuant to the notice and comment procedures . . . .

The . . . American Hospital Association ("AHA") . . . brought suit against HHS
in the District Court for the District of Columbia. Its complaint argued that HHS
had circumvented the notice and comment requirements of § 553 of the APA, and
asked that the court declare the transmittals and directives, as well as the RFPs
[Request for Proposals] and the contracts entered into by HHS and the PROs,
invalid for failure to comply with § 553. It also asked the court to order HHS to
promulgate all regulations implementing the PRO program in accordance with
notice and comment procedures. . . .

A. *The Analytic Framework of APA § 553*

Section 553 of the Administrative Procedure Act requires agencies to afford
notice of a proposed rulemaking and an opportunity for public comment prior to
a rule's promulgation, amendment, modification, or repeal. Congress, however,
crafted several exceptions to these notice and comment requirements, determining that they should not apply

> (A) to interpretive rules, general statements of policy, or rules of agency
> organization, practice or procedure; or

> (B) when the agency for good cause finds . . . that notice and public
> procedure thereon are impracticable, unnecessary, or contrary to the
> public interest.

Section 553(b). The issue in this case is whether the various pronouncements
made by HHS in the course of its implementation of the peer review program fall
within the first class of exception: those for interpretive rules, procedural rules, or
general statements of policy.

We begin our analysis by noting that Congress intended the exceptions to § 553's notice and comment requirements to be narrow ones. The purposes of according notice and comment opportunities were twofold: "to reintroduce public participation and fairness to affected parties after governmental authority has been delegated to unrepresentative agencies," and to "assure[] that the agency will have before it the facts and information relevant to a particular administrative problem, as well as suggestions for alternative solutions." In light of the obvious importance of these policy goals of maximum participation and full information, we have consistently declined to allow the exceptions itemized in § 553 to swallow the APA's well-intentioned directive. . . . The exceptions have a common theme in that they "accommodate situations where the policies promoted by public participation in rulemaking are outweighed by the countervailing considerations of effectiveness, efficiency, expedition and reduction in expense." . . . .

The function of § 553's first exemption, that for "interpretive rules," is to allow agencies to explain ambiguous terms in legislative enactments without having to undertake cumbersome proceedings. . . . While the spectrum between a clearly interpretive rule and a clearly substantive one is a hazy continuum, . . . our cases, deploying different verbal tests, have generally sought to distinguish cases in which an agency is merely explicating Congress' desires from those cases in which the agency is adding substantive content of its own. Substantive rules are ones which "grant rights, impose obligations, or produce other significant effects on private interests," or which "effect a change in existing law or policy." Interpretive rules, by contrast, "are those which merely clarify or explain existing law or regulations," are "essentially hortatory and instructional," and "do not have the full force and effect of a substantive rule but [are] in the form of an explanation of particular terms." . . . .

The function of the second § 553 exemption, for "general policy statements," is to allow agencies to announce their "tentative intentions for the future," see *Pacific Gas & Electric Co. v. FPC*, 506 F.2d 33 (D.C. Cir. 1974), without binding themselves. . . .

A useful articulation of the [procedural rule] exemption's critical feature is that it covers agency actions that do not themselves alter the rights or interests of parties, although it may alter the manner in which parties present themselves or their viewpoints to the agency. Over time, our circuit in applying the § 553 exemption for procedural rules has gradually shifted focus from asking whether a given procedure has a "substantial impact" on parties, to inquiring more broadly whether the agency action also encodes a substantive value judgment or puts a stamp of approval or disapproval on a given type of behavior. The gradual move away from looking solely into the substantiality of the impact reflects a candid recognition that even unambiguously procedural measures affect parties to some degree. . . .

PRO Manual IM85-2, promulgated by HHS in March, 1985, is a 70-page document that defines procedures governing many of the review functions of PROs. . . . [T]he statutes and preexisting regulations that deal with PRO review are relatively sketchy, and thus IM85-2 makes a significant contribution towards describing the daily functions of PROs. It requires, for instance, that the PRO review at least 5% of all hospital admissions, selected at random. Where a "significant pattern" of unnecessary admissions appears in a particular subcategory of medicine, the PRO is instructed to step up its review to 100% of hospital admissions in the area.

Other requirements of IM85-2 are that the PRO review all hospital admissions occurring within seven days of discharge; all permanent cardiac pacemaker implantation or reimplantation procedures; all other "invasive procedures" where a pattern of abuse has been identified; and all transfers from a hospital to a psychiatric, rehabilitation, or alcohol-drug treatment unit. The manual also bars PROs from delegating their "utilization review" activities unless provided for in the PRO's contract. Finally, it includes an array of rules about notice to hospitals and parties, about the timing of PRO review, and about jurisdictional disputes between hospitals in separate PRO-covered areas. . . .

While we share the view of the district court that the commands of IM85-2 are not valid as interpretive rules, we find this conclusion beside the point. The requirements set forth in the transmittal are classic *procedural* rules, exempt under that distinctive prong of § 553. The bulk of the regulations in the transmittal set forth an enforcement plan for HHS's agents in monitoring the quality of and necessity for various operations. They essentially establish a frequency and focus of PRO review, urging its enforcement agents to concentrate their limited resources on particular areas where HHS evidently believes PRO attention will prove most fruitful. . . .

The manual imposes no new burdens on hospitals that warrant notice and comment review. This is not a case in which HHS has urged its reviewing agents to utilize a different standard of review in specified medical areas; rather, it asks only that they examine a greater share of operations in given medical areas. Were HHS to have inserted a new standard of review governing PRO scrutiny of a given procedure, or to have inserted a presumption of invalidity when reviewing certain operations, its measures would surely require notice and comment, as well as close scrutiny to insure that it was consistent with the agency's statutory mandate. But that is not this case.

At worst, Manual IM85-2 burdens hospitals by (1) making it more likely that their transgressions from Medicare's standards will not go unnoticed and (2) imposing on them the incidental inconveniences of complying with an enforcement scheme. The former concern is patently illegitimate: Congress' very purpose in instituting peer review was to crack down on reimbursements for medical activity not covered by Medicare. As for the second burden, case law clearly establishes that such derivative burdens hardly dictate notice and comment review. Accordingly, we hold that PRO Manual IM85-2 is a procedural rule exempt from § 553's notice and comment requirements. . . .

[F]inally, we note that our decision today in no way forecloses the right of a hospital to bring a claim based on § 553 of the APA if in fact the contract objectives turn out to what HHS insists they are not: thinly veiled attempts to change the substantive standards of the Medicare Act. . . . But where, as here, the facts are so wholly ambiguous and unsharpened as not to present a purely legal question "fit . . . for judicial decision," *cf. Abbott Laboratories v. Gardner*, 387 U.S. 136 (1967), and where the agency's characterization of its action would fit them cleanly into a § 553 exemption, we think it the most prudent course to await the sharpened facts that come from the actual workings of the regulation in question before striking the objective down as violative of the APA. . . .

Underlying Case Documents

The case referenced:
The Peer Review Improvement Act of 1982
The Regulations on Peer Review

1. Normally, notice and comment is required when an agency issues a binding and final substantive rule or a new standard that announces a meaningful change in substantive obligations and responsibilities. The *American Hospital Association* case involved a change in procedure. In *Paralyzed Veterans of America v. D.C. Arena, 117 F.3d 579, 586 (D.C. Cir. 1997)*, the court held: "[I]f any agency's new interpretation [of its regulations] will result in significantly different rights and duties than existed under a prior interpretation, notice and comment is required." Notice and comment is not required when the new standard does no more than "advise the public of the agency's construction of the statutes and rules which it administers." *Shalala v. Guernsey Mem'l Hosp., 514 U.S. 87, 100 (1995)*. On the continuum between "advice" and "different rights and duties," where would you place *American Hospital Association*?

2. The *American Hospital Association* case is often cited for the proposition that the distinction between rules that trigger notice and comment process and those that

do not is cloudy at best. *See* <u>Air Transp. Ass'n of Am., Inc. v. FAA, 291 F.3d 49, 55</u> <u>(D.C. Cir. 2002)</u> ("The distinction between a substantive rule and an interpretive rule can be less than clear-cut."); <u>Syncor Int'l Corp. v. Shalala, 127 F.3d 90, 93 (D.C.</u> <u>Cir. 1997)</u> ("We have long recognized that it is quite difficult to distinguish between substantive and interpretative rules."); <u>Orengo Caraballo v. Reich, 11 F.3d</u> <u>186, 194 (D.C. Cir. 1993)</u> ("The distinction between rules or statements which are subject to the notice and comment requirements of 553 and rules or statements which are exempt from those procedures is notoriously 'hazy.'") (quoting *Am. Hosp. Ass'n*); <u>Cmty. Nutrition Inst. v. Young, 818 F.2d 943, 946 (D.C. Cir. 1987)</u> ("The distinction between legislative rules and interpretative rules or policy statements has been described at various times as 'tenuous,' 'fuzzy,' 'blurred,' and, perhaps most picturesquely, 'enshrouded in considerable smog.'").

Can you articulate a usable standard that would clear the haze?

3. Consider the problems raised in *American Hospital Association* in the context of privatization. Does a private corporation running a public assistance program, immigration program, educational system, or other aspect of traditionally public activities have any responsibility to conduct notice and comment? Ever?

> **Good Questions!**
>
> Assume your law school operates pursuant to the APA and has issued new rules for registration for classes. Would those be substantive? Procedural? Require notice and comment? Constitute internal policy decisions for which comments would have little value? You might find it useful to pose this question to the academic dean of your school.

In Professor Jody Freeman's <u>Public Value in an Era of Privatization: Extending Public</u> <u>Law Norms Through Privatization, 116 Harv. L. Rev. 1285, 1302-03 (2003)</u>, this problem is considered with great care:

> Adherents of the public law perspective begin with the observation that the Constitution, together with statutes like the federal Administrative Procedure Act (APA), imposes on government a host of obligations designed to render decisionmaking open, accountable, rational, and fair. While they recognize that such impositions generally apply only to government, they bristle at the notion that government would seek to avoid these obligations by systematically contracting out functions.
>
> As a result, the public law perspective asks not whether privatization is efficient, but whether it erodes the public law norms that these constitutional and statutory limits are designed to protect. In particular, this perspective prioritizes legally required procedures designed to guarantee public participation and due process, such as those required by the notice and comment and formal adjudication procedures of the APA. Compliance with these procedures has an inherent value in the public law view; it is part of the minimum obligation a state owes to its citizens. Procedural regularity is also instrumental, however – procedures designed to ensure public participation and individual fairness might improve the rationality of decisionmaking and legitimize the authority of the state.

To round out the comparison with the economic perspective described above, the relevant stakeholder in the public law perspective is the diffuse public, to which public law scholars ascribe an interest in such things as accountability, due process, and rationality in decisionmaking. They do this as a normative rather than an empirical matter, believing a commitment to such standards fundamental to a liberal democracy. In this same vein, public law scholars have traditionally sought to ensure that government engage in policymaking in the "public interest" – a notoriously ill-defined term, but one frequently invoked to convey a preference for deliberative, disinterested, and expert decisionmaking that does not merely serve the interests of a special few.

Public law scholars worry that privatization may enable government to avoid its traditional legal obligations, leading to an erosion of public law norms and a systematic failure of public accountability. How might this happen? First, Congress has wide discretion to delegate functions to both public and private actors. The nondelegation doctrine does little to limit Congress's prerogative in this regard, provided that Congress supplies the requisite "intelligible principle" to guide the exercise of private discretion. State-action doctrine insulates most private actors from constitutional obligations, including due process, that would apply to the government if it performed the same functions. Though the Supreme Court occasionally treats private actors as state actors for constitutional purposes, these instances are few.

Beyond constitutional limitations lie statutory imperatives designed to promote public law norms. Private actors may effectively escape these as well. First, the APA specifically excludes both grants and contracts from the demands of notice and comment rulemaking normally applicable to federal agencies. Moreover, the APA subjects only agency action to potential judicial review. As part of their inherent power, agencies may further delegate powers entrusted to them to other actors with virtually no constitutional limitation, provided that Congress does not prohibit them from doing so. While an agency's decision to contract with private providers may be subject to procurement regulations if the good or service purchased is for government consumption, the implementation of federal grants and run-of-the-mill discretionary funding decisions are not governed by the procurement process and generally receive considerable judicial deference. Courts consider decisions to award discretionary grants to be informal policymaking, a mode of agency action over which courts hesitate to tread too heavily. Moreover, courts have referred to federal grants as "gifts."

The bulk of privatization also remains beyond the reach of the subconstitutional discretion-constraining and accountability-forcing mechanisms of administrative law. Private actors need not comply with any of the APA's procedural requirements, nor must they, generally speaking, observe the disclosure provisions of the Freedom of Information Act (FOIA) or the open-meeting obligations of other sunshine laws that apply exclusively to government actors.

Good Questions!

Had the change in *American Hospital Association* been directed exclusively to practices within the agency, would the decision have been the same? What if an internal procedural change has explicit external consequences? The APA provides an exception for internal rules, *see, e.g.,* Nathan Katz Realty LLC v. NLRB, 251 F.3d 981 (D.C. Cir. 2001), but of course does not elaborate on the external effect problem.

This question is discussed in the context of international law in Laura A. Dickenson's *Government for Hire: Privatization Foreign Affairs, and the Problem Of Accountability Under International Law*, 47 W<small>M</small>. & M<small>ARY</small> L. R<small>EV</small>. 135 (2005).

HOCTOR V. UNITED STATES DEPARTMENT OF AGRICULTURE

82 F.3d 165 (7th Cir. 1996)

[J<small>UDGE</small> P<small>OSNER</small>] There are no formalities attendant upon the promulgation of an interpretive rule, but this is tolerable because such a rule is "only" an interpretation. Every governmental agency that enforces a less than crystalline statute must interpret the statute, and it does the public a favor if it announces the interpretation in advance of enforcement . . . . It would be no favor to the public to discourage the announcement of agencies' interpretations by burdening the interpretive process with cumbersome formalities.

The question presented [here] is whether a rule for the secure containment of animals, a rule promulgated by the Department [of Agriculture] under the Animal Welfare Act without compliance with the notice and comment requirements of the Administrative Procedure Act, is nevertheless valid because it is merely an interpretive rule. . . . The Act requires the licensing of dealers . . . and authorizes the Department to impose sanctions on licensees who violate either the statute itself or the rules promulgated by the Department under the authority of 7 U.S.C. § 2151 . . . . The Department has employed the notice and comment procedure to promulgate a regulation, the validity of which is not questioned, that is entitled "structural strength" and that provides that "the facility [housing the animals] must be constructed of such material and of such strength as appropriate for the animals involved. . . ."

Enter the petitioner, Patrick Hoctor, who in 1982 began dealing in exotic animals on his farm outside of Terre Haute. In a 25-acre compound he raised a variety of animals including "Big Cats" – a typical inventory included three lions, two tigers, seven ligers (a liger is a cross between a male lion and a female tiger, and is thus to be distinguished from a tigon), six cougars, and two snow leopards. . . . At the suggestion of a veterinarian employed by the Agriculture Department . . . Hoctor made the perimeter [surrounding the compound] fence six feet high.

The following year the Department issued an internal memorandum addressed to its force of inspectors in which it said that all "dangerous animals," defined as including . . . lions, tigers, and leopards, must be inside a perimeter fence at least eight feet high. This provision is the so-called interpretive rule [at issue]. On several occasions beginning in 1990, Hoctor was cited [and sanctioned for failure to have] an eight-foot perimeter fence. . . . He is a small dealer and it would cost him many thousands of dollars to replace his six-foot-high fence with an eight-foot-high fence. Indeed, we were told at argument that pending the resolution of his dispute over the fence he has discontinued dealing in Big Cats. . . .

We may assume, though we need not decide, that the Department of Agriculture has the statutory authority to require dealers in dangerous animals to enclose their compounds with eight-foot-high fences. . . . Since animals sometimes break out or are carelessly let out of their pens, a fail-safe device seems highly appropriate, to say the least. Two lions once got out of their pen on Hoctor's property, and he had to shoot them. . . . [W]e may also assume that the containment of dangerous animals is a proper concern of the Department in the enforcement of the Animal Welfare Act, even though the purpose of the Act is to protect animals from people rather than people from animals. . . . The internal memorandum also justifies the eight-foot requirement as a means of protecting the animals from animal predators, though one might have supposed the Big Cats able to protect themselves against the native Indiana fauna. . . .

The only ground on which the Department defends sanctioning Hoctor for not having a high enough fence is that requiring an eight-foot-high perimeter fence for dangerous animals is an interpretation of the Department's own structural-strength regulation, and "provided an agency's interpretation of its own regulations does not violate the Constitution or a federal statute, it must be given 'controlling weight unless it is plainly erroneous or inconsistent with the regulation.'" [*Auer v. Robbins*]. The regulation appears only to require that pens and other animal housing be sturdy enough in design and construction, . . . not that any enclosure, whether a pen or a perimeter fence, be high enough to prevent the animals from escaping by jumping *over* the enclosure. . . .

"Interpretation" in the narrow sense is the ascertainment of meaning. It is obvious that eight feet is not part of the meaning of secure containment. But "interpretation" is often used in a much broader sense. A process of "interpretation" has transformed the Constitution into a body of law undreamt of by the framers. To skeptics the *Miranda* rule is as remote from the text of the Fifth Amendment as the eight-foot rule is from the text of 9 C.F.R. § 3.125(a). But our task in this case is not to plumb the mysteries of legal theory; it is merely to give effect to a distinction that the Administrative Procedure Act makes, and we can do this by referring to the purpose of the distinction. The purpose is to separate the cases in which notice and comment rulemaking is required from the cases in which it is not required. As we noted at the outset, unless a statute or regulation is of crystalline transparency, the agency enforcing it cannot avoid interpreting it, and the agency would be stymied in its enforcement duties if every time it brought a case on a new theory it had to pause for a bout, possibly lasting several years, of notice and comment rulemaking. . . . [However, when] agencies base rules on arbitrary choices they are legislating, and so these rules are legislative or substantive and require notice and comment rulemaking, a procedure that is analogous to the procedure employed by legislatures in making statutes. . . .

The common sense of requiring notice and comment rulemaking for legislative rules is well illustrated by the facts of this case. There is no . . . reasoning by which the Department of Agriculture could have excogitated the eight-foot rule from the structural-strength regulation. The rule is arbitrary in the sense that it could well be different without significant impairment of any regulatory purpose. But this does not make the rule a matter of indifference to the people subject to it. There are thousands of animal dealers, and some unknown fraction of these face the prospect of having to tear down their existing fences and build new, higher ones at great cost. The concerns of these dealers are legitimate and since, as we are stressing, the rule could well be otherwise, the agency was obliged to listen to them before settling on a final rule and to provide some justification for that rule . . . . Notice and comment is the procedure by which the persons affected by legislative rules are enabled to communicate their concerns in a comprehensive and systematic fashion to the legislating agency. The Department's lawyer speculated that if the notice and comment route had been followed in this case the Department would have received thousands of comments. The greater the public interest in a rule, the greater reason to allow the public to participate in its formation.

We are not saying that an interpretive rule can never have a numerical component. There is merely an empirical relation between interpretation and generality on the one hand, and legislation and specificity on the other. Especially in scientific and other technical areas, where quantitative criteria are common, a rule that translates a general norm into a number may be justifiable as interpretation. . . . Even in a nontechnical area the use of a number as a rule of thumb to guide the application of a general norm will often be legitimately interpretive. Had the Department of Agriculture said in the internal memorandum that it could not imagine a case in which a perimeter fence for dangerous animals that was lower than eight feet would provide secure containment, and would therefore presume, subject to rebuttal, that a lower fence was insecure, it would have been on stronger ground. For it would have been tying the rule to the animating standard, that of secure containment, rather than making it stand free of the standard . . . .

The Department's position might seem further undermined by the fact that it has used the notice and comment procedure to promulgate rules prescribing perimeter fences for dogs and monkeys. 9 C.F.R. §§ 3.6(c)(2)(ii), 3.77(f). Why it proceeded differently for dangerous animals is unexplained. But we attach no weight to the Department's inconsistency, not only because it would be unwise to penalize the Department for having at least partially complied with the requirements of the Administrative Procedure Act, but also because there is nothing in the Act to forbid an agency to use the notice and comment procedure in cases in which it is not *required* to do so. . . . It is for the courts to say whether [an agency rule] is the kind of rule that is valid only if promulgated after notice and comment. It is that kind of rule if, as in the present case, it cannot be derived by interpretation. . . .

Vacated.

————————

Underlying Case Documents

The case referenced:
The Animal Welfare Act
The Structural Strength Regulation

For the original agency decision upholding the citation for the perimeter fence, as well as a number of other violations click HERE.

For more information on the liger click HERE.
For more information on the tigon click HERE.

After the opinion was issued the Department formalized the eight foot requirement.
For the proposed rule click HERE.
For the final rule click HERE.

1. Did the *Hoctor* case boil down to a technicality – does the agency behavior strike you as a major transgression? A clear rule required a "sturdy fence" – and when the agency concluded that eight feet was better than six, were they really out of line from your perspective? Was this truly a new rule or merely an interpretation of the existing standard?

2. There are good arguments for permitting agencies to use processes other than 553(c) rulemaking to both make clear agency-wide the standards to be applied and, on occasion, to advise the public of the standards the agency will follow. Rulemaking is notoriously expensive and time consuming. Furthermore, not everything an agency relies on for enforcement ought to be published.

Police departments may decide to issue speeding tickets only to drivers exceeding the posted speed limit by 10 miles per hour or more, but no one would expect them to announce or publish that information. *See, e.g.,* United States v. Ewig Bros., 502 F.2d 715, 724 (7th Cir. 1974), discussed in Dan L. Burk, The Milk Free Zone: Federal and Local Interests in Regulating RecombinantbST, 22 Colum. J. Envtl. L. 227 (1997). Professor Burk's discussion on RecombinantbST (rbST) involves interim guidelines which, he notes,

Food for Thought

For the most part, courts do not label agency action arbitrary without good reason. Whether the *Hoctor* facts compel this result is a legitimate question. Legislative rules can require OMB review, notice, comment, publication, possible congressional and judicial review – while guidance documents, interim guidelines, and other standards that are internal or published in the Federal Register (after they have been adopted), as a general rule, do not. Should they?

> offer mixed signals as to their status. Much like a proposed rule, the rbST guidelines were published in the Federal Register with a stated time period for written comments. At the same time, the extensive disclaimer included in the guidelines, stating that the agency does not intend the FDA or anyone else to be bound by the guidelines, further muddies their status. . . . [Thus, the] effect of the rbST guidelines is therefore difficult to ascertain. . . . [One] might argue that the publication of the interim guidelines simply constitutes fair notice of an internal agency standard as to the circumstances under which it may choose to initiate an enforcement proceeding, rather than an interpretation of exactly what the FDCA will or will not allow. . . .

Did the agency in *Hoctor* have the right – and the responsibility – to both clarify standards and enforce those standards? If so, why did the court find their action arbitrary?

3. There is a place for "publication rules" in agency practice. The promise of the APA did not include a guarantee that every standard the government uses would be produced through the notice and comment process. Interpretive rules, policy statements, and guidance documents are not "outlaw" administrative issuances. If anything, they should be encouraged – so long as they are published as a way of resolving regulatory policies that are murky at best. Should the trade off be that such issuances are presumptively final and ripe and thus subject to judicial review? *See* Peter L. Strauss, Publication Rules in the Rulemaking Spectrum: Assuring Proper Respect for an Essential Element, 53 Admin. L. Rev. 803, 808 (2001); William Funk, When IS a "Rule" a Regulation? Marking a Clear Line Between Nonlegislative Rules and Legislative Rules, 54 Admin. L. Rev. 659 (2002); and William Funk, A Primer on Nonlegislative Rules, 53 Admin. L. Rev. 1321, 1324-25 (2001).

4. Cases like *Hoctor* are not that unusual. In Perez v. Ashcroft, 236 F. Supp. 2d 899 (N.D. Ill. 2002), a church music director was denied a visa on the premise that

his training was insufficient under INS standards to qualify as a religious worker. As the court peeled away layer after layer of the government's case, they came to the following realization:

> Nowhere in its memoranda has INS offered any real explanation of how the formal training requirement can be derived from the Regulations. . . . [The government produced] I. R. Mem. 7 assert[ing] that it is not irrational for INS to require that religious worker visa applicants have formal training in their field and remind[ing] this Court that the Act delegates to INS the authority for determining visa eligibility procedures. But that is not what is at issue here. Perez has not disputed that INS authority extends to the establishment of visa eligibility procedures, nor has he contended – at least not for the sake of his challenge to INS procedures – that the formal training requirement is inherently irrational. Instead he contends that the formal training requirement amounts to a substantive rule that was impermissibly created informally – in violation of APA's requirements.

> This Court agrees: Nothing in the Regulations' definition of "religious occupation" suggests a reasonable "interpretation" that includes a formal training requirement. This opinion can assume without deciding that the implementation of a formal training requirement is within the scope of INS authority under the Act – but that in no way exempts INS from following the mandatory formal rulemaking procedures before implementing such a substantive rule. That it failed to do, and its failure is fatal to the principal gravamen of its denial of Perez' application.

> This Court therefore finds INS's denial of Perez' visa application on the ground that he lacks formal training as a music director to be invalid.

VI. A Second Look at Judicial Review

How review occurs for these less formal documents varies from case to case. The following two cases illustrate two different ways courts ask whether a given agency action should be considered a legislative rule, and therefore subject to the notice and comment requirements of 5 U.S.C. § 553.

DISMAS CHARITIES, INC. V. UNITED STATES DEPARTMENT OF JUSTICE, FEDERAL BUREAU OF PRISONS

401 F.3d 666 (6th Cir. 2005)

[JUDGE ROGERS] Dismas Charities, Inc. is a nonprofit corporation that owns and operates eighteen CCCs [community correction centers] in seven states. The majority of Dismas CCCs house only federal inmates. CCCs, such as Dismas, provide an alternative to traditional incarceration and attempt to facilitate the successful transition of prisoners back into society. While in a CCC, offenders must obtain employment, pay fines, restitution, child support, and subsistence, establish a budget, save money, and, if applicable, seek treatment of substance abuse and mental health issues, as well as attend classes in life skills, anger management, and wellness.

The Department of Justice's Bureau of Prisons chooses which inmates are sent to Dismas facilities. Before the change in policy, Dismas received two types of inmates – those on the "front end" of their sentences and those on the "back end." Front end placements usually involve offenders with relatively short sentences who serve their entire sentence at the CCC. Back end designations, by contrast, involve prisoners who have served the majority of their sentences in prison, but are sent to a CCC for a time before their release in order to provide transition of the offender back into society.

18 U.S.C. § 3621(b) grants the BOP [Bureau of Prisons] discretion to designate a prisoner's place of incarceration in "any available penal or correctional facility that meets minimum standards of health and habitability . . . ." . . . . On December 13, 2002, . . . the OLC [Department of Justice's Office of Legal Counsel] changed its interpretation of § 3621(b). . . . [U]nder the new interpretation . . ., front end placements are not authorized and back end offenders are only eligible for confinement in CCCs for the lesser of (i) ten percent of their sentence or (ii) six months – periods specifically authorized by 18 U.S.C. § 3624(c) (2000). The OLC reasoned that, while § 3621(b) gave the BOP the discretion to choose an inmate's place of imprisonment generally, a CCC did not constitute a place of imprisonment for purposes of that section. Instead, the OLC determined that the authority to transfer a prisoner to a CCC came solely from § 3624(c), which limits the time a prisoner may spend in a CCC to "a reasonable part, not to exceed six months, of the last 10 per centum of the term."

Shortly after the 2002 OLC opinion was issued, a memorandum written by Deputy Attorney General Larry Thompson instructed the BOP to transfer all offenders residing in CCCs with more than 150 days remaining on their sentence to a traditional prison facility because the use of CCCs was "unlawful." . . . .

. . . .

On December 20, 2000 the Director of the BOP issued a memorandum to all federal judges stating that the BOP would no longer honor judicial recommendations to place inmates in CCCs for the imprisonment portions of their sentences. Memorandum of BOP Director Kathleen Hawk Sawyer . . . . The memorandum explained briefly:

> This procedure change follows recent guidance from [OLC], finding that the term "community confinement" is not synonymous with "imprisonment." OLC has determined that the Bureau's practice of using CCCs as a substitute for imprisonment contravenes well-established caselaw, and is inconsistent with U.S.S.G. § 5C1.1.

The change in the interpretation of § 3621(b) has had a severe impact on Dismas. . . . [T]he number of front end offenders housed at CCCs operated by Dismas was drastically reduced . . . . The number of back end prisoners was also reduced . . . . In addition, the BOP cancelled the designations of many back end prisoners . . . . All told, the lost revenue amounted to $ 1,214,599. Dismas further argues that the BOP instruction interferes with its ability to help prisoners adjust to life outside prison, contending that offenders need at least 90-120 days in a CCC to adjust to outside life. Under the new policy, only people sentenced to imprisonment for 60 months or more can benefit from six months in a CCC, and many prisoners with sentences of less than 60 months would not be able to stay at a CCC for the necessary 120 days. . . . [Dismas brought suit, alleging that these new interpretations should have gone through the notice and comment process.]

. . . .

The rulemaking requirements of § 553 of the APA do not apply to "interpretative rules." § 553(a). Both the Thompson and Sawyer memoranda, assuming that either may be categorized as a "rule," clearly fall in the category of interpretative rule. The Attorney General's Manual on the Administrative Procedure Act, persuasive authority on the meaning of the APA, describes an interpretive rule as one "issued by an agency to advise the public of the agency's construction of the statutes and rules which it administers." . . . . "For purposes of the APA, substantive rules are rules that create law," while in contrast "interpretive rules merely clarify or explain existing law or regulations . . . ." . . . . The D.C. Circuit . . . in applying the interpretative rule exception, has "generally sought to distinguish cases in which an agency is merely explicating Congress' desires from those cases in which the agency is adding substantive content of its own."

It follows that the Thompson and Sawyer memoranda, assuming that either is a rule otherwise subject to the notice and comment requirements of the APA, are paradigm examples of interpretative rules. The memoranda each state that the statutory interpretation by the OLC will henceforth be implemented. The Thompson memorandum in its operative language relies specifically and directly on the unlawfulness of its previous practice as determined by the OLC. Even more clearly, the Sawyer memorandum does not make any kind of policy analysis or determine what is the better, or more effective, or less burdensome, rule. Instead, the BOP changed its procedure because the "OLC . . . determined that the practice of using CCCs as a substitute for imprisonment contravenes well-established case-law, and is inconsistent with U.S.S.G. § 5C1.1." . . . . Clearly, the memo simply determines what the law is, and does so by reliance upon a legal interpretation by the OLC. . . .

. . . We hold only that, under the interpretative rule exception, a rule that embodies a pure legal determination of what the applicable law already is does not require notice and comment under APA § 553(b). Because Dismas's claim based on § 553 of the APA fails as a matter of law, the district court properly dismissed that aspect of Dismas's case . . . .

———————

Underlying Case Documents

The case referenced:

18 U.S.C. § 3621(b)

The Thompson memo

The Sawyer memo

The policy in *Dismas* had been codified by the time the case was decided. For the Federal Register announcement of the final rule click HERE. For the newly codified rule click HERE.

1. This case holds, *inter alia*, that if an agency action is "a pure legal determination," the notice and comment requirements of 553(c) do not apply. Two obvious questions follow: (1) Does the "pure legal determination" standard make sense? And (2) Does this mean substantive and legislative rules cannot be "pure legal determinations"?

2. *Dismas* underscores two challenges in modern administrative law: (1) The APA exception to the notice and comment requirement for interpretive rules is expansive and likely to continue to grow in the future; and, (2) When public functions are privatized, procedural fairness entitlements that derive from the APA may well be subordinated to contracts.

3. Privatization.

a. Notwithstanding the directives in OMB CIRCULAR A-76 (Office of Mgmt. & Budget, Executive Office of the President, OMB Cir. No. A-76, Performance of Commercial Activities (2003), 68 Fed. Reg. 32,134 (May 29, 2003), available at http://www.whitehouse.gov/omb/circulars/a076/a76_rev2003.pdf), mandating that those activities and functions that are inherently governmental are undertaken by governmental entities, many "public activities" have been privatized. Private entities operate pursuant to government contracts – not necessarily to the APA. The failure to go through the notice and comment process in *Dismas*, however, was not the choice of the privatized party but of the governmental entity. Nonetheless, there is a sense that somehow things are different – the standard in issue may feel more like a contract amendment than a rule – and contract amendments are unlikely to be vetted through notice and comment.

b. In *American Hospital Association v. Bowen*, 834 F.2d 1037, 1053 (D.C. Cir. 1987), the court held, *inter alia*, that developing requests for proposals (RFPs) in privatized contracts do not require notice and comment process. As Professor Laura A. Dickenson points out in *Government for Hire: Privatizing Foreign Affairs and the Problem of Accountability Under International Law*, 47 Wm. & Mary L. Rev. 135, 168-69 (2005), basic protections provided by the legal system are by no means guaranteed in such a model. "Indeed, FOIA, FACA, inspector general oversight, whistle-blower protection statutes, civil service conflict of interest rules, notice and comment rulemaking, judicial review of agency decisionmaking under the APA, and even the First Amendment can be seen to embody concerns about transparency of governmental processes." For a discussion of notice and comment in a privatized context, see Alfred C. Aman, The Democracy Deficit: Taming Globalization Through Law Reform 150 et seq. (2004).

c. Private entities undertaking commercial functions, compelled to compete by conventional market pressures, will provide certain services efficiently. When those private entities engage in policy making, however, there is a potent and dangerous disconnect. A passing glance at Italian corporatism in the 1930s may be all that is required to be concerned about the risks of public/private partnerships. Moreover, there are grave risks when the government yields its law making function. Discussing the decision to allow ICANN to have massive power over Internet functions, Professor A. Michael Froomkin noted that the government yielded to the private sector

> some of the most important decisions relating to the near-term future of the Internet via research contracts rather than [to] agency adjudication or rulemaking, thus evading notice, comment, due process, and judicial review. . . . Although the ICANN-DoC contracts speak of cooperation and research, some of the most significant outputs from ICANN are government regulation in all but name. It is time to call them what they are." A. Michael Froomkin, *Thirteenth Annual Administrative Law Issue, Governance and the Internet: Wrong Turn in Cyberspace: Using ICANN to Route Around the APA and the Constitution*, 50 Duke L.J. 17 (2000).

4. Rationalizing the Use of Interpretive Rules.

a. *Dismas* centers on two memoranda, the Thompson memorandum and the Sawyer memorandum. The court finds these documents do not set policy but rather evaluate back-end or half-way houses as a substitute for imprisonment. This judgment, the court finds, is simply a legal conclusion based on the agency's perception of what would contravene caselaw and the sentencing guidelines. This, the court finds, is doing no more than "determining what the law is" – and that, it holds, is not up for public discussion.

b. An announcement that clarifies or explains a legal standard is perfect territory
for an interpretative rule. Was that the case here? Do you think this was a choice
driven by case analysis, not by policy considerations? In *Koenemann v. Marberry,*
2006 WL 1581431 (D. Mich. 2006), the court relies on *Dismas* for the proposition
that "[t]he interpretative rule exception reflects the idea that public input will not
help an agency make the legal determination of what the law already is." Was *Dis-*
mas an application of law to a complex and policy laden problem or was it solely
a matter of clarifying existing legal standards? Similarly, in *Holloway v. Marberry,*
2007 WL 2178314 (D. Mich. 2007), the court relied on this text in *Dismas:* "The
. . . primary purpose of Congress in imposing notice and comment requirements
for rulemaking [is] to get public input so as to get the wisest rules. That purpose
is not served when the agency's inquiry or determination is not 'what is the wisest
rule,' but 'what is the rule.'"

5. In *Beverly Health & Rehab. Servs. v. Thompson, Civil Action, 223 F. Supp. 2d 73*
(D.D.C. 2002), nursing home operators challenged a new

> survey protocol used by state and federal surveyors to monitor compliance with
> substantive statutory and regulatory requirements for nursing home participation in
> the Medicare and Medicaid programs.
>
> To decide this issue, the Court must determine whether the agency's guidelines set
> forth in Appendices P and Q are substantive or procedural. Substantive rules not
> promulgated in accordance with notice and comment rulemaking proceedings are
> invalid and will not be enforced. However, notice and comment rulemaking is not
> required under the APA for "interpretative rules, general statements of policy, or rules
> of agency organization, procedure, or practice."
>
> While "the distinction between a substantive rule and an interpretive rule can be less
> than clear-cut," the Court must nonetheless determine "whether the agency action . . .
> encodes a substantive value judgment or puts a stamp of approval or disapproval on
> a given type of behavior." *American Hosp. Ass'n*. Substantive rules create law, whereas
> interpretive rules are "statements as to what an administrative officer thinks the
> statute or regulation means. . . ."
>
> Based on the Court's review of the guidelines located at Appendices P and Q to the
> SOM, it must conclude that they do not contain substantive rules that may only be
> adopted through notice and comment rulemaking. They are procedural in nature, for
> Appendices P and Q merely "borrow[] the substantive standards of the statute and
> seek[] to channel agency enforcement resources toward ferreting out violations of the
> statute." *American Hosp. Ass'n*.
>
> In reaching this conclusion, the Court is persuaded [that the] survey protocol
> constituted procedural rules that were not subject to notice and comment
> rulemaking. . . . [T]here is no evidence that the rules do "more than 'announce[] how
> the agency believes the [Medicare] statute should be enforced. . . .'"
>
> Here, the regulations at issue involve "monitoring the quality [of care] provided . . .

and the protocol imposes "no new burdens on [nursing homes]." The only additional burdens imposed by the survey protocol are that it is "more likely that [plaintiffs'] transgressions from Medicare's standards will not go unnoticed" and "[the protocol] imposes on [nursing homes] the incidental inconveniences of complying with an enforcement scheme." Thus, notice and comment rulemaking is not necessary. . . .

Does this seem like double-speak to you? In light of the above, is substantive rulemaking about something other than making rules?

CENTER FOR AUTO SAFETY V. NATIONAL HIGHWAY TRAFFIC SAFETY ADMINISTRATION

452 F.3d 798 (D.C. Cir. 2006)

[JUDGE EDWARDS] The National Highway Traffic Safety Administration Authorization Act of 1991 ("Safety Act" or "Act") allows automakers to initiate voluntary "recalls" when a motor vehicle or its equipment contains a safety-related defect or does not comply with applicable safety standards. Generally, vehicle owners who are afforded recall notification of a safety-related defect or noncompliance are entitled to a free remedy from the manufacturer. The National Highway Traffic Safety Administration ("NHTSA") administers the Safety Act and monitors manufacturer-initiated recalls.

Beginning sometime in the mid-1980s, automakers adopted a practice of initiating "regional recalls." Under this practice, when a safety-related defect was caused by exposure to atypical climatic conditions, automakers gave notification and free remedies only in regions experiencing the climatic conditions that caused the identified safety-related defect. For example, if vehicle components corroded when exposed to salt, manufacturers limited their recalls to owners in states that used the most salt on their roads. In 1997, . . . NHTSA's Associate Administrator for Safety Assurance sent letters to some major automakers and a trade association, acknowledging that regional recalls had been authorized in the past, but stating that the agency now had "concerns" about the practice. In 1998, . . . other NHTSA officials sent letters to various motor vehicle manufacturers outlining NHTSA's "policy guidelines" for "regional recalls."

On March 10, 2004, Center for Auto Safety ("CAS") and Public Citizen, Inc. filed a lawsuit in District Court [claiming] that the 1998 policy guidelines constitute a "de facto legislative rule" that violates the Safety Act, and that, even if regional recalls are permissible in some circumstances, the policy statement violates the Administrative Procedure Act ("APA") "because it is arbitrary and capricious and was promulgated without public notice and comment." The District Court dismissed the complaint for failure to state a claim. . . .

In order to sustain their position, appellants must show that the 1998 policy guidelines either (1) reflect "final agency action," 5 U.S.C. § 704, or (2) constitute a de facto rule or binding norm that could not properly be promulgated absent the notice and comment rulemaking required by § 553 of the APA. . . . As the case law reveals, it is not always easy to distinguish between those "general statements of policy" that are unreviewable and agency "rules" that establish binding norms or agency actions that occasion legal consequences that are subject to review. Nevertheless, the distinction between "general statements of policy" and "rules" is critical. If the 1998 policy guidelines constitute a de facto rule, as appellants claim, then they would clearly meet [*Bennett v. Spear*'s] test for final agency action and § 553 of the APA would require the agency to afford notice of a proposed rulemaking and an opportunity for public comment prior to promulgating the rule. If the guidelines are no more than "general statements of policy," as NHTSA would have it, then they would neither determine rights or obligations nor occasion legal consequences and, thus, would be exempt from the APA's notice and comment requirement. . . .

On the record here . . . NHTSA's 1998 policy guidelines do not reflect final agency action and they do not constitute binding rules. . . . [U]nder *Bennett*, the 1998 policy guidelines cannot be viewed as "final agency action" under § 704 of the APA unless they "mark the consummation of the agency's decisionmaking process" *and* either determine "rights or obligations" or result in "legal consequences." *Bennett*. It is possible to view the guidelines as meeting the first part of the *Bennett* test, but not the second. The guidelines are nothing more than general policy statements with no legal force. They do not determine any rights or obligations, nor do they have any legal consequences. Therefore, the guidelines cannot be taken as "final agency action," nor can they otherwise be seen to constitute a binding legal norm.

There is no doubt that the guidelines reflect NHTSA's views on the legality of regional recalls. But this does not change the character of the guidelines from a policy statement to a binding rule. Indeed, the case law is clear that we lack authority to review claims under the APA "where 'an agency merely expresses its view of what the law requires of a party, even if that view is adverse to the party.'" . . . . NHTSA's position here is nothing more than a privileged viewpoint in the legal debate. The guidelines do not purport to carry the force of law. They have not been published in the Code of Federal Regulations. They do not define "rights or obligations." They are labeled "policy guidelines," not rules. And they read as *guidelines*, not binding regulations. For example, the generic letter states: "NHTSA has concluded that, *in general*, it is not appropriate for a manufacturer to limit the scope of a recall to a particular geographical area where the consequences of the defect can occur after a short-term exposure to a meteorological condition." (emphasis added). . . .

The 1998 policy guidelines certainly do not, as appellants contend, "read like a ukase." NHTSA has not commanded, required, ordered, or dictated. And there is nothing in the record to indicate that officials in NHTSA's Office of Defects Investigation are bound to apply the guidelines in an enforcement action. The agency remains free to exercise discretion in assessing proposed recalls and in enforcing the Act. There is also nothing to indicate that automakers can rely on the guidelines as "a norm or safe harbor by which to shape their actions," which might suggest that the guidelines are binding as a practical matter. And it does not matter that agency officials have *encouraged* automakers to comply with the guidelines. . . . In sum, the 1998 policy guidelines do not, as appellants claim, establish new rights and obligations for automakers. . . .

Take Note

A *ukase* is defined as: "1. Tsar's order: in pre-Revolutionary Russia, an order from the tsar that had the force of law; 2. Ruling: any order or ruling, especially one handed down by a self-styled expert or guru." ENCARTA WORLD ENGLISH DICTIONARY (2008) http://uk.encarta.msn.com/dictionary_1861740156/ukase.html, (last visited July 22, 2008.)

Appellants' final argument is that even if the guidelines do not determine rights and obligations, they had legal consequences. Appellants contend that the agency has altered the legal regime with consequence both for automakers – who now allegedly conform their practices to the agency's standards – and for automobile consumers – who allegedly own "defective" vehicles that do not qualify for recall remedies under the Act. . . . The flaw in appellants' argument is that the "consequences" to which they allude are practical, not legal. It may be that, to the extent that they actually prescribe anything, the agency's guidelines have been voluntarily followed by automakers and have become a de facto industry standard for how to conduct regional recalls. But this does not demonstrate that the guidelines have had *legal consequences*. The Supreme Court's decision in *Bennett* makes it quite clear that agency action is only final if it determines "rights or obligations" or occasions "*legal* consequences." (emphasis added) . . . .

As we explained only last term, "if the practical effect of the agency action is not a certain change in the legal obligations of a party, the action is non-final for the purposes of judicial review" under the APA. Here, the only consequences suggested by appellants are the automakers' voluntary compliance with NHTSA's guidelines on regional recalls, arguably in order to avoid any risk of the agency initiating a hearing . . . or bringing an enforcement action . . . . But de facto compliance is not enough to establish that the guidelines have had *legal* consequences. And there is nothing in the record here to indicate that NHTSA has "force[d the industry] to change its behavior, such that" NHTSA's position on regional recalls "may be deemed final agency action." . . . .

Appellants have no cause of action under the APA, because the contested 1998 policy guidelines do not reflect final agency action, and they do not otherwise constitute binding rules. We therefore affirm the District Court's judgment dismissing appellants' action.

Underlying Case Documents

The case referenced:
<u>One of the 1997 Letters</u>
<u>The 1998 Letter</u>

For information on what a ukase is click <u>HERE</u>.

---

1. Finality of Guidelines. The guidelines in *Center for Auto Safety* were deemed non-final and thus not subject to judicial review. How much more "final" did they need to be? The various tests that have been used to establish finality seem, at times, a bit of overkill. Shouldn't final mean, well, the end of agency action?

In <u>Southern Utah Wilderness Alliance v. Norton, 301 F.3d 1217 (10th Cir. 2002)</u>, a case later reversed by the Supreme Court in <u>Norton v. Southern Utah Wilderness Alliance, 542 U.S. 55 (2004)</u>, there was an attempt to give meaning to finality:

Good Questions!

In the continuous deconstruction of the term final, any semblance of the plain meaning of the term has been lost. Is something final only when it is legally binding? Practically binding? The last conceivable act an agency could undertake? Be honest – how many ways are there to interpret "consummation of agency action" that make sense?

> On appeal, the BLM also asserts that § 706(1) only applies to "final, legally binding actions that have been unlawfully withheld or unreasonably delayed." Apparently, the BLM believes that a court may only compel agency action under § 706(1) if the unlawfully withheld action would itself be considered a "final" action under § 704 of the APA, which limits judicial review to final agency actions. According to the BLM, § 706(1) is not available for "day-to-day management actions" . . . . In essence, the BLM seems to argue that, because it could prevent impairment by ORV [off-road vehicle] use through steps that might not themselves be considered a final agency action, federal courts lack subject matter jurisdiction under § 706(1) over these "day-to-day" decisions.

We find the BLM's finality argument unpersuasive, for it seems to read finality in an inappropriately cramped manner. Contrary to the implications of the BLM's argument, the APA treats an agency's inaction as "action." 5 U.S.C. § 551(13) (defining "agency action" as including a "failure to act"). Where, as here, an agency has an obligation to carry out a mandatory, nondiscretionary duty and either fails to meet an established statutory deadline for carrying out that duty or unreasonably delays in carrying out the action, the failure to carry out that duty is itself "final agency action." Once the agency's delay in carrying out the action becomes unreasonable, or once the established statutory deadline for carrying out that duty lapses, the agency's inaction under these circumstances is, in essence, the same as if the agency had issued a final order or rule declaring that it would not complete its legally required duty. . . . Consequently, contrary to the BLM's argument, the Bureau's alleged failure to comply with the FLPMA's nonimpairment mandate can be considered a final action under § 704 that is subject to compulsion under § 706(1). Therefore, the failure of an agency to carry out its mandatory, nondiscretionary duty either by an established deadline or within a reasonable time period may be considered final agency action. . . .

Take a look at JUSTICE SCALIA's decision, reversing the above case. Does it contravene the idea of finality articulated by the Tenth Circuit?

2. Are guidelines mandates? Do they establish criteria that command adherence? Assuming they do, what is the best argument that guidelines issued by agencies are presumptively final? *See* Peter L. Strauss, *Publication Rules in the Rulemaking Spectrum: Assuring Proper Respect for an Essential Element*, 53 ADMIN. L. REV. 803, 808 (2001).

3. Defining finality and then applying that definition can be difficult. In *Dunn-McCampbell Royalty Interest, Inc. v. Nat'l Park Serv.*, 2007 WL 1032346 (S.D. Tex. 2007), the court grappled with the finality (or lack thereof) of a guideline known as a Sensitive

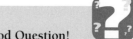

Good Question!

Should an agency be able to issue a guideline without complying with notice and comment process since it is interpretive in nature – and also avoid judicial review by asserting that guidelines are not final agency action? If so, what is the check on arbitrary agency action?

Resource Area Plan. The court relied in part on the *Center for Auto Safety* definition of finality for guidelines. The court examined whether the parties could meet the test in *Center for Auto Safety*, i.e., whether the guideline had "alter[ed] the legal character" of the rights and entitlements of the parties. The key, the court noted, was whether the plan had a "legal effect." Unfortunately, this test did not seem particularly helpful in resolving the apparently overwhelming task of defining the term "final." Even a comparison to the question of the finality of Environmental Impact Statements did not suggest how to resolve this challenge, the court noted that "some circuit courts have held that a final EIS constitutes final agency action – and some have not." In the end, while the court found the Plan final, marking "the consummation" of the agency process, it is a bit difficult to see what led them to that conclusion.

4. Regional Recalls. The *Center for Auto Safety* case involves the rather strained notion that automobile safety is a regional matter. Since cars are designed to be driven – as well as owned and operated – throughout the United States and beyond, what is the logic behind a regional recall? For a critique from a consumer perspective, take a look at Joe Benton, *Federal Court Upholds Regional Auto Recalls*, CONSUMERAFFAIRS.COM, June 26, 2006, http://www.consumeraffairs.com/news04/2006/06/nhtsa_regional_recalls.html (last visited May 26, 2008).

5. *Crowley's Yacht Yard, Inc. v. Pena,* 886 F. Supp. 98 (D.D.C. 1995):

> This case [concerns] the validity of a regulation restricting the movement of recreational vessels through the drawbridges crossing the Chicago River. . . . [T]he regulation previously in effect . . . provided that recreational vessels would be granted passage at virtually all times except for rush hours. At issue in the present case is a "temporary" rule . . . . The rule limits drawbridge openings for recreational vessels to: (1) Tuesdays and Thursdays from 10:30 a.m. to 1:30 p.m. and 6:30 p.m. to 11:30 p.m.; and (2) Saturdays and Sundays from 7:00 a.m. to 7:00 p.m. . . . The Coast Guard, a division of the Department of Transportation, issues temporary rules under the authority of 33 C.F.R. § 117.43 (1993), which provides: "In order to evaluate suggested changes . . . the District Commander may authorize temporary deviations . . . not to exceed 90 days. . . ."

> The Coast Guard, by publishing the notice of the proposed temporary rule in the Federal Register and accepting and considering comments thereon, satisfied the notice and comment requirements of § 553. The Court rejects plaintiff's characterization of the final temporary rule as a "substantial departure" from the proposed temporary rule which failed to provide adequate notice of the weekday restrictions to affected parties. . . . [S]ections of the notice . . . are clear that weekday daytime restrictions beyond the rush hour periods were foreseeable variations of the proposed rule that the Coast Guard might choose to implement. *See Chocolate Mfrs. Ass'n* . . . .

> Nonetheless, the temporary rule must be vacated [as] "arbitrary and capricious" . . . . For reasons the Court does not understand, the Coast Guard has chosen not to file the administrative record, instead filing [three] affidavits . . . . The APA, however, requires that judicial review be based on the full administrative record that was before the agency at the time the decision was made. Because the Coast Guard has declined to submit the administrative record in support of its rule, the Court concludes that the temporary rule must be vacated as arbitrary and capricious. . . .

6. *CropLife America v. Environmental Protection Agency,* 329 F.3d 876 (D.C. Cir. 2003):

> On December 14, 2001, EPA announced a broad moratorium on the use of third-party human test data [when approving a pesticide]. EPA publicly released a letter to the [National Academy of Sciences] in which the agency sought the Academy's recommendations regarding the ethical and scientific acceptability of third-party human pesticide tests. In a Press Release accompanying the letter's release, the agency

issued the following directive covering third-party human studies:

> During the Academy's consideration of the issues and until a policy is in place, the Agency will not consider or rely on any such human studies in its regulatory decision making . . . .

Petitioners now challenge this directive. . . . [The] clear and unequivocal language [in the Press Release], which reflects an obvious change in established agency practice, creates a "binding norm" that is "finally determinative of the issues or rights to which it is addressed." EPA's stated rule is binding on petitioners, who are now barred from relying on third-party human studies (even in cases where such studies formerly were approved), and is binding on the agency because EPA has made it clear that it simply "will not consider" human studies. . . .

EPA . . . also argue[s] that the directive in the Press Release is nothing more than a "policy statement" . . . . In the instant case, there is little doubt that the directive in the December 14 Press Release "binds private parties [or] the agency itself with the 'force of law,'" and thus constitutes a regulation rather than a policy statement. The directive clearly establishes a substantive rule declaring that third-party human studies are now deemed immaterial in EPA regulatory decisionmaking under FFDCA and FIFRA. . . .

Because the new rule effects a dramatic change in the agency's established regulatory regime, EPA was required to follow notice and comment procedures . . . . This was not done. Therefore, we vacate EPA's rule . . . .

———————

In *Gonzales v. Oregon*, below, an interpretive rule is reviewed in the emotionally charged area of physician assisted suicide. As you read the case, see if you find any flaws with the process by which the Rule was promulgated.

GONZALES V. OREGON

546 U.S. 243 (2006)

[JUSTICE KENNEDY] The question before us is whether the Controlled Substances Act allows the United States Attorney General to prohibit doctors from prescribing regulated drugs for use in physician-assisted suicide, notwithstanding a state law permitting the procedure. . . .

In 1994, Oregon became the first State to legalize assisted suicide when voters approved a ballot measure enacting the Oregon Death With Dignity Act (ODWDA). ODWDA . . . exempts from civil or criminal liability state-licensed physicians who, in compliance with the specific safeguards in ODWDA, dispense or prescribe a lethal dose of drugs upon the request of a terminally ill patient. The drugs Oregon physicians [can prescribe] are regulated under . . . the Controlled Substances Act (CSA or Act). The CSA allows these particular drugs to be available only by a written prescription from a registered physician. In the ordinary course the same drugs are prescribed in smaller doses for pain alleviation.

A November 9, 2001 Interpretive Rule issued by the Attorney General . . . determine[d] that using controlled substances to assist suicide is not a legitimate medical practice and that dispensing or prescribing them for this purpose is unlawful under the CSA. The Interpretive Rule's validity under the CSA is the issue before us.

I.

A.

We turn first to the text and structure of the CSA. . . . The CSA creates a comprehensive, closed regulatory regime criminalizing the unauthorized manufacture, distribution, dispensing, and possession of substances classified in any of the Act's five schedules. . . . Congress classified a host of substances when it enacted the CSA, but the statute permits the Attorney General to add, remove, or reschedule substances. He may do so, however, only after making particular findings, and on scientific and medical matters he is required to accept the findings of the Secretary of Health and Human Services (Secretary). These proceedings must be on the record after an opportunity for comment.

The present dispute involves controlled substances listed in Schedule II, substances generally available only pursuant to a written, nonrefillable prescription by a physician. . . . The CSA explicitly contemplates a role for the States in regulating controlled substances, as evidenced by its pre-emption provision.

> No provision of this subchapter shall be construed as indicating an intent on the part of the Congress to occupy the field in which that provision operates . . . to the exclusion of any State law on the same subject matter which would otherwise be within the authority of the State, unless there is a positive conflict between [the two].

B.

. . . For Oregon residents to be eligible to request a prescription under ODW-DA, they must receive a diagnosis from their attending physician that they have an incurable and irreversible disease that, within reasonable medical judgment, will cause death within six months. Attending physicians must also determine whether a patient has made a voluntary request, ensure a patient's choice is informed, and refer patients to counseling if they might be suffering from a psychological disorder or depression causing impaired judgment. A second "consulting" physician must examine the patient and the medical record and confirm the attending physician's conclusions. . . . In 2004, 37 patients ended their lives by ingesting a lethal dose of medication prescribed under ODWDA.

C.

In 1997, Members of Congress concerned about ODWDA invited the DEA to prosecute or revoke the CSA registration of Oregon physicians who assist suicide. They contended that hastening a patient's death is not legitimate medical practice, so prescribing controlled substances for that purpose violates the CSA. . . . [A bill was proposed to empower the Attorney General to prosecute] but it failed to pass.

In 2001, John Ashcroft was appointed Attorney General. . . . [As a senator] Mr. Ashcroft had supported efforts to curtail assisted suicide. . . . On November 9, 2001, without consulting Oregon or apparently anyone outside his Department, the Attorney General issued an Interpretive Rule [stating]:

> assisting suicide is not a "legitimate medical purpose" . . . and . . . prescribing, dispensing, or administering federally controlled substances to assist suicide violates the Controlled Substances Act. . . .

> . . . .

In response the State of Oregon, joined by a physician, a pharmacist, and some terminally ill patients, all from Oregon, challenged the Interpretive Rule in federal court. The United States District Court for the District of Oregon entered a permanent injunction against the Interpretive Rule's enforcement. A divided panel of the Court of Appeals for the Ninth Circuit . . . held the Interpretive Rule invalid. . . .

Executive actors often must interpret the enactments Congress has charged them with enforcing and implementing. . . . An administrative rule may receive substantial deference if it interprets the issuing agency's own ambiguous regulation. *Auer*. An interpretation of an ambiguous statute may also receive substantial deference. *Chevron*. Deference in accordance with *Chevron*, however, is warranted only "when it appears that Congress delegated authority to the agency generally to make rules carrying the force of law, and that the agency interpretation claiming deference was promulgated in the exercise of that authority." *Mead*. Otherwise, the interpretation is "entitled to respect" only to the extent it has the "power to persuade."

A.

The Government first argues that the Interpretive Rule is an elaboration of one of the Attorney General's own regulations, 21 C.F.R. § 1306.04 (2005), which requires all prescriptions be issued "for a legitimate medical purpose by an individual practitioner acting in the usual course of his professional practice."

As such, the Government says, the Interpretive Rule is entitled to considerable deference in accordance with *Auer*.

In our view *Auer* and the standard of deference it accords to an agency are inapplicable here. *Auer* involved a disputed interpretation of the Fair Labor Standards Act of 1938 as applied to a class of law enforcement officers. Under regulations promulgated by the Secretary of Labor, an exemption from overtime pay depended, in part, on whether the employees met the "salary basis" test. In this Court the Secretary of Labor filed an amicus brief explaining why, in his view, the regulations gave exempt status to the officers. We gave weight to that interpretation, holding that because the applicable test was "a creature of the Secretary's own regulations, his interpretation of it is, under our jurisprudence, controlling unless plainly erroneous or inconsistent with the regulation."

In *Auer*, the underlying regulations gave specificity to a statutory scheme the Secretary of Labor was charged with enforcing . . . . Here, on the other hand, the underlying regulation does little more than restate the terms of the statute itself. . . . The Government does not suggest that its interpretation turns on any difference between the statutory and regulatory language. . . . The regulation uses the terms "legitimate medical purpose" and "the course of professional practice," but this just repeats two statutory phrases and attempts to summarize the others. . . . Simply put, the existence of a parroting regulation does not change the fact that the question here is not the meaning of the regulation but the meaning of the statute. An agency does not acquire special authority to interpret its own words when, instead of using its expertise and experience to formulate a regulation, it has elected merely to paraphrase the statutory language.

Furthermore, as explained below, if there is statutory authority to issue the Interpretive Rule it comes from the 1984 amendments to the CSA that gave the Attorney General authority to register and deregister physicians based on the public interest. The regulation was enacted before those amendments . . . . That the current interpretation runs counter to the "intent at the time of the regulation's promulgation" is an additional reason why *Auer* deference is unwarranted. Deference under *Auer* being inappropriate, we turn to the question whether the Interpretive Rule, on its own terms, is a permissible interpretation of the CSA.

B.

Just as the Interpretive Rule receives no deference under *Auer*, neither does it receive deference under *Chevron*. . . . All would agree, we should think, that the statutory phrase "legitimate medical purpose" is . . . ambiguous . . . . *Chevron* deference, however, is not accorded merely because the statute is ambiguous and an administrative official is involved. To begin with, the rule must be promulgated pursuant to authority Congress has delegated to the official. The Attorney General has rulemaking power to fulfill his duties under the CSA. The specific respects in which he is authorized to make rules, however, instruct us that he is not authorized to make a rule declaring illegitimate a medical standard for care and treatment of patients that is specifically authorized under state law.

The starting point for this inquiry is, of course, the language of the delegation provision itself. In many cases authority is clear because the statute gives an agency broad power to enforce all provisions of the statute. . . . [However, the] CSA's express limitations on the Attorney General's authority . . . belie any notion that the Attorney General has been granted this implicit authority. . . .

We turn, next, to the registration provisions of the CSA. Before 1984, the Attorney General was required to register any physician who was authorized by his State. The Attorney General could only deregister a physician who falsified his application, was convicted of a felony relating to controlled substances, or had his state license or registration revoked. The CSA was amended in 1984 to allow the Attorney General to deny registration to an applicant "if he determines that the issuance of such registration would be inconsistent with the public interest." . . . . In determining consistency with the public interest, the Attorney General must . . . consider five factors, including: the State's recommendation; compliance with state, federal, and local laws regarding controlled substances; and public health and safety.

The Interpretive Rule cannot be justified under this part of the statute. It does not undertake the five-factor analysis and concerns much more than registration. . . . It is, instead, an interpretation of the substantive federal law requirements (under 21 C.F.R. § 1306.04 (2005)) for a valid prescription. It begins by announcing that assisting suicide is not a "legitimate medical purpose" under § 1306.04, and that dispensing controlled substances to assist a suicide violates the CSA. Violation is a criminal offense, and often a felony, under 21 U.S.C. § 841. The Interpretive Rule thus purports to declare that using controlled substances for physician-assisted suicide is a crime, an authority that goes well beyond the Attorney General's statutory power to register or deregister.

[I]f a physician dispenses a controlled substance after he is deregistered, he violates § 841. The Interpretive Rule works in the opposite direction, however: it declares certain conduct criminal, placing in jeopardy the registration of any physician who engages in that conduct. To the extent the Interpretive Rule concerns registration, it simply states the obvious because one of the five factors the Attorney General must consider in deciding the "public interest" is "compliance with applicable [laws]." 21 U.S.C. § 823(f)(4). . . .

. . . If the Attorney General's argument were correct, his power to deregister necessarily would include the greater power to criminalize . . . . This power to criminalize – unlike his power over registration, which must be exercised only after considering five express statutory factors – would be unrestrained. It would be anomalous for Congress to have so painstakingly described the Attorney General's limited authority to deregister a single physician or schedule a single drug, but to have given him, just by implication, authority to declare an entire class of activity outside "the course of professional practice," and therefore a criminal violation of the CSA. . . .

. . . In interpreting statutes that divide authority . . . ". . . we presume . . . that Congress intended to invest interpretive power in the administrative actor in the best position to develop these attributes." . . . . The Government contends the Attorney General's decision here is a legal, not a medical, one. This generality, however, does not suffice. The Attorney General's Interpretive Rule . . . place[s] extensive reliance on . . . the views of the medical community in concluding that assisted suicide is not a "legitimate medical purpose." This confirms that the authority claimed by the Attorney General is both beyond his expertise and incongruous with the statutory purposes and design.

. . . The importance of the issue of physician-assisted suicide . . . makes the oblique form of the claimed delegation all the more suspect. Under the Government's theory, [the Attorney General] could decide whether . . . a physician who administers any controversial treatment could be deregistered. . . . In light of the foregoing . . . the CSA does not give the Attorney General authority to issue the Interpretive Rule as a statement with the force of law.

If, in the course of exercising his authority, the Attorney General uses his analysis in the Interpretive Rule only for guidance in deciding when to prosecute or deregister, then the question remains whether his substantive interpretation is correct. Since the Interpretive Rule was not promulgated pursuant to the Attorney General's authority . . . it receives deference only in accordance with *Skidmore*. The deference here is tempered by the Attorney General's lack of expertise in this area and the apparent absence of any consultation with anyone outside the Department of Justice who might aid in a reasoned judgment. In any event, under *Skidmore*, we follow an agency's rule only to the extent it is persuasive, and . . . we do not find the Attorney General's opinion persuasive.

III.

As we have noted before, the CSA "repealed most of the earlier antidrug laws in favor of a comprehensive regime to combat the international and interstate traffic in illicit drugs." . . . . Beyond this, however, the statute manifests no intent to regulate the practice of medicine generally. The silence is understandable given the structure and limitations of federalism, which allow the States "great latitude under their police powers to legislate as to the protection of the lives, limbs, health, comfort, and quiet of all persons." The structure and operation of the CSA presume and rely upon a functioning medical profession regulated under the States' police powers. . . . Oregon's regime is an example of the state regulation of medical practice that the CSA presupposes. Rather than simply decriminalizing assisted suicide, ODWDA [places strict limits on it].

. . . .

In the face of the CSA's . . . recognition of state regulation of the medical profession it is difficult to defend the Attorney General's declaration that the statute impliedly criminalizes physician-assisted suicide. . . . The Government's attempt to meet this challenge rests, for the most part, on the CSA's requirement that every Schedule II drug be dispensed pursuant to a "written prescription of a practitioner." 21 U.S.C. § 829(a). A prescription, the Government argues, necessarily implies that the substance is being made available to a patient for a legitimate medical purpose. . . . The Government contends ordinary usage of [the word "medicine"] ineluctably refers to a healing or curative art, which . . . cannot embrace the intentional hastening of a patient's death. It also points to the teachings of Hippocrates . . . and the judgment of the 49 States that have not legalized physician-assisted suicide as further support for the proposition that the practice is not legitimate medicine. . . .

[This] reading of the prescription requirement . . . is persuasive only to the extent one scrutinizes the provision without the illumination of the rest of the statute. Viewed in its context, the prescription requirement is better understood as a provision that ensures patients use controlled substances under the supervision of a doctor so as to prevent addiction and recreational abuse. . . . To read prescriptions for assisted suicide as constituting "drug abuse" under the CSA is discordant with the phrase's consistent use throughout the statute, not to mention its ordinary meaning.

. . . For all these reasons, we conclude the CSA's prescription requirement does not authorize the Attorney General to bar dispensing controlled substances for assisted suicide in the face of a state medical regime permitting such conduct. . . .

[Justice Scalia, dissenting.]

Contrary to the Court's analysis, this case involves not one but *three* independently sufficient grounds for reversing the Ninth Circuit's judgment. First, the Attorney General's interpretation of "legitimate medical purpose" in 21 C.F.R. § 1306.04 (2005) is clearly valid, given the substantial deference we must accord it under *Auer v. Robbins* and his two remaining conclusions follow naturally from this interpretation. Second, even if this interpretation . . . is entitled to lesser deference or no deference at all, it is by far the most natural interpretation of the Regulation – whose validity is not challenged here. This interpretation is thus correct even upon de novo review. Third, even if that interpretation of the Regulation were incorrect, the Attorney General's independent interpretation of the *statutory* phrase "public interest" in 21 U.S.C. §§ 824(a) and 823(f), and his implicit interpretation of the statutory phrase "public health and safety" in § 823(f)(5), are entitled to deference under *Chevron*.

Underlying Case Documents

The case referenced:
The Controlled Substances Act
The Oregon Death With Dignity Act
The 2001 Interpretive Rule
21 C.F.R. § 1306.04

---

1. Parroting and *Auer*. *Auer* commands deference for an agency's interpretation of its own rules (unless the interpretation is clearly erroneous). Was this an *Auer* interpretation? If so, was anything more needed beyond the recitation of the prior rule? In the full opinion, the Court explains that there is a disconnect between the interpretation and the rule arguably interpreted. That said, what was wrong with the statutory reference used by the Attorney General?

a. One of the more overt messages in *Gonzales v. Oregon* is a condemnation of "parroting" – the arguably mindless restatement of a statute or a regulation as a foundation for and justification of a rule or interpretation designed to function as a standard that has the force of law. Lower courts picked up on this reading of *Oregon* with little difficulty. *See Pittsburg & Midway Coal Mining Co. v. Director, Office of Workers Compensation, 508 F.3d 975 (11th Cir. 2007)*, "where a regulation 'repeats two statutory phrases and attempts to summarize the others,' it is a parroting regulation," and unlikely to succeed in securing deference, respect, or anything close to it.

b. In *Groff v. United States, 493 F.3d 1343 (Fed. Cir. 2007)*, the court found that, "[w]hile an agency's interpretation of its own regulation is normally entitled to substantial deference, the *Auer* standard does not apply when the regulation does little more than restate the terms of the statute itself . . . . [T]he existence of a parroting regulation does not change the fact that the question . . . is not the meaning of the regulation but the meaning of the statute." If a statute authorizes specifically the issuance of a rule in a defined field (unlike *Oregon*, where – according to the majority – the Attorney General could not lay claim to such authority), how much more beyond recitation of that statute is required?

2. On expertise and experience: <u>Walker v. Eggleston, 2006 WL 2482619 (S.D.N.Y. 2006)</u>, "It is axiomatic that an agency interpretation of its own ambiguous regulation is 'controlling unless plainly erroneous or inconsistent with the regulation.'" *Auer v. Robbins*. However, "[a]n agency does not acquire special authority to interpret its own words when, instead of using its expertise and experience to formulate a regulation, it has elected merely to paraphrase the statutory language." *Gonzales v. Oregon*, 546 U.S. at 916.

3. Federal/State Relations. One reading of this case focuses on federalism since the rule in question regulates specific practices of state licensed physicians.

a. In <u>Raich v. Gonzales, 500 F.3d 850 (9th Cir. 2007)</u>, the Ninth Circuit explained its perspective on *Gonzales v. Oregon*:

> [The] Court invalidated an Interpretive Rule issued by the Attorney General on the basis of statutory construction, not on the basis of constitutional invalidity under the Tenth Amendment. Because the Attorney General's Rule was "incongruous with the statutory purposes and design" of the Controlled Substances Act, the Rule had to be nullified. Although *Gonzales v. Oregon* undoubtedly implicates federalism issues, its holding is inapposite [to a] Tenth Amendment claim.

Would you dismiss the federalism issue so bluntly? Wasn't the presence of state jurisdiction over doctors an important consideration?

b. The Controlled Substances Act is the responsibility of the Department of Health and Human Services, drug law enforcement is the responsibility of the states and the Attorney General, and medical practice – including the use of prescription drugs – is the responsibility of the states. In this setting, who has the ability to make rules that carry the "force of law" – and assuming the Attorney General has that power in some fields, does it exist here? What happens when there are multiple entities with coextensive power?

An excellent discussion of these issues – and of <u>Gonzales</u> – is in Professor Jacob E. Gersen's *Overlapping and Underlapping Jurisdiction in Administrative Law*, U. CHI. SUP. CT. REV. 201 (2006):

> *Gonzales* involved the intersection of a number of typically discrete administrative law doctrines. First, what deference is due an agency's interpretation of its own rule? Second, what deference ought to be given to a statutory interpretation issued by a federal agency that has the effect of displacing a state law? Third, should deference be

given to an agency's interpretation of a statute that gives authority to multiple federal agencies. . . ?

Much of JUSTICE KENNEDY's opinion relies on two ideas. First, when a statute shares authority between agencies, deference should be given to the agency that has the relevant expertise – here not the Attorney General, but the Secretary of Health and Human Services. Second, because the CSA shares authority between federal and state governments, no deference should be given to an interpretation that "displaces the States' general regulation of medical practice."

[At a more fundamental level is the question of an agency's authority to act or "step zero." (one doesn't get to *Chevron* or *Skidmore* or anything in between if the action of the agency is outside its delegated power)] In *Gonzales*, the Court first asserted that the Step Zero hurdle is cleared if "the statute gives an agency broad power to enforce all provisions of the statute." However, where the specific delegation provision fails to grant such broad authority to the agency, more analysis is required. Importantly, in overlapping jurisdiction statutes, this generally sufficient condition for *Chevron* deference will almost never be met unless authority is completely overlapping. This reading of *Mead* amounts to a bias against concurrent regulatory authority in the *Chevron* framework. The majority concluded that the CSA delegates to the Attorney General only "limited powers, to be exercised in specific ways" rather than the sufficient general authority. Because the CSA gives the Attorney General the authority to make rules and regulations to carry out "registration and control" and for the "efficient execution of his functions," the majority concluded that the Attorney General does not have general "force of law" authority to implement the entire statute. The Interpretive Rule could pass muster under Step Zero only if it was related to one of the two explicit delegation provisions, and the majority thought it inadequately tethered to either. In essence, the Court concluded that the statute does not create overlapping interpretive authority between the Attorney General and the Secretary on medical matters. The Interpretive Rule was not issued via notice and comment rulemaking, as required for rules promulgated under the relevant section. And, the majority concluded that the Interpretive Rule could not be "justified" under the registration portion of the statute because it failed to undertake the five-factor analysis required of such rules and concerned more than just registration.

Because dispensing controlled substances without being registered to do so is a crime, the majority concluded that the Interpretive Rule "purports to declare that using controlled substances for physician-assisted suicide is a crime, an authority that goes well beyond the Attorney General's statutory power to register or deregister." This would be "extraordinary authority." This part of the opinion connotes a series of cases in which the Court declined to give deference to agencies on "major questions." These cases were decided before *Mead*, and *Gonzales* indicates that the "major questions" exception fits neatly into the Step Zero analytic. . . .

Given the alleged breadth of the authority claimed by the Attorney General, and the silence or ambiguity of the CSA, the statute was best read to preclude *Chevron* deference because Congress does not confer broad authority through an implicit delegation. . . .

The Court seemed to adopt two interpretive presumptions that reduce the likelihood of deference for interpretations of shared jurisdiction statutes. The first presumes that

Congress gives law-interpreting authority to a single government entity. If real, the presumption makes the use of overlapping and underlapping jurisdictional schemes more costly and less effective. The second presumes that Congress does not implicitly grant law-interpreting authority to agencies with respect to interpretations that would impinge on state interests.

4. Is this nothing more than a case of an agency (in this instance, the Department of Justice) exceeding delegated authority, failing the so-called Step Zero test? The text of the case is on point: "Deference in accordance with *Chevron*, however, is warranted only when it appears that Congress delegated authority to the agency generally to make rules carrying the force of law, and that the agency interpretation claiming deference was promulgated in the exercise of that authority." 546 U.S. at 256.

5. Does the case undermine the ability of federal agencies to set policy? That is in part the argument in Professor David M. Wagner's Gonzales v. Oregon: *The Assisted Suicide of* Chevron *Deference*, 2007 MICH. ST. L. REV. 435. Professor Wagner sees the case in the broader context of post-*Mead* deference cases:

> Allowing administrative agencies, who are within the executive branch and accountable to the President, to change their minds within congressionally defined parameters is a way to keep the electorate in the administrative process – by choosing a President. But this solution has been diluted, first by *Christensen*, then by *Mead*, and now by *Oregon*, in the service of an inconsistent federalism and perhaps in the service of a "culture of death."

Do you read Oregon as strengthening the power of judiciary? Was the case a thinly veiled political diatribe endorsing euthanasia? Do you agree with JUSTICE SCALIA's dissent – was the majority simply wrong on the facts and the law?

FEDERAL COMMUNICATIONS COMMISSION V. FOX TELEVISION STATIONS, INC.

556 U.S. ____, 129 S. Ct. 1800, 173 L. Ed. 2d 738 (2009)

JUSTICE SCALIA delivered the opinion of the Court, except as to Part III–E.

Federal law prohibits the broadcasting of "any ... indecent ... language," 18 U. S. C. §1464, which includes expletives referring to sexual or excretory activity or organs. This case concerns the adequacy of the Federal Communications Commission's explanation of its decision that this sometimes forbids the broadcasting of indecent expletives even when the offensive words are not repeated.

Statutory and Regulatory Background I.

The Communications Act of 1934, 48 Stat. <u>1064, 47 U. S. C. §151</u> *et seq.* (2000 ed. and Supp. V), established a system of limited-term broadcast licenses subject to various "conditions" designed "to maintain the control of the United States over all the channels of radio transmission," §301 (2000 ed.). Twenty-seven years ago we said that "[a] licensed broadcaster is granted the free and exclusive use of a limited and valuable part of the public domain; when he accepts that franchise it is burdened by enforceable public obligations." *CBS, Inc. v. FCC,* <u>453 U. S. 367, 395</u> (1981) (internal quotation marks omitted).

One of the burdens that licensees shoulder is the indecency ban—the statutory proscription against "utter[ing] any obscene, indecent, or profane language by means of radio communication," <u>18 U. S. C. §1464</u>. . . .

The Commission first invoked the statutory ban on indecent broadcasts in 1975, declaring a daytime broadcast of George Carlin's "Filthy Words" monologue actionably indecent. *Pacifica Foundation,* 56 F. C. C. 2d 94. At that time, the Commission announced the definition of indecent speech that it uses to this day, prohibiting "language that describes, in terms patently offensive as measured by contemporary community standards for the broadcast medium, sexual or excretory activities or organs, at times of the day when there is a reasonable risk that children may be in the audience." *Id.,* at 98.

. . . .

In the ensuing years, the Commission took a cautious, but gradually expanding, approach to enforcing the statutory prohibition against indecent broadcasts. Shortly after *Pacifica,* the Commission expressed its "inten[tion] strictly to observe the narrowness of the *Pacifica* holding," which "relied in part on the repetitive occurrence of the 'indecent' words" contained in Carlin's monologue.   When the full Commission next considered its indecency standard, however, it repudiated the view that its enforcement power was limited to "deliberate, repetitive use of the seven words actually contained in the George Carlin monologue." The Commission determined that such a "highly restricted enforcement standard ... was unduly narrow as a matter of law and inconsistent with [the Commission's] enforcement responsibilities under Section 1464." The Court of Appeals for the District of Columbia Circuit upheld this expanded enforcement standard against constitutional and Administrative Procedure Act challenge.

Although the Commission had expanded its enforcement beyond the "repetitive use of specific words or phrases," it preserved a distinction between literal and non-literal (or "expletive") uses of evocative language.   The Commission explained that each literal "description or depiction of sexual or excretory functions must be examined in context to determine whether it is patently offensive," but that "deliberate and repetitive use … is a requisite to a finding of indecency" when a complaint focuses solely on the use of non-literal expletives. Ibid.

. . . "No single factor," the Commission said, "generally provides the basis for an indecency finding," but "where sexual or excretory references have been made once or have been passing or fleeting in nature, this characteristic has tended to weigh against a finding of indecency."

In 2004, the Commission took one step further by declaring for the first time that a nonliteral (expletive) use of the F- and S-Words could be actionably indecent, even when the word is used only once. The first order to this effect dealt with an NBC broadcast of the Golden Globe Awards, in which the performer Bono commented, " 'This is really, really, f***ing brilliant.' "

The Commission first declared that Bono's use of the F-Word fell within its indecency definition, even though the word was used as an intensifier rather than a literal descriptor. "[G]iven the core meaning of the 'F-Word,' " it said, "any use of that word … inherently has a sexual connotation." The Commission determined, moreover, that the broadcast was "patently offensive" because the F-Word "is one of the most vulgar, graphic and explicit descriptions of sexual activity in the English language," because "[i]ts use invariably invokes a coarse sexual image[]" . . . .

The Commission observed that categorically exempting such language from enforcement actions would "likely lead to more widespread use." Commission action was necessary to "safeguard the well-being of the nation's children from the most objectionable, most offensive language."

The order acknowledged that "prior Commission and staff action have indicated that isolated or fleeting broadcasts of the 'F-Word' … are not indecent or would not be acted upon." It explicitly ruled that "any such interpretation is no longer good law."

The Present Case II.

This case concerns utterances in two live broadcasts aired by Fox Television Stations, Inc., and its affiliates prior to the Commission's *Golden Globes Order*. The first occurred during the 2002 Billboard Music Awards, when the singer Cher exclaimed, "I've also had critics for the last 40 years saying that I was on my way out every year. Right. So f*** 'em." The second involved a segment of the 2003 Billboard Music Awards, during the presentation of an award by Nicole Richie and Paris Hilton, principals in a Fox television series called "The Simple Life." Ms. Hilton began their interchange by reminding Ms. Richie to "watch the bad language," but Ms. Richie proceeded to ask the audience, "Why do they even call it 'The Simple Life?' Have you ever tried to get cow s*** out of a Prada purse? It's not so f***ing simple." *Id.,* at 9–10. Following each of these broadcasts, the Commission received numerous complaints from parents whose children were exposed to the language.

On March 15, 2006, the Commission released Notices of Apparent Liability for a number of broadcasts that the Commission deemed actionably indecent, including the two described above. . . .

. . . .

. . . The Court of Appeals reversed the agency's orders, finding the Commission's reasoning inadequate under the Administrative Procedure Act. The majority was "skeptical that the Commission [could] provide a reasoned explanation for its 'fleeting expletive' regime that would pass constitutional muster," but it declined to reach the constitutional question. *Id.,* at 462. Judge Leval dissented. We granted certiorari, 552 U. S. ___ (2008).

Analysis III.

Governing Principles A.

The Administrative Procedure Act, which sets forth the full extent of judicial authority to review executive agency action for procedural correctness, , permits (insofar as relevant here) the setting aside of agency action that is "arbitrary" or "capricious" . Under what we have called this "narrow" standard of review, we insist that an agency "examine the relevant data and articulate a satisfactory explanation for its action." . We have made clear, however, that "a court is not to substitute its judgment for that of the agency," and should "uphold a decision of less than ideal clarity if the agency's path may reasonably be discerned[.]"

. . . .

We find no basis in the Administrative Procedure Act or in our opinions for a requirement that all agency change be subjected to more searching review. The Act mentions no such heightened standard. And our opinion in *State Farm* neither held nor implied that every agency action representing a policy change must be justified by reasons more substantial than those required to adopt a policy in the first instance. . . .

To be sure, the requirement that an agency provide reasoned explanation for its action would ordinarily demand that it display awareness that it *is* changing position. . . . But it need not demonstrate to a court's satisfaction that the reasons for the new policy are *better* than the reasons for the old one; it suffices that the new policy is permissible under the statute, that there are good reasons for it, and that the agency *believes* it to be better, which the conscious change of course adequately indicates. . . .

[T]he broadcasters' arguments have repeatedly referred to the First Amendment . If they mean to invite us to apply a more stringent arbitrary-and-capricious review to agency actions that implicate constitutional liberties, we reject the invitation. . . . We know of no precedent for applying it to limit the scope of authorized executive action. . . .

Application to This Case B.

Judged under the above described standards, the Commission's new enforcement policy and its order finding the broadcasts actionably indecent were neither arbitrary nor capricious. First, the Commission forthrightly acknowledged that its recent actions have broken new ground, taking account of inconsistent "prior Commission and staff action" and explicitly disavowing them as "no longer good law." To be sure, the (superfluous) explanation in its *Remand Order* of why the Cher broadcast would even have violated its earlier policy may not be entirely convincing. But that unnecessary detour is irrelevant. There is no doubt that the Commission knew it was making a change. That is why it declined to assess penalties; and it relied on the *Golden Globes Order* as removing any lingering doubt.

Moreover, the agency's reasons for expanding the scope of its enforcement activity were entirely rational. It was certainly reasonable to determine that it made no sense to distinguish between literal and non-literal uses of offensive words, requiring repetitive use to render only the latter indecent. . . . It is surely rational (if not inescapable) to believe that a safe harbor for single words would "likely lead to more widespread use of the offensive language[.]"

When confronting other requests for *per se* rules governing its enforcement of the indecency prohibition, the Commission has declined to create safe harbors for particular types of broadcasts. The Commission could rationally decide it needed to step away from its old regime where non-repetitive use of an expletive was *per se* non-actionable because that was "at odds with the Commission's overall enforcement policy."

The fact that technological advances have made it easier for broadcasters to bleep out offending words further supports the Commission's stepped-up enforcement policy. And the agency's decision not to impose any forfeiture or other sanction precludes any argument that it is arbitrarily punishing parties without notice of the potential consequences of their action.

. . . .

———————

1. *Political influence?* *Fox* involves a review of a relatively new agency policy implemented in an adjudication (an enforcement action). The policy involves indecency – expletives – and there is little question that its formulation was the consequence of political consider-ations. The dissenting opinions of Justices Breyer, Stevens, Ginsberg, and Souter reflect deep concern that policy choice of the agency was made for "purely political" reasons. The some-what passive review standard in the case that was the foundation for upholding the action of the FCC "seems to make it easier for agencies to change their policies due to changes in the political landscape." Kathryn A. Watts, *Proposing a Place for Politics in Arbitrary and Capricious Review*, 119 YALE L.J. 22 (2009).

Good Questions!

Access the full text of *Fox*, take a look at the dissenting opinions, and con-sider what you think are the "poli-tics" of the dissenting judges. Do the dissenting opinions reveal a rigorous assessment of precedent and statu-tory imperative – or do they reflect (appropriately or not) the politics of the dissenting judges? Is regulatory policy supposed to be pristine, di-vorced from political considerations?

2. *Rethinking judicial review.* We are just beginning to debate the ramifications of the *Fox* decision. According to the law clerk to Justice Kennedy, Scott A. Keller, *Fox*

> may be the watershed precedent that charts a new course for administrative law. The doctrinal culprits that have allowed judges to use their policy preferences to invalidate agency rulemaking are the Supreme Court's dicta on the Administrative Procedure Act's (APA) arbitrary and capricious standard of review in [*State Farm*] and the D.C. Circuit's hard look doctrine. While *Fox Television* did not explicitly reject the *State Farm* dicta and the hard look doctrine, the way *Fox Television* engaged in APA arbitrary and capricious review implicitly rejected both.

Scott A. Keller, *Depoliticizing Judicial Review of Agency Rulemaking*, 84 WASH. L. REV. 419, 424-26 (2009).

Keller asserts that post-*Fox* review of rules should involve only an examina-tion of

Good Questions!

Did you read *Fox* as a separation of powers case? Had the agency ac-tion in *Fox* been rejected, would that have been impermissible policymak-ing by the Court? Were the prob-lems in *Fox* about the expansion of judicial policy formulation or about the preservation of the ability of the executive to formulate policy?

> the agency's purpose in regulating and the means used . . . to achieve that purpose - instead of requiring the agency to use additional procedures and scouring the rulemaking record to make up insignificant problems with that record. . . ." Keller calls this form of review "[r]ational basis with bite. . .

[which] require[s] the agency . . . to articulate its actual statutory purpose in promulgating the rule and explain how the rule is rationally related to that purpose." This formulation would "significantly reduce the ability of judges to veto agency rules based on policy disagreements. . . .

3. *First Amendment concerns.* First Amendment concerns are on or lurking just below the surface in many FCC cases. Is there a way to read *Fox* that does not entail the regulation of speech? (Hint: we don't think so). While profound expressions regarding the First Amendment do not dominate the majority opinion, the argument surfaces in the concurrence of Justice Thomas, 556 U.S. __ (Apr. 28, 2009), 129 S. Ct. 1800, 1820-21, 173 L. Ed. 2d 738, 761-62 (2009), who characterizes the FCC action as a "deep intrusion into the First Amendment rights of broadcasters. . . ." Justice Thomas rejects the justification of the majority based on *Red Lion Broad. Co. v. FCC*, 395 U.S. 367 (1969) and *FCC v. Pacifica Foundation*, 438 U.S. 726 (1978) which Justice Thomas writes suffer from "logical weakness" and "doctrinal incoherence. . . ." He goes on to note that "dramatic technological advances have eviscerated the factual assumptions underlying those decisions. Broadcast spectrum is significantly less scarce than it was 40 years ago." He is unquestionably correct when it comes to scarcity. Kristen M. Formanek, *Critical Race Theory Speaker Series CRT 20: Honoring our Past, Charting our Future: Note: There's "No Such Thing as Too Much Speech": How Advertising Deregulation and the Marketplace of Ideas Can Protect Democracy in America*, 94 Iowa L. Rev. 1743 (2009); *Report on Gen. Fairness Doctrine Obligations of Broad. Licensees*, 102 F.C.C.2d 143, 146-47 (1985).

Food for Thought

Do you read the concurrence of Justice Thomas to be a strident defense of unfettered speech? For comparison, take at look at *Morse v. Frederick*, 127 S. Ct. 2618, 2630 (2007) (Thomas, J., concurring) (arguing that *Tinker v. Des Moines Independent Community School District*, 393 U.S. 503 (1969) is bad law since "the history of public education suggests that the First Amendment, as originally understood, does not protect student speech in public schools."

CONNECTICUT STATE MEDICAL SOCIETY V. CONNECTICUT BOARD OF EXAMINERS IN PODIATRY

<u>546 A.2d 830 (Conn. 1988)</u>

[Judge Hull] [The] Connecticut State Medical Society [initiated this proceeding after] the defendant Connecticut Board of Examiners in Podiatry (board) declared that "the ankle is part of the foot and the foot is part of the ankle."

[The board acted after a Medicare determination limited podiatric practice to] treatment of foot [and said] "services involving the ankle are not covered by Medicare." . . . . [T]he board sought an opinion from the attorney general [who] stated that the "question posed . . . is one which calls for a factual determination. In order to respond, analysis must first be conducted of the human anatomy to ascertain whether the ankle is . . . part of the foot." . . . . The board conducted [a] hearing on November 7, 1984, and received fifteen exhibits and heard testimony from eleven witnesses, both podiatrists and medical doctors, concerning the anatomical relationship between the foot and the ankle. It subsequently issued a declaratory ruling that the ankle is part of the foot and that podiatrists could, therefore, treat ankle ailments.

[The Medical Society went to court to challenge the decision of the Board. The court set aside the Board's decision, and the Board appealed. The members of the Board] claim that the court substituted its judgment for that of the [Board] as to the weight of the evidence on questions of fact . . . . They further claim that the court erred in failing to afford "special deference" to the board's factual findings, and to time-tested agency interpretations. . . .

[I]t is the function of the courts to expound and apply governing principles of law. This case presents a question of law turning upon the interpretation of a statute. Both the board and the trial court had to construe [the statute] to determine the permissible scope of podiatry practice in Connecticut. In our view, this is purely a question of law, requiring that the intent of the legislature be discerned. Such a question invokes a broader standard of review than is ordinarily involved in deciding whether, in light of the evidence, the agency has acted unreasonably, arbitrarily, illegally or in abuse of its discretion.

Ordinarily, we give great deference to the construction given a statute by the agency charged with its enforcement. . . . [However] in this case, the board's interpretation of [the statute] is not entitled to any special deference. . . . We have accorded deference to . . . a time-tested agency interpretation of a statute, but only when the agency has consistently followed its construction over a long period of time, the statutory language is ambiguous, and the agency's interpretation is reasonable. . . . [W]e do not consider the board's knowledge of and acquiescence in certain podiatric practices to rise to the level of statutory construction entitled to judicial deference.

Interpretation of [a] statute should effect the intent of the legislature and not expand the law's meaning to accommodate unauthorized practices simply because they have been performed in the past. . . . [The statute] defines podiatry as "the diagnosis, prevention and treatment of foot ailments . . . the practice of surgery upon the feet . . . the dressing, padding and strapping of the feet; the making of models of the feet and the palliative and mechanical treatment of functional and structural ailments of the feet, not including the amputation of the leg, foot or toes or the treatment of systemic diseases other than local manifestations in the foot." Our principal objective in construing statutory language is to ascertain the apparent intent of the legislature.

If the statutory language is clear and unambiguous, there is no room for construction [by the agency]. Webster's Third New International Dictionary defines "foot" as "[t]he terminal part of the vertebrate leg upon which an individual stands consisting in most bipeds (as man) and in many quadrupeds (as the cat) of all the structures (as heel, arches, and digits) below the ankle joint . . . ." The podiatrists argue, however, that the board's ruling, rather than the dictionary definition, is consistent with the legislative intent underlying the podiatry statutes. We are not so persuaded.

[O]ur examination of the statutory scheme [compels us to find the ankle is not part of the foot. The statute does not suggest an expansion of the area podiatrists can treat. Instead, it directs] specific limitations on the practice of podiatry. . . . General Statutes § 20-63 provides that "[n]o person granted a certificate under this chapter shall display or use the title 'Doctor' or its synonym without the designation 'Podiatrist.'" Further . . . grounds for revocation of a podiatrist's license or for disciplinary action [include] "undertaking or engaging in any medical practice beyond the privileges and rights accorded to the practitioner of podiatry by the provisions of this chapter . . . ." A final example of such a limitation is the provision . . . authorizing "the practice of surgery upon the feet, provided if an anesthetic other than a local anesthetic is required, such surgery shall be performed in a general hospital accredited by the Joint Commission on Accreditation of Hospitals by a licensed podiatrist who is accredited by the credentials committee of the medical staff of said hospital. . . . The subjection of podiatrists to hospital rules is a striking example of a legislative intent to restrain any expansion of the scope of podiatry practice that is not statutorily authorized. We conclude, therefore, that it was not the intention of the legislature to empower the board to define the scope of podiatry practice in Connecticut. . . . There is no error. . . .

———————————

Underlying Case Documents

The case referenced:
The Attorney General Opinion

Connecticut recently enacted a statute requiring the Commissioner of Public Health to use a panel to develop guidelines allowing qualified podiatrists to practice surgery on the ankle. For the report of the panel click HERE.

1. In *Tennessee Medical Ass'n v. Board of Registration in Podiatry*, 907 S.W.2d 820 (Tenn. App. 1995), the court faced nearly identical facts as in the *Connecticut State Medical Society* case – and came to the same conclusions:

> We are . . . of the opinion that the order of the Podiatry Board is not entitled to any deference because the Board's ruling is one of statutory construction, rather than a question of fact, and because the issue is one that does not require the special expertise of the Board. A question of whether the term "foot" includes the ankle is a matter of statutory interpretation and does not require the Board's knowledge of podiatric practices. This is not a question that falls within the sole expertise of podiatrist[s]. The Board's conclusion of law and reasons for the decision are inconsistent with the finding that an ankle sprain is an ailment of the human foot. The Board concluded that "to effectively treat ailments of the foot as outlined in T.C.A. § 63-3-103 will necessitate treatment and control of the adjacent structures." Tennessee Code Annotated section 63-3-103 defines podiatrist as one who "examines, diagnoses or treats medically, mechanically, or surgically, the ailments of the human foot . . . ." The law does not demarcate the anatomical barrier. The Board finds that all the soft tissue involved in an ankle sprain are within that definition. The Board, therefore, concluded that the ankle is an adjacent structure, not a part of the foot. The ankle cannot be both a part of the foot and an adjacent structure.
>
> As is pointed out by the appellees, the appellant and the Board of Podiatry are entitled to attempt to expand the scope of podiatry; however, the proper vehicle for that expansion is by legislative revision of the podiatry statute, not through a contested case hearing that disregards the clear and plain meaning of the statute. . . . The Board's decision was not based upon substantial and material evidence and exceeds the statutory authority of the Board. . . .

2. Why would the Tennessee and Connecticut courts find summarily that statutory construction is not entitled to deference? Doesn't *Chevron* involve giving deference to an agency's interpretation and application of a statute? If your answer is that interpretation of statutes is the essential task of courts – of judges and lawyers – you would be correct in terms of training and education – but what about in terms of administrative law? Are the Connecticut and Tennessee cases unique – or are they the norm?

a. In a dissenting opinion in *Ardestani v. INS*, 502 U.S. 129 (1991), decided seven years after *Chevron*, JUSTICES STEVENS and BLACKMUN expressed fairly conventional doctrine in this area.

> This Court has indicated . . . that reviewing courts do not owe deference to an agency's interpretation of statutes outside its particular expertise and special charge to administer. Because the [Equal Access to Justice Act] EAJA, like the APA, applies to all agencies and is not administered by any one in particular, deference to the interpretation by any particular agency is inappropriate.

The majority opinion was based on a "plain reading" of the statute – and did not rely on *Chevron*.

b. A year later, in *Estate of Cowart v. Nicklos Drilling Co.*, 505 U.S. 469 (1992), the Supreme Court held:

> The controlling principle in this case [regarding agency interpretation of a statute] is the basic and unexceptional rule that courts must give effect to the clear meaning of statutes as written. The principle can at times come into some tension with another fundamental principle of our law, one requiring judicial deference to a reasonable statutory interpretation by an administering agency. . . .

c. Very recently, in *Pulisir v. Mukasey*, 524 F.3d 302 (1st Cir. 2008), the First Circuit held that "[a]bstract legal points are reviewed *de novo*, but with some deference to the agency's reasonable interpretation of statutes and regulations that fall within its purview. *Pan v. Gonzales*, 489 F.3d 80, 85 (1st Cir. 2007). Is the interpretation of the meaning of a statute an "abstract legal point?" And what does the court mean by "some deference" – and why de novo review?

d. The *Pan v. Gonzales* case referred to above uses the following standard: "Rulings of law engender de novo review, but with some deference to the agency's reasonable interpretation of statutes and regulations that fall within its purview. . . ." 489 F.3d at 85.

e. How did de novo review and "some deference" slip in? Are these dilutions of deference based on the *Christensen*/*Mead* break from *Chevron*?

In *A.T. Massey Coal Co. v. Barnhart*, 472 F.3d 148, 166 (4th Cir. 2006), the Fourth Circuit provided one explanation:

> While Chevron analysis often results in affording deference to agency interpretations of statutes, that deference is limited to circumstances where (1) Congress has given the agency authority to make rules carrying the force of law and (2) the agency's interpretation is rendered in the exercise of that authority. *See* *Mead*. More precisely, *Mead* refined the standard for deference, describing the type of agency action deserving of *Chevron* deference this way:

> We hold that administrative implementation of a particular statutory
> provision qualifies for *Chevron* deference when it appears that Congress
> delegated authority to the agency generally to make rules carrying the
> force of law, and that the agency interpretation claiming deference was
> promulgated in the exercise of that authority. Delegation of such authority
> may be shown in a variety of ways, as by an agency's power to engage
> in adjudication or notice and comment rulemaking, or by some other
> indication of a comparable congressional intent. . . .

> Thus, the Court in *Mead* observed that even though agencies charged with applying
> statutes will make "all sorts of interpretive choices," "not all of those choices bind
> judges to follow them."

f. Is the *Connecticut State Medical Society* case about statutory interpretation – or is
it really about application of facts (the nature of the foot and ankle) to an unambiguous statutory term? If so, should the standard for fact finding in adjudication
– substantial evidence – be applied?

g. In <u>*AFGE, Local 2152 v. Principi,* 464 F.3d 1049, 1057 (9th Cir. 2006)</u>, the court
found that, as a rule, courts should give "great deference to . . . interpretations
involving statutes under which the
agency operates [unless] the agency's
decision was issued in the form of an
opinion letter and not as the result of
a formal proceeding. *See* <u>*Christensen v.*
Harris County</u>. . . ." Why great deference? Why not "some deference" as in
notes c and d above?

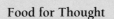

Food for Thought

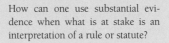

How can one use substantial evidence when what is at stake is an
interpretation of a rule or statute?

h. The deference question can also be varied by statutes that establish separate
interpretive preferences. For example, in <u>*Navajo Nation v. Department of Health and*
Human Services, 285 F.3d 864 (9th Cir. 2002)</u>, the court held:

> One could argue against the eligibility of *Chevron* deference in this case as conflicting
> with the general rule of interpretation of statutes enacted for the benefit of Indian
> tribes; namely, that such statutes "are to be construed liberally in favor of the Indians,
> with ambiguous provisions interpreted to their benefit." <u>*Montana v. Blackfeet Tribe*
> *of Indians,* 471 U.S. 759, 766 (1985)</u>. That is, even if the meaning of provisions of
> [legislation written for the benefit of Native Americans is] ambiguous, that statute
> was undoubtedly enacted for the benefit of Indian tribes, and, therefore, instead of
> deferring to agency interpretations in such circumstances, the court should construe
> the statute in a way that benefits Indians. Thus, to some extent, the *Chevron* rule of
> statutory interpretation and the *Blackfeet Tribe* rule of statutory interpretation conflict
> with one another in this case. We have dealt with this conflict by discarding the
> *Blackfeet Tribe* rule in favor of the *Chevron* rule whenever these two general rules of
> interpretation intersect in the same case. <u>*Williams v. Babbitt,* 115 F.3d 657, 663 n.5
> (9th Cir. 1997)</u>.

i. In <u>*E. & J. Gallo Winery v. Cantine Rallo*, 430 F. Supp. 2d 1064, 1081-82 (E.D. Cal. 2005)</u>, a trademark infringement case, the court, referring to *Ardestani* (note a above) found as follows:

> An agency's interpretation is entitled to deference under certain circumstances, such as when an agency is charged with the duty of interpreting and enforcing a regulation. Here, however, the target of the interpretation is a service-of-process provision, which is traditionally the province of the courts and not within the agency's special expertise. *See Ardestani.*

What is it about of service of process (and its relationship to in personam jurisdiction) that allows the court to ignore the decisions of the agency?

3. The *Connecticut State Medical Society* case involved a challenge by M.D.s to expansion of the domain of podiatrists. By fighting to limit the range of professional services the podiatrists can render, the M.D.s were protecting their market share. This is not an unusual motivation for professional associations – and the AMA and state medical societies are not unique in this quest. It took the legal profession some time to adjust to the presence of paralegals – and similar turf wars exist in other fields. Carol A. Heimer, <u>*Rethinking Health Law: Responsibility in Health Care: Spanning the Boundary Between Law and Medicine*, 41 WAKE FOREST L. REV. 465 (2006)</u>.

Major Theme

In the final analysis, is the *Connecticut State Medical Society* case about the most basic of all separation of powers principles: Public policy, expressed through legislation, is the province of the Legislature, not the Executive. Had the state legislature decided to redefine the foot, that would have been the end of it. Perhaps the case is merely one of many examples of the basic proposition that decisions of this nature should be made by elected representatives, not by administrative bodies. *See* <u>*Brown & Williamson*</u>, *infra* Chapter 5.

CHAPTER 4

Basic Reviewability Concerns

As has become evident, assuming you have read the cases that precede this section, judicial review of administrative action is one of the fundamental ways of developing and understanding administrative law. In the cases that follow, we explore the question of who can seek judicial review of the rules, regulations, and interpretations that agencies issue.

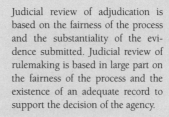

Bottom Line

Judicial review of adjudication is based on the fairness of the process and the substantiality of the evidence submitted. Judicial review of rulemaking is based in large part on the fairness of the process and the existence of an adequate record to support the decision of the agency.

The Administrative Procedure Act ("APA") allows any "aggrieved" person to seek out judicial review. It does not guarantee, however, that aggrieved persons will secure judicial review. Furthermore, it does not define what exactly is required to be "aggrieved." It does not state with specificity when a process is deemed "final" or "ripe" at the agency level. Nonetheless, a person can secure judicial review of agency action – or sue the government when they believe they are harmed by agency action – only if the agency matter is final and ripe, and if the party seeking review has standing.

It is inevitable that a decision regarding standing will be seen as political, activating debates regarding judicial restraint versus judicial activism and separation of powers. When a court reviews the action of an agency to determine the sufficiency of a record or when a court agrees to hear a claim under 28 U.S.C. § 1331, in which a party seeks damages for alleged harm caused by an agency, there are those who believe it impossible for a court to avoid second guessing the actions of the agency. That second guess is, to some, a violation of the clear constitu-

Key Concept

Standing, as one of the cases that follows suggests (*Frank Krasner Enterprise v. Montgomery County*, 401 F.3d 230 (4th Cir. 2005)) can be a "numbingly familiar" exercise. In guaranteeing "concrete adverseness," a party must show that it has an appropriate stake in the outcome and that it will not be wasting the court's time.

tional mandate of separation of power. To others, judicial review is a critical exercise of the constitutional mandate of checks and balances and a statutory mandate of the Administrative Procedure Act that requires, outside of certain exceptional circumstances, judicial review to ensure the fairness and efficacy of agency action.

In rulemaking cases, the question of standing is slightly more delicate than in adjudicatory proceedings. In an adjudicatory proceeding, the party who litigated the matter usually has a personal stake in the outcome and is able to ensure "concrete adverseness." In contrast, in rulemaking cases, many members of the public may be affected personally by a rule. Further, many members of the public who may not be affected by the rule may find the process or substance of the rule deeply offensive and violative of fundamental norms.

Quite obviously, it would be impossible to allow every member of the public who takes offense at the process or content of any rule issued by an agency to have his or her day in court. Judicial review is not an opportunity for general political critique of the actions of government. For that reason, determining standing in rulemaking cases becomes rather important. Legitimate standing doctrine must both provide an opportunity for judicial review to address those genuinely aggrieved and must also limit the use of judicial review as a political forum to air one's grievances against the regulatory state.

I. Review and Basic Jurisdictional Requirements: Standing

Since the Administrative Procedure Act guarantees anyone aggrieved by agency action a right to judicial review, one would think the basic jurisdictional questions are not all that complicated. However, even the most fundamental question – whether the APA constitutes an independent jurisdictional basis for judicial review – can leave one in a state of uncertainty. In *Califano v. Sanders*, 430 U.S. 99 (1977), the Supreme Court held that the APA does not form an independent jurisdictional bases for judicial review. *Califano*, however, dealt with a somewhat unique situation and, while it is cited occasionally (usually erroneously) for the aforementioned proposition, a far better statement of the jurisdictional nature of §701 of the APA is in *Bennett v. Spear*.

Bennett clarified that the APA is a critical component of the jurisdictional base for securing judicial review of agency action. Every administrative law decision (or at least every one that we can think of) involves an administrative agency – and it is the enabling statute (the substantive statute that empowers the agency to act) of that agency that provides the "federal question." The APA, however, plays a vital role in rounding out jurisdiction, leading some courts to characterize cases as an "APA cause of action." "An APA cause of action accrues at the time of the

Take Note

The term "enabling act" refers to the legislation that both establishes an agency and delegates the power to exercise authority. As a general rule, agencies, not courts, have the primary responsibility to interpret their enabling legislation.

individual agency action being challenged." *Pat Huval Rest. & Oyster Bar, Inc. v. United States Consol. Court*, 2008 WL 564646 CIT (Ct. Int'l Trade Mar. 3, 2008) (citing *Preminger v. Sec'y of Veterans Affairs*, 498 F.3d 1265, 1272 (Fed. Cir. 2007)). *See also Trudeau v. FTC*, 456 F.3d 178 (D.C. Cir. 2006); *Shinyei Corp. of Am. v. United States*, 355 F.3d 1297, 1304-05 (Fed. Cir. 2004); *Nat'l Wrestling Coaches Ass'n v. Dep't of Educ.*, 366 F.3d 930 (D.C. Cir. 2004); *and Viraj Forgings Ltd. v. United States*, 26 Ct of Int'l Tr. 513, 206 F. Supp. 2d 1288 (2002).

Jurisdiction requires not only a consideration of subject matter but also of venue. The "routing" of judicial review of agency action is often determined by statute. There are statutes that route appellants to a Court of Appeals and others that route parties to a District Court. While the Circuit Courts are the traditional venue for review, District Courts are the traditional forum for other lawsuits against the United States government. Further, District Courts hear cases where de novo review is appropriate. *See, e.g.*, *NVE Inc. v. HHS*, 436 F.3d 182 (3d Cir. 2006); *and Farrell v. Principi*, 366 F.3d 1066 (9th Cir. 2004).

Assuming one has identified the appropriate venue, the next set of obstacles are the questions that often dominate civil procedure and constitutional law classes: Standing, ripeness, finality, mootness, exhaustion of remedies, and primary jurisdiction. A number of the cases that follow discuss the many – and varied – rules pertaining to standing. We note preliminarily that if the plaintiff is not the object of the agency's action, but rather a third-party interested in using the court system to critique the work of the agency, the party will have a very difficult time obtaining standing. If the entity attacking the action of the agency is an association, organization, or public interest group, the require-

Practice Pointer

De novo trials can happen based on a statutory directive, a claim by the plaintiff that the agency action is unsupported – or grossly unwarranted – by the facts, an attempt by an agency to enforce an order or sanction where there was little or no fact finding before the order or sanction was issued, constitutional fact cases, and a limited number of other circumstances. Frank R. Strong, *Dilemmic Aspects of the Doctrine of "Constitutional Fact,"* 47 N.C. L. Rev. 311, 327 (1969); Steven Alan Childress, *Constitutional Fact and Process: A First Amendment Model of Censorial Discretion*, 70 Tul. L. Rev. 1229, 1240 (1996).

ments are also slightly different, as is discussed in the material that follows.

In addition to standing, a party challenging agency action must show that the decision under review is the "consummation of agency action" and demonstrate that legally binding consequences flow from that action. The more advisory the action of the agency, the less likely it is to be construed as final. Ripeness, often linked with finality, requires an identifiable legal question and a showing that the agency action will produce real – as opposed to theoretical or abstract – consequences.

A further consideration is exhaustion of administrative remedies. Exhaustion can be jurisdictional if it is required by the substantive statute governing the agency. Exhaustion allows an agency to "express" its expertise, correct its mistakes, develop a record suitable for review, and ensure that the agency process remains available long enough for those who are interested in participating in it. Exhaustion can be waived if an agency cannot give the requested relief, if continued agency action is futile or unconstitutional, if the agency action displays bias, or if the agency action is outside of the authority of the agency. While primary jurisdiction is often lumped in with exhaustion, it is a separate consideration. *See* Nicholas A. Lucchetti, Comment, _One Hundred Years of the Doctrine of Primary Jurisdiction: But What Standard of Review Is Appropriate for It_, 59 ADMIN. L. REV. 849 (2008).

The cases that follow show both the evolution of the standing doctrine and the problems the doctrine has produced.

ASSOCIATION OF DATA PROCESSING SERVICE ORGANIZATIONS, INC. V. CAMP

397 U.S. 150 (1970)

[JUSTICE DOUGLAS] Petitioners sell data processing services to businesses . . . . In this suit they seek to challenge a ruling by respondent Comptroller of the Currency that, as an incident to their banking services, national banks, including respondent American National Bank & Trust Company, may make data processing services available to other banks and to bank customers. The District Court dismissed the complaint for lack of standing . . . . The Court of Appeals affirmed. . . .

Generalizations about standing to sue are largely worthless as such. One generalization is, however, necessary and that is that . . . standing in the federal courts is to be considered in the framework of Article III which restricts judicial power to "cases" and "controversies." As we recently stated in *Flast v. Cohen*, "In terms of Article III limitations on federal court jurisdiction, the question of standing is related only to whether the dispute sought to be adjudicated will be presented in an adversary context and in a form historically viewed as capable of judicial resolution." *Flast* was a *taxpayer's* suit. The present is a *competitor's* suit. And while the two have the same Article III starting point, they do not necessarily track one another.

The first question is whether the plaintiff alleges that the challenged action has caused him injury in fact, economic or otherwise. There can be no doubt but that petitioners have satisfied this test. The petitioners not only allege that competition by national banks in the business of providing data processing services might entail some future loss of profits for the petitioners, they also allege that respondent American National Bank & Trust Company was performing or preparing to perform such services for two customers for whom petitioner Data Systems, Inc., had previously agreed or negotiated to perform such services. The petitioners' suit was brought not only against the American National Bank & Trust Company, but also against the Comptroller of the Currency. The Comptroller was alleged to have caused petitioners injury in fact by his 1966 ruling which stated:

> Incidental to its banking services, a national bank may make available its data processing equipment or perform data processing services on such equipment for other banks and bank customers.

. . . .

[In] *Tennessee Power Co. v. TVA*, [t]he Court denied the competitors' standing, holding that they did not have that status "unless the right invaded is a legal right, – one of property, one arising out of contract, one protected against tortious invasion, or one founded on a statute which confers a privilege."

The "legal interest" test goes to the merits. The question of standing is different. It concerns, apart from the "case" or "controversy" test, the question whether the interest sought to be protected by the complainant is arguably within the zone of interests to be protected or regulated by the statute or constitutional guarantee in question. Thus the Administrative Procedure Act grants standing to a person "aggrieved by agency action within the meaning of a relevant statute." 5 U.S.C. § 702. That interest, at times, may reflect "aesthetic, conservational, and recreational" as well as economic values. A person or a family may have a spiritual stake in First Amendment values sufficient to give standing to raise issues concerning the Establishment Clause and the Free Exercise Clause. We mention these noneconomic values to emphasize that standing may stem from them as well as from the economic injury on which petitioners rely here. Certainly he who is "likely to be financially" injured may be a reliable private attorney general to litigate the issues of the public interest in the present case. . . . Where statutes are concerned, the trend is toward enlargement of the class of people who may protest administrative action. . . .

That leaves the remaining question, whether judicial review of the Comptroller's action has been precluded. We do not think it has been. . . . We find no evidence that Congress in either the Bank Service Corporation Act or the National Bank Act sought to preclude judicial review of administrative rulings by the Comptroller as to the legitimate scope of activities available to national banks under those statutes. Both Acts are clearly "relevant" statutes within the meaning of § 702. The Acts do not in terms protect a specified group. But their general policy is apparent; and those whose interests are directly affected by a broad or narrow interpretation of the Acts are easily identifiable. It is clear that petitioners, as competitors of national banks which are engaging in data processing services, are within that class of "aggrieved" persons who, under § 702, are entitled to judicial review of "agency action."

Whether anything in the Bank Service Corporation Act or the National Bank Act gives petitioners a "legal interest" that protects them against violations of those Acts, and whether the actions of respondents did in fact violate either of those Acts, are questions which go to the merits and remain to be decided below.

We hold that petitioners have standing to sue and that the case should be remanded for a hearing on the merits.

———————————

1. The Fragility of the *Data Processing* Presumption of Reviewability. In <u>High Country Citizens Alliance v. Clarke, 454 F.3d 1177 (10th Cir. 2006)</u>, the court addressed what is required to overcome the presumption of judicial review in *Data Processing.* "[A]n intent to preclude judicial review must be 'fairly discernible' from the statutory scheme." The fact that a statute does not explicitly provide for judicial review is not outcome determinative. Rather, the Supreme Court set forth specific factors for courts to consider in analyzing whether, absent explicit language or explicit legislative history, the presumption of reviewability has been overcome:

> The congressional intent necessary to overcome the presumption [of reviewability] may . . . be inferred from contemporaneous judicial construction barring review and the congressional acquiescence in it . . . or from the collective import of legislative and judicial history behind a particular statute [or] by inferences of intent drawn from the statutory scheme as a whole. *Data Processing* (citing <u>Block v. Community Nutrition Institute</u>, 467 U.S. 340 (1984)).

The *Block* decision called into question the solid assumptions on which *Data Processing* was based. If Congress does not limit or prohibit review explicitly, can it be possible to do so by implication? The *Data Processing* decision holds that the bar must be explicit – fourteen years later, in *Block*, things changed: "[W]hether and to what extent a particular statute precludes judicial review is determined not only from its express language, but also from the *structure of the statutory scheme, its objectives, its legislative history, and the nature of the administrative action involved.*" 467 U.S. at 345. [Emphasis added.]

2. Since the Court allows review to be cut off based on the "structure of the statutory scheme, its objectives, [or] its legislative history", what remains of the promise of *Data Processing*? Does this permit courts to bend the intention of Congress? After all, if Congress wanted to prohibit review, it is quite capable of doing so expressly.

In *Bowen v. Michigan Academy of Family Physicians*, the Court provided a second wind for the *Data Processing* premise of access to the courts, holding that there is a "strong presumption that Congress intends judicial review of administrative action." 476 U.S. 667, 669 (1986). How strong can a presumption be if it can be set aside based on an analysis of the "structure of a statutory scheme"?

3. An excellent comment by Colin A. Olivers in 38 ENVTL. L. 243 (2008), *Has the Federal Courts Successive Undermining of the APA's Presumption of Reviewability Turned the Doctrine Into Fools Gold?*, discusses the Tenth Circuit's decision in *High Country Citizens Alliance v. Clarke* (note 1, above). Mr. Olivers notes that "contemporaneous decisions and the manner in which the courts have treated this [reviewability] presumption merits further consideration, as the apparent meaning of *Data Processing* was possibly not as clear as it seemed."

4. *Data Processing* in Context – The D.C. Gun Control Case. In *District of Columbia v. Heller*, 128 S. Ct. 2783 (2008), involving the constitutionality of the D.C. handgun ban, D.C. Code §§ 7-2502.02(a)(4), 7-2507.02, 22-4504, the Court passed up an opportunity to address some of the unanswered questions from *Data Processing*. While the Court directed its attention primarily to handgun ownership, in the underlying decision, the D.C. Circuit provided a valuable summary of the problems pertaining to the Second Amendment and standing/reviewability challenges as they relate to injury-in-fact:

> We note that the Ninth Circuit has recently dealt with a Second Amendment claim by first extensively analyzing that provision, determining that it does not provide an individual right, and then, and only then, concluding that the plaintiff lacked standing to challenge a California statute restricting the possession, use, and transfer of assault weapons. *See Silveira v. Lockyer*, 312 F.3d 1052, 1066-67 & n.18 (9th Cir. 2002). We think such an approach is doctrinally quite unsound. The Supreme Court has made clear that when considering whether a plaintiff has Article III standing, a federal court must assume arguendo the merits of his or her legal claim. *See Warth v. Seldin*, 422 U.S. 490, 501-02 (1975). . . . We have repeatedly recognized that proposition. . . . "Indeed, in reviewing the standing question, the court must be careful not to decide the questions on the merits for or against the plaintiff, and must therefore assume that on the merits the plaintiffs would be successful in their claims." (citing *Warth*, 422 U.S. at 502). This is no less true when, as here, the merits involve the scope of a constitutional protection.

Still, we have not always been so clear on this point. Although we recognized in _Claybrook v. Slater_, 111 F.3d 904 (D.C. Cir. 1997), that it was not necessary for a plaintiff to demonstrate that he or she would prevail on the merits . . . the rest of our discussion seems somewhat in tension with that proposition. We did recognize that in _Lujan v. Defenders of Wildlife_ [the following case in this text] when the Supreme Court used the phrase "legally protected interest" as an element of injury-in-fact, it made clear it was referring only to a "cognizable interest." The Court in _Lujan_ concluded that plaintiffs had a "cognizable interest" in observing animal species without considering whether the plaintiffs had a legal right to do so. We think it plain the _Lujan_ Court did not mean to suggest a return to the old "legal right" theory of standing rejected in _Association of Data Processing Service Organizations, Inc. v. Camp_. . . . Rather, the cognizable interest to which the Court referred would distinguish, to pick one example, a desire to observe certain aspects of the environment from a generalized wish to see the Constitution and laws obeyed. . . .

In sum, we conclude that Heller has standing to raise his § 1983 challenge to specific provisions of the District's gun control laws.

Parker v. District of Columbia, 478 F.3d 370 (D.C. Cir. 2007).

5. Reviewability and Competitive Injury. Among the most important continuing questions in this field are those pertaining to competitive injury. No one suggests that access to the courts is guaranteed if the sole ground for the claim is that a market is increasingly competitive. However, competitive injury and healthy competitive pressure are no easier to figure out in administrative law than in regulatory antitrust cases. Paul S. Dempsey, _Deregulation: A Decade Later, and the Band Played On_, 17 TRANSP. L.J. 31 (1988). In _Canadian Lumber Trade Alliance v. United States_, 425 F. Supp. 2d 1321 (U.S. Court of Int'l Trade 2006), _aff'd_ 517 F.3d 1319 (Fed. Cir. 2008), the court explored the matter.

> The United States Bureau of Customs and Border Protection . . . distributes to domestic producers who are competitors of the Plaintiff Canadian exporters the duties collected as a result of antidumping and countervailing orders on Canadian goods.
>
> [The government] contend[s] that economic injuries are not cognizable within the meaning of the injury-in-fact test. Specifically, relying on the Supreme Court's statement in _Hardin v. Ky. Utils. Co._, 390 U.S. 1, 5-6 (1968) that ". . . economic injury which results from lawful competition cannot, in and of itself, confer standing on the injured business to question the legality of any aspect of its competitor's operations. . . ." The court disagrees. . . .
>
> In _Data Processing_, the Supreme Court rejected the "legal interest" analysis which required claimants to demonstrate an injury to their legally protected rights. . . . In repudiating that earlier test, the Court noted that the "'legal interest' test [went] to the merits [whereas the] question of standing is different," and that the legal interest test conflicted with the "broadly remedial purpose" of the APA. The Supreme Court's rejection of the "legal interest" analysis was absolute and unqualified. _See_ Jonathan R. Siegel, _Zone of Interests_, 92 GEO. L.J. 317, 320 (2004). . . . Any remnants of this

analysis are now relevant only to prudential considerations in the context of the zone of interest test . . . .

Go back to the text of *Data Processing*. How does the Court limit or expand reviewability when the interest at stake is economic?

Food for Thought

These cases, and the many others that preceded *Data Processing*, raised but did not resolve questions regarding the nature of an injury-in-fact. Can it be solely economic? Can an injury extend beyond a personal interest to broader aesthetic and environmental concerns? Does an injury need to be "cognizable and recognized under existing law?" Who can bring such claims – is a living, breathing "injured or aggrieved person" required or can a group pursue such interests?

6. History. <u>Barlow v. Collins, 397 U.S. 159 (1970)</u>, decided along with *Data Processing*, includes a dissent by JUSTICES BRENNAN and WHITE in which they argue that *Data Processing* did not go far enough. They assert that the only element of the *Data Processing* test required for standing is injury-in-fact and that the statutory zone of interest test is not required as a matter of constitutional imperative. That is not to say that injury-in-fact is lacking in complexity or controversy. The triggering language for injury in administrative law cases comes from § 702 of the APA that provides a "right of review" to "a person suffering a legal wrong because of agency action, or adversely affected or aggrieved by agency action within the meaning of the relevant statute." During the New Deal, courts weighed in regularly on what it meant to be sufficiently injured or aggrieved. <u>Tennessee Electric Power v. TVA, 306 U.S. 118 (1939)</u>; <u>FCC v. Sanders Brothers, 309 U.S. 470 (1940)</u>; <u>Scripps Howard Radio v. FCC, 316 U.S. 4 (1942)</u>; and <u>Associated Industries of New York v. Ickes, 134 F.2d 694 (2d Cir. 1943)</u>, *vacated as moot* <u>320 U.S. 707 (1943)</u>.

As the cases that follow make clear, these questions were not resolved by *Data Processing*. Furthermore, just when it seems there is clarity, a new decision is handed down calling into question our understanding in the field.

Textual Note

We have selected the cases that follow based on our understanding that the vast majority of law students are exposed to reviewability, standing, and related doctrines prior to taking administrative law. However, we also know that law school curricula vary greatly. For those who spent months on this topic prior to taking this course, this should be a pleasant review. For those who have not seen these cases before, we urge you to read the full opinions of the main cases and to recognize that, while agency cases are of great value in the field, standing, ripeness, and mootness are of consequence beyond administrative law.

After the *Data Processing* case, one might have concluded that ascertaining the availability of judicial review of administrative action would be somewhat mechanical. After all, what could be so complicated about figuring out if there was an injury-in-fact to an interest arguably within the zone of a particular statute? Two cases decided shortly thereafter, *Sierra Club v. Morton*, 405 U.S. 727, 734 (1972), and *United States v. Students Challenging Regulatory Agency Procedures (SCRAP)*, 412 U.S. 669, 685-90 (1973), followed the ideas underlying *Data Processing* in terms of the nature of the injury. In *SCRAP*, the Court found that injury to a legally protected interest defined by "common law or statute" was not a formal requirement. In *Sierra Club*, the Court held that "injury" could extend to environmental and aesthetic concerns – and neither case appears to demand a clear causal connection between the harm alleged and the government action that was the apparent cause.

If one goal of the Court in *Data Processing* was to "open the courthouse doors," it was a short-lived objective. The cases that followed *Data Processing* reflect a slow and irregular, but real, set of limits on access to the courts. Some years after the decision, a student Comment noted the following:

> This new "zone of interests" test sought to reestablish separation of powers by providing relatively easy access to the courts for regulatory objects and beneficiaries. *Data Processing*, however, was the high water mark of the post-New Deal standing model. In a retreat from the pure "zone of interests" test, the Court subsequently introduced causation and redressability requirements into the standing analysis.

Christopher J. Sprigman, Comment, *Standing on Firmer Ground: Separation of Powers and Deference to Congressional Findings in the Standing Analysis*, 59 U. CHI. L. REV. 1645, 1649 (1992), referring to *Warth v. Seldin*, 422 U.S. 490, 498-501 (1975), and *Allen v. Wright*, 468 U.S. 737, 750-52 (1984).

The next step is to begin to think through the criteria for standing. "Standing to sue is part of the common understanding of what it takes to make a justiciable case." *Steel Co. v. Citizens for a Better Env't*, 523 U.S. 83, 102 (1990). Justiciability, however, turns out to be nothing resembling a singularity. In a fascinating piece on animal rights, an area where standing concerns are acute, Professor Elizabeth L. DeCoux notes that

> [s]tanding is a terrain in which a traveler can become lost, unless he begins his journey by looking out over the vista and locating several landmarks that will serve as reference points. . . . First, there is the distinction between standing and other rules of justiciability [e.g.] mootness, ripeness, [and] political question. . . . [There is also the] distinction between constitutional standing and prudential standing. . . . A claimant who meets the requirements of constitutional standing may nevertheless find the path barred by judge-made law regarding prudential standing. [From Elizabeth L. DeCoux, *In the Valley of Dry Bones: Reuniting the Word "Standing" with Its Meaning in Animal Cases*, 29 WM. & MARY ENVTL. L. & POL'Y REV. 720 (2005).]

Data Processing provided a workable theory for those who set out to challenge what they perceived as ill-conceived regulatory initiatives. As you read the cases that follow, pay attention to the fate of such challengers. Are these cases based genuinely on constitutional constraints, management-based concerns regarding access to the courts, prudential consideration, or other political considerations?

LUJAN V. DEFENDERS OF WILDLIFE

504 U.S. 555 (1992)

[JUSTICE SCALIA] The ESA (Endangered Species Act) seeks to protect species of animals against threats to their continuing existence caused by man. The ESA instructs the Secretary of the Interior to promulgate by regulation a list of those species which are either endangered or threatened under enumerated criteria, and to define the critical habitat of these species. Section 7(a)(2) of the Act then provides, in pertinent part:

> Each Federal agency shall, in consultation with and with the assistance of the Secretary [of the Interior], insure that any action authorized, funded, or carried out by such agency . . . is not likely to jeopardize the continued existence of any endangered species . . . or result in the destruction . . . of habitat of such species . . . .

In 1978, the Fish and Wildlife Service (FWS) and the National Marine Fisheries Service (NMFS) . . . promulgated a joint regulation stating that the obligations imposed by § 7(a)(2) extend to actions taken in foreign nations. The next year, however, the Interior Department began to reexamine its position. A revised joint regulation, reinterpreting § 7(a)(2) to require consultation only for actions taken in the United States or on the high seas, was . . . promulgated in 1986. Shortly thereafter, respondents, organizations dedicated to wildlife conservation and other environmental causes, filed this action against the Secretary of the Interior, seeking . . . an injunction requiring the Secretary to promulgate a new regulation restoring the initial interpretation. . . .

II.

. . . .

Over the years, our cases have established that the irreducible constitutional minimum of standing contains three elements. First, the plaintiff must have suffered an "injury in fact" – an invasion of a legally protected interest which is (a) concrete and particularized and (b) "actual or imminent, not 'conjectural' or 'hypothetical.'" Second, there must be a causal connection between the injury and the conduct complained of – the injury has to be "fairly . . . trace[able] to the challenged action of the defendant, and not . . . the result [of] the independent action of some third party not before the court." Third, it must be "likely," as opposed to merely "speculative," that the injury will be "redressed by a favorable decision."

. . . . .

When the suit is one challenging the legality of government action or inaction, the nature and extent of facts that must be averred (at the summary judgment stage) or proved (at the trial stage) in order to establish standing depends considerably upon whether the plaintiff is himself an object of the action (or forgone action) at issue. If he is, there is ordinarily little question that the action or inaction has caused him injury, and that a judgment preventing or requiring the action will redress it. When, however, as in this case, a plaintiff's asserted injury arises from the government's allegedly unlawful regulation (or lack of regulation) of *someone else*, much more is needed. In that circumstance, causation and redressability ordinarily hinge on the response of the regulated (or regulable) third party to the government action or inaction – and perhaps on the response of others as well. The existence of one or more of the essential elements of standing "depends on the unfettered choices made by independent actors not before the courts and whose exercise of broad and legitimate discretion the courts cannot presume either to control or to predict," and it becomes the burden of the plaintiff to adduce facts showing that those choices have been or will be made in such manner as to produce causation and permit redressability of injury. Thus, when the plaintiff is not himself the object of the government action or inaction he challenges, standing is not precluded, but it is ordinarily "substantially more difficult" to establish.

III.

We think the Court of Appeals failed to apply the foregoing principles in denying the Secretary's motion for summary judgment. Respondents had not made the requisite demonstration of (at least) injury and redressability.

A.

Respondents' claim to injury is that the lack of consultation with respect to certain funded activities abroad "increas[es] the rate of extinction of endangered and threatened species." Of course, the desire to use or observe an animal species, even for purely esthetic purposes, is undeniably a cognizable interest for purpose of standing. "But the 'injury in fact' test requires more than an injury to a cognizable interest. It requires that the party seeking review be himself among the injured." To survive the Secretary's summary judgment motion, respondents had to submit affidavits or other evidence showing, through specific facts, not only that listed species were in fact being threatened by funded activities abroad, but also that one or more of respondents' members would thereby be "directly" affected apart from their "'special interest' in the subject."

With respect to this aspect of the case, the Court of Appeals focused on the affidavits of two Defenders' members – Joyce Kelly and Amy Skilbred. Ms. Kelly stated that she traveled to Egypt in 1986 and "observed the traditional habitat of the endangered nile crocodile there and intend to do so again, and hope to observe the crocodile directly," and that she "will suffer harm in fact as the result of [the] American . . . role . . . in overseeing the rehabilitation of the Aswan High Dam on the Nile . . . ." Ms. Skilbred averred that she traveled to Sri Lanka in 1981 and "observed the habitat" of "endangered species such as the Asian elephant and the leopard" at what is now the site of the Mahaweli project funded by the Agency for International Development (AID), although she "was unable to see any of the endangered species"; "this development project," she continued, "will seriously reduce endangered, threatened, and endemic species habitat including areas that I visited[, which] may severely shorten the future of these species"; that threat, she concluded, harmed her because she "intend[s] to return to Sri Lanka in the future and hope[s] to be more fortunate in spotting at least the endangered elephant and leopard." When Ms. Skilbred was asked at a subsequent deposition if and when she had any plans to return to Sri Lanka, she reiterated that "I intend to go back to Sri Lanka," but confessed that she had no current plans: "I don't know [when]. There is a civil war going on right now. I don't know. Not next year, I will say. In the future."

We shall assume . . . that these affidavits contain facts showing that certain agency-funded projects threaten listed species – though that is questionable. They plainly contain no facts, however, showing how damage to the species will produce "imminent" injury to Mses. Kelly and Skilbred. That the women "had visited" the areas . . . before the projects commenced proves nothing. . . . And the affiants' profession of an "intent" to return to the places they had visited before – where they will presumably, this time, be deprived of the opportunity to observe animals of the endangered species – is simply not enough. Such "some day" intentions – without any description of concrete plans, or indeed even any specification of *when* the some day will be – do not support a finding of the "actual or imminent" injury that our cases require. . . .

Besides relying upon the Kelly and Skilbred affidavits, respondents propose a series of novel standing theories. The first, inelegantly styled "ecosystem nexus," proposes that any person who uses *any part* of a "contiguous ecosystem" adversely affected by a funded activity has standing even if the activity is located a great distance away. This approach, as the Court of Appeals correctly observed, is inconsistent with our opinion in *National Wildlife Federation*, which held that a plaintiff claiming injury from environmental damage must use the area affected by the challenged activity and not an area roughly "in the vicinity" of it. It makes no difference that the general-purpose section of the ESA states that the Act was intended in part "to provide a means whereby the ecosystems upon which endangered species and threatened species depend may be conserved." To say that the Act protects ecosystems is not to say that the Act creates . . . rights of action in persons who have not been injured in fact, that is, persons who use portions of an ecosystem not perceptibly affected by the unlawful action in question.

Respondents' other theories are called, alas, the "animal nexus" approach, whereby anyone who has an interest in studying or seeing the endangered animals anywhere on the globe has standing; and the "vocational nexus" approach, under which anyone with a professional interest in such animals can sue. Under these theories, anyone who goes to see Asian elephants in the Bronx Zoo, and anyone who is a keeper of Asian elephants in the Bronx Zoo, has standing to sue because the Director of the Agency for International Development (AID) did not consult with the Secretary regarding the AID-funded project in Sri Lanka. This is beyond all reason. Standing is not "an ingenious academic exercise in the conceivable," but . . . requires, at the summary judgment stage, a factual showing of perceptible harm. It is clear that the person who observes or works with a particular animal threatened by a federal decision is facing perceptible harm, since the very subject of his interest will no longer exist. It is even plausible – though it goes to the outermost limit of plausibility – to think that a person who observes or works with animals of a particular species in the very area of the world where that species is threatened by a federal decision is facing such harm, since some animals that might have been the subject of his interest will no longer exist. It goes beyond the limit, however, . . . to say that anyone who observes or works with an endangered species, anywhere in the world, is appreciably harmed by a single project affecting some portion of that species with which he has no more specific connection.

B.

The most obvious problem in the present case is redressability. Since the agencies funding the projects were not parties to the case, the District Court could accord relief only against the Secretary: He could be ordered to revise his regulation to require consultation for foreign projects. But this would not remedy respondents' alleged injury unless the funding agencies were bound by the Secretary's regulation, which is very much an open question. . . . When the Secretary promulgated the regulation at issue here, he thought it was binding on the agencies. The Solicitor General, however, has repudiated that position here, and the agencies themselves apparently deny the Secretary's authority. (During the period when the Secretary took the view that § 7(a)(2) did apply abroad, AID and FWS engaged in a running controversy over whether consultation was required with respect to the Mahaweli project, AID insisting that consultation applied only to domestic actions.)

Respondents assert that this legal uncertainty did not affect redressability (and hence standing) because the District Court itself could resolve the issue of the Secretary's authority as a necessary part of its standing inquiry. Assuming that it is appropriate to resolve an issue of law such as this in connection with a threshold standing inquiry, resolution by the District Court would not have remedied respondents' alleged injury anyway, because it would not have been binding upon the agencies. They were not parties to the suit, and there is no reason they should be obliged to honor an incidental legal determination the suit produced. The Court of Appeals tried to finesse this problem by simply proclaiming that "we are satisfied that an injunction requiring the Secretary to publish [respondents' desired] regulation . . . would result in consultation." We do not know what would justify that confidence, particularly when the Justice Department (presumably after consultation with the agencies) has taken the position that the regulation is not binding. The short of the matter is that redress of the only injury in fact respondents complain of requires action (termination of funding until consultation) by the individual funding agencies; and any relief the District Court could have provided in this suit against the Secretary was not likely to produce that action.

A further impediment to redressability is the fact that the agencies generally supply only a fraction of the funding for a foreign project. AID, for example, has provided less than 10% of the funding for the Mahaweli project. Respondents have produced nothing to indicate that the projects they have named will either be suspended, or do less harm to listed species, if that fraction is eliminated. . . . [I]t is entirely conjectural whether the non-agency activity that affects respondents will be altered or affected by the agency activity they seek to achieve. There is no standing.

IV.

The Court of Appeals found that respondents had standing for an additional reason: because they had suffered a "procedural injury." The so-called "citizen-suit" provision of the ESA provides, in pertinent part, that "any person may commence a civil suit on his own behalf (A) to enjoin any person, including the United States and any other governmental instrumentality or agency . . . who is alleged to be in violation of any provision of this chapter." The court held that, because § 7(a)(2) requires interagency consultation, the citizen-suit provision creates a "procedural right" to consultation in all "persons" – so that *anyone* can file suit in federal court to challenge the Secretary's (or presumably any other official's) failure to follow the assertedly correct consultative procedure, notwithstanding his or her inability to allege any discrete injury flowing from that failure. To understand the remarkable nature of this holding one must be clear about what it does *not* rest upon: This is not a case where plaintiffs are seeking to enforce a procedural requirement the disregard of which could impair a separate concrete interest of theirs (e.g., the procedural requirement for a hearing prior to denial of their license application, or the procedural requirement for an environmental impact statement before a federal facility is constructed next door to them). Nor is it simply a case where concrete injury has been suffered by many persons, as in mass fraud or mass tort situations. Nor, finally, is it the unusual case in which Congress has created a concrete private interest in the outcome of a suit against a private party for the Government's benefit, by providing a cash bounty for the victorious plaintiff. Rather, the court held that the injury-in-fact requirement had been satisfied by congressional conferral upon *all* persons of an abstract, self-contained, noninstrumental "right" to have the Executive observe the procedures required by law. We reject this view.

We have consistently held that a plaintiff raising only a generally available grievance about government – claiming only harm to his and every citizen's interest in proper application of the Constitution and laws, and seeking relief that no more directly and tangibly benefits him than it does the public at large – does not state an Article III case or controversy. . . .

To be sure, our generalized-grievance cases have typically involved Government violation of procedures assertedly ordained by the Constitution rather than the Congress. But there is absolutely no basis for making the Article III inquiry turn on the source of the asserted right. Whether the courts were to [ignore] the concrete injury requirement described in our cases, they would be discarding a principle fundamental to the separate and distinct constitutional role of the Third Branch – one of the essential elements that identifies those "Cases" and "Controversies" that are the business of the courts rather than of the political branches. "The province of the court," as CHIEF JUSTICE MARSHALL said in *Marbury v. Madison*, "is, solely, to decide on the rights of individuals." Vindicating the *public* interest (including the public interest in Government observance of the Constitution and laws) is the function of Congress and the Chief Executive. The question presented here is whether the public interest in proper administration of the laws (specifically, in agencies' observance of a particular, statutorily prescribed procedure) can be converted into an individual right by a statute that denominates it as such, and that permits all citizens (or, for that matter, a subclass of citizens who suffer no distinctive concrete harm) to sue. If the concrete injury requirement has the separation-of-powers significance we have always said, the answer must be obvious: To permit Congress to convert the undifferentiated public interest in executive officers' compliance with the law into an "individual right" vindicable in the courts is to permit Congress to transfer from the President to the courts the

Chief Executive's most important constitutional duty, to "take Care that the Laws be faithfully executed," Art. II, § 3. It would enable the courts, with the permission of Congress, "to assume a position of authority over the governmental acts of another and co-equal department," and to become "virtually continuing monitors of the wisdom and soundness of Executive action." We have always rejected that vision of our role:

> When Congress passes an Act empowering administrative agencies to carry on governmental activities, the power of those agencies is circumscribed by the authority granted. This permits the courts to participate in law enforcement entrusted to administrative bodies only to the extent necessary to protect justiciable individual rights against administrative action fairly beyond the granted powers. . . .

"Individual rights," within the meaning of this passage, do not mean public rights that have been legislatively pronounced to belong to each individual who forms part of the public.

Nothing in this contradicts the principle that "the . . . injury required by Art. III may exist solely by virtue of 'statutes creating legal rights, the invasion of which creates standing.'" [This happens by] Congress' elevating to the status of legally cognizable injuries concrete, de facto injuries that were previously inadequate in law (namely, injury to an individual's personal interest in living in a racially integrated community and injury to a company's interest in marketing its product free from competition).

We hold that respondents lack standing to bring this action and that the Court of Appeals erred in denying the summary judgment motion filed by the United States. The opinion of the Court of Appeals is hereby reversed, and the cause is remanded for proceedings consistent with this opinion. . . .

[JUSTICE KENNEDY, concurring in part.]

. . . With respect to the [nexus] theories . . . respondents' showing is insufficient to establish standing . . . . I am not willing to foreclose the possibility, however, that in different circumstances a nexus theory similar to those proffered here might support a claim to standing. . . . As Government programs and policies become more complex and far reaching, we must be sensitive to the articulation of new rights of action that do not have clear analogs in our common-law tradition. . . . In my view, Congress has the power to define injuries and articulate chains of causation that will give rise to a case or controversy where none existed before, and I do not read the Court's opinion to suggest a contrary view.

[JUSTICE BLACKMUN, dissenting.]

To survive petitioner's motion for summary judgment on standing, respondents need . . . show only a "genuine issue" of material fact as to standing. Fed. Rule Civ. Proc. 56(c). This is not a heavy burden. A "genuine issue" exists so long as "the evidence is such that a reasonable jury could return a verdict for the nonmoving party [respondents]." . . . . I think a reasonable finder of fact could conclude from the information in the affidavits and deposition testimony that either Kelly or Skilbred will soon return to the project sites, thereby satisfying the "actual or imminent" injury standard. . . .

The Court concludes that any "procedural injury" suffered by respondents is insufficient to confer standing. . . . Whatever the Court might mean with that very broad language, it cannot be saying that "procedural injuries" *as a class* are necessarily insufficient for purposes of Article III standing. Most governmental conduct can be classified as "procedural." . . . . When the Government, for example, "procedurally" issues a pollution permit, those affected by the permittee's pollutants are not without standing to sue. . . .

Under the Court's anachronistically formal view of the separation of powers, Congress legislates pure, substantive mandates and has no business structuring the procedural manner in which the Executive implements these mandates. . . . In complex regulatory areas, however, Congress often legislates, as it were, in procedural shades of gray. . . . Just as Congress does not violate separation of powers by structuring the procedural manner in which the Executive shall carry out the laws, surely the federal courts do not violate separation of powers when, at the very instruction and command of Congress, they enforce these procedures. . . . In conclusion, I cannot join the Court on what amounts to a slash-and-burn expedition through the law of environmental standing. . . .

Underlying Case Documents

The case referenced:
The affidavit of Ms. Skilbred
The affidavit of Ms. Kelly
The testimony of Ms. Skilbred

For a letter between the agencies discussing concerns over the proposed new rule click HERE.

1. How much is this case driven simply by facts – particularly the descriptions the plaintiffs provide of their interests in travel – and how much is it a change in

policy. Does the case simply clarify existing doctrine or does it articulate new standards? Compare Professor Wendy S. Albers' article, Lujan v. Defenders of Wildlife: *Closing the Courtroom Door to Environmental Plaintiffs – The Endangered Species Act Remains Confined to United States Borders*, 15 Loy. Int'l & Comp. L. Rev. 203 (1992), with Professor Cass Sunstein's *What's Standing After* Lujan? *Of Citizen Suits, "Injuries," and Article III*, 91 Mich. L. Rev. 163 (1992).

2. Most recently, the Court reiterated its concern about suits brought by those who are in stark disagreement with – but not personally harmed by – agency action. "We have consistently held that a plaintiff raising only a generally available grievance about government – claiming only harm to his and every citizen's interest in proper application of the Constitution and laws, and seeking relief that no more directly and tangibly benefits him than it does the public at large – does not state an Article III case or controversy." *Lance v. Coffman*, 549 U.S. 437 (2007) (per curiam).

3. What About Psychological Injury? In *Hein v. Freedom from Religion Found., 551 U.S. 587 (2007)*, the Court held that a taxpayer's "psychological disapproval" that government resources are being used unlawfully is never a concrete and particularized injury sufficient for Article III standing. "As a general matter, the interest of a federal taxpayer in seeing that Treasury funds are spent in accordance with the Constitution does not give rise to the kind of redressable 'personal injury' required for Article III standing." This approach is consistent with *Valley Forge Christian College v. Americans United for Separation of Church and State, Inc., 454 U.S. 464, 485-86 (1982)*:

Food for Thought

Should access to the courts be as demanding as the *Lujan* opinion suggests? Is there any proper role for courts vis-à-vis legal and statutory challenges to alleged agency misconduct by those citizens who are deeply concerned – but not personally affected? Maxwell L. Stearns, *Standing Back from the Forest: Justiciability and Social Choice*, 83 Cal. L. Rev. 1309 (1995). Keep these questions front and center – particularly when you read *Bennett v. Spear*, 520 U.S. 154, 163 (1997), *infra* Chapter 4, also involving the Endangered Species Act.

> [The complainants] fail to identify any personal injury suffered by them as a consequence of the alleged constitutional error, other than the psychological consequence presumably produced by observation of conduct with which one disagrees. That is not an injury sufficient to confer standing under Art. III, even though the disagreement is phrased in constitutional terms. . . . [S]tanding is not measured by the intensity of the litigant's interest or the fervor of his advocacy.

4. While there may have been some reason to think that the taxpayer standing from *Flast v. Cohen, 392 U.S. 83 (1968)*, possibly covered in both your civil

procedure course and in constitutional law, could serve to bypass the post-*Lujan* limitations on standing, that has been put to rest in the Court's most recent discussion of Lujan:

> It is significant that, in the four decades since its creation, the *Flast* exception has largely been confined to its facts. We have declined to lower the taxpayer standing bar in suits alleging violations of any constitutional provision apart from the Establishment Clause [and we] have similarly refused to extend *Flast* to permit taxpayer standing for Establishment Clause challenges that do not implicate Congress' taxing and spending power. . . . In effect, we have adopted the position set forth by JUSTICE POWELL in his concurrence in *United States v. Richardson*, 418 U.S. 166, 196 (1974), and have "limited the expansion of federal taxpayer and citizen standing in the absence of specific statutory authorization to an outer boundary drawn by the results in *Flast* . . . ." *Hein v. Freedom from Religion Found.*, 551 U.S. 587, 127 S. Ct. 2553, 2564, 168 L. Ed. 2d 424 (2007).

5. Separation of Powers and Standing. The standing requirement in *Lujan* appears to be targeted at keeping the federal courts free of claims where injuries are insufficiently personal or concrete. Limitations on standing, as a general rule, go well beyond definitions of "personal" or "concrete." They constitute "an essential ingredient of separation and equilibration of powers." *Steel Co. v. Citizens for Better Environment*, 523 U.S. 83, 101 (1998). The separation of powers link to standing is explicit. "Relaxation of standing requirements is directly related to the expansion of judicial power [and] would significantly alter the allocation of power at the national level, with a shift away from a democratic form of government." *Richardson*, 418 U.S. at 188 (POWELL, J., concurring).

6. Standing and *Chevron*. Can you find the connection between *Chevron* deference – or *Skidmore* respect – and standing? While the Court may be "improvising" administrative law and diluting or muddying aspects of *Chevron* in the post-*Christensen*/*Mead* era – in some instances expanding the role of the courts – the limitation on judicial interference that forms the foundation of *Chevron* is alive and well in standing. In recent cases the Court has said bluntly that standing requirements must be observed strictly to avoid "permanent judicial intervention in the conduct of governmental operations to a degree inconsistent with sound principles of federalism and the separation of powers." *Garcetti v. Ceballos*, 547 U.S. 410 (2006); *see Cheney v. United States Dist. Court for D.C.*, 542 U.S. 367, 382 (2004).

7. The Mystery of the Three Elements. Current case law relies on *Lujan*'s "simple statement" of standing. In *Stephens v. County of Albemarle*, 524 F.3d 485 (4th Cir. 2008), the court found that "[i]t is well-established that, to satisfy Article III's standing requirements, a plaintiff must show that: (1) [she] has suffered an 'injury in fact' that is (a) concrete and particularized and (b) actual or imminent, not conjectural or hypothetical; (2) the injury is fairly traceable to the challenged action

of the defendant; and (3) it is likely, as opposed to merely speculative, that the injury will be redressed by a favorable decision. *Friends of the Earth, Inc. v. Laidlaw Envtl. Servs., 528 U.S. 167, 180-81 (2000)* (*citing Lujan*, 504 U.S. at 560-61)." Our count of elements in this iteration of standing is seven, not three – but we may be missing one or two. . . .

8. Take a step back from the opinion and ask yourself whether the Court interpreted fairly the citizen-suit provision in the Endangered Species Act. Why would Congress include such a provision if not to facilitate claims of this type? *Compare Lujan* with *Federal Election Commission v. Akins, 524 U.S. 11 (1998)*. *Akins* granted standing to citizens challenging the decision of the FEC to deny "political committee" status to the American-Israel Public Affairs Committee, an organization in which they were not members. The plaintiffs based their challenge on the citizen-suit provision of the Act. The complainants claimed that by denying committee status to the organization, they, the citizens, would be denied information (and thereby aggrieved), since such committees had to report to the FEC and those reports could then become available to the plaintiffs. How is the potential denial of unspecified information regarding events that may or may not have occurred a distinct and palpable injury-in-fact? How is the potential denial of information anything but abstract? The answer to these questions lies in the Court's perception in *Akins* that the citizen-suit provision protects voters "from the kind of harm they say they have suffered." Fair enough – but why wouldn't the same apply in *Lujan*?

9. In the end, is this all about the quality of causation – or proximate cause? In *Friends of the Earth v. Laidlaw Environmental Services, 528 U.S. 167 (2000)*, the Court faced an environmental challenge involving the alleged unlawful discharge of mercury into the Tyger River. The district court and the Fourth Circuit found the discharges were insufficient to constitute the level of degradation required for sanctions or injunctive relief – and the Court reversed. The decision rested on the distinction between concerns about potentially adverse effects that were *reasonably* likely to occur as opposed to those where the likelihood of adverse effects was *unreasonable*. Is this the same hazy and subjective distinction that exists between foreseeable and unforeseeable events? Think back to torts – how many different ways can you list to determine the distinction between these terms?

10. In *Massachusetts v. EPA, 549 U.S. 497 (2007)*, *infra* Chapter 4, the Court granted standing to Massachusetts even though it asserted a claim common to many other states (various harms allegedly associated with global warming). Should the expansive vision in this case be limited to the states? *See* Bradford Mank, *Should States Have Greater Standing Rights than Ordinary Citizens?* Massachusetts v. EPA *New Standing Test for the States*, 49 WM. & MARY L. REV. 1701 (2008); *and* Jonathan Remy Nash, Essay, *Standing and the Precautionary Principle*, 108 COLUM. L. REV. 494 (2008): "[A] fundamental principle of environmental law – the

precautionary principle – should inform the question left unanswered in *Massachusetts v. EPA*. The precautionary principle . . . explains that the absence of certainty in the face of a large risk does not justify inaction. Application of the precautionary principle to the question of standing would suggest . . . 'precautionary-based standing' . . . in which it can be shown that there is uncertainty as to whether irreversible and catastrophic harms may occur."

Good Questions!

The *Massachusetts v. EPA* dissent characterized the harms as conjectural and, even if true, an injury common to all humanity – hardly the stuff of personal, concrete, distinct, palpable, and particularized injury. If standing was driven by a special provision in the statute – and it was – then why was the *Lujan* Court unwilling to hear the ecosystem, animal, and professional nexus arguments? Do you believe that the Supreme Court today is more inclined to open the courthouse doors than the *Lujan* Court decades earlier?

SUMMERS v. EARTH ISLAND INSTITUTE

__ U.S. __, 129 S. Ct. 1142, 173 L. Ed. 2d 1 (2009)

[JUSTICE SCALIA]

. . . .

In 1992, Congress enacted the Forest Service Decisionmaking and Appeals Reform Act (Appeals Reform Act or Act). Among other things, this required the Forest Service to establish a notice, comment, and appeal process for "proposed actions of the Forest Service concerning projects and activities implementing land and resource management plans developed under the Forest and Rangeland Renewable Resources Planning Act of 1974." Ibid.

The Forest Service's regulations implementing the Act provided that certain of its procedures would not be applied to projects that the Service considered categorically excluded from the requirement to file an environmental impact statement (EIS) or environmental assessment (EA). 36 CFR §§ 215.4(a) (notice and comment), 215.12(f) (appeal) (2008). Later amendments to the Forest Service's manual of implementing procedures, adopted by rule after notice and comment, provided that fire-rehabilitation activities on areas of less than 4,200 acres, and salvage-timber sales of 250 acres or less, did not cause a significant environmental impact and thus would be categorically exempt from the requirement to file an EIS or EA. This had the effect of excluding these projects from the notice, comment, and appeal process.

In the summer of 2002, fire burned a significant area of the Sequoia National Forest. In September 2003, the Service issued a decision memo approving the Burnt Ridge Project, a salvage sale of timber on 238 acres damaged by that fire. Pursuant to its categorical exclusion of salvage sales of less than 250 acres, the Forest Service did not provide notice in a form consistent with the Appeals Reform Act, did not provide a period of public comment, and did not make an appeal process available.

In December 2003, respondents [Earth Island] filed a complaint in the Eastern District of California, challenging the failure of the Forest Service to apply to the Burnt Ridge Project § 215.4(a) of its regulations implementing the Appeals Reform Act (requiring prior notice and comment), and § 215.12(f) of the regulations (setting forth an appeal procedure). . . .

The District Court granted a preliminary injunction against the Burnt Ridge salvage-timber sale [not in issue at the Supreme Court] . . . and proceeded . . . to adjudicate the merits of Earth Island's challenges. It invalidated five of the regulations . . . and entered a nationwide injunction against their application. . . .

The Ninth Circuit. . . affirmed . . .

The Government sought review of the question whether Earth Island could challenge the regulations at issue in the Burnt Ridge Project, and if so whether a nationwide injunction was appropriate relief. . . .

II

In limiting the judicial power to "Cases" and "Controversies," Article III of the Constitution restricts it to the traditional role of Anglo-American courts, which is to redress or prevent actual or imminently threatened injury to persons caused by private or official violation of law. Except when necessary in the execution of that function, courts have no charter to review and revise legislative and executive action. See Lujan v. Defenders of Wildlife. . . . This limitation "is founded in concern about the proper -- and properly limited -- role of the courts in a democratic society." Warth v. Seldin. . . .

The doctrine of standing is one of several doctrines that reflect this fundamental limitation. It requires federal courts to satisfy themselves that "the plaintiff has 'alleged such a personal stake in the outcome of the controversy' as to warrant his invocation of federal-court jurisdiction." He bears the burden of showing that he has standing for each type of relief sought. To seek injunctive relief, a plaintiff must show that he is under threat of suffering "injury in fact" that is concrete and particularized; the threat must be actual and imminent, not conjectural or hypothetical; it must be fairly traceable to the challenged action of the defendant; and it must be likely that a favorable judicial decision will prevent or redress the injury. This requirement assures that "there is a real need to exercise the power of judicial review in order to protect the interests of the complaining party," *Schlesinger v. Reservists Comm. to Stop the War*, 418 U.S. 208 (1974). Where that need does not exist, allowing courts to oversee legislative or executive action "would significantly alter the allocation of power . . . away from a democratic form of government. . . ."

The regulations under challenge here neither require nor forbid any action on the part of respondents. The standards and procedures that they prescribe for Forest Service appeals govern only the conduct of Forest Service officials engaged in project planning. "[W]hen the plaintiff is not himself the object of the government action or inaction he challenges, standing is not precluded, but it is ordinarily '*substantially more difficult*' to establish." [Lujan] [emphasis added]. . . .

It is common ground that the respondent organizations can assert the standing of their members. To establish the concrete and particularized injury that standing requires, respondents point to their members' recreational interests in the National Forests. While generalized harm to the forest or the environment will not alone support standing, if that harm in fact affects the recreational or even the mere esthetic interests of the plaintiff, that will suffice. Sierra Club v. Morton, 405 U.S. 727, 734-736 (1972).

Affidavits submitted to the District Court [were] sufficient to establish Article III standing with respect to Burnt Ridge. . . . [However, after] the District Court had issued a preliminary injunction . . . the parties settled their differences. . . . We know of no precedent for the proposition that when a plaintiff has sued to challenge the lawfulness of certain action or threatened action but has settled that suit, he retains standing to challenge the basis for that action (here, the regulation in the abstract), apart from any concrete application that threatens imminent harm to his interests. Such a holding would fly in the face of Article III's injury-in-fact requirement.

Respondents have identified no other application of the invalidated regulations that threatens imminent and concrete harm to the interests of their members. The only other affidavit relied on was that of Jim Bensman. [The Court refused to consider after-the-fact affidavits holding: "We do not consider these. If respondents had not met the challenge to their standing at the time of judgment, they could not remedy the defect retroactively.] He [Bensman] asserted, first, that he had suffered injury in the past from development on Forest Service land. That does not suffice for several reasons: because it was not tied to application of the challenged regulations, because it does not identify any particular site, and because it relates to past injury rather than imminent future injury that is sought to be enjoined.

Bensman's affidavit further asserts that he has visited many National Forests and plans to visit several unnamed National Forests in the future. Respondents describe this as a mere failure to "provide the name of each timber sale that affected [Bensman's] interests," Brief for Respondents 44. It is much more (or much less) than that. It is a failure to allege that any particular timber sale or other project claimed to be unlawfully subject to the regulations will impede a specific and concrete plan of Bensman's to enjoy the National Forests. The National Forests occupy more than 190 million acres, an area larger than Texas. . . . There may be a chance, but is hardly a likelihood, that Bensman's wanderings will bring him to a parcel about to be affected by a project unlawfully subject to the regulations. Indeed, without further specification it is impossible to tell which projects are (in respondents' view) unlawfully subject to the regulations. . . . Here we are asked to assume not only that Bensman will stumble across a project tract unlawfully subject to the regulations, but also that the tract is about to be developed by the Forest Service in a way that harms his recreational interests, and that he would have commented on the project but for the regulation. Accepting an intention to visit the National Forests as adequate to confer standing to challenge any Government action affecting any portion of those forests would be tantamount to eliminating the requirement of concrete, particularized injury in fact.

The Bensman affidavit does . . . not assert . . . any firm intention to visit their locations, saying only that Bensman "'want[s] to'" go there. . . . This vague desire to return is insufficient to satisfy the requirement of imminent injury: "Such 'some day' intentions -- without any description of concrete plans, or indeed any specification of when the some day will be -- do not support a finding of the 'actual or imminent' injury that our cases require." [Lujan]

Respondents argue that they have standing to bring their challenge because they have suffered procedural injury, namely that they have been denied the ability to file comments on some Forest Service actions and will continue to be so denied. But deprivation of a procedural right without some concrete interest that is affected by the deprivation -- a procedural right in vacuo -- is insufficient to create Article III standing. Only a "person who has been accorded a procedural right to protect his concrete interests can assert that right without meeting all the normal standards for redressability and immediacy." . . .

It makes no difference that the procedural right has been accorded by Congress. . . .

"[I]t would exceed [Article III's] limitations if, at the behest of Congress and in the absence of any showing of concrete injury, we were to entertain citizen suits to vindicate the public's non-concrete interest in the proper administration of the laws. . . . [T]he party bringing suit must show that the action injures him in a concrete and personal way. . . ."

III

The dissent proposes a hitherto unheard-of test for organizational standing: whether, accepting the organization's self-description of the activities of its members, there is a statistical probability that some of those members are threatened with concrete injury. . . . This novel approach to the law of organizational standing would make a mockery of our prior cases, which have required plaintiff-organizations to make specific allegations establishing that at least one identified member had suffered or would suffer harm. . . .

. . . ."Standing," we have said, "is not 'an ingenious academic exercise in the conceivable' . . . [but] requires . . . a factual showing of perceptible harm." In part because of the difficulty of verifying the facts upon which such probabilistic standing depends, the Court has required plaintiffs claiming an organizational standing to identify members who have suffered the requisite harm -- surely not a difficult task here, when so many thousands are alleged to have been harmed.

The dissent would have us replace the requirement of "'imminent'" harm, which it acknowledges our cases establish . . . with the requirement of " 'a realistic threat' that reoccurrence of the challenged activity would cause [the plaintiff] harm 'in the reasonably near future. . . .'" That language is taken, of course, from an opinion that did not find standing, so the seeming expansiveness of the test made not a bit of difference [and is rejected in this case as well].

Since we have resolved this case on the ground of standing, we need not reach the Government's contention that plaintiffs have not demonstrated that the regulations are ripe for review under the Administrative Procedure Act. We likewise do not reach the question whether, if respondents prevailed, a nationwide injunction would be appropriate. And we do not disturb the dismissal of respondents' challenge to the remaining regulations, which has not been appealed.

. . . .

[Finding a lack of standing, the Court reversed that part of the Court of Appeals decision that had found the Earth Island claims justiciable.]

[JUSTICE KENNEDY, concurred and JUSTICES BREYER, STEVENS, SOUTER, and GINSBURG dissented].

————————

1. The *Earth Island* decision is discussed in Jonathan H. Adler, Business, *The Environment, and the Roberts' Court: A Preliminary Assessment*, 49 SANTA CLARA L.

REV. 943 (2009). Professor Adler calls the case "a small and predictable win for the pro-business decision insofar as it reaffirmed the Court's long-standing requirement that citizen-suit plaintiffs suffer an injury-in-fact in order to satisfy the requirements of Article III standing. . . . Summers reaffirmed the Court's hostility to programmatic public interest litigation [making] it more difficult to challenge underlying policy changes. . . . Yet Summers broke no meaningfully new ground in the law of standing, and was thus not a particularly significant win for business interests."

2. Professor Timothy M. Mulvaney writes that *Summers* "drastically limited the ability of private persons and conservation organizations to seek redress for environmental wrongs." Timothy M. Mulvaney, *Instream Flows and the Public Trust*, 22 TUL. ENVTL. L.J. 315 (2009). He writes that the "Court more emphatically rejected the possibility of using probabilistic harms to establish standing. . . ."

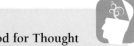

Food for Thought

Do you agree with Professor Adler or Professor Mulvaney? Is *Summers* an affirmation of existing standing requirements or does it increase the already substantial burdens on associational standing?

3. Probabilistic injury, rejected by the majority, sounds speculative. Keep in mind that this is a discussion about standing – determining if a party ought to have his or her day in court. Moreover, probability or the likelihood of harm is at the core of our jurisprudence. Much of tort law is predicated on notions of probability. The assessment of risk is by no means novel or controversial and is central to the most current notions of environmental law. Bradford Mank, *Standing and Statistical Persons: A Risk-Based Approach to Standing*, 36 Ecology L.Q. 665 (2009); Scott Michelman, *Who Can Sue Over Government Surveillance?* 57 UCLA L. Rev. 71 (2009). Take a look at *Shain v. Veneman*, 376 F.3d 815 (8th Cir. 2004) for an application of the concept.

Hypothetical

Assume that ten weeks into the semester, after being promised an open-book exam (and preparing accordingly), your professor announces that after thinking it over, the exam will be closed-book. You and your classmates, *en masse*, complain to your friendly academic dean that a great injustice has occurred. After listening, the dean responds: "You have no way of knowing what will happen on the exam. You are speculating. Probabilistically. There may be no harm at all. What if you all get "A's"? What if the exam is, by any measure, fair and manageable? What if after the exam you realize that having an open book exam would not have helped one iota? No blood, no foul. I am not interfering with a faculty member's discretion – our rules declare explicitly that testing procedures are a matter of academic freedom." Would you be content with this answer? If your response is that this change of policy is unfair procedurally, take a look at the full opinion in *Summers* where the Court finds procedural harms more often than not insufficient for purposes of standing.

II. Standing: Redressability

SIMON V. EASTERN KENTUCKY WELFARE RIGHTS ORGANIZATION

426 U.S. 26 (1976)

[JUSTICE POWELL] Several indigents and organizations composed of indigents brought this suit against the Secretary of the Treasury and the Commissioner of Internal Revenue. They asserted that the Internal Revenue Service (IRS) violated the Internal Revenue Code of 1954 (Code) and the Administrative Procedure Act (APA) by issuing a Revenue Ruling allowing favorable tax treatment to a nonprofit hospital that offered only emergency-room services to indigents. We conclude that these plaintiffs lack standing to bring this suit.

The Code . . . accords advantageous treatment to several types of nonprofit corporations, including exemption of their income from taxation and deductibility by benefactors of the amounts of their donations. Nonprofit hospitals have never received these benefits as a favored general category, but an individual nonprofit hospital has been able to claim them if it could qualify as a corporation "organized and operated exclusively for . . . charitable . . . purposes" . . . . As the Code does not define the term "charitable," the status of each nonprofit hospital is determined on a case-by-case basis by the IRS.

In recognition of the need of nonprofit hospitals for some guidelines on qualification as "charitable" corporations, the IRS in 1956 issued Revenue Ruling 56-185. This Ruling . . . set out four "general requirements" that a hospital had to meet . . . to be considered a charitable organization by the IRS. Only one of those requirements is important here, and it reads as follows:

> It must be operated to the extent of its financial ability for those not able to pay for the services rendered and not exclusively for those who are able and expected to pay. . . .

The fact that its charity record is relatively low is not conclusive that a hospital is not operated for charitable purposes to the full extent of its financial ability. It may furnish services at reduced rates which are below cost, and thereby render charity in that manner. It may also set aside earnings which it uses for improvements and additions to hospital facilities. It must not, however, refuse to accept patients in need of hospital care who cannot pay for such services. Furthermore, if it operates with the expectation of full payment from all those to whom it renders services, it does not dispense charity merely because some of its patients fail to pay for the services rendered.

Revenue Ruling 56-185 remained the announced policy . . . for 13 years, until the IRS issued Revenue Ruling 69-545 on November 3, 1969. This new Ruling described two unidentified hospitals . . . . The description of Hospital A included the following paragraph:

The hospital operates a full time emergency room and no one requiring emergency care is denied treatment. The hospital otherwise ordinarily limits admissions to those who can pay the cost of their hospitalization, either themselves, or through private health insurance, or with the aid of public programs such as Medicare. Patients who cannot meet the financial requirements for admission are ordinarily referred to another hospital in the community that does serve indigent patients.

Despite Hospital A's apparent failure to operate "to the extent of its financial ability for those not able to pay for the services rendered," as required by Revenue Ruling 56-185, the IRS in this new Ruling held Hospital A exempt as a charitable corporation under § 501(c)(3). Noting that Revenue Ruling 56-185 had set out requirements for serving indigents "more restrictive" than those applied to Hospital A, the IRS stated that "Revenue Ruling 56-185 is hereby modified to remove therefrom the requirements relating to caring for patients without charge or at rates below cost."

II

Issuance of Revenue Ruling 69-545 led to the filing of this suit . . . by a group of organizations and individuals. . . . The 12 individual plaintiffs described themselves as subsisting below the poverty income levels established by the Federal Government and suffering from medical conditions requiring hospital services. The organizations sued on behalf of their members, and each individual sued on his own behalf and as representative of all other persons similarly situated.

Each of the individuals described an occasion on which he or a member of his family had been disadvantaged in seeking needed hospital services because of indigency. Most involved the refusal of a hospital to admit the person because of his inability to pay a deposit or an advance fee, even though in some instances the person was enrolled in the Medicare program. At least one plaintiff was denied emergency-room treatment because of his inability to pay immediately. And another was treated in the emergency room but then billed and threatened with suit although his indigency had been known at the time of treatment.

According to the complaint, each of the hospitals involved in these incidents had been determined by the Secretary and the Commissioner to be a tax-exempt charitable corporation, and each received substantial private contributions. The Secretary and the Commissioner were the only defendants. The complaint alleged that by extending tax benefits to such hospitals despite their refusals fully to serve the indigent, the defendants were "encouraging" the hospitals to deny services to the individual plaintiffs and to the members and clients of the plaintiff organizations. . . .

The obvious interest of all respondents, to which they claim actual injury, is that of access to hospital services. In one sense, of course, they have suffered injury to that interest. The complaint alleges specific occasions on which each of the individual respondents sought but was denied hospital services solely due to his indigency, n.1 and in at least some of the cases it is clear that the needed treatment was unavailable, as a practical matter, anywhere else. . . . But injury at the hands of a hospital is insufficient by itself to establish a case or controversy in the context of this suit, for no hospital is a defendant. The only defendants are officials of the Department of the Treasury, and the only claims of illegal action respondents desire the courts to adjudicate are charged to those officials. "Although the law of standing has been greatly changed in [recent] years, we have steadfastly adhered to the requirement that, at least in the absence of a statute expressly conferring standing, federal plaintiffs must allege some threatened or actual injury resulting from the putatively illegal action before a federal court may assume jurisdiction." In other words, the "case or controversy" limitation of Art. III still requires that a federal court act only to redress injury that fairly can be traced to the challenged action of the defendant, and not injury that results from the independent action of some third party not before the court.

> n.1 One of the individual respondents complains, not that he was denied service, but that he was treated and then billed despite the hospital's knowledge of his indigency. This variation of the injury does not change the standing analysis.

The complaint here alleged only that petitioners, by the adoption of Revenue Ruling 69-545, had "encouraged" hospitals to deny services to indigents. The implicit corollary of this allegation is that a grant of respondents' requested relief, resulting in a requirement that all hospitals serve indigents as a condition to favorable tax treatment, would "discourage" hospitals from denying their services to respondents. But it does not follow from the allegation and its corollary that the denial of access to hospital services in fact results from petitioners' new Ruling, or that a court-ordered return by petitioners to their previous policy would result in these respondents' receiving the hospital services they desire. It is purely speculative whether the denials of service specified in the complaint fairly can be traced to petitioners' "encouragement" or instead result from decisions made by the hospitals without regard to the tax implications.

We do note, however, that it is entirely speculative whether even the earlier Ruling would have assured the medical care they desire. It required a hospital to provide care for the indigent only "to the extent of its financial ability," and stated that a low charity record was not conclusive that a hospital had failed to meet that duty. Thus, a hospital could not maintain, consistently with Revenue Ruling 56-185, a general policy of refusing care to all patients unable to pay. But the number of such patients accepted, and whether any particular applicant would be admitted, would depend upon the financial ability of the hospital to which admittance was sought.

It is equally speculative whether the desired exercise of the court's remedial powers in this suit would result in the availability to respondents of such services. So far as the complaint sheds light, it is just as plausible that the hospitals . . . would elect to forgo favorable tax treatment to avoid the undetermined financial drain of an increase in the level of uncompensated services. It is true that the individual respondents have alleged, upon information and belief, that the hospitals that denied them service receive substantial donations deductible by the donors. This allegation could support an inference that these hospitals, or some of them, are so financially dependent upon the favorable tax treatment afforded charitable organizations that they would admit respondents if a court required such admission as a condition to receipt of that treatment. But this inference is speculative at best. . . .

. . . .

[T]he complaint suggests no substantial likelihood that victory in this suit would result in respondents' receiving the hospital treatment they desire. A federal court, properly cognizant of the Art. III limitation upon its jurisdiction, must require more than respondents have shown before proceeding to the merits.

Our decision is also consistent with *Data Processing Serv. v. Camp*. . . . The complaint in Data Processing alleged injury that was directly traceable to the action of the defendant federal official, for it complained of injurious competition that would have been illegal without that action. . . . In the instant case respondents' injuries might have occurred even in the absence of the IRS Ruling that they challenge; whether the injuries fairly can be traced to that Ruling depends upon unalleged and unknown facts about the relevant hospitals.

Accordingly, the judgment of the Court of Appeals is vacated, and the cause is remanded to the District Court with instructions to dismiss the complaint. . . .

1. The complainants in *Simon* had at least three major problems: (1) associational standing – even though the "named plaintiffs" could each identify individual harm they had or would sustain; (2) redressability – the Court took the position that providing the requested remedy would not solve the problems about which the plaintiff complained; and (3) party designation – the focus of the Court and, to an extent, the plaintiffs' lawyers was the government. Had the case centered on hospitals, would that solve the redressability problem? Is the hospital the right party to attack if the gravamen of the complaint was a regulation issued by a government agency?

2. As with Lujan, it is useful to think about *Simon* in the familiar terminology of proximate cause. The U.S. Department of Treasury set in motion a course of events that led (according to plaintiff's theory) to hospitals making an independent decision that they either would (or would not) need to protect their tax-exempt status and therefore they would (or perhaps would not) provide additional health-care services. The decisionmaking of the hospital is an intervening event. If it is prompted by the "initial alleged breach" – the Treasury determination – is the hospital's decision reasonably foreseeable? Is it of "independent origin?" Is it the cause-in-fact of the plaintiff's injury? The more foreseeable an intervening event, the less likely it is to cut off the liability of the original actor, in this instance, the Treasury.

3. Is *Simon* less about the need of low-to-moderate-income individuals to secure necessary medical care than it is about access to federal courts? At the time the case was decided, the Court was narrowing the hallway to the courthouse door, if not closing it, to large numbers of claimants who wished to contest what they perceived as inappropriate or unlawful agency activity. It is the business of "prudential" considerations to exercise judgment that transcends the baseline constitutional requirements – is this case a fairly good example of that phenomenon? Broad concerns about associational standing and the activity of public interest groups were certainly part of the discourse surrounding this case.

4. Associational Standing. Associational standing cases raise unique and difficult challenges beyond the general admonition that the courts are not readily available to serve as a form for deeply concerned (but uninjured) persons to challenge the efficacy, legality, or even constitutionality of agency action. Fleck & Assocs. v. City of Phoenix, 471 F.3d 1100 (9th Cir. 2006). Deeply held beliefs and intense dedication to a cause are simply not part of the standing calculus.

a. For the last 30 years, the Court has tried to identify criteria for associational standing. In Warth v. Seldin, 422 U.S. 490, 511 (1975), the Court explained that an "association must allege that its members, or any one of them, are suffering immediate or threatened injury." Two years later, the Court found that even if a group or association has failed to demonstrate injury-in-fact, it may have "standing to bring suit on behalf of its members when: (a) its members would otherwise have standing to sue in their own right; (b) the interests it seeks to protect are germane to the organization's purpose; and (c) neither the claim asserted nor the relief requested requires the participation of individual members in the lawsuit." *Hunt v. Wash. State Apple Adver. Comm'n*, 432 U.S. 333, 343 (1977). The decision regarding the lack of essential participation by group members has been the basis of constant litigation. The Seventh Circuit recently interpreted the third *Hunt* test to require, as a matter of prudential screening, injury to an individual group member or a clearly defined injury affecting the whole group. In *Disability Rights Wisconsin v. Walworth County Board of Supervisors*, 522 F.3d 796 (7th Cir. 2008), the court found: "The third requirement does not derive from the Constitution. Instead, it is a judicially imposed limitation, *United Food & Commercial Workers Union Local 751 v. Brown Group, Inc.*, 517 U.S. 544, 556-57 (1996), which may be overridden by Congress. . . ."

b. If there is a requirement that one member be able to sue in his or her own right, what is the point of associational standing? Notice the language in *Seafood Exps. Ass'n of India v. United States*, 479 F. Supp. 2d 1367 (U.S. Court of Int'l Trade, 2007): "Plaintiff SEAI has met associational standing requirements, which require that at least *one member* of the association be able to sue in its own right, that the association seek to protect an interest central to its purpose, and that the relief sought not require individualized testimony by member plaintiffs." [Emphasis added.]

c. In a case involving the selection of judges in New York State, the court had to "peer inside New York State's political clubhouses and determine whether party leaders have arrogated to themselves a choice that belongs to the people." *Lopez Torres v. N.Y. State Bd. of Elections*, 462 F.3d 161 (2d Cir. 2006), *rev'd on other grounds*, *New York State Bd. of Elections v. Lopez Torres*, 260 Fed.Appx. 845 (6th Cir. 2008). Among others, Common Cause, an association, attacked the New York system of selection. On appeal, the court noted the following:

Although defendants do not challenge the associational standing of Common Cause/NY, and appear not to have done so below, we have considered the issue nostra sponte. At least at this point in the litigation, the record establishes that Common Cause/NY possesses associational standing because (1) there exists a clear likelihood that its members – 20,000 voters from across New York State – have suffered a concrete injury to their First Amendment rights that is fairly traceable to defendants' conduct

Take Note

The term "nostra sponte" conveys the same meaning as "sua sponte," and refers to a judicial act or inquiry initiated by (or on motion of) the court, as opposed to an action by the court in response to a request from counsel. Nostra sponte is used when the action is initiated by a judicial panel as opposed to an individual judge.

and can be remedied by court action; (2) the First Amendment associational interests that this suit seeks to vindicate are germane to Common Cause/NY's purpose of making "government more responsive and open to citizens, [restoring] ethics in government, and [curbing] the influence of special interest money in politics"; and (3) neither the claim asserted nor the injunctive and declaratory relief requested requires that Common Cause/NY's individual members participate in the suit. *See generally Hunt* [*supra*, note 4a].

While this case was reversed by the Supreme Court in 2008, the section on associational standing was untouched – so is there a requirement of an injury to an individual in these cases?

d. In *N.H. Motor Transportation Ass'n v. Rowe*, 448 F.3d 66 (1st Cir. 2006), *aff'd*, *Rowe v. N.H. Motor Transportation Ass'n*, 552 U.S. 364 (2008), a tobacco liability case, several nonprofit trade associations sought a declaration that federal law pertaining to tobacco preempted state law. On the question of associational standing, the court struggled with the third *Hunt* factor on injury to an individual in the group and

> acknowledged that "there is no well developed test in this circuit as to how the third prong of the *Hunt* test . . . applies in cases where injunctive relief is sought." *Pharmaceutical Care Mgmt. Ass'n v. Rowe*, 429 F.3d 294, 313-14 (1st Cir. 2005). . . . We concluded that representational standing is inappropriate if adjudicating the merits of an association's claim requires the court to engage in a "fact-intensive-individual inquiry. . . ."

Is this a new element of justiciability for associational standing?

e. In *Local 491 v. Gwinnett County*, 510 F. Supp. 2d 1271 (N.D. Ga. 2007), a case brought by Local 491 International Brotherhood of Police Officers regarding a prohibition against "off-duty police officers from wearing the Gwinnett County police uniform while attending meetings of the Gwinnett County Board of Commissioners," the court added yet another variable for associational standing: "Though an association may have standing to seek a 'declaration, injunction, or some other form of prospective relief' on behalf of its members, it does not enjoy standing to seek damages for monetary injuries peculiar to individual members where the fact and extent of injury will require individualized proof." (quoting *Warth v. Seldin*, 422 U.S. 490 (1975)).

f. In *Brady Campaign to Prevent Gun Violence United with the Million Mom March v. Ashcroft*, 339 F. Supp. 2d 68, 73-74 (D.C. Cir. 2004), plaintiff organization sued the Bureau of Alcohol, Tobacco, Firearms and Explosives (ATF), seeking to get ATF to require discontinuation of policies that made it possible for private citizens to get semiautomatic assault weapons (SAW). There were organization members living in neighborhoods where violent crimes involving SAWs had taken place.

After reciting the basic law of standing and the *Hunt* criteria, applicable to associations, the court turned to *Simon*.

> The "government argues both that the Brady Campaign fails to demonstrate that it has suffered actual injury that is fairly traceable to the ATF policy and conduct it challenges and sensitive to redress by a favorable judicial decision; and that the complaint presents a mere "generalized grievance" insufficient to satisfy prudential standing requirements. It is important to note that the requirement that the plaintiff allege an "injury in fact" is analytically distinct from the requirement that the alleged injury be "traceable" to the defendant's conduct and "redressable" by favorable judicial action. This Court finds that while the Brady Campaign has alleged a sufficient injury in fact to support standing, it has failed to allege sufficient facts to demonstrate traceability and redressability.

Now that you have read *Simon*, can you state with clarity what redressability means?

5. *Simon* and <u>*Chevron*</u>. Another consideration in *Simon* involves the question just below the surface in all public interest litigation: Where should the court draw the line? Is it the role of federal courts to be engaged in active and aggressive oversight of the decisions of federal agencies? Judgment regarding the wisdom of tax rulings that have broad and general applicability – as opposed to individual revenue rulings targeting a specific item and a specific tax payer – were, at the time, vested clearly in the discretion of the agency.

6. At the time *Simon* was decided, a pointed public controversy regarding the efficacy of federally funded "reform litigation" was under way. Should taxpayers support legal aid or legal services offices that are funded publicly when those offices engage in efforts to use Article III courts to change the law to suit the political agenda of a particular interest group? Even assuming a group could meet the requirements of standing (including, in appropriate instances, associational standing), should tax money be used? *See* Ingrid V. Eagley, *Community Education: Creating A New Vision of Legal Services Practice*, 4 CLIN. L. REV. 433 (1998); James P. Lorenz, Jr., <u>*Almost the Last Word on Legal Services: Congress Can Do Pretty Much What It Likes,* 17 ST. LOUIS U. PUB. L. REV. 295 (1998)</u>. *See also* Omnibus Consolidated Rescissions and Appropriations Act of 1996, <u>Pub. L. No. 104-134</u>, 504, <u>110 Stat. 1321</u>, 1321-53, re-enacted, Omnibus Consolidated Appropriations Act of 1997, <u>Pub. L. No. 104-208</u>, 502, <u>110 Stat. 3009</u>, 3009-59 (1996) (the "Act") (prohibiting reform litigation, lobbying, and class actions). This legislation was attacked (without success) in <u>*Legal Aid Society v. Legal Services Corp.*, 145 F.3d 1017, 1020 (9th Cir. 1998)</u>.

7. *Frank Krasner Enterprises v. Montgomery County, Maryland*, 401 F.3d 230 (4th Cir. 2005).

> Since 1990, Frank Krasner Enterprises, Ltd. ("Krasner") has been in the business of putting on gun shows in . . . Maryland. For his shows in Montgomery County, . . . Krasner has biannually leased between 13,000 to 18,000 square feet of space at . . . the Montgomery County Agricultural Center ("Ag Center"). . . .
>
> On May 16, 2001, the Montgomery County Council amended . . . section 57-13 of the [Montgomery County] Code, entitled "Use of Public Funds." It states "(a) The County must not give financial or in-kind support to any organization that allows the display and sale of guns at a facility owned or controlled by the organization. . . ." . . . . Less than a month after section 57-13 became law, the Ag Center sent a letter to Krasner stating that, "we have been forced to make financial decisions to stop conducting activities which would invoke the County to impose financial sanctions on the Ag Center." The letter made clear that this decision was a result of the County's funding restriction, not any problems with Krasner. . . . Krasner . . . responded to the Ag Center's decision by suing Montgomery County . . . . Importantly, the Ag Center is not a party to this lawsuit . . . .
>
> The requirements of Article III standing are numbingly familiar. . . . We have previously denied standing because the actions of an independent third party . . . stood between the plaintiff and the challenged actions. . . . We . . . find that the Appellees lack standing for failure to establish the causation and redressability prongs. The purported injury here . . . is not directly linked to the challenged law because an intermediary . . . (here, the Ag Center) stands directly between the plaintiffs and the challenged conduct in a way that breaks the causal chain. We freely acknowledge that the law makes it more expensive – perhaps prohibitively so – for the Ag Center to lease space to Krasner. . . . The record leaves no doubt that this was a deal-breaker; Krasner only rents space for perhaps four days a year, and the County has given the Ag Center over a half-million dollars in grants. But that the County's decision may have been easy does not alter the analysis. Likewise, even if we were to hear the case and hold for the Appellees, we could not compel the Ag Center to rent space to Krasner (nor, crucially, could we even direct the County to subsidize the Ag Center in the future). This would, then, be just the sort of advisory opinion federal courts must not give. . . .Thus, the Appellees lack standing.

———————

DUKE POWER CO. V. CAROLINA ENVIRONMENTAL STUDY GROUP, INC.

438 U.S. 59 (1978)

[CHIEF JUSTICE BURGER] These appeals present the question of whether Congress may, consistent with the Constitution, impose a limitation on liability for nuclear accidents resulting from the operation of private nuclear power plants licensed by the Federal Government.

I.

A.

When Congress passed the Atomic Energy Act of 1946, it contemplated that the development of nuclear power would be a Government monopoly. Within a decade, however, Congress concluded that the national interest would be best served if the Government encouraged the private sector to become involved . . . . The Atomic Energy Act of 1954 . . . implemented this policy decision, providing for licensing of private construction, ownership, and operation of commercial nuclear power reactors for energy production under strict supervision by the Atomic Energy Commission (AEC).

. . . It soon became apparent that profits from the private exploitation of atomic energy were uncertain and the accompanying risks substantial. Although the AEC offered incentives to encourage investment, there remained in the path of the private nuclear power industry various problems — the risk of potentially vast liability in the event of a nuclear accident of a sizable magnitude being the major obstacle. . . . Thus, while repeatedly stressing that the risk of a major nuclear accident was extremely remote, spokesmen for the private sector informed Congress that they would be forced to withdraw from the field if their liability were not limited by appropriate legislation.

Congress responded in 1957 by passing the Price-Anderson Act. . . . In its original form, the Act limited the aggregate liability for a single nuclear incident to $500 million plus the amount of liability insurance available on the private market — some $60 million in 1957. The nuclear industry was required to purchase the maximum available amount of [private] liability insurance, and the Act provided that if damages from a nuclear disaster exceeded [that amount], the Federal Government would indemnify the licensee . . . in an amount not to exceed $500 million. Thus, the actual ceiling on liability was the amount of private insurance coverage plus the Government's indemnification obligation which totaled $560 million.

Since its enactment, the Act has been [amended to require] those indemnified under the Act to waive all legal defenses in the event of a substantial nuclear accident. This provision was based on a congressional concern that state tort law dealing with liability for nuclear incidents was generally unsettled and that some way of insuring a common standard of responsibility for all jurisdictions — strict liability — was needed. A waiver of defenses was thought to be the preferable approach since it entailed less interference with state tort law than would the enactment of a federal statute prescribing strict liability.

In 1975 . . . a new provision was added requiring, in the event of a nuclear incident, each of the 60 or more reactor owners to contribute between $2 and

$5 million toward the cost of compensating victims. Since the liability ceiling remained at the same level, the effect . . . was to reduce the Federal Government's contribution to the liability pool. In its amendments to the Act in 1975, Congress also explicitly provided that "in the event of a nuclear incident involving damages in excess of [the] amount of aggregate liability, the Congress will . . . take whatever action is deemed necessary and appropriate to protect the public from the consequences of a disaster of such magnitude . . . ."

Under the Price-Anderson Act as it presently stands, liability in the event of a nuclear incident causing damages of $560 million or more would be spread as follows: $315 million would be paid from contributions by the licensees of the 63 private operating nuclear power plants; $140 million would come from private insurance (the maximum now available); [and the remaining] $105 million would be borne by the Federal Government.

B.

Duke Power Co. is an investor-owned public utility which is constructing one nuclear power plant in North Carolina and one in South Carolina. Duke Power, along with the NRC, was sued by appellees, two organizations – Carolina Environmental Study Group and the Catawba Central Labor Union – and 40 individuals who live within close proximity to the planned facilities. The action was commenced in 1973, and sought, among other relief, a declaration that the Price-Anderson Act is unconstitutional.

[T]he District Court held . . . that the Price-Anderson Act was unconstitutional in two respects: (a) it violated the Due Process Clause of the Fifth Amendment because it allowed injuries to occur without assuring adequate compensation to the victims; (b) the Act offended the equal protection component of the Fifth Amendment by forcing the victims of nuclear incidents to bear the burden of injury, whereas society as a whole benefits from the existence and development of nuclear power.

We . . . now reverse.

II.

. . . It is enough for present purposes that the claimed cause of action to vindicate appellees' constitutional rights is sufficiently substantial and colorable to sustain [subject matter] jurisdiction under § 1331(a).

III.

The District [Court's] factual findings form the basis for our analysis of these issues.

A.

The essence of the standing inquiry is whether the parties seeking to invoke the court's jurisdiction have "alleged such a personal stake in the outcome of the controversy as to assure that concrete adverseness which sharpens the presentation of issues upon which the court so largely depends for illumination of difficult constitutional questions." As refined by subsequent reformulation, this requirement of a "personal stake" has come to be understood to require not only a "distinct and palpable injury," to the plaintiff, but also a "fairly traceable" causal connection between the claimed injury and the challenged conduct. Application of these constitutional standards to the factual findings of the District Court persuades us that the Art. III requisites for standing are satisfied by appellees.

We turn first to consider the kinds of injuries the District Court found the appellees suffered. It discerned two categories of effects which resulted from the operation of nuclear power plants in potentially dangerous proximity to appellees' living and working environment. The immediate effects included: (a) the production of small quantities of non-natural radiation which would invade the air and water; (b) a "sharp increase" in the temperature of two lakes . . . resulting from the use of the lake waters to produce steam and to cool the reactor; . . . (d) threatened reduction in property values of land neighboring the power plants; (e) "objectively reasonable" present fear and apprehension regarding the "effect of the increased radioactivity . . . upon their descendants"; and (f) the continual threat of "an accident resulting in uncontrolled release of . . . radioactive material" with no assurance of adequate compensation for the resultant damage. Into a second category of potential effects were placed the damages ". . . from a core melt or other major accident in the operation of a reactor . . . ."

For purposes of the present inquiry, we need not determine whether all the putative injuries identified by the District Court, particularly those based on the possibility of a nuclear accident and the present apprehension generated by this future uncertainty, are sufficiently concrete to satisfy constitutional requirements. It is enough that several of the "immediate" adverse effects were found to harm appellees. Certainly the environmental and aesthetic consequences of the thermal pollution of the two lakes in the vicinity of the disputed power plants is the type of harmful effect which has been deemed adequate in prior cases to satisfy the "injury in fact" standard. And the emission of non-natural radiation into appellees' environment would also seem a direct and present injury, given our generalized concern about exposure to radiation and the apprehension flowing from the uncertainty about . . . even small emissions like those concededly emitted by nuclear power plants.

The more difficult step . . . is establishing that these injuries "fairly can be traced to the challenged action of the defendant," . . . or put otherwise, that the exercise of the Court's remedial powers would redress the claimed injuries. The District Court discerned a "but for" causal connection between the Price-Anderson Act, which appellees challenged as unconstitutional, "and the construction of the nuclear plants . . . ." Particularizing that causal link to the facts of the instant case, the District Court concluded that "there is a substantial likelihood that Duke would not be able to complete [and operate] the McGuire and Catawba Nuclear Plants but for the protection provided by the Price-Anderson Act."

These findings . . . are challenged on two grounds. First, it is argued that the evidence presented at the hearing, contrary to the conclusion reached by the District Court, indicated that the McGuire and Catawba nuclear plants would be completed and operated without the Price-Anderson Act's limitation on liability. And second, it is contended that the Price-Anderson Act is not, in some essential sense, the "but for" cause . . . since if the Act had not been passed Congress may well have chosen to pursue the nuclear program as a Government monopoly as it had from 1946 until 1954. We reject both of these arguments.

The District Court's finding of a "substantial likelihood" that the McGuire and Catawba nuclear plants would be neither completed nor operated absent the Price-Anderson Act rested in major part on the testimony of corporate officials before the Joint Committee on Atomic Energy (JCAE) . . . . During the 1956-1957 hearings, industry spokesmen . . . expressed a categorical unwillingness to participate in the development of nuclear power absent guarantees of a limitation on their liability. By 1975, the tenor of the testimony had changed only slightly. While large utilities and producers were somewhat more equivocal . . . the smaller producers of component parts and architects and engineers – all of whom are essential to the building of the reactors and generating plants – considered renewal of the Act as the critical variable in determining their continued involvement with nuclear power. Duke Power itself, in its letter to the Committee urging extension of the Act, cited recent experiences with suppliers and contractors who were requiring the inclusion of cancellation clauses in their contracts to take effect if the liability-limitation provisions were eliminated. . . . Considering the [evidence] in the record, we cannot say we are left with "the definite and firm conviction that" the finding by the trial court . . . is clearly erroneous; and, hence, we are bound to accept it.

The second attack . . . warrants only brief attention. Essentially the argument is . . . that Price-Anderson is not a "but for" cause of the injuries appellees claim since, if Price-Anderson had not been passed, the Government would have undertaken development of nuclear power on its own and the same injuries would likely have accrued to appellees from such Government-operated plants as from privately operated ones. Whatever the ultimate accuracy of this speculation, it is not responsive to the simple proposition that private power companies now do in fact operate the nuclear-powered generating plants injuring appellees, and that their participation would not have occurred but for the enactment and implementation of the Price-Anderson Act. Nothing in our prior cases requires a party seeking to invoke federal jurisdiction to negate the kind of speculative and hypothetical possibilities suggested in order to demonstrate the likely effectiveness of judicial relief.

B.

It is further contended that in addition to proof of injury and of a causal link between such injury and the challenged conduct, appellees must demonstrate a connection between the injuries they claim and the constitutional rights being asserted. . . . Since the environmental and health injuries claimed by appellees are not directly related to the constitutional attack on the Price-Anderson Act, such injuries, the argument continues, cannot supply a predicate for standing. n.3 We decline to accept this argument.

> n.3 The only injury that would possess the required subject-matter nexus to the due process challenge is the injury that would result from a nuclear accident causing damages in excess of the liability limitation provisions of the Price-Anderson Act.

. . . No cases have been cited outside the context of taxpayer suits where we have demanded this type of subject-matter nexus between the right asserted and the injury alleged, and we are aware of none. . . . We . . . cannot accept the contention that, outside the context of taxpayers' suits, a litigant must demonstrate something more than injury in fact and a substantial likelihood that the judicial relief requested will prevent or redress the claimed injury to satisfy the "case or controversy" requirement of Art. III. . . . Where a party champions his own rights, and where the injury alleged is a concrete and particularized one which will be prevented or redressed by the relief requested, the basic practical and prudential concerns underlying the standing doctrine are generally satisfied when the constitutional requisites are met.

We conclude that appellees have standing to challenge the constitutionality of the Price-Anderson Act.

C.

. . . Since we are persuaded that "we will be in no better position [in the event of a nuclear catastrophe] than we are now" to decide this question, we hold that it is presently ripe for adjudication.

IV.

The District Court held that the Price-Anderson Act contravened the Due Process Clause because "[the] amount of recovery is not rationally related to the potential losses"; because "[the] Act tends to encourage irresponsibility in matters of safety and environmental protection . . ."; and finally because "[there] is no quid pro quo" for the liability limitations. An equal protection violation was also found because the Act "places the cost of [nuclear power] on an arbitrarily chosen segment of society, those injured by nuclear catastrophe." Application of the relevant constitutional principles forces the conclusion that these holdings of the District Court cannot be sustained.

A.

Our due process analysis properly begins with a discussion of the appropriate standard of review. Appellants . . . urge that the Price-Anderson Act be accorded the traditional presumption of constitutionality generally accorded economic regulations and that it be upheld absent proof of arbitrariness or irrationality on the part of Congress. Appellees, however, urge a more elevated standard of review on the ground that the interests jeopardized by the Price-Anderson Act "are far more important than those in the economic due process and business-oriented cases" . . . . An intermediate standard . . . is thus recommended for our use here.

As we read the Act and its legislative history, it is clear that Congress' purpose was to remove the economic impediments in order to stimulate the private development of electric energy by nuclear power while simultaneously providing the public compensation in the event of a catastrophic nuclear incident. The liability-limitation provision thus emerges as a classic example of an economic regulation – a legislative effort to structure and accommodate "the burdens and benefits of economic life." "It is by now well established that [such] Acts . . . come to the Court with a presumption of constitutionality, and that the burden is on one complaining of a due process violation to establish that the legislature has acted in an arbitrary and irrational way." That the accommodation struck may have profound and far-reaching consequences, contrary to appellees' suggestion, provides all the more reason for this Court to defer to the congressional judgment unless it is demonstrably arbitrary or irrational.

B.

When examined in light of this standard of review, the Price-Anderson Act, in our view, passes constitutional muster. The record before us fully supports the need for . . . a statutory limit on liability to encourage private industry participation and hence bears a rational relationship to Congress' concern for stimulating the involvement of private enterprise in the production of electric energy through the use of atomic power; nor do we understand appellees or the District Court to be of a different view. Rather their challenge is to the alleged arbitrariness of the particular figure of $560 million, which is the statutory ceiling on liability. . . .

Assuming, arguendo, that the $560 million fund would not insure full recovery in all conceivable circumstances – and the hard truth is that no one can ever know – it does not by any means follow that the liability limitation is therefore irrational and violative of due process. The legislative history clearly indicates that the $560 million figure was not arrived at on the supposition that it alone would necessarily be sufficient to guarantee full compensation in the event of a nuclear incident. Instead, it was conceived of as a "starting point" or a working hypothesis. The reasonableness of the statute's assumed ceiling on liability was predicated on two corollary considerations – expert appraisals of the exceedingly small risk of a nuclear incident involving claims in excess of $560 million, and the recognition that in the event of such an incident, Congress would likely enact extraordinary relief provisions to provide additional relief, in accord with prior practice. . . . [C]andor requires acknowledgment that whatever ceiling figure is selected will, of necessity, be arbitrary in the sense that any choice of a figure based on imponderables like those at issue here can always be so characterized. This is not, however, the kind of arbitrariness which flaws otherwise constitutional action. . . .

[The] District Court's further conclusion that the Price-Anderson Act "tends to encourage irresponsibility . . . on the part of builders and owners" of the nuclear power plants simply cannot withstand careful scrutiny. We recently outlined the multitude of detailed steps involved in the review of any application for a license to construct or to operate a nuclear power plant, *Vermont Yankee Nuclear Power Corp. v. NRDC*; nothing in the liability-limitation provision [alters] that process. Moreover, in the event of a nuclear accident the utility itself would suffer perhaps the largest damages. While obviously not to be compared with the loss of human life and injury to health, the risk of . . . bankruptcy to the utility is in itself no small incentive to avoid the kind of irresponsible and cavalier conduct implicitly attributed to licensees by the District Court.

The remaining due process objection to the liability-limitation provision is that it fails to provide those injured by a nuclear accident with a satisfactory quid pro quo for the common-law rights of recovery which the Act abrogates. Initially, it is not at all clear that the Due Process Clause in fact requires that a legislatively enacted compensation scheme either duplicate the recovery at common law or provide a reasonable substitute remedy. However, we need not resolve this question here since the Price-Anderson Act does, in our view, provide a reasonably just substitute for the common-law or state tort law remedies it replaces. n.4

n.4 We reject at the outset appellees' contention that . . . prior to the enactment of the Price-Anderson Act, appellees had some right, cognizable under the Due Process

> Clause, to be free of nuclear power or to take advantage of the state of uncertainty which inhibited the private development of nuclear power. . . . Appellees' only relevant right prior to the enactment of the Price-Anderson Act was to utilize their existing common-law and state-law remedies to vindicate any particular harm visited on them from whatever sources. After the Act was passed, that right . . . was replaced by the compensation mechanism of the statute, and it is only the terms of that substitution which are pertinent to the quid pro quo inquiry which appellees insist the Due Process Clause requires.

. . . We view the congressional assurance of a $560 million fund for recovery, accompanied by an express statutory commitment, to "take whatever action is deemed necessary and appropriate to protect the public from the consequences of" a nuclear accident to be a fair and reasonable substitute for the uncertain recovery of damages of this magnitude from a utility or component manufacturer, whose resources might well be exhausted at an early stage. The record in this case raises serious questions about the ability of a utility or component manufacturer to satisfy a judgment approaching $560 million – the amount guaranteed under the Price-Anderson Act. Nor are we persuaded that the mandatory waiver of defenses required by the Act is of no benefit to potential claimants. Since there has never been, to our knowledge, a case arising out of a nuclear incident like those covered by the Price-Anderson Act, any discussion of the standard of liability that state courts will apply is necessarily speculative. . . . Further, even if strict liability were routinely applied, the common-law doctrine is subject to exceptions for acts of God or of third parties – two of the very factors which appellees emphasized in the District Court in the course of arguing that the risks of a nuclear accident are greater than generally admitted. All of these considerations belie the suggestion that the Act leaves the potential victims of a nuclear disaster in a more disadvantageous position than they would be in if left to their common-law remedies – not known in modern times for either their speed or economy.

Appellees' remaining objections can be briefly treated. The claim-administration procedures under the Act provide that in the event of an accident with potential liability exceeding the $560 million ceiling, no more than 15% of the limit can be distributed pending court approval of a plan of distribution taking into account the need to assure compensation for "possible latent injury claims which may not be discovered until a later time." Although some delay might follow from compliance with this statutory procedure, we doubt that it would approach that resulting from routine litigation of the large number of claims caused by a catastrophic accident. Moreover, the statutory scheme insures the equitable distribution of benefits to all who suffer injury – both immediate and latent; under the common-law route, the proverbial race to the courthouse would instead determine who had "first crack" at the diminishing resources of the tortfeasor, and fairness could well be sacrificed in the process. The remaining contention that recovery is uncertain because of the aggregate rather than individualized nature of the liability ceiling is but a thinly disguised version of the contention that the $560 million figure is inadequate, which we have already rejected.

. . . The Price-Anderson Act not only provides a reasonable, prompt, and equitable mechanism for compensating victims of a catastrophic nuclear incident, it also guarantees a level of net compensation generally exceeding that recoverable in private litigation. Moreover, the Act contains an explicit congressional commitment to take further action to aid victims of a nuclear accident in the event that the $560 million ceiling on liability is exceeded. This panoply of remedies and guarantees is at the least a reasonably just substitute for the common-law rights replaced by the Price-Anderson Act. Nothing more is required by the Due Process Clause.

[T]he equal protection arguments largely track and duplicate those made in support of the due process claim. . . . The general rationality of the Price-Anderson Act liability limitations – particularly with reference to the important congressional purpose of encouraging private participation in the exploitation of nuclear energy – is ample justification for the difference in treatment between those injured in nuclear accidents and those whose injuries are derived from other causes. . . .

Accordingly, the decision of the District Court is reversed, and the cases are remanded for proceedings consistent with this opinion. . . .

Underlying Case Documents

The case referenced:
The Atomic Energy Act of 1946
The Price-Anderson Act
Testimony before the Joint Committee in 1956–1957
Testimony before the Joint Committee in 1975
Duke's Statement

1. Declaring the Price-Anderson Act unconstitutional would have been an act of some moment in the nuclear power field – and required dozens of massive private investor owned utilities to make judgments about their plans to continue construction on nuclear power plants throughout the United States. But would it mandate cessation of construction or operation? How is this different from *Simon*? *Simon* requires that the harm about which the plaintiffs complain is "likely to be redressed by a favorable decision" while *Duke* requires a "substantial likelihood" that the remedy will address the plaintiff's alleged injuries. Do you see a significant

difference in those two standards? *See* Richard H. Fallon, *Of Justiciability, Remedies, and Public Law Litigation: Notes on the Jurisprudence of* Lyons, 59 N.Y.U. L. Rev. 1, 18 (1984).

2. Is this case about "but for" causation, attenuated causation theory, or pure politics? Justice Stewart's concurring opinion notes that a desire to declare constitutional the Price-Anderson Act is not a basis to determine that the constitutional and prudential requirements of standing have been met.

> Even assuming that but for the Act the plant would not exist and therefore neither would its effects on the environment, I cannot believe that it follows that the appellees have standing to attack the constitutionality of the Act. Apart from a "but for" connection in the loosest sense of that concept, there is no relationship at all between the injury alleged for standing purposes and the injury alleged for federal subject-matter jurisdiction. . . . Surely there must be some direct relationship between the plaintiff's federal claim and the injury relied on for standing. [From 438 U.S. 94-95.]

Make the Connection

The Energy Policy Act of 2005 extends the liability limitation under the Price-Anderson Act for 20 years, until 2025. Pub. L. No. 109-58, §§ 601-610, 119 Stat. 594 (2005). The maximum on liability for cognizable harms related to nuclear power generation, viewing all likely insurance sources, is now $10 billion. Should the federal government be responsible for damages in excess of $10 billion? For an overview of the basics of the legislation, see Fact Sheet on Nuclear Insurance and Disaster Relief Funds, http://www.nrc.gov/reading-rm/doc-collections/fact-sheets/funds-fs.html, site last visited July 27, 2008.

Justice Stevens expressed a similar concern:

> The string of contingencies that supposedly holds this litigation together is too delicate for me. We are told that but for the Price-Anderson Act there would be no financing of nuclear power plants, no development of those plants by private parties, and hence no present injury to persons such as appellees; we are then asked to remedy an alleged due process violation that may possibly occur at some uncertain time in the future, and may possibly injure the appellees in a way that has no significant connection with any present injury. It is remarkable that such a series of speculations is considered sufficient either to make this litigation ripe for decision or to establish appellees' standing. [From 438 U.S. 103-04.]

Does it seem possible that the majority was determined to resolve a dispute to insure nuclear power generation, coming down on one side of a controversial political issue? What about the Court's historic commitment to steer clear of political disputes? Courts in this country have a long history of refusing to decide "political questions." *Nixon v. United States*, 506 U.S. 224, 228-29 (1993); *Luther v. Borden*, 48 U.S. (7 How.) 1, 46-47 (1849). *But see, Bush v. Gore*, 531 U.S. 98, 104

(2000), *and* Louis Michael Seidman, *The Secret Life of the Political Question Doctrine*, 37 J. MARSHALL L. REV. 441, 460 (2004).

3. Declaring that the complainants had standing in *Duke* allowed the Court to put to rest the constitutionality challenge to the Price Anderson Act – a decision that the dissenting opinions suggest may have been based more on national energy policy than the law of standing. That said, think about the timing of this case and the energy issues in the United States at the time. An oil embargo had created a national crisis not long before this case

Take Note

"How." in *Luther v. Borden*, the case cited in the comments adjacent to this box, refers to Howard, a reporter for the Supreme Court at the time of that decision. For those seeking an authoritative discussion of citation format for early Supreme Court cases, see Anne Ashmore, Library of Congress, *Dates of Supreme Court Decisions and Arguments, United States Reports, Volumes 2 – 107 (1791 – 1882)*. http://www.supremecourtus. gov/opinions/datesofdecisions.pdf, last visited July 27, 2008.

was decided and nuclear power may well have seemed one important way to lessen the demand for fossil fuel in the United States. Assuming this is true, is it an appropriate consideration in a case that assesses constitutional and prudential standing requirements? How would you distinguish prudential and political considerations?

4. In *Allen v. Wright*, 468 U.S. 737 (1984), a group of parents brought suit against the Internal Revenue Service, demanding that IRS cease to provide tax exempt status to those private schools that discriminated on the basis of race. In part because the parents involved had children in public schools and in part because

For More Information

Other cases allowing standing despite relatively attenuated chains of causation include *Heckler v. Mathews*, 465 U.S. 728, 737-38 (1984); *Larson v. Valente*, 456 U.S. 228, 239-42 (1982); *Bryant v. Yellen*, 447 U.S. 352, 366-68 (1980); *Village of Arlington Heights v. Metropolitan Hous. Dev. Corp.*, 429 U.S. 252, 261-64 (1977); and *United States v. SCRAP*, 412 U.S. 669, 687-90 (1973)." *See also* Steven L. Winter, *The Metaphor of Standing and the Problem of Self-Governance*, 40 STAN. L. REV. 1371, 1477 (1988).

the Court believed that the denial of a tax exemption might not change the admissions of purely private schools – and probably would not change the pace of integrating public schools – the Court denied standing. Do the claims in *Allen* seem more highly attenuated than those in *Duke*? In Professor Cass R. Sunstein's *Standing and the Privatization of Public Law*, 88 COLUM. L. REV. 1432, n.163 (1988), he notes that, "the claim of a causal connection was quite speculative; it was hardly certain that such effects would occur, and their consequences for any particular plaintiff were highly uncertain.

5. The Court has held that "clear precedent requir[es] that the allegations of future injury be particular and concrete." *Steel Co. v. Citizens for a Better Env't, 523 U.S. 83, 109 (1998)*. Years earlier, in *Laird v. Tatum, 408 U.S. 1 (1972)*, the Court rejected speculation of future harm as a sufficient injury in a speech case. Recently, the Sixth Circuit dealt with warrantless wiretapping in *ACLU v. United States National Security Agency, 493 F.3d 644 (6th Cir. 2007)*. Although the wiretapping program was operating, the harms complained of by the ACLU (invasion of privacy, First Amendment concerns, etc.) were seen as speculative. The court held: "[T]he injury alleged here is just as attenuated as the future harm in *Laird*; the present injury derives solely from the fear of secret government surveillance, not from some other form of direct government regulation, prescription, or compulsion."

Good Questions!

A note on the *ACLU* decision, *Sixth Circuit Denies Standing to Challenge Terrorist Surveillance Program*, 121 HARV. L. REV. 922 (2008), discusses the role of "probability-based" standing for future harms. How strong a probability must be established in order to have standing? How imminent the harm? Does the Court's decision in *Duke* provide a basis for probability-based standing?

6. *White Tail Park, Inc. v. Stroube, 413 F.3d 451 (10th Cir. 2004)*.

AANR-East is one of several regional organizations affiliated with the American Association for Nude Recreation, a national social nudism organization. In June 2003, AANR-East opened a week-long juvenile nudist camp at a licensed nudist campground ("White Tail Park") operated . . . near Ivor, Virginia. AANR-East leased the 45-acre campground that ordinarily attracts about 1000 weekend visitors who come to engage in nude recreation . . . .

Virginia law requires any person who owns or operates a summer camp or campground facility in Virginia to be licensed by the Food and Environmental Services Division of the Virginia Department of Health ("VDH"). *See* Va. Code § 35.1-18. Prior to the scheduled start of AANR-East's 2004 youth camp, the Virginia General Assembly amended the statute governing the licensing of summer camps specifically to address youth nudist camps. The amended statute requires a parent, grandparent or guardian to accompany any juvenile who attends a nudist summer camp . . . .

AANR-East contends that the amended statute will reduce the size of the camp every year because not all would-be campers have parents or guardians who are available to register and attend a week of camp during the summer, as evidenced by the fact that 24 campers who would have otherwise attended camp by themselves in June 2004 were unable to do so because of their parents' inability or unwillingness to attend. AANR-East contends that the statute encroached on its First Amendment right by reducing the size of the audience for its message of social nudism and will continue to do so as long as it is enforced. We think this is sufficient for purposes of standing. A regulation that reduces the size of a speaker's audience can constitute an invasion of a legally protected interest . . . .

Bennett v. Spear is of interest both because of its contribution to the standing dialogue and to questions of finality. The excerpted section below pertains primarily to questions of standing. In particular, based on what you have read thus far, how would you define "zone of interest"? What happens when an individual or entity is affected by the action of an agency, but their interests – while affected by the agency action – are at odds with the goals of the statute?

Good Questions!

The Consumer Product Safety Act (CPSA), 86 Stat. 1207, as amended, 15 U.S.C. § 2051 et seq., for example, empowers the Consumer Product Safety Commission (CPSC) to issue orders, interpretations, policy statements, and other steps pertaining to product safety. The purpose of the CPSA is to enhance the quality of consumer goods. Are the interests of manufacturers who produce allegedly defective goods within the "zone of interest" of the CPSA? Are the interests of retailers who sell products that are defective and cause harm within the "zone of interest" of the CPSA? In other words, does a determination of standing pertaining to the zone of interest test require that the complainant have interests that are consistent with the regulatory goals the statute embodies? Does it make sense to allow those who oppose the implementation of a statute to benefit from not only the regulatory process but also the court system?

BENNETT V. SPEAR

520 U.S. 154 (1997)

[JUSTICE SCALIA] This is a challenge to a biological opinion issued by the Fish and Wildlife Service in accordance with the Endangered Species Act of 1973 (ESA) concerning the [impact of the] operation of the Klamath Irrigation Project . . . on two varieties of endangered fish. The question for decision is whether the petitioners, who have [a] competing economic . . . interest[] in Klamath Project water, have standing to seek judicial review of the biological opinion under the citizen-suit provision of the ESA and the Administrative Procedure Act (APA).

I.

The ESA requires the Secretary of the Interior to promulgate regulations listing those species of animals that are "threatened" or "endangered" . . . . The ESA further requires each federal agency to "insure that any action authorized, funded, or carried out by such agency . . . is not likely to jeopardize the continued existence of any endangered . . . or threatened species . . . ." If an agency determines that action it proposes to take may adversely affect a listed species, it must engage in formal consultation with the Fish and Wildlife Service, . . . after which the Service must provide the agency with a written statement (the Biological Opinion) explaining how the proposed action will affect the species or its habitat. If the Service concludes that the proposed action will "jeopardize the continued existence of any species . . .," the Biological Opinion must outline any "reasonable and prudent alternatives" that the Service believes will avoid that consequence. . . .

The Klamath Project, one of the oldest federal reclamation schemes, is a series of lakes, rivers, dams and irrigation canals in northern California and southern Oregon. The project . . . is administered by the Bureau of Reclamation, which is under the [Secretary of the Interior's] jurisdiction. In 1992, the Bureau notified the Service that operation of the project might affect the Lost River Sucker (*Deltistes luxatus*) and Shortnose Sucker (*Chasmistes brevirostris*), species of fish that were listed as endangered in 1988. After formal consultation with the Bureau . . . the Service issued a Biological Opinion which concluded that the "long-term operation of the Klamath Project was likely to jeopardize the continued existence of the Lost River and shortnose suckers." The Biological Opinion identified "reasonable and prudent alternatives" the Service believed would avoid [this problem], which included the maintenance of minimum water levels on Clear Lake and Gerber reservoirs. The Bureau later notified the Service that it intended to operate the project in compliance with the Biological Opinion.

Petitioners, two Oregon irrigation districts that receive Klamath Project water and the operators of two ranches within those districts, filed the present action against the director . . . of the Service and the Secretary of the Interior. Neither the Bureau nor any of its officials is named as [a] defendant. The complaint asserts that the Bureau "has been following essentially the same procedures for storing and releasing water from Clear Lake and Gerber reservoirs throughout the twentieth century," that "there is no scientifically or commercially available evidence indicating that the populations of endangered suckers in Clear Lake and Gerber reservoirs have declined, are declining, or will decline as a result" . . ., that "there is no commercially or scientifically available evidence indicating that the restrictions on lake levels imposed in the Biological Opinion will have any beneficial effect on the . . . populations of suckers in Clear Lake and Gerber reservoirs," and that the Bureau nonetheless "will abide by the restrictions imposed by the Biological Opinion."

Petitioners[] allege that the Service's jeopardy determination with respect to Clear Lake and Gerber reservoirs, and the ensuing imposition of minimum water levels, violated § 7 of the ESA. . . . [They also] claim . . . that the imposition of minimum water elevations constituted an implicit determination of critical habitat for the suckers, which violated § 4 of the ESA, because it failed to take into consideration the designation's economic impact. Each of the claims also states that the relevant action violated the APA's prohibition of agency action that is "arbitrary, capricious, an abuse of discretion, or otherwise not in accordance with law." 5 U.S.C. § 706(2)(A).

The complaint asserts that petitioners' use of the reservoirs and related waterways for ". . . their primary sources of irrigation water[]" will be "irreparably damaged" by the actions complained of, and that the restrictions on water delivery "recommended" by the Biological Opinion "adversely affect plaintiffs by substantially reducing the quantity of available irrigation water." In essence, petitioners claim a competing interest in the water the Biological Opinion declares necessary for the preservation of the suckers.

The District Court dismissed the complaint for lack of jurisdiction. It concluded that petitioners did not have standing because their ". . . interests . . . do not fall within the zone of interests sought to be protected by ESA." The Court of Appeals for the Ninth Circuit affirmed. It held that . . . "only plaintiffs who allege an interest in the *preservation* of endangered species fall within the zone of interests protected by the ESA." We granted certiorari.

In this Court, petitioners raise two questions: first, whether the prudential standing rule known as the "zone of interests" test applies to claims brought under the citizen-suit provision of the ESA; and second, if so, whether petitioners have standing under that test notwithstanding that the interests they seek to vindicate are economic rather than environmental. In this Court, the Government has made no effort to defend the reasoning of the Court of Appeals. Instead, it [argues] (1) that petitioners fail to meet the standing requirements imposed by Article III of the Constitution [and] (2) that the ESA's citizen-suit provision does not authorize judicial review of the types of claims advanced by petitioners . . . .

II.

We first turn to the question the Court of Appeals found dispositive: whether petitioners lack standing by virtue of the zone-of-interests test. Although petitioners contend that their claims lie both under the ESA and the APA, we look first at the ESA because it may permit petitioners to recover their litigation costs and because the APA by its terms independently authorizes review only when "there is no other adequate remedy in a court."

. . . In addition to the immutable requirements of Article III, "the federal judiciary has also adhered to a set of prudential principles that bear on the question of standing." Like their constitutional counterparts, these "judicially self-imposed limits on the exercise of federal jurisdiction," are "founded in concern about the proper – and properly limited – role of the courts in a democratic society," but unlike their constitutional counterparts, they can be modified or abrogated by Congress. Numbered among these prudential requirements is the doctrine of particular concern in this case: that a plaintiff's grievance must arguably fall within the zone of interests protected or regulated by the statutory provision or constitutional guarantee invoked in the suit.

The "zone of interests" formulation was first employed in *Association of Data Processing Service Organizations, Inc. v. Camp*. There, certain data processors sought to invalidate a ruling by the Comptroller of the Currency authorizing national banks to sell data processing services . . . . In reversing [the Court of Appeals], we stated the applicable prudential standing requirement to be "whether the interest sought to be protected by the complainant is arguably within the zone of interests to be protected or regulated by the statute or constitutional guarantee in question." *Data Processing* . . . applied the zone-of-interests test to suits under the APA, but later cases have . . . specifically listed it among other prudential standing requirements of general application. We have made clear, however, that the breadth of the zone of interests varies according to the provisions of law at issue, so that what comes within the zone of interests of a statute for purposes of obtaining judicial review of administrative action under the . . . APA may not do so for other purposes.

Congress legislates against the background of our prudential standing doctrine, which applies unless it is expressly negated. The first question in the present case is whether the ESA's citizen-suit provision . . . expands the zone of interests. We think it does. The first operative portion of the provision says that "any person may commence a civil suit" – an authorization of remarkable breadth when compared with the language Congress ordinarily uses. Even in some other environmental statutes, Congress has used more restrictive formulations, such as "[any person] having an interest which is or may be adversely affected," (Clean Water Act) . . . or "any person having a valid legal interest which is or may be adversely affected . . . whenever such action constitutes a case or controversy" (Ocean Thermal Energy Conversion Act). And in contexts other than the environment, Congress has often been even more restrictive. In statutes concerning unfair trade practices and other commercial matters, for example, it has authorized suit only by "any person injured in his business or property," . . . or only by "competitors, customers, or subsequent purchasers."

Our readiness to take the term "any person" at face value is greatly augmented by two interrelated considerations: that the overall subject matter of this legislation is the environment (a matter in which it is common to think all persons have an interest) and that the obvious purpose of the particular provision in question is to encourage enforcement by so-called "private attorneys general" – evidenced by its elimination of the usual amount-in-controversy and diversity-of-citizenship requirements, its provision for recovery of the costs of litigation (including even expert witness fees), and its reservation to the Government of a right of first refusal to pursue the action initially and a right to intervene later. Given these factors, we think the conclusion of expanded standing follows a fortiori from our decision in *Trafficante v. Metropolitan Life Ins. Co.*, which held that standing was expanded to the full extent permitted under Article III by a provision of the Civil Rights Act of 1968 that authorized "any person who claims to have been injured by a discriminatory housing practice" to sue for violations of the Act. There also we relied on textual evidence of a statutory scheme to rely on private litigation to ensure compliance with the Act. The statutory language here is even clearer, and the subject of the legislation makes the intent to permit enforcement by everyman even more plausible.

It is true that the plaintiffs here are seeking to prevent application of environmental restrictions rather than to implement them. But the "any person" formulation applies to all the causes of action authorized by § 1540(g) – not only to actions against private violators of environmental restrictions, and not only to actions against the Secretary asserting underenforcement under § 1533, but also to actions against the Secretary asserting overenforcement under § 1533. . . . [T]he citizen-suit provision does favor environmentalists in that it covers all private violations of the Act but not all failures of the Secretary to meet his administrative responsibilities; but there is no textual basis for saying that its expansion of standing requirements applies to environmentalists alone. The Court of Appeals therefore erred in concluding that petitioners lacked standing under the zone-of-interests test to bring their claims under the ESA's citizen-suit provision.

III.

[The petitioners have an injury in fact because] it is easy to presume specific facts under which petitioners will be injured – for example, the Bureau's distribution of the reduction pro rata among its customers. . . . The Government also contests compliance with the second and third Article III standing requirements, contending that any injury suffered by petitioners is neither "fairly traceable" to the Service's Biological Opinion, nor "redressable" by a favorable judicial ruling, because the "action agency" (the Bureau) retains ultimate responsibility for determining whether and how a proposed action shall go forward. . . . This wrongly equates injury "fairly traceable" to the defendant with injury as to which the defendant's actions are the very last step in the chain of causation. . . .

The judgment of the Court of Appeals is reversed, and the case is remanded . . . .

Underlying Case Documents

For a picture of the Lost River Sucker (*Deltistes luxatus*) and the Short-nose Sucker (*Chasmistes brevirostris*) click <u>HERE</u>.

1. In determining the zone of interests a statute protects, does the court use an analysis that focuses on congressional intent? What options are there for statutory interpretation beyond legislative intent? *Bennett* holds that the matter of zone of interests "is to be determined not by reference to the overall purpose of the Act in question . . . but by reference to the particular provision of law upon which the plaintiff relies. . . ." What canon of statutory construction is in play? See <u>Interfaith Community Organization v. Honeywell International, Inc., 399 F.3d 248, 253-54, 257-58, 264, 268 (3d Cir. 2005)</u>, and <u>Sierra Club v. El Paso Gold Mines, Inc., 421 F.3d 1133 (10th Cir. 2005)</u>, for expansive readings of citizen suit provisions.

2. Is the focus of the Court on the environmental protection aspects of the Endangered Species Act – or on the citizen suit provision of that legislation? It bears noting that while some citizen suit provisions can be restricted to certain interests, the language in the ESA provides simply that "any person may commence a civil suit." The Court finds that this produces a "remarkable breadth when compared with the language Congress ordinarily uses." Does that mean that *Bennett's* holding is limited to broadly written citizen suit provisions? The Clean Water Act permits "any citizen" to sue any person "who is alleged to be in violation of an effluent standard or limitation. . . ." <u>Clean Water Act, 33 U.S.C. 1365(a)(1)(2)</u>. The Court has held that this provision is designed to further the enforcement goals of the act (as opposed to displacing federal agency enforcement efforts). <u>Gwaltney of Smithfield, Ltd. v. Chesapeake Bay Found., 484 U.S. 49, 60 (1987)</u>. Can you envision a business that generates pollutants availing itself of this provision? *See* Michael S. Greve, <u>The Private Enforcement of Environmental Law, 65 Tul. L. Rev. 339, 340 (1990)</u> (opining that "citizen suit provisions are an off-budget entitlement program for the environmental movement").

3. At one point in the opinion, the Court discusses the "any person" citizen suit provision and notes that this language provides "zone of interest" coverage to "all persons" who are affected by environmental determinations – and that is extremely broad. In that same passage in the opinion, the Court refers to the role of "private attorneys general" and the importance of that term in interpreting this legislation. Noting that Congress has eliminated the normal diversity and amount-in-controversy requirements to facilitate access to federal courts for performing the role of private attorneys general, one has to wonder how it is that a litigant *opposed* to achieving the protections the ESA promises is empowered to initiate the litiga-

tion in *Bennett*? The Court answers that directly, holding that the "any person" language is applicable "to all causes of action . . . not only to actions against private violators of environmental restrictions . . . but also to actions against the secretary asserting over-enforcement. . . ."

4. While *Bennett* may be somewhat aberrant, it does not depart from the requirement or the necessity of establishing cognizable injury. The injury asserted in this case is entirely commercial: Plaintiffs charge that the action of the Secretary will result in a reduction of water used in the irrigation process. No one doubts that losing a resource constitutes an injury – the question is whether that was the type of injury the statute (even vaguely) contemplates. If you assume for the moment that the Endangered Species Act was not designed to maximize water available to commercial agriculture, why would the Court find that the plaintiffs have standing? Is this, like *Duke*, a case in which the standing determination is

Good Question!

Does it make sense to allow anyone to use a private attorneys general provision – including those who are seeking to thwart the goals of the statute in question? *See* Matthew C. Stephenson, *Public Regulation of Private Enforcement: The Case for Expanding the Role of Administrative Agencies*, 91 Va. L. Rev. 93 (2005). For two classic examinations of the role of citizen enforcement, see Louis L. Jaffe, *The Citizen as Litigant in Public Actions: The Non-Hohfeldian or Ideological Plaintiff*, 116 U. Pa. L. Rev. 1033 (1968), and Abram Chayes, *The Role of the Judge in Public Law Litigation*, 89 Harv. L. Rev. 1281 (1976).

made to get to a substantive question that the Court is anxious to resolve? Could it be that the Court wants to send the message that, to the extent the courthouse doors are open at all, those seeking to protect environmental resources and those who are in the business of exploiting the environment are equally welcome? Most legal scholarship suggests a contrary perspective on citizen suits. Myriam E. Gilles, *Reinventing Structural Reform Litigation: Deputizing Private Citizens in the Enforcement of Civil Rights*, 100 Colum. L. Rev. 1384, 1390-91 (2000); Charles F. Sabel & William H. Simon, *Destabilization Rights: How Public Law Litigation Succeeds*, 117 Harv. L. Rev. 1016 (2004). For a parallel analysis of qui tam actions, see Richard A. Bales, *A Constitutional Defense of Qui Tam*, 2001 Wis. L. Rev. 381; and Evan Caminker, Comment, *The Constitutionality of Qui Tam Actions*, 99 Yale L.J. 341, 341-42 (1989). In qui tam cases, private citizens seek penalties and fees to enforce statutory obligations.

5. In the term following *Bennett*, the Court decided *National Credit Union Administration v. First National Bank*, 522 U.S. 479 (1998). At issue was the meaning of statutory terms in the Federal Credit Union Act – and the competitive relationship between commercial banks and credit unions. As in *Bennett*, there is little question that the Federal Credit Union Act was designed to regulate credit unions,

not to protect commercial banks. Nonetheless, the Court found that the Commercial Banking Association had "an interest in limiting the markets that federal credit unions can serve." Taking *Credit Union* and *Bennett* together, it is fair to ask whether the "zone of interest" test has ceased to have meaning. Since these two cases, the injury-in-fact requirement has consumed far more attention than the "zone of interest" test itself.

6. One interpretation of the standing component of *Bennett* involves a procedural assessment of what took place in the District Court and the Court of Appeals. The initial complaint had been dismissed for lack of standing before the plaintiffs had an opportunity to put forward evidence regarding the impact of the application of the Endangered Species Act. Granting summary judgment before providing plaintiffs an opportunity to put forward any evidence on the impact of the enforcement of the ESA may have been one of the decisive factors in the case – and may be a limit on the applicability of *Bennett* to future decisions. *See* Peter M. Shane, *Returning Separation of Powers Analysis to Its Normative Roots: The Constitutionality of Qui Tam Actions and Other Private Suits to Enforce Civil Penalties*, 20 ENVTL. L. REP. 11,081, 11,089-90 (2000).

Good Questions!

Based on the *Bennett* opinion, would an Oregon association of retail grocery stores have standing to attack the potential implementation of the ESA on the premise that the cost that retailers will have to pay for food products will go up if inexpensive water is not made readily available for irrigation purposes in the district in question? What about an organization that supports and promotes farmers who grow organic crops – the application of the ESA in the irrigation district in question will have an effect on the cost of organically grown goods? What about individual consumers – could anyone challenge the application of the ESA on the premise that the implementation of the statute will cause an increase in the price of food they wish to purchase? Does the language "any person may commence a civil suit" expand the "zone of interest" test this broadly? *See Nulankeyutmonen Nkihtaqmikon v. Impson*, 462 F. Supp. 2d 86 (D. Me. 2006); and *Springs v. Stone*, 362 F. Supp. 2d 686 (E.D. Va. 2005).

III. Ripeness

ABBOTT LABORATORIES V. GARDNER

387 U.S. 136 (1967)

[JUSTICE HARLAN] In 1962 Congress amended the Federal Food, Drug, and Cosmetic Act to require manufacturers of prescription drugs to print the "established name" of the drug "prominently and in type at least half as large as that used thereon for any proprietary name or designation for such drug," on labels and other printed material. The "established name" is one designated by the Secretary of Health, Education, and Welfare[;] the "proprietary name" is usually a trade name under which a particular drug is marketed. The underlying purpose of the 1962 amendment was to bring to the attention of doctors and patients the fact that many of the drugs sold under familiar trade names are actually identical to drugs sold under their "established" or less familiar trade names at significantly lower prices. The Commissioner of Food and Drugs [properly] promulgated the following regulation for the "efficient enforcement" of the Act: "[T]he established name . . . corresponding to [the] proprietary name . . . shall accompany each appearance of such proprietary name . . . ." A similar rule was made applicable to advertisements for prescription drugs.

The present action was brought by a group of 37 individual drug manufacturers and by the Pharmaceutical Manufacturers Association, of which all the petitioner companies are members, and which includes manufacturers of more than 90% of the Nation's supply of prescription drugs. They challenged the regulations on the ground that the Commissioner exceeded his authority under the statute by promulgating an order requiring . . . printed matter relating to prescription drugs to designate the established name of the particular drug involved every time its trade name is used anywhere in such material.

[The Court granted certiorari to determine whether pre-enforcement review of the regulations was authorized.] n.1

> n.1 That is, a suit brought by one before any attempted enforcement of the statute or regulation against him.

I.

The first question . . . is whether Congress . . . intended to forbid pre-enforcement review of this sort of regulation promulgated by the Commissioner. The question is phrased in terms of "prohibition" rather than "authorization" because a survey of our cases shows that judicial review of a final agency action by an aggrieved person will not be cut off unless there is persuasive reason to believe that such was the purpose of Congress. Early cases in which this type of judicial review was entertained have been reinforced by the enactment of the Administrative Procedure Act, which embodies the basic presumption of judicial review to one "suffering legal wrong because of agency action, or adversely affected or aggrieved by agency action within the meaning of a relevant statute," 5 U.S.C. § 702, so long as no statute precludes such relief or the action is not one committed by law to agency discretion, 5 U.S.C. § 701(a). The Administrative Procedure Act provides specifically not only for review of "agency action made reviewable by statute" but also for review of "final agency action for which there is no other adequate remedy in a court," 5 U.S.C. § 704. The legislative material elucidating that seminal act manifests a congressional intention that it cover a broad spectrum of administrative actions, and this Court has echoed that theme by noting that the Administrative Procedure Act's "generous review provisions" must be given a "hospitable" interpretation. Again in *Rusk v. Cort*, the Court held that only upon a showing of "clear and convincing evidence" of a contrary legislative intent should the courts restrict access to judicial review.

Given this standard, we are wholly unpersuaded that the statutory scheme in the food and drug area excludes this type of action. The Government relies on no explicit statutory authority for its argument that pre-enforcement review is unavailable, but insists instead that because the statute includes a specific procedure for such review of certain enumerated kinds of regulations, not encompassing those of the kind involved here, other types were necessarily meant to be excluded from any pre-enforcement review. The issue, however, is not so readily resolved; we must go further and inquire whether in the context of the entire legislative scheme the existence of that circumscribed remedy evinces a congressional purpose to bar agency action not within its purview from judicial review. As a leading authority in this field has noted, "The mere fact that some acts are made reviewable should not suffice to support an implication of exclusion as to others. The right to review is too important to be excluded on such slender and indeterminate evidence of legislative intent."

. . . .

II.

A further inquiry must, however, be made. The injunctive and declaratory judgment remedies are discretionary, and courts traditionally have been reluctant to apply them to administrative determinations unless these arise in the context of a controversy "ripe" for judicial resolution. Without undertaking to survey the intricacies of the ripeness doctrine it is fair to say that its basic rationale is to prevent the courts, through avoidance of premature adjudication, from entangling themselves in abstract disagreements over administrative policies, and also to protect the agencies from judicial interference until an administrative decision has been formalized and its effects felt in a concrete way by the challenging parties. The problem is best seen in a twofold aspect, requiring us to evaluate both the fitness of the issues for judicial decision and the hardship to the parties of withholding court consideration.

As to the former factor, we believe the issues presented are appropriate for judicial resolution at this time. First, all parties agree that the issue tendered is a purely legal one: whether the statute was properly construed by the Commissioner to require the established name of the drug to be used *every time* the proprietary name is employed. Both sides moved for summary judgment in the

District Court, and no claim is made here that further administrative proceedings are contemplated. It is suggested that the justification for this rule might vary with different circumstances, and that the expertise of the Commissioner is relevant to passing upon the validity of the regulation. This of course is true, but the suggestion overlooks the fact that both sides have approached this case as one purely of congressional intent, and that the Government made no effort to justify the regulation in factual terms.

Second, the regulations in issue we find to be "final agency action" within the meaning of § 10 of the Administrative Procedure Act, 5 U.S.C. § 704, as construed in judicial decisions. . . . The regulation challenged here, promulgated in a formal manner after announcement in the Federal Register and consideration of comments by interested parties is quite clearly definitive. . . . It was made effective upon publication, and the Assistant General Counsel for Food and Drugs stated in the District Court that compliance was expected.

The Government argues, however, that the present case can be distinguished from [prior] cases . . . on the ground that in those instances the agency involved could implement its policy directly, while here the Attorney General must authorize criminal and seizure actions for violations of the statute. In the context of this case, we do not find this argument persuasive. These regulations are not meant to advise the Attorney General, but purport to be directly authorized by the statute. Thus, if within the Commissioner's authority, they have the status of law and violations of them carry heavy criminal and civil sanctions. Also, there is no representation that the Attorney General and the Commissioner disagree in this area; the Justice Department is defending this very suit. . . .

This is also a case in which the impact of the regulations upon the petitioners is sufficiently direct and immediate as to render the issue appropriate for judicial review at this stage. These regulations purport to give an authoritative interpretation of a statutory provision that has a direct effect on the day-to-day business of all prescription drug companies; its promulgation puts petitioners in a dilemma that it was the very purpose of the Declaratory Judgment Act to ameliorate. As the District Court found on the basis of uncontested allegations, "Either they must comply with the every time requirement and incur the costs of changing over their promotional material and labeling or they must follow their present course and risk prosecution." The regulations are clear-cut, and were made effective immediately upon publication; as noted earlier the agency's counsel represented to the District Court that immediate compliance with their terms was expected. If petitioners wish to comply they must change all their labels, advertisements, and promotional materials; they must destroy stocks of printed matter; and they must invest heavily in new printing type and new supplies. The alternative to compliance – continued use of material which they believe in good faith meets the statutory requirements, but which clearly does not meet the regulation of the Commissioner – may be even more costly. That course would risk serious criminal and civil penalties for the unlawful distribution of "misbranded" drugs.

It is relevant at this juncture to recognize that petitioners deal in a sensitive industry, in which public confidence in their drug products is especially important. To require them to challenge these regulations only as a defense to an action brought by the Government might harm them severely and unnecessarily. Where the legal issue presented is fit for judicial resolution, and where a regulation requires an immediate and significant change in the plaintiffs' conduct of their affairs with serious penalties attached to noncompliance, access to the courts under the Administrative Procedure Act and the Declaratory Judgment Act must be permitted, absent a statutory bar or some other unusual circumstance, neither of which appears here.

. . . .

Finally, the Government urges that to permit resort to the courts in this type of case may delay or impede effective enforcement of the Act. We fully recognize the important public interest served by assuring prompt and unimpeded administration of the Pure Food, Drug, and Cosmetic Act, but we do not find the Government's argument convincing. First, in this particular case, a pre-enforcement challenge by nearly all prescription drug manufacturers is calculated to speed enforcement. If the Government prevails, a large part of the industry is bound by the decree; if the Government loses, it can more quickly revise its regulation.

The Government contends, however, that if the Court allows this consolidated suit, then nothing will prevent a multiplicity of suits in various jurisdictions challenging other regulations. The short answer to this contention is that the courts are well equipped to deal with such eventualities. The venue transfer provision may be invoked by the Government to consolidate separate actions. Or, actions in all but one jurisdiction might be stayed pending the conclusion of one proceeding. A court may even in its discretion dismiss a declaratory judgment or injunctive suit if the same issue is pending in litigation elsewhere. In at least one suit for a declaratory judgment, relief was denied with the suggestion that the plaintiff intervene in a pending action elsewhere.

Further, the declaratory judgment and injunctive remedies are equitable in nature, and other equitable defenses may be interposed. If a multiplicity of suits are undertaken in order to harass the Government or to delay enforcement, relief can be denied on this ground alone. The defense of laches could be asserted if the Government is prejudiced by a delay. And courts may even refuse declaratory relief for the nonjoinder of interested parties who are not, technically speaking, indispensable.

In addition to all these safeguards against what the Government fears, it is important to note that the institution of this type of action does not by itself stay the effectiveness of the challenged regulation. There is nothing in the record to indicate that petitioners have sought to stay enforcement of the "every time" regulation pending judicial review. If the agency believes that a suit of this type will significantly impede enforcement or will harm the public interest, it need not postpone enforcement of the regulation and may oppose any motion for a judicial stay on the part of those challenging the regulation. It is scarcely to be doubted that a court would refuse to postpone the effective date of an agency action if the Government could show, as it made no effort to do here, that delay would be detrimental to the public health or safety.

Lastly, although the Government presses us to reach the merits of the challenge to the regulation in the event we find the District Court properly entertained this action, we believe the better practice is to remand the case to the Court of Appeals for the Third Circuit to review the District Court's decision that the regulation was beyond the power of the Commissioner.

[JUSTICE FORTAS, concurring in *Toilet Goods* – the next case, and dissenting in *Abbott Labs*.]

The Court, by today's decisions . . . has opened Pandora's box. Federal injunctions will now threaten programs of vast importance to the public welfare. . . . [The majority] appear[s] to proceed on the principle that . . . exercise of judicial power to enjoin allegedly erroneous regulatory action is permissible unless Congress has explicitly prohibited it, provided only that the controversy is "ripe" for judicial determination. . . . I believe that this approach . . . unwisely gives individual federal district judges a roving commission to halt the regulatory process, and to do so on the basis of abstractions and generalities instead of concrete fact situations. . . .

The Court . . . moved by petitioners' claims as to the expense and inconvenience of compliance . . . says that this confronts the manufacturer with a "real dilemma." But the fact of the matter is that the dilemma is no more than citizens face in connection with countless statutes and with the rules of the . . . other regulatory agencies. . . . Somehow, the Court has concluded that the damage to petitioners . . . outweighs the damage to the public of deferring during the tedious months and years of litigation a cure for the possible danger and asserted deceit of peddling plain medicine under fancy trademarks and for fancy prices which, rightly or wrongly, impelled the Congress to enact this legislation. I submit that a much stronger showing is necessary than the expense and trouble of compliance and the risk of defiance. . . . We should confine ourselves – as our jurisprudence dictates – to actual, specific, particularized cases and controversies . . . .

TOILET GOODS ASSOCIATION, INC. V. GARDNER

387 U.S. 158 (1967)

[JUSTICE HARLAN] Petitioners in this case are the Toilet Goods Association, an organization of cosmetics manufacturers accounting for some 90% of annual American sales in this field, and 39 individual cosmetics manufacturers and distributors. They brought this action seeking declaratory and injunctive relief against the Secretary of Health, Education, and Welfare and the Commissioner of Food and Drugs, on the ground that certain regulations promulgated by the Commissioner exceeded his statutory authority . . . . The District Court held that the Act did not prohibit this type of preenforcement suit, that a case and controversy existed, that the issues presented were justiciable, and that no reasons had been presented by the Government to warrant declining jurisdiction on discretionary grounds. . . .

. . . .

The regulation in issue here was promulgated under the Color Additive Amendments of 1960, a statute that revised . . . the authority of the Commissioner to control the ingredients added to foods, drugs, and cosmetics that impart color to them. The Commissioner of Food and Drugs, exercising power . . . "to promulgate regulations for the efficient enforcement" of the Act, issued the following regulation after due public notice and consideration of comments submitted by interested parties:

> (a) When it appears to the Commissioner that a person has: . . . .
>
> > (4) Refused to permit duly authorized employees of the Food and Drug Administration free access to all manufacturing facilities, processes, and formulae involved in the manufacture of color additives and intermediates from which such color additives are derived;
>
> he may immediately suspend certification service to such person and may continue such suspension until adequate corrective action has been taken.

The petitioners maintain that this regulation is an impermissible exercise of authority, that the FDA has long sought congressional authorization for free access to facilities, processes, and formulae, but that Congress has always denied the agency this power except for prescription drugs. Framed in this way, we agree with petitioners that a "legal" issue is raised, but nevertheless we are not persuaded that the present suit is properly maintainable.

In determining whether a challenge to an administrative regulation is ripe for review a twofold inquiry must be made: first to determine whether the issues tendered are appropriate for judicial resolution, and second to assess the hardship to the parties if judicial relief is denied at that stage.

As to the first of these factors, we agree with the Court of Appeals that the legal issue as presently framed is not appropriate for judicial resolution. This is not because the regulation is not the agency's considered and formalized determination, for we are in agreement with petitioners that . . . there can be no question that this regulation – promulgated in a formal manner after notice and evaluation of submitted comments – is a "final agency action" under § 10 of the Administrative Procedure Act, 5 U.S.C. § 704. Also, we recognize the force of petitioners' contention that the issue as they have framed it presents a purely legal question: whether the regulation is totally beyond the agency's power under the statute, the type of legal issue that courts have occasionally dealt with without requiring a specific attempt at enforcement, or exhaustion of administrative remedies.

These points which support the appropriateness of judicial resolution are, however, outweighed by other considerations. The regulation serves notice only that the Commissioner *may* under certain circumstances order inspection of certain facilities and data, and that further certification of additives *may* be refused to those who decline to permit a duly authorized inspection until they have complied in that regard. At this juncture we have no idea whether or when such an inspection will be ordered and what reasons the Commissioner will give to justify his order. The statutory authority asserted for the regulation is the power to promulgate regulations "for the efficient enforcement" of the Act. Whether the regulation is justified thus depends not only, as petitioners appear to suggest, on whether Congress refused to include a specific section of the Act authorizing such inspections, although this factor is to be sure a highly relevant one, but also on whether the statutory scheme as a whole justified promulgation of the regulation. This will depend not merely on an inquiry into statutory purpose, but concurrently on an understanding of what types of enforcement problems are encountered by the FDA, the need for various sorts of supervision in order to effectuate the goals of the Act, and the safeguards devised to protect legitimate trade secrets. We believe that judicial appraisal of these factors is likely to stand on a much surer footing in the context of a specific application of this regulation than could be the case in the framework of the generalized challenge made here.

We are also led to this result by considerations of the effect on the petitioners of the regulation, for the test of ripeness, as we have noted, depends not only on how adequately a court can deal with the legal issue presented, but also on the degree and nature of the regulation's present effect on those seeking relief. The regulation challenged here is not [one] where the impact of the administrative action could be said to be felt immediately by those subject to it in conducting their day-to-day affairs.

This is not a situation in which primary conduct is affected – when contracts must be negotiated, ingredients tested or substituted, or special records compiled. This regulation merely states that the Commissioner may authorize inspectors to examine certain processes or formulae; no advance action is required of cosmetics manufacturers, who since the enactment of the 1938 Act have been under a statutory duty to permit reasonable inspection of a "factory, warehouse, establishment, or vehicle and all pertinent equipment, finished and unfinished materials; containers, and labeling therein." Moreover, no irremediable adverse consequences flow from requiring a later challenge to this regulation by a manufacturer who refuses to allow this type of inspection. Unlike the other regulations challenged in this action, in which seizure of goods, heavy fines, adverse publicity for distributing "adulterated" goods, and possible criminal liability might penalize failure to comply, a refusal to admit an inspector here would at most lead only to a suspension of certification services to the particular party, a determination that can then be promptly challenged through an administrative procedure, which in turn is reviewable by a court. Such review will provide an adequate forum for testing the regulation in a concrete situation. . . .

Underlying Case Documents

The case referenced:
The FDA regulations
Various provisions of the United States Code, available in the appendix to the opinion.

Hypothetical

Concerned about the burgeoning rates of childhood obesity, the US Department of Agriculture in partnership with the US Food and Drug Administration (a sub-agency of the Department of Health and Human Services) promulgate a regulation requiring that all foods advertised primarily to children 16 years of age and under (including sugary breakfast cereals and convenience snack foods) contain new labeling disclosing detailed nutritional information and portion recommendations calibrated to children at ages 5, 10 and 15. The regulation includes penalty provisions that include the seizure and forfeiture by the manufacturers of all covered products in interstate commerce that fail to comply with

> the new labeling requirements. Assume that you are the attorney for the trade association representing the five largest producers of the food products covered by this new regulation and that your client wants to challenge the regulation immediately, before it is enforced. Is pre-enforcement judicial review available in this case? Why or why not?

1. In *National Park Hospitality Association v. DOI*, 538 U.S. 803, 807-08 (2003), the Court was asked to review a challenge to a National Park Service rule (found at 36 C.F.R. § 51.3) that requires concession operators to resolve all contractual disputes under Contract Disputes Act of 1978, 41 U.S.C. § 601 et seq. The rule stated the Park Service's policy but, arguably, did not change rights, contracts, licenses, or subject parties to civil or criminal liability. It did produce uncertainty for concessionaires, raise a purely legal issue, and constitute final agency action – but did not provide the facts needed to facilitate judicial review. A challenge to policy not applied in a specific case raises ripeness concerns. Given the absence of any current hardship or change in rights and the absence of a good factual record, the Court declared the matter to lack ripeness. The doctrine the Court provided – its most recent statement on ripeness – is straightforward:

> Ripeness is a justiciability doctrine designed "to prevent the courts, through avoidance of premature adjudication, from entangling themselves in abstract disagreements over administrative policies, and also to protect the agencies from judicial interference until an administrative decision has been formalized and its effects felt in a concrete way by the challenging parties." *Abbott Laboratories v. Gardner*, accord, *Ohio Forestry Ass'n v. Sierra Club*, 523 U.S. 726, 732-33 (1998). The ripeness doctrine is "drawn both from Article III limitations on judicial power and from prudential reasons for refusing to exercise jurisdiction." *Reno v. Catholic Social Services, Inc.*, 509 U.S. 43, 57 n.18 (1993).
>
> Determining whether administrative action is ripe for judicial review requires us to evaluate (1) the fitness of the issues for judicial decision and (2) the hardship to the parties of withholding court consideration. *Abbott Laboratories.* "Absent [a statutory provision providing for immediate judicial review], a regulation is not ordinarily considered

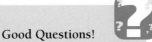

Good Questions!

Ripeness assessments are both judicial self-protection measures (waiting for cases to "be reduced to manageable proportions") and based on the importance of avoiding interference with agency proceedings – much like finality, exhaustion, and primary jurisdiction. In *Abbott Labs*, was the proceeding manageable? How can review of an as-yet unenforced regulation be manageable? While the petitioners in *Abbott Labs* convinced the Court that they were in a tough position (expensive compliance or running the risk of a damaging enforcement proceeding), wouldn't the case have been more focused had the Court waited for the dispute to ripen?

the type of agency action 'ripe' for judicial review under the [APA] until the scope of the controversy has been reduced to more manageable proportions, and its factual components fleshed out, by some concrete action applying the regulation to the claimant's situation in a fashion that harms or threatens to harm him. (The major exception, of course, is a substantive rule which as a practical matter requires the plaintiff to adjust his conduct immediately . . . .)" <u>Lujan v. National Wildlife Federation</u>, 497 U.S. 871, 891 (1990).

Hypothetical

The Federal Communications Commission receives a large number of complaints from citizens and civic organizations urging the agency to require broadcast television and radio stations to air a minimum amount of public affairs programming. They argue that as FCC licensees and public trustees transmitting over publicly owned airwaves, broadcasters are required by statute to air programming that covers local civic affairs and governance issues. Studies show that there has been a steep reduction in such local public affairs programming over the last two decades, leaving some localities with no such programming at all.

In response, the FCC establishes "Public Affairs Programming Enforcement Thresholds," which vary according to the size of the local community served by the broadcaster, and are the amounts above which the FCC will deem the broadcast licensee to be in compliance with its statutory obligations. Broadcast licensees who fail to air a quantity of local public affairs programming *at or below* the relevant enforcement threshold may be subjected to an FCC enforcement action, which could include a financial penalty or even revocation of the station license.

There are three potential plaintiffs: One is a trade association representing local broadcasters who argue that because local public affairs programming attracts very small audiences, compliance with the enforcement thresholds will cost local broadcasters unreasonably large amounts of lost advertising revenue. Another potential plaintiff is a coalition of citizens and local civic organizations, arguing that the enforcement thresholds are too low and will result in too modest of an increase in local public affairs programming. A third potential plaintiff is a coalition of libertarian free speech activists, which argues that the FCC's new enforcement thresholds are obsolete in light of the vibrant new digital media marketplace and a violation of the First Amendment. If all three plaintiffs file court challenges against the FCC's new enforcement thresholds, which of the three cases – if any – would be ripe for pre-enforcement review? Why? What additional information might you need?

2. Recently, in <u>New York Civil Liberties Union v. Grandeau, 2008 WL 2311584 (2d Cir., June 6, 2008)</u>, the court set out the distinction between the constitutional and prudential components of ripeness:

> Both [criteria] are concerned with whether a case has been brought prematurely, but they protect against prematureness in different ways and for different reasons. The first of these ripeness requirements has as its source the Case or Controversy Clause of Article III of the Constitution, and hence goes, in a fundamental way, to the existence of jurisdiction. The second is a more flexible doctrine of judicial prudence, and constitutes an important exception to the usual rule that where jurisdiction exists a federal court must exercise it.
>
> > These two forms of ripeness are not coextensive in purpose. Constitutional ripeness is a doctrine that, like standing, is a limitation on the power of the judiciary. It prevents courts from declaring the meaning of the law in a vacuum and from constructing generalized legal rules unless the resolution of an actual dispute requires it. But when a court declares that a case is not prudentially ripe, it means that the case will be better decided later and that the parties will not have constitutional rights undermined by the delay. It does not mean that the case is not a real or concrete dispute affecting cognizable current concerns of the parties within the meaning of Article III. . . . Prudential ripeness is, then, a tool that courts may use to enhance the accuracy of their decisions and to avoid becoming embroiled in adjudications that may later turn out to be unnecessary or may require premature examination of, especially, constitutional issues that time may make easier or less controversial. <u>Simmonds v. INS, 326 F.3d 351, 356-57 (2d Cir. 2003)</u>.

This distinction is evident also in <u>Suitum v. Tahoe Regional Planning Agency, 520 U.S. 725, 733 n.7 (1997)</u> (ripeness is assessed "both from Article III limitations on judicial power and from prudential reasons for refusing to exercise jurisdiction").

3. Can ripeness be used as an affirmative measure to compel judicial review? In <u>Central Delta Water Agency v. Bureau of Reclamation (Central Delta III), 452 F.3d 1021 (9th Cir. 2006)</u>, the Plaintiffs, state agencies and commercial farmers, alleged that a plan approved by the U.S. Bureau of Reclamation violated the <u>Central Valley Project Improvement Act (CVPIA), Pub. L. 102-575, 106 Stat. 4600 (1992)</u>, by creating a water control system that would, at some future point, contravene the

Good Questions!

Is the prudential side of the ripeness calculus shorthand for "political" considerations? How are prudential considerations anything other than discretionary and subjective? Is there much of a difference between the discretion inherent in the power to grant or deny certiorari and in the prudential side of ripeness? If the prudential side of ripeness is a matter of judgment and discretion on the part of reviewing courts, does that undermine the APA "right" to judicial review for those aggrieved by agency action?

Vernalis Salinity Standard. Using a finality analysis, the court found that despite the Bureau's acknowledgment that they would likely violate the salinity standard, until the standard was actually violated the case was not final and not justiciable. In a note discussing this case, it is suggested that the court should have used a ripeness analysis, not finality. Had they done so, they would have realized that allowing the agency action to go forward, unchecked by judicial intervention, would lead to significant hardship. Elisabeth Skillen, Note, Central Delta Water Agency v. Bureau of Reclamation: How the Ninth Circuit Paved the Way for the Next Fish Kill, 34 ECOLOGY L.Q. 979 (2007). Is the hardship element likely to be helpful to those seeking review – or to agencies claiming that they have done little more than announce a standard? What kind of hardship is required? Are costs alone enough? What about competitive disadvantage? What about damage to commercial reputation?

4. Ripeness issues at both the state and federal levels focus often on pre-enforcement reviews of agency policy statements and guidance documents. *See, e.g.*, Christopher R. Pieper, Note, No Harm, No Rule: The Muddy Waters of Agency Policy Statements and Judicial Review Under the Missouri Administrative Procedure Act, 69 MO. L. REV. 731 (2004); Stephen M. Johnson, Good Guidance, Good Grief!, 72 MO. L. REV. 695 (2007). *Abbott Labs* opened the door to pre-enforcement review – but how do courts decide if the moment is right? In AT&T Corp. v. FCC, 349 F.3d 692, 699-700 (D.C. Cir. 2003), the court considered the adverse consequences of facing downstream litigation in the event a pre-enforcement review was not granted and held:

> [T]he primary focus of the ripeness doctrine is to balance the petitioners' interest in prompt consideration of allegedly unlawful agency action against the agency's interest in crystallizing its policy before that policy is subject to review and the court's interest in avoiding unnecessary adjudication and in deciding issues in a concrete setting. . . .
> If the only hardship a claimant will endure as a result of delaying consideration of the disputed issue is the burden of having to engage in another suit, this will not suffice to overcome an agency's challenge to ripeness.

Interim plans, even those of great consequence and interest to a state and its citizens, are, more often than not, deemed unripe. For example, in Nevada v. DOE, 457 F.3d 78 (D.C. Cir. 2006), *dismissed as moot*, Nev. v. DOE, 2006 U.S. App. LEXIS 20689 (D.C. Cir., Aug. 9, 2006), the interim transportation plan to move hazardous plutonium across the State of Nevada to be stored in Yucca Mountain was deemed to be unripe. Based on the *AT&T* standard, what more is required for the harm to be "crystallized"?

5. In some areas, including election law and other first amendment fields, pre-enforcement review is more likely to be granted. In Shays v. FEC, 414 F.3d 76 (D.C. Cir. 2005), JUDGE TATEL set the stage for a pre-enforcement review:

A landmark reform to the nation's campaign finance laws, the <u>Bipartisan Campaign Finance Reform Act (BCRA) of 2002, Pub. L. No. 107-155, 116 Stat. 81</u>, took aim at two perceived demons of federal electoral contests: "soft money," i.e., use of unregulated political party activities to influence federal elections, and "sham issue ads," i.e., ostensibly issue-related advocacy functioning in practice as unregulated campaign advertising. These two tactics, given broad scope by permissive Federal Election Commission rulings, infused federal campaigns with hundreds of millions of dollars in federally unregulated funds, much of it contributed by corporations and labor unions. Now BCRA's House sponsors (joined by Senate sponsors as amici) claim the FEC has undone their hard work, resurrecting in its regulations practices BCRA eradicated and thus forcing them to seek reelection in illegally constituted electoral contests. If true, given the pace of the electoral process, damage could have been irreparable in terms of the 2006 mid-term election. Moreover, there were "safe harbor" provisions in the law [that would ensure] that these questionable practices "will never be subject to enforcement proceedings." (As noted earlier, good-faith reliance on FEC regulations affords a defense against FEC sanction, see <u>2 U.S.C. § 438(e)</u>.) For that very reason, moreover, the regulations also cause hardship. By removing certain conduct from any risk of enforcement, the challenged safe harbors establish "legal rights" to engage in that conduct, thus "creating adverse effects of a strictly legal kind." *See* <u>Ohio Forestry Ass'n v. Sierra Club, 523 U.S. 726, 733 (1998)</u>.

6. While we are absolutely certain you will see immediately the difference between *Toilet Goods* and <u>*Abbott Labs*</u>, keep in mind that the *Toilet Goods* Court found a matter unripe that was a purely legal question regarding an undeniably final agency action – and finality is all the APA requires. Nevertheless, the Court decided to see what kinds of "enforcement problems are encountered by the FDA, the need for various sorts of supervision in order to effectuate the goals of the Act, and the safeguards devised to protect legitimate trade secrets." When would reasoning of this type not be applicable? Wouldn't a court always have a better sense of "enforcement problems" after an enforcement action?

7. The options available to manufacturers the Court enumerates in *Toilet Goods* require considerable costs – denying an inspector admission, fighting out licensing cases at FDA, and risking suspension of certification are all risky – and yet they are characterized by the Court as merely an "inconvenience and possibly [a] hardship." If there are clear legal questions with a newly announced standard, why wait for its first application? Every enforcement action can have reputational consequences – and for publicly held businesses, a pronounced effect on the value of its stock. If a regulation is problematic, are you convinced that judges in Article III courts should be free to balance multiple facts and deny review in the only forum available to challenge the executive assertions of power?

8. <u>*Texas Independent Producers & Royalty Owners Ass'n v. EPA*, 413 F.3d 479 (5th Cir. 2005)</u>:

On March 9, 2005, EPA published a final rule . . . postponing the requirement for obtaining permit coverage for discharges associated with oil and gas construction activity that disturbs one to five acres of land from March 10, 2005 to June 12, 2006. Along with this rule, EPA published a statement that "within six months of [this] action, EPA intends to publish a notice of proposed rulemaking in the Federal Register for addressing these discharges and to invite public comments". . . . EPA urges this Court to dismiss the petition for review as unripe because it has never issued a final rule with respect to the oil and gas exemption and, further, the Deferral Rule contemplates an additional evaluation and assessment of Section 402(l)(2) during the Deferral Period. . . .

[T]his case is not ripe for review. . . . [I]t is clear to us that our ruling on this case would inappropriately interfere with administrative action. Given that EPA has specifically stated its intent to examine, during the Deferral Period, the issue of "how best to resolve questions posed by outside parties regarding section 402(l)(2) of the <u>Clean Water Act</u>", any interpretation we would provide would necessarily prematurely cut off EPA's interpretive process.

We are also unpersuaded that . . . the hardship faced by Petitioners at this time is sufficient to override the administrative body's right to interpret the law. Given that the effective date of the permit requirement for Petitioners is now a year away, we are not convinced that Petitioners will suffer significant hardship if we decline to supersede the administrative process. Petitioners themselves, when discussing the nature of oil and gas exploration and production activities, explain that planning cannot be done far in advance, but rather that "the potential number and approximate location of the oil and gas wells is not known for a comparatively long time after drilling commences". . . . Further, Petitioners state that "oil and gas activities do not have a long planning process, and instead proceed in a series of stops and starts dictated by the results of the last well and market conditions". . . . Given this uncertain nature of the oil and gas industry, Petitioners have not demonstrated how a possible change in permitting requirements a year from now could seriously affect an industry that, by its own admission, is unable to plan far in advance.

IV. Finality

Section 704 of the Administrative Procedure Act permits judicial review of "final agency action." The Act permits challenges to intermediate and procedural matters decided in the course of an agency proceeding – but only at the conclusion of that proceeding. In <u>Lujan v. National Wildlife Federation</u>, 497 U.S. 871 (1990), the Department of the Interior's Bureau of Land Management issued a "land withdrawal review" pertaining to the use of public land for certain commercial purposes, including resource exploitation, mineral removal, and agricultural purposes. When the Federation went to court to

Key Concept

Beyond the necessity of a "final agency action," the finality doctrine generally requires action taken by one who can speak on behalf of and conclusively for the agency. Thus, determinations made by intermediary agency officials, regardless of their immediate effect, may well be deemed to lack finality.

stop the Bureau of Land Management from facilitating the use of public land for private commercial gain, the agency responded by arguing that the land withdrawal system did not constitute final agency action. The Supreme Court agreed, holding that there was no "identifiable agency action" and equated the set of rules to general program announcements regarding "drug interdiction." Presumably, in *National Wildlife Federation*, there was more to come – specifically the permission to individual contractors to make use of the specified land in question.

In *National Automatic Laundry & Cleaning Council v. Schultz*, 443 F.2d 689 (D.C. Cir. 1971), the court held that an advice letter, even one that had significant consequences in an on-going proceeding, would not be presumed final if it had been signed by anyone other than the head of the agency. The court went on to note that an agency could, if it so chose, affirm the decision of an intermediary – but in the absence of that affirmation, the action is lacking in finality. The greater the latitude an agency has after the decision in question, the less likely the decision will be construed as final. Even if the decision comes from the head of the agency, if, in the end, it is a recommendation to the White House to take a particular action (a recommendation that can be accepted or rejected), then the action is construed to lack finality. *See Franklin v. Massachusetts*, 505 U.S. 788 (1992); *and Dalton v. Specter*, 511 U.S. 462 (1964).

If one is free to choose between compliance and noncompliance, it would be difficult to argue that one is "bound" by the decision of the agency. *See Franklin v. Massachusetts*, 505 U.S. 788, 798 (1992); *Invention Submission Corp. v. Rogan*, 357 F.3d 452 (4th Cir. 2004), and *Ipharmacy.md v. Mukasey*, 2008 WL 638240 (11th Cir. Fla., Mar. 11, 2008). In *Flue-Cured Tobacco Cooperative Stabilization v. EPA*, 313 F.3d 852 (4th Cir. 2002), the Fourth Circuit found nonreviewable an EPA report that determined that exposure to "second hand smoke" produces a profound health hazard. After the report issued, a number of states began programs to ban smoking in restaurants and other places of public accommodation, predicated in part on the report. Nevertheless, when the report was challenged by the tobacco industry, the court found that the report had no immediate legal effect but was rather a presentation of information.

The Bottom Line

The bottom line in finality cases is straightforward: In order to constitute a final determination that can be reviewed judicially, the decision must "mark the consummation of agency decisionmaking [and] be one by which rights and obligations have been determined or from which legal consequences flow." *Bennett*, 520 U.S. at 177-78. Further, in order to be final, an agency action has to have an actual "legal effect." In this regard, terms like "force of law" and "binding" are very much center-stage. If an agency action has a profound economic consequence, that might only be considered a "practical effect" and not a legal effect.

NATIONAL ASSOCIATION OF HOMEBUILDERS V. UNITED STATES ARMY CORPS OF ENGINEERS

417 F.3d 1272 (D.C. Cir. 2005)

[JUDGE HENDERSON] The [Clean Water Act] CWA aims to "restore and maintain the chemical, physical, and biological integrity of the Nation's waters" . . . . The CWA divides the authority to issue permits to discharge pollutants between the United States Environmental Protection Agency and the . . . Army . . . Corps [of Engineers]. Responsibility for the day-to-day administration of the permitting . . . falls to the Corps . . . .

[To issue] a permit under section 404 of the CWA . . . on a class-wide ("general permit") . . . basis . . . the Corps must "determine that the activities . . . will cause only minimal adverse environmental effects . . . and will have only minimal cumulative adverse effect on the environment." 33 U.S.C. § 1344(e)(1). A general permit has a statutorily-limited lifespan i.e., no longer than five years . . . . The Corps' individual permit process is, by contrast, "a longer, more comprehensive procedure." . . . .

[A] party desiring to discharge fill or dredged material into our nation's navigable waters may do so in either of two ways. If the proposed discharge activity is covered by a general permit, the party may proceed without obtaining an individual permit or, in some cases, even without giving the Corps notice of the discharge. On the other hand, if the proposed discharge is not covered by a general permit, the party must secure an individual permit before undertaking the discharge . . . . There are currently 43 [Nationwide Permits (NWPs) in force. NWPs are a type of general permit. They cover] activities ranging from "Single-family Housing" (NWP 29) to "Mining Activities" (NWP 44) to "Cranberry Production Activities" (NWP 34) . . . . In 1996, the Corps proposed to reissue a number of existing NWPs, albeit with modifications, that were otherwise set to expire on January 21, 1997. . . .

Following public comment, the Corps decided to replace NWP 26[, which had allowed discharge of fill material in up to ten acres of wetlands,] with "activity-specific" general permits. To allow ample time to develop replacement permits, however, it reissued NWP 26 for a two-year period but with more stringent conditions. In July 1998, the Corps published a proposed suite of activity-specific general permits to replace NWP 26, and extended, once more, the life of NWP 26 until December 30, 1999 "or the effective date of the new and modified NWPs, whichever comes first" . . . . [T]he Corps also reissued the NWP regarding single-family housing (NWP 29), but reduced the authorized maximum acreage impact from one-half to one-quarter acre.

. . . In March 2000, following another round of public comment, the Corps promulgated activity-specific permits consisting of five new NWPs and six modified NWPs, all intended to replace NWP 26. With some of the activity-specific NWPs, the Corps reduced the authorized maximum per-project acreage impact from ten acres to one-half acre and required preconstruction notification for impacts greater than one-tenth acre . . . . [The effect of these new regulations was to limit opportunity to develop commercial and residential property, pleasing environmentalists and frustrating developers.]

. . . The National Resources Defense Council and the Sierra Club . . . intervened in the district court [challenge] in support of the Corps. . . . In November 2003, the district court granted summary judgment to the Corps, concluding that "the Corps' issuance of the new NWPs and general conditions, while constituting the completion of a decisionmaking process, does not constitute a 'final' agency action because no legally binding action has taken place as to any given project until either an individual permit application is denied or an enforcement action is instituted." . . . . The appellants now appeal the district court's judgment . . . .

. . . .

Where, as here, no more specific statute provides for judicial review, the APA empowers a federal court to review a "final agency action for which there is no other adequate remedy in a court." 5 U.S.C. § 704. "Two conditions," the United States Supreme Court tells us, "must be satisfied for agency action to be 'final.'" *Bennett v. Spear*. "First, the action must mark the consummation of the agency's decisionmaking process – it must not be of a merely tentative or interlocutory nature. And second, the action must be one by which rights or obligations have been determined, or from which legal consequences will flow." In other words, an agency action is final if, as the Supreme Court has said, it is "'definitive' and has a 'direct and immediate . . . effect on the day-to-day business' of the party challenging it"; or if, as our court has said, "it imposes an obligation, denies a right or fixes some legal relationship." There can be little doubt that under these standards the Corps' issuance of the NWPs challenged by the appellants constitutes final agency action subject to judicial review.

We need not tarry long on the finality test's first prong; plainly, the Corps' issuance of the revised NWPs "marks the consummation of decisionmaking process." *Bennett*. There is nothing "tentative" or "interlocutory" about the issuance of permits allowing any party who meets certain conditions to discharge fill and dredged material into navigable waters. The intervenors argue, however, that, by "setting terms and conditions for NWPs, the Corps did not finally decide that a would-be discharger must comply with those terms and conditions, nor did the Corps finally deny authorization for discharges that exceed those terms and conditions." . . . . The district court similarly opined that a party whose activities do not meet the conditions set by the NWPs has not been "denied anything until [she] has exhausted all of [her] permit options." . . . .

But the NWPs do not simply work a change in the Corps' permitting procedures, thereby disadvantaging some within the class of would-be dischargers. The NWPs are not a definitive, but otherwise idle, statement of agency policy – they carry easily-identifiable legal consequences for the appellants and other would-be dischargers. Admittedly, our precedent announces no self-implementing, bright-line rule in this regard; the finality inquiry is a "pragmatic" and "flexible" one. . . .

[T]he Corps' issuance of NWPs likewise satisfies the second prong of the finality test. To our mind, all three constitute challenges to agency action "with legal consequences that are binding on both petitioners and the agency." The Corps' NWPs create legal rights and impose binding obligations insofar as they authorize certain discharges of dredged and fill material into navigable waters without any detailed, project-specific review by the Corps' engineers. The "direct and immediate" consequence of these authorizations for the appellants' "day-to-day business" is not hard to understand: While some builders can discharge immediately, others cannot. . . .

. . . Because the Corps' NWPs mark the completion of the Corps' decision-making process and affect the appellants' day-to-day operations, they constitute final agency action regardless of the fact that the Corps' action might carry different (or no) consequences for a different challenger, such as an environmental group. In any event, the notion that "would-be dischargers" like the appellants nevertheless "remain free to pursue an individual or general permit" suggests a ripeness – not a finality – problem. . . .

---

1. *SEC v. Medical Committee for Human Rights*, 404 U.S. 403 (1972).

> The Medical Committee for Human Rights acquired by gift five shares of stock in Dow Chemical Co. In March 1968, the Committee's national chairman wrote a letter to the company . . . request[ing] that there be included in the company's proxy statement for 1968 a proposal to amend Dow's Certificate of Incorporation to prohibit the sale of napalm unless the purchaser gives reasonable assurance that the napalm will not be used against human beings. Dow replied that the proposal was too late for inclusion in the 1968 proxy statement . . ., but that it would be reconsidered the following year. . . . On February 7, 1969, Dow responded that it intended to omit the proposal . . . from the 1969 statement under the authority of . . . the SEC Rule . . . that permitted omission of shareholder proposals . . . "[i]f it clearly appears that the proposal is submitted by the security holder primarily for the purpose of . . . promoting . . . social . . . causes" . . . .

The Committee requested that Dow's decision be reviewed by the . . . SEC. On February 18, 1969, the Chief Counsel for the Division of Corporation Finance wrote both Dow and the Committee to inform them that "this Division will not recommend any action to the Commission if this proposal is omitted from the management's proxy material." The SEC Commissioners granted a request by the Committee that they review the Division's decision and affirmed it. . . .

On July 8, 1970, the Court of Appeals held that the decision of the SEC was reviewable [but] that the case should be remanded to the Commission for reconsideration and a statement of reasons. The Commission petitioned for review here, and we granted certiorari . . . . [However, in] January 1971, the Medical Committee again submitted its napalm resolution for inclusion in Dow's 1971 proxy statement. This time Dow acquiesced . . . . Less than 3% of all voting shareholders supported it, and [so] Dow may exclude the same or substantially the same proposal from its proxy materials for the next three years. We find that this series of events has mooted the controversy.

2. *Kixmiller v. Securities and Exchange Commission, 492 F.2d 641 (D.C. Cir. 1974)*.

On November 19, 1971, petitioner, a . . . stockholder of the Washington Post Company, informed the company[] of his intention to submit three proposals . . . for consideration at the 1972 annual meeting of stockholders. . . . The company, following [proper] procedure . . ., informed the [Securities and Exchange] Commission's Division of Corporate Finance of its intention to omit petitioner's proposals from its 1972 proxy statements, and sought confirmation that the Division would not urge action by the Commission on that account. Petitioner filed memoranda and supporting materials in opposition to the request for a no-action decision.

The Division issued a letter opinion on March 8, 1972, stating that it would not recommend that the Commission take enforcement action . . . . Petitioner then asked the Commission to reexamine the Division's ruling; but was later informed that the Commission "declined to review the staff's position . . . ." This petition for review followed.

Our authority to directly review Commission action springs solely from Section 25(a) of the Securities Exchange Act of 1934, which confines our jurisdiction to "[orders] issued by the Commission. . . ." We think members of the Commission's staff, like staff personnel of other agencies, "have no authority individually or collectively to make 'orders,'" and that, on the contrary, "only the Commission makes orders." Here the Commission made no order on the merits of petitioner's claim; rather, it emphatically "declined to review the staff's position." It follows that what petitioner seeks to have reviewed in this court is not an "order issued by the Commission." *See National Automatic Laundry & Cleaning Council v. Shultz, 443 F.2d 689 (1971)*, wherein we drew a clear line between opinions reflecting the definitive views of an agency head and the considerably less authoritative rulings by subordinate officials.

We are mindful that administrative inaction may become judicially cognizable [b]ut assuming, without deciding, that the refusal is otherwise encompassed by [the statute], we are not at liberty to override it.

"Agency action," as defined in the Administrative Procedure Act, "includes . . . failure to act," 5 U.S.C. § 551(13), and the Act commands the reviewing court to "compel agency action unlawfully withheld or unreasonably delayed." § 706(1). . . .

An agency's decision to refrain from an investigation or an enforcement action is generally unreviewable and, as to the agency before us, the specifications of the Act leave no doubt on that score. . . . The Commission offers informal advice by its staff on a vast number of proxy solicitations. Sheer volume of this wholesome activity belies Commission review in every such instance. . . . And finding no legal fault in the Commission's discretionary exercise here, we are powerless to upset it.

V. Preclusion of Judicial Review

The Administrative Procedure Act sets out two situations where judicial review is precluded: Where agency action is committed to the discretion of the agency by law, and statutory preclusion. The study of preclusion is focused on the exceptional circumstance in which the protections promised in §§ 701-706 of the APA are limited or blocked completely.

While Congress anticipated that in some instances agency action would not be subject to judicial scrutiny, that does not address the constitutional argument that a judicial "check" ought to be available to "balance" against arbitrary or unsubstantiated executive action. In _United States v. Mendoza-Lopez, 481 U.S. 828 (1987)_, the Court found that where fundamental interests were at stake – in that instance a deportation case – exclusion of all judicial review was arguably unconstitutional. That case notwithstanding, the Supreme Court has not declared unconstitutional on its face a statute that precludes judicial review. The D.C. Circuit has held that a statute would be constitutionally suspect if it precludes all judicial review in "any forum – federal, state or agency – [required] for the resolution of a federal constitutional claim.") _Bartlett v. Bowen, 816 F.2d 695, 703 (D.C. Cir. 1987)_; _Adair v. Winter, 451 F. Supp. 2d 210, 216-17 (D.C. Cir. 2006)_.

For More Information

A good starting point for looking at the preclusion of judicial review is an article by former Justice Sandra Day O'Connor, _Reflections on Preclusions of Judicial Review in England and the United States_, 27 Wm. & Mary L. Rev. 643, 658-67 (1986).

There is then a "strong presumption" that judicial review of administrative action will be available. _INS v. St. Cyr, 533 U.S. 289 (2001)_; _McNary v. Haitian Refugee Center, Inc., 498 U.S. 479, 498 (1991)_; _Webster v. Doe, 486 U.S. 592, 603 (1988)_; _and Artichoke Joe's v. Norton, 216 F. Supp. 2d 1084 (E.D. Cal. 2002)_. That "strong presumption" is capable of being set aside if there is a "persuasive reason" to believe that Congress meant to limit or prohibit entirely judicial review. _Love v. Thomas, 858 F.2d 1347 (9th Cir. 1988)_. For a recent discussion of this, see _Bredesen v. Rumsfeld, 500 F. Supp. 2d 752 (M.D. Tenn. 2007)_.

Since *Abbott Labs*, an agency needs to show by "clear and convincing evidence" if judicial review is precluded. Later cases suggest an agency must put forward a "persuasive reason" to demonstrate that review should not be available. Even in those cases where judicial review appears to be limited by statute, there has always been the possibility of attacking the general scheme of decisionmaking, as opposed to individual determinations.

In *Johnson v. Robison*, 415 U.S. 361 (1974), the Court dealt with a statute that gave the Veterans Administration the right to make "final and conclusive" determinations regarding certain benefits. The statute went on to note that no court would have the "power or jurisdiction" to review such decisions. Even with that language, the *Robison* Court permitted limited judicial review by allowing the claimant to challenge the entire scheme for allocating certain veterans' benefits, as opposed to merely review of an individual benefit determination.

Ten years after *Robison*, the Court decided that preclusion of review required an assessment of whether the intention to limit review was "fairly discernible" from the statute in issue. (*Block*, below.) The "fairly discernible" test is fuzzier than the earlier "clear and convincing" language, and has given rise to a good deal of litigation regarding the extent to which Congress intends to block completely access to the courts.

One of the areas where preclusion of judicial review is most likely is in allocation of individual financial benefits in various federally funded programs, such as Medicare, veterans' claims, and other forms of public assistance. The idea is fairly straight-forward: If the sole basis for a challenge is that the claimant believes an insufficient amount of money has been allocated, the appellate process will devolve into nothing more than a factual review – de novo – of an agency determination.

In *Shalala v. Illinois Council on Long Term Care*, 529 U.S. 1 (2000), the Court produced a new test for analyzing congressional intent regarding preclusion of judicial review, the "channeling" test. In effect, *Shalala* asks courts to determine if Congress "channeled" claimants into a specific administrative process that was either terminal or required completion (exhaustion) prior to consideration of judicial review.

The discussion thus far has focused on statutory preclusion. Review can also be precluded where there is "agency action committed to agency discretion by law" – a standard that seems counter-intuitive. After all, a great deal of this field involves determinations committed to the discretion of the agency (outside of clear and unambiguous statutory directives). Accordingly, abuse of discretion (§706 of the APA) is one of the fundamental tests used for judicial review.

Generally speaking, this is an extremely limited exception applicable only when there is "no law to apply," i.e., no measure to determine the efficacy of the action of the agency. *See Heckler v. Chaney*, *infra* Chapter 4, *and Lincoln v. Vigil*, 508 U.S. 182 (1993).

Finally, preclusion of judicial review questions are linked directly with the problems associated with compelling an agency to act. For the most part, the decision to move forward with an enforcement action or with a rulemaking is vested to the

> **Good Question!**
>
> How can the APA limit judicial review when action is "committed to the discretion of the agency by law" when so much of the behavior that is the focus of judicial review is discretionary?

discretion of the agency and is nonreviewable. *Heckler v. Chaney*. Most mandamus cases explore the expansive discretion permitted for agency action, and agonize over the question whether a court should step in and compel an agency to act when it has delayed or otherwise resisted what it is required to do. *Telecommunications Research & Action Center v. FCC, 750 F.2d 70 (D.C. Cir. 1984)* ("TRAC").

As you read the cases that follow, keep in mind that preclusion of judicial review is the exception, not the norm.

BOWEN V. MICHIGAN ACADEMY OF FAMILY PHYSICIANS

476 U.S. 667 (1986)

[JUSTICE STEVENS] The question presented in this case is whether Congress [statutorily] barred judicial review of regulations promulgated under Part B of the Medicare program.

Respondents, who include an association of family physicians and several individual doctors, filed suit to challenge the validity of 42 C.F.R. § 405.504(b) (1985) . . . . The District Court held that the regulation contravened several provisions of the statute governing the Medicare program:

> There is no basis to justify the segregation of allopathic family physicians from all other types of physicians. Such segregation is not rationally related to any legitimate purpose of the Medicare statute. To lump MDs who are family physicians, but who have chosen not to become board certified family physicians for whatever motive, with chiropractors, dentists, and podiatrists for the purpose of determining Medicare reimbursement defies all reason. . . .

The Court of Appeals agreed with the District Court that the Secretary's regulation was "[obviously inconsistent] with the plain language of the Medicare statute" and held that "this regulation is irrational and is invalid. . . ."

The Secretary of Health and Human Services . . . renews the contention, rejected by both the District Court and the Court of Appeals, that Congress has forbidden judicial review of all questions affecting the amount of benefits payable under Part B of the Medicare program. . . . We [disagree].

I

We begin with the strong presumption that Congress intends judicial review of administrative action. From the beginning "our cases [have established] that judicial review of a final agency action by an aggrieved person will not be cut off unless there is persuasive reason to believe that such was the purpose of Congress." In *Marbury v. Madison*, a case itself involving review of executive action, CHIEF JUSTICE MARSHALL insisted that "very essence of civil liberty certainly consists in the right of every individual to claim the protection of the laws." . . . . Committees of both Houses of Congress have endorsed this view. . . . [During] the passage of the Administrative Procedure Act (APA), the Senate Committee on the Judiciary remarked:

> Very rarely do statutes withhold judicial review. It . . . could not be otherwise, for in such a case statutes would in effect be blank checks drawn to the credit of some administrative officer or board.

[It is understood] that "only upon a showing of 'clear and convincing evidence' of a contrary legislative intent should the courts restrict access to judicial review." This standard has been invoked time and again when considering whether the Secretary has discharged "the heavy burden of overcoming the strong presumption that Congress did not mean to prohibit all judicial review of his decision."

Subject to constitutional constraints, Congress can, of course, make exceptions to the historic practice whereby courts review agency action. The presumption of judicial review is, after all, a presumption, and "like all presumptions used in interpreting statutes, may be overcome by," *inter alia*, "specific language or specific legislative history that is a reliable indicator of congressional intent," or a specific congressional intent to preclude judicial review that is "'fairly discernible' in the detail of the legislative scheme." n.4

> n.4 The congressional intent necessary to overcome the presumption may also be inferred from contemporaneous judicial construction barring review and the congressional acquiescence in it or from the collective import of legislative and judicial history behind a particular statute. . . .

In this case, the Government asserts that two statutory provisions remove the Secretary's regulation from review under the grant of general federal-question jurisdiction found in 28 U.S.C. § 1331. First, the Government contends that 42 U.S.C. § 1395ff(b), which authorizes "Appeal by individuals," impliedly forecloses administrative or judicial review of any action taken under Part B of the Medicare program by failing to authorize such review while simultaneously authorizing administrative and judicial review of "any determination . . . as to . . . the amount of benefits under part A." Second, the Government asserts that 42 U.S.C. § 1395ii . . . expressly precludes all administrative or judicial review not otherwise provided in that statute. We find neither argument persuasive.

II

Section 1395ff on its face is an explicit authorization of judicial review, not a bar. As a general matter, "[the] mere fact that some acts are made reviewable should not suffice to support an implication of exclusion as to others. The right to review is too important to be excluded on such slender and indeterminate evidence of legislative intent."

In the Medicare program, however, the situation is somewhat more complex. Under Part B of that program, which is at issue here, the Secretary contracts with private health insurance carriers to provide benefits for which individuals voluntarily remit premiums. This optional coverage, which is federally subsidized, supplements the mandatory institutional health benefits (such as coverage for hospital expenses) provided by Part A. Subject to an amount-in-controversy requirement, individuals aggrieved by delayed or insufficient payment with respect to benefits payable under Part B are afforded an "opportunity for a fair hearing by the *carrier*," in comparison, and subject to a like amount-in-controversy requirement, a similarly aggrieved individual under Part A is entitled "to a hearing thereon by the *Secretary* . . . and to judicial review." "In the context of the statute's precisely drawn provisions," we held in *United States v. Erika, Inc.*, that the failure "to authorize further review for determinations of the amount of Part B awards . . . provides persuasive evidence that Congress deliberately intended to foreclose further review of such claims." . . . .

Respondents' federal-court challenge to the validity of the Secretary's regulation is not foreclosed by § 1395ff as we construed that provision in *Erika*. The reticulated statutory scheme, which carefully details the forum and limits of review of . . . the "amount of . . . payment" of benefits under Part B, simply does not speak to challenges mounted against the *method* by which such amounts are to be determined rather than the *determinations* themselves. As the Secretary has made clear, "the legality, constitutional or otherwise, of any provision of the Act or regulations relevant to the Medicare Program" is not considered in a "fair hearing" held by a carrier to resolve a grievance related to a determination of the amount of a Part B award. As a result, an attack on the validity of a regulation is not the kind of administrative action . . . with respect to which the Act impliedly denies judicial review.

That Congress did not preclude review of the method by which Part B awards are computed (as opposed to the computation) is borne out by the very legislative history we found persuasive in *Erika*. The Senate Committee Report on the original 1965 legislation reveals an intention to preclude "judicial review of a determination concerning the *amount of benefits* under part B where claims will probably be for substantially smaller amounts than under part A." . . . . The legislative history of the pertinent 1972 amendment likewise reveals that judicial review was precluded only as to controversies regarding determinations of amounts of benefits. . . . Senator Bennett's introductory explanation to the amendment confirms that preclusion of judicial review of Part B awards – designed "to avoid overloading the courts with quite minor matters" – embraced only "decisions on a claim for payment for a given service." . . . . As we found in *Erika*, Congress has precluded judicial review only "of adverse hearing officer determinations of the amount of Part B payments."

Careful analysis of the governing statutory provisions and their legislative history thus reveals that Congress intended to bar judicial review only of determinations of the amount of benefits to be awarded under Part B. Congress delegated this task to carriers who would finally determine such matters in conformity with the regulations and instructions of the Secretary. We conclude, therefore, that those matters which Congress did *not* leave to be determined in a "fair hearing" conducted by the carrier – including challenges to the validity of the Secretary's instructions and regulations – are not impliedly insulated from judicial review by 42 U.S.C. § 1395ff.

III

[M]atters which Congress did *not* delegate to private carriers, such as challenges to the validity of the Secretary's instructions and regulations, are cognizable in courts of law. . . . [W]e will not indulge the Government's assumption that Congress contemplated review by carriers of "trivial" monetary claims, but intended no review at all of substantial statutory and constitutional challenges to the Secretary's administration of Part B of the Medicare program. This is an extreme position . . . . We ordinarily presume that Congress intends the executive to obey its statutory commands and, accordingly, that it expects the courts to grant relief when an executive agency violates such a command. That presumption has not been surmounted here. The judgment of the Court of Appeals is affirmed.

1. In <u>Giesse v. Sec'y of the HHS, 522 F.3d 697 (6th Cir. 2008)</u>, the

> [p]laintiff . . . filed a suit [for] wrongful termination of medical care. Plaintiff . . . alleges constitutional claims, and because these claims are "wholly collateral" to his administrative claims, plaintiff contends that his federal claims do not "arise under" the Medicare Act, and [are reviewable]. . . . We disagree. . . .

> Plaintiff . . . argues that . . . *Bowen v. Michigan Academy of Family Physicians* . . . provides for judicial review of his claim. "Under the narrow reading of *Bowen* adopted in <u>Shalala v. Illinois Council on Long Term Care, Inc., 529 U.S. 1 (2000)</u>, parties affected by Medicare administrative determinations may sue in federal court under <u>28 U.S.C. § 1331</u>, bypassing § 405 preclusion, only where requiring agency review pursuant to § 405(h) 'would mean no review at all.'" This exemption, however, should not serve to circumvent established mechanisms of judicial review. In determining whether the *Michigan Academy* exception applies to a particular case, this court "must examine whether [the plaintiff] is simply being required to seek review first through the agency or is being denied altogether the opportunity for judicial review." . . . .

A constitutional challenge is not likely to succeed unless review is denied in every "forum, federal, state or agency. . . ." <u>Adair v. Winter, 451 F. Supp. 2d 210, 216 (D.D.C. 2006)</u>. Of what value is administrative review of administrative agency action – and how does that provide a check?

2. In <u>High Country Citizens Alliance v. Clarke, 454 F.3d 1177 (10th Cir. 2006)</u>, the court found:

> To overcome the presumption of reviewability, an intent to preclude judicial review must be "fairly discernible" from the statutory scheme. <u>Ass'n of Data Processing Serv. Orgs., Inc. v. Camp</u>, 397 U.S. 150 (1970). . . . [That can be] inferred from contemporaneous judicial construction barring review and the congressional acquiescence in it . . . or from the collective import of legislative and judicial history behind a particular statute [or] by inferences of intent drawn from the statutory scheme as a whole. <u>Block, 467 U.S. at 349</u>.

Why trust something of such great consequence as preclusion of judicial review to an analysis of something as easily manipulated as legislative history? This is not an area about which Congress is unaware – why not block review only when the preclusion is explicit? In <u>Exxon Mobil Corp. v. Allapattah Servs., 545 U.S. 546, 568-69 (2005)</u>, the Court noted: "Judicial investigation of legislative history has a tendency to become, to borrow JUDGE LEVENTHAL's memorable phrase, an exercise in 'looking over a crowd and picking out your friends.'" *See* Wald, <u>Some Observations on the Use of Legislative History in the 1981 Supreme Court Term, 68 IOWA L. REV. 195, 214 (1983)</u>.

3. <u>Trustees in Bankruptcy of North American Rubber Thread Co. v. United States, 464 F. Supp. 2d 1350 (Ct. Int'l Trade 2006)</u>:

> When a court considers . . . preclusion . . . judicial review . . . will not be cut off unless

there is persuasive reason to believe that such was the purpose of Congress." *Abbott Labs. v. Gardner*. . . .

[In footnotes, the court explained that to test if preclusion is present, courts use the] "clear and convincing evidence" [test, which] is not meant in the strict evidentiary sense . . . but rather serves as a reminder that courts should decline to review a cause of action only where Congress has clearly exhibited its intent to preclude that cause of action. . . .

[However, the] Supreme Court has recognized the "longstanding principle that a statute whose provisions are finely wrought may support the preclusion of judicial review, even though that preclusion is only by negative implication." *Shalala v. Ill. Council on Long Term Care, Inc.*, 529 U.S. 1, 34 n.3 (2000). . . .

How do you define "negative implication"? It cannot mean that if review is not mentioned it is precluded – but what does it mean? *See, e.g., United States v. Fausto*, 484 U.S. 439, 452 (1988).

BLOCK V. COMMUNITY NUTRITION INSTITUTE

467 U.S. 340 (1984)

[JUSTICE O'CONNOR] This case presents the question whether ultimate consumers of dairy products may obtain judicial review of milk market orders issued by the Secretary of Agriculture (Secretary) under the authority of the Agricultural Marketing Agreement Act of 1937 (Act) . . . .

I

A

[T]he 1937 Act authorizes the Secretary to issue milk market orders setting the minimum prices that handlers (those who process dairy products) must pay to producers (dairy farmers) for their milk products. 7 U.S.C. § 608c. The "essential purpose [of the milk market order scheme is] to raise producer prices," S. Rep. No. 1011, 74th Cong., 1st Sess., 3 (1935) . . . . [T]he Secretary must conduct an appropriate rulemaking proceeding before issuing a milk market order. The public must be notified of these proceedings and provided an opportunity for public hearing and comment. . . . [B]efore any market order may become effective, it must be approved by the handlers of at least 50% of the volume of milk covered by the proposed order and at least two-thirds of the affected dairy producers in the region. If the handlers withhold their consent, the Secretary may nevertheless impose the order. But the Secretary's power to do so is conditioned upon at least two-thirds of the producers consenting to its promulgation and upon his making an administrative determination that the order is "the only practical means of advancing the interests of the producers."

. . . .

[Under this statutory scheme], the Secretary has regulated the price of "reconstituted milk" – that is, milk manufactured by mixing milk powder with water – since 1964. The Secretary's orders assume that handlers will use reconstituted milk to manufacture surplus milk products. . . . The compensatory payment is equal to the difference between the Class I and Class II milk product prices. Handlers make . . . payments [pursuant to the orders of the Secretary] to the regional pool, from which moneys are then distributed to producers of fresh fluid milk in the region where the reconstituted milk was manufactured and sold.

B

In December 1980, respondents brought suit in District Court, contending that the compensatory payment requirement makes reconstituted milk uneconomical for handlers to process. Respondents . . . included three individual consumers of fluid dairy products, a handler regulated by the market orders, and a nonprofit organization. The District Court concluded that the consumers and the nonprofit organization did not have standing to challenge the market orders. In addition, it found that Congress had intended by the Act to preclude such persons from obtaining judicial review. . . . The Court of Appeals . . . reversed [and w]e granted certiorari to resolve the conflict in the Circuits. We now reverse the judgment of the Court of Appeals in this case.

[T]he APA confers a general cause of action upon persons "adversely affected or aggrieved by agency action within the meaning of a relevant statute," 5 U.S.C. § 702, but withdraws that cause of action to the extent the relevant statute "[precludes] judicial review," 5 U.S.C. § 701(a)(1). Whether and to what extent a particular statute precludes judicial review is determined not only from its express language, but also from the structure of the statutory scheme, its objectives, its legislative history, and the nature of the administrative action involved. Therefore, we must examine this statutory scheme "to determine whether Congress precluded all judicial review, and, if not, whether Congress nevertheless foreclosed review to the class to which the [respondents belong]."

It is clear that Congress did not intend to strip the judiciary of all authority to review the Secretary's milk market orders. . . . [It did, however,] limit the classes entitled to participate in the development of market orders. . . . Nowhere in the Act . . . is there an express provision for participation by consumers in any proceeding. In a complex scheme of this type, the omission of such a provision is sufficient reason to believe that Congress intended to foreclose consumer participation in the regulatory process.

To be sure, the general purpose sections of the Act allude to general consumer interests. But the preclusion issue does not only turn on whether the interests of a particular class like consumers are implicated. Rather, the preclusion issue turns ultimately on whether Congress intended for that class to be relied upon to challenge agency disregard of the law. The structure of this Act indicates that Congress intended only producers and handlers, and not consumers, to ensure that the statutory objectives would be realized. . . . Congress channeled disputes concerning marketing orders to the Secretary in the first instance because it believed that only he has the expertise necessary to illuminate and resolve questions about them. Had Congress intended to allow consumers to attack provisions of marketing orders, it surely would have required them to pursue the administrative remedies provided in § 608c(15)(A) as well. The restriction of the administrative remedy to handlers strongly suggests that Congress intended a similar restriction of judicial review of market orders.

Allowing consumers to sue the Secretary would . . . provide handlers with a convenient device for evading the statutory requirement that they first exhaust their administrative remedies. A handler may also be a consumer and, as such, could sue in that capacity. Alternatively, a handler would need only to find a consumer who is willing to join in or initiate an action in the district court. The consumer or consumer-handler could then raise precisely the same exceptions that the handler must raise administratively. Consumers or consumer-handlers could seek injunctions against the operation of market orders that "impede, hinder, or delay" enforcement actions, even though such injunctions are expressly prohibited in proceedings properly instituted under 7 U.S.C. § 608c(15). Suits of this type would effectively nullify Congress' intent to establish an "equitable and expeditious procedure for testing the validity of orders, without hampering the Government's power to enforce compliance with their terms." For these reasons, we think it clear that Congress intended that judicial review of market orders issued under the Act ordinarily be confined to suits brought by handlers . . . .

. . . .

The presumption favoring judicial review of administrative action is just that – a presumption. This presumption, like all presumptions used in interpreting statutes, may be overcome by specific language or specific legislative history that is a reliable indicator of congressional intent. . . . [T]he presumption favoring judicial review of administrative action may be overcome by inferences of intent drawn from the statutory scheme as a whole. *See, e.g., Morris v. Gressette*, 432 U.S. 491 (1977). In particular, at least when a statute provides a detailed mechanism for judicial consideration of particular issues at the behest of particular persons, judicial review of those issues at the behest of other persons may be found to be impliedly precluded.

. . . .

In this case, the Court of Appeals did not [follow] *Morris* . . . . Rather, it recited this Court's oft-quoted statement that "only upon a showing of 'clear and convincing evidence' of a contrary legislative intent should the courts restrict access to judicial review." *Abbott Laboratories v. Gardner*. . . . This Court has, however, never applied the "clear and convincing evidence" standard in the strict evidentiary sense the Court of Appeals thought necessary in this case. Rather, the Court has found the standard met, and the presumption favoring judicial review overcome, whenever the congressional intent to preclude judicial review is "fairly discernible in the statutory scheme." *Data Processing Service v. Camp*. In the context of preclusion analysis, the "clear and convincing evidence" standard is not a rigid evidentiary test but a useful reminder to courts that, where substantial doubt about the congressional intent exists, the general presumption favoring judicial review of administrative action is controlling. That presumption does not control in cases such as this one, however, since the congressional intent to preclude judicial review is "fairly discernible" in the detail of the legislative scheme. . . .

. . . .

[The] preclusion of consumer suits will not threaten realization of the fundamental objectives of the statute. Handlers have interests similar to those of consumers. Handlers, like consumers, are interested in obtaining reliable supplies of milk at the cheapest possible prices. Handlers can therefore be expected to challenge unlawful agency action and to ensure that the statute's objectives will not be frustrated. Indeed, as noted above, consumer suits might themselves frustrate achievement of the statutory purposes. . . .

. . . Accordingly, the judgment of the Court of Appeals is reversed.

———————————

1. *Shalala v. Illinois Council on Long Term Care*, 529 U.S. 1, 34 (2000), cites *Block* for the proposition that a "statute whose provisions are finely wrought may support the preclusion of judicial review, even though that preclusion is only by negative implication. . . ." Both *United States v. Fausto*, 484 U.S. 439, 452 (1988), and *Block* discerned the intent to preclude based on "inferences of intent" in the statutory schemes taken as a whole.

The uncertainty inherent in "negative implication" and "inferences" is obvious. The terms "inference" and "implication" leave little doubt: Courts are given considerable latitude to determine the intention to preclude review notwithstanding the premise that agency actions are presumed reviewable unless there is solid evidence that Congress decided affirmatively to limit access to the courts.

2. Preclusion of judicial review is only one possible limitation on conventional Article III "checks" on executive action. There are also situations where review is confined to a single court or where the remedial potential is limited. In the majority opinion in <u>Hamdan v. Rumsfeld, 548 U.S. 557 (2006)</u>, the Court found that it had the power to review a claim brought by a detainee, giving a somewhat strained interpretation of the <u>Detainee Treatment Act, Pub. L. No. 109-148</u>, Div. A, Tit. X, 119 Stat. 2739, 2680 (signed into law on December 30, 2005), which vests the D.C. Circuit with exclusive jurisdiction to review final classification decisions and other determinations related to detainees at the Guantanamo Bay detention facility.

Although *Hamdan* appears to reinforce the notion that judicial review is of great consequence, it seems of limited effect when read in conjunction with the evisceration of habeas corpus under the <u>Military Commissions Act</u> (which may well lead to unreviewable confinements of detainees in other U.S. military bases located outside the United States such as the Bagram facility). Military Commissions Act of 2006, <u>Pub. L. No. 109-366</u>, <u>120 Stat. 2600</u>. On August 6, 2008, a military jury convened under the Military Commissions Act rendered a split decision, finding Mr. Hamdan guilty of lesser offenses but not guilty of conspiracy to commit acts of terrorism. Mr. Hamdan, the personal driver for Osama Bin Laden, the alleged "mastermind" of the 9/11 attacks on the United States, was sentenced to five and one-half years. Given credit for the time already served at Guantanamo, Mr. Hamdan was released in November 2008, and returned to Yemen in January 2009.

For More Information

Important Note Regarding Military Commissions Proceedings and Administrative Law

The *Hamdan* trial was underway as this text went to the publisher. While proceedings of this type are not easily classified, many rights available in Article III courts are not available to Mr. Hamdan. Pursuant to the Military Commissions Act, while Mr. Hamdan is entitled to a trial by a military jury, the rules of evidence are greatly relaxed, discovery is limited at best, and documents critical to the defense were, in large part, redacted. Accordingly, these proceedings can be seen as an exercise of executive power and therefore worthy of study in administrative law. In a number of places in this text, particularly Chapter 11, we have provided cases and materials regarding military proceedings. We do so with the understanding that these are unique tribunals with rules unlike most other conventional agency proceedings. If you are interested in a human rights critique of the *Hamdan* trial, we suggest: *US:* Hamdan *Trial Exposes Flaws in Military Commissions, Tribunal Handicaps the Defense*, Guantanamo Bay, August 5, 2008, Human Rights News, <u>http://hrw.org/english/docs/2008/08/05/usint19540.htm</u>, (last visited August 5, 2008).

The War Powers/judicial review cases are perhaps the most difficult to categorize. Professor Robert J. Pushaw recently commented: "[T]he quest for a coherent jurisprudential framework is futile because the Constitution's text and history do not clearly reveal any single proper way to reconcile judicial review with war powers. This uncertainty has led the Court to eschew black-letter rules in favor of a flexible approach that reflects political and practical considerations." Robert J. Pushaw, Jr., *The Enemy Combatant Cases in Historical Context: The Inevitability of Pragmatic Judicial Review*, 82 NOTRE DAME L. REV. 1005, 1013 (2007).

3. What about the decisions of the Office of the President? In *Franklin v. Massachusetts*, 505 U.S. 788, 800-01 (1992), and *Dalton v. Specter*, 511 U.S. 462 (1994), the Court found that APA conventions, including judicial review, are generally not available for presidential decisions since the President is not an agency. However, not everything related to the presidency is immune from either APA process or judicial review. *See* Kevin M. Stack, *The Statutory President*, 90 IOWA L. REV. 539 (2005), *and* Neal Kumar Katyal, *Internal Separation of Powers: Checking Today's Most Dangerous Branch from Within*, 115 YALE L.J. 2314 (2006).

4. Do you believe (as *Block* appears to hold) that Congress actually meant to keep the public from having any involvement, judicial or otherwise, in the regulation of milk?

Not surprisingly, among the most controversial of all agency decisions is the determination to cease funding of existing programs. Denying those in need what they perceive as essential resources is predictably characterized as arbitrary and capricious by those who will suffer upon the termination of benefits. The question posed in the next case is whether that deprivation is reviewable, as opposed to falling under the statutory exemption for agency action committed to agency discretion by law.

LINCOLN V. VIGIL

508 U.S. 182 (1993)

[JUSTICE SOUTER] The Indian Health Service . . . provides health care for some 1.5 million American Indian and Alaska Native people. The Service receives yearly lump-sum appropriations from Congress [and is authorized] to "expend such moneys as Congress may from time to time appropriate, for the benefit, care, and assistance of the Indians," for the "relief of distress and conservation of health." . . . . This case concerns a collection of related services, commonly known as the Indian Children's Program, that the Service provided from 1978 to 1985. . . . Congress never expressly appropriated funds for [the Program]. In 1978, however, the Service allocated approximately $ 292,000 from its fiscal year 1978 appropriation to its office in Albuquerque, New Mexico, for the planning and development of a pilot project for handicapped Indian children, which became known as the

Indian Children's Program. The pilot project apparently convinced the Service that a building was needed, and, in 1979, the Service requested $ 3.5 million from Congress to construct a diagnostic and treatment center for handicapped Indian children. The appropriation for fiscal year 1980 did not expressly provide the requested funds, however, and legislative reports indicated only that Congress had increased the Service's funding by $ 300,000 for nationwide expansion and development of the Program in coordination with the Bureau.

Plans for a national program to be managed jointly by the Service and the Bureau were never fulfilled, however, and the Program continued simply as an offering of the Service's Albuquerque office . . . . The Program's staff provided "diagnostic, evaluation, treatment planning and followup services" for Indian children with emotional, educational, physical, or mental handicaps." . . . . Congress never authorized or appropriated moneys expressly for the Program, and the Service continued to pay for its regional activities out of annual lump-sum appropriations from 1980 to 1985, during which period the Service repeatedly apprised Congress of the Program's continuing operation.

Nevertheless, the Service had not abandoned the proposal for a nationwide treatment program, and in June 1985 it notified those who referred patients to the Program that it was "re-evaluating [the Program's] purpose . . . as a national mental health program for Indian children and adolescents." In August 1985, the Service determined that Program staff hitherto assigned to provide direct clinical services should be reassigned as consultants to other nationwide Service programs and discontinued the direct clinical services to Indian children in the Southwest. The Service announced its decision in a memorandum, dated August 21, 1985, addressed to Service offices and Program referral sources:

> As you are probably aware, the Indian Children's Program has been involved in planning activities focusing on a national program effort. This process has included the termination of all direct clinical services to children in the Albuquerque, Navajo and Hopi reservation service areas. During the months of August and September, . . . staff will [see] children followed by the program in an effort to . . . identify alternative resources . . . . In communities where there are no identified resources, meetings with community service providers will be scheduled to facilitate the networking between agencies to secure or advocate for appropriate services.

. . . .

Respondents, handicapped Indian children eligible to receive services through the Program, subsequently brought this action for declaratory and injunctive relief against petitioners, [alleging it was unlawful to] discontinue direct clinical services [and that this decision] violated the federal trust responsibility to Indians, . . . the Administrative Procedure Act, various agency regulations, and the Fifth Amendment's Due Process Clause.

. . . .

II

First is the question whether it was error for the Court of Appeals to hold the substance of the Service's decision to terminate the Program reviewable under the APA. The APA provides that "[a] person suffering legal wrong because of agency action, or adversely affected or aggrieved by agency action within the meaning of a relevant statute, is entitled to judicial review thereof," 5 U.S.C. § 702, and we have read the APA as embodying a "basic presumption of judicial review," *Abbott Laboratories v. Gardner*. This is "just" a presumption, however, *Block v. Community Nutrition Institute*, 467 U.S. 340 (1984), and under § 701(a)(2) agency action is not subject to judicial review "to the extent that" such action "is committed to agency discretion by law." As we explained in *Heckler v. Chaney*, § 701 (a)(2) makes it clear that "review is not to be had" in those rare circumstances where the relevant statute "is drawn so that a court would have no meaningful standard against which to judge the agency's exercise of discretion." "In such a case, the statute ('law') can be taken to have 'committed' the decisionmaking to the agency's judgment absolutely." *Heckler*.

Over the years, we have read § 701(a)(2) to preclude judicial review of certain categories of administrative decisions that courts traditionally have regarded as "committed to agency discretion." . . . . [We have] held an agency's decision not to institute enforcement proceedings to be presumptively unreviewable under § 701(a)(2). . . . [Similarly,] an agency's refusal to grant reconsideration of an action because of material error [is unreviewable]. . . . Finally . . . § 701(a)(2) precludes judicial review of a decision . . . to terminate an employee in the interests of national security, an area of executive action "in which courts have long been hesitant to intrude."

The allocation of funds from a lump-sum appropriation is another administrative decision traditionally regarded as committed to agency discretion. After all, the very point of a lump-sum appropriation is to give an agency the capacity to adapt to changing circumstances and meet its statutory responsibilities in what it sees as the most effective or desirable way. . . . Put another way, a lump-sum appropriation reflects a congressional recognition that an agency must be allowed "flexibility to shift . . . funds within a particular . . . appropriation account so that" the agency "can make necessary adjustments for 'unforeseen developments'" and "changing requirements."

Like the decision against instituting enforcement proceedings, then, an agency's allocation of funds from a lump-sum appropriation requires "a complicated balancing of a number of factors which are peculiarly within its expertise": whether its "resources are best spent" on one program or another; whether it "is likely to succeed" in fulfilling its statutory mandate; whether a particular program "best fits the agency's overall policies"; and, "indeed, whether the agency has enough resources" to fund a program "at all." *Heckler*. As in *Heckler*, so here, the "agency is far better equipped than the courts to deal with the many variables involved in the proper ordering of its priorities." Of course, an agency is not free simply to disregard statutory responsibilities: Congress may always circumscribe agency discretion to allocate resources by putting restrictions in the operative statutes . . . . And, of course, we hardly need to note that an agency's decision to ignore congressional expectations may expose it to grave political consequences. But as long as the agency allocates funds from a lump-sum appropriation to meet permissible statutory objectives, § 701(a)(2) gives the courts no leave to intrude. "To [that] extent," the decision to allocate funds "is committed to agency discretion by law."

The Service's decision to discontinue the Program is accordingly unreviewable under § 701(a)(2). . . . It is true that the Service repeatedly apprised Congress of the Program's continued operation, but, as we have explained, these representations do not translate . . . into legally binding obligations. . . . The Court of Appeals saw a separate limitation on the Service's discretion in the special trust relationship existing between Indian people and the Federal Government. . . . Whatever the contours of that relationship, though, it could not limit the Service's discretion to reorder its priorities from serving a subgroup of beneficiaries to serving the broader class of all Indians nationwide. . . .

———————

1. The termination action in this case was embodied in a policy statement. Section 553(b)(A) of the APA exempts "interpretative rules, general statements of policy, or rules of agency organization, procedure, or practice" from the notice and comment requirements. Was the basis for this decision rooted in the fact that policy statements are issued without public process from the outset? If the idea behind this particular exemption is that agencies should be free to set policy – and that such statements are designed primarily to communicate with the public the general perspective of the agency (as opposed to articulating an enforceable rule or standard) – then the exception might make a sound basis for the action of the Court.

The problem with this argument is that the issuance in question in *Lincoln* was dispositive of the fate of an entire

For More Information

Is it fair to conclude that the substantive content of policy statements generally should not be subjected to judicial review? See Stephen M. Johnson, *Good Guidance, Good Grief!, 2007, 72* Mo. L. Rev. 695 (2007), and, for a state law perspective, Christopher R. Pieper, Note, *No Harm, No Rule: The Muddy Waters of Agency Policy Statements and Judicial Review Under the Missouri Administrative Procedure Act,* 69 Mo. L. Rev. 731 (2004).

program and could hardly be characterized as a simple attempt to keep the public informed.

2. Should the decision to terminate a federally funded program ever be subject to judicial review? The *Lincoln* decision characterized the process of decision-making as "committed to the discretion" of the agency and thus nonreviewable. Certainly, the Executive branch is charged with making these types of decisions regularly – but are they always nonreviewable?

What happens if the decision to terminate a program is a patent abuse of authority or is otherwise driven by inappropriate political motives – or worse? What if an ethnic or racial bias appears to be the motivation of a public official – what recourse is available under *Lincoln*? What if a personal moral or religious belief is the motivating force? *See* Joanna K. Sax, *The States "Race" with the Federal Government for Stem Cell Research*, 15 ANN. HEALTH L. 1 (2006), *and* Francesca Crisera, Note, *Federal Regulation of Embryonic Stem Cells: Can Government Do It? An Examination of Potential Regulation Through the Eyes of California's Recent Legislation*, 31 HASTINGS CONST. L.Q. 355 (2004).

3. Not every program termination case escapes judicial review, notwithstanding the general notion that lump sum funding decisions are committed to agency discretion and inherently political. In *Castellini v. Lappin*, 365 F. Supp. 2d 197 (D. Mass. 2005), a prisoner was sentenced to serve a 21 month sentence in a facility that was characterized as a "boot camp" and where, presumably, some level of career training and personal growth were more likely than in a conventional prison setting. When the Board of Prisons (BOP) decided to close down the boot camp program in question, the prisoner brought suit, claiming, *inter alia*, that his rights to a notice and comment process under the APA had been violated. The court compared his situation to *Lincoln* and held:

> Here, unlike in *Lincoln*, Congress enabled and authorized funding for the program at issue. . . . [However] Congress intended to authorize the BOP to operate a boot camp program but did not intend to require the operation of such a program. . . . Thus, BOP has the authority to reallocate boot camp resources. . . .
>
> Regardless of its authority to reallocate resources, however, the BOP's termination of the boot camp program violated the APA. The APA "provides generally that an agency must publish notice of a proposed rulemaking in the Federal Register and afford interested persons an opportunity to participate . . . through submission of written data, views, or arguments. . . ." "Numerous courts have found that the APA applies to BOP rulemaking." *Iacaboni v. United States*, 251 F. Supp. 2d 1015, 1036 (D. Mass. 2003). . . .
>
> In *Lincoln*, the Supreme Court held that termination of the program at issue was exempt from APA notice and comment requirements, potentially as a rule of agency organization and certainly as a general statement of policy. . . .

However, unlike the Indian Health Service in *Lincoln*, the BOP established the program at issue here, which Congress enabled, through regulation subject to notice and comment. 61 Fed. Reg. at 18,658 ("The Bureau is publishing this regulation as an interim rule in order to provide for public comment. . . ."). The APA requires notice and comment "when an agency adopts a new position inconsistent with any of the [agency's] existing regulations." . . . . Where an agency's "interpretation [of a regulation] has the practical effect of altering the regulation, a formal amendment – almost certainly prospective and after notice and comment – is the proper course." *United States v. Hoyts Cinemas Corp.*, 380 F.3d 558, 569 (1st Cir. 2004). . . .

The BOP's abrupt termination of the boot camp program is inconsistent with, and effectively repudiates, the regulations by which the BOP established the program.

Had the health care program in *Lincoln* been "established" through a notice and comment process, would the outcome of the judicial review issue have been different? Think back to <u>*Long Island Care at Home v. Coke*</u>. The notice and comment process in that case appeared to be part of the basis for compelling *Chevron* deference. If the agency involved decided to change its rules on in-home elder care by contract employees from a registered assisted living company, would it be required to do so through notice and comment?

WEBSTER V. DOE

<u>486 U.S. 592 (1988)</u>

[JUSTICE REHNQUIST] Section 102(c) of the National Security Act of 1947 provides that:

> The Director of Central Intelligence may, in his discretion, terminate the employment of any officer or employee of the Agency whenever he shall deem such termination necessary or advisable in the interests of the United States . . . .

In this case we decide whether, and to what extent, the termination decisions of the Director under § 102(c) are judicially reviewable.

Respondent John Doe was first employed by the Central Intelligence Agency (CIA or Agency) in 1973 as a clerk-typist. He received periodic fitness reports that consistently rated him as an excellent or outstanding employee. By 1977, respondent had been promoted to a position as a covert electronics technician.

In January 1982, respondent voluntarily informed a CIA security officer that he was a homosexual. Almost immediately, the Agency placed respondent on paid administrative leave pending an investigation of his sexual orientation and conduct. On February 12 and again on February 17, respondent was extensively questioned by a polygraph officer concerning his homosexuality and possible security violations. Respondent denied having sexual relations with any foreign nationals and maintained that he had not disclosed classified information to any of his sexual partners. . . .

On April 14, 1982, a CIA security agent informed respondent that the Agency's Office of Security had determined that respondent's homosexuality posed a threat to security, but declined to explain the nature of the danger. Respondent was then asked to resign. When he refused to do so, the Office of Security recommended to the CIA Director (petitioner's predecessor) that respondent be dismissed. After reviewing respondent's records and the evaluations of his subordinates, the Director "deemed it necessary and advisable in the interests of the United States to terminate [respondent's] employment with this Agency pursuant to section 102(c) of the National Security Act . . . ." . . . .

Respondent then filed an action against petitioner in the United States District Court for the District of Columbia. Respondent's amended complaint asserted a variety of statutory and constitutional claims against the Director. Respondent alleged that the Director's decision to terminate his employment violated the Administrative Procedure Act (APA), 5 U.S.C. § 706, because it was arbitrary and capricious, represented an abuse of discretion, and was reached without observing the procedures required by law and CIA regulations. He also complained that the Director's termination of his employment deprived him of constitutionally protected rights to property, liberty, and privacy in violation of the First, Fourth, Fifth, and Ninth Amendments. Finally, he asserted that his dismissal transgressed the procedural due process and equal protection of the laws guaranteed by the Fifth Amendment. . . .

Petitioner moved to dismiss respondent's amended complaint on the ground that § 102(c) of the National Security Act (NSA) precludes judicial review of the Director's termination decisions under the provisions of the APA . . . . The scope of judicial review under § 702, however, is circumscribed by § 706 and its availability . . . is predicated on satisfying the requirements of § 701, which provides:

> (a) This chapter applies, according to the provisions thereof, except to the extent that –
>
> (1) statutes preclude judicial review; or
>
> (2) agency action is committed to agency discretion by law.

. . . .

In *Citizens to Preserve Overton Park, Inc. v. Volpe*, this Court explained the distinction between §§ 701(a)(1) and (a)(2). Subsection (a)(1) is concerned with whether Congress expressed an intent to prohibit judicial review; subsection (a)(2) applies "in those rare instances where 'statutes are drawn in such broad terms that in a given case there is no law to apply.'"

We further explained what it means for an action to be "committed to agency discretion by law" in *Heckler v. Chaney*. *Heckler* required the Court to determine whether the Food and Drug Administration's decision not to undertake an enforcement proceeding against the use of certain drugs in administering the death penalty was subject to judicial review. We noted that, under § 701(a)(2), even when Congress has not affirmatively precluded judicial oversight, "review is not to be had if the statute is drawn so that a court would have no meaningful standard against which to judge the agency's exercise of discretion." Since the statute conferring power on the Food and Drug Administration to prohibit the unlawful misbranding or misuse of drugs provided no substantive standards on which a court could base its review, we found that enforcement actions were committed to the complete discretion of the FDA to decide when and how they should be pursued.

Both *Overton Park* and *Heckler* emphasized that § 701(a)(2) requires careful examination of the statute on which the claim of agency illegality is based (the Federal-Aid Highway Act of 1968 in *Overton Park* and the Federal Food, Drug, and Cosmetic Act in *Heckler*). In the present case, respondent's claims against the CIA arise from the Director's asserted violation of § 102(c) of the NSA. As an initial matter, it should be noted that § 102(c) allows termination of an Agency employee whenever the Director "shall *deem* such termination necessary or advisable in the interests of the United States" (emphasis added), not simply when the dismissal *is* necessary or advisable to those interests. This standard fairly exudes deference to the Director, and appears to us to foreclose the application of any meaningful judicial standard of review. Short of permitting cross-examination of the Director concerning his views of the Nation's security and whether the discharged employee was inimical to those interests, we see no basis on which a reviewing court could properly assess an Agency termination decision. The language of § 102(c) thus strongly suggests that its implementation was "committed to agency discretion by law."

So too does the overall structure of the NSA. Passed shortly after the close of the Second World War, the NSA created the CIA and gave its Director the responsibility "for protecting intelligence sources and methods from unauthorized disclosure." Section 102(c) is an integral part of that statute, because the Agency's efficacy, and the Nation's security, depend in large measure on the reliability and trustworthiness of the Agency's employees. As we [previously] recognized . . ., employment with the CIA entails a high degree of trust that is perhaps unmatched in Government service.

. . . .

We thus find that the language and structure of § 102(c) indicate that Congress meant to commit individual employee discharges to the Director's discretion, and that § 701(a)(2) accordingly precludes judicial review of these decisions under the APA. . . .

III

In addition to his claim that the Director failed to abide by the statutory dictates of § 102(c), respondent also alleged a number of constitutional violations in his amended complaint. Respondent charged that petitioner's termination of his employment deprived him of property and liberty interests under the Due Process Clause of the Fifth Amendment, denied him equal protection of the laws, and unjustifiably burdened his right to privacy. Respondent asserts that he is entitled, under the APA, to judicial consideration of these claimed violations.

. . . .

Petitioner maintains that, no matter what the nature of respondent's constitutional claims, judicial review is precluded by the language and intent of § 102(c). In petitioner's view, all Agency employment termination decisions, even those based on policies normally repugnant to the Constitution, are given over to the absolute discretion of the Director, and are hence unreviewable under the APA. We do not think § 102(c) may be read to exclude review of constitutional claims. We [previously] emphasized . . . that where Congress intends to preclude judicial review of constitutional claims its intent to do so must be clear. . . . We require this heightened showing in part to avoid the "serious constitutional question" that would arise if a federal statute were construed to deny any judicial forum for a colorable constitutional claim.

Our review of § 102(c) convinces us that it cannot bear the preclusive weight petitioner would have it support. As detailed above, the section does commit employment termination decisions to the Director's discretion, and precludes challenges to these decisions based upon the statutory language of § 102(c). A discharged employee thus cannot complain that his termination was not "necessary or advisable in the interests of the United States," since that assessment is the Director's alone. Subsections (a)(1) and (a)(2) of § 701, however, remove from judicial review only those determinations specifically identified by Congress or "committed to agency discretion by law." Nothing in § 102(c) persuades us that Congress meant to preclude consideration of colorable constitutional claims arising out of the actions of the Director pursuant to that section; we believe that a constitutional claim based on an individual discharge may be reviewed by the District Court. . . .

   . . . .

[JUSTICE SCALIA, dissenting.]

I agree with the Court's apparent holding in Part II of its opinion, that the Director's decision to terminate a CIA employee is "committed to agency discretion by law" within the meaning of 5 U.S.C. § 701(a)(2). But because I do not see how a decision can, either practically or legally, be both unreviewable and yet reviewable for constitutional defect, I regard Part III of the opinion as essentially undoing Part II. I therefore respectfully dissent from the judgment of the Court. . . .

Underlying Case Documents

The case referenced:
The National Security Act of 1947

For the affidavit of "John Doe" click HERE.
For the letter sent by "John Doe's" attorney to the CIA in an attempt to prevent the agency from firing "John Doe" click HERE.
For the letter of termination from the CIA click HERE.

1. One of the more powerful issues in *Webster* is whether the presence of a "constitutional issue," as opposed to a statutory or common law claim, creates a separate constitutional right to and basis for judicial review. *See* Richard H. Fallon, Jr., *Of Legislative Courts, Administrative Agencies, and Article III*, 101 HARV. L. REV. 915, 950-70 (1988), *and* Henry P. Monaghan, *Constitutional Fact Review*, 85 COLUM. L. REV. 229, 267 (1985) (asserting that constitutional issues are no more or less important than other issues). The problem becomes pronounced when, as in *Webster*, there is a basis to deny review completely (the government's position) or to conclude the substantive review summarily on the premise that the agency decision was soundly vested to the discretion of the agency.

The issue was raised – and then passed over – in *United States v. Erika, Inc.*, 456 U.S. 201, 211 n.14 (1982). In his full dissent, JUSTICE SCALIA dismisses the matter directly. Is he right?

a. If an administrative action is arguably unconstitutional, is it unreviewable if there is a statute precluding review? If so, the preclusion statute becomes a shield for unconstitutional action undertaken by those charged with defending and implementing the Constitution's protections. If not, many actions government officials take that are vested explicitly in their discretion are subject to challenge. After all, due process claims are often part of the arguments made by those who challenge agency action.

b. What if an administrative action vested to the discretion of the agency is arguably unconstitutional – is it unreviewable? The same pro and con arguments apply – with this twist: If there is "no law to apply" to judge whether the agency action is proper (a basis to conclude the matter is nonreviewable), the public is left with an executive empowered to act without legislative standards to gauge the propriety of the action and without an opportunity to challenge that action in an Article III court.

2. Based on the Court's opinion, *Webster* involved a "perfect storm" of nonreviewability: The statute fairly "exudes" deference to the Director of the CIA, the agency is involved in activity that involves national security, and there are apparently no "law[s] to apply" to employment actions (including dismissals). That meant that a challenge based on the APA standards for judicial review would not be permitted. Do these arguments ring true? *See* Ronald M. Levin, *Understanding Unreviewability in Administrative Law*, 74 Minn. L. Rev. 689, 730 (1990), *and* Kenneth Culp Davis, *No Law to Apply*, 25 San Diego L. Rev. 1 (1988). Even assuming the unavailability of the APA, was there a constitutional question? The employee was allegedly dismissed based on sexual orientation/preference. There were standards for hiring and retention of government employees (and thus some law to apply) as well as associational rights issue that could have been raised.

3. How would *Webster* be decided today? *See* Harel Arnon, *Legal Reasoning: Justifying Tolerance in the U.S. Supreme Court*, 2 N.Y.U. J.L. & Liberty 262 (2007).

4. The statute that was the basis for the dismissal in *Webster* gave the Director authority to terminate employees as "necessary or advisable." *See* 50 U.S.C. 403(c). Is this "unbridled discretion" . . . or is this "law to apply" to judge whether the action of the Director was arbitrary, capricious, or an abuse of discretion?

VI. Review of Agency Inaction

In most administrative agencies – as well in the domain of civil and criminal justice – those charged with promulgating rules and policies, overseeing regulatory systems, and enforcing specific legal standards are vested with considerable (although not unlimited) discretion. Agency enforcement officials as well as those charged with rulemaking tasks – and, outside the administrative law system, criminal prosecutors – are expected to make judgment calls regarding the best use of governmental resources, the overall enforcement scheme, and the prioritization of various policy imperatives. *See* Daniel P. Selmi, *Jurisdiction to Review Agency Inaction Under Federal Environmental Law*, 72 IND. L.J. 65 (1996). There is little question that great deference is due the decision to issue (or not issue) regulations or policies or to enforce (or not enforce) a particular statute. This exercise of discretion is an essential choice made by the executive branch. *See* Cass R. Sunstein, *Reviewing Agency Inaction After* Heckler v. Chaney, 52 U. CHI. L. REV. 653 (1985).

Notwithstanding the deference due discretionary choices in the enforcement and rulemaking domain, there are instances where the decision not to act has significant and adverse consequences. *See* Christina Larsen, *Is the Glass Half Empty or Half Full? Challenging Incomplete Agency Action Under Section 706(1) of the Administrative Procedure Act*, 25 PUB. LAND & RESOURCES L. REV. 113 (2004).

In the criminal justice system, it is easy to understand the anger and frustration the victim of a crime will experience if a prosecutor chooses not to go after a perpetrator. Similarly, in the agency context, it takes little imagination to understand the frustration members of the public experience when an agency simply takes no action – or decides affirmatively not to act – allowing a hazard, risk, nuisance, or environmental degradation to continue. This phenomenon was evident in *Norton v. Southern Utah Wilderness Alliance*, 542 U.S. 55, 60 (2004), which articulated (to the great disappointment of very vocal parties and interest groups) the basic noninterference policy courts follow in most instances.

The fact of an apparent violation of regulatory standards or norms does not create an absolute (or anything close to absolute) obligation, enforceable in court, to go forward. Because agency inaction is generally vested in the discretion of the agency, courts are hesitant to interfere. Similarly, the Office of Management and Budget and the important and somewhat secretive Office of Information and Regulatory Affairs, entities with direct power over certain agency activity, have done next to nothing in the last ten years about agency inaction other than issue occasional informal letters "prompting" agencies to exercise their authority.

There are times, however (rare though they may be) when the inaction or unreasonable delay on the part of an agency can be challenged successfully in court. The most dramatic recent example of this occurred in *Massachusetts v. EPA*, *infra* Chapter 4. Frustrated with EPA's failure to address the interrelationship between arguably unacceptable levels of greenhouse gasses (including carbon dioxide), automobile emissions, and global warming, various States brought suit against EPA.

Unlike *Southern Utah Wilderness Alliance*, the Court found EPA's inaction unacceptable. "In short, EPA has offered no reasoned explanation for its refusal to decide whether greenhouse gases cause or contribute to climate change. Its action was therefore 'arbitrary, capricious, . . . or otherwise not in accordance with law.' . . . . We hold . . . that EPA must ground its reasons for action or inaction in the statute." 127 S.Ct. at 1444.

For More Information

In the vast majority of cases, courts – and particularly the Supreme Court – have refused to issue a Writ of Mandamus or other type of injunctive relief to compel an agency to act, even in light of unconscionable delay. The scholarship in this area is plentiful and of great value. *See, e.g.*, Jacob E. Gersen & Anne Joseph O'Connell, *Deadlines in Administrative Law*, 156 U. PA. L. REV. 923 (2008); Eric Biber, *Two Side of the Same Coin: Judicial Review of Administrative Agency Action and Inaction*, 26 VA. ENVTL. L.J. 461 (2008); Nicholas Bagley & Richard L. Revesz, *Centralized Oversight of the Regulatory State*, 106 COLUM. L. REV. 1260 (2006); Lisa S. Bressman, *Judicial Review of Agency Inaction: An Arbitrariness Approach*, 79 N.Y.U. L. REV. 1657, 1668 (2004); Catherine Zaller, Note, *The Case for Strict Statutory Construction of Mandatory Agency Deadlines Under § 706(1)*, 42 WM. & MARY L. REV. 1545, 1545 (2001).

Finally, there is one line of cases that establishes criteria to determine if agency delay has finally reached the point where a court ought to invade the otherwise sacrosanct, discretionary province of the agency and to issue an order directing the agency to act. These criteria, referred to as the *TRAC* factors, are discussed *infra* Chapter 6. *Telecommunications Research & Action Ctr. [TRAC] v. F.C.C.*, 750 F.2d 70, 79-80 (D.C. Cir. 1984). *TRAC* analysis is not without its problems – and contrary case law. *See Forest Guardians v. Babbitt*, 174 F.3d 1178, 1191 (10th Cir. 1999).

The cases that follow allow you to explore some of the parameters surrounding judicial review of inaction.

HECKLER V. CHANEY

470 U.S. 821 (1985)

[JUSTICE REHNQUIST] This case presents the question of the extent to which a decision of an administrative agency to exercise its "discretion" not to undertake certain enforcement actions is subject to judicial review under the Administrative Procedure Act (APA). Respondents are several prison inmates convicted of capital offenses and sentenced to death by lethal injection of drugs. They petitioned the Food and Drug Administration (FDA), alleging that . . . the use of these drugs for capital punishment violated the Federal Food, Drug, and Cosmetic Act (FDCA), and requesting that the FDA take various enforcement actions to prevent these violations. The FDA refused their request. . . . [T]he Court of Appeals for the District of Columbia Circuit . . . held the FDA's refusal to take enforcement actions both reviewable and an abuse of discretion, and remanded the case with directions that the agency be required "to fulfill its statutory function."

I

Respondents have been sentenced to death by lethal injection of drugs under the laws of the States of Oklahoma and Texas. . . . Respondents first petitioned the FDA, claiming that the drugs used by the States for this purpose, although approved by the FDA for [other uses], were not approved for use in human executions [and] given that the drugs would likely be administered by untrained personnel, it was also likely that the drugs would not induce the quick and painless death intended. . . . Accordingly, respondents claimed that the FDA was required to approve the drugs as "safe and effective" for human execution before they could be distributed in interstate commerce. They therefore requested the FDA to take various investigatory and enforcement actions to prevent these perceived violations; they requested the FDA to affix warnings to the labels of all the drugs stating that they were unapproved and unsafe for human execution, to send statements to the drug manufacturers and prison administrators stating that the drugs should not be so used, and to adopt procedures for seizing the drugs from state prisons and to recommend the prosecution of all those in the chain of distribution who knowingly distribute or purchase the drugs with intent to use them for human execution.

The FDA Commissioner responded, refusing to take the requested actions. The Commissioner first detailed his disagreement with respondents' understanding of the scope of FDA jurisdiction . . . . He went on to state:

> Were FDA clearly to have jurisdiction in the area, moreover, we believe we would be authorized to decline to exercise it under our inherent discretion to decline to pursue certain enforcement matters. . . . Generally, enforcement proceedings in this area are initiated only when there is a serious danger to the public health or a blatant scheme to defraud. We cannot conclude that those dangers are present under State lethal injection laws, which are duly authorized statutory enactments in furtherance of proper State functions. . . .

. . . .

II

. . . For us, this case turns on the . . . extent to which determinations by the FDA *not to exercise* its enforcement authority . . . may be judicially reviewed. That decision in turn involves the construction of two separate but necessarily inter-related statutes, the APA and the FDCA.

[Under the APA any] person "adversely affected or aggrieved" by agency action, including a "failure to act," is entitled to "judicial review thereof," as long as the action is a "final agency action for which there is no other adequate remedy in a court." The standards to be applied on review are governed by the provisions of § 706. But before any review at all may be had, a party must first clear the hurdle of § 701(a). That section provides that the chapter on judicial review "applies, according to the provisions thereof, except to the extent that – (1) statutes preclude judicial review; or (2) agency action is committed to agency discretion by law." Petitioner urges that the decision of the FDA to refuse enforcement is an action "committed to agency discretion by law" under § 701(a)(2).

. . . .

[Section 701(a)(1)] applies when Congress has expressed an intent to preclude judicial review. . . . [Section 701(a)(2)] applies in different circumstances; even where Congress has not affirmatively precluded review, review is not to be had if the statute is drawn so that a court would have no meaningful standard against which to judge the agency's exercise of discretion. . . . This construction avoids conflict with the "abuse of discretion" standard of review in § 706 – if no judicially manageable standards are available for judging how and when an agency should exercise its discretion, then it is impossible to evaluate agency action for "abuse of discretion." In addition, this construction [gives effect to every clause in the statute] by identifying a separate class of cases to which § 701(a)(2) applies.

To this point our analysis does not differ significantly from that of the Court of Appeals. That court purported to apply the "no law to apply" standard of *Overton Park*. We disagree, however, with that court's insistence that . . . § (a)(2) required application of a presumption of reviewability even to an agency's decision not to undertake certain enforcement actions. Here we think the Court of Appeals broke with tradition, case law, and sound reasoning.

Overton Park did not involve an agency's refusal to take requested enforcement action. It involved an affirmative act of approval under a statute that set clear guidelines for determining when such approval should be given. Refusals to take enforcement steps generally involve precisely the opposite situation, and in that situation we think the presumption is that judicial review is not available. This Court has recognized on several occasions over many years that an agency's decision not to prosecute or enforce, whether through civil or criminal process, is a decision generally committed to an agency's absolute discretion. This recognition of the existence of discretion is attributable in no small part to the general unsuitability for judicial review of agency decisions to refuse enforcement.

The reasons for this general unsuitability are many. First, an agency decision not to enforce often involves a complicated balancing of a number of factors which are peculiarly within its expertise. Thus, the agency must not only assess whether a violation has occurred, but whether agency resources are best spent on this violation or another, whether the agency is likely to succeed if it acts, whether the particular enforcement action requested best fits the agency's overall policies, and, indeed, whether the agency has enough resources to undertake the action at all. An agency generally cannot act against each technical violation of the statute it is charged with enforcing. The agency is far better equipped than the courts to deal with the many variables involved in the proper ordering of its priorities. Similar concerns animate the principles of administrative law that courts generally will defer to an agency's construction of the statute it is charged with implementing, and to the procedures it adopts for implementing that statute.

In addition to these administrative concerns, we note that when an agency refuses to act it generally does not exercise its *coercive* power over an individual's liberty or property rights, and thus does not infringe upon areas that courts often are called upon to protect. Similarly, when an agency *does* act to enforce, that action itself provides a focus for judicial review, inasmuch as the agency must have exercised its power in some manner. The action at least can be reviewed to determine whether the agency exceeded its statutory powers. Finally, we recognize that an agency's refusal to institute proceedings shares to some extent the characteristics of the decision of a prosecutor in the Executive Branch not to indict – a decision which has long been regarded as the special province of the Executive Branch, inasmuch as it is the Executive who is charged by the Constitution to "take Care that the Laws be faithfully executed." U.S. Const., Art. II, § 3.

We of course only list the above concerns to facilitate understanding of our conclusion that an agency's decision not to take enforcement action should be presumed immune from judicial review under § 701(a)(2). For good reasons, such a decision has traditionally been "committed to agency discretion," and we believe that the Congress enacting the APA did not intend to alter that tradition. In so stating, we emphasize that the decision is only presumptively unreviewable; the presumption may be rebutted where the substantive statute has provided guidelines for the agency to follow in exercising its enforcement powers. Thus, in establishing this presumption in the APA, Congress did not set agencies free to disregard legislative direction in the statutory scheme that the agency administers. Congress may limit an agency's exercise of enforcement power if it wishes, either by setting substantive priorities, or by otherwise circumscribing an agency's power to discriminate among issues or cases it will pursue. . . .

Dunlop v. Bachowski, relied upon heavily by respondents and the majority in the Court of Appeals, presents an example of statutory language which supplied sufficient standards to rebut the presumption of unreviewability. . . . [The statute] provided that, upon filing of a complaint by a union member, "[the] Secretary shall investigate such complaint and, if he finds probable cause to believe that a violation . . . has occurred . . . he shall . . . bring a civil action. . . ." After investigating the plaintiff's claims the Secretary of Labor declined to file suit, and the plaintiff sought judicial review under the APA. This Court held that review was available. It rejected the Secretary's argument that the statute precluded judicial review [and was] content to rely on the Court of Appeals' opinion to hold that the § (a)(2) exception did not apply. The Court of Appeals, in turn, had found the "principle of absolute prosecutorial discretion" inapplicable, because the language of the LMRDA (Labor-Management Reporting and Disclosure Act of 1959) indicated that the Secretary was required to file suit if certain "clearly defined" factors were present. The decision therefore was not "beyond the judicial capacity to supervise."

Dunlop is thus consistent with a general presumption of unreviewability of decisions not to enforce. The statute being administered quite clearly withdrew discretion from the agency and provided guidelines for exercise of its enforcement power. Our decision that review was available was not based on "pragmatic considerations," such as those cited by the Court of Appeals that amount to an assessment of whether the interests at stake are important enough to justify intervention in the agencies' decisionmaking. The danger that agencies may not carry out their delegated powers with sufficient vigor does not necessarily lead to the conclusion that courts are the most appropriate body to police this aspect of their performance. That decision is in the first instance for Congress, and we therefore turn to the FDCA to determine whether in this case Congress has provided us with "law to apply." . . . .

III

[The FDCA grants the FDA discretion whether to take action in a given case.]

IV

We therefore conclude that the presumption that agency decisions not to institute proceedings are unreviewable under 5 U.S.C. § 701(a)(2) is not overcome by the enforcement provisions of the FDCA. . . . In so holding, we essentially leave to Congress, and not to the courts, the decision as to whether an agency's refusal to institute proceedings should be judicially reviewable. No colorable claim is made in this case that the agency's refusal to institute proceedings violated any constitutional rights of respondents, and we do not address the issue that would be raised in such a case. The fact that the drugs involved in this case are ultimately to be used in imposing the death penalty must not lead this Court or other courts to import profound differences of opinion over the meaning of the Eighth Amendment to the United States Constitution into the domain of administrative law.

The judgment of the Court of Appeals is reversed.

[JUSTICE BRENNAN, concurring.]

[T]he Court properly does not decide today that nonenforcement decisions are unreviewable in cases where (1) an agency flatly claims that it has no statutory jurisdiction to reach certain conduct; (2) an agency engages in a pattern of non-enforcement of clear statutory language . . . ; (3) an agency has refused to enforce a regulation lawfully promulgated and still in effect or (4) a nonenforcement decision violates constitutional rights. It is possible to imagine other nonenforcement decisions made for entirely illegitimate reasons, for example, nonenforcement in return for a bribe, judicial review of which would not be foreclosed by the nonreviewability presumption. . . .

[JUSTICE MARSHALL, concurring.]

Easy cases at times produce bad law . . . . [T]he "presumption of unreviewability" announced today is a product of that lack of discipline that easy cases make all too easy. The majority . . . creates out of whole cloth the notion that agency decisions not to take "enforcement action" are unreviewable unless Congress has rather specifically indicated otherwise. Because this "presumption of unreviewability" is fundamentally at odds with rule-of-law principles firmly embedded in our jurisprudence . . . one can only hope that it will come to be understood as a relic of [this] particular factual setting . . . .

Underlying Case Documents

The case referenced:
The petition to FDA seeking agency action
The FDA response to the petition declining to act

1. JUSTICE BRENNAN's concurrence identified a series of circumstances where the general principle of unreviewability of agency inaction may not block judicial review: (1) When an agency "flatly claims" that it is without authority to address particular conduct – when in fact, it has precisely that authority – the nonreview-

ability prohibition does not apply; and (2) If an agency engages in a "pattern of nonenforcement" or a refusal to enforce a rule that is "lawfully promulgated and still in effect" or undertakes action that is otherwise unconstitutional or illegal (for example accepting a bribe in exchange for inaction) the nonreviewability premise can be overcome. These exceptions to the nonreviewability presumption require some thought.

a. If an agency claims it has no authority to reach a particular area or engages in a pattern of nonenforcement, how is that not defensible as an exercise of discretion? Regardless of the inaccuracy underlying the claim of "no authority," the essence of the assertion is that the agency has chosen not to act. What remedy would emerge if an agency claims it has no authority when a plain reading of the statute suggests that it does have such authority? Would a court be limited to interpreting the statute accurately? And then what?

b. "Pattern of enforcement" cases are equally perplexing. The majority in *Chaney* holds that because agencies have the best sense of their resources, regulatory and enforcement priorities, personnel and time limitations, and expertise in a particular field, their decisions regarding enforcement or regulatory priorities are entitled to deference. If an agency decides – repeatedly – that it will not proceed in a particular direction, presumably that would constitute a "pattern of non-enforcement." Why is a pattern of nonenforcement less subject to the prohibition on judicial review? Outside of those circumstances where the pattern of nonen-forcement can be linked with inappropriate behavior (either discriminatory action or patently illegal behavior), what is the breadth of this exception?

In *Schering v. Heckler, 779 F.2d 683 (D.C. Cir. 1985)*, after the FDA approved a new drug by one manufacturer, a second manufacturer began to market a similar drug without securing FDA approval. The FDA initiated an enforcement proceed-ing that was soon settled. Shortly thereafter, unsatisfied with the settlement, the first manufacturer brought suit claiming that the FDA had not done its job. It contended that the FDA had not made a determination about whether the sec-ond manufacturer's product was a new drug, nor had it issued guidelines for the type of product the second manufacturer was producing. When the FDA took no further action, the first manufacturer went to court seeking to compel the FDA to do its job. While the FDA had jurisdiction, the court noted that the agency had "elected not to pursue enforcement activities. . . ." These choices, noted the court, were committed to the discretion of the agency and not readily reviewable. The court went on to note however, that had this practice been part of a "policy or pattern of nonenforcement that amounts [to an] abdication of statutory respon-sibility," it might have taken action. Further, the court noted that it might have been motivated to act had there been an assertion that the activity of the agency violated "any constitutional rights." Seeing neither a pattern of nonenforcement nor a violation of constitutional rights, the case was dismissed.

Hypothetical

Assume that a federal communications statute authorizes "the chairman of the Federal Communications Commission, at his or her discretion, to place cities, towns and other population centers across the nation on a National Broadband Priority List." Localities on the NBPL are targeted for significant federal resources, including subsidies and technical support, designed to promote universal access to high speed residential and commercial broadband Internet services. After two years of petitioning the chairman of the FCC to place metropolitan Sloverlook, TX, on the NBPL, the Sloverlook Town Council has decided to sue the FCC chairman. Is his decision not to place Sloverlook, TX, on the NBPL subject to judicial review?

---

2. If Congress articulates clear and unequivocal standards for enforcement, and an agency fails to act when those criteria are met, *Chaney* suggests the possibility of bypassing the deference accorded generally to agency inaction. Likewise, where Congress requires an agency to act as a predicate for a party to secure judicial review or to initiate an independent claim in court, and the agency fails to do so, the prohibition against judicial interference with agency inaction can be set aside. *Dunlop v. Bachoski, 421 U.S. 560 (1975)*. In the area of unfair labor practices and employment discrimination, a claimant cannot easily initiate a proceeding in federal court to secure relief from allegedly unlawful conduct unless the agency has considered and acted upon the claim initially. These requirements are statutory in nature and differ from the general obligation to exhaust administrative remedies. Exhaustion, as a predicate for judicial action, is often not a jurisdictional necessity – unless a specific statute commands a party to exhaust his or her remedies prior to filing suit.

3. Section 553(e) of the APA allows any interested person to request or petition an agency to issue a rule in a particular field. Section 555(e) requires an agency to respond to such petitions and set forth reasons why they will either go forward with some type of rulemaking proceeding – or not. *Chaney* seems to suggest that the decision to initiate a rulemaking is so solidly vested to the discretion of the agency that parties should have no expectation of judicial review when agencies take no action after such petitions are filed. After *Massachusetts v. EPA, infra* Chapter 4 decided in 2007, an agency's obligation to respond to such petitions seems more straightforward.

4. While *Chaney* affirms the principle that agency inaction is usually nonreviewable, it also raises the possibility of a court finding that the agency's behavior "consciously and expressly . . . represents an abdication of the agency's statutory responsibilities." Evidence of lower courts using the "abdication of responsibility" as a foundation to compel agencies to act is scarce at best. <u>River-keeper Inc. v. Collins, 359 F.3d 156 (2d Cir. 2004)</u>. In some areas, however, the abdication discourse is becoming more pronounced. *See* George Cameron Coggins, *"Devolution" in Federal Land Law: Abdication by Any Other Name*, 14 HASTINGS W.-NW. J. ENVTL. L. & POL'Y 485 (2008).

Good Question!

The FDA's stated position in *Chaney* was that it could not be compelled to act unless there was "a serious danger to the public health or a blatant scheme to defraud." If an approved pharmaceutical product is used for a purpose that is outside of any of the uses the FDA approved, how is that not a danger to public health?

5. <u>Norton v. Southern Utah Wilderness Alliance, 542 U.S. 55 (2004)</u>:

> Almost half the State of Utah, about 23 million acres, is federal land administered by the Bureau of Land Management (BLM) . . . . Protection of wilderness has come into increasing conflict with . . . recreational use of so-called off-road vehicles (ORVs) . . . . [S]ome 42 million Americans participate in off-road travel each year, more than double the number two decades ago. . . .

> All . . . claims at issue here involve assertions that BLM failed to take action with respect to ORV use that it was required to take. Failures to act are sometimes remediable under the APA, but not always. . . . [T]he only agency action that can be compelled under the APA is action legally *required*. . . . Thus, a claim under § 706(1) can proceed only where a plaintiff asserts that an agency failed to take a *discrete* agency action that it is *required to take*. . . . [W]hen an agency is compelled by law to act within a certain time period, but the manner of its action is left to the agency's discretion, a court can compel the agency to act, but has no power to specify what the action must be. . . .

> With these principles in mind, we turn to SUWA's first claim, that by permitting ORV use in certain [Wilderness Study Areas], BLM violated its mandate to "continue to manage . . . in a manner so as not to impair the suitability of such areas for preservation as wilderness." . . . . Section 1782(c) is mandatory as to the object to be achieved, but it leaves BLM a great deal of discretion in deciding how to achieve it. It assuredly does not mandate, with the clarity necessary to support judicial action under § 706(1), the total exclusion of ORV use.

> SUWA . . . contends that a federal court could simply enter a general order compelling compliance . . . without suggesting any particular manner of compliance. . . . If courts were empowered to enter general orders compelling compliance with broad statutory mandates, they would necessarily be empowered, as well, to determine whether compliance was achieved – which would mean that it would ultimately become the task of the supervising court, rather than the agency, to work out compliance with

the broad statutory mandate. . . . [A]llowing general enforcement of plan terms would lead to pervasive interference with BLM's own ordering of priorities [and we will not do it].

6. *Drake v. Federal Aviation Administration*, 291 F.3d 59 (D.C. Cir. 2002):

FAA regulations require that air carriers administer periodic drug tests on employees who perform certain safety-sensitive functions. . . . Delta Airlines required its flight attendants to undergo random drug tests as a condition of their employment. In 1993, Drake was selected for testing . . . . His urine sample was sent to Delta's designated laboratory, CompuChem Laboratories, Inc., which pronounced it "unsuitable for testing" . . . . A subsequent report suggested that this initial result was "indicative of adulteration with glutaraldehyde," a substance often used to mask the presence of drugs in the body. . . . [A]fter Delta learned of this result, Drake was removed from active flight status. One month later, he was asked to resign, and was fired when he refused. . . .

In September 1998, Drake formally requested that the FAA investigate Delta for its allegedly unlawful actions in processing his urine sample. . . . On March 25, 1999 . . . the FAA . . . reported that it had found no evidence to support Drake's allegations against Delta. . . . The instant case commenced on October 20, 1999, when Drake filed a second pro se action [alleging] that the FAA's determination that Delta had not violated [federal regulations on employee drug testing] was unreasonable, and the product of a conspiracy between the agency and the airline. . . . The District Court then dismissed Drake's action [and] Drake appealed . . . .

We reject this challenge, because we find that the FAA's decision to dismiss Drake's complaint without a hearing is "committed to agency discretion by law," and thus excluded from review under the APA. 5 U.S.C. § 701(a)(2). . . . [T]he FAA's decision to dismiss Drake's complaint without a hearing was equivalent to a decision not to commence an enforcement action. . . . The FAA's action in this case was thus analogous to an exercise of "prosecutorial discretion" of the sort discussed in *Chaney*. And, as *Chaney* makes clear, when prosecutorial discretion is at issue, the matter is presumptively committed to agency discretion by law.

7. *Sierra Club v. Whitman*, 268 F.3d 898 (9th Cir. 2001):

The Nogales International Wastewater Treatment Plant . . . is located in Rio Rico, Arizona . . . . In 1991 the EPA granted a permit to the City of Nogales, Arizona and the United States Section of the Boundary Commission, the joint operators of the Treatment Plant. . . . [T]he Treatment Plant violated its permit limitations 128 times between January 1995 and January 2000. The Clean Water Act provides that, whenever "the Administrator finds that any person is in violation" of permit conditions, the Administrator "shall issue an order requiring such person to comply . . . or . . . shall bring a civil action" against the violator. The EPA Administrator, however, has not made a finding of a violation by the Treatment Plant, nor has she taken any of the enforcement actions authorized by the Act. The Sierra Club brought this action against the EPA to compel it to initiate enforcement action. . . .

The EPA has many plants to monitor and must be able to choose which violations are the most egregious. . . . [H]owever, the presumption that the EPA has discretion to decide when to enforce is only a presumption and can be overcome by indications that Congress intended otherwise. . . . It is . . . the word "shall," upon which the Sierra Club principally relies. It is true that "shall" in a statute generally denotes a mandatory duty. Nonetheless, the use of "shall" is not conclusive . . . "shall" is sometimes the equivalent of "may." . . . . [Our analysis] of the structure and the legislative history of the Clean Water Act leads to the conclusion that subsection 1319(a)(3) does not create mandatory enforcement duties.

First, the structure of section 1319 suggests that Congress did not intend the enforcement provisions . . . to be mandatory. . . . Subsection (b) merely states that "the Administrator is *authorized* to commence a civil action . . . ." (emphasis added). The language of authorization . . . shows congressional intent to give the Administrator . . . options, not to require their use in all instances. . . . Another aspect of the statutory structure that suggests that the enforcement mechanisms are discretionary is the availability of citizen suits to enforce the <u>Clean Water Act</u>. . . . By allowing citizens to sue to bring about compliance with the Clean Water Act, Congress implicitly acknowledged that there would be situations in which the EPA did not act. . . . [Therefore the] presumption that it is within the EPA's discretion whether to enforce or not enforce in any given case has not been overcome. . . .

VII. Agency Action Without Written Opinion

N*GURE* v. A*SHCROFT*

<u>367 F.3d 975 (8th Cir. 2004)</u>

[J*UDGE* C*OLLOTON*] On August 30, 1995, Joseph Ngure, a native and citizen of Kenya, entered the United States . . . to attend Principia College in Elsah, Illinois. The terms of his J-1 visa permitted him to stay in the United States until June 15, 1996. On January 25, 2000, the INS issued a Notice to Appear charging that Ngure was removable . . . . Ngure admitted that he was removable, and . . . applied for asylum . . . and relief under the Convention Against Torture.

Ngure is a member of the Kikuyu tribe, which is the largest tribe in Kenya. While Ngure was a student at the University of Nairobi in 1987, he participated in a week-long pro-democracy demonstration . . . . Ngure was arrested while he was in his room. Soon after he arrived at the police station, he secured his release because he knew the superintendent of police. . . . Again, in 1990, Ngure participated in a pro-democracy demonstration that became riotous [and] was arrested. . . . [H]e was hit with batons and truncheons. He was detained at a police station for one week, during which time he was interrogated, "roughed up," and subjected to cold and crowded conditions. . . .

Ngure is a follower of the Christian Science faith. In 1993, his Christian Science group met in the park, but police officials advised them that they needed to have a permit to meet in the park and ordered them to disperse. The police took names, but none of the meeting attendees were harmed or arrested.

[I]n 1994 [Ngure] was arrested as he passed by a demonstration-turned-riot at a park. He was . . . released . . . on a recognizance bond. . . . After Ngure left Kenya . . . the Kenyan police went to the home of Ngure's family because he failed to report as scheduled pursuant to the bond. . . . [A]n arrest warrant was issued on February 5, 1996, . . . ordering him to be brought before the court to answer the charge that he "participated in illegal demonstrations . . . ."

. . . The IJ concluded that Ngure was ineligible for asylum because he did not file his application within one year of arriving in the United States and did not demonstrate any "changed" or "extraordinary circumstances" that caused his failure to apply within that time period. Alternatively, the IJ found that although Ngure's testimony was credible, he did not suffer past persecution or have a well-founded fear of future persecution on account of his membership in the Kikuyu tribe, political opinions, or religious beliefs [and] denied his requests for withholding of removal and relief under the Convention Against Torture. The BIA subsequently affirmed the IJ's decision without opinion, pursuant to 8 C.F.R. § 3.1(e)(4) (2003). Pursuant to agency regulations, the IJ's decision became the final agency determination.

[In 1999, after] concluding that the rapidly growing caseload of the Board of Immigration Appeals was impeding its ability to provide fair, timely, and uniform adjudications, Attorney General Reno instituted the BIA's affirmance without opinion ("AWO") procedure . . . . [In 2002, Attorney General Ashcroft amended the AWO process to streamline it further.] The streamlining regulations provide that a single board member shall "affirm without opinion" an IJ's decision . . . if the member finds that the result reached by the IJ was correct, that any errors by the IJ were harmless or nonmaterial, and that either "the issues on appeal . . . do not involve the application of precedent to a novel factual situation" or "the factual and legal issues raised on appeal are not so substantial that the case warrants the issuance of a written opinion . . . ." The decision to affirm without opinion does not necessarily approve the reasoning of the IJ, but it does signify that the BIA agrees that the result was correct because any errors were harmless or nonmaterial. Once the BIA affirms a decision without opinion, the IJ's decision becomes the final agency determination.

. . . .

There is a "basic presumption of judicial review" of agency action. "This is 'just' a presumption, however," and in certain instances, agency action is deemed committed to agency discretion by law, and thus unreviewable by the courts. Over the years, the Supreme Court has held that judicial review is precluded for certain administrative decisions that are "traditionally left to agency discretion" . . . . *Heckler v. Chaney*. These discretionary actions include such matters as whether to institute an enforcement action, how to allocate funds from a lump-sum appropriation, and whether to grant reconsideration of an action because of material error.

The Supreme Court typically has held that actions are committed to agency discretion where it is not possible to devise an adequate standard of review for an agency action . . . . *Chaney*. Courts often ask whether there is sufficient "law to apply" in reviewing the agency's action. *Citizens to Preserve Overton Park, Inc. v. Volpe*. An important factor in discerning whether there is a "meaningful standard" for judicial review is whether the agency decision "involves a complicated balancing of a number of factors which are peculiarly within its expertise." . . . .

There is no statute that requires the BIA to issue a written opinion in any particular case, and Ngure does not contend that a statute provides the requisite "law to apply." As noted, however, the judiciary may in certain contexts review an agency's compliance with its own regulations . . . . The Supreme Court has conducted judicial review, for example, where agency rules were "intended primarily to confer important procedural benefits upon individuals in the face of otherwise unfettered discretion" . . . . On the other hand, where a procedural rule is designed primarily to benefit the agency in carrying out its functions, judicial review may be circumscribed.

. . . .

The Attorney General's explanation for the AWO procedure demonstrates the applicability of these principles to the immigration review process:

> To operate effectively in an environment where over 28,000 appeals and motions are filed yearly, the Board must have discretion over the methods by which it handles its cases. . . . Even in routine cases in which all Panel Members agree that the result reached below was correct, disagreements concerning the rationale or style of a draft decision can require significant time to resolve. The . . . Board's resources are better spent on cases where there is a reasonable possibility of reversible error in the result reached below.

We believe that the tradition of agency discretion over internal procedures is particularly strong in this case, because "judicial deference to the Executive Branch is especially appropriate in the immigration context where officials 'exercise especially sensitive political functions that implicate questions of foreign relations.'"

. . . .

. . . It is . . . a basic principle of administrative law that where agency action is subject to judicial review, the agency must provide [a] reasoned explanation of its decision. The Attorney General's streamlining regulations, however, *explicitly prohibit* the BIA from providing any explanation for its decision to affirm without opinion. The reason seems evident: If the BIA were required to explain in each case why the result reached by the IJ was correct, why any errors were harmless or nonmaterial, why the issues on appeal are squarely controlled by precedent and do not involve application of precedent to a novel factual situation, and why the issues are not so substantial that the case warrants issuance of a written opinion, then the BIA would be required to write the functional equivalent of a written opinion on the merits in every adjudication. . . .

. . . Like other decisions committed to agency discretion by law, the BIA's streamlining determination "involves a complicated balancing of a number of factors which are peculiarly within its expertise," *Chaney*, including the size of the BIA's caseload and the limited resources available to the BIA. . . . Accordingly, we hold that the BIA's decision to affirm without opinion in Ngure's case is not subject to judicial review. . . .

Underlying Case Documents

The case referenced:
The Convention Against Torture
The statute governing asylum
The statute governing removal of aliens
The regulation governing asylum
The regulation governing removal of aliens
The regulation governing affirmance without opinion
The 1999 Federal Register publication of the rule allowing summary affirmation
The 2002 Federal Register publication of the streamlining of the summary affirmation rule

1. In a student piece on the situation in *Ngure*, Jessica R. Hertz, Comment, *Appellate Jurisdiction Over the Board of Immigration Appeals's Affirmance Without Opinion Procedure*, 73 U. Chi. L. Rev. 1019 (2006), the basic framework in the case is set out succinctly:

> In 2002, the Department of Justice issued administrative reforms that dramatically altered the procedures governing appeals before the BIA. This controversial

restructuring changed the traditional system of review by a three-member panel to permit review by a single Board member. This member may now issue an Affirmance Without Opinion (AWO) if he or she finds that the initial factfinder – the Immigration Judge (IJ) – reached the correct result. . . . The First, Third, and Ninth circuits hold that judicial review is proper because the BIA's decision to affirm without opinion is not committed to agency discretion by law. . . . The [Second,] Eighth and Tenth circuits disagree, finding . . . the AWO procedure . . . discretionary and thus exempt from the APA's general presumption of review.

How should this split be resolved? Is it possible to issue a decision without an opinion and comply with the requirements of *State Farm*? What protection against arbitrary action can you identify in *Ngure*?

2. Another student piece, Martin S. Krezalek, Note, *How to Minimize the Risk of Violating Due Process Rights While Preserving the BIA's Ability to Affirm Without Opinion*, 21 GEO. IMMIGR. L.J. 277, 317 (2007), compares the two approaches on the "decision without opinion" issue in *Ngure* by looking at *Ekasinta v. Gonzales*, 415 F.3d 1188, 1189 (10th Cir. 2005) (which found the practice acceptable), and *Lanza v. Ashcroft*, 389 F.3d 917, 920 (9th Cir. 2004) (which found the practice unacceptable). The Note concludes that:

> The mere implementation of the affirmance without opinion procedure has not infringed noncitizens' statutory right to judicial review . . . . [T]he summary affirmance has been a valuable tool in the Attorney General's efforts to improve the efficiency of immigration adjudication. . . . However, the BIA's use of the summary affirmance in cases where the IJ's decision rests on both reviewable and non-reviewable grounds has created an area of jurisdictional ambiguity for the circuit courts. Remanding every questionable affirmance for clarification is inconsistent with the regulatory scheme of adjudicating immigration appeals efficiently. On the other hand, the outright denial of jurisdiction may violate procedural due process. . . .

3. There is some question whether BIA's practice of issuing decisions without opinions accounts for the large number of appeals of BIA determinations. John R. B. Palmer, *Seeking Review: Immigration Law and Federal Court Jurisdiction: Article: The Nature and Causes of the Immigration Surge in the Federal Courts of Appeals: A Preliminary Analysis*, 51 N.Y.L. SCH. L. REV. 13, 33 (2007).

There is also uncertainty whether the "streamlined process" adopted for BIA decisions is vested in the discretion of the agency. *Chen v. Ashcroft*, 378 F.3d 1081, 1088 (9th Cir. 2004), holds that

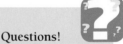

Good Questions!

Try putting this in the context of law students. Are you owed an explanation of a grade you receive in a class? Must it be in writing? Presumably your professor has considerable discretion (subject to a curve your school might impose) in grading. Are grade decisions reviewable at your school? What would be the effect on grades of an automatic review by someone other than the professor who entered the grade initially?

the court can review the matter – meaning that it is not committed to agency discretion, while the Second, Eighth, and Tenth Circuits have taken the position that this choice of process is consistent with the agency's legislative mandate, and thus vested in its discretion. *Ngure* is testament to that perspective.

Food for Thought

To be clear, these are adjudicatory decisions, not rulemaking cases. They are relevant at this point because they illuminate the extent to which agency action – and process – is vested to the discretion of administrative bodies. Since they are adjudicatory – and the standard for review in formal adjudication is typically "substantial evidence" – how can any review take place? If there is no record, what would a reviewing court assess?

The decision of an agency not to act is generally vested to the discretion of that agency. The following case challenges that notion.

VIII. Extraordinary Remedies for Inaction

MASSACHUSETTS V. ENVIRONMENTAL PROTECTION AGENCY

549 U.S. 497 (2007)

[JUSTICE STEVENS] A well-documented rise in global temperatures has coincided with a significant increase in the concentration of carbon dioxide in the atmosphere. Respected scientists believe the two trends are related. For when carbon dioxide is released into the atmosphere, it acts like . . . a greenhouse, trapping solar energy and retarding the escape of reflected heat. It is therefore a species – the most important species – of . . . "greenhouse gas." . . . .

[In 1987, Congress] enacted the Global Climate Protection Act. Finding that "manmade pollution – the release of carbon dioxide, chlorofluorocarbons, methane, and other trace gases into the atmosphere – may be producing a long-term and substantial increase in the average temperature on Earth," Congress directed EPA to propose to Congress a "coordinated national policy on global climate change" . . . .

II.

On October 20, 1999, a group of 19 private organizations filed a rulemaking petition asking EPA to regulate "greenhouse gas emissions from new motor vehicles under § 202 of the Clean Air Act." Petitioners maintained that 1998 was the "warmest year on record"; that carbon dioxide, methane, nitrous oxide, and hydrofluorocarbons are "heat trapping greenhouse gases"; that greenhouse gas emissions have significantly accelerated climate change; and that the [Intergovernmental Panel on Climate Change's] 1995 report warned that "carbon dioxide remains the most important contributor to [man-made] forcing of climate change." The petition further alleged that climate change will have serious adverse effects on human health and the environment [and] observed that the agency itself had already confirmed that it had the power to regulate carbon dioxide. . . .

Fifteen months after the petition's submission, EPA requested public comment on "all the issues raised in [the] petition," adding a "particular" request for comments on "any scientific, technical, legal, economic or other aspect of these issues that may be relevant to EPA's consideration of this petition." EPA received more than 50,000 comments over the next five months. Before the close of the comment period, the White House sought "assistance in identifying the areas in the science of climate change where there are the greatest certainties and uncertainties" from the National Research Council, asking for a response "as soon as possible." The result was a 2001 report titled Climate Change: An Analysis of Some Key Questions (NRC Report), which . . . concluded that "greenhouse gases are accumulating in Earth's atmosphere as a result of human activities, causing surface air temperatures and subsurface ocean temperatures to rise. . . ."

On September 8, 2003, EPA entered an order denying the rulemaking petition. The agency gave two reasons for its decision: (1) that contrary to the opinions of its former general counsels, the Clean Air Act does not authorize EPA to issue mandatory regulations to address global climate change; and (2) that even if the agency had the authority to set greenhouse gas emission standards, it would be unwise to do so at this time.

EPA observed that Congress "was well aware of the global climate change issue when it last comprehensively amended the [Clean Air Act] in 1990," yet it declined to adopt a proposed amendment establishing binding emissions limitations. Congress instead chose to authorize further investigation into climate change. EPA further reasoned that Congress' "specially tailored solutions to global atmospheric issues," in particular, its 1990 enactment of a comprehensive scheme to regulate pollutants that depleted the ozone layer, counseled against reading the general authorization of § 202(a)(1) to confer regulatory authority over greenhouse gases. . . .

Even assuming that it had authority over greenhouse gases, EPA explained in detail why it would refuse to exercise that authority. The agency began by recognizing that the concentration of greenhouse gases has dramatically increased as a result of human activities, and acknowledged the attendant increase in global surface air temperatures. EPA nevertheless gave controlling importance to the NRC Report's statement that a causal link between the two "cannot be unequivocally established." Given that residual uncertainty, EPA concluded that regulating greenhouse gas emissions would be unwise. . . .

III.

Petitioners, now joined by intervenor States and local governments, sought review of EPA's order . . . . [The court first rejected EPA's claim that the petitioners lacked standing. It then reviewed the agency's rejection of the rulemaking petition.]

V.

. . . As we have repeated time and again, an agency has broad discretion to choose how best to marshal its limited resources and personnel to carry out its delegated responsibilities. That discretion is at its height when the agency decides not to bring an enforcement action. . . . Some debate remains, however, as to the rigor with which we review an agency's denial of a petition for rulemaking. There are key differences between a denial of a petition for rulemaking and an agency's decision not to initiate an enforcement action. In contrast to nonenforcement decisions, agency refusals to initiate rulemaking "are less frequent, more apt to involve legal as opposed to factual analysis, and subject to special formalities, including a public explanation." They moreover arise out of denials of petitions for rulemaking which (at least in the circumstances here) the affected party had an undoubted procedural right to file in the first instance. Refusals to promulgate rules are thus susceptible to judicial review, though such review is "extremely limited" and "highly deferential." . . . .

EPA . . . argues that it cannot regulate carbon dioxide emissions from motor vehicles because doing so would require it to tighten mileage standards, a job (according to EPA) that Congress has assigned to DOT. But that DOT sets mileage standards in no way licenses EPA to shirk its environmental responsibilities. EPA has been charged with protecting the public's "health" and "welfare," a statutory obligation wholly independent of DOT's mandate to promote energy efficiency. The two obligations may overlap, but there is no reason to think the two agencies cannot both administer their obligations and yet avoid inconsistency. . . . Because greenhouse gases fit well within the Clean Air Act's capacious definition of "air pollutant," we hold that EPA has the statutory authority to regulate the emission of such gases from new motor vehicles.

. . . .

VII.

The alternative basis for EPA's decision – that even if it does have statutory authority to regulate greenhouse gases, it would be unwise to do so at this time – rests on reasoning divorced from the statutory text. While the statute does condition the exercise of EPA's authority on its formation of a "judgment," that judgment must relate to whether an air pollutant "causes, or contributes to, air pollution which may reasonably be anticipated to endanger public health or welfare." Put another way, the use of the word "judgment" is not a roving license to ignore the statutory text. It is but a direction to exercise discretion within defined statutory limits.

If EPA makes a finding of endangerment, the Clean Air Act requires the agency to regulate emissions of the deleterious pollutant from new motor vehicles. 42 U.S.C. § 7521(a)(1) (stating that "[EPA] shall by regulation prescribe . . . standards applicable to the emission of any air pollutant from any class of new motor vehicles"). EPA no doubt has significant latitude as to the manner, timing, content, and coordination of its regulations with those of other agencies. But once EPA has responded to a petition for rulemaking, its reasons for action or inaction must conform to the authorizing statute. Under the clear terms of the Clean Air Act, EPA can avoid taking further action only if it determines that greenhouse gases do not contribute to climate change or if it provides some reasonable explanation as to why it cannot or will not exercise its discretion to determine whether they do. To the extent that this constrains agency discretion . . ., this is the congressional design.

EPA has refused to comply with this clear statutory command. Instead, it has offered a laundry list of reasons not to regulate. For example, EPA said that a number of voluntary executive branch programs already provide an effective response to the threat of global warming, that regulating greenhouse gases might impair the President's ability to negotiate with "key developing nations" to reduce emissions, and that curtailing motor-vehicle emissions would reflect "an inefficient, piece-meal approach to address the climate change issue." Although we have neither the expertise nor the authority to evaluate these policy judgments, it is evident they have nothing to do with whether greenhouse gas emissions contribute to climate change. Still less do they amount to a reasoned justification for declining to form a scientific judgment. . . .

Nor can EPA avoid its statutory obligation by noting the uncertainty surrounding various features of climate change and concluding that it would therefore be better not to regulate at this time. If the scientific uncertainty is so profound that it precludes EPA from making a reasoned judgment as to whether greenhouse gases contribute to global warming, EPA must say so. That EPA would prefer not to regulate greenhouse gases because of some residual uncertainty . . . is irrelevant. The statutory question is whether sufficient information exists to make an endangerment finding.

In short, EPA has offered no reasoned explanation for its refusal to decide whether greenhouse gases cause or contribute to climate change. Its action was therefore "arbitrary, capricious, . . . or otherwise not in accordance with law." 42 U.S.C. § 7607(d)(9)(A). We need not and do not reach the question whether on remand EPA must make an endangerment finding, or whether policy concerns can inform EPA's actions in the event that it makes such a finding. *Chevron*. We hold only that EPA must ground its reasons for action or inaction in the statute. . . .

[JUSTICE SCALIA, dissenting.]

I join THE CHIEF JUSTICE's [dissent] in full, and would hold that this Court has no jurisdiction . . . because petitioners lack standing. The Court having decided otherwise, it is appropriate for me to note my dissent on the merits.

. . . § 202(a)(1) of the Clean Air Act (CAA) . . . provides that the Administrator of the Environmental Protection Agency (EPA) "shall by regulation prescribe . . . standards applicable to the emission of any air pollutant from any class or classes of new motor vehicles or new motor vehicle engines, which *in his judgment* cause, or contribute to, air pollution . . . ." There is no dispute that the Administrator has made no such judgment in this case. The question thus arises: Does anything *require* the Administrator to make a "judgment" whenever a petition for rulemaking is filed? Without citation of the statute or any other authority, the Court says yes. . . . The Court points to no . . . provision because none exists.

Instead, the Court invents a multiple-choice question that the EPA Administrator must answer when a petition for rulemaking is filed. The Administrator must exercise his judgment in one of three ways: (a) by concluding that the pollutant *does* cause, or contribute to, air pollution that endangers public welfare (in which case EPA is required to regulate); (b) by concluding that the pollutant *does not* cause, or contribute to, air pollution that endangers public welfare (in which case EPA is *not* required to regulate); or (c) by "providing some reasonable explanation as to why it cannot or will not exercise its discretion to determine whether" greenhouse gases endanger public welfare (in which case EPA is *not* required to regulate).

I am willing to assume, for the sake of argument, that the Administrator's discretion in this regard is not entirely unbounded . . . . The Court, however, with no basis in text or precedent, rejects all of EPA's stated "policy judgments" . . . effectively narrowing the universe of potential reasonable bases to a single one:

Judgment can be delayed *only* if the Administrator concludes that "the scientific uncertainty is profound." . . . . As the Administrator acted within the law in declining to make a "judgment" for the policy reasons above set forth, I would uphold the decision to deny the rulemaking petition on that ground alone. . . .

The Court's alarm over global warming may or may not be justified, but it ought not distort the outcome of this litigation. This is a straightforward administrative-law case, in which Congress has passed a malleable statute giving broad discretion, not to us but to an executive agency. No matter how important the underlying policy issues at stake, this Court has no business substituting its own desired outcome for the reasoned judgment of the responsible agency.

───────────

Underlying Case Documents

The case referenced:
The Global Climate Protection Act
The Clean Air Act
The October 1999 petition
The EPA request for public comment
The EPA denial of the petition for rulemaking

While it is only indirectly referenced in the opinion, for the full 1995 report on climate change click HERE.

For a site devoted to the Clean Air Act click HERE.

For a recent update on the case click HERE.

1. It is too early to judge the full effect of *Massachusetts v. EPA*. The case certainly raises far more questions than it answers. To what extent does the decision limit the deference due agency decisionmaking – has another hunk of *Chevron* been lopped off? *See* Dru Stevenson, *Special Solicitude for State Standing*: Massachusetts v. EPA, 112 PENN ST. L. REV. 1, 74-75 (2007).

> Massachusetts v. EPA [redraws] the boundaries of judicial deference and agency discretion. In seeming contrast to earlier precedents, the Court held that agencies have substantially less discretion regarding their refusal to regulate than they do about when and how to enforce regulations. This distinction further tips the scales toward the states, who not only have assurances of standing, but also have an invitation

to compel federal agencies to regulate new areas where they have been previously silent. . . .

2. a. Is the *Chaney* doctrine regarding the general presumption of nonreviewability of agency inaction now confined exclusively to enforcement actions?

b. Has Section 553(e) of the APA regarding the petitioning process undergone a radical transformation?

c. Since the case appears to give favorable status, in terms of standing, to states seeking to force federal agencies into action, will the states play a more significant role in the federal regulatory process in the future?

d. Will the courts play a more significant role monitoring the allocation of agency time and resources?

3. One certain consequence of the case has been overtly political. In Spring 2008, subpoenas from various congressional committees issued to EPA, ostensibly to learn why, within a year of the decision, no new significant regulatory initiatives have been put into place. The subpoenas seek EPA internal working papers and communication between EPA and the Office of the President, and thus far the agency has not complied.

Press Release, Select Committee on Energy Independence and Global Warming, Anniversary Gift: Markey, Select Committee to Issue Subpoena to EPA for Global Warming Docs Today (Apr. 2, 2008) http://globalwarming.house.gov/mediacenter/pressreleases?id=0197.

4. In May, 2008, EPA announced it would issue an advance notice of proposed rulemaking [Federal News Service, May 20, 2008, Tuesday, *Hearing of the Oversight and Government Reform Committee: Subject: EPA's New Ozone Standards, Testimony of Stephen L. Johnson, Administrator, EPA*] – but nothing more concrete has been done in response to the *Massachusetts v. EPA* opinion. *See* Katherine Boyle, *Dems Say Johnson Is a Puppet for White House*, 10 ENV'T & ENERGY DAILY, 9 (2008). Not to put too fine an edge on this, but is it inappropriate for the Administrator of EPA, a cabinet-level officer, to be responsive to the Office of the President?

5. Assuming the agency does little or nothing, there is one potentially devastating interpretation. If a cabinet-level official – with the approval of the White House – does not appear to be bound to the mandates of the Supreme Court, what are the consequences for the power of the court and the rule of law? If EPA decides to take no further steps, are we back to President Andrew Jackson's comments (or so legend goes) following *Worcester v. Georgia*? 31 U.S. (6 Pet.) 515 (1832). (After the Court found the Cherokee Nation entitled to mine ownership and proceeds

flowing from the discovery of gold in the State of Georgia on Cherokee land and directed the State to insure those resources stayed with the Cherokees – an order the State did not follow – President Jackson is said to have refused to send federal troops to enforce the Court's order, commenting: "John Marshall has made his decision; now let him enforce it." Brian M. Feldman, *Evaluating Public Endorsement of the Weak and Strong Forms of Judicial Supremacy*, 89 VA. L. REV. 979, 989 (2003), *citing* Charles Warren, 1 THE SUPREME COURT IN UNITED STATES HISTORY, 1789-1835, at 759 (rev. ed. 1926) (suggesting the Jackson story may be apocryphal).)

a. Problems implementing *Massachusetts v. EPA* abound as this text goes to press. On July 11, 2008, the D.C. Circuit threw out the newly promulgated EPA Clean Air Interstate Rule, *Rule to Reduce Interstate Transport of Fine Particulate Matter and Ozone (Clean Air Interstate Rule); Revisions to Acid Rain Program; Revisions to the $NO_{[x]}$ SIP Call*, 70 Fed. Reg. 25,162 (May 12, 2005) ("CAIR"). The rule derives its authority from 42 U.S.C. § 7410(a)(2)(D)(i)(I). The rule took a regional approach and would have obligated more than half the states and the District of Columbia to takes steps to lower vehicle generated sulfur dioxide and nitrogen oxides levels and to reduce power plant emissions. *North Carolina v. EPA*, 531 F.3d 896 (D.C. Cir. 2008). Finding the complex rules the agency issued "unseverable," the court threw out the entire rule, in all likelihood requiring the agency to commence anew the rulemaking process, a decision certain to delay any further regulatory initiatives in this area until well into 2009.

The announcement of the court's decision coincided with a statement from the White House that "it would take no steps under the Clean Air Act to regulate greenhouse gas emissions that contribute to global warming, even though the EPA formally announced that it would seek public comment on the issue." Del Quentin Wilber & Marc Kaufman, *Judges Toss EPA Rule to Reduce Smog, Soot; It Was Agency's Most Aggressive Air Measure*, WASH. POST, July 12, 2008, at A1.

b. There is a "toehold" theory in administrative law: Every meaningful regulatory initiative needs to start somewhere (i.e., with a toehold). Once an entry point is established, further amendments, revisions, interpretations, or guidances are possible – and may well attract far less attention than the initial rule. Even if the initial rule is less than ideal, in some areas, something is better than nothing. Read *North Carolina v. EPA* (above) in the full version: For those supporting a cleaner environment, would a less-than-perfect rule have been better than no rule at all?

c. The White House's position in the above note is not subtle. Was President Jackson right? Can the President simply refuse to implement a Supreme Court decision?

d. On January 26, 2009, President Obama issued two memoranda regarding federal rules and policy on fuel efficiency and energy use. In one, he instructed the EPA to "take all measures" to issue a final rule that would implement administration policies on fuel consumption. In the second, the President asked EPA to reconsider the issuance of waivers to the State of California regarding compliance with fuel efficiency rules. To read those memoranda, click HERE and HERE.

6. The Endangerment Finding. How should EPA respond after the "endangerment" finding in *Massachusetts v. EPA* set out in the full text version of this case?

a. The partisan response has not been subtle *See Waxman Accuses White House of Thwarting EPA On CO$_2$*, NAT'L JOURNAL'S CONGRESS DAILY, Mar. 12, 2008.

> House Oversight and Government Reform Chairman Waxman today accused the White House of stopping an EPA effort to regulate carbon dioxide and other greenhouse gases from motor vehicles. In a letter to EPA Administrator Johnson, Waxman said that senior EPA officials had told his committee that the White House has not acted on an "endangerment finding" that EPA provided to the OMB in December. The finding, Waxman said, argues that vehicular greenhouse gas emissions pose a public health risk and should be reduced.

b. The focus on endangerment is, itself, a change from EPA's asserted position that regulations were not required or even appropriate in the absence of scientific certainty regarding the harm a pollutant will cause. That change is noted in Professor Sidney A. Shapiro's Symposium, <u>OMB and the Politicization of Risk Assessment, 37 ENVTL. L. 1083, 1088 (2007)</u>:

> The state of Massachusetts and other parties sued the Environmental Protection Agency (EPA) after it rejected a petition from the parties to regulate greenhouse emissions . . . . The Court held that EPA's rejection of the petition was "arbitrary and capricious." EPA defended its rejection of the petition in part on the ground that . . . a causal link between greenhouse gases and global warming could not be "unequivocally" established. The Court concluded that the absence of scientific certainty was "irrelevant" because the question under the statute was whether the scientific evidence was sufficient to make an endangerment finding. Section 202 mandates [EPA to prescribe regulations when an air pollutant] may reasonably be anticipated to endanger the public health or welfare. . . .

Good Question!

At a basic level, *Massachusetts v. EPA* is of consequence because it is one of very few cases in which the Supreme Court expressed neither deference, respect, nor even much tolerance for agency inaction. Does the case signal a genuine change in policy – or does the fact that it was brought by various states suggest only limited applicability in future challenges to agency inaction brought by private parties, public interest organizations, businesses, or other nongovernmental entities?

7. <u>*Sierra Club v. Larson*, 882 F.2d 128 (4th Cir. 1989)</u>.

> Pursuant to the [<u>Highway Beautification Act</u> (HBA)], each state that participates in [the] highway beautification program is responsible for . . . exercising "effective control" over outdoor advertising. . . . It is up to the Secretary, acting through the FHWA, to monitor compliance. If the Secretary determines . . . that a state is not maintaining "effective control," she may institute formal enforcement proceedings and ultimately withhold 10% of federal highway funds until compliance is achieved. . . . The withholding decisions and the decision to commence enforcement proceedings are reserved exclusively to the Secretary . . . .
>
> In early 1981, the FHWA conducted a fact-finding investigation in South Carolina, based partially on complaints by Dr. Charles Floyd . . . . The resultant report indicated that South Carolina was not maintaining "effective control" over its outdoor advertising and recommended that corrective steps be taken. . . . On January 7, 1982, the Regional Administrator wrote Dr. Floyd to notify him that . . . no further action, outside routine monitoring, would be taken. . . .
>
> [The government claims] that the agency made an unreviewable decision not to recommend a formal penalty action and that <u>*Overton Park*</u> is inapplicable. We agree. *Overton Park* is inapposite because it involved a decision by the Secretary to provide funds under a statute that required a specific determination to be made before those funds could be released. In this case South Carolina already receives federal highway funds and the decision by the Regional Administrator was a non-coercive one declining to proceed toward further action to withhold a portion of these funds. . . . In this instance, the agency exercised its discretion . . . by declining to proceed any further against South Carolina. This is clearly a decision not to enforce the statute as opposed to an affirmative decision of compliance. Since we have determined that this was an agency decision not to seek enforcement of a statute, it is presumptively unreviewable under <u>*Chaney*</u>. . . .
>
> This case aptly demonstrates the separation of powers underpinning of the presumption of the unreviewability of administrative agency decisions not to pursue enforcement in particular instances. The judiciary is ill-equipped to oversee executive enforcement decisions, whereas the agency is equipped to decide where to focus scarce resources, how to handle delicate federal-state relations and how to evaluate the strengths and weaknesses of particular cases. A decision by this Court to review such agency actions could lead to court intervention in all decisions not to pursue further action after preliminary investigations. The appropriate place for changes of the type sought by appellant is through Congress, not through the judiciary. . . .

Reread the last paragraph in the case above. Why was that not the winning argument in <u>*Massachusetts v. EPA*</u>?

8. Securing a Writ of Mandamus.

a. A writ of mandamus is one option to address agency inaction. While such writs issue rarely, filing a claim to secure a writ may have a strategic value: At a minimum, it will guarantee that the agency, a judge, and (depending on one's approach) the press all focus on the fact that an agency has either failed to act in an area where it would seem action is warranted or delayed unreasonably, causing harm to those either subject to the agency's jurisdiction or who must proceed with the agency to secure a right, benefit, or entitlement.

Section 706(1) of the APA permits a court to "compel agency action unlawfully withheld or unreasonably delayed." This language ostensibly addresses "failure to act" cases but generates some tough issues. For example, to be in court, a plaintiff must establish that they have standing and that matter is both ripe and final. *Bennett v. Spear*, *supra* Chapter 4, holds that finality requires that: "(1) the action should mark the consummation of the agency's decisionmaking process; and (2) the action should be one by which rights or obligations have been determined or from which legal consequences flow."

For More Information

Under the All Writs Statute, 28 U.S.C. § 1651, there are fairly severe limits on the use of the extraordinary Writ of Mandamus. Accordingly, from time to time, a federal court will issue a "writ in the nature of mandamus" to compel the desired response. For a discussion of mandamus, see Jessica H. Roark, *No Duty to End the Frustration: Petitioning for Mandamus Relief from the Director of the USPTO*, 15 FED.CIR. B.J. 487 (2005 / 2006).

b. If the "action" under attack is inaction, it is quite difficult to show that it is the final action of the agency. For example, even in the face of massive delay, if an agency issues a vague interim interpretive rule, it can claim it is "underway" or "in process" and therefore the matter is not final. Assuming one can show that the action the agency has taken is completely insufficient – or virtually nonexistent – the agency will likely argue that if the writ were to issue, it would be a crude and unconstitutional intrusion into the range of discretion *Chevron* deference (or some variety thereof) demands.

c. One response to this is well expressed in *Intermodal Techs., Inc. v. Mineta*, 413 F. Supp. 2d 834 (E.D. Mich. 2006), where the court held:

> [A]n agency's inaction may itself amount to an exercise of discretion if responsibilities for a particular subject area have been entrusted to the agency without any plainly defined mandate to act, or where construction or application of a particular statute has been left to agency discretion." The court went on to explain that pushing the agency to act was not an intrusion into the domain of agency decisionmaking: "[E]ven if the outcome of that exercise rests within the agency's discretion, the agency can be compelled to exercise its discretion [without dictating a substantive response to the matter before the agency]. . . ."

d. Mandamus directed to an individual in an agency responsible for a specific task might be available if that person is not following clear and unambiguous rules. See *Dillard v. Yeldell,* 334 A.2d 578, 579 (D.C. 1975), and *Yeager v. Greene,* 502 A.2d 980, 981 n.3 (D.C. 1985), for the traditional standards applicable to nondiscretionary acts that are performed improperly – or not at all. One last and perhaps most important point: "A writ of mandamus is an extraordinary writ and should only be issued in 'exceptional circumstances amounting to a judicial usurpation of power. . . .'" *See In re M.O.R.,* 851 A.2d 503 (D.C. App. 2004). Thus, this is a strategy with a low probability of success – though certainly worthy of consideration when delay and inaction cause significant harm. See *Erspamer v. Derwinski,* 1 Vet. App. 3 (U.S. Vet. App. 1990), for an interesting contrast in approach to the writ.

IN RE BLUEWATER NETWORK & OCEAN ADVOCATES

234 F.3d 1305 (D.C. Cir. 2000)

[CHIEF JUDGE EDWARDS] On March 24, 1989, the *Exxon Valdez* supertanker [spilled] nearly eleven million gallons of oil into Alaska's once-pristine coastal ecosystem. Congress responded with the Oil Pollution Act of 1990 ("OPA" or "Act"). The Act not only broadened federal liability for oil spills, it also established [tanker] requirements to prevent such spills from occurring in the first place. The Oil Pollution Act of 1990 is now more than ten-years old, but the Coast Guard, the enforcing agency, still has failed to promulgate regulations required by the Act. Citing the agency's failures on this score, petitioners Bluewater Network and Ocean Advocates now seek a writ of mandamus to compel the Coast Guard to finally make good on Congress' commitments. . . .

. . . What makes this case somewhat unusual, albeit not difficult, is the fact that the Coast Guard has episodically engaged in some rulemaking, and promulgated some regulations [as required by the statute]. Approximately three months before the statutorily-imposed deadline [in 1991], the Coast Guard issued an advanced notice of proposed rulemaking seeking comments and suggestions regarding possible proposed rules for complying with §§ 4110(a) and (b). The Coast Guard also commissioned a technical feasibility study of existing [tank level or pressure monitoring (TLPM)] devices . . . which . . . found that "attainable accuracy is expected to be within 1.0-2.0% of the actual level." Concerned that a 1.0 to 2.0 percent error margin, which translates to between 36,075 and 72,150 gallons of oil for a 400,000 ton tanker, would provide "insufficient warning to allow prompt action by the crew," the Coast Guard called for a public hearing to augment comments to the original advanced notice.

In its August 1995 notice of proposed rulemaking, the Coast Guard limited its proposed rule to the establishment of *standards* for TLPM devices pursuant to

§ 4110(a), leaving questions of *installation and use* of compliant devices, pursuant to § 4110(b), for another day. . . . In March 1997, nearly six years after the statutory deadline, the Coast Guard adopted the proposed standards in the form of a *temporary* rule, effective for two years beginning April 28, 1997. The rule did not require installation or use of TLPM devices unless and until § 4110(a) compliant technology had been invented and the appropriate § 4110(b) rulemaking undertaken. . . . The temporary regulations did, in fact, sunset on April 28, 1999. In November of that year, the Coast Guard [said if it] "ever receives information about a device that is accurate enough to meet the standard, the rulemaking will be reinitiated." . . . . [No further regulations issued.]

The temporary regulations questioned whether, in light of [tanker] phaseout schedules, it would be "economically feasible" to require installation of tank level and pressure monitoring devices if such devices were not developed within two years. But this question was raised because the agency knew that the temporary regulations . . . arguably embodied technology-forcing requirements that were beyond the current capacity of the affected industry. The Coast Guard never suggested, however, that the standards proposed in the temporary regulations were the *only* viable options to address the statutory mandate *compelling* the agency to establish some sort of rules as to both *compliance* standards and *use* requirements. . . .

The Coast Guard is correct that petitioners cannot use the present mandamus action to challenge the substance of the 1997 temporary regulations. . . . [They were non-final and have expired.] Rather, petitioners challenge what the Coast Guard has since failed to do: it has never established permanent § 4110(a) regulations; and it has put off, and now disregards, addressing § 4110(b)'s use and installation requirements.

"An agency's failure to regulate more comprehensively [than it has] is not ordinarily a basis for concluding that the regulations already promulgated are invalid." Likewise, an agency's pronouncement of its intent to defer or to engage in future rulemaking generally does not constitute final agency action reviewable by this court. . . . [However, what] is at issue in this case is the *absence of any regulations* under § 4110. The statute *compels* the agency to establish both compliance standards and use requirements. There are no such standards or requirements in existence – none – and the agency has no present intention to promulgate any. Petitioners argue, rather convincingly, that the agency's current "we-will-not-promulgate-regulations" position is a blatant violation of the Act. That is the question that is before this court. . . .

Our consideration of any and all mandamus actions starts from the premise that issuance of the writ is an extraordinary remedy, reserved only for the most transparent violations of a clear duty to act. In the case of agency inaction, we not only must satisfy ourselves that there indeed exists such a duty, but that the agency has "unreasonably delayed" the contemplated action. *See* Administrative Procedure Act, 5 U.S.C. § 706(1) (1994). This court analyzes unreasonable delay claims under the now-familiar criteria set forth in *Telecommunications Research & Action Center v. FCC*, 750 F.2d 70 (D.C. Cir. 1984) ("*TRAC*"):

> (1) the time agencies take to make decisions must be governed by a "rule of reason"; (2) where Congress has provided a timetable or other indication of the speed with which it expects the agency to proceed in the enabling statute, that statutory scheme may supply content for this rule of reason; (3) delays that might be reasonable in the sphere of economic regulation are less tolerable when human health and welfare are at stake; (4) the court should consider the effect of expediting delayed action on agency activities of a higher or competing priority; (5) the court should also take into account the nature and extent of the interests prejudiced by delay; (6) the court need not "find any impropriety lurking behind agency lassitude in order to hold that agency action is unreasonably delayed."

. . . The statute indisputably commands the Coast Guard to establish *some sort of* compliance standards *and* use requirements *by August 1991*. There are no such standards or requirements, and the Coast Guard has disavowed any further action. The Coast Guard contends only that any attempt now to promulgate compliance standards and use requirements will run into the same practical problems encountered in the 1997 rulemaking – namely, that no equipment currently exists to meet the necessary standards. This argument misses the point. . . . Neither the Coast Guard in its prior rulemakings, nor government counsel at argument, dispute that functioning TLPM devices are available on the market. Nor, as a result, do they dispute that *some sort of* minimum § 4110(a) standard is possible – whether it be a less-stringent numbers standard or a simple technology-based standard.

The Coast Guard has not disputed petitioners' arguments regarding the specific *TRAC* factors, and we do not pause to analyze them. Suffice it to say that all favor granting mandamus: a nine-year delay is unreasonable given a clear one-year time line and the Coast Guard's admission that it will do no more; the delayed regulations implicate important environmental concerns; and the Coast Guard has not shown that expedited rulemaking here will interfere with other, higher priority activities. We will, therefore, retain jurisdiction over the case until final agency action disposes of the Coast Guard's obligations under § 4110 of the OPA.

Mandamus pursuant to *TRAC* is an extraordinary remedy, reserved only for extraordinary circumstances. This is just such a circumstance. . . . For the foregoing reasons, we hereby direct the Coast Guard to undertake prompt § 4110 rulemaking.

———

Underlying Case Documents

The case referenced:

The Oil Pollution Act of 1990

The 1991 notice of proposed rulemaking

The 1995 notice of proposed rulemaking

The 1997 temporary rule

The 1999 notice that rules will be issued only if the technology improves enough to make them feasible

For more information on the Exxon Valdez spill click HERE or HERE.

---

1. The basic requirements for mandamus in *Bluewater* – and in *TRAC* – are not hard to articulate. This extraordinary remedy should be considered when (a) there is a legislative timetable, (b) the delay is egregious, (c) the action sought is arguably nondiscretionary, (d) an important interest (like public health) is at stake, (e) the delay is unreasonable and has a prejudicial effect, and (f) the issuance of the writ would serve not only an individual client interest but also the public interest.

Were all these factors present in *Bluewater*? What makes a delay unreasonable? If the test of reasonability requires a measure against which the delay of the agency can be judged, what measure is appropriate? Generalizing about delay in government is not useful – some processes take longer than others. That said, what facts and evidence would you need to demonstrate that a delay in a specific case is at a level that justifies issuance of the writ?

2. Is a three-year delay in having the FBI complete a "name and background check" unreasonable? Those lawfully present in the United States who seek a visa adjustment for a family member (to change the status of a spouse or children) must have their application processed by the U.S. Citizenship and Immigration Services (USCIS). The backlog in this area is the subject of a number of decisions where applicants have challenged USCIS in court, seeking writs of mandamus, claiming that these delays are unreasonable and destructive. Here is a glimpse of two opinions involving similar claims – and opposite results:

a. In *Sayyadinejad v. Chertoff*, 2007 WL 4410356 (S.D. Cal. 2007),

> plaintiff Servati, a citizen of the United States, filed a visa petition [in 2004] to bring his then fiancé, now wife . . . into the United States . . . under 8 U.S.C. § 1101(a)(15)(K). . . . [More than three years passed and, as of the date of this decision, no action has been taken on the adjustment petition.]

District courts have original jurisdiction over any action in the nature of mandamus [under] 28 U.S.C. § 1361 if . . . (1) the individual's claim is clear and certain; (2) the official's duty is nondiscretionary, ministerial, and so plainly prescribed as to be free from doubt, and (3) no other adequate remedy is available. *Kildare v. Saenz*, 325 F.3d 1078, 1084 (9th Cir. 2003). . . .

[S]ome district courts have concluded that the pace that U.S. Citizenship and Immigration Services ("USCIS") adjudicates an adjustment of status application is discretionary [and outside] § 1361. . . . In contrast, other district courts have concluded that courts have jurisdiction to hear a mandamus suit alleging that USCIS [as failed] to adjudicate an immigration application within a reasonable period of time. . . .

Victoria Porto ("Porto") [an] Officer [with] USCIS . . . explains that since the terrorist attacks on September 11, 2001, there is a need to conduct more rigorous background checks of those who are seeking immigration status. Because this process is more thorough, it sometimes results in the delay of requested documentation and immigration benefits. However, because of public safety, it is imperative that background checks are conducted properly. . . . [T]he Court finds that the USCIS is properly adjudicating Plaintiff's application [and therefore the writ will not issue].

b. In *Tang v. Chertoff*, 2007 WL 2462187 (E.D. Ky. 2007),

[t]he plaintiffs . . . are married citizens of China [and] researchers at the University of Kentucky. Along with their daughter . . ., they [sought] Adjustment Status . . . with USCIS to obtain permanent resident status. . . . [More than three years have passed since the applications for adjustment were filed.]

The parties agree that the plaintiffs' I-485 applications, along with thousands of other unrelated applications, are still being processed while the United States Federal Bureau of Investigation ("FBI") conducts a routine background security check. . . . [A]ccording to the [government], the FBI has received "millions of name check requests" from CIS since September 11, 2001, "thus taxing that agency's resources and creating a backlog in FBI's performance of complete security checks. . . ."

The court is persuaded by the reasoning of those courts that have found mandamus jurisdiction exists to review such claims. Although USCIS's ultimate decision on the merits . . . . is discretionary, and therefore beyond the scope of mandamus jurisdiction, USCIS has a non-discretionary duty to reach its decision . . . within a reasonable time. Put another way, the defendants' alleged failure to take timely action on the plaintiffs' application is not itself a decision, let alone a discretionary decision, but rather unreasonable inaction, which is the proper subject of mandamus relief. . . .

3. *Marathon Oil Company v. Lujan*, 937 F.2d 498 (10th Cir. 1991).

On April 4, 1986, the plaintiffs-appellees, . . . ("Marathon"), filed a Mineral Application with the Colorado State office of the Bureau of Land Management ("BLM"). The application covered six oil shale placer mining claims . . . in western Rio Blanco County, Colorado. . . . On June 9, 1987, Marathon was notified that the Colorado division of the BLM would conduct a mineral examination of their claims to determine whether there was a sufficient amount of oil shale to justify the awarding of patents for the claims. . . . The field work for the examination was completed by late July, 1987. By December 9, 1987, Marathon had filed all the necessary papers required to process its application . . . . [O]n February 1, 1989, the Department prepared a draft of its Final Mineral Report. The report unequivocally stated that Marathon's mineral claims were valid and that the patents should issue. However, by October of 1989, the patents still had not been issued. Marathon . . . filed suit in the United States District Court for the District of Colorado requesting that the court order the defendants to grant the patents. On June 20, 1990, the district court ruled in favor of Marathon and [issued the writ at issue here].

Congress intended the defendants to process oil shale mining patent applications. Therefore, the writ of mandamus ordering appellants to "expeditiously complete administrative action" was entirely appropriate. . . . [The appellants do not contest this.] What the appellants do dispute is the district court's order that the department complete its review of the patent application within thirty days. Although the party seeking issuance of a writ of mandamus has a heavy burden of showing that the conditions are clearly met the issuance of the writ is a matter of the issuing court's discretion. After reviewing the record, we cannot agree with the defendants that the district court abused its discretion in ordering the agency to take action within thirty days.

When the district court issued the writ, more than four years had elapsed since Marathon had filed its application with the BLM. By December 9, 1987, Marathon had met its obligations . . . . It took the BLM almost three years from the filing of Marathon's application to complete the mineral report. The report was completed on February 1, 1989, and recommended that the patents be issued. As of February 1, 1989, the only thing standing between Marathon and its patents was the absence of signature "under the authority of the Director [of the Bureau of Land Management] and signed in the name of the United States." Eight months later when Marathon filed suit in district court, the patent still had not issued. When the district court finally issued the writ of mandamus ordering the Department to finish the process, approximately fourteen months had elapsed since the mineral report recommending approval had been issued.

The district court, however, exceeded its authority when it ordered the defendants to approve the application and to issue the patents. The Department has not yet determined officially that all conditions to issuance of the patents have occurred. Thus, the Department has not yet reached the point when it is left only with the purely ministerial act of issuing the patent. Therefore, the approval of the application should not yet be compelled by a writ of mandamus. . . . In other words, while the district court can compel the defendants to exercise their discretion, it cannot dictate how that discretion is to be exercised. . . .

IX. Judicial Review of Retroactive Agency Action

Our legal system places a high value on notice. At the core of due process is the concept that adverse action cannot be taken unless one has notice and an opportunity to be heard. This is expressed by the historical disfavor with ex post facto laws and the prohibition against Bills of Attainder.

The premise is fairly straightforward: One should not be sanctioned for behavior that, when it occurred, had not been deemed unlawful. When individuals and entities act, they are subject only to those standards (in the statute, regulation, rule, or common law) that exist.

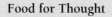

Food for Thought

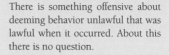

There is something offensive about deeming behavior unlawful that was lawful when it occurred. About this there is no question.

As a general rule, agencies cannot make rules that condemn theretofore lawful behavior that has already occurred and sanction parties for engaging in that behavior. Were it that simple, there would be no need to study the cases that follow. The complexity arises from both the essential generality of legislation and the necessity of meaningful enforcement of statutes.

Neither statutes nor regulations can articulate with specificity every infraction that might occur. For example, statutes that require fairness in the trading of securities or prohibit activity that contaminates the air and water cannot set forth every conceivable unfair action or every type of polluting event. Some latitude must be provided to allow for definitions to emerge over time. The question, of course, is whether the emergence of a new definition of prohibited conduct will allow for retroactive enforcement or whether such clarification by regulation allows only for prospective enforcement of the newly articulated sanctions.

As the cases demonstrate, balancing the interests of the government in effective enforcement against the interests of the individual in avoiding unfair retroactive application of standards requires a careful assessment of multiple factors.

SECURITIES & EXCHANGE COMMISSION V. CHENERY CORPORATION

332 U.S. 194 (1947)

[JUSTICE MURPHY] This case is here for the second time. . . . [The first time around] we held that an order of the Securities and Exchange Commission could not be sustained on the grounds upon which that agency acted. We therefore directed that the case be remanded to the Commission for such further proceedings as might be appropriate. On remand, the Commission reexamined the problem, recast its rationale and reached the same result. The issue now is whether the Commission's action is proper in light of the principles established in our prior decision.

When the case was first here, we emphasized a simple but fundamental rule of administrative law. That rule is to the effect that a reviewing court, in dealing with a determination or judgment which an administrative agency alone is authorized to make, must judge the propriety of such action solely by the grounds invoked by the agency. If those grounds are inadequate or improper, the court is powerless to affirm the administrative action by substituting what it considers to be a more adequate or proper basis. To do so would propel the court into the domain which Congress has set aside exclusively for the administrative agency. We also emphasized in our prior decision an important corollary of the foregoing rule. If the administrative action is to be tested by the basis upon which it purports to rest, that basis must be set forth with such clarity as to be understandable. It will not do for a court to be compelled to guess at the theory underlying the agency's action . . . . Applying this rule and its corollary, the Court was unable to sustain the Commission's original action. . . .

During [a] period when successive reorganization plans proposed by the [Federal Water Service Corporation (Federal)] management were before the Commission, the officers, directors and controlling stockholders of Federal purchased a substantial amount of Federal's preferred stock on the over-the-counter market. Under the fourth reorganization plan, this preferred stock was to be converted into common stock of a new corporation; on the basis of the purchases of preferred stock, the management would have received more than 10% of this new common stock. It was frankly admitted that the management's purpose in buying the preferred stock was to protect its interest in the new company. It was also plain that there was no fraud or lack of disclosure in making these purchases.

But the Commission would not approve the fourth plan so long as the preferred stock purchased by the management was to be treated on a parity with the other preferred stock. It felt that the officers and directors of a holding company in process of reorganization under the Act were fiduciaries and were under a duty not to trade in the securities of that company during the reorganization period. And so the plan was amended to provide that the preferred stock acquired by the management, unlike that held by others, was not to be converted into the new common stock; instead, it was to be surrendered at cost plus dividends accumulated since the purchase dates. As amended, the plan was approved by the Commission over the management's objections.

The Court interpreted the Commission's order approving this amended plan as grounded solely upon . . . what [the Commission] thought were standards theretofore recognized by courts. . . . On that basis, the order could not stand. The opinion pointed out that courts do not impose upon officers and directors of a corporation any fiduciary duty to its stockholders which precludes them, merely because they are officers and directors, from buying and selling the corporation's stock. . . . And the only judge-made rule of equity which might have justified the

Commission's order related to fraud or mismanagement of the reorganization by the officers and directors, matters which were admittedly absent in this situation.

After the case was remanded to the Commission, Federal Water and Gas Corp. (Federal Water), the surviving corporation under the reorganization plan, made an application for . . . an amendment to the plan to provide for the issuance of new common stock of the reorganized company. This stock was to be distributed to the members of Federal's management on the basis of the shares of the old preferred stock which they had acquired during the period of reorganization, thereby placing them in the same position as the public holders of the old preferred stock. . . . The Commission denied the application in an order issued on February 8, 1945. That order was reversed by the Court of Appeals, which felt that our prior decision precluded such action by the Commission.

The latest order of the Commission definitely avoids the fatal error of relying on judicial precedents which do not sustain it. This time, after a thorough reexamination of the problem in light of the purposes and standards of the Holding Company Act, the Commission has concluded that the proposed transaction is inconsistent with the standards of §§ 7 and 11 of the Act. It has drawn heavily upon its accumulated experience in dealing with utility reorganizations. And it has expressed its reasons with a clarity and thoroughness that admit of no doubt as to the underlying basis of its order.

The argument is pressed upon us, however, that the Commission was foreclosed from taking such a step following our prior decision. . . . Under this view, the Commission would be free only to promulgate a general rule outlawing such profits in future utility reorganizations; but such a rule would have to be prospective in nature and have no retroactive effect upon the instant situation.

We reject this contention, for it grows out of a misapprehension of our prior decision and of the Commission's statutory duties. We held no more and no less than that the Commission's first order was unsupportable for the reasons supplied by that agency. But when the case left this Court, the problem whether Federal's management should be treated equally with other preferred stockholders still lacked a final and complete answer. It was clear that the Commission could not give a negative answer by resort to prior judicial declarations. . . . Still unsettled, however, was the answer the Commission might give were it to bring to bear on the facts the proper administrative and statutory considerations, a function which belongs exclusively to the Commission in the first instance. The administrative process had taken an erroneous rather than a final turn. Hence we carefully refrained from expressing any views as to the propriety of an order rooted in the proper and relevant considerations. . . . The fact that the Commission had committed a legal error in its first disposition of the case certainly gave Federal's management no vested right to receive the benefits of such an order. . . .

The absence of a general rule or regulation governing management trading during reorganization did not affect the Commission's duties in relation to the particular proposal before it. . . . Indeed, if the Commission rightly felt that the proposed amendment was inconsistent with [the Act], an order giving effect to the amendment merely because there was no general rule or regulation covering the matter would be unjustified.

It is true that our prior decision explicitly recognized the possibility that the Commission might have promulgated a general rule dealing with this problem under its statutory rulemaking powers, [b]ut we did not mean to imply thereby that the failure of the Commission to anticipate this problem and to promulgate a general rule withdrew all power from that agency to perform its statutory duty in this case. To hold that the Commission had no alternative in this proceeding but to approve the proposed transaction, while formulating any general rules it might desire for use in future cases of this nature, would be to stultify the administrative process. That we refuse to do.

Since the Commission, unlike a court, does have the ability to make new law prospectively through the exercise of its rulemaking powers, [t]he function of filling in the interstices of the Act should be performed, as much as possible, through this quasi-legislative promulgation of rules to be applied in the future. But any rigid requirement to that effect would make the administrative process inflexible and incapable of dealing with many of the specialized problems which arise. . . . To insist upon one form of action to the exclusion of the other is to exalt form over necessity. In other words, problems may arise in a case which the administrative agency could not reasonably foresee, problems which must be solved despite the absence of a relevant general rule. Or the agency may not have had sufficient experience with a particular problem to warrant rigidifying its tentative judgment into a hard and fast rule. Or the problem may be so specialized and varying in nature as to be impossible of capture within the boundaries of a general rule. In those situations, the agency must retain power to deal with the problems on a case-to-case basis if the administrative process is to be effective. . . . And the choice . . . between proceeding by general rule or by individual, ad hoc litigation is one that lies primarily in the informed discretion of the administrative agency.

Hence we refuse to say that the Commission, which had not previously been confronted with the problem of management trading during reorganization, was forbidden from utilizing this particular proceeding for announcing and applying a new standard of conduct. That such action might have a retroactive effect was not necessarily fatal to its validity. Every case of first impression has a retroactive effect, whether the new principle is announced by a court or by an administrative agency. But such retroactivity must be balanced against the mischief of producing a result which is contrary to a statutory design or to legal and equitable principles. If that mischief is greater than the ill effect of the retroactive application of a new standard, it is not the type of retroactivity which is condemned by law.

And so in this case, the fact that the Commission's order might retroactively prevent Federal's management from securing the profits and control which were the objects of the preferred stock purchases may well be outweighed by the dangers inherent in such purchases from the statutory standpoint. If that is true, the argument of retroactivity becomes nothing more than a claim that the Commission lacks power to enforce the standards of the Act in this proceeding. Such a claim deserves rejection.

The problem in this case thus resolves itself into a determination of whether the Commission's action in denying effectiveness to the proposed amendment to the Federal reorganization plan can be justified on the basis upon which it clearly rests. As we have noted, the Commission avoided placing its sole reliance on inapplicable judicial precedents. Rather it has derived its conclusions from the particular facts in the case, its general experience in reorganization matters and its informed view of statutory requirements. It is those matters which are the guide for our review.

The Commission concluded that it could not find that the reorganization plan, if amended as proposed, would be "fair and equitable to the persons affected thereby" within the meaning of § 11(e) of the Act, under which the reorganization was taking place. Its view was that the amended plan would involve the issuance of securities on terms "detrimental to the public interest or the interest of investors" . . . and would result in an "unfair or inequitable distribution of voting power" among the Federal security holders within the meaning of § 7(e). It was led to this result "not by proof that the interveners [Federal Water's management] committed acts of conscious wrongdoing but by the character of the conflicting interests created by the interveners' program of stock purchases carried out while plans for reorganization were under consideration."

The Commission noted that Federal's management controlled a large multistate utility system and that its influence permeated down to the lowest tier of operating companies. . . . The broad range of business judgments vested in Federal's management multiplied opportunities for affecting the market price of Federal's outstanding securities and made the exercise of judgment on any matter a subject of greatest significance to investors. Added to these normal managerial powers, the Commission pointed out that a holding company management obtains special powers in the course of a voluntary reorganization under § 11(e) of the Holding Company Act. The management represents the stockholders in such a reorganization, initiates the proceeding, draws up and files the plan, and can file amendments thereto at any time. These additional powers may introduce conflicts between the management's normal interests and its responsibilities to the various classes of stockholders which it represents in the reorganization. Moreover, because of its representative status, the management has special opportunities to obtain advance information of the attitude of the Commission.

Drawing upon its experience, the Commission indicated that all these normal and special powers of the holding company management during the course of a § 11(e) reorganization placed in the management's command "a formidable battery of devices that would enable it, if it should choose to use them selfishly, to affect in material degree the ultimate allocation of new securities among the various existing classes, to influence the market for its own gain, and to manipulate or obstruct the reorganization required by the mandate of the statute." In that setting, the Commission felt that a management program of stock purchase would give rise to the temptation and the opportunity to shape the reorganization proceeding so as to encourage public selling on the market at low prices. . . . The Commission further felt that its answer should be the same even where proof of intentional wrongdoing on the management's part is lacking. Assuming a conflict of interests, the Commission thought that the absence of actual misconduct is immaterial; injury to the public investors and to the corporation may result just as readily. . . . Moreover, the Commission was of the view that the delays and the difficulties involved in probing the mental processes and personal integrity of corporate officials do not warrant any distinction on the basis of evil intent, the plain fact being "that an absence of unfairness or detriment in cases of this sort would be practically impossible to establish by proof." . . . .

The scope of our review of an administrative order wherein a new principle is announced and applied is no different from that which pertains to ordinary administrative action. The wisdom of the principle adopted is none of our concern. Our duty is at an end when it becomes evident that the Commission's action is based upon substantial evidence and is consistent with the authority granted by Congress. . . . The Commission's conclusion here rests squarely in that area where administrative judgments are entitled to the greatest amount of weight by appellate courts. It is the product of administrative experience, appreciation of the complexities of the problem, realization of the statutory policies, and responsible treatment of the uncontested facts. It is the type of judgment which administrative agencies are best equipped to make and which justifies the use of the administrative process. Whether we agree or disagree with the result reached, it is an allowable judgment which we cannot disturb.

[JUSTICE JACKSON, dissenting.]

. . . As the Court correctly notes, the Commission has only "recast its rationale and reached the same result." There being no change in the order, no additional evidence in the record and no amendment of relevant legislation, it is clear that there has been a shift in attitude between that of the controlling membership of the Court when the case was first here and that of those who have the power of decision on this second review. . . . The Court's reasoning adds up to this: The Commission must be sustained because of its accumulated experience in solving a problem with which it had never before been confronted! . . .

I suggest that administrative experience is of weight in judicial review only [in that] it is a persuasive reason for deference to the Commission in the exercise of its discretionary powers under and within the law. It cannot be invoked to support action outside of the law. And what action is, and what is not, within the law must be determined by courts, when authorized to review, no matter how much deference is due to the agency's fact finding. . . .

———————

1. While *Chenery* is an adjudication, it is a basic administrative law case and is often referred to in rulemaking cases, in part because the case is about what many see as the articulation of a new rule in an adjudication. "A time-honored principle of administrative law is that the label an agency puts on its actions 'is not necessarily conclusive.'" *Columbia Broadcasting System, Inc. v. United States, 316 U.S. 407, 416 (1942)*. Equally true, however, is the fact that agencies can issue rules through adjudication (the process by which orders are normally issued) and orders through rulemaking. *San Diego Air Sports Center, Inc. v. Federal Aviation Administration, 887 F.2d 966 (9th Cir. 1989)*. Was the agency issuing a rule in *Chenery*? Did the agency – and thereafter the Court – announce a standard that has the force of law? Was there, prospectively, a prohibition on insiders purchasing preferred stock during a period of corporate reorganization?

2. *Chenery's* mandate to judge an agency by what it claims to be the basis of its action is referenced frequently as the rule the case sets forth regarding retroactivity. It is not a controversial concept but is of use in client representation. It is, technically speaking, a ban on post hoc rationalization by lawyers charged with the responsibility of defending an agency decision and, at first blush, makes sense. There has always been a prohibition on making appellate arguments "not raised below." In agency practice, however, particularly with rulemaking, there is no requirement that a statement of basis and purpose include all evidence, comments, arguments, and policies that are relevant.

3. In a recent decision, *Utah Environmental Congress (UEC) v. Richmond, 483 F.3d 1127 (10th Cir. 2007)*, the UEC challenged a Forest Service plan to permit logging in an ecologically sensitive area. On appeal, the UEC argued that the Forest

Service had not relied on the best available science to make its decision, an argument not made below. In response, the Forest Service sought to demonstrate the efficacy of its decision, using arguments that were not part of the agency decision. Based on *Chenery*, the court noted as follows:

> The fact that UEC never argued that the Forest Service failed to use the "best available science" standard brings into conflict two established lines of precedent. The first is that we will not, absent manifest injustice, vacate or reverse a district court decision based on an argument not made by the plaintiff. *See Sussman v. Patterson, 108 F.3d 1206, 1210 (10th Cir. 1997)*. The second [is that] we may not affirm an agency decision based on reasoning that the agency itself never considered. . . . *Citing SEC v. Chenery*.

4. Rulemaking is legislative, and if there is enough to understand the statutory and regulatory context, regulatory history, legal and factual basis for the rule, and purpose of the rule, § 553(c) is satisfied. On appeal, the attack on a rule can be expansive, and it is not necessarily bound by the content of the rule itself and may go to areas the agency did not address.

In that moment, would the agency's ability to respond be hampered by the prohibition on raising arguments not found in the agency decision?

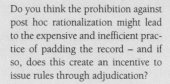

Food for Thought

Do you think the prohibition against post hoc rationalization might lead to the expensive and inefficient practice of padding the record — and if so, does this create an incentive to issue rules through adjudication?

5. In *Yale-New Haven Hosp. v. Leavitt, 470 F.3d 71 (2d Cir. 2006)*, the Department of Health and Human Services (HHS) sought to apply a revised Medicare manual (which HHS treated as having the force of law) as a basis to deny coverage in a treatment program "involving investigational cardiac devices provided to 48 patients." The appellate issue centered on the very limited record used by HHS when the agency completed the revisions to its manual — and the more elaborate information HHS wanted considered in court to explain the basis for the earlier revisions. The court held as follows:

> Generally speaking, after-the-fact rationalization for agency action is disfavored. . . . At the same time, an agency may supplement the administrative record before the reviewing court in some circumstances — among them, if "the absence of formal administrative findings makes such investigation necessary in order to determine the reasons for the agency's choice." . . . . Some tension is evident between the general principle (disfavoring the after-the-fact rationalization of agency action) and the exceptions. . . . [The court then decided to follow the D.C. Circuit rule] that "new materials should be merely explanatory of the original record and should contain no new rationalizations."

Under the D.C. Circuit standard, how easy would it be to distinguish between new materials not present in a rulemaking record and new materials that "merely" explain the rule? Once the court opens the door to new explanatory materials, does the basic principle in *Chenery* vanish?

6. *Utah Environmental Congress v. Troyer*, 479 F.3d 1269 (10th Cir. 2007).

> Plaintiff Utah Environmental Congress (UEC) brought this action alleging that defendants, representatives of the United States Forest Service . . . violated federal law by authorizing six separate projects in four national forests in the State of Utah. . . . [While the] Forest Service on appeal asks us to adopt the same approach as the district court and conclude that the analysis actually engaged in by the Forest Service effectively satisfies the best available science standard, UEC takes this position to task, correctly noting that "the reviewing court may not supply the basis for the agency's decision that the agency itself has not given." . . . . [S]*ee Chenery* (holding that a reviewing "court is powerless to affirm the administrative action by substituting what it considers to be a more adequate or proper basis") . . . .

———————

The applicability of *Chenery* to rulemaking is longstanding and uncontroversial. If anything, the restrictions on retroactive action are more explicit in rulemaking than in adjudication, as becomes obvious in the following case.

BOWEN V. GEORGETOWN UNIVERSITY HOSPITAL

488 U.S. 204 (1988)

[JUSTICE KENNEDY] Under the Medicare program, health care providers are reimbursed by the Government for expenses incurred in providing medical services to Medicare beneficiaries. Congress has authorized the Secretary of Health and Human Services to promulgate regulations setting limits on the levels of Medicare costs that will be reimbursed. The question presented here is whether the Secretary may exercise this rulemaking authority to promulgate cost limits that are retroactive.

I

The Secretary's authority to adopt cost-limit rules is established by . . . the Social Security Amendments of 1972.

On June 30, 1981, the Secretary issued a cost-limit schedule that [changed] the method for calculating the "wage index," a factor used to reflect the salary levels for hospital employees in different parts of the country. Under the prior rule, the wage index for a given geographic area was calculated by using the average salary levels for all hospitals in the area; the 1981 rule provided that wages paid by

Federal Government hospitals would be excluded from that computation.

Various hospitals in the District of Columbia area brought suit . . . seeking to have the 1981 schedule invalidated. On April 29, 1983, the District Court struck down the 1981 wage-index rule, concluding that the Secretary had violated the [APA] by failing to provide notice and an opportunity for public comment before issuing the rule. The court did not enjoin enforcement of the rule, however, finding it lacked jurisdiction to do so because the hospitals had not yet exhausted their administrative reimbursement remedies. The court's order stated:

> If the Secretary wishes to put in place a valid prospective wage index, she should begin proper notice and comment proceedings; any wage index currently in place that has been promulgated without notice and comment is invalid as was the 1981 schedule.

The Secretary did not pursue an appeal. Instead, . . . the Secretary settled the hospitals' cost reimbursement reports by applying the pre-1981 wage-index method.

In February 1984, the Secretary published a notice seeking public comment on a proposal to reissue the 1981 wage-index rule, retroactive to July 1, 1981. Because Congress had subsequently amended the Medicare Act to require significantly different cost reimbursement procedures, the readoption of the modified wage-index method was to apply exclusively to a 15-month period commencing July 1, 1981. After considering the comments received, the Secretary reissued the 1981 schedule in final form on November 26, 1984, and proceeded to recoup sums previously paid as a result of the District Court's ruling . . . . In effect, the Secretary had promulgated a rule retroactively, and the net result was as if the original rule had never been set aside.

Respondents, a group of seven hospitals who had benefited from the invalidation of the 1981 schedule, were required to return over $ 2 million in reimbursement payments. After exhausting administrative remedies, they sought judicial review under . . . the APA, claiming that the retroactive schedule was invalid under both the APA and the Medicare Act.

The United States District Court for the District of Columbia granted summary judgment for respondents. . . . [T]he court held that retroactive application was not justified under the circumstances of the case. The Secretary appealed to . . . the District of Columbia Circuit, which affirmed . . . on the alternative grounds that the APA, as a general matter, forbids retroactive rulemaking, and that the Medicare Act, by specific terms, bars retroactive cost-limit rules. . . . [W]e now affirm.

II

It is axiomatic that an administrative agency's power to promulgate legislative regulations is limited to the authority delegated by Congress. In determining the validity of the Secretary's retroactive cost-limit rule, the threshold question is whether the Medicare Act authorizes retroactive rulemaking.

Retroactivity is not favored in the law. Thus, congressional enactments and administrative rules will not be construed to have retroactive effect unless their language requires this result. By the same principle, a statutory grant of legislative rulemaking authority will not, as a general matter, be understood to encompass the power to promulgate retroactive rules unless that power is conveyed by Congress in express terms. Even where some substantial justification for retroactive rulemaking is presented, courts should be reluctant to find such authority absent an express statutory grant.

. . . .

A

The authority to promulgate cost-reimbursement regulations is set forth in § 1395x(v)(1)(A). That subparagraph also provides that:

> Such regulations shall . . . (ii) provide for the making of suitable retroactive corrective adjustments where, for a provider of services for any fiscal period, the aggregate reimbursement produced by the methods of determining costs proves to be either inadequate or excessive.

This provision on its face permits some form of retroactive action. We cannot accept the Secretary's argument, however, that it provides authority for the retroactive promulgation of cost-limit rules. To the contrary, we agree with the Court of Appeals that clause (ii) directs the Secretary to establish a procedure for making case-by-case adjustments to reimbursement payments where the regulations prescribing computation methods do not reach the correct result in individual cases. The structure and language of the statute require the conclusion that the retroactivity provision applies only to case-by-case adjudication, not to rulemaking.

. . . .

B

The statutory provisions establishing the Secretary's general rulemaking power contain no express authorization of retroactive rulemaking. Any light that might be shed on this matter by suggestions of legislative intent also indicates that no such authority was contemplated. . . .

The legislative history of the cost-limit provision directly addresses the issue of retroactivity. . . . [T]he House and Senate Committee Reports expressed a desire to forbid retroactive cost-limit rules:

> The proposed new authority to set limits on costs . . . would be exercised on a prospective, rather than retrospective, basis so that the provider would know in advance the limits to Government recognition of incurred costs and have the opportunity to act to avoid having costs that are not reimbursable.

The Secretary's past administrative practice is consistent with this interpretation of the statute. The first regulations promulgated under § 223(b) provided that "[t]hese limits will be imposed prospectively . . . ." . . . . Other examples of similar statements by the agency abound. . . .

The Secretary nonetheless suggests that, whatever the limits on his power to promulgate retroactive regulations in the normal course of events, judicial invalidation of a prospective rule is a unique occurrence that creates a heightened need, and thus a justification, for retroactive curative rulemaking. The Secretary warns that congressional intent and important administrative goals may be frustrated unless an invalidated rule can be cured of its defect and made applicable to past time periods. The argument is further advanced that the countervailing reliance interests are less compelling than in the usual case of retroactive rulemaking, because the original, invalidated rule provided at least some notice to the individuals and entities subject to its provisions.

Whatever weight the Secretary's contentions might have in other contexts, they need not be addressed here. The case before us is resolved by the particular statutory scheme in question. Our interpretation of the Medicare Act compels the conclusion that the Secretary has no authority to promulgate retroactive cost-limit rules.

The 1984 reinstatement of the 1981 cost-limit rule is invalid. The judgment of the Court of Appeals is Affirmed.

[JUSTICE SCALIA, concurring.]

I agree with the Court that . . . § 223(b) of the Medicare Act does not permit retroactive application of the Secretary of Health and Human Service's 1984 cost-limit rule. I write separately because I find it incomplete to discuss general principles of administrative law without reference to the basic structural legislation which is the embodiment of those principles, the Administrative Procedure Act . . . .

The first part of the APA's definition of "rule" states that a rule

means the whole or a part of an agency statement of general or particular applicability *and future effect* designed to implement, interpret, or prescribe law or policy or describing the organization, procedure, or practice requirements of an agency . . . .

5 U.S.C. § 551(4) (emphasis added).

The only plausible reading of the italicized phrase is that rules have legal consequences only for the future. It could not possibly mean that merely *some* of their legal consequences must be for the future, though they may also have legal consequences for the past, since that description would not enable rules to be distinguished from "orders," see 5 U.S.C. § 551(6), and would thus destroy the entire dichotomy upon which the most significant portions of the APA are based. (Adjudication – the process for formulating orders, see § 551(7) – has future as well as past legal consequences, since the principles announced in an adjudication cannot be departed from in future adjudications without reason.) . . . .

[The House Report accompanying the APA] states that "[t]he phrase 'future effect' does not preclude agencies from considering and, so far as legally authorized, dealing with past transactions in prescribing rules for the future." The Treasury Department might prescribe, for example, that for purposes of assessing future income tax liability, income from certain trusts that has previously been considered nontaxable will be taxable – whether those trusts were established before or after the effective date of the regulation. That is not retroactivity in the sense at issue here, i.e., in the sense of altering the *past* legal consequences of past actions. Rather, it is what has been characterized as "secondary" retroactivity. A rule with exclusively future effect (taxation of future trust income) can unquestionably *affect* past transactions (rendering the previously established trusts less desirable in the future), but it does not for that reason cease to be a rule under the APA. Thus, with respect to the present matter, there is no question that the Secretary could have applied her new wage-index formulas to respondents in the future, even though respondents may have been operating under long-term labor and supply contracts negotiated in reliance upon the pre-existing rule. . . .

Underlying Case Documents

The case referenced:

The Social Security Amendments of 1972

The 1984 notice seeking comment to reissue the 1981 schedule

The 1984 final rule reissuing the 1981 schedule

1. Since the *Bowen* opinion issued, the argument has surfaced from time to time that the Court's decision in <u>*Smiley v. Citibank*, 517 U.S. 735 (1996)</u>, is a retreat from its clear prohibition against primary retroactivity. The argument was raised – and debunked – in <u>*Pauly v. United States Department of Agriculture*, 348 F.3d 1143 (9th Cir. 2003)</u>. The Ninth Circuit noted that

> [t]he Supreme Court has observed that "retroactivity is generally disfavored in the law." <u>*Eastern Enters. v. Apfel*, 524 U.S. 498, 532 (1998)</u> (plurality opinion). In *Bowen* the Court held that "administrative rules will not be construed to have retroactive effect unless their language requires this result." The district court recognized *Bowen's* limitation on retroactivity, but nonetheless concluded that *Smiley v. Citibank* "effectively limited" *Bowen*. . . . The district court's reliance on *Smiley* was misplaced. . . . No other court has read . . . *Smiley* [that way and] we refuse to do so today.

> **Bottom Line**
>
> It is difficult to read *Bowen* as anything other than a prohibition against primary retroactivity, i.e., a rule that would alter past consequences of past action. As to its affect on secondary retroactivity (a rule that affects future consequences of past action), *Bowen* does not necessarily resolve the debate. Secondary retroactivity involves "a new rule that legally has only [a] 'future effect,' and is therefore not subject to doctrines limiting retroactive effect, [but] may still have a serious impact on pre-existing transactions." <u>*Indep. Petroleum Ass'n of Am. v. DeWitt*, 279 F.3d 1036 (D.C. Cir. 2002)</u>.

2. In <u>*Mobile Relay Associates v. FCC*, 457 F.3d 1 (D.C. Cir. 2006)</u>, two licensees claimed that the FCC's rules directing reconfiguration of the electromagnetic spectrum's 800 MHz band (designed to reduce interference with public safety communications) were unlawful. They argued, *inter alia*, that the rebanding created a "different communications system architecture[,]" relied on a standard that was not in place at the time their initial licenses were granted, and constituted a taking. The court addressed the retroactivity argument as follows:

> Secondary retroactivity – which occurs if an agency's rule affects a regulated entity's investment made in reliance on the regulatory status quo before the rule's promulgation – will be upheld "if it is reasonable," i.e., if it is not "arbitrary" or "capricious." <u>*DIRECTV v. FCC*, 110 F.3d 816 (D.C. Cir. 1996)</u>. The Rebanding Decision was reasonable because . . . the Commission sought to segregate incompatible mobile communications architectures to reduce interference . . ., pursuant to its public interest mandate. . . . A change in policy "is not arbitrary or capricious merely because it alters the current state of affairs. The Commission is entitled to reconsider and revise its views as to the public interest and the means needed to protect that interest if it gives a reasoned explanation for the revision." [Id.]

Good Questions!

The Court held in *Bowen v. Georgetown University Hospital* that primary retroactive rule-making is generally unacceptable in the absence of explicit Congressional authorization. Assume the Clean Air Act *does not* have that authorization. Which if any of the following situations would be prohibited under *Bowen*:

    a. EPA issues a rule capping CO_2 emissions from existing power plants and only a few plants can meet the standard.

    b. EPA issues the rule but says it will become effective in 2 years; virtually all plants will have to install major new scrubbers.

    c. EPA publishes a new rule that changes the interpretation of an existing rule; as a result, many power plants have been out of compliance for years and face significant penalties if the EPA were to enforce the new interpretation.

    d. A plant applies for an operating permit that would have been granted but for the new rule. Many millions have been spent getting the facility in compliance in anticipation of the review of the license application – but the standards by which these changes were made derived from the old rule.

3. The question of retroactivity for rulemaking is resolved differently than retroactivity for adjudication. In enforcement actions, retroactivity problems are not necessarily resolved as decisively as in *Bowen*. If a statute gives broad and general authority in a field, the fact that an agency has not yet condemned a specific practice will not prevent the agency from going forward in an enforcement action. As the D.C. Circuit noted in <u>*AT&T v. FCC*, 454 F.3d 329, 332 (D.C. Cir. 2006)</u>,

> [r]etroactivity is the norm in agency adjudications no less than in judicial adjudications. . . . For our part we have drawn a distinction between agency decisions that "substitut[e] new law for old law that was reasonably clear" and those which are merely "new applications of existing law, clarifications, and additions." The latter carry a presumption of retroactivity that we depart from only when to do otherwise would lead to "manifest injustice."

For the most part, agencies do not have difficulty confronting the manifest injustice standard in adjudications. But see <u>*Qwest Services Corp. v. FCC*, 509 F.3d 531, 539-40 (D.C. Cir. 2007)</u>, where the court held that an agency's "finding of manifest injustice is completely unconvincing."

Practice Pointer

Questions to contemplate in retroactivity cases:

1. Did Congress intend the agency to issue retroactive rules or adjudicatory orders?
2. Did Congress prohibit the agency from issuing retroactive rules or adjudicatory orders?
3. Is the application of the new rule (to past facts) going to create a manifest injustice?

4. Was the agency action unexpected – did the parties have de facto or de jure notice?

5. Was there justifiable reliance (a settled expectation) on the existing rules or standards prior to the issuance of the retroactive rule or order?

6. Is there a new liability, sanction, legal consequence/obligation, or fine that did not exist before?

7. Were there easy and available other means to change the government policy/program without the harsh effect of a retroactive rule or order?

8. Would the statutory goals be frustrated if the agency is prohibited from issuing the retroactive rule or order?

9. Will "law breakers" go unpunished (thus compromising deterrence and the statutory purpose) if the agency is prohibited from issuing the retroactive rule or order?

10. When you evaluate the retroactive rule or order, consider the level of misconduct or harm the agency is trying to address – which is worse – the fact of a retroactive action or the behavior seeking to be prevented?

11. Is this primary retroactivity (alters past consequences of past action) or secondary (affects future consequences of past action)

12. Is the challenged retroactivity central to the rights, interests or entitlements of the parties or is it collateral, e.g., procedural?

13. Does the retroactivity respond to an emergency or correct a critical error?

LANDGRAF V. *USI FILM PRODUCTS*

511 U.S. 244 (1994)

[JUSTICE STEVENS] From September 4, 1984, through January 17, 1986, petitioner Barbara Landgraf was employed in the USI Film Products (USI) plant in Tyler, Texas . . . operating a machine that produced plastic bags. A fellow employee named John Williams repeatedly harassed her with inappropriate remarks and physical contact. Petitioner's complaints to her immediate supervisor brought her no relief, but when she reported the incidents to the personnel manager, he conducted an investigation, reprimanded Williams, and transferred him to another department. Four days later petitioner quit her job.

Petitioner filed a timely charge with the Equal Employment Opportunity Commission (EEOC or Commission). The Commission . . . issued a notice of right to sue. . . . After a bench trial, the District Court found that Williams had sexually harassed petitioner causing her to suffer mental anguish. However, the court concluded that she had not been constructively discharged. . . . Because . . . Title VII did not then authorize any other form of relief, the court dismissed her complaint.

On November 21, 1991, while petitioner's appeal was pending, the President signed into law the Civil Rights Act of 1991. The Court of Appeals rejected petitioner's argument that her case should be remanded for a jury trial on damages pursuant to the 1991 Act. Its decision not to remand rested on the premise that "a court must 'apply the law in effect at the time it renders its decision, unless doing so would result in manifest injustice or there is statutory direction or legislative history to the contrary.'"

We assume . . . that if the same conduct were to occur today, petitioner would be entitled to a jury trial and that the jury might find that . . . her mental anguish or other injuries would support an award of damages against her former employer. Thus, the controlling question is whether the Court of Appeals should have applied the law in effect at the time the discriminatory conduct occurred, or at the time of its decision in July 1992. . . .

[T]he antiretroactivity principle finds expression in several provisions of our Constitution. The Ex Post Facto Clause flatly prohibits retroactive application of penal legislation. Article I, § 10, cl. 1, prohibits States from passing another type of retroactive legislation, laws "impairing the Obligation of Contracts." . . . . The prohibitions on "Bills of Attainder" in Art. I, §§ 9-10, prohibit legislatures from singling out disfavored persons and meting out summary punishment for past conduct. The Due Process Clause also protects the interests in fair notice and repose that may be compromised by retroactive legislation. . . .

The Constitution's restrictions, of course, are of limited scope. Absent a violation of one of those specific provisions, the potential unfairness of retroactive civil legislation is not a sufficient reason for a court to fail to give a statute its intended scope. Retroactivity provisions often serve entirely benign and legitimate purposes, whether to respond to emergencies, to correct mistakes, to prevent circumvention of a new statute in the interval immediately preceding its passage, or simply to give comprehensive effect to a new law Congress considers salutary. However, a requirement that Congress first make its intention clear helps ensure that Congress itself has determined that the benefits of retroactivity outweigh the potential for disruption or unfairness. . . .

A statute does not operate "retrospectively" merely because it is applied in a case arising from conduct antedating the statute's enactment, or upsets expectations based in prior law. Rather, the court must ask whether the new provision attaches new legal consequences to events completed before its enactment. . . . Even absent specific legislative authorization, application of new statutes passed after the events in suit is unquestionably proper in many situations. When the intervening statute authorizes or affects the propriety of prospective relief, application of the new provision is not retroactive.

. . . .

When a case implicates a federal statute enacted after the events in suit, the court's first task is to determine whether Congress has expressly prescribed the statute's proper reach. . . . [The Civil Rights Act of 1991 did not address retro- activity. In fact, the court notes, the absence of language empowering retroactive enforcement may be the reason the Act garnered the votes needed to pass. For that reason, the presumption prohibiting retroactivity application stands and the claimant is denied the benefit of the newly passed law.]

[JUSTICE SCALIA, concurring.]

I of course agree with the Court that . . . a legislative enactment affecting sub- stantive rights does not apply retroactively absent *clear statement* to the contrary. The Court, however, is willing to let that clear statement be supplied, not by the text of the law in question, but by individual legislators who participated in the enactment of the law, and even legislators in an earlier Congress which tried and failed to enact a similar law. For the Court not only combs the floor debate and Committee Reports of the statute at issue, the Civil Rights Act of 1991, but also reviews the procedural history of an earlier, unsuccessful, attempt by a *different* Congress to enact similar legislation, the Civil Rights Act of 1990.

This effectively converts the "clear statement" rule into a "discernible legisla- tive intent" rule – and even that understates the difference. The Court's rejection of the floor statements of certain Senators because they are "frankly partisan" and "cannot plausibly be read as reflecting any general agreement," reads like any other exercise in the soft science of legislative historicizing, undisciplined by any distinctive "clear statement" requirement. If it is a "clear statement" we are seeking, surely it is not enough to insist that the statement can "plausibly be read as reflecting general agreement"; the statement must *clearly* reflect general agreement. No legislative history can do that, of course, but only the text of the statute itself. . . .

Underlying Case Documents

The case referenced:
The Civil Rights Act of 1991
The notice of right to sue

For a letter Ms. Landgraf sent to her fellow employees upon leaving click HERE.

For the initial administrative determination click HERE.

1. JUSTICE SCALIA's concurrence highlights a split of opinion regarding the use of legislative history – and the legislative history disagreement is just the tip of the iceberg. The controversy regarding proper authority embraces various types of secondary source material and most international material (including foreign case law, statutes, and regulations).

The split regarding the use of legislative history and floor debates came up in the 2007 Supreme Court term. In a dissent in *Zuni Public School District No. 89 v. Department of Education*, 551 U.S. 1110 (2007), JUSTICE SCALIA accused JUSTICE BREYER of relying on "nothing other than . . . judge-supposed legislative intent [as opposed to] clear statutory text."

The disagreement on legislative history is reflected in JUSTICE SCALIA's majority opinion – and JUSTICE BREYER's dissent – in *FCC. v. NextWave Personal Communications*, 537 U.S. 293 (2003). In JUSTICE BREYER's dissent in *Arlington Central School District v. Murphy*, 548 U.S. 291, 323 (2006), he notes: "I cannot agree with the majority's conclusion. Even less can I agree with its failure to consider fully the statute's legislative history."

In *Landgraf*, the majority opinion does not need to rely on legislative history for the most part. Its focus on the general presumption against retroactivity – absent congressional intent to the contrary – is fairly standard, though as the Court notes, any hard retroactivity case "will leave room for disagreement."

2. *Landgraf* remains a reliable basis for determining whether a retroactivity problem exists in a particular case. Among other things, it makes it clear that the application of a statute to antecedent conduct requires analysis, not a knee-jerk negative reaction. The presence of reasonable notice, foreseeable reliance, and settled expectations are part of the equation unless Congress has spoken expressly on retroactive application. *See Campos v. INS*, 16 F.3d 118, 122 (6th Cir. 1994), *and Patel v. Gonzales*, 432 F.3d 685, 690 (6th Cir. 2005).

3. In *Republic of Austria v. Altmann*, 541 U.S. 677, 692-700 (2004), the Court returned to the retroactivity field, discussing the impact of various "pre-statute" activities in a Foreign Sovereign Immunities Act (FSIA) case. 28 U.S.C. § 1330(a). Altmann sued the Austrian government (including the state-owned museum) to recover artwork (including Klimt paintings) that came into possession of the gallery as a result of the Nazi occupation. The Court found the *Landgraf* anti-retroactivity principles required a careful look at FSIA – and that while not an "express command," the text of FSIA (relevant, of course, to Austria's assertion of immunity) anticipated claims based on prior conduct, finding that Congress intended resolution on FSIA principles, without reference to the date of the acts that gave rise to the claim in the first instance.

4. For a very recent – and comprehensive – application of *Landgraf*, see <u>Martinez v. INS, 523 F.3d 365 (2d Cir. 2008)</u>. There the court dealt with revised "stop time" rules applicable to those seeking to fulfill the seven-year, in-country requirement to secure citizenship status. The claimant was accused of committing a felony one month before completing his seven years. Under the rules in place at the time he entered the United States, it was at least arguable that the "clock" could continue to run until a judgment was entered, either by conviction or plea. Under the revised rules, the date of the crime stops the clock and deportation proceedings can commence. The claimant argued that the new rules should not apply – but the court disagreed.

> *Landgraf* . . . confirmed the continuing viability of the centuries-old presumption against retroactive legislation, emphasizing that "[e]lementary considerations of fairness dictate that individuals should have an opportunity to know what the law is and to conform their conduct accordingly. . . ." At the same time, the Court acknowledged that Congress had the power, within constitutional limits, to enact laws with retroactive effect . . . to respond to emergencies, to correct mistakes, to prevent circumvention of a new statute in the interval immediately preceding its passage, or simply to give comprehensive effect to a new law Congress considers salutary.

> Based on the above principles, the *Landgraf* Court articulated a two-step test for determining when a statute could be applied retroactively. In the first step, the court must ascertain, using the ordinary tools of statutory construction, "whether Congress has expressly prescribed the statute's proper reach." If the answer is yes, the inquiry is over. If, however, "the statute contains no such express command," the court must move on to the second step and decide "the nature and extent of the change in the law and the degree of connection between the operation of the new rule and a relevant past event," and determine "whether the new provision attaches new legal consequences to events completed before its enactment." . . . . [The court did not find an express prescription for retroactivity and the analysis moved to step two.]

> [T]aking into account "familiar considerations of fair notice . . . and settled expectations," we fail to see how either of these guiding principles was contravened in the instant case. Fair notice was not violated because the law was certain at the time Zuluaga acted. He would have been deportable without possibility of discretionary relief had he been convicted before he accrued seven years [under the existing rules as well as the amended statute]. And settled expectations were not disrupted because, assuming that Zuluaga expected anything with respect to deportation when he committed the offense, his expectation could not have been anything other than that he was subject to deportation without the opportunity for discretionary relief.

IMMIGRATION AND NATURALIZATION SERVICE v. St. CYR

<u>533 U.S. 289 (2001)</u>

[JUSTICE STEVENS] Both the Antiterrorism and Effective Death Penalty Act of 1996 (AEDPA), . . . and the Illegal Immigration Reform and Immigrant Responsibility Act of 1996 (IIRIRA) . . . contain comprehensive amendments to the Immigration and Nationality Act (INA), 8 U.S.C. § 1101 et seq. . . .

Respondent, Enrico St. Cyr, is a citizen of Haiti who was admitted to the United States as a lawful permanent resident in 1986. Ten years later . . . he pled guilty in a state court to a charge of selling a controlled substance in violation of Connecticut law. That conviction made him deportable. Under pre-AEDPA law applicable at the time of his [plea and] conviction, St. Cyr would have been eligible for a waiver of deportation at the discretion of the Attorney General. . . . [It was, arguably, the reason for St. Cyr's plea.] However, removal proceedings against him were not commenced until . . . after both AEDPA and IIRIRA became effective, and, as the Attorney General interprets those statutes, he no longer has discretion to grant such a waiver. . . .

Section 212 of the Immigration and Nationality Act of 1952 . . . excluded from the United States several classes of aliens, including those convicted of offenses involving moral turpitude or the illicit traffic in narcotics. . . . [T]his section was subject to a proviso granting the Attorney General broad discretion to admit excludable aliens. . . . § 212(c) was literally applicable only to exclusion proceedings, but it . . . has been interpreted by the Board of Immigration Appeals (BIA) to authorize any permanent resident alien with "a lawful unrelinquished domicile of seven consecutive years" to apply for a discretionary waiver from deportation. If relief is granted, the deportation proceeding is terminated and the alien remains a permanent resident. . . . [A] substantial percentage of . . . applications for § 212(c) relief have been granted [and,] in the period between 1989 and 1995 alone, § 212(c) relief was granted to over 10,000 aliens. . . .

[The question is] whether depriving removable aliens of consideration for § 212(c) relief produces an impermissible retroactive effect for aliens who, like respondent, were convicted pursuant to a plea agreement at a time when their plea would not have rendered them ineligible for § 212(c) relief.

. . . As we have repeatedly counseled, the judgment whether a particular statute acts retroactively "should be informed and guided by 'familiar considerations of fair notice, reasonable reliance, and settled expectations.'" IIRIRA's elimination of any possibility of § 212(c) relief for people who entered into plea agreements with the expectation that they would be eligible for such relief clearly "attaches a new disability, in respect to transactions or considerations already past." *Landgraf*. Plea agreements involve a quid pro quo between a criminal defendant and the government. In exchange for some perceived benefit, defendants waive several of their constitutional rights (including the right to a trial) and grant the government numerous "tangible benefits, such as promptly imposed punishment without the expenditure of prosecutorial resources." There can be little doubt that, as a general matter, alien defendants considering whether to enter into a plea agreement are acutely aware of the immigration consequences of their convictions. Given the frequency with which § 212(c) relief was granted in the years leading up to AEDPA and IIRIRA, preserving the possibility of such relief would have been one of the principal benefits sought by defendants deciding whether to accept a plea offer or instead to proceed to trial.

. . . The potential for unfairness in the retroactive application of IIRIRA § 304(b) to people like . . . St. Cyr is significant and manifest. Relying upon settled practice, the advice of counsel, and perhaps even assurances in open court that the entry of the plea would not foreclose § 212(c) relief, a great number of defendants in . . . St. Cyr's position agreed to plead guilty. Now that prosecutors have received the benefit of these plea agreements, agreements that were likely facilitated by the aliens' belief in their continued eligibility for § 212(c) relief, it would surely be contrary to "familiar considerations of fair notice, reasonable reliance, and settled expectations," *Landgraf*, to hold that IIRIRA's subsequent restrictions deprive them of any possibility of such relief.

The INS argues that deportation proceedings (and the Attorney General's discretionary power to grant relief from deportation) are "inherently prospective" and that, as a result, application of the law of deportation can never have a retroactive effect. Such categorical arguments are not particularly helpful in undertaking [a] commonsense, functional retroactivity analysis. Moreover, although we have characterized deportation as "look[ing] prospectively to the respondent's right to remain in this country in the future," *INS v. Lopez-Mendoza*, 468 U.S. 1032 (1984), we have done so in order to reject the argument that deportation is punishment for past behavior and that deportation proceedings are therefore subject to the "various protections that apply in the context of a criminal trial." As our cases make clear, the presumption against retroactivity applies far beyond the confines of the criminal law. And our mere statement that deportation is not punishment for past crimes does not mean that we cannot consider an alien's reasonable reliance on the continued availability of discretionary relief from deportation when deciding whether the elimination of such relief has a retroactive effect.

Finally, the fact that § 212(c) relief is discretionary does not affect the propriety of our conclusion. There is a clear difference, for the purposes of retroactivity analysis, between facing possible deportation and facing certain deportation. Prior to AEDPA and IIRIRA, aliens like St. Cyr had a significant likelihood of receiving § 212(c) relief. Because respondent, and other aliens like him, almost certainly relied upon that likelihood in deciding whether to forgo their right to a trial, the elimination of any possibility of § 212(c) relief by IIRIRA has an obvious and severe retroactive effect. . . .

We find nothing in IIRIRA unmistakably indicating that Congress considered the question whether to apply its repeal of § 212(c) retroactively to such aliens. We therefore hold that § 212(c) relief remains available for aliens, like respondent, whose convictions were obtained through plea agreements and who, notwithstanding those convictions, would have been eligible for § 212(c) relief at the time of their plea under the law then in effect.

———

Underlying Case Documents

The case referenced:
The Antiterrorism and Effective Death Penalty Act of 1996
The Illegal Immigration Reform and Immigrant Responsibility Act of 1996
The Immigration and Nationality Act of 1952

A month after his victory, St. Cyr was released from prison. For more information click HERE.

1. The legal issues associated with criminal misconduct for those seeking citizenship are complex. When and whether to "stop the clock" during the seven-year in-country "good conduct" period pursuant to 8 U.S.C. § 1229b(d) is the subject of a number of federal court decisions in cases not unlike *St. Cyr. Jimenez-Angeles v. Ashcroft*, 291 F.3d 594 (9th Cir. 2002); *Castello-Diaz v. United States*, 174 Fed. Appx. 719 (3d Cir. 2006); *Campbell v. Ashcroft*, 2004 WL 1563022 (E.D. Pa. 2004); *Falconi v. INS*, 240 F. Supp. 2d 215 (E.D.N.Y. 2002).

2. Which crimes "stop the clock?" All crimes? State and federal? Felonies only? Acts of moral turpitude? In 2006, the Court decided *Lopez v. Gonzales*, 549 U.S. 47 (2006), in part to create workable standards to determine whether a plea or conviction in a drug trafficking case under state criminal law should be treated the same as a conviction under federal law for immigration purposes. "[A] state offense constitutes a 'felony punishable under the Controlled Substances Act' only if it proscribes conduct punishable as a felony under that federal law." Unfortunately the clarity of *Lopez v. Gonzales* is not the norm.

3. Section 8 U.S.C. § 1446 requires an FBI "name check" before the Bureau of Immigration Affairs process can go forward. Since September 11, 2001, the number of checks the FBI has been asked to make is in the "millions." *Ibrahim v. Chertoff*, 529 F. Supp. 2d 611, 614 (E.D.N.C. 2007). As a consequence of such

volume, the delays in processing these checks are staggering. Are the retroactivity policies in *Landgraf* and *St. Cyr* likely to compound the problem? Regulations change regularly – and compliance with them can be tricky. With each change, the retroactivity issue must be addressed.

4. Given the problems discussed above, those with sufficient resources trying to make their way through the immigration maze secure the assistance of counsel – all too often leading to claims that they have been poorly advised on problems relating to various aspects of the process, not the least of which are the *St. Cyr* issues pertaining to the effect of the commission of a crime during the seven-year good conduct period.

a. The First Circuit recently discussed the general right to legal advice in *Zeru v. Gonzales*, 503 F.3d 59 (1st Cir. 2007): "While aliens in deportation proceedings do not enjoy a Sixth Amendment right to counsel, they have due process rights in deportation proceedings. As an 'integral part' of this procedural due process [they] have a statutory right [8 U.S.C. § 1362] to be represented by counsel at their own expense. . . ."

b. An earlier First Circuit decision weighed in on the problem of questionable legal advice: "Ineffective assistance of counsel in a deportation proceeding is a denial of due process only if the proceeding was so fundamentally unfair that the alien was prevented from reasonably presenting his case". *Lozada v. INS*, 857 F.2d 10, 13 (1st Cir. 1988). This claim can only succeed if the claimant can show "a reasonable probability of prejudice" as a consequence of the former representation. *Saakian v. INS*, 252 F.3d 21, 25 (1st Cir. 2001).

c. For more information on this topic, see John J. Francis, *Failure to Advise Non-Citizens of Immigration Consequences of Criminal Convictions: Should this Be Grounds to Withdraw a Guilty Plea?*, 36 U. Mich. J.L. Reform 691 (2003); *Hill v. Lockhart*, 474 U.S. 52, 56 (1985) (on ineffective assistance of counsel); *Magallanes-Damian v. INS*, 783 F.2d 931, 933 (9th Cir. 1986) (linking effective counsel and a baseline right to fundamental fairness); and *In re Cecilia Rivera-Claros*, 21 I. & N. Dec. 232 (BIA 1996) (discussing ineffective assistance and reporting obligations). *In re Cecilia Rivera-Claros* requires an applicant claiming ineffective assistance to:

> (1) file an affidavit explaining the agreement between the applicant and former counsel and listing what actions counsel failed to take; (2) grant former counsel an opportunity to respond; and (3) *indicate whether former counsel's error was reported to disciplinary authorities*. [Emphasis added.]

Does it seem reasonable to require one claiming ineffective assistance of counsel to initiate a legal proceeding against his or her attorney?

d. *Lu v. Ashcroft, 259 F.3d 127, 131 (3d Cir. 2001)*, and *Fadiga v. United States, 488 F.3d 142 (3d Cir. 2007)*, discuss the so-called "bar complaint" requirement in an ineffective assistance claim, noting the interests served by requiring claimants to report an ineffective assistance allegation to bar or disciplinary authorities:

> These interests include providing a "means of identifying and correcting possible misconduct" in the immigration bar . . . deter[ring] meritless claims of ineffective assistance of counsel [and] highlight[ing] the standards which should be expected of attorneys who represent aliens in immigration proceedings[,] increas[ing] the Board's] confidence in the validity of the particular claim[,] reduc[ing] the likelihood that an evidentiary hearing will be needed[,] serv[ing the Board's] long-term interests in policing the immigration bar[, a]nd . . . protect[ing] against possible collusion between counsel and the alien client. [*From Fadiga*, 488 F.3d at 156.]

Take Note

Not only must a person claiming ineffective assistance report his or her lawyer to the proper judicial or state bar authorities, a difficult task at best, but the claim may not even be raised until the administrative proceeding at the Bureau of Immigration Appeals has been completed. *See Ontiveros-Lopez v. INS*, 213 F.3d 1121, 1124 (9th Cir. 2000); and *Liu v. Waters*, 55 F.3d 421, 426 (9th Cir. 1995).

What effect will the reporting requirement have on ineffective assistance claims?

5. There are many, many retroactivity cases. Distinguishing between them can be next to impossible. Can you explain the results in the following two decisions?

a. In *Hernandez-Rodriguez v. Pasquarell, 118 F.3d 1034 (5th Cir. 1997)*, the Board of Immigration Appeals denied a permanent resident alien discretionary INA 212(c) relief from exclusion and denied his motion to reopen exclusion proceedings. While his subsequent habeas corpus petition was pending, the agency promulgated new regulations more favorable to him. Because the language of the new regulations did not require retroactivity, however, they did not apply to his case.

b. In *Mountain Solutions, Ltd., Inc. v. FCC, 197 F.3d 512, 521 (D.C. Cir. 1999)*, the FCC refused to allow a radio license bidder to benefit from a fee deadline rule change instituted while the bidder's request for waiver of late payment rules was pending. The court noted that it would be "an unusual procedure for rulemaking" if it allowed the retroactive rule application urged by the radio license bidder.

CHAPTER 5

Rulemaking – Delegation, Limitations, and Alternatives

I. Expansion/Limitation of Agency Control and Power

The rulemaking process allows agencies to define and clarify standards. Furthermore, there is no question that the general nature of most legislation requires agencies to "fill in the gaps" and give specificity to behaviors that are sanctioned or required. Agencies are invested with considerable discretion to both clarify and articulate regulatory standards and, as _Chevron_ and its progeny demonstrate, accorded deference when the interpretations the agency provides are reasonable and consistent with congressional intent.

There are limitations on the scope and nature of the regulations agencies may articulate and there are limitations on the enforcement power agencies possess. Central to these limitations is the notion that an agency may not expand its power by virtue of regulation beyond what was contemplated by Congress. However, so long as the agency practice is generally consistent with congressional mandate, it may well be that some level of expansion of power or modification of procedure is inherent in a rule the agency articulates. The cases that follow explore some of these problems.

Delegation – Separation of Powers

Panama Refining and _Schechter Poultry_ raise basic questions regarding limits on the capacity of Congress to delegate power to the President, administrative agencies, or other organizations. At a superficial level, the limitations inherent in these cases are self-evident. Congress cannot delegate to an agency a power it does not have. When Congress delegates responsibility to implement a program to an agency, it must do so with some level of clarity so that the agency is not put in the position of making fundamental public policy choices – that being the domain of Congress. Congress cannot delegate unlimited power to an agency and, correspondingly, to the President, since that would impinge on the constitutional responsibility of Congress to make public policy on behalf of those it represents. Finally, Congress cannot delegate power or responsibility that it, Congress, is required to perform, e.g., taxation or impeachment. These principles are not particularly controversial. However, the question of the clarity of a delegation or the legitimacy of a delegation to a private entity have been litigated over and over again.

The argument regarding congressional delegation has at its base the principle of separation of powers. An unduly broad delegation to an administrative agency cedes the congressional responsibility to make public policy. Likewise, when a court reviews and rejects an agency formulation of public policy, it may well be undertaking a task more properly assigned to Congress. At this introductory level, suffice it to say that one is never far from the separation of powers problem.

Take Note

Formalists in the field believe that powers should be separated explicitly and with clarity. Functionalists take the position that powers were meant to be blended and it is inevitable that the Executive (through agencies) will perform policymaking functions, and that courts, from time to time, will do likewise.

PANAMA REFINING COMPANY V. RYAN

293 U.S. 388 (1935)

[CHIEF JUSTICE HUGHES] On July 11, 1933, the President, by Executive Order, prohibited "the transportation in interstate and foreign commerce of petroleum . . . produced or withdrawn from storage in excess of the amount permitted . . . by any State law or valid regulation or order prescribed thereunder . . . ." This action was based on § 9(c) of Title I of the National Industrial Recovery Act of June 16, 1933. That section provides:

> Sec. 9 . . .
>
> (c) The President is authorized to prohibit the transportation in interstate and foreign commerce of petroleum . . . produced or withdrawn from storage in excess of the amount permitted . . . by any state law or valid regulation or order prescribed thereunder . . . . Any violation of any order of the President issued under the provisions of this subsection shall be punishable by fine of not to exceed $ 1,000, or imprisonment for not to exceed six months, or both.

> . . . .

Section 9(c) is assailed upon the ground that it is an unconstitutional delegation of legislative power. The section purports to authorize the President to pass a prohibitory law. The subject to which this authority relates is defined [explicitly]. Assuming for the present purpose, without deciding, that the Congress has power to interdict the transportation of that excess in interstate and foreign commerce, the question whether that transportation shall be prohibited by law is obviously one of legislative policy. Accordingly, we look to the statute to see whether the Congress has declared a policy with respect to that subject. . . .

Section 9(c) is brief and unambiguous. . . . It does not qualify the President's authority by reference to the basis, or extent, of the State's limitation of production. Section 9(c) does not state whether, or in what circumstances or under what conditions, the President is to prohibit the transportation of the amount of petroleum or petroleum products produced in excess of the State's permission. It establishes no criterion to govern the President's course. It does not require any finding by the President as a condition of his action. The Congress in § 9(c) thus declares no policy as to the transportation of the excess production. . . . [I]t gives to the President an unlimited authority to determine the policy and to lay down the prohibition, or not to lay it down, as he may see fit. And disobedience to his order is made a crime punishable by fine and imprisonment.

. . . .

[The] general outline of policy [in the statute] contains nothing as to the circumstances or conditions in which transportation of petroleum or petroleum products should be prohibited – nothing as to the policy of prohibiting, or not prohibiting, the transportation of production exceeding what the States allow. The general policy declared is "to remove obstructions to the free flow of interstate and foreign commerce." As to production, the section lays down no policy of limitation. It favors the fullest possible utilization of the present productive capacity of industries. It speaks, parenthetically, of a possible temporary restriction of production, but of what, or in what circumstances, it gives no suggestion. . . . It is manifest that this broad outline is simply an introduction of the Act, leaving the legislative policy as to particular subjects to be declared and defined, if at all, by the subsequent sections.

It is no answer to insist that deleterious consequences follow the transportation of "hot oil" – oil exceeding state allowances. The Congress did not prohibit that transportation. The Congress did not undertake to say that the transportation of "hot oil" was injurious. The Congress did not say that transportation of that oil was "unfair competition." The Congress did not declare in what circumstances that transportation should be forbidden, or require the President to make any determination as to any facts or circumstances. Among the numerous and diverse objectives broadly stated, the President was not required to choose. The President was not required to ascertain and proclaim the conditions prevailing in the industry which made the prohibition necessary. The Congress left the matter to the President without standard or rule, to be dealt with as he pleased. . . .

The question whether such a delegation of legislative power is permitted by the Constitution is not answered by the argument that it should be assumed that the President has acted, and will act, for what he believes to be the public good. The point is not one of motives but of constitutional authority, for which the best of motives is not a substitute. . . .

The Constitution provides that "All legislative powers herein granted shall be vested in a Congress of the United States . . . ." Art. I, § 1. . . . The Congress manifestly is not permitted to abdicate, or to transfer to others, the essential legislative functions with which it is thus vested . . . . Thus, in every case in which the question has been raised, the Court has recognized that there are limits of delegation which there is no constitutional authority to transcend. We think that § 9(c) goes beyond those limits. As to the transportation of oil production in excess of state permission, the Congress has declared no policy, has established no standard, has laid down no rule. There is no requirement, no definition of circumstances and conditions in which the transportation is to be allowed or prohibited.

If § 9(c) were held valid, it would be idle to pretend that anything would be left of limitations upon the power of the Congress to delegate its law-making function. The reasoning of the many decisions we have reviewed would be made vacuous and their distinctions nugatory. Instead of performing its law-making function, the Congress could at will and as to such subjects as it chose transfer that function to the President or other officer or to an administrative body. The question is not of the intrinsic importance of the particular statute before us, but of the constitutional processes of legislation which are an essential part of our system of government.

Reversed.

[JUSTICE CARDOZO, dissenting.]

I am unable to assent to the conclusion that § 9(c) . . . is to be nullified upon the ground that his discretion is too broad or for any other reason. . . . I concede that to uphold the delegation there is need to discover in the terms of the act a standard reasonably clear whereby discretion must be governed. I deny that such a standard is lacking . . . when the act . . . is considered as a whole. . . . The Act as a whole is entitled as one "To encourage national industrial recovery, to foster fair competition, and to provide for the construction of certain useful public works, and for other purposes"; and the heading of Title I, which includes §§ 1 to 10, is "Industrial Recovery."

I am persuaded that a reference, express or implied, to the policy of Congress as declared in § 1 is a sufficient definition of a standard to make the statute valid. Discretion is not unconfined and vagrant. It is canalized within banks that keep it from overflowing. . . . Under these decisions the separation of powers between the Executive and Congress is not a doctrinaire concept to be made use of with pedantic rigor. There must be sensible approximation, there must be elasticity of adjustment, in response to the practical necessities of government, which cannot foresee today the developments of tomorrow in their nearly infinite variety. . . .

Underlying Case Documents

The case referenced:
Executive Order 6199
The National Industrial Recovery Act

Since *Panama Refining* was decided, most courts have been disinclined to express the minimum linguistic precision requirements for delegation. That is not to say that the delegation question is – or ought to be – set aside. Two recent cases raise questions pertaining to agency authority worthy of your consideration.

1. The First Circuit dealt with a dispute between the Secretary of the Interior, the State of Rhode Island, and the Narragansett Tribe "over a parcel of land taken into trust [by the federal government] and designated for Indian housing." In *Carcieri v. Kempthorne*, 497 F.3d 15 (1st Cir. 2007), *cert. granted*, 128 S. Ct. 1443 (2008), the court had to decide, *inter alia*, whether Section 5 of the Indian Reorganization Act of 1934 (IRA), 25 U.S.C. § 465, was sufficiently clear – or whether it was an unconstitutional delegation. Section 465 authorized the Secretary "in his discretion" to acquire and take into trust for Indian tribes "any interest in lands . . . within or without existing reservations . . . for the purpose of providing land for Indians." On the delegation question, the court found as follows:

> Congress "is not permitted to abdicate, or to transfer to others, the essential legislative functions with which it is . . . vested." *Panama Refining*. Yet, the Supreme Court has recognized that "in our increasingly complex society, replete with ever changing and more technical problems, Congress simply cannot do its job absent an ability to delegate power under broad general directives." *Mistretta v. United States*, *infra* Chapter 10. As a result, the Supreme Court has repeatedly held that Congress may confer decision-making authority on agencies as long as it "lay[s] down by legislative act an intelligible principle to which the person or body authorized to [act] is directed to conform." *Whitman v. Am. Trucking Ass'ns*, 531 U.S. 457, 472 (2001). The Court "has deemed it 'constitutionally sufficient if Congress clearly delineates the general policy, the public agency which is to apply it, and the boundaries of this delegated authority.'" *Mistretta*, [488 U.S. 361, 372-73 (1989)].

[In] *Confederated Tribes of Siletz Indians of Oregon v. United States*, 110 F.3d 688 (9th Cir. 1997), [the Ninth Circuit held] "[t]he general delegation of power to the Executive to take land into trust for the Indians is a valid delegation because Congress has decided under what circumstances land should be taken into trust and has delegated to the Secretary of the Interior the task of deciding when this power should be used." *Id. at 698*.

The Supreme Court has upheld the constitutionality of statutes authorizing regulation in the "public interest" as well as statutes authorizing regulation to ensure fairness and equity. As the Court stated in its most recent nondelegation decision, it has "almost never felt qualified to second-guess Congress regarding the permissible degree of policy judgment that can be left to those executing or applying the law." *Am. Trucking Assn's.* We similarly decline to do so here. We hold that § 465 is not an unconstitutional delegation of legislative authority.

Given the legislation in question, what land would the Secretary be prohibited from acquiring? What are the intelligible standards? Section 465 allows a taking in "his discretion" for "any interest in lands" "within or without existing reservations" "for the purpose of providing land for Indians."

2. In *Save Our Heritage Organization v. Gonzales*, 533 F. Supp. 2d 58 (D.C. Cir. 2008), the court dealt with several pieces of legislation pertaining to homeland security. The case involved opposition to the construction of barriers, concrete and otherwise, at and near various border locations. The delegation question involves the Illegal Immigration Reform and Immigrant Responsibility Act, which gives the Secretary of Homeland Security the power to "to install additional physical barriers and roads . . . in the vicinity of the United States border to deter illegal crossings. . . ." 8 U.S.C. § 1103.

To the extent that such barriers may have an adverse effect on endangered species – or the environment – the Act gives the Secretary the power

> to waive the requirements of the Endangered Species Act of 1973 and the National Environmental Policy Act of 1969 upon making a determination that the waiver is "necessary to ensure expeditious construction of the barriers and roads under this section. . . . The REAL ID Act of 2005 expanded the Secretary's waiver . . . such that "[n]otwithstanding any other provision of law, the Secretary . . . shall have the authority to waive all legal requirements" that the Secretary, in his "sole discretion, determines necessary to ensure expeditious construction of the barriers and roads under this section." . . . .

> In determining whether a delegation of authority from Congress to the Executive Branch is impermissibly broad, a court asks whether the statute in question sets forth "an intelligible principle to which the person or body authorized to [exercise the delegated authority] is directed to conform." Congress's ability to delegate power is broad and a statute need only "clearly delineate[] the general policy, the public agency which is to apply it, and the boundaries of this delegated authority."

The last Supreme Court cases expressly relying on . . . nondelegation [were] *Schechter Poultry* and *Panama Refining*. In describing those cases the Supreme Court has stated: "In the history of the Court we have found the requisite 'intelligible principle' lacking in only two statutes, one of which provided literally no guidance for the exercise of discretion, and the other of which conferred authority to regulate the entire economy on the basis of no more precise standard than stimulating the economy by assuring 'fair competition.'" *Am. Trucking Ass'ns*. The Supreme Court "[has] almost never felt qualified to second-guess Congress regarding the permissible degree of policy judgment that can be left to those executing or applying the law." . . . . [T]his Court finds that the Secretary's waiver authority is not an impermissible delegation of power to the Executive Branch. . . .

How can it be that giving the Secretary of Homeland Security the "authority to waive all legal requirements" is intelligible? Has Congress simply yielded to the Executive the responsibility to issue – or repeal – or suspend – all laws? Parenthetically, a year before the *Save Our Heritage* case, the district court considered a similar question in *Defenders of Wildlife v. Chertoff*, 527 F. Supp. 2d 119 (D.C. Cir. 2007), and affirmed the expansive power of the Secretary of Homeland Security.

Good Question!

For examples of use of executive power without notice or public participatory process, click HERE and HERE.

Do you see any Establishment Clause problems with the Council for Faith (referred to as part of the faith-based initiative of the prior administration)?

For More Information

There is wonderful current scholarship in the delegation field. *See, e.g.*, Patrick M. Garry, *The Unannounced Revolution: How the Court Has Indirectly Effected a Shift in the Separation of Powers*, 57 Ala. L. Rev. 689 (2006); Ronald J. Krotoszynski, Jr., *Reconsidering the Nondelegation Doctrine: Universal Service, the Power to Tax, and the Ratification Doctrine*, 80 Ind. L.J. 239 (2005); Michael Herz, *The Rehnquist Court and Administrative Law*, 99 Nw. U.L. Rev. 297 (2004); Saikrishna B. Prakash, *Branches Behaving Badly: The Predictable and Often Desirable Consequences of the Separation of Powers*, 12 Cornell J.L. & Pub. Pol'y 543 (2003); Peter M. Shane, *When Inter-Branch Norms Break Down: Of Arms-for-Hostages, "Orderly Shutdowns," Presidential Impeachments, and Judicial "Coups"*, 12 Cornell J.L. & Public Pol'y 503 (2003); Richard W. Murphy, *Separation of Powers and the Horizontal Force of Precedent*, 78 Notre Dame L. Rev. 1075 (2003); John F. Manning, *The Nondelegation Doctrine as a Canon of Avoidance*, 2000 Sup. Ct. Rev. 223 (2000); and the classic Cass R. Sunstein, *Constitutionalism After the New Deal*, 101 Harv. L. Rev. 421 (1987).

A. L. A. Schechter Poultry Corp. v. United States

<u>295 U.S. 495 (1935)</u>

[Chief Justice Hughes] Petitioners . . . were convicted [of] eighteen . . . violations of . . . the "Live Poultry Code," and on an additional count for conspiracy to commit such violations. . . . [T]he defendants contend[] that the Code had been adopted pursuant to an unconstitutional delegation by Congress of legislative power . . . .

The "Live Poultry Code" was promulgated under § 3 of the National Industrial Recovery Act. That section . . . authorizes the President to approve "codes of fair competition." Such a code may be approved for a trade or industry, upon application by one or more trade . . . associations . . ., if the President finds (1) that such associations . . . "impose no inequitable restrictions on admission to membership therein and are truly representative," and (2) that such codes are not designed "to promote monopolies or to eliminate or oppress small enterprises and will not operate to discriminate against them, and will tend to effectuate the policy" of Title I of the Act. . . . [T]he President may "impose . . . conditions . . . for the protection of consumers, competitors, employees, and others, and in furtherance of the public interest, and may provide such . . . exemptions from the provisions of such code as the President in his discretion deems necessary to effectuate the policy herein declared." Where such a code has not been approved, the President may prescribe one, either on his own motion or on complaint. . . .

The Code fixes the number of hours for work-days. . . . The article containing "general labor provisions" prohibits the employment of any person under sixteen years of age, and declares that employees shall have the right of "collective bargaining" . . . . The minimum number of employees, who shall be employed by slaughterhouse operators, is fixed. . . .

. . . We are told that the provision of the statute authorizing the adoption of codes must be viewed in the light of the grave national crisis with which Congress was confronted. . . . But [e]xtraordinary conditions do not create or enlarge constitutional power. . . . Accordingly, we look to the statute to see whether Congress has . . . attempted to transfer [the formulation of policy] to others. . . . The Act does not define "fair competition." "Unfair competition," as known to the common law, is a limited concept. . . . But . . . in its widest range, "unfair competition," as it has been understood in the law, does not reach the objectives of the codes which are authorized by the National Industrial Recovery Act. . . .

Under § 3, whatever "may tend to effectuate" the[] general purposes [of the Act] may be included in the "codes of fair competition." We think the conclusion is inescapable that the authority sought to be conferred by § 3 was not merely to deal with "unfair competitive practices". . . . Rather, the purpose is . . . to authorize new and controlling prohibitions through codes of laws which would embrace what the formulators would propose, and what the President would approve . . . as wise and beneficient measures for the government of trades and industries in order to bring about their rehabilitation, correction and development. . . .

[One could not] seriously contend[] that Congress could delegate its legislative authority to trade . . . associations . . . so as to empower them to enact the laws they deem to be wise and beneficent for the rehabilitation and expansion of their trade . . . . Could trade . . . associations . . . be [considered] legislative bodies for that purpose because such associations . . . are familiar with the problems of their enterprises? And, could an effort of that sort be made valid by such a preface of generalities as to permissible aims as we find in section 1 of title I? The answer is obvious. Such a delegation of legislative power is unknown to our law and is utterly inconsistent with the constitutional prerogatives and duties of Congress. . . .

Accordingly we turn to the Recovery Act to ascertain what limits have been set to the exercise of the President's discretion. . . . [The Act's] restrictions leave virtually untouched the field of policy. . . . [The President] may roam at will and . . . approve or disapprove . . . proposals as he may see fit. . . .

. . . The Act provides for the creation by the President of administrative agencies to assist him, but the action or reports of such agencies . . . have no sanction beyond the will of the President, who may accept, modify or reject them as he pleases. Such recommendations or findings in no way limit [the President's] authority . . . . And this authority relates to a host of different trades and industries, thus extending the President's discretion to all the varieties of laws which he may deem to be beneficial in dealing with the vast array of commercial and industrial activities throughout the country.

Such a sweeping delegation of legislative power finds no support in the decisions upon which the Government especially relies. . . .

———————————

Underlying Case Documents

The case referenced:
The Live Poultry Code
The National Industrial Recovery Act

Of course, the story of the Schechters did not end with the case. For a
NEW YORK TIMES book review on THE FORGOTTEN MAN: A NEW HISTORY OF
THE GREAT DEPRESSION, which discusses the Schechters in more detail,
click HERE. The book review links to the first chapter of the book as well
as original NEW YORK TIMES articles about the Schechters, some of which
can also be directly accessed HERE, HERE, and HERE.

---

1. In *Carter v. Carter Coal Co.*, 298 U.S. 238, 311 (1936), the Court expressed
concern about delegation without meaningful metes and bound, particularly to a
private group:

> "This is legislative delegation in its most obnoxious form; for it is not even
> delegation to an official or an official body, presumptively disinterested, but to
> private persons. . . ." In *Schechter Poultry*, the Court wondered if Congress would
> have the audacity not only to yield unrestricted power to the executive but to permit
> private "trade or industrial associations or groups be constituted legislative bodies
> [solely because] such associations or groups are familiar with the problems of their
> enterprises. . . ? Such a delegation of legislative power is unknown to our law and
> is utterly inconsistent with the constitutional prerogatives and duties of Congress."

Privatization is so common at present that it may seem odd to consider the questions raised in *Carter Coal* and *Schechter* – but one has to wonder whether, in
the absence of "intelligible standards" and in the presence of seemingly limitless
privatized governance (if there is such a thing) the balance is somewhat askew.
What functions of government cannot be delegated to private entities? If your
answer is national defense, think again.

2. In February 2008, Professor Laura A. Dickinson testified before the Senate
Homeland Security and Governmental Affairs Committee. *U.S. Use of Private Security Firms Overseas*, CQ Congressional Testimony, February 27, 2008.

> It is extremely important that Congress move forward with this Committee's efforts
> to impose greater contractual standards and monitoring requirements on private
> security contractors.

This testimony was directed at the activities of Blackwater, Inc., a private contractor responsible for a number of conventional governmental functions including

armed protection of embassy, consular, and diplomatic personnel. As of February 2008, "[t]he Defense Department ha[d] 163,590 contractors in Iraq and 36,520 in Afghanistan. . . ." Faith Bremner, *Tester Takes on War Contracting*, GREAT FALLS TRIB., Feb. 28, 2008, available at http://tester.senate.gov/Newsroom/02282008 tribune contracting.cfm (last visited July 31, 2008). As this casebook goes to press, there are 159,000 troops in Iraq and 34,000 in Afghanistan, meaning there is an approximately equal number of U.S. troops and U.S. contractors in these areas.

3. On the civilian side, "[t]here are currently fewer than 1.9 million civilian employees of the federal government" and six times that number of private contract employees. Paul Verkuil, *Public Law Limitations on Privatization of Government Functions*, 84 N.C.L. REV. 397, n.1, n.2 (2006). Professor Sacha M. Coupet cautions about the risks associated with privatizing child welfare in *The Subtlety of State Action in Privatized Child Welfare Services*, 11 CHAP. L. REV. 85 (2007), leading with a quote from the 19th Century:

> He [who] acts in the name and for the State, and is clothed with the State's power, his act is that of the State. This must be so, or the constitutional prohibition [against government deprivation of property, life or liberty] has no meaning. Then the State has clothed one of its agents with power to annul or to evade it. *Ex parte Commonwealth of Virginia*, 100 U.S. 339, 347 (1879).

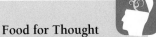

Food for Thought

When private actors perform historically public functions, what constitutional constraints are imposed? In privately run "charter schools," prisons, and immigration detention centers (to name but a very small number of privatized public functions) what rights and entitlements apply in contested individual cases (adjudication)? What are the standards for rulemaking?

4. Any delegation of power without intelligible standards or meaningful limits is – or ought to be – a matter worthy of consideration. *Schechter* and *Panama Refining* lay the foundation for such inquiry but, for better or worse, little has been built on that foundation. In *Massieu v. Reno*, 91 F. Supp. 416 (3d Cir. 1996), *rev'd on other grounds*, 91 F.3d 416 (3d Cir. 1996), the court threw out a deportation rule that allowed a person to be excluded if their presence had "adverse foreign policy consequences." The statute, 8 U.S.C. § 1251(a)(4)(C)(i), reads: "An alien whose presence or activities in the United States the Secretary of State has reasonable grounds to believe would have potentially serious adverse foreign policy consequences for the United States is deportable."

A few years later a federal district court explained that the statute was flawed because: "In such circumstances, aliens had no way of knowing when the Secretary would deem their presence to have 'potentially serious adverse foreign policy consequences.'" *Humanitarian Law Project v. Reno*, 9 F. Supp. 2d 1176 (C.D. Cal.

1998). So that you are not in any way misled, *Massieu v. Reno*, the first of the two cases in this note, is one of a tiny number of cases that follow this line of analysis.

5. In a variety of dissenting opinions, various Justices have set out the arguments for nondelegation, i.e., either forcing Congress to exercise its constitutionally mandated decisional responsibility without fobbing it off on the Executive branch or on some nongovernmental entity, or delegating power only after the fundamental policy choices have been made by drafting legislation that communicates these choices with precision and clarity. The counter argument appears to be dominant: It is neither wise nor possible, given the complexity of governance, for Congress to decide all the choices that are and will become necessary to any sophisticated regulatory endeavor. Agencies have rulemaking and adjudicatory power precisely for that reason – and their action must be reasoned, supported by records, and subject to judicial review.

In case it has not become obvious, this is a matter of some political sensitivity. Those who believe deeply in permitting agencies to achieve the laudable goals underlying environmental, civil rights, human rights, social welfare, and public safety may well believe that revival of nondelegation is a smokescreen for suppression of progressive interests. Another group may well believe that the Executive (in the form of an agency) has garnered excessive power at the invitation of a captive Congress that has been all-too-willing to cede its responsibility in the name of national security, free market theory, or (dare we suggest it) laziness and political horse-trading. Still others take the position that all of the above is inconsequential: The Constitution vests in Congress the responsibility to act on behalf of the people, to make law and set policy – and it abdicates that responsibility when it yields power to governmental agencies (or nongovernmental entities) but does so without meaningful limits or guidance.

Good Questions!

For a very quick and admittedly unsophisticated self-analysis, ask yourself whether you would be content to have your professor give your final exams to a couple of her or his research assistants who have already taken administrative law (for the entry of your final grade). First, does this seem a proper group to handle this task? Second, assume your professor provides no grade scale and no model answer – but trusts that the assistants are bright and have good judgment – is this a satisfactory delegation? Is this a task that can properly even *be* delegated?

6. In *Skinner v. Mid-American Pipeline, 490 U.S. 212 (1989)*, the Court upheld legislation that allowed an agency to establish a pricing structure with "user fees" without further guidance. Decisions of this type derive their juridical sustenance more from *Yakus v. United States, 321 U.S. 414 (1944)*, than from *Schechter* and

Panama. *Yakus* upheld the Emergency Price Control Act of 1942, legislation that established a comprehensive program to control prices to limit excess profits during a time of war with little more congressional direction than a mandate to put into place a "comprehensive scheme" that would cap prices if they rise in a manner "inconsistent with the purposes of the Act." The Court went on to note that a standard would become suspect – or unintelligible – only if there were an "absence of standards" such that it would be "impossible" to ascertain the will of Congress. Did the *Yakus* Court apply its own standard?

7. *United States v. Dhafir*, 461 F.3d 211 (2d Cir. 2006).

> Defendant-Appellant Osameh Al Wahaidy pled guilty to transferring money into Iraq on three specific occasions in 1999 and 2000, in violation of Executive Orders and regulations issued pursuant to the IEEPA [International Emergency Economic Powers Act], but preserved his right to bring a constitutional challenge to the statute. . . .
>
> The IEEPA, enacted in 1977 . . . confers on the President certain powers to respond to any threat to the national security, foreign policy or economy of the United States that is "unusual and extraordinary" and that "has its source in whole or substantial part outside the United States." The President is granted the power to "investigate, regulate, or prohibit" various commercial activities, including "any transactions in foreign exchange" . . . only if and when the President declares a national emergency with respect to the threat. . . . The violation of an Executive Order or regulation promulgated pursuant to the IEEPA is punishable by a fine of not more than $50,000 and imprisonment for not more than twenty years.
>
> The IEEPA reserves a continuing role for Congress. Thus, the IEEPA provides that "[t]he President, in every possible instance, shall consult with the Congress before exercising any of the authorities granted," that he "shall consult regularly with the Congress so long as such authorities are exercised," and that he shall report periodically concerning any actions taken in the exercise of the delegated authority. Congress can terminate the President's declaration of emergency "by concurrent resolution . . . ."
>
> Following the Iraqi invasion of Kuwait in August, 1990, President George H.W. Bush issued four emergency Executive Orders declaring a national emergency, and prohibiting trade, transportation and financial transactions with Iraq and Kuwait. . . . [That day] the Senate passed a resolution commending the measures taken and urging the President to act immediately to enforce the IEEPA and to impose sanctions against Iraq . . . .
>
> Al Wahaidy argues that the IEEPA is an improper delegation to the President of the Congressional authority to create criminal offenses . . . . The Constitution vests in Congress the legislative power to define criminal conduct . . . . Delegations of congressional authority are upheld "[s]o long as Congress 'shall lay down by legislative act an intelligible principle to which the person or body authorized to [exercise the delegated authority] is directed to conform.'" . . . . [In] foreign affairs, . . . delegation

is afforded even broader deference. *United States v. Curtiss-Wright Export Corp.* . . . .

IEEPA "meaningfully constrains the [President's] discretion," by requiring that "[t]he authorities granted to the President . . . may only be exercised to deal with an unusual and extraordinary threat with respect to which a national emergency has been declared." . . . . Significantly, the IEEPA relates to foreign affairs – an area in which the President has greater discretion. Additionally, Congress endorsed the President's actions and enacted legislation codifying the sanctions. There is thus no question that "the will of Congress has been obeyed."

8. As you read the next main case – referred to as the "*Benzene*" decision – see if you can fit it in with one of the jurisprudential and ideological strands in this field. Do you have a sense of the meaning of terms like "feasible" and "reasonable" – or, at a minimum, would you know where to turn to get useful and reliable definitions and parameters for these words?

———————

Hypothetical

Concerned about the low nutritional content and overabundance of fat and calories in public school lunches, Congress enacted the Fit, Healthy and Nutritious School Lunch Act, popularly known as the "Healthy Lunch Act." The statute requires that existing public school lunches comply with minimum levels of enumerated nutrients (*e.g.*, iron, calcium, several vitamins and minerals) and stay within specified limits on calories, fat and sugar depending on the specific food item. The statute also authorizes the Department of Education to promulgate subsequent regulations that would "add to the list of required nutrients provided in this Act, providing minimum required quantities of the respective newly enumerated nutrients, adjust the minimum required quantities of the already enumerated nutrients, and modify the already enumerated limits for fat and calories in the foods covered by this statute or other foods identified by the Department as requiring nutritional controls." The statute fails to specify how the agency should go about making these additions, modifications and adjustments to the lists and levels provided in the statute. Is the Healthy Lunch Act consistent with the Nondelegation Doctrine?

INDUSTRIAL UNION DEPARTMENT, AFL-CIO V. AMERICAN PETROLEUM INSTITUTE

448 U.S. 607 (1980)

[JUSTICE STEVENS] The Occupational Safety and Health Act of 1970 was enacted for the purpose of ensuring safe and healthful working conditions for every working man and woman in the Nation. This litigation concerns a standard promulgated by the Secretary of Labor to regulate occupational exposure to benzene, a substance which has been shown to cause cancer at high exposure levels. The principal question is whether such a showing is a sufficient basis for a standard that places the most stringent limitation on exposure to benzene that is technologically and economically possible.

. . . The basic definition of an "occupational safety and health standard" is found in § 3(8), which provides:

> The term "occupational safety and health standard" means a standard which requires conditions . . . *reasonably necessary or appropriate* to provide safe or healthful employment . . . .

Where toxic materials or harmful physical agents are concerned, a standard must also comply with § 6(b)(5), which provides:

> The Secretary . . . shall set the standard which most adequately assures, *to the extent feasible*, on the basis of the *best available evidence*, that no employee will suffer material impairment of health or functional capacity even if such employee has regular exposure to the hazard dealt with by such standard for the period of his working life. . . . [Emphasis added.]

Wherever the toxic material to be regulated is a carcinogen, the Secretary has taken the position that no safe exposure level can be determined and that § 6(b)(5) requires him to set an exposure limit at the lowest technologically feasible level that will not impair the viability of the industries regulated. In this case, after having determined that there is a causal connection between benzene and leukemia (a cancer of the white blood cells), the Secretary set an exposure limit on airborne concentrations of benzene of one part benzene per million parts of air (1 ppm), regulated dermal and eye contact with solutions containing benzene, and imposed complex monitoring and medical testing requirements on employers whose workplaces contain 0.5 ppm or more of benzene.

On pre-enforcement review . . . the Fifth Circuit held the regulation invalid. The court concluded that the Occupational Safety and Health Administration (OSHA) had exceeded its standard-setting authority because it had not shown that the new benzene exposure limit was "reasonably necessary or appropriate to provide safe or healthful employment" as required by § 3(8), and because § 6(b)(5) does "not give OSHA the unbridled discretion to adopt standards designed to create absolutely risk-free workplaces regardless of costs." Reading the two provisions together, the Fifth Circuit held that the Secretary was under a duty to determine whether the benefits expected from the new standard bore a reasonable relationship to the costs that it imposed. The court noted that OSHA had made an estimate of the costs of compliance, but that the record lacked substantial evidence of any discernible benefits.

We agree with the Fifth Circuit's holding that § 3(8) requires the Secretary to find, as a threshold matter, that the toxic substance in question poses a significant health risk in the workplace and that a new, lower standard is therefore "reasonably necessary or appropriate to provide safe or healthful employment and places of employment." Unless and until such a finding is made, it is not necessary to address the further question whether the Court of Appeals correctly held that there must be a reasonable correlation between costs and benefits, or whether, as the federal parties argue, the Secretary is then required by § 6(b)(5) to promulgate a standard that goes as far as technologically and economically possible to eliminate the risk. . . .

. . . The Government interprets "feasible" as meaning technologically achievable at a cost that would not impair the viability of the industries subject to the regulation. The respondent industry representatives, on the other hand, argue that the Court of Appeals was correct in holding that the "reasonably necessary and appropriate" language of § 3(8), along with the feasibility requirement of § 6(b)(5), requires the Agency to quantify both the costs and the benefits of a proposed rule and to conclude that they are roughly commensurate.

In our view, it is not necessary to decide whether either the Government or industry is entirely correct. For we think it is clear that § 3(8) does apply to all permanent standards promulgated under the Act and that it requires the Secretary, before issuing any standard, to determine that it is reasonably necessary and appropriate to remedy a significant risk of material health impairment. . . . Because the Secretary did not make the required threshold finding in these cases, we have no occasion to determine whether costs must be weighed against benefits in an appropriate case. . . .

By empowering the Secretary to promulgate standards that are "reasonably necessary or appropriate to provide safe or healthful employment and places of employment," the Act implies that, before promulgating any standard, the Secretary must make a finding that the workplaces in question are not safe. But "safe" is not the equivalent of "risk-free." There are many activities that we engage in every day – such as driving a car or even breathing city air – that entail some risk of accident or material health impairment; nevertheless, few people would consider these activities "unsafe." Similarly, a workplace can hardly be considered "unsafe" unless it threatens the workers with a significant risk of harm.

Therefore, before he can promulgate *any* permanent health or safety standard, the Secretary is required to make a threshold finding that a place of employment is unsafe – in the sense that significant risks are present and can be eliminated or lessened by a change in practices. This requirement applies to permanent standards promulgated pursuant to § 6(b)(5), as well as to other types of permanent standards. For there is no reason why § 3(8)'s definition of a standard should not be deemed incorporated by reference into § 6(b)(5). . . . That section repeatedly uses the term "standard" without suggesting any exception from, or qualification of, the general definition; on the contrary, it directs the Secretary to select "*the standard*" – that is to say, one of various possible alternatives that satisfy the basic definition in § 3(8) – that is most protective. Moreover, requiring the Secretary to make a threshold finding of significant risk is consistent with the scope of the regulatory power granted to him by § 6(b)(5), which empowers the Secretary to promulgate standards, not for chemicals and physical agents generally, but for "*toxic* materials" and "*harmful* physical agents." . . . .

If the Government were correct in arguing that neither § 3(8) nor § 6(b)(5) requires that the risk from a toxic substance be quantified sufficiently to enable the Secretary to characterize it as significant in an understandable way, the statute would make such a "sweeping delegation of legislative power" that it might be unconstitutional under the Court's reasoning in *Schechter Poultry* and *Panama Refining*. A construction of the statute that avoids this kind of open-ended grant should certainly be favored. . . .

Finally, with respect to the legislative history, it is important to note that Congress repeatedly expressed its concern about allowing the Secretary to have too much power over American industry. . . . This effort by Congress to limit the Secretary's power is not consistent with a view that the mere possibility that some employee somewhere in the country may confront some risk of cancer is a sufficient basis for the exercise of the Secretary's power to require the expenditure of hundreds of millions of dollars to minimize that risk. . . .

. . . As we read the statute, the burden was on the Agency to show, on the basis of substantial evidence, that it is at least more likely than not that long-term exposure to 10 ppm of benzene presents a significant risk of material health impairment. Ordinarily, it is the proponent of a rule or order who has the burden of proof in administrative proceedings. . . . In this case OSHA did not even attempt to carry its burden of proof. The closest it came to making a finding that benzene presented a significant risk of harm in the workplace was its statement that the benefits to be derived from lowering the permissible exposure level from 10 to 1 ppm were "likely" to be "appreciable." . . . . The inadequacy of the Agency's findings can perhaps be illustrated best by its rejection of industry testimony . . . that, even under the most conservative extrapolation theory, current exposure levels would cause at most two deaths out of a population of about 30,000 workers every six years. . . .

. . . It is the Agency's responsibility to determine, in the first instance, what it considers to be a "significant" risk. Some risks are plainly acceptable and others are plainly unacceptable. If, for example, the odds are one in a billion that a person will die from cancer by taking a drink of chlorinated water, the risk clearly could not be considered significant. On the other hand, if the odds are one in a thousand that regular inhalation of gasoline vapors that are 2% benzene will be fatal, a reasonable person might well consider the risk significant and take appropriate steps to decrease or eliminate it. . . .

While the court below may have been correct in holding that, under the peculiar circumstances of this case, OSHA was required to obtain more information, there is no need for us to reach that issue. For, in order to justify a ban on dermal contact, the Agency must find that such a ban is "reasonably necessary and appropriate" to remove a significant risk of harm from such contact. The Agency did not make such a finding, but rather acted on the basis of the absolute, no-risk policy that it applies to carcinogens. Indeed, on this issue the Agency's position is even more untenable, inasmuch as it was required to assume not only that benzene in small doses is a carcinogen, but also that it can be absorbed through the skin in sufficient amounts to present a carcinogenic risk. These assumptions are not a proper substitute for the findings of a significant risk of harm required by the Act. . . .

[JUSTICE REHNQUIST, concurring.]

. . . I would . . . suggest that the widely varying positions advanced in the briefs of the parties and in the [opinion] of [the majority] demonstrate, perhaps better than any other fact, that Congress, the governmental body best suited and most obligated to make the choice confronting us in this litigation, has improperly delegated that choice to the Secretary of Labor and, derivatively, to this Court. . . . "That Congress cannot delegate legislative power to the President is a principle universally recognized as vital to the integrity and maintenance of the system of government ordained by the Constitution". *Marshall Field & Co. v. Clark*, 143 U.S. 649 (1892). The rule against delegation of legislative power is not, however, so cardinal a principle as to allow for no exception. . . .

Viewing the legislation at issue here in light of these principles, I believe that it fails to pass muster. Read literally, the relevant portion of § 6(b)(5) is completely precatory, admonishing the Secretary to adopt the most protective standard if he can, but excusing him from that duty if he cannot. In the case of a hazardous substance for which a "safe" level is either unknown or impractical, the language of § 6(b)(5) gives the Secretary absolutely no indication where on the continuum of relative safety he should draw his line. Especially in light of the importance of the interests at stake, I have no doubt that the provision at issue, standing alone, would violate the doctrine against uncanalized delegations of legislative power. . . .

––––––––––––––

1. JUSTICE REHNQUIST's concurring opinion emphasizes the necessity for Congress to make critical public policy choices and articulate those choices with an intelligible standard, thereby relieving the agencies (the Executive) and the courts from making public policy determinations. He distinguishes filling in gaps where expertise is necessary from making substantive policy determinations. The challenge is, of course, in deciding when a particular determination constitutes a new policy versus when a decision is simply the implementation or logical extension of existing public policy.

2. In *Whitman v. American Trucking Associations, Inc.*, 531 U.S. 457, 475-76 (2001), the Court rejected the notion that Congress must use a "determinate criterion" to be sure that policy choices of the legislature are made in Congress and merely carried out (as opposed to being invented) in the agencies. In dealing with fairly vague air quality standards, the Court held as follows:

Good Questions!

Does the relevant terminology in *Benzene*, "reasonably necessary or appropriate to provide a safe or healthful [place of] employment" and "set the standard which most adequately assures, to the extent feasible," fail to communicate in a way that you understand? Is it unintelligible? Is it less precise than the *Yakus* statute the Court upheld (discussed in the notes following *Schechter Poultry*) that permitted the government to concoct a nationwide price and rent control scheme that was "fair and equitable?" For a useful critique of nondelegation jurisprudence at the close of the 20th Century, you might take a look at the Symposium, *The Phoenix Rises Again: The Nondelegation Doctrine from Constitutional and Policy Perspectives*, 20 CARDOZO L. REV. 731 (1999).

It is true enough that the degree of agency discretion that is acceptable varies according to the scope of the power congressionally conferred. . . . [Congress] must provide substantial guidance on setting air standards that affect the entire national economy. But even in sweeping regulatory schemes we have never demanded . . . that statutes provide a "determinate criterion" for saying "how much [of the regulated harm] is too much." . . . . [In prior cases] we did not require the statute to decree how "imminent" was too imminent, or how "necessary" was necessary enough, or even – most relevant

> here – how "hazardous" was too hazardous . . . . [A] certain degree of discretion . . .
> inheres in most executive or judicial action." . . . . [Thus the term] "requisite" . . . fits
> comfortably within the scope of discretion permitted by our precedent.

Like *Benzene*, <u>Whitman</u> is an air quality case. How is "requisite" acceptable when "feasible" is not? For an interesting perspective on *Whitman*, see David M. Wagner, <u>American Trucking: The "New Non-Delegation Doctrine" is Dead (Long Live the Old One)</u>, 11 U. Balt. J. Envtl. L. 25 (2003).

The "determinate criterion," standard rejected in *Whitman* was used recently by the D.C. District Court in <u>Sierra Club v. Mainella, 459 F. Supp. 2d 76 (D.D.C. 2006)</u>, *appeal dismissed,* <u>Sierra Club v. Mainella, 2007 WL 1125716 (D.C. Cir., Mar. 30, 2007)</u>.

3. Justice Stevens' plurality opinion in *Benzene* expresses concern that OSHA will have "power to impose enormous costs that might produce little, if any, discernible benefit. . . ." Is this a concern about the precision of the delegation or about the insufficiency of the cost/benefit analysis in the agency standards? Given that the plurality appeared disinclined to deal head-on with the issue of imprecise delegation, were they driven by the potentially arbitrary nature of the cost/benefit analysis? As much as a cost/benefit formula appears to mimic scientific or mathematical objectivity, there is good reason to think that such a formulation is fraught with portent; political and personal priorities are as easily inserted into a cost/benefit calculus as they are in the interpretation of vague legislative text (e.g., fair and equitable, reasonable, or in the public interest). Granted, however, the point is debatable. Start with David M. Driesen, <u>Is Cost-Benefit Analysis Neutral?, 77 U. Colo. L. Rev. 335 (2006)</u>, and Lewis A. Kornhauser, <u>On Justifying Cost-Benefit Analysis, 29 J. Legal Stud. 1037 (2000)</u>

Take Note

The Kaldor-Hicks theory (or more accurately, insight) is that economic analysis does not benefit when one uses a personal comparative model as a basis to define efficiency. The theory presupposes that each actor or entity may well have assigned different values to "winning" or "losing" in any transaction and that there may well be transfers between winners and losers that balance efficiency. See Lawson, *Efficiency and Individualism,* 42 Duke L.J. 53, 89-90 (1992)

(cost benefit is "at best suspect and at worst in ruins"). On the other side of the cost/benefit aisle, see Cass R. Sunstein, <u>Cognition and Cost-Benefit Analysis, 29 J. Legal Stud. 1059 (2000)</u>, and Richard A. Posner, <u>Cost-Benefit Analysis: Definition, Justification, and Comment on Conference Papers, 29 J. Legal Stud. 1153 (2000)</u>. If you are schooled in <u>Kaldor-Hicks theory</u> and use that as a lens through which to assess cost/benefit, take a look at Guido Calabresi, <u>The Pointlessness of Pareto: Carrying Coase Further, 100 Yale L.J. 1211, 1212, 1218-19 (1991)</u>; C. Edwin Baker, *The Ideology of the Economic Analysis of Law,* 5 Phil. & Pub. Aff. 3 (1975);

and Ronald Dworkin, *Is Wealth a Value?*, 9 J. LEGAL STUD. 191 (1980).

4. If you sense that nondelegation is a bit slippery, you are not alone. Does it seem unreasonable to ask Congress to develop standards that are understandable, reflect fundamental policy choices, and include limits that prevent agencies from engaging in congressionally authorized arbitrary action? After all, how would a court know if an agency is acting in an arbitrary manner if it has been provided no meaningful limits on what it can sanction? Nonetheless, merely raising the topic can evoke an argument that one is anti-agency (we, your authors, certainly are not). The best evidence of this phenomenon lies in the fact that nondelegation has found its way into the ideological black hole knows as the canon of avoidance. *See* John F. Manning, *The Nondelegation Doctrine as a Canon of Avoidance*, 2000 SUP. CT. REV. 223, 244-46.

5. Delegation challenges often involve the question of whether the action of the executive is consistent with a legislative grant of power. On occasion, Congress provides not only a statute but other information setting forth expectations for and conditions of executive action. There is a debate, referenced in various places in the text, about the extent to which language not in the statute (e.g., the legislative history) can be used by the executive as a basis for action. Putting aside the question of the efficacy of the use of non-textual material, it is valuable to see the different ways the legislative branch can signal expectations to the executive. In anticipation of the largest single domestic expenditure in U.S. history, the American Investment and Recovery Act (the so-called February 2009 "stimulus package") the Speaker of the House issued a preliminary Conference Report setting out the goals and expectations for that legislation. To read that report, click HERE

Insufficiency in delegation is a failure of legislative process. If an agency is given general authority and need only fill in gaps (even if the putty used to fill the gaps includes major new substantive rules and policy) the nondelegation cases will not, in all likelihood, be a primary obstacle to agency action. If the delegation is so imprecise as to call into question the very authority to act, a separate doctrine emerges: An agency cannot cure a lack of delegated authority by promulgating new authority. It's a simple rule – but its application, the subject of the next case, is anything but simple.

FOOD AND DRUG ADMINISTRATION V. BROWN & WILLIAMSON TOBACCO CORPORATION

529 U.S. 120 (2000)

[JUSTICE O'CONNOR] In 1996, the Food and Drug Administration (FDA), after having expressly disavowed any such authority since its inception, asserted jurisdiction to regulate tobacco products. . . .

I.

The [Food, Drug, and Cosmetic Act (FDCA)] grants the FDA . . . the authority to regulate . . . "drugs" and "devices." The Act defines "drug" to include "articles (other than food) intended to affect the structure or any function of the body." It defines "device," in part, as "an instrument . . . which is . . . intended to affect the structure or any function of the body." The Act also grants the FDA the authority to regulate so-called "combination products," which "constitute a combination of a drug, device, or biologic product." The FDA has construed this provision as giving it the discretion to regulate combination products as drugs, as devices, or as both.

On August 11, 1995, the FDA published a proposed rule . . . designed to reduce the availability and attractiveness of tobacco products to young people. A public comment period followed, during which the FDA received over 700,000 submissions, more than "at any other time in its history on any other subject."

On August 28, 1996, the FDA issued a final rule entitled "Regulations Restricting the Sale and Distribution of Cigarettes and Smokeless Tobacco to Protect Children and Adolescents." The FDA determined that nicotine is a "drug" and that cigarettes and smokeless tobacco are "drug delivery devices," and therefore it had jurisdiction under the FDCA to regulate tobacco products . . . . First, the FDA found [that] nicotine "exerts psychoactive, or mood-altering, effects on the brain" that cause and sustain addiction, have both tranquilizing and stimulating effects, and control weight. Second, the FDA determined that these effects were "intended" under the FDCA because . . . consumers use tobacco products . . . to obtain these effects [and] manufacturers revealed that they "have 'designed' cigarettes to provide pharmacologically active doses of nicotine to consumers." Finally, the agency concluded that cigarettes and smokeless tobacco are "combination products" because, in addition to containing nicotine, they include device components that deliver a controlled amount of nicotine to the body.

Having resolved the jurisdictional question, the FDA next explained the policy justifications for its regulations. . . . It found that tobacco consumption was "the single leading cause of preventable death in the United States." . . . . The agency also determined that the only way to reduce the amount of tobacco-related illness and mortality was to reduce the level of addiction, a goal that could be accomplished only by preventing children and adolescents from starting to use tobacco. . . .

Based on these findings, the FDA promulgated regulations concerning tobacco products' promotion, labeling, and accessibility to children and adolescents. The access regulations prohibit the sale of cigarettes or smokeless tobacco to persons younger than 18; . . . prohibit the sale of cigarettes in quantities smaller than 20; . . . and prohibit sales through self-service displays and vending machines except in adult-only locations. The promotion regulations . . . prohibit outdoor advertising within 1,000 feet of any public playground or school; prohibit the distribution of any promotional items . . . bearing the manufacturer's brand name; and prohibit a manufacturer from sponsoring any athletic . . . or cultural event using its brand name. The labeling regulation requires that the statement, "A Nicotine-Delivery Device for Persons 18 or Older," appear on all tobacco product packages.

. . . Given the greater flexibility in the FDCA for the regulation of devices, the FDA determined that "the device authorities provide the most appropriate basis for regulating cigarettes and smokeless tobacco." Under 21 U.S.C. § 360j(e), the agency may "require that a device be restricted to sale [under certain] conditions . . . if, because of its potentiality for harmful effect . . ., [the FDA] determines that there cannot otherwise be reasonable assurance of its safety and effectiveness." The FDA reasoned that its regulations fell within the authority granted by § 360j(e) because they related to the sale or distribution of tobacco products and were necessary for providing a reasonable assurance of safety.

Respondents, a group of tobacco manufacturers, retailers, and advertisers, filed suit . . . . We granted the Government's petition for certiorari to determine whether the FDA has authority under the FDCA to regulate tobacco products as customarily marketed.

II.

The FDA's assertion of jurisdiction to regulate tobacco products is founded on its conclusions that nicotine is a "drug" and that cigarettes and smokeless tobacco are "drug delivery devices." . . . . [T]he FDA's claim to jurisdiction contravenes the clear intent of Congress.

. . . Because this case involves an administrative agency's construction of a statute that it administers, our analysis is governed by *Chevron* . . . . In determining whether Congress has specifically addressed the question at issue, a reviewing court should not confine itself to examining a particular statutory provision in isolation. The meaning – or ambiguity – of certain words or phrases may only become evident when placed in context. . . . Similarly, the meaning of one statute may be affected by other Acts, particularly where Congress has spoken subsequently and more specifically to the topic at hand. In addition, we must be guided . . . by common sense as to the manner in which Congress is likely to delegate a policy decision of such economic and political magnitude to an administrative agency. . . .

A.

Viewing the FDCA as a whole, it is evident that one of the Act's core objectives is to ensure that any product regulated by the FDA is "safe" and "effective" for its intended use. . . . Thus, the Act generally requires the FDA to prevent the marketing of any drug or device where the "potential for inflicting death or physical injury is not offset by the possibility of therapeutic benefit." In its rulemaking proceeding, the FDA quite exhaustively documented that "tobacco products are unsafe," "dangerous," and "cause great pain and suffering from illness." . . . . Indeed, the FDA characterized smoking as "a pediatric disease" because "one out of every three young people who become regular smokers . . . will die prematurely as a result."

These findings logically imply that, if tobacco products were "devices" under the FDCA, the FDA would be required to remove them from the market. Consider, first, the FDCA's provisions concerning . . . misbranding . . . . The Act prohibits "the introduction . . . into interstate commerce of any food, drug, device, or cosmetic that is . . . misbranded." In light of the FDA's findings, two distinct FDCA provisions would render cigarettes and smokeless tobacco misbranded devices. First, § 352(j) deems a drug or device misbranded "if it is dangerous to health when used [as] suggested in the labeling thereof." The FDA's findings make clear that tobacco products are "dangerous to health" when used in the manner prescribed. Second, a drug or device is misbranded under the Act "unless its labeling bears . . . adequate directions for use . . . ." Given the FDA's conclusions concerning the health consequences of tobacco use, there are no directions that could adequately protect consumers. That is, there are no directions that could make tobacco products safe for obtaining their intended effects. Thus, were tobacco products within the FDA's jurisdiction, the Act would deem them misbranded devices that could not be introduced into interstate commerce. Contrary to the dissent's contention, the Act admits no remedial discretion once it is evident that the device is misbranded.

Second, the FDCA requires the FDA to place all devices that it regulates into one of three classifications. . . . The FDA has yet to classify tobacco products. Instead, the regulations at issue here represent so-called "general controls," which the Act entitles the agency to impose in advance of classification. . . . [T]he FDA has stated that it will classify tobacco products "in a future rulemaking" as required by the Act. Given the FDA's findings regarding the health consequences of tobacco use, the agency would have to place cigarettes and smokeless tobacco in Class III because, even after the application of the Act's available controls, they would "present a potential unreasonable risk of illness or injury." As Class III devices, tobacco products would be subject to the FDCA's premarket approval process. Under these provisions, the FDA would be prohibited from approving an application for premarket approval without "a showing of reasonable assurance that such device is safe under the conditions of use prescribed . . . on the labeling thereof." In view of the FDA's conclusions regarding the health effects of tobacco use, the agency would have no basis for finding any such reasonable assurance of safety. Thus, once the FDA fulfilled its statutory obligation to classify tobacco products, it could not allow them to be marketed.

The FDCA's misbranding and device classification provisions therefore make evident that were the FDA to regulate cigarettes and smokeless tobacco, the Act would require the agency to ban them. In fact . . . the FDA itself has previously taken the position that if tobacco products were within its jurisdiction, "they would have to be removed from the market because it would be impossible to prove they were safe for their intended use."

Congress, however, has foreclosed the removal of tobacco products from the market. . . . [T]he United States Code . . . states that "the marketing of tobacco constitutes one of the greatest basic industries of the United States . . . and stable conditions therein are necessary to the general welfare." More importantly, Congress has directly addressed the problem of tobacco and health through legislation on six occasions since 1965. When Congress enacted these statutes, the adverse health consequences of tobacco use were well known, as were nicotine's pharmacological effects. . . . Congress' decisions to regulate labeling and advertising and to adopt the express policy of protecting "commerce and the national economy . . ." reveal its intent that tobacco products remain on the market. . . . A ban of tobacco products by the FDA would therefore plainly contradict congressional policy.

The FDA apparently recognized this dilemma and concluded, somewhat ironically, that tobacco products are actually "safe" within the meaning of the FDCA. In promulgating its regulations, the agency conceded that "tobacco products are unsafe, as that term is conventionally understood." Nonetheless, the FDA reasoned that, in determining whether a device is safe under the Act, it must consider "not only the risks presented by a product but also . . . the consequences of not permitting the product to be marketed." Applying this standard, the FDA found that, because of the high level of addiction among tobacco users, a ban would likely be "dangerous." In particular, current tobacco users could suffer from extreme withdrawal, the health care system and available pharmaceuticals might not be able to meet the treatment demands of those suffering from withdrawal, and a black market offering cigarettes even more dangerous than those currently sold legally would likely develop. The FDA therefore concluded that, "while taking cigarettes and smokeless tobacco off the market could . . . reduce death and disease . . ., the record does not establish that such a ban is the appropriate public health response under the act."

. . . But [that] judgment . . . is no substitute for the specific safety determinations required by the FDCA[]. Several provisions in the Act require the FDA to determine that the *product itself* is safe as used by consumers. That is, the product's probable therapeutic benefits must outweigh its risk of harm. In contrast, the FDA's conception of safety would allow the agency, with respect to each provision of the FDCA that requires the agency to determine a product's "safety" or "dangerousness," to compare the aggregate health effects of alternative administrative actions. This is a qualitatively different inquiry. Thus, although the FDA has concluded that a ban would be "dangerous," it has *not* concluded that tobacco products are "safe" as that term is used throughout the Act. . . .

. . . The FDA . . . may clearly regulate many "dangerous" products without banning them. Indeed, virtually every drug or device poses dangers under certain conditions. What the FDA may not do is conclude that a drug or device cannot be used safely for any therapeutic purpose and yet, at the same time, allow that product to remain on the market. Such regulation is incompatible with the FDCA's core objective of ensuring that every drug or device is safe and effective. . . . The inescapable conclusion is that there is no room for tobacco products within the FDCA's regulatory scheme. If they cannot be used safely for any therapeutic purpose, and yet they cannot be banned, they simply do not fit.

B.

In determining whether Congress has spoken directly to the FDA's authority to regulate tobacco, we must also consider in greater detail the tobacco-specific legislation that Congress has enacted over the past 35 years. At the time a statute is enacted, it may have a range of plausible meanings. Over time, however, subsequent acts can shape or focus those meanings. . . . This is particularly so where the scope of the earlier statute is broad but the subsequent statutes more specifically address the topic at hand. . . .

Congress has enacted six separate pieces of legislation since 1965 addressing the problem of tobacco use and human health. . . . In adopting each statute, Congress has acted against the backdrop of the FDA's consistent and repeated statements that it lacked authority under the FDCA to regulate tobacco absent claims of therapeutic benefit by the manufacturer. In fact, on several occasions over this period, . . . Congress considered and rejected bills that would have granted the FDA such jurisdiction. Under these circumstances, it is evident that Congress' tobacco-specific statutes have effectively ratified the FDA's long-held position that it lacks jurisdiction under the FDCA to regulate tobacco products. Congress has created a distinct regulatory scheme to address the problem of tobacco and health, and that scheme, as presently constructed, precludes any role for the FDA. . . .

Although the dissent takes issue with our discussion of the FDA's change in position, our conclusion does not rely on the fact that the FDA's assertion of jurisdiction represents a sharp break with its prior interpretation of the FDCA. Certainly . . . agencies "must be given ample latitude to 'adapt their rules and policies to the demands of changing circumstances.'" The consistency of the FDA's prior position is significant in this case for a different reason: it provides important context to Congress' enactment of its tobacco-specific legislation. When the FDA repeatedly informed Congress that the FDCA does not grant it the authority to regulate tobacco products, its statements were consistent with the agency's unwavering position since its inception, and with the position that its predecessor agency had first taken in 1914. Although not crucial, the consistency of the FDA's prior position bolsters the conclusion that when Congress created a distinct regulatory scheme addressing the subject of tobacco and health, it understood that the FDA is without jurisdiction to regulate tobacco products and ratified that position.

The dissent also argues that the proper inference to be drawn from Congress' tobacco-specific legislation is "critically ambivalent." We disagree. In that series of statutes, Congress crafted a specific legislative response to the problem of tobacco and health, and it did so with the understanding, based on repeated assertions by the FDA, that the agency has no authority under the FDCA to regulate tobacco products. Moreover, Congress expressly preempted any other regulation of the labeling of tobacco products concerning their health consequences, even though the oversight of labeling is central to the FDCA's regulatory scheme. And in addressing the subject, Congress consistently evidenced its intent to preclude any federal agency from exercising significant policymaking authority in the area. Under these circumstances, we believe the appropriate inference – that Congress intended to ratify the FDA's prior position that it lacks jurisdiction – is unmistakable. . . .

C.

. . . Deference under <u>*Chevron*</u> to an agency's construction of a statute that it administers is premised on the theory that a statute's ambiguity constitutes an implicit delegation from Congress to the agency to fill in the statutory gaps. In extraordinary cases, however, there may be reason to hesitate before concluding that Congress has intended such an implicit delegation.

This is hardly an ordinary case. . . . Owing to its unique place in American history and society, tobacco has its own unique political history. Congress, for better or for worse, has created a distinct regulatory scheme for tobacco products, squarely rejected proposals to give the FDA jurisdiction over tobacco, and repeatedly acted to preclude any agency from exercising significant policymaking authority in the area. Given this history and the breadth of the authority that the FDA has asserted, we are obliged to defer not to the agency's expansive construction of the statute, but to Congress' consistent judgment to deny the FDA this power. . . .

By no means do we question the seriousness of the problem that the FDA has sought to address. . . . Nonetheless, no matter how "important, conspicuous, and controversial" the issue, and regardless of how likely the public is to hold the Executive Branch politically accountable, an administrative agency's power to regulate in the public interest must always be grounded in a valid grant of authority from Congress. And "in our anxiety to effectuate the congressional purpose of protecting the public, we must take care not to extend the scope of the statute beyond the point where Congress indicated it would stop." Reading the FDCA as a whole, as well as in conjunction with Congress' subsequent tobacco-specific legislation, it is plain that Congress has not given the FDA the authority that it seeks to exercise here. For these reasons, the judgment . . . is affirmed. . . .

[JUSTICE BREYER, dissenting.]

[T]he majority nowhere denies the following two salient points. First, tobacco products (including cigarettes) fall within the scope of [the] statutory definition, read literally. Cigarettes achieve their mood-stabilizing effects through the interaction of the chemical nicotine and the cells of the central nervous system. Both cigarette manufacturers and smokers alike know of, and desire, that chemically induced result. Hence, cigarettes are "intended to affect" the body's "structure" and "function," in the literal sense of these words. Second, the statute's basic purpose – the protection of public health – supports the inclusion of cigarettes within its scope. Unregulated tobacco use causes "more than 400,000 people [to] die each year from tobacco-related illnesses, such as cancer, respiratory illnesses, and heart disease." . . . .

[T]he majority nonetheless reads the statute as *excluding* tobacco products for two basic reasons:

> (1) the FDCA does not "fit" the case of tobacco because the statute requires the FDA
> to prohibit dangerous drugs or devices (like cigarettes) outright, and the agency

concedes that simply banning the sale of cigarettes is not a proper remedy; and

(2) Congress has enacted other statutes, which, when viewed in light of the FDA's long history of denying tobacco-related jurisdiction and considered together with Congress' failure explicitly to grant the agency tobacco-specific authority, demonstrate that Congress did not intend for the FDA to exercise jurisdiction over tobacco.

In my view, neither of these propositions is valid. Rather, the FDCA does not significantly limit the FDA's remedial alternatives. And the later statutes do not tell the FDA it cannot exercise jurisdiction, but simply leave FDA jurisdictional law where Congress found it. *Cf.* Food and Drug Administration Modernization Act of 1997 (statute "shall" *not* "be construed to affect the question of whether" the FDA "has any authority to regulate any tobacco product").

. . . In short, I believe that the most important indicia of statutory meaning – language and purpose – along with the FDCA's legislative history . . . are sufficient to establish that the FDA has authority to regulate tobacco. . . . The inferences that the majority draws from later legislative history are not persuasive, since . . . one can just as easily infer from the later laws that Congress did not intend to affect the FDA's tobacco-related authority at all. And the fact that the FDA changed its mind about the scope of its own jurisdiction is legally insignificant because the agency's reasons for changing course are fully justified. Finally, the degree of accountability that likely will attach to the FDA's action in this case should alleviate any concern that Congress, rather than an administrative agency, ought to make this important regulatory decision.

Underlying Case Documents

The case referenced:
The Food, Drug, and Cosmetic Act
The FDA proposed rule to regulate tobacco
The FDA assertion of authority to regulate tobacco
The FDA rule regulating the sale of tobacco products
Food and Drug Administration Modernization Act of 1997

1. *Martin v. Vermont*, 819 A.2d 742 (Vt. 2003).

[The Department of Motor Vehicles denied Carol Ann Martin's request for IRISH or IRISH1 vanity plates, relying on a regulation prohibiting references to ethnic heritage.] Neither DMV in refusing to grant the "IRISH" plate, nor the State in its argument before this Court, have asserted that "IRISH" is a word that might be offensive to the public – undoubtedly because the general public would find the assertion more offensive than the word. . . .

Courts have generally upheld broad delegations of authority to administrative agencies, but agency action that "transcends the delegation will not be sustained." Here . . . Section 304(d) provides that vanity plates "shall be issued" in any combination of seven or less numbers and letters that do not duplicate or resemble a regular-issue plate. The Commissioner may, however, refuse to honor or revoke "any request that might be offensive or confusing to the general public." . . . . Notably, [this] sentence does not give the Commissioner the discretion to refuse to honor any request – period. Rather, the Commissioner "may" refuse to honor only those requests that might be confusing or offensive. . . .

[T]he challenged regulation extends beyond the statutory language and permits the Commissioner to reject requests for vanity plates that are themselves inoffensive but belong in one of several designated categories that include words with the potential to offend. Indeed . . . Martin's request for "IRISH" was refused, not because it might be offensive – there was no evidence or argument to that effect – but rather because it refers to ethnicity, a topic that would also include offensive ethnic slurs. . . . DMV is imposing its own policy with respect to vanity plate requests – one that is distinct from, and inconsistent with, the one adopted by the Legislature [and that is therefore beyond the delegated authority]."

Two years before *Martin*, the Second Circuit dealt with the broad First Amendment question involved with vanity plates. In <u>Perry v. McDonald, 280 F.3d 159 (2d Cir. 2001)</u>,

Perry submitted an application to the Vermont DMV for vanity plates for her motor vehicle. . . . [The relevant statute regarding such plates states:] "The commissioner may refuse to honor any request [for a vanity plate] that might be offensive or confusing to the general public." <u>Vt. Stat. Ann. 23, § 304(d) (2000)</u>. . . . [The] requested vanity plates [bore] the letters "SHTHPNS," which stand for "Shit Happens." . . . . Perry's inspiration in choosing this message was an asserted Alcoholics Anonymous slogan, "Shit happens (so don't let life's problems drive you to drink.") . . . . Although Perry's brief on appeal, and her counsel at oral argument, note that "SHTHPNS" may also be read as "Shout Happiness," Perry's own complaint in this lawsuit states that the letters at issue stand for "Shit Happens." . . . . [The court found that] (1) Vermont's license plates are a nonpublic forum for purposes of the First Amendment; (2) Vermont's prohibition on the use of automobile license plates bearing scatological terms that might be deemed offensive or confusing by the general public is reasonable and viewpoint-neutral; (3) Vermont's actions in revoking Perry's vanity plates did not constitute a prior restraint on speech, and Vermont's current vanity-plate regime is not an unconstitutional prior restraint on speech because its restrictions and procedures are reasonable and viewpoint-neutral; (4) Vermont's revocation of Perry's vanity plates prior to a hearing and Vermont's current revocation procedures do not infringe Perry's constitutional right to due process of law.

a. How is it that banning a phrase used in Alcoholics Anonymous – and extensively in popular culture (we believe no additional references are required to make this point) – is acceptable and within the scope of "confusing and offensive," whereas an ethnic term is not? What if instead of IRISH, the request was for LIMEY? What principle or canon of statutory construction is in play? *See* KENT GREENWALT, LEGISLATION: STATUTORY INTERPRETATION: 20 QUESTIONS 77 et. seq. (1999).

b. Take another look at finding four above. If you believe there is some First Amendment content in this case (which seems reasonable enough), is it appropriate to take adverse action prior to a hearing? What would have been lost by holding a hearing first?

c. The license plate issue raised in *Martin* surfaced in April 2009 when a Colorado resident with a fondness for tofu was advised that the letters on her license plate, "ILVTOFU," were beyond the bounds of decency at the Colorado Division of Motor Vehicles would permit. For an online account of the controversy, click HERE.

2. <u>*American Library Association v. Federal Communications Commission*, 406 F.3d 689 (D.C. Cir. 2005)</u>.

> [D]igital television service ("DTV") . . . permits broadcasters to transmit more information over a channel of electromagnetic spectrum than is possible through analog broadcasting. . . . In August 2002 . . . the Commission issued a notice of proposed rulemaking to inquire, *inter alia*, whether rules were needed to prevent the unauthorized copying and redistribution of digital television programming. Thousands of comments were filed in response . . . . In November 2003, the Commission adopted "broadcast flag" regulations, requiring that . . . devices capable of receiving digital television broadcast signals, manufactured on or after July 1, 2005, include technology allowing them to recognize the broadcast flag. The broadcast flag is a digital code embedded in a DTV broadcasting stream, which prevents digital television reception equipment from redistributing broadcast content. . . .

> The FCC argues here that the court should defer to the agency's interpretation of its ancillary jurisdiction under <u>*Chevron*</u>, because, in its view, the regulations promulgated in the Flag Order reflect a reasonable application of the agency's ancillary authority under the <u>Communications Act</u>. The agency's self-serving invocation of *Chevron* leaves out a crucial threshold consideration, i.e., whether the agency acted pursuant to delegated authority. As the court explained in <u>*Motion Picture Association of America, Inc. v. FCC*, 309 F.3d 796, 801 (D.C. Cir. 2002)</u>, an "agency's interpretation of statute is not entitled to deference absent a *delegation of authority* from Congress to regulate in the areas at issue." . . . .

> Because the Flag Order does not require demodulator products to give effect to the broadcast flag until *after* the DTV broadcast has been completed, the regulations adopted in the Flag Order do not fall within the scope of the Commission's general jurisdictional grant. . . . We can find nothing in the statute, its legislative history, the applicable case law, or agency practice indicating that Congress meant to provide the sweeping authority the FCC now claims over receiver apparatus. . . .

Is it really so far-fetched to think that the FCC does not have jurisdiction over the equipment in question? *See* Rob Frieden, *Internet Packet Sniffing and Its Impact on the Network Neutrality Debate and the Balance of Power Between Intellectual Property Creators and Consumers*, 18 FORD. INTEL. PROP. MEDIA & ENT. L.J. 633, 660 (2008).

Consider the consumer problem of interconnection capability involving various types of telecommunications equipment (like cell phones and PDAs) – most equipment is configured to limit the extent to which consumers can change brands for peripheral parts.

3. Are *Library Association* (note 2 above) and *Brown & Williamson* delegation cases? Are they more like *Chevron* step-zero decisions similar to *Gonzales v. Oregon*: "To begin with, the rule must be promulgated pursuant to authority Congress has delegated to the official. . . ." 546 U.S. 243, 258 (2006). *See* Cass R. Sunstein, *Chevron Step Zero*, 92 VA. L. REV. 187 (2006)? If you read the case to hold that the FDA was without authority over tobacco – completely – why the long opinion – and why wasn't the case unanimous? Can you read the statute in question in *Brown & Williamson* in a way that would include nicotine as a drug and cigarettes as a drug-delivery device?

4. After decades of debate and disagreement regarding the role of the FDA, in summer 2009 the Congress passed and the President signed legislation that gives the FDA regulatory responsibility for tobacco products. To see this legislation, click HERE.

WYETH V. LEVINE

555 U.S.   , 129 S. Ct. 1187, 173 L. Ed. 2d 51 (2009)

OPINION BY JUSTICE STEVENS

Directly injecting the drug Phenergan into a patient's vein creates a significant risk of catastrophic consequences. A Vermont jury found that petitioner Wyeth, the manufacturer of the drug, had failed to provide an adequate warning of that risk and awarded damages to respondent Diana Levine to compensate her for the amputation of her arm. The warnings on Phenergan's label had been deemed sufficient by the federal Food and Drug Administration (FDA) when it approved Wyeth's new drug application in 1955 and when it later approved changes in the drug's labeling. The question we must decide is whether the FDA's approvals provide Wyeth with a complete defense to Levine's tort claims. We conclude that they do not.

I

. . . .

[Levine prevailed at trial and was awarded $7.4 million in damages which was later reduced by the trial judge. The award was affirmed by the Vermont Supreme Court.]

II

. . . . The [narrow] question presented is whether federal law pre-empts Levine's claim that <u>Phenergan's</u> label did not contain an adequate warning about using the IV-push method of administration.

Our answer to that question must be guided by two cornerstones of our pre-emption jurisprudence. First, "the purpose of Congress is the ultimate touchstone in every pre-emption case." <u>Medtronic, Inc. v. Lohr, 518 U.S. 470, 485, 116 S.Ct. 2240, 135 L.Ed.2d 700 (1996)</u> (internal quotation marks omitted). Second, "[i]n all pre-emption cases, and particularly in those in which Congress has 'legislated ... in a field which the States have traditionally occupied,' ... we 'start with the assumption that the historic police powers of the States were not to be superseded by the Federal Act unless that was the clear and manifest purpose of Congress.' " <u>Lohr, 518 U.S., at 485, 116 S.Ct. 2240</u> (quoting <u>Rice v. Santa Fe Elevator Corp., 331 U.S. 218, 230, 67 S.Ct. 1146, 91 L.Ed. 1447 (1947)</u>). . . .

As it enlarged the FDA's powers to "protect the public health" and "assure the safety, effectiveness, and reliability of drugs," *id.,* at 780, Congress took care to preserve state law. The 1962 amendments added a saving clause, indicating that a provision of state law would only be invalidated upon a "direct and positive conflict" with the FDCA. . . . And when Congress enacted an express pre-emption provision for medical devices in 1976, . . . it declined to enact such a provision for prescription drugs.

. . . .

III

Wyeth first argues that Levine's state-law claims are pre-empted because it is impossible for it to comply with both the state-law duties underlying those claims and its federal labeling duties. The FDA's premarket approval of a new drug application includes the approval of the exact text in the proposed label. Generally speaking, a manufacturer may only change a drug label after the FDA approves a supplemental application. There is, however, an FDA regulation that permits a manufacturer to make certain changes to its label before receiving the agency's approval. Among other things, this "changes being effected" (CBE) regulation provides that if a manufacturer is changing a label to "add or strengthen a contraindication, warning, precaution, or adverse reaction" or to "add or strengthen an instruction about dosage and administration that is intended to increase the safe use of the drug product," it may make the labeling change upon filing its supplemental application with the FDA; it need not wait for FDA approval.

Wyeth argues that the CBE regulation is not implicated in this case because a 2008 amendment provides that a manufacturer may only change its label "to reflect newly acquired information." 73 Fed.Reg. 49609. Resting on this language (which Wyeth argues simply reaffirmed the interpretation of the regulation in effect when this case was tried), Wyeth contends that it could have changed Phenergan's label only in response to new information that the FDA had not considered. And it maintains that Levine has not pointed to any such information concerning the risks of IV-push administration. Thus, Wyeth insists, it was impossible for it to discharge its state-law obligation to provide a stronger warning about IV-push administration without violating federal law. Wyeth's argument misapprehends both the federal drug regulatory scheme and its burden in establishing a preemption defense.

. . . . As the FDA explained in its notice of the final rule, " 'newly acquired information' " is not limited to new data, but also encompasses "new analyses of previously submitted data." Id., at 49604. . . .

. . . . [A]s amputations continued to occur, Wyeth could have analyzed the accumulating data and added a stronger warning about IV-push administration of the drug.

Wyeth argues that if it had unilaterally added such a warning, it would have violated federal law governing unauthorized distribution and misbranding. Its argument that a change in Phenergan's labeling would have subjected it to liability for unauthorized distribution rests on the assumption that this labeling change would have rendered Phenergan a new drug lacking an effective application. But strengthening the warning about IV-push administration would not have made Phenergan a new drug. Nor would this warning have rendered Phenergan misbranded. . . . And the very idea that the FDA would bring an enforcement action against a manufacturer for strengthening a warning pursuant to the CBE regulation is difficult to accept-neither Wyeth nor the United States has identified a case in which the FDA has done so.

. . . .

Impossibility pre-emption is a demanding defense. On the record before us, Wyeth has failed to demonstrate that it was impossible for it to comply with both federal and state requirements. The CBE regulation permitted Wyeth to unilaterally strengthen its warning, and the mere fact that the FDA approved Phenergan's label does not establish that it would have prohibited such a change.

IV

Wyeth also argues that requiring it to comply with a state-law duty to provide a stronger warning about IV-push administration would obstruct the purposes and objectives of federal drug labeling regulation. Levine's tort claims, it maintains, are pre-empted because they interfere with "Congress's purpose to entrust an expert agency to make drug labeling decisions that strike a balance between competing objectives." Brief for Petitioner 46. We find no merit in this argument, which relies on an untenable interpretation of congressional intent and an overbroad view of an agency's power to pre-empt state law.

Wyeth contends that the FDCA establishes both a floor and a ceiling for drug regulation: Once the FDA has approved a drug's label, a state-law verdict may not deem the label inadequate, regardless of whether there is any evidence that the FDA has considered the stronger warning at issue. The most glaring problem with this argument is that all evidence of Congress' purposes is to the contrary. Building on its 1906 Act, Congress enacted the FDCA to bolster consumer protection against harmful products. Congress did not provide a federal remedy for consumers harmed by unsafe or ineffective drugs in the 1938 statute or in any subsequent amendment. Evidently, it determined that widely available state rights of action provided appropriate relief for injured consumers. . . .

If Congress thought state-law suits posed an obstacle to its objectives, it surely would have enacted an express pre-emption provision at some point during the FDCA's 70-year history. But despite its 1976 enactment of an express pre-emption provision for medical devices, see § 521, 90 Stat. 574 (codified at 21 U.S.C. § 360k(a)), Congress has not enacted such a provision for prescription drugs. Its silence on the issue, coupled with its certain awareness of the prevalence of state tort litigation, is powerful evidence that Congress did not intend FDA oversight to be the exclusive means of ensuring drug safety and effectiveness. . . .

Despite this evidence that Congress did not regard state tort litigation as an obstacle to achieving its purposes, Wyeth nonetheless maintains that, because the FDCA requires the FDA to determine that a drug is safe and effective under the conditions set forth in its labeling, the agency must be presumed to have performed a precise balancing of risks and benefits and to have established a specific labeling standard that leaves no room for different state-law judgments.

In advancing this argument, Wyeth relies not on any statement by Congress, but instead on the preamble to a 2006 FDA regulation governing the content and format of prescription drug labels. In that preamble, the FDA declared that the FDCA establishes "both a 'floor' and a 'ceiling,' " so that "FDA approval of labeling ... preempts conflicting or contrary State law." *Id., at 3934-3935*. It further stated that certain state-law actions, such as those involving failure-to-warn claims, "threaten FDA's statutorily prescribed role as the expert Federal agency responsible for evaluating and regulating drugs." *Id., at 3935*.

This Court has recognized that an agency regulation with the force of law can pre-empt conflicting state requirements. In such cases, the Court has performed its own conflict determination, relying on the substance of state and federal law and not on agency proclamations of pre-emption. We are faced with no such regulation in this case, but rather with an agency's mere assertion that state law is an obstacle to achieving its statutory objectives. Because Congress has not authorized the FDA to pre-empt state law directly, . . . the question is what weight we should accord the FDA's opinion.

. . . .

In keeping with Congress' decision not to pre-empt common-law tort suits, it appears that the FDA traditionally regarded state law as a complementary form of drug regulation. The FDA has limited resources to monitor the 11,000 drugs on the market, and manufacturers have superior access to information about their drugs, especially in the post-marketing phase as new risks emerge. State tort suits uncover unknown drug hazards and provide incentives for drug manufacturers to disclose safety risks promptly. They also serve a distinct compensatory function that may motivate injured persons to come forward with information. Failure-to-warn actions, in particular, lend force to the FDCA's premise that manufacturers, not the FDA, bear primary responsibility for their drug labeling at all times. Thus, the FDA long maintained that state law offers an additional, and important, layer of consumer protection that complements FDA regulation. The agency's 2006 preamble represents a dramatic change in position.

. . . .

In short, Wyeth has not persuaded us that failure-to-warn claims like Levine's obstruct the federal regulation of drug labeling. Congress has repeatedly declined to pre-empt state law, and the FDA's recently adopted position that state tort suits interfere with its statutory mandate is entitled to no weight. Although we recognize that some state-law claims might well frustrate the achievement of congressional objectives, this is not such a case.

V

We conclude that it is not impossible for Wyeth to comply with its state and federal law obligations and that Levine's common-law claims do not stand as an obstacle to the accomplishment of Congress' purposes in the FDCA. Accordingly, the judgment of the Vermont Supreme Court is affirmed.

It is so ordered.

[JUSTICE BREYER's concurring opinion is omitted.]

JUSTICE THOMAS, concurring.

. . . . I cannot join the majority's implicit endorsement of far-reaching implied pre-emption doctrines. In particular, I have become increasingly skeptical of this Court's "purposes and objectives" pre-emption jurisprudence. . . .

. . . . Under the vague and "potentially boundless" doctrine of "purposes and objectives" pre-emption . . . the Court has pre-empted state law based on its interpretation of broad federal policy objectives, legislative history, or generalized notions of congressional purposes that are not contained within the text of federal law.

. . . . Because such a sweeping approach to pre-emption leads to the illegitimate-and thus, unconstitutional-invalidation of state laws, I can no longer assent to a doctrine that pre-empts state laws merely because they "stan[d] as an obstacle to the accomplishment and execution of the full purposes and objectives" of federal law, *Hines,* 312 U.S., at 67, 61 S.Ct. 399, as perceived by this Court. I therefore respectfully concur only in the judgment.

JUSTICE ALITO, with whom THE CHIEF JUSTICE and JUSTICE SCALIA join, dissenting.

. . . .

To be sure, state tort suits can peacefully coexist with the FDA's labeling regime, and they have done so for decades. But this case is far from peaceful coexistence. The FDA told Wyeth that Phenergan's label renders its use "safe." But the State of Vermont, through its tort law, said: "Not so."

The state-law rule at issue here is squarely pre-empted. Therefore, I would reverse the judgment of the Supreme Court of Vermont.

Notes, Comments, and Questions

1. The politics of preemption are not entirely predictable. Those favoring aggressive federal regulation (sometimes characterized as liberal) will, on occasion, oppose co-extensive application of state tort law on the premise that it is at odds with the federal regulatory effort. Marin R. Scordato, *Federal Preemption of State Tort Claims*, 35 U.C. Davis L. Rev. 1, 3 (2001); Jean Macchiaroli Eggen, *The Normalization of Product Preemption Doctrine*, 57 Ala. L. Rev. 725 (2006).

2. *Wyeth* is one of a series of recent decisions that attempt to balance federal regulation and state tort liability. In rejecting defendant Wyeth's claim for preemption protection and upholding the Vermont judgment, the Court allowed to stand a "failure to warn" case – and failure to warn cases are most assuredly problematic. Any time one is harmed by a product, in hindsight, it is not all that unusual to assert that a warning might have helped. When there is a governmentally approved warning, as in *Wyeth*, it is understandable that a defendant would argue it has done all it is supposed to do – but, according to this decision, the defendant would be wrong. Richard L. Cupp, *Symposium: The Products Liability Restatement: Was It a Success?: Preemption's Rise (and Bit of a Fall) as Products Liability Reform, Wyeth, Riegel, Altria, and the Restatement (Third)'s Prescription Product Design Defect Standard*, 74 Brooklyn L. Rev. 727 (2009) (discussing the Restatement (Third) provision on pharmaceuticals, Sec. 6(c) and the impact of *Wyeth* and other recent preemption cases).

3. In Riegel v. Medtronic, 552 U.S. 312, ___, 128 S. Ct. 999, 1004, 1007 (2008), decided less than a year before Wyeth, the court *found* express preemption for Class III products approved under the Medical Devices Amendment Act of 1976, 21 U.S.C. § 360k(a) (2006) (MDA). Preemption of state tort law was premised in part on the extensive testing required prior to FDA approval under the MDA and the fact that subsequent manufacture of a product approved under this provision could not vary from the specifications established in the MDA review process. The Court found that Class III devices undergo a "rigorous regime of premarket approval." In the premarket approval process, the FDA reviews the device design, labeling, and manufacturing specifications and makes a determination as to whether the specifications provide a "reasonable assurance of safety and effectiveness."

Good Question!

Can one generalize about consumer protection and conclude that a comprehensive federal regulatory scheme is superior to state tort law if the goal is to protect the consumer? Take a look at the *Medtronic* case and ask yourself if the process the Court describes is more likely to protect consumer interests than the incentives for safer and more efficacious products generated by the possibility of a multi-million dollar damage award.

Based on Wyeth, one could conclude that the presence of state tort litigation options played a role in protecting the consumer. Interestingly enough, some commentators find the exact opposite to be true in Medtronic.

> [T]he opinion reflects a concern for consumer welfare. In Justice Antonin Scalia's majority opinion, the Court stressed that expert regulators are better-suited than juries to balance the safety risks of a particular medical device against the potential health benefits of the product. The Court pointed out that state tort litigation might very well force life-saving products off the market and thus hurt public health. From this perspective, Riegel . . . reflects the Court's skepticism of litigation as an effective tool for regulation and for protecting consumer welfare.

Robin S. Conrad, The Roberts Court and the Myth of a Pro-Business Bias, 49 SANTA CLARA L. REV. 997, 1007 (2009).

WHITMAN V. AMERICAN TRUCKING ASSOCIATIONS

531 U.S. 457 (2001)

[JUSTICE SCALIA] Section 109(a) of the CAA [Clean Air Act] requires the Administrator of the EPA to promulgate NAAQS for each air pollutant for which "air quality criteria" have been issued under § 108. Once a NAAQS has been promulgated, the Administrator must review the standard (and the criteria on which it is based) "at five-year intervals" and make "such revisions . . . as may be appropriate." These cases arose when, on July 18, 1997, the Administrator revised the NAAQS for particulate matter (PM) and ozone. American Trucking Associations, Inc., and . . . the States of Michigan, Ohio, and West Virginia challenged the new standards . . . .

. . . .

Section 109(b)(1) of the CAA instructs the EPA to set "ambient air quality standards the attainment and maintenance of which in the judgment of the Administrator, based on criteria [documents of § 108] and allowing an adequate margin of safety, are requisite to protect the public health." The Court of Appeals held that this section as interpreted by the Administrator did not provide an "intelligible principle" to guide the EPA's exercise of authority in setting NAAQS. . . . The court hence found that the EPA's interpretation (but not the statute itself) violated the nondelegation doctrine. We disagree.

In a delegation challenge, the constitutional question is whether the statute has delegated legislative power to the agency. Article I, § 1, of the Constitution vests "all legislative Powers herein granted . . . in a Congress of the United States." This text permits no delegation of those powers and so we repeatedly have said that when Congress confers decisionmaking authority upon agencies *Congress* must "lay down by legislative act an intelligible principle to which the person or body authorized to [act] is directed to conform." We have never suggested that an agency can cure an unlawful delegation of legislative power by adopting in its discretion a limiting construction of the statute. . . . [This idea] seems to us internally contradictory. The very choice of which portion of the power to exercise – that is to say, the prescription of the standard that Congress had omitted – would *itself* be an exercise of the forbidden legislative authority. Whether the statute delegates legislative power is a question for the courts, and an agency's voluntary self-denial has no bearing upon the answer.

We agree with the Solicitor General that the text of § 109(b)(1) of the CAA at a minimum requires that "for a discrete set of pollutants and based on published air quality criteria that reflect the latest scientific knowledge, EPA must establish uniform national standards at a level that is requisite to protect public health from the adverse effects of the pollutant in the ambient air." Requisite, in turn, "means sufficient, but not more than necessary." These limits on the EPA's discretion are strikingly similar to the ones we approved in *Touby v. United States*, which permitted the Attorney General to designate a drug as a controlled substance for purposes of criminal drug enforcement if doing so was "necessary to avoid an imminent hazard to the public safety." They also resemble the Occupational Safety and Health Act provision requiring the agency to "set the standard which most adequately assures, to the extent feasible, on the basis of the best available evidence, that no employee will suffer any impairment of health" – which the Court upheld in <u>*Industrial Union Dep't., AFL-CIO v. American Petroleum Institute*</u> . . . .

The scope of discretion § 109(b)(1) allows is in fact well within the outer limits of our nondelegation precedents. In the history of the Court we have found the requisite "intelligible principle" lacking in only two statutes, one of which provided literally no guidance for the exercise of discretion, and the other of which conferred authority to regulate the entire economy on the basis of no more precise a standard than stimulating the economy by assuring "fair competition." We have, on the other hand, upheld the validity of § 11(b)(2) of the Public Utility Holding Company Act of 1935, which gave the Securities and Exchange Commission authority to modify the structure of holding company systems so as to ensure that they are not "unduly or unnecessarily complicated" and do not "unfairly or inequitably distribute voting power among security holders." We have approved the wartime conferral of agency power to fix the prices of commodities at a level that "will be generally fair and equitable and will effectuate the [in some respects conflicting] purposes of the Act." And we have found an "intelligible principle" in various statutes authorizing regulation in the "public interest." In short, we have "almost never felt qualified to second-guess Congress regarding the permissible degree of policy judgment that can be left to those executing or applying the law."

It is true enough that the degree of agency discretion that is acceptable varies according to the scope of the power congressionally conferred. . . . But even in sweeping regulatory schemes we have never demanded, as the Court of Appeals did here, that statutes provide a "determinate criterion" for saying "how much [of the regulated harm] is too much." In *Touby*, for example, we did not require the statute to decree how "imminent" was too imminent, or how "necessary" was necessary enough, or even – most relevant here – how "hazardous" was too hazardous. . . . It is therefore not conclusive for delegation purposes that, as respondents argue, ozone and particulate matter are "nonthreshold" pollutants that inflict a continuum of adverse health effects at any airborne concentration greater than zero, and hence require the EPA to make judgments of degree. "[A] certain degree of discretion, and thus of lawmaking, inheres in most executive or judicial action." Section 109(b)(1) of the CAA, which to repeat we interpret as requiring the EPA to set air quality standards at the level that is "requisite" – that is, not lower or higher than is necessary – to protect the public health with an adequate margin of safety, fits comfortably within the scope of discretion permitted by our precedent.

We therefore reverse the judgment of the Court of Appeals remanding for reinterpretation that would avoid a supposed delegation of legislative power. It will remain for the Court of Appeals – on the remand that we direct for other reasons – to dispose of any other preserved challenge to the NAAQS. . . .

. . . .

[JUSTICE STEVENS, concurring in part.]

The Court has two choices. We could choose to articulate our ultimate disposition of this issue by frankly acknowledging that the power delegated to the EPA is "legislative" but nevertheless conclude that the delegation is constitutional because adequately limited by the terms of the authorizing statute. Alternatively, we could pretend, as the Court does, that the authority delegated to the EPA is somehow not "legislative power." Despite the fact that there is language in our opinions that supports the Court's articulation of our holding, I am persuaded that it would be both wiser and more faithful to what we have actually done in delegation cases to admit that agency rulemaking authority is "legislative power."

The proper characterization of governmental power should generally depend on the nature of the power, not on the identity of the person exercising it. . . . [A]n executive agency's exercise of rulemaking authority pursuant to a valid delegation from Congress is "legislative." As long as the delegation provides a sufficiently intelligible principle, there is nothing inherently unconstitutional about it. . . .

> ## Underlying Case Documents
>
> The case referenced:
> Section 108 of the Clean Air Act
> Section 109 of the Clean Air Act
> The revised NAAQS for particulate matter
> The revised NAAQS for ozone

1. Does the *Whitman* standard, "adequate margin of safety . . . requisite to protect the public health," 42 U.S.C. § 7409(a), seem imprecise? Does the term "adequate margin" provide the agency any more guidance than the term "feasible" in the *Benzene* case? The post-*Whitman* case law suggests that the guidance requirement is not all that demanding. In *Shivwits Band of Paiute Indians v. Utah*, 428 F.3d 966 (10th Cir. 2005), the court focused on this text from *Whitman*: "[T]he constitutional question is whether the statute has delegated legislative power to the agency[, and the Court has] 'almost never felt qualified to second-guess Congress.'" This is a minimalist perspective on the "intelligible standard" notion. In contrast, the court in *United States v. Martinez-Flores*, 428 F.3d 22, 27 (1st Cir. 2005), saw *Whitman* thusly: "[I]f Congress delegates a relatively narrow task, it need not cabin the actor's discretion as to how to accomplish that task, whereas if it delegates a broad duty – for example, setting national air quality standards – it must provide 'substantial guidance.'" How substantial was the guidance in *Whitman*?

2. After the decision, the case was remanded and the focus shifted to the substantive standard set by the EPA. In *American Trucking Associations v. EPA*, 283 F.3d 355, 369 (D.C. Cir. 2002), the court found that the agency had chosen primary and secondary ozone levels through a process that was neither arbitrary, capricious, nor an abuse of discretion. It was, the court found, a rational choice. Furthermore, the permissive tone of the opinion suggests that for the future, projection of air quality levels bordering on a "best guess" might be all that is required, as these few excerpts of the *Whitman* remand demonstrate:

> Although we recognize that the Clean Air Act and circuit precedent require EPA qualitatively to describe the standard governing its selection of particular NAAQS, [National Ambient Air Quality Standards, § 307(d)(9) of the Clean Air Act (42 U.S.C.S. § 7401 et seq.), and § 7607(d)(9)] we have expressly rejected the notion that the Agency must "establish a measure of the risk to safety it considers adequate to protect public health every time it establishes a [NAAQS]." *Natural Res. Def. Council, Inc. v. EPA*, 902 F.2d 962, 973 (D.C. Cir. 1990). . . . Such a rule would compel EPA to leave hazardous pollutants unregulated unless and *until it completely understands every risk* they pose, thus thwarting the Clean Air Act's requirement that the Agency

err on the side of caution by setting primary NAAQS that "allow[] an adequate margin of safety[.]" 42 U.S.C. § 7409(b)(1). The Act requires EPA to promulgate protective primary NAAQS even where, as here, the pollutant's risks cannot be quantified or "precisely identified as to nature or degree. . . ."

EPA cannot determine [with certainty the specific peak exposure risks and has made a calculated judgment]. We think this expert judgment worthy of *deference*, at least until formerly polluted areas come into compliance with the new . . . standard[s].

[N]othing in the Clean Air Act requires EPA to wait until it has perfect information before adopting a protective secondary NAAQS. Rather, the Act mandates promulgation of secondary standards requisite to protect public welfare from any "anticipated adverse effects associated with" regulated pollutants . . . suggesting that EPA must act as soon as it has enough information (even if crude) to "anticipate[]" such effects – just as it did here. . . .

a. How can the court give deference to a standard that EPA acknowledges is uncertain? We (your authors) urge you to consider this point carefully. Deference to agency action on review requires an act of faith – and not a decision (even in setting standards that, as in *Whitman*, carry the force of law) that is supported by substantial evidence, the manifest weight of the evidence, a preponderance of the evidence – or anything close to it. The congressionally-delegated power to issue rules is not just the power to find facts and draw conclusions – it is often the remarkable power to promulgate binding standards that are a best guess.

b. The full text of the circuit court's decision does not reveal a very "hard look" at the substance of the finding. One commentator characterizes such reviews as a "soft look." *See* William H. Rodgers, *The Most Creative Moments in the History of Environmental Law*, 39 WASHBURN L.J. 1, 2 (1999). Others see the opinion differently. *See, e.g.*, Heath A. Brooks, American Trucking Associations v. EPA: *The D.C. Circuit's Missed Opportunity to Unambiguously Discard the Hard Look Doctrine*, 27 HARV. ENVTL. L. REV. 259 (2003).

3. One of the most fundamental components of the Clean Air Act, central to *Whitman* and more recent Clean Air Act cases, is the mandate to assess environmental regulations without being constrained by a required cost/benefit analysis. The prohibition on consideration of costs was first expressed in *Lead Industries Association v. Environmental Protection Agency*, 647 F.2d 1130, 1148 (D.C. Cir. 1980), *cert. denied*, 449 U.S. 1042 (1980). While considerations of cost are often part of the regulatory discourse (the Regulatory Flexibility Act, 5 U.S.C. §§ 601-12, set out in full in the Statutory Supplement, usually compels such considerations), the Clean Air Act's mandate is to the contrary. In response to the argument that Congress must have meant costs should be considered, JUSTICE SCALIA noted that inclusion of costs is simply not something that Congress either overlooked or implied:

Congress, we have held, does not alter the fundamental details of a regulatory scheme in vague terms or ancillary provisions – it does not, one might say, hide elephants in mouseholes. . . . Respondents' . . . claim is that . . . "adequate margin" and "requisite" leave room to pad health effects with cost concerns. . . . [W]e find it implausible that Congress would give to the EPA . . . the power to determine whether implementation costs should moderate national air quality standards [implicitly] "delegating" its resolution [of the cost question] to the administering agency. . . . [The insertion of cost into standards] is both so indirectly related to public health and so full of potential for canceling the conclusions drawn from direct health effects that it would surely have been expressly mentioned . . . had Congress meant it to be considered.

Take Note

Many of the executive orders and statutes discussed in adjacent notes and comments are set out in full in the Statutory Supplement accompanying this text. The REGULATORY FLEXIBILITY ACT, Pub. L. No. 96-354, 94 Stat. 1164 (1980) (codified as amended at 5 U.S.C. § 601 et seq. (2000)), the SMALL BUSINESS REGULATORY ENFORCEMENT FAIRNESS ACT, 5 U.S.C. §§ 801-808 (Supp. 1999), and the TRUTH IN REGULATING ACT OF 2000, Pub. L. No. 106-302, 114 Stat. 1248 (2000) were designed to lessen the impact of agency rules on small businesses by giving Congress unprecedented direct review of major rules.

4. The scientific basis for making specific determinations comes in part from information provided by the Clean Air Scientific Advisory Committee (42 U.S.C. § 7409(d)(2)(A) & (B) (2000)). Advisory committees are central to the EPA and other federal agencies (e.g., the Nuclear Regulatory Commission's Advisory Committee on Reactor Safeguards, 10 C.F.R. § 1.11 (2008)). These committees function pursuant to the mandates of the Federal Advisory Committee Act (FACA), 5 U.S.C. app. (2000). *See generally* SHEILA JASANOFF, THE FIFTH BRANCH: SCIENCE ADVISERS AS POLICYMAKERS 1 (1990).

5. While *Whitman* focused on the regulation itself, always in the background is the specter of civil liability. Once a federal standard is in place, it can become a basis for demonstrating due care. For example, in California, the federal statute challenged in *Whitman* was raised in *California v. GMC*, 2007 U.S. Dist. LEXIS 68547 (N.D. Cal. 2007), an unsuccessful attempt to hold the automobile industry liable for broadly defined harms to the environment. The state filed a complaint, alleging "(1) public nuisance under federal common law; and, alternatively (2) public nuisance under California Law," which was dismissed. Other attacks continue. *See, e.g., Ctr. for Biological Diversity v. Nat'l Highway Traffic Safety Admin., 508 F.3d 508 (2007)* (9th Cir. 2007) (using a NHTSA standard). Accordingly, these cases can become "knock down, drag out" brawls with the full arsenal of both industry and environmental/plaintiffs lawyers and lobbyists in full battle gear. *See* DAVID M. DRIESEN, THE ECONOMIC DYNAMICS OF ENVIRONMENTAL LAW (2003). Special interest funding, media manipulation, and political "hardball" are the norm. *See* John M. Stanton, *Environmental Attorneys and the Media: Guidelines for Effectiveness, 33 B.C.*

ENVTL. AFF. L. REV. 593 (2006); Zygmunt J.B. Plater, Essay, *Law and the Fourth Estate: Endangered Nature, the Press, and the Dicey Game of Democratic Governance*, 32 ENVTL. L. 1 (2002); Kirsten H. Engel & Scott R. Saleska, *"Facts Are Stubborn Things": An Empirical Reality Check in the Theoretical Debate Over the Race-to-the-Bottom in State Environmental Standard-Setting*, 8 CORNELL J.L. & PUB. POL'Y 55, 64 (1998) ("According to the economic theory of regulation, laws tend to respond to the wants of small, cohesive special interest groups, such as industry, at the expense of the wants of the larger, more diffuse public.").

6. *Whitman* may lead one to think that the capacity of an agency to articulate new regulatory norms is unbounded. That is, of course, not true – but it is the case that legislation is unlikely to be struck down based on imprecision in delegation merely because it leaves open important details best ironed out by agencies with both the expertise and time to do so. Those details can be cavernous – and the regulations that fill them in can be what the public experiences as major public policy leading quite naturally to separation of powers questions. Shouldn't Congress take care of such important matters as permissible levels for the most common pollutants? Shouldn't elected representatives, accountable to the electorate, decide on ozone, carbon monoxide, and other types of automobile pollution? After all, the economy, the very essence of personal and business mobility, hangs in the balance. The simple fact is that notwithstanding the counterarguments in *Whitman*, agencies are in the best position to make those decisions and to implement some of the hard choices (such as not taking cost directly into account in air pollution cases) that the legislation requires. The hard business of regulation takes place at the agency level.

To the extent there are clear limits on agencies, they have less to do with tough and controversial regulatory decisions agencies must make than with agency failures to adhere to the most basic instructions Congress provides. Conformity with the basic set of instructions will likely result in favorable treatment in court, assuming there is judicial review. Refusal to follow basic instructions, however, will produce a very different result, as happened in *Natural Resources Defense Council v. Abraham*, 355 F.3d 179 (2d Cir. 2004):

> [T]he Energy Policy and Conservation Act . . . was passed following the oil embargo imposed by [OPEC]. . . . [A]mong its stated purposes was the reduction of demand for energy through such measures as conservation plans and improved energy efficiency of consumer products. . . . [T]en years after the passage of the original Act . . . Congress adopted legislation . . . known as the National Appliance Energy Conservation Act, in 1987. . . . [T]he 1987 Act set [an efficiency] standard[] for central air conditioners . . . .
>
> The NAECA also added a significant provision to section 325 that is at the heart of these proceedings. The new provision mandated that, when it came time for DOE to undertake its periodic review of the efficiency standards, DOE could decide no amendment was necessary but it could not amend the standards so as to weaken

efficiency requirements. In other words, it built an "anti-backsliding" mechanism into the EPCA: efficiency standards for consumer appliances could be amended in one direction only, to make them more stringent.

Pursuant to [this] provision[], DOE published an advanced notice of proposed rulemaking ("ANOPR") on September 8, 1993 [eventually] DOE promulgated a final rule amending the efficiency standards originally set by Congress for central air conditioners. The new rule . . . was published in the Federal Register on January 22, 2001. . . . [NOTE: George W. Bush was sworn in as President on January 20, 2001.] Consistent with the five-year timeframe between publication and compliance contemplated by the EPCA, the rule provided that manufacturers would be subject to these standards as of January 23, 2006. The final rule listed its "effective date" as February 21, 2001.

[O]n February 2, 2001, without any prior notice or comment, DOE published what it denoted a "final rule" delaying the effective date of the efficiency standards to April 23, 2001. The . . . President's Chief of Staff, Andrew H. Card, [had previously published a memo asking the] heads of executive agencies to postpone the effective dates of any federal regulations already published in the Federal Register, but not yet effective, for a period of sixty days . . . . On April 20, 2001, again without notice and comment, DOE issued yet another "final rule" [that] suspended the effective date of the amended standards indefinitely . . . . [In May, 2001] following public comment and a public hearing on this proposed new course of action, DOE announced three final rulemaking determinations [including the] withdrawal of the January 22, 2001, final rule [and adopting] new efficiency standards for central air conditioners and heat pumps. . . .

Throughout section 325, publication of final rules amending efficiency standards is used as the relevant act for purposes of circumscribing DOE's discretion to conduct rulemakings. . . . [T]he language of the statute also reflects the fact that Congress considered publication as the terminal act effectuating an amendment. Under the terms of the EPCA consumer appliance procedural provisions, publication in the Federal Register – not modification of the Code of Federal Regulations – is the culminating event in the rulemaking process. . . .

Thus, once [a] new standard[] [is] published, . . . regardless of the fact that manufacturers have a number of years to bring themselves into compliance, it becomes the "established" standard in the statute's own language, or, in other terms, the "required" minimum efficiency standard. . . . In other words, publication must be read as the triggering event for the operation of section 325(o)(1). . . . [Any other] reading would effectively render section 325(o)(1)'s "anti-backsliding" mechanism inoperative, or a nullity, in these circumstances. . . . Consequently, we agree with petitioners that the replacement standards promulgated by DOE on May 23, 2002, were prescribed in violation of section 325 of the EPCA and are thus invalid.

II. Presidential Power

Mayors, governors, and the President of the United States all share a common problem. After a political campaign during which candidates articulate their platform and specify the goals and objectives they will seek to implement, executives take office and discover that their actual power to implement new standards has real limitations. First, there is the recognition that while political appointees may be in top positions at agencies at any level of government, the professional staff of most agencies play a powerful – if not dominant – role in shaping the activity of the agency. Furthermore, the legislative and judicial branches of government play a controlling role in many respects. The President, like a mayor or governor, can be completely neutralized if the legislative body with which that individual works is diametrically opposed to all actions the executive proposes. Furthermore, courts can block the action of the executive if there is a constitutional or statutory basis to deem the agency action inappropriate.

That said, it requires little political sophistication to realize that presidents, governors, and mayors exert enormous force on the regulatory state. The means by which that force is exerted is the subject of endless debate that predated *Panama Refining* and *Schechter Poultry* and continues to the present.

One of the most direct forms of executive governance is the issuance of <u>Executive Orders. Executive Order 12866</u>, (see Statutory Supplement) established the basis for presidential review of agency action. <u>Exec. Order No. 12,866</u>, <u>58 Fed. Reg. 51,735</u> (1993) (signed by President Clinton). The Order empowers the Office of Information and Regulatory Affairs (OIRA) to review all rules an agency considers, assessing whether the benefits the rule provides are greater than the costs the rule exacts. The Order also is the basis for expanding the role of the Vice President to include regulatory review and agency oversight. 12866 and its predecessors were the dominant executive edict for most of the Reagan, Bush I, Clinton, and the first part of the Bush II administrations. In conjunction with § 610 of the Regulatory Flexibility Act, a "look back" provision, federal agencies must develop a plan both to assess the economic consequences of proposed regulations as well as to re-evaluate prior regulations to eliminate those that have a significant negative economic impact, particularly on small businesses.

By 2005, the administration of George W. Bush sought to further increase regulatory review of agency action, directing the Office of Management and Budget (OMB–the executive agency that houses the OIRA) to evaluate guidance documents agencies were issuing.

Starting in the mid-1990s, federal agencies increased the use of "guidances" as a way to set forth regulatory policy without the time-consuming and expensive notice and comment process required for substantive rules. Guidance documents had previously both avoided judicial review because of their advisory nature and slipped under the radar of OIRA. The 2005 initiatives sought to place significant executive control (through OIRA) on guidance documents that were complex, controversial, had an economic impact of $100,000,000 or more on a defined market, or had a noticeable effect on small business.

In response to the efforts of the administration, various groups contended that OIRA interference with guidance documents would provide a significant impediment to federal agencies with a particularly negative effect in the area of environmental protection and consumer rights. The 2005 OMB initiative did not produce the results the administration desired and in January 2007, the White House issued Executive Order 13422, an initiative designed to ensure the implementation of the President's 2005 policy initiative. That Order was repealed, January 20, 2009.

Executive Order 13422 required that all regulatory initiatives that have a significant economic effect ($100,000,000 or more) be cleared by a political appointee within a federal agency. Exec. Order No. 13,422, 72 Fed. Reg. 2763 (2007). *See* http://www.whitehouse.gov/news/releases/2007/01/20070118.html, (last visited July 31, 2008). It further required that regulations issue only when there has been a market failure. Finally, it imposed the same cost/benefit test that Executive Order 12866 required. The OMB circular following the Executive Order, *see* 72 Fed. Reg. 16, at 3432 (2007); Rob Portman, Exec. Office of the President, Memorandum M-07-13, Implementation of Executive Order 13422, *amending* Executive Order 12866; Exec. Office of the President, Office of Mgmt. & Budget, Bulletin on Good Guidance Practices, April 25, 2007, available at www.whitehouse.gov/OMB/memoranda/fy2007-m07-13, clarified the goals of the Order. Executive Order 13422 was repealed on January 20, 2009.

The caselaw regarding Executive power presents additional challenges:

CLINTON V. CITY OF NEW YORK

524 U.S. 417 (1998)

[JUSTICE STEVENS] The Line Item Veto Act (Act) . . . was enacted in April 1996. . . . [The next year] the President exercised his authority to cancel [certain provisions]. We now hold that . . . the cancellation procedures set forth in the Act violate the Presentment Clause, Art. I, § 7, cl. 2, of the Constitution.

I

. . . .

Title XIX of the Social Security Act . . . authorizes the Federal Government to transfer huge sums of money to the States to help finance medical care for the indigent. In 1991, Congress directed that those federal subsidies be reduced by the amount of certain taxes levied by the States on health care providers. In 1994, the Department of Health and Human Services (HHS) notified the State of New York that . . . the statute . . . required New York to return $955 million to the United States. . . . New York turned to Congress for relief. On August 5, 1997, Congress enacted a law that resolved the issue in New York's favor. Section 4722(c) of the Balanced Budget Act of 1997 identifies the disputed taxes and provides that they "are deemed to be permissible health care related taxes and in compliance with the requirements" of the relevant provisions of the 1991 statute.

On August 11, 1997, the President sent identical notices to the Senate and to the House of Representatives canceling "one item of new direct spending," specifying § 4722(c) as that item, and stating that he had determined that "this cancellation will reduce the Federal budget deficit.". . . .

In . . . 1997, Congress amended § 1042 of the Internal Revenue Code to permit owners of certain food refiners and processors to defer the recognition of gain if they sell their stock to eligible farmers' cooperatives. . . . [T]he President . . . canceled this limited tax benefit. In his explanation of that action, the President endorsed the objective . . . but concluded that the provision lacked safeguards and also "failed to target its benefits to small-and-medium-size cooperatives."

. . . .

III

[The appellees have standing and the court has subject matter jurisdiction.]

IV

The Line Item Veto Act gives the President the power to "cancel in whole" three types of provisions that have been signed into law: "(1) any dollar amount of discretionary budget authority; (2) any item of new direct spending; or (3) any limited tax benefit." . . . .

The Act requires the President to adhere to precise procedures whenever he exercises his cancellation authority. In identifying items for cancellation he must consider the legislative history, the purposes, and other relevant information about the items. He must determine, with respect to each cancellation, that it will "(i) reduce the Federal budget deficit; (ii) not impair any essential Government functions; and (iii) not harm the national interest." Moreover, he must transmit a special message to Congress notifying it of each cancellation within five calendar days (excluding Sundays) after the enactment of the canceled provision. . . .

A cancellation takes effect upon receipt by Congress of the special message from the President. If, however, a "disapproval bill" pertaining to a special message is enacted into law, the cancellations set forth in that message become "null and void." The Act sets forth a detailed expedited procedure for the consideration of a "disapproval bill," but no such bill was passed for either of the cancellations involved in these cases. A majority vote of both Houses is sufficient to enact a disapproval bill. The Act does not grant the President the authority to cancel a disapproval bill but he does, of course, retain his constitutional authority to veto such a bill.

[U]nder the plain text of the statute, the two actions of the President that are challenged in these cases prevented one section of the Balanced Budget Act of 1997 and one section of the Taxpayer Relief Act of 1997 "from having legal force or effect." The remaining provisions of those statutes . . . continue to have the same force and effect as they had when signed into law.

In both legal and practical effect, the President has amended two Acts of Congress by repealing a portion of each. "Repeal of statutes, no less than enactment, must conform with Art. I." There is no provision in the Constitution that authorizes the President to enact, to amend, or to repeal statutes. . . . The President "shall from time to time give to the Congress Information on the State of the Union, and recommend to their Consideration such Measures as he shall judge necessary and expedient . . . ." Art. II, § 3. Thus, he may initiate and influence legislative proposals. Moreover, after a bill has passed both Houses of Congress, but "before it becomes a Law," it must be presented to the President. If he approves it, "he shall sign it, but if not he shall return it, with his Objections to that House in which it shall have originated, who shall enter the Objections at large on their Journal, and proceed to reconsider it." Art. I, § 7, cl. 2. His "return" of a bill, which is usually described as a "veto," is subject to being overridden by a two-thirds vote in each House.

There are important differences between the President's "return" of a bill pursuant to Article I, § 7, and the exercise of the President's cancellation authority pursuant to the Line Item Veto Act. The constitutional return takes place before the bill becomes law; the statutory cancellation occurs after the bill becomes law. The constitutional return is of the entire bill; the statutory cancellation is of only a part. Although the Constitution expressly authorizes the President to play a role in the process of enacting statutes, it is silent on the subject of unilateral Presidential action that either repeals or amends parts of duly enacted statutes.

There are powerful reasons for construing constitutional silence on this profoundly important issue as equivalent to an express prohibition. The procedures governing the enactment of statutes set forth in the text of Article I were the product of the great debates and compromises that produced the Constitution itself.

Familiar historical materials provide abundant support for the conclusion that the power to enact statutes may only "be exercised in accord with a single, finely wrought and exhaustively considered, procedure." Our first President understood the text of the Presentment Clause as requiring that he either "approve all the parts of a Bill, or reject it in [its entirety]." What has emerged in these cases from the President's exercise of his statutory cancellation powers, however, are truncated versions of two bills that passed both Houses of Congress. They are not the product of the "finely wrought" procedure that the Framers designed.

At oral argument, the Government suggested that the cancellations at issue in these cases do not effect a "repeal" of the canceled items because under the special "lockbox" provisions of the Act, a canceled item "retains real, legal budgetary effect" insofar as it prevents Congress and the President from spending the savings that result from the cancellation. . . . That a canceled item may have "real, legal budgetary effect" as a result of the lockbox procedure does not change the fact that by canceling the items at issue in these cases, the President made them entirely inoperative as to appellees. . . . Such significant changes do not lose their character simply because the canceled provisions may have some continuing financial effect on the Government. . . .

V

The Government advances two related arguments to support its position that despite the unambiguous provisions of the Act, cancellations do not amend or repeal properly enacted statutes in violation of the Presentment Clause. First, relying primarily on *Marshall Field & Co. v. Clark* the Government contends that the cancellations were merely exercises of discretionary authority granted to the President by the Balanced Budget Act and the Taxpayer Relief Act read in light of the previously enacted Line Item Veto Act. Second, the Government submits that the substance of the authority to cancel tax and spending items "is, in practical effect, no more and no less than the power to 'decline to spend' specified sums of money, or to 'decline to implement' specified tax measures." Neither argument is persuasive.

In *Marshall Field & Co. v. Clark*, the Court upheld the constitutionality of the Tariff Act of 1890. That statute contained a "free list" of almost 300 specific articles that were exempted from import duties . . . . Section 3 was a special provision that directed the President to suspend that exemption for sugar, molasses, coffee, tea, and hides "whenever, and so often" as he should be satisfied that any country producing and exporting those products imposed duties on the agricultural products of the United States that he deemed to be "reciprocally unequal and unreasonable . . . ." The section then specified the duties to be imposed on those products during any such suspension. . . .

[There were] three critical differences between the power to suspend the exemption from import duties and the power to cancel portions of a duly enacted statute. First, the exercise of the suspension power was contingent upon a condition that did not exist when the Tariff Act was passed: the imposition of "reciprocally unequal and unreasonable" import duties by other countries. In contrast, the exercise of the cancellation power within five days after the enactment of the Balanced Budget and Tax Reform Acts necessarily was based on the same conditions that Congress evaluated when it passed those statutes. Second, under the Tariff Act, when the President determined that the contingency had arisen, he had a duty to suspend; in contrast, while it is true that the President was required by the Act to make three determinations before he canceled a provision those determinations did not qualify his discretion to cancel or not to cancel. Finally, whenever the President suspended an exemption under the Tariff Act, he was executing the policy that Congress had embodied in the statute. In contrast, whenever the President cancels an item of new direct spending or a limited tax benefit he is rejecting the policy judgment made by Congress and relying on his own policy judgment. Thus, the conclusion in *Marshall Field & Co. v. Clark* that the suspensions mandated by the Tariff Act were not exercises of legislative power does not undermine our opinion that cancellations pursuant to the Line Item Veto Act are the functional equivalent of partial repeals of Acts of Congress that fail to satisfy Article I, § 7.

. . . .

[Furthermore,] this Court has recognized that in the foreign affairs arena, the President has "a degree of discretion and freedom from statutory restriction which would not be admissible were domestic affairs alone involved." "Moreover, he, not Congress, has the better opportunity of knowing the conditions which prevail in foreign countries." More important, when enacting the statutes discussed in *Field*, Congress itself made the decision to suspend or repeal the particular provisions at issue upon the occurrence of particular events subsequent to enactment, and it left only the determination of whether such events occurred up to the President. The Line Item Veto Act authorizes the President himself to effect the repeal of laws, for his own policy reasons, without observing the procedures set out in Article I, § 7. The fact that Congress intended such a result is of no moment. . . . Congress cannot alter the procedures set out in Article I, § 7, without amending the Constitution.

Neither are we persuaded by the Government's contention that the President's authority to cancel new direct spending and tax benefit items is no greater than his traditional authority to decline to spend appropriated funds. . . . [Traditionally] the President was given wide discretion with respect to both the amounts to be spent and how the money would be allocated among different functions.

It is argued that the Line Item Veto Act merely confers comparable discretionary authority over the expenditure of appropriated funds. The critical difference between this statute and all of its predecessors, however, is that unlike any of them, this Act gives the President the unilateral power to change the text of duly enacted statutes. None of the Act's predecessors could even arguably have been construed to authorize such a change.

VI

Although they are implicit in what we have already written, the profound importance of these cases makes it appropriate to emphasize three points.

First, we express no opinion about the wisdom of the procedures authorized by the Line Item Veto Act. Many members of both major political parties who have served in the Legislative and the Executive Branches have long advocated the enactment of such procedures for the purpose of "ensuring greater fiscal accountability in Washington." . . . . We do not lightly conclude that their action was unauthorized by the Constitution. We have, however, . . . concluded that our duty is clear.

Second, although appellees challenge the validity of the Act on alternative grounds, the only issue we address concerns the "finely wrought" procedure commanded by the Constitution. . . . Thus . . . we find it unnecessary to consider [whether] the Act "impermissibly disrupts the balance of powers among the three branches of government."

Third, our decision rests on the narrow ground that the procedures authorized by the Line Item Veto Act are not authorized by the Constitution. . . . Something that might be known as "Public Law 105-33 as modified by the President" may or may not be desirable, but it is surely not a document that may "become a law" pursuant to the procedures designed by the Framers of Article I, § 7, of the Constitution.

. . . .

The judgment of the District Court is affirmed. . . .

[JUSTICE KENNEDY, concurring.]

. . . I write to respond to my Colleague JUSTICE BREYER, who observes that the statute does not threaten the liberties of individual citizens, a point on which I disagree. The argument is related to his earlier suggestion that our role is lessened here because the two political branches are adjusting their own powers between themselves. To say the political branches have a somewhat free hand to reallocate their own authority would seem to require acceptance of two premises: first, that the public good demands it, and second, that liberty is not at risk. The former premise is inadmissible. The Constitution's structure requires a stability which transcends the convenience of the moment. . . . The latter premise, too, is flawed. Liberty is always at stake when one or more of the branches seek to transgress the separation of powers.

. . . It is no answer, of course, to say that Congress surrendered its authority by its own hand; nor does it suffice to point out that a new statute, signed by the President or enacted over his veto, could restore to Congress the power it now seeks to relinquish. That a congressional cession of power is voluntary does not make it innocuous. The Constitution is a compact enduring for more than our time, and one Congress cannot yield up its own powers, much less those of other Congresses to follow. . . . Abdication of responsibility is not part of the constitutional design.

————————

Underlying Case Documents

The case referenced:
The Line Item Veto Act
The Balanced Budget Act of 1997
The Taxpayer Relief Act of 1997

For a text version of the joint appendix click HERE.

1. While legend has it that the Continental Congress was willing to make George Washington king (probably on the condition that John Adams was not), they were not willing to give him line item veto authority. Although presidents since Washington have sought line-item veto power, it was not until the Clinton presidency that Congress actually granted that authority, Line Item Veto Act, Public Law 104-130, 110 Stat. 1200, 2 U.S.C. §§ 621 et. seq. (1996), and, as the case you have just read demonstrates, that power was never realized. It was not a matter of the substance of the items stricken – the Line Item Veto Act permitted the President to excise from the budget "pork" – though one person's pork is another's sine qua non of political support in his or her home district. *See* Rick Klein, *House GOP Leaders Decry Pork, But Back It*, BOSTON GLOBE, July 08, 2006, at A1.

The history in the field is revealing – Presidents seek this power and Congress resists. *See, e.g.*, Staff of House Comm. on the Budget, 98th Cong., THE LINE ITEM

VETO: AN APPRAISAL 11-12 (Comm. Print 1984); *Symposium on the Line Item Veto*, 1 NOTRE DAME J.L. ETHICS & PUB. POL'Y 157 (1985); Anthony R. Petrilla, Note, *The Role of the Line-Item Veto in the Federal Balance of Power*, 31 HARV. J. ON LEGIS. 469 (1994).

2. The presidential quest for a line-item veto continues. In July 2007, Congressman Udall of Colorado introduced H.R. 4699, a bill entitled: "Stimulating Leadership in Cutting Expenditures," or the SLICE Act of 2006. If passed, the bill would permit the President to identify specific items in a proposed budget that the President believes should be eliminated. Thereafter, the bill would obligate Congress to vote specifically on each item designated by the White House. *Cf. A Practical and Constitutional Version of the Line Item Veto*, U.S. FED. NEWS, July 6, 2007. H.R. 4699 is but one of several attempts to secure the elusive line item authority presidents seek. *See, e.g.*, Legislative Line Item Veto Act of 2007, H.R. 689, 110th Cong. (2007). For two articles from spring 2009 regarding the line-item veto, Click HERE and HERE.

3. Other proposals designed to get around the prohibition on the line-item veto have been referred to as "enhanced" or "expedited" rescission authority. Presumably, the President ought to be able to identify excessive spending items in a federal budget and refer them back to Congress without undoing the whole of the budget approval process. *See* Seema Mittal, Note, *The Constitutionality of an Expedited Rescission Act: The New Line Item Veto or a New Constitutional Method of Achieving Deficit Reduction?*, 76 GEO. WASH. L. REV. 125 (2007). Unfortunately, the Constitution does not give the President the power to pick and choose among budget items, notwithstanding the argument that such authority is essential to deal with "pork" or "earmarks." *See* Ronald D. Utt, *The Congressional Earmark Moratorium: Will It Last the Year?*, HERITAGE FOUND. REPS., BACKGROUNDER, No. 2016 (2007).

4. Part of the reasoning underlying *Clinton* involves the very basic matter of how laws are made. Short of a full veto, the President does not have the power to modify or suspend laws – for the most part. *See* Michael B. Rappaport, *The Selective Nondelegation Doctrine and the Line Item Veto: A New Approach to the Nondelegation Doctrine and Its Implications for* Clinton v. City of New York, 76 TUL. L. REV. 265 (2001).

Key Concept

In the area of foreign affairs, the President *is* accorded a considerable degree of discretion and freedom to modify existing legal obligations, a power not permitted for domestic matters. *See, e.g.*, United States v. Curtiss-Wright Export, 299 U.S. 304, 320 (1936).

5. The prohibition with the line-item veto is a federal phenomenon. Some years ago, it was estimated that governors in 43 of the 50 states had something resem-

bling line-item veto power. Richard Briffault, *The Item Veto in State Courts*, 66 TEMP. L. REV. 1171, 1175 (1993). What explains this difference? Is it that the system of separation of powers so significantly different at the state level? For a look at the issue in California, see Jonathan Zasloff, *Taking Politics Seriously: A Theory of California's Separation of Powers*, 51 UCLA L. REV. 1079 (2004).

6. Executive Transition. One of the most important and interesting events to assess is the transition from one presidential administration to the next. Presidents are elected, in part, based on a political platform. For an election to have validity, the newly elected President must be able to implement those planks – in essence, to govern. This raises a myriad of issues addressed in Chapters One through Four.

The first public acts begin before the presidential inauguration and involve the power of appointment as the newly elected President replaces political appointees (as opposed to long-term "career" federal employees) with new office holders who can implement the policies of the President. Appointments to leadership positions in executive agencies (e.g., cabinet level officers) are an obvious starting point. Appointments at independent agencies (see Chapter One for the distinction) are more difficult. Take a second look at the *Myers*, *Humphrey's Executor*, and *Wiener* cases in Chapter One. Those cases affect directly the power of the President to "hit the ground running."

7. a. On the first day in office, on behalf of President Barack Obama, Chief of Staff Rahm Emanuel issued a *Memorandum* to the heads of all "departments and agencies" revoking Executive Order 13422, theretofore the baseline for all regulatory decisions made during the administration of President George W. Bush. The *Emanuel Memorandum*, in effect, reinstated Executive Order 12896, the baseline Executive Order in use during the administration of President William Clinton. As of December 2009, no new Executive Order has been issued by the Obama administration. The *Emanuel Memorandum* follows:

THE WHITE HOUSE – WASHINGTON - January 20, 2009

MEMORANDUM FOR HEADS OF EXECUTIVE DEPARTMENTS AND AGENCIES

FROM :   Rahm Emanuel

          Assistant to the President and Chief of Staff

SUBJECT :   Regulatory Review

President Obama has asked me to communicate to each of you his plan for managing the Federal regulatory process at the beginning of his Administration. It is important that President Obama's appointees and designees have the opportunity to review and approve any new or pending regulations. Therefore, at the direction of the President, I am requesting that you immediately take the following steps:

1. Subject to any exceptions the Director or Acting Director of the Office of Management and Budget (the "OMB Director") allows for emergency situations or other urgent circumstances relating to health, safety, environmental, financial, or national security matters, or otherwise, no proposed or final regulation should be sent to the Office of the Federal Register (the 'IOFR") for publication unless and until it has been reviewed and approved by a department or agency head appointed or designated by the President after noon on January 20, 2009, or in the case of the Department of Defense, the Secretary of Defense. The department or agency head may delegate this review and approval power to any other person so appointed or designated by the President, consistent with applicable law.

2. Withdraw from the OFR all proposed or final regulations that have not been published in the *Federal Register* so that they can be reviewed and approved by a department or agency head as described in paragraph 1. This withdrawal is subject to the exceptions described in paragraph 1 and must be conducted consistent with OFR procedures.

3. Consider extending for 60 days the effective date of regulations that have been published in the *Federal Register* but not yet taken effect, subject to the exceptions described in paragraph 1, for the purpose of reviewing questions of law and policy raised by those regulations. Where such an extension is made for this purpose, you should immediately reopen the notice and comment period for 30 days to allow interested parties to provide comments about issues of law and policy raised by those rules. Following the 60-day extension: a. for those rules that raise no substantial questions of law or policy, no further action needs to be taken; and b. for those rules that raise substantial questions of law or policy, agencies should notify the OMB Director and take appropriate further action.

4. The requested actions set forth in paragraphs 1-3 do not apply to any regulations subject to statutory or judicial deadlines. Please immediately notify the OMB Director of any such regulations.

5. Notify the OMB Director promptly of any regulations that you believe should not be subject to the directives in paragraphs 1-3 because they affect critical health, safety, environmental, financial, or national security functions of the department or agency, or for some other reason. The OMB Director will review all such notifications and determine whether an exception is appropriate.

6. Continue in all instances to comply with any applicable Executive Orders concerning regulatory management.

As used in this memorandum, "regulation" has the meaning set forth in section 3(e) of Executive Order 12866 of September 30, 1993, as amended; this memorandum covers "any substantive action by an agency (normally published in the Federal Register) that promulgates or is expected to lead to the promulgation of a final rule or regulation, including notices of inquiry, advance notices of proposed rulemaking, and notices of proposed rulemaking."

This regulatory review will be implemented by the OMB Director, and communications regarding any matters pertaining to this review should be addressed to that official.

The OMB Director is authorized and directed to publish this memorandum in the Federal Register.

b. For a partial list of executive orders, presidential memoranda, and proclamations pertaining to the transition, click HERE.

c. Homeland security was a dominant consideration from the moment President Obama took office. On the second day in office, the Secretary of Homeland Security issued a press release detailing the initial actions to be taken. To access that press release, click HERE.

d. Beyond homeland security and national defense, another critical challenge facing the new administration was the declining state of the U.S. economy. After Congress passed a massive economic stimulus package without conducting notice and comment proceeding, the Office of Management and Budget issued guidelines to implement the new legislation. To view those guidelines, click HERE.

e. President Barack Obama's exercise of presidential power during his first few months in office was noteworthy. For an example of the volume of policy documents and decisions made by the White House (without any administrative process) click HERE.

f. Presidential performance is assessed in many different ways. One measure, made famous during the first term of Franklin Delano Roosevelt, is a critique of the "First 100 days." The web sites below provide a useful snapshot of the changes and developments in administrative agencies during the first 100 days of the administration of President Barack Obama.

> Department of Agriculture
>
> Department of Commerce
>
> Department of Defense
>
> Department of Education
>
> Department of the Interior
>
> Department of Health and Human Services
>
> Department of Homeland Security
>
> Department of Housing and Urban Development
>
> Department of Labor
>
> Department of Transportation
>
> Department of the Treasury
>
> Environmental Protection Agency

III. Rulemaking by Adjudication – When Is It An Option?

The Administrative Procedure Act appears to create dual regimes, one for adjudication and one for rulemaking. It has been clear for the last quarter-century (at least) that the division between rulemaking and adjudication is at best muddled.

Practice Pointer

While some may be troubled by reference to the presence of federal common law or administrative common law, the fact remains that major agency enforcement actions resulting in fines or sanctions communicate directly with the entire regulated community – who will at least consider avoiding a similar fate. Thus, agency adjudication informally creates a common law that guides other actors.

Every adjudicatory announcement made public, whether issued by an Article III court or a regulatory agency, communicates with the public at large. In fact, we are charged with knowing the content of the action of courts and agencies. Once an adjudication is concluded, it is fair to assume that all those similarly situated will take notice of the adjudication and contemplate conforming their behavior to the apparent mandates of the agency or court, even though they were not parties to the proceeding.

Beyond the presence of prior adjudicatory determinations that one can assess to determine the likely approach an agency will follow, there are situations where an agency will announce in an adjudicatory proceeding a new policy or standard. The National Labor Relations Board explicitly uses the adjudicatory process as a vehicle for articulating new standards.

Adjudication is certainly more efficient than notice and comment rulemaking. However, the public is not advised of the potential new rule nor does the agency benefit from the information the public might provide through the comment process. Consequently, rules made through the adjudicatory model run the risk of being perceived as profoundly unfair. Lacking the vetting that the comment process provides, rules announced through adjudication can be seen as authoritarian, efficient though they may be.

NATIONAL LABOR RELATIONS BOARD V. BELL AEROSPACE COMPANY

<u>416 U.S. 267 (1974)</u>

[JUSTICE POWELL] On July 30, 1970, [a union] petitioned the National Labor Relations Board (Board) for a representation election to determine whether the union would be certified as the bargaining representative of the 25 buyers in the purchasing and procurement department at [Bell Aerospace's] plant. The company opposed the petition on the ground that the buyers were "managerial employees" and thus were not covered by the National Labor Relations Act. . . . The purchasing and procurement department . . . is responsible for purchasing all of the company's needs from outside suppliers. . . . Buyers execute all purchase orders up to $ 50,000. They may place or cancel orders of less than $ 5,000 on their own signature. On commitments in excess of $ 5,000, buyers must obtain the approval of a superior, with higher levels of approval required as the purchase cost increases. . . . After the representation hearing, the Regional Director transferred the case to the Board. On May 20, 1971, the Board issued its decision holding that the company's buyers constituted an appropriate unit for purposes of collective bargaining and directing an election. . . . The company stood by its contention that the buyers, as "managerial employees," were not covered by the Act, and refused to bargain with the union. An unfair labor practice complaint resulted in a Board finding that the company had violated §§ 8(a)(5) and (1) of the Act, 29 U.S.C. §§ 158(a)(5) and (1), and an order compelling the company to bargain with the union. Subsequently, the company petitioned the United States Court of Appeals for the Second Circuit for review of the order and the Board cross-petitioned for enforcement.

. . . .

The Court of Appeals . . . held that, although the Board was not precluded from determining that buyers or some types of buyers were not "managerial employees," it could do so only by invoking its rulemaking procedures under § 6 of the Act. We disagree.

. . . The Court of Appeals thought that rulemaking was required because *any* Board finding that the company's buyers are not "managerial" would . . . presumably be in the nature of a general rule designed "to fit all cases at all times." . . . . *Chenery II* and <u>Wyman-Gordon</u> make plain that the Board is not precluded from announcing new principles in an adjudicative proceeding and that the choice between rulemaking and adjudication lies in the first instance within the Board's discretion. Although there may be situations where the Board's reliance on adjudication would amount to an abuse of discretion or a violation of the Act, nothing in the present case would justify such a conclusion. Indeed, there is ample indication that adjudication is especially appropriate in the instant context. As the Court of Appeals noted, "there must be tens of thousands of manufacturing, wholesale and retail units which employ buyers, and hundreds of thousands of the latter." Moreover, duties of buyers vary widely depending on the company or industry. It is doubtful whether any generalized standard could be framed which would have more than marginal utility. The Board thus has reason to proceed with caution, developing its standards in a case-by-case manner with attention to the specific character of the buyers' authority and duties in each company. The Board's judgment that adjudication best serves this purpose is entitled to great weight.

The possible reliance of industry on the Board's past decisions with respect to buyers does not require a different result. It has not been shown that the adverse consequences ensuing from such reliance are so substantial that the Board should be precluded from reconsidering the issue in an adjudicative proceeding. Furthermore, this is not a case in which some new liability is sought to be imposed on individuals for past actions which were taken in good-faith reliance on Board pronouncements. Nor are fines or damages involved here. . . .

It is true, of course, that rulemaking would provide the Board with a forum for soliciting the informed views of those affected in industry and labor before embarking on a new course. But surely the Board has discretion to decide that the adjudicative procedures in this case may also produce the relevant information necessary to mature and fair consideration of the issues. Those most immediately affected, the buyers and the company in the particular case, are accorded a full opportunity to be heard before the Board makes its determination.

The judgment of the Court of Appeals is therefore . . . reversed in part [as to the issue of rulemaking by adjudication], and the cause remanded . . . .

Underlying Case Documents

The case referenced:
The May 20, 1971, decision of the Board
The order compelling the company to bargain with the union
§ 6 of the Act

For the decision on remand click HERE.

1. The Supreme Court made clear the year after the APA was adopted that the choice of process (between rulemaking and adjudication) is a matter best left to the discretion of the agency, barring a statutory directive. *SEC v. Chenery Corp.*, 332 U.S. 194 (1947). If an agency chooses to proceed by adjudication, the question is whether new standards may be both announced – and applied – in that proceeding. In *Chenery*, the Court held:

> Not every principle essential to the effective administration of a statute can or should be cast immediately into the mold of a general rule. Some principles must await their own development, while others must be adjusted to meet particular, unforeseeable situations. In performing its important functions in these respects, therefore, an administrative agency must be equipped to act either by general rule or by individual order. To insist upon one form of action to the exclusion of the other is to exalt form over necessity.

332 U.S. at 202. Was the new standard in *Bell Aerospace* a surprise to the parties? If not, what is the real objection?

2. Announcing standards in an adjudication – and applying them – can require a careful balancing of interests. *See Clark-Cowlitz Joint Operating Agency v. FERC*, 826 F.2d 1074, 1081 (D.C. Cir. 1987) (en banc). In the 1970s and 80s, the D.C. Circuit set out a series of factors to determine whether the rule could be applied in the adjudication in which it was announced:

> (1) whether the particular case is one of first impression

> (2) whether the new rule represents an abrupt departure from well established practice or merely attempts to fill a void in an unsettled area of law

> (3) the extent to which the party against whom the new rule is applied relied on the former rule

> (4) the degree of the burden which a retroactive order imposes on a party, and

> (5) the statutory interest in applying a new rule despite the reliance of a party on the old standard.

Retail, Wholesale & Dep't Store Union v. NLRB, 466 F.2d 380, 390 (D.C. Cir. 1972). Could the agency assure the Court in *Bell* that these conditions were met?

3. There is a Supreme Court case holding that if the new rule interprets a statute as opposed to interpreting an agency regulation, the agency should first conduct

Food for Thought

Were you counseling a company in circumstances similar to *Bell Aerospace*, would you be comfortable assuring them that the policy announced by the agency in *Bell* is not binding and that there is no obligation to adhere to its strictures?

a notice and comment rulemaking. *Shalala v. Guernsey Mem'l Hosp.*, 514 U.S. 87, 100 (1995). Moreover, in *Wyman-Gordon*, the decision following *Bell Aerospace* in this text, the language of the Court is less than a full endorsement of this practice: "Adjudicated cases may and do, of course, serve as vehicles for the formulation of agency policies, which are applied and announced therein. *See* HENRY FRIENDLY, THE FEDERAL ADMINISTRATIVE AGENCIES 36-52 (1962). They generally provide a guide to action that the agency may be expected to take in future cases. Subject to the qualified role of stare decisis in the administrative process, they may serve as precedents. But this is far from saying . . . that commands, decisions, or policies announced in adjudication are "rules" in the sense that they must, without more, be obeyed by the affected public." *NLRB v. Wyman-Gordon*.

4. New standards announced in guidances (generally without notice and comment) evoke some of the same issues as new standards announced in adjudication. A recent OMB "best practices" publication directed at agency guidance documents expresses these concerns: "[R]ules which do not merely interpret existing law or announce tentative policy positions but which establish new policy positions that the agency treats as binding must comply with the APA's notice and comment requirements, regardless of how they initially are labeled." Office of Mgmt & Budget, Final Bulletin for Agency Good Guidance Practices, 72 Fed. Reg. 3432 (issued January 25, 2007). Would NLRB be better off using policy statements (exempt from notice and comment requirements based on §553(b)(A)) rather than adjudications as a way to short-cut the notice and comment process?

5. In *Epilepsy Foundation v. NLRB*, 268 F.3d 1095 (D.C. Cir. 2001), the court rejected a fine the NLRB imposed in a case where the Foundation had failed to conform with standards that did not appear to be expressly articulated – in any form – at the time the alleged unfair practice took place. Relying on *Public Service Company of Colorado v. FERC*, 91 F.3d 1478, 1488 (D.C. Cir. 1996), the court found that "the governing principle is that when there is a "substitution of new law for old law that was reasonably clear," the new rule may justifiably be given prospective-only effect in order to "protect the settled expectations of those who had relied on the preexisting rule." *Williams Natural Gas Co. v. FERC*, 3 F.3d 1544, 1554 (D.C. Cir. 1993). By contrast, retroactive effect is appropriate for "new applications of [existing] law, clarifications, and additions."

Clear? Does it matter whether the party attempting to apply a newly announced standard is the government or the person or entity subject to the regulation?

Good Question!

How would you decide the following: Your law school convenes an honor code proceeding, charging a student with academic dishonesty. The charge is based on the student's failure to cite a source used (repetitively) in a research paper. The student cited the authority once but in two subsequent uses of *the ideas* from the source, no reference or attribution was provided. In the course of the honor code proceeding, a new edition of the GRAY BOOK issued. The GRAY BOOK is the manual used for citation at your school (your school prefers Gray over both Red and Blue). Under the new standards, the citation the student used is now acceptable. Should the new GRAY BOOK rule be applied retroactively?

One does not have to look hard for the variables *Bell* articulated: Applying a new standard in adjudication is acceptable if the diversity and complexity of the regulatory problem make it well-suited for a case-by-case evolution of standards, if there is a lack of detrimental reliance, and if there are no new liabilities or sanctions. The next case, decided five years earlier, provided the foundation for *Bell* but produced a different set of conditions applicable to the retroactivity problem.

NATIONAL LABOR RELATIONS BOARD V. WYMAN-GORDON CO.

394 U.S. 759 (1969)

[JUSTICE FORTAS] On the petition of the International Brotherhood of Boilermakers . . . the National Labor Relations Board ordered an election among the production and maintenance employees of the respondent [Wyman-Gordon]. At the election, the employees were to select one of two labor unions as their exclusive bargaining representative, or to choose not to be represented by a union at all. In connection with the election, the Board ordered the respondent to furnish a list of the names and addresses of its employees who could vote in the election, so that the unions could use the list for election purposes. The respondent refused to comply with the order, and the election was held without the list. Both unions were defeated . . . .

The Board upheld the unions' objections to the election because the respondent had not furnished the list, and the Board ordered a new election. The respondent again refused to obey a Board order to supply a list of employees, and the Board issued a subpoena ordering the respondent to provide the list . . . . The Board filed an action in the United States District Court for the District of Massachusetts [to mandate compliance]. The District Court held the Board's order valid and directed the respondent to comply. The United States Court of Appeals for the First Circuit reversed. The Court of Appeals thought that the order in this case was invalid because it was based on a rule laid down in an earlier decision by the Board, *Excelsior Underwear Inc.*, and the *Excelsior* rule had not been promulgated in accordance with the requirements that the Administrative Procedure Act prescribes for rule making. We granted certiorari to resolve a conflict among the circuits concerning the validity and effect of the *Excelsior* rule.

I.

. . . *Excelsior* [like the present case, was an adjudication in which "management" referred to an address list. The NLRB not only ordered the address list produced but] purported to establish the general rule that such a list must be provided [in future elections]. Section 6 of the National Labor Relations Act empowers the Board "to make . . ., in the manner prescribed by the Administrative Procedure Act, such rules and regulations as may be necessary to carry out the provisions of this Act." . . . . [Rulemaking pursuant to Section 6] requires . . . publication in the Federal Register of notice of proposed rule making and of hearing; opportunity to be heard; a statement in the rule of its basis and purposes; and publication in the Federal Register of the rule as adopted. The Board asks us to hold that it has discretion to promulgate new rules in adjudicatory proceedings, without complying with the requirements of the Administrative Procedure Act.

The rule-making provisions of that Act, which the Board would avoid, were designed to assure fairness and mature consideration of rules of general application. They may not be avoided by the process of making rules in the course of adjudicatory proceedings. There is no warrant in law for the Board to replace the statutory scheme with a rule-making procedure of its own invention. . . . The "rule" created in *Excelsior* was not published in the Federal Register, which is the statutory and accepted means of giving notice of a rule as adopted; only selected organizations were given notice of the "hearing," [thus failing to allow] all interested parties . . . an opportunity to participate in the rule making.

[Notwithstanding the lack of notice in *Excelsior*, the government argued that it produced a rule that is binding on Wyman-Gordon. In light of the failure of the NLRB to comply with the NLRA or APA requirements, the court found *Excelsior* could not serve as a basis to order Wyman-Gordon to produce the address lists in question. However, the Court held that there] is no question that, in an adjudicatory hearing, the Board could validly decide the issue whether the employer must furnish a list of employees to the union. . . .

Adjudicated cases may . . . serve as vehicles for the formulation of agency policies, which are applied and announced therein. They generally provide a guide to action that the agency may be expected to take in future cases. Subject to the qualified role of stare decisis in the administrative process, they may serve as precedents. But this is far from saying, as the Solicitor General suggests, that commands, decisions, or policies announced in adjudication are "rules" in the sense that they must, without more, be obeyed by the affected public. In the present case . . . the respondent [was] directed . . . to submit a list of the names and addresses of its employees . . . in connection with the election. This direction . . . is unquestionably valid. Even though the direction to furnish the list was followed by citation to "*Excelsior Underwear Inc.*," it is an order in the present case that the respondent was required to obey. . . .

II.

The respondent also argues that it need not obey the Board's order because the requirement of disclosure of employees' names and addresses is substantively invalid. This argument lacks merit. . . . All of the [appellate courts] that have passed on the question have upheld the substantive validity of the disclosure requirement, and the court below strongly intimated a view that the requirement was substantively a proper one. . . . Congress granted the Board a wide discretion to ensure the fair and free choice of bargaining representatives . . . by encouraging an informed employee electorate and by allowing unions the right of access to employees . . . .

The judgment of the Court of Appeals is reversed, and the case is remanded to the District Court with directions to reinstate its judgment. . . .

[JUSTICE HARLAN, dissenting.]

. . . One cannot always have the best of both worlds. Either the rule-making provisions are to be enforced or they are not. Before the Board may be permitted to adopt a rule that so significantly alters pre-existing labor-management understandings, it must be required to conduct a satisfactory rule-making proceeding, so that it will have the benefit of wide-ranging argument before it enacts its proposed solution to an important problem. . . .

Since the *Excelsior* rule was invalidly promulgated . . . the Board is obliged on remand to recanvass all of the competing considerations before it may properly announce its decision in this case. We cannot know what the outcome of such a reappraisal will be. Surely, it cannot be stated with any degree of certainty that the Board will adopt precisely the same solution as the one which was embraced in *Excelsior*. The plurality simply usurps the function of the National Labor Relations Board when it says otherwise.

> ### Underlying Case Documents
>
> The case referenced:
> The NLRB's *Excelsior* decision

1. What is the effect of a rule, interpretation, or standard announced in an adjudication on future preemption claims? In *Good v. Altria Group, Inc.*, 501 F.3d 29, 53 (1st Cir. 2007), defendant Altria, a tobacco conglomerate, was sued after plaintiffs alleged that the terms "light" and "lowered tar and nicotine" on cigarette packages failed to mention tar and nicotine ratings as required under the rules of the Federal Trade Commission (FTC). Defendant argued, *inter alia*, that various FTC determinations – not issued as rules – in the tobacco area (including an FTC consent decree) created a basis for a federal preemption argument, sufficient to stave off civil liability based in part on *Wyman-Gordon*. The court held: "We acknowledge . . . that an agency often prefers to formulate policy through case-by-case adjudication. . . . *NLRB v. Wyman-Gordon Co*. But this is far from saying . . . that commands, decisions, or policies announced in adjudications are 'rules' in the sense that they must, without more, be obeyed by the affected public."

2. Are agency adjudicatory determinations written with the purpose – or at least an awareness – that such decisions could become something resembling a rule, or at a minimum, precedent? Professor Charles H. Koch writes that

> policy is made in administrative adjudications just as it is made in common-law judicial processes. The common-law system recognizes the value of this interstitial policymaking. Because adjudicative policymaking takes place within administrative structures exercising considerable policymaking responsibility, administrative adjudicators have both a richer opportunity and graver responsibility than their counterparts in the conventional judiciary.

Charles H. Koch, *Policy Making by the Administrative Judiciary*, 56 ALA. L. REV. 693 (2005). This perspective in reflected in a concurring opinion in *Wyman-Gordon* by JUSTICE BLACK, who weighed in on the precedential import of policy decisions announced in adjudicatory proceedings:

> In exercising its quasi-judicial function an agency must frequently decide controversies on the basis of new doctrines, not theretofore applied to a specific problem, though drawn to be sure from broader principles reflecting the purposes of the statutes involved and from the rules invoked in dealing with related problems. If the agency decision reached under the adjudicatory power becomes a precedent, it guides future conduct in much the same way as though it were a new rule promulgated under the rule-making power.

What would motivate an agency to conduct a rulemaking when they can announce standards in an adjudication?

3. What is the difference between precedent and authority? A prior agency decision may be a good indication of future agency policy and may be a solid source to support an argument – but can it be formal authority? Does it constitute an enforceable standard? Does it have the force of law? Does it bind the agency? Does it bind those members of the public subject to the jurisdiction of the agency?

4. Can you articulate the actual holding in *Wyman-Gordon*? Do policies set in adjudications bind the agency and other employers? Can the NLRB issue rules in adjudications? Henceforth is there a requirement to release address lists? If you feel like you are on the brink of an answer – but not quite sure – you are in very good company. See Michael I. Meyerson, *The Irrational Supreme Court*, 84 NEB. L. REV. 895, 957 (2006), for a fascinating look at important Supreme Court cases, including *Wyman-Gordon*, where the Court has left the public with clear issues and uncertain answers.

>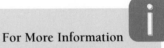
> **For More Information**
>
> The FERC and the NLRB are among the agencies that formulate policy in adjudicatory proceedings on a case-by-case basis. *See* M. Elizabeth Magill, *Agency Choice of Policymaking Form*, 71 U. CHI. L. REV. 1383 (2004); Jim Rossi, *Redeeming Judicial Review: The Hard Look Doctrine and the Federal Regulatory Efforts to Restructure the Electric Utility Industry*, 1994 WIS. L. REV. 763, 833.

5. Should one subject to the jurisdiction of an agency conform to standards set in adjudicatory proceedings? What if the standard is simply an interpretation of agency policy? Professor Richard Murphy noted that "an 'interpretation' of an agency organic statute adopted through formal adjudication acquires whatever prospective force it might possess not because it writes a new 'law' that binds regulated parties, regulators, and courts, but rather because a sensible regulated party should expect that the agency will likely stick to this interpretation in later cases." Richard W. Murphy, *Judicial Deference, Agency Commitment, and Force of Law*, 66 OHIO ST. L.J. 1013, 1041-42 (2005).

6. What is the proper standard for judicial review applicable to those cases where new polices or interpretations are announced in adjudicatory proceedings? Section 706 of the APA makes clear that adjudicatory hearings conducted pursuant to § 556-57 are reviewed under the substantial evidence test. How would a court review a policy decision based on proffered traditional evidence?

In *Association of Data Processing Organization v. Board of Governors*, 745 F.2d 677,

<u>683-84 (D.C. Cir. 1984)</u>, an opinion by JUSTICE SCALIA (written prior to his appointment to the Supreme Court) takes on this problem and discussed the interrelationship between substantial evidence and arbitrary and capricious review:

> [I]n their application to the requirement of factual support the substantial evidence test and the arbitrary or capricious test are one and the same. The former is only a specific application of the latter, separately recited in the APA not to establish a more rigorous standard of factual support but to emphasize that in the case of formal proceedings the factual support must be found in the closed record as opposed to elsewhere. . . .
>
> The "scope of review" provisions of the APA, <u>5 U.S.C. § 706(2)</u>, are cumulative. Thus, an agency action which is supported by the required substantial evidence may in another regard be "arbitrary, capricious, an abuse of discretion, or otherwise not in accordance with law" . . . . Thus, in those situations where paragraph (E) has no application (informal rulemaking, for example, which is not governed by §§ 556 and 557 to which paragraph (E) refers), paragraph (A) takes up the slack, so to speak, enabling the courts to strike down, as arbitrary, agency action that is devoid of needed factual support. When the arbitrary or capricious standard is performing that function of assuring factual support, there is no substantive difference between what it requires and what would be required by the substantial evidence test, since it is impossible to conceive of a "nonarbitrary" factual judgment supported only by evidence that is not substantial in the APA sense. . . .

7. Finally, there are times when the limits on the apparent power to articulate new standards in adjudication become apparent and a notice and comment process is mandated. In <u>*Shell Offshore, Inc. v. Babbitt*, 238 F.3d 622 (5th Cir. 2001)</u>, "Plaintiff-appellant Shell . . . sued the Department of the Interior . . . challenging Interior's denial of Shell's request to use its Federal Energy Regulatory Commission [existing] tariff rate. . . ." Assuming that each of Interior's interpretations of their regulation are valid interpretive rules, a significant issue remains: Can Interior switch from one consistently long followed permissible interpretation [found in their rules] to a new one without providing an opportunity for notice and comment? The court held:

> In a line of recent cases, the D.C. Circuit has addressed this very issue. In <u>*Alaska Professional Hunters Ass'n v. FAA*</u>, a regional office of the FAA had for many years been advising Alaskan hunting and fishing guides that they were exempt from FAA regulations governing commercial pilots. . . . At some point in the early 1990's, the FAA discovered [this] and in 1998 the FAA published a "Notice to Operators" which announced that Alaskan guides who transport customers by aircraft were no longer considered exempt from the FAA's safety regulations. . . . The court ruled that the FAA's action required notice and comment, and that the new interpretation of their regulation was invalid without it. . . .
>
> If a new agency policy represents a significant departure from long established and consistent practice that substantially affects the regulated industry, the new policy is a new substantive rule and the agency is obliged, under the APA, to submit the change for notice and comment. If Interior wishes to change its established practices and

procedures in a manner that . . . affects . . . lessees, it must give them notice and an opportunity to comment on the proposed change. Interior's new practice . . . places a new and substantial requirement on many OCS lessees, was a significant departure from long established and consistent past practice, and should have been submitted for notice and comment before adoption. . . . Since Shell cannot lawfully be affected by this new requirement, until Interior properly promulgates a new regulation it cannot require more of Shell than filing their tariff with FERC. . . .

ALLENTOWN MACK SALES & SERVICE, INC. V. NATIONAL LABOR RELATIONS BOARD

<u>522 U.S. 359 (1998)</u>

[JUSTICE SCALIA] Under longstanding precedent of the National Labor Relations Board, an employer who believes that an incumbent union no longer enjoys the support of a majority of its employees has three options: to request a formal, Board-supervised election, to withdraw recognition from the union and refuse to bargain, or to conduct an internal poll of employee support for the union. The Board has held that the latter two are unfair labor practices unless the employer can show that it had a "good faith reasonable doubt" about the union's majority support. We must decide whether the Board's standard for employer polling is rational and consistent with the National Labor Relations Act, and whether the Board's factual determinations in this case are supported by substantial evidence in the record.

I

Mack Trucks, Inc., had a factory branch in Allentown, Pennsylvania, whose service and parts employees were represented by Local Lodge 724 of the . . . AFL-CIO. Mack notified its Allentown managers . . . that it intended to sell the branch, and several of those managers formed Allentown Mack Sales, Inc., the petitioner here, which purchased the assets of the business . . . and began to operate it as an independent dealership. . . . Allentown hired 32 of the original 45 Mack employees.

During the period [surrounding] the sale, a number of Mack employees made statements to the prospective owners of Allentown Mack Sales suggesting that the incumbent union had lost support among employees . . . . In job interviews, eight employees made statements indicating, or at least arguably indicating, that they personally no longer supported the union. In addition, Ron Mohr, a member of the union's bargaining committee . . . told an Allentown manager that it was his feeling that the employees did not want a union, and that "with a new company, if a vote was taken, the Union would lose." And Kermit Bloch, who worked for Mack Trucks . . . on the night shift, told a manager that the entire night shift (then

5 or 6 employees) did not want the union.

On January 2, 1991, Local Lodge 724 asked Allentown Mack Sales to recognize it as the employees' collective-bargaining representative, and to begin negotiations for a contract. The new employer rejected that request . . . claiming a "good faith doubt as to support of the Union among the employees" [and announcing] that Allentown had "arranged for an independent poll by secret ballot of its hourly employees to be conducted under guidelines prescribed by the National Labor Relations Board." The poll [was] supervised by a Roman Catholic priest . . .; the union lost 19 to 13. Shortly thereafter, the union filed an unfair-labor-practice charge with the Board.

The Administrative Law Judge (ALJ) concluded that Allentown was a "successor" employer to Mack Trucks, Inc., and therefore inherited Mack's bargaining obligation and a presumption of continuing majority support for the union. The ALJ held that Allentown's poll was conducted in compliance with the procedural standards enunciated by the Board . . ., but that it violated §§ 8(a)(1) and 8(a)(5) of the National Labor Relations Act (Act) because Allentown did not have an "objective reasonable doubt" about the majority status of the union. The Board adopted the ALJ's findings and agreed with his conclusion . . . .

On review . . . Allentown challenged both the facial rationality of the Board's test for employer polling and the Board's application of that standard to the facts of this case. . . .

. . . .

III

The Board held Allentown guilty of an unfair labor practice in its conduct of the polling because it "had not demonstrated that it held a reasonable doubt, based on objective considerations, that the Union continued to enjoy the support of a majority of the bargaining unit employees." We must decide whether that conclusion is supported by substantial evidence on the record as a whole. . . . Before turning to that issue, we must clear up some semantic confusion. . . . [Doubt means not knowing, and there were enough questions raised that Allentown might have doubted, might not have known, whether the Union still had support.] The question presented for review . . . is whether, on the evidence presented to the Board, a reasonable jury could have found that Allentown lacked a genuine, reasonable uncertainty about whether Local 724 enjoyed the continuing support of a majority of unit employees.

In our view, the answer is no. . . .

. . . .

Accepting the Board's apparent (and in our view inescapable) concession that Allentown received reliable information that 7 of the bargaining-unit employees did not support the union, the remaining 25 would have had to support the union by a margin of 17 to 8 – a ratio of more than 2 to 1 – if the union commanded majority support. . . . The Board cannot covertly transform its presumption of continuing majority support into a working assumption that all of a successor's employees support the union until proved otherwise. Giving fair weight to Allentown's circumstantial evidence, we think it quite impossible for a rational fact-finder to avoid the conclusion that Allentown had reasonable, good-faith grounds to doubt – to be uncertain about – the union's retention of majority support.

IV

That conclusion would make this a fairly straightforward administrative-law case, except for the contention that the Board's factfinding here was not an aberration. . . . The Board . . . defend[s] its factfinding in this case by saying that it has regularly rejected similarly persuasive demonstrations of reasonable good-faith doubt in prior decisions. The Court of Appeals in fact accepted that defense, relying on . . . earlier, similar decisions to conclude that the Board's findings were supported by substantial evidence here. . . .

It is certainly conceivable that an adjudicating agency might consistently require a particular substantive standard to be established by a quantity or character of evidence so far beyond what reason and logic would require as to make it apparent that the *announced* standard is not *really* the effective one. And it is conceivable that in certain categories of cases an adjudicating agency which purports to be applying a preponderance standard of proof might so consistently demand in fact more than a preponderance, that all should be on notice from its case law that the genuine burden of proof is more than a preponderance. The question arises, then, whether, if that should be the situation that obtains here, we ought to measure the evidentiary support for the Board's decision against the standards consistently applied rather than the standards recited. As a theoretical matter (and leaving aside the question of legal authority), the Board could certainly have raised the bar for employer polling or withdrawal of recognition by imposing a more stringent requirement than the reasonable-doubt test, or by adopting a formal requirement that employers establish their reasonable doubt by more than a preponderance of the evidence. Would it make any difference if the Board achieved precisely the same result by formally leaving in place the reasonable-doubt and preponderance standards, but consistently applying them as though they meant something other than what they say? We think it would.

The Administrative Procedure Act . . . establishes a scheme of "reasoned deci-sionmaking." Not only must an agency's decreed result be within the scope of its lawful authority, but the process by which it reaches that result must be logical and rational. Courts enforce this principle with regularity when they set aside agency regulations which, though well within the agencies' scope of authority, are not supported by the reasons that the agencies adduce. The National Labor Rela-tions Board, uniquely among major federal administrative agencies, has chosen to promulgate virtually all the legal rules in its field through adjudication rather than rulemaking. . . . But adjudication is subject to the requirement of reasoned decisionmaking as well. It is hard to imagine a more violent breach of that require-ment than applying a rule of primary conduct or a standard of proof which is in fact different from the rule or standard formally announced. And the consistent repetition of that breach can hardly mend it.

Reasoned decisionmaking, in which the rule announced is the rule applied, promotes sound results, and unreasoned decisionmaking the opposite. The evil of a decision that applies a standard other than the one it enunciates spreads in both directions, preventing both consistent application of the law by subordinate agency personnel (notably administrative law judges), and effective review of the law by the courts. . . .

Because reasoned decisionmaking demands it, and because the systemic con-sequences of any other approach are unacceptable, the Board must be required to apply in fact the clearly understood legal standards that it enunciates in principle, such as good-faith reasonable doubt and preponderance of the evidence. Review-ing courts are entitled to take those standards to mean what they say, and to conduct substantial-evidence review on that basis. Even the most consistent and hence predictable Board departure from proper application of those standards will not alter the legal rule by which the agency's factfinding is to be judged. . . .

For the foregoing reasons, we need not determine whether the Board has consistently rejected or discounted probative evidence so as to cause "good faith reasonable doubt" . . . to mean something more than what the term[] connote[s]. The line of precedents relied on by the ALJ and the Court of Appeals could not render irrelevant to the Board's decision, and hence to our review, any evidence that tends to establish the existence of a good-faith reasonable doubt. It was there-fore error, for example, for the ALJ to discount Ron Mohr's opinion about lack of union support because of "the Board's historical treatment of unverified assertions by an employee about another employee's sentiments." . . . . Assuming that those assessments of the Board's prior behavior are true, they nonetheless provide no justification for the Board's factual inferences here. Of course the Board is entitled to be skeptical about the employer's claimed reliance on second-hand reports when the reporter has little basis for knowledge, or has some incentive to mislead.

But that is a matter of logic and sound inference from all the circumstances, not an arbitrary rule of disregard to be extracted from prior Board decisions. . . .

We conclude that the Board's "reasonable doubt" test for employer polls is facially rational and consistent with the Act. But the Board's factual finding that Allentown Mack Sales lacked such a doubt is not supported by substantial evidence on the record as a whole. The judgment of the Court of Appeals . . . is therefore reversed, and the case is remanded with instructions to deny enforcement.

———

Underlying Case Documents

The case referenced:
<u>The decision of the Administrative Law Judge</u>
<u>The decision of the Board</u>

For the anticlimactic decision on remand click <u>HERE</u>.

Take Note

Using adjudication to formulate policy allows the NLRB to evolve rules over time, bypass notice and comment entirely, and change the meaning of the standards by which it assesses unfair labor practices in proceedings that have a very limited number of parties and interests represented.

1. While *Allentown Mack* is a basic judicial review of an NLRB adjudication, the implications and unanswered questions the case presents are interesting. First, what would have prompted the court to engage in such a comprehensive, line-by-line review of the record? Did you sense an "edge" in the opinion? Is it possible, at least from the perspective of the majority, that the interest in taking apart the agency process has something to do with the fact that the NLRB has long announced new standards through adjudication instead of rulemaking? The Court notes this practice can "impede judicial review, and even political review, by disguising policymaking as fact finding."

2. The basic standard for review of adjudication has been the substantial evidence test (a somewhat unencumbered and straightforward measure) set out in <u>*Universal Camera Corp. v. NLRB*, 340 U.S. 474, 492-97 (1951)</u>. Without saying it is making a basic change, the *Allentown Mack* Court finds that the substantial evidence stan-

dard means something akin to the standard of proof jurors are instructed to use when assessing testimony and other evidence in Article III trials. 522 U.S. at 367.

a. The Court notes that the jury-equivalent test is biased in favor of the agency "since it requires not the degree of evidence which satisfies the court that the requisite fact exists, but merely the degree that could satisfy a reasonable factfinder." Does that include the role jurors play in civil case only? What about the role jurors perform in criminal cases where the standard "beyond a reasonable doubt" guides jury decisions?

b. The Court defines its task thusly: "We must decide whether on this record it would have been possible for a reasonable jury to reach the Board's conclusion." Does that seem right? Does the Supreme Court, as a general rule, engage in extensive factual analysis? Is this case aberrant – or a lead-in to the *Christensen*/*Mead* departure from *Chevron*?

3. The basic standard announced by the Court for review seems simple enough: "We examine the Board's decisions to ensure that they are rational, consistent with the National Labor Relations Act, and supported by substantial evidence." Using that standard, the majority concludes the agency erred in giving little credence to statements that had "undeniable and substantial probative value on the issue of reasonable doubt." Functioning almost like a first-level internal agency review board, the Court sizes up one witness, concluding that the NLRB should have paid more attention to the fact that "he was not hostile to the union, and was in a good position to assess union sentiment [and that his] statement has undeniable and substantial probative value. . . ." 522 U.S. at 372.

a. Is an appellate court the proper venue to decide the underlying motivations of witnesses? Why are the findings of the hearing officer or the Board regarding this witness not entitled to deference?

b. *Chevron* deference, *Mead* tells us, applies to notice and comment rulemaking and formal adjudication. Is *Allentown* a formal adjudication? The dissent in *Allentown* notes that the majority has "rewritten a Board decision without adequate justification . . . and has failed to give the kind of leeway . . . the Court's precedent mandates." Did the Court fail to give deference where deference was due, as the dissent suggests? After all, the "standard setting" piece of this case (defining standard setting very broadly) involved the "reasonable doubt" standard the NLRB adopted – which was upheld, but its application was not. Was that a failure of deference or a disagreement about witness credibility?

c. It is one thing to defer to the Board's judgment to use a "reasonable doubt" test – that decision is subject to arbitrary and capricious review – but what about the factual conclusions? In a case where both facts are found and policy is announced, the review questions are complicated and the Court's resolution unsettling. *See* Paul R. Verkuil, *An Outcomes Analysis of Scope of Review Standards*, 44 WM. & MARY L. REV. 679, 695 (2002).

IV. Negotiated Rulemaking

The criticism of "command and control" regulation reached a high point in the late 1980s. Admittedly, it over-simplifies the problem to note that people do not enjoy being told what to do. Nonetheless, the time and expense of notice and comment rulemaking is prohibitive. The need for rules is undeniable. One response to this collision in forces is to attempt a negotiation in advance of the notice and comment rulemaking that allows for the formulation of a proposed rule that will have a greater chance of success as it goes through the notice and comment process and a lower probability of attack if the rule is adopted.

Take Note

The concept underlying negotiated rulemaking is simple: If those most affected by a rule agree with its content, the chances for both compliance and reduced enforcement costs increases. The risk, of course, is that a rule negotiated by those who are regulated will be at best a lowest common denominator rule and at worst an ugly example of what happens when one allows a fox to take residence in a hen house.

When an agency contemplates the need for a rule where there is some possibility of a negotiation, it must comply with the Negotiated Rulemaking Act (see the Statutory Supplement). Assuming the basic requirements of the Act are met, the agency will then designate a "convener" who will facilitate the negotiation. The convener's responsibility includes selecting representatives for the different interests that will be affected by the rule to participate in a negotiation in which a rule can be written in a collaborative way. In this negotiation, the government representative has but one vote, as does each of the interests represented in the dialogue. At the conclusion of the process, assuming consensus can be reached, a proposed rule emerges that should be supported by those who participated in the negotiation.

Quite obviously, those who are not selected to participate in the negotiation are excluded from the process and left only with the remedy of commenting on the rule once it is put forward as a proposed rule during the notice and comment process that follows the negotiation. The cases and materials that follow highlight the positive and negative aspects of negotiated rulemaking.

USA GROUP LOAN SERVICES V. RILEY

<u>82 F.3d 708 (7th Cir. 1996)</u>

[CHIEF JUDGE POSNER] The federal government has an enormous program, administered by the Department of Education, of subsidizing student loans. The loans are made by banks but are guaranteed by state and private agencies that have reinsurance contracts with the Department, making it the indirect guarantor of the loans and thus inducing banks to make what would otherwise be risky loans. . . . Like so many government programs, the student loan program places heavy administrative burdens on the entities involved in it – the lenders, the guarantors, and the institutions. A whole industry of "servicers" has arisen to relieve these entities of some of the administrative burdens. . . . [T]he servicers maintain records of the institution's student loans . . ., they collect the loans from the students as the loans come due and dun (sic.) the students when they are slow in paying . . ., [and they] keep track of defaults and make sure that the banks comply with the various conditions for triggering the guarantees. In any of these roles a servicer who makes a mistake can end up costing the federal government money. . . .

Mistakes and outright fraud by servicers, some resulting in large losses of federal money, led Congress in 1992 to amend Title IV of the Higher Education Act to authorize the Secretary of Education to "prescribe . . . regulations applicable to third party servicers (including regulations concerning . . . the assessment of liabilities for program violations . . .) . . . ." The Secretary has done this, and the servicers have brought this suit to invalidate portions of the regulations on substantive and procedural grounds. The district court rejected the challenge, and the servicers appeal.

. . . .

. . . The 1992 amendment to the Higher Education Act, under which the regulation was promulgated, required that the Secretary submit any draft regulation to a process of negotiated rulemaking, to be conducted in accordance with . . . the Negotiated Rulemaking Act[, which] is to expire later this year but was applicable to the servicer rulemaking. The Act . . . authorize[s] the agency, in advance of the notice and comment rulemaking proceeding, to submit draft regulations to the industry or other groups that are likely to be significantly affected by the regulations and to negotiate with them over the form and substance of the regulations. The hope is that these negotiations will produce a better draft as the basis for the notice and comment proceeding. . . .

The servicers argue that the Department negotiated in bad faith with them. . . . During the negotiations, an official of the Department of Education promised the servicers that the Department would abide by any consensus reached by them unless there were compelling reasons to depart. The propriety of such a promise may be questioned. It sounds like an abdication of regulatory authority to the regulated, the full burgeoning of the interest-group state, and the final confirmation of the "capture" theory of administrative regulation. At all events, although the servicers reached a firm consensus that they should not be liable for their mistakes the Department refused to abide by its official's promise. What is more, the draft regulations that the Department submitted to the negotiating process capped the servicers' liability at the amount of the fees they received from their customers, yet when it came time to propose a regulation as the basis for the notice and comment rulemaking the Department abandoned the cap. The breach of the promise to abide by consensus in the absence of compelling reasons not here suggested, and the unexplained withdrawal of the Department's proposal to cap the servicers' liability, form the basis for the claim that the Department negotiated in bad faith.

We have doubts about the propriety of the official's promise to abide by a consensus of the regulated industry, but we have no doubt that the Negotiated Rulemaking Act did not make the promise enforceable. The practical effect of enforcing it would be to make the Act extinguish notice and comment rulemaking in all cases in which it was preceded by negotiated rulemaking; the comments would be irrelevant if the agency were already bound by promises that it had made to the industry. There is no textual or other clue that the Act meant to do this. Unlike collective bargaining negotiations, . . . the Act does not envisage that the negotiations will end in a binding contract. The Act simply creates a consultative process in advance of the more formal arms' length procedure of notice and comment rulemaking.

The complaint about the Secretary's refusal to adhere to the proposal to cap the servicers' liability misconceives the nature of negotiation. The Secretary proposed the cap in an effort to be accommodating . . . . The industry, in retrospect improvidently, rejected the proposal, holding out for no liability. So, naturally, the Secretary withdrew the proposal. A rule that a rejected offer places a ceiling on the offeror's demands would destroy negotiation. Neither party would dare make an offer, as the other party would be certain to reject it in order to limit the future demands that his opponent could make. This concern lies behind the principle that settlement offers are not admissible in litigation if the settlement effort breaks down. Fed. R. Evid. 408. By the same token, the negotiating position of the parties in negotiated rulemaking ought not be admissible in a challenge to the rule eventually promulgated when the negotiation failed.

The servicers argue that they should be allowed to conduct discovery to uncover the full perfidy of the Department's conduct in the negotiations. Discovery is rarely proper in the judicial review of administrative action. The court is supposed to make its decision on the basis of the administrative record, not create its own record. There are exceptions, . . . and the main one has some potential applicability here: discovery is proper when it is necessary to create a record without which the challenge to the agency's action cannot be evaluated. Negotiated rulemaking does not usually produce a comprehensive administrative record, such as notice and comment rulemaking, or a cease and desist order proceeding, or a licensing proceeding would do, any more than a settlement conference will usually produce a full record. Some discovery was conducted in the district court in order to present a picture of what went on at the negotiations between the servicers and the Department. The servicers argue that if only they could get access to the notes of certain participants in the negotiating sessions they could demonstrate additional instances of bad faith on the part of the Department.

[The servicers'] conception of "bad faith" reflects, as we have noted, a misconception of the negotiation process. It is not bad faith to withdraw an offer after the other side has rejected it. If as we doubt the Negotiated Rulemaking Act creates a remedy as well as a right, we suppose that a refusal to negotiate that really was in bad faith, because the agency was determined to stonewall, might invalidate the rule eventually adopted by the agency. But we do not think that the Act was intended to open the door wide to discovery in judicial proceedings challenging regulations issued after the notice and comment proceeding that followed the negotiations. If as in this case the public record discloses no evidence of bad faith on the part of the agency, that should be the end of the inquiry. A contrary conclusion would stretch out such judicial proceedings unconscionably. The Act's purpose – to reduce judicial challenges to regulations by encouraging the parties to narrow their differences in advance of the formal rulemaking proceeding – would be poorly served if the negotiations became a source and focus of litigation.

Affirmed.

Underlying Case Documents

The case referenced:
The 1992 amendment to the Higher Education Act
The Negotiated Rulemaking Act
Federal Rule of Evidence 408
The proposed rule

1. Is regulatory negotiation worth the time and expense? The debate is pitched – and extends over the last quarter-century.

a. The initial presentation – and defense – of the field comes from Professor Philip J. Harter's seminal work, *Negotiating Regulations: A Cure for Malaise*, 71 GEO. L.J. 1, 28-29 (1982):

> The parties participate directly and immediately in the decision. They share in its development and concur with it, rather than "participate" by submitting information that the decisionmaker considers in reaching the decision. Frequently, those who participate in the negotiation are closer to the ultimate decisionmaking authority of the interest they represent than traditional intermediaries that represent the interest in an adversarial proceeding. Thus, participants in negotiations can make substantive decisions, rather than acting as experts in the decisionmaking process. In addition, negotiation can be a less expensive means of decisionmaking because it reduces the need to engage in defensive research in anticipation of arguments made by adversaries.

b. Professor William Funk, in *Bargaining Toward the New Millennium: Regulatory Negotiation and the Subversion of the Public Interest*, 46 DUKE L.J. 1351, 1374-75 (1997), argued that such negotiations actually limit and in some instance silence the public because the number of participants and groups must be limited. Furthermore, he notes that this process will marginalize the capacity of an agency to undertake the hard business of regulation (after all, the agency is not in control of the negotiation).

> To the extent that negotiated rulemaking is the model for rulemaking, its theory and principles subvert the principles and theory of normal rulemaking. Moreover, the incentives to make negotiated rulemaking succeed themselves undermine and subvert the principles underlying traditional administrative law by elevating the importance of consensus among the parties above the law, the facts, or the public interest.

c. Andrew P. Morriss, et al., *Choosing How to Regulate*, 29 HARV. ENVTL. L. REV. 179 (2005):

> Regulation-by-negotiation failed to live up to its proponents' initial enthusiastic predictions but . . . provides agencies with significant advantages. . . . [In some circumstances] regulation-by-negotiation [is] genuinely cheaper to implement than regulation-by-rulemaking. . . . [Furthermore,] agencies may need the negotiation process to allow one set of interests to make credible commitments or disclosures to another set of interests that enable the regulation to be recognized as a Pareto improvement. . . .
>
> The key characteristics of regulation-by-negotiation are: (1) early and continuous negotiation amongst included affected interests over the substance of the rule; (2) the requirement of unanimous consent to the final negotiated rule proposal; (3) increased costs for the agency involved; and (4) continuation of the notice and comment procedures for those not participating in the negotiation.

[However,] the great failing of regulation-by-negotiation from the point of view of the agency is that institutionally negotiated rulemaking reduces the agency's power relative to the regulated entities and other interest groups by granting them a veto over the consensus required. Nonetheless it may offer agencies important benefits. . . .

d. Cary Coglianese, *Assessing the Advocacy of Negotiated Rulemaking: A Response to Philip Harter*, 9 NYU ENVTL. L.J. 386 (2001):

> Despite nearly twenty years of experimentation, negotiated rulemaking has yet to achieve a demonstrable reduction in the time it takes to develop regulations nor in the frequency or intensity of subsequent litigation over those regulations. . . . [N]egotiated rulemaking actually demands more effort and results in more litigation than other comparable rulemaking processes. . . .
>
> Indeed, there are good reasons to doubt that negotiated rulemaking will in fact lead to any systematic improvement at all in regulatory policy. Making consensus a precondition for policymaking will only likely exacerbate problems such as ambiguity, lowest common denominator results, and an undue emphasis on tractability. . . . Negotiated rulemaking's failure to achieve its goals of reducing rulemaking time and preventing litigation is simply not offset by any demonstrated improvements in the quality of regulatory policy. . . .

2. If a standard emerges as the rule or end product of a negotiation, it is still subject to notice and comment – and to comprehensive revision. A negotiated rulemaking does not bind the agency. Some case excerpts are illuminating:

a. In *City of Portland v. Environmental Protection Agency*, 507 F.3d 706 (D.C. Cir. 2007), the most recent circuit opinion in the field, the court held:

> In this case Portland and New York City challenge an Environmental Protection Agency rule regulating microbial contaminants in drinking water. The rule requires the two cities to take . . . steps to eliminate the parasite Cryptosporidium from their drinking water. . . .
>
> The cities claim that because the proposed rule flowed from a negotiated rulemaking and exactly mirrored the stakeholders' suggestions, EPA should have given clearer notice that the rule might be revised. This argument, however, ignores that the Agreement in Principle EPA executed with the stakeholders in this rulemaking expressly reserved the Agency's right to modify the final rule in response to comments. Moreover, neither the Negotiated Rulemaking Act, 5 U.S.C. §§ 561-570a, nor any other statute we know of requires an agency to provide more detailed notice of possible changes in its draft rules just because they evolve from negotiated rulemaking. Indeed, adopting the cities' suggestion would make it easier for disappointed parties to overturn negotiated rules than non-negotiated rules, thus discouraging agencies from engaging in negotiated rulemaking – exactly the opposite of what Congress intended. *See id.* § 569 (encouraging negotiated rulemaking).

b. *Raymond Proffitt Foundation v. Environmental Protection Agency*, 930 F. Supp. 1088, 1093 (E.D. Pa. 1996), involved a protracted dispute over the failure of the

State and EPA to promulgate an adequate plan to abate degradation of various water sources. Claims and counter claims were brought by environmental groups, developers, citizens associations, and land holders, all of whom had an interest in the plan. In part to respond to the inexplicable delays by EPA and the State, the state Department of Environmental Resources proposed a regulatory negotiation. The goal was

> to utilize public and internal input to develop a report on program issues and outline a range of options for change. At that point, we plan to initiate focused, facilitated discussions with representatives of the regulated community, the environmental community, and general public interest groups. These structured discussions will be facilitated by a professional environmental mediator and will be designed to generate consensus on program modifications that will be incorporated into water quality standards rulemaking. This consensus-building approach to revising Pennsylvania's water quality standard is called a regulatory-negotiation, or "reg-neg," process.

After excoriating the government for its failure to put forward a timely anti-degradation plan, the court noted the following: "[D]espite the few informational gaps in the record, the court . . . can . . . discern the basis for Defendants' decision not to propose and publish a water quality standard for Pennsylvania, but rather to permit the state to engage in a reg-neg process that might or might not culminate in promulgation of a standard that complies with the Act."

The court noted that the "reg-neg" was a basis to discount some damaging information in the record regarding delay, and the results may be worth the wait. At what point does a negotiation have value? Is it only when some form of agreement has been reached – or is the process itself of sufficient intrinsic value to put on hold the ordinary legal processes used to protect individual rights and interests?

c. *Central Arizona Water Conservation District v. Environmental Protection Agency, 990 F.2d 1531 (9th Cir. 1993),* involved one of a number of disputes regarding air quality in the Grand Canyon. As in the *Proffitt* case above, the use of regulatory negotiation as a means to try to come to some type of consensus between various interest groups played a positive role in the decision of the court. For a general discussion of this situation, see D. Michael Rappoport & John F. Cooney, *Visibility at the Grand Canyon: Regulatory Negotiations Under the Clean Air Act,* 24 ARIZ. ST. L.J. 627 (1992).

d. There are many situations where negotiated rulemaking does not succeed. See, for example, *Allied Local & Regional Manufacturers Caucus v. Environmental Protection Agency,* 215 F.3d 61 (D.C. Cir. 2000), where a negotiation to develop standards for volatile compound in coating materials (architectural paint) failed to produce consensus, or anything close to it. Similarly, because the process is optional – "[a]n agency *may* establish a negotiated rulemaking committee" 5 U.S.C. § 563(b) (emphasis added) – it is simply not used in many cases. *See, e.g., Tex. Office of Pub.*

<u>Util. Counsel v. FCC, 265 F.3d 313 (5th Cir. 2001)</u>. Moreover, negotiation is only one step in the rulemaking process. A notice and comment process will follow the negotiation – and in some cases, that will be followed by interpretations that may well change the focus or impact of the initial agreement. *See, e.g.,* <u>Ass'n of Am. RRs v. DOT, 198 F.3d 944 (D.C. Cir. 1999)</u>. Along the same lines, the value of a negotiation lies in the expectation that it will produce consensus and that thereafter, compliance rates will increase and enforcement cost will decline – but these are not guarantees – they are (in our judgment) well-founded hopes. Courts understand fully the nature of this process. *See, e.g.,* <u>Fort Peck Hous. Auth. v. United States HUD, 435 F. Supp. 2d 1125 (D. Colo. 2006)</u> ("The fact that the regulatory scheme was developed through a negotiated rulemaking procedure is of no relevance to this determination.").

e. As *USA Group Loan v. Reily* points out, a consensus derived through negotiated rulemaking can get bumped aside as the post-negotiation notice and comment process unfolds. Challenges are limited, however. In <u>Center for Law and Education v. Department of Education, 315 F. Supp. 2d 15 (D.D.C. 2004)</u>, the challenge focused on the composition of the group selected to participate in the rulemaking:

> Two advocacy groups . . . challenge the composition of a negotiated rulemaking committee assembled by the Department of Education ("Education") to propose regulations as required by the <u>No Child Left Behind Act, 20 U.S.C. § 6301</u> et seq. ("NCLBA"). . . . Specifically, plaintiffs object to Education's designation of some educators as representatives of parents and students, given NCLBA's command that Education select committee members "in such numbers as will provide an equitable balance between representatives of parents and students and representatives of educators and education officials.". . . . The NCLBA . . . provides support for education programs designed to help disadvantaged children meet high academic standards. . . .
>
> [The] persons selected to participate in the negotiated rulemaking committee . . . included . . . seven individuals "representing students . . . ." Of the seven individuals set forth as representatives of students, two were described in the notice simply as "parents," one was identified as a "teacher," and four appeared to be state or local education officials. . . . [The committee reached] consensus on proposed rules, which were published for further comment. . . . [T]he advocacy group plaintiffs submitted extensive recommendations and comments. . . .
>
> Plaintiffs [rely] on the second sentence of Section 570 – "nothing in this section shall bar judicial review of a rule if such judicial review is otherwise provided by law" – and on the strong traditional presumption that final agency action is reviewable absent a clear expression of Congressional intent to the contrary.
>
> An overarching goal of the NRA was "to reduce judicial challenges to regulations by encouraging the parties to narrow their differences in advance of the formal rulemaking proceeding." Reading Section 570 to multiply the grounds for attacking final rules would thus seem inconsistent with the spirit of the NRA. . . . Agencies would have little incentive to convene negotiated rulemaking committees if doing so made their final rules more vulnerable to legal challenge. This conclusion accords

no greater judicial deference to rules that flow from negotiated rulemaking – such rules remain subject to all other challenges on the same basis as other rules. It merely recognizes Congress' intent to bar judicial review of a narrow category of potential procedural flaws in the interest of more efficient rulemaking.

3. The two excerpts that follow highlight some of the more important considerations in the negotiated rulemaking area.

a. Daniel P. Selmi, *The Promise and Limits of Negotiated Rulemaking: Evaluating the Negotiation of a Regional Air Quality Rule*, 35 ENVTL. L. 415 (2005):

I. Introduction

For almost 25 years the possibility of utilizing negotiation as a means of breaking deadlocks over administrative rulemaking has attracted the attention of academic commentators. Even after all this time, however, the prospects for negotiated rulemaking remain very much subject to debate. Proponents see negotiated rulemaking as providing a variety of benefits, including a non-adversarial, creative approach to environmental problem solving. They view negotiation as facilitating improved outcomes that are less likely to result in litigation. Some envision negotiated rulemaking as part of a much larger trend toward either a "contractarian" or "pragmatic" approach to administrative lawmaking.

In contrast, opponents of negotiated rulemaking primarily raise concerns relating to the integrity of the administrative process. The overarching criticism is that bargained agreements between government and private interests will be treated as elements of public law rather than as private contracts. Some also claim negotiated rulemaking fails to meet the two prominent efficiency goals promoted for it: preventing litigation and saving time in the regulatory process.

Traditionally, the literature on negotiated rulemaking has largely centered on case-by-case evaluations. Many are "first-person" accounts by participants, often in the context of rulemakings undertaken by federal agencies. The participants analyze and describe their reactions to the process, and many of these evaluations have been favorable to negotiated rulemaking. Others, however, criticize these studies as too narrow and as not providing a systematic comparison of negotiated rules with non-negotiated rules. Critics also label some of the favorable case studies as focused only on the successful negotiations and note that they typically are not written by independent observers.

At least partially in response to this body of criticism, academics have begun to employ empirical research as a tool for reaching more general conclusions about whether negotiated rulemaking achieves the benefits it advertises. These empirical studies have tried to compare outcomes by relying on interviews and questionaires filled out by participants in those regulatory negotiations. However, as was the case with the previous debates over negotiated rulemaking, the literature is in sharp conflict. Two recent empirical studies found broad benefits in negotiated rulemaking, while another concluded that the suggested benefits of negotiated rulemaking are overstated.

The recent trend toward empirical research is a natural and welcome evolution in the study of negotiated rulemaking. Sufficient experience with regulatory negotiation now exists to begin drawing tentative conclusions about its overall efficacy. Nonetheless, case-specific studies of regulatory negotiations still can serve important purposes. By focusing on a specific negotiation, such studies shed light on whether and how the interaction among the parties to a negotiated rulemaking is different from the interaction in a normal notice and comment rulemaking. Case-specific studies also can illumine whether the negotiation format fosters the exercise of creativity beyond that found in the usual administrative process. Moreover, broad based empirical comparisons of negotiated rulemakings face significant barriers. For example, the data base – the actual number of negotiated rulemakings – is not large, despite the lengthy period of time negotiated rulemaking has been in use.

. . . .

IV. Regulatory Negotiation: A Brief Summary

Some background on regulatory negotiation will set the stage before discussion of the actual negotiation. The academic literature exhausts the subject of regulatory negotiation. Accordingly, the process will be described only briefly here.

A negotiated rulemaking begins when a "convener," often someone employed by a public agency, canvasses interested parties to determine their willingness to participate in a negotiation as an alternative to the agency simply proposing a rule. If a sufficient number of parties indicate a willingness to participate, then the agency formally convenes the negotiating process. At the federal level, the Negotiated Rulemaking Act of 1990, as reauthorized in 1996, governs the negotiation process. Under this law, if the negotiation ultimately succeeds, it culminates in a proposed rule, which the agency then formally proposes for adoption under the Administrative Procedure Act.

An impartial facilitator, normally compensated by the agency but not a full-time employee of it, presides over the negotiation. The facilitator may have some expertise in the subject of the negotiation, but more often does not. Instead, the facilitator brings the parties together, establishes ground rules governing the negotiations, and then guides the negotiations. Ground rules may, for example, particularly emphasize civility among the negotiating parties by requiring each party to commit to listening to the other parties and to adhere to various other rules designed to prevent adversarial behavior.

The agency acts as a participant in the negotiations along with the other interested parties. During the process, the facilitator may appoint various subcommittees to examine specific aspects of the rule. Ultimately, the parties either agree to a proposal or acknowledge that agreement is impossible. A successful negotiation normally culminates in a written document which the parties agree to support, or at least not to oppose.

Thereafter, the formal rulemaking process begins. Under standard administrative law, the agency must take comments from the public on the rule; it cannot commit to adoption of the negotiated rule before the public process concludes. All parties to the negotiation, however, understand that the agency is highly committed to the outcome of the negotiation. Thus, as a practical matter, any substantial change in the negotiated rule during the actual rulemaking process is unlikely.

. . . .

VI. Evaluating the Negotiations:

. . . .

A. The Role of Information: Gathering and Exchange

1. The Debate on the Availability of Information

The traditional administrative law model envisions that agency experts will propose a regulation and then provide opportunity for public comment before final adoption of the rule. While the "reformation" of administrative law called into question the model of administrative action based on agency expertise, the fact remains that agencies exercising regulatory power do so on the basis of their presumed expertise. That expertise, however, requires an information base, and a principal difficulty faced by environmental regulatory agencies is lack of information about the industries they regulate. . . .

Some commentators also have suggested that negotiation is an ineffective means of resolving factual matters. Others go even further, arguing that an agency should not undertake a negotiation where technical support for the rule does not exist, or alternatively that in negotiations, data becomes a "bargaining chip" rather than the foundation for deliberation. Still other commentators disagree, asserting that negotiation provides the agency with a more complete understanding of the factual grounds for the regulation.

In theory, the negotiation model allows for information gathering where necessary to fill in gaps in the design of regulation. Regulatory negotiation emphasizes cooperative learning, and the pragmatism of the negotiation process should lead to a meaningful exchange of information. By committing to negotiate in good faith, the parties agree that they will make every effort to provide sought-after data. In this process the facilitator serves as an enforcement officer of sorts, refereeing disputes and reminding parties of their commitment. In contrast, notice and comment rulemaking contains no similar cooperative dynamic among the parties.

2. The Effective Exchange of Information

. . . .

Because of the data exchange, by the end of the negotiation [in the examples studied] there was little dispute over the technical basis for the rule. In contrast, the normal rulemaking process often does not resolve technical disputes, as the process is not designed to facilitate the kinds of good faith exchanges that might lead to such a resolution. Instead, the rule adoption is likely to be preceded by the submission of lengthy comment letters designed to exhaust administrative remedies, and thus lay the groundwork for litigation, rather than to clarify and possibly to resolve issues.

A recent empirical study concluded that negotiated rule participants "are far more likely to say that they gained new technical information, better knowledge of the issue, and new information about the positions of other parties." . . . . The new data [can serve] to clarify existing contentious issues, rather than to raise new disputes.

Thus, to the extent that one asks whether negotiated rulemaking "has demonstrated a capability for alleviating the adversarialism that plagues the pluralist interactions of interest groups," the answer . . . is positive. In [the case studied], the information allowed the parties to understand the true costs that would be imposed on industry if the rule required enhanced regulation of plating facilities near sensitive receptors. In short, it was not a psychological benefit of negotiation that led the parties to accept the outcome (although those benefits did exist); it was the concrete data obtained through the process. To employ a term found in one article raising the issue of the legitimacy of negotiation, the technical data was a "legitimacy benefit" produced by the negotiation.

3. Affording Technical Assistance to Parties

. . . .

This type of request poses a problem for the agency that is rooted in public regulatory theory. In a notice and comment rulemaking, agencies expect participants in agency processes to bear their own expenses. The assumption is that a party's interest in a given issue will cause the party to generate sufficient resources for effective participation. Furthermore, the agency's impartiality can be questioned if it seems to favor one particular interest group by taking steps to ensure that the group's position is fully articulated.

However, a negotiated rulemaking is quite different from a normal rulemaking proceeding. It emphasizes personal interaction, and thus allows confrontation of technical questions in a detailed way that a priori cannot occur in a notice and comment rulemaking. Furthermore, because the negotiation places demands on parties that normal rulemaking does not, some parties invited to participate by the agency may have difficulty marshalling the necessary resources. These parties can plausibly claim that, because regulatory negotiations place extraordinary demands on participants, the agency could fairly bear some of the costs involved.

. . . .

[O]ther factors can interfere with the pursuit of creative solutions in a regulatory negotiation. For example, if the agency is under a statutory deadline to act, it may opt for a rule taking the easier or more familiar path. Embarking on a time-consuming effort to create alternative solutions would put the agency in legal jeopardy if the negotiations fail and the legal deadline to act passes. Similarly, if a statute compels the agency to adopt a plan or rules securing specific emission reductions, and a technology-forcing rule is the agency's only option, little room to negotiate is likely to exist. These constraints are quite serious under the <u>Clean Air Act</u>, which obligates states to carry out their implementation plans. The failure to do so can result in a judicial order compelling implementation.

In contrast, successful negotiation is an attempt to create the proverbial "win-win" situation in which all parties benefit from the agreement. It also works to foster a framework in which parties seek new solutions that would not otherwise exist. In the context of a rulemaking, this expansion of possible solutions may lead to a broader consensus that includes, but is not limited to, agreement on what the rule should contain. Moreover, where an entire industry faces a proposed rule that seems only to impose additional costs, the chances that the industry will voluntarily agree to the rule are small unless it will receive other benefits not related to the rule. Indeed, without the possibility of those additional benefits, an industry might decide that other options are preferable, such as an all-out political offensive opposing the rule or, if that effort is unsuccessful, the initiation of litigation. . . .

[R]ule implementation questions normally are seen as secondary to the rulemaking adoption process. In contrast, the informality of the negotiation process, and the availability of the facilitator, combine to provide a broader, more creative framework in which the parties can present their views and concerns. . . .

Whether industry representation in a negotiation can be skewed so that certain segments of a particular industry unduly benefit to the exclusion of others remains a lurking question. Standard economic theory suggests that industry negotiators might well seek to benefit themselves at the expense of competitors. . . . Still, agencies must assure that industry representation is sufficiently robust and widespread to avoid any charges that the outcome of the negotiations benefits some parts of an industry over others.

More importantly, for too long the debate over negotiated rulemaking has revolved around extreme conclusions about its benefits or failures. It is portrayed either as a panacea or a totally misguided venture. In fact, it is neither. It will certainly not be a complete "cure" for administrative malaise, and it will not be effective in many situations where the proposed rule affects a wide range of interests. It can, however, be quite useful in some instances. Accordingly, the expectations for regulatory negotiation need to be re-calibrated, and, to be effective, its use must be targeted. . . .

b. Phillip J. Harter, *In Search of Goldilocks: Democracy, Participation, and Government*, 10 PENN. ST. ENVTL. L. REV. 113 (2002):

Very few people of any stripe would actively advocate a return to the expert model of administration in which we are to simply trust the agencies to make the right decision with very little input from the public or oversight or involvement from the political branches of the government. The administrative law developments of the 1960s-1970s largely remain in place and the procedures serve to legitimize many of the decisions:

agencies must develop an extensive factual background for their decisions and explain in detail how you get from that to the rule, members of the public must be able to participate in the process at minimum by commenting on proposals that are considered by the agency, the agency must examine the implications of the rules on a whole host of issues, the decision is reviewed politically at the White House both as a preliminary matter and before issuing the final decision, and, finally, courts will review to make sure the facts are straight, but will provide considerable deference to the policy decisions.

Agencies have now broadly accepted public participation. It serves a number of quite different functions in the regulatory process. First, it fosters a type of citizenship and buy-in that result when members of the public take the time to be involved in making their government work and seeing the decisions made. Second, it provides direct accountability since the agency has to tell the people what it is up to and justify why it is taking the action it is. Third, it develops better information for the agency's consideration. Fourth, it helps ward off capture by interests that have preferential access to decisionmakers, and discourages agencies from being unresponsive to important issues because public participation serves as a means by which these issues are presented squarely for resolution.

But note, even though agencies widely follow and advocate public participation in a broad spectrum of matters, the mere fact that the public participates does not answer the essential question: Who decides and how. As we have seen from history, public participation can still be grafted onto the expert model, so that all this outpouring from the public as it participates is really designed to supply information to the agency so that it, and it alone, can decide the issue, subject, of course, to the accountability to Congress and the courts. Thus, public participation often does not mean a sharing in the decision; rather, it means an opportunity to tell your views to those who will decide, with or without any dialogue or other feedback. Or, the agency can use public participation to try to defuse the whole situation and come up with an answer to maximize the overall benefits to the participants. Seen another way, public participation minimizes the discomfort to the agency. In short, through the participation, the agency seeks to make a deal. . . .

As a number of people have recently pointed out, however, there is a third model of administrative decision-making called "deliberative democracy." It is reaching governmental decisions through a dialogue based on communication and reason, not simply assertions of desires and positions met by counter positions. The goal is not just the aggregate of individual preferences, but rather a group quest for what is the public good or, as it is more commonly expressed, the public interest. Each of these theories has been used to legitimize various agency decisions. While fostering a deliberative democracy is certainly a key element of the developments of administrative law and has many direct supporters, it has not been given enough attention.

IV. A Discussion of Deliberative Democracy

What are the basic requirements of this approach? First, it is deliberative and that requires for its legitimacy a conversation, discussion, dialogue, or negotiation based on reason, and not just the raw preferences of the aggregated interests. In effect, it is a search for what is the best, appropriate thing to do when reaching a decision. The deliberation could, of course, take place solely within the agency. And, indeed, that is how the term is commonly used – the deliberations are within the agency and do not include members of the public. But, that would ignore its democratic dimension – a deliberative democracy is perforce a democracy, and that means citizens need to participate by some means or another. The question then becomes: Just what is the form of participation? Is it solely in choosing a government – picking a king or queen – that will then make all the decisions, or is the participation in making the actual, individual decisions? . . .

. . . .

If the process is to meet constitutional requirements, it is clear the agency cannot delegate its authority to even a democratically elected group, and it must make, or at least be able to review and control, the decisions that are binding on others. This is important not only for legal legitimacy but also as a practical matter in how the system works. If the deliberations break down, the agency will still be called upon to make the final decision. Indeed, even if the deliberations among the representatives do not break down, the agency still has the authority under the constitution to make the decision and, hence, might change the consensus of the deliberations. Thus, the default is not the status quo, but rather what the agency will do if the deliberators hit an impasse. . . .

. . . .

The experience over the past 20 years has shown that using a form of direct participation by representatives of those substantially affected by the decision can solve many [problems that result when multiple groups in a single field have disparate views and goals]. This has indeed been the case for a number of negotiations in which I have served as the mediator or been a close observer of the process. This is also the observation of those who have actually studied the processes and talked to a diverse sample of participants – from personal discussions with participants themselves and from discussions with senior agency officials who have used them.

While a direct democratic process for resolving these contentious issues has proven itself time and time again and there are a number of ways that the process can be organized, its use is not appropriate for all decisions and there are some basic requirements that should be followed. There needs to be sufficiently diverse representation so that virtually anyone with an interest in the issue can be confident that his or her perspective will be raised at the table. The flip side of that requirement is that there also needs to be some process to ensure that no interest is left out or purposefully excluded.

Many critically important decisions can and are made with less than a consensus. Indeed, that is the entire function of any committee that operates under Robert's Rules of Order as do most Federal Advisory Committees. Important guidance can stem from policy dialogues and other forms of cooperation and collaboration. But, for the types of decisions we are talking about here, consensus in which each interest has a veto, or at least needs to be able to live with the decision when viewed as whole, plays a fundamental, irreducible role. First, it makes it safe to come to the table; otherwise each party would likely continue to build support and make its case in other forums. Under consensus, however, each party knows it cannot be out-voted and, hence, that an adverse decision will not be imposed on it; as a result, that interest can relax the power-building while the talks are productive. Consensus also forces the parties to deal with each other and to look at the entire decision and not just its individual parts. This, in turn, can lead to sophisticated trade-offs that are simply unavailable under a less rigorous mode of decision. The use of consensus, therefore, stimulates a "deliberative democracy" approach.

The agency plays a crucial role in the deliberations. First, the private parties need to recognize that if they do not reach an agreement, the agency will impose one. Thus, when assessing their "Best Alternative To a Negotiated Agreement" or BATNA, the parties must take into account what the agency will do. Simply doing nothing or avoiding a decision will not be helpful to a private party. Because the agency will eventually make some decision, the negotiations provide the participants with the opportunity to actually control the outcome. Further, the agency will represent in the negotiations whatever interests it has in the subject. It will then use the creative ideas and information available to the private parties to enhance those interests. Importantly for the constitutional theory, no decision will be imposed on the agency. Rather the agency, like the others, agrees that when considered as a whole and when compared to what it can achieve otherwise, it concurs in the decision. Thus, the entire decision can be viewed as that of the agency alone, even though the others agree with the agency. When these processes are followed, the results have largely been very good time wise, substantively, and as measured by the parties' satisfaction.

It can, moreover, be viewed as a deliberative democratic approach to administrative decisionmaking. It is a representative democracy: Representation is based on interests and not geography. And it is deliberative: One of the main issues is how much information, data, or scientific certainty is needed to make a responsible decision, not trying to gather everything possible nor trying to decide who is right to the exclusion of others. Further, the parties and their technical experts can engage in a form of peer review with the scientists discussing science with other scientists. That can clarify assumptions and limitations and deepen the mutual understanding of the science and its uncertainties. The parties may continue to disagree about the science, but the question then becomes: What are we collectively going to do about solving the issue at hand? The role of science is different in this process than in the traditional process. Here, science is not being used to corral the decision precisely because the parties themselves make the actual decision. The end result is likely to be a more scientifically accurate picture since it does not try to force precision where there is none. Instead, it recognizes the disagreements and uncertainty.

Moreover, the process still meets the requirements for accountability. First, the decision of the agency can be envisioned as the decision of the requisite Officer of the United States because the agency did indeed concur in the outcome and decided that it would be better off with the decision than without it. Courts can review the decision, and it must meet the statute and have the necessary underpinnings. This prevents logrolling and makes sure no one is zapped. Congress continues to have oversight and the White House remains involved, preferably through the political appointees in the agency.

. . . .

Agencies need to recognize that reg neg [regulatory negotiation – another name for negotiated rulemaking] can be a powerful tool in addressing difficult cases. Agency management needs to set goals, provide resources, and follow through. People whether senior managers, line officers, or staff, do not want to be second-guessed and criticized. For example, someone may be criticized for cooperating with industry, which would, of course, be a quite legitimate complaint if it were done to the exclusion of others. It is not legitimate, however, when others who would be affected by the outcome participate as well and the resulting decision clearly meets the public goals defined by agency management. We need to provide the means for getting clearances and blessings along the way and to hold people accountable for not paying attention to details and doing it right. And, if some staff member decides to buck senior directives, one would think the senior manager would require explicit reasons for not following through. Much, indeed most, depends on sensitive agency management.

Using a deliberative democratic approach to make these decisions requires the agency to charter the committee as an advisory committee. Because hell hath no fury as a regulated regulator and chartering is just that, it would help greatly if the process of chartering were streamlined and made far easier than it has been, or at least agency officials have to understand that it is not such a big deal. It would also help if agency staff understood that participating in these processes is a way to greatly leveraging their expertise and insights by taking advantage of the insights and information of the private sector on all sides of an issue.

If this is done, reg neg and other forms of consensus processes has a promising future; without it, they are likely to be used only when a[n] agency gets really "stuck" and must get something out the door.

. . . .

V. ISO Goldilocks

Much of the criticism of these procedures is based on assertions, not data, that the mediation procedure does not work, that someone might be excluded from the process, that mediation does not comport with some mid-level guy's views as to what it should be, that business always wins, that the only role of the agency is to make a deal no matter what the substance, or some other conjured up view. Then, based on these views, the process as a whole is rejected as a sell out. The other opposing political theory would be to embrace technocratic decisions – trusting the agency alone to make the right decisions unfettered by dirty old politics.

There is here, as in the story of Goldilocks, a middle ground that relies on careful attention to detail as to how the processes operate and how the government participates in them that can lead to mutually beneficial results, especially when the issues are particularly difficult as in the types of issues being discussed here. In these cases, the agency plays the central role of assembling the representatives together to solve a difficult problem and ensures that the decision is faithful to the criteria that are to enter into the resolution. That is a powerful role indeed for an agency to play. It is to be sure somewhat different from the one envisioned under a technocratic theory but one that comports more to what actually happens in these terribly difficult cases.

To address the grave malaise facing administrative law today, those who would wish agencies were better able to address problems based on complex scientific and technical issues should join Goldilocks in her search for a reasonable middle ground based on careful attention to detail.

CHAPTER 6

Adjudication – Basic Principles and Entitlements

I. An Overview of the Adjudicatory Process

Agencies use the adjudicatory process to resolve disputes, enforce statutes and regulations, and grant or deny licenses or benefits. The process for formal adjudication is set out in the Administration Procedure Act (5 U.S.C. §§ 554, 556-57), but the rules and procedures for informal adjudication are not found in any one place in the APA. It is not that members of Congress or state legislatures are incapable of establishing the ground rules for informal adjudication. It is rather that the range and nature of adjudicatory determinations is so broad and varied that it is simply impossible to articulate a "one size fits all" set of rules to cover informal adjudicatory action.

While there is no definitive APA provision for informal adjudication – the most common of all agency processes – there are certain principles worth noting at the outset. First, it is not a foregone conclusion that Fifth or Fourteenth Amendment Due Process protections will apply to adjudication. The initial cases in this section will allow you to determine whether and the extent to which those protections are applicable in agency adjudication. That said, the denial of timely notice – a bedrock due process entitlement and a right guaranteed for formal adjudication in 5 U.S.C. § 554(b) – is generally unacceptable. Vague as the rules may be for informal action, some type of notice is fundamental to any proceeding where meaningful interests are at stake.

As to the format, rules, participatory rights, and evidentiary principles in informal and formal adjudicatory proceedings, the process varies considerably from agency to agency – and often within an agency, depending on the right, entitlement, sanction, or interest at stake.

> **Take Note**
>
> At a basic level, unlike rulemaking, neither formal nor informal adjudicatory proceedings are open-ended public processes in which any interested person can participate. While the rules are less demanding than the constitutional and prudential restrictions regarding access to courts, agencies limit participation in adjudications, permitting only the parties to the proceeding and those interveners the agency determines will be of value in the decisionmaking process.

Procedural comparisons with rulemaking, like comparisons with trials in Article III tribunals, can be misleading. For example, there is no general right to discovery in agency practice – although many agencies have elaborate procedures for depositions and interrogatories. Even the basic premise that those charged with fact finding ought not also perform in a decisionmaking capacity (the separation of functions doctrine) is not applied in all adjudicatory matters.

Furthermore, the rules and principles you may have learned in Evidence, on the presentation of witnesses, documents, and other mechanisms of proof, are generally not applicable in agency litigation. Again, while agencies often characterize their evidentiary rules as "relaxed," many agencies have complex and occasionally formal processes to determine what information to admit and what information is unacceptable.

> **Bottom Line**
>
> In formal adjudication, evidence must be reliable, probative, and substantive–terms to be discussed in the cases that follow. This test is also referred to by some courts as the "clear error" test. "The difference [between clear error and substantial evidence] is a subtle one – so fine that . . . we have failed to uncover a single instance in which a reviewing court conceded that the use of one standard rather than the other would in fact have produced a different outcome." *Dickinson v. Zurko*, 527 U.S. 150, 162-63 (1999).

1. When is a Formal Hearing Required?

a. When does the APA mandate a formal hearing? Much like *Florida East Coast*, *supra* Chapter 6, which is applicable to rulemaking, Section 554(a) of the APA requires formal adjudication when the statute being implemented requires agency determinations to be made "on the record after opportunity for an agency hearing . . . ." 5 U.S.C. § 554(a). *Crestview Parke Care Ctr. v. Thompson*, 373 F.3d 743, 748 (6th Cir. 2003). Legislation that uses phrases such as "hearing" or "public hearing" does not, without more, mandate formality.

b. Moreover, much the same as in the rulemaking materials, the APA created exceptions for circumstances where formal hearings might otherwise seem the appropriate process. Section 5 U.S.C. § 554(a) (regarding adjudication) reads:

> This section applies, according to the provisions thereof, in every case of adjudication required by statute to be determined on the record after opportunity for an agency hearing, except to the extent that there is involved: (1) a matter subject to a subsequent trial of the law and the facts de novo in a court; (2) the selection or tenure of an employee, except a[n] administrative law judge appointed under section 3105 of this title [5 U.S.C. § 3105]; (3) proceedings in which decisions rest solely on inspections, tests, or elections; (4) the conduct of military or foreign affairs functions; (5) cases in which an agency is acting as an agent for a court; or (6) the certification of worker representatives.

c. In many instances, an agency will have an option to proceed with formal adjudication, using an enforcement action to apply and interpret its own rules as well as statutes, or to proceed with a rulemaking (formal, informal, hybrid, interpretive, or otherwise). The choice, unless mandated by statute, between rulemaking and adjudication "lies primarily in the informed discretion of the administrative agency. . . ." *Chenery*, 332 U.S. at 203, *supra* Chapter 4. The Fourth Circuit noted recently that this principle allows agencies to proceed in adjudication "without spelling out their interpretations beforehand through notice and comment rulemaking. . . . A contrary rule would 'stultify the administrative process,' ignoring the benefits of adjudicatory development that have led courts to recognize 'a very definite place for the case-by-case evolution of statutory standards.'" *West Virginia v. Thompson, 475 F.3d 204, 210 (4th Cir. 2007)*.

d. Assuming the agency proceeds by adjudication, the process can appear far more complicated than any Article III proceeding. A case is initiated in most courts of general jurisdiction by filing a complaint. Consider, by comparison, the situation in *Joseph v. FTC, 505 F.3d 1380, 1381-83 (Fed. Cir. 2007)*, and the procedural journey required to get to a hearing and initial decision. The petitioner, a veteran, applied unsuccessfully for a job at the Federal Trade Commission. Petitioner "contend[ed] that the agency's procedure in filling the vacancy denied him his veterans' preference rights. The Merit Systems Protection Board ("Board") rejected this contention. . . . After unsuccessfully challenging his non-appointment before the Department of Labor pursuant to *5 U.S.C. § 3330(a)(1)* as violating his veterans' preference rights, [petitioner] appealed his non-selection to the Board. Because he was a Board employee, the Board referred the complaint to the National Labor Relations Board for adjudication by one of that agency's administrative law judges. In his initial decision the administrative law judge sustained [petitioner's] contention and ordered his selection. The Board, however, reversed. . . ."

2. Basic Deference and Substantial Evidence

a. There are some important similarities between rulemaking and formal adjudication pertaining to *Chevron* that you will recognize immediately (assuming you have completed the rulemaking materials in this text). The Court's holdings in this area are not quite as "improvised" (a term we have used a number of times, based on JUSTICE SCALIA's dissents in *Mead*, *supra* Chapter 3, and *Nat'l Cable & Telecomms. Ass'n v. Brand X Internet Servs.*, *supra* Chapter 3). In *Thomas Jefferson University v. Shalala, 512 U.S. 504, 512 (1994)*, the Court found that an agency's interpretation of its own regulations in an adjudication, "must be given controlling weight unless it is plainly erroneous or inconsistent with the regulation," a ruling the Court repeated in *Auer v. Robbins* and *Christensen v. Harris County*.

b. This deference to interpretations in adjudication extends to certain positions taken for the first time in the adjudication itself. In <u>Martin v. OSHRC, 499 U.S. 144, 157 (1991)</u>, the Court found that the "Secretary's interpretation of [the Occupational Safety and Health] Act regulations in an administrative adjudication, however, is agency action, not a post hoc rationalization of it . . . . [The] Secretary's litigating position before the Commission is as much an exercise of delegated lawmaking powers as is the Secretary's promulgation of a workplace health and safety standard." Consider further that Congress can – and on occasion does – limit judicial review of such cases. In <u>Ballesteros v. Ashcroft, 452 F.3d 1153, 1156 (10th Cir. 2006)</u>, the court noted:

> Our review of immigration decisions is limited by statute. Congress has eliminated judicial review of both the BIA's discretionary decisions, <u>8 U.S.C. § 1252(a)(2)(B)</u>, and of any "final order of removal against an alien who is removable by reason of having committed" certain offenses, among them aggravated felonies and controlled substance offenses, <u>8 U.S.C. § 1252(a)(2)(C)</u>. . . . [In addition, the] Court has "acknowledged the power of administrative agencies to announce 'new rules' through adjudication rather than formal rulemaking and placed the burden of proving detrimental reliance on the opponents of the new rule."

c. One distinction between rulemaking and adjudication that should be obvious involves the decisionmaker. In rulemaking cases, the commissioners or administrator heading the agency bear primary responsibility. In adjudication, there are a range of decisionmakers involved – and a range of titles, each with varying powers and obligations. In addition to administrative law judges, there are hearing officers, field specific judges (e.g., immigration judges), boards, panels, and a number of other roles and titles involved in the process.

Take Note

Regardless of title, hearing officers responsible for adjudicatory decisionmaking benefit from tort immunity for their actions as judges. <u>Butz v. Economou, 438 U.S. 478, 511 (1978)</u>. They do not, however, share the same tenure protections, compensation, and benefits of federal district court judges.

3. Right to Counsel?

a. Another important difference between Article III tribunals and adjudicatory proceedings at administrative agencies involves the right to counsel. <u>Section 555(b)</u> provides: "A person compelled to appear in person before an agency or representative thereof is entitled to be accompanied, represented, and advised by counsel or, if permitted by the agency, by other qualified representative. . . . This subsection does not grant or deny a person who is not a lawyer the right to appear for or represent others before an agency or in an agency proceeding." This section has not been read to create an across-the-board right to counsel in all adjudicatory proceedings.

b. There is a right to have counsel (or, in some instances a non-lawyer representative) present in many adjudicatory hearings, particularly where a statute clarifies the entitlement. *See, e.g.*, 42 U.S.C. § 406, 20 C.F.R. § 404.1700. For example, in situations covered by the "Individuals with Disabilities Education Act" (IDEA) involving placement of students with learning differences in various programs, 20 U.S.C. § 1415(h) provides: "Any party . . . shall be accorded (1) the right to be accompanied and advised by counsel and by individuals with special knowledge or training with respect to the problems of children with disabilities. . . ." In Social Security disability cases, the courts have held there is no *constitutional* right to counsel but there is a "statutory and regulatory" entitlement. *Skinner v. Astrue*, 478 F.3d 836, 841 (7th Cir. 2007).

Practice Pointer

While *Gideon v. Wainwright*, 372 U.S. 335 (1963), created the foundation for the right to counsel, as a general rule, its protections do not extend to civil and administrative cases.

c. Waiver. Even in statutory cases, the right can be and often is waived. "If properly informed of the right [to attorney representation at a social security hearing], the claimant may waive it." *Binion v. Shalala*, 13 F.3d 243, 245 (7th Cir. 1994). A waiver must, "explain . . . : (1) the manner in which an attorney can aid in the proceedings (2) the possibility of free counsel or a contingency arrangement, and (3) the limitation on attorney fees to 25 percent of past due benefits and required court approval of the fees." *Thompson v. Sullivan*, 933 F.2d 581, 584 (7th Cir. 1991).

Where a claimant asserts that the waiver was ineffective, a burden may exist to show that the absence of counsel was prejudicial or unfair in order to have the matter remanded. *Hall v. Secretary of Health, Educ. & Welfare*, 602 F.2d 1372, 1378 (9th Cir. 1979). In this instance, the burden falls on the administrative law judge (ALJ) "to conscientiously and scrupulously probe into, inquire of, and explore for all the relevant facts" in order to protect the plaintiff's interest. *Vidal v. Harris*, 637 F.2d 710, 713 (9th Cir. 1981). One measure would be to assess if a full factual record was developed at the hearing. *Key v. Heckler*, 754 F.2d 1545, 1551 (9th Cir. 1985). The burden on the ALJ is to be "especially diligent in exploring for all relevant facts."

d. In other areas, refusal to permit counsel can be a basis for a remand even in the absence of prejudicial effect. In *Picca v. Mukasey*, 512 F.3d 75, 78-79 (2d Cir. 2008), the court held that "because immigration cases are civil, not criminal, proceedings[, a]n asylum applicant . . . enjoys no specific right to counsel, but only a general right to due process of law under the Fifth Amendment of the Constitution." *Zheng v. DOJ*, 409 F.3d 43, 46 (2d Cir. 2005). "Nonetheless, the

Due Process clause and the Immigration and Nationality Act afford[] an alien the right to counsel of his own choice at his own expense." <u>Montilla v. INS, 926 F.2d 162, 166 (2d Cir. 1991)</u>.

> The government has adopted various regulations in order to give procedural safeguard to this right to counsel. *See* 38 U.S.C. § 1229a(b)(4)(A) (directing the Attorney General to adopt regulations ensuring that "the alien shall have the privilege of being represented, at no expense to the Government, by counsel of the alien's choosing who is authorized to practice in such proceedings"). . . .
>
> [We have] held that the failure of the IJ to follow these established procedures can constitute "reversible error," without a showing of prejudice, because, among other reasons, the right to counsel concerns "fundamental notions of fair play underlying the concept of due process," and "remand[ing] for agency compliance with its own rules would actively encourage such compliance." *Montilla.* . . . Accordingly, to warrant remand, all a petitioner need show is that "the subject regulations were for the alien's benefit and that the INS failed to adhere to them." [From *Picca v. Mukasey*]

e. The right to counsel is by no means certain, and while *Gideon* lives on in criminal cases, the Court has not applied it to agency practice. In some cases, the Court has even implied that the sensitive nature of a proceeding militates against the presence of counsel. <u>Wolff v. McDonnell, 418 U.S. 539 (1974)</u>. In most instances, however, counsel can be present – although that right does not include a requirement that the agency provide counsel if the party involved in the adjudication is unable to afford a lawyer.

In <u>*Lassiter v. Department of Social Services,* 452 U.S. 18, 26 (1981)</u>, the Court found that:

> [t]he dispositive question . . . is whether [the interests of the state, the individual, and the likelihood of error,] when weighed against the presumption that there is no right to appointed counsel in the absence of at least a potential deprivation of physical liberty, suffice to rebut that presumption and thus to lead to the conclusion that the Due Process Clause requires the appointment of counsel when a State seeks to terminate an indigent's parental status.

Two years later, in <u>*INS v. Chadha,* 462 U.S. 919, 966 (1983)</u>, in a concurring opinion, JUSTICE POWELL suggested there was a "right to counsel and a hearing before an impartial tribunal . . . when [an] agency adjudicates individual rights." A year later, however, the Court held that the right to appointed counsel (as opposed to counsel provided by a claimant) was limited to criminal cases. <u>*United States v. Gouveia,* 467 U.S. 180 (1984)</u>. In <u>*Walters v. National Association of Radiation Survivors,* 473 U.S. 305 (1985)</u>, the Court concluded that for certain veterans benefit's claims, there was no particular right to have counsel present.

II. Due Process: Individual Interests and Procedural Entitlements

The starting point for the study of adjudication is the Due Process Clause. It is important to understand to whom the Due Process Clause applies and what protections the Due Process Clause provides.

Before getting to the cases, we have inserted below those sections of the APA that are central to the adjudicatory process:

Textual Note

Following the due process material, the cases examine the basic obligations that agencies have when they adjudicate claims, the role of courts in reviewing adjudication, the activities of agencies in conducting adjudication, both pre-hearing and during the hearing, and some of the unique evidentiary and ethical problems that are inherent in the adjudicatory process.

§ 551. Definitions

(6) "order" means the whole or a part of a final disposition, whether affirmative, negative, injunctive, or declaratory in form, of an agency in a matter other than rule making but including licensing;

(7) "adjudication" means agency process for the formulation of an order;

(8) "license" includes the whole or a part of an agency permit, certificate, approval, registration, charter, membership, statutory exemption or other form of permission;

(9) "licensing" includes agency process respecting the grant, renewal, denial, revocation, suspension, annulment, withdrawal, limitation, amendment, modification, or conditioning of a license;

§ 554. Adjudications

(a) This section applies, according to the provisions thereof, in every case of adjudication required by statute to be determined on the record after opportunity for an agency hearing, except to the extent that there is involved –

(1) a matter subject to a subsequent trial of the law and the facts de novo in a court;

(2) the selection or tenure of an employee, except [an] administrative law judge appointed under section 3105 of this title [5 U.S.C. § 3105];

(3) proceedings in which decisions rest solely on inspections, tests, or elections;

(4) the conduct of military or foreign affairs functions;

(5) cases in which an agency is acting as an agent for a court; or

(6) the certification of worker representatives.

(b) Persons entitled to notice of an agency hearing shall be timely informed of –

(1) the time, place, and nature of the hearing;

(2) the legal authority and jurisdiction under which the hearing is to be held; and

(3) the matters of fact and law asserted.

When private persons are the moving parties, other parties to the proceeding shall give prompt notice of issues controverted in fact or law; and in other instances agencies may by rule require responsive pleading. In fixing the time and place for hearings, due regard shall be had for the convenience and necessity of the parties or their representatives.

(c) The agency shall give all interested parties opportunity for –

(1) the submission and consideration of facts, arguments, offers of settlement, or proposals of adjustment when time, the nature of the proceeding, and the public interest permit; and

(2) to the extent that the parties are unable so to determine a controversy by consent, hearing and decision on notice and in accordance with sections 556 and 557 of this title [5 U.S.C. §§ 556 and 557].

(d) The employee who presides at the reception of evidence pursuant to section 556 of this title [5 U.S.C. § 556] shall make the recommended decision or initial decision required by section 557 of this title [5 U.S.C. § 557], unless he becomes unavailable to the agency. Except to the extent required for the disposition of ex parte matters as authorized by law, such an employee may not –

(1) consult a person or party on a fact in issue, unless on notice and opportunity for all parties to participate; or

(2) be responsible to or subject to the supervision or direction of an employee or agent engaged in the performance of investigative or prosecuting functions for an agency.

An employee or agent engaged in the performance of investigative or prosecuting functions for an agency in a case may not, in that or a factually related case, participate or advise in the decision, recommended decision, or agency review pursuant to section 557 of this title [5 U.S.C. § 557], except as witness or counsel in public proceedings. This subsection does not apply –

(A) in determining applications for initial licenses;

(B) to proceedings involving the validity or application of rates, facilities, or practices of public utilities or carriers; or

(C) to the agency or a member or members of the body comprising the agency.

(e) The agency, with like effect as in the case of other orders, and in its sound discretion, may issue a declaratory order to terminate a controversy or remove uncertainty.

Due process claims require a traditionally cognizable interest, entitlement or right. Absent that, one can assert protection from arbitrary government action through statutes, regulations, or common law. However, if the claim is that the right to Fifth or Fourteenth Amendment Due Process has been violated, the claimant must demonstrate an interest, right, or entitlement the Constitution actually protects, and that is neither automatic nor facile, as the cases that follow demonstrate.

CAFETERIA & RESTAURANT WORKERS UNION V. MCELROY

367 U.S. 886 (1961)

[JUSTICE STEWART] In 1956 the petitioner Rachel Brawner was a short-order cook at a cafeteria operated by her employer, M & M Restaurants, Inc., on the premises of the Naval Gun Factory in the city of Washington. She had worked there for more than six years, and from her employer's point of view her record was entirely satisfactory. The Gun Factory was engaged in . . . the development of weapons systems of a highly classified nature. . . . Access to it was restricted, and guards were posted at all points of entry. Identification badges were issued to persons authorized to enter the premises by the Security Officer . . . . Rachel

Brawner had been issued such a badge.

The cafeteria where she worked was operated by M & M under a contract with the Board of Governors of the Gun Factory. Section 5(b) of the contract provided:

> . . . In no event shall the Concessionaire engage, or continue to engage, for operations under this Agreement, personnel who . . . .

> (iii) fail to meet the security requirements or other requirements under applicable regulations of the Activity, as determined by the Security Officer . . . .

On November 15, 1956, Mrs. Brawner was required to turn in her identification badge because of [a] determination that she had failed to meet the security requirements of the installation. . . . The petitioners brought this action . . . seeking, among other things, to compel the return to Mrs. Brawner of her identification badge, so that she might be permitted to enter the Gun Factory and resume her former employment. . . . [The district court granted the motion and the court of appeals affirmed.]

As the case comes here, two basic questions are presented. Was the commanding officer of the Gun Factory authorized to deny Rachel Brawner access to the installation in the way he did? If he was so authorized, did his action in excluding her operate to deprive her of any right secured to her by the Constitution?

I.

[T]he plain words of Article 0734 made absolute the commanding officer's power to withdraw her permission to enter the Gun Factory at any time.

II.

The question remains whether . . . summarily denying Rachel Brawner access to the site of her former employment violated the requirements of the Due Process Clause of the Fifth Amendment. This question cannot be answered by easy assertion that, because she had no constitutional right to be there in the first place, she was not deprived of liberty or property by the Superintendent's action. "One may not have a constitutional right to go to Baghdad, but the Government may not prohibit one from going there unless by means consonant with due process of law." It is the petitioners' claim that due process in this case required that Rachel Brawner be advised of the specific grounds for her exclusion and be accorded a hearing at which she might refute them. We are satisfied, however, that under the circumstances of this case such a procedure was not constitutionally required.

The Fifth Amendment does not require a trial-type hearing in every conceivable case of government impairment of private interest. . . . The very nature of due process negates any concept of inflexible procedures universally applicable to every imaginable situation. "'Due process,' unlike some legal rules, is not a technical conception with a fixed content unrelated to time, place and circumstances." It is "compounded of history, reason, the past course of decisions . . . ."

[C]onsideration of what procedures due process may require under any given set of circumstances must begin with a determination of the precise nature of the government function involved as well as of the private interest that has been affected by governmental action. Where it has been possible to characterize that private interest (perhaps in oversimplification) as a mere privilege subject to the Executive's plenary power, it has traditionally been held that notice and [a] hearing are not constitutionally required.

What, then, was the private interest affected by [the commanding officer's] action in the present case? It most assuredly was not the right to follow a chosen trade or profession. Rachel Brawner remained entirely free to obtain employment as a short-order cook or to get any other job, either with M & M or with any other employer. All that was denied her was the opportunity to work at one isolated and specific military installation. Moreover, the governmental function operating here was not the power to regulate or license, as lawmaker, an entire trade or profession, or to control an entire branch of private business, but, rather, as proprietor, to manage the internal operation of an important federal military establishment. In that proprietary military capacity, the Federal Government . . . has traditionally exercised unfettered control. . . . It has become a settled principle that government employment, in the absence of legislation, can be revoked at the will of the appointing officer. . . .

. . . We may assume that Rachel Brawner could not constitutionally have been excluded from the Gun Factory if the announced grounds for her exclusion had been patently arbitrary or discriminatory – that she could not have been kept out because she was a Democrat or a Methodist. It does not follow, however, that she was entitled to notice and a hearing when the reason advanced for her exclusion was, as here, entirely rational and in accord with the contract with M & M.

Finally, it is to be noted that this is not a case where government action has operated to bestow a badge of disloyalty or infamy, with an attendant foreclosure from other employment opportunity. All this record shows is that, in the opinion of the Security Officer of the Gun Factory, concurred in by the Superintendent, Rachel Brawner failed to meet the particular security requirements of that specific military installation. There is nothing to indicate that this determination would in any way impair Rachel Brawner's employment opportunities anywhere else. As pointed out by JUDGE PRETTYMAN, speaking for the Court of Appeals, "Nobody has said that Brawner is disloyal or is suspected of the slightest shadow of intentional wrongdoing. 'Security requirements' at such an installation, like such requirements under many other circumstances, cover many matters other than loyalty." For all that appears, the Security Officer and the Superintendent may have simply thought that Rachel Brawner was garrulous, or careless with her identification badge.

For these reasons, we conclude that the Due Process Clause of the Fifth Amendment was not violated in this case. Affirmed.

[JUSTICE BRENNAN, dissenting.]

[T]he Court . . . holds that the mere assertion by government that exclusion is for a valid reason forecloses further inquiry. That is, unless the government official is foolish enough to admit what he is doing – and few will be so foolish after today's decision – he may employ "security requirements" as a blind behind which to dismiss at will for the most discriminatory of causes. . . . One further circumstance makes this particularly a case where procedural requirements of fairness are essential. Petitioner was not simply excluded from the base summarily, without a notice and chance to defend herself. She was excluded as a "security risk," that designation most odious in our times. The Court consoles itself with the speculation that she may have been merely garrulous, or careless with her identification badge [b]ut, in the common understanding . . ., the term "security risk" carries a much more sinister meaning. . . .

——————————

1. This case is sometimes presented in constitutional law courses as an example of the use of the outdated right-privilege distinction as a basis for making the threshold determination regarding the applicability of due process – and of course, to an extent, that is true. That the notion of privilege is passé is another matter.

a. A "privileged based" exclusion, which should not be confused with the typical right/privilege analysis, is at the core of cases involving various types of limited access rules for military bases, often relying on *Cafeteria Workers*. *See, e.g.*, *Greer v. Spock*, 424 U.S. 828 (1976); *Tokar v. Hearne*, 699 F.2d 753 (5th Cir. 1983); *Bechtel Constructors Corp. v. Detroit Carpenters Dist. Council*, 610 F. Supp. 1550 (E.D. Mich. 1985); and Major Lisa L. Turner & Major Lynn G. Norton, *Civilians at the Tip of the Spear*, 51 A.F. L. REV. 1, 36 (2001).

b. The limitations on the right to a hearing before a federal administrative tribunal (as opposed to a state court of general jurisdiction) in *Cafeteria Workers* is central to – and cited with favor in – *Lujan v. G & G Fire Sprinklers*, 532 U.S. 189, 196-97 (2001).

The very nature of due process negates any concept of inflexible procedures universally applicable to every imaginable situation. Due process, "unlike some legal rules, is not a technical conception with a fixed content unrelated to time, place and circumstances." It is "compounded of history, reason, the past course of decisions . . . ."

2. Though note 1 above suggests that there is more to *Cafeteria Workers* than the basic pedagogical exercise of comparison with the cases that follow, there is little question that the Court subsequently distanced itself from using right-privilege as a test to determine the applicability of due process. As JUSTICE BRENNAN noted in *Goldberg, infra* Chapter 6, "constitutional challenge cannot be answered by an argument that public assistance benefits are a privilege and not a right . . . ."

We wonder, however, whether the Court – and Congress – have in fact abandoned the crude algorithm of *Cafeteria Workers*. What are we to make of CHIEF JUSTICE REHNQUIST's opinion in <u>DeShaney v. Winnebago County Department of Social Services, 489 U.S. 189, 196 (1989)</u>: "[T]he Due Process Clauses generally confer no affirmative right to governmental aid, even where . . . necessary to secure life, liberty or property interests of which the government itself may not deprive the individual."

> **ℹ For More Information**
>
> For further thoughts on the broad questions raised in *Cafeteria Workers*, see Karima Bennoune, <u>Terror/ Torture, 26 BERKELEY J. INT'L L. 1 (2008)</u>; Ingrid Detter, <u>Symposium on the New Face of Armed Conflict: Enemy Combatants After Hamdan v. Rumsfeld: The Law of War and Illegal Combatants, 75 GEO. WASH. L. REV. 1049 (2007)</u>; David Abraham, <u>The Uses and Abuses of Executive Power: The Bush Regime from Elections to Detentions: A Moral Economy of Carl Schmitt and Human Rights, 62 U. MIAMI L. REV. 249 (2008)</u>; Vincent-Joel Proulx, <u>If the Hat Fits, Wear It, If the Turban Fits, Run for your Life: Reflections on the Indefinite Detention and Targeted Killing of Suspected Terrorists, 56 HASTINGS L.J. 801 (2005)</u>; and Daniel J. Steinbock, <u>Designating the Dangerous: From Blacklists to Watch Lists, 30 SEATTLE UNIV. L. R. 659 (2006)</u>.

3. The questions surrounding detainee treatment are hard to avoid when thinking through whether characterizing an arguable entitlement as a privilege has ceased to be part of our jurisprudence. <u>Hamdan v. Rumsfeld, 548 U.S. 557 (2006)</u>; <u>Bismullah v. Gates, 514 F.3d 1291 (D.C. Cir. 2008)</u>; the <u>Detainee Treatment Act of 2005, Pub. L. No. 109-148</u>, § 1005(e)(1), <u>119 Stat. 2739, 2742</u> (to be codified at <u>28 U.S.C. § 2241(e)</u>) and the Detainee Treatment Act of 2005 § 1005(e)(3), <u>10 U.S.C. § 801</u> note (West Supp. 2007); Memorandum from Paul Wolfowitz, Deputy Sec'y of Def., to the Sec'y of the Navy (July 7, 2004), available at <u>http://www.defenselink.mil/news/Jul2004/d20040707review.pdf</u> (last visited June 8, 2008).

Good Questions!

Do you find convincing the rationale in *Cafeteria Workers* that Ms. Brawner was not denied much of anything other than her right to engage in her profession at a particular location? How much would national security have been compromised had there been a hearing on the questions Ms. Brawner raised prior to taking adverse action? Is it fair to presume that such a hearing would have thrown open the doors to important state secrets?

Few cases created more controversy – and hope – regarding adjudicary process than *Goldberg v. Kelly*. Government agencies feared that *Goldberg* would require countless full trial-like hearings, a process that would cost untold millions of dollars. Representatives of those affected by government action hoped that *Goldberg* signaled the dawn of a new era of fairness and impartiality in decision-making. Neither prediction was accurate.

GOLDBERG V. KELLY

397 U.S. 254 (1970)

[JUSTICE BRENNAN] The question for decision is whether a State that terminates public assistance payments to a particular recipient without affording him the opportunity for an evidentiary hearing prior to termination denies the recipient procedural due process in violation of the Due Process Clause of the Fourteenth Amendment.

This action was brought . . . by residents of New York City receiving financial aid under the federally assisted program of Aid to Families with Dependent Children (AFDC) or under New York State's general Home Relief program. n.1 Their complaint alleged that the New York State and New York City officials administering these programs terminated, or were about to terminate, such aid without prior notice and hearing, thereby denying them due process of law. At the time the suits were filed there was no requirement of prior notice or hearing of any kind before termination of financial aid. However, the State and city adopted procedures for notice and hearing after the suits were brought, and the plaintiffs, appellees here, then challenged the constitutional adequacy of those procedures.

> n.1 AFDC . . . is a categorical assistance program supported by federal grants-in-aid but administered by the States according to regulations of the Secretary of Health, Education, and Welfare. Home Relief is a general assistance program financed and

administered solely by New York state and local governments. . . .

. . . .

[Under the regulations a] caseworker who has doubts about the recipient's continued eligibility must first discuss them with the recipient. If the caseworker concludes that the recipient is no longer eligible, he recommends termination of aid to a unit supervisor. If the latter concurs, he sends the recipient a letter stating the reasons for proposing to terminate aid and notifying him that within seven days he may request that a higher official review the record, and may support the request with a written statement prepared personally or with the aid of an attorney or other person. If the reviewing official affirms the determination of ineligibility, aid is stopped immediately and the recipient is informed by letter of the reasons for the action. Appellees' challenge to this procedure emphasizes the absence of any provisions for the personal appearance of the recipient before the reviewing official, for oral presentation of evidence, and for confrontation and cross-examination of adverse witnesses. However, the letter does inform the recipient that he may request a post-termination "fair hearing." n.5 This is a proceeding before an independent state hearing officer at which the recipient may appear personally, offer oral evidence, confront and cross-examine the witnesses against him, and have a record made of the hearing. If the recipient prevails at the "fair hearing" he is paid all funds erroneously withheld. A recipient whose aid is not restored by a "fair hearing" decision may have judicial review. The recipient is so notified.

> n.5 . . . In both AFDC and Home Relief the "fair hearing" must be held within 10 working days of the request with decision within 12 working days thereafter. It was conceded in oral argument that these time limits are not in fact observed.

I.

The constitutional issue to be decided, therefore, is the narrow one whether the Due Process Clause requires that the recipient be afforded an evidentiary hearing *before* the termination of benefits. The District Court held that only a pre-termination evidentiary hearing would satisfy the constitutional command . . . . We affirm.

Appellant does not contend that procedural due process is not applicable to the termination of welfare benefits. Such benefits are a matter of statutory entitlement for persons qualified to receive them. n.8 . . . . [Nor can the] constitutional challenge . . . be answered by an argument that public assistance benefits are "a 'privilege' and not a 'right.'" Relevant constitutional restraints apply as much to the withdrawal of public assistance benefits as to disqualification for unemployment compensation . . . or to discharge from public employment. The extent to *balancing test.*

which procedural due process must be afforded the recipient is influenced by the extent to which he may be "condemned to suffer grievous loss" and depends upon whether the recipient's interest in avoiding that loss outweighs the governmental interest in summary adjudication. Accordingly, as we said in Cafeteria & Restaurant Workers Union v. McElroy, "consideration of what procedures due process may require under any given set of circumstances must begin with a determination of the precise nature of the government function involved as well as of the private interest that has been affected by governmental action."

> n.8 . . . Much of the existing wealth in this country takes the form of rights that do not fall within traditional common-law concepts of property. . . . [S]ociety today is built around entitlement. The automobile dealer has his franchise, the doctor and lawyer their professional licenses . . . . Many of the most important of these entitlements now flow from government: subsidies to farmers and businessmen, routes for airlines and channels for television stations; long term contracts for defense, space, and education; social security pensions for individuals. Such sources of security, whether private or public, are no longer regarded as luxuries or gratuities; to the recipients they are essentials, fully deserved, and in no sense a form of charity. It is only the poor whose entitlements, although recognized by public policy, have not been effectively enforced.

It is true, of course, that some governmental benefits may be administratively terminated without affording the recipient a pre-termination evidentiary hearing. But we agree with the District Court that when welfare is discontinued, only a pre-termination evidentiary hearing provides the recipient with procedural due process. For qualified recipients, welfare provides the means to obtain essential food, clothing, housing, and medical care. Thus the crucial factor in this context – a factor not present in [any other case where] governmental entitlements are ended – is that termination of aid pending resolution of a controversy over eligibility may deprive an *eligible* recipient of the very means by which to live while he waits. Since he lacks independent resources, his situation becomes immediately desperate. His need to concentrate upon finding the means for daily subsistence, in turn, adversely affects his ability to seek redress from the welfare bureaucracy.

rationale

Moreover, important governmental interests are promoted by affording recipients a pre-termination evidentiary hearing. . . . We have come to recognize that forces not within the control of the poor contribute to their poverty. . . . Welfare, by meeting the basic demands of subsistence, can help bring within the reach of the poor the same opportunities that are available to others to participate meaningfully in the life of the community. At the same time, welfare guards against the societal malaise that may flow from a widespread sense of unjustified frustration and insecurity. Public assistance, then, is not mere charity, but a means to "promote the general Welfare, and secure the Blessings of Liberty to ourselves and our Posterity." The same governmental interests that counsel the provision of welfare, counsel as well its uninterrupted provision to those eligible to receive it;

policy

pre-termination evidentiary hearings are indispensable to that end.

Appellant does not challenge the force of these considerations but argues that they are outweighed by countervailing governmental interests in conserving fiscal and administrative resources. . . . Summary adjudication protects the public fisc by stopping payments promptly upon discovery of reason to believe that a recipient is no longer eligible. Since most terminations are accepted without challenge, summary adjudication also conserves both the fisc and administrative time and energy by reducing the number of evidentiary hearings actually held.

We agree with the District Court, however, that these governmental interests are not overriding in the welfare context. The requirement of a prior hearing doubtless involves some greater expense, and the benefits paid to ineligible recipients pending decision at the hearing probably cannot be recouped, since these recipients are likely to be judgment-proof. But the State is not without weapons to minimize these increased costs. Much of the drain on fiscal and administrative resources can be reduced by . . . prompt pre-termination hearings . . . . Thus, the interest of the eligible recipient in uninterrupted receipt of public assistance, coupled with the State's interest that his payments not be erroneously terminated, clearly outweighs the State's competing concern to prevent any increase in its fiscal and administrative burdens. . . .

II.

We also agree with the District Court, however, that the pre-termination hearing need not take the form of a judicial or quasi-judicial trial. . . . [T]he [post termination] statutory "fair hearing" will provide the recipient with a full administrative review. Accordingly, the pre-termination hearing has one function only: to . . . protect a recipient against an erroneous termination of his benefits. Thus, a complete record and a comprehensive opinion, which would serve primarily to facilitate judicial review and to guide future decisions, need not be provided at the pre-termination stage. We recognize, too, that both welfare authorities and recipients have an interest in relatively speedy resolution of questions of eligibility, that they are used to dealing with one another informally, and that some welfare departments have very burdensome caseloads. These considerations justify the limitation of the pre-termination hearing to minimum procedural safeguards, adapted to the particular characteristics of welfare recipients, and to the limited nature of the controversies to be resolved. We wish to add that we, no less than the dissenters, recognize the importance of not imposing . . . any procedural requirements beyond those demanded by rudimentary due process.

"The fundamental requisite of due process of law is the opportunity to be heard." The hearing must be "at a meaningful time and in a meaningful manner."

In the present context these principles require that a recipient have timely and adequate notice detailing the reasons for a proposed termination, and an effective opportunity to defend by confronting any adverse witnesses and by presenting his own arguments and evidence orally. . . .

We are not prepared to say that the seven-day notice currently provided by New York City is constitutionally insufficient per se, although there may be cases where fairness would require that a longer time be given. Nor do we see any constitutional deficiency in the content or form of the notice. New York employs both a letter and a personal conference with a caseworker to inform a recipient of the . . . legal and factual bases for the Department's doubts. This combination is probably the most effective method of communicating with recipients.

The city's procedures presently do not permit recipients to appear personally with or without counsel before the official who finally determines continued eligibility. Thus a recipient is not permitted to present evidence to that official orally, or to confront or cross-examine adverse witnesses. These omissions are fatal to the constitutional adequacy of the procedures.

The opportunity to be heard must be tailored to the capacities and circumstances of those who are to be heard. It is not enough that a welfare recipient may present his position to the decisionmaker in writing or secondhand through his caseworker. Written submissions are an unrealistic option for most recipients, who lack the educational attainment necessary to write effectively and who cannot obtain professional assistance. Moreover, written submissions do not afford the flexibility of oral presentations; they do not permit the recipient to mold his argument to the issues the decisionmaker appears to regard as important. Particularly where credibility and veracity are at issue, as they must be in many termination proceedings, written submissions are a wholly unsatisfactory basis for decision. The secondhand presentation to the decisionmaker by the caseworker has its own deficiencies; since the caseworker usually gathers the facts upon which the charge of ineligibility rests, the presentation of the recipient's side of the controversy cannot safely be left to him. Therefore a recipient must be allowed to state his position orally. Informal procedures will suffice; in this context due process does not require a particular order of proof or mode of offering evidence.

In almost every setting where important decisions turn on questions of fact, due process requires an opportunity to confront and cross-examine adverse witnesses. What we said in *Greene v. McElroy* is particularly pertinent here:

> [Confrontation] is even more important where the evidence consists of the testimony of individuals whose memory might be faulty or who, in fact, might be perjurers or persons motivated by malice, vindictiveness, intolerance, prejudice, or jealousy. . . . This Court has been zealous to protect these rights from erosion. It has spoken out

not only in criminal cases, . . . but also in all types of cases where administrative . . . actions were under scrutiny.

Welfare recipients must therefore be given an opportunity to confront and cross-examine the witnesses relied on by the department.

. . . We do not say that counsel must be provided at the pre-termination hearing, but only that the recipient must be allowed to retain an attorney if he so desires. Counsel can help delineate the issues, present the factual contentions in an orderly manner, conduct cross-examination, and generally safeguard the interests of the recipient. We do not anticipate that this assistance will unduly prolong or otherwise encumber the hearing. . . .

Finally, the decisionmaker's conclusion as to a recipient's eligibility must rest solely on the legal rules and evidence adduced at the hearing. To demonstrate compliance with this elementary requirement, the decisionmaker should state the reasons for his determination and indicate the evidence he relied on, though his statement need not amount to a full opinion or even formal findings of fact and conclusions of law. And, of course, an impartial decisionmaker is essential. We agree with the District Court that prior involvement in some aspects of a case will not necessarily bar a welfare official from acting as a decisionmaker. He should not, however, have participated in making the determination under review. Affirmed.

[JUSTICE BLACK, dissenting.]

The Court apparently feels that this decision will benefit the poor and needy. In my judgment the eventual result will be just the opposite. While today's decision requires only an administrative, evidentiary hearing . . . I would be surprised if the weighing process did not compel the conclusion that termination without full judicial review would be unconscionable. After all, at each step, as the majority seems to feel, the issue is only one of weighing the government's pocketbook against the actual survival of the recipient, and surely that balance must always tip in favor of the individual. . . . [T]he inevitable result of such a constitutionally imposed burden will be that the government will not put a claimant on the rolls initially until it has made an exhaustive investigation to determine his eligibility. While this Court will perhaps have insured that no needy person will be taken off the rolls without a full "due process" proceeding, it will also have insured that many will never get on the rolls, or at least that they will remain destitute during the lengthy proceedings followed to determine initial eligibility.

Underlying Case Documents

The case referenced:
The complaint of Ester Lett
The complaint of John Kelly
The regulations

1. The public assistance program that was the basis of the claim for relief in *Goldberg*, Aid to Families With Dependent Children (AFDC), was replaced in 1996 with the Personal Responsibility and Work Opportunity Reconciliation Act (PRWORA). PRWORA is drafted so as to limit the hearing rights implicit in *Goldberg* for those receiving public assistance, as the note case below suggests. For a recent statement on what *Goldberg* still provides in terms of a right to a fair hearings, see *Jonathan C. v. Hawkins*, 2006 WL 3498494 (E.D. Tex. 2006).

Marchwinski v. Howard, 309 F.3d 330 (6th Cir. 2002), vacated on other grounds, 319 F.3d 258 (6th Cir. 2003), provides a brief history of the current system:

> In 1996, Congress passed the Personal Responsibility and Work Opportunity Reconciliation Act ("PRWORA") that replaced the previous welfare entitlement program with the Temporary Assistance for Needy Families program ("TANF"). Among the general purposes for the PRWORA is the goal of increasing the flexibility of the states in providing assistance to needy families "so that children may be cared for in their own homes or in the homes of relatives." A state participating in the TANF program must submit to the Secretary of Health and Human Services a written document that includes, among other things, the state's plan for a program that will "provide assistance to needy families with (or expecting) children and provide parents with job preparation, work, and support services to enable them to leave the program and become self-sufficient." Only needy families who have or are expecting children are eligible for benefits under this program. . . . [The Act] explicitly provides that the Act "shall not be interpreted to entitle any individual or family to assistance under any State program funded under this part." TANF permits states to drug test applicants for and recipients of these benefits and to impose sanctions where use of controlled substances is found.

2. The full hearing the *Goldberg* Court envisioned undoubtedly provided comprehensive protection of individual interests. These procedural entitlements are summarized in JUDGE FRIENDLY's remarkable article, *Some Kind of Hearing*, 123 U. PA. L. REV. 1267, 1279-95 (1975), are comprehensive and include:

1. An unbiased tribunal;

2. Notice of proposed action and the grounds asserted for that action in advance of a hearing;

3. A full opportunity to present the reasons why the proposed action should not be undertaken;

4. The right to call witnesses by an individual who is either being denied a benefit or seeking a benefit;

5. The right to know in advance the evidence that will be used against an individual's interest;

6. The right to have a decision based only on the evidence presented in the record in the *Goldberg* hearing;

7. The right to have counsel present, although there is no right to have counsel paid for as in criminal cases;

8. The right to have a full record maintained;

9. The right to a statement of reasons that explain the decision of the agency;

10. The right to public attendance at the hearing;

11. The right to judicial review of the hearing.

What justified this level of procedural protection? Are rights this comprehensive based on a distrust of caseworkers and the system of public assistance?

3. In a 1990 symposium on *Goldberg*, Professor Lucie E. White wrote:

> In the twenty years since [*Goldberg*] was decided, the plaintiffs' skepticism about their own remedial theory has proved well-founded. Welfare hearings have offered no panacea to the problems inherent in our ossified and bureaucratic system of public assistance administration.

> Welfare hearings have not compelled welfare bureaucrats to treat poor people with dignity. The experience of present-day welfare advocates shows just how inadequate the [*Goldberg*] remedy has proved to be.

Lucie E. White, *Symposium: The Legacy of* Goldberg v. Kelly: *A Twenty Year Perspective:* Goldberg v. Kelly *on the Paradox of Lawyering for the Poor,* 56 BROOK. L. REV. 861, 867 (1990). White's critique of *Goldberg* is not quite as harsh as Professor Richard A. Epstein's. Writing in the same symposium, Professor Epstein concluded: "Notwithstanding JUSTICE BRENNAN's impassioned defense, *Goldberg* amounts in the end to another regulatory misadventure, albeit one of constitutional dimensions." Richard A. Epstein, *Symposium: The Legacy of* Goldberg v. Kelly: *A Twenty Year Perspective: No New Property,* 56 BROOK. L. REV. 747, 775 (1990).

What would have been a better system? In the absence of counsel paid for by the government, what is the benefit of a "fair hearing?"

4. In working through the application of *Goldberg* in the 21st Century, consider the stunning case of McWaters v. Federal Emergency Management Agency, 436 F. Supp. 2d 802, 817-19 (E.D. La., 2006). This decision involves the apparent failure of FEMA to provide prompt, fair, and legitimate process to assess claims of victims after Hurricane Katrina.

> In *Goldberg v. Kelly*, the Supreme Court held that because persons meeting state AFDC eligibility criteria automatically qualified for benefits, those individuals deemed eligible per the standards had a protected property interest in the receipt of welfare benefits. However, where final determination of which eligible individuals receive benefits was left to the "unfettered discretion" of administrators, no constitutionally protected property interest existed. . . . [Citing Roth, the next case in this text.]

> Applying these principles in order to answer the question as to whether [the legislation FEMA administers] creates a constitutionally protected entitlement to disaster assistance, the Court must determine whether, under current regulations, hurricane disaster victims meeting the statutory qualifications for assistance are indeed automatically entitled to receive it. If so, as in Goldberg, eligible persons would have a constitutionally protected property interest in assistance. However, if FEMA has discretion to choose whom to assist from among otherwise eligible persons, then no constitutionally protected interest in disaster assistance exists. . . .

> FEMA's discretion in providing assistance . . . is tempered in many important ways. Firstly . . . the agency has no discretion regarding provision of Temporary Housing Assistance to eligible persons and families. . . . Additionally, while the ultimate resources allocated to FEMA from the federal government and Congress may be finite in monetary amount, its provision of those resources must be done . . . equitably under the law and in accordance with regulations. . . . As such the Court finds that the mandatory and non-discretionary policies and regulations . . . creates a reasonable expectation of the benefit of federal disaster assistance in these applicants, and this expectation rises to the level of a property interest protectable under the Due Process Clause. . . .

> However, despite FEMA's lack of discretion . . . as well as the seemingly interminable delays in provision of such assistance, and despite the fact that a protected interest [exists] under the Due Process Clause . . . the Court finds that plaintiffs have failed to prove . . . a deprivation of that right. Evidence adduced throughout the course of this litigation reveals that FEMA was definitely unprepared to quickly and efficiently deal with the multitude of applications. . . .

> However, despite FEMA's lack of preparation, and regardless of the property interest implicated . . . the Court must find that the delay faced by FEMA in processing the voluminous number of Katrina-related housing applications was inevitable due to the sheer practicalities of the circumstances wrought by the aftermath of the storm. . . . [A]s a practical matter the Court cannot hold that FEMA's delay in the provision of these services equates to a denial or deprivation of plaintiffs' property rights. FEMA did and is taking action, albeit at a rather excruciatingly slow place. Accordingly, because

the Court finds no actionable violation of the constitutional standard applicable to this claim, it must be dismissed.

How would you advise a client seeking to challenge FEMA, suffering as a consequence of what the court refers to as an excruciating delay? What part of *Goldberg* is in play in the above case? What good is the entitlement if there is no remedy?

5. Two articles by Professor Vicki Lens provide a unique and interesting perspective on public assistance and hearing entitlements a third of a century after *Goldberg*: Vicki Lens, *Bureaucratic Disentitlement After Welfare Reform: Are Fair Hearings the Cure?*, 12 GEO. J. POVERTY L. & POL'Y 13 (2005); and Vicki Lens, *In the Fair Hearing Room: Resistance and Confrontation in the Welfare Bureaucracy*, 32 L. & SOC. INQUIRY 309 (2007). Since *Goldberg* was decided, it has not been clear whether the high cost of a formal *Goldberg* hearing could be justified by the benefits such hearings provide. However, in the last few years, the debate has shifted to removing the bureaucracy entirely from the administration of public assistance programs. Jacob S. Hacker, *Privatizing Risk Without Privatizing the Welfare State: The Hidden Politics of Social Policy Retrenchment in the United States*, 98 AM. POL. SCI. REV. 243, 250 (2004); Dru Stevenson, *Privatization of Welfare Services: Delegation by Commercial Contract*, 45 ARIZ. L. REV. 83 (2003); Michele Estrin Gilman, *Legal Accountability in an Era of Privatized Welfare*, 89 CALIF. L. REV. 569 (2001).

Would privatization resolve any of the problems raised in the above notes? What would be the driving force in a privately administered program that allocated public assistance? Assuming profit maximization plays a role, what is the likely fate of *Goldberg* hearings in a privatized public assistance system?

6. A *Goldberg* hearing functions best when the individuals participating are fully aware of their rights and are skilled in presenting their side of the story. While *Goldberg* provided the opportunity to secure counsel of one's choice, it did not provide a right to have that counsel paid for. For that reason, more often than not, individuals go forward without counsel, reducing the likelihood that all the rights to which the individual is entitled will actually be asserted.

It is worth asking whether the absence of a lawyer renders comprehensive procedural entitlements of limited or even no value. It is also worth asking what the cost would be of providing counsel to every person who has an arguable entitlement to a fair hearing. Congress considered the question in a

Good Question!

At the core of due process is the right to notice and the opportunity to be heard – in a complex proceeding, can one be heard without counsel?

hearing focused on the *Indian Child Welfare Program*: Hearings Before the Subcommittee on Indian Affairs of the Committee on Interior and Insular Affairs,

93d Cong., 2d Sess. 29 (1974), but never in the context of broad-based public assistance programs involving thousands upon thousands of hearings.

7. Even with a lawyer present, the nature of the underlying right, interest, or entitlement is the triggering element to activate a due process claim. Clarifying the interest has been challenging. The *Cafeteria Workers* right/privilege distinction seems to have been set aside by *Goldberg's* use of liberty and property. The case that follows begins the long task of defining the parameters of liberty and property and the consequences that attach as a result of those designations.

BOARD OF REGENTS OF STATE COLLEGES V. ROTH

408 U.S. 564 (1972)

[JUSTICE STEWART] In 1968 the respondent, David Roth, was hired for his first teaching job as assistant professor of political science at Wisconsin State University-Oshkosh. He was hired for a fixed term of one academic year. . . . The respondent completed that term. But he was informed that he would not be rehired for the next academic year.

The respondent had no tenure rights to continued employment. Under Wisconsin statutory law a state university teacher can acquire tenure as a "permanent" employee only after four years of year-to-year employment. Having acquired tenure, a teacher is entitled to continued employment "during efficiency and good behavior." A relatively new teacher without tenure, however, is under Wisconsin law entitled to nothing beyond his one-year appointment. There are no statutory or administrative standards defining eligibility for re-employment. State law thus clearly leaves the decision whether to rehire a nontenured teacher for another year to the unfettered discretion of university officials.

[A] tenured teacher cannot be "discharged except for cause upon written charges" and pursuant to certain procedures. A nontenured teacher, similarly, is protected to some extent *during* his one-year term. . . . But the [Wisconsin] Rules provide no real protection for a nontenured teacher who simply is not re-employed for the next year. He must be informed by February 1 "concerning retention or nonretention for the ensuing year." But "no reason for non-retention need be given. No review or appeal is provided in such case."

In conformance with these Rules, the President of Wisconsin State University-Oshkosh informed the respondent before February 1, 1969, that he would not be rehired for the 1969-1970 academic year. He gave the respondent no reason for the decision and no opportunity to challenge it at any sort of hearing.

The respondent then brought this action . . . alleging that the decision not to rehire him for the next year infringed his Fourteenth Amendment rights. He attacked the decision both in substance and procedure. First, he alleged that the true reason for the decision was to punish him for certain statements critical of the University administration, and that it therefore violated his right to freedom of speech. n.5 Second, he alleged that the failure of University officials to give him notice of any reason for nonretention and an opportunity for a hearing violated his right to procedural due process of law.

> n.5 . . . The District Court came to no conclusion whatever regarding the true reason for the University President's decision. "In the present case," it stated, "it appears that a determination as to the actual bases of decision must await amplification of the facts at trial. . . . Summary judgment is inappropriate."

The District Court granted summary judgment for the respondent on the procedural issue, ordering the University officials to provide him with reasons and a hearing. The Court of Appeals . . . affirmed this partial summary judgment. . . . The only question presented to us at this stage in the case is whether the respondent had a constitutional right to a statement of reasons and a hearing on the University's decision not to rehire him for another year. We hold that he did not.

I.

. . . The District Court . . . concluded that the respondent's interest in re-employment at Wisconsin State University-Oshkosh outweighed the University's interest in denying him re-employment summarily. . . . But, to determine whether due process requirements apply in the first place, we must look not to the "weight" but to the *nature* of the interest at stake. We must look to see if the interest is within the Fourteenth Amendment's protection of liberty and property.

[T]he Court has fully . . . rejected the wooden distinction between "rights" and "privileges" that once seemed to govern the applicability of procedural due process rights. The Court has also made clear that the property interests protected by procedural due process extend well beyond actual ownership of real estate, chattels, or money. By the same token, the Court has required due process protection for deprivations of liberty beyond the sort of formal constraints imposed by the criminal process.

Yet, while the Court has eschewed rigid or formalistic limitations on the protection of procedural due process, it has at the same time observed certain boundaries. For the words "liberty" and "property" in the Due Process Clause of the Fourteenth Amendment must be given some meaning.

we
due process:
substantive
What in
interest

II.

[Liberty] denotes not merely freedom from bodily restraint but also the right of the individual to contract, to engage in any of the common occupations of life, to acquire useful knowledge, to marry, establish a home and bring up children, to worship God according to the dictates of his own conscience, and generally to enjoy those privileges long recognized . . . as essential to the orderly pursuit of happiness by free men." In a Constitution for a free people, there can be no doubt that the meaning of "liberty" must be broad indeed.

There might be cases in which a State refused to reemploy a person under such circumstances that interests in liberty would be implicated. But this is not such a case. The State, in declining to rehire the respondent, did not make any charge against him that might seriously damage his standing and associations in his community. It did not base the nonrenewal of his contract on a charge, for example, that he had been guilty of dishonesty, or immorality. . . . Similarly, there is no suggestion that the State, in declining to re-employ the respondent, imposed on him a stigma or other disability that foreclosed his freedom to take advantage of other employment opportunities. . . . [n.13]

> n.13 The District Court made an *assumption* "that non-retention by one university or college creates concrete and practical difficulties for a professor in his subsequent academic career." . . . . But even assuming, arguendo, that [this] would constitute a state-imposed restriction on liberty, the record contains no support for these assumptions. . . . Mere proof, for example, that his record of nonretention in one job, taken alone, might make him somewhat less attractive to some other employers would hardly establish the kind of foreclosure of opportunities amounting to a deprivation of "liberty."

To be sure, the respondent has alleged that the nonrenewal of his contract was based on his exercise of his right to freedom of speech. But this allegation is not now before us. The District Court stayed proceedings on this issue, and the respondent has yet to prove that the decision not to rehire him was, in fact, based on his free speech activities. n.14

> n.14 The Court of Appeals, nonetheless, argued that opportunity for a hearing and a statement of reasons were required here "as a *prophylactic* against non-retention decisions improperly motivated by exercise of protected rights."
>
> [T]his Court has on occasion held that opportunity for a fair adversary hearing must precede the action, whether or not the speech or press interest is clearly protected under substantive First Amendment standards. Thus, we have required fair notice and opportunity for an adversary hearing before an injunction is issued against the holding of rallies and public meetings. Similarly, we have indicated the necessity of procedural safeguards before a State makes a large-scale seizure of a person's allegedly obscene books, magazines, and so forth.

In the respondent's case, however, the State has not directly impinged . . . in any way comparable to a seizure of books or an injunction against meetings. Whatever may be a teacher's rights of free speech, the interest in holding a teaching job at a state university, simpliciter, is not itself a free speech interest.

Hence, on the record before us, all that clearly appears is that the respondent was not rehired for one year at one university. It stretches the concept too far to suggest that a person is deprived of "liberty" when he simply is not rehired in one job but remains as free as before to seek another. *Cafeteria Workers v. McElroy.*

III.

The Fourteenth Amendment's procedural protection of property is a safeguard of the security of interests that a person has already acquired in specific benefits. . . . Thus, the Court has held that a person receiving welfare benefits . . . has an interest in continued receipt of those benefits that is safeguarded by procedural due process. *Goldberg v. Kelly.* Similarly, in the area of public employment, the Court has held that a public college professor dismissed from an office held under tenure provisions and college professors and staff members dismissed during the terms of their contracts have interests in continued employment that are safeguarded by due process. . . .

Certain attributes of "property" interests protected by procedural due process emerge from these decisions. To have a property interest in a benefit, a person clearly must have more than an abstract need or . . . a unilateral expectation of it. He must, instead, have a legitimate claim of entitlement to it. It is a purpose of the ancient institution of property to protect those claims upon which people rely in their daily lives . . . . It is a purpose of the constitutional right to a hearing to provide an opportunity for a person to vindicate those claims.

Property interests, of course, are not created by the Constitution. Rather, they are created and their dimensions are defined by existing rules or understandings that stem from an independent source such as state law . . . . Thus, the welfare recipients in *Goldberg v. Kelly* had a claim of entitlement to welfare payments that was grounded in the statute defining eligibility for them. . . . Just as the welfare recipients' "property" interest in welfare payments was created and defined by statutory terms, so the respondent's "property" interest in employment at Wisconsin State University-Oshkosh was created and defined by the terms of his appointment. Those terms secured his interest in employment up to June 30, 1969. But the important fact in this case is that they specifically provided that the respondent's employment was to terminate on June 30. They did not provide for contract renewal absent "sufficient cause." Indeed, they made no provision for renewal whatsoever.

Thus, the terms of the respondent's appointment secured absolutely no interest in re-employment for the next year. . . . Nor, significantly, was there any state statute or University rule or policy that secured his interest in re-employment or that created any legitimate claim to it. n.16 In these circumstances, the respondent surely had an abstract concern in being rehired, but he did not have a *property* interest sufficient to require the University authorities to give him a hearing when they declined to renew his contract of employment.

> n.16 To be sure, the respondent does suggest that most teachers hired on a year-to-year basis by Wisconsin State University-Oshkosh are, in fact, rehired. But the District Court has not found that there is anything approaching a "common law" of re-employment . . . .

IV.

. . . .

We must conclude that the summary judgment for the respondent should not have been granted, since the respondent has not shown that he was deprived of liberty or property protected by the Fourteenth Amendment. The judgment of the Court of Appeals, accordingly, is reversed and the case is remanded . . . .

[JUSTICE MARSHALL, dissenting.]

This Court has long maintained that

> the right to work for a living in the common occupations of the community is of the very essence of the personal freedom and opportunity that it was the purpose of the [Fourteenth] Amendment to secure.

[T]he denial of public employment is a serious blow to any citizen. . . . Employment is one of the greatest, if not the greatest, benefits that governments offer in modern-day life. . . . I would . . . hold that respondent was denied due process when his contract was not renewed and he was not informed of the reasons and given an opportunity to respond. . . . As long as the government has a good reason for its actions it need not fear disclosure. It is only where the government acts improperly that procedural due process is truly burdensome. And that is precisely when it is most necessary. It might also be argued that to require a hearing and a statement of reasons is to require a useless act, because a government bent on denying employment to one or more persons will do so regardless of the procedural hurdles that are placed in its path. Perhaps this is so, but a requirement of procedural regularity at least renders arbitrary action more difficult. Moreover, proper procedures will surely eliminate some of the arbitrariness that results, not from malice, but from innocent error.

[JUSTICE DOUGLAS, dissenting.]

Respondent Roth . . . was rated by the faculty as an excellent teacher, [but] had publicly criticized the administration for suspending an entire group of 94 black students without determining individual guilt. . . . In this case [Roth claimed] in part that the decision of the school authorities not to rehire was in retaliation for his expression of opinion. . . . No more direct assault on academic freedom can be imagined than for the school authorities to be allowed to discharge a teacher because of his or her philosophical, political, or ideological beliefs. . . .

Underlying Case Documents

The case referenced:

<u>The notice of appointment</u>

<u>The Wisconsin Rules</u> (as stated by the president of the university)

---

1. *Roth* is the "seminal case defining the boundaries of constitutionally protected property rights under the Fourteenth Amendment . . . ." <u>*Jan Rubin Assocs. v. Hous. Auth.*, 2007 WL 1035016 (E.D. Ky. 2007)</u>. *Roth* also makes clear that state law is the primary source for determining the nature of a property interest. Applying *Roth*, however, is becoming increasingly difficult, particularly in the less-than-crystal clear world of at-will employment. *See* <u>*Mt. Healthy City Sch. Dist. Bd. of Educ. v. Doyle*, 429 U.S. 274, 283-84 (1977)</u> (at-will employees cannot be fired for unconstitutional reasons); <u>*Callantine v. Staff Builders*, 271 F.3d 1124 (8th Cir. 2001)</u>; <u>*Ross v. Clayton County*, 173 F.3d 1305 (11th Cir. 1999)</u>.

Food for Thought

Take a look at the list of courses offered at your law school for a one year period (assuming it is available). Do you know how many faculty, including legal writing, clinic, and academic support faculty are on tenure-track lines? Does it seem to you this makes a difference in the quality of teaching, scholarship, or professional and institutional service?

In legal academia, short term appointments have become more prevalent than traditional tenure track appointments. Andy Guess, *Threat to Tenure at Law Schools*, INSIDE HIGHER ED.COM, http://www.insidehighered.com/news/2007/05/04/abatenure (last visited June 8, 2008) ("The American Bar Association – at the urging of some law deans and to the dismay of many law professors – is considering an end to having tenure systems be one requirement for law school accreditation.");

Suzanne Ehrenberg, *Embracing the Writing-Centered Legal Process*, 89 IOWA L. REV. 1159 (2004); Peter Brandon Bayer, *A Plea for Rationality and Decency: The Disparate Treatment of Legal Writing Faculties as a Violation of Both Equal Protection and Professional Ethics*, 39 DUQ. L. REV. 329 (2001). Most contracts, other than those for tenure-track or tenured faculty, are written to avoid creating any expectation of re-appointment, much like the contract between Professor Roth and his university.

2. In *Minch v. City of Chicago*, 486 F.3d 294 (7th Cir. Ill. 2007), a collective bargaining agreement allowed the city to discharge firefighters *exclusively* for cause. After the agreement was in place, the city adopted an ordinance that made retirement by age 63 compulsory. The ordinance was challenged as a deprivation of due process raising the question of whether the retirement mandate infringed on a *Roth*-based liberty or property interest.

> The plaintiffs contend that the CBA's identification of just cause as the sole basis for discipline or discharge gave them a property interest in continued employment of which the City deprived them when it compelled them to retire at age 63. . . . [The question is whether] the plaintiffs had a protected interest in working beyond the age of 63. . . . Compelled retirement, like a discharge, severs the employment relationship between employer and employee. Nonetheless, there are intuitive distinctions between being fired and being forced to retire. Retirement is necessarily linked to the employee's age and/or tenure with the employer; and whether voluntary or not, retirement often bestows certain benefits on the employee (e.g., a pension and/or continued receipt of insurance and other employee benefits) that he would not enjoy if simply fired. (There is the same intuitive distinction between quitting and retiring voluntarily). Being fired and being forced to retire indubitably have in common the fact that the employer unilaterally terminates the employment relationship. But only a broad understanding of the term "discharge" that brings within its reach any and all forms of involuntary termination would demand just cause even for an unwilling retirement. . . . The collective bargaining agreement between the City and its firefighters did not preclude the City from subsequently adopting a mandatory retirement age. Because the CBA did not give the plaintiffs a protected property interest in continued employment regardless of their age, the plaintiffs cannot show that they were deprived of procedural due process when the City adopted the [ordinance] and enforced it by compelling their retirement at age 63. . . .

What do you think of the reasoning of the court – do you buy the distinction between forced retirement and discharge? At the time the CBA was consummated, there was no mandatory retirement. How can the imposition of an ordinance that appears to modify the contract by limiting the span of a career be anything other than a deprivation of property? Based on *Roth*, what would have been the best argument for firefighters unwillingly discharged at age 63?

3. *Roth* was a procedural due process case, not a substantive due process claim. The case can be misread since Professor Roth asserted he had been stigmatized by the university. In *Holthaus v. Board of Education, Cincinnati Public Schools*, 986 F.2d 1044 (6th Cir. 1993), the plaintiff Holthaus was discharged after allegedly making

racist remarks.

> In support of this theory of his case, Holthaus relies primarily on *Board of Regents v. Roth*. Initially, we note that *Roth* is not a substantive due process case; it is clearly a procedural due process case. . . . We recognize that the very theory of Holthaus' lawsuit is that . . . the termination of his one year coaching contract did cast a stigma on his name that would affect his other employment opportunities. Even so, *Roth* makes clear that this would only amount to a denial of procedural due process even if Holthaus had not been given an opportunity to be heard. Holthaus . . . has been given abundant opportunities to be heard. . . .

On appeal, Professor Roth argued that the content of his speech was the basis for the refusal of the university to reappoint him – a fairly clear liberty interest. How is that not a substantive due process claim?

4. Roth may have no clear contractual right to be re-appointed – but did the state, by its silence, interfere with his capacity to have a meaningful negotiation to secure reappointment? Assume, as JUSTICE DOUGLAS did, that Roth had good reason to think he was denied reappointment because of his speech activity. If Roth was the effective teacher that JUSTICE DOUGLAS assumed him to be, and the denial of his reappointment was based on his political/substantive criticism of the university (a speech claim), how is that not a denial of a liberty interest necessitating a pre-adverse action hearing? Furthermore, if there is right to – or freedom of – contract (*Meyer v. Nebraska*, 262 U.S. 390, 399 (1923) (holding that liberty includes the "right of the individual to contract, to engage in the common occupations of life . . .")) how can Professor Roth determine if the state decided against renewing his contract on unconstitutional grounds?

Good Question!

In *Rampey v. Allen*, 501 F.2d 1090 (10th Cir. 1974), a number of faculty members were fired after holding a press conference during which they were critical of the university president. The court set aside the district court's dismissal of their complaint, noting that dismissal "on account of disapproved associations, or disapproval of statements made," would violate their speech interest. Why not the same outcome in *Roth*?

5. How is the liberty/property analysis applied when dealing with private parties engaged in publicly funded or government licensed activity?

a. *Merritt v. Mackey*, 827 F.2d 1368 (9th Cir. 1987).

> Knowlton Merritt began working for KADA as a counselor in 1976. . . . KADA had contracts with both Klamath County and the Indian Health Services ("IHS"), a federal agency, to provide alcohol and drug abuse services. In 1981 state and federal officials, including defendant[] John Mackey . . . began evaluating KADA's management. . . . The report conditioned further funding of KADA on the requirement that Merritt . . .

"must not be employed by KADA".

KADA, fearing the loss of funds, fired Merritt on March 17, 1983. . . . KADA [then] informed . . . Mackey that its personnel policies gave it the burden of proving the reasons for Merritt's termination and requested such an explanation . . . . No explanation was ever provided. In September 1983 [Merritt] filed this action under 42 U.S.C. § 1983 and the Fifth Amendment, alleging liberty and property deprivations without due process.

It is indisputable that an individual may have a protected property interest in private employment. . . . [W]here the actions of private individuals operate to deprive an individual of his employment, a suit for interference with private contractual relationships would lie, but where government officials are involved, the nature of the interest at stake in private employment is a property interest. . . . The inquiry does not end here, however. For the purpose of due process, Merritt must . . . demonstrate a "legitimate claim of entitlement." . . . . KADA's personnel policies stated that permanent employees could be fired only "for cause." Under Oregon law "just cause" policies can form part of the employment contract. We conclude therefore . . . that Merritt had a protected property interest in his continued employment with KADA. Thus, the Due Process Clause entitled Merritt to a meaningful hearing at a meaningful time to challenge any deprivation of that interest by the . . . government. . . .

That KADA and not the government officials themselves terminated Merritt's employment does not change the nature of his protected property interest. Liability under 42 U.S.C. § 1983 attaches to any person who, under color of state law, "subjects or causes to be subjected" any person to a deprivation of protected rights . . . . Mackey's order to KADA to fire Merritt or lose state and federal funding was not random and the authorities could easily predict the injury to Merritt that would result . . . .

b. *Ulrich v. City and County of San Francisco*, 308 F.3d 968 (9th Cir. 2002).

[In 1998] Dr. Ulrich . . . learned that, for budgetary reasons, the San Francisco Department of Health had begun to lay off physicians at the hospital. His own higher pay classification was not affected. . . . Dr. Ulrich protested the layoffs . . . . On August 28, Dr. Ulrich received a written notice . . . stating that the hospital[] was opening a formal investigation of him into allegations of professional incompetence. . . . On September 30, Dr. Ulrich posted a notice of his resignation, effective November 1, 1998.

Thereafter, Dr. Ulrich's lawyer advised him that his resignation could trigger a reporting requirement . . . . The federal Health Care Quality Improvement Act requires that a health care entity submit an adverse action report . . . if the entity "accepts the surrender of clinical privileges of a physician . . . while the physician is under an investigation by the entity relating to possible incompetence or improper professional conduct." . . . . Dr. Ulrich wrote to Dr. Rivero on October 16, rescinding his resignation pending the completion of the . . . investigation. . . . Dr. Rivero sent Dr. Ulrich a letter stating that "we" would not honor the revocation of the resignation . . . . On November 6, Dr. Rivero filed adverse action reports . . . . [A]ccording to the presidents of two medical associations in California, it will be virtually impossible for Dr. Ulrich to obtain employment as a practicing physician at any hospital in the country if the report . . . is not voided. . . .

The district court found that Dr. Ulrich could not proceed to trial because, given that he voluntarily resigned his job, he could not show that he was denied any property interest by . . . the hospital's decision not to accept his rescission of resignation. We agree. . . . Under California law, an employee has a right to rescind a resignation . . . only prior to its acceptance. . . . The phrase does not create an absolute right to rescind an accepted resignation simply because the request is made before the resignation's effective date. . . . [O]nce the hospital accepted Dr.Ulrich's resignation, which Dr. Rivero did on October 1, whether to reinstate him lay in the discretion of the hospital's decisionmakers. No constitutionally protected property interest can exist in the outcome of a decision "unmistakably committed . . . to the discretion of the [public entity].

Perry v. Sindermann

408 U.S. 593 (1972)

[Justice Stewart] From 1959 to 1969 the respondent, Robert Sindermann, was a teacher in the state college system of the State of Texas. After teaching for two years at the University of Texas and for four years at San Antonio Junior College, he became a professor of Government and Social Science at Odessa Junior College in 1965. He was employed at the college for four successive years, under a series of one-year contracts. He was successful enough to be appointed, for a time, the cochairman of his department.

During the 1968-1969 academic year, however, controversy arose between the respondent and the college administration. The respondent was elected president of the Texas Junior College Teachers Association. In this capacity, he left his teaching duties on several occasions to testify before committees of the Texas Legislature, and he became involved in public disagreements with the policies of the college's Board of Regents. In particular, he aligned himself with a group advocating the elevation of the college to four-year status – a change opposed by the Regents. And, on one occasion, a newspaper advertisement appeared over his name that was highly critical of the Regents.

Finally, in May 1969, the respondent's one-year employment contract terminated and the Board of Regents voted not to offer him a new contract for the next academic year. The Regents issued a press release setting forth allegations of the respondent's insubordination. n.1 But they provided him no official statement of the reasons for the nonrenewal of his contract. And they allowed him no opportunity for a hearing to challenge the basis of the nonrenewal.

n.1 The press release stated, for example, that the respondent had defied his superiors by attending legislative committee meetings when college officials had specifically refused to permit him to leave his classes for that purpose.

The respondent then brought this action . . . . He alleged primarily that the Regents' decision not to rehire him was based on his public criticism of the policies of the college administration and thus infringed his right to freedom of speech. He also alleged that their failure to provide him an opportunity for a hearing violated the Fourteenth Amendment's guarantee of procedural due process. The petitioners – members of the Board of Regents and the president of the college – denied that their decision was made in retaliation for the respondent's public criticism and argued that they had no obligation to provide a hearing. On the basis of these bare pleadings and three brief affidavits filed by the respondent, the District Court granted summary judgment for the petitioners. It concluded that the respondent had "no cause of action against the [college] since his contract of employment terminated May 31, 1969, and Odessa Junior College has not adopted the tenure system."

The Court of Appeals reversed . . . . First, it held that, despite the respondent's lack of tenure, the nonrenewal of his contract would violate the Fourteenth Amendment if it in fact was based on his protected free speech. Since the actual reason for the Regents' decision was "in total dispute" in the pleadings, the court remanded the case for a full hearing on this contested issue of fact. Second, the Court of Appeals held that, despite the respondent's lack of tenure, the failure to allow him an opportunity for a hearing would violate the constitutional guarantee of procedural due process if the respondent could show that he had an "expectancy" of re-employment. It, therefore, ordered that this issue of fact also be aired upon remand. . . . [W]e have considered this case along with *Board of Regents v. Roth*.

I.

The first question presented is whether the respondent's lack of a contractual or tenure right to re-employment, taken alone, defeats his claim that the nonrenewal of his contract violated the First and Fourteenth Amendments. We hold that it does not.

For at least a quarter-century, this Court has made clear that [government] may not deny a benefit to a person on a basis that infringes his constitutionally protected interests – especially, his interest in freedom of speech. . . . We have applied the principle regardless of the public employee's contractual or other claim to a job. Thus, the respondent's lack of a contractual or tenure "right" to re-employment for the 1969-1970 academic year is immaterial to his free speech claim. Indeed, twice before, this Court has specifically held that the nonrenewal of a nontenured public school teacher's one-year contract may not be predicated on his exercise of First and Fourteenth Amendment rights. We reaffirm those holdings here.

In this case, of course, the respondent has yet to show that the decision not to renew his contract was, in fact, made in retaliation for his exercise of the constitutional right of free speech. The District Court foreclosed any opportunity to make this showing when it granted summary judgment. Hence, we cannot now hold that the Board of Regents' action was invalid. But we agree with the Court of Appeals that there is a genuine dispute as to "whether the college refused to renew the teaching contract on an impermissible basis – as a reprisal for the exercise of constitutionally protected rights." . . . . For this reason we hold that the grant of summary judgment against the respondent, without full exploration of this issue, was improper.

II.

The respondent's lack of formal contractual or tenure security in continued employment at Odessa Junior College, though irrelevant to his free speech claim, is highly relevant to his procedural due process claim. But it may not be entirely dispositive.

We have held today in *Board of Regents v. Roth* that the Constitution does not require opportunity for a hearing before the nonrenewal of a nontenured teacher's contract, unless he can show that the decision not to rehire him somehow deprived him of an interest in "liberty" or that he had a "property" interest in continued employment, despite the lack of tenure or a formal contract. In *Roth* the teacher had not made a showing on either point to justify summary judgment in his favor.

Similarly, the respondent here has yet to show that he has been deprived of an interest that could invoke procedural due process protection. . . . But the respondent's allegations – which we must construe most favorably to the respondent at this stage of the litigation – do raise a genuine issue as to his interest in continued employment at Odessa Junior College. . . . In particular, the respondent alleged that the college had a de facto tenure program, and that he had tenure under that program. He claimed that he and others legitimately relied upon an unusual provision that had been in the college's official Faculty Guide for many years:

> Teacher Tenure: Odessa College has no tenure system. The Administration of the College wishes the faculty member to feel that he has permanent tenure as long as his teaching services are satisfactory and as long as he displays a cooperative attitude toward his co-workers and his superiors, and as long as he is happy in his work.

Moreover, the respondent claimed legitimate reliance upon guidelines promulgated by the Coordinating Board of the Texas College and University System that provided that a person, like himself, who had been employed as a teacher in the state college and university system for seven years or more has some form of job tenure. Thus, the respondent offered to prove that [he] had no less a "property" interest in continued employment than a formally tenured teacher at other colleges, and had no less a procedural due process right to a statement of reasons and a hearing before college officials upon their decision not to retain him.

We have made clear in *Roth* that "property" . . . denotes a broad range of interests that are secured by "existing rules or understandings." A person's interest in a benefit is a "property" interest for due process purposes if there are such rules or mutually explicit understandings that support his claim of entitlement to the benefit and that he may invoke at a hearing. A written contract with an explicit tenure provision clearly is evidence of a formal understanding that supports a teacher's claim of entitlement to continued employment unless sufficient "cause" is shown. Yet absence of such an explicit contractual provision may not always foreclose the possibility that a teacher has a "property" interest in re-employment. . . . Explicit contractual provisions may be supplemented by other agreements implied from "the promisor's words and conduct in the light of the surrounding circumstances." . . . .

A teacher, like the respondent, who has held his position for a number of years, might be able to show . . . that he has a legitimate claim of entitlement to job tenure. Just as this Court has found there to be a "common law of a particular industry or of a particular plant" that may supplement a collective-bargaining agreement so there may be an unwritten "common law" in a particular university that certain employees shall have the equivalent of tenure. . . . [n.7]

> n.7 We do not now hold that the respondent has any such legitimate claim of entitlement to job tenure. . . . If it is the law of Texas that a teacher in the respondent's position has no contractual or other claim to job tenure, the respondent's claim would be defeated.

In this case, the respondent has alleged the existence of rules and understandings, promulgated and fostered by state officials, that may justify his legitimate claim of entitlement to continued employment absent "sufficient cause." We disagree with the Court of Appeals insofar as it held that a mere subjective "expectancy" is protected by procedural due process, but we agree that the respondent must be given an opportunity to prove the legitimacy of his claim of such entitlement in light of "the policies and practices of the institution." Proof of such a property interest would not, of course, entitle him to reinstatement. But such proof would obligate college officials to grant a hearing at his request, where he could be informed of the grounds for his nonretention and challenge their sufficiency.

Therefore, while we do not wholly agree with the opinion of the Court of Appeals, its judgment remanding this case to the District Court is Affirmed.

———

> ### Underlying Case Documents
>
> The case referenced:
> The guidelines promulgated by the Coordinating Board of the Texas College and University System
> The press release setting forth Sindermann's insubordination

1. In the notes following *Roth*, we discussed the increasing frequency of at-will employment. As you read the following note case, can you tell why Mr. Sindermann was not treated as an at-will employee?

In *Neva v. Multi Agency Communications Center*, 2005 WL 1677530 (E.D. Wash. 2005), the plaintiff was the director – and an at-will employee – of a governmental agency that consolidated requests for emergency assistance from police, fire, and medical rescue services. Plaintiff was summarily terminated and filed suit, claiming that statements made to her as well as various actions by the agency gave her a constitutionally protected interest in her job. The court found that absent written policies or action that reflected detrimental reliance on binding promises allegedly made, plaintiff's at-will status was insufficient to allow a court to find a liberty or property interest. The court held as follows:

> A person's property interest in employment is created and defined by state law, but protected by the due process clause of the state and federal constitutions. *Roth*. . . . Plaintiff contends her protected property interest exists because there was a mutual understanding that supported her claim of entitlement. . . . [S]he argues that even absent an express written provision, a property interest can be implied by the words and conduct of the employer. *Perry v. Sindermann*. . . . [A] due process property interest exists "if there are such rules or mutually explicit understandings that support (an individual's) claim of entitlement." . . . . The Board minutes submitted by plaintiff do not include any explicit promises that plaintiff would only be terminated after the creation of a job description and evaluation. Plaintiff also states that . . . she spoke to [Board members] about a new job description and evaluation [and received] assurances about continued employment. . . . She stated [she was] "left . . . feeling that [a Board member] was definitely not in favor of firing me. . . ."
>
> It is settled law in Washington state that at-will employment may be modified (1) by an express or implied agreement subject to the rules of contract formation (offer, acceptance, consideration), or (2) by an implied contract, without the traditional contract elements, based on the specific written policies announced by the employer in a written employee handbook. . . . The foregoing of another job opportunity is not sufficient consideration to defeat an employer's right to terminate at will. . . . To be considered sufficient, consideration must be in addition to required services and result in a detriment to the employee and benefit to the employer. . . . [Plaintiff] states only that she refrained from seeking alternative employment at the time based on alleged assurances from individual Board members in private conversations that

she would not be summarily discharged. This is not adequate consideration to form a contract. . . .

In the absence of a written policy promising specific treatment in specific circumstances, oral representations made by an employee's supervisor are insufficient to establish an enforceable promise. . . . The court finds as a matter of law plaintiff was an at-will employee at the time of her termination. Consequently, she has not shown there is a genuine issue of material fact with regard to the § 1983 claim.

a. List the factors that led the Court to conclude that Mr. Sindermann had met the threshold requirements to assert a constitutionally protected interest. Are those interests less compelling than assurances by an employer coupled with passing up a career change (demonstrating one's reasonable belief in a right to continued employment)?

b. Why was the plaintiff's claim in the above note case based on 42 U.S.C. § 1983? Of what civil right was plaintiff deprived?

2. Mr. Sindermann was able to get into the record the content of his comments that he claimed were the driving force behind the decision of the school system to deny him a new contract. Put aside the de facto tenure argument. Was the speech claim raised in *Sindermann* of greater concern than the claim in *Roth*? Why is Mr. Sindermann's speech of more interest to the Court than Professor Roth's? *See* Marvin F. Hill, Jr. & James A. Wright, *"Riding with the Cops and Cheering for the Robbers": Employee Speech, Doctrinal Cubbyholes, and the Duty of Loyalty*, 25 Pepp. L. Rev. 721 (1998).

As you know from constitutional law, notwithstanding the fact that the First Amendment instructs Congress to make "no law" abridging freedom of speech, we have many laws (including defamation; criminal conspiracy; threatening speech that constitutes an assault, creates a public danger, or is directed at a public officials, etc.) that limit speech. What if the basis for a dismissal is speech that is patently offensive but not explicitly deemed criminal or otherwise in violation of established norms? Consider the following note cases:

a. *Locurto v. Giuliani*, 269 F. Supp. 2d 368 (S.D.N.Y. 2003), *rev'd and remanded on other grounds*, *Locurto v. Giuliani*, 447 F.3d 159 (2d Cir. 2006).

In September 1998, following their terminations, plaintiffs . . . brought suit pursuant to 42 U.S.C. § 1983, alleging they were terminated illegally from their positions of public employment – specifically, that they were terminated without due process of law and in retaliation for engaging in offensive speech. . . . Plaintiffs claim that their participation in the "Black to the Future: Broad Channel 2098" float was a comment on racial integration of a white community for the purpose of entertainment and, as such, was protected by the First Amendment. Regarding their subsequent termination, plaintiffs maintain that defendants did not dismiss them out of a reasonable concern for anticipated disruption but rather in retaliation for the content of their speech. . . . [P]laintiffs urge that their termination was nonetheless impermissible because, given the circumstances, any concern over disruption was insufficient as a matter of law.

It does not take much imagination to understand the speech content of the plaintiff's "float" and the defendant's concern regarding "anticipated disruption." You decide – is this protected speech? If so, do plaintiffs have a due process interest that was contravened?

b. In *Sizemore v. City of Dallas, 443 F. Supp. 2d 1201 (D. Ore. 2006)*, the court dealt with speech that was blatantly racist and brought suit.

> [P]laintiff established he was subjected to such conduct . . . considered abusive and hostile to a reasonable Hispanic. . . . The Findings [also show] that plaintiff had used similar racist terms in reference to his Hispanic heritage and that he waited . . . four years after he was hired, to complain. . . .
>
> When government employees speak about corruption, wrongdoing, misconduct, wastefulness, or inefficiency by other government employees, including speech about invidious discrimination, whether it is a single act or a pattern of conduct, that speech is inherently a matter of public concern. . . . Accordingly, plaintiff's speech regarding the racial discrimination of public officials is a matter of public concern. . . .
>
> Moreover, the critical question in the analysis of a governmental employee's claim of First Amendment retaliation is identifying the motive for the speech – whether the point of the speech was to bring wrongdoing to light, to raise issues of public concern, or solely to further a purely private interest. . . . Plaintiff argues that his speech . . . was a protest against ongoing unlawful racial harassment and discrimination and the fact that a public agency was allowing a superior officer to engage in such unlawful behavior. . . . That is a question of fact more appropriately decided by a jury.

Is the court correct – is the level of constitutional import in speech tested by the "motive" of the speaker? What if Mr. Sindermann's motives boiled down to a personal vendetta – would that matter?

c. The Supreme Court recently dealt with a case involving the alleged retaliatory discharge of a district attorney who claimed that language he wrote in a memo was protected since it was meant to call into question official misconduct. In *Garcetti v. Ceballos, 547 U.S. 410 (2006)*, the Court held:

> [The Court] has recognized that [a] citizen who works for the government is nonetheless a citizen. The First Amendment limits the ability of a public employer to leverage the employment relationship to restrict, incidentally or intentionally, the liberties employees enjoy in their capacities as private citizens. *See Perry v. Sindermann.* So long as employees are speaking as citizens about matters of public concern, they must face only those speech restrictions that are necessary for their employers to operate efficiently and effectively. . . .

Yet the First Amendment interests at stake extend beyond the individual speaker. The Court has acknowledged the importance of promoting the public's interest in receiving the well-informed views of government employees engaging in civic discussion. Pickering again provides an instructive example. The Court characterized its holding as rejecting the attempt of school administrators to "'limi[t] teachers' opportunities to contribute to public debate." 391 U.S. at 573. It also noted that teachers are "the members of a community most likely to have informed and definite opinions" about school expenditures. The Court's approach acknowledged the necessity for informed, vibrant dialogue in a democratic society. It suggested, in addition, that widespread costs may arise when dialogue is repressed. . . .

"The Court's decisions, then, have sought both to promote the individual and societal interests that are served when employees speak as citizens on matters of public concern and to respect the needs of government employers attempting to perform their important public functions. . . . Underlying our cases has been the premise that while the First Amendment invests public employees with certain rights, it does not empower them to "constitutionalize the employee grievance." Connick, 461 U.S. at 154. . . .

How are any of these cases anything other than "constitutionalizing the employee grievance[s]?" Why would the Court be concerned about giving constitutional protection to the speech interests of public sector employees – and not the interests in Professor Roth's speech regarding racism?

3. To what extent did the relative professional status of the primary actors in *Roth* and *Sindermann* enter into the decision of the Court? JUSTICE STEWART began both opinions with descriptions of the complainants:

From *Sindermann*

From 1959 to 1969 the respondent, Robert Sindermann, was a teacher in the state college system of the State of Texas. After teaching for two years at the University of Texas and for four years at San Antonio Junior College, he became a professor of Government and Social Science at Odessa Junior College in 1965. He was employed at the college for four successive years, under a series of one-year contracts. He was successful enough to be appointed, for a time, the cochairman of his department.

During the 1968-1969 academic year, however, controversy arose between the respondent and the college administration. The respondent was elected president of the Texas Junior College Teachers Association. In this capacity, he left his teaching duties on several occasions to testify before committees of the Texas Legislature [and] on one occasion, a newspaper advertisement appeared over his name that was highly critical of the Regents."

From *Roth*

In 1968 the respondent, David Roth, was hired for his first teaching job as assistant professor of political science at Wisconsin State University-Oshkosh. He was hired for a fixed term of one academic year. The notice of his faculty appointment specified that his employment would begin on September 1, 1968, and would end on June 30, 1969. The respondent completed that term. But he was informed that he would not be rehired for the next academic year. The respondent had no tenure rights to continued employment.

If, as the at-will cases make clear, the bottom line is the written contract, are these cases really that different?

Hypothetical

Assume that you are a graduate student at a state university and

a. Your research assistant position and its associated $5,000 stipend, upon which you rely for living expenses, have been terminated because of deep cuts to the university's budget made by the state legislature (which is trying to close a large deficit in the state's budget). You received notice of the termination by e-mail message on a Monday. The message indicated that your last stipend payment would be made to you on the following Monday. All of your friends with similar research assistant positions received the same message. You want to fight the termination. What process, if any, are you due in this circumstance? Should the university have afforded you a pre-termination hearing? If not, should it give you the opportunity for a post-termination hearing? Any other process?

b. The chief resident advisor (RA) of your dormitory files a report with the campus housing office accusing you of playing loud music late into the night, relating to your roommates in a belligerent manner, and refusing to take direction from the RA. Upon receipt of the report, the director of campus housing sends you a letter indicating that you have lost on-campus housing privileges and that you must move to off-campus housing at the end of the current semester. You report to the director's office immediately after reading his letter and request a meeting with him, which he gives you. Although you respond to all of the RA's allegations at that meeting, the director tells you that his decision to terminate your housing privileges is firm. You ask to be given an impartial hearing. He replies: "This was it." Was it? Do you have a constitutional right to additional process in this circumstance? If so, what form should it take and why?

4. <u>*Vail v. Bd. of Educ. of Paris Union School*, 706 F.2d 1435 (7th Cir. 1983)</u>.

> This case arose because of the efforts of the Board of Education of Paris Union School District No. 95 (Board) to secure the services of the plaintiff-appellee Jesse A. Vail (Vail) as an athletic director and football coach. At the time the Board sought his services Vail was employed as supervisor of recreation and physical education for the Stateville Correctional Center in Joliet, Illinois. . . .

> Vail was concerned about . . . giving up his job at Stateville. In response [the] Board instructed Dr. James Cherry, the superintendent, to convey an offer to Vail and to explain the Board's intention to renew the one-year contract at the end of the first year. Vail was informed of the offer and told that while the Board could not offer him more than a one year contract, it could assure him of extending the contract for a second year. Vail accepted . . . and subsequently assumed the duties of athletic director and football coach. On March 2, 1981 the Board met in public session and voted not to renew Vail's contract for the ensuing year. Vail was not given any explanation as to the reason for his termination, nor was he given any sort of a hearing. On these findings of fact the district court held that Vail had a constitutionally protected property interest in his continued employment with the Board. . . .

> Vail had a two-year employment promise rather than a commitment for indefinite employment, as in the case of tenure. The length of time that an individual retains an asset affects the weight or value of the interest, but not the nature of the interest. . . . We affirm the finding that the Board deprived Vail of his legitimate expectation of continued employment in terminating him without cause before the expiration of his employment period, and that such deprivation is a violation of due process and actionable under the <u>Civil Rights Act</u>.

While statutes can create property rights, the same is not always true of less formal administrative action.

5. <u>*Washington Legal Clinic for the Homeless v. Barry, Jr.*, 107 F.3d 32 (D.C. Cir. 1997)</u>.

> In early 1994, the Shelter Office abandoned the first-come, first-served system, replacing it with the wait-list procedures currently in effect. Now, all eligible families remaining on the waiting list eventually receive shelter. If this procedure were mandated by statute or regulation, eligible homeless families might well have a constitutionally protected entitlement to shelter, even though delay between application and shelter would almost always occur.

> We agree with the dissent that in certain circumstances property rights may arise from administrative "rules or understandings." <u>*Roth*</u>; [*Sindermann*]. Equally clear, however, administrative actions may not create property rights where that result would "contravene the intent of the legislature." Here, the City Council's intent is plain: "Nothing in this chapter shall be construed to create an entitlement in any homeless person or family to emergency shelter. . . ." D.C. Code § 3-206.9(a). While we doubt that blanket "no-entitlement" disclaimers can by themselves strip entitlements from individuals in the face of statutes or regulations unequivocally conferring them, the District's "no-entitlement" disclaimer reinforces our conclusion that District of Columbia law, by leaving allocation of limited shelter among eligible

families to administrative discretion, creates no constitutionally protected entitlement to emergency shelter.

Moreover, outside the employment context, we have found no decision of the Supreme Court or of this Circuit holding that administrative rules or understandings existing wholly apart from legislation or regulations may create a property interest. We are not surprised by the lack of such decisions. In the absence of special circumstances neither alleged nor present in this case, such as where reliance on administrative action creates contractual responsibilities, obligations enforceable against the public fisc, i.e., entitlements, may arise only from the people acting through their legislators, not from administrative fiat.

MATHEWS, SECRETARY OF HEALTH, EDUCATION, AND WELFARE V. ELDRIDGE

424 U.S. 319 (1976)

[JUSTICE POWELL] The issue in this case is whether the Due Process Clause of the Fifth Amendment requires that prior to the termination of Social Security disability benefit payments the recipient be afforded an opportunity for an evidentiary hearing.

I.

Cash benefits are provided to workers during periods in which they are completely disabled under the disability insurance benefits program created by the 1956 amendments to Title II of the Social Security Act. Respondent Eldridge was first awarded benefits in June 1968. In March 1972, he received a questionnaire from the state agency charged with monitoring his medical condition. Eldridge completed the questionnaire, indicating that his condition had not improved and identifying the medical sources, including physicians, from whom he had received treatment recently. The state agency then obtained reports from his physician and a psychiatric consultant. After considering these reports and other information in his file the agency informed Eldridge by letter that it had made a tentative determination that his disability had ceased in May 1972. The letter included a statement of reasons for the proposed termination of benefits, and advised Eldridge that he might request reasonable time in which to obtain and submit additional information pertaining to his condition.

In his written response, Eldridge disputed one characterization of his medical condition and indicated that the agency already had enough evidence to establish his disability. n.2 The state agency then made its final determination that he had ceased to be disabled in May 1972. This determination was accepted by the Social Security Administration (SSA), which notified Eldridge in July that his benefits would terminate after that month. The notification also advised him of his right to seek reconsideration by the state agency of this initial determination within six months.

> n.2 Eldridge originally was disabled due to chronic anxiety and back strain. He subsequently was found to have diabetes. The tentative determination letter indicated that aid would be terminated because available medical evidence indicated that his diabetes was under control, that there existed no limitations on his back movements which would impose severe functional restrictions, and that he no longer suffered emotional problems that would preclude him from all work for which he was qualified. In his reply letter he claimed to have arthritis of the spine rather than a strained back.

Instead of requesting reconsideration Eldridge commenced this action challenging the constitutional validity of the administrative procedures established by the Secretary of Health, Education, and Welfare for assessing whether there exists a continuing disability. He sought an immediate reinstatement of benefits pending a hearing on the issue of his disability. The Secretary moved to dismiss on the grounds that Eldridge's benefits had been terminated in accordance with valid administrative regulations and procedures and that he had failed to exhaust available remedies. In support of his contention that due process requires a pretermination hearing, Eldridge relied exclusively upon this Court's decision in _Goldberg v. Kelly_ . . . . The Secretary contended that _Goldberg_ was not controlling since eligibility for disability benefits, unlike eligibility for welfare benefits, is not based on financial need and since issues of credibility and veracity do not play a significant role in the disability entitlement decision, which turns primarily on medical evidence.

The District Court concluded that the administrative procedures pursuant to which the Secretary had terminated Eldridge's benefits abridged his right to procedural due process. The court viewed the interest of the disability recipient in uninterrupted benefits as indistinguishable from that of the welfare recipient in _Goldberg_. It further noted that decisions subsequent to _Goldberg_ demonstrated that the due process requirement of pretermination hearings is not limited to situations involving the deprivation of vital necessities. Reasoning that disability determinations may involve subjective judgments based on conflicting medical and nonmedical evidence, the District Court held that prior to termination of benefits Eldridge had to be afforded an evidentiary hearing of the type required for welfare beneficiaries under Title IV of the Social Security Act. . . . [T]he Court of Appeals for the Fourth Circuit affirmed the injunction barring termination of Eldridge's benefits prior to an evidentiary hearing. We reverse.

II.

[The Court has jurisdiction.]

III.

A.

. . . The Secretary does not contend that procedural due process is inapplicable to terminations of Social Security disability benefits. . . . Rather, the Secretary contends that the existing administrative procedures . . . provide all the process that is constitutionally due before a recipient can be deprived of that interest. . . .

B.

[I]dentification of the specific dictates of due process generally requires consideration of three distinct factors: First, the private interest that will be affected by the official action; second, the risk of an erroneous deprivation of such interest through the procedures used, and the probable value, if any, of additional or substitute procedural safeguards; and finally, the Government's interest, including the function involved and the fiscal and administrative burdens that the additional or substitute procedural requirement would entail. . . .

C.

. . . Since a recipient whose benefits are terminated is awarded full retroactive relief if he ultimately prevails, his sole interest is in the uninterrupted receipt of this source of income pending final administrative decision on his claim. . . . Only in *Goldberg* has the Court held that due process requires an evidentiary hearing prior to a temporary deprivation. . . . Eligibility for disability benefits, in contrast, is not based upon financial need [so the] potential deprivation here is generally likely to be less than in *Goldberg*, although [a]s the District Court emphasized, to remain eligible for benefits a recipient must be "unable to engage in substantial gainful activity." . . . .

. . . The Secretary concedes that the delay between a request for a hearing before an administrative law judge and a decision on the claim is currently between 10 and 11 months. Since a terminated recipient must first obtain a reconsideration decision as a prerequisite to invoking his right to an evidentiary hearing, the delay between the actual cutoff of benefits and final decision after a hearing exceeds one year. In view of the torpidity of this administrative review process and the typically modest resources of the family unit of the physically disabled worker, the hardship imposed upon the erroneously terminated disability recipient may be significant. Still, the disabled worker's need is likely to be less than that of a welfare recipient. In addition to the possibility of access to private resources, other forms of government assistance will become available where the termination of disability benefits places a worker or his family below the subsistence level . . . .

D.

An additional factor to be considered here is the fairness and reliability of the existing pretermination procedures, and the probable value, if any, of additional procedural safeguards. . . . [T]he decision whether to discontinue disability benefits will turn, in most cases, upon "routine, standard, and unbiased medical reports by physician specialists," *Richardson v. Perales*, concerning a subject whom they have personally examined. n.28 In *Richardson* the Court recognized the "reliability and probative worth of written medical reports," emphasizing that while there may be "professional disagreement with the medical conclusions" the "specter of questionable credibility and veracity is not present." To be sure, credibility and veracity may be a factor in the ultimate disability assessment in some cases. But procedural due process rules are shaped by the risk of error inherent in the truthfinding process as applied to the generality of cases, not the rare exceptions. The potential value of an evidentiary hearing, or even oral presentation to the decisionmaker, is substantially less in this context than in *Goldberg*.

> n.28 The decision is not purely a question of the accuracy of a medical diagnosis since the ultimate issue which the state agency must resolve is whether in light of the particular worker's "age, education, and work experience" he cannot "engage in any . . . substantial gainful work which exists in the national economy . . . ." Yet information concerning each of these worker characteristics is amenable to effective written presentation. . . . Similarly, resolution of the inquiry as to the types of employment opportunities that exist in the national economy for a physically impaired worker with a particular set of skills would not necessarily be advanced by an evidentiary hearing. The statistical information relevant to this judgment is more amenable to written than to oral presentation.

The decision in *Goldberg* also was based on the Court's conclusion that written submissions were an inadequate substitute for oral presentation because they did not provide an effective means for the recipient to communicate his case to the decisionmaker. . . . In the context of the disability-benefits-entitlement assessment the administrative procedures under review here fully answer these objections.

The detailed questionnaire which the state agency periodically sends the recipient identifies with particularity the information relevant to the entitlement decision, and the recipient is invited to obtain assistance from the local SSA office in completing the questionnaire. More important, the information critical to the entitlement decision usually is derived from medical sources, such as the treating physician. Such sources are likely to be able to communicate more effectively through written documents than are welfare recipients or the lay witnesses supporting their cause. The conclusions of physicians often are supported by X-rays and the results of clinical or laboratory tests, information typically more amenable to written than to oral presentation.

A further safeguard against mistake is the policy of allowing the disability recipient's representative full access to all information relied upon by the state agency. In addition, prior to the cutoff of benefits the agency informs the recipient of its tentative assessment, the reasons therefor, and provides a summary of the evidence that it considers most relevant. Opportunity is then afforded the recipient to submit additional evidence or arguments, enabling him to challenge directly the accuracy of information in his file as well as the correctness of the agency's tentative conclusions. These procedures, again as contrasted with those before the Court in *Goldberg*, enable the recipient to "mold" his argument to respond to the precise issues which the decisionmaker regards as crucial.

Despite these carefully structured procedures, amici point to the significant reversal rate for appealed cases as clear evidence that the current process is inadequate. Depending upon the base selected and the line of analysis followed, the relevant reversal rates urged by the contending parties vary from a high of 58.6% for appealed reconsideration decisions to an overall reversal rate of only 3.3%. Bare statistics rarely provide a satisfactory measure of the fairness of a decisionmaking process. Their adequacy is especially suspect here since the administrative review system is operated on an open file basis. A recipient may always submit new evidence, and such submissions may result in additional medical examinations. . . . In this context, the value of reversal rate statistics as one means of evaluating the adequacy of the pretermination process is diminished. Thus, although we view such information as relevant, it is certainly not controlling in this case.

E.

In striking the appropriate due process balance the final factor to be assessed is the public interest. This includes the administrative burden and other societal costs that would be associated with requiring, as a matter of constitutional right, an evidentiary hearing upon demand in all cases prior to the termination of disability benefits. The most visible burden would be the incremental cost resulting from the increased number of hearings and the expense of providing benefits to ineligible recipients pending decision. No one can predict the extent of the increase, but the fact that full benefits would continue until after such hearings would assure the exhaustion in most cases of this attractive option. . . . [E]xperience with the constitutionalizing of government procedures suggests that the ultimate additional cost in terms of money and administrative burden would not be insubstantial.

Financial cost alone is not a controlling weight in determining whether due process requires a particular procedural safeguard prior to some administrative decision. But the Government's interest, and hence that of the public, in conserving scarce fiscal and administrative resources is a factor that must be weighed. . . .

Significantly, the cost of protecting those whom the preliminary administrative process has identified as likely to be found undeserving may in the end come out of the pockets of the deserving since resources available for any particular program of social welfare are not unlimited. . . .

We conclude that an evidentiary hearing is not required prior to the termination of disability benefits and that the present administrative procedures fully comport with due process.

[JUSTICE BRENNAN, dissenting.]

[T]he Court's consideration that a discontinuance of disability benefits may cause the recipient to suffer only a limited deprivation is no argument. It is speculative. Moreover, the very legislative determination to provide disability benefits, without any prerequisite determination of need in fact, presumes a need by the recipient which is not this Court's function to denigrate. Indeed, in the present case, it is indicated that because disability benefits were terminated there was a foreclosure upon the Eldridge home and the family's furniture was repossessed, forcing Eldridge, his wife, and their children to sleep in one bed. . . .

———————

1. *Mathews* is about process. Assuming a liberty or property is extant, what process is due? Will a hearing *after* adverse action has been taken be sufficient – or is a hearing a pre-condition to adverse action? The importance of a timely hearing is central – particularly at moments in our history when efficiency and the capacity to proceed, unimpeded by the effort a hearing entails, seem justified by external forces. This was thematic in JUSTICE FRANKFURTER'S concurring opinion in *Joint Anti-Fascist Refugee Committee v. McGrath*, 341 U.S. 123, 171-72 (1951):

> No better instrument has been devised for arriving at truth than to give a person in jeopardy of serious loss notice of the case against him and opportunity to meet it. . . . That a hearing has been thought indispensable in so many other situations, leaving the cases of denial exceptional, does not of itself prove that it must be found essential here. But it does place upon the Attorney General the burden of showing weighty reason for departing in this instance from a rule so deeply imbedded in history and in the demands of justice.

Are there "weighty reasons" to act first and permit a fair hearing thereafter in *Mathews? See* Jerry L. Mashaw, *The Supreme Court's Due Process Calculus for Administrative Adjudication in* Mathews v. Eldridge: *Three Factors in Search of a Theory of Value*, 44 U. CHI. L. REV. 28, 44 (1976).

2. *Mathews* announced a balancing test to determine the nature of the process due. Several years earlier, the Court focused on the due process entitlements in

repossession cases in <u>*Fuentes v. Shevin*, 407 U.S. 67, 80 (1972)</u> (citing <u>*Baldwin v. Hale*, 68 U.S. 223 (1864)</u>. The *Fuentes* Court found that the "central meaning of procedural due process [is the] right to notice and an opportunity to be heard . . . at a meaningful time and in a meaningful manner."

Are the processes that are affirmed in *Mathews* provided at a "meaningful time?"

3. Random generalities regarding constitutionally driven procedural entitlements are of little value. Rather, as you proceed through this material, it is worthwhile to develop some type of orderly way to organize a series of factors to be used to determine the impact of the constitution in a particular setting. *Mathews* provided three factors to determine the level of process to which one was entitled – and, doctrinally speaking, they are central to any due process analysis of an individual or entity interest.

Good Questions!

No matter how you distill the opinion, *Mathews* makes clear that the costs of various processes are of consequence – the opinion can be seen as a cost-benefit analysis of procedural due process. Are you comfortable with that proposition? The Constitution provides a threshold level of protection for those affected by government action – but did the founders envision the balancing this case entails?

Major Theme

From a counseling perspective, however, we want to suggest a more complete list. The following questions provide a workable approach to determining whether the Constitution is applicable and to what extent the process ought to change by virtue of a constitutional right or entitlement:

1. What is the nature of the client's right, interest, request, or asserted entitlement?

2. Does the client's interest touch on an area that is historically construed as fundamental, such as speech, travel, or the right to vote?

3. Is the interest or entitlement one that is defined by categories that immediately raise constitutional concerns such as race, religion, national origin, gender, age, or economic power?

4. Is the interest one that is defined in conventional constitutional law terms as a property or liberty interest?

5. What is the nature of the government's interest in the process the government wishes to implement and in the substance of the governmental program involved? Process-based interests might include the speed and efficiency of a decisionmaking system or the necessity to proceed summarily in order to process a large number of claims. Substantive interests often include the degree of importance placed on a regulatory goal, for example the protection of national security, environmental quality, or education.

6. Viewing the governmental process objectively, how likely is it that "mistakes will be made"? To what extent, if any, would additional procedural protections add to the accuracy and fairness of the process?

7. What is the status of the interests your client asserts? Is your client seeking a new privilege or benefit or are they trying to keep from losing an existing entitlement?

8. Is the interest one that is available to all parties within a defined class?

9. How many other individuals and entities are in the same position as your client? Are the needs of your client unique or are they indistinguishable from large numbers of other individuals or entities?

10. Is the government seeking to protect property in which it has a "trust" interest?

11. Does the government have a direct fiscal obligation for the protection and maintenance of this property or does it serve in the role of a guarantor? When the government's "own property" is in play, the tendency is for the government to use those procedures most likely to allow it to protect those assets to which it has been entrusted.

12. What remedies, beyond an improvement in procedural due process, are available to your client?

13. Are the interests your client asserts capable of being protected by remedies available in the civil justice system?

14. To what extent is public safety implicated? Where the tangible, physical needs of the public are in play, where risk from epidemic, poisoning, or violence is imminent, the nature of the procedural entitlement may be diluted.

15. From a temporal perspective, is the right your client asserts one that can only be protected if a more comprehensive process occurs before that right, interest, or entitlement is affected? Will the protection be adequate if the additional process (usually a hearing) takes place after the fact?

3. The APA provides some guidance on the quantum of process due. For example, on cross-examination, Section 556(d) states: "A party is entitled to present his case or defense by oral or documentary evidence, to submit rebuttal evidence, and to conduct such cross-examination as may be required for a full and true disclosure of the facts." The APA also cautions against the admission of "irrelevant, immaterial, or unduly repetitious evidence," focusing on relevancy and materiality. It does not preclude the admission of hearsay so long as it has probative value.

Why not use these principles (and a number of other standards set out in §§ 554, 556-57), to answer the question *Mathews* raised?

4. *Perkowski v. Stratford Bd. of Educ.*, 455 F. Supp. 2d 91 (D. Conn. 2006)

Plaintiff Perkowski, an assistant in the human resources field, was fired by her employer (the Board), as part of a budgetary reduction. She was given no notice prior to her dismissal and brought a civil rights action pursuant to 42 U.S.C. § 1983. Plaintiff asserted she was covered under a union agreement that permitted dismissal exclusively for "just cause." Though not a member of the union, plaintiff claimed that the benefits of the agreement covered her position. She did not seek the grievance process the agreement provided for arbitration of disputes. Plaintiff claimed her dismissal was pretextual though she did not make that assertion until she filed suit. Relying on *Dwyer v. Regan*, 777 F.2d 825 (2d Cir. 1985), *modified*, 793 F.2d 457 (2d Cir. 1986), the court found that "as a general matter the removal of a tenured employee from his position requires some kind of preremoval hearing" and that a state employer could not avoid its obligation to provide a hearing by engaging in a sham or pretextual elimination of the employee's position. *Dwyer*, 777 F.2d at 831. However, the Second Circuit was not persuaded that a state employer has an obligation to "routinely" provide hearings whenever it eliminates or consolidates workforce positions. *See, e.g.*, *Matthews v. Eldridge*. . . . [A] pretermination hearing is required only when, first, the employee alleges that the reduction in force was pretextual and second, the employee demonstrates that she timely requested a pretermination hearing. Plaintiff Perkowski did neither.

> As the Second Circuit stated in *Dwyer*, if "an employee who has received notice that his position is to be eliminated protests that notice and contends that it is but a sham and pretext . . . the state must be prepared to grant the employee some kind of hearing prior to the termination of his employment." Here, the Board of Education can not be faulted for failing to give Perkowski a pretermination hearing on a claim of pretext when she never protested the notice of her termination, never told . . . anyone else that the stated reason for her termination was a sham and pretext and never asked for a pretermination hearing of any kind.

On whom does the *Mathews* burden lie? If a hearing is a matter of right, why must the party who is the subject of adverse governmental action be the moving party?

5. As *Mathews* demonstrates, the nature and vigor of constitutional protection varies considerably, based on the interest or entitlement affected and the task the government undertakes. Compromise is inevitable; when vital interests affecting national security are in play, courts occasionally approve the limitation of the nature and range of procedural protections to which an individual might be entitled. One could argue, however, that heightened national security concerns are a test for the most important values the Constitution enshrines. The Constitution is of greatest consequence when real and potent pressures are raised to justify summary procedures and the limitation of procedural due process.

a. Balancing interests counts most when powerful forces are in play – and in conflict. Note the balancing in *Hamdi v. Rumsfeld*, 542 U.S. 507, 535 (2004):

> In sum, while the full protections that accompany challenges to detentions in other

settings may prove unworkable and inappropriate in the enemy-combatant setting, the threats to military operations posed by a basic system of independent review are not so weighty as to trump a citizen's core rights to challenge meaningfully the Government's case and to be heard by an impartial adjudicator.

Consider due process in the context of the "War on Terror." George W. Bush, Remarks on the War on Terror, 42 WEEKLY COMP. PRES. DOC. 1569, 1571, 1573 (Sept. 11, 2006), available at http://www.whitehouse.gov/news/releases/2006/09/20060906-3.html. For citizens and non-citizens alike, the caselaw is complex and evolving rapidly, particularly as it applies to those outside the United States.

b. Generally speaking, the regime of constitutional protection for non-citizens is limited. *Hamdi v. Rumsfeld*, 542 U.S. 507 (2004), gives citizens designated as enemy combatants protection under the Due Process clause – but *Hamdan v. Rumsfeld*, 548 U.S. 557 (2006), involving non-citizen enemy combatants outside the United States but in U.S. custody, does not, although it finds certain military tribunals violative of the Uniform Code of Military Justice and the Geneva Convention. *Rasul v. Bush*, 542 U.S. 466 (2004), suggests that non-citizens held outside of the United States appear to have no claim to procedural due process, and *Parker v. District of Columbia*, 478 F.3d 370 (D.C. Cir. 2007), holds the Fourth Amendment inapplicable to non-citizens outside the United States.

For More Information

To learn more about this area, *see* Stephen Vladeck, Hirota: Habeas Corpus, Citizenship, and Article III, 95 GEO. L.J. 1497 (2007); Anthony J. Colangelo, *Constitutional Limits on Extraterritorial Jurisdiction: Terrorism and the Intersection of National and International Law*, 48 HARV. INT'L L.J. 121 (2007); and Jared A. Goldstein, Habeas Without Rights, 2007 WIS. L. REV. 1165.

c. Some of the questions raised above were addressed – though not exactly resolved – in *Boumediene v. Bush*, 553 U.S. 723 (2008), as this book was in the final stage of preparation:

Petitioners are aliens designated as enemy combatants and detained at the United States Naval Station at Guantanamo Bay, Cuba. There are others detained there, also aliens, who are not parties to this suit.

Petitioners present a question not resolved by our earlier cases relating to the detention of aliens at Guantanamo: whether they have the constitutional privilege of habeas corpus, a privilege not to be withdrawn except in conformance with the Suspension Clause, Art. I, § 9, cl. 2. We hold these petitioners do have the habeas corpus privilege. Congress has enacted a statute, the Detainee Treatment Act of 2005 (DTA), 119 Stat. 2739, that provides certain procedures for review of the detainees' status. We hold that those procedures are not an adequate and effective substitute for habeas corpus. Therefore § 7 of the Military Commissions Act of 2006 (MCA), 28 U.S.C. § 2241(e)

(Supp. 2007), operates as an unconstitutional suspension of the writ. We do not address whether the President has authority to detain these petitioners nor do we hold that the writ must issue. These and other questions regarding the legality of the detention are to be resolved in the first instance by the District Court. . . .

Where a person is detained by executive order, rather than, say, after being tried and convicted in a court, the need for collateral review is most pressing. A criminal conviction in the usual course occurs after a judicial hearing before a tribunal disinterested in the outcome and committed to procedures designed to ensure its own independence. These dynamics are not inherent in executive detention orders or executive review procedures. In this context the need for habeas corpus is more urgent. The intended duration of the detention and the reasons for it bear upon the precise scope of the inquiry. Habeas corpus proceedings need not resemble a criminal trial, even when the detention is by executive order. But the writ must be effective. The habeas court must have sufficient authority to conduct a meaningful review of both the cause for detention and the Executive's power to detain.

Because our Nation's past military conflicts have been of limited duration, it has been possible to leave the outer boundaries of war powers undefined. If, as some fear, terrorism continues to pose dangerous threats to us for years to come, the Court might not have this luxury. This result is not inevitable, however. The political branches, consistent with their independent obligations to interpret and uphold the Constitution, can engage in a genuine debate about how best to preserve constitutional values while protecting the Nation from terrorism. *Cf. Hamdan, 548 U.S., at 636* (BREYER, J., concurring) ("[J]udicial insistence upon that consultation does not weaken our Nation's ability to deal with danger. To the contrary, that insistence strengthens the Nation's ability to determine – through democratic means – how best to do so").

It bears repeating that our opinion does not address the content of the law that governs petitioners' detention. That is a matter yet to be determined. We hold that petitioners may invoke the fundamental procedural protections of habeas corpus. The laws and Constitution are designed to survive, and remain in force, in extraordinary times. Liberty and security can be reconciled; and in our system they are reconciled within the framework of the law. The Framers decided that habeas corpus, a right of first importance, must be a part of that framework, a part of that law.

The determination by the Court of Appeals that the Suspension Clause and its protections are inapplicable to petitioners was in error.

For More Information

We recommend the following for a critique of the use of executive power in the first decade of the 21st Century: David J. Barron & Martin S. Lederman, *The Commander-in-Chief at the Lowest Ebb – A Constitutional History*, 121 HARV. L. REV. 941 (2008); Mark C. Rahdert, *Double Checking Executive Emergency Power: Lessons From Hamdi and Hamdan*, 80 TEMP. L. REV. 451 (2007); Bradley J. Wyatt, *Even Aliens Are Entitled to Due Process: Extending Mathews v. Eldridge Balancing to Board of Immigration Procedural Reforms*, 12 WM. & MARY BILL OF RTS. J. 605 (2004); Ricardo J. Bascuas, *The Unconstitutionality of "Hold Until Cleared": Reexamining Material Witness Detentions in the Wake of the September 11th*

Dragnet, 58 VAND. L. REV. 677, 682-94 (2005); Jesselyn A. Radack, *You Say Defendant, I Say Combatant: Opportunistic Treatment of Terrorism Suspects Held in the United States and the Need for Due Process*, 29 NYU REV. L. & SOC. CHANGE 525, 536-41 (2005); and Leti Volpp, *The Citizen and the Terrorist*, 49 UCLA L. REV. 1575, 1577-84 (2002).

Providing a full panoply of procedural rights when little is at stake is easy; providing those same rights when national defense or significant governmental interests are at stake is a far more legitimate test of the power and force underlying a constitutional imperative.

Hypothetical

The Federal Communications Commission, by means of a APA § 553 notice and comment rulemaking proceeding with no opportunity for a hearing, decides to revoke the television station licenses of Washington, DC's WJRG-TV (channel 8) and New York City's WGLV-TV (channel 10), citing repeated violations of the FCC's indecency and obscenity rules. What, if any, legal recourse is available to the owners of the two stations?

CLEVELAND BOARD OF EDUCATION V. LOUDERMILL

470 U.S. 532 (1985)

[JUSTICE WHITE] In these cases we consider what pretermination process must be accorded a public employee who can be discharged only for cause.

I.

In 1979 the Cleveland Board of Education . . . hired respondent James Loudermill as a security guard. On his job application, Loudermill stated that he had never been convicted of a felony. Eleven months later, as part of a routine examination of his employment records, the Board discovered that in fact Loudermill had been convicted of grand larceny in 1968. By letter dated November 3, 1980, the Board's Business Manager informed Loudermill that he had been dismissed because of his dishonesty in filling out the employment application. Loudermill was not afforded an opportunity to respond to the charge of dishonesty or to challenge his dismissal. On November 13, the Board adopted a resolution officially approving the discharge.

Under Ohio law, Loudermill was a "classified civil servant." Such employees can be terminated only for cause, and may obtain administrative review if discharged. Pursuant to this provision, Loudermill filed an appeal with the Cleveland Civil Service Commission on November 12. The Commission appointed a referee, who held a hearing on January 29, 1981. Loudermill argued that he had thought that his 1968 larceny conviction was for a misdemeanor rather than a felony. The referee recommended reinstatement. On July 20, 1981, the full Commission heard argument and orally announced that it would uphold the dismissal. Proposed findings of fact and conclusions of law followed on August 10, and Loudermill's attorneys were advised of the result by mail on August 21.

Although the Commission's decision was subject to judicial review in the state courts, Loudermill instead brought the present suit in the Federal District Court . . . . The complaint alleged that § 124.34 was unconstitutional on its face because it did not provide the employee an opportunity to respond to the charges against him prior to removal. As a result, discharged employees were deprived of liberty and property without due process. The complaint also alleged that the provision was unconstitutional as applied because discharged employees were not given sufficiently prompt postremoval hearings.

Before a responsive pleading was filed, the District Court dismissed for failure to state a claim on which relief could be granted. It held that because the very statute that created the property right in continued employment also specified the procedures for discharge, and because those procedures were followed, Loudermill was, by definition, afforded all the process due. The . . . District Court [also] concluded that, in light of the Commission's crowded docket, the delay in processing Loudermill's administrative appeal was constitutionally acceptable.

The other case before us arises on similar facts and followed a similar course. Respondent Richard Donnelly was a bus mechanic for the Parma Board of Education. In August 1977, Donnelly was fired because he had failed an eye examination. . . .

A divided panel of the Court of Appeals for the Sixth Circuit reversed in part and remanded. . . . It . . . concluded that the compelling private interest in retaining employment, combined with the value of presenting evidence prior to dismissal, outweighed the added administrative burden of a pretermination hearing. With regard to the alleged deprivation of liberty, and Loudermill's 9-month wait for an administrative decision, the court affirmed the District Court, finding no constitutional violation. . . . We . . . now affirm in all respects.

II.

Respondents' federal constitutional claim depends on their having had a property right in continued employment. If they did, the State could not deprive them of this property without due process. . . . The Ohio statute plainly creates such an interest. Respondents were "classified civil service employees," entitled to retain their positions "during good behavior and efficient service," who could not be dismissed "except . . . for . . . misfeasance, malfeasance, or nonfeasance in office" . . . . Indeed, this question does not seem to have been disputed below.

The Parma Board argues, however, that the property right is defined by, and conditioned on, the legislature's choice of procedures for its deprivation. The Board stresses that in addition to specifying the grounds for termination, the statute sets out procedures by which termination may take place. The procedures were adhered to in these cases. According to petitioner, "[t]o require additional procedures would in effect expand the scope of the property interest itself." . . . . In *Vitek v. Jones*, we pointed out that "minimum requirements [are] a matter of federal law, they are not diminished by the fact that the State may have specified its own procedures that it may deem adequate for determining the preconditions to adverse official action." This conclusion was reiterated in *Logan v. Zimmerman Brush Co.*, where we reversed the lower court's holding that because the entitlement arose from a state statute, the legislature had the prerogative to define the procedures to be followed to protect that entitlement.

. . . If a clearer holding is needed, we provide it today. The . . . Due Process Clause provides that certain substantive rights – life, liberty, and property – cannot be deprived except pursuant to constitutionally adequate procedures. The categories of substance and procedure are distinct. Were the rule otherwise, the Clause would be reduced to a mere tautology. "Property" cannot be defined by the procedures provided for its deprivation any more than can life or liberty. The right to due process "is conferred, not by legislative grace, but by constitutional guarantee. While the legislature may elect not to confer a property interest in employment, it may not constitutionally authorize the deprivation of such an interest, once conferred, without appropriate procedural safeguards." In short, once it is determined that the Due Process Clause applies, "the question remains what process is due." The answer to that question is not to be found in the Ohio statute.

III.

An essential principle of due process is that a deprivation of life, liberty, or property "be preceded by notice and opportunity for hearing appropriate to the nature of the case." We have described "the root requirement" of the Due Process Clause as being "that an individual be given an opportunity for a hearing *before* he is deprived of any significant property interest." n.7 This principle requires "some kind of a hearing" prior to the discharge of an employee who has a constitutionally protected property interest in his employment. . . .

> n.7 There are, of course, some situations in which a postdeprivation hearing will satisfy due process requirements.

The need for some form of pretermination hearing . . . is evident from a balancing of the competing interests at stake. These are the private interest in retaining employment, the governmental interest in the expeditious removal of unsatisfactory employees and the avoidance of administrative burdens, and the risk of an erroneous termination.

First, the significance of the private interest in retaining employment cannot be gainsaid. . . . While a fired worker may find employment elsewhere, doing so will take some time and is likely to be burdened by the questionable circumstances under which he left his previous job. Second, some opportunity for the employee to present his side of the case is . . . of obvious value in reaching an accurate decision. Dismissals for cause will often involve factual disputes. Even where the facts are clear, the appropriateness or necessity of the discharge may not be; in such cases, the only meaningful opportunity to invoke the discretion of the decisionmaker is likely to be before the termination takes effect.

The cases before us illustrate these considerations. Both respondents had plausible arguments to make that might have prevented their discharge. The fact that the Commission saw fit to reinstate Donnelly suggests that an error might have been avoided had he been provided an opportunity to make his case to the Board. As for Loudermill, given the Commission's ruling we cannot say that the discharge was mistaken. Nonetheless, . . . the termination involved arguable issues, n.9 and the right to a hearing does not depend on a demonstration of certain success.

> n.9 Loudermill's dismissal turned not on the objective fact that he was an ex-felon . . . but on the subjective question whether he had lied on his application form. His explanation for the false statement is plausible in light of the fact that he received only a suspended 6-month sentence and a fine on the grand larceny conviction.

The governmental interest in immediate termination does not outweigh these interests. As we shall explain, affording the employee an opportunity to respond prior to termination would impose neither a significant administrative burden nor intolerable delays. Furthermore, the employer shares the employee's interest in avoiding disruption and erroneous decisions; and until the matter is settled, the employer would continue to receive the benefit of the employee's labors. It is preferable to keep a qualified employee on than to train a new one. A governmental employer also has an interest in keeping citizens usefully employed rather than taking the possibly erroneous and counterproductive step of forcing its employees onto the welfare rolls. Finally, in those situations where the employer perceives a significant hazard in keeping the employee on the job, it can avoid the problem by suspending with pay.

IV.

The foregoing considerations indicate that the pretermination "hearing," though necessary, need not be elaborate. . . . In general, "something less" than a full evidentiary hearing is sufficient prior to adverse administrative action. Under state law, respondents were later entitled to a full administrative hearing and judicial review. The only question is what steps were required before the termination took effect. In only one case, _Goldberg v. Kelly_, has the Court required a full adversarial evidentiary hearing prior to adverse governmental action. However, as the *Goldberg* Court itself pointed out, that case presented significantly different considerations than are present in the context of public employment. Here, the pretermination hearing need not definitively resolve the propriety of the discharge. It should be an initial check against mistaken decisions – essentially, a determination of whether there are reasonable grounds to believe that the charges against the employee are true and support the proposed action.

The essential requirements of due process, and all that respondents seek or the Court of Appeals required, are notice and an opportunity to respond. The opportunity to present reasons . . . why proposed action should not be taken is a fundamental due process requirement. The tenured public employee is entitled to oral or written notice of the charges against him, an explanation of the employer's evidence, and an opportunity to present his side of the story. To require more than this prior to termination would intrude to an unwarranted extent on the government's interest in quickly removing an unsatisfactory employee.

V.

Our holding rests in part on the provisions in Ohio law for a full post-termination hearing. In his cross-petition Loudermill asserts, as a separate constitutional violation, that his administrative proceedings took too long. n.11 The Court of Appeals held otherwise, and we agree. n.12 The Due Process Clause requires provision of a hearing "at a meaningful time." At some point, a delay in the post-termination hearing would become a constitutional violation. In the present case, however, the complaint merely recites the course of proceedings and concludes that the denial of a "speedy resolution" violated due process. This reveals nothing about the delay except that it stemmed in part from the thoroughness of the procedures. A 9-month adjudication is not, of course, unconstitutionally lengthy per se. Yet Loudermill offers no indication that his wait was unreasonably prolonged other than the fact that it took nine months. . . .

n.11 Loudermill's hearing before the referee occurred two and one-half months after he filed his appeal. The Commission issued its written decision six and one-half months after that. . . . Section 124.34 provides that a hearing is to be held within 30 days of the appeal, though the Ohio courts have ruled that the time limit is not mandatory. The statute does not provide a time limit for the actual decision.

n.12 It might be argued that once we find a due process violation in the denial of a pretermination hearing we need not and should not consider whether the post-termination procedures were adequate. We conclude that it is appropriate to consider this issue, however, for three reasons. First, the allegation of a distinct due process violation in the administrative delay is not an alternative theory supporting the same relief, but a separate claim altogether. Second, it was decided by the court below and is raised in the cross-petition. Finally, the existence of post-termination procedures is relevant to the necessary scope of pretermination procedures.

VI.

We conclude that all the process that is due is provided by a pretermination opportunity to respond, coupled with post-termination administrative procedures as provided by the Ohio statute. Because respondents allege in their complaints that they had no chance to respond, the District Court erred in dismissing for failure to state a claim. The judgment of the Court of Appeals is affirmed, and the case is remanded for further proceedings consistent with this opinion. . . .

[JUSTICE BRENNAN, concurring in part.]

Recognizing the limited scope of the holding in Part V, I must still dissent from its result, because the record in this case is insufficiently developed to permit an informed judgment on the issue of overlong delay. . . . Loudermill alleged that it took the Commission over two and one-half months simply to hold a hearing in his case, over two months *more* to issue a nonbinding interim decision, and more than three and one-half months after *that* to deliver a final decision. The Commission provided no explanation for these significant gaps in the administrative process . . . . We do know, however, that under Ohio law the Commission is obligated to hear appeals like Loudermill's "within thirty days." Although this statutory limit has been viewed only as "directory" by Ohio courts, those courts have also made it clear that when the limit is exceeded, "[the] burden of proof [is] placed on the [Commission] to illustrate to the court that the failure to comply with the 30-day requirement . . . was reasonable." . . . . [A]ll of our precedents [on] administrative delays under the Due Process Clause . . . have been decided only after more complete proceedings in the District Courts. . . .

[JUSTICE REHNQUIST, dissenting.]

In *Arnett v. Kennedy*, six Members of this Court agreed that a public employee could be dismissed for misconduct without a full hearing prior to termination. A plurality of Justices agreed that the employee was entitled to exactly what Congress gave him, and no more. . . . We ought to recognize the totality of the State's definition of the property right in question, and not merely seize upon one of several paragraphs in a unitary statute to proclaim that in that paragraph the State has inexorably conferred upon a civil service employee something which it is powerless under the United States Constitution to qualify in the next paragraph of the statute. This practice ignores our duty under _Roth_ to rely on state law as the source of property interests for purposes of applying the Due Process Clause of the Fourteenth Amendment. . . .

Underlying Case Documents

The current version of the Ohio law provides that no appeal can be taken for dismissal for committing a felony and can be accessed HERE.

---

1. Timing, notice, and the opportunity to be heard are at the core of *Loudermill*. The case appears to ensure "some kind of hearing" prior to adverse action (assuming a public non-probationary, non-at-will employee). In a recent decision, the First Circuit explored just what kind of hearing that might be.

Chmielinski v. Mass. Office of the Comm'r of Prob., 513 F.3d 309 (1st Cir. 2008).

> Andrew Chmielinski, the Chief Probation Officer of the Milford, Massachusetts, District Court, was fired by the Commissioner of Probation after a hearing on charges he had abused his office. . . . [The Commissioner contended that] Chmielinski had shoplifted . . . improperly obtained a "blue light permit" and mounted the light in his personal vehicle . . . made improper disclosures of court records [and] was involved in improper interactions with other employees. . . . A two-day hearing on the allegations was conducted. . . . At this hearing, Chmielinski . . . presented evidence . . . and had the opportunity to question the evidence against him.

> Chmielinski does not contest that he received adequate notice here or that he was given an explanation. . . . Rather, Chmielinski's allegations of procedural due process all concern the adequacy of the hearing he was provided. The standard the defendant must meet here is not high: the U.S. Constitution requires only "some pretermination opportunity to respond." *Loudermill.* . . . Most of Chmielinski's allegations are a call to transpose the procedural protections of a court of law into his termination hearing: his desire for pre-hearing discovery, his request that the witnesses be sworn and sequestered, and his assertion of various improprieties in the admission and consideration of evidence. These are easily dismissed. The termination hearing is not a court of law, and the same level of process is not required. The U.S. Constitution requires only that Chmielinski was provided notice and a meaningful opportunity to respond, a requirement that was clearly met on the facts of this case. . . . [T]he Constitution requires only an initial check against erroneous decisions, not that the state follow best practices.

Why not provide the protections Mr. Chmielinski seeks? Is there any doubt that the quality of the hearing would have improved had the full panoply of evidentiary processes been available? *See* J. Michael McGuinness, *Procedural Due Process Rights of Public Employees: Basic Rules and a Rationale for a Return to Rule-Oriented Process*, 33 NEW ENG. L. REV. 931, 935 (1999).

The less-than-full process Mr. Chmielinski received has come to be known as a "*Loudermill* hearing." *Marable v. Nitchman*, 511 F.3d 924 (9th Cir. 2007); *Piscottano v. Murphy*, 511 F.3d 247 (2d Cir. 2007). Did the Court envision such a rudimentary, "bare bones" proceeding?

2. Does *Loudermill* actually guarantee a pre-termination hearing for a public non-probationary, non-at-will employee?

In *Gilbert v. Homar*, 520 U.S. 924 (1997), a campus law enforcement officer was suspended without pay and ultimately demoted, all without a prior hearing, after he was indicted on narcotics charges. In upholding adverse action prior to a hearing, the Court noted that the employee was entitled to a post-suspension hearing, was in a high profile and security sensitive position, and that the risk of error was low since an "independent third party" found probable cause regarding a crime that had been committed. In effect, the state's interests trumped the employee's due process rights.

How does this decision square with *Loudermill*? Is a grand jury an unbiased tribunal? What rights are present to "notice and an opportunity to be heard" in the grand jury setting? Rule 6(d) of the Federal Rules of Criminal Procedure provides that "no person other than the jurors may be present while the grand jury is deliberating or voting." Rule 6(d). *See United States v. Sells Engineering, Inc.*, 463 U.S. 418 (1983).

For a useful discussion on the hearing rights of public employees, see Cameron Argetsinger, Note, *Procedural Bungling in Disciplinary Actions Against Federal Employees: Harmless Error or Due Process Violation?*, 15 FED. CIR. B.J. 445 (2005/2006).

3. Compare *Gilbert* (note 2, above) with *Barry v. Barchi*, 443 U.S. 55 (1979).

> Be Alert, a harness race horse trained by . . . John Barchi, finished second in a race at Monticello Raceway. Two days later . . . a post-race urinalysis had revealed a drug in Be Alert's system. Barchi proclaimed his innocence, and two lie-detector tests supported his lack of knowledge of the drugging [but] the steward suspended Barchi for 15 days. . . . Under § 8022 of the New York Unconsolidated Laws, a suspended licensee is entitled to a post-suspension hearing, but the section ordains that "[pending] such hearing and final determination thereon, the action of the [Board] in . . . suspending a license . . . shall remain in full force and effect." The section specifies no time in which the hearing must be held, and it affords the Board as long as 30 days after the conclusion of the hearing in which to issue a final order adjudicating a case.

[The Court held that § 8022 was constitutional.] It . . . seems clear to us that the procedural mechanism selected to mitigate the threats to the public interest arising in the harness racing context is rationally related to the achievement of that goal. The State could reasonably conclude that swift suspension of harness racing trainers was necessary to protect the public from fraud and to foster public confidence in the harness racing sport. . . .

JUSTICE BRENNAN's concurrence saw the matter differently:

[T]he State has failed to identify any substantial interest in postponing Barchi's opportunity for a full hearing. . . . Furthermore . . . in harness racing, even a temporary suspension can irreparably damage a trainer's livelihood. . . . Where, as here, even a short temporary suspension threatens to inflict substantial and irreparable harm, an "initial" deprivation quickly becomes "final," and the procedures afforded either before or immediately after suspension are de facto the final procedures. A final full hearing . . . after Barchi had been barred from racing his horses and had lost his clients to other trainers . . . would certainly not qualify as a "meaningful opportunity to be heard at a meaningful time." To be meaningful, an opportunity for a full hearing and determination must be afforded at least at a time when the potentially irreparable and substantial harm caused by a suspension can still be avoided – i.e., either before or immediately after suspension.

a. Does the basic promise in *Loudermill*, decided a few years after *Barchi*, include a "meaningful opportunity to be heard at a meaningful time?" Notwithstanding JUSTICE BRENNAN's concurrence, and the use of the phrase in *Mathews*, 424 U.S. at 333, the Supreme Court has used the "meaningful time" qualifier sparingly since *Loudermill* (three times in the last 20 years). *See City of Los Angeles v. David, 538 U.S. 715 (2003)* (permitting a 27-day delay before a "pay-recovery" hearing regarding an allegation that a vehicle was towed illegally); *Gray v. Netherland, 518 U.S. 152 (1996)* (JUSTICE GINSBURG, dissenting); *and McKesson Corp. v. Div. of Alcoholic Bevs. & Tobacco, 496 U.S. 18 (1990)*.

b. A temporary suspension, as JUSTICE BRENNAN notes in his concurrence, can have devastating consequences. The *Loudermill* decision raises the same problem, noting that adverse employment action can make it very difficult to secure a new position, particularly if there is no record to clarify "questionable circumstances under which [an employee] left his previous job." In *Federal Deposit Insurance Corporation v. Mallen*, the Court held that a job "ought not be interrupted without substantial justification." 486 U.S. 230 (1988).

4. The rights secured in *Loudermill*, such as they are, are available only to public sector employees "who possess property interests in continued public employment." *Maymi v. P.R. Ports Auth., 515 F.3d 20 (1st Cir. 2008); Marrero-Gutierrez v. Molina, 491 F.3d 1, 8 (1st Cir. 2007)*. The *Roth* requirement is not subtle: In the absence of a cognizable liberty or property interest, a probationary employee may have common law, regulatory, and statutory entitlements, but not rights secured

by Fifth or Fourteenth Amendment Due Process. *See, e.g., Silva v. Bieluch*, 351 F.3d 1045 (11th Cir. 2003); *Trejo v. Shoben*, 319 F.3d 878 (7th Cir. 2003); *Kyle v. Morton High School*, 144 F.3d 448 (7th Cir. 1998).

Key Concept

Credibility. Can *Loudermill* be explained in part based on the initial decisionmaker's belief of the statement in question – the "misunderstanding" that the underlying criminal act was a misdemeanor, not a felony? There is a line of cases in the Federal Circuit holding that credibility determinations in administrative cases are "virtually unreviewable." *Frey v. DOL*, 359 F.3d 1355, 1361 (Fed. Cir. 2004); *King v. HHS*, 133 F.3d 1450, 1453 (Fed. Cir. 1998); *Hambsch v. Dep't of the Treasury*, 796 F.2d 430, 436 (Fed. Cir. 1986). Similarly, the Federal Circuit has held that an ALJ's decision based primarily on demeanor is due "special deference." *Chauvin v. Dep't of Navy*, 38 F.3d 563, 566 (Fed. Cir. 1994).

III. Basic Agency Obligations in the Adjudicatory Process

1. Due Process, A Record, and Exceptions

When an agency exercises adjudicatory power it must produce a record demonstrating that the agency has evaluated the evidence the parties submitted and made its decision based on some meaningful standards. Appeals of adjudicatory decisions within agencies also require a written decision – for the most part.

The "Streamlining" Example

In certain immigration cases decided by the Board of Immigration Appeals, review of the decisions of Immigrations Judges result in no opinion, a matter of some concern in the various circuit courts that ultimately have the authority to review such decisions. This is part of the general practice of "streamlining regulations" in the immigration field. *See Board of Immigration Appeals: Procedural Reforms to Improve Case Management*, 67 Fed. Reg. 54,878, 54,893 (Aug. 26, 2002), codified at 8 C.F.R. § 1003.1 (2002).

Streamlining is on its face risky – decisions that shortchange the standard process ought to be examined closely – and these have been. In *Kambolli v. Gonzales*, 449 F.3d 454, 459 (2d Cir. 2006), the court noted that while these rules have generated multiple challenges, the "streamlining program has uniformly withstood challenges based on the Due Process Clause," citing *Zhang v. Department of Justice*, 362 F.3d 155, 156-59 (2d Cir. 2004). *Yu* examined a series of circuit court decisions and concluded that there was consensus: These procedures shortcut conventional and important hearing rights – and thus far, have withstood constitutional scrutiny, though the appeals continue. *See* John R.B. Palmer et al., *Why Are So Many People Challenging Board of Immigration Appeals Decisions in Federal Court? An Empirical Analysis of the Recent Surge in Petitions for Review*, 20 Geo. Immigr. L.J. 1, 28 (2005).

Whether such decisions are reviewable when written by a single Board member is a matter of some controversy. *Kambolli v. Gonzales*, 449 F.3d 454, 463 (2d Cir. 2006). Overall, however, the case law is not encouraging for those who believe that this model is at odds with a sense of fairness. *See Ngure v. Ashcroft*, 367 F.3d 975 (8th Cir. 2004); and *Mendoza v. U.S. Att'y Gen.*, 327 F.3d 1283 (11th Cir. 2003).

It is not that challenges are rejected uniformly. *See Smriko v. Ashcroft*, 387 F.3d 279 (3d Cir. 2004). It is more a matter of struggling to figure out what the role of judicial review of agency action should be in "streamlined" cases. The Second Circuit has held that questions of law are reviewed de novo, *Khouzam v. Ashcroft*, 361 F.3d 161, 164 (2d Cir. 2004), and credibility assessments and factual findings are reviewed using the substantial evidence test. *See Gao v. U.S. Att'y Gen.*, 400 F.3d 963, 964 (2d Cir. 2005), explaining that courts "look to see if the [Immigration Judge] has provided 'specific, cogent' reasons for the adverse credibility finding and whether those reasons bear a 'legitimate nexus' to the finding." Just how one reviews the unwritten part of the record remains a bit of a mystery.

At a more general level, the study of adjudication involves, as *Loudermill* made clear, a close assessment of the *timing* – when is delay a denial of fairness and justice? Based on *Mathews*, we know that *cost* and *efficiency* play roles in determining the process due – but when is the cost-benefit trade-off too great a compromise?

What kind of evidence must be adduced by the government to support an adjudicatory decision? What if a decision in an adjudication is made based on a predetermined formula? Does every person who may be affected adversely by agency action have a right to a full hearing? Whether the agency develops a record independently or relies on a predetermined formula, it must at a minimum present a record that allows the public – and a reviewing court – to understand the basis for the action chosen by the agency.

Good Question!

Think about the basic rules. Deference is due agency interpretation of statutes. Agencies are free (for the most part) to choose between rule-making and adjudication. Courts are supposed to give a "hard look" and review the substantiality of the evidence when assessing adjudicatory actions. How can a court be deferential while taking a hard look and reviewing the substantiality of the evidence – in a case where an agency adjudicates and in so doing implements an important policy?

Finally, since agencies use the adjudicatory process to apply – and interpret – statutes, such decisions often reflect very clear policy preferences of the executive. Much as in rulemaking, judicial review of adjudicatory decisions that express and elaborate policy raise separation of powers problems.

CITIZENS TO PRESERVE OVERTON PARK V. VOLPE

401 U.S. 402 (1971)

[JUSTICE MARSHALL] The growing public concern about the quality of our natural environment has prompted Congress in recent years to enact legislation designed to curb the accelerating destruction of our country's natural beauty. We are concerned in this case with § 4(f) of the Department of Transportation Act of 1966 . . . and § 18(a) of the Federal-Aid Highway Act of 1968. These statutes prohibit the Secretary of Transportation from authorizing the use of federal funds to finance the construction of highways through public parks if a "feasible and prudent" alternative route exists. If no such route is available, the statutes allow him to approve construction through parks only if there has been "all possible planning to minimize harm" to the park.

Petitioners, private citizens as well as local and national conservation organizations, contend that the Secretary has violated these statutes by authorizing the expenditure of federal funds for the construction of a six-lane interstate highway through a public park in Memphis, Tennessee. Their claim was rejected by the District Court, which granted the Secretary's motion for summary judgment, and the Court of Appeals for the Sixth Circuit affirmed. . . . We now reverse . . . .

Overton Park is a 342-acre city park located near the center of Memphis. The park contains a zoo, a nine-hole municipal golf course, an outdoor theater, nature trails, a bridle path, an art academy, picnic areas, and 170 acres of forest. The proposed highway, which is to be a six-lane, high-speed, expressway, will sever the zoo from the rest of the park. Although the roadway will be depressed below ground level except where it crosses a small creek, 26 acres of the park will be destroyed. . . .

Although the route through the park was approved by the Bureau of Public Roads in 1956 and by the Federal Highway Administrator in 1966, the enactment of § 4(f) . . . prevented distribution of federal funds for the section of the highway designated to go through Overton Park until the Secretary of Transportation determined whether the requirements of § 4(f) had been met. . . . In April 1968, the Secretary announced that he concurred in the judgment of local officials that I-40 should be built through the park. . . . [This announcement was not] accompanied by a statement of the Secretary's factual findings. He did not indicate why he believed there were no feasible and prudent alternative routes or why design changes could not be made to reduce the harm to the park.

Petitioners contend that the Secretary's action is invalid without such formal findings and that the Secretary did not make an independent determination but merely relied on the judgment of the Memphis City Council. . . . [The only record of the deliberations of the Memphis City Council was in the form of some notes and an "account" of the meetings given by former Federal Highway Administrator Birdwell.] Respondents argue that it was unnecessary for the Secretary to make formal findings, and that he did, in fact, exercise his own independent judgment which was supported by the facts. In the District Court, respondents introduced affidavits, prepared specifically for this litigation, which indicated that the Secretary had made the decision and that the decision was supportable. These affidavits were contradicted by affidavits introduced by petitioners, who also sought to take the deposition of a former Federal Highway Administrator who had participated in the decision to route I-40 through Overton Park.

The District Court and the Court of Appeals found that formal findings by the Secretary were not necessary . . . . And, believing that the Secretary's authority was wide and reviewing courts' authority narrow in the approval of highway routes, the lower courts held that the affidavits contained no basis for a determination that the Secretary had exceeded his authority. We agree that formal findings were not required. But we do not believe that in this case judicial review based solely on litigation affidavits was adequate.

. . . .

[Judicial Review is appropriate here since the statute does not specifically disallow it and the decision] does not fall within the exception for action "committed to agency discretion." This is a very narrow exception. The legislative history of the Administrative Procedure Act indicates that it is applicable in those rare instances where "statutes are drawn in such broad terms that in a given case there is no law to apply."

Section 4(f) of the Department of Transportation Act and § 138 of the Federal-Aid Highway Act are clear and specific directives. Both the Department of Transportation Act and the Federal-Aid Highway Act provide that the Secretary "shall not approve any program or project" that requires the use of any public parkland "unless (1) there is no feasible and prudent alternative to the use of such land, and (2) such program includes all possible planning to minimize harm to such park . . . ." This language is a plain and explicit bar to the use of federal funds for construction of highways through parks – only the most unusual situations are exempted. . . . For this exemption to apply the Secretary must find that as a matter of sound engineering it would not be feasible to build the highway along any other route. Respondents argue, however, that the requirement that there be no other "prudent" route requires the Secretary to . . . weigh the detriment resulting from the destruction of parkland against the cost of other routes, safety considerations, and other factors, and determine on the basis of the importance that he attaches to these other factors whether, on balance, alternative feasible routes would be "prudent."

But no such wide-ranging endeavor was intended. It is obvious that in most cases considerations of cost, directness of route, and community disruption will indicate that parkland should be used for highway construction whenever possible. . . . [Furthermore,] there will always be a smaller outlay required from the public purse when parkland is used since the public already owns the land and there will be no need to pay for right-of-way. And since people do not live or work in parks, if a highway is built on parkland no one will have to leave his home or give up his business. Such factors are common to substantially all highway construction. Thus, if Congress intended these factors to be on an equal footing with preservation of parkland there would have been no need for the statutes.

Congress clearly did not intend that cost and disruption of the community were to be ignored by the Secretary. But the very existence of the statutes indicates that protection of parkland was to be given paramount importance. The few green havens that are public parks were not to be lost unless there were truly unusual factors present in a particular case or the cost or community disruption resulting from alternative routes reached extraordinary magnitudes. If the statutes are to have any meaning, the Secretary cannot approve the destruction of parkland unless he finds that alternative routes present unique problems.

Plainly, there is "law to apply" and thus the exemption for action "committed to agency discretion" is inapplicable. But the existence of judicial review is only the start: the standard for review must also be determined. . . . [Under the APA] agency action must be set aside if the action was "arbitrary, capricious, an abuse of discretion, or otherwise not in accordance with law" or if the action failed to meet statutory, procedural, or constitutional requirements. In certain narrow, specifically limited situations, the agency action is to be set aside if the action was not supported by "substantial evidence." And in other equally narrow circumstances the reviewing court is to engage in a de novo review of the action and set it aside if it was "unwarranted by the facts."

Petitioners argue that the Secretary's approval of the construction of I-40 through Overton Park is subject to one or the other of these latter two standards of limited applicability. First, they contend that the "substantial evidence" standard of § 706(2)(E) must be applied. In the alternative, they claim that § 706(2)(F) applies and that there must be a de novo review to determine if the Secretary's action was "unwarranted by the facts." Neither of these standards is, however, applicable.

[The substantial evidence test does not apply here. This was not a rulemaking and the only hearing was] a public hearing conducted by local officials for the purpose of informing the community about the proposed project and eliciting community views on the design and route. The hearing [was] nonadjudicatory, quasi-legislative in nature. It [was] not designed to produce a record that is to be the basis of agency action – the basic requirement for substantial-evidence review.

Petitioners' alternative argument also fails. De novo review of whether the Secretary's decision was "unwarranted by the facts" is authorized by § 706(2)(F) in only two circumstances. First . . . when the action is adjudicatory in nature and the agency factfinding procedures are inadequate. . . . [Second] when issues that were not before the agency are raised in a proceeding to enforce nonadjudicatory agency action. Neither situation exists here.

[Therefore the] generally applicable standards of § 706 require the reviewing court to engage in a substantial inquiry. Certainly, the Secretary's decision is entitled to a presumption of regularity. But that presumption is not to shield his action from a thorough, probing, in-depth review.

The court is first required to decide whether the Secretary acted within the scope of his authority. . . . The reviewing court must consider whether the Secretary properly construed his authority to approve the use of parkland as limited to situations where there are no feasible alternative routes or where feasible alternative routes involve uniquely difficult problems. And the reviewing court must be able to find that the Secretary could have reasonably believed that in this case there are no feasible alternatives or that alternatives do involve unique problems.

Scrutiny of the facts does not end, however, with the determination that the Secretary has acted within the scope of his statutory authority. Section 706(2)(A) requires a finding that the actual choice made was not "arbitrary, capricious, an abuse of discretion, or otherwise not in accordance with law." To make this finding the court must consider whether the decision was based on a consideration of the relevant factors and whether there has been a clear error of judgment. Although this inquiry into the facts is to be searching and careful, the ultimate standard of review is a narrow one. The court is not empowered to substitute its judgment for that of the agency.

The final inquiry is whether the Secretary's action followed the necessary procedural requirements. Here the only procedural error alleged is the failure of the Secretary to make formal findings and state his reason for allowing the highway to be built through the park. Undoubtedly, review of the Secretary's action is hampered by his failure to make such findings, but the absence of formal findings does not necessarily require that the case be remanded to the Secretary. Neither [statute] requires such formal findings. Moreover, the Administrative Procedure Act requirements that there be formal findings in certain rulemaking and adjudicatory proceedings do not apply to the Secretary's action here. And, although formal findings may be required in some cases in the absence of statutory directives when the nature of the agency action is ambiguous, those situations are rare. Plainly, there is no ambiguity here; the Secretary has approved the construction of I-40 through Overton Park and has approved a specific design for the project.

. . . .

[Under these circumstances, a court should have access to] an administrative record that allows the full, prompt review of the Secretary's action . . . without additional delay. . . . That administrative record is not, however, before us. The lower courts based their review on the litigation affidavits that were presented. These affidavits were merely "post hoc" rationalizations, which have traditionally been found to be an inadequate basis for review. And they clearly do not constitute the "whole record" compiled by the agency: the basis for review required by § 706 of the Administrative Procedure Act.

Thus it is necessary to remand this case to the District Court for plenary review of the [full record on which the] Secretary's decision [was based]. But since the bare record may not disclose the factors that were considered or the Secretary's construction of the evidence it may be necessary for the District Court to require some explanation in order to determine if the Secretary acted within the scope of his authority and if the Secretary's action was justifiable under the applicable standard.

The court may require the administrative officials who participated in the decision to give testimony explaining their action. Of course, such inquiry into the mental processes of administrative decisionmakers is usually to be avoided. *United States v. Morgan.* And where there are administrative findings that were made at the same time as the decision, as was the case in *Morgan*, there must be a strong showing of bad faith or improper behavior before such inquiry may be made. But here there are no such formal findings and it may be that the only way there can be effective judicial review is by examining the decisionmakers themselves.

The District Court is not, however, required to make such an inquiry. It may be that the Secretary can prepare formal findings including the information required by DOT Order 5610.1 that will provide an adequate explanation for his action. Such an explanation will, to some extent, be a "post hoc rationalization" and thus must be viewed critically. If the District Court decides that additional explanation is necessary, that court should consider which method will prove the most expeditious so that full review may be had as soon as possible.

Underlying Case Documents

The case referenced:

The Department of Transportation Act of 1966

The Federal-Aid Highway Act of 1968

For a press release announcing the original decision to approve the highway through the park click HERE.

For an internal agency report on the impact of the road on the park click HERE.

---

1. The background of the *Overton Park* case is set forth in Professor Serena M. Williams' *Sustaining Urban Green Spaces: Can Public Parks be Protected Under the Public Trust Doctrine?*, 10 S.C. ENVTL. L.J. 23, 28-29 (2002):

> Overton Park . . . was designed at the turn of the twentieth century by landscape architect George Kessler. . . . Kessler, following the principles of the City Beautiful movement, created a park with a lake, monuments, a formal garden, and a dance pavilion. . . . A public golf course and a zoo were built in 1906 . . . and in 1916, an art gallery was constructed. . . . Beginning in 1956, the tranquility and openness of Overton Park were threatened by a proposed six-lane high-speed expressway that would sever the zoo from the rest of the park and destroy twenty-six acres of parkland. . . . In 1968, the Secretary concurred with local officials that the highway, Interstate 40, should be built through the Park. . . . [The] Secretary merely relied upon the judgment of the Memphis City Council, ignoring the "feasible and prudent" alternatives that existed. . . .

Was the agency decision truly without support? The routing question had been under review for twelve years – and the action the Secretary selected was very much consistent with prior agency actions. Why should the Supreme Court make the final decision in this case?

2. It is hard to read this case as anything other than a "hard look" at the decision of the agency. Did the Court substitute its judgment for the considered judgment

of the Secretary?

Professor Mariano-Florentino Cuellar writes that *Overton Park* "firmly establishes close judicial scrutiny of a discretionary decision as a presumptive means of policing executive decisions. Mariano-Florentino Cuellar, *Auditing Executive Discretion*, 82 Notre Dame L. Rev. 227 (2006). Should the judiciary give such close scrutiny to decisions that reflect a policy choice?

The decision of the Secretary represents a political option of sorts – there were many competing forces in play and a choice needed to be made. Isn't that what the Secretary is supposed to do – and precisely what the Court is not to do? Barry Friedman, *The Politics of Judicial Review*, 84 Tex. L. Rev. 257 (2005); and James E. Pfander, *Article I Tribunals, Article III Courts, and the Judicial Power of the United States*, 118 Harv. L. Rev. 643, 653 (2004).

3. The seminal article on *Overton Park* is Peter L. Strauss' *Revisiting Overton Park: Political and Judicial Controls Over Administrative Actions Affecting the Community*, 39 UCLA L. Rev. 1251 (2002), in which he concludes:

> The risks created by accepted judicial participation in the political process should lead judges to pay serious attention to the realities of political controls over administrative action before acting on the assumption that such controls will not prove effective. . . . Even if the court concludes that political controls cannot be relied upon to encourage balanced outcomes, it would be preferable for it directly to address the institutional causes of imbalance – seeking to restore the effectiveness of the political controls, rather than transforming the judicial review process into a surrogate political process. "Originally published in 39 UCLA L. Rev. 1251 (1992).

Was the Court engaged in political judgment as opposed to a simple review of a patently inadequate record?

4. Beyond the generalization that a court engaged in judicial review should not be "probing the mind of the administrator" or substituting its judgment for that of the agency, what does it mean to take a "hard look" at the action of the agency? Keep in mind that the question of the depth and intensity of judicial review involves a basic separation of powers problem: The more penetrating the review, the more likely it is that the judiciary is engaging in tasks that are the province of the executive and legislative branches.

Professor Patrick M. Garry noted that:

> *Overton Park* employed a version of the hard look standard of judicial review that was developing in the D.C. Circuit. Even though the action at issue was the product of informal adjudication, which had traditionally been accorded great deference under the APA, the Court in *Overton Park* articulated a new standard of judicial review, requiring it to conduct a "substantial inquiry [that does not] shield [the Agency] from

a thorough, probing, in-depth review" exploring "whether the decision was based on a consideration of the relevant factors."

Patrick M. Garry, *Judicial Review and the "Hard Look" Doctrine*, 7 Nev. L.J. 151 (2006).

Consider that this was, as Professor Garry notes, informal adjudication involving a policy choice. Is it appropriate for courts to look this closely at the basis for informal agency action?

5. Challenges to findings based on *Overton Park* require some level of clarity on the nature of the requisite underlying findings. *Port of Jacksonville*, a case challenging a Coast Guard permit to allow bridge construction, illuminates that requirement. *Port of Jacksonville Maritime Ad Hoc Committee, Inc. v. U.S. Coast Guard*, 788 F.2d 705 (11th Cir. 1986).

> The appellants urge that the Coast Guard was required to look beyond the two factors mentioned in the Bridge Manual, and to consider such matters as these [to determine whether construction had commenced by the regulatory deadline]: . . . the final plans and design drawings for the Dame Point Bridge had not been approved; there were no funds available for construction of the bridge; the Cabinet of the State of Florida had not approved construction of the bridge; the Cabinet of the State of Florida had not approved the issuance of bonds necessary to finance construction of the bridge; [and] there was not a contract for the construction of the bridge in its entirety. . . .
>
> Assuming that the facts are such as this list alleges, there is nothing in the statute or regulations that requires the Coast Guard to make [such a] wide-ranging inquiry in order to determine whether construction has commenced. The concern underlying the permit procedure is to assure that navigation is not unduly impeded by bridges or other obstructions. Even in the initial permit procedure this concern does not require a determination that a bridge project undertaken by a public authority is desirable, affordable, practical, wise, politically do-able or designed in any particular fashion so long as the project if built will not have an unacceptable impact on navigational needs. The Coast Guard has interpreted its self-imposed time limitations regulation in a way that allows it to make a relatively rough-and-ready determination whether construction has commenced. This interpretation is due to be upheld if it is reasonable. We hold that it is.

The government's use of records of a discussion of the Memphis City Council as a basis for its findings led to the Court's decision to remand in *Overton Park*. The use of inappropriate considerations, unconventional data, or non-record information in *Overton Park* has given rise to a "bad faith" doctrine.

6. *TRAC*. The final note case both explores the "bad faith" doctrine and the "*TRAC*" factors. In *Tummino v. Von Eschenbach*, 427 F. Supp. 2d 212 (E.D.N.Y. 2006), the plaintiffs pushed for expansive discovery to learn more about the basis for the government's failure to go forward with over-the-counter access to "Plan B" birth

control. When the government argued that the record it produced should be the sole basis for review, the court responded as follows:

> Despite the general "record rule," an extra-record investigation by the reviewing court may be appropriate when there has been a strong showing in support of a claim of bad faith or improper behavior on the part of agency decisionmakers or where the absence of formal administrative findings makes such investigation necessary in order to determine the reasons for the agency's choice. . . .

> A showing of bad faith or improper behavior is by no means the only basis for inquiry beyond the administrative record. Thus, the court's review of agency conduct is not limited to the record in an action to "compel agency action unlawfully withheld or unreasonably delayed." In such cases, to determine the reasonableness of a delay the court is guided by the following considerations, known as the *TRAC* factors:

> (1) the time agencies take to make decisions must be governed by a "rule of reason";

> (2) where Congress has provided a timetable or other indication of the speed with which it expects the agency to proceed in the enabling statute, that statutory scheme may supply content for this rule of reason;

> (3) delays that might be reasonable in the sphere of economic regulation are less tolerable when human health and welfare are at stake;

> (4) the court should consider the effect of expediting delayed action on agency activities of a higher or competing priority;

> (5) the court should also take into account the nature and extent of the interests prejudiced by delay; and

> (6) the court need not "find any impropriety lurking behind agency lassitude in order to hold that agency action is 'unreasonably delayed.'"

> Of particular significance, given the issues in this case, is the observation made by the District of Columbia Circuit when examining an earlier claim of unreasonable delay by the FDA in a matter concerning over-the-counter drugs:

> > The agency must justify its delay to the court's satisfaction. If the court determines that the agency delays in bad faith, it should conclude that the delay is unreasonable. . . .

> Given these considerations, discovery beyond the administrative record is appropriate in this case. First, discovery concerning matters relating to the *TRAC* factors above must be allowed. Specifically, given that a "rule of reason" ultimately governs the issue of unreasonable delay, some inquiry into the legitimacy of the reasons offered for the delay must be permitted. Moreover, because a delay that is the result of bad faith – that is, a delay for improper reasons – is a delay that is per se unreasonable, inquiry into whether the reasons offered by the agency are the actual reasons for the delay must also be permitted.

Inquiry which includes testimony by agency personnel, including the senior level personnel who overruled the professional staff, is particularly appropriate in this case because the court finds that a strong preliminary showing of "bad faith or improper behavior" has been made. *See, e.g., Overton Park.* The finding rests on a number of facts. First, the length of the delay in deciding the Citizen Petition, now five years, alone raises questions about the good faith of the FDA. Moreover, the actions of the FDA . . . strongly suggest that the delay is a calculated "filibuster" designed to avoid making a decision subject to judicial review. . . .

By its inaction in making a final determination on the Citizen Petition, one way or the other, the agency has evaded judicial review of its decisionmaking concerning [over-the-counter (OTC)] access for Plan B. . . . Although the court is not in a position now to decide whether OTC access to Plan B is appropriate, the overwhelming support of the professional staff of the FDA for OTC access, as detailed above, provides substantial evidence to question the agency's failure to authorize OTC access. . . .

The prospect that the agency's senior decisionmakers were resting on improper concerns about the morality of adolescent sexual activity is buttressed by the statements of many involved in the process that the decision not to approve the first [application] had already been made and communicated to the professional staff as early as December 2003 and January 2004. . . .

Finally, the conclusions of the [Government Accountability Office (GAO)] Report that the FDA's decisionmaking processes were unusual in four significant respects satisfies the court that the necessary showing of bad faith or improper behavior has been made by the plaintiffs here. . . .

For the foregoing reasons the defendant's motion for a protective order is denied and discovery shall proceed in accordance with this order.

PENSION BENEFIT GUARANTY CORPORATION V. LTV CORPORATION

496 U.S. 633 (1990)

[JUSTICE BLACKMUN] Petitioner PBGC is a wholly owned United States Government corporation modeled after the Federal Deposit Insurance Corporation. . . . The PBGC administers and enforces Title IV of ERISA. Title IV includes a mandatory Government insurance program that protects the pension benefits of over 30 million private-sector American workers who participate in plans covered by the Title. . . . When a plan covered under Title IV terminates with insufficient assets . . . the PBGC becomes trustee of the plan . . . . The PBGC then [adds] its own funds to ensure payment of . . . "nonforfeitable" benefits, i.e., those benefits to which participants have earned entitlement under the plan terms as of the date of termination. ERISA does place limits on the benefits PBGC may guarantee upon plan termination, however, even if an employee is entitled to greater benefits under the terms of the plan. In addition, benefit increases resulting from plan amendments adopted within five years of the termination are not paid in full. Finally, active plan participants (current employees) cease to earn additional benefits under the plan upon its termination, and lose entitlement to most benefits not yet fully earned as of the date of plan termination.

The cost of the PBGC insurance is borne primarily by employers that maintain ongoing pension plans. Sections 4006 and 4007 of ERISA require these employers to pay annual premiums. The insurance program is also financed by statutory liability imposed on employers who terminate underfunded pension plans. Upon termination, the employer becomes liable to the PBGC for the benefits that the PBGC will pay out. Because the PBGC historically has recovered only a small portion of that liability, Congress repeatedly has been forced to increase the annual premiums. Even with these increases, the PBGC in its most recent Annual Report noted liabilities of $ 4 billion and assets of only $ 2.4 billion, leaving a deficit of over $ 1.5 billion.

As noted above, plan termination is the insurable event under Title IV. Plans may be terminated "voluntarily" by an employer or "involuntarily" by the PBGC. An Employer may terminate a plan voluntarily in one of two ways. It may proceed with a "standard termination" only if it has sufficient assets to pay all benefit commitments. A standard termination thus does not implicate PBGC insurance responsibilities. If an employer wishes to terminate a plan whose assets are insufficient to pay all benefits, the employer must demonstrate that it is in financial "distress" as defined in 29 U.S.C. § 1341(c). Neither a standard nor a distress termination by the employer, however, is permitted if termination would violate the terms of an existing collective-bargaining agreement.

The PBGC, though, may terminate a plan "involuntarily," notwithstanding the existence of a collective-bargaining agreement. Section 4042 of ERISA provides that the PBGC may terminate a plan whenever it determines that:

(1) the plan has not met the minimum funding standard required under section 412 of title 26, . . .

(2) the plan will be unable to pay benefits when due,

. . . .

(4) the possible long-run loss of the [PBGC] with respect to the plan may reasonably be expected to increase unreasonably if the plan is not terminated.

Termination can be undone by PBGC. Section 4047 of ERISA provides:

In the case of a plan which has been terminated under section 1341 or 1342 of this title the [PBGC] is authorized in any such case in which [it] determines such action to be appropriate and consistent with its duties under this subchapter, to take such action as may be necessary to restore the plan to its pretermination status, including, but not limited to, the transfer to the employer or a plan administrator of control of part or all of the remaining assets and liabilities of the plan.

When a plan is restored, full benefits are reinstated, and the employer, rather than the PBGC, again is responsible for the plan's unfunded liabilities.

II.

This case arose after respondent The LTV Corporation (LTV Corp.) and many of its subsidiaries, including LTV Steel Company Inc. (LTV Steel) (collectively LTV), in July 1986 filed petitions for reorganization under Chapter 11 of the Bankruptcy Code. At that time, LTV Steel was the sponsor of three defined benefit pension plans (the Plans) covered by Title IV of ERISA. . . . Chronically underfunded, the Plans . . . had unfunded liabilities for promised benefits of almost $ 2.3 billion. Approximately $ 2.1 billion of this amount was covered by PBGC insurance.

It is undisputed that one of LTV Corp's principal goals in filing the Chapter 11 petitions was the restructuring of LTV Steel's pension obligations, a goal which could be accomplished if the Plans were terminated and responsibility for the unfunded liabilities was placed on the PBGC. . . . LTV, however, could not voluntarily terminate the Plans because two of them had been negotiated in collective bargaining. LTV therefore sought to have the PBGC terminate the Plans.

To that end, LTV advised the PBGC in 1986 that it could not continue to provide complete funding for the Plans. PBGC estimated that, without continued funding, the Plans' $ 2.1 billion underfunding could increase by as much as $ 65 million by December 1987 . . . unless the Plans were terminated. Moreover, extensive plant shutdowns were anticipated. These shutdowns, if they occurred before the Plans were terminated, would have required the payment of significant "shutdown benefits." The PBGC estimated that such benefits could increase the Plans' liabilities by as much as $ 300 million to $ 700 million, of which up to $ 500 million was covered by PBGC insurance. Confronted with this information, the PBGC, invoking § 4042(a)(4) of ERISA, determined that the Plans should be terminated in order to protect the insurance program from the unreasonable risk of large losses, and commenced termination proceedings in the District Court. With LTV's consent, the Plans were terminated effective January 13, 1987.

Because the Plans' participants lost some benefits as a result of the termination, the Steelworkers filed an adversary action against LTV in the Bankruptcy Court . . . . This action was settled, with LTV and the Steelworkers negotiating an interim collective-bargaining agreement that included new pension arrangements intended to make up benefits that plan participants lost as a result of the termination. . . . Retired participants were . . . placed in substantially the same positions they would have occupied had the old Plans never been terminated. . . . [For active plan participants, with] respect to shutdown benefits, LTV stated in Bankruptcy Court that the new benefits totaled "75% of benefits lost as a result of plan termination." With respect to some other kinds of benefits for active participants, the new arrangements provided 100% or more of the [lost] benefits.

The PBGC objected to these new pension agreements, characterizing them as "follow-on" plans. It defines a follow-on plan as a new benefit arrangement designed to wrap around the insurance benefits provided by the PBGC in such a way as to provide both retirees and active participants substantially the same benefits as they would have received had no termination occurred. The PBGC's policy against follow-on plans stems from the agency's belief that such plans are "abusive" of the insurance program and result in the PBGC's subsidizing an employer's ongoing pension program in a way not contemplated by Title IV. The PBGC consistently has made clear its policy of using its restoration powers under § 4047 if an employer institutes an abusive follow-on plan. . . . LTV ignored the PBGC's objections to the new pension arrangements and asked the Bankruptcy Court for permission to fund the follow-on plans. The Bankruptcy Court granted LTV's request. In doing so, however, it noted that the PBGC "may have legal options or avenues that it can assert administratively . . . to implement its policy goals. Nothing done here tonight precludes the PBGC from pursuing these options. . . ."

In early August 1987, the PBGC determined that the financial factors on which it had relied in terminating the Plans had changed significantly. Of particular significance to the PBGC was its belief that the steel industry, including LTV Steel, was experiencing a dramatic turnaround. As a result, the PBGC concluded it no longer faced the imminent risk, central to its original termination decision, of large unfunded liabilities stemming from plant shutdowns. Later that month, the PBGC's internal working group made a recommendation, based upon LTV's improved financial circumstances and its follow-on plans, to the PBGC's Executive Director to restore the Plans under the PBGC's § 4047 powers. After consulting the PBGC's Board of Directors, which agreed with the working group that restoration was appropriate, the Executive Director decided to restore the Plans. n.4

n.4 Thereafter, the Executive Director offered to meet with LTV to "consider any additional information [it] might wish to supply." . . . . At these meetings, LTV officials expressed concern about the timing of the restoration decision and indicated that restoration would give rise to time-consuming litigation, which would cast doubt on the bankruptcy reorganization, thereby imposing hardship on other creditors.

The Director issued a Notice of Restoration on September 22, 1987, indicating the PBGC's intent to restore the terminated Plans. The PBGC Notice explained that the restoration decision was based on (1) LTV's establishment of "a retirement program that results in an abuse of the pension plan termination insurance system established by Title IV of ERISA," and (2) LTV's "improved financial circumstances." Restoration meant that the Plans were ongoing, and that LTV again would be responsible for administering and funding them. LTV refused to comply with the restoration decision[, an informal adjudication].

. . . .

[The question is whether] the agency procedures were inadequate . . . . Relying upon a passage in *Bowman Transportation, Inc. v. Arkansas-Best Freight System, Inc., 419 U.S. 281 (1974)*, the [lower] court held that the PBGC's decision was arbitrary and capricious because the "PBGC neither apprised LTV of the material on which it was to base its decision, gave LTV an adequate opportunity to offer contrary evidence, proceeded in accordance with ascertainable standards . . ., nor provided [LTV] a statement showing its reasoning in applying those standards." The court suggested that on remand the agency was required to do each of these things.

The PBGC argues that this holding conflicts with *Vermont Yankee Nuclear Power Corp. v. Natural Resources Defense Council, Inc.*, where, the PBGC contends, this Court made clear that when the Due Process Clause is not implicated and an agency's governing statute contains no specific procedural mandates, the Administrative Procedure Act establishes the maximum procedural requirements a reviewing court may impose on agencies. Although *Vermont Yankee* concerned additional procedures imposed by [a court on an agency] in informal rulemaking, the PBGC argues that the informal adjudication process by which the restoration decision was made should be governed by the same principles.

Respondents counter by arguing that courts, under some circumstances, do require agencies to undertake additional procedures. As support for this proposition, they rely on *Citizens to Preserve Overton Park, Inc. v. Volpe.* In *Overton Park*, the Court concluded that the Secretary of Transportation's "post hoc rationalizations" regarding a decision to authorize the construction of a highway did not provide "an adequate basis for [judicial] review" for purposes of § 706 of the APA. Accordingly, the Court directed the District Court on remand to consider evidence that shed light on the Secretary's reasoning at the time he made the decision. Of particular relevance for present purposes, the Court in *Overton Park* intimated that one recourse for the District Court might be a remand to the agency for a fuller explanation of the agency's reasoning at the time of the agency action. Subsequent cases have made clear that remanding to the agency in fact is the preferred course. Respondents contend that the instant case is controlled by *Overton Park* rather than *Vermont Yankee*, and that the Court of Appeals' ruling was thus correct.

We believe that respondents' argument is wide of the mark. We begin by noting that although one initially might feel that there is some tension between *Vermont Yankee* and *Overton Park*, the two cases are not necessarily inconsistent. *Vermont Yankee* stands for the general proposition that courts are not free to impose upon agencies specific procedural requirements that have no basis in the APA. At most, *Overton Park* suggests that § 706(2)(A) of the APA, which directs a court to ensure that an agency action is not arbitrary and capricious or otherwise contrary to law, imposes a general "procedural" requirement of sorts by mandating that an agency take whatever steps it needs to provide an explanation that will enable the court to evaluate the agency's rationale at the time of decision.

Here, unlike in *Overton Park*, the Court of Appeals did not suggest that the administrative record was inadequate to enable the court to fulfill its duties under § 706. Rather, to support its ruling, the court focused on "fundamental fairness" to LTV. . . . But the court did not point to any provision in ERISA or the APA which gives LTV the procedural rights the court identified. Thus, the court's holding runs afoul of *Vermont Yankee* and finds no support in *Overton Park*.

Nor is *Arkansas-Best*, the case on which the Court of Appeals relied, to the contrary. The statement relied upon (which was dictum) said: "A party is entitled, of course, to know the issues on which decision will turn and to be apprised of the factual material on which the agency relies for decision so that he may rebut it." That statement was entirely correct in the context of *Arkansas-Best*, which involved a formal adjudication . . . pursuant to the trial-type procedures set forth in §§ 5, 7 and 8 of the APA, which include requirements that parties be given notice of "the matters of fact and law asserted," an opportunity for "the submission and consideration of facts [and] arguments," and an opportunity to submit "proposed findings and conclusions" or "exceptions". The determination in this case, however, was lawfully made by informal adjudication, the minimal requirements for which are set forth in § 555 of the APA, and do not include such elements. A failure to provide them where the Due Process Clause itself does not require them (which has not been asserted here) is therefore not unlawful.

IV.

We conclude that the PBGC's failure to consider all potentially relevant areas of law did not render its restoration decision arbitrary and capricious. We also conclude that the PBGC's anti-follow-on policy, an asserted basis for the restoration decision, is not contrary to clear congressional intent and is based on a permissible construction of § 4047. Finally, we find the procedures employed by the PBGC to be consistent with the APA. Accordingly, the judgment of the Court of Appeals is reversed and the case is remanded for further proceedings consistent with this opinion.

. . . .

> ## Underlying Case Documents
>
> The case referenced:
> The notice of restoration

1. Importantly, this case reflects a sound view of *Overton Park* – but the comprehensive deference shown the agency action would likely not be repeated were the case heard in 2008. As the court notes in *In re UAL*, 468 F.3d 444, 450-51 (7th Cir. 2006), "after *Mead* and *Christensen*, the sort of opinion letters to which the Court deferred in *LTV* would receive, not *Chevron* deference, but respectful consideration under *Skidmore v. Swift & Co.*, 323 U.S. 134 (1944)." Do you find the reasoning of the PBGC valid, thorough, and persuasive?

2. There are limits on the necessity and capacity of agencies to consider every – or even most – alternatives to a particular regulatory solution that evolves in an adjudicatory process. Recent Executive Order 13,422 demands consideration of regulatory options, though as Professor Roger G. Noll notes, there is good reason to doubt the ability of agencies to do so. Roger G. Noll, *Reflections on Executive Order 13,422: The Economic Significance of Executive Order 13,422*, 25 YALE J. ON REG. 113, 122-23 (2008):

> [A]gencies do not effectively analyze reasonable regulatory alternatives. Section 1(a) [of E.O. 13,422] states the agencies "should assess all costs and benefits of available regulatory alternatives." Section 1(b)(8) states that agencies "shall identify and assess alternative forms of regulation," and section 6(a)(3)(C)(iii) requires that agencies consider "potentially effective and reasonably feasible alternatives" to a proposed regulation. Agencies rarely implement the "best practice" version of this requirement, which is to consider a small but significant increase and decrease in the stringency of the regulation they propose.

This is a rather dim view of agency competence and creativity. What would you think makes the assessment of alternatives inefficient, as noted above? *LTV* certainly does not compel consideration of every option – but how much is enough? Furthermore, there is a cost in considering multiple options – why not defer to an agency's judgment in this area?

3. Compulsory consideration of "less restrictive (regulatory) alternatives" is common in a number of fields – and probably not far from the motivation behind the sections of 13,422 just mentioned. When it comes to health and safety and minimizing regulatory intrusion into the marketplace, consider Professor Thomas A. Lambert's commentary on efficiency based regulation.

> [E]fficiency-minded regulatory theorists have suggested that regulators should adopt

the "least restrictive alternative" when regulating to correct a market failure. But sometimes the regulatory option that is literally least restrictive will not be socially optimal, because more restrictive regulatory alternatives, though more costly to implement, will provide higher net benefits. Similarly, the "most effective alternative" is a flawed regulatory criterion because the regulatory alternative that is most effective at eliminating market failure will not be most desirable if it costs significantly more than slightly less effective alternatives. . . . Sometimes, the optimal regulatory option will be neither the least restrictive nor the most effective alternative.

Thomas A. Lambert, *Avoiding Regulatory Mismatch in the Workplace: An Informational Approach to Workplace Safety Regulation*, 82 NEB. L. REV. 1006, 1033 (2004).

HORNSBY V. ALLEN

326 F.2d 605 (5th Cir. 1964)

[CHIEF JUDGE TUTTLE] Appellant Mrs. Hornsby is an unsuccessful applicant for a license to operate a retail liquor store in Atlanta, Georgia. She brings this action under 28 U.S.C. § 1343 to redress an alleged deprivation of civil rights and under 28 U.S.C. § 2201 to obtain a declaration of her rights. The Mayor, the City Clerk, and the Aldermen of Atlanta are defendants. In her complaint, Mrs. Hornsby alleges that although she met all the requirements and qualifications, as to moral character of the applicant and proposed location of the store, prescribed for the holder of a retail liquor dealer's license, her application was denied "without a reason therefor" by the Mayor and Board of Aldermen. This action is characterized as "arbitrary, unreasonable, unjust, capricious, discriminatory" and in contravention of the due process and equal protection clauses of the 14th Amendment. The complaint also charges that a system of ward courtesy was followed in the issuance of liquor licenses; under this system licenses allegedly would be granted only upon the approval of one or both of the aldermen of the ward in which the store was to be located. This too is said to constitute a violation of the 14th Amendment.

. . . .

At the outset, we note our disagreement with the district court's classification of the challenged actions as purely those of a legislative body; we do not conceive the denial of an application for a license to be an act of legislation. . . . [Rather,] we prefer the view that licensing proper is an adjudicative process. Thus when a municipal or other governmental body grants a license it is an adjudication that the applicant has satisfactorily complied with the prescribed standards for the award of that license. Similarly the denial of a license is based on an adjudication that the applicant has not satisfied those qualifications and requirements. On the other hand, the prescription of standards which must be met to obtain a license is legislation, since these standards are authoritative guides for future conduct derived from an assessment of the needs of the community. A governmental agency entrusted with . . . licensing power therefore functions as a legislature when it prescribes these standards, but the same agency acts as a judicial body when it makes a determination that a specific applicant has or has not satisfied them.

Since licensing consists in the determination of factual issues and the application of legal criteria to them – a judicial act – the fundamental requirements of due process are applicable to it. Due process in administrative proceedings of a judicial nature has been said generally to be conformity to fair practices of Anglo-Saxon jurisprudence, which is usually equated with adequate notice and a fair hearing. Although strict adherence to the common-law rules of evidence at the hearing is not required, the parties must generally be allowed an opportunity to know the claims of the opposing party, to present evidence to support their contentions, and to cross-examine witnesses for the other side. Thus it is not proper to admit ex parte evidence, given by witnesses not under oath and not subject to cross-examination by the opposing party. A fortiori, the deciding authority may not base its decision on evidence which has not been specifically brought before it, the findings must conform to the evidence adduced at the hearing. Furthermore, the Supreme Court has said that an administrative order "cannot be upheld merely because findings might have been made and considerations disclosed which would justify its order . . . . There must be such a responsible finding." Thus where the Secretary of State indicated that passport regulations precluded the issuance of a passport to the applicant in question, but did not specify the applicable subsection or set out the findings on which the conclusion was based, it was held that factual findings would be required before the Secretary could deny the application.

Also, the Supreme Court has held that the arbitrary refusal to grant a license or permit to one group when other groups have obtained permits under similar circumstances constitutes a denial of equal protection of the law. Although this case raised the problem of freedom of religion, state action and hence, necessarily, the 14th Amendment were involved. The Court concluded that a "completely arbitrary and discriminatory refusal to grant" park permits sought by Jehovah's Witnesses constituted a denial of equal protection of the law where other religious organizations had customarily been allowed to use the park.

The appellees here, however, seek to place liquor in a special category, and argue that since Georgia has declared a license to sell spirituous liquor to be a privilege, the licensing authority has an unreviewable discretion to grant or deny licenses. It is firmly established, of course, that the state has the right to regulate or prohibit traffic in intoxicating liquor in the valid exercise of its police power, but this is something quite different from a right to act arbitrarily and capriciously.

Merely calling a liquor license a privilege does not free the municipal authorities from the due process requirements in licensing and allow them to exercise an uncontrolled discretion. . . . The public has the right to expect its officers to observe prescribed standards and to make adjudications on the basis of merit. The first step toward insuring that these expectations are realized is to require adherence to the standards of due process; absolute and uncontrolled discretion invites abuse.

. . . .

We find in this case that Mrs. Hornsby's allegations, if borne out by the evidence, are sufficient to show a violation of her 14th Amendment rights. If her application actually was denied because the delegation from her ward decided, from their own knowledge of the circumstances, that Mrs. Hornsby should not be issued a liquor license, then she was deprived of the hearing which due process requires, since she could not discover the claims of those opposing her and subject their evidence to cross-examination. In addition, Mrs. Hornsby was not afforded an opportunity to know, through reasonable regulations promulgated by the board, of the objective standards which had to be met to obtain a license. Next, the alleged failure of the board to reveal the basis for denying her application would, if true, be a denial of her right to have the board make findings based on the evidence adduced at a hearing. Moreover, appellees themselves indicate that the mandates of equal protection were not observed in the awarding of liquor licenses:

> In granting a mere privilege, appellant cites no authority which would prevent the defendants (appellees) from arbitrarily accepting one eligible application while denying others; otherwise they would, of necessity, be forced to grant licenses to every eligible citizen upon application.

If there are too many qualified applicants, then the proper remedy is for the Board of Aldermen to adopt reasonable rules and regulations which will raise the standards of eligibility or fix limits on the number of licenses which may be issued in an area; the solution is not to make arbitrary selections among those qualified. . . .

---

1. Many – if not most – of the adjudication cases studied in administrative law focus on federal agencies. *Hornsby*, in contrast, does not. Part of the value of this case involves the fact that a state entity is the agency in question – and, perhaps more importantly – that a purely political agency is under scrutiny. All politics may be local – and much of administrative law is practiced at the state and local level – but that does not relieve the state government of basic obligation to provide a fair process for adjudicatory determinations, including articulating "ascer-

tainable standards" prior to making adjudicatory determinations.

Take Note

Simply calling a licensing decision a legislative enactment where no standards are needed and no particular process is due is not going to fool anyone. *Carico Invs., Inc. v. Tex. Alcoholic Bev. Comm'n, 439 F. Supp. 2d 733 (S.D. Tex. 2006)*. That said, many decisions that might seem adjudicatory are in fact legislative. For example, in the land use and zoning areas, single parcel zoning is often construed as a legislative action. Carlos A. Ball & Laurie Reynolds, *Exactions and Burden Distribution in Takings Law*, 47 WM. & MARY L. REV. 1513, 1531 (2006); Todd W. Prall, Comment, *Dysfunctional Distinctions in Land Use: The Failure of Legislative/Adjudicative Distinctions in Utah and the Case for a Uniform Standard of Review*, 2004 B.Y.U. L. REV. 1049; Brian W. Blaesser, *Substantive Due Process Protection at the Outer Margins of Municipal Behavior*, 3 WASH. U. J.L. & POL'Y 583, 595 (2000).

2. In some ways, the Fifth Circuit was ahead of its time. Rejection of the notion of "privilege" as well as some of the basic entitlements in *Hornsby* are consistent with the holding in *Goldberg v. Kelly*, decided some years later. That said, since the property interest asserted in *Hornsby* is fuzzy, there are some questions of the direct applicability of the holding in due process cases, particularly after *Roth* and *Perry*.

How should courts treat license applicants? Does a property interest vest only after a license is granted? A *Roth* property interest requires that one "must have more than an abstract need or desire for it. He must have more than a unilateral expectation of it. He must, instead, have a legitimate claim of entitlement to it." 408 U.S. at 577. Did the plaintiff in *Hornsby* have a "legitimate claim of entitlement?" For a comparison of the different perspectives on this, compare the majority and dissenting opinions in *Hamby v. Neel, 368 F.3d 549 (6th Cir. 2004)*. Remember, what constitutes property is defined, in most instances, by state law – and if the claim is speculative, unilateral, or abstract, then chances are it will not rise to the level of a cognizable property interest. *Banks v. Block, 700 F.2d 292, 296-97 (6th Cir. 1983)*.

3. The lack of discernible standards, central to the holding in *Hornsby*, continues to be a subject of considerable interest. JUSTICE MARSHALL's dissent in *Board of Regents v. Roth* cites the *Hornsby* standard with favor: "With respect to occupations controlled by the government, one lower court has said that 'the public has the right to expect its officers . . . to make adjudications on the basis of merit. The first step toward insuring that these expectations are realized is to require adherence to the standards of due process; absolute and uncontrolled discretion invites abuse.'" 408 U.S. 564, 587 (1972), citing *Hornsby v. Allen*. Take another look at *Morton v. Ruiz*, *supra* Chapter 2. Was that case based in part on the lack of standards?

JUSTICE MARSHALL's theme repeats regularly. For example, in a deportation case involving a person who had been convicted of a narcotics offense and who asserted, *inter alia*, that he had been rehabilitated, the Ninth Circuit observed:

> The BIA's failure to consider any of this pertinent evidence may be due in part to its lack of discernible standards regarding what constitutes rehabilitation. In order for us to give meaningful review to a finding regarding rehabilitation, we must understand what factors the INS considers in making such a determination. [From *Yepes-Prado v. United States*, 10 F.3d 1363, 1372, n.19 (9th Cir. 1993).]

Hornsby, then, raises a fairly nuanced problem: On the one hand, administrative agencies in the United States cannot – and do not – issue standards governing every conceivable enforcement action. On the other hand, *notice* and an opportunity to be heard are at the core of due process – and one way to think about notice is in terms of the requirement for publication of standards. What level of detail is required to make a standard discernible? How can an agency evolve standards through the adjudicatory process if it must first articulate standards?

4. The lack of a meaningful standard is the focus of a number of First Amendment cases involving agency or executive action. In *Lakewood v. Plain Dealer Publishing Co.*, 486 U.S. 750, 755-56 (1988), the Court was faced with a set of regulations that provided no standards regarding the detail of newsrack designs, in effect giving the executive "unbridled" discretion over licensing. The Court found that its "cases have long held that when a licensing statute allegedly vests unbridled discretion in a government official over whether to permit or deny expressive activity, one who is subject to the law may challenge it facially without the necessity of first applying for, and being denied, a license." E.g., *Freedman v. Maryland*, 380 U.S. 51, 56 (1965); *Lovell v. Griffin*, 303 U.S. 444, 452-53 (1938) ("As the ordinance [providing for unbridled licensing discretion] is void on its face, it was not necessary for appellant to seek a permit under it."). The burden to demonstrate that a regulation vested unbridled discretion in an agency rests with the party challenging the regulation. *Preminger v. VA*, 517 F.3d 1299 (Fed. Cir. 2008).

NORTH AMERICAN COLD STORAGE COMPANY V. CITY OF CHICAGO

211 U.S. 306 (1908)

[JUSTICE PECKHAM] [The Illinois statute in question read:]

> Every person being the owner, lessee or occupant of any . . . cold storage house or other place, other than a private dwelling, where any meat, fish, poultry, game, vegetables, fruit, or other perishable article adapted or designed to be used for human food, shall be stored or kept . . . shall put, preserve and keep such article of food supply in a clean and wholesome condition, and shall not allow the same, nor any

part thereof, to become putrid, decayed, poisoned, infected, or in any other manner rendered or made unsafe or unwholesome for human food; and it shall be the duty of the meat and food inspectors and other duly authorized employees of the health department of the city to enter any and all such premises above specified at any time of any day, and to forthwith seize, condemn and destroy any such putrid, decayed, poisoned and infected food, which any such inspector may find in and upon said premises.

[The statute provides] for no notice to the complainant or opportunity for a hearing before the seizure and destruction of the food. A constitutional question was thus presented to the court, over which it had jurisdiction, and it was bound to decide the same on its merits.

[Counsel for the complainant states:]

There is but one question in this case, [is] section 1161 of the Revised Municipal Code of Chicago in conflict with the due process of law provision of the Fourteenth Amendment, in . . . that it does not provide for notice and an opportunity to be heard before the destruction of the food products therein referred to?

. . . We are of [the] opinion . . . that provision for a hearing before seizure and condemnation and destruction of food which is unwholesome and unfit for use, is not necessary. The right to so seize is based upon the right and duty of the State to protect and guard, as far as possible, the lives and health of its inhabitants, and that it is proper to provide that food which is unfit for human consumption should be summarily seized and destroyed to prevent the danger which would arise from eating it. The right to so seize and destroy is, of course, based upon the fact that the food is not fit to be eaten. Food that is in such a condition, if kept for sale or in danger of being sold, is in itself a nuisance, and a nuisance of the most dangerous kind, involving, as it does, the health, if not the lives, of persons who may eat it.

A determination on the part of the seizing officers that food is in an unfit condition to be eaten is . . . not in any way binding upon those who own or claim the right to sell the food. If a party cannot get his hearing in advance of the seizure and destruction he has the right to have it afterward, which right may be claimed upon the trial in an action brought for the destruction of his property, and in that action those who destroyed it can only successfully defend if the jury shall find the fact of unwholesomeness as claimed by them. . . .

. . . .

Miller v. Horton is in principle like the case before us. It was an action brought for killing the plaintiff's horse. The defendants admitted the killing but justified the act under an order of the board of health, which declared that the horse had the glanders, and directed it to be killed. The court held that the decision of the board of health was not conclusive as to whether or not the horse was diseased, and said that:

> Of course there cannot be a trial by jury before killing an animal supposed to have a contagious disease, and we assume that the legislature may authorize its destruction in such emergencies without a hearing beforehand. But it does not follow that it can throw the loss upon the owner without a hearing. If he cannot be heard beforehand he may be heard afterward. . . .

. . . .

Complainant, however, contends that there was no emergency requiring speedy action for the destruction of the poultry in order to protect the public health from danger resulting from consumption of such poultry. It is said that the food was in cold storage, and that it [would] continue in the same condition it then was [in] for three months, if properly stored, and that therefore the defendants had ample time in which to give notice to complainant or the owner and have a hearing of the question as to the condition of the poultry, and as the ordinance provided for no hearing, it was void. But we think this is not required. The power of the legislature to enact laws in relation to the public health being conceded, as it must be, it is to a great extent within legislative discretion as to whether any hearing need be given before the destruction of unwholesome food which is unfit for human consumption. If a hearing were to be always necessary, even under the circumstances of this case, the question at once arises as to what is to be done with the food in the meantime. Is it to remain with the cold storage company, and if so under what security that it will not be removed? To be sure that it will not be removed during the time necessary for the hearing, which might frequently be indefinitely prolonged, some guard would probably have to be placed over the subject-matter of investigation, which would involve expense, and might not even then prove effectual. What is the emergency which would render a hearing unnecessary?

We think when the question is one regarding the destruction of food which is not fit for human use the emergency must be one which would fairly appeal to the reasonable discretion of the legislature as to the necessity for a prior hearing, and in that case its decision would not be a subject for review by the courts. As the owner of the food or its custodian is amply protected against the party seizing the food, who must in a subsequent action against him show as a fact that it was within the statute, we think that due process of law is not denied the owner or custodian by the destruction of the food alleged to be unwholesome and unfit for human food without a preliminary hearing. . . .

Affirmed.

———————

1. There is little question in *North American Cold Storage* that a *Roth*-like property interest – or, looking to a seemingly bygone test, a <u>*Cafeteria Workers*</u> right (as opposed to a privilege) – was subordinated. The pre-hearing summary action – informal adjudicatory action – was based on protecting the public from serious harm. This is a basic, easily understood – and potentially hazardous – doctrine.

2. Can you tell what tests should be used to determine whether due process should be trumped by the fear of some type of injury or grave risk? How does an agency make a decision this important, this fundamental, in the absence of notice and an opportunity to be heard? Consider a recent application of the doctrine in the following case excerpt from <u>*Camuglia v. City of Albuquerque*, 448 F.3d 1214 (10th Cir. 2006)</u>:

> [An] employee of the Albuquerque Environmental Health Department (EHD), inspected Paisano's Restaurant, owned by Mr. Camuglia . . . and cited the restaurant for several violations, including cockroaches. . . . [The restaurant's operating permit was, shortly thereafter, summarily suspended and notice of the suspension faxed to local papers. No hearing was held prior to the suspension.]
>
> Mr. Camuglia contended . . . that his procedural-due-process rights were "violated . . . when [the city] closed Paisano's and notified the media without providing Mr. Camuglia with any level of process. . . ."
>
> In matters of public health and safety, the Supreme Court has long recognized that the government must act quickly. Quick action may turn out to be wrongful action, but due process requires only a post-deprivation opportunity to establish the error. . . . [citing] *North American Cold Storage Co.* . . . "We are of opinion, however, that provision for a hearing before seizure and condemnation and destruction of food which is unwholesome and unfit for use is not necessary. . . ." This holding has been repeatedly reaffirmed. *See, e.g.,* <u>*Mackey v. Montrym*, 443 U.S. 1, 17 (1979)</u> ("We have traditionally accorded the states great leeway in adopting summary procedures to protect public health and safety. . . .") . . . . [T]he City, acting through its inspectors, may close a restaurant to protect the health of patrons and workers without first providing a hearing to the restaurant owner. . . .
>
> At one point in the hearing, counsel for Mr. Camuglia stated: "They can close [the restaurant] if there's an imminent danger, but if there's not an imminent danger, then [the Ordinance] provides differently."
>
> This argument misses the point. It concedes that limiting the owner to a post-deprivation hearing comports with due process when the government has acted

properly, but contends that a pre-deprivation hearing is required when the government has erred. In other words, the government can delay the hearing until after the deprivation only when the deprivation was in fact lawful. We might ask why even a post-deprivation hearing is required in that circumstance, when one is conceding that the government did nothing wrong. The purpose of a hearing, after all, is to determine whether government conduct has been (or would be) unlawful. When the Supreme Court states that granting just a post-deprivation hearing is constitutionally adequate, it is saying that determining the propriety of government action can wait. . . .

The process one is due is not dependent on whether the government was right or wrong in the particular case but on whether, in general, constitutional norms require particular procedures to balance private and public interests. Postponing the hearing may, as Mr. Camuglia contends happened here, cause harm. The Supreme Court, however, has recognized that possibility and ruled that the public interest in prompt action permits that action to precede a hearing in public-health matters. Mr. Camuglia may have a remedy for a governmental error, but he cannot claim that he has been deprived of procedural due process.

The statute in this case provides no meaningful guidance. If an inspector "finds" unsafe conditions, the permit to operate can be suspended. The constitutional protection from unwarranted suspension is in the post-deprivation hearing. Are there harms that cannot be addressed after-the-fact? It is understandable that the city wanted to advise the public of the apparent risk – hence the fax to the media – but how would you calculate harm in a post-deprivation hearing if the inspector was simply wrong?

3. Summary suspension, seizure, and destruction of property are not vestiges of the early 20th Century. For a defense of a North Carolina law that permits summary deprivation of property when there is a suspicion that cattle may carry "mad cow" disease (Bovine spongiform encephalopathy), see Andrew H. Nelson, Comment, *High Steaks: Defending North Carolina's Response to Contagious Animal Diseases*, 83 N.C. L. REV. 238, 239 (2004), describing legislation that flew through the state house, senate, and was signed into law in 48 hours.

> [T]he bill authorized the state veterinarian, after receiving the approval of the Governor, to quarantine large areas of the state, to conduct warrantless searches and seizures of people and animals, and to destroy potentially infected animals without notifying the owner. This authorization greatly expanded the power of the state veterinarian, an unelected official, and authorized a dramatic exercise of the state's police power.

4. Emergency property seizures – summary informal adjudicatory acts – are easily compared with warrantless inspections. In a case exploring the use of warrantless searches to implement New York's "smoking ban," *Players, Inc. v. City of New York*, 371 F. Supp. 2d 522 (S.D.N.Y. 2005), the court found a warrantless inspection is permissible. Generally, a warrantless search will be permitted if the following fac-

tors are present: (1) a substantial government interest; (2) warrantless inspections that further the regulatory scheme; and (3) a constitutionally adequate substitute for a warrant provided by the regulatory program.

> The . . . City clearly has a substantial government interest in ensuring the health of its food supply, and of customers of food service establishments. . . . [citing *North American Cold Storage.*] [P]rotecting the safety of the food supply represents an important governmental interest. . . . Both food safety and the health of food service workers and patrons may be endangered by the consumption of tobacco products in and around food preparation areas; the Court has previously noted that the concern for the safety of individuals exposed to secondhand smoke represented an "important government interest."

There are many "important governmental interests," ranging from the competency of teachers, doctors, lawyers, architects, engineers, and numerous other occupations, to the quality of air and water, the fuel efficiency of automobiles, and many, many more. If an inspector "finds" a problem with anyone associated with the aforementioned careers or uses, should there be the power to suspend summarily one's career or seize one's property? To suspend the operation of any school or office? The power to search without warrant or a finding of probable cause?

In the criminal justice field, presumably the deprivation of liberty through an arrest constitutes adverse action – for which a probable cause standard must be met. What is the civil/administrative equivalent? In his dissent in *Skinner v. Railway Labor Executives' Association*, 489 U.S. 602, 640 (1989), JUSTICE MARSHALL asserted that the idea that any legitimate government basis could justify warrantless search eliminated any notion of civil probable cause – and he was right.

> **Take Note**
>
> In administrative searches, the standard used to determine the efficacy of a search is reasonable belief, not probable cause.

5. Can summary action or other forms of expedited decisionmaking be justified in the name of efficiency as opposed to physical hazard? Isn't that partly the premise of *Mathews v. Eldridge*? If so, what is the promise of due process? For property deprivation, post-adverse action hearings are common.

We, your authors, do not dismiss as antiquated cases like *North American Cold Storage* (although others might). In fact, executive action to suspend the right to a hearing in the interest of public safety is very much front and center as this text goes to press. Claims of national security or an epidemic as a basis for taking summary action are hard to resist – and can be an acid test of administrative process. There is reason to study how the executive governs, how it responds to public outcry, and how it implements the constitutional guarantees of due process. In the last few years, the Supreme Court has decided a half dozen cases on warrantless detention alone. *See, e.g.*, *Boumediene v. Bush*, 553 U.S. 723 (2008).

BOWLES V. WILLINGHAM

321 U.S. 503 (1944)

[JUSTICE DOUGLAS] Appellee, Mrs. Willingham of Macon, Georgia, sued . . . to restrain the issuance of certain rent orders under the Emergency Price Control Act of 1942 on the ground that the orders and the statutory provisions on which they rested were unconstitutional. The state court issued, ex parte, a temporary injunction and a show cause order. . . . [The] Administrator of the Office of Price Administration, brought this suit in the federal District Court . . . to restrain Mrs. Willingham from . . . prosecution of the state proceedings . . . and to restrain [the] sheriff, from executing or attempting to execute any orders in the state proceedings. . . .

. . . .

[History]

[T]he Administrator [of the Office of Price Administration] issued a declaration designating twenty-eight areas . . . including Macon, Georgia, as defense-rental areas. That declaration stated that defense activities had resulted in increased housing rents in those areas and that it was necessary and proper in order to effectuate the purposes of the Act to stabilize and reduce such rents. It also contained a recommendation . . . that the maximum rent for housing accommodations rented on April 1, 1941, should be [capped as of the rent effective on] April 1, 1941. . . . As respects housing . . . rented for the first time between that date and the effective date of the regulation, July 1, 1942 – the situation involved in this case – it was provided that the maximum rent should be the first rent charged after April 1, 1941 [but] that the Rent Director . . . might order a [further] decrease on his own initiative on the ground, among others, that the rent was higher than that generally prevailing in the area for comparable housing accommodations on April 1, 1941. . . . Within 60 days of the final action of the Rent Director the landlord might file an application for review by the regional administrator for the region [with further administrative review by] the Administrator [and judicial review by] the Emergency Court of Appeals. . . .

In June, 1943, the Rent Director gave written notice to Mrs. Willingham that he proposed to decrease the maximum rents for three apartments owned by her . . . on the ground that the first rents for these apartments . . . were in excess of those generally prevailing in the area for comparable accommodations on April 1, 1941. Mrs. Willingham filed objections to that proposed action together with supporting affidavits. The Rent Director thereupon advised her that he would proceed to issue an order reducing the rents. . . . [She responded by filing suit.]

. . . .

. . . The controls adopted by Congress [are] necessary "in the interest of the national defense and security" and for the "effective prosecution of the present war." They have as their aim the effective protection of our price structures against the forces of disorganization and the pressures created by war . . . . Thus the policy of the Act is clear. The maximum rents fixed by the Administrator are those which "in his judgment" will be "generally fair and equitable and will effectuate the purposes of this Act." . . . . There is no grant of unbridled administrative discretion as appellee argues. Congress has not told the Administrator to fix rents whenever and wherever he might like and at whatever levels he pleases. Congress has directed that maximum rents be fixed in those areas where defense activities have resulted or threaten to result in increased rentals inconsistent with the purpose of the Act. And it has supplied the standard and the base period to guide the Administrator in determining what the maximum rentals should be in a given area. . . .

. . . .

It is finally suggested that the Act violates the Fifth Amendment because it makes no provision for a hearing to landlords before the order or regulation fixing rents becomes effective. Congress would have been under no necessity to give notice and provide a hearing before it acted, had it decided to fix rents on a national basis. . . . We agree with the Emergency Court of Appeals that Congress need not make that requirement when it delegates the task to an administrative agency. In <u>Bi-Metallic Investment Co . v. State Board</u> . . . JUSTICE HOLMES, speaking for the Court, stated:

> Where a rule of conduct applies to more than a few people it is impracticable that every one should have a direct voice in its adoption. The Constitution does not require all public acts to be done in town meeting or an assembly of the whole. . . .

Here Congress has provided for judicial review of the Administrator's action. To be sure, that review comes after the order has been promulgated; and no provision for a stay is made. . . . [However, that] review satisfies the requirements of due process. . . . [The question is one of timing.] As stated by . . . JUSTICE BRANDEIS for a unanimous Court in *Phillips v. Commissioner*:

> Where only property rights are involved, mere postponement of the judicial enquiry is not a denial of due process, if the opportunity given for the ultimate judicial determination of the liability is adequate. Delay in the judicial determination of property rights is not uncommon where it is essential that governmental needs be immediately satisfied.

. . . Congress was dealing here with the exigencies of wartime conditions and the insistent demands of inflation control. . . . Congress . . . adopted [a process] with the view of eliminating the necessity for "lengthy and costly trials with concomitant dissipation of the time and energies of all concerned in litigation rather than in the common war effort." . . . . To require hearings for thousands of landlords before any rent control order could be made effective might have defeated the program of price control. . . . National security might not be able to afford the luxuries of litigation and the long delays which preliminary hearings traditionally have entailed. . . . [W]here Congress has provided for judicial review after the regulations or orders have been made effective it has done all that due process under the war emergency requires. . . .

Underlying Case Documents

The case referenced:

The Emergency Price Control Act of 1942

For a sample maximum rent designations click HERE and HERE.

1. Was *Bowles* predicated on the failure of counsel to pursue available agency review or predetermined judicial remedies? After all, Mrs. Willingham jumped to state court and sought to enjoin a process for which there were further statutory remedies: "The machinery for a hearing on a protest . . . was designed to provide the basis of judicial review by the Emergency Court of Appeals . . . ." What might have motivated Mrs. Willingham to bypass the final administrative reviews and the Emergency Court of Appeals?

a. How would you characterize the Court's reaction to the decision to seek a state court injunction? Was it a failure to exhaust administrative remedies? Exhaustion is certainly part of the calculus – but it is a jurisdictional requirement only when the substantive statute specifies (e.g., 8 U.S.C. § 1252(d)(1)) – and no such provision applied in *Bowles*. The dialogue regarding exhaustion is complex and will be covered later in this text. Even the basic question whether exhaustion is a jurisdictional or prudential limitation on review is the subject of controversy. *See Darby v. Cisneros, 509 U.S. 137 (1993); and* Professor Colin Miller's *Manifest Destiny?: How Some Courts Have Fallaciously Come to Require a Greater Showing of Congressional Intent for Jurisdictional Exhaustion Than They Require for Preemption,* 2008 B.Y.U. L. REV. 169. Finally, if you were thinking why didn't they just use the APA – the APA § 704 requirements are riddled with exceptions – and, of course, the APA was adopted after the *Bowles* decision.

b. Was the review Mrs. Willingham sought unsuccessful because the Emergency Court of Appeals had primary jurisdiction? Was there a lack of finality – i.e., was there "more to be done" at the agency as well as in the special court set up for review?

c. In the last moments of the Emergency Court of Appeals (TECA):

> Congress [re]established the Temporary Emergency Court of Appeals in December 1971 (85 Stat. 474) and granted it exclusive jurisdiction to hear appeals from the decisions of the U.S. district courts in cases arising under the wage and price control program of the Economic Stabilization Act of 1970 (84 Stat. 799). Congress authorized the Chief Justice of the United States to appoint to the temporary court three or more district and appeals court judges, each of whom was to serve on a part-time basis for an indefinite term. The court exercised the same powers as a U.S. court of appeals, and it was authorized to prescribe its own rules of practice, which it did when its three district and six circuit court judges convened for the first time in February 1972. The Temporary Emergency Court of Appeals was modeled on the Emergency Court of Appeals, which was established in 1942 to hear appeals in cases involving various wartime price control measures and which heard its last case in 1961.

> Although the Economic Stabilization Act expired in 1974, Congress extended the operation of the Temporary Emergency Court of Appeals in the Emergency Petroleum Allocation Act of 1973. The court exercised the judicial review provisions of the energy price stabilization program established by the act. The temporary court's jurisdiction was further expanded in the Energy Policy and Conservation Act of 1975 and the Emergency Natural Gas Act of 1977. In 1992 Congress abolished the Temporary Emergency Court of Appeals and transferred both its jurisdiction and its pending cases to the U.S. Court of Appeals for the Federal Circuit. [From *History of TECA*, http://www.fjc.gov/history/home.nsf/page/temp_appeals (last visited, June 14, 2008).]

Was TECA an agency or a court? The blending of executive, legislative, and judicial functions is evident in entities of this nature. The Independent Counsel legislation that was used to investigate allegations of misconduct by President Clinton spawned a similar non-branch specific entity, the "Special Commission." Ethics in Government Act of 1978 (Ethics Act) 92 Stat. 1824, 2 U.S.C.A. § 701 et seq., as amended in 1988.

2. Was *Bowles* based on the economic pressures and risks the war produced? Was this a "national security" case in which the Court was willing to by-pass ordinary process to assist members of the armed forces by limiting wartime profiteering?

3. Did Mrs. Willingham lack a constitutional interest or entitlement sufficient to justify a hearing prior to adverse action? Property rights, *Bowles* makes clear, do not uniformly require a hearing prior to adverse action. As you already know, this is not an absolute rule (*Loudermill*) but certainly a factor of consequence when the right involved is a question of property valuation as opposed to employment. The

basic standard pre-dates *Bowles*: "Where only property rights are involved, mere postponement of the judicial enquiry is not a denial of due process, if the opportunity given for the ultimate judicial determination of the liability is adequate." *Phillips v. Commissioner*, 283 U.S. 589, 596-97 (1931).

a. In *Bowles*, part of the attack was based on the "class-rate" nature of the downward rent adjustments. This raises a basic adjudicatory argument: Rates are inherently regulatory, i.e., legislative. When a state or federal agency establishes a rate, it usually does so for all those engaged in that specific product or service, across the board. This will often provoke a challenge since rates – the prices one charges for a service or product – seem rather individuated. Ratemaking, however, is specifically designed as a rule-like function in the APA, § 551(4).

b. In *Chevron USA, Inc. v. Cayetano*, 224 F.3d 1030 (9th Cir. 2000), Chevron attacked Hawaii Rev. Stat. § 486H-10.4, which capped the rent a petroleum wholesaler could charge service stations, arguing that the limitation on pricing constituted an unconstitutional "taking."

> Chevron . . . argues that Act 257 is unconstitutional because it fails to provide for any individualized consideration and contains no mechanism for obtaining relief from the confiscatory rent limitation provisions. In support of this argument, Chevron relies on two state . . . cases. . . . The precedents established in these cases do not bind us. . . . [In] *Permian Basin Area Rate Cases*, 390 U.S. 747, 770 (1968), [the Court] refused to decide whether individualized consideration and administrative relief were "constitutionally imperative." Earlier Supreme Court cases, however, have suggested that there are no such constitutional requirements. In *Bowles v. Willingham* . . . the Court stated that otherwise valid price-fixing was not improper because it was on a class rather than an individual basis. . . . [As in *Bowles*,] Chevron was not denied an opportunity to seek judicial review of Act 257.

c. While the Supreme Court denied certiorari in *Chevron USA, Inc. v. Cayetano* (above), it heard a similar challenge to the same statute four years later in *Lingle v. Chevron, U.S.A.*, 544 U.S. 528 (2005). There, the claim was that regulations that devalue property can be constitutional only when they substantially advance a legitimate state interest – an argument that failed and thereby changed the formula for attacking regulatory takings. Justice O'Connor wrote:

> We hold that the "substantially advances" formula is not a valid takings test, and indeed conclude that it has no proper place in our takings jurisprudence. In so doing, we reaffirm that a plaintiff seeking to challenge a government regulation as an uncompensated taking of private property may proceed . . . by alleging a "physical" taking, a *Lucas*-type "total regulatory taking" [*Lucas v. South Carolina Coastal Council*, 505 U.S. 1003 (1992)], a *Penn Central* taking [*Penn Central Transport Co. v. New York*, 438 U.S. 104 (1978)], or a land-use exaction violating the standards set forth in *Nollan* and *Dolan* [*Nollan v. California Coastal Commission*, 483 U.S. 825 (1987), and *Dolan v. City of Tigard*, 512 U.S. 374 (1994)]. Because Chevron argued only a "substantially advances" theory in support of its takings claim, it was not entitled to summary judgment on that claim.

d. As to compulsory rent control or stabilization (the regulatory hope of lessees including many, many law students), the case law is encouraging – assuming such a program exists in a particular locale. In *Federal Home Loan Mortgage Corp. (FHLMC) v. New York State Division of Housing & Community Renewal, 83 F.3d 45 (2d Cir. 1996)*, the court held that the case law does not

> support the view that application of the Rent Stabilization Law constitutes a regulatory taking. *See Keystone Bituminous Coal Assoc. v. DeBenedictis, 480 U.S. 470, 485 (1987).* Rent stabilization does not deprive FHLMC of economically viable use of the property. Although FHLMC will not profit as much as it would under a market-based system, it may still rent apartments and collect the regulated rents. *See Bowles v. Willingham, 321 U.S. at 517; Park Ave. Tower Assocs. v. City of New York, 746 F.2d 135, 139-40 (2d Cir. 1984),* cert. denied, *470 U.S. 1087 (1985)* (regulation may not preclude property owner "from realizing any profit whatsoever" but owner is not guaranteed "reasonable return" on investment); *Rent Stabilization Ass'n v. Dinkins, 805 F. Supp. 159, 163 (S.D.N.Y. 1992) (rent control does not constitute regulatory taking simply because it denies owners reasonable return on property), aff'd 5 F.3d 591 (2d Cir. 1993);* cf. *Higgins, 83 N.Y.2d at 173* (where owner's right to receive regulated rents is not impaired, regulation expanding the definition of "protected family members" for noneviction purposes does not deprive owners of all economically beneficial uses of their property).

HECKLER v. CAMPBELL

461 U.S. 458 (1983)

[JUSTICE POWELL] The issue is whether the Secretary of Health and Human Services may rely on published medical-vocational guidelines to determine a claimant's right to Social Security disability benefits.

I.

The Social Security Act . . . provides disability benefits only to persons who are unable "to engage in any substantial gainful activity by reason of any medically determinable physical or mental impairment." And it specifies that a person must "not only [be] unable to do his previous work but [must be unable], considering his age, education, and work experience, [to] engage in any other kind of substantial gainful work which exists in the national economy, regardless of whether such work exists in the immediate area in which he lives, or whether a specific job vacancy exists for him, or whether he would be hired if he applied for work."

. . . .

[Prior to 1978 this determination was made individually in each case based in part on expert testimony.] To improve both the uniformity and efficiency of this determination, the Secretary promulgated medical-vocational guidelines as part of the 1978 regulations. These guidelines relieve the Secretary of the need to rely on vocational experts by establishing through rulemaking the types and numbers of jobs that exist in the national economy. They consist of a matrix of the four factors identified by Congress – physical ability, age, education, and work experience – and set forth rules that identify whether jobs requiring specific combinations of these factors exist in significant numbers in the national economy. n.4 Where a claimant's qualifications correspond to the job requirements identified by a rule, the guidelines direct a conclusion as to whether work exists that the claimant could perform. If such work exists, the claimant is not considered disabled.

> n.4 For example, Rule 202.10 provides that a significant number of jobs exist for a person who can perform light work, is closely approaching advanced age, has a limited education but who is literate and can communicate in English, and whose previous work has been unskilled.

II.

In 1979, Carmen Campbell applied for disability benefits because a back condition and hypertension prevented her from continuing her work as a hotel maid. After her application was denied, she requested a hearing de novo before an Administrative Law Judge. He determined that her back problem was not severe enough to find her disabled without further inquiry, and accordingly considered whether she retained the ability to perform either her past work or some less strenuous job. He concluded that even though Campbell's back condition prevented her from returning to her work as a maid, she retained the physical capacity to do light work. In accordance with the regulations, he found that Campbell was 52 years old, that her previous employment consisted of unskilled jobs, and that she had a limited education. He noted that Campbell, who had been born in Panama, experienced difficulty in speaking and writing English. She was able, however, to understand and read English fairly well. Relying on the medical-vocational guidelines, the Administrative Law Judge found that a significant number of jobs existed that a person of Campbell's qualifications could perform. Accordingly, he concluded that she was not disabled.

This determination was upheld by both the Social Security Appeals Council and the District Court . . . . The Court of Appeals for the Second Circuit reversed. . . . The court found that the medical-vocational guidelines did not provide the specific evidence that it previously had required. It explained that in the absence of such a showing, "the claimant is deprived of any real chance to present evidence showing that she cannot in fact perform the types of jobs that are administratively noticed by the guidelines." . . . . We now reverse.

III.

. . . .

A.

The Court of Appeals held that "[by] failing to show suitable available alternative jobs for Ms. Campbell, the Secretary's finding of 'not disabled' is not supported by substantial evidence" . . . and remanded for the Secretary to put into evidence "particular types of jobs suitable to the capabilities of Ms. Campbell." . . . . Accordingly, we think the decision below requires us to consider whether the Secretary may rely on medical-vocational guidelines in appropriate cases.

The Social Security Act directs the Secretary to "adopt reasonable and proper rules and regulations to regulate and provide for the nature and extent of the proofs and evidence and the method of taking and furnishing the same" in disability cases. . . . We do not think that the Secretary's reliance on medical-vocational guidelines is inconsistent with the Social Security Act. It is true that the statutory scheme contemplates that disability hearings will be individualized determinations based on evidence adduced at a hearing. But this does not bar the Secretary from relying on rulemaking to resolve certain classes of issues. The Court has recognized that even where an agency's enabling statute expressly requires it to hold a hearing, the agency may rely on its rulemaking authority to determine issues that do not require case-by-case consideration. A contrary holding would require the agency continually to relitigate issues that may be established fairly and efficiently in a single rulemaking proceeding.

[I]n determining whether a claimant can perform less strenuous work, the Secretary must make two determinations. She must assess each claimant's individual abilities and then determine whether jobs exist that a person having the claimant's qualifications could perform. The first inquiry involves a determination of historic facts, and the regulations properly require the Secretary to make these findings on the basis of evidence adduced at a hearing. We note that the regulations afford claimants ample opportunity both to present evidence relating to their own abilities and to offer evidence that the guidelines do not apply to them. The second inquiry requires the Secretary to determine an issue that is not unique to each claimant – the types and numbers of jobs that exist in the national economy. This type of general factual issue may be resolved as fairly through rulemaking as by introducing the testimony of vocational experts at each disability hearing.

As the Secretary has argued, the use of published guidelines brings with it a uniformity that previously had been perceived as lacking. To require the Secretary to relitigate the existence of jobs in the national economy at each hearing would hinder needlessly an already overburdened agency. We conclude that the Secretary's use of medical-vocational guidelines does not conflict with the statute, nor can we say on the record before us that they are arbitrary and capricious.

. . . .

IV.

. . . Accordingly, the judgment of the Court of Appeals is Reversed.

Underlying Case Documents

The case referenced:
The 1978 regulations including medical-vocational guidelines
The decision of the Administrative Law Judge
The decision of the Appeals Council

1. The post-*Heckler* grid cases demonstrate the difficulties in bypassing the conventional presentation of fact, substituting predetermined conclusions. In *Sykes v. Apfel*, the court sets forth some of the different perspectives focused just on exertional and nonexertional impairments.

Sykes v. Apfel, 228 F.3d 259 (3d Cir. 2000).

After suffering several job-related injuries, Sykes filed for Disability . . . . The Commissioner . . . found Sykes to be not disabled within the meaning of the Social Security Act. Sykes then requested a hearing before an Administrative Law Judge ("ALJ"). The ALJ concluded that Sykes had several severe impairments, at least one of which (left-eye blindness) is a nonexertional impairment under the regulations. The ALJ nevertheless denied Sykes's application. Applying the medical-vocational guidelines "as a framework" (and without referring to a vocational expert or other evidence), the ALJ concluded that Sykes's exertional impairments left him able to perform light work, and that the exclusion of jobs requiring binocular vision from light work positions in consideration of his nonexertional impairment did not significantly compromise Sykes's broad occupational base under the guidelines. . . .

There is . . . considerable variety among the courts of appeals regarding . . . the use of the grids when a claimant has exertional and nonexertional impairments. . . . The Commissioner frequently relies on vocational expert testimony [but,] as we have held, the Commissioner can rely on evidence other than vocational expert testimony to establish that a claimant's nonexertional limitation does not diminish residual functional capacity. Moreover, we read *Heckler v. Campbell*, to leave open the question whether the Commissioner could formally notice a fact such as that the loss of binocular vision does not significantly erode the job base for light work, giving the claimant the opportunity to respond to the fact to be noticed.

> The flaw in the government's argument is simple. Campbell permits the government to establish through a rulemaking rather than an individualized fact-finding the fact that there are jobs in the economy for claimants with particular types of impairments. But it does not permit the government to avoid its burden to establish this fact. To hold otherwise would be to eviscerate the requirement that disability hearings will be individualized determinations based on evidence adduced at a hearing. . . . The Commissioner cannot establish that there are jobs in the national economy that Sykes can perform by relying on the grids alone, even if he uses the grids only as a framework instead of to direct a finding of no disability. . . .

2. Contrast the above case with _Barnhart v. Thomas_, 540 U.S. 20 (2003), in which the Supreme Court affirmed the denial of disability benefits based on a perceived – and arguably questionable – assumption. *Barnhart*, like *Campbell v. Heckler* asserts that the size of the Social Security system justifies procedural shortcuts, including basing decisions on conclusions that are both of great consequence – and not adduced by direct testimony. "The need for efficiency is self-evident. . . ."

When the need for efficiency is coupled (as it is in *Heckler*) with the fact that "agencies with statutory enforcement responsibilities enjoy broad discretion in allocating investigative and enforcement resources . . ." the ability to challenge a streamlined adjudicatory process is somewhat constrained. *Compare* _Magnola Metallurgy, Inc. v. United States_, 464 F. Supp. 2d 1376 (Ct. Intl. Trade 2006), _aff'd, Magnola Metallurgy, Inc. v. United States_, 508 F.3d 1349 (Fed. Cir. 2007), *with* _Anderson v. United States Sec'y of Agric._, 469 F. Supp. 2d 1300 (Ct. Intl. Trade 2006), _aff'd, Anderson v. United States Sec'y of Agric._, 469 F. Supp. 2d 1300 (Ct. Int'l Trade 2007) (expressing a somewhat more skeptical perspective on the practice of either ignoring or refusing to admit evidence).

3. Determining the availability of benefits based on a grid developed in a prior rulemaking has become the norm. If the grid criteria matches the claimant's circumstances, the caselaw follows *Heckler*. There are options, however. In _Hoopai v. Astrue_, 499 F.3d 1071, 1075-76 (9th Cir. 2007), the court explained that

> [w]hen the grids match the claimant's qualifications, "the guidelines direct a conclusion as to whether work exists that the claimant could perform." When the grids do not match the claimant's qualifications, the ALJ can either (1) use the grids as a framework and make a determination of what work exists that the claimant can perform . . . or (2) rely on a vocational expert when the claimant has significant nonexertional limitations. _Desrosiers v. Secretary of Health & Human Services._, 846 F.2d 573, 577 (9th Cir. 1988).

The *Hoopai* court also address the oft-litigated question of the circumstances that would justify permitting the claimant to present expert testimony to show that the variables in the grid are not applicable. The court found that "a vocational expert is required only when there are significant and 'sufficiently severe' nonexertional limitations not accounted for in the grid." On the other hand

> [i]f the claimant suffers from nonexertional impairments or a combination of exertional and nonexertional impairments, then the Commissioner must rely on a vocational expert to establish that suitable jobs exist in the economy. Therefore, before applying the grids, it must be determined whether nonexertional factors, such as mental illness, significantly affect a claimant's RFC [residual functional capacity]. <u>Woods v. Barnhart, 458 F. Supp. 2d 336, 352 (S.D. Tex. 2006)</u>.

Why the hesitancy to permit expert testimony?

4. What is the virtue in a system that claims to adjudicate individually but resolves cases mechanistically? In <u>Banks v. Gonzales, 453 F.3d 449, 454-55 (7th Cir. 2006)</u>, the court was faced with a situation in which asylum claims were handled individually – and as a result inconsistently. The court's resolution was to urge the government to consider the benefits of uniformity inherent in the decisional system upheld in *Campbell v. Heckler*:

> The immigration system's consideration of asylum claims today is in much the situation as the Social Security disability system before the introduction of vocational experts. It relies on hearing officers to do the work of both creating rules (for there is no equivalent to the Grid) and supplying analysis (for there is no equivalent to the vocational expert). That requires entirely too much of a lawyer who should be a neutral adjudicator rather than a rulemaker and expert rolled together.
>
> Many disputes about asylum are recurring and could be resolved once and for all by the Secretary of Homeland Security, the Attorney General, and their delegates. . . . [Asylum r]egulation 1208.13(b)(2)(iii) cries out for systemic decisions. . . . [The parties in this case suffer from similar circumstances and] should have been treated the same way. . . . Many asylum claims . . . could be handled by the sort of detailed regulations that the Social Security Administration uses. Others, of the kind that arise less frequently, could be resolved with the assistance of country specialists along the lines of vocational experts. What cannot continue, however, is administrative refusal to take a stand on recurring questions, coupled with the reliance on IJs to fill in for the expertise missing from the record. The immigration bureaucracy has much to learn from the experience of other federal agencies that handle large numbers of comparable claims with individual variations.

5. Shortly after the *Heckler* decision, there was reason to question the fairness of this end-run around the normal adjudicatory process. *See* Mark S. Smith, Heckler v. Campbell *and the Grid: Are Disability Claimants Entitled to Examples of Suitable Jobs?*, 9 AM. J.L. & MED. 501 (1984); John J. Capowski, <u>Accuracy and Consistency in Categorical Decision-Making: A Study of Social Security's Medical-Vocational Guidelines – Two Birds with One Stone or Pigeon-Holing Claimants?, 42 MD. L. REV. 329 (1983)</u>. More recently, the process has not been front and center in the discourse regarding disability. *See, e.g.*, Frank S. Block, <u>Symposium, Social Security in Transi-</u>

tion: Medical Proof, Social Policy, and Social Security's Medically Centered Definition of Disability, 92 Cornell L. Rev. 189 (2007).

6. The following case presents a separate question: What is the interrelationship of state remedies and federal administrative remedies when both are available?

Lujan v. G & G Fire Sprinklers, Inc.

532 U.S. 189 (2001)

[Chief Justice Rehnquist] Petitioners are the California Division of Labor Standards Enforcement (DLSE) . . . and several state officials in their official capacities. Respondent G & G Fire Sprinklers, Inc. (G & G) is a fire-protection company that installs fire sprinkler systems. G & G served as a subcontractor on several California public works projects. . . . The California Labor Code requires that contractors and subcontractors on such projects pay their workers a prevailing wage that is determined by the State. At the time relevant here, if workers were not paid the prevailing wage, the contractor was required to pay each worker the difference between the prevailing wage and the wages paid, in addition to forfeiting a penalty to the State. The awarding body [for a public works contract] was required to include a clause in the contract so stipulating.

The Labor Code provides that "before making payments to the contractor . . . the awarding body shall withhold and retain therefrom all wages and penalties which have been forfeited pursuant to any stipulation in a contract for public work, and the terms of this chapter." If money is withheld from a contractor because of a subcontractor's failure to comply with the Code's provisions, "it shall be lawful for [the] contractor to withhold from [the] subcontractor under him sufficient sums to cover any penalties withheld."

The Labor Code permits the contractor, or his assignee, to bring suit against the awarding body "on the contract . . ." to recover the wages or penalties withheld. The suit must be brought within 90 days of completion of the contract and acceptance of the job. Such a suit "is the exclusive remedy of the contractor or his or her assignees." The awarding body retains the wages and penalties "pending the outcome of the suit." . . . . G & G sued petitioners . . . claiming that the issuance of withholding notices without a hearing constituted a deprivation of property without due process of law in violation of the Fourteenth Amendment. The District Court granted respondent's motion for summary judgment . . . . [T]he Ninth Circuit affirmed. The court concluded that . . . because subcontractors were "afforded neither a pre- nor post-deprivation hearing when payments [were] withheld," the statutory scheme violated the Due Process Clause of the Fourteenth Amendment.

. . . .

Where a state law such as this is challenged on due process grounds, we inquire whether the State has deprived the claimant of a protected property interest, and whether the State's procedures comport with due process. We assume, without deciding, that the withholding of money due respondent under its contracts occurred under color of state law, and that, as the Court of Appeals concluded, respondent has a property interest . . . in its claim for payment under its contracts. Because we believe that California law affords respondent sufficient opportunity to pursue that claim in state court, we conclude that the California statutory scheme does not deprive G & G of its claim for payment without due process of law.

. . . .

[R]espondent has not been denied any present entitlement. . . . G & G has only a claim that it [complied with the contract] terms and therefore that it is entitled to be paid in full. Though we assume for purposes of decision here that G & G has a property interest in its claim for payment, it is an interest . . . that can be fully protected by an ordinary breach-of-contract suit. In *Cafeteria & Restaurant Workers v. McElroy*, we said ". . . . '"Due process," unlike some legal rules, is not a technical conception with a fixed content unrelated to time, place and circumstances.' It is 'compounded of history, reason, the past course of decisions . . . .'" We hold that if California makes ordinary judicial process available to respondent for resolving its contractual dispute, that process is due process.

The California Labor Code provides that "the contractor or his or her assignee" may sue the awarding body "on the contract for alleged breach thereof" for "the recovery of wages or penalties." There is no basis here to conclude that the contractor would refuse to assign the right of suit to its subcontractor. In fact, respondent stated at oral argument that it has sued awarding bodies in state superior court pursuant to . . . the Labor Code to recover payments withheld on previous projects where it served as a subcontractor. Presumably, respondent brought suit as an assignee of the contractors on those projects, as the Code requires. Thus, the Labor Code, by allowing assignment, provides a means by which a subcontractor may bring a claim for breach of contract to recover wages and penalties withheld.

Respondent complains that a suit under the Labor Code is inadequate because the awarding body retains the wages and penalties "pending the outcome of the suit," which may last several years. A lawsuit of that duration, while undoubtedly something of a hardship, cannot be said to deprive respondent of its claim for payment under the contract. Lawsuits are not known for expeditiously resolving claims, and the standard practice in breach-of-contract suits is to award damages, if appropriate, only at the conclusion of the case.

. . . .

. . . As the party challenging the statutory withholding scheme, respondent bears the burden of demonstrating its unconstitutionality. We therefore conclude that the relevant provisions of the California Labor Code do not deprive respondent of property without due process of law. Accordingly, the judgment of the Court of Appeals is reversed. . . .

————————————

1. The principles in *Lujan* are of consequence not only in terms of remedy but also in terms of access to the courts for judicial review of agency action for adjudicatory decisions. In <u>Suburban Mortgage v. HUD, 480 F.3d 1116 (Fed. Cir. 2007)</u>, the federal government (HUD) insured a mortgage issued by Suburban Mortgage to a nursing home. When the borrower defaulted, the government refused to "accept assignment" of the debt. The mortgage company brought an "APA" suit for breach of contract and damages against HUD. On appeal, the court found as follows:

> We have considered the . . . arguments raised by Suburban, including its argument that it has been denied due process and that that alone entitles it to APA review in the district court. We agree with the Government that a claim that a government agency has violated a party's right to due process by refusing performance under a contract is substantively indistinguishable from a breach of contract claim. The process to which plaintiff is due on these facts is a post-deprivation suit for breach of the contract. *See Lujan v. G&G Fire Sprinklers Inc.* . . . Because an adequate remedy is available under the <u>Tucker Act</u> in the Court of Federal Claims, this case cannot proceed in the district court under the APA.

a. The <u>Tucker Act</u>, mentioned above, provides the Court of Federal Claims jurisdiction to "render judgment upon any claim against the United States founded either upon the Constitution, or any Act of Congress or any regulation of an executive department, or upon any express or implied contract with the United States, or for liquidated or unliquidated damages in cases not sounding in tort." <u>28 U.S.C. § 1491(a)(1)</u>. The jurisdiction is exclusive unless Congress has designated another forum for the resolution of claims. The <u>Little Tucker Act, 28 U.S.C. § 1346(a)(2)</u>, gives the Court of Federal Claims, as well as district courts, jurisdiction for "federal small claims" involving amounts under $10,000.

b. Also mentioned above is the specter of an "APA cause-of-action." There were many purposes underlying the adoption of the APA – including standardizing (to an extent) agency practice and facilitating judicial review of agency action – but probably not creating an independent basis for lawsuits for money damages in contract. Even assuming that might have been a purpose of the APA, until 1976, the government claimed sovereign immunity (successfully), a practice made considerably more difficult after the APA was amended to waive that defense. 5 U.S.C. §§ 701-706, amended by Pub. L. No. 94-574, 90 Stat. 2721 (1976). Those amendments, coupled with federal question (28 U.S.C. § 1331) jurisdiction – which is likely to exist since most of these cases involve a federal agency – give the district courts power to hear APA based claims for civil damages.

In 1988, *Bowen v. Massachusetts*, 487 U.S. 879 (1988), affirmed the idea of an APA claim, but did little to clarify the actual expanse of the jurisdiction of the district courts, the relationship of APA cases to the Tucker Act, and similar matters of some importance. Commentators in the field have not been kind to *Bowen* and have urged the Court to overrule the case – or at least give meaningful guidance in the field. Gregory C. Sisk, *The Tapestry Unravels: Statutory Waivers of Sovereign Immunity and Money Claims Against the United States*, 71 GEO. WASH. L. REV. 602, 707 (2003).

One matter seems on the way to resolution: Claims for money damages for breach of contract are relegated to the Claims Court under the Tucker Act – not the district court. Claims for injunctive relief or other exercises of equitable power are matters for the district courts. Further development of these problems is detailed nicely in *Suburban Mortg. Assocs. v. United States HUD*, noted above.

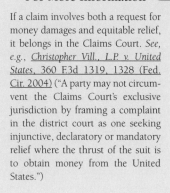

For More Information

If a claim involves both a request for money damages and equitable relief, it belongs in the Claims Court. *See, e.g.*, *Christopher Vill., L.P. v. United States*, 360 F.3d 1319, 1328 (Fed. Cir. 2004) ("A party may not circumvent the Claims Court's exclusive jurisdiction by framing a complaint in the district court as one seeking injunctive, declaratory or mandatory relief where the thrust of the suit is to obtain money from the United States.")

2. The Mystery of Present Entitlement.

a. In *Baird v. Board of Education for Warren Cmty. Unit Sch. Dist. No. 205*, 389 F.3d 685 (7th Cir. Ill. 2004), Baird, a school superintendent, brought suit alleging breach of contract and a violation of due process after he was fired in the first year of a three year contract. Prior to his dismissal, the Board amassed insulting and negative comments directed at Baird – but did not conduct a hearing. At a post-termination hearing, Baird appeared only to protest the breach of contract, raise a due process claim, and get the names of those who had besmirched him, but the Board refused to disclose the authors of the offending comments. Thereafter, Baird filed a § 1983 action for violation of his due process interests and a claim for breach of contract.

> The issue . . . is whether a post-termination lawsuit for breach of contract can remedy the full due process deficiency in the pre-termination proceedings. *Lujan v. G&G Fire*

Sprinklers, Inc., is the leading Supreme Court case addressing this question. With respect to *Lujan*, the question of when a judicial remedy like this provides adequate post-termination due process, as the district court found, is elusive. A fine line distinguishes factual scenarios in which a judicial remedy for breach of contract is adequate from those in which it is not. Not all injuries are equal, and not all parties can be made whole through a breach of contract action. The somewhat obscure quality that separates one from the other is important and yet eludes precise definition. The Supreme Court has referred to this mysterious element as a "present entitlement," and identifies cases involving this factor as ones in which "the claimant was denied a right by virtue of which he was *presently entitled* either to exercise ownership dominion over real or personal property, or to pursue a gainful occupation." *Lujan*. . . .

A *present entitlement* is immediately distinguishable from the contractual interests dealt with in *Lujan* and its progeny. In *Lujan*, the . . . Supreme Court characterized the subcontractor's interest as merely a contractual interest . . . protected through a breach of contract suit. . . . The post-deprivation remedies appropriate to the deprivation of an interest to which there is a present entitlement are characterized by promptness and by the ability to restore the claimant to possession. The underlying concept seems to be that the remedy is available before the loss has become complete and irrevocable.

A state law breach of contract action is not an adequate post-termination remedy for a terminated employee who possesses a present entitlement and who has been afforded only a limited pre-termination hearing. While it does provide a species of due process, a lawsuit does not satisfy the requirement of promptness, which is essential if the employee is to pursue time-sensitive remedies such as reinstatement. While there is no specific time frame within which a hearing must be held to qualify as "prompt," lack of a speedy resolution to proceedings may result in a denial of due process. *Loudermill*. . . . Similarly, while there is no automatic right to reinstatement, it is "normally an integral part of the remedy for a constitutionally impermissible employment action." . . . . Further, as the Sixth Circuit has noted, "employment, especially in a career such as education, is more than a way to make money; it is a profession with significant non-monetary rewards," and consequently money damages may be a "hollow victory." Thus, when a public employee terminated for cause has a present entitlement, and when the only available post-termination remedy is the opportunity to bring a state breach of contract suit, the pre-termination hearing to which such an employee is entitled must fully satisfy the due process requirements of confrontation and cross-examination in addition to the minimal *Loudermill* requirements of notice and an opportunity to be heard.

After reviewing the facts of this case, we conclude that Baird has established his present entitlement. Baird's interest is distinguishable from those in *Lujan* and its progeny; he was terminated in the first year of a three-year contract, and had a protected property interest in remaining in office under his contract for its full term and in being compensated accordingly. Baird's present entitlement also meant that he was entitled to pursue reinstatement promptly if his rights had been violated. Accordingly, the Board was obligated to provide a pre-termination hearing that fully complied with due process. This it failed to do.

b. In <u>*DeBoer v. Pennington*, 287 F.3d 748, 750 (9th Cir. 2002)</u>, the Ninth Circuit held that "[t]he common law breach of contract claim provides adequate process for the deprivation of a property right derived from a contract, unless the deprivation constitutes a denial of a present entitlement." A "present entitlement," the court noted, involves the right to possess presently personal or real property or pursue gainful employment, "a greater interest than the contract itself."

3. Can you think of a circumstance where a breach of contract does give rise to a constitutional deprivation? What if the underlying basis for the breach involves racial animus? What if the underlying basis for the breach involves age or gender considerations that violate federal statutes? "It is well established that a simple breach of contract does not rise to the level of a constitutional deprivation." *Dover Elevator Co. v. Ark. State Univ., 64 F.3d 442, 446 (8th Cir. 1995)* (quoting *Medical Laundry Serv. v. Board of Trustees of Univ. of Ala., 906 F.2d 571, 573 (11th Cir. 1990)*). Do you agree? See *Scott v. Bd. of Comm'rs of the County of Los Alamos, 785 P.2d 221, 223 (1989)* on the adequacy of state court contract remedies for a breach of contract coupled with a due process claim.

What about a state court tort remedy? Will a post-deprivation tort action satisfy an apparent procedural due process claim? *See Parratt v. Taylor, 451 U.S. 527 (1981)*.

2. Intervening – How Open Is the Agency Door?

In the first part of this book, we discuss at some length the question of standing to challenge rules or regulations promulgated by an agency in court. In the cases that follow, we explore a more fundamental problem: When does a party have standing to intervene in an agency adjudication? Are the general rules for standing used in Article III courts the same as those used by administrative agencies?

While agencies unquestionably have broader standards for intervention allowing more members of the public to participate than would be the case in a court of general jurisdiction, there are limits on public participation in order to make it possible for agencies to make decisions at all. The cases that follow explore these standards and limits.

OFFICE OF COMMUNICATION OF THE UNITED CHURCH OF CHRIST V. FEDERAL COMMUNICATIONS COMMISSION

359 F.2d 994 (D.C. Cir. 1966)

[JUDGE BURGER] This is an appeal from a decision of the Federal Communications Commission granting to the Intervenor a one-year renewal of its license to operate television station WLBT in Jackson, Mississippi. Appellants [United Church of Christ] filed with the Commission a timely petition to intervene to present evidence and arguments opposing the renewal application. The Commission dismissed Appellants' petition and, without a hearing, took the unusual step of [limiting] the license to one year . . . and impos[ing] what it characterizes . . . as "strict conditions" on WLBT's operations in that one-year probationary period.

. . . .

Background

The complaints against Intervenor embrace charges of discrimination on racial and religious grounds . . . . As the Commission's order indicates, the first complaints go back to 1955 when it was claimed that WLBT had deliberately cut off a network program about race relations problems on which the General Counsel of the NAACP was appearing and had flashed on the viewers' screens a "Sorry, Cable Trouble" sign. In 1957 another complaint was made to the Commission that WLBT had presented a program urging the maintenance of racial segregation and had refused requests for time to present the opposing viewpoint. Since then numerous other complaints have been made. When WLBT sought a renewal of its license in 1958, the Commission at first deferred action because of complaints of this character but eventually granted the usual three-year renewal because it found that, while there had been failures . . . the failures were isolated instances . . . and did not warrant denial of WLBT's renewal application.

Shortly after the outbreak of prolonged civil disturbances . . . in September 1962, the Commission again received complaints that various . . . stations, including WLBT, had presented programs concerning racial integration in which only one viewpoint was aired. In 1963 the Commission investigated and requested the stations to submit detailed factual reports on their programs dealing with racial issues. On March 3, 1964, while the Commission was considering WLBT's responses, WLBT filed the license renewal application presently under review.

To block license renewal, Appellants filed a petition in the Commission urging denial of WLBT's application and asking to intervene in their own behalf and as representatives of "all other television viewers in the State of Mississippi." The petition stated that the Office of Communication of the United Church of Christ is an instrumentality of the United Church of Christ, a national denomination with substantial membership within WLBT's prime service area. It listed Appellants Henry and Smith as individual residents of Mississippi . . .; both are described as leaders in Mississippi civic and civil rights groups. Dr. Henry is president of the Mississsppi NAACP. . . . The petition claimed that WLBT failed to serve the general public because it . . . did not give a fair and balanced presentation of controversial issues, especially those concerning Negroes, who comprise almost forty-five per cent of the total population within its prime service area; it also claimed discrimination against local activities of the Catholic Church. . . . The Commission denied the petition to intervene on the ground that . . . "petitioners . . . can assert no greater interest or claim of injury than members of the general public." The Commission stated in its denial, however, that as a general practice it "does consider the contentions advanced in circumstances such as these . . . and argues that it did so in this proceeding."

. . . .

Appellants contend that, against the background of complaints since 1955 and the Commission's conclusion that WLBT was in fact guilty of "discriminatory programming," the Commission could not properly renew the license even for one year without a hearing to resolve factual issues raised by their petition and vitally important to the public. The Commission argues, however, that it in effect accepted Petitioners' view of the facts, took all necessary steps to insure that the practices complained of would cease, and for this reason granted a short-term renewal . . . . [But the] Commission seems to have based [this decision] on a blend of what the Appellants alleged, what its own investigation revealed, its hope that WLBT would improve, and its view that the station was needed.

The Commission's denial of standing to Appellants was based on the theory that . . . the only types of effects sufficient to support standing are economic injury and electrical interference. It asserted its traditional position that members of the listening public do not suffer any injury peculiar to them and that allowing them standing would pose great administrative burdens. . . . What the Commission apparently fails to see in the present case is that the courts have resolved questions of standing as they arose . . . . [Although] some Congressional reports have expressed . . . that standing should not be accorded lightly[,] the recurring theme in the legislative reports is not so much fear of a plethora of parties in interest as apprehension that standing might be abused by persons with no *legitimate* interest in the proceedings but with a desire only to delay the granting of a license for some private selfish reason. The Congressional Committee which voiced the apprehension of a "host of parties" seemingly was willing to allow standing to anyone who could show economic injury or electrical interference. Yet these criteria are no guarantee of the legitimacy of the claim sought to be advanced . . . .

. . . .

The Commission's rigid adherence to a requirement of direct economic injury . . . denies standing to spokesmen for the listeners, who are most directly concerned with and intimately affected by the performance of a licensee. Since the concept of standing is a practical and functional one designed to insure that only those with a genuine and legitimate interest can participate in a proceeding, we can see no reason to exclude those with such an obvious and acute concern as the listening audience. This much seems essential to insure that the holders of broadcasting licenses be responsive to the needs of the audience, without which the broadcaster could not exist.

. . . .

The theory that the Commission can always effectively represent the listener interests in a renewal proceeding without the aid and participation of legitimate listener representatives fulfilling the role of private attorneys general is . . . no longer a valid assumption . . . . The gradual expansion and evolution of concepts of standing in administrative law attests that experience rather than logic or fixed rules has been accepted as the guide. . . . We cannot believe that the Congressional mandate of public participation . . . was meant to be limited to . . . the Commission's grace in considering listener claims . . . . [T]he long history of complaints against WLBT beginning in 1955 had left the Commission virtually unmoved in the subsequent renewal proceedings, and it seems not unlikely that the 1964 renewal application might well have been routinely granted except for the determined and sustained efforts of Appellants at no small expense to themselves. . . .

. . . .

We [understand that] regulatory agencies, the Federal Communications Commission in particular, would ill serve the public interest if the courts imposed such heavy burdens on them as to overtax their capacities. The competing consideration is that experience demonstrates consumers are generally among the best vindicators of the public interest. In order to safeguard the public interest in broadcasting, therefore, we hold that some "audience participation" must be allowed in license renewal proceedings . . . but it does not necessarily follow that "hosts" of protestors must be granted standing to challenge a renewal application or that the Commission need allow the administrative processes to be obstructed or overwhelmed by captious or purely obstructive protests. . . . Although [the Commission] denied Appellants standing, it employed ad hoc criteria in determining that these Appellants were responsible spokesmen for representative groups having significant roots in the listening community. These criteria can afford a basis for developing formalized standards to regulate and limit public intervention to spokesmen who can be helpful. A petition for such intervention must "contain specific allegations of fact sufficient to show that the petitioner is a party in interest and that a grant of the application would be prima facie inconsistent" with the public interest. 47 U.S.C. 309(d)(1) (1964).

The responsible and representative groups eligible to intervene cannot here be enumerated or categorized specifically; such community organizations as civic associations, professional societies, unions, churches, and educational institutions or associations might well be helpful to the Commission. These groups . . . usually concern themselves with a wide range of community problems and tend to be representatives of broad . . ., public . . . interests. The Commission should be accorded broad discretion in establishing and applying rules for such public participation . . . . The usefulness of any particular petitioner for intervention must be judged in relation to other petitioners and the nature of the claims it asserts as [a] basis for standing. Moreover it is no novelty in the administrative process to require consolidation of petitions and briefs to avoid multiplicity of parties and duplication of effort.

The fears of regulatory agencies that their processes will be inundated by expansion of standing criteria are rarely borne out. . . . [L]egal and related expenses of administrative proceedings are such that even those with large economic interests find the costs burdensome. Moreover, the listening public seeking intervention in a license renewal proceeding cannot attract lawyers to represent their cause by the prospect of lucrative contingent fees, as can be done, for example, in rate cases. We are aware that there may be efforts to exploit the enlargement of intervention . . . . But this problem, as we have noted, can be dealt with by the Commission under its inherent powers and by rulemaking. In line with this analysis, we do not now hold that all of the Appellants have standing to challenge WLBT's renewal. We do not reach that question. As to these Appellants we limit ourselves to holding that the Commission must allow standing to one or more of them as responsible representatives to assert and prove the claims they have urged in their petition.

Underlying Case Documents

The case referenced:
The decision of the Commission

For additional background on the push to integrate television in the South click HERE.

1. Standing to intervene in a judicial proceeding, and intervention in agency adjudicatory proceedings raise some similar questions.

Rainbow/PUSH Coalition v. Federal Communications Commission, 330 F.3d 539 (D.C. Cir. 2003).

> Rainbow/PUSH Coalition petitioned the Federal Communications Commission to deny certain applications to transfer control of television broadcasting licenses. The Commission, having determined that some of Rainbow's objections relating to the licensees' prior dealings had merit, imposed forfeitures upon the licensees but nevertheless granted their applications without holding a hearing. We hold that Rainbow lacks standing to appeal that decision. . . .

It was perfectly clear in [*United Church of Christ*] that the appellants would be injured, and substantially so, by the Commission's grant of the renewal license. The appellants had complained that "Negro individuals and institutions are given very much less television exposure than others are given and that programs are generally disrespectful toward Negroes." This allegation was "particularized and accompanied by a detailed presentation of the results of Appellants' monitoring of a typical week's programming." . . . . In short, the appellants' proffer demonstrated that the Commission's renewal of the license would adversely affect them.

Rainbow has not made a comparable showing. . . . In its initial brief Rainbow stated broadly that it "is an organization committed to furthering social, racial, and economic justice" and that it "seeks to ensure that professional opportunities in broadcasting expand for minorities and that communities have access to diverse broadcasting sources." . . . . [In] two declarations in the record compiled before the agency . . . the declarant alleges she is a Rainbow member and a "regular viewer" of either KOKH or KRRT. Each declarant also alleges that if the relevant application were granted, then "members of Rainbow/PUSH, including myself, would be deprived of job opportunities and program service in the public interest." These statements do not establish the declarants' standing. They merely identify rather than document two potential types of injury: loss of "job opportunities" and deprivation of "program service in the public interest." Rainbow's briefs say nothing at all about job opportunities, and therefore neither shall we. Rainbow's real claim of injury goes to the alleged deprivation of "program service in the public interest," but that claim is not sufficiently "concrete and particularized" to pass constitutional muster.

2. *United Church of Christ* works well as a foundation to assess intervention before administrative agencies. It is less workable as a basis to argue standing in an Article III court, as the following note cases suggests. <u>Fund Democracy, LLC v. Securities and Exchange Commission, 278 F.3d 21 (D.C. Cir. 2002)</u>.

Fund Democracy argues that it has standing because it is an "interested person" for purposes of Rule 270.0-5, which allows "interested persons" to request a hearing on an application. That petitioner is an "interested person" is a most tenuous proposition. But, even assuming that Fund Democracy is an "interested person" under the rule and therefore eligible to participate in the SEC proceedings, this does not mean that Fund Democracy has Article III standing. Participation in agency proceedings is alone insufficient to satisfy judicial standing requirements. Because agencies are not constrained by Article III, they may permit persons to intervene in the agency proceedings who would not have standing to seek judicial review of the agency action. For this reason, we agree with the Second Circuit which has expressly rejected the argument that an individual's status as an "interested person" is sufficient to confer standing to petition for review of an SEC order under the Act. . . . [On review, the court upheld the agency action.]

3. Compulsory agency participation and <u>28 U.S.C. § 2348</u>. As the note case above points out, there is a considerable difference between the standard for intervention at the agency level and the standard for standing to intervene in a district court or court of appeals. There is also a very real and important relationship between intervention at the agency level and in an Article III court.

We urge you to read carefully the following section of the United States Code, 28 U.S.C. § 2348.

Representation in proceeding; intervention

> The Attorney General is responsible for and has control of the interests of the Government in all court proceedings under this chapter [28 U.S.C. §§ 2341 et seq.]. *The agency, and any party in interest in the proceeding before the agency whose interests will be affected if an order of the agency is or is not enjoined, set aside, or suspended, may appear as parties thereto of their own motion and as of right, and be represented by counsel in any proceeding to review the order.* Communities, associations, corporations, firms, and individuals, whose interests are affected by the order of the agency, may intervene in any proceeding to review the order. The Attorney General may not dispose of or discontinue the proceeding to review over the objection of any party or intervenor, but any intervenor may prosecute, defend, or continue the proceeding unaffected by the action or inaction of the Attorney General. [Emphasis added.]

Does this mean that intervention at the agency is compulsory? If one hopes to intervene "as a matter of right," the terms of Section 2348 are of consequence. In *Alabama Power Co. v. FCC, 311 F.3d 1357 (11th Cir. 2002)*, the Eleventh Circuit was explicit: "Under 28 U.S.C. § 2348, only parties to the agency proceeding can intervene as of right, while intervention by a nonparty is discretionary."

Consider the following disposition from *Commodity Carriers, Inc. v. Fed. Motor Carrier Safety Admin, 434 F.3d 604 (D.C. Cir. 2006)*.

> Under the Hobbs Act, a petition for review of a Federal Motor Carrier Safety Administration order requires that the one seeking review be a "party aggrieved." 28 U.S.C. § 2348. As that term has been uniformly interpreted, a party aggrieved *must have been a party to the agency proceeding under review.* See *Alabama Power Co. v. ICC, 852 F.2d 1361, 1367 (D.C. Cir. 1988).* . . . Because petitioner . . . did not participate before the agency [in the underlying proceeding] it is not a party aggrieved and therefore must be dismissed. [Emphasis added.]

Why would there be a requirement for agency participation? Isn't Article III standing a matter for the courts to decide? By failing to participate in the agency proceeding, a party will not be able to add to the record or evaluate administrative remedies that might have made judicial review unnecessary. *See Rio Grande Pipeline Co. v. FERC, 178 F.3d 533 (D.C. Cir. 1999); and* Note, *Federal Courts – Intervention – D.C. Circuit Holds That Article III Standing Is a Prerequisite to Intervention Under 28 U.S.C. 2348 –* Rio Grande Pipeline Co. v. FERC, 113 HARV. L. REV. 1557 (2000).

4. Standing before an agency is not necessarily broader than in an Article III court.

Envirocare of Utah, Inc. v. Nuclear Regulatory Commission, 194 F.3d 72 (D.C. Cir. 1999).

Envirocare was the first commercial facility in the nation the Commission licensed to dispose of certain radioactive by-product material from offsite sources. . . . In the late 1990s, the Commission granted the applications of two [new] companies. . . . In both licensing proceedings . . . Envirocare requested a hearing and sought leave to intervene . . . . Envirocare's basic complaint was "that the license amendment permits [the company] to become a general commercial facility like Envirocare, but . . . the NRC did not require [the company] to meet the same regulatory standards the agency imposed upon Envirocare when Envirocare sought its license to become a commercial disposal facility for" radioactive waste. The Licensing Board rejected Envirocare's requests . . . in both cases . . . . [In one case] the Commission ruled that Envirocare did not come within the following "standing" provision in the Atomic Energy Act: when . . . granting or amending . . . a license, "the Commission shall grant a hearing upon the request of any person whose interest may be affected by the proceeding, and shall admit any such person as a party to such proceeding." . . . .

The Commission . . . is not an Article III court and thus is not bound to follow the law of standing derived from the "case or controversy" requirement. . . . Whether the Commission erred in excluding Envirocare from participating . . . therefore turns not on judicial decisions dealing with standing to sue, but on familiar principles of administrative law regarding an agency's interpretation of the statutes it alone administers. Chevron. . . . Because we cannot be confident of what kinds of interests the 1954 Congress meant to recognize . . . because, in other words, the statute is ambiguous – the Commission's interpretation of this provision must be sustained if it is reasonable. We think it is. For one thing, excluding competitors who allege only economic injury from the class of persons entitled to intervene in licensing proceedings is consistent with the Atomic Energy Act. The Act meant to increase private competition in the industry, not limit it. . . . Allowing new competitors to enter the market strengthens competition. Permitting current license holders to initiate hearings for the purpose of imposing burdens on potential competitors does the opposite. . . .

5. Agency adjudicatory proceedings can become unmanageable if there are too many participants, including parties before the agency and intervenors. Presumably, most agencies will exercise some level of control to ensure that those who are designated as parties and intervenors have some meaningful and arguably personal stake in the proceedings, can contribute to the proceedings in ways that are different than the parties before the agency, have no other ready remedial opportunity, or other good reason to participate.

As noted above, nonparticipation could, in some instances, be problematic. That said, there are cost factors to be considered for individuals and groups of modest means. Representation by experienced, competent counsel is often vital to public interest groups – and expensive – and a cost that may have to be borne both at the agency level and in court. Even if a client has limited resources and believes the dispositive determination will not occur until the parties are in court, there may be no choice but to engage in the agency process.

CHAPTER 7

Judicial Review of Facts, Law, and Agency Policy in Adjudication

I. The Exhaustion Requirement

Exhaustion of administrative remedies is a perfectly logical doctrine. Agencies were set up to handle an enormous range, variety, and number of situations and (in our opinion), when given sufficient resources, do so effectively and efficiently. Permitting contested matters to move prematurely to the strained dockets of Article III courts makes little sense. The argument is straightforward: Agencies should first be given the opportunity to implement the legislation entrusted to them, apply their expertise, maintain some level of continuity, resolve (when possible) the dispute avoiding the need to go to court, and provide a forum for those who will not be able to meet the more demanding standing requirements in the court system. Courts should be – and are – hesitant to hear a case that is within the jurisdiction of an agency, particularly when the record at the agency is underdeveloped and there are more "facts to be found."

On the other hand, there are circumstances where spending any more time and money at an agency is unreasonable because the agency is mired in delay, has a long history of rejecting similar claims, or demonstrates bias against an interest or individual. If staying at an agency ends up subjecting one to criminal liability or produces an irreparable limitation on speech (e.g., a case gets bogged down at the FCC or FEC as an election approaches), then compelling exhaustion seems unjust.

Given the wisdom of requiring exhaustion – and the periodic need to get into court directly – should exhaustion be considered a jurisdictional requirement? Should it instead be considered part of the "prudential" considerations involved in deciding who can have access to the court and under what circumstances?

McCARTHY v. MADIGAN

503 U.S. 140 (1992)

[JUSTICE BLACKMUN] The issue in this case is whether a federal prisoner must resort to the internal grievance procedure promulgated by the Federal Bureau of Prisons before he may initiate a suit, pursuant to the authority of *Bivens v. Six Unknown Fed. Narcotics Agents*, 403 U.S. 388 (1971), solely for money damages. . . .

While he was a prisoner in the federal penitentiary at Leavenworth, petitioner John J. McCarthy filed a pro se complaint in the United States District Court for the District of Kansas against four prison employees: the hospital administrator, the chief psychologist, another psychologist, and a physician. McCarthy alleged that respondents had violated his constitutional rights under the Eighth Amendment by their deliberate indifference to his needs and medical condition resulting from a back operation and a history of psychiatric problems. On the first page of his complaint, he wrote: "This Complaint seeks Money Damages Only."

The District Court dismissed the complaint on the ground that petitioner had failed to exhaust prison administrative remedies. Under 28 C.F.R. Part 542 (1991), setting forth the general "Administrative Remedy Procedure for Inmates" at federal correctional institutions, a prisoner may "seek formal review of a complaint which relates to any aspect of his imprisonment. . . ."

The doctrine of exhaustion of administrative remedies is one among related doctrines – including abstention, finality, and ripeness – that govern the timing of federal-court decisionmaking. Of "paramount importance" to any exhaustion inquiry is congressional intent. Where Congress specifically mandates, exhaustion is required. But where Congress has not clearly required exhaustion, sound judicial discretion governs. Nevertheless, even in this field of judicial discretion, appropriate deference to Congress' power to prescribe the basic procedural scheme under which a claim may be heard in a federal court requires fashioning of exhaustion principles in a manner consistent with congressional intent and any applicable statutory scheme.

[T]he exhaustion doctrine recognizes the notion, grounded in deference to Congress' delegation of authority to coordinate branches of Government, that agencies, not the courts, ought to have primary responsibility for the programs that Congress has charged them to administer. Exhaustion concerns apply with particular force when the action under review involves exercise of the agency's discretionary power or when the agency proceedings in question allow the agency to apply its special expertise. The exhaustion doctrine also acknowledges the commonsense notion of dispute resolution that an agency ought to have an opportunity to correct its own mistakes with respect to the programs it administers before it is haled into federal court. Correlatively, exhaustion principles apply with special force when "frequent and deliberate flouting of administrative processes" could weaken an agency's effectiveness by encouraging disregard of its procedures.

As to the second of the purposes, exhaustion promotes judicial efficiency in at least two ways. When an agency has the opportunity to correct its own errors, a judicial controversy may well be mooted, or at least piecemeal appeals may be avoided. And even where a controversy survives administrative review, exhaustion of the administrative procedure may produce a useful record for subsequent judicial consideration, especially in a complex or technical factual context.

This Court's precedents have recognized at least three broad sets of circumstances in which the interests of the individual weigh heavily against requiring administrative exhaustion. First, requiring resort to the administrative remedy may occasion undue prejudice to subsequent assertion of a court action. . . . Second, an administrative remedy may be inadequate "because of some doubt as to whether the agency was empowered to grant effective relief. . . ." Third, an administrative remedy may be inadequate where the administrative body is shown to be biased or has otherwise predetermined the issue before it. . . .

In light of these general principles, we conclude that petitioner McCarthy need not have exhausted his constitutional claim for money damages. . . .

. . . To be sure, the Bureau has a substantial interest in encouraging internal resolution of grievances and in preventing the undermining of its authority by unnecessary resort by prisoners to the federal courts. But other institutional concerns relevant to exhaustion analysis appear to weigh in hardly at all. The Bureau's alleged failure to render medical care implicates only tangentially its authority to carry out the control and management of the federal prisons. Furthermore, the Bureau does not bring to bear any special expertise on the type of issue presented for resolution here.

. . . No formal factfindings are made [and] the grievance procedure does not create a formal factual record of the type that can be relied on conclusively by a court for disposition of a prisoner's claim on the pleadings or at summary judgment without the aid of affidavits. . . . The judgment of the Court of Appeals is reversed.

Underlying Case Documents

The case referenced:

Bivens v. Six Unknown Fed. Narcotics Agents

The pro se complaint

28 C.F.R. Part 542

1. In *Booth v. Churner*, 532 U.S. 731 (2001), an inmate filed a 42 U.S.C. § 1983 claim seeking money damages for alleged mistreatment. He contended he was physically abused and denied medical care. He filed an administrative grievance that was unsuccessful and, rather than appealing administratively as the statute directed, he sought judicial relief. He argued (correctly) that the administrative system could not provide the requested remedy – money damages – raising the question whether remedies must be exhausted if the agency cannot provide the remedy sought.

> In the aftermath of the Prison Litigation Reform Act of 1995, 42 U.S.C. § 1997e(a) provides that "no action shall be brought with respect to prison conditions under section 1983 of this title, or any other Federal law, by a prisoner confined in any jail, prison, or other correctional facility until such administrative remedies as are available are exhausted."

> The meaning of the phrase "administrative remedies . . . available" is the crux of the case. . . . The dispute . . . comes down to whether or not a remedial scheme is "available" where . . . the administrative process has authority to take some action in response to a complaint, but not the remedial action an inmate demands. . . .

> When Congress replaced the text of the statute as construed in *McCarthy* with the exhaustion requirement at issue today, it presumably understood that under *McCarthy*, the term "effective" in the former § 1997e(a) eliminated the possibility of requiring exhaustion of administrative remedies when an inmate sought only monetary relief and the administrative process offered none. It has to be significant that Congress removed the very term we had previously emphasized in reaching the result. . . . [The] fair inference to be drawn is that Congress meant to preclude the *McCarthy* result. Congress's imposition of an obviously broader exhaustion requirement makes it highly implausible that it meant to give prisoners a strong inducement to skip the administrative process simply by limiting prayers for relief to money damages not offered through administrative grievance mechanisms. . . . Thus, we think that Congress has mandated exhaustion clearly enough, regardless of the relief offered through administrative procedures. . . . Here, we hold only that Congress has provided in § 1997e(a) that an inmate must exhaust irrespective of the forms of relief sought and offered through administrative avenues. . . .

2. There is a general rule: Unlike standing, exhaustion is not automatically a constitutionally driven jurisdictional requirement – though Congress may mandate, by statute, that a party exhaust all administrative remedies before going to court, as note 1, above, suggests. Furthermore, Congress may actually limit exhaustion explicitly. *Patsy v. Board of Regents*, 457 U.S. 496 (1982). The scholarship in the field is expansive and valuable. *See* Colin Miller, *"Manifest" Destiny?: How Some Courts Have Fallaciously Come to Require a Greater Showing of Congressional Intent for Jurisdictional Exhaustion Than They Require for Preemption*, 2008 B.Y.U. L. Rev. 169 (2008); Robin L. Dull, *Understanding Proper Exhaustion: Using the Special-Circumstances Test to Fill the Gaps Under* Woodford v. Ngo *and Provide Incentives for Effective Prison Grievance Procedures*, 92 Iowa L. Rev. 1929 (2007); Charles Donefer, Note, Sarei v. Rio Tinto *and the Possibility of Reading an Exhaustion Requirement*

<u>*into the Alien Tort Claims Act*</u>, 6 Nw. U. J. Int'l Hum. Rts. 155 (2007); Eugene Novikov, Comment, <u>*Tacking the Deck: Futility and the Exhaustion Provision of the Prison Litigation Reform Act*</u>, 156 U. Pa. L. Rev. 817 (2008).

3. <u>*Jones v. Zenk*, 495 F. Supp. 2d 1289, 1298-1300 (N.D. Ga. 2007)</u>, is a habeas case where the court was again required to assess whether exhaustion was compelled by statute pursuant to <u>28 U.S.C. § 2241</u>. Finding the matter not mandated by law, meaning the decision on exhaustion was discretionary, the court focused on the futility exception. There was little question that the factual basis to claim futility existed – the issue was the extent to which the magistrate could make a purely discretionary determination on futility. The court noted that in the Eleventh Circuit, one group of cases suggests that "[t]he current state of the law in this Circuit does not leave room for this Court to engraft a futility

> **Key Concept**
>
> "Prudential" exhaustion, as the term implies, involves discretion. The criteria vary, but the following are a good start. Prudential exhaustion is advisable when "(1) agency expertise makes agency consideration necessary to generate a proper record and reach a proper decision; (2) relaxation of the requirement would encourage the deliberate bypass of the administrative scheme; and (3) administrative review is likely to allow the agency to correct its own mistakes and to preclude the need for judicial review." <u>*El Rescate Legal Servs., Inc. v. Executive Office of Immigration Review*, 959 F.2d 742, 747 (9th Cir. 1991)</u>.

exception onto the requirement that § 2241 petitioners exhaust administrative remedies," while another group holds that "exhaustion of administrative remedies is prudential and not mandatory. . . ." The resolution of this intra-circuit conflict was direct:

> The Eleventh Circuit has held, however, that a prisoner seeking habeas relief pursuant to § 2241 is subject to a judicially-imposed [meaning discretionary, prudential, or nonstatutory] administrative-exhaustion requirement. . . . Petitioner claims that he should be excused from "tilting at the administrative windmills" . . . because the adoption of <u>28 C.F.R. § 570.21(a)</u> makes clear that such an effort would be futile. . . . [citing] *McCarthy v. Madigan*. . . . Delineating the bounds of "sound judicial discretion," the Court noted that "at least three broad sets of circumstances" excused administrative exhaustion: (1) where prejudice to the prisoner's subsequent court action "may result, for example, from an unreasonable or indefinite timeframe for administrative action"; (2) where the administrative agency may not have the authority "to grant effective relief"; or (3) "where the administrative body is shown to be biased or has otherwise predetermined the issue before it." . . . .
>
> More recently, the Supreme Court has stated that [a] party may not be required to exhaust administrative procedures from which there is no possibility of receiving any type of relief. *See* <u>*Booth v. Churner*, 532 U.S. 731, 741 n.6 (2001)</u>. . . .
>
> [The state] counters that such an exception is not available . . . because the Eleventh Circuit has repeatedly referred to the judicial requirement of exhaustion in § 2241

cases as "jurisdictional."

[T]he question whether the Eleventh Circuit considers the exhaustion requirement in § 2241 subject to judicial waiver is, at best, unsettled. . . . But the Eleventh Circuit's occasional labeling of the § 2241 exhaustion requirement as "jurisdictional" does not, in this Court's view, resolve the question of whether judicial waiver is ever available in § 2241 cases. . . . Thus, while courts have often described statutorily imposed exhaustion requirements as jurisdictional, and judicially imposed exhaustion requirements as prudential, both requirements concern a court's exercise of jurisdiction. The important difference, as explained in *McCarthy*, is that the failure to comply with the statutory exhaustion requirement precludes jurisdiction, whereas failure to exhaust a judicially-imposed requirement counsels the Court to decline jurisdiction except in its "sound judicial discretion."

What is more, any doubt left by *McCarthy* . . . has been resolved by the Supreme Court's recent opinion in *Bowles v. Russell*, 551 U.S. 205 (2007). There, the Court determined that the deadlines for filing a federal notice of appeal were mandatory and jurisdictional because they were statutorily, and not judicially, imposed; thus, no exceptions, such as waiver or equitable tolling, could apply. . . . The Court reasoned that, under Article III, Section 1 of the Constitution, "[o]nly Congress may determine a lower federal court's subject-matter jurisdiction" and thus "it was improper for courts to use the term 'jurisdictional' to describe [judicially imposed] time prescriptions in rules of court."

The exhaustion requirement imposed in § 2241 cases has judicial, and not statutory, underpinnings. . . . Because the exhaustion requirement is judicially fashioned, a court has discretion to waive the requirement in its "sound judicial discretion." Thus, the exceptions recognized in *McCarthy*, including the futility exception, apply to the exhaustion requirement in § 2241 cases.

In sum, the Court concludes that, although the Eleventh Circuit has occasionally labeled the exhaustion requirement in § 2241 cases as "jurisdictional," it has not uprooted the exhaustion requirement from its judicial, and thus, prudential foundation.

4. Would the same reasoning used in *Jones v. Zenk* for a habeas case be applicable to immigration cases?

Zhong v. United States Department of Justice, 480 F.3d 104 (2d Cir. 2007).

The principal issue in this case concerns whether the mandatory requirement of issue exhaustion in asylum cases is also jurisdictional. The Supreme Court . . . recently cautioned lower federal courts against conflating mandatory with jurisdictional prerequisites to review. We take the Court's caveat to heart. . . . The use of "jurisdictional" language in [previous] cases . . ., none of which expressly considered the question of whether the Attorney General might waive an argument as to issue exhaustion, cannot, without more, be held to govern cases in which the government has failed to raise an exhaustion argument. Today we hold (a) that 8 U.S.C. § 1252(d)(1) does not make issue exhaustion a statutory jurisdictional requirement (b) that as a result, a failure to exhaust specific issues may be waived by the Attorney General (c) that in the case before us such a waiver occurred, and (d) that, therefore, in our discretion we may choose to review Lin's arguments not previously made to the [Board of Immigration Appeals (BIA)].

Our conclusion in this regard rests primarily on the language of § 1252(d)(1), which, as the Eighth Circuit has noted, does not expressly proscribe judicial review of issues not raised in the course of exhausting all administrative remedies. In contrast, as the Supreme Court observed in *Sims*, Congress has, in other contexts, expressly written issue exhaustion requirements into statutes. . . . [Also in *Sims*,] the Supreme Court . . . said that it is "not necessarily" the case that "an issue-exhaustion requirement is 'an important corollary' of any requirement of exhaustion of remedies." Moreover, the High Court has also suggested that the same distinction applied to exhaustion requirements for federal habeas review. . . .

We are persuaded, both on the language of § 1252(d)(1) and [from other cases], that the exhaustion of "all administrative remedies available to [an] alien as of right" under 8 U.S.C. § 1252(d)(1) does not require – as a statutory matter – that a petitioner for relief from removal raise to the BIA each issue presented in his or her petition for judicial review. Therefore, in the context of 8 U.S.C. § 1252(d)(1), the failure to exhaust individual issues before the BIA does not deprive this court of subject matter jurisdiction to consider those issues.

That conclusion does not mean, however, that petitioners seeking review of their removal orders are ordinarily excused from issue exhaustion. Quite the contrary. Usually, the requirement of § 1252(d)(1) that federal courts review only "final orders of removal" has the effect of imposing a bar to the review of issues not raised to the BIA. That requirement has been read by us, by the Supreme Court, and by other circuits to mean that when the BIA issues an opinion in a petitioner's administrative appeal, and that opinion constitutes the final agency determination, we may consider only those issues that formed the basis for that decision. It follows that, when an applicant for asylum or withholding of removal has failed to exhaust an issue before the BIA, and that issue is, therefore, not addressed in a reasoned BIA decision, we are, by virtue of the "final order" requirement of § 1252(d)(1), usually unable to review the argument.

But such is not the case when, as here, the BIA order is not the agency determination we review. When the BIA invokes its summary affirmance authority pursuant to its streamlining regulations, the decision of the [Immigration Judge] constitutes the "final agency determination" and the entirety of that decision – containing both issues that were and issues that were not raised to the BIA – is before us on review. . . .

5. How is exhaustion different from finality? Finality requires the decision in question to be the "consummation" of the agency's process, producing consequences that are binding on the agency and the parties. It exists, in part, for all the reasons set out in the brief introduction to this section and in *McCarthy*. The classical decision conflating finality and exhaustion is *Myers v. Bethlehem Shipbuilding Corp.*, 303 U.S. 41 (1938), in which the Court valued the fact-finding function of agencies and the notion that if parties are compelled to conclude agency options, they may well find a resolution that avoids the necessity of any judicial action.

———

DARBY V. CISNEROS

509 U.S. 137 (1993)

[JUSTICE BLACKMUN] This case presents the question whether federal courts have the authority to require that a plaintiff exhaust available administrative remedies before seeking judicial review under the Administrative Procedure Act (APA), 5 U.S.C. § 701 et seq., where neither the statute nor agency rules specifically mandate exhaustion as a prerequisite to judicial review. At issue is the relationship between the judicially created doctrine of exhaustion of administrative remedies and the statutory requirements of § 10(c) of the APA. n.1

> n.1 Section 10(c), 80 Stat. 392-393, 5 U.S.C. § 704, provides:
>
> Agency action made reviewable by statute and final agency action for which there is no other adequate remedy in a court are subject to judicial review. A preliminary, procedural, or intermediate agency action or ruling not directly reviewable is subject to review on the review of the final agency action. Except as otherwise expressly required by statute, agency action otherwise final is final for the purposes of this section whether or not there has been presented or determined an application for a declaratory order, for any form of reconsideration, or, unless the agency otherwise requires by rule and provides that the action meanwhile is inoperative, for an appeal to superior agency authority. . . .

I.

Petitioner R. Gordon Darby is a self-employed South Carolina real estate developer who specializes in the development and management of multifamily rental projects. . . . Darby obtained financing for three separate multiunit projects [and] single-family mortgage insurance from HUD. Although Darby successfully rented the units, a combination of low rents, falling interest rates, and a generally depressed rental market forced him into default in 1988. HUD became responsible for the payment of over $6.6 million in insurance claims. HUD . . . initiated an audit [and] concluded that [Darby] had done [nothing] wrong . . . . Nevertheless, in June 1989, HUD issued a limited denial of participation (LDP) . . . for one year [and proposed] to debar [Darby and others] from further participation in all HUD procurement contracts and in any nonprocurement transaction with any federal agency.

[Darby's] appeals of the LDP and of the proposed debarment were consolidated, and an Administrative Law Judge (ALJ) conducted a hearing on the consolidated appeals in December 1989. The judge issued an "Initial Decision and Order" in April 1990, finding that the financing method used by petitioners was a sham[, but that Darby] lacked criminal intent, and . . . genuinely "cooperated with HUD to try [to] work out his financial dilemma and avoid foreclosure." In light of these mitigating factors, the ALJ concluded that an indefinite debarment would be punitive and that it would serve no legitimate purpose . . . . [Darby saw this as final and took no additional action at that point although there were sanctions beyond debarment imposed.]

. . . .

On May 31, 1990, [Darby] filed suit in . . . District Court [seeking an] injunction and a declaration that the administrative sanctions were imposed for purposes of punishment, in violation of HUD's own debarment regulations, and therefore were "not in accordance with law" within the meaning of § 10(e)(B)(1) of the APA, 5 U.S.C. § 706 (2)(A). . . . [The District Court found Darby had exhausted his administrative remedies and the case could go forward but the Court of Appeals reversed.]

. . . .

. . . The last sentence of § 10(c) reads:

> Except as otherwise expressly required by statute, agency action otherwise final is final for the purposes of this section whether or not there has been presented or determined an application for a declaratory order, for any form of reconsideration, or, unless the agency otherwise requires by rule and provides that the action meanwhile is inoperative, for an appeal to superior agency authority. 5 U.S.C. § 704.

[Darby] argue[s] that this provision means that a litigant seeking judicial review of a final agency action under the APA need not exhaust available administrative remedies unless such exhaustion is expressly required by statute or agency rule. According to [Darby], since § 10(c) contains an explicit exhaustion provision, federal courts are not free to require further exhaustion as a matter of judicial discretion.

Respondents contend that § 10(c) is concerned solely with timing, that is, when agency actions become "final," and that Congress had no intention to interfere with the courts' ability to impose conditions on the timing of their exercise of jurisdiction to review final agency actions. . . . We have recognized that the judicial doctrine of exhaustion of administrative remedies is conceptually distinct from the doctrine of finality:

> The finality requirement is concerned with whether the initial decisionmaker has arrived at a definitive position on the issue that inflicts an actual, concrete injury; the exhaustion requirement generally refers to administrative and judicial procedures by which an injured party may seek review of an adverse decision and obtain a remedy if the decision is found to be unlawful or otherwise inappropriate.

Whether courts are free to impose an exhaustion requirement as a matter of judicial discretion depends, at least in part, on whether Congress has provided otherwise, for "of 'paramount importance' to any exhaustion inquiry is congressional intent." We therefore must consider whether § 10(c), by providing the conditions under which agency action becomes "final for the purposes of" judicial review, limits the authority of courts to impose additional exhaustion requirements as a prerequisite to judicial review.

It perhaps is surprising that it has taken over 45 years since the passage of the APA for this Court definitively to address this question. . . . [Under § 10(c) when] an aggrieved party has exhausted all administrative remedies expressly prescribed by statute or agency rule, the agency action is "final for the purposes of this section" and therefore "subject to judicial review" . . . . While federal courts may be free to apply, where appropriate, other prudential doctrines of judicial administration to limit the scope and timing of judicial review, § 10(c), by its very terms, has limited the availability of the doctrine of exhaustion of administrative remedies to what the statute or rule clearly mandates.

The last sentence of § 10(c) refers explicitly to "any form of reconsideration" and "an appeal to superior agency authority." Congress clearly was concerned with making the exhaustion requirement unambiguous so that aggrieved parties would know precisely what administrative steps were required before judicial review would be available. If courts were able to impose additional exhaustion requirements beyond those provided by Congress or the agency, the last sentence of § 10(c) would make no sense. To adopt respondents' reading would transform § 10(c) from a provision designed to "remove obstacles to judicial review of agency action," into a trap for unwary litigants. Section 10(c) explicitly requires exhaustion of all intra-agency appeals mandated either by statute or by agency rule; it would be inconsistent with the plain language of § 10(c) for courts to require litigants to exhaust optional appeals as well.

. . . .

The purpose of § 10(c) was to permit agencies to require an appeal to "superior agency authority" before an examiner's initial decision became final. This was necessary because, under § 8(a), initial decisions could become final agency decisions in the absence of an agency appeal. *See* 5 U.S.C. § 557(b). Agencies may avoid the finality of an initial decision, first, by adopting a rule that an agency appeal be taken before judicial review is available, and, second, by providing that the initial decision would be "inoperative" pending appeal. Otherwise, the initial decision becomes final and the aggrieved party is entitled to judicial review. . . . [In this case, neither the statute nor regulation mandates a determination by a superior agency authority.]

. . . .

We noted just last Term in a non-APA case that

> appropriate deference to Congress' power to prescribe the basic procedural scheme
> under which a claim may be heard in a federal court requires fashioning of exhaustion
> principles in a manner consistent with congressional intent and any applicable
> statutory scheme.

Appropriate deference in this case requires the recognition that, with respect
to actions brought under the APA, Congress effectively codified the doctrine of
exhaustion of administrative remedies in § 10(c). Of course, the exhaustion doctrine continues to apply as a matter of judicial discretion in cases not governed
by the APA. But where the APA applies, an appeal to "superior agency authority"
is a prerequisite to judicial review *only* when expressly required by statute or
when an agency rule requires appeal before review and the administrative action
is made inoperative pending that review. Courts are not free to impose an exhaustion requirement as a rule of judicial administration where the agency action has
already become "final" under § 10(c).

The judgment of the Court of Appeals is reversed, and the case is remanded
for further proceedings consistent with this opinion.

Underlying Case Documents

The case referenced:
The HUD initial decision and order

For more information on Darby Development Co. click HERE.

1. *Darby* begins with a simple premise: Administrative exhaustion is a prerequisite
to judicial review if "expressly required by statute or . . . agency rule." Where there
is no statute or rule, exhaustion is not required.

Should an agency be able to make so important a decision by rule? Consider
the reasoning in <u>Dismas</u>, *supra* Chapter 3. If the only question before the agency
involves the meaning of a legal premise, *Dismas* holds that there is little to be
gained from the notice and comment process. A federal district court recently
repeated that theme regarding certain rules issues by the Bureau of Prisons in
<u>Ahmed v. AG of United States, 2007 WL 397045 (N.D. Ohio 2007)</u>.

> [A] change in BOP policy regarding placement of federal offenders . . . based on a legal interpretation that the statute limited BOP's authority was an "interpretive rule" and, as such, was not subject to notice and comment rulemaking under the APA.

Add to that the respect due under *Skidmore* and it would appear that the power of the agency to determine the necessity of exhaustion may be unchecked in certain circumstances.

2. The APA requires a party to exhaust only those administrative remedies that are made mandatory by a statute or agency rule. 5 U.S.C. § 704 (2000) ("Except as otherwise expressly required by statute, agency action otherwise final is final for the purposes of this section whether or not there has been presented or determined an application for a declaratory order, for any form of reconsideration, or, unless the agency otherwise requires by rule and provides that the action meanwhile is inoperative, for an appeal to superior agency authority."). *Darby* affirms this concept finding the APA "has limited the availability of the doctrine of exhaustion of administrative remedies to that which the statute or rule clearly mandates." Where an appeal is optional, the APA does not require a plaintiff to exhaust that remedy before seeking judicial review of the agency's decision. *Bangura v. Hansen*, 434 F.3d 487, 498 (6th Cir. 2006). Moreover, the Sixth Circuit has gone further and stated that not only is an APA plaintiff not required to exhaust administrative remedies not required by statute, but also that courts do not have the discretion to require such exhaustion. *See Dixie Fuel Co. v. Comm'r of Soc. Sec.*, 171 F.3d 1052, 1059 (6th Cir. 1999), *and Town of Smyrna v. United States Army Corps of Eng'rs*, 517 F. Supp. 2d 1026 (M.D. TN 2007).

3. At the risk of stating the obvious, exhaustion – where required – is about more than concluding a matter and receiving a "final order," the general end product of agency adjudication. It includes the administrative appellate process as well, mandating exhaustion of intra-agency appeals, where compelled by statute or agency rule. In the absence of a rule or statute, "it would be inconsistent with the plain language of [§ 704] for courts to require litigants to exhaust optional appeals as well." *See Aleutian Pribilof Islands Ass'n, Inc. v. Kempthorne*, 537 F. Supp. 2d 1, 8 (D.D.C. 2008). The matter of statutory interpretation, then, is central to exhaustion – and many of the various canons of construction are twisted by litigants to achieve the desired result, perhaps due to the Court's unhelpful language in *Weinberger v. Salfi*, 422 U.S. 749 (1975). There the Court found "[s]weeping and direct statutory language indicating that there is no federal jurisdiction prior to exhaustion. . . ." Without putting too fine an edge on it, the qualifier "sweeping and direct" is not particularly useful.

4. Cases involving the Individuals with Disabilities Education Act have often focused on exhaustion issues. Dissatisfied with decisions made by schools after initial hearings, the impulse to "go to court" is strong as the following note case

demonstrates. <u>McQueen v. Colorado Springs School District No. 11, 488 F.3d 868</u>
<u>(10th Cir. 2007)</u>.

Joshua McQueen, formerly a student in Colorado Springs School District Number
11 (the District), suffers from autism. Under the <u>Individuals with Disabilities</u>
<u>Education Act (IDEA), 20 U.S.C. §§ 1400-1482</u>, he is entitled to a free appropriate
public education [FAPE]. Joshua, through his parents, claims that the District's policy
limiting extended-school-year (ESY) services (provided during the summer) to
maintenance of previously learned skills violates the IDEA because such services must
be designed to meet the unique need of autistic children for continual development
of new skills. . . .

[Joshua's parents filed an administrative complaint with the school system, contesting
the allegedly restrictive ESY policy. However, rather] than continue to an evidentiary
hearing, Joshua's parents . . . filed on his behalf a complaint in the United States
District Court for the District of Colorado [asking] the court to rule that the District's
ESY policy violates the IDEA and then remand to the hearing officer (1) to determine
how much to reimburse Joshua's parents for costs and expenses incurred by them in
providing ESY services to Joshua over the summer of 2003, [and] (2) to determine
what compensatory educational services should be provided to Joshua. . . .

Before bringing suit under the IDEA, Joshua and his parents had to exhaust their
administrative remedies. *See* <u>Cudjoe ex rel. Cudjoe v. Indep. Sch. Dist. No. 12, 297 F.3d</u>
<u>1058 (10th Cir. 2002)</u>. "As part of the bargain of providing children with educational
rights and parents with procedural safeguards to protect those rights, Congress
required that parents turn first to the [IDEA's] administrative framework to resolve any
conflicts they had with the school's educational services." Requiring administrative
exhaustion of IDEA claims advances several objectives:

> (1) permitting the exercise of agency discretion and expertise on issues
> requiring these characteristics;

> (2) allowing the full development of technical issues and a factual record
> prior to court review;

> (3) preventing deliberate disregard and circumvention of agency procedures
> established by Congress; and

> (4) avoiding unnecessary judicial decisions by giving the agency the first
> opportunity to correct any error.

. . . . Section 1415 grants the right to present to the school district a complaint
"with respect to any matter relating to the identification, evaluation, or educational
placement of [a child with a disability], or the provision of a [FAPE] to such child."
. . . . The complaint, if not settled through mediation . . . is resolved through an
impartial due-process hearing . . . . Either party may appeal the hearing officer's
decision to the state educational agency . . . . Only after the state agency has issued
its decision may a party bring "a civil action with respect to the complaint" in state
or federal court.

[However], as noted by the hearing officer, still to be decided was "whether [Joshua's individualized education program (IEP)] as implemented during the school year or extended school year provided a [FAPE]." We see no barrier to an "interlocutory appeal" within the administrative process, as occurred in this case; but the IDEA does not provide for judicial review of such an interlocutory determination before resolution of the entire administrative complaint. Accordingly, we hold that Joshua has not fully exhausted the administrative remedies available under § 1415.

5. A similar set of issues arose in <u>Munsell v. Department of Agriculture, 509 F.3d 572 (D.C. Cir. 2007)</u>.

Montana Quality Foods [MQF] filed a lawsuit . . . against the Department of Agriculture . . . and Nathaniel Clark, . . . the District Office Manager of United States Department of Agriculture's (USDA) Food Safety and Inspection Service (FSIS) . . . . [Munsell] claimed that FSIS officials used . . . enforcement powers to retaliate against Munsell for statements he made concerning USDA's handling of an E. coli outbreak in 2002. . . .

Congress enacted the <u>Federal Meat Inspection Act</u> in 1907 in response to unsanitary conditions in the nation's meat packing industry. . . . [The program is now overseen by USDA, and more specifically the FSIS, which inspects and approves meat processing plants.]

Munsell's family first started operating a meat processing plant in Montana in 1946. . . . For a time preceding the events leading to this litigation, Munsell had been displeased with USDA's oversight of MQF's meat processing operation. In September 2001, he urged agency officials to adopt two procedural changes[:] the segregation of large plant meat products and the creation of a record of source beef to facilitate the traceback of adulterated meat . . . . FSIS officials declined to adopt Munsell's recommendations.

Roughly five months later, on January 28, 2002, FSIS alerted Munsell that a ground beef sample taken from MQF's facilities five days prior tested positive for E. coli contamination. Munsell voluntarily agreed to recall 270 pounds of ground beef . . . . Two days later, Munsell asked FSIS officials to test unopened chubs of beef[, but] FSIS officials declined . . . . Munsell . . . complained to . . . Clark, the District Office Manager . . . of the FSIS, about how FSIS was handling the E. coli outbreak [and] requested FSIS officials to test an unopened chub [from ConAgra, but] FSIS officials refused. . . .

Munsell also communicated with congressional officials concerning his own plant and his fears of an E. coli threat at a large meat processor. . . . [The complaints to members of Congress allegedly upset FSIS officials and] Munsell alleges that [thereafter] FSIS inspectors . . . took retaliatory action against him. . . .

On June 30, 2002, ConAgra announced a recall of 350,000 pounds of contaminated beef. . . . On October 13, 2004, Munsell and MQF filed suit in the District Court [seeking] injunctive [relief] and [damages] against . . . District Manager Clark, under a <u>Bivens</u> theory of liability [<u>Bivens v. Six Unknown Named Agents of Federal Bureau of Narcotics, 403 U.S. 388 (1971)</u>].

FSIS actions are indisputably subject to review under the APA. 5 U.S.C. §§ 702, 704. . . . "When an aggrieved party [seeking judicial review under the APA] has exhausted all administrative remedies expressly prescribed by statute or agency rule, the agency action is final . . . and therefore subject to judicial review." The question here is whether Congress' enactment of 7 U.S.C. § 6912(e) imposes a jurisdictional or nonjurisdictional prerequisite to Munsell/MQF's and AAMP's actions and, in either event, whether appellants satisfied the prescribed exhaustion requirements. . . 7 U.S.C. § 6912(e) — states: "Notwithstanding any other provision of law, a person shall exhaust all administrative appeal procedures established by the Secretary or required by law before the person may bring an action in a court . . . ."

For More Information

Bivens v. Six Unknown Named Agents of Federal Bureau of Narcotics, 403 U.S. 388 (1971) recognized a civil cause of action for damages when a person's Fourth Amendment rights were violated by federal officers or agents and no other remedies, administrative or otherwise, were available. For a quick overview of *Bivens,* see Susan Bandes, *Reinventing* Bivens: *The Self-Executing Constitution,* 68 S. Cal. L. Rev. 289, 345-50 (1995); John E. Nordin, II, The *Constitutional Liability of Federal Employees:* Bivens *Claims,* 41 Fed. B. News & J. 342 (1994); Gene R. Nichol, Bivens, Chilicky, *and Constitutional Damages Claims,* 75 Va. L. Rev. 1117 (1989).

[T]here is no doubt that Munsell/MQF were bound by 7 U.S.C. § 6912(e) and therefore subject to the administrative appeals requirement under 9 C.F.R. § 306.5. The only question is whether the statute imposes a jurisdictional requirement which determines subject matter jurisdiction. . . . Under established precedent, we must assume that an exhaustion requirement is nonjurisdictional unless we find "sweeping and direct statutory language indicating that there is no federal jurisdiction prior to exhaustion."

For several reasons, we hold that the exhaustion requirement in the 1994 Reorganization Act is nonjurisdictional. First, it is noteworthy that the language of 7 U.S.C. § 6912(e) is very similar to the statutory exhaustion requirement under the [Prison Litigation Reform Act (PLRA)]. Second, we also find it noteworthy that every other circuit that has directly considered whether the 1994 Reorganization Act creates a jurisdictional exhaustion provision has found that 7 U.S.C. § 6912(e) is nonjurisdictional. We see no reason to part ways with our sister circuits.

In sum, we find that the 1994 Reorganization Act did not create a jurisdictional bar to judicial review of USDA actions. Rather, § 6912(e) establishes a mandatory, but nonjurisdictional, exhaustion requirement. There is no clear, sweeping, or direct language within the 1994 Reorganization Act that would indicate a congressional intent to create a jurisdictional limit on the courts. . . . [A]bsent a clear statement from Congress, exhaustion requirements will be found to be nonjurisdictional. Accordingly, we reverse the decision of the District Court and hold that there is subject matter jurisdiction over this case under 28 U.S.C. § 1331.

The administrative process in this case is not burdensome. . . . Munsell took advantage of that process for his claims that the agency was acting unreasonably by failing to require the traceback of contaminated meat . . . . He did not, however, raise his constitutional claims while pursuing challenges to the enforcement action. . . . Therefore, even assuming that there might be a cognizable *Bivens* action in a case of this sort – a matter that we do not decide – appellants' failure to exhaust their administrative remedies is dispositive. . . . For the foregoing reasons, appellants' actions are hereby dismissed.

II. Judicial Review Standards

In the first part of this book we explored the general question of the deference owed by courts to regulatory determinations made by agencies. As a general rule, after a notice and comment rulemaking, assuming the agency's action is reasonable in analyzing an ambiguity Congress has created in a statute, the decision of the agency will be entitled to deference. In the adjudicatory area, questions of deference become slightly more complex.

The basic standard for judicial review of adjudicatory determinations is "substantial evidence." The Administrative Procedure Act requires that agencies use evidence that is substantial, reliable, and probative. Neither the APA nor the case law requires that courts defer to agencies when their decisions are unreasonable or when they lack support in the record. Furthermore, when courts review adjudicatory determinations, while they are obligated to look carefully at the action of the agency, they may decide that a particular adjudication was not the type in which broad agency policy ought to be articulated. For that reason, the necessity of deferring to the agency is less.

A party who has been "aggrieved" by the action of an agency in an adjudication has a reasonable expectation that judicial review will be provided and that it will be more than a gesture deferring to the agency. The scope and depth of judicial review of adjudicatory determinations is the subject of the cases that follow.

UNIVERSAL CAMERA CORP. V. NATIONAL LABOR RELATIONS BOARD

340 U.S. 474 (1951)

[JUSTICE FRANKFURTER] The essential issue raised by this case . . . is . . . the duty of Courts of Appeals when called upon to review orders of the National Labor Relations Board.

The Court of Appeals for the Second Circuit granted enforcement of an order directing . . . that petitioner reinstate with back pay an employee found to have been discharged because he gave testimony under the Wagner Act and cease and desist from discriminating against any employee who files charges or gives testimony under that Act. . . .

. . . .

The Wagner Act provided: "The findings of the Board as to the facts, if supported by evidence, shall be conclusive." This Court read "evidence" to mean "substantial evidence," and we said that "substantial evidence is more than a mere scintilla. It means such relevant evidence as a reasonable mind might accept as adequate to support a conclusion." . . . . But . . . the phrasing of this Court's process of review readily lent itself to the notion that it was enough that the evidence supporting the Board's result was "substantial" when considered by itself. . . . [This] led to the assumption that the requirements of the Wagner Act were met when the reviewing court could find in the record evidence which, when viewed in isolation, substantiated the Board's findings. . . . [In time protests] against "shocking injustices" and intimations of judicial "abdication" with which some courts granted enforcement of the Board's orders stimulated pressures for legislative relief from alleged administrative excesses.

[An] investigation [was] conducted . . . . The final report of the Attorney General's Committee was submitted in January, 1941. . . . Departure from the "substantial evidence" test, it thought, would either create unnecessary uncertainty or transfer to courts the responsibility for ascertaining and assaying matters the significance of which lies outside judicial competence. Accordingly, it recommended against legislation embodying a general scheme of judicial review. Three members of the Committee registered a dissent. . . . Their view led them to recommend that Congress enact principles of review applicable to all agencies . . . . One of these principles was expressed by the formula that judicial review could extend to "findings, inferences, or conclusions of fact unsupported, upon the whole record, by substantial evidence." . . . . [T]his formula for judicial review found its way into the statute books when Congress . . . enacted the Administrative Procedure Act.

. . . .

Similar dissatisfaction with too restricted application of the "substantial evidence" test is reflected in the legislative history of the Taft-Hartley Act. . . . [A]s the Senate Committee Report relates,

> it was finally decided to conform the statute to the corresponding section of the Administrative Procedure Act where the substantial evidence test prevails. In order to clarify any ambiguity in that statute, however, the committee inserted the words "questions of fact, if supported by substantial evidence *on the record considered as a whole* . . . ."

. . . . Congress has left no room for doubt as to the kind of scrutiny which a Court of Appeals must give the record before the Board to satisfy itself that the

Board's order rests on adequate proof. . . . Whether or not it was ever permissible for courts to determine the substantiality of evidence supporting a Labor Board decision . . . without taking into account contradictory evidence or evidence from which conflicting inferences could be drawn, the new legislation definitively precludes such a theory of review and bars its practice. The substantiality of evidence must take into account whatever in the record fairly detracts from its weight. . . .

To be sure, the requirement for canvassing "the whole record" . . . does [not] mean that . . . a court may displace the Board's choice between two fairly conflicting views, even though the court would justifiably have made a different choice had the matter been before it de novo. Congress has merely made it clear that a reviewing court is not barred from setting aside a Board decision when it cannot conscientiously find that the evidence supporting that decision is substantial, when viewed in the light that the record in its entirety furnishes, including the body of evidence opposed to the Board's view.

. . . .

[C]ourts must now assume more responsibility for the reasonableness and fairness of Labor Board decisions than some courts have shown in the past. Reviewing courts must be influenced by a feeling that they are not to abdicate the conventional judicial function. Congress has imposed on them responsibility for assuring that the Board keeps within reasonable grounds. . . . The Board's findings are entitled to respect; but they must nonetheless be set aside when the record before a Court of Appeals clearly precludes the Board's decision from being justified by a fair estimate of the worth of the testimony of witnesses or its informed judgment on matters within its special competence . . . .

[The court next addressed the question of how to evaluate the findings of the initial hearing examiner. Are those findings accorded special value since the examiner observed "first hand" the testimony of the witnesses, or should the findings of the Board, the final arbiter of the agency, be afforded inherently greater weight.] Section 10(c) of the Labor Management Relations Act provides that "If upon the preponderance of the testimony taken the Board shall be of the opinion that any person named in the complaint has engaged in or is engaging in any such unfair labor practice, then the Board shall state its findings of fact . . . ." The responsibility for decision thus placed on the Board is wholly inconsistent with the notion that it has power to reverse an examiner's findings only when they are "clearly erroneous." . . . . [But the] Attorney General's Committee on Administrative Procedure [states that]

> on matters which the hearing commissioner, having heard the evidence and seen the witnesses, is best qualified to decide, the agency should be reluctant to disturb his findings unless error is clearly shown.

. . . . Nothing in the statutes suggests that the Labor Board should not be influenced by the examiner's opportunity to observe the witnesses he hears and sees and the Board does not. Nothing suggests that reviewing courts should not give to the examiner's report such probative force as it intrinsically commands. . . .

. . . .

We do not require that the examiner's findings be given more weight than in reason and in the light of judicial experience they deserve. The "substantial evidence" standard is not modified in any way when the Board and its examiner disagree. We intend only to recognize that evidence supporting a conclusion may be less substantial when an impartial, experienced examiner who has observed the witnesses and lived with the case has drawn conclusions different from the Board's than when he has reached the same conclusion. The findings of the examiner are to be considered along with the consistency and inherent probability of testimony. . . . To give it this significance does not seem to us materially more difficult than to heed the other factors which in sum determine whether evidence is "substantial."

. . . .

We therefore remand the cause to the Court of Appeals. On reconsideration of the record it should accord the findings of the trial examiner the relevance that they reasonably command in answering the comprehensive question whether the evidence supporting the Board's order is substantial. But the court need not limit its reexamination of the case to the effect of that report on its decision. We leave it free to grant or deny enforcement as it thinks the principles expressed in this opinion dictate.

Underlying Case Documents

The case referenced:

The Wagner Act

The Board's order

The final report of the Attorney General's Committee

For the report of the agency trial examiner click HERE.

1. *Universal Camera* is the bottom line source for generalizations on evidence in adjudicatory proceedings. Notice the language in the APA, (5 U.S.C. § 556(d)), regarding evidence:

> A sanction may not be imposed or [an] order issued except on consideration of the whole record or those parts thereof cited by a party and supported by and in accordance with the reliable, probative, and substantial evidence. . . . A party is entitled to present his case or defense by oral or documentary evidence, to submit rebuttal evidence, and to conduct such cross-examination as may be required for a full and true disclosure of the facts. . . .

The trick is to discern the meaning of substantial evidence – and the starting point is to look at who gets to decide factual matters.

2. The basic premise regarding credibility determinations is somewhat primitive. Can you tell when someone is lying by listening to or looking at them? An accomplished liar may be far more poised than a nervous witness telling the truth. That said, the case law in this area gives a nod in the direction of the initial factfinder. As a rule "[c]redibility determinations are peculiarly the province of the finder of fact, and . . . will not [be] upset . . . when supported by substantial evidence." _Diaz v. Secretary of Health & Human Servs._, 898 F.2d 774, 777 (10th Cir. 1990). This entitles initial factfinders to "special deference" for assessments of credibility. _Williams v. Bowen_, 844 F.2d 748, 755 (10th Cir. 1988).

Good Questions!

What value should be given to assessments of credibility made by those who are present when evidence is presented? Are findings by an ALJ or otherwise-titled hearing officer inviolate? Does the value of these assessments vary according to the nature of the testimony? Is there a difference in the worth of the finding of the initial decisionmaker between technical information and "who, what, where, when" factual testimony? Is there a difference between factfindings based on documentary evidence proffered (and admitted) and oral presentation of information by question and answer?

In _Huston v. Bowen_, 838 F.2d 1125, 1132-33 (10th Cir.1988), the same court cautioned that "an ALJ's findings as to credibility should be closely and affirmatively linked to substantial evidence and not just a conclusion in the guise of findings." So which is it – special deference or close scrutiny?

3. The ALJ appears to be the primary actor, looking at these cases from the standpoint of credibility assessments. The elevated position on ALJ's noted above is reasoned thusly: The ALJ is "optimally positioned to observe and assess witness credibility." _Adams v. Chater_, 93 F.3d 712, 715 (10th Cir. 1996) (quoting _Casias v. Sec'y of Health & Human Servs._, 933 F.2d 799, 801 (10th Cir. 1991)). This perspec-

tive leads directly to the nature of judicial review – a court "may overturn such a credibility determination only when there is a conspicuous absence of credible evidence to support it." *Patterson v. Apfel*, 62 F. Supp. 2d 1212, 1217 (D. Kan. 1999) (citing *Trimiar v. Sullivan*, 966 F.2d 1326, 1329 (10th Cir. 1992)). The court characterizes such findings as "binding" on reviewing courts. *See Talley v. Sullivan*, 908 F.2d 585, 587 (10th Cir. 1990). This concept seems generally accepted – if the decision is "consistent with the law and is supported by substantial evidence," it is "conclusive and it is immaterial that the facts permit the drawing of diverse inferences." *Mikels v. United States Dep't of Labor*, 870 F. 2d 1407, 1409 (8th Cir. 1989). *Hays v. Sullivan*, 907 F.2d 1453, 1456 (4th Cir. 1990), finds that making such conclusive determinations is the "duty" of the initial factfinder. The task of factfinding is vested to the ALJ and is not the province of the courts. *King v. Califano*, 599 F.2d 597, 599 (4th Cir. 1979). The discretion allocated to the ALJ seems vast – including the opportunity (if the ALJ so chooses) to admit almost any kind of evidence proffered including "probative hearsay." *Crawford v. United States Dep't of Agric.*, 50 F.3d 46, 48-50 (D.C. Cir. 1995).

4. In light of the above, what happens to the obligation of courts to take a "hard look" at agency decisions? How can the right to judicial review be meaningful if courts are prevented from studying a record and coming to their own conclusions? The answer, of course, is that judicial review can be penetrating and the above generalizations are a guideline only.

Consider the following from *Environmental Defense Fund v. Ruckelshaus*, 439 F.2d 584, 597-98 (D.C. Cir. 1971):

> We stand on the threshold of a new era in the history of the long and fruitful collaboration of administrative agencies and reviewing courts. For many years, courts have treated administrative policy decisions with great deference . . . with a nod in the direction of the "substantial evidence" test, and a bow to the mysteries of administrative expertise. . . . To protect [fundamental interests] from administrative arbitrariness, it is necessary . . . to insist on strict judicial scrutiny of administrative action.

5. The meaning of "substantial evidence," as a matter of doctrine, is not particularly hard to pin down. Substantial evidence is "enough that [a] reasonable mind might accept it as adequate to support [a] decision." *Pyland v. Apfel*, 149 F.3d 873, 876 (8th Cir. 1998). This is so even if "it is possible to draw two inconsistent conclusions from the evidence." *Bourns, Inc. v. Raychem*, 331 F.3d 704, 714 (9th Cir. 2003). Substantial evidence consists of more than a "mere scintilla" of evidence, may be somewhat less than a preponderance, and ought to be sufficient "to direct a verdict were the case before a jury. . . ." *Laws v. Celebrezze*, 368 F.2d 640, 642 (4th Cir. 1966). The jury parallel is derived from the pre-APA case *NLRB v. Columbian Enameling & Stamping Co.*, 306 U.S. 292, 300 (1939), where the

Court held that the evidence must be "enough to justify, if the trial were to a jury, a refusal to direct a verdict when the conclusion sought to be drawn from it is one of fact for the jury."

6. As *Universal Camera* made clear, the "substantiality of the evidence must be based upon the record taken as a whole." Thus, on review, a court is to look not just at the evidence on which the ALJ, board, or commission relied, but the "whole of the record." *NLRB v. Cal-Maine Farms*, 998 F.2d 1336, 1339 (5th Cir. 1993). This means looking at the "the totality of evidence in the record, including 'that which fairly detracts from the decision.'" *Mikels v. United States Dep't of Labor*, 870 F. 2d 1407, 1409 (8th Cir. 1989); *Garcia v. Califano*, 463 F. Supp. 1098, 1105 (N.D. Ill. 1979).

7. What happens to scientific evidence in an administrative record? Is it treated with the same meta-deference suggested above? Since agencies are free to admit evidence without being confined by the Federal Rules of Evidence, technical evidence becomes the source of some debate. Should ALJ's perform the same gatekeeping role as trial court judges, making sure that the evidence on which they rely is supported by accepted scientific principles? Independently tested? Supported by the literature in peer reviewed journals? This, as you may have guessed, is the *Daubert* debate, which is very much alive in administrative law. *Daubert v. Merrell Dow Pharmaceuticals*, 509 U.S. 579, 593 (1993). In the absence of jurors who presumably are not expert, and in the presence of hearing officers who presumably are, do the limits on scientific evidence in *Daubert* make sense?

In Claire R. Kelly's *The Dangers of* Daubert *Creep in the Regulatory Realm*, 14 J.L. & Pol'y 165, 208 (2006), the author notes:

> It is difficult to have that debate in a meaningful way if regulatory *Daubert* is allowed to creep into the law, operating as shadow authority and installing a new framework. This new framework is less deferential to agencies than the current framework. . . . [A]s it stands now this framework is ill-defined and creates a host of predictable problems, including confusion and abuse. It also promises unique problems because it lacks any administrative law grounding. It is ill-suited to apply across the board to all agencies, it is likely to be used in a rhetorical and meaningless way, and it is likely to be overused, morphed, and stretched to fit any conceivable situation.

For a contrary position focused on the Endangered Species Act, see J. Tavener Holland, Comment, *Regulatory* Daubert: *A Panacea for the Endangered Species Act's "Best Available Science" Mandate?*, 39 McGeorge L. Rev. 299 (2008):

> Regulatory *Daubert* has much to offer the ESA's "best available science" standard. By instituting a new framework for judicial review of the methodologies behind agency science, regulatory *Daubert* will help agencies effect a needed separation between policy and science. . . .

Regulatory *Daubert* can clarify the judicial role in existing administrative law doctrines by providing judges with a familiar framework to assess scientific evidence and by clarifying the protocol and procedure for engaging in searching, "hard look" review, while maintaining appropriate deference to well-defined policy choices. This would have the added benefit of providing some independent significance to the "best available science" standard apart from the APA's "arbitrary and capricious" standard. . . .

While both positions are intriguing, we pose for you only one question: Should agencies be limited to the "best available science"?

NATIONAL LABOR RELATIONS BOARD V. HEARST PUBLICATIONS, INC.

322 U.S. 111 (1944)

[JUSTICE RUTLEDGE] The proceedings before the National Labor Relations Board were begun with the filing of four petitions for investigation and certification by Los Angeles Newsboys Local Industrial Union No. 75. Hearings were held in a consolidated proceeding after which the Board made findings of fact and concluded that the regular full-time newsboys selling each paper were employees within the Act and that questions affecting commerce concerning the representation of employees had arisen. It designated appropriate units and ordered elections. At these the union was selected as their representative by majorities of the eligible newsboys. After the union was appropriately certified the respondents refused to bargain with it. Thereupon proceedings under § 10 were instituted, a hearing was held and respondents were found to have violated §§ 8(1) and 8(5) of the Act. They were ordered to cease and desist from such violations and to bargain collectively with the union upon request.

. . . .

In addition to questioning the sufficiency of the evidence to sustain [the Board's] findings, respondents . . . urge that on the entire record the [newsboys] cannot be considered their employees. They base this conclusion on the argument that by common-law standards the extent of their control and direction of the newsboys' working activities creates no more than an "independent contractor" relationship and that common-law standards determine the "employee" relationship under the Act. They further urge that the Board's selection of a collective bargaining unit is neither appropriate nor supported by substantial evidence.

I.

The principal question is whether the newsboys are "employees." Because Congress did not explicitly define the term, respondents say its meaning must be determined by reference to common-law standards. In their view "common-law standards" are those the courts have applied in distinguishing between "employees" and "independent contractors" when working out various problems unrelated to the Wagner Act's purposes and provisions.

The argument assumes that there is some simple, uniform and easily applicable test . . . . Unfortunately this is not true. . . . Few problems in the law [create more conflict] than the cases arising in the borderland between what is clearly an employer-employee relationship and what is clearly one of independent, entrepreneurial dealing. . . . [W]ithin a single jurisdiction a person who, for instance, is held to be an "independent contractor" for the purpose of imposing vicarious liability in tort may be an "employee" for the purposes of particular legislation, such as unemployment compensation. . . . Persons who might be "employees" in one state would be "independent contractors" in another. . . . Persons working across state lines might fall in one class or the other, possibly both, depending on whether the Board and the courts would be required to give effect to the law of one state or of the adjoining one, or to that of each in relation to the portion of the work done within its borders.

Both the terms and the purposes of the statute, as well as the legislative history, show that Congress had in mind no such patchwork plan for securing freedom of employees' organization and of collective bargaining. The Wagner Act is federal legislation, administered by a national agency, intended to solve a national problem on a national scale. . . .

II.

. . . .

To eliminate the causes of labor disputes and industrial strife, Congress thought it necessary to create a balance of forces in certain types of economic relationships. These do not embrace simply employment associations in which controversies could be limited [by common law]. On the contrary, Congress recognized those economic relationships cannot be fitted neatly into the containers designated "employee" and "employer" which an earlier law had shaped for different purposes. . . . [T]he broad language of the Act's definitions . . . leaves no doubt that its applicability is to be determined broadly . . . rather than technically and exclusively by previously established legal classifications.

It is not necessary in this case to make a completely definitive limitation around the term "employee." That task has been assigned primarily to the agency created by Congress to administer the Act. Determination of "where all the conditions of the relation require protection" involves inquiries for the Board charged with this duty. Everyday experience in the administration of the statute gives it familiarity with the circumstances and backgrounds of employment relationships in various industries, with the abilities and needs of the workers for self-organization and collective action, and with the adaptability of collective bargaining for the peaceful settlement of their disputes with their employers. The experience thus acquired must be brought frequently to bear on the question who is an employee under the Act. Resolving that question, like determining whether unfair labor practices have been committed, "belongs to the usual administrative routine" of the Board.

In making that body's determinations as to the facts in these matters conclusive, if supported by evidence, Congress entrusted to it primarily the decision whether the evidence establishes the material facts. Hence in reviewing the Board's ultimate conclusions, it is not the court's function to substitute its own inferences of fact for the Board's, when the latter have support in the record. Undoubtedly questions of statutory interpretation, especially when arising in the first instance in judicial proceedings, are for the courts to resolve, giving appropriate weight to the judgment of those whose special duty is to administer the questioned statute. But where the question is one of specific application of a broad statutory term in a proceeding in which the agency administering the statute must determine it initially, the reviewing court's function is limited. Like the commissioner's determination under the Longshoremen's & Harbor Workers' Act, that a man is not a "member of a crew" or that he was injured "in the course of employment" and the Federal Communications Commission's determination that one company is under the "control" of another, the Board's determination that specified persons are "employees" under this Act is to be accepted if it has "warrant in the record" and a reasonable basis in law.

In this case the Board found that the designated newsboys work continuously and regularly, rely upon their earnings for the support of themselves and their families, and have their total wages influenced in large measure by the publishers, who dictate their buying and selling prices, fix their markets and control their supply of papers. Their hours of work and their efforts on the job are supervised and to some extent prescribed by the publishers or their agents. Much of their sales equipment and advertising materials is furnished by the publishers with the intention that it be used for the publisher's benefit. Stating that "the primary consideration in the determination of the applicability of the statutory definition is whether effectuation of the declared policy and purposes of the Act comprehend securing to the individual the rights guaranteed and protection afforded by the Act," the Board concluded that the newsboys are employees. The record sustains the Board's findings and there is ample basis in the law for its conclusion.

. . . .

Underlying Case Documents

The case referenced:
The Board's decision ordering elections

---

1. Like *Universal Camera*, *Hearst* provided very general principles that were to guide courts in reviewing agency action. The idea that a court should not substitute its judgment for that of an agency is attributed occasionally to *Hearst*. In *Cabana v. United States Secretary of Agriculture*, the court announced that it was not permitted to "substitute its judgment for the agency's." 427 F. Supp. 2d 1232, 1234 (Ct. Int'l Trade 2006) ("[A] court must defer to an agency's reasonable interpretation of a statute even if the court might have preferred another.") (citing *Koyo Seiko Co. v. United States*, 36 F.3d 1565, 1570 (Fed. Cir. 1994)). Furthermore, *Hearst* provides additional text to determine when a record is sufficient to support a decision, using the phrase "warrant in the record" and a "reasonable basis in law." This is standard language in a number of settings. *Allied Chem. & Alkali Workers of America, Local Union No. 1 v. Pittsburgh Plate Glass*, 404 U.S. 157 (1971); *BPS Guard Servs. v. NLRB*, 942 F.2d 519 (8th Cir. 1991). The words, however, are not free of controversy.

2. "Warrant in the record" is simple enough, but "reasonable basis in law" is a bit more dicey. Does that reasonability assessment render *Hearst* inconsistent with *Chevron*? While seemingly deferential, the task of reviewing courts begins with the following assessment: "[Q]uestions of statutory interpretation, especially when arising in the first instance in judicial proceedings, are for the courts to resolve, giving appropriate weight to the judgment of those whose special duty is to administer the questioned statute." Doesn't *Chevron* involve deferring to the "permissible" interpretations of statutes by agencies? Or do you read *Hearst* to be a "step-zero" assessment – whether there is any authority to act in the first instance?

3. In *Batterton v. Francis*, 432 U.S. 416, 425-26 (1977), the Court held that "Congress entrusted [to administrative agencies], rather than to the courts, the primary responsibility for interpreting the statutory term[s.]" Is this an application of *Hearst* or a departure from it? Does *Hearst* interpret the law and then check to see if the agency "got it right"? Does an agency decide on the meaning of a statute in an adjudication – a decision to which courts must defer only if, in the judgment of the court, there is a "reasonable basis in law"? *See* Doug Geyser, Note, *Courts Still "Say What the Law Is": Explaining the Functions of the Judiciary and Agencies After Brand X*, 106 COLUM. L. REV. 2129 (2006).

4. *Air Brake Systems, Inc. v. Mineta*, 357 F.3d 632 (6th Cir. 2004).

> This case arises from a longstanding dispute between the National Highway Traffic Safety Administration (NHTSA) and Air Brake Systems, Inc. (Air Brake). Air Brake manufactures a "non-electronic" antilock brake system for trucks and trailers, which purports to comply with Federal Motor Vehicle Safety Standard 121, a NHTSA regulation concerning antilock brakes. When an Air Brake customer asked NHTSA whether a vehicle with Air Brake's brake system – the only non-electronic antilock brake system on the market – would comply with Standard 121, NHTSA's Acting Chief Counsel issued two opinion letters stating that the brake system would not satisfy the standard. NHTSA posted the letters on its website (with negative consequences for Air Brake's business) . . . .

> The . . . question is whether the letters . . . occasion sufficient "legal consequences" to make them reviewable. One reliable indicator that an agency interpretation still has the requisite legal consequence . . . is whether the agency may claim *Chevron* deference for it. . . . If the Supreme Court's recent decisions concerning administrative deference signal any change, it is that less agency action will qualify for *Chevron* deference and less agency action accordingly may qualify for federal-court review. Cases will arise involving informal agency actions that once received, but no longer receive, *Chevron* deference in the aftermath of *Mead* and *Christensen*. Correspondingly, cases will now arise involving agency action that we once might have considered "final" for APA-review purposes as a result of *Chevron*'s legal effect but that we will no longer consider final because *Chevron* does not apply. . . .

> Air Brake, however, cannot rely [on *Chevron*, *Mead*, or *Christensen*] because the Chief Counsel's legal interpretations have no claim to deference of any sort. For one reason, they are too informal. Congress does not generally expect agencies to make law through general counsel opinion letters. For another reason, the letters interpret a regulation (Standard 121), not the statute that the agency is charged with enforcing (the Safety Act). *Chevron* does not apply in this setting.

Why not defer? The decision seems logical – but is it consistent with *Hearst*?

The next group of note cases all involve judicial review of adjudications.

a. In each case, try to define the task of the reviewing court. Are they assessing process? Interjecting their own perspective on substance? Second-guessing initial decisionmakers? Second-guessing commissions or boards?

b. These cases are exemplars of various approaches, doctrines, and theories regarding judicial review of adjudication – and each was intensely fought by the parties. What was the case theory of the parties who were the subject of the agency action? Try to distill down to a few sentences their best arguments as they moved from the agency into court. The "story line" of each of these cases is quite revealing.

1. *Penasquitos Village, Inc. v. National Labor Relations Board*, 565 F.2d 1074 (9th Cir. 1977).

The National Labor Relations Board (the Board), reversing the decision of an administrative law judge, held that Penasquitos Village, Inc. and affiliated companies (Penasquitos) had engaged in coercive interrogation of employees in violation of section 8(a)(1) of the National Labor Relations Act (the Act) and had wrongfully discharged employees in violation of section 8(a)(3) of the Act. Penasquitos petitioned us to review and set aside the Board's order, alleging that it was not supported by substantial evidence. . . .

We treat as conclusive the factual determinations in a Board decision if they are "supported by substantial evidence on the record considered as a whole." . . . . Nevertheless, the administrative law judge's findings of fact constitute a part of that whole record which we must review. We give those initial findings some weight, whether they support or contradict the Board's factual conclusions. *See Universal Camera Corp. v. NLRB*. . . . The most difficult problem facing the reviewing court arises when, as in this case, the Board and the administrative law judge disagree on the facts. . . .

[E]ven when the record contains independent, credited evidence supportive of the Board's decision, a reviewing court will review more critically the Board's findings of fact if they are contrary to the administrative law judge's factual conclusions. This more rigorous review follows necessarily from the Supreme Court's statement in *Universal Camera Corp. v. NLRB* that the "substantiality of evidence [in support of the Board's decision] must take into account whatever in the record fairly detracts from its weight. . . . "

[There is a distinction] between credibility determinations based on demeanor – sometimes referred to as *testimonial inferences* – and inferences drawn from the evidence itself – sometimes referred to as *derivative inferences*. . . .

Weight is given the administrative law judge's determinations of credibility for the obvious reason that he or she "sees the witnesses and hears them testify, while the Board and the reviewing court look only at cold records." All aspects of the witness's demeanor – including the expression of his countenance, how he sits or stands, whether he is inordinately nervous, his coloration during critical examination, the modulation or pace of his speech and other non-verbal communication – may convince the observing trial judge that the witness is testifying truthfully or falsely. These same . . . factors, however, are entirely unavailable to a reader of the transcript, such as the Board or the Court of Appeals. But it should be noted that the administrative law judge's opportunity to observe the witnesses' demeanor does not, by itself, require deference with regard to his or her derivative inferences. Observation of demeanor makes weighty only the observer's testimonial inferences.

Deference is accorded the Board's factual conclusions for a different reason – Board members are presumed to have broad experience and expertise in labor–management relations. . . . We emphasize that we do not hold that the administrative law judge's determinations of credibility based on demeanor are conclusive on the Board. . . . We simply observe that the special deference deservedly afforded the administrative law judge's factual determinations based on testimonial inferences will weigh heavily in our review of a contrary finding by the Board. [Citing] *Universal Camera Corp. v. NLRB*.

Recognition of the distinction between testimonial inferences and derivative inferences, and an appreciation of the different sources of deference accorded the Board and the administrative law judge, provide helpful guidance in those cases where the Board and the administrative law judge disagree about the facts. That recognition and appreciation do not, however, eliminate all difficulty for the reviewing court. Cases may still arise where the administrative law judge's position is well supported by testimonial inferences, while the contrary position of the Board is equally well supported by valid derivative inferences. . . .

B. *The Discharges.* It is axiomatic that an employer's discharge of an employee because of his union activities or sympathies violates section 8(a)(3) of the Act. . . . The determinative factual issue, therefore, is the employer's motive.

In this case, the administrative law judge and the Board disagreed on Penasquitos' motive. Whether, in light of this disagreement, the Board's conclusion is sustainable because it is based on substantial evidence is an extremely close question. . . .

The keystone of the administrative law judge's finding of proper motive was his conviction that Zamora told the truth. Zamora testified that he observed Rios and Martinez working slowly and watching several women sunbathe in bikinis some distance from the employees' worksite. Upset with their performance, Zamora approached Rios and Martinez and stated that "if you want to see girls wearing bikinis there were some better ones at the beach." Zamora then left, verified with his superior that he had authority to fire, returned and discharged the two men. At the hearing before the administrative law judge, Martinez admitted that he was working at a slow pace on the day he was fired.

The administrative law judge relied on other evidence also. Several months prior to the discharge, Zamora and another supervisor watched for 5 or 10 minutes while Rios and two other employees stood under a tree, doing no work. When Zamora approached and demanded an explanation, the employees stated that they had no work to do and were waiting for quitting time. Zamora then suspended them – a fact initially denied by the mendacious Rios during cross-examination but later clearly established.

In reaching a contrary conclusion regarding Zamora's motive, the Board [found] Zamora's action in discharging Rios and Martinez [revealed] anti-union animus [based on] his alleged threats and unlawful interrogations. But, as we [separately found], that finding of anti-union animus was not supported by substantial evidence. The Board also ascribed an improper motive to Zamora for the discharge because of his alleged statements at the timeclock. . . . [However], the witnesses testifying about that incident were not credited by the administrative law judge, thus vitiating the inference the Board attempted to draw from it.

The Board also relied on the fact that Martinez and Rios had signed authorization cards for the union and that Cuevas had informed Zamora that those two, among others, were the leaders of the organizing effort. But against this must be placed the credited testimony of Zamora that he was unconcerned about who was doing the organizing because "I thought they were all in the Union. . . ."

The Board drew two inferences, however, from uncontroverted facts. First, the discharge was abrupt. Rios and Martinez received no warning prior to their discharge. . . . Second, the discharge came only two days after the Board's Regional Director issued a Decision and Direction of Election ordering an election among the Penasquitos employees under Zamora's supervision. These derivative inferences undoubtedly carry weight, which is not diminished by the fact that the administrative law judge drew a contrary inference from the timing of the discharge. As noted before, special deference is accorded the Board when, in the application of its expertise and experience, it derives such inferences from the facts of a labor dispute.

But in this case, credibility played a dominant role. The administrative law judge's testimonial inferences reduce significantly the substantiality of the Board's contrary derivative inferences. Particularly, removing the Board's finding of anti-union animus based upon alleged unlawful threats and interrogations, leaves poorly substantiated the Board's other conclusion that the discharges were improperly motivated. Considering the record as a whole, we conclude that the Board's conclusion that Penasquitos committed unlawful labor practices is not supported by substantial evidence and must, therefore, be set aside.

Can you explain – beyond the labels given by the court – the distinction between the court's assessment of the value to be given to the initial hearing officer and the Board? In *W.F. Bolin Co. v. NLRB*, 70 F.3d 863, 872-73 (6th Cir. 1995), the court relied on *Penasquitos* and found that an "ALJ's opportunity to observe witnesses' demeanor does not, by itself, require deference with regard to his or her derivative inferences. Observation of demeanor makes weighty only the observer's testimonial inferences." In that case, after a contractor complained about performance, the petitioner threw the relevant collective bargaining agreement on the ground and said, "[I]f you guys keep complaining I'm going to fire the whole crew." In an unfair labor case, would you think the problem involved the derivative inference or the testimonial?

2. *Strycker's Bay Neighborhood Council, Inc. v. Karlen*, 444 U.S. 223 (1980).

At the center of this dispute is the site of a proposed low-income housing project to be constructed on Manhattan's Upper West Side. . . . As originally written, the plan called for a mix of 70% middle-income housing and 30% low-income housing and designated the site at issue here as the location of one of the middle-income projects. . . . [Suits were filed challenging the lack of low-income housing.]

The District Court entered judgment in favor of petitioners[, finding] that petitioners had not violated the National Environmental Policy Act of 1969 (NEPA) On respondents' appeal, the Second Circuit affirmed all but the District Court's treatment of the NEPA claim. . . . [T]he Court of Appeals held that HUD had not complied with § 102(2)(E), which requires an agency to "study, develop, and describe appropriate alternatives to recommended courses of action in any proposal which involves unresolved conflicts concerning alternative uses of available resources." . . . .

On remand, HUD prepared a lengthy report . . . . [But] the Second Circuit vacated and remanded again. The appellate court focused upon that part of HUD's report where the agency considered and rejected alternative sites, and in particular upon HUD's reliance on the delay such a relocation would entail. The Court of Appeals purported to recognize that its role in reviewing HUD's decision was defined by the Administrative Procedure Act (APA), 5 U.S.C. § 706(2)(A), which provides that agency actions should be set aside if found to be "arbitrary, capricious, an abuse of discretion, or otherwise not in accordance with law. . . ." Additionally, however, the Court of Appeals looked to "[the] provisions of NEPA" for "the substantive standards necessary to review the merits of agency decisions. . . ." . . . . According to the court, when HUD considers such projects, "environmental factors, such as crowding low-income housing into a concentrated area, should be given determinative weight."
 . . . .

In *Vermont Yankee Nuclear Power Corp. v. NRDC*, we stated that NEPA . . . imposes upon agencies duties that are "essentially procedural." As we stressed in that case, NEPA was designed "to insure a fully informed and well-considered decision," but not necessarily "a decision the judges of the Court of Appeals or of this Court would have reached had they been members of the decisionmaking unit of the agency." *Vermont Yankee* cuts sharply against the Court of Appeals' conclusion that an agency, in selecting a course of action, must elevate environmental concerns over other appropriate considerations. On the contrary, once an agency has made a decision subject to NEPA's procedural requirements, the only role for a court is to insure that the agency has considered the environmental consequences; it cannot "interject itself within the area of discretion of the executive as to the choice of the action to be taken."

In the present litigation there is no doubt that HUD considered the environmental consequences of its decision to redesignate the proposed site for low-income housing. NEPA requires no more. The petitions for certiorari are granted, and the judgment of the Court of Appeals is therefore, Reversed.

While *Chevron* applies to formal adjudication and notice and comment rulemaking, did this case involve the interpretation of a statute or rule – or was it about the interjection of preferences by the Court regarding the substance of the agency action? Did the Court defer to the derivative inferences?

3. *Mayo Foundation v. Surface Transportation Board*, 472 F.3d 545 (8th Cir. 2006).

The petitioners challenge the decision of the Surface Transportation Board, which . . . approved a proposal of the Dakota, Minnesota & Eastern Railroad Corporation (DM&E) to construct approximately 280 miles of new rail line to reach the coal mines of Wyoming's Powder River Basin and to upgrade nearly 600 miles of existing rail line . . . . Because granting such approval is "a major Federal action significantly affecting the quality of the human environment," NEPA requires the Board to evaluate the environmental impact of the project. The Board therefore prepared both a draft environmental impact statement (DEIS) and a final environmental impact statement (FEIS) . . . and after imposing 147 conditions designed to mitigate the project's environmentally adverse effects[, approved the project]. Rochester and Olmsted

County [contend] that the Board . . . should have required DM&E . . . to build sound walls in Rochester and Chester . . . .

In <u>Marsh v. Oregon Natural Res. Council, 490 U.S. 360 (1989)</u>, the . . . Court noted that the agency action required a high level of technical expertise, and concluded that "review of the narrow question" was "controlled by the 'arbitrary and capricious' standard of § 706(2)(A)."

The Board's conclusion with respect to . . . the construction of sound walls in Rochester and Chester is [adequately] supported . . . . [T]he discussion of sound walls encompassed nearly five pages in the FSEIS . . . . The FSEIS ultimately recommended against sound walls as a mitigating alternative for horn noise "in light of the safety concerns for motorists, train crews, and pedestrians; questions regarding the ultimate effectiveness of sound walls; and significant costs associated with sound wall construction and maintenance." The Board also specifically addressed the issue of sound walls in Chester, stating . . . that "no sound barriers in Chester, Minnesota warranted consideration due to the minimal length of residential development along the existing line through this community."

We thus believe the Board's rejection of the sound wall mitigating condition, was not arbitrary and capricious, but rather a reasoned consideration of an ultimately unavailing proposition.

4. <u>Vermont Yankee</u> prevents a court from second-guessing the policy choices an agency makes in establishing procedures for a licensing hearing. The choices in play in <u>Strycker's Bay</u> are substantive and go to the content of a record, factual conclusions, and references that could be drawn from testimony submitted during an adjudication. Deference to factual inference is a very different matter than deference to broad policy determinations. Think back to <u>Mead</u> – did *Mead* involve an argument regarding deference to policy determination (*Chevron*), selection of process (*Vermont Yankee*), or judgments regarding inferences to be drawn from evidence – from facts and information in the record (*Strycker's Bay*)? Is it the nature of the choice (policy, process, or fact) that dictates the difference in outcome?

5. <u>Garcia-Quintero v. Gonzales, 455 F.3d 1006 (9th Cir. 2006)</u>.

Garcia-Quintero, a citizen of Mexico, entered the United States unlawfully in 1986, and has resided here for the last twenty years. He is married to a lawful permanent resident ("LPR"), and has four LPR children . . . . He has no criminal record. In 1993, Garcia-Quintero was accepted into the FUP. The Family Unity Program . . . permits qualified alien spouses or unmarried children of legalized aliens . . . to apply for the benefits of the program, which include protection from deportation and authorization to work in the United States.

Garcia-Quintero . . . became an LPR in 1998. In June 2001, Garcia-Quintero received a Notice to Appear in Removal Proceedings, which charged him with being removable as an alien smuggler . . . . Based upon Garcia-Quintero's testimony, the IJ determined that he knowingly participated in alien smuggling, and was therefore subject to removal. Garcia-Quintero appealed the IJ's decision to the BIA, arguing that . . . the IJ forced Garcia-Quintero to incriminate himself in violation of the Fifth Amendment. . . . He also requested that his appeal be reviewed by a three-member panel of the BIA. . . . In a one-member unpublished order, the BIA dismissed Garcia-Quintero's appeal and denied his motion to remand.

[T]he initial question presented is whether we should accord the BIA's decision in this case the deferential review prescribed by the Supreme Court in *Chevron*. . . . [B]ecause the BIA's decision was an unpublished disposition, issued by a single member of the BIA, which does not bind third parties, we conclude that it does not carry the force of law. . . . [Therefore, under *Mead*] we must examine the validity of the BIA's reasoning, its thoroughness, and overall persuasiveness. To do so, we turn to the heart of Garcia-Quintero's appeal . . . whether acceptance into the Family Unity Program renders Garcia-Quintero "admitted in any status" for cancellation of removal purposes. . . . Because Garcia-Quintero was already in the United States, the BIA determined that his entrance into the FUP did not constitute an admission into this country, and therefore he was not "admitted in any status." . . . . [But] the plain meaning of "admitted in any status" . . . leads us to hold that acceptance into the Family Unity Program [qualifies]. We therefore grant Garcia-Quintero's petition regarding his motion to remand, and we remand to the BIA for further proceedings as it deems appropriate.

Is this *Skidmore* respect? Why not "respect" the derivative inferences and interpretations of the Board?

6. *Navarro v. Pfizer Corp.*, 261 F.3d 90 (1st Cir. 2001).

On October 14, 1997, [Navarro] requested an unpaid leave of absence . . . to travel to Germany so that she might minister to her adult daughter (Gladys Hernandez) . . . . At the time she made this request, the appellant provided Pfizer with a note from her daughter's attending physician which reported that "Mrs. Hernandez is pregnant in 36th week. Because of high blood pressure bed rest is recommended to carry the baby to full term. So she cannot watch her other children." Pfizer denied the appellant's request. She implored the company to reconsider. On October 25, having received no further response from her employer, the appellant departed for Germany. On November 6 . . . Pfizer direct[ed] her to return to work forthwith. The appellant remained at her daughter's bedside and Pfizer terminated her employment . . . . Eleven months later, the appellant sued. . . . [Her claim, based on the Family Medical Leave Act (FMLA), required reference to an EEOC interpretive guidance that defined "temporary non-chronic impairment."]

In holding that a "temporary, non-chronic impairment" did not constitute a disability, the lower court relied entirely on an EEOC interpretive guidance thereby implicitly if not explicitly granting *Chevron* deference to the EEOC's interpretation of its own rules. This was error . . . . Pertinently, the *Mead* Court warned that "where statutory circumstances indicate no intent to delegate general authority to make rules with force of law, or where such authority was not invoked," a court must review agency interpretations under a less tolerant standard. . . . [S]uch an agency interpretation is entitled to respect only to the extent that the interpretation has the power to persuade. . . .

The EEOC never had any authority to promulgate regulations pursuant to the FMLA. To the contrary, Congress explicitly delegated to the Secretary of Labor the *sole* authority to promulgate such regulations. . . . Indeed, it borders on the Kafkaesque to suggest that the EEOC, acting some three years before Congress passed the FMLA, had invoked the authority delegated to the Secretary of Labor and written interpretations to govern an as-yet-unenacted statute. Accordingly, we decline to grant *Chevron* deference to the EEOC's interpretive guidance and instead apply the *Skidmore* standard. . . .

7. *Singh v. Gonzales*, 451 F.3d 400 (6th Cir. 2006).

Surrinder Singh . . . entered the United States in 1989 under a visa in the name of his deceased cousin, Lal Singh. Lal had passed away in 1988 shortly before appearing at the United States Embassy in India to receive his immigration visa. Surrinder fraudulently assumed the identity of his deceased cousin and secured a visa that allowed him to enter the United States. . . . Surrinder [then] obtained a divorce from Parveen. They remarried in India shortly thereafter, with Surrinder assuming the name of Lal Singh. The purpose of this second marriage was to obtain admission to the United States for Parveen and Amandeep as the spouse and daughter, respectively, of a lawful permanent resident (LPR). Parveen later admitted that . . . the three Singhs had entered the country "on false pretenses." . . . .

The government initiated removal proceedings against Parveen and Amandeep in June of 2001, asserting that both of them were removable under § 237(a)(1)(A) . . . which . . . allows aliens to be removed [if they] obtained their immigrant visas or admission "by fraud or by willfully misrepresenting a material fact" . . . . The BIA . . . "reject[ed] the argument that the parents' fraudulent entry cannot be imputed to their minor daughter . . ." . . . even though that conduct occurred when Amandeep was only five years old. . . .

The first question of law before us is whether the BIA's decision to impute the fraudulent conduct of Amandeep's parents to Amandeep is a reasonable interpretation of the INA. In deciding this question, we accord the BIA's interpretation of the statute deference under *Chevron* . . . . [Finding ambiguity, the court moved to step two.] We believe . . . that imputing fraudulent conduct – which necessarily includes both *knowledge* of falsity and an *intent to deceive* . . . is a far cry from imputing knowledge of ineligibility for admission, which is the only type of imputation specifically [within the prior decisions of BIA or caselaw]. Fraudulent conduct carries heightened moral and legal culpability and is sanctioned both civilly (as an intentional tort) and criminally (by state and federal laws). These strong . . . sanctions, in turn, require proof of an intent to deceive. . . . As a general matter, however, not even a parent's *negligence* is typically imputed to a minor child. . . . We therefore [find the BIA's] decision to impute the fraudulent conduct of Amandeep's parents to Amandeep herself [unreasonable].

8. *G&T Terminal Packaging Co., Inc. v. United States Department of Agriculture*, 468 F.3d 86 (2d Cir. 2006).

In late 1996, the USDA . . . and the FBI launched an investigation into allegations of corruption in the USDA office in Hunts Point[, New York]. The investigators discovered that "corrupt inspectors . . . were taking cash payments . . . from produce wholesalers in exchange for agreeing to 'downgrade' produce on inspection certificates, to the substantial financial detriment of growers." . . . . William Cashin was one of the unscrupulous USDA inspectors. After his arrest, Cashin cooperated with the ongoing investigation . . . . Cashin's cooperation . . . ensnared several merchants . . . including Spinale, who was indicted . . . and charged with nine counts of bribing a public official . . . . Spinale admitted that ". . . I paid Mr. Cashin $ 100 per inspection to influence the outcome of the report." . . . . On June 3, 2003, the government filed an administrative complaint charging G&T and Tray-Wrap with having "willfully, flagrantly, and repeatedly violated Section 2(4) of the PACA by . . . making payments, through Spinale, to Cashin. . . ."

The petitioners challenge two conclusions [from the Order of the Judicial Officer]. They argue that because a USDA inspector's duty is to provide timely and accurate inspections, [and the evidence did not show reporting was compromised by the money paid the agents,] the Secretary's construction is unreasonable. Second, they challenge the Secretary's case-specific determination, unaccompanied by a comprehensive discussion of the meaning of "reasonable cause," that the inspectors' actions did not constitute "reasonable cause" for Spinale's payments. The petitioners claim that Spinale reasonably feared that the petitioners would suffer significant economic loss if he did not pay regular gratuities to the inspectors, and that such a fear must be encompassed by the term "reasonable cause."

We consider both of the petitioners' arguments [under] *Chevron*. . . . Our task at the first step of the *Chevron* analysis is a simple one. . . . [The statute] provides that "[i]t shall be unlawful in or in connection with any transaction in interstate or foreign commerce . . . (4) For any commission merchant, dealer, or broker . . . to fail, without reasonable cause, to perform any specification or duty, express or implied, arising out of any undertaking in connection with any [transaction involving any perishable agricultural commodity]." This statutory language [is ambiguous].

We affirm as reasonable the Secretary's conclusion that the PACA imposes an implied duty upon licensees to refrain from making payments to USDA inspectors in connection with produce inspections, irrespective of whether those payments induce, or are intended to induce, the inspectors to issue inaccurate inspection certificates. Indeed, given a statutory scheme which assigns government inspectors to protect the financial interests of distant shippers by providing impartial assessments of the condition of the produce upon arrival, we can hardly conceive of a duty more clearly implicated than the obligation of recipients not to make side-payments to these inspectors. As the Judicial Officer noted, such payments give rise to a strong inference that the inspector's loyalty has been purchased by the payor, and therefore "undermine the trust a produce seller places in the accuracy of the inspection certificate and the integrity of the inspector." The facts of this case do not belie that presumption. . . .

We also affirm the Secretary's conclusion that the inspectors' practice of withholding "fast, fair and accurate" inspections from merchants who refused to pay illegal gratuities does not excuse the petitioners' decision to breach the implied duties owed under the PACA by making such payments. . . . [A]gencies are generally accorded *Chevron* deference when they give "ambiguous statutory terms concrete meaning through a process of case-by-case adjudication." . . . .

The facts in the record reveal that the "extortion" practiced by Cashin and his cohorts, while real, was indeed "soft" enough to support the view that no reasonable cause existed for the petitioners' breach of duty. Spinale has never suggested that he was physically threatened [n]or did the inspectors threaten Spinale with . . . the outright denial of produce inspections. . . . [Furthermore,] Spinale never attempted to report the illegal activities at Hunts Point . . . . While we need not and do not address whether he bore an affirmative obligation to do so, we simply point out that there were clearly available – and potentially anonymous – means of resisting the inspectors' illegal scheme that Spinale never explored. We think this fact serves to bolster the Secretary's decision to reject the petitioners' assertion that Spinale had no choice but to make cash payments to the inspectors for over a decade. . . . Therefore, for the reasons set forth above . . .the decision of the Secretary of Agriculture is hereby affirmed.

————————

Read the following case carefully: Is the decision to grant deference to the action of the agency based on ineluctable principles of administrative law or on the court's "judgment" about the meaning of an apparently ambiguous term, and if it is the latter, is the court substituting its judgment for that of the agency?

IMMIGRATION AND NATURALIZATION SERVICE V. CARDOZA-FONSECA

480 U.S. 421 (1987)

[JUSTICE STEVENS] Since 1980, the Immigration and Nationality Act has provided two methods through which an otherwise deportable alien who claims that he will be persecuted if deported can seek relief. Section 243(h) of the Act requires the Attorney General to withhold deportation of an alien who demonstrates that his "life or freedom would be threatened" on account of one of the listed factors if he is deported. In *INS v. Stevic*, we held that to qualify for this entitlement to withholding of deportation, an alien must demonstrate that "it is more likely than not that the alien would be subject to persecution" in the country to which he would be returned. The Refugee Act of 1980 also established a second type of broader relief. Section 208(a) of the Act authorizes the Attorney General, in his discretion, to grant asylum to an alien who is unable or unwilling to return to his home country "because of persecution or a well-founded fear of persecution on account of race, religion, nationality, membership in a particular social group, or political opinion."

In *Stevic*, we rejected an alien's contention that the § 208(a) "well-founded fear" standard governs applications for withholding of deportation under § 243(h). Similarly, today we reject the Government's contention that the § 243(h) standard, which requires an alien to show that he is more likely than not to be subject to persecution, governs applications for asylum under § 208(a). Congress used different, broader language to define the term "refugee" as used in § 208(a) than

it used to describe the class of aliens who have a right to withholding of deportation under § 243(h). The Act's establishment of a broad class of refugees who are
eligible for a discretionary grant of asylum, and a narrower class of aliens who are
given a statutory right not to be deported to the country where they are in danger,
mirrors the provisions of the United Nations Protocol Relating to the Status of
Refugees, which provided the motivation for the enactment of the Refugee Act
of 1980. In addition, the legislative history of the 1980 Act makes it perfectly
clear that Congress did not intend the class of aliens who qualify as refugees to be
coextensive with the class who qualify for § 243(h) relief.

I.

Respondent is a 38-year-old Nicaraguan citizen who entered the United States
in 1979 as a visitor. After she remained in the United States longer than permitted,
and failed to take advantage of the Immigration and Naturalization Service's (INS)
offer of voluntary departure, the INS commenced deportation proceedings against
her. Respondent conceded that she was in the country illegally, but requested
withholding of deportation pursuant to § 243(h) and asylum as a refugee pursuant to § 208(a).

To support her request under § 243(h), respondent attempted to show that
if she were returned to Nicaragua her "life or freedom would be threatened" on
account of her political views; to support her request under § 208(a), she attempted to show that she had a "well-founded fear of persecution" upon her return. The
evidence supporting both claims related primarily to the activities of respondent's
brother who had been tortured and imprisoned because of his political activities
in Nicaragua. Both respondent and her brother testified that they believed the
Sandinistas knew that the two of them had fled Nicaragua together and that even
though she had not been active politically herself, she would be interrogated about
her brother's whereabouts and activities. Respondent also testified that because of
her brother's status, her own political opposition to the Sandinistas would be
brought to that government's attention. Based on these facts, respondent claimed
that she would be tortured if forced to return.

The Immigration Judge applied the same standard in evaluating respondent's
claim for withholding of deportation under § 243(h) as he did in evaluating her
application for asylum under § 208(a). He found that she had not established "a
clear probability of persecution" and therefore was not entitled to either form of
relief. On appeal, the Board of Immigration Appeals (BIA) agreed that respondent
had "failed to establish that she would suffer persecution within the meaning of
section 208(a) or 243(h) of the Immigration and Nationality Act."

In the Court of Appeals for the Ninth Circuit, respondent did not challenge the BIA's decision that she was not entitled to withholding of deportation under § 243(h), but argued that she was eligible for consideration for asylum under § 208(a), and contended that the Immigration Judge and BIA erred in applying the "more likely than not" standard of proof from § 243(h) to her § 208(a) asylum claim. Instead, she asserted, they should have applied the "well-founded fear" standard, which she considered to be more generous. The court agreed. . . . We granted certiorari to resolve a Circuit conflict on this important question.

II.

The Refugee Act of 1980 . . . added a new § 208(a) to the Immigration and Nationality Act of 1952, reading as follows:

> The Attorney General shall establish a procedure for an alien physically present in the United States or at a land border or port of entry, irrespective of such alien's status, to apply for asylum, and the alien may be granted asylum in the discretion of the Attorney General if the Attorney General determines that such alien is a refugee within the meaning of section 1101(a)(42)(A) of this title.

Under this section, eligibility for asylum depends entirely on the Attorney General's determination that an alien is a "refugee," as that term is defined in § 101(a)(42), which was also added to the Act in 1980. That section provides:

> The term "refugee" means (A) any person who is outside any country of such person's nationality . . . and who is unable or unwilling to return to . . . that country because of persecution or a well-founded fear of persecution on account of race, religion, nationality, membership in a particular social group, or political opinion . . . .

Thus, the "persecution or well-founded fear of persecution" standard governs the Attorney General's determination whether an alien is eligible for asylum. In addition to establishing a statutory asylum process, the 1980 Act . . . removed the Attorney General's discretion in § 243(h) proceedings.

. . . .

The Government argues, however, that even though the "well-founded fear" standard is applicable, there is no difference between it and the "would be threatened" test of § 243(h). It asks us to hold that the only way an applicant can demonstrate a "well-founded fear of persecution" is to prove a "clear probability of persecution." The statutory language does not lend itself to this reading. To begin with, the language Congress used to describe the two standards conveys very different meanings. The "would be threatened" language of § 243(h) has no subjective component, but instead requires the alien to establish by objective evidence that it is more likely than not that he or she will be subject to persecution upon deportation. In contrast, the reference to "fear" in the § 208(a) standard obviously makes the eligibility determination turn to some extent on the subjective mental state of the [a]lien. "The linguistic difference between the words 'well-founded fear' and 'clear probability' may be as striking as that between a subjective and an objective frame of reference. . . . We simply cannot conclude that the standards are identical."

. . . .

III.

The message conveyed by the plain language of the Act is confirmed by an [extensive] examination of its history. . . .

IV.

. . . .

. . . The INS argues that the BIA's construction of the Refugee Act of 1980 is entitled to substantial deference, even if we conclude that the Court of Appeals' reading of the statutes is more in keeping with Congress' intent. This argument is unpersuasive. The question whether Congress intended the two standards to be identical is a pure question of statutory construction for the courts to decide. . . . The narrow legal question whether the two standards are the same is, of course, quite different from the question of interpretation that arises in each case in which the agency is required to apply either or both standards to a particular set of facts. . . . We do not attempt to set forth a detailed description of how the "well-founded fear" test should be applied. Instead, we merely hold that the Immigration Judge and the BIA were incorrect in holding that the two standards are identical. . . . Whether or not a "refugee" is eventually granted asylum is a matter which Congress has left for the Attorney General to decide. But it is clear that Congress did not intend to restrict eligibility for that relief to those who could prove that it is more likely than not that they will be persecuted if deported.

The judgment of the Court of Appeals is Affirmed.

[JUSTICE SCALIA, concurring.]

. . . I concur in the judgment rather than join the Court's opinion . . . for two reasons. First, despite having reached the above conclusion, the Court undertakes an exhaustive investigation of the legislative history of the Act. . . . [T]hat is . . . an ill-advised deviation from the venerable principle that if the language of a statute is clear, that language must be given effect — at least in the absence of a patent absurdity. . . . I am far more troubled, however, by the Court's discussion of the question whether the INS's interpretation of "well-founded fear" is entitled to deference. Since the Court quite rightly concludes that the INS's interpretation is clearly inconsistent with the plain meaning of that phrase and the structure of the Act, there is simply no need and thus no justification for a discussion of whether the interpretation is entitled to deference. . . . Even more unjustifiable, however, is the Court's use of this superfluous discussion as the occasion to express controversial, and I believe erroneous, views on the meaning of this Court's decision in *Chevron*. *Chevron* stated that where there is no "unambiguously expressed intent of Congress, a court may not substitute its own construction of a statutory provision for a reasonable interpretation made by the administrator of an agency." This Court has consistently interpreted *Chevron* . . . as holding that courts must give effect to a reasonable agency interpretation of a statute unless that interpretation is inconsistent with a clearly expressed congressional intent. The Court's discussion is flatly inconsistent with this well-established interpretation. The Court first implies that courts may substitute their interpretation of a statute for that of an agency whenever, "[e]mploying traditional tools of statutory construction," they are able to reach a conclusion as to the proper interpretation of the statute. But this approach would make deference a doctrine of desperation, authorizing courts to defer only if they would otherwise be unable to construe the enactment at issue. This is not an interpretation but an evisceration of *Chevron*.

Underlying Case Documents

The case referenced:
The Refugee Act of 1980
The United Nations Protocol Relating to the Status of Refugees
The opinion of the Immigration Judge
The opinion of the Board of Immigration Appeals

1. Putting this case in a neat category is a challenge. Is the absence of deference justified if an agency has provided a reasoned "best interpretation" of the relevant statute?

There is a clean doctrinal and somewhat linear principle in the *Cardoza-Fonseca* opinion that can be used at this juncture: "The judiciary is the final authority on issues of statutory construction and must reject administrative constructions which are contrary to clear congressional intent." That is quite true – and a bit difficult to line up with *Chevron*, which is, after all, about an agency interpretation of a statute. Statutory interpretation in an adjudication is a way of life in administrative law. Are the rules of deference different from those applicable to interpretations in rulemakings?

2. In <u>Good Samaritan Hospital v. Sha-</u>
<u>lala</u>, 508 U.S. 402, 417 (1993), the
Supreme Court found that "where the
agency's interpretation of a statute is at
least as plausible as competing ones,
there is little, if any, reason not to defer
to its construction." Why would that
principle not apply in *Cardoza-Fonseca*? The break-point varies, depending
on the way one frames the analysis.

3. The statutory provisions in question
were not clearly identical, as the government contends, but they were not
wildly dissimilar. A "well-founded
fear" and a "clear probability of persecution" are different – but are they so
different that the compulsory deference <u>Chevron</u> demands should have

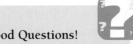

Good Questions!

Does <u>Chevron</u> permit reviewing
courts to engage in a parallel analysis
of a statute interpreted by an agency, opting for what the court finds
"most consistent" with congressional
intent? (Hint: No, *Chevron* does not
seem to allow such an analysis.) Do
you buy into the argument that *Cardoza-Fonseca* was an early *Chevron*
step-zero opinion – that there is no
possible way this action is within the
authority of the agency? (Again the
answer should be no.) Is it a step-
one *Chevron* application – the statute
is clearly unambiguous and thus the
agency is due no deference? (Another hint: we, your authors, don't buy
that one either, though this puts us
in the minority.)

been side-stepped? Section 243(h) and section 208(a) are not exactly the yin and
yang of immigration and asylum law – and deciding on the distinction is a "question of statutory construction" – but so are volumes and volumes of other agency
interpretations. Why is this one different?

Two hapless explanations surface on occasion: (1) The guild perspective:
Cardoza-Fonseca affirms the complexities of statutory interpretation, matters so

overwhelmingly difficult and intellectually demanding that only judges
(professionals of great skill and training) can undertake the task; and (2)
The separation of powers perspective:
It is the function of Article III courts
to interpret the law. We will leave to
you the task of dismantling the above
perspectives – with one reminder:
<u>Chevron</u>.

4. In a recent piece, William N.
Eskridge and Lauren E. Baer note
that, "*Cardoza-Fonseca* revealed the
rhetorical tilt toward deference. . . .
JUSTICE STEVENS' opinion for the Court

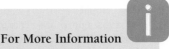

For More Information

There is outstanding scholarship discussing *Cardoza-Fonseca* that for the
most part reads it to be consistent
with *Chevron*. Richard J. Pierce, <u>Two</u>
<u>Problems in Administrative Law: Politi-</u>
<u>cal Polarity on the District of Columbia</u>
<u>Circuit and Judicial Deference of Agen-</u>
<u>cy Rulemaking</u>, 1988 DUKE L.J. 300;
Robert A. Anthony, <u>Which Agency</u>
<u>Interpretations Should Bind Citizens</u>
<u>and the Courts?</u>, 7 YALE J. ON REG. 1
<u>(1990)</u>: Thomas W. Merrill, <u>Judicial</u>
<u>Deference to Executive Precedent</u>, 101
<u>YALE L.J. 969 (1992)</u>.

in *Cardoza-Fonseca* closed with a concession that the agency had considerable leeway in implementing the asylum standard the Court found in the statute. Even as they sought to narrow *Chevron*, the Justices were publicly ceding the details of statutory policymaking to agencies." Eskridge & Baer, *The Continuum of Deference: Supreme Court Treatment of Agency Statutory Interpretations from* Chevron *to* Hamdan, 96 Geo. L.J. 1083, 1088-89 (2008).

Few cases have the temerity to suggest that *Cardoza-Fonseca* is either aberrant or a reflection of the Court's wistful desire to back away from the limitations on review imposed by *Chevron* – though there are a few. *See, e.g., Union of Concerned Scientists v. Nuclear Regulatory Comm'n, 824 F.2d 108, 113 (D.C. Cir. 1987).*

5. Consistent with *Chevron* or not, *Cardoza-Fonseca* is far from moribund. In *National Wildlife Federation v. Nat'l Marine Fisheries Service, 524 F.3d 917 (9th Cir. 2008),* the court dealt with the

> complex and long-running battle over salmon and steelhead listed under the Endangered Species Act. . . . In this ESA action brought by the National Wildlife Federation . . . we consider a November 2004 Biological Opinion addressing the effects of proposed operations of Federal Columbia River Power System dams and related facilities on listed fish in the lower Columbia and Snake Rivers. . . . [T]he district court [determined] that the 2004 BiOp was structurally flawed. . . . We affirm. . . .
>
> Our conclusion is not altered by the Supreme Court's recent decision in *National Association of Home Builders v. Defenders of Wildlife, 127 S. Ct. 2518 (2007),* [in] which . . . the Supreme Court granted *Chevron* deference to the regulation which provides that Section 7 consultation applies "to all actions in which there is discretionary Federal involvement or control," 50 C.F.R. § 402.03 (emphasis added). . . .
>
> [F]ederal agencies . . . have not previously taken such a cramped view of § 402.03's reference to "discretionary" federal action. Indeed, such an approach is a drastic change from [the agency's] own approach in the 1995 and 2000 BiOps. Because [this] approach is a novel one, completely at odds with . . . prior scientific approaches, it merits little deference. *INS v. Cardoza-Fonseca* . . . ("An agency interpretation of a relevant provision which conflicts with the agency's earlier interpretation is entitled to considerably less deference . . . .") . . . . Because the agency has so dramatically changed its approach, its new interpretation is entitled to less deference than we might usually give. Citing *Cardoza-Fonseca.*

A radical change in agency policy *is* due deference if it is the result of a notice and comment process, a formal adjudication, or, if neither, is valid, thorough, and persuasive – but not if it is outside the range of interpretations permitted under the relevant statute or improperly supported by a record. What was, in the end, the real agency failing in *Cardoza-Fonseca*?

6. In *Chen v. Ashcroft, 381 F.3d 221 (3d Cir. 2004),* the court was faced with personal circumstances at least as compelling as *Cardoza-Fonseca.*

Chen and his fiancee, Chen Gui, are both . . . citizens of the People's Republic of China. Chen and Chen Gui started living together at Chen's parents' house in July 1994. At the time, Chen was 19 and Chen Gui was 18. In September 1995, the couple discovered that Chen Gui was pregnant, and they then applied for a marriage license at the local government office . . . . However, the office told them that their application could not be approved, since the legal age to marry was 25 for men and 23 for women.

Government officials soon became aware of the pregnancy and told Chen Gui that the child would have to be aborted [and came to get her]. Chen Gui, having been warned of the visit, was not there when the officials arrived, and Chen was accordingly asked to disclose Chen Gui's whereabouts. When Chen refused, the officials started hitting him with "sticks," and Chen fought back with a "plumbing tool." Finally, Chen's parents intervened to end the scuffle. The officials left, warning Chen that he would be arrested if Chen Gui did not report for an abortion in three days. . . . [C]hen left the country shortly thereafter. . . . About two months later, Chen . . . was told that Chen Gui had ultimately been found and had been forced to submit to an abortion in the eighth month of the pregnancy. . . . [Chen sought asylum based on the persecution of Chen Gui and lost. He appealed.]

The respondent in this case (hereinafter "the government") contends that the BIA's interpretation of 8 U.S.C. § 1101(a)(42) as covering the spouses but not the unmarried partners of persons who have been forced to undergo abortions or sterilization is entitled to deference under *Chevron*. . . . Chen's argument [is] that the BIA's interpretation of the 1996 amendment, by drawing a distinction between married and unmarried couples, "evinces such a lack of rationality as to be arbitrary and capricious." n.5

> n.5 While this argument bears some similarity to a rational-basis *Equal Protection Clause* argument, it is clear that Chen is not attempting to make a constitutional argument here. . . .

[Chen argued that the fact that he and Chen Gui are not married is arbitrary. Unfortunately for Chen, the court disagreed. T]his use of marital status as a proxy is undoubtedly both over- and under-inclusive to some extent, but neither over- nor under-inclusiveness is alone sufficient to render the use of a metric like marital status irrational. . . . Moreover, the BIA might reasonably have decided that, *in general*, forced abortions and sterilization procedures tend to have a more severe impact on spouses than on unmarried partners. The BIA might also have been concerned that unmarried asylum-seekers would falsely claim to have had an intimate relationship with a person who suffered a forced abortion or sterilization, and the BIA might have felt that it would be too difficult to distinguish between those unmarried persons who had a truly close relationship with the person who underwent the medical procedure and those unmarried asylum seekers who did not. . . . For these reasons, we conclude that the BIA's decision not to extend [protection to] unmarried partners satisfies step two of *Chevron*. . . .

Is *Chen* consistent with *Cardoza-Fonseca*? The interpretation of the regulations and statutes was questionable. Why is the BIA interpretation in *Chen* more entitled to deference?

Deference to an agency determination regarding process had been a central issue in administrative law for many decades. The case below (unlike *Vermont Yankee*, which struggled with whole sections of regulations to determine proper process) focuses on the term "public hearing" in its statutory context. The term "hearing," like the term "record," may have once had a clear and unequivocal meaning, but that was not true in 1978 when *Seacoast* was decided, and it is not true today. This case should be read together with *Dominion*.

SEACOAST ANTI-POLLUTION LEAGUE V. COSTLE

572 F.2d 872 (1st Cir. 1978)

[CHIEF JUDGE COFFIN] This case is before us on a petition by the Seacoast Anti-Pollution League and the Audubon Society of New Hampshire (petitioners) to review a decision by the Administrator of the Environmental Protection Agency (EPA). . . . The petition presents several important issues relating to the applicability and effect of the Administrative Procedure Act (APA) . . . and the interpretation of the Federal Water Pollution Control Act of 1972 (FWPCA). . . .

The Public Service Company of New Hampshire (PSCO) filed an application with the EPA for permission to discharge heated water into the Hampton-Seabrook Estuary which runs into the Gulf of Maine. The water would be taken from the Gulf of Maine, be run through the condenser of PSCO's proposed nuclear steam electric generating station at Seabrook, and then be directly discharged back into the Gulf at a temperature 39 degrees Fahrenheit higher than at intake. The water is needed to remove waste heat . . . generated by the nuclear reactor but not converted into electrical energy by the turbine. Occasionally, in a process called backflushing, the water will be recirculated through the condenser, and discharged through the intake tunnel . . . in order to kill whatever organisms may be living in the intake system.

Section 301(a) of the FWPCA prohibits the discharge of any pollutant unless the discharger, the point source operator, has obtained an EPA permit. Heat is a pollutant. . . . The parties agree that the cooling system PSCO has proposed does not meet the EPA standards because PSCO would utilize a once-through open cycle system – the water would not undergo any cooling process before being returned to the sea. Therefore, in August, 1974, PSCO applied not only for a discharge permit under § 402 of the FWPCA, but also an exemption from the EPA standards pursuant to § 316 of the FWPCA. Under § 316(a) a point source operator who "after opportunity for public hearing, can demonstrate to the satisfaction of the Administrator" that the EPA's standards are "more stringent than necessary to assure the projection and propagation of a balanced, indigenous population of shellfish, fish, and wildlife in and on the body of water" may be allowed to meet a lower standard. . . .

. . . .

Applicability of the Administrative Procedure Act

Petitioners assert that the proceedings by which the EPA decided this case contravened certain provisions of the APA governing adjudicatory hearings, 5 U.S.C. §§ 554, 556, and 557. Respondents answer that the APA does not apply to proceedings held pursuant to § 316 or § 402 of the FWPCA. The dispute centers on the meaning of the introductory phrases of § 554(a) of the APA:

> This section applies . . . in every case of adjudication required by statute to be determined on the record after opportunity for an agency hearing. . . .

Both § 316(a) and § 402(a)(1) of the FWPCA provide for public hearings, but neither states that the hearing must be "on the record." We are now the third court of appeals to face this issue. The Ninth Circuit and the Seventh Circuit have each found that the APA does apply to proceedings pursuant to § 402. We agree.

At the outset we reject the position of intervenor PSCO that the precise words "on the record" must be used to trigger the APA. The Supreme Court has clearly rejected such an extreme reading . . . . Rather, we think that the resolution of this issue turns on the substantive nature of the hearing Congress intended to provide.

We begin with the nature of the decision at issue. The EPA Administrator must make specific factual findings about the effects of discharges from a specific point source. On the basis of these findings the Administrator must determine whether to grant a discharge permit to a specific applicant. . . . As the instant proceeding well demonstrates, the factual questions involved in the issuance of section 402 permits will frequently be sharply disputed. Adversarial hearings will be helpful, therefore, in guaranteeing both reasoned decisionmaking and meaningful judicial review. In summary, the proceedings below were conducted in order "to adjudicate disputed facts in particular cases," not "for the purposes of promulgating policy-type rules or standards."

This is exactly the kind of quasi-judicial proceeding for which the adjudicatory procedures of the APA were intended. . . . One of the developments that prompted the APA was the "multiplication of federal administrative agencies and expansion of their functions to include adjudications which have serious impact on private rights." This is just such an adjudication. The panoply of procedural protections provided by the APA is necessary not only to protect the rights of an applicant for less stringent pollutant discharge limits, but is also needed to protect the public for whose benefit the very strict limitations have been enacted. If determinations such as the one at issue here are not made on the record, then the fate of the Hampton-Seabrook Estuary could be decided on the basis of evidence that a court would never see or, what is worse, that a court could not be sure existed. We cannot believe that Congress would intend such a result. . . .

In short, we . . . are willing to presume that, unless a statute otherwise specifies, an adjudicatory hearing subject to judicial review must be on the record . . . . Here the statute certainly does not indicate that the determination need *not* be on the record, and we find no indication of a contrary congressional intent. Therefore, we will judge the proceedings below according to the standards set forth in §§ 554, 556, and 557 of the APA.

Compliance with the Administrative Procedure Act

Petitioners contend that two steps in the EPA's proceedings in this case violated the APA. We will look at each in turn.

1. The Post-hearing Submissions; The Request for Information

The Regional Administrator, in his initial decision, had determined that the record was insufficient to properly evaluate the environmental effects of back-flushing. . . . The Administrator asked PSCO to submit supplemental information on that subject. Other parties were given permission to comment on PSCO's submission. . . . PSCO submitted the requested information. Other parties, including petitioners, submitted comments, and petitioners requested a hearing. The Administrator denied the hearing . . . . Petitioners argue, first, that the Administrator could not rely on this information because it was not part of the exclusive record for decision. 5 U.S.C. § 556(e). Second, petitioners argue that even if the information was legitimately part of the record, the Administrator was obligated to provide an opportunity for cross-examination pursuant to 5 U.S.C. § 556(d). . . . [W]e can find no fault with the Administrator's decision to seek further evidence. Indeed we think this procedure was a most appropriate way to gather the necessary information without the undue delay that would result from a remand.

The question remains, however, whether the procedures by which the Administrator gathered the information conformed to the governing law. The first point is whether the Administrator was empowered to require that the new evidence be submitted in written form. The Administrator may, under 5 U.S.C. § 556(d), so require in cases of initial licensing. This is an initial licensing. But just as the APA does not impose procedures excused by a governing statute, so the APA does not excuse procedures compelled by the governing statute. In this case § 316(a) of the FWPCA requires the EPA to afford an opportunity for a *public hearing*. We do not believe that an opportunity to submit documents constitutes a public hearing. Nor do we believe that the Administrator can comply with the statute merely by taking some evidence at a public hearing and then taking the rest in written form. If that were the law, nothing would prevent the Administrator from holding a ten minute hearing to establish compliance and then requiring the submission of the rest of the evidence. Therefore, we interpret the closing lines of § 556(d) of the APA to mean that the Administrator can require evidence to be submitted in written form in initial licensings unless the governing statute requires a public hearing. The public hearing can be especially important in cases such as this one which turn not so much upon the actual baseline data (which presumably all parties will be happy to have submitted in written form) as upon experts' interpretation of the data. The experts' credibility is, therefore, very much at issue here.

While we believe that it was error for the Administrator not to hold a hearing to receive the responses to his request for Information, . . . we cannot be sure that any purpose would be served by ordering a hearing on this issue at this stage in these proceedings. Petitioners' principal complaints are that either the Administrator could not take any evidence or that he was required to afford an opportunity for cross-examination. The latter complaint has no more basis than the former. A party to an administrative adjudicatory hearing does not have an absolute right to cross-examine witnesses. The plain language of 5 U.S.C. § 556(d) limits that right to instances where cross-examination is "required for a full and true disclosure of the facts."

We will order a remand for the limited purpose of allowing the Administrator to determine whether cross-examination would be useful. . . . If the Administrator finds that cross-examination would help disclose the facts a hearing must be provided at which cross-examination would be available. If, however, the Administrator concludes that cross-examination would not serve any useful purpose then we will not require him to hold a hearing merely to have the already submitted statements read into the record.

2. Participation of the Technical Review Panel

Petitioners object to the Administrator's use of a panel of EPA scientists to assist him in reviewing the Regional Administrator's initial decision. The objection is two-fold: first, that the Administrator should not have sought such help at all; and, second, that the panel's report (the Report) to the Administrator included information not in the administrative record.

. . . The Administrator is charged with making highly technical decisions in fields far beyond his individual expertise. . . . Therefore, "evidence . . . may be sifted and analyzed by competent subordinates." *Morgan v. United States*. The decision ultimately reached is no less the Administrator's simply because agency experts helped him to reach it. A different question is presented, however, if the agency experts do not merely sift and analyze but also add to the evidence properly before the Administrator. . . . To the extent the technical review panel's Report included information not in the record on which the Administrator relied, § 556(e) was violated. . . .

Our review of the Report indicates that such violations did occur. The most serious instance is on page 19 of the Report where the technical panel rebuts the Regional Administrator's finding that PSCO had failed to supply enough data on species' thermal tolerances by saying:

> There is little information in the record on the thermal tolerances of marine organisms . . . . However, the scientific literature does contain many references to the thermal sensitivity of members of the local biota.

. . . . What is important is that the record did not support the conclusion until supplemented by the panel. The panel's work found its way directly into the Administrator's decision at page 27 where he . . . concludes, "On the recommendation of the panel, however, I find that . . . local indigenous populations will not be significantly affected." This conclusion depends entirely on what the panel stated about the scientific literature.

Similar, though less egregious, examples occur [a number of times] in the Report [and found] their way into the Administrator's decision . . . . The panel did not say that the information missing was unavailable or irrelevant; instead they supplied the information. They are free to do that as witnesses, but not as deciders.

The appropriate remedy under these circumstances is to remand the decision to the Administrator because he based his decision on material not part of the record. We are compelled to treat the use of the Report more severely than the use of the PSCO post-hearing submission because no party was given any opportunity to comment on the panel's Report. By contrast, all parties were given the opportunity to comment on PSCO's submission, and these comments were considered equally part of the record by the Administrator. . . . The Administrator will have the options of trying to reach a new decision not dependent on the panel's supplementation of the record; of holding a hearing at which all parties will have the opportunity to cross-examine the panel members and at which the panel will have an opportunity to amplify its position; or of taking any other action within his power and consistent with this opinion. . . .

> ## Underlying Case Documents
>
> The case referenced:
> The Federal Water Pollution Control Act of 1972
> The Administrator's decision
>
> For the Administrator's decision on remand click HERE.

1. *Seacoast* and the Problem of Extra-Record Information.

a. Looking first to the question of the record on which the agency relied, what standard does the court use to determine whether the consideration of data not included in the record "contaminates" the proceedings and renders the process at odds with the mandates of due process or the APA?

The legitimacy of the use of non-record information is varied by the nature of the hearing the agency provides. The greater the formality, the less the agency ought to use information that cannot be confronted. The less formal the adjudicatory process, the greater the acceptability of such information. Given that the mission of every agency is, first and foremost, to implement its statute, why not allow an agency to use any and all sources that contribute to an understanding of the problem it faces?

b. In this brief excerpt from *Connecticut Natural Gas Corporation v. Public Utilities Control Authority*, 439 A.2d 282 (D. Conn. 1981), the court was faced with non-record information and held as follows:

> On October 3, 1977, the plaintiff, Connecticut Natural Gas Corporation, . . . requested that the defendant Public Utilities Control Authority (PUCA) permit amendments to the plaintiff's existing rate schedule . . . to increase the plaintiff's annual revenues by $ 9,612,396 . . . . [T]he PUCA held public hearings [on this request and] hired James Rothschild . . . to participate in considering the application and to cross-examine some of the witnesses who appeared at the hearings before the PUCA. Rothschild did not testify, had no role in enforcing the PUCA's orders, and was not associated with any party to the proceedings. . . . At the close of the hearings, PUCA employees, including Rothschild, submitted their reports to the PUCA. Rothschild's report discussed the plaintiff's cost of capital, cost of common equity, capital structure, tax credits and rate of return. The report specifically attacked the testimony [of] one of the plaintiff's witnesses, and said that the corporation's requested return on equity appeared to be excessive.
>
> At the PUCA's subsequent public deliberations the Rothschild report came to the plaintiff's attention. On February 6, 1978, the plaintiff wrote to the PUCA objecting to Rothschild's methodology for calculating a rate of return on common equity.

[Among many other issues, the court considered the PUCA's use of Rothschild's report since it was not readily available as part of the original hearing record.] Part of the Rothschild report . . . may contain extra-record evidence. . . . The inclusion of improper evidence in the record upon which the decision is based does not, however, by itself, invalidate the decision. . . . [T]he use of improper evidence requires a remand only if a party has affirmatively shown substantial prejudice. . . . Nevertheless, although the PUCA stipulated that it considered the Rothschild report during the ratemaking process, a reviewing court must assume, unless the contrary appears from the record, that the PUCA's final decision did not rely upon whatever extra-record evidence the report may contain. This presumption is particularly strong when, as here, a party alerted the PUCA to possible extra-record evidence in the report. . . . On remand, the trial court may reexamine the question of prejudice.

c. Not every procedural misstep dooms an administrative proceeding. The *Seacoast* standard is fairly straightforward – the mistake must cause substantial prejudice, an injury to an interest that the "statute, regulation, or rule in question was designed to protect." *See Hernandez-Luis v. INS, 869 F.2d 496, 498 (9th Cir. 1989); United States v. Cerda-Pena, 799 F.2d 1374, 1377 (9th Cir. 1986); Aero Mayflower Transit, Inc. v. ICC, 711 F.2d 224, 232 (D.C. Cir. 1983); and Ka Fung Chan v. INS, 634 F.2d 248, 258 (5th Cir. 1981).*

If there is evidence of substantial prejudice, a remand is the normal remedy. *Dixon Ticonderoga Co. v. U.S. Customs & Border Prot., 366 F. Supp. 2d 1352, 1357 (Ct. Int'l Trade 2005).*

The Supreme Court has not defined with precision the concept of substantial prejudice as the term was used in *Seacoast*, although in *American Farm Lines v. Black Ball Freight Serv*ice, 397 U.S. 532 (1970), and *Vitarelli v. Seaton, 359 U.S. 535 (1959)*, the Court provided some general guidelines. *American Farm* relates more to agency practice (from the agency's perspective) and *Vitarelli* relates more to the rights of those subject to agency action.

d. Keep in mind that the protections of the Sixth Amendment Confrontation Clause are not applicable to civil proceedings. *Austin v. United States, 509 U.S. 602, 608 n.4 (1993).* Even in those proceedings where liberty interests are at stake, courts have been careful to define procedural entitlements based on due process or statute, but not in terms of the Confrontation Clause. *See United States v. Sahhar, 917 F.2d 1197, 1205-06 (9th Cir. 1990),* a civil commitment case where the Sixth Amendment was not applicable.

e. What if an administrative proceeding has ramifications that are likely to be central to – or even activate – a criminal proceeding? There are many fields where facts found in agency cases (tax, antitrust, immigration, securities, and environmental law, for starters) may not only be relevant to a subsequent criminal case, they may be admissible (at a minimum for impeachment purposes) in the criminal proceeding. If one can show that a subsequent criminal proceeding is on the immediate horizon, should different rules apply? For a discussion of the Court's general perspective on confrontation, see *Crawford v. Washington*, 541 U.S. 36 (2004).

2. Does "Public Hearing" Mean Formal Hearing?

a. Until 2006 and the court's decision in *Dominion Energy Brayton Point v. Johnson*, 443 F.3d 12 (1st Cir. 2006), which follows in this text after the *Chemical Waste* case, the more controversial part of *Seacoast* involved the question of whether the term "public hearing" meant a formal hearing bounded by §§ 554, 556-557 of the APA or something less formal. Two schools of thought emerged – by far, the dominant perspective was that if Congress wanted to direct the agency to conduct a formal adjudicatory proceeding, they would have either said so directly or at least used the phrase "on the record." The other perspective was that the term "public hearing," when used in the context of adjudication (and licensing is inherently adjudicatory), could mean a formal hearing, depending on the nature of the interests of those affected by agency action, the interests of the government, and the risk that an informal process would likely result in erroneous decisionmaking – in other words, *Mathews v. Eldridge*.

b. As a matter of policy, pragmatically speaking, what are the benefits of an informal process? Is the agency likely to be better informed – or likely to receive less reliable information? Is public confidence likely to be enhanced by the ease of participation – or diminished when it becomes clear that the agency is ignoring the core of what was presented in the informal process? When you read *Londoner v. City and County of Denver*, 210 U.S. 373 (1908), at the start of the semester (assuming it was assigned), what kind of hearing did you envision? What is your preconceived notion of the rights and processes that are extant in the course of a hearing?

c. In *Union of Concerned Scientists v. NRC*, 735 F.2d 1437, 1444 n.12 (D.C. Cir. 1984), the court faced a question similar to that in *Seacoast*. What follows is a brief excerpt of footnote 12 from that opinion:

> Although section 189(a)'s hearing provision lacks the magic words "on the record," there is much to suggest that the Administrative Procedure Act's (APA) "on the record" procedures, 5 U.S.C. §§ 554, 556, 557 (1982), apply. . . . *First, licensing is adjudication, and when a statute calls for a hearing in an adjudication the hearing is presumptively governed by "on the record" procedures. See Seacoast Anti-Pollution League v. Costle.* Second, in 1961, the AEC specifically requested Congress to relieve it of its burden of "on the record" adjudications under 189(a) [and Congress refused]. Third, more recently in amending section 189(a) to allow hearings after (rather than prior to) a license amendment where the NRC determines that the amendment involves no significant hazards, Congress again assumed that the amendment hearings were "on

the record." *See, e.g.*, H.R. Rep. No. 22, Part 2, 97th Cong., 1st Sess. 9 (1982). Finally, over the past twenty years the NRC has consistently taken the position that section 189(a) calls for "on the record" hearings in adjudications. . . . [Emphasis added.]

d. The Ninth Circuit reached a similar conclusion in *Marathon Oil Co. v. EPA*, 564 F.2d 1253, 1263 (9th Cir. 1977), holding that formal procedures are anticipated notwithstanding the lack of the phrase "on the record" in the statutory text. In contrast, in *U.S. Lines, Inc. v. Federal Maritime Commission*, 584 F.2d 519, 536 (D.C. Cir. 1978), JUDGE SKELLY WRIGHT found

the exact phrase "on the record" is not an absolute prerequisite to application of the formal hearing requirements, [but] the Supreme Court has made clear that these provisions do not apply unless Congress has clearly indicated that the "hearing" required by statute must be a trial-type hearing on the record.

e. Keep in mind that *Seacoast* is pre-*Chevron* and *Mead*. The court in *Seacoast*, therefore, was not limited to assessing if the agency action was within the statutory authority of the EPA and therefore "permissible."

CHEMICAL WASTE MANAGEMENT, INC. v. U.S. ENVIRONMENTAL PROTECTION AGENCY

873 F.2d 1477 (D.C. Cir. 1989)

[JUDGE D.H. GINSBURG] Petitioners . . . seek review of Environmental Protection Agency regulations, 40 C.F.R. Part 24 (1988), that establish informal procedures for administrative hearings concerning the issuance of corrective action orders under § 3008(h) of the Resource Conservation and Recovery Act (RCRA), as modified by the Hazardous and Solid Waste Amendments of 1984. . . .

Congress enacted RCRA in 1976 to establish a comprehensive program for regulation of hazardous waste management and disposal. The statute requires generally that the operator of any hazardous waste treatment, storage, or disposal facility obtain a permit . . . . Subsection (a) of RCRA § 3008 authorizes EPA to enter orders assessing civil penalties, including suspension or revocation of permits, for violation of RCRA regulations. Subsection (b) provides that, upon request made within thirty days of the issuance of a subsection (a) order, EPA "shall promptly conduct a public hearing." . . . . In 1978, EPA promulgated procedural regulations to implement the "public hearing" provision of subsection (a). 40 C.F.R. Part 22. These procedures conform to the provisions of the Administrative Procedure Act for formal adjudication. 5 U.S.C. §§ 556 & 557. . . .

. . . .

In the Hazardous and Solid Waste Amendments of 1984, Congress added to § 3008 a new subsection (h), authorizing the Administrator of EPA to issue "an order requiring corrective action" whenever he "determines that there is or has been a release of hazardous waste into the environment" from an interim facility. Such orders must indicate "the nature of the required corrective action or other response measure, and . . ." may assess a civil penalty of up to $ 25,000 per day for noncompliance with a corrective action order. The 1984 Amendments also modified subsection (b) to make it clear that those subject to corrective action orders . . . have the right to a "public hearing."

. . . EPA . . . regulations . . . provide that the formal adjudicatory procedures of Part 22 shall be applicable only to challenges to subsection (h) corrective action orders that include a suspension or revocation of interim status or an assessment of civil penalties for noncompliance. If the order calls upon the interim facility operator merely to undertake an investigation or to do so in combination with interim corrective measures, then, depending upon the burden entailed by such measures, the agency will use [the Part 24] informal adjudicatory procedures . . . .

[Under the informal procedures the] operator . . . may submit written information and argument for inclusion in the record; make an oral presentation at the hearing itself; and be assisted at [the] hearing by legal and technical advisors. *Direct examination and cross-examination of witnesses is not permitted*, but the Presiding Officer may direct questions to either party. The Presiding Officer is to be either "the Regional Judicial Officer [not an administrative law judge (ALJ), as would be the case for a formal hearing] or another attorney employed by the Agency, who has had no prior connection with the case, including performance of any investigative or prosecuting functions." With respect to both Subpart B and Subpart C proceedings, EPA, when issuing a corrective action order, shall deliver to the operator "all relevant documents and oral information . . . the Agency considered in the process of developing and issuing the order . . . ."

. . . .

Petitioners argue initially that [the] informal procedures of Part 24 are inconsistent with the intent of Congress in enacting and amending § 3008. To this end, petitioners [argue that the term "public hearing" requires a formal hearing]. Petitioners point to our statement in a footnote in *Union of Concerned Scientists v. NRC*, 735 F.2d 1437 (D.C. Cir. 1984) (*UCS*), that "when a statute calls for a hearing in an adjudication the hearing is presumptively governed by 'on the record' procedures," notwithstanding omission of the phrase "on the record" in the statute. *See also Seacoast Anti-Pollution League v. Costle*. For the reasons set out below, however, we decline to adhere any longer to the presumption raised in *UCS*.

For perspective, we note first . . . that "we refrain[ed] from holding outright that [the hearing provision in question there] require[d] 'on the record' hearings." Our statement about the presumption to that effect was therefore dicta. We did not actually rely on the presumption we announced, but rather inferred that Congress intended the use of formal adjudicatory procedures based both upon NRC's unsuccessful efforts to convince Congress to do away with such procedures and upon NRC's consistent position, over a twenty year period, that the statute required formal procedures. No such contextual circumstances exist here.

More important, *UCS* and its kin, *Seacoast* and *Marathon*, all predate the Supreme Court's decision in *Chevron*. Under that decision, it is not our office to presume that a statutory reference to a "hearing," without more specific guidance from Congress, evinces an intention to require formal adjudicatory procedures, since such a presumption would arrogate to the court what is now clearly the prerogative of the agency, *viz.*, to bring its own expertise to bear upon the resolution of ambiguities in the statute that Congress has charged it to administer. In effect, the presumption in *UCS* truncates the *Chevron* inquiry at the first step by treating a facially ambiguous statutory reference to a "hearing" as though it were an unambiguous constraint upon the agency. We will henceforth make no presumption that a statutory "hearing" requirement does or does not compel the agency to undertake a formal "hearing on the record," thereby leaving it to the agency, as an initial matter, to resolve the ambiguity. . . . [A]n agency that *reasonably* reads a simple requirement that it hold a "hearing" to allow for informal hearing procedures must prevail under the second step of *Chevron*. . . .

. . . .

Finally, petitioners contend that [the informality of the process] denies them due process of law . . . . [The court found that, since the EPA continued to use formal adjudication when the private interest was substantial, no significant private interest was at stake. Meanwhile, the government benefited greatly from the use of an informal adjudication when the private interest was minimal.]

[A portion of the court's discussion of the risk-of-error element of the *Mathews* test follows.] Petitioners fail to explain how [formal adjudicatory] procedures will significantly advance the accuracy of an adjudicative process in which the issues typically do not require determinations of witness credibility but turn instead upon technical data and policy judgments. In [*Mathews*] itself, the Court states that such proceedings present less of a need for trial-type procedures.

According to petitioners, due process requires that an ALJ conduct a subsection (h) hearing. Petitioners are particularly critical of the provisions of Part 24 that allow agency attorneys to serve as Presiding Officers, provided only that they have "had no prior connection with the case, including the performance of any investigative or prosecuting functions." . . . . [I]ndeed, the Presiding Officer might, for all that the regulation requires, be a subordinate of the prosecuting attorney within EPA's internal hierarchy.

[However, the] Supreme Court has held that even the combination, in a single administrative decisionmaker, of investigative and adjudicative functions – which the EPA regulations plainly forbid – "does not, without more, constitute a due process violation"; rather, "the special facts and circumstances of the case [must indicate] that the risk of unfairness is intolerably high." *Withrow v. Larkin*. Moreover, in challenging a particular adjudication on this ground, the complaint must "overcome the presumption of honesty and integrity in those serving as adjudicators" by showing "a risk of actual bias or prejudgment." In light of *Withrow's* stringent standard for an "as applied" attack on procedures that allow the combination of investigative and adjudicative functions, we find no basis for petitioners' broad facial challenge, which by its nature deprives us of the particularized information necessary to evaluate a claim of probable bias.

Finally, petitioners attack the regulations on the ground that the Presiding Officer will be unable to resolve the intricate technical issues that may arise in a subsection (h) proceeding. They do not, however, explain why an agency attorney would be any less equal to that task than would be the ALJ they prefer.

In sum, petitioners have shown little if any avoidable risk of error arising from the procedural regulations they challenge.

. . . .

Underlying Case Documents

The case referenced:
The Hazardous and Solid Waste Amendments of 1984

1. In *Bowles v. Seminole Rock & Sand Co.*, 325 U.S. 410, 414 (1945), the precursor to *Auer v. Robbins*, *supra* Chapter 3, the Court held that an agency's interpretation of its regulations "becomes of controlling weight unless it is plainly erroneous or inconsistent with the regulation." Is *Chemical Waste* a *Seminole Rock* decision? Was this a meaningful review of the interests of the individuals affected, the interests of the government, and the probability of erroneous decisionmaking (*Mathews v.*

Eldridge), or an affirmation of the ability of agencies to determine their own procedures absent congressional directive? See John F. Manning, *Constitutional Structure and Judicial Deference to Agency Interpretations of Agency Rules*, 96 COLUM. L. REV. 612 (1996), for a penetrating and useful discussion of *Seminole Rock*.

2. Refer back to the notes following the *Seacoast* decision. Quite obviously, the *Chemical Waste* court was disinclined to compel a more formal process. If the basis for the *Seacoast* decision was the statute under which EPA operated as well as fairness concerns, what was the basis for the *Chemical Waste* decision?

Citing *MCI Cellular Telephone Company v. FCC*, 738 F.2d 1322, 1333 (D.C. Cir. 1984), the *Chemical Waste* court held that it was "guided by two fundamental principles. The first is that an agency's interpretation of its own regulations will be accepted unless it is plainly wrong [and the] second is that on a highly technical question . . . courts necessarily must show considerable deference to an agency's expertise. . . . Taken together, these principles counsel extreme circumspection in our review of the agency's action."

Was the court referring to expertise with the science involved – or was it referring to expertise regarding the nature of hearings, and the need – or lack thereof – for formality?

3. What is the "check" on the agency, given the kind of hearing that the court found permissible in *Chemical Waste*? How would one avoid a situation in which non-record information became central to the decisionmaking of the agency? What kind of judicial review – including review of the record – is likely in this setting? *See* Cooley R. Wowarth, Jr., *Restoring the Applicability of the APA's Adjudicatory Procedures*, 56 ADMIN. L. REV. 1043, 1048 (2004).

4. In *Friends of Earth v. Reilly*, 966 F.2d 690, 693-94 (D.C. Cir. 1992), the state administered a hazardous waste program pursuant to EPA rules. While the program was underway, a state legislative proposal surfaced that, in the opinion of some, was at odds with the Resource Conservation and Recovery Act (RCRA), 42 U.S.C. § 6926(e), an action that would "subject the state to withdrawal." A hearing was held before an administrative law judge and an order issued stating that there was no incompatibility between RCRA and the proposed state regulation, after which the *Friends of Earth* claimed a right to attorneys fees on the premise that the hearing was – or should have been – an "adversary adjudication," and so therefore, under the Equal Access to Justice Act (EAJA), they were entitled to fees. Of interest is the portion of the opinion dealing with formality in the adjudicatory process:

> Friends gives several reasons for arguing that Congress intended withdrawal proceedings to be subject to Section 554 [of the APA]. First, Friends argues that

because RCRA recognizes the states' traditional police power in environmental manners, Congress could not have intended to allow for withdrawal without a Section 554 hearing. Second, Friends argues that, because withdrawal upsets both a state's interest as well as the public's expectation in the state's administration of its hazardous waste program and is a draconian remedy, Congress must have intended that Section 554 procedures be used. Third, Friends argues that because withdrawal prevents a state from enacting more stringent requirements and is tantamount to preemption, Congress must have intended to require Section 554 procedures.

Undoubtedly, a state's interest in the continued administration of its hazardous waste program is substantial. But even so, it does not follow that a Section 554 hearing is necessary to ensure that the state's interest is adequately protected. A Section 554 hearing, with its attendant procedural protections, has as its primary purpose the determination of "adjudicative facts," i.e., those facts which "usually answer the questions of who did what, where, when, how, why, with what motive or intent [and] are roughly the kind of facts that go to a jury in a jury case." A section 554 hearing is, in short, like a trial proceeding. But it does not necessarily follow that the nature of the interests at stake in a withdrawal proceeding requires a Section 554 proceeding. . . . [T]he nature of the interests at stake in a withdrawal proceeding hardly seems to be dispositive of the question whether Congress intended to require a Section 554 hearing. Rather, it seems to us that it is the nature of the issues to be resolved in the withdrawal proceeding which is determinative. *Cf. Chemical Waste Management.* . . .

While factual issues may arise in the course of addressing these issues, these factual issues can be classified as involving "legislative facts" – those "general facts which help the tribunal decide questions of law and policy." A Section 554 hearing is rarely necessary to determine such facts. . . . In short, neither the interests involved nor the issues likely to arise in a withdrawal proceeding suggest that a Section 554 hearing is required. We thus conclude that Congress, in providing for a "public hearing," did not intend that the withdrawal hearing be "subject to or governed by" Section 554.

The case below continues the dialogue begun in *Seacoast*. Significantly, and unlike *Seacoast*, *Dominion* is a post-*Chevron*, post-*Brand X* case.

DOMINION ENERGY BRAYTON POINT, LLC V. JOHNSON

443 F.3d 12 (1st Cir. 2006)

[JUDGE SELYA] USGen New England, Inc., now Dominion Energy Brayton Point, LLC (Dominion), filed suit against the U.S. Environmental Protection Agency, its administrator, and its regional office (collectively, the EPA), alleging that the EPA failed to perform a non-discretionary duty when it refused to grant Dominion's request for a formal evidentiary hearing after issuing a proposed final National Pollution Discharge Elimination System (NPDES) permit. The district court dismissed the case for want of subject matter jurisdiction. On appeal, the central question presented concerns the effect of this court's decision in *Seacoast*

Anti-Pollution League v. Costle, in light of the Supreme Court's subsequent decision in *Chevron*. Concluding, as we do, that *Seacoast* does not control, we affirm the judgment below.

I. BACKGROUND

Dominion owns an electrical generating facility in Somerset, Massachusetts (the station). The station opened in the 1960s and, like most power plants of its era, utilizes an "open-cycle" cooling system. Specifically, the station withdraws water from the Lees and Taunton Rivers, circulates that water through the plant's generating equipment as a coolant, and then discharges the water (which, by then, has attained an elevated temperature) into Mount Hope Bay. The withdrawals and discharges of water are regulated by the Clean Water Act (CWA) . . . .

In 1998, the station applied for renewal of its NPDES permit and thermal variance authorization. The EPA issued a proposed final permit on October 6, 2003, in which it rejected the requested thermal variance. On November 4, Dominion sought review before the Environmental Appeals Board (the Board), and asked for an evidentiary hearing. The Board accepted the petition for review but declined to convene an evidentiary hearing. On August 11, 2004, Dominion notified the EPA of its intent to file a citizen's suit under section 505(a)(2) of the CWA, to compel the Board to hold an evidentiary hearing. Receiving no reply, Dominion proceeded to file its complaint in the United States District Court for the District of Massachusetts. The EPA moved to dismiss.

The district court granted the motion . . . . [I]t concluded that it was without subject matter jurisdiction because the suit, though billed as a citizen's suit, constituted a direct challenge to the EPA's hearing rule and, thus, came within the exclusive jurisdiction of the circuit court under 33 U.S.C. § 1369(b)(1)(E). This timely appeal followed.

II. THE LEGAL LANDSCAPE

. . . Before the EPA either issues an NPDES permit or authorizes a thermal variance, n.2 it must offer an "opportunity for public hearing." 33 U.S.C. §§ 1326(a), 1342(a). No definition of "public hearing" is contained within the four corners of the CWA. The Administrative Procedure Act['s] (APA) [formal adjudication] procedures apply "in every case of adjudication required by statute to be determined on the record after opportunity for an agency hearing." The APA does not directly address whether these procedures apply when a statute simply calls for an "opportunity for public hearing" without any specific indication that the hearing should be "on the record."

n.2 . . . The fact that Dominion is seeking a permit renewal rather than a new permit
is . . . irrelevant [as] the application procedure is the same.

In *Seacoast* [e]xamining the legislative history of the APA, we adopted a
presumption that "unless a statute otherwise specifies, an adjudicatory hearing
subject to judicial review must be [an evidentiary hearing] on the record." Applying that presumption to the CWA, we concluded that "the statute certainly does
not indicate that the determination need not be on the record." . . . . Acquiescing
in this construction, the EPA promulgated regulations that memorialized the use
of formal evidentiary hearings in the NPDES permit process.

In 1984, a sea change occurred in administrative law and, specifically, in
the interpretation of organic statutes such as the CWA. The Supreme Court
[decided *Chevron*]. Armed with the *Chevron* decision and a presidential directive to streamline regulatory programs, the EPA advanced a proposal to eliminate
formal evidentiary hearings from the NPDES permitting process. In due course,
the EPA adopted that proposal as a final rule. This revision depended heavily
on a *Chevron* analysis. The agency began by "finding no evidence that Congress
intended to require formal evidentiary hearings or that the text [of section 402(a)]
precludes informal adjudication of permit review petitions." Then, it weighed the
risks and benefits of employing informal hearing procedures for NPDES permit
review, "determining that these procedures would not violate the Due Process
Clause." Finally, it "concluded that informal hearing procedures satisfy the hearing requirement of section 402(a)."

It was under this new regulatory scheme that the EPA considered Dominion's
request to renew its NPDES permit and to authorize a thermal variance. Thus, it
was under this scheme that the EPA denied Dominion's request for an evidentiary
hearing.

III. ANALYSIS

The court of appeals reviews a dismissal for want of subject matter jurisdiction de novo. . . . [T]he statute invoked by Dominion grants federal district courts
jurisdiction over any citizen's suit brought "against the Administrator [of the EPA]
where there is alleged a failure of the Administrator to perform any act or duty
under [the CWA] which is not discretionary." . . . . The crux of the case, therefore,
is whether Dominion has pleaded the flouting of a non-discretionary duty.

One thing is crystal clear: on their face, the current EPA regulations do not
establish a non-discretionary duty to provide the evidentiary hearing that Dominion seeks. Prior to the date of Dominion's request, the EPA vitiated the preexisting rule introducing evidentiary hearings into the NPDES permitting process.
Dominion concedes this fact, but nonetheless relies on *Seacoast* as the source

of a non-discretionary duty to convene an evidentiary hearing. This reliance is misplaced. . . .

. . . .

For present purposes, the critical precedent is *National Cable & Telecommunications Ass'n v. Brand X Internet Services*. There, the Court examined the relationship between the stare decisis effect of an appellate court's statutory interpretation and the *Chevron* deference due to an administrative agency's subsequent, but contrary, interpretation. Echoing *Chevron*, the Court reiterated that "filling gaps . . . involves difficult policy choices that agencies are better equipped to make than courts." Then, concluding that *Chevron*'s application should not turn on the order in which judicial and agency interpretations issue, the Justices held squarely that "[a] court's prior judicial construction of a statute trumps an agency construction otherwise entitled to *Chevron* deference only if the prior court decision holds that its construction follows from the unambiguous terms of the statute and thus leaves no room for agency discretion." . . . .

Brand X demands that we reexamine pre-*Chevron* precedents through a *Chevron* lens. . . . At the first step, a court "must look primarily to the plain meaning of the statute, drawing its essence from the particular statutory language at issue, as well as the language and design of the statute as a whole." . . . . If the precedent at issue finds clarity at step one – that is, if the holding of the case rests on a perception of clear and unambiguous congressional intent – that precedent will govern. *See Brand X*. If, however, the precedent operates at *Chevron* step two – that is, if the case holds, in effect, that congressional intent is less than pellucid and proceeds to choose a "best reading" rather than "the only permissible reading," [i]ts stare decisis effect will, through *Chevron* deference, yield to a contrary but plausible agency interpretation.

Once this mode of analysis is understood and applied, Dominion's argument collapses. *Seacoast* simply does not hold that Congress clearly intended the term "public hearing" in sections 402(a) and 316(a) of the CWA to mean "evidentiary hearing." To the contrary, the *Seacoast* court based its interpretation of the CWA on a presumption derived from the legislative history of the APA – a presumption that would hold sway only in the absence of a showing of a contrary congressional intent. *Seacoast*. In other words, the . . . *Seacoast* court, faced with an opaque statute, settled upon what it sensibly thought was the best construction of the CWA's "public hearing" language. Such a holding is appropriate at step two of the *Chevron* pavane, not at step one. Consequently, under *Brand X*, *Seacoast* must yield to a reasonable agency interpretation of the CWA's "public hearing" requirement.

The only piece left to this puzzle is to confirm that the EPA's new regulations are, in fact, entitled to *Chevron* deference. This inquiry is a straightforward one. As our earlier discussion suggests (and as the *Seacoast* court correctly deduced), Congress has not spoken directly to the precise question at issue here. Accordingly, we must defer to the EPA's interpretation of the CWA as long as that interpretation is reasonable. In this instance, the administrative interpretation took into account the relevant universe of factors. *See* 65 Fed. Reg. at 30,898-30,900 (considering "(1) the private interests at stake (2) the risk of erroneous decisionmaking, and (3) the nature of the government interest," and concluding that its new regulation was a reasonable interpretation of the CWA). The agency's conclusion that evidentiary hearings are unnecessary and that Congress, in using the phrase "opportunity for public hearing," did not mean to mandate evidentiary hearings seems reasonable – and Dominion, to its credit, has conceded the point.

Dominion makes two final attempts to resuscitate *Seacoast*. First, it asseverates that a refusal to follow *Seacoast* offends the "law of the circuit" rule. That rule (a branch of the stare decisis doctrine) holds that, "ordinarily, newly constituted panels in a multi-panel circuit should consider themselves bound by prior panel decisions" closely on point. However, the "law of the circuit" rule, like most rules of general application, is subject to exceptions. One such exception "comes into play when a preexisting panel opinion is undermined by subsequently announced controlling authority, such as a decision of the Supreme Court." In this instance, the Supreme Court's decisions in *Chevron* and *Brand X* counsel against a mechanical application of *Seacoast*.

Second, Dominion exhorts us to find that *Seacoast*'s holding is actually an interpretation of the APA, not the CWA (and, therefore, the EPA's regulation is also an interpretation of the APA, not entitled to *Chevron* deference). Such a reading of *Seacoast* is plainly incorrect. While the *Seacoast* court relied on a presumption borrowed from the APA, the court's holding is an interpretation of the CWA and, specifically, of the term "public hearing" contained in sections 402(a) and 316(a). The EPA's regulations are also derived from the CWA. Because those changes implicate the statute that the EPA administers (i.e., the CWA), *Chevron* deference is appropriate.

IV. CONCLUSION

We summarize succinctly. Although we in no way disparage the soundness of *Seacoast*'s reasoning, the *Chevron* and *Brand X* opinions and the interposition of a new and reasonable agency interpretation of the disputed statutory language have changed the picture. Because we, like the *Seacoast* court, cannot discern a clear and unambiguous congressional intent behind the words "public hearing" in the CWA and because the EPA's interpretation of that term constitutes a reasonable construction of the statute, deference is due. It follows inexorably that no non-discretionary duty to grant Dominion an evidentiary hearing on its permit application exists. Consequently, the jurisdictional requirements of section 505(a)(2) have not been satisfied. We need go no further. For the reasons elucidated above, we conclude that the district court did not err in dismissing Dominion's action.

———————

Underlying Case Documents

The case referenced:
The EPA publication of the factors in its decision to not use evidentiary hearings
The Board's denial of Dominion's request for an evidentiary hearing

For information on the eventual agreement reached regarding Dominion click HERE.

1. Refer back to the notes following *Seacoast* and *Chemical Waste*. In neither case did the court find that the term "public hearing" mandated a formal hearing – but in an almost identical factual setting, the *Seacoast* court (the same circuit court) interpreted the statute in play in *Dominion* to require formality, raising the obvious question: Why did the *Dominion* court ignore precedent – what about the "rule of the circuit" that obligates courts within a federal circuit to follow precedent, outside of Supreme Court cases to the contrary?

We recognize (as the next section in this text points out) the very limited role of stare decisis in administrative law – is the same true in Article III courts? *See* Amy Coney Barrett, *Stare Decisis and Due Process*, 74 U. COLO. L. REV. 1011 (2003); Oona Hathaway, *Path Dependence in the Law: The Course and Pattern of Legal Change in a Common Law System*, 86 IOWA L. REV. 601, 605 (2001); Richard Fallon, Jr., *Stare Decisis and the Constitution: An Essay on Constitutional Methodology*, 76 N.Y.U. L. REV. 570, 570 (2001); James C. Rehnquist, Note, *The Power That Shall Be Vested in a Precedent: Stare Decisis, the Constitution and the Supreme Court*, 66 B.U. L. REV. 345, 347 (1986); Larry Alexander, *Constrained by Precedent*, 63 S. CAL. L. REV. 1 (1989).

2. *Dominion* has not yet generated a great deal of scholarship – but what has been done is useful. *See* Melissa M. Berry, *Beyond* Chevron's *Domain: Agency Interpretations of Statutory Procedural Provisions*, 30 SEATTLE UNIV. L. REV. 541 (2007). There is also a well-done summary of the case in *Pepperdine University School of Law Legal*

Summaries, 27 J. NAT'L ASS'N L. JUD. 723 (2007).

3. The *Dominion* opinion could not be more clearly written: There is no presumptive entitlement to a formal process, absent congressional mandate – or at least none that the court chose to recognize. There are, as noted after the last two cases, a few courts that see things differently. Recall the text from *Union of Concerned Scientists v. NRC, 735 F.2d 1437, 1444 n.12 (D.C. Cir. 1984)*: "[W]hen a statute calls for a hearing in an adjudication the hearing is presumptively governed by 'on the record' procedures." Most courts, however, will follow the approach in *Dominion*. See, e.g., *Buttrey v. United States, 690 F.2d 1170, 1174-75 (5th Cir. 1982)* (affirming a decision of the Army Corps of Engineers' to deny a formal hearing under the Clean Water Act because of a lack of a congressional directive mandating formality); and *United States v. Indep. Bulk Transp., 480 F. Supp. 474, 479, 481 (S.D.N.Y. 1979)* (a similar set of assumptions regarding the Coast Guard).

4. Retrace the application of *Mathews v. Eldridge* in *Dominion*. Can you think of a viable case theory in which the three steps the court assessed would come out differently? Furthermore, given the fact-laden context in which decisions were made regarding requests for exceptions from the thermal sensitivity rule, isn't there an argument that a more formal hearing would have produced a better record? Assume that is true – does it matter?

In one of the few applications of this case, the First Circuit held in *Harvey v. Johanns, 494 F.3d 237, 240 (1st Cir. 2007)*, that "[i]f the statute is found to be unclear . . . an inquiring court should defer to the Secretary's reasonable interpretation. See *Chevron U.S.A. Inc. v. NRDC, 467 U.S. 837 (1984)*; and *Dominion Energy Brayton Point, LLC v. Johnson*." Accordingly, even if a formal hearing would seem a better idea, so long as the process the agency adopted conforms with the minimum required, it is very hard to attack. Is that *Chevron* deference – or the holding in *Vermont Yankee*?

5. Had EPA announced its decision through notice and comment rulemaking or formal adjudication, there would be no question about the deference due based on *Mead* – that case made clear that those procedures get *Chevron* deference. What was the procedure by which the decision was made to proceed with an informal process in *Dominion*?

6. A Note on Stare Decisis and Administrative Law.

a. *Dominion*, *Seacoast Anti-Pollution*, and, in the rulemaking materials, *Brand X*, directly raise the question of stare decisis. All agencies must maintain records of the decisions they announce. Fundamental to judicial review of the action of any agency is an examination of the record the agency produces.

b. Some agencies make clear that they will be bound by their own precedent while others take the position that there is nothing in the Administrative Procedure Act that compels the agency to follow its own precedent. Importantly, all administrative agencies are capable of changing policy, so long as the proper procedures are followed. Unlike Article III courts, administrative agencies must have the ability to shift position in order to meet changing social and economic needs. While agencies may not be bound by their own prior decisions, under certain circumstances they may well be bound by the prior decisions of courts.

Food for Thought

At an introductory level, it is worth asking what effect the decisions of the agencies have on future agency action. The question is fairly basic: Does *stare decisis* apply in administrative law?

c. There is no generic requirement that agencies adhere to their own precedent. "There is, of course, no rule of administrative stare decisis. Agencies frequently adopt one interpretation of a statute and then, years later, adopt a different view. This and other courts have approved such administrative 'changes in course,' as long as the new interpretation is consistent with congressional intent." *Bankamerica Corp. v. United States*, 462 U.S. 122 (1983) (dissenting opinion of JUSTICE WHITE) (approving new agency statutory interpretation despite many years of contrary interpretation) (citing *United States v. Generix Drug Corp.*, 460 U.S. 453 (1983)); *NLRB v. J. Weingarten, Inc.*, 420 U.S. 251 (1975) (same); *NLRB v. Seven-Up Bottling Co.*, 344 U.S. 344 (1953). This is a basic – and time-tested – premise in the administrative law field. *See FCC v. WOKO, Inc.*, 329 U.S. 223, 228 (1946) (the year the APA was adopted); *and Virginian Railway Co. v. United States*, 272 U.S. 658 (1926).

d. The fact that the Court did not find stare decisis to be a binding rule in administrative law does not mean agency precedent is irrelevant. Quite the contrary, as *State Farm* made clear. When an agency makes a change in a rule, at a minimum, it needs to set out the reason for the new rule. This is true at the state level as well. *See Vergeyle v. Employment Sec. Dep't*, 623 P.2d 736 (Wa. App. 1981) ("Although stare decisis plays only a limited role in the administrative agency context, agencies should strive for equality of treatment."); *330 Concord St. Neighborhood Ass'n v. Campsen*, 424 S.E.2d 538 (S.C. App. 1992) ("An administrative agency is generally not bound by the principle of stare decisis but it cannot act arbitrarily in failing to follow established precedent.").

e. Neither *Seacoast* nor *Dominion* resolve the question of "minimum adjudicatory rights" that are present when an agency must conduct a formal hearing but has no "on the record" requirement.

7. *Citizens Awareness Network, Inc. v. United States of America*, 391 F.3d 338 (1st Cir. 2004).

Disenchanted with its existing procedural framework for the conduct of adjudicatory hearings, the Nuclear Regulatory Commission (NRC or Commission) promulgated new rules designed to make its hearing processes more efficient. . . . The petitioners and petitioner-intervenors are public interest groups. . . . [T]hey claim that the new rules violate a statutory requirement that all reactor licensing hearings be conducted in accordance with sections 554, 556, and 557 of the Administrative Procedure Act (APA). In the alternative, they claim that the Commission has not put forth an adequate justification for so substantial a departure from prior practice and that, therefore, the new rules must be set aside as arbitrary and capricious. . . .

The NRC is the federal agency charged with regulating the use of nuclear energy, including the licensing of reactors used for power generation. The Atomic Energy Act requires . . . the Commission, "upon the request of any person whose interest may be affected" by certain agency actions, to hold "a hearing." It does not explicitly require that the hearing be on the record. . . . For years, the courts of appeals have avoided the question of whether section 2239 requires reactor licensing hearings to be on the record. We too decline to resolve this issue. Because the new rules adopted by the Commission meet the requirements of the APA it does not matter what type of hearing the NRC is required to conduct in reactor licensing cases. . . .

The APA lays out only the most skeletal framework for conducting agency adjudications, leaving broad discretion to the affected agencies in formulating detailed procedural rules. . . . The petitioners urge that the magnitude of the risks involved in reactor licensing proceedings warrant the imposition of a more elaborate set of safeguards. It is beyond cavil, however, that, short of constitutional constraints, a court may not impose procedural requirements in administrative cases above and beyond those mandated by statute (here, the APA). [*Vermont Yankee*.] Accordingly, we are not at liberty to impress on the Commission (or any other agency, for that matter) a procedural regime not mandated by Congress. . . .

CHAPTER 8

Administrative Judging

At a basic level, those who serve as decisionmakers in administrative adjudication are expected to be informed, impartial, and fair. They are expected to evaluate the evidence submitted and make determinations based on that information. If they pre-judge a matter, relying on non-record information or on bias, they are presumably engaged in behavior that will be seen as unfair and lacking impartiality. Furthermore, if they have a specific interest of a personal or financial nature in the matter before them, one would assume that they would be deemed inappropriate decisionmakers.

The fairness and impartiality of those who are required to adjudicate claims is a matter of considerable debate. Take, for example, the question of the expertise of the decisionmaker. On one hand, it seems only logical that the best decisions will be made by those skilled and well-educated in the particular field in which decisions are made. It would be ridiculous to assert that we seek decisionmakers who are uninformed or uneducated about the area in which they adjudicate. On the other hand, skilled, educated, and informed decisionmakers may well have formulated distinct ideas and beliefs regarding a particular field. They may have "heard it all before." An individual who knows the field well enough to have developed a particular point of view could be seen as one who might pre-judge a particular case. At a minimum, a highly informed decisionmaker might, consciously or unconsciously, rely on data secured through a lifetime of research, and not necessarily rely exclusively on the data submitted for the record.

The cases that follow explore the question of administrative judging, fairness, bias, and partiality.

MORGAN v. UNITED STATES

298 U.S. 468 (1936)

[CHIEF JUSTICE HUGHES] These are fifty suits, consolidated for the purpose of trial, to restrain the enforcement of an order of the Secretary of Agriculture, fixing the maximum rates to be charged by market agencies for buying and selling livestock at the Kansas City Stock Yards. . . . After the taking of voluminous testimony . . . the order in question was made on June 14, 1933. Rehearing was refused . . . . Plaintiffs then brought these suits attacking the order, so far as it prescribed maximum charges for selling livestock, as illegal and arbitrary and as depriving plaintiffs of their property without due process of law in violation of the Fifth Amendment of the Constitution. The District Court of three judges entered decrees sustaining the order . . . . Plaintiffs bring this direct appeal.

claim

[Plaintiffs assert] that the Secretary made the rate order without having heard or read any of the evidence, and without having heard the oral arguments or having read or considered the briefs which the plaintiffs submitted. That the only information which the Secretary had as to the proceeding was what he derived from consultation with employees of the Department.

[I]t cannot be said that . . . the fundamental question [is] one of mere delegation of authority. The Government urges that the Acting Secretary who heard the oral argument was in fact the Assistant Secretary of Agriculture whose duties are prescribed by the Act of February 9, 1889, providing for his appointment and authorizing him to perform such duties in the conduct of the business of the Department of Agriculture as may be assigned to him by the Secretary. If the Secretary had assigned to the Assistant Secretary the duty of holding the hearing, and the Assistant Secretary accordingly had received the evidence taken by the examiner, had heard argument thereon and had then found the essential facts and made the order upon his findings, we should have had simply the question of delegation. But while the Assistant Secretary heard argument he did not make the decision. The Secretary who, according to the allegation, had neither heard nor read evidence or argument, undertook to make the findings and fix the rates. The Assistant Secretary, who had heard, assumed no responsibility for the findings or order, and the Secretary, who had not heard, did assume that responsibility.

We may likewise put aside the contention as to the circumstances in which an Acting Secretary may take the place of his chief. In the course of administrative routine, the disposition of official matters by an Acting Secretary is frequently necessary and the integrity of administration demands that credit be given to his action in that capacity. We have no such question here. The Acting Secretary did not assume to make the order.

What is a "hearing"? Why purpose of hearing.

. . . The "hearing" is designed to afford the safeguard that the one who decides shall be bound in good conscience to consider the evidence, to be guided by that alone, and to reach his conclusion uninfluenced by extraneous considerations which in other fields might have play in determining purely executive action. The "hearing" is the hearing of evidence and argument. If the one who determines the facts which underlie the order has not considered evidence or argument, it is manifest that the hearing has not been given.

There is thus no basis for the contention that the authority conferred by § 310 of the Packers and Stockyards Act is given to the Department of Agriculture, as a department in the administrative sense, so that one official may examine evidence, and another official who has not considered the evidence may make the findings and order. In such a view, it would be possible, for example, for one official to hear the evidence and argument and arrive at certain conclusions of fact, and another official who had not heard or considered either evidence or argument to overrule those conclusions and for reasons of policy to announce entirely different ones. It is no answer to say that the question for the court is whether the evidence supports the findings and the findings support the order. For the weight ascribed by the law to the findings – their conclusiveness when made within the sphere of the authority conferred – rests upon the assumption that the officer who makes the findings has addressed himself to the evidence and upon that evidence has conscientiously reached the conclusions which he deems it to justify. That duty cannot be performed by one who has not considered evidence or argument. It is not an impersonal obligation. It is a duty akin to that of a judge. The one who decides must hear.

This necessary rule does not preclude practicable administrative procedure in obtaining the aid of assistants in the department. Assistants may prosecute inquiries. Evidence may be taken by an examiner. Evidence thus taken may be sifted and analyzed by competent subordinates. Argument may be oral or written. The requirements are not technical. But there must be a hearing in a substantial sense. And to give the substance of a hearing, which is for the purpose of making determinations upon evidence, the officer who makes the determinations must consider and appraise the evidence which justifies them. That duty undoubtedly may be an onerous one, but the performance of it in a substantial manner is inseparable from the exercise of the important authority conferred.

The decree is reversed and the cause is remanded for further proceedings in conformity with this opinion. . . .

Underlying Case Documents

The case referenced:
The Act of February 9, 1889
The Packers and Stockyards Act
The order in question parts 1, 2, 3, 4, 5

For the decision on remand click HERE.

1. What does it mean to allow assistants – or law clerks – to "sift and analyze" masses of evidence? Could sifting and analyzing, done in good faith, stack the deck in one direction or another? Realistically speaking, commissioners, administrators, and other senior agency decisionmakers are unlikely to have the time to organize hundreds of thousands – or millions – of documents. Even the most competent and thorough agency head will need help – and that help can have a major effect on the outcome of the case.

2. In *Gomes v. University of Maine*, 365 F. Supp. 2d 6 (D. Me. 2005), several students were expelled after allegations of sexual assault. The university director of judicial affairs, Fiacco, was the hearing officer designated to make the initial decision of whether to refer the matter to a Hearing Committee. He received information from the police department confirming a complaint of sexual assault and thereafter referred the case to a Hearing Committee. Mr. Fiacco "failed to turn documents over to the Plaintiffs when requested to do so [and had] ex parte contact with the Appeal Committee . . . . [The court found this could] "shadow the impartiality, or at least the appearance of impartiality. . . ."

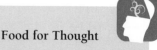

Food for Thought

Technology has created the capacity to organize and access vast amounts of data – but it has also made it easier to include vast amounts of data. Is the idea underlying *Morgan* antiquated – do decisionmakers actually "hear" evidence in most cases? In the common setting of "paper" hearings, where oral presentations are limited or non-existent, how does one implement the axiom "the one who decides must hear?"

Noting that ex parte communication will render a hearing unfair only if the process is "irrevocably tainted by the communications," citing *Springfield Terminal Railway Co. v. United Transportation Union*, 767 F. Supp. 333, 349 (D. Me. 1991), the court assessed:

> (1) the gravity of the contact; (2) whether the contact may have influenced the decision; (3) whether the party making the contact benefited from the decision; (4) whether the contents of the communications were unknown to the opposing parties, who had no opportunity to respond; and (5) whether vacation of the decision and remand for further proceedings would serve a useful purpose. *Prof'l Air Traffic Controllers Org. v. Fed. Labor Relations Auth*, *infra* Chapter 9. . . . [The court found this communication short of "irrevocable taint" and turned to the "tone" of the interaction with Mr. Fiacco. In the footnotes of the opinion, the court indicated it was "unimpressed with the adversary tone" of the argument and noted that, generally speaking, due process did not require a "neutral tone"] .

It is unclear whether the Plaintiffs object to any separate communication between the Appeal Committee and Mr. Fiacco. The law has long allowed administrative officers to rely on subordinates to sift and analyze the record and prepare summaries and confidential recommendations. *Morgan; Normile v. McFague*, 685 F.2d 9, 12 (1st

Cir. 1982). . . . [The Appeals Committee] asked for background information about "standard practices" and "procedures in place" for handling disciplinary matters. Demonstrating the dangers inherent in this practice, Mr. Fiacco's responses strayed beyond the University's general procedures into their application to this case. The Appeal Committee should have informed the parties of all its contacts with Mr. Fiacco to give them an opportunity to understand and object, if necessary. The Plaintiffs have not, however, raised any specific objections to the accuracy of the background material Mr. Fiacco provided. . . . Upon analysis, the Plaintiffs fall far short of demonstrating that Mr. Fiacco's statements rendered the appeal process irrevocably tainted with fundamental unfairness."

The absence of direct objection was fatal to the plaintiffs' claim – but the case is nonetheless a useful reminder of the risks of undue ex parte communication, even if it consists of sifting, analyzing, and summarizing facts and procedures.

3. In *De la Llana-Castellon v. INS*, 16 F.3d 1093 (10th Cir. 1994), the court reviewed the claim of an individual seeking asylum. INS had denied the claim and given "official notice" – the equivalent of judicial notice – to the contention that Nicaragua's general elections had brought about a change in government such that the claimant could no longer claim a "well-founded fear of persecution." Giving notice to a claim means, in effect, making a finding of fact without reviewing independently the evidence regarding that fact. The court held as follows:

[D]ue process entitles a person to fact-finding based on a record produced before the decisionmaker and disclosed to that person [and] it requires that the decisionmaker actually consider the evidence and argument that a party presents. *See, Morgan v. United States.* On the facts of this case, we conclude that the BIA's denial of asylum to Petitioners based on facts administratively noticed violated their right to due process. . . .

In the circumstances of this case, where the BIA noticed facts and made disputable inferences based on those facts which not only directly contradicted the findings of the immigration judge but were dispositive of Petitioners' appeal, we hold that due process requires the BIA to give Petitioners advance notice and an opportunity to be heard. Whatever the ambit of "administrative notice," it is meant to facilitate fair and reasoned decision making and not to substitute for it.

4. Not every shortcut to factfinding – or even substitution of intermediate decisionmakers – is problematic, as *Bates v. Sponberg*, 547 F.2d 325 (6th Cir. 1976), demonstrates:

Professor Bates, as Director of the Center for Aquatic Biology of [Eastern Michigan] University, . . . was obliged to submit certain reports in 1971. . . . Bates . . . withheld submission of them . . . "to protest the University's accounting practices which caused irreparable injury to his professional reputation and reputation in the community." As a result, . . . the Board of Regents directed its president, the defendant Sponberg, to initiate suspension procedures against Bates . . . . [After a grievance committee review, the matter went to President Sponberg who reviewed the record and then recommended Professor Bates' dismissal to the Board of Regents]. . . . [P]resident Sponberg did not transmit to the Board the actual transcript or tapes of the proceedings, which covered over 60 hours of recordings, nor did he transmit . . . some 600 pages of exhibits. His failure to do so, and the Board's failure to have the record available and to consider that evidence, claims Bates, was a violation by the Board of Regents of Rule C.6. of its own regulations. . . .

It is important to recognize that the sole issue presented [is] whether the circumstances . . . violated Bates' rights to due process under the Fourteenth Amendment . . . . While courts have generally invalidated adjudicatory actions by federal agencies which violated their own regulations promulgated to give a party a procedural safeguard, we conclude that the basis for such reversals is not, as Bates asserts, the Due Process Clause, but rather a rule of administrative law. . . . [T]he Administrative Procedure Act does not apply to Eastern Michigan University, a state agency. . . .

We think the crux of the issue, in terms of due process . . . is not whether the [hearing] was held in the presence of the authority having final responsibility to determine his discharge, but instead whether the hearing accorded him was meaningful. . . . [T]he Board of Regents' consideration and action upon the report of the Grievance Committee met the minimal requirements of due process. Nothing in the record . . . suggests that the Grievance Committee's report was deficient, contained factual inaccuracies or did not fairly summarize the evidence before it. . . .

5. There were actually three cases that went to the Supreme Court in the *Morgan* series. In <u>United States v. Morgan, 313 U.S. 409, 421-22 (1941)</u>, the Court dealt with the nature of judicial review and the extent to which a reviewing court can examine the actual thought processes of the agency decisionmaker, as opposed to drawing conclusions exclusively from the record put forward to support the decision. The Court decided that a reviewing court must use the record as the primary vehicle to determine whether a decision was supported by substantial evidence or was arbitrary, capricious, or an abuse of discretion. It is "not the function of the court to probe the mental processes" of the decisionmakers. *See* <u>Nat'l Nutritional Foods Ass'n v. FDA, 491 F.2d 1141 (2d Cir. 1974)</u>; <u>Steffan v. Perry, 41 F.3d 677, 700 (D.C. Cir. 1994)</u> (Buckley, J, concurring). The exception to the rule – permitting inquiry into extra-record sources – is allowed when "there has been a strong showing in support of a claim of bad faith or improper behavior on the part of agency decisionmakers or where the absence of formal administrative findings makes such investigation necessary in order to determine the reasons for the agency's choice." <u>Nat'l Audubon Soc'y v. Hoffman, 132 F.3d 7, 14 (2d Cir. 1997)</u>.

———

Are you convinced that an independent administrative law judge is genuinely independent? Would aggressive oversight of administrative law judges compromise their independence?

NASH V. BOWEN

869 F.2d 675 (2d Cir. 1989)

[JUDGE ALTIMARI] The principal issue raised . . . is whether efforts by the Secretary of Health and Human Services (the "Secretary") to improve the quality and efficiency of the work of Administrative Law Judges ("ALJs") impaired their asserted right to "decisional independence" under the Administrative Procedure Act (the "APA"). [W]e agree with the district court that the Secretary's practices did not infringe on the decisional independence of ALJs. . . .

issue

> holding

Plaintiff-appellant, pro se, Simon Nash is an Administrative Law Judge ("ALJ") with some thirty years experience in the Social Security Administration. In 1967, he became an ALJ in charge ("ALJIC") . . . . By 1975, the Social Security Administration (the "agency") was faced with an administrative crisis due to a backlog of over 100,000 cases. In order to eliminate the backlog and the concomitant delays in processing appeals, former director . . . Robert L. Trachtenberg instituted a series of reforms which appellant contends interfered with the "decisional independence" of ALJs under the APA, the Social Security Act and the due process clause of the fifth amendment. Nash initially protested the new policies within the agency only to be summarily demoted from his position as ALJIC to ALJ. . . .

II.

Turning, then, to plaintiff's "decisional independence" claims, the challenged practices are threefold. . . . [T]he first allegedly unlawful practice is the "Peer Review Program" (a/k/a the "Appellate Appraisal System") which directed the Office of Hearings and Appeals to review decisions of ALJs outside of the usual appeals procedure . . . . The second practice concerns the imposition of allegedly arbitrary monthly production quotas . . . . The third alleged threat to ALJs' decisional independence is the "Quality Assurance System," which attempted to control the number of ALJ decisions reversing previous state-level determinations declining to award benefits.

B.

The district court explicitly determined that "although the defendants may have engaged in some questionable practices . . . they did not infringe on the decisional independence of ALJs." The factual components of this conclusion, as with all findings of fact, cannot be set aside on appeal unless they are clearly erroneous.

std of review

The district court held that the "Peer Review Program" was intended to respond to the "wide disparity in legal and factual determinations among ALJs."

. . . . Policies designed to insure a reasonable degree of uniformity among ALJ decisions are not only within the bounds of legitimate agency supervision but are to be encouraged. In this case, "extra-appellate" review of "dead" cases aimed at improving the quality of ALJ decisionmaking is entirely consistent with the prerogative of the agency which retains "all the powers which it would have in making the initial decision." It is, after all, the Secretary who ultimately is authorized to make final decisions in benefit cases. . . . Thus, the Secretary's efforts through peer review to ensure that ALJ decisions conformed with his interpretation of relevant law and policy were permissible so long as such efforts did not directly interfere with "live" decisions (unless in accordance with the usual administrative review performed by the Appeals Council). *See* § 554(d)(2) (ALJ shall not be "subject to . . . supervision or direction" concerning pending matters). The efforts complained of in this case for promoting quality and efficiency do not infringe upon ALJs' decisional independence. Since JUDGE ELFVIN concluded that the "Peer Review Program" was intended to be, and operated as, a quality control measure, we see no reason to disturb his determination.

Regarding the Secretary's policy of setting a minimum number of dispositions an ALJ must decide in a month, we agree with the district court that reasonable efforts to increase the production levels of ALJs are not an infringement of decisional independence. In a memorandum dated July 1, 1975, then Director Trachtenberg indicated that while he was opposed to the fixing of *quotas*, he was recommending a *goal* of 26 dispositions per four-week period. . . . The setting of reasonable production goals, as opposed to fixed quotas, is not in itself a violation of the APA. The district court explicitly found that the numbers at issue constituted reasonable goals as opposed to unreasonable quotas. JUDGE ELFVIN explained that

> [a] minimum number of dispositions an ALJ must decide in a given period, provided this number is reasonable and not "etched in stone", is not a prescription of how, or how quickly, an ALJ should decide a particular case. It does not dictate the content of the decision.

Moreover, in view of the significant backlog of cases, it was not unreasonable to expect ALJs to perform at minimally acceptable levels of efficiency. Simple fairness to claimants awaiting benefits required no less. Accordingly, we agree with the district court that the decisional independence of ALJs was not in any way usurped by the Secretary's setting of monthly production goals.

The Secretary's "reversal" rate policy embodied in the "Quality Assurance System," however, is cause for concern. To coerce ALJs into lowering reversal rates – that is, into deciding more cases against claimants – would, if shown, constitute in the district court's words "a clear infringement of decisional independence." . . . . The Secretary concedes that he was very concerned about reversal rates, but only to the extent that they might indicate errors in the decisionmaking of ALJs. Testimony in the record revealed that reversal rates were used as a benchmark in deciding whether there *might* be problems in the adjudicatory methods of particularly high (or low) reversal rate ALJs. Statistical record evidence supported the agency's proffered correlation between actual errors of law or policy in ALJs decisions and extremes in their reversal rates. . . .

In view of the foregoing record evidence, therefore, we cannot say that the district court's determination was clearly erroneous. Whatever legitimate concerns there may be about the soundness of the Secretary's practices regarding "reversal" rates, those concerns are more appropriately addressed by Congress or by courts through the usual channels of judicial review in Social Security cases. The bottom line in this case is that it was entirely within the Secretary's discretion to adopt reasonable administrative measures in order to improve the decisionmaking process. Since the district court found no direct pressure on ALJs to maintain a fixed percentage of reversals, we conclude that the Secretary's policy in this regard did not infringe upon the "decisional independence" of ALJs. . . . For all of the foregoing reasons, the judgment of the district court is [a]ffirmed.

Underlying Case Documents

For a GAO report at the time of the case on ALJ disfavor with the productivity initiatives click <u>HERE</u>.

For a 2004 letter expressing ALJ disfavor with "quotas" click <u>HERE</u>.

1. In <u>*Henriquez v. Astrue*, 482 F. Supp. 2d 50 (D. Mass. 2007)</u>, when the claimant in a disability case argued "that the ALJ should have treated her job as a 'trial work period,'" the court responded by noting that the claimant's position was at odds with the view of the Secretary, who ultimately is authorized to make final decisions in benefit cases. In support of this finding, the court cited the following language from *Nash*: "An ALJ is a creature of statute and, as such, is subordinate to the Secretary in matters of policy and interpretation of law." Does this mean that an ALJ, an "impartial decisionmaker" charged with conducting proceedings that are fair and objective, is bound to the perspectives of the political appointees at the top of the agency or administration for which the ALJ works?

The idea that an agency undertakes review of all employees, including ALJ's, to insure efficiency and effectiveness is not controversial – that the reviews could be a means to impose political or ideological preferences is a far more problematic proposition. Accordingly, a number of courts have determined that the system for review of ALJ's approved in *Nash* was inappropriate. *See Barry v. Bowen, 825 F.2d 1324, 1330-31 (9th Cir. 1987)* ("Administrative decisionmakers do not bear all the badges of independence that characterize an Article III judge, but they are held to the same standard of impartial decisionmaking."); *Salling v. Bowen, 641 F. Supp. 1046, 1055-56, 1073-74 (W.D. Va. 1986)* ("If there ever was a chilling of judicial independence, this is it. This is like threatening a lawyer with disbarment if he takes a case of a controversial nature. This is the same as saying that every law judge in the country should be deciding a certain percentage of cases against the claimant."); Jeffrey S. Lubbers, *The Federal Administrative Judiciary: Establishing an Appropriate System of Performance Evaluation for ALJs,* 7 ADMIN. L.J. AM. U. 589 (1994).

2. Concern about the independence of administrative law judges goes beyond the issue of performance reviews raised in *Nash*. In *Grant v. Shalala, 989 F.2d 1332 (3d Cir. 1993)*:

> [P]laintiffs made very extensive efforts to probe the thinking and decision making processes of an officer occupying a position described by the Supreme Court as "functionally comparable" to that of a judge. . . .

> Such efforts to probe the mind of an ALJ, if allowed, would pose a substantial threat to the administrative process. Every ALJ would work under the threat of being subjected to such treatment if his or her pattern of decisions displeased any administrative litigant or group with the resources to put together a suit charging bias. Every ALJ would know that his or her staff members could be deposed and questioned in detail about the ALJ's decision making and thought processes, that co-workers could be subpoenaed and questioned about social conversations, that the ALJ's notes and papers could be ordered produced in discovery, and that any evidence gathered by these means could be used, in essence, to put the ALJ on trial in district court to determine if he or she should be barred from performing the core functions of his or her office. This would seriously interfere with the ability of many ALJs to decide the cases that come before them based solely on the evidence and the law. . . .

> [W]e are convinced that the plaintiffs' right to an impartial administrative determination can be fully protected through the process of judicial review of the Secretary's determination.

How would one prove that an ALJ is biased? Are the mechanisms in *Nash* designed to reveal bias – or ineptitude? *See* Richard J. Pierce, Jr., *Political Control Versus Impermissible Bias in Agency Decisionmaking: Lessons from* Chevron *and* Mistretta, 57 U. CHI. L. REV. 481 (1990).

3. The very independence of the administrative judiciary is subject of dispute. While many scholars – and certainly ALJ's – are troubled by any incursion into the independence of ALJ's, Professor James E. Moliterno takes a contrary view:

> To perform this critical role in the most effective way, administrative judges are not to function in a judicially independent way. Instead, they must recognize that their role demands adherence to agency policy and goals. Judges of the judicial branch, acting independently of the executive and legislative branches, will apply contested legal principles and rules to executive agency action, including that taken by the administrative judiciary. [From James E. Moliterno, *The Administrative Judiciary's Independence Myth,* 41 WAKE FOREST L. REV. 1191, 1192 (2006).]

For a somewhat different perspective, see Harold J. Krent & Lindsay DuVall, *Accommodating ALJ Decision Making Independence with Institutional Interests of the Administrative Judiciary,* 25 J. NAALJ 1 (2005).

In *Tunik v. MSPB,* 407 F.3d 1326, 1340-45 (Fed. Cir. 2005), the court wrote at length on the issue of the independence of ALJ's, focused in large part on 5 U.S.C. § 7521, the section of the U.S. Code dealing with the removal of ALJ's. The case involved a Merit Systems Protections Board regulation pertaining to removal of ALJ's that had been adopted without notice and comment. The court expressed initially some ambivalence on the matter of absolute independence. "[T]he ALJs argue that interference with their decisional independence causes them to perform their duties in an unfair manner, which is inconsistent with their duties as ALJs. It is unclear, however, how an agency's interference with an ALJ's decisional independence causes an ALJ to perform a duty that is inconsistent with the ALJ's duties and responsibilities as an ALJ." However, the court ultimately decided with the ALJ's on the question of process. "Given the importance of the independence of ALJs to the framework of the APA, it would be unreasonable to conclude that regulations promulgated pursuant to section 7521, which is a cornerstone of decisional independence for ALJs, were of so little concern to the public at large that they should not be subject to notice and comment rulemaking."

4. Related to the issue of independence of ALJ's is the question of whether ALJ's should be assigned permanently to one agency – with the expectation that over time the ALJ will become an expert in the legal and regulatory issues at that agency – or whether it is better to have ALJ's on a centralized panel, assigned to various agencies as the need arises, increasing the probability of independence but decreasing the likelihood of specific expertise.

For More Information

See James F. Flanagan, *Redefining the Role of the State Administrative Law Judge Central Panels and Their Impact on State ALJ Authority and Standards of Agency Review,* 54 ADMIN. L. REV. 1355 (2002); Christopher B. McNeil, *Symposium, Maximizing Judicial Fairness & Efficiency: Should Indiana Consider Creating an Office of Administrative Hearings?: Executive Branch Adjudications in Public Safety Laws: Assessing the Costs and Identifying the Benefits of ALJ Utilization in Public Safety Legislation,* 38 IND. L. REV. 435 (2005); John W. Hardwicke, *The Central Panel Movement A Work in Progress,* 53 ADMIN. L. REV. 419 (2001); William Swent, *South Carolina's ALJ: Central Panel, Administrative Court, or a Little of Both?,* 48 S.C. L. REV. 1 (1996).

The decision at issue in the deportation case below, *Wong Yang Sung*, was made by the same individual who prosecuted the case. Investigators make initial decisions in many types of cases. What is different about this case?

WONG YANG SUNG V. MCGRATH

339 U.S. 33 (1950)

[JUSTICE JACKSON] This habeas corpus proceeding involves a single ultimate question – whether administrative hearings in deportation cases must conform to requirements of the Administrative Procedure Act of June 11, 1946 [the "APA"].

Wong Yang Sung, native and citizen of China, was arrested by immigration officials on a charge of being unlawfully in the United States through having overstayed shore leave as one of a shipping crew. A hearing was held before an immigrant inspector who recommended deportation. The Acting Commissioner approved; and the Board of Immigration Appeals affirmed.

Wong Yang Sung then sought release from custody by habeas corpus proceedings in District Court for the District of Columbia, upon the sole ground that the administrative hearing was not conducted in conformity with §§ 5 and 11 of the [APA]. The Government admitted noncompliance, but asserted that the Act did not apply. The court, after hearing, discharged the writ and remanded the prisoner to custody, holding the Administrative Procedure Act inapplicable to deportation hearings. The Court of Appeals affirmed. Prisoner's petition for certiorari was not opposed by the Government and, because the question presented has obvious importance in the administration of the immigration laws, we granted review.

I.

The [APA] is a basic and comprehensive regulation of procedures in many agencies, more than a few of which can advance arguments that its generalities should not or do not include them. . . . Multiplication of federal administrative agencies and expansion of their functions to include adjudications which have serious impact on private rights has been one of the dramatic legal developments of the past half-century.

II.

Of the several administrative evils sought to be cured or minimized, [one was to] change the practice of embodying in one person or agency the duties of prosecutor and judge. . . . The Committee's report . . . said

. . . the independent commission is obliged to carry on judicial functions under conditions which threaten the impartial performance of that judicial work. . . . [T]he same men are obliged to serve both as prosecutors and as judges. This not only undermines judicial fairness; it weakens public confidence in that fairness. . . .

Another study was made by a distinguished committee named by the Secretary of Labor, whose jurisdiction at the time included the Immigration and Naturalization Service. . . . It said

[m]erely to provide that in particular cases different inspectors shall investigate and hear is an insufficient guarantee of insulation and independence of the presiding official. . . . A genuinely impartial hearing, conducted with critical detachment, is psychologically improbable if not impossible, when the presiding officer has at once the responsibility of appraising the strength of the case and of seeking to make it as strong as possible. Nor is complete divorce between investigation and hearing possible so long as the presiding inspector has the duty himself of assembling and presenting the results of the investigation. . . .

. . . .

III.

Turning now to the case before us, we find the administrative hearing a perfect exemplification of the practices so unanimously condemned. This hearing, which followed the uniform practice of the Immigration Service, was before an immigrant inspector, who, for purposes of the hearing, is called the "presiding inspector." Except with consent of the alien, the presiding inspector may not be the one who investigated the case. But the inspector's duties include investigation of like cases . . . . The presiding inspector . . . is required to "conduct the interrogation of the alien and the witnesses in behalf of the Government and shall cross-examine the alien's witnesses and present such evidence as is necessary to support the charges in the warrant of arrest." . . . . Then, as soon as practicable, he is to prepare a summary of the evidence, proposed findings of fact, conclusions of law, and a proposed order. . . .

The Administrative Procedure Act did not go so far as to require a complete separation of investigating and prosecuting functions from adjudicating functions. But that the safeguards it did set up were intended to ameliorate the evils from the commingling of functions as exemplified here is beyond doubt. And this commingling, if objectionable anywhere, would seem to be particularly so in the deportation proceeding, where we frequently meet with a voteless class of litigants who not only lack the influence of citizens, but who are strangers to the laws and customs in which they find themselves involved and who often do not even understand the tongue in which they are accused. . . .

. . . .

We hold that deportation proceedings must conform to the requirements of the Administrative Procedure Act if resulting orders are to have validity. Since the proceeding in the case before us did not comply with these requirements, we sustain the writ of habeas corpus and direct release of the prisoner.

Reversed.

Underlying Case Documents

The case referenced:
The Habeas petition

---

1. The law changed after *Wong Yang Sung*, and undid the separation of functions aspect of the case. In *Jonal Corp. v. District of Columbia*, 533 F.2d 1192, 1195-96 (D.C. Cir. 1976), a disgruntled contractor sought payment in a proceeding before the Contract Appeals Board for the District of Columbia. Board members were appointed through the Corporation Counsel of the District – the same office that defends contact claims on behalf of the City. The contractor claimed that the system in place violated due process because it allowed adjudicative and prosecutorial functions to be vested in one agency. Although the matter was remanded to allow for further fact finding, to address the separation of functions issue, the court recited the post-*Wong Yang Sung* history:

> In a matter involving a deportation proceeding, the Supreme Court held in *Marcello v. Bonds*, 349 U.S. 302 (1955), that due process was not violated by the supervision of adjudicating officers by officials charged with investigating and prosecuting functions. . . .

> Prior to the *Marcello* case, the Supreme Court had interpreted the [APA] to require the separation of administrative functions in deportation cases. *Wong Yang Sung*. Six months thereafter, Congress expressly excluded deportation proceedings from specified sections of the Act so as to reinstate the proceedings suspended by the Supreme Court. Supplemental Appropriation Act of 1951, 64 Stat. 1068. In 1962 Congress enacted the Immigration Act, 8 U.S.C. § 1252, which specifically provided for various combinations of judicial, prosecutorial and investigative functions that seemingly ran counter to the Administrative Procedure Act. The Supreme Court in *Marcello* specifically held that the Immigration Act was intended by Congress to supersede the Administrative Procedure Act on the question of separation of functions, and denied the petitioner's claim of a due process violation. The case has consistently been interpreted to stand for the general proposition that the combination

in administrative procedures of judging with prosecuting or investigating functions is not, per se, a denial of due process.

Should an investigator be permitted to make deportation or confinement decisions? The general notion of impartiality after *Wong Yang Sung* continues to be a basic part of our expectations in adjudicatory hearings. *See Daniels v. Wadley*, 926 F. Supp. 1305 (M.D. Tenn. 1996).

2. The basic holding in *Wong Yang Sung*, that one is entitled to a fair hearing prior to deportation, is very much still in place. In *Samirah v. Mukasey*, 2008 WL 450823 (N.D. Ill. 2008), the court held "that deportation involves a loss of liberty and thus the government cannot permanently remove aliens from the United States without a removal hearing." The court relied on *Reno v. Flores*, 507 U.S. 292, 306 (1993), and *Wong Yang Sung v. McGrath*, quoting *Wong Yang Sung* for its reference to another case saying: "It was under the compulsion of the Constitution that this Court long ago held that an antecedent deportation statute must provide a hearing at least for aliens who had not entered clandestinely and who had been here some time even if illegally." (citing The *Japanese Immigrant Case*, 189 U.S. 86, 100-01 (1903)).

There is, of course, a difference between a right to remain in the United States and a right to a hearing to determine if one is entitled to remain. The Seventh Circuit noted recently that there is "a significant difference between saying one has a right to obtain discretionary relief and saying that one has a right to seek discretionary relief." *Johnson v. Gonzales*, 478 F.3d 795, 798 (7th Cir. 2007) (citing *United States v. Roque-Espinoza*, 338 F.3d 724, 729 (7th Cir. 2003)). As to the type of hearing *Wong Yang Sung* contemplated, see William Funk, *The Rise and Purported Demise of* Wong Yang Sung, 58 ADMIN. L. REV. 881 (2006), discussing agency aversion to formality in the hearing process.

3. How much can an agency decisionmaker know about a case outside of what is presented in the course of a hearing? On the one hand, information possessed by the decisionmaker is "phantom evidence"; it cannot be confronted, cross-examined, or assessed on judicial review, much like bias or prejudice. On the other hand, informed decisionmakers do not live in isolation. In *Schacht v. Wisconsin Department of Corrections*, 175 F.3d 497 (7th Cir. 1999), the court found that "[o]ne of the most basic guarantees of fair procedure is an unbiased decisionmaker. This does not necessarily mean a decisionmaker who knows nothing of the facts . . . but it does imply honesty in the process."

In the inquisitorial model used by the Bureau of Prisons for disciplinary sanctions, the investigative and the decisional roles are not separated. *See, e.g.*, *Kikumura v. Osagie*, 461 F.3d 1269, 1284 (10th Cir. 2006). In what other areas are investigation and decisionmaking – including sanctions – linked? Would you consider qualifying examinations (e.g., a road test for a driver's license) an improperly merged function?

4. The *Wong Yang Sung* decision was based on Section 554(d) of the APA:

> [A]n employee or agent engaged in the performance of investigative or prosecuting functions for an agency in a case may not, in that or a factually related case, participate or advise in the decision, recommended decision, or agency review pursuant to section 557 of this title, except as witness or counsel in public proceedings.

Why was it not based on constitutional imperative? Immigration cases often rely on this premise. *See, e.g.*, *Yosd v. Mukasey*, 514 F.3d 74, 77 (1st Cir. 2008); *Marincas v. Lewis*, 92 F.3d 195, 203-04 (3d Cir. 1996) (one of the "most basic of due process protections" is "a hearing before a neutral immigration judge").

WITHROW V. LARKIN

421 U.S. 35 (1975)

[JUSTICE WHITE] The statutes of the State of Wisconsin forbid the practice of medicine without a license from an Examining Board composed of practicing physicians. The statutes also define and forbid various acts of professional misconduct . . . . To enforce these provisions, the Examining Board is empowered under [Wisconsin law] to warn and reprimand, temporarily to suspend the license, and "to institute criminal action or action to revoke [a] license when it finds probable cause [therefore]." . . . .

I

Appellee['s] practice . . . consisted of performing abortions at an office in Milwaukee. . . . On September 18, 1973, the Board sent to appellee a notice that a "contested hearing" would be held . . . to determine whether appellee had engaged in certain prohibited acts and that based upon the evidence adduced at the hearing the Board would determine whether his license would be suspended temporarily. Appellee moved for a restraining order against the contested hearing. The District Court granted the motion. . . . The Board complied and did not go forward with the contested hearing. Instead, it noticed and held a final investigative session . . . at which appellee's attorney, but not appellee, appeared. The Board thereupon . . . found that appellee had engaged in specified conduct proscribed by the statute. The operative portion of its "Decision" was the following:

> [I]t is hereby determined that there is probable cause to believe that licensee has violated the criminal provisions of [the statute] and that there is probable cause for an action to revoke the license of the licensee for engaging in unprofessional conduct.

Therefore, it is the decision of this Board that the secretary verify this document and file it as a verified complaint with the District Attorney of Milwaukee County . . . for the purpose of initiating an action to revoke the license of Duane R. Larkin, M.D., to practice medicine and surgery in the State of Wisconsin and initiating appropriate actions for violation of the criminal laws relating to the practice of medicine.

On November 19, 1973, the three-judge District Court found . . . that [the statute] was unconstitutional as a violation of due process guarantees and enjoined the Board from enforcing it. . . .

III

The District Court framed the constitutional issue . . . as being whether "for the board temporarily to suspend Dr. Larkin's license at its own contested hearing on charges evolving from its own investigation would constitute a denial to him of his rights to procedural due process." . . . .

Concededly, a "fair trial in a fair tribunal is a basic requirement of due process." This applies to administrative agencies which adjudicate as well as to courts. Not only is a biased decisionmaker constitutionally unacceptable but "our system of law has always endeavored to prevent even the probability of unfairness." In pursuit of this end, various situations have been identified in which experience teaches that the probability of actual bias on the part of the judge or decisionmaker is too high to be constitutionally tolerable. Among these cases are those in which the adjudicator has a pecuniary interest in the outcome and in which he has been the target of personal abuse or criticism from the party before him.

The contention that the combination of investigative and adjudicative functions necessarily creates an unconstitutional risk of bias in administrative adjudication has a much more difficult burden of persuasion to carry. It must overcome a presumption of honesty and integrity in those serving as adjudicators; and it must convince that, under a realistic appraisal of psychological tendencies and human weakness, conferring investigative and adjudicative powers on the same individuals poses such a risk of actual bias or prejudgment that the practice must be forbidden if the guarantee of due process is to be adequately implemented.

That is not to say that there is nothing to the argument that those who have investigated should not then adjudicate. . . . For the generality of agencies, Congress has been content with § 5 of the Administrative Procedure Act, which provides that no employee engaged in investigating or prosecuting may also participate or advise in the adjudicating function . . . ." . . . . [However, the] incredible variety of administrative mechanisms in this country will not yield to any single organizing principle.

Appellee relies heavily on *In re Murchison* [349 U.S. 133 (1955)] in which a state judge, empowered under state law to sit as a "one-man grand jury" and to compel witnesses to testify before him in secret about possible crimes, charged two such witnesses with criminal contempt, one for perjury and the other for refusing to answer certain questions, and then himself tried and convicted them. This Court found the procedure to be a denial of due process of law not only because the judge in effect became part of the prosecution and assumed an adversary position, but also because as a judge, passing on guilt or innocence, he very likely relied on "his own personal knowledge and impression of what had occurred in the grand jury room," an impression that "could not be tested by adequate cross-examination."

[But] *Murchison* has not been understood to stand for the broad rule that the members of an administrative agency may not investigate the facts, institute proceedings, and then make the necessary adjudications. . . . Nor is there anything in this case that comes within the strictures of *Murchison*. When the Board instituted its investigative procedures, it stated only that it would investigate . . . . Later in noticing the adversary hearing, it asserted only that it would determine if violations had been committed . . . . Without doubt, the Board then anticipated that the proceeding would eventuate in an adjudication of the issue; but there was no more evidence of bias or the risk of bias or prejudgment than inhered in the very fact that the Board had investigated and would now adjudicate.

Of course, we should be alert to the possibilities of bias that may lurk in the way particular procedures actually work in practice. The processes utilized by the Board, however, do not in themselves contain an unacceptable risk of bias. The investigative proceeding had been closed to the public, but appellee and his counsel were permitted to be present throughout; counsel actually attended the hearings and knew the facts presented to the Board. No specific foundation has been presented for suspecting that the Board had been prejudiced by its investigation . . . . The mere exposure to evidence presented in nonadversary investigative procedures is insufficient in itself to impugn the fairness of the Board members at a later adversary hearing. . . .

We are of the view, therefore, that the District Court was in error when it entered the restraining order . . . . The contested hearing should have been permitted to proceed.

IV

Nor do we think the situation substantially different because the Board, when it was prevented from going forward with the contested hearing, [still found] that there was probable cause to believe that appellee had engaged in various acts prohibited by the Wisconsin statutes. These findings and conclusions were verified and filed with the district attorney for the purpose of initiating revocation and criminal proceedings. . . .

Judges repeatedly issue arrest warrants on the basis that there is probable cause to believe that a crime has been committed and that the person named in the warrant has committed it. Judges also preside at preliminary hearings where they must decide whether the evidence is sufficient to hold a defendant for trial. Neither of these pretrial involvements has been thought to raise any constitutional barrier against the judge's presiding over the criminal trial and, if the trial is without a jury, against making the necessary determination of guilt or innocence. . . . It is also very typical for the members of administrative agencies to receive the results of investigations, to approve the filing of charges or formal complaints instituting enforcement proceedings, and then to participate in the ensuing hearings. This mode of procedure does not violate the Administrative Procedure Act, and it does not violate due process of law. We should also remember that it is not contrary to due process to allow judges and administrators who have had their initial decisions reversed on appeal to confront and decide the same questions a second time around.

Here, the Board stayed within the accepted bounds of due process. . . . Indeed, just as there is no logical inconsistency between a finding of probable cause and an acquittal in a criminal proceeding, there is no incompatibility between the agency filing a complaint based on probable cause and a subsequent decision, when all the evidence is in, that there has been no violation of the statute. Here, if the Board now proceeded after an adversary hearing to determine that appellee's license to practice should not be temporarily suspended, it would not implicitly be admitting error in its prior finding of probable cause. Its position most probably would merely reflect the benefit of a more complete view of the evidence afforded by an adversary hearing.

. . . .

That the combination of investigative and adjudicative functions does not, without more, constitute a due process violation, does not, of course, preclude a court from determining from the special facts and circumstances present in the case before it that the risk of unfairness is intolerably high. Findings of that kind made by judges with special insights into local realities are entitled to respect, but injunctions resting on such factors should be accompanied by at least the minimum findings required by Rules 52(a) and 65(d).

The judgment of the District Court is reversed and the case is remanded to that court for further proceedings consistent with this opinion. . . .

Underlying Case Documents

The case referenced:
The decision of the Board
The decision of the three-judge district court

1. Reading *Wong Yang Sung*, one could conclude that merging prosecution and investigation runs a grave risk of an actual or perceived lack of impartiality and constitutes a combination of functions to be avoided unless deemed necessary by Congress to implement a specific regulatory program. Reading *Withrow*, one could conclude that merging prosecution and investigation is normal, ordinary, and necessary. Is it just the passage of 25 years?

Consider the regulatory setting 1950 and compare it to 1975. The number of employees in government – and the number of pages in the Federal Register – tripled. "The federal government began to regulate oil prices and other aspects of energy production; to impose significant controls upon environmental pollution; and to regulate the safety of the workplace, of the highway, and of consumer products. It increased regulatory protection of investors, including pension holders and commodities traders." Stephen Breyer, Regulation and Its Reform 1 (1982). The demand for efficient regulation, the initial driving force behind deregulation, may have led the *Withrow* Court to conclude that the "incredible variety of administrative mechanisms in this country will not yield to any single organizing principle." Of course, the forces driving deregulation in the 1970s and 1980s went well beyond a quest for maximizing employee output by having one person performing both investigation and decision-making. *See* Alfred E. Kahn, *Deregulation: Looking Backward and Looking Forward, 7* Yale J. on Reg. 325, 329 (1990) ("The case for deregulation has been that direct regulation typically suppressed competition, or at least severely distorted it, and that competition, freed of such direct restraints, is a far preferable system of economic control."); R. Litan & W. Nordhaus, Reforming Federal Regulation 1-2 (1983).

Was *Withrow* driven by efficiency? Was it a matter of maximizing resources?

2. The conflation of responsibilities in *Withrow* is no longer a matter of controversy. In *AFGE v. Gates, 486 F.3d 1316 (D.C. Cir. 2007)*, dealing with a collective bargaining dispute, the court noted that "[n]othing in the statute or in logic requires a separation of functions within the 'independent third party.' *See Withrow v. Larkin*, 421 U.S. at 47; *United Steelworkers of Am., AFL-CIO-CLC v. Marshall, 647 F.2d 1189, 1215 n.28 (D.C. Cir. 1980)*. What is more, many independent federal

agencies combine these functions. *See, e.g.*, 15 U.S.C. §§ 45(b), 46 (Federal Trade Commission); 47 U.S.C. §§ 204, 208 (Federal Communications Commission)."

There are, however, instances where the combination goes too far. In *Wildberger v. AFGE*, 86 F.3d 1188, 1195-96 (D.C. Cir. 1996), a national union president investigated a local union leader, and thereafter appointed a trial committee to hear the charges. The national president also had the power to make a final decision to unseat the local official. The court assessed the process as follows:

> In non-criminal proceedings, such an overlap of functions does not always violate due process. . . . Requiring administrative agencies to maintain a rigid separation of functions . . . would deprive agencies of the flexibility needed to conduct their complex and varied functions. . . . In the case before us . . . the union constitution's combination of investigative, prosecutorial, and adjudicatory functions in the President does not, by itself, violate the Labor-Management Reporting and Disclosure Act (LMRDA). *Withrow* directs us to assume that the President is a person "of conscience and intellectual discipline capable of judging a particular controversy fairly on the basis of its own circumstances." . . . . The fact that the President makes the initial probable cause determination, therefore, does not mean that, after reviewing all the evidence and the recommendations of an impartial trial committee, he cannot fairly make the ultimate decision. Nor does the fact that the President and his staff selected the trial committee mean that the committee is biased against the accused.
>
> Where, however, evidence casts doubt on the partiality of the President, the combination of prosecutorial and adjudicatory functions in a single person can present due process concerns. Although we do not presume that the mere combination of prosecutorial and adjudicatory functions leads to bias, "we should be alert to the possibilities of bias that may lurk in the way particular procedures actually work in practice." *Withrow*. . . . We believe that this is such a case.

Obviously, if the combination of functions also included a financial interest, the problem is entirely different. *See Haas v. County of San Bernardino*, 119 Cal. Rptr. 2d 341, 347 (Cal. 2002). "While adjudicators challenged for reasons other than financial interest have in effect been afforded a presumption of impartiality, adjudicators challenged for financial interest have not." *See Aetna Life Ins. Co. v. Lavoie*, 475 U.S. 813, 820 (1986).

3. Are there ethical problems with a system where investigation and decision-making are either unified — or simply in such close proximity that pre-decisional knowledge — ex parte — is almost inevitable? See Jeff Bush & Kristal Wiitala Knutson, *The Building and Maintenance of "Ethics Walls" in Administrative Adjudicatory Proceedings*, 24 J. NAALJ 1 (2004), discussing the ethical issues and the potential "central panel" solution.

4. In *Nightlife Partners, Ltd. v. City of Beverly Hills*, 133 Cal. Rptr. 2d 234 (Cal. Ct. App. 2003), operators of an adult entertainment facility ran into opposition when they sought to renew their permit. After the agency refused to renew their

license, they requested and received a hearing to contest the denial. At the hearing, the hearing officer was in close proximity to the city attorney/investigator. There was evidence the attorney "advised" the hearing officer during the course of the proceeding. On review, the trial court found the attorney had "taken an 'active and significant' part in Petitioners' unsuccessful application renewal process, and that when Petitioners sought administrative review of that process, [the attorney] participated in the administrative hearing by advising and assisting . . . the hearing officer[, constituting] actual bias." On appeal of the order of the trial judge, the court held as follows:

> [T]he provisions of the APA are helpful as indicating what the Legislature believes are the elements of a fair and carefully thought out system of procedure for use in administrative hearings.
>
> One of the basic tenets of the APA, as well as the Model State Administrative Procedure Act . . . is that, to promote both the appearance of fairness and the absence of even a probability of outside influence on administrative hearings, the prosecutory and, to a lesser extent, investigatory, aspects of administrative matters must be adequately separated from the adjudicatory function. . . . While the combination of investigative and adjudicative functions standing alone generally does not create a due process violation in the absence of some showing of bias . . . the same cannot be so said when prosecutory and adjudicative functions are too closely combined.
>
> Thus, when, as here, "counsel . . . performs as an advocate in a given case[, he or she] is generally precluded from advising a decision-making body in the same case." . . . . This is because "the due process rule of overlapping functions in administrative disciplinary proceedings applies to prevent the participant from being in the position of reviewing his or her own decision or adjudging a person whom he or she has either charged or investigated."
>
> Here . . . there was a confounding of the functions of advocacy and adjudication – a situation always fraught with more problems that when there is some combination of investigatory and adjudicatory functions. Furthermore, these dual functions were not held by different sections of a single office, but by a single individual. . . . [Accordingly, the] hearing here . . . violated due process.

For a useful article on this case, see Kelli Shope, *Balancing Administrative Efficiency and Fairness: Restrictions on Local Hearing Advisors Post-Nightlife Partners, Ltd. v. City of Beverly Hills 2004*, 24 J. NAALJ 51 (2004).

Good Questions!

In many administrative proceedings, particularly zoning cases, it is not unusual for the "staff" of the office responsible for the issuance of a sanction, license, permit, exemption, or similar adjudicatory order to have a somewhat preferred position in the process. In some instances, by law or regulation, the staff opinion is entitled to "great weight." It is also not usual to see whole chunks of a staff pre-hearing report appear as the hearing officer's final decision. Are such practices unconstitutional? Inadvisable? Essential to the continuity of what the agency administers?

5. Related to the question of whether one who investigates can also adjudicate impartially is the matter of personal relationships between decisionmakers and others involved in matters that must be judged. Should the "appearance of impropriety" standard apply? Should a judge recuse himself or herself any time they know the parties before them well? Obviously, if there is a financial relationship between the judge and the parties, the risk of the judge being co-opted is greater than if it is a simple friendship. The case that follows explores some of these concerns bluntly.

CHENEY V. UNITED STATES DISTRICT COURT FOR THE DISTRICT OF COLUMBIA

541 U.S. 913 (2004)

[JUSTICE SCALIA] I have before me a motion to recuse in these cases consolidated below. The motion is filed on behalf of respondent Sierra Club. The other private respondent, Judicial Watch, Inc., does not join the motion and has publicly stated that it "does not believe the presently-known facts about the hunting trip satisfy the legal standards requiring recusal." . . . .

I

. . . .

For five years or so, I have been going to Louisiana during the Court's long December-January recess, to the duck-hunting camp of a friend . . . Wallace Carline . . . . During my December 2002 visit, I learned that Mr. Carline was an admirer of Vice President Cheney. Knowing that the Vice President, with whom I am well acquainted (from our years serving together in the Ford administration), is an enthusiastic duck-hunter, I asked whether Mr. Carline would like to invite him to our next year's hunt. The answer was yes; I conveyed the invitation . . . and received an acceptance (subject, of course, to any superseding demands on the Vice President's time) . . . . The Vice President said that if he did go, I would be welcome to fly down to Louisiana with him. (Because of national security requirements, of course, he must fly in a Government plane.) That invitation was later extended – if space was available – to my son-in-law and to a son who was joining the hunt for the first time; they accepted. . . .

We departed from Andrews Air Force Base . . . on Monday, January 5 . . . . [At the hunting camp there were] about 13 hunters in all; also present during our time there were about 3 members of Mr. Carline's staff, and, of course, the Vice President's staff and security detail. It was not an intimate setting. The group hunted that afternoon and Tuesday and Wednesday mornings; it fished (in two boats) Tuesday afternoon. All meals were in common. Sleeping was in rooms of two or three, except for the Vice President, who had his own quarters. Hunting was in two- or three-man blinds. As it turned out, I never hunted in the same blind with the Vice President. Nor was I alone with him at any time during the trip, except, perhaps, for instances so brief and unintentional that I would not recall them – walking to or from a boat, perhaps, or going to or from dinner. Of course we said not a word about the present case. The Vice President left the camp Wednesday afternoon, about two days after our arrival. I stayed on to hunt (with my son and son-in-law) until late Friday morning, when the three of us returned to Washington on a commercial flight from New Orleans.

II

Let me respond, at the outset, to Sierra Club's suggestion that I should "resolve any doubts in favor of recusal." That might be sound advice if I were sitting on a Court of Appeals. There, my place would be taken by another judge, and the case would proceed normally. On the Supreme Court, however, the consequence is different: The Court proceeds with eight Justices, raising the possibility that, by reason of a tie vote, it will find itself unable to resolve the significant legal issue presented by the case. . . . Moreover, granting the motion is (insofar as the outcome of the particular case is concerned) effectively the same as casting a vote against the petitioner. . . .

. . . .

A

My recusal is required if, by reason of the actions described above, my "impartiality might reasonably be questioned." Why would that result follow from my being in a sizable group of persons, in a hunting camp with the Vice President, where I never [had any] opportunity for private conversation? The only possibility is that it would suggest I am a friend of his. But while friendship is a ground for recusal of a Justice where the personal fortune or the personal freedom of the friend is at issue, it has traditionally *not* been a ground for recusal where *official action* is at issue . . . . A rule that required Members of this Court to remove themselves from cases in which the official actions of friends were at issue would be utterly disabling. Many Justices have reached this Court precisely because they were friends of the incumbent President or other senior officials . . . . John Quincy Adams hosted dinner parties featuring such luminaries as CHIEF JUSTICE MARSHALL, JUSTICES JOHNSON, STORY, and TODD, . . . and Daniel Webster. . . .

It is said, however, that this case is different because the federal officer (Vice President Cheney) is actually a *named party*. That is by no means a rarity. At the beginning of the current Term, there were before the Court (excluding habeas actions) no fewer than 83 cases in which high-level federal Executive officers were named in their official capacity – more than 1 in every 10 federal civil cases then pending. . . . Regardless of whom they name, such suits . . . when the officer is the defendant, seek relief not against him personally, but against the Government. . . . Richard Cheney's name appears in this suit only because he was the head of a Government committee that allegedly did not comply with the Federal Advisory Committee Act (FACA) and because he may, by reason of his office, have custody of some or all of the Government documents that the plaintiffs seek. If some other person were to become head of that committee or to obtain custody of those documents, the plaintiffs would name that person and Cheney would be dismissed. . . .

The recusal motion, however, asserts the following ". . . this is not a run-of-the-mill legal dispute about an administrative decision . . . . [T]he Vice President's 'reputation and his integrity are on the line.'" I think not. Certainly as far as the legal issues immediately presented to me are concerned, this *is* "a run-of-the-mill legal dispute about an administrative decision." . . . . Nothing this Court says on those subjects will have any bearing upon the reputation and integrity of Richard Cheney. Moreover, even if this Court affirms the decision below and allows discovery to proceed in the District Court, the issue . . . . would be, quite simply, whether some private individuals were de facto members of the National Energy Policy Development Group (NEPDG). It matters not whether they were caused to be so by Cheney or someone else . . . .

. . . .

To be sure, there could be political consequences from disclosure of the fact (if it be so) that the Vice President favored . . . a sector of business with which he was formerly connected. But political consequences are not my concern, and the possibility of them does not convert an official suit into a private one. That possibility exists to a greater or lesser degree in virtually all suits involving agency action. To expect judges to take account of political consequences – and to assess the high or low degree of them – is to ask judges to do precisely what they should not do. It seems to me quite wrong (and quite impossible) to make recusal depend upon what degree of political damage a particular case can be expected to inflict.

In sum, I see nothing about this case which takes it out of the category of normal official-action litigation, where my friendship, or the appearance of my friendship, with one of the named officers does not require recusal.

B

The recusal motion claims that "the fact that JUSTICE SCALIA and his daughter were the Vice President's guest on Air Force Two on the flight down to Louisiana" means that I "accepted a sizable gift from a party in a pending case," a gift "measured in the thousands of dollars."

Let me speak first to the value, though that is not the principal point. Our flight down cost the Government nothing, since space-available was the condition of our invitation. And, though our flight down on the Vice President's plane was indeed free, since we were not returning with him we purchased (because they were least expensive) round-trip tickets that cost precisely what we would have paid if we had gone both down and back on commercial flights. In other words, none of us saved a cent by flying on the Vice President's plane. The purpose of going with him was not saving money, but avoiding some inconvenience to ourselves (being taken by car from New Orleans to Morgan City) and considerable inconvenience to our friends, who would have had to meet our plane in New Orleans, and schedule separate boat trips to the hunting camp, for us and for the Vice President's party. . . .

The principal point, however, is that social courtesies, provided at Government expense by officials whose only business before the Court is business in their official capacity, have not hitherto been thought prohibited. Members of Congress and others are frequently invited to accompany Executive Branch officials on Government planes, where space is available. That this is not the sort of gift thought likely to affect a judge's impartiality is suggested by the fact that the Ethics in Government Act of 1978, which requires annual reporting of transportation provided or reimbursed, excludes from this requirement transportation provided by the United States. I daresay that, at a hypothetical charity auction, much more would be bid for dinner for two at the White House than for a one-way flight to Louisiana on the Vice President's jet. . . .

III

When I learned that Sierra Club had filed a recusal motion in this case, I assumed that the motion would be replete with citations of legal authority . . . . In fact, however, the motion cites only two Supreme Court cases assertedly relevant to the issue here discussed, and nine Court of Appeals cases. Not a single one of these even involves an official-action suit. . . . Instead, the Argument section of the motion consists almost entirely of references to, and quotations from, newspaper editorials. . . . Many of them do not even have the facts right. The length of our hunting trip together was said to be several days (San Francisco Chronicle), four days (Boston Globe), or nine days (San Antonio Express-News). . . . And these are just the inaccuracies pertaining to the *facts*. With regard to the *law*, the vast majority of the editorials display no recognition of the central proposition that a federal officer is not ordinarily regarded to be a personal party in interest in an official-action suit. . . .

. . . .

Since I do not believe my impartiality can reasonably be questioned, I do not think it would be proper for me to recuse. . . . There are, I am sure, those who believe that my friendship with persons in the current administration might cause me to favor the Government in cases brought against it. That is not the issue here. Nor is the issue whether personal friendship with the Vice President might cause me to favor the Government in cases in which *he* is named. None of those suspicions regarding my impartiality (erroneous suspicions, I hasten to protest) bears upon recusal here. The question, simply put, is whether someone who thought I could decide this case impartially despite my friendship with the Vice President would reasonably believe that I *cannot* decide it impartially because I went hunting with that friend and accepted an invitation to fly there with him on a Government plane. If it is reasonable to think that a Supreme Court Justice can be bought so cheap, the Nation is in deeper trouble than I had imagined.

Underlying Case Documents

The case referenced:
The motion to recuse
Various newspaper editorials
The Ethics in Government Act of 1978
The Federal Advisory Committee Act

1. The underlying decision that led to the above opinion by JUSTICE SCALIA is *In re Cheney*, 334 F.3d 1096, 1098-99 (D.C. Cir. 2003). The case involved a discovery request. Environmental groups were seeking to learn who – in addition to the Vice President – participated in executive office meetings that led to the announcement of an energy policy the environmental groups found repugnant, and on what did they rely? JUDGE TATEL began that case as follows:

> The Vice President of the United States and others, all defendants in this suit under the Federal Advisory Committee Act, petition for a writ of mandamus vacating the district court's discovery orders, directing the district court to rule on the basis of the administrative record, and ordering dismissal of the Vice President as a party. . . .

Shortly after his inauguration, President George W. Bush issued a memorandum establishing the National Energy Policy Development Group (NEPDG), a task force charged with "developing . . . a national energy policy designed to help the private sector, and government at all levels, promote dependable, affordable, and environmentally sound production and distribution of energy for the future." MEM. ESTABLISHING NATIONAL ENERGY POLICY DEVELOPMENT GROUP, Jan. 29, 2001, available at http://www.whitehouse.gov/energy/National-Energy-Policy.pdf. Established within the Office of the President and chaired by Vice President Richard B. Cheney, the task force consisted of six cabinet secretaries, as well as several agency heads and assistants to the President. The memorandum authorized the Vice President to invite "other officers of the Federal Government" to participate "as appropriate." Five months later, the NEPDG issued a final report recommending a set of energy policies. . . ."

2. On the matter of recusal, 28 U.S.C. § 455(a) sets out the standard for recusal for Article III judges: "Any justice, judge or magistrate of the United States shall disqualify himself in any proceeding in which his impartiality might reasonably be questioned."

Food for Thought

Was there anything in the *Cheney* opinion that caused you to question JUSTICE SCALIA's partiality? Is JUSTICE SCALIA correct that the "appearance of impropriety" test applicable to attorneys is inapplicable to judges in Article III courts? How different are the "appearance of impropriety" and the "reasonable basis to question" tests?

In *Liteky v. United States*, 510 U.S. 540, 544 (1994), the Court recites the history of the recusal legislation – which has been amended often. One amendment is noteworthy. In 1821, the basis for recusal was expanded "to include all judicial relationship or connection with a party that would in the judge's opinion make it improper to sit." Act of Mar. 3, 1821, ch. 51, 3 Stat. 643 (1821). Were one to apply this standard to the *Cheney* case, would the outcome have to be different?

In *Liljeberg v. Health Services Acquisition*, 486 U.S. 847, 858-60 (1988), decided six years before *Liteky*, the Court found that when applying § 455 the question is not "whether a judge is in fact biased or prejudiced, but whether a judge's impartiality might reasonably be questioned." However, in *Liteky*, the court qualified that somewhat, prompting JUSTICE STEVENS to comment in his concurring opinion that the majority opinion "announces a mistaken, unfortunate precedent [in that] it accords nearly dispositive weight to the source of a judge's alleged partiality, to the point of stating that disqualification for intrajudicial partiality is not required unless it would make a fair hearing impossible . . . ." With this backdrop, does JUSTICE SCALIA's opinion strike you as in any way controversial?

Later cases have held that § 455(a) mandates recusal only when a neutral third person would reasonably question a judge's impartiality. *See United States v. Cole,*

293 F.3d 153, 164 (4th Cir. 2002). The less important the relationship, the more extensive the time difference between contacts, the less likely a judge's impartiality will be at issue. In *United States v. Lovaglia, 954 F.2d 811, 815-17 (2d Cir. 1992)*, the court refused to mandate recusal even though the judge was a personal friend of the victim of the crime in question.

3. Do the standards in *Cheney* and in note 2, above, apply to administrative agencies? In *Bunnell v. Barnhart, 336 F.3d 1112 (9th Cir. 2003)*, after plaintiff's request for disability payments was denied, she went to court to challenge the ALJ's decision. She claimed, *inter alia*, that the fact of the judicial challenge (her lawsuit) created an appearance of impropriety that compelled recusal of the ALJ:

> Our holding finds further support in the federal regulation concerning the recusal of an administrative law judge. 20 C.F.R. § 404.940. The regulation provides that an administrative law judge "shall not conduct a hearing if he or she is prejudiced or partial with respect to any party or has any interest in the matter pending for decision." This regulation mentions only actual prejudice; *nothing in this regulation mandates recusal for the mere appearance of impropriety.* [Emphasis added.]

In *Greenberg v. Board of Governors of Federal Reserve System, 968 F.2d 164, 167 (2d Cir. 1992)*, the court held that the § 455 standard, "cannot apply to administrative law judges who, after all, are employed by the agency whose actions they review. Otherwise, ALJs would be forced to recuse themselves in every case." Not surprisingly, the court in *Greenberg* rejected the "appearance of impropriety" principle for ALJs.

When there is a question about recusal, the starting point is often *Withrow v. Larkin*, in which the Supreme Court instructed that "a heavy presumption of honesty and integrity in those serving as adjudicators" was in order when dealing with actual or perceived bias. 421 U.S. 35, 47 (1975).

4. Are you convinced the appearance of impropriety principle is inapplicable? Consider the MODEL CODE OF JUDICIAL CONDUCT FOR STATE ADMINISTRATIVE LAW JUDGES. Canon 2 of that code states that an ALJ should "avoid impropriety and the appearance of impropriety in all activities." Canon 2B states that an "administrative law judge shall not allow family, social, political or other relationships to influence judicial conduct or judgment. A judge shall not lend the prestige of the office to advance the private interests of the judge or others, nor convey or permit others to convey the impression that they are in a special position of influence." http://www.naalj.org/modelcode.html, last visited July 28, 2008.

5. *Board of Trustees of the University of Arkansas v. Secretary of Health and Human Services, 354 F. Supp. 2d 924, 937-38 (E.D. Ark. 2005)*, is a complex case involving the Secretary's refusal to pay Medicare in a chemotherapy case involving stem cell transplantation. In the course of the proceeding, an ALJ had an ex parte meet-

ing regarding the issues in the case. The court held, in part, as follows:

Improper ex parte communications do not render an ALJ's proceedings automatically void. . . . *Prof'l Air Traffic Controllers Org.*, 685 F.2d at 564-65 [infra Chapter 9].

[T]he ALJ did not comply with 5 U.S.C. § 557(d)(1)(C)(ii) because he did not place on the public record of the proceeding memoranda stating the substance of his communications. The Court will not reverse based solely on the ex parte communication. However, on remand, the case should be assigned to a different ALJ to avoid the appearance of impropriety. . . .

For More Information

For a lucid and thorough discussion of the need for a model code of ethics for state administrative law judges, see *Judging Ethics for Administrative Law Judges: Adoption of a Uniform Code of Conduct for the Administrative Judiciary*, by Associate Dean and Professor Patricia E. Salkin, available at http://www.governmentlaw.org/files/WJPL-Judging_ethics.pdf, (last visited August 1, 2008).

Can you guess why a recusal is mandated in the above case for an ALJ based on the appearance of impropriety test?

For More Information

For more information on the *Cheney* case, see Deborah Goldberg et al., *The Best Defense: Why Elected Courts Should Lead Recusal Reform*, 46 WASHBURN L.J. 503 (2007); Debra Lyn Bassett, *Recusal and the Supreme Court*, 56 HASTINGS L.J. 657 (2005); Brian Fletcher, *Cheney v. United States District Court for the District of Columbia*, 28 HARV. ENV'T L. REV. 605 (2004); Timothy J. Goodson, Comment, *Duck, Duck, Goose: Hunting for Better Recusal Practices in the United States Supreme Court in Light of Cheney v. United States District Court*, 84 N.C.L. REV. 181 (2005); Caprice L. Roberts, *The Fox Guarding the Henhouse? Recusal and the Procedural Void in the Court of Last Resort*, 57 RUTGERS L. REV. 107 (2004); Michael J. Mongan, Note, *Fixing FACA: The Case for Exempting Presidential Advisory Committees from Judicial Review Under the Federal Advisory Committee Act*, 58 STAN. L. REV. 895 (2005).

———

Another question pertaining to judging involves whether a judge should be held to a higher standard of impartiality when the decisions they render are not subject to judicial review. As you read the case below consider both the effect of nonreviewability and, arguably, the interest of the judge in making determinations that limit the funds expended for Medicare Part B benefits.

SCHWEIKER V. MCCLURE

<u>456 U.S. 188 (1982)</u>

[JUSTICE POWELL] The question is whether Congress, consistently with the requirements of due process, may provide that hearings on disputed claims for certain Medicare payments be held by private insurance carriers, without a further right of appeal.

I

Title XVIII of the Social Security Act, commonly known as the Medicare program, is administered by the Secretary of Health and Human Services. It consists of two parts. Part A, which is not at issue in this case, provides insurance against the cost of institutional health services, such as hospital and nursing home fees. Part B . . . covers a portion (typically 80%) of the cost of certain physician services, outpatient physical therapy, X-rays, laboratory tests, and other medical and health care. Only persons 65 or older or disabled may enroll, and eligibility does not depend on financial need. Part B is financed by . . . appropriations from the Treasury, together with monthly premiums paid by the individuals who choose voluntarily to enroll in the Part B program. Part B consequently resembles a private medical insurance program that is subsidized in major part by the Federal Government.

Part B is a social program of substantial dimensions. More than 27 million individuals presently participate, and the Secretary pays out more than $ 10 billion in benefits annually. In 1980, 158 million Part B claims were processed. In order to make the administration of this sweeping program more efficient, Congress authorized the Secretary to contract with private insurance carriers to administer on his behalf the payment of qualifying Part B claims. (In this case, for instance, the private carriers that performed these tasks in California for the Secretary were Blue Shield of California and the Occidental Insurance Co.) The congressional design was to take advantage of such insurance carriers' "great experience in reimbursing physicians."

The Secretary pays the participating carriers' costs of claims administration. In return, the carriers act as the Secretary's agents. They review and pay Part B claims for the Secretary according to a precisely specified process. Once the carrier has been billed for a particular service, it decides initially whether the services were medically necessary, whether the charges are reasonable, and whether the claim is otherwise covered by Part B. If it determines that the claim meets all these criteria, the carrier pays the claim out of the Government's Trust Fund – not out of its own pocket.

Should the carrier refuse on behalf of the Secretary to pay a portion of the claim, the claimant has one or more opportunities to appeal. First, all claimants are entitled to a "review determination," in which they may submit written evidence and arguments of fact and law. A carrier employee, other than the initial decision-maker, will review the written record de novo and affirm or adjust the original determination. If the amount in dispute is $ 100 or more, a still-dissatisfied claimant then has a right to an oral hearing. An officer chosen by the carrier presides over this hearing. The hearing officers "do not participate personally, prior to the hearing, in any case they adjudicate."

Hearing officers receive evidence and hear arguments pertinent to the matters at issue. As soon as practicable thereafter, they must render written decisions based on the record. Neither the statute nor the regulations make provision for further review of the hearing officer's decision.

II

This case arose as a result of decisions by hearing officers against three claimants. The claimants, here appellees, sued to challenge the constitutional adequacy of the hearings afforded them. The District Court . . . certified appellees as representatives of a nationwide class of individuals whose claims had been denied by carrier-appointed hearing officers. On cross-motions for summary judgment, the court concluded that the Part B hearing procedures violated appellees' right to due process "insofar as the final, unappealable decision regarding claims disputes is made by carrier appointees . . . ."

. . . .

III
A

The hearing officers involved in this case serve in a quasi-judicial capacity, similar in many respects to that of administrative law judges. As this Court repeatedly has recognized, due process demands impartiality on the part of those who function in judicial or quasi-judicial capacities. We must start, however, from the presumption that the hearing officers who decide Part B claims are unbiased. . . .

Fairly interpreted, the factual findings made in this case do not reveal any disqualifying interest under the standard of our cases. The District Court relied almost exclusively on generalized assumptions of possible interest, placing special weight on the various connections of the hearing officers with the private insurance carriers. The difficulty with this reasoning is that these connections would be relevant only if the carriers themselves are biased or interested. We find no basis in the record for reaching such a conclusion. As previously noted, the carriers pay all Part B claims from federal, and not their own, funds. Similarly, the salaries of the hearing officers are paid by the Federal Government. Further, the carriers operate under contracts that require compliance with standards prescribed by the statute and the Secretary. In the absence of proof of financial interest on the part of the carriers, there is no basis for assuming a derivative bias among their hearing officers.

B

Appellees further argued, and the District Court agreed, that due process requires an additional administrative or judicial review by a Government rather than a carrier-appointed hearing officer. Specifically, the District Court ruled that "Part B procedures might remain intact so long as aggrieved beneficiaries would be entitled to appeal carrier appointees' decisions to Part A administrative law judges." In reaching this conclusion, the District Court applied the familiar test prescribed in *Mathews v. Eldridge*. We may assume that the District Court was correct in viewing the private interest in Part B payments as "considerable," though "not quite as precious as the right to receive welfare or social security benefits." We likewise may assume, in considering the third *Mathews* factor, that the additional cost and inconvenience of providing administrative law judges would not be unduly burdensome. n.13

> n.13 [P]erhaps this conclusion would have been difficult to prove. It is known that in 1980 about 158 million Part B claims . . . were filed. Even though the additional review would be available only for disputes in excess of $ 100, a small percentage of the number of claims would be large in terms of number of cases.

We focus narrowly on the second *Mathews* factor that considers the risk of erroneous decision and the probable value, if any, of the additional procedure. The District Court's reasoning on this point consisted only of this sentence:

> In light of [the] undisputed showing that carrier-appointed hearing officers receive little or no formal training and are not required to satisfy any threshold criteria such as having a law degree, it must be assumed that additional safeguards would reduce the risk of erroneous deprivation of Part B benefits.

Again, the record does not support these conclusions. The Secretary has directed carriers to select as a hearing office[r]

> an attorney or other *qualified* individual with the ability to conduct formal hearings and with a general understanding of medical matters and terminology. The [hearing officer] must have a *thorough knowledge* of the Medicare program and the statutory authority and regulations upon which it is based, as well as rulings, policy statements, and general instructions pertinent to the Medicare Bureau.

The District Court did not identify any specific deficiencies in the Secretary's selection criteria. By definition, a "qualified" individual already possessing "ability" and "thorough knowledge" would not require further training. The court's further general concern that hearing officers "are not required to satisfy any threshold criteria" overlooks the Secretary's quoted regulation. Moreover, the District Court apparently gave no weight to the qualifications of hearing officers about whom there is information in the record. Their qualifications tend to undermine rather than to support the contention that accuracy of Part B decisionmaking may suffer by reason of carrier appointment of unqualified hearing officers. n.15

> n.15 The record contains information on nine hearing officers. Two were retired administrative law judges with 15 to 18 years of judging experience, five had extensive experience in medicine or medical insurance, one had been a practicing attorney for 20 years, and one was an attorney with 42 years' experience in the insurance industry who was self-employed as an insurance adjuster.

Process is flexible and calls for such procedural protections as the particular situation demands." We have considered appellees' claims in light of the strong presumption in favor of the validity of congressional action and consistently with this Court's recognition of "congressional solicitude for fair procedure . . . ." Appellees simply have not shown that the procedures prescribed by Congress and the Secretary are not fair or that different or additional procedures would reduce the risk of erroneous deprivation of Part B benefits.

IV

The judgment of the District Court is reversed, and the case is remanded for judgment to be entered for the Secretary.

———————

1. *Amundsen v. The Chicago Park District*, 218 F.3d 712 (7th Cir. 2000):

> Amundsen was employed by the Chicago Park District as a physical fitness instructor . . . to teach athletic skills to park patrons. . . . On . . . March 24, 1995, the Park . . . Manager . . . informed Amundsen that a couple had accused him of striking a park patron (their child) during a class. . . . Amundsen was suspended as a result . . . . Amundsen initially accuses the hearing officer of being biased in favor of the Park District as "it is apparent that a hearing officer who consistently rules against the Park District will not continue to enjoy his place on the Park District payroll."

> The plaintiff has failed to present any evidence of actual bias on the part of the hearing officer. Amundsen's bald accusation is based solely on the fact that the hearing officer was employed by the Park District, which of itself is insufficient to establish actual bias. Thus, we hold that Amundsen has failed to satisfy his burden of overcoming the well-established "presumption of honesty and integrity in those serving as adjudicators. . . ."

Quite clearly, status alone is insufficient to establish bias. Based on *Schweiker*, what is required? What assumptions can be made? Impartiality is an obvious component of fundamental fairness – but how is it protected?

2. *Independence Public Media of Philadelphia, Inc. v. Pennsylvania Public Television Network Commission*, 808 F. Supp. 416 (D. Pa. 1992):

> Nine in-state public television stations currently serve the citizens of Pennsylvania. Plaintiff Independence Public Media of Philadelphia, Inc. operates the infant of these nine, WYBE in Philadelphia . . . . Plaintiff alleges that WYBE's eight Pennsylvania sister stations jealously share in a state-funded network known as the Pennsylvania Public Television Network ("PPTN"), which links the stations via microwave relay and produces statewide public television programming. The PPTN is . . . operated by defendant Pennsylvania Public Television Network Commission ("PPTNC"), a commonwealth entity consisting of 22 commissioners, eight of whom are closely affiliated with . . . WYBE's sister stations. . . . [O]ver the past four years, WYBE has unsuccessfully attempted to join the PPTN family . . . . [P]laintiff asserts that the eight PPTNC commissioners affiliated with the TV Defendants necessarily labor under a pecuniary conflict of interest when considering plaintiff's application for interconnection and funding. . . .
>
> Plaintiff likens the instant situation to . . . *Gibson v. Berryhill*, 411 U.S. 564 (1973). There, the Alabama Board of Optometry (the "Board") intended to revoke the licenses to practice required of all optometrists employed by corporations, a group comprising about one-half of all the optometrists in the state. . . . [Membership on] the Board . . . was limited to independent practitioners. The district court found that the independent practitioners in the state, including the Board members, would benefit substantially if the licenses of the corporate practitioners were revoked [thus creating] a financial conflict of interest, disqualifying the Board members. The Supreme Court affirmed, holding that "those with substantial pecuniary interest in legal proceedings should not adjudicate these disputes."
>
> Plaintiff contends that [PPTNC] is not significantly different from the Board found to be unconstitutionally biased in *Gibson*. I agree. . . . PPTNC is a state agency adjudicating significant rights – the rights . . . of a new station like WYBE to receive PPTN interconnection and funding. . . . [D]ue process requires PPTNC impartiality. *Schweiker*. . . . The commissioners affiliated with the TV Defendants have a substantial pecuniary interest in the outcome of the PPTNC's decision on plaintiff's request. There is no dispute among the parties that if the PPTNC provides funding to plaintiff, each of the TV Defendants will receive fewer funds from the PPTNC as a consequence. . . . These undisputed facts suggest strongly that the TV Defendants have a significant financial interest in opposing plaintiff's request for interconnection and funding. . . .
>
> When the PPTNC sits down to consider plaintiff's request, the presence of these eight financially biased commissioners presents precisely the type of situation prohibited . . . as a violation of due process. . . . In sum, I conclude that plaintiff has carried its burden of demonstrating the presence of a disqualifying conflict of interest among the eight PPTNC commissioners affiliated with the TV Defendants. . . .

Those who are a position to act as initial or final decisionmakers who have a financial stake in the outcome have a patent conflict. Do you accept the Court's premise in *McClure* that those who administer public health programs are without any interest in limiting payouts in cases under what was then Part B?

3. In *Simpson v. Macon County, 132 F. Supp. 2d 407-10 (W.D.N.C. 2001)*

> plaintiff was dismissed from employment as the Macon County Health Director . . . . [Plaintiff] claims that four members of the Board of Health, the body which made the final decision to fire Plaintiff, harbored a personal bias against him [and] alleges that one member of the Board harbored and concealed a fixed bias against him. . . . Plaintiff bears the heavy burden of proving bias or a *high risk thereof*. (citing *Schweiker v. McClure*, 456 U.S. at 196).

What are the risks to which the court (above) refers? The system of publicly funded health care in *Schweiker v. McClure* has undergone extensive change (as the note below suggests), but the difficulty of establishing bias has not changed. *See* Jennifer L. Wright, *Unconstitutional or Impossible: The Irreconcilable Gap Between Managed Care and Due Process in Medicaid and Medicare*, 17 J. CONTEMP. HEALTH L. & POL'Y 135, 168 (2000) ("The most basic requirement of procedural due process under the Fifth and Fourteenth Amendments is that of an unbiased decision-maker. No matter what other procedural protections may exist, a determination cannot meet the minimum requirements of fairness if the decision is made by someone who has a financial stake in the outcome.").

4. Public health care has never been a simple matter in the United States – if anything, it is becoming more complicated, which thereby widens the already generous deference due hearing officers in the field. "The Court of Appeals for this Circuit has made clear that in framing the scope of review, the court takes special note of the tremendous complexity of the Medicare statute. That complexity adds to the deference which is due to the Secretary's decision." *Dialysis Clinic, Inc. v. Leavitt, 518 F. Supp. 2d 197 (D.D.C. 2007)* (*quoting Methodist Hosp. of Sacramento v. Shalala, 38 F.3d 1225, 1229 (D.C. Cir. 1994)*).

The current Medicare legislation pertaining to parts A-D is distributed throughout Title 42. Roughly, Part A is at 42 U.S.C. § 1395c, Part B at § 1395k, Part C at § 1395w – as is Part D, and § 1395b-9 provides statutory guidelines regarding management and operation of Medicare. By comparison, the regulatory environment in *Schweiker v. McClure* looks primitive.

5. The current iteration of privatized decisionmaking in the publicly financed health care field provides no safe harbor for those concerned about the potential deprivation of due process and the impartiality of hearing officers. Professor Nan D. Hunter's *Managed Process, Due Care: Structures of Accountability in Health Care*, 6 YALE J. HEALTH POL'Y L. & ETHICS 93 (2006), provides a clear picture of the current

regulatory environment:

> In forty-one states and the District of Columbia, special entities have been established to resolve contract and tort claims. State law created and mandates each system; these are not arbitrations agreed to by contract between the parties. Despite their public nature, however, these systems are not offered or operated by courts; the public function of adjudication is entirely outsourced to private actors. The decisionmakers . . . do not write opinions, and . . . neither establish nor follow precedent.

> These new entities are the external review systems set up to resolve disputes between patients and managed care organizations (MCOs), which arise when such organizations deny coverage for medical treatment, services, or equipment that the patient, generally upon the recommendation of a physician, believes to be medically necessary. . . . the Supreme Court has decided that only three component rights of procedural due process are essential: adequate notice, a hearing at a meaningful time, and a hearing before an impartial decisionmaker. . . . Many aspects of health law process, however, became an exception to the normal operations of procedural due process requirements.

In light of Professor Hunter's critique, the holding in *Schweiker*, and the probability that 42 U.S.C. §1395w-26(b)(3) et. seq., arguably preempts all state common law claims pertaining to Medicare, where is the "check" on biased administration of the Medicare program? *See* Jonathan Oberlander, *Through the Looking Glass: The Politics of the Medicare Prescription Drug, Improvement, and Modernization Act*, 32 J. HEALTH POL. POL'Y & L. 187, 204 (2007).

6. In *Duchesne* (above), the court concluded that if there was "animosity" between a decisionmaker and a party, the impartiality of the decision was inherently suspect. Pre-judgment (unless explicit and overt), unlike overt animosity, is problematic. As *Withrow* cautions, there is a presumption of honesty and integrity that should be observed. There are problems in "penalizing" for past accomplishments highly experienced professionals who agree to serve in government. There are challenges in both insuring fairness in fact and perceptually in the hearing process – and insuring an open discourse between agencies, the press, and public.

The following notes and note cases continue the dialogue on appearance of impropriety, conflict of interest, bias, and other factors that can affect the actual and perceived fairness of adjudicatory proceedings.

a. Ex parte communications are disfavored in the APA, Section 5 U.S.C. § 557 (d) (1) – but fairly common, given the nature of administrative agencies and the role played by top-level agency officials (who are public figures). Agency leaders are expected to engage in public discourse – but also serve as final decisionmakers in adjudication. If an ex parte communication "substantially taints" a record (a test that will be developed more in this text), it can become the basis for a remand – or even a "show cause" order. *See PATCO*, infra Chapter 9.

Ex parte communication is so common that it is written into the rules of most agencies. In most instances, so long as the communication is disclosed in a timely way, giving others an opportunity to respond, there are few, if any, consequences. Often the debate is not over sanctioning ex parte communication (as is the case in Article III courts), but rather whether the communication can be part of the record. *See Nat'l Ass'n of State Util. Consumer Advocates v. FCC, 457 F.3d 1238 (11th Cir. 2006)*.

In *Guenther v. Commissioner, 939 F.2d 758, 760 (9th Cir. 1991)*, the court held that an ex parte communication can be tolerated if the parties involved can demonstrate "compelling justification" for the dialogue. Those fighting the use of such communications must show they have been "unfairly prejudiced."

On occasion, agencies try, through the issuance of rules, orders, or guidelines, to deal with ex parte dialogue. In *Electric Power Supply Association v. FERC, 391 F.3d 1255 (2004)*, FERC exempted ex parte communications between market monitors and the staff at FERC where the monitor was neither a party nor appearing on behalf of a party. Such communications would be memorialized only if relied on in reaching an on-the-record decision. On review, the court found the FERC rule violated the 557(d) prohibition on ex parte communications. An agency can interpret a statute – but it cannot, de jure, amend it.

b. How does one assess if a decision-maker has pre-judged a matter? Must you prove "an unalterably closed mind" or will something less suffice?

Antoniu v. Securities and Exchange Commission, 877 F.2d 721 (8th Cir. 1989):

> **Food for Thought**
>
> How can an agency increase the probability of impartiality without chilling the essential dialogue between agency leaders and the public?

> Adrian Antoniu (Antoniu) [originally] worked [with] Morgan Stanley & Co., Inc. [as] a broker-dealer registered with the Securities and Exchange Commission (SEC or Commission). Antoniu entered into an insider trading conspiracy with . . . Newman[,] a securities trader. Antoniu would obtain the non-public information about imminent takeover bids by Morgan Stanley's clients. Newman would then buy large blocks of stock of the targeted companies and later sell the stock at a profit. Antoniu shared in the profits.
>
> Morgan Stanley asked Antoniu to resign and he took a position at Kuhn Loeb & Co. (later Lehman Brothers Kuhn Loeb, Inc.). . . . Antoniu continued to receive market-sensitive non-public information [and] Antoniu repeated the pattern: he misappropriated the information and passed it to Newman, who bought and sold stocks of target companies. . . . Kuhn Loeb fired Antoniu in 1978 when he was investigated for insider trading violations. Antoniu then moved to Italy.

On November 13, 1980, Antoniu pled guilty to two counts of misappropriating information in securities markets . . . . He was sentenced to three months' imprisonment, thirty-six months' suspended sentence and a $ 5000 fine . . . . [T]he sentence was [later] reduced to thirty-nine months' unsupervised probation and a $ 5000 fine.

In 1984, Antoniu moved to Minnesota to take a job with M.H. Novick & Co. Due to Antoniu's criminal conviction, Antoniu and Novick sought approval for the employment from the National Association of Securities Dealers (NASD). After an evidentiary hearing, *NASD approved the employment on June 3, 1985.* Antoniu went to work for Novick later that summer.

On September 3, 1985, the SEC vetoed NASD's approval . . . . One of the participating commissioners was Charles C. Cox. On September 19, 1985, the SEC started a second set of proceedings (. . . *Antoniu II*). . . . The purpose of this second set of proceedings was to determine . . . whether it was in the public interest to exclude Antoniu from *any* employment in the securities business.

While *Antoniu II* was pending, on October 18, 1985, Commissioner Cox gave a speech in Denver entitled "Making the Punishment Fit the Crime – A Look at SEC Enforcement Remedies." The speech outlined two recent cases before the SEC in which the Commission had imposed sanctions on firms or persons. Commissioner Cox said that each of the sanctioned entities was an "indifferent violator" and further expounded:

> Mr. Antoniu, on the other hand, can be appropriately termed a violator, for he pled guilty to criminal violations of the federal securities laws. . . . [He] provided inside information on several occasions to accomplices who traded while in possession of that information. Although he was prosecuted for this conduct, Mr. Antoniu recently applied to become associated with a broker-dealer. Apparently, Mr. Antoniu believed that, since his rehabilitation was complete, there was no further reason to prevent his future dealings in the securities industry. . . . One issue that frequently arises with respect to individuals whom I call "indifferent violators" is the length of time that a Commission remedy should remain in effect. . . . *In the case of Mr. Antoniu, his bar from association with a broker-dealer was made permanent.*

Cox's words describing Antoniu's bar as permanent can only be interpreted as a prejudgment of the issue. We emphasize that the speech was made while the *Antoniu II* proceedings were pending. The text of the speech was also printed and distributed by the SEC. . . . [In light of Cox's speech] Antoniu . . . made a motion . . . to disqualify the whole Commission. The motion was denied and specifically, Commissioner Cox refused to recuse himself. . . .

> [From *Antoniu II*] Due in part to Commissioner Cox's remarks about Antoniu made in the Denver speech, Antoniu claims that the proceedings were biased or at least that they were impermissibly tainted with the appearance of impropriety. . . . The relevant inquiry is thus whether Commissioner Cox's post-speech participation in the *Antoniu II* proceedings comported with the appearance of justice. . . .

> The test for [disqualification] has been succinctly stated as being whether "a disinterested observer may conclude that [the agency] has in some measure adjudged the facts as well as the law of a particular case in advance of hearing it."

We turn again to the case before us. . . . After reviewing the statements made by Commissioner Cox, we can come to no conclusion other than that Cox had "in some measure adjudged the facts as well as the law of a particular case in advance of hearing it." Even though Cox recused himself prior to the filing of the SEC's final decision, there is no way of knowing how Cox's participation affected the Commissioner's deliberations. Accordingly, we nullify all Commission proceedings (including the Commission's rejection of Antoniu's proposed settlement) in which Commissioner Cox participated occurring after Commissioner Cox's speech was given and remand the case to the Commission with directions to make a de novo review of the evidence, without any participation by Commissioner Cox. . . . [Cox recused himself the day *Antoniu II* was decided.]

c. *Haas v. County of San Bernardino*, 45 P.3d 280 (Cal. 2002):

> Plaintiff . . . Haas operates a massage clinic in San Bernardino . . . under a license issued by the County. When a deputy sheriff reported that a massage technician had exposed her breasts and proposed a sexual act, the County Board of Supervisors (the Board) revoked Haas's license. Haas timely appealed . . . and the Board set the matter for hearing. The notice identified a local attorney, Abby Hyman, as the hearing officer. . . .
>
> Haas's attorney, . . . Diamond, argued that Hyman had an impermissible financial interest in the case . . . and moved that she recuse herself. . . . Deputy County Counsel Alan Green [had said], "The intent is that we will use Ms. Hyman on assignment, as the occasion suggests, in the future if she's interested in doing it and if the case should arise." . . . . Diamond asked Green, "And so certainly you've advised that she might be needed on future hearings." Green responded, "I probably have. . . ." Diamond then asked, "But you, as the moving party, are, in effect, paying the hearing officer?" Green responded, "So?" . . . . Hyman interjected, "Would you like to split my bill? I don't care . . . . [Hyman denied the motion to recuse and the hearing was held. She] rendered a brief written decision 47 days later recommending revocation.
>
> The question presented is whether a temporary administrative hearing officer has a pecuniary interest requiring disqualification when the government unilaterally selects and pays the officer on an ad hoc basis and the officer's income from future adjudicative work depends entirely on the government's goodwill. We conclude the answer is yes. . . . While the rules governing the disqualification of administrative hearing officers are in some respects more flexible than those governing judges, the rules are not more flexible on the subject of financial interest. . . . The "possible temptation" not to be scrupulously fair, alone and in itself, offends the Constitution. That such a temptation can arise from the hope of future employment as an adjudicator is easy to understand and impossible in good faith to deny. . . . [The situation in this case created unconstitutional financial bias on the part of the hearing officer.]

d. *Municipal Services Corporation v. North Dakota, 483 N.W.2d 560 (N.D. 1992)*:

MSC petitioned the Department for modification of its landfill permit to include changes in the construction . . . and for permission to dispose of municipal waste combuster (incinerator) ash in the modified landfill. . . . The Department held a public hearing . . . . On December 20, 1990, Dr. Wentz [denied] MSC's application for modification of its permit. MSC petitioned for rehearing and also petitioned to disqualify Dr. Wentz as the hearing officer, based upon a November 19, 1990, letter from Dr. Wentz to Governor George A. Sinner [stating]:

> . . . I am firmly opposed to permitting the landfill and, in fact, my preference would be to approach the public hearing with an announced intent to deny the permit. My primary areas of concern are as follows:
>
> > 1. While there is debate regarding . . . municipal solid waste ash, it is clear that this ash does contain what I consider to be substantial amounts of heavy metals including lead, mercury and cadmium.
> >
> > 2. If one just focuses on the issue of lead in the ash, the health risks, in my opinion, are substantial. . . . Lead is so highly toxic that no threshold level is believed to exist for toxic effects, especially in children. . . .

[In this case,] rather than an issue of actual bias, we are faced with an issue about prejudgment, "an area closely akin to bias." . . . . Dr. Wentz appears to have prejudged and precommitted himself to some adjudicative facts, which has been held to be disqualifying or violative of due process. . . . Dr. Wentz's undisclosed intent to deny MSC's permit application taints the procedure employed in this case. . . . If administrators disclose their opinions on relevant issues, "interested parties are at least aware of which opinions they must persuade an administrator to change." . . . . In our view, the Department's deviation from its usual practice of issuing a notice of intent to grant or deny an environmental permit before conducting a permit hearing [when] Dr. Wentz was firmly opposed to granting MSC's application [and the Department's] failure to disclose the bases of Dr. Wentz's opposition . . . do not give the appearance of being fair. We conclude that the Department's procedure did not afford MSC a fair hearing . . . .

e. *First Savings & Loan Association of Borger v. Vandygriff (Vandygriff I), 605 S.W.2d 740 (Tex. Civ. App. 1980)*:

Appellant is First Savings and Loan Association, and appellees are [Citizens Security Savings and Loan Association] and L. Alvis Vandygriff, Savings and Loan Commissioner of Texas. . . . The crucial issue on appeal is [whether] the district court erred in failing to hold that the course of ex parte actions and conduct pursued by the organizers of [Citizens] invalidated the Commissioner's order [granting the bank charter].

The organizers of [Citizens] filed a charter application in 1978. The Commissioner . . . entered an order denying the application in August . . . . During the first week in September . . . five of the disappointed organizers came to Austin and visited with the Commissioner, giving him a "different view" of economic conditions of the Borger area than that reflected in the order . . . . Those persons told the Commissioner . . .

that two new shopping centers were going to be located in Borger and . . . about the expansion of the Phillips Petroleum Company in the Borger area. No one representing appellant was advised of or was present at this parley with the Commissioner. After their conference . . . the organizers [refiled] the application . . . . In March, 1979, the Commissioner entered his order approving the charter application. The Commissioner's order recited the fact that the organizers had met with him in September, 1978 [but said]: "The Commissioner would note the existence of that meeting only in order to say that his decision in this case was based only upon the record as complied by all of the parties at the January 31 and February 1, 1979, hearing."

An administrative order must be grounded upon evidence taken at the hearing and upon facts officially noticed by the hearings officer in the record of such hearing. Recognition of this fundamental rule necessarily means that ex parte communications may not be a basis for such order. . . . It is true, as urged by appellees, that at the time of the meeting the organizers had no formal contested case pending before the Commission. Nevertheless, it is also true that shortly after the parley with the Commissioner, the same organizers once again filed with the Commissioner their application for a charter for an association with the same name for the same location, Borger, Texas. . . . The organizers placed in no new capital funds because the capital funds from the first application were still placed on account to the credit of the proposed association. The applicants also used the stock subscription forms from the prior application in the second application. This Court agrees with the organizers that, indeed, the first and second proceedings before the Commissioner were, in effect, "just one ongoing application" . . . .

It is not the burden of the complaining party to demonstrate harm by showing the extent, if any, to which the official was persuaded by the secret information. Instead, it is presumed that the separate meeting resulted in findings that precipitated the administrative order . . . even though the administrative order may recite the opposite. . . . The judgment of the district court is reversed . . . .

f. *Vandygriff v. First Savings and Loan Association of Borger (Vandygriff II), 617 S.W.2d 669 (Tex. 1981)*.

This is an appeal from [the case you just read]. We reverse the judgment of the court of civil appeals and remand the cause to that court for further consideration. . . . [T]he applications were not the same. There are different organizers and stockholders and the location was different. This was stated in the Commissioner's order granting Citizens' charter. The organizers and stockholders not participating in the second application withdrew their money from the capital account. The new participants deposited new funds. The organizers paid a new and additional filing fee and new notices were given as required by statute and regulation. The hearing examiner refused to admit the record from the first application because it had no bearing on the record in the subsequent new application. The facts establish that no application was pending before the Savings and Loan Commission when the meeting between the Commissioner and the organizers occurred. There was no contested case at the time. We hold the meeting was not an ex parte communication . . . .

The court of civil appeals' opinion presumes that substantial harm resulted from the meeting. The court concludes the discussions with the Commissioner precipitated the order granting the charter. . . . [But appeals] are subject to review under the substantial evidence rule [meaning] the Commissioner's order may be overturned only upon showing that "substantial rights of the appellant have been prejudiced."

[The standards are in note 4, which lists the factors as follows:] Substantial prejudice may be found if the order is: 1) in violation of constitutional or statutory provisions, 2) in excess of the statutory authority of the agency, 3) made upon unlawful procedure, 4) affected by other error of law, 5) not reasonably supported by substantial evidence in view of the reliable and probative evidence in the record as a whole, or, 6) arbitrary or capricious or characterized by an abuse of discretion or clearly unwarranted exercise of discretion.

The court presumes the Commissioner performed his duties in compliance with the law, and the appellants have the burden to show he did not. . . .

Courts have not been reluctant to criticize the administrative decisionmakers, as the holding in *Antoniu* suggests. The following case explores both pre-judgment and the extent to which a reviewing administrative body is bound to factfinding in an initial decision.

g. *Cinderella Career and Finishing Schools, Inc. v. Federal Trade Commission*, 425 F.2d 583 (D.C. Cir. 1970):

This is a petition to review orders of the Federal Trade Commission which required petitioners Cinderella Career College and Finishing Schools . . . to cease and desist from engaging in certain practices which were allegedly unfair and deceptive.

After the Commission filed its complaint under section 5 of the Federal Trade Commission Act, which charged Cinderella with making representations and advertising in a manner which was false, misleading and deceptive, a hearing examiner held a lengthy series of hearings [eventually ruling] that the charges in the complaint should be dismissed. Complaint counsel appealed the hearing examiner's initial decision to the full Commission[, which] reversed the hearing examiner as to six of the original thirteen charges and entered a cease and desist order against the petitioners, who then brought this appeal. . . .

We are faced with two principal issues on this appeal: whether the action of the Commission in reversing the hearing examiner comports with standards of due process, and whether then Chairman Paul Rand Dixon should have recused himself from participation in the review of the initial decision due to public statements he had previously made which allegedly indicated pre-judgment of the case on his part.

I. Procedural Irregularity and Due Process. . . . [The] full Commission, in reviewing an initial decision, may consider the advertisements de novo . . . and arrive at independent findings of fact and conclusions of law . . . . In their final decision the Commissioners [stated]: "In view of our decision to independently analyze – and without assistance from consumer or other witnesses – the challenged advertisements and their impact . . . it becomes *unnecessary to review the testimony of these expert and consumer witnesses.*" Later in the opinion they again noted that "for the reasons stated above *the Commission will rely on its own reading and study of the advertisements to*

hearing officer
vs.
Commissioner
decision-
maker

determine whether the questioned representation has the capacity to deceive." The hearing examiner in a Federal Trade Commission proceeding has both the right and the duty to make determinations concerning the credibility of witnesses and the exclusion of hearsay evidence; while the Commissioners may review those determinations on appeal, in light of the record, they may not choose to ignore completely the testimony adduced at the hearing. n.3

> n.3 It is clear that what the Commissioners did here was to review selected parts of the record (the advertisements) while ignoring other matters of record (the testimony of consumer and expert witnesses). . . .

We think it as preposterous for the Commission to claim a right to ignore [the testimony] and . . . to decide a case de novo as it would be for this court to claim a right to ignore the findings of fact and conclusions of law of a district court in a proceeding here, substituting the judgment of this court on a cold record for that of the finder of the fact below. . . . We [also] hardly think it permissible for the Commission to draw . . . independent conclusions, while ignoring the record and consequently converting the entire hearing proceeding into a meaningless exercise, leaving it for the court to review the record to find whether there is evidence to support those conclusions.

[The] Commissioners [have] great latitude to disagree with their hearing examiner; [they do not have] the option of completely ignoring the testimony of many witnesses and the findings of the examiner . . . . If they choose to modify or set aside his conclusions they must state that they are doing so and they must give reasons for so doing. To hold otherwise is to ignore the objectives of adversary proceedings before the Commission. Only if such rules are carefully adhered to can a reviewing court properly analyze the action taken by the Commission; only then can the wheat of meaningful agency action be separated from the chaff of arbitrary and capricious conduct. . . .

II. Disqualification of Chairman Dixon. . . . [O]n March 15, 1968, while the appeal from the examiner's decision was pending before him, Chairman Dixon made a speech before the Government Relations Workshop of the National Newspaper Association in which he stated:

> What kind of vigor can a reputable newspaper exhibit? . . . How about ethics on the business side of running a paper? . . . What would be the attitude toward accepting good money for advertising by a merchant who conducts a "going out of business" sale every five months? *What about carrying ads that offer college educations in five weeks . . . or becoming an airline's hostess by attending a charm school?* . . . Without belaboring the point, I'm sure you're aware that advertising acceptance standards could stand more tightening by many newspapers. *Granted that newspapers are not in the advertising policing business, their advertising managers are savvy enough to smell deception when the odor is strong enough.* And it is in the public interest, as well as their own, that their sensory organs become more discriminating. . . .

It requires no superior olfactory powers to recognize that the danger of unfairness through prejudgment is not diminished by a cloak of self-righteousness. . . . There is a marked difference between the issuance of a press release which states that the Commission has filed a complaint because it has "reason to believe" that there have been violations, and statements by a Commissioner after an appeal has been filed which give the appearance that he has already prejudged the case and that the ultimate determination of the merits will move in predestined grooves. . . .

We find it hard to believe that former Chairman Dixon is so indifferent to the dictates of the Courts of Appeals that he has chosen once again to put his personal determination . . . ahead of what the courts have time and again told him the law requires. . . . We . . . will spell out for him once again, . . . in no uncertain terms, exactly what those requirements are, in the fervent hope that this will be the last time we have to travel this wearisome road.

The test for disqualification has been succinctly stated as being whether "a disinterested observer may conclude that [the agency] has in some measure adjudged the facts as well as the law of a particular case in advance of hearing it." . . . . We further stated that such an administrative hearing "must be attended, not only with every element of fairness but with the very appearance of complete fairness" . . . .

It is appalling to witness such insensitivity to the requirements of due process . . . . We are constrained to this harshness of language because of Mr. Dixon's flagrant disregard of prior decisions. The rationale for remanding the case despite the fact that former Chairman Dixon's vote was not necessary for a majority is well established:

 Litigants are entitled to an impartial tribunal whether it consists of one man or twenty and there is no way which we know of whereby the influence of one upon the others can be quantitatively measured. . . .

For the reasons set forth above we vacate the order of the Commission and remand with instructions that the Commissioners consider the record and evidence in reviewing the initial decision, without the participation of Commissioner Dixon.

Do the prior professional affiliations of a judge affect the capacity or probability of rendering fair and impartial decisions?

ANDREWS V. AGRICULTURAL LABOR RELATIONS BOARD

623 P.2d 151 (Cal. 1981)

[JUDGE MOSK] [P]etitioners seek a writ of review to set aside a decision and order of the Agricultural Labor Relations Board (Board). The Board's general counsel initiated the underlying proceeding by filing complaints . . . alleging that petitioners – agricultural employers of workers covered by the Agricultural Labor Relations Act (ALRA) – had committed various unfair labor practices in connection with a union representation election held among petitioners' employees.

The Board appointed Armando Menocal as a temporary ALO [administrative law officer] to conduct the hearings . . . . At [the] time, Menocal was an attorney in private practice with Public Advocates, Inc., a public interest law firm in San Francisco. Petitioners' counsel first learned of this fact approximately one hour before the hearing commenced. He immediately moved to disqualify Menocal under the then current [California] regulation on disqualification of ALOs. . . . [T]he ALO permitted counsel to make an oral affidavit as follows:

> Mr. Brown: . . . I understand Mr. Menocal is employed by Public Advocates which . . . does a good deal of work in the area of employment discrimination [and] on behalf of labor unions. It is my understanding that they do not work on behalf of employers. I understand the Hearing Officer is presently involved in an employment discrimination case . . . against the J. C. Penney Company . . . and on those grounds and other grounds which I am sure I could possibly find out with further inquiry . . . there is certainly the appearance of bias, and I do not feel that my client can get the type of unbiased hearing that he is entitled to.

[The ALO denied the motion.] The hearings proceeded to the merits of the unfair labor practice charges, and the ALO filed a recommended decision adverse to petitioners on most of the major issues. The Board issued its final decision without treating the disqualification issue; it essentially adopted the ALO's findings and recommendations. The Board did declare that it had considered and made an independent review of the entire record in the case. . . . [P]etitioners . . . major contention [is] that the ALO improperly failed to disqualify himself . . . . [W]e conclude that contention lacks both legal and factual support. . . .

II

Petitioners imply that a ground for bias was the ALO's practice of law with a firm which in the past had represented individual farm workers [and] Mexican-Americans. From this, it appears we are to infer that the ALO has some philosophical or political inclination that would make it impossible for him to conduct hearings impartially. Even if the nature of a lawyer's practice could be taken as evidence of his political or social outlook, n.3 such evidence . . . is irrelevant to prove bias. . . .

> n.3 Amici assert persuasively that imputing the values of a client to a lawyer is an improper exercise inevitably fraught with dangers of erroneous conclusions. That view is consistent with the American Bar Association Code of Professional Responsibility which urges every lawyer to accept representation of "unpopular clients and causes . . . ."

The right to an impartial trier of fact is not synonymous with the claimed right to a trier completely indifferent to the general subject matter of the claim before him. . . . "Bias in the sense of crystallized point of view about issues of law or policy is almost universally deemed no ground for disqualification." This long established, practical rule is merely a recognition of the fact that anyone acting in a judicial role will have attitudes and preconceptions toward some of the legal and social issues that may come before him. . . . Therefore, even if the viewpoint attributed to an ALO could be inferred from the nature of his legal practice or his clients – which we do not concede – that would be no ground for disqualification. . . . The more politically or socially sensitive a matter, the more likely it is that the ALO, like most intelligent citizens, will have at some time reached an opinion on the issue. This is an unavoidable feature of a legal system dependent on human beings rather than robots for dispute resolution.

III

Even assuming, arguendo, the political or legal views of an ALO could result in an appearance of bias, we cannot hold, as requested by petitioners, that a mere appearance of bias is a ground for the disqualification of a judicial officer. Code of Civil Procedure section 170, subdivision 5, requires disqualification "when it is made to appear probable that, by reason of bias or prejudice of such justice or judge a fair and impartial trial cannot be had before him." . . . . [N]o court in California has ever interpreted [this section] to mean that an appearance of bias, in the sense of a subjective belief in its existence, is a sufficient ground for disqualification. . . . [Instead, a] party must allege concrete facts that demonstrate the challenged judicial officer is contaminated with bias or prejudice. "Bias and prejudice are never implied and must be established by clear averments."

Thus, our courts have never required the disqualification of a judge unless the moving party has been able to demonstrate concretely the actual existence of bias. n.5 We cannot now exchange this established principle for one as vague, unmanageable and laden with potential mischief as an "appearance of bias" standard, despite our deep concern for the objective and impartial discharge of all judicial duties in this state.

> n.5 Of course, there are some situations in which the probability or likelihood of the existence of actual bias is so great that disqualification of a judicial officer is required . . . even without proof that the judicial officer is actually biased towards a party. In California, these situations are codified in Code of Civil Procedure section 170, subdivisions 1-4. They include cases in which the judicial officer either has a personal or financial interest, has a familial relation to a party or attorney, or has been counsel to a party. . . .

The foregoing considerations, of course, are equally [if not more] applicable to the disqualification of a judicial officer in the administrative system. . . . For example, in an unfair labor practice proceeding the Board is the ultimate fact-finder, not the ALO. We therefore fail to see how a mere subjective belief in the ALO's appearance of bias, as distinguished from actual bias, can prejudice either party when the Board is responsible for making factual determinations, upon an independent review of the record. In the case at bar the Board declared it did undertake such an independent review of the entire record.

IV

Appellants further contend that the temporary status of the ALO herein should be recognized as a factor in the disqualification analysis . . . . However, we know of no case, nor have we been cited to any, that stands for the proposition that a pro tempore judicial officer is peculiarly vulnerable to a disqualification challenge because he is engaged in the practice of law before and after his temporary public service.

V

Petitioners finally contend that bias appears on the face of the ALO's findings and recommended decision. . . . The fallacy of this assertion is explained in Gellhorn et al., Administrative Law – Cases and Comments:

> If the fact finder has allegedly credited unsubstantial evidence while disregarding utterly irrefutable evidence, the issue before a reviewing court should not be whether the fact finder was biased, but whether his findings of fact are supported by substantial evidence on the whole record.

. . . . To hold otherwise would encourage a losing party to raise the specter of bias indiscriminately, whenever he could demonstrate that one finding of fact in a large administrative record was not sufficiently supported. . . .

But, petitioners assert, . . . bias may be established where the record shows the hearing officer uniformly believed evidence introduced by the union and uniformly disbelieved evidence produced by the employer. This contention is contrary to the great weight of authority. . . . To fulfill his duty, an ALO must make choices when conflicting evidence is offered; thus, his reliance on certain witnesses and rejection of others cannot be evidence of bias no matter how consistently the ALO rejects or doubts the testimony produced by one of the adversaries.

JUDGE CLARK [dissenting].

I dissent. The appearance of bias . . . is not only a sufficient but a compelling ground for disqualification. . . . Only in truly rare cases will . . . bias be openly disclosed. . . . Bias, unlike other deprivations of due process which may be clearly determined on the record, is generally an invisible influence and for that reason must be particularly guarded against. . . . The majority agree that the nature of the ALO's law practice is irrelevant to prove bias . . . . However, when an ALO's law firm consistently represents the same limited class of clients, it may be reasonably concluded the ALO is programmed not only to a particular viewpoint on legal and social issues but also to a bias in favor of the particular class he represents and, correspondingly, to a predisposition against those classes generally cast in an opposing role. Bias against a class of which a party is a member is sufficient grounds for disqualification.

Underlying Case Documents

The case referenced:
The order of the Administrative Law Officer
The order of the Agricultural Labor Relations Board

---

1. *Andrews* continues the discussion on bias and presumptions. Do you believe a person with decades of experience in a field in which they gave every indication of commitment and dedication can detach from the policies and preferences on which they worked and assume a role as an objective decisionmaker? Is the record in a case – the acid test against which one can judge bias – a valid indicator? Does it matter if the record is produced in a less-than-formal adjudication? Keep in mind that with the rules of evidence relaxed and limited cross examination (if any), the record in an informal administrative adjudication may be no more than a collection of random information – some valid and some of questionable probative worth.

In *Tug Valley Recovery Center v. Watt*, 703 F.2d 796, 802 (4th Cir. 1983), the court held that

> [t]here is no due process right to have one's claims heard before a court purged of ideology. One is certainly entitled to a tribunal untainted by monetary inducements or evident personal bias, but a litigant may not hold a judge's experience and education against him or her. A criminal defendant may be tried before a judge who was once a prosecutor, and a former legal aid attorney appointed to the bench may preside over a food stamp entitlement case.

2. In *Andrews*, the claim was that the background and experience of the hearing officer rendered him biased. Bias, if proven, leads to recusal. What if one of the parties believes the hearing officer, by prior experience or prior rulings, is predisposed to a particular point of view at odds with that party's best interests – how far can one go to push an allegedly biased hearing officer off the bench?

In *In re BellSouth*, 334 F.3d 941, 958 (11th Cir. 2003), the court was called upon "to consider the appropriate course of action where a party [was] accused of contriving to engineer the recusal of a district judge by hiring a close relative of the judge as counsel." The case reached the Court of Appeals after the lawyers who were allegedly involved in forcing recusal were disqualified from representing their client, BellSouth. The majority reminded the lawyers that "[it] is unethical conduct for a lawyer to tamper with the court system or to arrange disqualifications, selling the lawyer's family relationship rather than professional services. A lawyer who joins a case as co-counsel, and whose principal activity on the case is to provide the recusal, is certainly subject to discipline. Although only a few courts have addressed the issue, it has been said that 'attempts to manipulate the random case assignment process are subject to universal condemnation.' *United States v. Phillips*, 59 F. Supp. 2d 1178, 1180 (D. Utah 1999)." In an exhaustive opinion detailing the law of recusal and the significant burden placed on one seeking a writ of mandamus, the court held that the disqualification order would stand. In an equally lengthy and powerful dissent, JUDGE TJOFLAT asserted that the action of the majority had deprived BellSouth of its counsel of choice.

3. Sometimes bias is simply overt and not a matter of assumptions regarding prior experience. *Duchesne v. Williams, Jr.*, 849 F.2d 1004 (6th Cir. 1988):

> Plaintiff Duchesne was hired in 1982 as the Chief Building Inspector for the City of Inkster (the City). Something over a year later, in 1983, a dispute developed between Duchesne and defendant Williams, then the Inkster City Manager. Duchesne refused to approve payments for repair work done on the Inkster Ice Arena, stating that work did not conform to city standards. Williams insisted that the work should be approved. The dispute erupted in public at a September 6, 1983, city council meeting. On September 12, 1983, Duchesne was terminated. . . .

> We must . . . consider whether Duchesne received the process due him. . . . In the district court's view, the pre-existing animosity between Williams and Duchesne, and the fact that it was Williams who initially fired Duchesne, who developed many of the charges against Duchesne, who testified against Duchesne at the hearing, and who thereafter weighed the evidence and decided that it supported Duchesne's termination, sufficed to destroy the fairness of the termination hearing. . . . [We agree.]

> No characterization of the nature of the hearing can alter the fact that Williams was assigned to conduct a factual inquiry into the very same incidents he had previously investigated and acted upon. Furthermore, there is no construction of the facts of this case that could support the view that Williams was not too biased to give Duchesne a fair hearing. . . . [T]he record clearly shows the existence of personal animosity between Williams and Duchesne such that Williams' subsequent [decision] was, at a minimum, suspect. This, taken together with Williams' in-depth involvement in every stage of the proceedings, forbids the conclusion that Williams was a suitable hearing officer. Williams was involved in some of the incidents that formed the basis for Duchesne's termination, and he was principally responsible for accusing, trying, and deciding the issues at Duchesne's hearing. Under the circumstances, the hearing provided to Duchesne was constitutionally deficient. . . .

4. One way to deal with fairness in decisionmaking is to establish clear rules regarding burden of proof and persuasion. Are agency rules regarding proof requirements entitled to *Chevron* deference, assuming they are issued in conformity with the APA's minimum procedural requirements – the basic rule from the *Vermont Yankee* case? In *Director, Office of Workers' Compensation Programs v. Greenwich Collieries, 512 U.S. 267 (1994)*, a disability case, the Court addressed what conclusions can be drawn from an "evenly balanced" record. While the case does not involve a claim of bias, the discussion is instructive. It is not unusual in cases in which recusal is sought for the facts favoring recusal and those against to be in equipoise, in part because the claims – on both sides – are often based on assumptions. How should such a matter be resolved? In *Greenwich Collieries*, the Department of Labor devised what it calls the "true doubt" rule:

> [W]hen the evidence is evenly balanced, the benefits claimant wins. This litigation presents the question whether the rule is consistent with § 7(c) of the Administrative Procedure Act (APA), which states that "except as otherwise provided by statute, the proponent of a rule or order has the burden of proof." 5 U.S.C. § 556(d). . . .

> For many years the term "burden of proof" was ambiguous because the term was used to describe two distinct concepts. Burden of proof was frequently used to refer to what we now call the burden of persuasion – the notion that if the evidence is evenly balanced, the party that bears the burden of persuasion must lose. But it was also used to refer to what we now call the burden of production – a party's obligation to come forward with evidence to support its claim. . . . We . . . presume Congress intended the phrase to have the meaning generally accepted in the legal community at the time of enactment. These principles lead us to conclude that the drafters of the APA used the term "burden of proof" to mean the burden of persuasion. . . .

> In part due to Congress' recognition that claims such as those involved here would be difficult to prove, claimants in adjudications under these statutes benefit from certain statutory presumptions easing their burden. . . . But with the true doubt rule the Department attempts to go one step further. In so doing, it runs afoul of the APA, a statute designed "to introduce greater uniformity of procedure and standardization of administrative practice among the diverse agencies whose customs had departed widely from each other." . . . . Under the Department's true doubt rule, when the evidence is evenly balanced the claimant wins. Under § 7(c), however, when the evidence is evenly balanced, the benefits claimant must lose. Accordingly, we hold that the true doubt rule violates § 7(c) of the APA.

CHAPTER 9

Evidence: Before, Beyond, and in the Record

I. Discovery

There is no question that effective discovery helps ensure a fair trial and avoids unnecessary surprise in any adjudicatory proceeding. When lawyers are well-informed about both the evidence they will submit as well as the evidence they are likely to confront, the quality of the adjudicatory process will improve. Good discovery not only allows a lawyer to prepare their case better, but helps limit the issues. Discovery might reveal agreement regarding basic facts thus eliminating the need to present evidence about these facts in the adjudication.

APA § 556 provides the authority to conduct depositions and allow interrogatories to issue – but it does not compel either. In pertinent part, it reads as follows:

Key Concept

The basic doctrine is easily summarized: "There is no basic constitutional right to pretrial discovery in administrative proceedings. . . . The extent of discovery that a party engaged in an administrative hearing is entitled to is primarily determined by the particular agency . . . . Nevertheless, because the [D]ue [P]rocess [C]lause ensures that an administrative proceeding will be conducted fairly, discovery must be granted if in the particular situation a refusal to do so would so prejudice a party as to deny him due process." *Mohilef v. Janovici*, 58 Cal. Rptr. 2d 721 (Cal. App. Ct. 1996). [Internal quotes omitted.]

(c) Subject to published rules of the agency and within its powers, employees presiding at hearings [ALJ's or other hearing officers] may –

(1) administer oaths and affirmations;

(2) issue subpoenas authorized by law;

(3) rule on offers of proof and receive relevant evidence;

(4) take depositions or have depositions taken when the ends of justice would be served;

(5) regulate the course of the hearing;

(6) hold conferences for the settlement or simplification of the issues by consent of the parties or by the use of alternative means of dispute resolution as provided in subchapter IV of this chapter;

(7) inform the parties as to the availability of one or more alternative means of dispute resolution, and encourage use of such methods;

(8) require the attendance at any conference held pursuant to paragraph (6) of at least one representative of each party who has authority to negotiate concerning resolution of issues in controversy. . . .

Quite simply, the Administrative Procedure Act confers no right to discovery. *Frilette v. Kimberlin*, 508 F.2d 205, 208 (3d Cir. 1974) (en banc), *cert. denied*, 421 U.S. 980 (1975); *Kelly v. EPA*, 203 F.3d 519, 523 (7th Cir. 2000). However, the APA permits discovery – and it is a major part of the adjudicatory process. Recent focus has been on electronic discovery, primarily paperless document requests and interrogatories. *See, e.g.*, Merit Systems Protection Board, Discovery Rules, available at http://www.afge.org/Documents/DiscoveryInMeritSystems.pdf and http://edocket.access.gpo.gov/2008/E8-6934.htm (last visited June 18, 2008) (regarding the revised interim rules (with request for comments) for discovery, pertaining to 5 C.F.R. Part 1201 et. seq.); Kristopher Stark & Thomas R. Mulroy, *A Suggested Rule for Electronic Discovery in Illinois Administrative Proceedings*, 3 DePaul Bus. & Comm. L.J. 1 (2004).

While it makes sense to allow parties to serve interrogatories, conduct depositions, and participate in pre-hearing conferences with administrative law judges or other decisionmakers to bring into sharp focus the issues to be litigated in an adjudication, these practices often do not take place. In some areas, the time and expense of interrogatories and depositions simply make it impossible to utilize those discovery mechanisms. Furthermore, the fact that the rules of evidence are relaxed in administrative law and that, as a general matter, hearsay is admissible, makes the impeachment function of discovery less important. Finally, there is the very real fact that some agencies, particularly those dealing with public benefits or entitlements, must adjudicate enormous numbers of claims. Permitting extensive discovery in each instance would bring the agency process to a grinding halt.

The note cases that follow provide a quick look into agency discovery and pre-hearing process.

1. *McClelland v. Andrus*, 606 F.2d 1278 (D.C. Cir. 1979):

[For 17 years] B. Riley McClelland, appellant, a professional ecologist, was [employed by] the Department of Interior, National Park Service. . . . Appellant's record with the Park Service was unblemished . . . . In July 1969 William Briggle became the superintendent of Glacier National Park. . . . At his request an unusual number of employees were transferred out of Glacier. . . . Briggle and appellant [had] a philosophical difference . . . . Briggle was concerned with overall management of the Park whereas appellant was concerned with preservation of resources. . . . [Briggle ultimately transferred appellant to another park.]

[Appellant challenged this action and a hearing was held.] Pursuant to the ALJ's recommendation, the Department of Interior undertook a study of Briggle's management and personnel practices and procedures. . . . [A]ppellant requested a copy of the report. However, the hearing examiner held that he had no power to subpoena it and, further, that it need not be produced because it had not been relied upon in the adverse action against appellant. Appellant also asked . . . the Department of Interior to release the report, but they too refused. In support of its refusal the Department of Interior relied on various exemptions to the Freedom of Information Act (FOIA) . . . . We find this reliance on the FOIA to be misplaced. Appellant requested the report not as a member of the public entitled to it under the FOIA, but as a private individual in the throes of agency proceedings adjudicating his claim of arbitrary removal. . . . The extent of discovery that a party engaged in an administrative hearing is entitled to is primarily determined by the particular agency [but] the agency is bound to ensure that its procedures meet due process requirements. . . .

The . . . report is uniquely relevant to appellant's case. . . . The manner in which Briggle dealt with other employees would be probative on the manner in which he dealt with appellant. The report might identify individuals that appellant may wish to call as witnesses [or] lead appellant to additional evidence supportive of his claim. Any remaining doubts . . . are foreclosed by its germination from the very administrative proceeding . . . in which the propriety of the transfer order was first adjudicated. The ALJ recommended the investigation which resulted in the . . . report. . . . [T]o deny appellant access to the results of that investigation could do violence to our conception of fair procedure and due process. . . .

2. *Hi-Tech Furnace Systems, Inc. v. Federal Communications Commission*, 224 F.3d 781 (D.C. Cir. 2000).

Sprint, a common carrier regulated under the Communications Act of 1934, provides long distance telephone service to the public. . . . On December 14, 1995, Sprint filed tariff provisions proposing to offer . . . customers a promotion under which they would be able to make free domestic and international long distance calls on one day of the week for twelve months [called] "Fridays Free." . . . . On February 29, 1996, Hi-Tech enrolled in the Fridays Free program by signing Sprint's standard agreement form. . . . Shortly after initiating Fridays Free, Sprint began experiencing a substantial increase in international call volume on Fridays. The growth was so pronounced that it . . . threatened to crash Sprint's international network. . . . On April 4, 1996, in an effort to ameliorate the overload problem, Sprint . . . removed 10 countries with high numbers of calls from the list of approximately 220 foreign locations to which free calling was permitted . . . . In lieu of free Friday calling to the deleted countries, Sprint offered subscribers a 25% discount on calls to those countries every day of the week. . . .

On April 17, 1998, Hi-Tech filed a complaint against Sprint with the FCC, alleging that Sprint's curtailment of the Fridays Free program violated . . . the Communications Act because it was unjust and unreasonable, and . . . in breach of Sprint's existing tariffs. . . . After filing its complaint with the FCC, Hi-Tech served Sprint with a set of seven interrogatories. Sprint objected and . . . FCC counsel declined to direct the carrier to respond. Instead, the Commission undertook its own investigation. . . . Hi-Tech's real dispute is not with the discovery measures the FCC took, but . . . that the Commission should have permitted Hi-Tech itself to take discovery from Sprint . . . in order to test Sprint's responses "through normal adversarial proceedings." But Hi-Tech's demand misapprehends the nature of the administrative process . . . . "The extent of discovery that a party engaged in an administrative hearing is entitled to is primarily determined by the particular agency: . . . agencies need not observe all the rules and formalities applicable to courtroom proceedings."

Nothing in either the Communications Act or the APA entitles a party to the specific procedures Hi-Tech demands. To the contrary, and as the FCC properly emphasizes, section 208 of the Communications Act expressly authorizes the Commission "to investigate the matters complained of in such manner and by such means as it shall deem proper. . . .

3. *Silverman v. Commodity Futures Trading Commission*, 549 F.2d 28 (7th Cir. 1977).

On March 13, 1973, a complaint was brought before the Secretary of Agriculture, alleging violations by the petitioner, Jeffrey L. Silverman of section 4b of the CFTC Act. On May 5, 1976, a final order was entered by the CFTC [Commodity Futures Trading Commission], prohibiting the petitioner from trading on or subject to the rules of any contract market for a period of two years. The petitioner was also ordered to permanently cease and desist from placing, or causing to be placed, in any customer's account, any contracts of sale of any commodity for future delivery, without the prior knowledge, consent or authorization of such customer. . . . The petitioner has argued that he was denied due process during the administrative proceedings in several ways, many of which relate to the pre-hearing production of documents by the CFTC.

There is no basic constitutional right to pretrial discovery in administrative proceedings. The Administrative Procedure Act contains no provision for pretrial discovery in the administrative process and the Federal Rules of Civil Procedure for discovery do not apply to administrative proceedings. The regulations of the [CFTC] did not provide, at the time of the administrative hearing, for pre-hearing discovery.

The petitioner was provided in advance of the hearing with copies of all proposed exhibits, a list of all proposed witnesses, the identity of the government employees who had investigated the case and copies of memoranda reflecting petitioner's own statements to administrative representatives. The petitioner also sought . . . the agency's internal non-public guidelines relating to the conduct of investigations. The three such guidelines which were applicable to the investigation . . . were furnished . . . . [We see nothing wrong with the agency procedures.]

4. *Bender v. Dudas*, 2006 WL 89831 (D.D.C. 2006).

The plaintiff, S. Michael Bender ("Bender"), brings this action against the defendant, Jon W. Dudas ("Dudas"), Director of the United States Patent and Trademark Office ("PTO"), . . . challenging the Director's Final Decision precluding him from practicing law before the PTO. . . .

In 1993, Bender assumed the prosecution of a large number of patents before the PTO formerly handled by . . . Leon Gilden ("Gilden"). At that time, Gilden was involved in disciplinary proceedings which stemmed from Gilden's filing of over 1000 patent applications "under the auspices" of American Inventor's Corporation ("AIC"), an invention marketing company. . . . [The PTO discovered] that Gilden, or someone associated with his office, had "embellished the drawings in each application with a unique decorative pattern of surface indicia," a tactic allegedly employed for the purpose of obtaining a patent for each application and "avoiding a refund of AIC's service fee under a guarantee clause contained in some . . . of the contracts between each inventor and AIC." . . . . At some point, the PTO discovered Bender's relationship with AIC . . . . [A]n administrative Complaint . . . was served on Bender [in June, 2000, related to] Bender's representation of nine AIC related clients. . . .

The ALJ found that Bender had violated several provisions of the PTO's rules on attorney conduct, which resulted in his exclusion from practice before the PTO. Bender appealed the ALJ Decision . . . . Bender argues that the ALJ's pre-hearing decision not to allow him to take the testimony of certain PTO employees "adversely affected [his] ability to put on an effective defense thereby denying him a full and fair hearing. . . .

[T]he extent of discovery that a party engaged in an administrative hearing is entitled to is primarily determined by the particular agency. . . ." 37 C.F.R. § 10.152(b) states that "discovery shall not be authorized . . . of any matter which: (1) will be used by another party solely for impeachment or cross-examination." In seeking the testimony . . . Bender's very purpose was to illicit admissions that the PTO's investigation and complaint against him . . . was unfair and flawed on multiple levels. Therefore, the discovery sought by Bender was reasonably construed as designed to develop "impeachment or cross-examination" material, and according deference . . . the Court declines to disturb the agency's decision. . . .

5. *Dorris v. Federal Deposit Insurance Corporation*, 1994 WL 774535 (D.D.C. 1994).

On March 26, 1992, plaintiff Dorris submitted to the Federal Deposit Insurance Corporation ("FDIC") a Notification [informing] the FDIC that Dorris wished to serve as a director and senior executive officer of the Bank of Arizona . . . . [T]he FDIC disapproved Dorris' Notification. The FDIC based its decision on Dorris' lack of competence . . . based on Dorris' performance at National Bank in Phoenix, Arizona [and] at Sun State Savings and Loan Association. . . . Dorris appealed [and] requested a hearing . . . . [T]he FDIC granted plaintiff a hearing and appointed retired ADMINISTRATIVE LAW JUDGE DANIEL HANSCOM as the Presiding Officer ("PO") for the hearing.

Although 12 C.F.R. § 308.155(c)(4) specifically prohibits discovery in a Section 32 hearing, . . . plaintiff filed a Request for More Specific Statement and a Request for Documents. . . . PO Hanscom ruled that "discovery" would be limited to those documents which the FDIC chose to offer into evidence at the hearing to support its allegations of incompetence. . . . Dorris [then] forwarded to PO Hanscom a subpoena duces tecum directed to the FDIC . . . . PO Hanscom denied the application for issuance of the subpoenas based on provision § 308.155(c)(4) that there shall be no discovery. . . . Dorris applied to PO Hanscom for the issuance of [additional] subpoena duces tecum . . . . PO Hanscom denied the applications in all respects relying on the no discovery provision of 12 C.F.R. § 308.155(c)(4). . . .

Plaintiff states that PO Hanscom's denial of his request for subpoenas duces tecum and the FDIC's subsequent review and denial of the request (after the hearing) violates plaintiff's due process rights. 12 C.F.R. § 308.155(c)(6) provides that the presiding officer has the power to issue subpoenas duces tecum. Although the presiding officer has this power, it is not mandatory that he exercise it, especially if the exercise thereof would violate other provisions of the statute. It is a clear principle that the court must defer to the agency's own interpretation of its rules [unless] the decision is "plainly erroneous or inconsistent with the regulations." Given that 12 C.F.R. § 308.155(c)(4) explicitly bars any discovery under Section 32 hearings, it is not at all unreasonable that neither PO Hanscom nor the FDIC would issue plaintiff subpoenas duces tecum.

6. For additional examples and information relating to agency discovery, click HERE.

II. Beyond the Record: Ex Parte Communication

One of the fundamental goals of agency process, both in the adjudication and rulemaking domain, is to provide the agency with a maximum flow of information to permit the agency to carry out its statutory mandate. In rulemaking, agency decisionmakers use information both from the comments submitted as well as from other sources. So long as the agency proceeds with some level of openness and disclosure, accessing information not submitted through the comment process is both normal and, in some instances, expected. Were one to analogize that to the activities of Article III courts, it might sound like the rulemaking process is one that encourages ex parte communication. Such an analogy would be inappropriate, however, because the task of rulemaking is fundamentally a legislative process whereas the task of Article III courts is primarily adjudicatory.

When agencies make adjudicatory determinations, the lax rules extant for ex parte communication with rulemaking do not necessarily apply. An ex parte exchange in the course of an adjudicatory proceeding that is not disclosed constitutes a serious breach. It creates the possibility of a "phantom record" on which a decision might be based and is potentially quite unfair to the party or parties not involved in the ex parte dialogue or information exchange.

Food for Thought

If hearings require an opportunity to confront the evidence being used, even at a basic level, ex parte communications are, at a minimum, suspect.

That said, given the objective of optimizing the flow of information to allow for the best possible implementation of the statutes agencies are mandated to enforce, the prohibition on ex parte communication is not as explicit in agency adjudication as it is in Article III tribunals. Ex parte communication is sometimes tolerated, particularly if it is "noticed" in the record and other parties are given the opportunity to respond.

There are instances, however, where ex parte communication involves inappropriate content as well as inappropriate political or financial pressure that renders the entire process unfair and violative of the rights of the other participants in the adjudication. The cases that follow explore the area of ex parte communication in the adjudicatory process.

PROFESSIONAL AIR TRAFFIC CONTROLLERS ORGANIZATION V. FEDERAL LABOR RELATIONS AUTHORITY

685 F.2d 547 (D.C. Cir. 1982)

[JUDGE EDWARDS] [On August 3, 1981, 11,350 air traffic controllers, employees of the Federal Aviation Administration, went on strike over debilitating workplace stress as well as salary and benefits issues. This action caused the cancellation of thousands of flights and prompted President Ronald Reagan to issue a statement directing the controllers (represented by the Professional Air Traffic Controllers Organization or PATCO) to return to work or face dismissal. The White House took the position that strikes by public employees were inherently unlawful and refused to bargain. PATCO officers instructed the membership to hold fast and not return to work.

After 48 hours, all 11,350 controllers were fired. At one point, PATCO leaders were jailed for contempt. Within a week, more than half of the scheduled flights resumed as FAA administrators and members of the military took over air traffic control tasks. An executive order issued banning rehiring of the fired employees. Several weeks after the strike, a union decertification fight erupted when the regional director of the Federal Labor Relations Authority (FLRA) sought revocation of PATCO's certification under the Civil Service Reform Act. By early fall, the dispute came before the FLRA.

The battle over the decertification of PATCO drew in the White House, Congress, the FAA, and leaders of public labor unions (e.g., teachers and postal worker unions). At stake was nothing less than the future of the public labor movement. At one point, there was a discussion between a public labor advocate and one of the administrative law judges charged with rendering an initial decision in the decertification case. That discussion, among others, was at issue in this case.

Within a year, the PATCO decertification dispute reached the D.C. Circuit, but not on the question of the right of public employees to strike. Rather, the case involved a challenge to the numerous ex parte discussions that had taken place including a dinner between two long-time friends: an administrative law judge on the FLRA panel in the case and an AFL-CIO council member. At the direction of the FLRA, an administrative fact-finder was appointed to determine whether the discussions had violated the rules regarding ex parte communication in the contested administrative adjudication. The report of the administrator was submitted to the court and became the basis for the court's opinion.]

C. Applicable Legal Standards

1. The Statutory Prohibition of Ex parte Contacts and the FLRA Rules

. . . Since FLRA unfair labor practice hearings are formal adjudications within the meaning of the APA, section 557(d) governs ex parte communications. Section 557(d) was enacted by Congress as part of the Government in the Sunshine Act. The section prohibits ex parte communications "relevant to the merits of the proceeding" between an "interested person" and an agency decisionmaker . . . . The FLRA has adopted rules that, with minor variations, parallel the requirements of section 557(d).

Three features of the prohibition on ex parte communications in agency adjudications are particularly relevant to the contacts here at issue. First, by its terms, section 557(d) applies only to ex parte communications to or from an "interested person." Congress did not intend, however, that the prohibition on ex parte communications would therefore have only a limited application. A House Report explained:

> The term "interested person" is intended to be a wide, inclusive term . . . . The term includes, but is not limited to, parties, competitors, public officials, and nonprofit or public interest organizations and associations with a special interest in the matter regulated. The term does not include a member of the public at large who makes a casual or general expression of opinion about a pending proceeding.

Second, the Government in the Sunshine Act defines an "ex parte communication" as "an oral or written communication not on the public record [but] not including requests for status reports on any matter or proceeding. . . ." . . . . Third, and in direct contrast to status reports, section 557(d) explicitly prohibits communications "relevant to the merits of the proceeding." . . . .

In sum, Congress sought to establish common-sense guidelines to govern ex parte contacts in administrative hearings, rather than rigidly defined and woodenly applied rules. The disclosure of ex parte communications serves two distinct interests. Disclosure is important in its own right to prevent the appearance of impropriety . . . . Disclosure is also important as an instrument of fair decision-making; only if a party knows the arguments presented to a decisionmaker can the party respond effectively and ensure that its position is fairly considered. . . .

2. Remedies for Ex parte Communications

Section 557(d) contains two possible administrative remedies for improper ex parte communications. The first is disclosure of the communication and its content. The second requires the violating party to "show cause why his claim or interest in the proceeding should not be dismissed . . . or otherwise adversely affected on account of [the] violation. Congress did not intend, however, that an agency would . . . dismiss a party's interest more than rarely. Indeed, the statutory language clearly states that a party's interest in the proceeding may be adversely affected only "to the extent consistent with the interests of justice and the policy of the underlying statutes." n.30

> n.30 By way of example, the Senate Report suggested that:
>
> > The interests of justice might dictate that a claimant for an old age benefit not lose his claim even if he violates the ex parte rules. On the other hand, where two parties have applied for a license and the applications are of relatively equal merit, an agency may rule against a party who approached an agency head in an ex parte manner in an effort to win approval of his license.

. . . .

Under the case law in this Circuit, improper ex parte communications, even when undisclosed during agency proceedings, do not necessarily void an agency decision. Rather, agency proceedings that have been blemished by ex parte communications have been held to be *voidable*. . . . [A]ny such decision must of necessity be an exercise of equitable discretion. . . . [At various points in the opinion, the court suggests further standards for review of ex parte determinations in formal adjudication. Special attention would be in order if:

one has benefited from the ex parte communication,

the contents of the communication were unknown to the opposing parties,

the communication compromises judicial review because facts and arguments "vital to the agency decision" are only communicated to the agency off the record,

the ex parte communication constitutes a "corrupt tampering with the adjudicatory process,"

the "contacts are of such severity that an agency decisionmaker should have disqualified himself,"

the communication "materially influenced the action ultimately taken," or the communication otherwise substantially prejudices the other parties to the proceeding.]

D. Analysis of the Alleged Ex parte Communications with FLRA Members

[T]he vast majority of the reported contacts between FLRA Members and persons outside the Authority are not troubling. They relate to inquiries about the expected date of issuance of the FLRA's opinion . . . and other communications unrelated to the merits of the case. After extensive review of the three troubling incidents we believe that they too provide insufficient reason to vacate the FLRA Decision . . . . We conclude that at least one and possibly two of the contacts documented by the A.L.J. probably infringed the statutory prohibitions on ex parte communications. . . . Nevertheless, we agree with A.L.J. Vittone that the ex parte contacts here at issue had no effect on the ultimate decision of the FLRA. Moreover, we conclude that . . . to vacate and remand would be a gesture of futility.

[Discussion section of the report by A.L.J. Vittone.]

I have found that the telephone calls on August 13, 1981 from Secretary Lewis to Members Frazier and Applewhaite may have had some undetermined effect on their decision to limit the time for filing exceptions to the administrative law judge's decision. Both members testified that the calls had no effect on their August 18, 1981 decision. However, the Secretary told Member Frazier that he wanted expeditious processing of the case within the FLRA's rules and he stated his concern to Member Applewhaite that the case not be delayed. Both members described the Secretary's call as unusual. Later that same day, August 13, the FAA filed a motion to limit the time for filing exceptions from 25 to 7 days. It is quite likely that the FAA motion was filed in accordance with the advice concerning the FLRA regulations given to Mr. Lewis by Member Applewhaite. . . . However, it should be noted that I do not believe that the Secretary's calls had any effect on the merits of [the] final decision in the PATCO case.

. . . I find that the meeting between Member Applewhaite, General Counsel Gordon, and Ellen Stern on August 10, 1981 may have been a prohibited ex parte communication. It is clear that the Stern memorandum concerned the PATCO case. . . . As noted, Mr. Gordon is the FLRA General Counsel. The General Counsel is defined as a "person outside this agency" when his representative is prosecuting an unfair labor practice proceeding. . . . Even Member Applewhaite testified at that time that he expected exceptions to be filed to the judge's decision. In view of all of the above, and even though Applewhaite and Gordon described the discussion as abstract, the discussion may have been a prohibited ex parte communication. However, the discussion was very short, general in nature, and very early in the processing of the PATCO case. Accordingly, I do not believe that it had any effect upon Member Applewhaite's deliberations and final decision in the PATCO case.

. . . .

Mr. Shanker is closely associated with the AFL-CIO. He is president of one of the AFL-CIO's affiliated unions and sits on the Executive Council of the AFL-CIO. The AFL-CIO was an amicus curiae party to the proceeding and participated in the oral argument before the FLRA. The AFL-CIO is clearly an interested party in the PATCO proceeding. Therefore Mr. Shanker may also be an interested party outside the FLRA. It is for those reasons that the Shanker-Applewhaite dinner may have been an unauthorized communication in violation of the FLRA ex parte communications regulations . . . . It is clear that Mr. Shanker's message to Mr. Applewhaite was that revocation of certification was a drastic remedy out of proportion to the violation. However, as stated in my findings, I do not believe that the dinner had any effect on the final decision of the FLRA in the PATCO case. . . .

The most troubling part of this proceeding has been the conflict between the testimony of Members Frazier and Applewhaite with respect to the Shanker-Applewhaite dinner. On the whole, I find Mr. Shanker's testimony regarding that dinner to be credible. There is no direct evidence that Mr. Shanker . . . made any promises or threats to Applewhaite. . . . I believe that Member Frazier was troubled by Member Applewhaite's statements at the September 22 meeting and left that meeting with the impression that the events at the dinner has caused Applewhaite to change his position from revocation to suspension of PATCO's certification. . . . On the other hand, Member Applewhaite's testimony, in substantial parts, was confusing, contradictory, and in some respects, incredible. . . .

. . . Member Applewhaite disputed many of the statements attributed to him in the FBI report. However, . . . both agents who interviewed Member Applewhaite testified credibly that it was an accurate reflection of the interview. Member Applewhaite testified that he never thought about reappointment until last December or January, 1982. Yet he . . . raised the subject with Mr. Shanker on September 21. Further, he discussed the possibility of becoming Chairman with Senator Laxalt's Administrative Aide on August 6, 1981. . . . Further, Member Applewhaite could not recall any of the details of his 12 minute phone call with Mr. Frazier on October 7. Finally, Member Applewhaite testified that the FBI agents appeared to understand his situation and . . . praised him and told him he had courage. Agent Knisley denied making any such statements, and it is extremely doubtful that FBI agents praise the people they are investigating.

SUMMARY

Accordingly, it is found that the possible ex parte contacts and approaches described at the hearing did not have any effect on the final decision of the members of the FLRA in the PATCO case.

[JUDGE MACKINNON, concurring.]

The number of ex parte contacts that were disclosed at the remand hearing is appalling, as are the statements by counsel that such contacts were nothing more than what is normal and usual in administrative agencies . . . . In deciding such cases the government officials act in a quasi-judicial capacity and ex parte contacts that attempt to "back door" the adjudicative process, with respect to the merits or discipline, are highly improper and illegal. In this connection 18 U.S.C. § 1505 should be noted. This section of the Criminal Code provides that it is an offense if one "corruptly . . . *endeavors to influence*, obstruct or impede the due and proper administration of the law under which proceeding is being had before [an] agency of the United States . . ." (emphasis added). . . . Shanker argues that his dinner with . . . Applewhaite "had no effect on the decision" and hence is of no moment. That is like the man charged with attempted murder asserting the indictment should be dismissed because his shot missed the intended victim. . . .

[Some years after the PATCO strike, the order banning rehiring of the fired controllers was lifted. Few controllers ever returned to their previous positions.]

Underlying Case Documents

The case referenced:
The Government in the Sunshine Act

For a 1981 news broadcast of the PATCO strike, which includes the statement by President Reagan that the striking workers were required to return to their job within 48 hours click HERE (as this clip includes sound we strongly recommend you do not open it during class).

For a look back on the strike after 25 years click HERE.

1. Section 554(d) of the APA sets out the general rule for ex parte communications:

> Except to the extent required for the disposition of ex parte matters as authorized by law . . . an [ALJ or other hearing officer] may not – (1) consult a person or party on a fact in issue, unless on notice and opportunity for all parties to participate. . . .

The cases that follow are from both state and federal agencies because, as you will see, the treatment of ex parte communication does not vary in any significant way. However, in some respects, the setting for state officials in decisionmaking roles presents a more challenging problem than for federal officials. In the zoning area, for example, the difficulties faced by local zoning board members who are residents in the communities they serve are substantial. Professor Michael Asimow makes a powerful case that certain land use proceedings, while necessarily bounded by standard notions of fairness, are simply not a good match for the restrictions and conventions of a formalized adjudicatory process. Michael Asimow & Edward Sullivan, _Due Process in Local Land Use Decision Making: Is the Imperfect Way of Doing Business Good Enough or Should We Radically Reform It?_, 29 ZONING & PLAN. L. REP. 1 (2006).

2. _New Jersey Racing Commission v. Silverman, 696 A.2d 771 (N.J. Super. Ct. 1997)_.

[R]ichard Silverman is a driver and trainer of harness racing horses licensed by the respondent New Jersey Racing Commission. On October 23, 1993, appellant [Silverman] was the driver of "Tidewater Trick" in Garden State Park's eleventh race. The horse was the third favorite in a field of eight . . . . However, the horse finished in fifth place. . . . [T]he Board of Judges at Garden State Racetrack determined that appellant had violated N.J.A.C. 13:71-20.10(b) by using poor judgment and carelessness in the race and imposed a forty-five day suspension of his license. Appellant appealed . . . .

Phyllis DeVitis, one of the three members of the Board of Judges . . . described four rule violations that appellant committed . . . . First, appellant allowed the No. 6 horse to get in front of him and go to the rail, without attempting to close the gap. Second, appellant allowed a gap of two to two and one half lengths behind the horse in front of him to exist for about a half a mile . . . . Third, appellant seesawed the bit in the horse's mouth, effectively holding the horse back. Fourth, appellant did not use sufficient effort in driving his horse down the stretch. . . . Appellant testified in his defense that he . . . discovered that Tidewater Trick was not running the same as he had two weeks earlier. . . . He tapped . . . but refused to beat the horse to finish better than fifth when he could not win. . . .

Appellant also presented the testimony of Donato Latessa, the presiding judge on the Board of Judges . . . . [Latessa] testified that the judges had agreed to impose a fifteen day suspension . . . but that the Executive Director . . . had [called] and instructed them to impose a forty-five day suspension. As a result, the other two judges changed [to] a forty-five day suspension. Latessa testified that there had been two other occasions when the Executive Director had recommended . . . a particular suspension . . . and that when the judges failed to follow his recommendation . . . the Executive Director had threatened to fire him. Latessa . . . refused to join in the decision . . . . Shortly thereafter, Latessa was [fired]. Latessa also testified that a fifteen day suspension was the usual sanction for [this type of] violation.

[O]ur review of the record in this case convinces us that the Executive Director's actions infected the Commission's deliberations and resulted in an arbitrary and capricious decision. . . . Accordingly, we . . . reduce the . . . suspension from forty-five to fifteen days.

3. The case below is a classical hard line statement on ex parte communication. Do you agree with the prohibitions the court announces?

Portland Audubon Society v. Oregon Lands Coalition, 984 F.2d 1534 (9th Cir. 1993).

> [P]etitioners Portland Audubon Society et al. (collectively "the environmental groups") challenge the decision of the statutorily-created Endangered Species Committee ("the Committee"), known popularly as "<u>The God Squad</u>", to grant an exemption from the requirements of the Endangered Species Act . . . for thirteen timber sales in western Oregon. . . . [T]he environmental groups seek . . . leave to conduct discovery into allegedly improper ex parte communications between the White House and individual Committee members . . . .
>
> It is of no consequence that the sections of the Endangered Species Act governing the operations of the Committee fail to mention the APA. . . . By its terms, section 554 of the APA, which pertains to formal adjudications, applies . . . whenever the three requirements set forth in [section] 554(a) are satisfied . . . . Because Committee decisions are adjudicatory in nature, are required to be on the record, and are made after an opportunity for an agency hearing, we conclude that the APA's ex parte communication prohibition is applicable. . . .
>
> The government . . . argues that the President's broader policy role places him beyond the reach of the "interested person" language. We strongly disagree. In fact, we believe [that as] the head of government . . . the President necessarily has an interest in *every* agency proceeding. No ex parte communication is more likely to influence an agency than one from the President or a member of his staff. . . . The government's next argument – that . . . the President and the members of the Committee are all members of the executive branch . . . amounts to a contention that the President is not "outside the agency" for the purposes of APA § 557(d)(1). The Supreme Court soundly rejected the basic logic of this argument in <u>United States ex rel. Accardi v. Shaughnessy, 347 U.S. 260 (1954)</u>. . . . The government [finally] contends that any construction of APA § 557(d)(1) that includes presidential communications . . . would constitute a violation of the separation of powers doctrine. . . . We reject this argument out of hand. . . . Congress' important objectives reflected in the enactment of the APA would, in any event, outweigh any de minimis impact on presidential power. . . .

A number of agencies have promulgated rules pertaining to ex parte communication, though several have been found to be ultra vires – beyond the authority of the agency to act. An agency can interpret a statute – it cannot by rule invalidate a statute. *See, e.g.,* <u>Ctr. for Law & Educ. v. Dep't of Educ., 396 F.3d 1152 (D.C. Cir. 2005)</u> and <u>Electric Power Supply Ass'n v. FERC, 391 F.3d 1255 (D.C. Cir. 2004)</u>. In some areas, Congress has developed ex parte rules, beyond § 554(d) addressing ex parte communication. *See* <u>19 U.S.C. § 1677f(a)(3) (1999)</u>, obligating the Department of Commerce to maintain records of ex parte communications if they related to "factual information in connection with a proceeding."

4. *Ortiz v. Eichler, 616 F. Supp. 1046 (D. Del. 1985)*:

> Plaintiffs . . . complain that DES [Division of Economic Services of the Delaware Department of Health and Social Services] employees have . . . initiated and considered ex parte communications [when determining public assistance eligibility]. Plaintiffs have placed in the record several cases in which the Hearing Representative or the Director received ex parte communications relating to a claim before rendering a decision. For example, in Ms. Ortiz's case, the Director, after receiving the recommended decision, asked her case supervisor about the case and examined Ms. Ortiz's case file, including documents not contained in the hearing record. The Director's decision, which rejected a recommended decision favorable to Ms. Ortiz, was based in part on documents contained in the case file which were not in the hearing record. In Mr. Benson's case, the Director received a two-page, single-spaced memorandum after the hearing from three employees objecting to the Hearing Representative's recommended decision in favor of Mr. Benson. In neither case was the claimant made aware of these ex parte contacts or given an opportunity to respond to the facts or arguments presented in them.

> Defendants . . . argue that the mere occurrence of ex parte contacts is not forbidden as long as the decisionmaker does not rely on evidence outside the record. This position is unacceptable. First, plaintiffs have demonstrated, at least in Ms. Ortiz's case, that the Director has based his decision on evidence outside the record. In the case[] of Charles Benson . . . the only credible inference is that the final decisions were based in part on ex parte communications. Second, defendants cite no authority for their distinction between considering ex parte communications and relying on them. . . . The Hearing Representative testified at his deposition that he would "like to think" that his decisions were based solely on the record evidence, but that he could not block out ex parte conversations from his mind. Moreover, the Director's mere consideration of ex parte argument, as occurred in the Benson case, would violate the claimant's right to refute any testimony or evidence. . . . [D]efendants' practice of considering ex parte communications concerning the merits of a case violates the claimant's rights, under federal regulations, to a decision based solely on the evidence adduced at the hearing, and to be confronted with, cross-examine, and refute all adverse evidence.

5. The source for ex parte communication is of consequence. What if the source is internal to the office of the decisionmaker, e.g., a special assistant or counsel to the decision making body?

Appeal of Atlantic Connections, Ltd. (New Hampshire Public Utilities Commission), 608 A.2d 861 (N.H. 1992).

> Atlantic Connections, Ltd. (Atlantic) appeals from a public utilities commission (PUC) order that it cease and desist from intrastate telecommunications resale operations, pay a $ 5,000 fine, and apply to the PUC for a certificate of service. We affirm. In 1988, Atlantic commenced business in Portsmouth as a reseller of long-distance telephone services without obtaining a franchise from the PUC . . . .

> The record indicates that Atlantic conducted business in a manner typical of long-distance resellers. It owned a telecommunications switch in New England Telephone's

(NET) Portsmouth local exchange area. It leased interexchange facilities from NET for intrastate calls, and from AT&T, Sprint and MCI for interstate calls. When a call entered Atlantic's switch via the Portsmouth local exchange network, Atlantic would identify the destination of the call and select the leased line that offered the least cost route. On March 23, 1990, the PUC opened a docket to investigate whether Atlantic was a public utility operating without the commission's authority. . . . After five days of hearings, the PUC found that Atlantic was a "public utility. . . ."

In its report and order rejecting Atlantic's motion for a rehearing [based on ex parte communication between staff assistants and the commission], the PUC stated that its "normal practice is to deliberate orally first either during a public meeting or in executive session and then to reduce its decision to writing subject to approval and signing at a public meeting . . . ." It then stated that this practice was followed after the Atlantic hearing and that "to the extent staff members assisted the commission by drafting orders in this docket, they acted subject to the commission's direction and final approval." Finally, it noted "that this practice serves to preserve the commission's impartiality and allows expeditious resolution of matters before the commission."

Here, the decision had already been made by the time the staff attorneys became involved. The staff attorneys simply reduced the commissioners' decision to writing. In so doing, they were acting as "personal assistants" to the commissioners. This function is deemed essential to the agency's adjudicative role and [does not violate the ex parte prohibition].

6. *Electric Power Supply Association v. Federal Energy Regulatory Commission*, 391 F.3d 1255 (D.C. Cir. 2004).

In January 2003, the Commission . . . amended its ex parte regulations, purporting to exempt from the Sunshine Act communications between Commission-approved market monitors and Commission decisional staff in those situations in which a market monitor is not a party to and does not appear on behalf of a party to the on-the-record proceeding to which the ex parte communication relates. Under this purported exemption, an ex parte communication will only be memorialized and included in the official record of the relevant proceeding if the Commission determines that it relied on the ex parte communication in reaching a decision in an on-the-record proceeding. . . . "Market monitors must report to the Commission objective information about RTO markets, evaluate the behavior of market participants, and recommend how markets can operate more competitively and efficiently." It is undisputed, however, that market monitors are private parties who work outside the agency. They are not hired, paid, or directly managed by FERC in their work. . . .

Following the Commission's issuance of the initial order purporting to amend its ex parte regulations, petitioner EPSA [Electric Power Supply Association] sought rehearing, asserting, *inter alia*, that the market monitor exemption was contrary to [the ban on ex parte contact]. The Commission conceded that a market monitor may have an "interest in the outcome of a particular proceeding" to which his or her communication may be relevant, but contended that such an interest "does not make him [or her] an 'interested person' as that term is used in APA § 706(d)." . . . . According to the Commission, "communications with market monitors are similar to communications between Commission staff, which give no appearance of impropriety, nor lead to biased decision-making." . . . . On the merits, it is clear that the orders creating the market monitor exemption violate the explicit and sweeping proscription against ex parte communications contained in § 557(d). . . . Consequently, FERC's orders modifying its ex parte regulations must be reversed and vacated. . . .

III. Estoppel

As a general rule, government agencies are required to implement the statutes and regulations that have been promulgated and that they are charged with enforcing. Those who are subject to the jurisdiction of the agency often seek clarification regarding the nature of those statutes and regulations so that they can conform their behavior accordingly. When members of the public seek out information from an agency, they have some reasonable expectation that the information they receive will be reliable. Unfortunately, mistakes can and do occur.

Where a senior agency official acting on behalf of the agency provides information on which a reasonable person can rely, someone does rely on that information to his or her detriment, and it turns out the information is incorrect, it is reasonable to ask whether the government should be estopped from taking adverse action and bound by the initial inaccurate information the agency has provided. For the most part, courts have been unwilling to permit a private party to prevent the government from implementing the correct interpretation of a regulation or standard, simply because an agency official, in a prior communication, gave incorrect information on which a citizen relied to his or her detriment. That general rule, however, has exceptions. The cases that follow explore the basic prohibition against governmental estoppel as well as exceptions to the rule.

Schweiker v. Hansen

450 U.S. 785 (1981)

[Per Curiam] On June 12, 1974, respondent met for about 15 minutes with Don Connelly, a field representative of the Social Security Administration (SSA), and orally inquired of him whether she was eligible for "mother's insurance benefits" under § 202(g) of the Social Security Act (Act). Connelly erroneously told her that she was not, and she left the SSA office without having filed a written application. By the Act's terms, such benefits are available only to one who, among other qualifications, "has filed [an] application." By a regulation promulgated pursuant to the Act, only written applications satisfy the "filed application" requirement. The SSA's Claims Manual, an internal Administration handbook, instructs field representatives to advise applicants of the advantages of filing written applications and to recommend to applicants who are uncertain about their eligibility that they file written applications. Connelly, however, did not recommend to respondent that she file a written application; nor did he advise her of the advantages of doing so. The question is whether Connelly's erroneous statement and neglect of the Claims Manual estop petitioner, the Secretary of Health and Human Services, from denying retroactive benefits to respondent for a period in which she was eligible for benefits but had not filed a written application.

Respondent eventually filed a written application after learning in May 1975 that in fact she was eligible. She then began receiving benefits. Pursuant to § 202(j)(1) of the Act she also received retroactive benefits for the preceding 12 months, which was the maximum retroactive benefit allowed by the Act. Respondent contended, however, that she should receive retroactive benefits for the 12 months preceding her June 1974 interview with Connelly. An Administrative Law Judge rejected this claim, concluding that Connelly's erroneous statement and neglect of the Claims Manual did not estop petitioner from determining respondent's eligibility for benefits only as of the date of respondent's written application. The Social Security Appeals Council affirmed.

Respondent then brought this lawsuit in the District Court for the District of Vermont, which held that the written-application requirement was "unreasonably restrictive" as applied to the facts of this case. A divided panel of the Court of Appeals for the Second Circuit affirmed. . . . We agree with the dissent. This Court has never decided what type of conduct by a Government employee will estop the Government from insisting upon compliance with valid regulations governing the distribution of welfare benefits. . . . The Court has recognized, however, "the duty of all courts to observe the conditions defined by Congress for charging the public treasury." Lower federal courts have recognized that duty also, and consistently have relied on *Merrill* in refusing to estop the Government where an eligible applicant has lost Social Security benefits because of possibly erroneous replies to oral inquiries. This is another in that line of cases, for we are convinced that Connelly's conduct – which the [Court of Appeals] majority conceded to be less than "affirmative misconduct" – does not justify the abnegation of that duty.

Connelly erred in telling respondent that she was ineligible for the benefit she sought. It may be that Connelly erred because he was unfamiliar with a recent amendment which afforded benefits to respondent. Or it may be that respondent gave Connelly too little information for him to know that he was in error. But at worst, Connelly's conduct did not cause respondent to take action, or fail to take action, that respondent could not correct at any time.

Similarly, there is no doubt that Connelly failed to follow the Claims Manual in neglecting to recommend that respondent file a written application and in neglecting to advise her of the advantages of a written application. But the Claims Manual is not a regulation. It has no legal force, and it does not bind the SSA.

Rather, it is a 13-volume handbook for internal use by thousands of SSA employees, including the hundreds of employees who receive untold numbers of oral inquiries like respondent's each year. If Connelly's minor breach of such a manual suffices to estop petitioner, then the Government is put "at risk that every alleged failure by an agent to follow instructions to the last detail in one of a thousand cases will deprive it of the benefit of the written application requirement which experience has taught to be essential to the honest and effective administration of the Social Security Laws."

Finally, the majority's distinction between respondent's "substant[ive] eligib[ility]" and her failure to satisfy a "procedural requirement" does not justify estopping petitioner in this case. Congress expressly provided in the Act that only one who "has filed [an] application" for benefits may receive them, and it delegated to petitioner the task of providing by regulation the requisite manner of application. A court is no more authorized to overlook the valid regulation requiring that applications be in writing than it is to overlook any other valid requirement for the receipt of benefits.

In sum, Connelly's errors "[fall] far short" of conduct which would raise a serious question whether petitioner is estopped from insisting upon compliance with the valid regulation. Accordingly, we grant the motion of respondent for leave to proceed in forma pauperis and the petition for certiorari and reverse the judgment of the Court of Appeals. . . .

[JUSTICE MARSHALL, dissenting.]

A summary reversal is a rare disposition, usually reserved by this Court for situations in which the law is settled and stable, the facts are not in dispute, and the decision below is clearly in error. Because this is not such a case, I dissent . . . . [T]o conclude that Connelly's incorrect assessment of respondent's eligibility did not cause her to act to her detriment in a manner that she "could not correct at any time" is to blink in the face of the obvious. . . . While not necessarily free of error, such preliminary advice is inevitably accorded great weight by applicants who – like respondent – are totally uneducated in the intricacies of the Social Security laws. Hence, . . . the fault for respondent's failure to file a timely application for benefits that she was entitled to must rest squarely with the Government, first, because its agent incorrectly advised her that she was ineligible for benefits, and, second, because the same agent breached his duty to encourage [her] to file a written application regardless of his views on her eligibility.

In my view, when this sort of governmental misconduct directly causes an individual's failure to comply with a purely procedural requirement established by the agency, it may be sufficient to estop the Government from denying that individual benefits that she is substantively entitled to receive. . . . At the very least, the question deserves more than the casual treatment it receives from the majority today.

———————

Underlying Case Documents

The case referenced:
The <u>denial</u> of longer retroactive benefits by the administrative law judge
The <u>appeal</u> of that denial by the Appeals Council

1. The idea that a citizen ought to be able to rely on direct instruction provided by one who appears to be acting on behalf of a government agency is reasonable enough – but it somewhat misunderstands the very notion of government. The government is not a singularity – it consists of thousands of identifiable agencies, departments, branches, divisions, units, commissions, and more. Taken as a whole, the government is, quite simply, not like any other party in a transaction, as the Court made clear more than 60 years ago.

In *Federal Crop Insurance Corp. v. Merrill, 332 U.S. 380 (1947)*, the claimant had been assured that a winter wheat crop was covered by the Federal Crop Insurance Corporation (FCIC). FCIC later refused to pay out on a claim for failed winter wheat since the pertinent regulations actually prohibited the issuance of such insurance.

> The case no doubt presents phases of hardship. We take for granted that . . . the respondents reasonably believed that their entire crop was covered by petitioner's insurance. . . . It is too late in the day to urge that the Government is just another private litigant, for purposes of charging it with liability. . . . [A]nyone entering into an arrangement with the Government takes the risk of having accurately ascertained that he who purports to act for the Government stays within the bounds of his authority. The scope of this authority may be explicitly defined by Congress or be limited by delegated legislation, properly exercised through the rule-making power. . . .
>
> If the Federal Crop Insurance Act had by explicit language prohibited the insurance of spring wheat which is reseeded on winter wheat acreage, the ignorance of such a restriction . . . would be immaterial. . . .
>
> Accordingly, the Wheat Crop Insurance Regulations were binding on all who sought to come within the Federal Crop Insurance Act, regardless of actual knowledge of what is in the Regulations or of the hardship resulting from innocent ignorance. The oft-quoted observation in *Rock Island, Arkansas & Louisiana Railroad Co. v. United States, 254 U.S. 141, 143 (1920)*, that "Men must turn square corners when they

deal with the Government," does not reflect a callous outlook. It merely expresses the duty of all courts to observe the conditions defined by Congress for charging the public treasury.

Even when the Court comes to the conclusion that the assurances of an authorized government representative ought to be something on which a person can rely, it tends not to use the language of detrimental reliance or estoppel.

In *Moser v. United States*, 341 U.S. 41 (1951), a Swiss national came to the United States and was informed that he did not have to register for military service. Some time thereafter, he learned that his failure to register could have dire consequences. In deciding that, in this one instance, the government would not be permitted to renege on its assurances, the Court noted that

> [t]here is no need to evaluate these circumstances on the basis of any estoppel of the Government. . . . [Petitioner] never had an opportunity to make an intelligent election between the diametrically opposed courses required as a matter of strict law. Considering all the circumstances of the case, we think that to bar petitioner, nothing less than an intelligent waiver is required by elementary fairness. . . . To hold otherwise would be to entrap petitioner.

Comparing *Merrill* and *Moser* will not yield readily useable doctrine – but it does provide a back-drop and context both for *Schweiker v. Hansen* and the following note cases.

2. *Federal Deposit Insurance Corporation (FDIC) v. Harrison*, 735 F.2d 408 (11th Cir. 1984).

> In 1977 Bell, Harrison and Rixey formed Real Estate Marketing Corporation. Southern National Bank agreed to loan the corporation slightly more than $30,000.00 . . . . In March 1978, primarily to lower their individual income tax liabilities, the three incorporators divided the corporation's 1977 note into three parts, with each person becoming primarily liable on one of the three notes and signing a limited guaranty agreement on the notes of the other two. . . .

> When Southern National Bank was declared insolvent in June 1979, FDIC was appointed receiver of the bank. . . . In October 1979, FDIC made a demand on Bell, Harrison and Rixey for payment of the three notes . . . . After receiving his demand notice, Rixey contacted FDIC . . . . He testified, and the district court agreed, that an FDIC agent assured him that Harrison and Bell were paying off their loans and that he need pay only the amount stated on his own note. Rixey paid off his note shortly thereafter. Harrison also contacted FDIC when he received his demand notice. He spoke to a liquidator named Marcia Carrigan . . . and was told by her that Rixey and Bell were paying their notes [and] that he need pay only his own note and that he would not be held liable on his guaranty. . . . [Harrison paid off his note the next day.]

In April 1981 . . . FDIC sent demand letter to Harrison and Rixey to enforce their guaranty contracts . . . . FDIC [then] filed suit against Bell, Harrison and Rixey . . . alleging that Bell had failed to pay all that was due on two notes and that Harrison and Rixey were liable as guarantors of Bell's debt up to $ 11,277.50. The court entered a default judgment against Bell . . . . It concluded, however, that FDIC was equitably estopped from asserting its claim against Harrison and Rixey as guarantors of Bell. . . .

Despite the reluctance of the Supreme Court to estop the government when it has performed a sovereign function, the circuit courts generally have held that the federal government may be estopped when it serves an essentially proprietary role and its agents act within the scope of their delegated authority. . . . Whereas in its sovereign role, the government carries out unique governmental functions for the benefit of the whole public, in its proprietary capacity the government's activities are analogous to those of a private concern. After reviewing the role of FDIC in this case, we conclude that it acted in a proprietary capacity and therefore is subject to the rules of equitable estoppel.

FDIC was created as part of the Federal Deposit Insurance Corporation Act as an instrument for insuring to a limited extent the deposits of the banks participating in the plan. . . . FDIC in this case was acting as receiver of Southern National Bank, and in its corporate capacity purchased the notes of Bell, Harrison and Rixey and demanded their payment. In its dealings with Harrison and Rixey, the Corporation performed essentially the same function as any other assuming bank that may have acquired some of the assets of a failed bank. . . . As would any other receiver or liquidating agent, FDIC should be required to deal fairly with its debtors and should be held accountable for the representations of its agents. . . .

In holding the principles of equitable estoppel applicable to FDIC in this case, we note that FDIC does not claim that the representations of its agents were unauthorized or contrary to statute or regulation. Thus, cases involving representations of government officers that were beyond the scope of their authority are distinguishable. . . .

Reviewing the conclusions of the district court and the record in this case, we find sufficient evidence to support the district court's finding that all of the elements of estoppel were proved. . . .

Schweiker was decided three years earlier and was not dispositive in the above case. On what exception to *Schweiker* did the Court rely?

3. *Socop-Gonzalez v. Immigration and Naturalization Service (INS), 272 F.3d 1176 (9th Cir. 2001).*

In November 1991, Oscar A. Socop-Gonzalez ("Socop"), a native and citizen of Guatemala, entered the United States as a nonimmigrant visitor. He [remained past his authorized time]. On October 19, 1995, the INS initiated deportation proceedings against Socop . . . . Socop filed a timely appeal with the BIA. . . . [W]hile his [appeal] was pending, Socop married . . . a United States citizen [and] went to [an] INS office . . . to inquire about how to submit a petition to immigrate based on his marriage. The INS officer staffing the information booth instructed Socop to withdraw his asylum appeal and to file an application for adjustment of status with the INS. Socop followed these instructions: that very day, he sent a letter to the BIA withdrawing his appeal. . . .

Unfortunately, the INS officer provided incorrect advice to Socop. . . . Instead of instructing Socop to withdraw his asylum petition, the INS officer should have told Socop to file an immediate relative visa petition with the INS and wait until it was approved. . . . [T]he INS sent Socop a "Bag and Baggage" letter instructing him to report for deportation. . . . With a lawyer's assistance . . . Socop moved the BIA to reopen his case and to reinstate his asylum appeal. . . . The BIA denied Socop's motion . . . because it was not filed within ninety days of the BIA's decision. . . .

These facts . . . are precisely those needed to support an equitable tolling argument. Unfortunately, . . . Socop requested relief based on the doctrine of equitable estoppel, which is similar to, but distinct from, equitable tolling. . . . [W]hile tolling "focuses on the plaintiff's excusable ignorance of the limitations period and on lack of prejudice to the defendant," estoppel "focuses on the actions of the defendant." Equitable estoppel cannot serve as the basis for relief in this case because Socop would have to show that the INS officer engaged in "affirmative misconduct" when she provided him with incorrect advice. . . . Negligently providing misinformation to an alien does not meet [the requirement], so Socop cannot prevail on an estoppel theory. . . . [However, even] though Socop's lawyer mistakenly invoked equitable estoppel instead of equitable tolling as the basis for relief, . . . Socop is not barred from presenting a meritorious tolling argument on appeal. . . .

The "affirmative misconduct" exception is widely accepted but rarely occurs. Instead, most situations where a person is affected adversely by a misstatement of law or regulation by a government official involve innocent mistakes or simple negligence. Another approach used to get around the restrictive use of equitable estoppel involves the claim that reliance on erroneous information has led to the permanent deprivation of a clear legal right or entitlement.

4. *Fredericks v. Commissioner of Internal Revenue, 126 F.3d 433 (3d Cir. 1997)*.

Barry I. Fredericks appeals . . . a deficiency assessed . . . in July 1992 for Fredericks' 1977 income tax return. The IRS action requires the taxpayer to pay an additional tax of $ 28,361 and approximately $ 158,000 in interest on the basis of a disallowed tax-shelter deduction. . . . The IRS' assessment was filed long after the three-year statute of limitations had expired. However, at the request of the IRS Fredericks signed various consent agreements extending the time for the government to assess his 1977 tax return. The taxpayer's estoppel contention is based on alleged . . . misconduct by the IRS regarding . . . these consent forms. . . .

First, the IRS misrepresented in 1981 that it never received a Form 872-A (Special Consent to Extend the Time to Assess Taxes), which Fredericks had signed to authorize an indefinite extension of the statute of limitations. Second, the IRS confirmed this misrepresentation in 1981, 1982 and 1983, by soliciting and executing three separate Forms 872, which extend the statute of limitations for one year. Third, the IRS discovered that it possessed the Form 872-A sometime before June 30, 1984, the date the last one-year extension expired, decided to rely on that form in continuing its investigation of Fredericks' tax return and failed to notify the taxpayer of its changed course of action. Fourth, the IRS used the Form 872-A to assess a deficiency in 1992, 11 years after informing the taxpayer that the Form 872-A did not exist, and eight years after the final one-year extension expired. Finally, the IRS imposed interest penalties totaling over five times the amount of the tax and covering the entire duration of its protracted investigation of the tax shelter. . . .

We believe that the misrepresentations here were . . . egregious . . . . The government's misrepresentation went beyond mere erroneous oral advice . . .; it consisted of affirmative, authorized acts inducing Fredericks to sign and rely on the terms of the Form 872 on three different occasions . . . . Moreover, the IRS' misleading silence after finding and deciding to rely on the Form 872-A, coupled with its failure to notify Fredericks of its decision and its effective revocation of the third Form 872, constitute affirmative misconduct. . . . and gives rise to the most impressive case for estoppel against the IRS that our research has disclosed. . . . Fredericks acted reasonably in relying on the IRS' misrepresentation that the Form 872-A was not in his file, and in relying on the subsequent Forms 872 executed by him and the IRS. . . .

5. *Rider v. United States Postal Service*, 862 F.2d 239 (9th Cir. 1988).

A Postal Service employee promised Dr. Rider that political materials that Dr. Rider wanted to send by third-class bulk mail would be delivered within forty-eight hours. In reliance on this promise Dr. Rider paid $ 34,200.00 to have the materials delivered. Some of the materials were not delivered within forty-eight hours. These materials lost their value because they were not delivered until during or after the election to which they pertained.

Under the relevant postal regulations postal employees do not have actual authority to guarantee the time of delivery of third class mail. Thus, unless the Postal Service is estopped from denying the authority of its employee to bind the Postal Service, Dr. Rider can prove no set of facts which would entitle him to relief. . . . The conduct in this case is not more egregious than in many cases in which no affirmative misconduct has been found. . . . A simple misstatement is not affirmative misconduct. The fact that the incorrect information is given orally makes it even less likely to rise to the level of affirmative misconduct. . . .

Dr. Rider does not claim that the government conduct in this case is more serious than an incorrect oral representation. Thus, this is not an appropriate case for estoppel.

6. *Dawkins v. Witt*, 318 F.3d 606 (4th Cir. 2003).

On September 5, 1996, the plaintiffs' insured property was damaged as a result of Hurricane Fran. . . . The plaintiffs . . . notified FEMA, who responded with a letter . . . indicating that it had received the notice of claim and had assigned it to Bellmon Adjusters, Inc. . . . An adjuster from Bellmon Adjusters, Bob Hughes, met with the plaintiffs . . . on September 13, 1996. . . . While Hughes informed the plaintiffs that they could only make claims for losses that were verified by a proof of loss, he also told them that with major disasters, FEMA was not concerned with the 60 day deadline . . . and that it would reopen the claim if the plaintiffs found any further verifiable flood damage after that time. . . . [Plaintiffs sent in their proof of loss] in December 1996. The 60 day period for filing a proof of loss had expired November 4, 1996. . . . Despite the late filing, FEMA paid the claim amount indicated . . . . The plaintiffs then hired a contractor who proceeded to repair the property beginning in December 1996. . . . During the repair process [another adjuster] determined that damage to the window frames in the upper floors of the home had occurred as a result of the flood waters twisting and uplifting the home and its decks. . . . [FEMA denied this claim] because the repairs to the property had compromised its ability to investigate. . . .

The behavior the plaintiffs must rely on in this case to demonstrate affirmative misconduct consists of the following: Hughes representing to the plaintiffs that FEMA was not concerned about the 60 day requirement with major disasters, FEMA accepting the plaintiffs' initial proof of loss well after the 60 day deadline, and FEMA proceeding to continue to address their [first] claim after the 60 day deadline. We agree with the district court that while the plaintiffs may have shown "unprofessional and misleading conduct . . ." this conduct is no worse than that the Supreme Court has determined does not rise to a level to justify estoppel against the government. . . .

IV. Evidence in Adjudicatory Proceedings

Many students taking administrative law during their second year of law school have not yet taken Evidence. While we certainly advise you to take Evidence before finishing law school, the materials that follow do not require a sophisticated understanding of the Federal Rules of Evidence, including the many and varied rules regarding hearsay evidence. For starters, the evidence rules matter less because most agencies do not closely follow the Federal Rules of Evidence including the rules regarding hearsay evidence which, for the most part, is both admissible and can become an important part of the record supporting a particular decision.

As you can see, the rules of evidence are "relaxed" in administrative proceedings. Administrative law judges, panel members, commissioners, administrators, and other individuals charged with making adjudicatory determinations are, however, in the position of having to evaluate the probative value, substantial weight, and reliability of the evidence put before them.

In the course of an adjudication evidentiary problems are common. First, one must attempt to discern what rules of evidence will apply, if any. Next, one must evaluate whether to respond and object when evidence is proffered that is either inherently unreliable or otherwise objectionable. After a hearing is concluded and the decision announced, lawyers must decide whether to attack the decision based on the nature of the evidence submitted and relied upon or the substantive content of that evidence. Lawyers must evaluate whether the processes used in the course of the adjudication are rational, fair, and consistent with the procedural and evidentiary standards the agency either has articulated or otherwise, by statute, must follow.

The cases that follow explore some of the questions of the use of evidence in administrative adjudication.

CARROLL V. KNICKERBOCKER ICE COMPANY

113 N.E. 507 (N.Y. 1916)

[JUDGE CUDDEBACK] This is an appeal by the Knickerbocker Ice Company from an order affirming the decision and award of the workmen's compensation commission in the matter of the claim of Bridget Carroll for compensation for the death of her husband, Myles Carroll, which was occasioned as it is alleged by injuries received while he was in the employ of the appellant. . . . The decedent was employed by the ice company as driver on an ice wagon, and the claim is that he suffered an injury on September 22, 1914, while delivering ice. The commission made certain findings of fact upon which it based an award to the claimant. One of such findings of fact is as follows:

> On said date while said Carroll was putting ice in the cellar of a saloon at 20 East Forty-second street, borough of Manhattan, city of New York, the ice tongs slipped and a 300-lb. cake of ice fell upon him, striking him in the abdomen, causing an epigastric hemorrhage and a rigidity of the abdomen. He was taken to a hospital and there developed delirium tremens and died on the 28th day of September, 1914.

Section 21 of the Workmen's Compensation Law provides that in any proceeding upon a claim for compensation under the law, "it shall be presumed in the absence of substantial evidence to the contrary . . . that the claim comes within the provisions of this chapter." There was in this case substantial evidence to overcome this statutory presumption. A helper on the ice wagon and two cooks employed in the saloon where the ice was delivered, testified before the commission that they were present at the time and place when it was alleged the plaintiff was injured, and that they did not see any accident whatsoever happen to him, and that they did not see any cake of ice fall. The physicians who subsequently examined the decedent testified that there were no bruises, discolorations or abrasions on the surface of his body.

The finding of the commission is based solely on the testimony of witnesses who related what Carroll told them as to how he was injured. Carroll's wife testified that when he came home from his work he told her that he was putting a 300 pound cake of ice in Daly's cellar and the tongs slipped and the ice came back on him. The physician who was called to treat the injured man at his home, a neighbor who dropped in, and the physicians at the hospital, where he was taken later in the day, testified that he made like statements to them.

The question is presented whether this hearsay testimony is sufficient under the circumstances of the case to sustain the finding of the commission. . . . We have only to consider whether the law of this state excluding such testimony has been changed in cases coming within the Workmen's Compensation Law by section 68 of that law. That section is as follows:

> Section 68. Technical rules of evidence or procedure [are] not required. The commission or a commissioner or deputy commissioner in making an investigation or inquiry or conducting a hearing shall not be bound by common law or statutory rules of evidence or by technical or formal rules of procedure, except as provided in this chapter; but may make such investigation or inquiry or conduct such hearing in such manner as to ascertain the substantial rights of the parties.

This section has plainly changed the rule of evidence in all cases affected by the act. It gives the workmen's compensation commission free rein in making its investigations and in conducting its hearings and authorizes it to receive and consider not only hearsay testimony, but any kind of evidence that may throw light on a claim pending before it. The award of the commission cannot be overturned on account of any alleged error in receiving evidence.

This is all true, but, as I read it, section 68 as applied to this case does not make the hearsay testimony offered by the claimant sufficient ground to uphold the award which the commission made. That section does not declare the probative force of any evidence, but it does declare that the aim and end of the investigation by the commission shall be "to ascertain the substantial rights of the parties." . . . . The act may be taken to mean that while the commission's inquiry is not limited by the common law or statutory rules of evidence or by technical or formal rules of procedure, and it may in its discretion accept any evidence that is offered; still in the end there must be a residuum of legal evidence to support the claim before an award can be made. . . .

The only substantial evidence before the workmen's compensation commission was to the effect that no cake of ice slipped and struck the decedent, and there were no bruises or marks upon his body which indicated that he had been so injured. The findings to the contrary rest solely on the decedent's statement made at a time when he was confessedly in a highly nervous state, which ended in his death from delirium tremens. Such hearsay testimony is no evidence. . . .

I recommend that the order appealed from be reversed and the claim for compensation be dismissed, with costs against [the] state industrial commission . . . .

1. *Altschuller v. Bressler*, 46 N.E.2d 886 (N.Y. 1943).

> The State Industrial Board has found that the claimant's total disability is the result of accidental injuries sustained by the claimant on May 9, 1939, and that the injuries arose out of and in the course of his employment. The Appellate Division has unanimously affirmed . . . . [T]he finding of the Industrial Board that the claimant's condition is the result of accidental injuries arising out of and in the course of his employment rests solely upon the "hearsay testimony," perhaps corroborated, by "circumstances or other evidence." This court granted leave to appeal in order to review the question whether under the terms of section 118 of the Workmen's Compensation Law, such hearsay testimony may be accepted as sufficient to establish the accident and the injury. . . .
>
> If the claimant had testified under oath and subject to cross-examination, that "all of a sudden he got a heartburn," while lifting the heavy boiler, findings of the Industrial Board that the claimant suffered a coronary occlusion "due to the strain and unusual effort used in the lifting of said heavy kettle" and that "the total disability of Nathan Altschuller was the natural and unavoidable result of the accidental injuries sustained by him" would not be subject to serious challenge. There is ample medical testimony that such "strain and unusual effort" would be a competent producing cause of the occlusion . . . . The question remains whether testimony of narration of the alleged accident by the claimant can be accepted as sufficient to prove that the alleged accident did occur. . . .
>
> The [*Carroll v. Knickerbocker Ice Co.*] rule . . . has been criticised by many scholars as the product of judicial reluctance to depart from long accepted but technical common law rules and concepts . . . . Nonetheless, this court has never overruled its decision . . . nor has the Legislature amended the statute . . . . The . . . decision [in this case] is not inconsistent with *Carroll v. Knickerbocker Ice Co.* There, as the court pointed out, all the substantial evidence contradicted the "hearsay" statements. . . . Here . . . there is no substantial testimony to show that an accident did not occur as narrated by the injured employee, and [the] established "facts and circumstances" leave little reasonable doubt that the narration is substantially true. . . .

2. Is it wise to base a decision entirely on hearsay? Should there be, as *Carroll* held, "a residuum of legal evidence?" While the rule is often seen as an anachronism, it continues to be followed in some states. *Mayes v. Dep't of Employment Sec.*, 754 P.2d 989, 992 (Utah Ct. App. 1988), holds that: "Under the residuum rule, findings of fact . . . must be supported by a residuum of legal evidence competent in a court of law, quoting *Yacht Club v. Utah Liquor Control Comm'n*, 681 P.2d 1224, 1226 (Utah 1984)." This was clarified recently in *Prosper, Inc. v. Department of Workforce Services*, 168 P.3d 344 (Utah App. 2007): "While it is true that findings of fact must be supported by a residuum of legally competent evidence, and therefore cannot be based solely on inadmissible hearsay, it is equally true that hearsay can constitute legally competent evidence. In *Mayes*, then, we should have clarified that findings of fact 'cannot be based exclusively on inadmissible hearsay evidence' because admissible hearsay evidence is 'evidence competent in a court of law'. . . . The residuum rule requires that findings be supported by a residuum

of legally competent evidence, not that they be supported by 'non-hearsay' evidence. . . ."

3. *Shepp v. Uehlinger, 775 F.2d 452 (1st Cir. 1985)*, was a contract dispute brought by an unpaid drummer. In the course of the initial trial, the drummer's lawyer failed to object to some damaging hearsay evidence. When the drummer argued that the lower court should not have relied exclusively on hearsay, the court responded that "the 'residuum' rule . . . arose in the context of administrative proceedings where counsel has no general right to object to the admission of hearsay evidence. . . . *Levins v. Bucholtz, 2 A.D.2d 351 (1956).* . . . And, recent [New York] cases repudiate the 'residuum' rule even in the field of administrative law. *Eagle v. Paterson, 442 N.E.2d 56 (N.Y. 1982); 300 Gramatan Ave. Associates v. State Division of Human Rights, 379 N.E.2d 1183 (N.Y. 1978).*"

> ### For More Information
>
> For a different point of view, see John Gedid, *Hearsay Evidence in Administrative Proceedings – Pro and Con Views on the "Legal Residuum" Rule: The "Legal Residuum" Rule Should be Retained in Pennsylvania Because of Its Function to Insure Fundamental Fairness and Due Process*, 75 PA. BAR ASSN. QTLY. 1 (2004); and Gary Muldoon, *To What Extent is the "Residuum of Legal Evidence" Rule Applicable in Criminal Proceedings?* 2 ISSUES IN N.Y. CRIM. L. (March 2000), http://www.mcacp.org/issue12.htm (last visited June 17, 2008).

RICHARDSON V. PERALES

402 U.S. 389 (1971)

[JUSTICE BLACKMUN] In 1966 Pedro Perales, a San Antonio truck driver . . . filed a claim for disability insurance benefits under the Social Security Act. . . . The issue here is whether physicians' written reports of medical examinations they have made of a disability claimant may constitute "substantial evidence" supportive of a finding of nondisability, within the § 205(g) standard, when the claimant objects to the admissibility of those reports and when the only live testimony is presented by his side and is contrary to the reports.

I

In his claim Perales asserted that on September 29, 1965, he became disabled as a result of an injury to his back sustained in lifting an object at work. He was seen by a neurosurgeon, Dr. Ralph A. Munslow, who first recommended conservative treatment. When this provided no relief . . . surgery for a possible protruded intervertebral disc . . . was advised. The patient at first hesitated . . . . On recurrence of pain, however, he consented to the recommended procedure. . . . No disc protrusion or other definitive pathology was identified at surgery. . . . The patient was discharged . . . with a final diagnosis of "Neuritis, lumbar, mild." Mr. Perales continued to complain, but Dr. Munslow and . . . a neurologist called in consultation were still unable to find any objective neurological explanation for his complaints. Dr. Munslow advised that he return to work. In April 1966 Perales consulted Dr. Max Morales, Jr., a general practitioner . . . . Dr. Morales hospitalized the patient from April 15 to May 2. His final discharge diagnosis was: "Back sprain, lumbo-sacral spine."

Perales then filed his claim. . . . The agency obtained the hospital records and a report from Dr. Morales. The report set forth no physical findings or laboratory studies, but the doctor again gave as his diagnosis: "Back sprain – lumbo-sacral spine," this time "moderately severe," with "Ruptured disk not ruled out." The agency arranged for a medical examination . . . by Dr. John H. Langston, an orthopedic surgeon. . . .

Dr. Langston's ensuing report to the Division of Disability Determination was devastating from the claimant's standpoint. The doctor . . . noted a slightly edematous condition in the legs, attributed to "inactivity and sitting around" . . . and "a very mild sprain [of those muscles] which would resolve were he actually to get a little exercise and move." Apart from this . . . Dr. Langston found no abnormalities of the lumbar spine. Otherwise, he described Perales as a

> big physical healthy specimen . . . obviously holding back and limiting all of his motions, intentionally. . . . His upper extremities, though they are completely uninvolved by his injury, he holds very rigidly as though he were semiparalyzed. His reach and grasp are very limited but intentionally so. . . . Neurological examination is entirely normal . . . .

> The state agency denied the claim. Perales requested reconsideration. Dr. Morales submitted a further report to the agency. The doctor concluded that the patient had not made a complete recovery from his surgery, that he was not malingering . . . and that he was totally and permanently disabled. . . . The state agency then arranged for an examination by Dr. James M. Bailey, a board-certified psychiatrist . . . . Dr. Bailey's report to the agency . . . concluded with the following diagnosis:

> Paranoid personality, manifested by hostility, feelings of persecution and long history of strained interpersonal relationships. I do not feel that this patient has a separate psychiatric illness at this time. It appears that his personality is conducive to anger, frustrations, etc.

The agency again reviewed the file. . . . The claim was again denied.

Perales requested a hearing before a hearing examiner. The agency then referred the claimant to Dr. Langston and to Dr. Richard H. Mattson for electromyography studies. . . . [These doctors] verified what Dr. Langston had found on the earlier physical examination. The requested hearing was set . . . . The notice . . . advised the claimant that he should bring all medical and other evidence not already presented, afforded him an opportunity to examine all documentary evidence on file prior to the hearing, and told him that he might bring his own physician or other witnesses and be represented at the hearing by a lawyer.

The hearing took place [and a] supplemental hearing was held March 31. The claimant appeared at the first hearing with his attorney and with Dr. Morales. The attorney formally objected to the introduction of the several reports of [the state's doctors] and of the hospital records. Various grounds of objection were asserted, including hearsay, . . . absence of proof the physicians were licensed to practice in Texas . . . and the conclusory nature of the reports. These objections were overruled and the reports and hospital records were introduced. The reports of Dr. Morales and of Dr. Munslow were then submitted by the claimant's counsel and admitted.

At the two hearings oral testimony was submitted by claimant Perales, by Dr. Morales, by a former fellow employee of the claimant, by a vocational expert, and by Dr. Lewis A. Leavitt . . . . Dr. Leavitt was called by the hearing examiner as an independent "medical adviser," that is, as an expert who does not examine the claimant but who hears and reviews the medical evidence and who may offer an opinion. The adviser is paid a fee by the Government. The claimant, through his counsel, objected to any testimony by Dr. Leavitt not based upon examination or upon a hypothetical. Dr. Leavitt testified over this objection and was cross-examined by the claimant's attorney. He stated that the consensus of the various medical reports was that Perales had a mild low-back syndrome of musculo-ligamentous origin.

The hearing examiner . . . found that the claimant "is suffering from a low back syndrome of musculo-ligamentous origin, and of mild severity"; that while he "has an emotional overlay to his medical impairment it does not require psychiatric treatment . . ."; that "neither his medical impairment nor his emotional overlay, singly or in combination, constitute a disability as defined" in the Act; and that the claimant is capable of engaging . . . in work . . . . The hearing examiner's decision, then, was that the claimant was not entitled to a period of disability or to disability insurance benefits.

It is to be noted at this point that § 205(d) of the Act provides that . . . a claimant may request the issuance of subpoenas. Perales, however, who was represented by counsel, did not request subpoenas for either of the two hearings.

The claimant then made a request for review by the Appeals Council . . . . The Appeals Council [affirmed the decision]. Upon this adverse ruling the claimant instituted the present action . . . . Each side moved for summary judgment on the administrative transcript. The District Court stated that it was reluctant to accept as substantial evidence the opinions of medical experts submitted in the form of unsworn written reports, the admission of which would have the effect of denying the opposition an opportunity for cross-examination; that the opinion of a doctor who had never examined the claimant is entitled to little or no probative value, especially when opposed by substantial evidence including the oral testimony of an examining physician; and that what was before the court amounted to hearsay upon hearsay. . . . On appeal the Fifth Circuit noted the absence of any request by the claimant for subpoenas and held that . . . he was [therefore] not in a position to complain that he had been denied the rights of confrontation and of cross-examination. It held that the hearsay evidence in the case was admissible [and] that Dr. Leavitt's testimony also was admissible; but that [this] did not constitute substantial evidence when it was objected to and when it was contradicted by evidence from the only live witnesses. . . .

II

We therefore are presented with . . . a system which produces a mass of medical evidence in report form. May material of that kind ever be "substantial evidence" when it stands alone and is opposed by live medical evidence and the client's own contrary personal testimony? The courts below have held that it may not.

III

Section 205(b) . . . provides:

> Evidence may be received at any hearing before the Secretary even though inadmissible under rules of evidence applicable to court procedure.

[T]he Secretary has adopted regulations that state, among other things:

> The hearing examiner . . . shall receive in evidence the testimony of witnesses and any documents which are relevant and material to such matters. . . . The . . . procedure at the hearing . . . shall be in the discretion of the hearing examiner and of such nature as to afford the parties a reasonable opportunity for a fair hearing.

From this [t]here emerges an emphasis upon the informal rather than the formal. . . . This is the obvious intent of Congress so long as the procedures are fundamentally fair.

IV

With this background and this atmosphere in mind, we turn to the statutory standard of "substantial evidence" prescribed by § 205(g). . . . The Court [has] said [this is] "more than a mere scintilla. It means such relevant evidence as a reasonable mind might accept as adequate to support a conclusion." . . . .

V

. . . .

We conclude that a written report by a licensed physician who has examined the claimant . . . may be received as evidence in a disability hearing and, despite its hearsay character and an absence of cross-examination, and despite the presence of opposing direct medical testimony and testimony by the claimant himself, may constitute substantial evidence supportive of a finding by the hearing examiner adverse to the claimant, when the claimant has not exercised his right to subpoena the reporting physician and thereby provide himself with the opportunity for cross-examination of the physician.

We are prompted to this conclusion by a number of factors that, we feel, assure underlying reliability and probative value:

1. . . . Each report presented here was prepared by a practicing physician who had examined the claimant. . . . Although each received a fee, that fee is recompense for his time and talent otherwise devoted to private practice or other professional assignment. We cannot, and do not, ascribe bias to the work of these independent physicians, or any interest on their part in the outcome of the administrative proceeding beyond the professional curiosity a dedicated medical man possesses.

2. The vast workings of the social security administrative system make for reliability and impartiality in the consultant reports. . . . [T]he agency operates essentially . . . as an adjudicator and not as an advocate or adversary. This is the congressional plan. We do not presume on this record to say that it works unfairly.

3. . . . These are routine, standard, and unbiased medical reports by physician specialists concerning a subject whom they had seen. That the reports were adverse to Perales' claim is not in itself bias or an indication of nonprobative character.

4. The reports present the impressive range of examination to which Perales was subjected. A specialist in neurosurgery, one in neurology, one in psychiatry, one in orthopedics, and one in physical medicine and rehabilitation add up to definitive opinion in five medical specialties . . . . It is fair to say that the claimant received professional examination and opinion on a scale beyond the reach of most per-

sons and that this case reveals a patient and careful endeavor by the state agency and the examiner to ascertain the truth.

5. So far as we can detect, there is no inconsistency whatsoever in the reports of the five specialists. Yet each result was reached by independent examination in the writer's field of specialized training.

6. Although the claimant complains of the lack of opportunity to cross-examine the reporting physicians, he did not take advantage of the opportunity afforded him under 20 C.F.R. § 404.926 to request subpoenas for the physicians. . . . This inaction on the claimant's part supports the Court of Appeals' view that the claimant as a consequence is to be precluded from now complaining that he was denied the rights of confrontation and cross-examination.

7. Courts have recognized the reliability and probative worth of written medical reports even in formal trials and . . . have admitted them as an exception to the hearsay rule. . . .

8. . . . Until the decision in this case, the courts of appeals, including the Fifth Circuit . . . uniformly recognized [the] value in [medical] reports. The courts have reviewed administrative determinations, and upheld many adverse ones, where the only supporting evidence has been reports of this kind . . . . In these cases admissibility was not contested, but the decisions do demonstrate traditional and ready acceptance of the written medical report in social security disability cases.

9. There is an additional and pragmatic factor which, although not controlling, deserves mention. . . . With over 20,000 disability claim hearings annually, the cost of providing live medical testimony at those hearings, where need has not been demonstrated by a request for a subpoena, over and above the cost of the examinations requested by hearing examiners, would be a substantial drain on the trust fund and on the energy of physicians already in short supply.

VI

1.

Perales relies heavily on . . . *Goldberg v. Kelly*, particularly the comment that due process requires notice "and an effective opportunity to defend by confronting any adverse witnesses . . . ." . . . . [However, in this case the] physicians' reports were on file and available for inspection by the claimant and his counsel. And the authors of those reports were known and were subject to subpoena and to the very cross-examination that the claimant asserts he has not enjoyed. Further, the specter of questionable credibility and veracity is not present; there is professional disagreement with the medical conclusions, to be sure, but there is no attack here upon the doctors' credibility or veracity. *Goldberg v. Kelly* affords little comfort to the claimant.

2.

Perales also [describes] the medical reports in question as "mere uncorroborated hearsay" and would relate this to CHIEF JUSTICE HUGHES' sentence in *Consolidated Edison Co. v. NLRB*: "Mere uncorroborated hearsay or rumor does not constitute substantial evidence." . . . . [W]e feel that the claimant and the Court of Appeals read too much into the single sentence from *Consolidated Edison*. The contrast the Chief Justice was drawing . . . was not with material that would be deemed formally inadmissible in judicial proceedings but with material "without a basis in evidence having rational probative force." This was not a blanket rejection by the Court of administrative reliance on hearsay irrespective of reliability and probative value. The opposite was the case.

3.

The claimant, the District Court, and the Court of Appeals also criticize the use of Dr. Leavitt as a medical adviser. Inasmuch as medical advisers are used in approximately 13% of disability claim hearings, comment as to this practice is indicated. We see nothing "reprehensible" in the practice, as the claimant would describe it. The trial examiner is a layman; the medical adviser is a board-certified specialist. He is used primarily in complex cases for explanation of medical problems in terms understandable to the layman-examiner. He is a neutral adviser. This particular record discloses that Dr. Leavitt explained the technique and significance of electromyography. He did offer his own opinion on the claimant's condition. That opinion, however, did not differ from the medical reports. Dr. Leavitt did not vouch for the accuracy of the facts assumed in the reports. No one understood otherwise. We see nothing unconstitutional or improper in the . . . presence of Dr. Leavitt in this administrative hearing.

4.

Finally, the claimant complains . . . that in any event the hearing procedure is invalid on due process grounds. . . . The matter comes down to the question of the procedure's integrity and fundamental fairness. We see nothing that works in derogation of that integrity and of that fairness in the admission of consultants' reports, subject as they are to being material and to the use of the subpoena and consequent cross-examination. This precisely fits the statutorily prescribed "cross-examination as may be required for a full and true disclosure of the facts." That is the standard. It is clear and workable and does not fall short of procedural due process. . . .

We therefore reverse and remand for further proceedings. We intimate no view as to the merits. It is for the District Court now to determine whether the

Secretary's findings, in the light of all material proffered and admissible, are supported by "substantial evidence" within the command of § 205(g). . . .

———————

Underlying Case Documents

The case referenced:
Dr. Munslow's <u>recommendation</u> for surgery
The <u>discharge report</u> of Dr. Munslow
The <u>report</u> from Dr. Morales
The <u>report</u> from Dr. Langstron
The state's <u>initial denial</u> of the claim
Dr. Bailey's <u>report</u> to the agency
The <u>second denial</u> by the agency
The <u>notice of the hearing</u>
The <u>report of the hearing examiner</u>
Perales' <u>request for reconsideration</u>
The denial by the Appeals Council's <u>affirmance</u> of the decision of the hearing examiner

For the transcript of the first hearing click <u>HERE</u>.

For the transcript of the supplemental hearing click <u>HERE</u>.

1. The failure of the claimant in *Richardson* has produced multiple conflicting opinions regarding the meaning of the case. It is fair to read *Richardson* as a case about waiver, i.e., Perales's failure to subpoena the physicians constituted a waiver to cross-examine witnesses whose testimony was central to the agency determination. *Richardson* can also be seen as a case in which the individual's interest in disability payments (which the court finds to be something short of sustenance or survival resources) is sufficient for purposes of activating due process, but insufficient to provide a full range of procedural protections including unimpeded cross-examination. In <u>*Wallace v. Bowen*, 869 F.2d 187, 193, 194 (3d Cir. 1989)</u>, the court held that *Richardson* affirms the right to subpoena and that the "question of whether to issue a subpoena to compel cross-examination . . . is a question entrusted to the ALJ who is obligated to develop the record fully."

Richardson also makes clear that it is possible for a decision to be based entirely on hearsay, although it is not clear whether that is a universal principle applicable in all formal adjudicatory proceedings or whether it is limited to those situations where there has been a right to cross-examine and secure corroborating evidence that has been waived by the parties affected by the decision. *See* William H. Kuehnle, *Standards of Evidence in Administrative Proceedings*, 49 N.Y.L. Sch. L. Rev. 829 (2005).

2. *Brown Tire Company v. Underwriters Adjusting Company*, 573 N.E.2d 901 (Ind. Ct. App. 1991).

> On August 3, 1987, Mark McKim was injured during the course of his employment with Brown Tire Company while lifting a tire into the back of a pickup truck. At the time of the injury, Brown Tire was insured by Meridian Mutual. After hospitalization, surgery, physical therapy, and bed rest, McKim returned to work . . . . On May 31, 1988, while trying to stop a falling tire, McKim reinjured his back. . . . After a hearing before the Workers' Compensation Board, McKim was assigned a rating of 42% permanent partial impairment, 15% of which was attributed to the first injury . . . . Meridian Mutual appeals, arguing that the evidence did not support a finding that any of the 42% impairment could be attributed to the first injury.
>
> Meridian . . . contends that the Board erred in considering a letter from Dr. Beghin, an expert retained by Underwriters[, as the letter was hearsay]. In the letter, Dr. Beghin stated in pertinent part:
>
> > I would note that surgical excision of disk with no fusion, good results, and no persistent sciatic pain would receive a ten per cent whole body permanent physical impairment . . . . Since Mr. McKim did suffer a dural tear . . . I would recommend increasing the impairment rating to at least a 15 per cent whole body permanent physical impairment . . . .
>
> Indiana has implemented the "modified residuum rule" with respect to hearsay at workers' compensation hearings. . . . If properly objected to, preserved on review, and not falling within a recognized exception to the hearsay rule, then an award may not be based solely upon hearsay evidence. Thus, as long as there is some "thread of legal evidence" to support the award, it will be sustained, even if the thread is of no great weight, as to weigh the evidence is not the province of this court. . . . [I]n order for the Board's finding of 15% permanent partial impairment to be sustained, there must be some evidence in the record besides Dr. Beghin's report that McKim suffered a permanent loss of function from the first accident. Our search of the record reveals none. . . . All of the evidence indicates that McKim's impairment was temporary and had resolved itself prior to the second injury. As a result, McKim's doctor had released him to perform his prior job involving heavy lifting without restrictions. . . . [We therefore] hold that the admission of Dr. Beghin's report was erroneous. . . .

3. While agencies may be permitted to make use of documents that are little more than "hearsay upon hearsay," the practice comes at a price, as the opinion below suggests.

Niam v. Ashcroft, 354 F.3d 652 (7th Cir. 2004).

> Our second case involves Peter Blagoev, a professional musician in Chicago who, accompanied by his wife and his stepdaughter, was admitted to the United States from Bulgaria . . . in 1993 . . . . All three . . . seek asylum . . . . Blagoev comes from a prominent anticommunist family. The communists sentenced his grandfather to death when they took power in Bulgaria in 1944, although the sentence was not carried out. . . . [A]n attack on [Blagoev's parent's] home with acetone, a powerful corrosive chemical, caused permanent injury to Blagoev's mother. As for Blagoev himself, he was first beaten . . . when at age 16 he asked a guest lecturer at his school "how come . . . if it's so nice here everybody is trying to get out of here and go West." . . . . His wife, who was active in the same causes as he, was assaulted, and her cousin was murdered after filing a claim to recover land that had been stolen from him by the communists. When an attempt was made to abduct Blagoev's stepdaughter, the family had had enough and left the country. . . .

> In nevertheless denying the Blagoevs' petition for asylum, the immigration judge relied heavily on [a Bulgarian country report], where we read that "political conditions have so altered in the past eight years as to remove any presumption that past mistreatment under the Communists will lead to future difficulties" for people (like the Blagoevs) . . . . The immigration judge concluded that the Blagoevs had no well-founded fear of persecution should they be returned to Bulgaria. . . .

> The immigration judge's finding that the Blagoevs were not victims of persecution thus cannot be sustained. But if he reasonably found that they won't be persecuted if they return to Bulgaria, his decision must still be upheld. There was some evidence of this, namely the country report. We and other courts have expressed concern about the immigration service's chronic overreliance on such reports. The State Department naturally is reluctant to level harsh criticisms against regimes with which the United States has friendly relations [such as] the former communist states of central and eastern Europe, and so the country report on Bulgaria can be expected to emphasize the bright side of Bulgarian politics. Furthermore, the authors of these reports are anonymous and there is no opportunity for the asylum-seeker to cross-examine any of them. That doesn't make the reports inadmissible as evidence. . . . Nevertheless the evidentiary infirmities of the country reports are important in placing in perspective a startling evidentiary ruling of which the Blagoevs complain. . . . So, [based on this and other problems,] the Blagoevs' case must be returned to the agency for further proceedings consistent with this opinion.

While JUDGE POSNER's suggestion to find different and presumably better immigration judges stands as a personal condemnation of shoddy decisionmaking practices, it does not resolve the problem of the widespread use of compound hearsay in asylum cases.

4. *DeBartolomeis v. Board of Review, 775 A.2d 87 (N.J. Super. Ct. App. Div. 2001).*

> Petitioner appeals from a decision of the Board of Review holding him to be disqualified for unemployment compensation benefits. . . . The only evidence received in the hearing before the Appeal Tribunal was petitioner's testimony, in which he made an effort to establish the medical basis for his inability to work at the job assigned by

the employer. Petitioner testified about his health history, particularly concerning a back injury which had been recognized as a basis for workers' compensation benefits and a medical-surgical leave. When he requested an opportunity to submit medical records in support of his contentions, the appeals examiner replied: "No, just sworn testimony here."

Petitioner has supplied us with the medical records and related documents he contends he attempted to introduce at the hearing before the Appeal Tribunal, but which were rejected. These include four workplace injury reports, apparently copies of employment records. Each is entitled "first report of injury." They memorialize two incidents in June 1995, one in April 1999, and another in May 1999, in which petitioner reported on-the-job back injuries from moving items such as benches, a baby grand piano, shop equipment, and chairs and tables. . . . The remaining medical records . . . tend to establish that, after unavailing courses of conservative treatment for his back pain, petitioner underwent surgery on January 27, 1999, a lumbar laminotomy, for a herniated disc at L5-S1. . . .

The appeals examiner erred in declining to receive the medical reports and related documents in support of petitioner's contention that he left the job because he was medically unable to do the work assigned to him. . . . It may be that once all the proofs are analyzed, petitioner will fail in his quest for unemployment compensation. He may be unable to explain apparent inconsistencies in the documentation he submits, or between those documents and the account he offers. . . . [However, with] whatever shortcomings his proffers may embody, petitioner is entitled to a full evaluation of all the proofs available before a ruling is made on the validity of his claim, and we remand for a new hearing toward that end. . . .

The court in *Debartolomeis* suggests that the "residuum rule" is required "in our state as well as in many other jurisdictions." We (your authors) would urge caution in accepting that premise as the Delaware note case, below, implies.

5. *Munyori v. Division of Long Term Care Residents Protection*, 2005 WL 2158508 (2005).

On January 16, 2004, the victim, Ruth Wintrop, alleged an incident of abuse against the Appellant, who was working . . . at Millcroft Assisted Living Facility. . . . At approximately 5 a.m., Wintrop rang her call bell and the Appellant responded. The Appellant [Munyori] provided Wintrop with a bedpan and then left the room. When the Appellant returned, she spilled some of the contents of the bedpan on the sheets, became frustrated, and flipped the sheet over Wintrop's head. At approximately 7 a.m., Sharon Harrop, the charge nurse . . . spoke to Wintrop while completing her rounds. Harrop testified that Wintrop was very tearful and became more so as she told Harrop about the incident. . . . Harrop reported the incident to . . . the Director of Health Services at Millcroft, [who] went to speak with Wintrop . . . . She testified that Wintrop was still visibly upset and described her demeanor as agitated, frustrated and disappointed. . . . Thereafter . . . the Appellant was terminated. . . . Following a review of the evidence, the Hearing Officer concluded that Appellant was guilty of emotional abuse [and] the State's [recommendation] for a two year listing on the Adult Abuse Registry was reasonable. The Appellant timely appealed to this Court. . . .

[Ruth Winthrop did not testify at the hearing.] Appellant asserts that her state and federal constitutional due process right to a fair hearing was violated by a decision unjustifiably based exclusively on hearsay. Appellant further argues that the legal residuum rule must be satisfied regardless of the admissibility of Wintrop's statement. . . . The Division argues that Wintrop's description of the events in question fell within an exception to the hearsay rule, Rule 803 of the Delaware Rules of Evidence, because her statement constitutes an excited utterance. . . .

In *Barnett v. Division of Motor Vehicles,* [514 A.2d 1145 (Del. Super. Ct. 1986),] the Court determined that the decision of an Administrative Hearing Officer cannot be based solely on legally inadmissible evidence. However, the ruling in *Barnett* does not apply to this case because the evidence in question in this case is legally admissible under the Delaware Rules of Evidence [as an excited utterance. Further, this c]ourt has repeatedly ruled that no residuum of legal evidence is required in administrative proceedings. . . . Considering the foregoing, the Division's decision to place the Appellant on the Registry for a period of two years after a finding of abuse is affirmed.

6. *Compton v. District of Columbia Board of Psychology,* 858 A.2d 470 (D.C. 2004).

John W. Compton petitions this court for review of an order issued by the District of Columbia Board of Psychology ("Board") revoking his license to practice psychology . . . . He asks us to decide whether evidence almost exclusively hearsay in nature constituted the critical mass of "substantial evidence" required under principles of administrative law to sustain the Board's decision. . . .

Dr. Compton has been a practicing psychologist since 1969. . . . In 1986, Dr. Compton began treating F.M.K., a licensed professional counselor herself. . . . Beginning in 1991, F.M.K. was additionally [seen] by Dr. Lynn . . . . In October 1995, . . . F.M.K. revealed to Dr. Lynn . . . that she "had some sort of sexual connection" with Dr. Compton, vaguely implying that he had engaged in sexual intercourse with her. . . . [This] prompted Dr. Lynn to write a letter to F.M.K. [asking] that F.M.K. release Dr. Lynn from her duty of confidentiality so that Dr. Lynn could report the matter to the appropriate authorities. F.M.K. did not respond to the letter, and Dr. Lynn did not make a report to the licensing authorities. . . . F.M.K. filed a lawsuit in 1997 . . . alleging that Dr. Compton's sexual misconduct constituted medical malpractice and that Dr. Lynn had negligently failed to protect F.M.K. from the abuse. . . . The case ultimately settled before trial.

Thereafter, [F.M.K.'s current therapists, Drs. Zinner and Lazar] filed . . . a joint complaint with the Board regarding Dr. Compton's alleged misconduct. The Board [issued] a notice of intent to bring disciplinary proceedings . . . . [T]he matter was assigned to a D.C. Department of Health administrative law judge ("ALJ"). . . . To prove its allegations, the government relied almost exclusively on F.M.K.'s deposition testimony. . . . [The transcript of a deposition is hearsay.] Drs. Zinner and Lazar also testified during the government's case-in-chief to corroborate F.M.K.'s deposition. They both indicated that . . . at no point did either detect an inconsistency in her account despite multiple and repeated discussions of the subject over the course of their respective treatment sessions. . . .

[T]he ALJ found [based on the deposition of F.M.K.] that, over the course of his therapeutic relationship with F.M.K. and in the privacy of their sessions together, Dr.

Compton . . . engaged in sexual intercourse [and other sexual acts] with F.M.K. [and thus] transgressed . . . the standards of acceptable conduct and prevailing practice within his profession. The ALJ accordingly recommended that Dr. Compton's license . . . be revoked because "no sanction less than revocation . . . provides an adequate assurance that other clients will not become victims of his disregard of the clear ethical mandates of his profession." . . . . [T]he ALJ determined that the reliability of F.M.K.'s deposition was diminished by (1) F.M.K.'s failure to testify in person . . .; (2) Dr. Compton's live testimony contradicting the deposition; and (3) the potential bias inhering in a deposition prepared in anticipation of a civil trial for damages. He nonetheless credited the deposition as being trustworthy because it was sworn and because it was corroborated by other evidence. . . .

Our examination of the corroboration relied upon to credit the hearsay evidence in this case leads us to conclude that F.M.K.'s deposition was given greater weight than warranted. . . . [T]he government built its case-in-chief solely on F.M.K.'s hearsay deposition, and, due to the private nature of allegations of sexual misconduct, credibility was the critical issue in this case. . . . The importance of live testimony was driven home here where the ALJ decided to discredit Dr. Compton's testimony based partly on personal observation of his demeanor, yet decided to credit F.M.K.'s testimony based on the cold record, without having a similar opportunity to observe her demeanor on the stand. . . .

[T]he ALJ [erroneously] found corroboration in Drs. Zinner's and Lazar's . . . testimony that F.M.K. "consistently adhered to her story of abuse . . . and that the details of her story have not changed." This finding suffers from a critical flaw of logic. . . . "[R]epetition does not imply veracity." Although it is popularly thought that the liar will often stumble over the forgotten details of earlier deceits, it is also equally true that the liar may "consistently adhere to" a well-rehearsed untruth. This is not to suggest that we have an opinion on the truth or falsity of F.M.K.'s allegations, because we surely do not. Rather, we state only that consistent repetition is not a sufficient basis upon which to evaluate the reliability of testimonial evidence in administrative proceedings, hearsay or otherwise. . . . Accordingly the revocation order is reversed on the present record and the case remanded for further proceedings not inconsistent with this opinion.

7. *Calhoun v. Bailar*, 626 F.2d 145 (9th Cir. 1980).

Plaintiff [worked for] the United States Post Office . . . . His duties included the supervision of several postal clerks engaged in compiling and reporting [information] on the volume of mail handled by various distribution operations . . . . He was charged with the falsification of mail volume records, or with directing his subordinates to falsify the records and, after an administrative hearing and appeal, discharged. The Notice of Removal served upon Appellant relied upon the affidavits of four of his subordinates. . . .

On direct examination each of the affiants attempted to disavow his or her affidavit. Affiant Scroggins completely disavowed the affidavit on direct examination but refused to answer any questions on cross examination, presumably on self-incrimination grounds. Evidence was later admitted that clearly contradicted his statement on direct examination that he had never reweighed mail. . . . Affiant Whitley totally disavowed her affidavit and testified that she was coerced into signing it. Inspector Johns was the only other major witness. He testified that he had observed widespread falsification during Appellant's tenure as supervisor, and introduced statistical evidence that tended to show falsification in Appellant's unit. Other evidence corroborated Johns' testimony that falsification was occurring, although this testimony, like Johns', did not directly tie the falsification to Appellant. . . .

Appellant did not challenge the admissibility of the affidavits at any time during the administrative process. At most, he argued the weight that should be given to the affidavits. The hearing examiner found that the affidavits were more credible evidence than the statements made on direct examination, in part because of the witnesses' refusal to answer questions put in cross examination and because portions of the affidavit were corroborated by other evidence. . . . Appellant concedes that the affidavits themselves would be sufficient to support a finding if they were uncontradicted. Appellant argues, however, that hearsay statements disavowed by a declarant can never supply substantial evidence. . . .

[T]he affidavits clearly provide substantial evidence to support the discharge. Although the affidavits are contradicted . . . by other testimony, we have long held that credibility issues should be resolved by the trier of fact . . . and that where "there is conflicting evidence sufficient to support either outcome, we must affirm the decision actually made."

Food for Thought

Is it more likely that a factual conclusion will be reliable, probative, and substantial if it is based on direct observation – or if it is based on the testimony of witnesses who claim they saw or experienced the event or activity in question?

8. The use of direct observation as a means of fact finding is problematic for both agencies and courts. Are the on-site observations of a decisionmaker hearsay? Valuable evidence? Evidence at all? If an observation cannot be "confronted," can it be the basis of a decision? How we visually assess a situation is a complex process – one might draw conclusions and make judgments based on observations affected (knowingly or unknowingly) by preconceived notions about the event or activity.

a. *Cowan v. Bunting Glider Co.*, 49 A.2d 270 (Pa. Super. Ct. 1946).

On October 28, 1942, claimant, who was employed in defendant's "dipping department", [went] to the men's room. Before he left his station he washed his hands in naphtha in an effort to remove paint from them. Upon arriving at the men's room, . . . he struck a match preparatory to lighting a cigarette, his sweater caught fire and he was severely burned, losing the industrial use of his right hand. These facts are not disputed, and the case presents only one controverted question: Was the act of smoking such a violation of the employer's direct and positive order as to take claimant out of the course of his employment and thereby preclude him from compensation?

The record shows that defendant had promulgated a general rule forbidding smoking and had placed "No Smoking" signs at various points in the plant. However, [t]here is evidence to the effect that claimant, on numerous occasions and in the company of others, used the men's room as a smoking rendezvous, and that this practice was known to defendant's supervisory officials. . . . [T]he board deemed it advisable to make a personal visit to the plant . . . . While there it observed that the floor of the men's room was littered with cigarette butts, and, partly, perhaps mainly on that ground, the board found that the company had condoned smoking, at least in the men's room.

This, the court below properly condemned because the personal observations of the board were not buttressed by evidence introduced into the record, and because they related to a time too remote from the date of the accident. Triers of fact, be they judges, jurors, viewers, board or commissions, may always visit and inspect the locus in quo to secure a better understanding of the evidence and to enable them to determine the relative weight of conflicting testimony. But a view cannot replace testimony; . . . the only legitimate purpose of an inspection is to illustrate the evidence and provide a base for understanding and comprehending testimony upon the record. . . . The privilege to confront witnesses, to cross-examine them, to refute them, and to have a record of their testimony is not a mere technical rule. It is a fundamental right, without which the prime essentials of a fair trial, according to Anglo-American standards of justice, are not preserved. . . .

b. *Tarpley v. Hornyak*, 174 S.W.3d 736 (Tenn. Ct. App. 2004).

This dispute involves a [bridge] built by Wilson County landowners Bert and Dorothy Hornyak. Their upstream neighbors, Ernest and Mary Nell Tarpley, claimed that the drainage culverts under the structure were inadequate to carry the volume of water flowing down the creek in wet and rainy times, causing the Tarpleys' fields to flood . . . . The Tarpleys filed a Complaint to Abate Nuisance in the Chancery Court of Wilson County alleging that because of its faulty construction, the bridge essentially functioned as a dam for creek waters. The plaintiffs asked the court to order the structure removed . . . . A trial was begun. . . .

During [the first cross examination] the chancellor interrupted . . . . [T]he judge announced . . . that he would be happy for the parties to put on all the proof they wanted, but that from their opening statements, it appeared they were going to testify in direct contradiction to each other on the question of whether the bridge caused flooding. The judge reasoned that a continuance of the case would not cause either party any harm, and declared that he did not want to make a decision until he or the Clerk and Master had the opportunity to witness the flooding in person. He accordingly instructed the plaintiffs' attorney to contact the [court] when and if flooding occurred again . . . .

Eight months after the trial began, the Tarpleys reported an incident of flooding . . . . Their attorney notified the [court]. The Clerk and Master and the Chancellor drove to the site, as did the Tarpleys' attorney. . . . The Chancellor spent about half an hour viewing the creek and the flooding . . . . The Chancellor subsequently placed a three-way call between himself and the two attorneys, in which he announced his judgment. . . . He declared that the bridge was a nuisance, ordered its removal, and stated that he would hold all other matters in abeyance pending a party setting a hearing on the issue of damages and attorney fees. . . .

> [A] trial judge has the inherent discretion to [view a site], where such a view will enable the judge to assess the credibility of witnesses, to resolve conflicting evidence, or to obtain a clearer understanding of the issues. However, the view cannot . . . replace the requirement that evidence be produced at trial . . . . Applying those principles to the case before us, it is clear that the judgment of the trial court must be reversed. The trial court's finding that the bridge or crossover caused the property to flood is unsupported by any evidence in the record other than [the first witness], and his cross-examination was cut short. . . .

There is a modest constitutional dimension to the question of the general use of hearsay and the "relaxed" evidentiary standards an agency follows. The case below examines some of the diluted evidentiary precepts agencies follow from the perspective of the Due Process Clause.

BROCK V. ROADWAY EXPRESS, INC.

481 U.S. 252 (1987)

[JUSTICE MARSHALL] Appellee Roadway Express, Inc., is a large interstate trucking company engaged primarily in cargo transportation . . . . On November 22, 1983, Roadway discharged one of its drivers, Jerry Hufstetler, alleging that he had disabled several lights on his assigned truck in order to obtain extra pay while waiting for repairs. Hufstetler filed a grievance, contending that he had not been discharged for an "act of dishonesty" . . . but rather . . . in retaliation for having previously complained of safety violations. The grievance was submitted to arbitration, which ultimately resulted in a ruling on January 30, 1984, that Hufstetler had been properly discharged.

On February 7, 1984, Hufstetler filed a complaint with the Department of Labor alleging that his discharge had violated § 405. . . . An OSHA field investigator interviewed Hufstetler and other Roadway employees and obtained statements substantiating Hufstetler's retaliatory discharge claim. Roadway was afforded an opportunity to meet with the investigator and submit a written statement detailing the basis for Hufstetler's discharge, but it was not provided with the names of the other witnesses or the substance of their statements. . . . Following review of [this] evidence . . . the Department of Labor Regional Administrator . . . issued a preliminary decision ordering Hufstetler's immediate reinstatement with backpay. Without detailing the evidence relied upon for this decision, the order stated that the Secretary of Labor had found reasonable cause to believe Hufstetler had been discharged in violation of § 405 for having previously complained about the safety of Roadway's trucks. . . .

Roadway then filed the present action . . . seeking an injunction against enforcement of the Secretary's order and a declaratory judgment that § 405 was unconstitutional to the extent it empowered the Secretary to order temporary reinstatement without first conducting an evidentiary hearing. . . .

. . . .

Section 405 was enacted in 1983 to encourage employee reporting of non-compliance with safety regulations governing commercial motor vehicles. Congress recognized that employees in the transportation industry are often best able to detect safety violations and yet, because they may be threatened with discharge for cooperating with enforcement agencies, they need express protection against retaliation for reporting these violations. Section 405 protects employee "whistle-blowers" by forbidding discharge, discipline, or other forms of discrimination by the employer in response to an employee's complaining about or refusing to operate motor vehicles that do not meet the applicable safety standards.

Congress also recognized that the employee's protection against having to choose between operating an unsafe vehicle and losing his job would lack practical effectiveness if the employee could not be reinstated pending complete review. The longer a discharged employee remains unemployed, the more devastating are the consequences to his personal financial condition and prospects for reemployment. Ensuring the eventual recovery of backpay may not alone provide sufficient protection to encourage reports of safety violations. Accordingly, § 405 incorporates additional protections, authorizing temporary reinstatement based on a preliminary finding of reasonable cause to believe that the employee has suffered a retaliatory discharge. . . .

The statute does not specify procedures for employer participation in the Secretary's investigation, other than to require that the employer be notified of the employee's complaint. . . . The standard procedures which governed the investigation of Hufstetler's complaint against Roadway in this case required that Roadway be notified "of the complaint and of the substance of the allegation" and . . . that the . . . investigator consult with Roadway to obtain its explanation for the discharge before the Secretary made any findings and issued a preliminary reinstatement order. The current implementing rules [include] an opportunity to . . . submit statements from witnesses supporting the employer's position.

Neither set of procedures, however, requires that . . . the Secretary . . . hold an evidentiary hearing and allow the employer to cross-examine the witnesses from whom the investigator has obtained statements supporting the employee's complaint [or] divulge the names of these individuals or the substance of their statements before the preliminary reinstatement order takes effect. Roadway claims that the lack of an evidentiary hearing and the confidentiality of the investigator's evidence operate to deny employers procedural due process under the Fifth Amendment. . . . [T]he Secretary concedes that the contractual right to discharge an employee for cause constitutes a property interest protected by the Fifth Amendment.

[T]he Court has upheld procedures affording less than a full evidentiary hearing if "some kind of a hearing" ensuring an effective "initial check against mistaken decisions" is provided before the deprivation occurs, and a prompt opportunity for complete administrative and judicial review is available. _Loudermill_. Determining the adequacy of predeprivation procedures requires consideration of the Government's interest in imposing the temporary deprivation, the private interests of those affected by the deprivation, the risk of erroneous deprivations through the challenged procedures, and the probable value of additional or substitute procedural safeguards. _Mathews_. In the present case, the District Court assessed these factors and determined that § 405 was "unconstitutional and void to the extent that it empowers [the Secretary] to order reinstatement of discharged employees prior to conducting an evidentiary hearing which comports with the minimum requirements of due process." . . . . Our consideration of the relevant factors leads us to a different conclusion.

We begin by accepting as substantial the Government's interests in promoting highway safety and protecting employees from retaliatory discharge. Roadway does not question the legislative determination that noncompliance with applicable state and federal safety regulations in the transportation industry is sufficiently widespread to warrant enactment of specific protective legislation encouraging employees to report violations. . . .

We also agree with the District Court that Roadway's interest in controlling the makeup of its work force is substantial. In assessing the competing interests, however, the District Court failed to consider . . . Hufstetler's interest in not being discharged for having complained about the allegedly unsafe condition of Roadway's trucks. This Court has previously acknowledged the "severity of depriving a person of the means of livelihood." _Loudermill_. . . . The statute reflects a careful balancing of "the strong Congressional policy that persons reporting health and safety violations should not suffer because of this action" and the need "to assure that employers are provided protection from unjustified refusal by their employees to perform legitimate assigned tasks."

Reviewing this legislative balancing of interests, we conclude that the employer is sufficiently protected by procedures that do not include an evidentiary hearing before the discharged employee is temporarily reinstated [s]o long as the prereinstatement procedures establish a reliable "initial check against mistaken decisions," *Loudermill*, and complete and expeditious review is available . . . .

We thus confront the . . . question whether the Secretary's procedures implementing § 405 reliably protect against the risk of erroneous deprivation, even if only temporary, of an employer's right to discharge an employee. We conclude that minimum due process for the employer in this context requires notice of the employee's allegations, notice of the substance of the relevant supporting evidence, an opportunity to submit a written response, and an opportunity to meet with the investigator and present statements from rebuttal witnesses. . . . [C]ross-examination of the employee's witnesses need not be afforded at this stage of the proceedings.

. . . .

The Secretary represents that it is the practice of Department of Labor investigators to inform employers of the substance of the evidence supporting employees' allegations. Though we do not find this practice expressed in the field manuals for OSHA investigators or in the Secretary's new regulations, we accept the representation as embodying an established, official procedure for implementing § 405 of which employers are specifically made aware. It is undisputed, however, that in this case the procedure was not followed, for Roadway requested and was denied access to the information upon which the Secretary based the order for Hufstetler's preliminary reinstatement. Given this circumstance, the District Court correctly held that Roadway had been denied a due process protection to which it was entitled, and we affirm the order of summary judgment in that respect.

Notice of an employee's complaint of retaliatory discharge and of the relevant supporting evidence would be of little use if an avenue were not available through which the employer could effectively articulate its response. On this score, assuming the employer is informed of the substance of the evidence supporting the employee's complaint, the Secretary's current procedures allowing the employer to submit a written response, including affidavits and supporting documents, and to meet with the investigator to respond verbally to the employee's charges and present statements from the employer's witnesses, satisfy the due process requirements for reliability. Except for the Secretary's failure to inform Roadway of the evidence supporting Hufstetler's complaint, similar procedures were followed in this case. . . . To allow the employer and employee an opportunity to test the credibility of opposing witnesses during the investigation would not increase the reliability of the preliminary decision sufficiently to justify the additional delay. Moreover, the primary function of the investigator is not to make credibility determinations, but rather to determine simply whether reasonable cause exists to believe that the employee has been discharged for engaging in protected conduct. Ensuring the employer a meaningful opportunity to respond to the employee's complaint and supporting evidence maintains the principal focus on the employee's conduct and the employer's reason for his discharge. . . .

Roadway finally argues that requiring an evidentiary hearing as part of the process leading to preliminary reinstatement would not impose a significant additional burden on the Secretary since a subsequent evidentiary hearing must be "expeditiously conducted" in any event. Again, however, Roadway's suggested approach would undoubtedly delay issuance of the Secretary's order of reinstatement. In addition to the extra time required for the hearing itself, this approach would provide an incentive for employers to engage in dilatory tactics. Added delay at this stage of the Secretary's proceedings would further undermine the ability of employees to obtain a means of livelihood, and unfairly tip the statute's balance of interests against them. This is not to say, however, that the employer's interest in an expeditious resolution of the employee's complaint can never provide a basis for a due process violation. . . . [However, because] the procedural posture of this case has not allowed factual development on the issue, we decline to decide whether the delay Roadway has encountered, or the delays authorized in the Secretary's new regulations, are so excessive as to constitute a violation of due process.

. . . .

Affirmed in part and reversed in part.

Underlying Case Documents

The case referenced:
Section 405
The notice of discharge
The grievance
The ruling that Hufstetler had been properly discharged
The preliminary decision by the department of labor

1. *Brock* raises important questions that go to the core of a fair hearing – and also to the heart of various disputes in the private and public labor law fields. Assume that prior to the imposition of a sanction (which in *Brock* included an order to rehire an employee an employer deemed unfit) there is a right to a hearing. *Loudermill* makes clear there is a right to notice and an opportunity to be heard based on fundamental fairness and due process – but more specifically, what does that

entail? While *Mathews v. Eldridge* is a good starting point, it may not help you come to closure.

Brock poses the question of the extent to which one is entitled to investigative reports, witness lists, and similar information that would reveal the backbone of an opponent's case.

In *Bechtel v. Competitive Techs., Inc (CTI).*, 448 F.3d 469 (2d Cir. 2006), plaintiff sued to enforce an order of reinstatement issued by the Secretary of Labor after it was determined that plaintiff's discharge was in violation of 18 U.S.C.S. § 1514(A). That statute is part of the Sarbanes-Oxley legislation and is designed to protect whistleblowers employed by privately owned, publically traded companies. The statute read: "No company with a class of securities registered under section 12 of the Securities Exchange Act of 1934 (15 U.S.C. 78l) . . . may discharge, demote, suspend, threaten, harass, or in any other manner discriminate against an employee in the terms and conditions of employment because of any lawful act done by the employee. . . ." The employee, Bechtel, claimed he was fired because "he had raised concerns with management about CTI's financial reporting." The majority concluded that the statute involved conferred no direct enforcement authority to the courts at the point the case was brought by Bechtel and refused to consider the due process questions discussed below. The concurring and dissenting opinions, however, are good examples of the due process issues *Brock* raises.

First is an excerpt from JUDGE LEVAL's concurrence:

> In *Brock*, a majority of the Justices held that due process did not require an evidentiary hearing prior to the preliminary reinstatement order. However, a different majority held that Roadway's due process rights had been violated because it was not informed, prior to the preliminary reinstatement order, what evidence had been submitted to the Secretary in support of the employee's allegations. . . . [M]inimum due process for the employer in this context requires notice of the employee's allegations, notice of the substance of the relevant supporting evidence, an opportunity to submit a written response, and an opportunity to meet with the investigator and present statements from rebuttal witnesses . . . . [D]ue process required the Secretary of Labor to inform the employer of the substance of the evidence supporting the employee's allegations. [Quotations omitted.]
>
> [The] Secretary gave CTI a copy of Bechtel's initial complaint, a description of the allegations, and opportunities to submit written responses to those allegations and to present statements from rebuttal witnesses. An OSHA investigator also met with CTI's counsel on at least two occasions. However, based on the record before us, CTI was not given reasonable notice of the evidence against it. CTI repeatedly asked OSHA to provide it with copies of statements by Bechtel or witness statements that supported Bechtel's allegations. On July 2, 2004, CTI was provided with a two-page purported summary of witness statements. The document, however, does not name any of the witnesses against CTI. Nor does it mention the undisclosed oral revenue-sharing agreements or whistleblowing regarding those agreements – the very grounds for the

preliminary order of reinstatement. Most important, the "summary" is not a summary at all, but a mishmash of disconnected sentences that does not provide a coherent or comprehensible picture of the evidence against CTI. . . .

I express no view on this question – that summaries of witness statements, redacted to maintain the confidentiality of witnesses' identities, are consistent with Brock's requirements. But even assuming this to be the case, the summaries must be sufficient to provide an employer with reasonable notice of the evidence against it – a standard that was not satisfied here. Moreover, confidentiality interests cannot explain the Secretary's failure to provide CTI with copies, or even coherent summaries, of Bechtel's own statements, as his identity as a source of complaints about his employer was known. . . .

Dissenting JUDGE STRAUB saw things differently:

Brock . . . explained that, in determining how much process is due, courts must weigh three sets of "substantial" interests: 1) the government's interest in encouraging whistleblowing; 2) the employer's interest in controlling the makeup of its staff; and 3) the employee's interest in his livelihood (which depends not merely on receiving backpay but also on being able to find another job). Although an employer's interests must be protected by a pre-reinstatement investigative procedure that ensures a minimum degree of reliability, after a certain point the value of additional reliability is outweighed by the cost of "extending inordinately the period in which the employee must suffer unemployment." Ultimately, in the context of whistleblower actions, the inquiry boils down to whether "the pre-reinstatement procedures establish a reliable initial check against mistaken decisions, and complete and expeditious review is available."

In my view, this record reflects a methodical investigation and ample notice to CTI of the evidence, as well as the allegations, against it. Whether . . . the Department . . . should have provided any further information to CTI, its investigation constituted "a reliable initial check against mistaken decisions," . . . and therefore merits enforcement.

Can you tell after reading *Brock* and *Bechtel* whether an employer has a right to witness lists? Can you prepare for a hearing without that information? Is the goal of whistleblower protection compromised by providing more data for the hearing? Would other whistleblowers be intimidated?

2. *McCombs v. Barnhart*, 2004 WL 1662304 (7th Cir. 2004).

Ruth McCombs applied for disability benefits and supplemental security income, claiming that constant pain in her back and legs prevented her from working. . . . [A]n administrative law judge ("ALJ") concluded that she was not disabled. . . . McCombs then brought this action . . . . McCombs . . . argues that the ALJ erred when he discredited her subjective complaints of pain, because he failed to provide specific reasons for his credibility finding. . . .

[T]he ALJ's opinion does not mention any of the . . . extensive evidence in the record showing that numerous doctors both diagnosed and treated McCombs for pain in her lower back and legs. In 1995 McCombs saw Dr. Claude Foreit, Sr., a general physician, . . . he diagnosed scoliosis and mild degenerative changes in the spine . . . . Dr. Gordon Shaw . . . diagnosed "Mild Lumbar Scoliosis with Mild Degenerative Changes in LS Spine with Nerve Involvement." . . . . Dr. Niles diagnosed arthritis and degenerative disk disease at L5-S1. . . . Dr. Gonzalo Magsaysay . . . prescribed Propoxyphene and Chlorzoxazone to relieve her pain. In September 1998 an MRI was conducted after McCombs went to the emergency room . . . the physician reviewing the MRI diagnosed osteoarthritic and discogenic degenerative change with mild effacement at L4-L5 as well as mild encroachment on the left lateral recess at L3-L4. In November 2000 Dr. Antonela Svetic, a neurologist, prescribed Prednisone, Klonopin, Paxil, and Elavil for pain relief.

Since Social Security Ruling 96-7p specifically directs an ALJ to consider the consistency of a claimant's complaints and her treatment history, the ALJ's failure to discuss any of these records in his order makes it difficult at best for a reviewing court. . . . We conclude that the ALJ failed to connect the evidence before him with his conclusions. His apparent decision to discredit McCombs's testimony about her pain did not explain why he dismissed the substantial evidence corroborating the existence of that pain. . . . We have no choice but to remand her case to the agency for further proceedings. . . .

What was the affirmative obligation of the government in this case in terms of proof? Was the failure to correlate the record and the decision the fault of the government or the ALJ?

3. The case below is a starting point to deal with the question of technically generated evidence as it relates to the basic questions posed in *Brock*. When conclusions are made based on a computer program, who is the real witness – and what needs to be disclosed?

<u>*Wirtz v. Baldor Electric Company*, 337 F.2d 518 (D.C. Cir. 1963).</u>

[T]he Department of Labor instituted an administrative proceeding for the purpose of determining minimum wages [in] the electric motors and generators industry . . . . In connection with this proceeding, the Bureau of Labor Statistics ("BLS") of the Department of Labor [sent out a questionnaire,] which contained a pledge of confidentiality . . . . [From this information] BLS compiled six tables summarizing the wage data of 216 firms . . . . Of these firms, 212 had answered the questionnaire circulated by BLS and the data as to the other 4 firms (which had declined to answer) was estimated.

After the tables had been compiled, a hearing to determine the prevailing minimum wages in the industry . . . was scheduled . . . . Copies of the BLS wage tables were furnished to the National Electrical Manufacturers Association ("NEMA," appellees' trade association) about five weeks before the hearing date. Eight days before the hearing NEMA informed the Bureau that it had obtained from 61 companies . . . copies of their [questionnaire] answers and also independent data as to the wages paid by the companies; and that it (NEMA) had found discrepancies between the wage data given to it and the data reported to the Bureau. The Bureau examined the discrepancies cited and found that only two would affect the result. These lowered . . . the original estimates in the tables as to prevailing minimum wages. The day before the hearing NEMA applied to the Hearing Examiner for a subpoena duces tecum requiring the Commissioner of Labor Statistics to produce for inspection [t]he completed questionnaire forms [and other relevant information]. The Hearing Examiner denied the subpoena application.

At the hearing, the Government introduced . . . the six wage tables. . . . Counsel for NEMA thereupon unsuccessfully attempted to introduce affidavits by officials of several establishments stating that data had been erroneously reported to BLS by their companies. NEMA then moved to strike the . . . BLS wage tables, on the ground that [the] testimony "was based on a perusal of records which have not been made available to us and on the further ground that we are not being allowed to impeach [this] testimony . . . by offering these affidavits." This motion was denied. The affidavits were however admitted by agreement. On the basis of the affidavits BLS agreed to further revisions in the wage tables.

Secretary Goldberg, the predecessor of the appellant, . . . upheld the Hearing Examiner's rulings refusing to issue the subpoena, and denying NEMA's motion to strike the BLS wage tables . . . . The Secretary stated that –

> [T]he nearly universal response the Bureau was able to obtain in this survey . . . depends on giving and honoring assurances of confidential treatment – such as those involved here. . . .

There is of course no question as to the admissibility of the summary tabulations compiled by the Bureau. But it is also the general requirement that where tables of this kind are received in evidence, the documents supporting the tables and on which they are based must also be introduced or at least be made available to the opposing party to the extent that they are necessary for purposes of rebuttal and cross-examination. . . . The exhibits are admissible under the broad rule that administrative agencies are not bound by the ordinary rules of evidence. All the more scrupulous should be the effort on the part of the agency to extend to the litigant the right to test evidence thus admitted by the fullest possible cross-examination.

We are not without sympathy for the problems faced by the Secretary, but we have found nothing in the [relevant acts] which would empower us to release the Secretary from conforming to the procedural commands of the controlling statutes because of such considerations. . . . It does not follow, however, that courts will generally force the Government to reveal information it seeks to keep confidential. The Government, in situations of the present sort, has an option: it can hold back confidential material, and take the risk of not being able to prove its case, or it can produce the material and allow it to be the subject of direct and cross-examination. . . .

We must necessarily conclude that the admission of the wage tabulations compiled from undisclosed confidential data, as to which we will not compel disclosure, failed to accord to appellees the adequate opportunity for rebuttal and cross-examination that the Congress prescribed. . . .

a. We see *Wirtz* as the start of long and interesting journey regarding the far broader topic of computer generated evidence. Between 1963 and 2008, there have been hundreds of cases, articles, and treatises dealing with the topic, and yet in *Lorraine v. Markel American Insurance Co.*, 241 F.R.D. 534, 537 (D. Md. 2007), the court noted:

> Although cases abound regarding the discoverability of electronic records, research has failed to locate a comprehensive analysis of the many interrelated evidentiary issues associated with electronic evidence. Because there is a need for guidance to the bar regarding this subject, this opinion undertakes a broader and more detailed analysis of these issues. . . .

Indeed, the court goes on for 85 pages to discuss the topic – an opinion worth reading if the need arises.

b. In some ways, Federal Rule of Evidence 901(b)(9) addresses the question of validity, authentication, and foundational requirements. Authentication requires "[e]vidence describing a process or system used to produce a result and showing that the process or system produces an accurate result." This rule is meant for circumstances in which the validity and probative value of the evidence is affected primarily by the legitimacy of the system used to develop that evidence. The Advisory Committee notes for 901(b)(9) state

> it is common for the proponent to provide evidence of the input procedures and their accuracy, and evidence that the computer was regularly tested for programming errors. At a minimum, the proponent should present evidence sufficient to warrant a finding that the information is trustworthy. . . .

c. In *American Export Travel Related Services v. Vinhnee (Re Vee Vinhnee)*, 336 B.R. 437, 446 (B.A.P. 9th Cir. 2005), the court set out an eleven-step process for "foundational authentication" for computer generated records, relying on EDWARD J. IMWINKELRIED, EVIDENTIARY FOUNDATIONS § 4.03[2] (5th ed. 2002). We note two important caveats: (1) These rules – including the Federal Rules of Evidence – are useful guidance but do not bind administrative agencies and (2) an eleven-step process is probably more than any agency requires – but valuable to study and think through.

d. We leave for your Evidence class and beyond the question of whether computer generated evidence is hearsay – and if so, whether it is admissible as a public or business record, *compare* Adam Wolfson, Note, *"Electronic Fingerprints": Doing Away with the Conception of Computer-Generated Records as Hearsay*, 104 MICH. L. REV. 151 (2005), *with* Leach Voigt Romano, *Developments in the Law IV: Electronic Evidence and the Federal Rules*, 38 LOYOLA L.A.L. REV. 1745 (2005), or whether such evidence is not hearsay. *See United States v. Hamilton*, 413 F.3d 1138, 1142 (10th Cir. 2005); *United States v. Khorozian*, 333 F.3d 498, 505 (3d Cir. 2003); *State v. Armstead*, 432 So.2d 837, 842-43 (La. 1983).

4. The release of the names of survey respondents in *Wirtz* allows for the verification of information vital to the resolution of a claim but does not resolve many issues pertaining to the release of underlying data, not the least of which are privacy concerns, as the following case suggests.

<u>United States Department of Defense v. Federal Labor Relations Authority</u>, 510 U.S. 487 (1994).

> The controversy underlying this case arose when two local unions requested the petitioner federal agencies to provide them with the names and home addresses of the agency employees in the bargaining units represented by the unions. The agencies supplied the unions with the employees' names and work stations, but refused to release home addresses [arguing] that disclosure of the home addresses was prohibited by the Privacy Act of 1974. . . .
>
> It is true that home addresses often are publicly available through sources such as telephone directories and voter registration lists, but [a]n individual's interest in controlling the dissemination of information regarding personal matters does not dissolve simply because that information may be available to the public in some form. Here, for the most part, the unions seek to obtain the addresses of nonunion employees who have decided not to reveal their addresses to their exclusive representative. . . . Whatever the reason that these employees have chosen not to become members of the union or to provide the union with their addresses, however, it is clear that they have some nontrivial privacy interest in nondisclosure, and in avoiding the influx of union-related mail, and, perhaps, union-related telephone calls or visits, that would follow disclosure. . . . We are reluctant to disparage the privacy of the home, which is accorded special consideration in our Constitution, laws, and traditions. . . .
>
> [R]espondents contend that our decision creates an unnecessary and unintended disparity between public and private sector unions. While private sector unions assertedly are entitled to receive employee home address lists from employers under the <u>National Labor Relations Act</u> . . . respondents claim that federal sector unions now will be needlessly barred from obtaining this information, despite the lack of any indication that Congress intended such a result. . . . We do not question that, as a general matter, private sector labor law may provide guidance in parallel public sector matters. This fact has little relevance here, however, for unlike private sector employees, federal employees enjoy the protection of the Privacy Act, and that statute prohibits the disclosure of the address lists sought in this case. To the extent that this prohibition leaves public sector unions in a position different from that of their private sector counterparts, Congress may correct the disparity.
>
> While there is little question about the prevalence of electronic evidence both in Article III tribunals and agencies, there is some healthy discussion about both the uniform reliability and admissibility of such information.

There is an interesting and not particularly uniform group of cases regarding disclosure of similar lists and FOIA. *See <u>Nat'l Ass'n of Home Builders v. Norton</u>, 309 F.3d 26 (D.C. Cir. 2002)*; <u>*Hughes Salaried Retirees Action Comm. v. Adm'r of the Hughes Non-Bargaining Ret. Plan*</u>, 72 F.3d 686 (9th Cir. 1995); <u>*Consumers' Check-*</u>

book v. United States Health and Human Services, 502 F. Supp. 2d 79 (D.D.C. 2007); Martin E. Halstuk, *When Secrecy Trumps Transparency: Why the Open Government Act of 2007 Falls Short*, 16 COMMLAW CONSPECTUS 427 (2008).

The materials that follow briefly raise the question of conflict of interest in the practice of administrative law. It is not unusual in the course of a career for a lawyer to move from the private sector to government or from government practice to the private sector. When these career transitions occur, the potential for a conflict of interest arises. Obviously, if one has had a substantial and personal involvement in a pending case on one side, it is unethical to jump ship and serve as counsel to the other side, thereby making use of confidential information or attorney work product secured in one's initial role. Beyond that obvious conflict, however, are more subtle questions. The cases that follow allow for a discussion of the conflict of interest challenges for those involved in government service and in private practice.

LASALLE NATIONAL BANK V. COUNTY OF LAKE

703 F.2d 252 (7th Cir. 1983)

[JUDGE CUDAHY] This case confronts us with some of the ethical problems involved when a former government attorney takes up the practice of law with a large law firm. Lake County, Illinois, one of the parties to this appeal, is the former employer of an attorney now practicing law with the firm representing the plaintiffs-appellants. Lake County moved to disqualify the plaintiffs' law firm because of the County's former relationship with one of the firm's associates. The district court granted the motion . . . . We affirm . . . .

I

. . . On December 1, 1976, Mr. Seidler was appointed Chief of the Civil Division of the Lake County State's Attorney's office . . . . As such, he had general supervisory responsibility with respect to all civil cases handled by the State's Attorney's office. On February 2, 1981, Mr. Seidler joined the Chicago law firm of Rudnick & Wolfe as an associate . . . .

On June 5, 1981, Rudnick & Wolfe filed suit against the County of Lake and the Village of Grayslake, on behalf of its clients, the LaSalle National Bank as Trustee ("LaSalle National") and Lake Properties Venture ("Lake Properties"). LaSalle National and Lake Properties are the owners of a tract of land, known as Heartland, located in the Village of Round Lake Park, an Illinois municipal corporation situated in Lake County. Rudnick & Wolfe has represented these two clients since January 1976 in connection with plans to develop the Heartland property as a mixed-use, low-density development. This representation has included all legal work necessary for implementing the development . . . . After failing in a 1979 attempt to secure annexation of the Heartland property to the Village of Grayslake, the plaintiffs negotiated annexation of the property by the Village of Round Lake Park, a process which was completed on January 9, 1981. The plaintiffs allege that on the date of the annexation, they were already planning a law suit to challenge the probable denial by the Village of Grayslake of their request for access to the County's interceptor sewer system. . . . [This was the] complaint filed on June 5, 1981 . . . .

The Lake County-Grayslake Sewage Disposal Agreement was signed prior to Mr. Seidler's association with the State's Attorney's office, and he was not involved in consideration of the validity or impact of the Agreement upon the Heartland property in particular. However, the Lake County-Grayslake Agreement was one of several similar agreements executed between the County and various municipalities. Mr. Seidler was, moreover, in charge of the Civil Division in a [six person] legal department during the period when the Grayslake Agreement was in effect and was privy to discussions about the validity of such sewage agreements in general. Specifically, it is alleged that Mr. Seidler had access to . . . an opinion letter about the validity of the Agreement prepared by bond counsel for the County and a memorandum expressing the views of one County Board member on the Agreement. Some of these documents were subsequently made public. When County officials requested that the State's Attorney's office prepare a formal legal opinion about the Agreement, Seidler was assigned responsibility for its preparation. The request was subsequently withdrawn and the opinion never written, but Seidler did review the relevant documents in preparation for writing it. He was also involved in consideration of the validity of similar agreements in relation to sewer service for property other than Heartland and participated in discussion about, and the formulation of legal strategies concerning, those agreements. On the basis of Seidler's involvement in these matters, the County moved to disqualify both Seidler and the entire Rudnick & Wolfe firm.

Mr. Seidler has submitted a sworn affidavit stating that he has not disclosed to his law firm or any of its personnel any information about the Agreement, about the County's legal strategy or about any other matter relevant to the present litigation. In addition, Theodore J. Novak, a partner at Rudnick & Wolfe involved in the representation of Lake Properties, has filed an affidavit swearing that Mr. Seidler had been screened from all involvement in the litigation since the motion to disqualify was filed.

II

. . . We will therefore consider, first, whether the district court abused its discretion in holding that Mr. Seidler must be disqualified, and second, whether, if he was properly disqualified, the law firm of Rudnick & Wolfe must also be disqualified from representing the plaintiffs in its suit against Mr. Seidler's former employer.

III

The standard for disqualification of an attorney who undertakes litigation against a former client is the so-called "substantial relationship" test . . . . The test has been described by this circuit as embodying the substance of Canon 4 of the A.B.A. Code of Professional Responsibility, which protects the confidences of a client against disclosure and possible use against him, and of Canon 9, which provides that an attorney must avoid even the appearance of impropriety. Thus, the question before a district court considering a motion for disqualification is "whether it could reasonably be said that during the former representation the attorney might have acquired information related to the subject matter of the subsequent representation." . . . . [To determine this] a three-level inquiry [must] be undertaken . . . . First, the trial judge must make a factual reconstruction of the scope of the prior legal representation. Second, it must be determined whether it is reasonable to infer that the confidential information allegedly given would have been given to a lawyer representing a client in those matters. Third, it must be determined whether that information is relevant to the issues raised in the litigation pending against the former client. . . . If . . . we find that such a substantial relationship did exist, we are entitled to presume that the attorney received confidential information during his prior representation. This presumption, however, is a rebuttable one. . . . [W]ith respect to all these determinations, we must accept the conclusions of the district court unless we find that there has been an abuse of discretion.

A

. . . As to the first prong of the substantial relationship test, . . . Seidler contends that the scope of [his] prior representation did not include the subject of the present litigation because he was not substantially involved in the particular matter at issue – the application of the Lake County-Grayslake Agreement to the Heartland property. However, Seidler was the County's principal legal advisor with respect to all civil matters, supervising an office with only six attorneys in it. Although he may not have been involved in the precise subject of this litigation, he was clearly privy to a substantial amount of discussion and strategic thinking about the various sewage agreements negotiated and signed by Lake County with various municipalities over a period of time when the validity of such agreements was being challenged. The validity of one of those substantially identical agreements is the subject of a broad-based challenge in the lawsuit at hand. We therefore [agree] that the subject matter of the present litigation fell within the scope of Mr. Seidler's previous representation.

Applying the second prong . . . we find that it is reasonable to infer that confidential information about the County's legal analysis and strategies relating to the validity of the various sewage agreements would have been given to an attorney who was the chief of the civil division of the State's Attorney's office during that time. In fact, the record contains uncontroverted evidence that Mr. Seidler's advice was sought on the very Agreement in question in the present litigation. He does not deny, moreover, that he was substantially involved in representation of the County regarding the sewage agreements signed with other municipalities or applied to other parcels of land. His own affidavits and the evidence of memoranda contained within his files at the State's Attorney's office make clear that he received a great deal of information about the Grayslake Agreement. The substantial relationship standard does not require that a party moving to disqualify point to or reveal a particular piece of confidential information which the attorney challenged actually received; its receipt will be presumed in circumstances which make it a likely possibility. We therefore [agree] that it was reasonable to infer that confidential information . . . would have been given to an attorney in Mr. Seidler's former position.

Applying the third prong . . . we have no difficulty finding that information about the validity of the various sewage agreements signed by Lake County is relevant to the issues raised in the litigation now pending against the County. . . . Mr. Seidler not only had information about the Agreement challenged here but would presumably be a likely person, as principal legal advisor to the County on civil matters, to have knowledge about the County's attitude or policy toward the extension of sewer services in general. We therefore [agree] that the subjects of his past and present representation were substantially related.

. . . Mr. Seidler submitted an affidavit that he had received no information specific to the Grayslake Agreement or to application of the Agreement to the Heartland property. However, after considering the pleadings in this case, we have decided that information relating to any of the similar sewage agreements or to the attitude or policies of Lake County toward provision of sewer service in general to new developments is relevant to the issues in the present litigation. Mr. Seidler does not deny that he was privy to information about these other matters. Moreover, considering the small size of the State's Attorney's office and Mr. Seidler's position as supervisor of all the civil legal work there, we cannot say that the presumption raised by the substantial relationship test has been clearly and persuasively rebutted. Since we are required to resolve any doubts in favor of disqualification, we therefore hold that the district court did not abuse its discretion by disqualifying Marc Seidler from representing the plaintiffs in this litigation.

IV

Having found that Mr. Seidler was properly disqualified from representation of the plaintiffs in this case, we must now address whether this disqualification should be extended to the entire law firm of Rudnick & Wolfe. Although the knowledge possessed by one attorney in a law firm is presumed to be shared with the other attorneys in the firm this court has held that this presumption may be rebutted. . . . [Seidler was screened from the date of the motion to disqualify.]

Although this court has rejected screening in a situation involving simultaneous representation of adverse interests by different offices of a large law firm, it has never directly confronted this issue in a situation such as that presented here. Other circuits, however, have begun to address the problems which arise when attorneys leaving government service join large law firms [and allowed screening to prevent disqualification of the entire firm]. Scholarly commentary has also generally approved screening as a device to avoid the wholesale disqualification of law firms with which former government attorneys are associated.

The screening arrangements which courts and commentators have approved, however, contain certain common characteristics. The attorney involved in [one] case, for example, was denied access to relevant files and did not share in the profits or fees derived from the representation in question; discussion of the suit was prohibited in his presence and no members of the firm were permitted to show him any documents relating to the case; and both the disqualified attorney and others in his firm affirmed these facts under oath. The screening approved in [another] case was similarly specific: all other attorneys in the firm were forbidden to discuss the case with the disqualified attorney and instructed to prevent any documents from reaching him; the files were kept in a locked file cabinet, with the keys controlled by two partners and issued to others only on a "need to know" basis. In both cases, moreover . . . the screening arrangement was set up at the time when the potentially disqualifying event occurred, either when the attorney first joined the firm or when the firm accepted a case presenting an ethical problem.

In the case at hand, by contrast, Mr. Seidler joined the firm of Rudnick & Wolfe on February 2, 1981; yet screening arrangements were not established until the disqualification motion was filed in August 1981. Although Mr. Seidler states in his affidavit that he did not disclose to any person associated with the firm any information about the validity of the Agreement or the County's strategy on any matter relevant to this litigation, no specific institutional mechanisms were in place to insure that that information was not shared, even if inadvertently, between the months of February and August. Recognizing that this is an area in which the relevant information is singularly within the ken of the party defending against the motion to disqualify . . . we hold that the district court did not abuse its discretion in extending the disqualification of Marc Seidler to the entire firm of Rudnick & Wolfe. The district court order is therefore affirmed.

———————

1. Switching from public to private sector practice (or vice-versa) is guided by a variety of ethical considerations as well as 18 U.S.C. § 207, a criminal statute that sets out guidelines for those contemplating such a change. The rule is not all that difficult: If one has "participated personally and substantially as such officer or employee," in a case, they are barred from involvement in that same matter on the other side. There is a two-year period for lesser involvement and also fairly new regulations at 5 C.F.R. § 2637.205 that detail a "cooling off period" for federal employees moving to the private sector. *See* http://edocket.access.gpo. gov/C.F.R._2007/janqtr/5C.F.R.2637.205.htm (last visited June 20, 2008).

As clear as these limitations appear at first blush, in practice, they can be the source of significant interpretive challenges. Recent case law and state law advisory opinions in the area on conflict and disqualification are abundant. *See, e.g., Sorci v. Iowa Dist. Court, 671 N.W.2d 482 (Iowa 2007); In re Advisory Committee on Professional Ethics Opinion 705, A-74, 926 A.2d 839 (N.J. 2007); In re Application of the Okla. Bar Ass'n to Amend the Rules of Prof'l Conduct, 171 P.3d 780 (Okla. 2007).*

2. Is the problem one of incentives? Do those contemplating a career in government need assurances that they will be able to participate in private practice if they decide to bring their public service to a close? More than a half-century ago, Judge Kaufman framed the debate: "If the Government service will tend to sterilize an attorney in too large an area of law for too long a time, or will prevent [one] from engaging in the practice of a technical specialty which [one] had devoted years in acquiring, and if that sterilization will spread to the firm with which [one] becomes associated, the sacrifice of entering government service will be too great for most . . . to make. Irving R. Kaufman, *The Former Government Attorney and the Canons of Professional Ethics, 70 Harv. L. Rev. 657, 668 (1957). See* Benjamin Civiletti, *Disqualifying Former Government Lawyers, 7 Lit. 8 (1981);* Philip A. Lacovara, *Restricting the Private Practice of Former Government Lawyers, 20 Ariz. L. Rev. 369, 387-90 (1978).*

The mechanism of screening plays a role of consequence in addressing Judge Kaufman's concerns, as the *LaSalle* case points out. For comparison, see *Armstrong v. McAlpin, 625 F.2d 433, 443-44 (2d Cir. 1980)* (screening private section lawyers after a period of government service), *vacated on other grounds*, 449 U.S. 1106 (1981). Parenthetically, the American Bar Association's Code of Professional Responsibility discusses screening devices only in terms of former government lawyers.

3. These two excerpts provide a comparison to assess conflict solely in the private sector.

a. *Cobb Publishing v. Hearst Corporation, and Dow Jones & Co.*, 907 F. Supp. 1038 (D. Mich. 1995).

> Plaintiffs Cobb Publishing, Inc. . . . filed suit charging Defendants Hearst Corporation, and Dow Jones and Co., with . . . violation of copyright protection laws, and breach of contract. Defendants . . . retained the law firm of Miller, Canfield, Paddock and Stone (hereinafter MC) to represent them. . . . Plaintiff Cobb filed a Motion to Disqualify Defendants' Counsel as a result of MC's hiring of BK attorney Steven Cohen on August 8, 1994, during the pendency of this litigation. . . . Plaintiff Cobb was initially represented by three BK attorneys [including] Cohen. Cohen spent the greatest amount of time on the case, approximately 300 hours, and had an extensive amount of contact with Plaintiff Cobb. . . .
>
> During the first week of July 1994, Cohen informed Vanderkloot, MC's recruiting coordinator, that his practice at BK created a conflict of interest since MC represented an adversary party on a case. No comprehensive firm-wide screen or wall was erected at MC . . . when Cohen was hired on August 8, 1994 [or] on August 15th when Cohen began work . . . . Plaintiff's Motion to Disqualify Defendants' Counsel was filed on August 22, 1994. . . . MC erected and noticed a firm-wide screen or wall to its staff on August 26, 1994. . . .
>
> The Sixth Circuit set forth two independent issues for determination. First, it must be demonstrated by the firm to which the "infected" attorney transfers, that the transferee has not shared his prior firm's confidences with members of his new firm. In the instant case this Court finds that MC has demonstrated through Cohen's testimony and [various] affidavits . . . that Cohen did not share Cobb's confidences with others at MC.
>
> Second, the transferee firm, MC must demonstrate that it, "in a timely fashion, implemented screening procedures which will be effective in preventing any disclosures of these confidences." The Court finds that MC did not timely implement comprehensive, effective screening procedures. . . . In the instant case, the problem had been clearly noticed to MC when Cohen was first contacted by Vanderkloot, MC's hiring coordinator. Yet, there was no timely institutional screening mechanism in place when Cohen joined MC. . . .

b. *Coburn v. DaimlerChrysler Services North America*, 289 F. Supp. 2d 960 (D. Ill. 2003).

> Karen Bradley . . . processed all legal documents received by Chrysler Financial, including confidential . . . and privileged documents, and typed confidential letters

. . . . She also had access to Chrysler Financial's litigation files. On February 6 Bradley purchased a Jeep Grand Cherokee from Rochester Jeep . . . . [Unhappy with the financing she received from Chrysler Financial through Rochester Jeep, she decided to sue.] On June 11, Bradley's husband called Edward Vrdolyak . . . . Bradley and Vrdolyak spoke the next day. . . . As soon as Vrdolyak learned about Bradley's employment at Chrysler Financial, Vrdolyak told her not to tell him anything about her work . . . . The following day . . . Bradley informed Chrysler Financial that she had hired Vrdolyak, and Chrysler Financial promptly transferred her to the insurance department. . . .

Chrysler Financial argues that Plaintiffs' counsel should be disqualified because . . . Bradley was the administrative assistant to Defendant's assistant general counsel . . . . Plaintiffs do not even attempt to rebut the presumption that Bradley possessed confidential information. . . . The only disputed issue is whether Plaintiffs can rebut the presumption that Bradley provided or is likely to provide their counsel with confidential information.

A lawyer can only discover that a client has confidential information through discussion. Appropriately, this Court focuses on Vrdolyak's actions taken *after* he learned where Bradley worked . . . . As soon as Vrdolyak learned that Bradley worked for Chrysler Financial's assistant general counsel, he told her not to tell him anything about her work. This instruction does not "clearly and effectively" demonstrate that Vrdolyak did not receive and is not likely to receive any confidential information. First, Bradley, as a potential plaintiff in this case, has a personal incentive to transmit confidential information. Second, the information Vrdolyak requested (everything about the two cars Chrysler Financial financed for Bradley) and the information Vrdolyak prohibited (anything about the pending discriminatory financing case) are closely related. . . . Finally, Bradley is not a lawyer, so . . . she is not qualified to determine confidentiality. The effectiveness of Vrdolyak's screen – asking her not to tell him anything about her work – hinges on her ability to identify confidential information. . . . Accordingly, we resolve these doubts in favor of Defendant and disqualify the law firm of Edward R. Vrdolyak, Ltd. . . .

————————

CHAPTER 10

Adjudication and Separation of Powers

There is little question that Article I of the Constitution places in Congress the responsibility for the formulation of public policy. The representatives that serve in Congress are accountable to the people for the public policy choices they make. Agency professional staff and courts are not generally accountable through the electoral process. For that reason, when courts and agencies make public policy it can be argued that they are transgressing the constitutional mandate and violating separation of powers principles.

The cases that follow explore some of the dimensions of the separation of powers problem. This is an area of rich and continuous debate; these cases simply provide a background and structure for the field.

Food for Thought

While there are numerous ways of describing the government of the United States, all entail an understanding that public policy is primarily the domain of Congress, enforcement the domain of the Executive, and judicial review the domain of the courts. Agreement stops there. Those characterized as formalists take the position that the division between the branches of government must be pristine and that any crossover in function creates a serious constitutional problem. Those characterized as pragmatists take the position that it is inevitable and probable that the branches of government will overlap.

IMMIGRATION AND NATURALIZATION SERVICE v. CHADHA

<u>462 U.S. 919 (1983)</u>

[CHIEF JUSTICE BURGER] Chadha is an East Indian who was born in Kenya and holds a British passport. He was lawfully admitted to the United States in 1966 on a nonimmigrant student visa. His visa expired on June 30, 1972. On October 11, 1973, the District Director of the Immigration and Naturalization Service ordered Chadha to show cause why he should not be deported for having "remained in the United States for a longer time than permitted." . . . . [A] deportation hearing was held . . . . Chadha conceded that he was deportable . . . and the hearing was adjourned to enable him to file an application for suspension of deportation under § 244(a)(1) of [the Immigration and Nationality] Act. . . . After Chadha submitted his application . . . the hearing . . . resumed . . . . On the basis of evidence adduced at the hearing, affidavits submitted with the application, and the results of a character investigation conducted by the INS, the Immigration Judge . . . ordered that Chadha's deportation be suspended [finding] that Chadha met the requirements of § 244(a)(1): he had resided continuously in the United States for over seven years, was of good moral character, and would suffer "extreme hardship" if deported.

Pursuant to § 244(c)(1) of the Act, . . . a report of the suspension was transmitted to Congress [as a report of the Attorney General]. Congress [then] had the power under § 244(c)(2) of the Act to veto the Attorney General's determination that Chadha should not be deported. Section 244(c)(2) provides:

> (2) In the case of an alien specified in paragraph (1) of subsection (a) of this subsection–
>
>> if . . . either the Senate or the House of Representatives passes a resolution stating . . . that it does not favor the suspension of such deportation, the Attorney General shall thereupon deport such alien or authorize the alien's voluntary departure at his own expense . . . in the manner provided by law. . . .

The . . . order of the Immigration Judge suspending Chadha's deportation remained outstanding . . . for a year and a half. For reasons not disclosed by the record, Congress did not exercise the veto authority reserved to it [until] the final session in which Congress, pursuant to § 244(c)(2), could act to veto the Attorney General's determination that Chadha should not be deported. The session ended on December 19, 1975. Absent congressional action, Chadha's deportation proceedings would have been canceled after this date and his status adjusted to that of a permanent resident alien.

On December 12, 1975, Representative Eilberg, Chairman of the Judiciary Subcommittee on Immigration, Citizenship, and International Law, introduced a resolution opposing "the granting of permanent residence in the United States to aliens," including Chadha. . . . On December 16, 1975, the resolution was . . . submitted to the House of Representatives for a vote. . . . So far as the record before us shows, the House consideration of the resolution was based on Representative Eilberg's statement from the floor that

> [it] was the feeling of the committee, after reviewing 340 cases, that [Chadha and five others] did not meet these statutory requirements, particularly as it relates to hardship; and it is the opinion of the committee that their deportation should not be suspended.

The resolution was passed without debate or recorded vote. Since the House action was pursuant to § 244(c)(2), the resolution was not . . . submitted to the Senate or presented to the President for his action.

After the House veto of the Attorney General's decision to allow Chadha to remain in the United States, the Immigration Judge reopened the deportation proceedings to implement the House order deporting Chadha. Chadha moved to terminate the proceedings on the ground that § 244(c)(2) is unconstitutional. The Immigration Judge held that he had no authority to rule on the constitutional validity of § 244(c)(2). . . . Chadha appealed the deportation order to the Board of Immigration Appeals . . . . The Board [also] held that it had "no power to declare unconstitutional an act of Congress" and Chadha's appeal was dismissed.

. . . Chadha filed a petition for review of the deportation order in . . . the Ninth Circuit. The Immigration and Naturalization Service . . . joined him in arguing that § 244(c)(2) is unconstitutional. In light of the importance of the question, the Court of Appeals invited both the Senate and the House of Representatives to file briefs amici curiae. . . . [T]he Court of Appeals held that . . . § 244(c)(2) violates the constitutional doctrine of separation of powers. We . . . now affirm. . . .

III

A

. . . JUSTICE WHITE undertakes to make a case for the proposition that the one-House veto is a useful "political invention" . . . . But . . . even useful "political inventions" are subject to the demands of the Constitution which defines powers and, with respect to this subject, sets out just how those powers are to be exercised. . . .

B

The Presentment Clauses

The records of the Constitutional Convention reveal that [p]resentment to the President and the Presidential veto were considered so imperative that the draftsmen took special pains to assure that these requirements could not be circumvented. During the final debate on Art. I, § 7, cl. 2, James Madison expressed concern that it might easily be evaded by the simple expedient of calling a proposed law a "resolution" or "vote" rather than a "bill." As a consequence, Art. I, § 7, cl. 3 was added. The decision to provide the President with a limited and qualified power to nullify proposed legislation by veto was based on the profound conviction of the Framers that the powers conferred on Congress were the powers to be most carefully circumscribed. . . .

. . . The Court also has observed that the Presentment Clauses serve the important purpose of assuring that a "national" perspective is grafted on the legislative process:

> [I]t may be, at some times, on some subjects, that the President elected by all the people is rather more representative of them all than are the members of either body of the Legislature whose constituencies are local and not countrywide . . . .

C

Bicameralism

The bicameral requirement of Art. I, §§ 1, 7, was of scarcely less concern to the Framers than was the Presidential veto and indeed the two concepts are interdependent. . . . In the Constitutional Convention . . ., James Wilson, later to become a Justice of this Court, commented ". . . . If the Legislative authority be not restrained, there can be neither liberty nor stability; and it can only be restrained by dividing it within itself, into distinct and independent branches. . . ." . . . . However familiar, it is [also] useful to recall that . . . the Great Compromise, under which one House was viewed as representing the people and the other the states, allayed the fears of both the large and small states. . . .

IV

The Constitution sought to divide the delegated powers of the new Federal Government into three defined categories, Legislative, Executive, and Judicial . . . . The hydraulic pressure inherent within each of the separate Branches to exceed the outer limits of its power, even to accomplish desirable objectives, must be resisted. . . . Whether actions taken by either House are, in law and fact, an exercise of legislative power depends not on their form but upon "whether they contain matter which is properly to be regarded as legislative in its character and effect."

Examination of the action taken here by one House pursuant to § 244(c)(2) reveals that it was essentially legislative in purpose and effect. . . . The one-House veto operated in these cases to overrule the Attorney General and mandate Chadha's deportation; absent the House action, Chadha would remain in the United States. Congress has *acted* and its action has altered Chadha's status.

The legislative character of the one-House veto . . . is confirmed by the character of the congressional action it supplants. Neither the House of Representatives nor the Senate contends that, absent the veto provision in § 244(c)(2), either of them, or both of them acting together, could effectively require the Attorney General to deport an alien once the Attorney General . . . had determined the alien should remain in the United States. Without the challenged provision in

§ 244(c)(2), this could have been achieved, if at all, only by legislation requiring deportation. . . .

The nature of the decision . . . further manifests its legislative character. After long experience with the clumsy, time-consuming private bill procedure, Congress made a deliberate choice to delegate . . . the authority to allow deportable aliens to remain in this country in certain specified circumstances. . . . Disagreement with the Attorney General's decision on Chadha's deportation – that is, Congress' decision to deport Chadha – no less than Congress' original choice to delegate to the Attorney General the authority to make that decision, involves determinations of policy that Congress can implement in only one way; bicameral passage followed by presentment to the President. Congress must abide by its delegation of authority until that delegation is legislatively altered or revoked.

Finally, [t]here are four provisions in the Constitution . . . by which one House may act alone with the unreviewable force of law, not subject to the President's veto:

> (a) The House of Representatives alone was given the power to initiate impeachments. Art. I, § 2, cl. 5;
>
> (b) The Senate alone was given the power to conduct trials following impeachment on charges initiated by the House and to convict following trial. Art. I, § 3, cl. 6;
>
> (c) The Senate alone was given final unreviewable power to approve or to disapprove Presidential appointments. Art. II, § 2, cl. 2;
>
> (d) The Senate alone was given unreviewable power to ratify treaties negotiated by the President. Art. II, § 2, cl. 2.

Clearly, when the Draftsmen sought to confer special powers on one House, independent of the other House, or of the President, they did so in explicit, unambiguous terms. . . . [N]one of [these exceptions] authorize the action challenged here. On the contrary, they provide further support for the conclusion that congressional authority is not to be implied and for the conclusion that the veto provided for in § 244(c)(2) is not authorized by the constitutional design of the powers of the Legislative Branch.

Since it is clear that the action by the House under § 244(c)(2) was not within any of the express constitutional exceptions authorizing one House to act alone, and equally clear that it was an exercise of legislative power, that action was subject to the standards prescribed in Art. I. . . .

The veto authorized by § 244(c)(2) doubtless has been in many respects a convenient shortcut; the "sharing" with the Executive by Congress of its authority over aliens in this manner is, on its face, an appealing compromise. . . . [B]ut it is crystal clear from the records of the Convention, contemporaneous writings and debates, that the Framers ranked other values higher than efficiency. . . . The choices we discern as having been made in the Constitutional Convention impose burdens on governmental processes that often seem clumsy, inefficient, even unworkable, but those hard choices were consciously made by men who had lived under a form of government that permitted arbitrary governmental acts to go unchecked. . . . With all the obvious flaws of delay, untidiness, and potential for abuse, we have not yet found a better way to preserve freedom than by making the exercise of power subject to the carefully crafted restraints spelled out in the Constitution.

V

We hold that the congressional veto provision in § 244(c)(2) is severable from the Act and that it is unconstitutional. Accordingly, the judgment of the Court of Appeals is Affirmed.

[JUSTICE WHITE, dissenting.]

The prominence of the legislative veto mechanism in our contemporary political system and its importance to Congress can hardly be overstated. It has become a central means by which Congress secures the accountability of executive and independent agencies. Without the legislative veto, Congress is faced with a Hobson's choice: either to refrain from delegating the necessary authority, leaving itself with a hopeless task of writing laws with the requisite specificity to cover endless special circumstances across the entire policy landscape, or in the alternative, to abdicate its law-making function to the Executive Branch and independent agencies. To choose the former leaves major national problems unresolved; to opt for the latter risks unaccountable policymaking by those not elected to fill that role. Accordingly, over the past five decades, the legislative veto has been placed in nearly 200 statutes. The device is known in every field of governmental concern: reorganization, budgets, foreign affairs, war powers, and regulation of trade, safety, energy, the environment, and the economy. . . .

———

Underlying Case Documents

The case referenced:

The show cause order
The application for suspension of deportation
The immigration judge's order the Chadha's deportation be suspended
Representative Eilberg's statement from the floor and the House vote
The deportation order from the immigration judge
The Board's order affirming the deportation order of the immigration judge

1. The Supreme Court's most recent rote recitation of the values underlying separation of powers is in <u>Boumediene v. Bush, 553 U.S. 723 (2008)</u>.

The Framers' inherent distrust of governmental power was the driving force behind the constitutional plan that allocated powers among three independent branches. This design serves not only to make Government accountable but also to secure individual liberty. *See* <u>Loving v. United States, 517 U.S. 748 (1996)</u> (noting that "[e]ven before the birth of this country, separation of powers was known to be a defense against tyranny"); *cf.* <u>Youngstown Sheet & Tube Co. v. Sawyer, 343 U.S. 579 (1952)</u> (Jackson, J., concurring) ("[T]he Constitution diffuses power the better to secure liberty"); <u>Clinton v. City of New York</u>, 524 U.S. 417, 450 (1998) (Kennedy, J., concurring) ("Liberty is always at stake when one or more of the branches seek to transgress the separation of powers"). Because the Constitution's separation-of-powers structure, like the substantive guarantees of the Fifth and Fourteenth Amendments, see <u>Yick Wo v. Hopkins, 118 U.S. 356 (1886)</u>, protects persons as well as citizens, foreign nationals who have the privilege of litigating in our courts can seek to enforce separation-of-powers principles, see, e.g., *INS v. Chadha*, 462 U.S. at 958-59.

Good Questions!

Why not take JUSTICE WHITE's approach in the *Chadha* dissent? The legislative veto solved a host of practical problems, created a transparent process, allowed representatives from every state and district to vote, and produced an efficient outcome. Why stick so staunchly to such an unbending interpretation of bicameralism and presentment? Did the Founders intend such a formalistic view of separation of powers?

2. *Chadha* involved immigration, an exclusively federal area. In <u>Metropolitan Washington Airports Authority v. Citizens for Abatement of Airport Noise, 501 U.S. 252 (1991)</u>, the Court dealt with a far more unique situation: Control of airports in the Washington, D.C. area is subject to both local and federal law – and at the time, particularly in terms of airport noise, was a source of great controversy.

An Act of Congress authorizing the transfer of operating control of two major airports from the Federal Government to the Metropolitan Washington Airports Authority (MWAA) conditioned the transfer on the creation by MWAA of a unique "Board of Review" composed of nine Members of Congress. . . . The principal question presented is whether this unusual statutory condition violates the constitutional principle of separation of powers, as interpreted in *INS v. Chadha*, and *Springer v. Philippine Islands*, 277 U.S. 189 (1928). We conclude . . . that the condition is unconstitutional. . . .

Congress cannot directly vest the Federal Board with authority to veto decisions made by the Airports Authority any more than it can authorize one House, one committee, or one officer to overturn the Attorney General's decision to allow a deportable alien to remain in the United States, to reject rules implemented by an executive agency pursuant to delegated authority, to dictate mandatory budget cuts to be made by the President, or to overturn any decision made by a state agency.

The question is whether the maintenance of federal control over the airports by means of the Board of Review, which is allegedly a federal instrumentality, is invalid, not because it invades any state power, but because Congress' continued control violates the separation-of-powers principle, the aim of which is to protect not the States but "the whole people from improvident laws." *Chadha*. Nothing in our opinion in *Dole* implied that a highway grant to a State could have been conditioned on the State's creating a "Highway Board of Review" composed of Members of Congress. We must therefore consider whether the powers of the Board of Review may, consistent with the separation of powers, be exercised by an agent of Congress.

To forestall the danger of encroachment "beyond the legislative sphere," the Constitution imposes two basic and related constraints on the Congress. It may not "invest itself or its Members with either executive power or judicial power." *J.W. Hampton, Jr., & Co. v. United States*, 276 U.S. 394 (1928). And, when it exercises its legislative power, it must follow the "single, finely wrought and exhaustively considered, procedures" specified in Article I. *Chadha*. . . .

If the power is executive, the Constitution does not permit an agent of Congress to exercise it. If the power is legislative, Congress must exercise it in conformity with the bicameralism and presentment requirements of Art. I, § 7. In short, when Congress "[takes] action that has the purpose and effect of altering the legal rights, duties, and relations of persons . . . outside the Legislative Branch," it must take that action by the procedures authorized in the Constitution. *Chadha*.

JUSTICE WHITE's dissent, once again, has a very different perspective:

For the first time in its history, the Court employs separation-of-powers doctrine to invalidate a body created under state law. The majority justifies this unprecedented step on the ground that the Board of Review "exercises sufficient federal power . . . to mandate separation-of-powers scrutiny." This conclusion follows, it is claimed, because the Board, as presently constituted, would not exist but for the conditions set by Congress in the Metropolitan Washington Airports Act of 1986 (Transfer Act). This unprecedented rationale is insufficient on at least two counts. The Court's reasoning fails first because it ignores the plain terms of every instrument relevant to this case. The Court further errs because it also misapprehends the nature of the Transfer Act as a lawful exercise of congressional authority under the Property Clause. U.S. CONST.,

Art. IV, § 3, cl. 2.

While the majority's insistence that Congress should not perform an Executive task (read: Review an action of a federal agency) is familiar and comfortable, particularly to administrative lawyers, what about the power of the states? Is JUSTICE WHITE right – does Congress have the power to transfer to the states certain powers and then have members of Congress serve in a review capacity?

3. In <u>Bowsher v. Synar, 478 U.S. 714, 721-22, 733-34 (1986)</u>, the Court assessed a program by which Congress attempted to curb expenditures through a budget review process and arrogated to itself the power to dismiss the budget officer who exercised this power.

> The declared purpose of separating and dividing the powers of government, of course, was to "[diffuse] power the better to secure liberty." <u>Youngstown Sheet & Tube Co. v. Sawyer, 343 U.S. 579, 635 (1952)</u> (Jackson, J., concurring). JUSTICE JACKSON's words echo the famous warning of Montesquieu, quoted by James Madison in <u>THE FEDERALIST NO. 47</u>, that "'there can be no liberty where the legislative and executive powers are united in the same person, or body of magistrates'. . . ." . . . .

> [O]nce Congress makes its choice in enacting legislation, its participation ends. Congress can thereafter control the execution of its enactment only indirectly – by passing new legislation. By placing the responsibility for execution of the Balanced Budget and Emergency Deficit Control Act in the hands of an officer who is subject to removal only by itself, Congress in effect has retained control over the execution of the Act and has intruded into the executive function. The Constitution does not permit such intrusion.

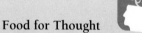

Food for Thought

Is the power to remove an officer from his or her job for "good cause only" the power to control the substantive decisions made in that position? While courts often make that assumption, is it correct?

4. Since 2001, one of the separation of powers questions attracting considerable attention has focused on presidential signing statements. After legislation is passed and presented, is the President "legislating" by issuing a signing statement when the bill is signed into law? On the one hand, such statements do not bind courts and cannot amend legislation. On the other hand, such statements can significantly affect the meaning the public gives new legislation and the enforcement priorities of the agencies responsible for implementing the new law. Can you envision a circumstance where a President might sign a bill to secure the funding the new law promises – but then issue a signing statement directing absolute non-enforcement of the majority of the new law? For a discussion of these and related issues, see Peter L. Strauss, <u>*Within Marbury: The Importance of Judicial Limits on the Executive's Power To Say What the Law Is*, 116 YALE L.J. Pocket Part 59 (2006)</u>; AM.

BAR ASS'N, TASK FORCE ON PRESIDENTIAL SIGNING STATEMENTS AND THE SEPARATION OF POWERS DOCTRINE, RECOMMENDATION AND REPORT 5 (2006), available at http://www.abanet.org/op/signingstatements/aba_final_signing_statements_recommendation-report_7-24-06.pdf; Peter L. Strauss, *Overseer, or "The Decider"? The President in Administrative Law*, 75 GEO. WASH. L. REV. 696 (2007); Thomas J. Cleary, *A Wolf in Sheep's Clothing: The Unilateral Executive and the Separation of Powers*, 6 PIERCE L. REV. 265 (2007). Also look at the entire symposium beginning with Charles Savage, *Introduction Symposium, The Last Word: The Constitutional Implications of Presidential Signing Statements*, 16 WM. & MARY BILL OF RTS. J. 1 (2007).

5. The formalism of *Chadha* should not prevent necessary discourse between branches of government. In a terrific article on the importance of the interchange, Professor Amanda Frost notes that "[w]hen a federal court must construe a statute that leaves important issues about its application unclear, the court should have the option to stay the case and refer the question to Congress, much in the same way that courts now use abstention and certification to obtain answers about the meaning of state law from state courts. Congress may then resolve the ambiguity by amending the law in accordance with Article I's bicameralism and presidential presentment requirements, after which the court can (in fact, usually must) apply the new law to the pending case." Amanda Frost, *Certifying Questions to Congress*, 101 NW. U.L. REV. 1, 3 (2007).

Professor Frost notes these cases, *inter alia*, as examples of her thesis, at note 3:

Good Questions!

After *Chadha* held that the only way Congress can alter policy is by enacting a bill that is passed by both chambers of Congress and signed by the President, can Congress:

a. Require that before an agency rule becomes effective, the agency must send a copy of it to Congress and wait 60 days?

b. Provide that if a committee expresses a concern over a proposed rule in a letter to the agency head, the agency will delay the effective date of the rule by at least 60 days?

c. Require that before an agency issues a new rule, it must consult with the chairs of the relevant committees of both houses of Congress? What if instead of "consult," the operative term is "secure the approval of?"

d. Require that before an agency spends any funds on a particular project it must consult with the chairs of the committees? Or again, could Congress require that the agency secure the approval of those chairs?

Exxon Mobil Corp. v. Allapattah Servs., Inc., 545 U.S. 546, 2624 (2005) (noting that 28 U.S.C. § 1367 may contain an "unintentional drafting gap" but concluding that "if that is the case, it is up to Congress rather than the courts to fix it. . . ."); *Gustafson v. Alloyd Co.*, 513 U.S. 561, 603-04 (1995) (Ginsburg, J., dissenting) ("If adjustment [of the statute] is in order, as the Court's opinion powerfully suggests it is,

Congress is equipped to undertake the alteration."); <u>*Reves v. Ernst & Young*, 494 U.S. 56, 63 n.2 (1990)</u> ("If Congress erred, however, it is for that body, and not this Court, to correct its mistake."); <u>*Abdul-Malik v. Hawk-Sawyer*, 403 F.3d 72, 76 (2d Cir. 2005)</u> (noting that sentencing statutes raise separation of powers and federalism concerns, and "inviting congressional consideration of these statutes. . . .").

Mistretta v. United States

<u>488 U.S. 361 (1989)</u>

[Justice Blackmun] [W]e granted certiorari . . . in order to consider the constitutionality of the Sentencing Guidelines promulgated by the United States Sentencing Commission. . . .

This Litigation

On December 10, 1987, John M. Mistretta (petitioner) and another were indicted in the United States District Court for the Western District of Missouri on three counts centering in a cocaine sale. . . . Petitioner was sentenced under the Guidelines to 18 months' imprisonment, to be followed by a 3-year term of supervised release. . . .

Delegation of Power

Petitioner argues that in delegating the power to promulgate sentencing guidelines for every federal criminal offense to an independent Sentencing Commission, Congress has granted the Commission excessive legislative discretion in violation of the constitutionally based nondelegation doctrine. We do not agree.

[W]e long have insisted that "the integrity and maintenance of the system of government ordained by the Constitution" mandate that Congress generally cannot delegate its legislative power to another Branch. *Marshall Field & Co. v. Clark*, 143 U.S. 649, 692 (1892). We also have recognized, however, that . . . in our increasingly complex society, replete with ever changing and more technical problems, Congress simply cannot do its job absent an ability to delegate power under broad general directives. . . . Accordingly, this Court has deemed it "constitutionally sufficient if Congress clearly delineates the general policy, the public agency which is to apply it, and the boundaries of this delegated authority." *American Power & Light Co. v. SEC*, 329 U.S. 90, 105 (1946). . . . After invalidating in 1935 two statutes as excessive delegations, we have upheld, . . . without deviation, Congress' ability to delegate power under broad standards. . . .

[W]e [therefore] harbor no doubt that Congress' delegation of authority to the Sentencing Commission is sufficiently specific and detailed to meet constitutional requirements. Congress charged the Commission with three goals: to "assure the meeting of the purposes of sentencing as set forth" in the Act; to "provide certainty and fairness in meeting the purposes of sentencing, avoiding unwarranted sentencing disparities among defendants with similar records . . . while maintaining sufficient flexibility to permit individualized sentences," where appropriate; and to "reflect, to the extent practicable, advancement in knowledge of human behavior as it relates to the criminal justice process." Congress further specified four "purposes" of sentencing that the Commission must pursue in carrying out its mandate: "to reflect the seriousness of the offense, to promote respect for the law, and to provide just punishment for the offense"; "to afford adequate deterrence to criminal conduct"; "to protect the public from further crimes of the defendant"; and "to provide the defendant with needed . . . correctional treatment."

In addition, Congress prescribed the specific tool – the guidelines system – for the Commission to use in regulating sentencing. More particularly, Congress directed the Commission to develop a system of "sentencing ranges" applicable "for each category of offense involving each category of defendant." Congress instructed the Commission that these sentencing ranges must be consistent with pertinent provisions of Title 18 of the United States Code . . . . Congress also required that for sentences of imprisonment, "the maximum of the range established for such a term shall not exceed the minimum of that range by more than the greater of 25 percent or 6 months, except that, if the minimum term of the range is 30 years or more, the maximum may be life imprisonment." . . . .

To guide the Commission in its formulation of offense categories, Congress directed it to consider seven factors: the grade of the offense; the aggravating and mitigating circumstances of the crime; the nature and degree of the harm caused by the crime; the community view of the gravity of the offense; the public concern generated by the crime; the deterrent effect that a particular sentence may have on others; and the current incidence of the offense. Congress set forth 11 factors for the Commission to consider in establishing categories of defendants. These include the offender's age, education, vocational skills, mental and emotional condition, physical condition (including drug dependence), previous employment record, family ties and responsibilities, community ties, role in the offense, criminal history, and degree of dependence upon crime for a livelihood. Congress also prohibited the Commission from considering the "race, sex, national origin, creed, and socioeconomic status of offenders" . . . . Congress also enumerated various aggravating and mitigating circumstances, such as, respectively, multiple offenses or substantial assistance to the Government, to be reflected in the guidelines. In other words, although Congress granted the Commission substantial discretion in formulating guidelines, in actuality it legislated a full hierarchy of punishment . . . .

We cannot dispute petitioner's contention that the Commission enjoys significant discretion in formulating guidelines. The Commission does have discretionary authority to determine the relative severity of federal crimes and to assess the relative weight of the offender characteristics that Congress listed for the Commission to consider. . . . [But the] Act sets forth more than merely an "intelligible principle" or minimal standards. . . . Having determined that Congress has set forth sufficient standards for the exercise of the Commission's delegated authority, we turn to Mistretta's claim that the Act violates the constitutional principle of separation of powers.

This Court consistently has given voice to, and has reaffirmed, the central judgment of the Framers of the Constitution that, within our political scheme, the separation of governmental powers into three coordinate Branches is essential to the preservation of liberty. . . . [But we have adopted a] flexible understanding of separation of powers, [recognizing] Madison's teaching that the greatest security against tyranny – the accumulation of excessive authority in a single Branch – lies not in a hermetic division among the Branches, but in a carefully crafted system of checked and balanced power within each Branch. . . .

Mistretta argues that . . . in delegating to an independent agency within the Judicial Branch the power to promulgate sentencing guidelines, Congress unconstitutionally has required the Branch, and individual Article III judges, to exercise not only their judicial authority, but legislative authority – the making of sentencing policy – as well. . . . At the same time, petitioner asserts, Congress unconstitutionally eroded the integrity and independence of the Judiciary by requiring Article III judges to sit on the Commission, by requiring that those judges share their rulemaking authority with nonjudges, and by subjecting the Commission's members to appointment and removal by the President. According to petitioner, Congress, consistent with the separation of powers, may not upset the balance among the Branches by co-opting federal judges into the quintessentially political work of establishing sentencing guidelines . . . .

. . . .

The Sentencing Commission unquestionably is a peculiar institution within the framework of our Government. Although placed by the Act in the Judicial Branch, it is not a court and does not exercise judicial power. Rather, the Commission is an "independent" body comprised of seven voting members including at least three federal judges, entrusted by Congress with the primary task of promulgating sentencing guidelines. Our constitutional principles of separated powers are not violated, however, by mere anomaly or innovation. . . . [I]t hardly can be argued in this case that Congress has impaired the functioning of the Executive Branch. In the field of sentencing, the Executive Branch never has exercised the kind of authority that Congress has vested in the Commission. Moreover, since Congress has empowered the President to appoint and remove Commission members, the President's relationship to the Commission is functionally no different from what it would have been had Congress not located the Commission in the Judicial Branch. . . .

[C]onsistent with the separation of powers, Congress may delegate to the Judicial Branch nonadjudicatory functions that do not trench upon the prerogatives of another Branch and that are appropriate to the central mission of the Judiciary. Following this approach, we specifically have upheld not only Congress' power to confer on the Judicial Branch the rulemaking authority contemplated in the various enabling Acts, but also to vest in judicial councils authority to "make 'all necessary orders for the effective and expeditious administration of the business of the courts.'" . . . . In light of this precedent and practice, we can discern no separation-of-powers impediment to the placement of the Sentencing Commission within the Judicial Branch. . . .

[The] President's removal power over Commission members poses a similarly negligible threat to judicial independence. The Act does not, and could not under the Constitution, authorize the President to remove, or in any way diminish the status of Article III judges, as judges. Even if removed from the Commission, a federal judge appointed to the Commission would continue, absent impeachment, to enjoy tenure "during good Behaviour" and a full judicial salary. . . . In order to safeguard the independence of the Commission from executive control, Congress specified in the Act that the President may remove the Commission members only for good cause. . . .

. . . .

Petitioner's most fundamental and far-reaching challenge to the Commission is that Congress' commitment of such broad policy responsibility to any institution is an unconstitutional delegation of legislative power. It is difficult to imagine a principle more essential to democratic government than that upon which the doctrine of unconstitutional delegation is founded. . . . But while the doctrine of unconstitutional delegation is unquestionably a fundamental element of our constitutional system, it is not an element readily enforceable by the courts. Once it is conceded, as it must be, that no statute can be entirely precise, and that some judgments, even some judgments involving policy considerations, must be left to the officers executing the law and to the judges applying it, the debate over unconstitutional delegation becomes a debate not over a point of principle but over a question of degree. . . .

. . . .

. . . The Constitution's structural protections do not prohibit Congress from delegating to an expert body located within the Judicial Branch the intricate task of formulating sentencing guidelines consistent with such significant statutory direction as is present here. Nor does our system of checked and balanced authority prohibit Congress from calling upon the accumulated wisdom and experience of the Judicial Branch in creating policy on a matter uniquely within the ken of judges. Accordingly, we hold that the Act is constitutional. The judgment of United States District Court for the Western District of Missouri is affirmed.

[JUSTICE SCALIA, dissenting.]

By reason of today's decision, I anticipate that Congress will find delegation of its lawmaking powers much more attractive in the future. . . . How tempting to create an expert Medical Commission (mostly M.D.'s, with perhaps a few Ph.D.'s in moral philosophy) to dispose of such thorny, "nowin" political issues as the withholding of life-support systems in federally funded hospitals, or the use of fetal tissue for research. This is an undemocratic precedent that we set – not because of the scope of the delegated power, but because its recipient is not one of the three Branches of Government. The only governmental power the Commission possesses is the power to make law; and it is not the Congress. . . . I think the Court errs, in other words, . . . because it fails to recognize that this case is not about commingling, but about the creation of a new Branch altogether, a sort of junior varsity Congress. It may well be that in some circumstances such a Branch would be desirable; perhaps the agency before us here will prove to be so. But there are many desirable dispositions that do not accord with the constitutional structure we live under. And in the long run the improvisation of a constitutional structure on the basis of currently perceived utility will be disastrous. . . .

Underlying Case Documents

The case referenced:

The Sentencing Reform Act

For a brief overview of the Sentencing Commission click HERE.

1. The sentencing guidelines have been affected by several major decisions since *Mistretta* was announced. The effect of those cases has been to declare the guidelines more advisory than mandatory. The separation of powers resolution regarding the power of the sentencing commission in *Mistretta*, however, remains

unchanged. The principle case affecting the sentencing guidelines post-*Mistretta*, is <u>United States v. Booker, 543 U.S. 220 (2005)</u>. *Booker* found that "Congress did not exceed constitutional limitations in creating the Commission . . . ." *Booker* left the sentencing commission in place but permitted courts limited flexibility in certain situations, notwithstanding the fact that the sentencing guidelines continue to be a primary advisory tool. On separation of powers, *Booker* left *Mistretta* unscathed.

> Our holding today does not call into question any aspect of our decision in *Mistretta*. That decision was premised on an understanding that the Commission, rather than performing adjudicatory functions, instead makes political and substantive decisions. We noted that the promulgation of the Guidelines was much like other activities in the Judicial Branch, such as the creation of the Federal Rules of Evidence, all of which are non-adjudicatory activities.

This is a functionalist approach. Would the Court have made the same decision using a formalist approach? For a wonderful discussion of a possible common ground between living constitutionalists and originalists, see Bernadette Meyler, <u>*Towards a Common Law Originalism*, 59 STAN. L. REV. 551 (2006)</u>.

If the Court had decided to apply strictly the lines of separation between the various branches in *Mistretta*, would the Sentencing Commission be out of business?

2. In <u>United States v. Hook, 471 F.3d 766 (7th Cir. 2006)</u>, the defendant, Hook, attacked the <u>DNA Analysis Backlog Elimination Act of 2000, Pub. Law No. 106-546, 114 Stat. 2726</u> (codified at <u>42 U.S.C. §§ 14135-14135e</u>) (collectively "DNA Act"), that requires probation officers to collect DNA samples as part of their administrative work with released prisoners pursuant to the <u>Justice for All Act of 2004, Pub. Law No. 108-405, 118 Stat. 2260</u>:

> Hook asserts that the DNA Act violates the separation of powers doctrine. The separation of the three branches of government is essential to liberty, however that separation is not complete and entire. *Mistretta.* While law enforcement is an executive function and a probation officer serves a supervisory function of the judicial branch, a probation officer's collection of DNA does not violate the separation of powers. The probation officer neither analyzes the DNA nor conducts investigations in collecting DNA pursuant to the DNA Act. Moreover, such collection is analogous to a probation officer in his supervisory capacity preventing a supervisee from using drugs by means of drug testing. <u>*United States v. Sczubelek*, 402 F.3d 175, 188-89 (3d Cir. 2005)</u>. Further, as the Third Circuit noted, there is no encroachment on the executive's ability to perform law enforcement functions by virtue of the probation officer's collection of DNA because the probation officer has no role in how the information is used once he submits the sample to the FBI.

Can you define the line separating the Executive and the Judicial branches in the enforcement and oversight of probationers?

3. Separation of powers is discussed often as a nondelegation standard. In <u>United States v. Martinez-Flores, 428 F.3d 22, 26-27 (1st Cir. 2005)</u>, the court reviewed the basics of the doctrine:

> The nondelegation doctrine is rooted in the principle of separation of powers that underlies our tripartite system of Government. *Mistretta.* Because the Constitution states that all federal legislative power "shall be vested in a Congress of the United States," U.S. CONST. art. I, § 1, the Supreme Court "long has insisted that 'the integrity and maintenance of the system of government ordained by the Constitution' mandate that Congress generally cannot delegate its legislative power to another Branch. *Mistretta,* quoting <u>Marshall Field & Co. v. Clark, 143 U.S. 649 (1892)</u>. The Court, however, also has recognized that this principle does not prevent Congress from obtaining the assistance of its coordinate Branches, and that how it may go about obtaining that assistance in a particular case must be fixed according to common sense and the inherent necessities of the government co-ordination, quoting <u>J. W. Hampton, Jr., & Co. v. United States, 276 U.S. 394 (1928)</u>). The Court developed the following rule: "So long as Congress 'shall lay down by legislative act an *intelligible principle* to which the person or body authorized to [exercise the delegated authority] is directed to conform, such legislative action is not a forbidden delegation of legislative power." (Citations omitted)

> [If Congress] delegates a broad duty – for example, setting national air quality standards – it must provide "substantial guidance." . . . . [For more on the "intelligible principle" concept see Cass R.] Sunstein, <u>Nondelegation Canons, 67 U. CHI. L. REV. 315, 322 (2000)</u> (describing the nondelegation doctrine as having had "one good year, and 211 bad ones (and counting))" . . . .

4. In <u>ACLU v. National Security Agency/Central Security Service, 438 F. Supp. 2d 754 (E.D. Mich. 2006)</u>, *vacated and remanded,* <u>ACLU v. NSA, 493 F.3d 644 (6th Cir. 2007)</u>, the court assessed the constitutionality of

> a secret program (hereinafter "TSP") undisputedly inaugurated by the National Security Agency (hereinafter "NSA") at least by 2002 and continuing today, which intercepts without benefit of warrant or other judicial approval, prior or subsequent, the international telephone and internet communications of numerous persons and organizations within this country. The TSP has been acknowledged by this Administration to have been authorized by the President's secret order during 2002 and reauthorized at least thirty times since. [Available at http://www.white-house.gov//news/releases/2005/12/20051219-2.html.]

> Plaintiffs have alleged that the TSP violates [*inter alia*] the principle of the Separation of Powers because the TSP has been authorized by the President in excess of his Executive Power under Article II of the United States Constitution. . . .

> In this case, the President has acted, undisputedly, as FISA forbids. FISA is the expressed statutory policy of our Congress. The presidential power, therefore, was exercised at its lowest ebb and cannot be sustained.

This decision, clear as it seems, was vacated by the Sixth Circuit, and in June, 2008, the House passed a bill that would continue the wiretapping program and immunize the phone companies that participated in the activity the Michigan District Court condemned above. James Risen, *New Scrutiny for Executive Power; Bush Era of Expanding Presidential Authority Grinds to an End*, INT'L HERALD TRIB., June 23, 2008, at 6.

Adherence to a coherent view – whether formalist or functionalist – of separation of powers, is best assessed when there are hard choices at hand. On less critical issues, one's good faith adherence to constitutional norms is of consequence, but not a measure of the true force of the specific constitutional doctrine in issue. In the above case, the matter of the questionable exercise of executive power is in play – as is national security. The difficulty of the balance is obvious – no one wants a repeat of September 11, 2001 – but is the trade-off appropriate?

MORRISON V. OLSON

487 U.S. 654 (1988)

[CHIEF JUSTICE REHNQUIST] This case presents us with a challenge to the independent counsel provisions of the Ethics in Government Act of 1978. We hold today that these provisions . . . do not violate the Appointments Clause of the Constitution, Art. II, § 2, cl. 2, or the limitations of Article III, nor do they impermissibly interfere with the President's authority under Article II in violation of the constitutional principle of separation of powers.

I

Briefly stated, Title VI of the Ethics in Government Act (Title VI or the Act) allows for the appointment of an "independent counsel" to investigate and, if appropriate, prosecute certain highranking Government officials for violations of federal criminal laws. The Act requires the Attorney General, upon receipt of information that he determines is "sufficient to constitute grounds to investigate whether [a highranking government official] may have violated any Federal criminal law," to conduct a preliminary investigation of the matter. When the Attorney General has completed this investigation, or 90 days has elapsed, he is required to report to a special court (the Special Division) created by the Act . . . . If the Attorney General determines that "there are no reasonable grounds to believe that further investigation is warranted," then . . . "the division of the court shall have no power to appoint an independent counsel." If, however, the Attorney General has determined that there are "reasonable grounds to believe that further investigation or prosecution is warranted," then he "shall apply to the division of the court for the appointment of an independent counsel." . . . . Upon receiving this application, the Special Division "shall appoint an appropriate independent counsel and shall define that independent counsel's prosecutorial jurisdiction."

With respect to all matters within the independent counsel's jurisdiction, the Act grants the counsel "full power and independent authority to exercise all investigative and prosecutorial functions and powers of the Department of Justice . . ." [including] "initiating and conducting prosecutions in any court of competent jurisdiction, framing and signing indictments, filing informations, and handling all aspects of any case, in the name of the United States." The counsel may appoint employees, may request and obtain assistance from the Department of Justice, and may accept referral of matters from the Attorney General if the matter falls within the counsel's jurisdiction as defined by the Special Division. The Act also states that an independent counsel "shall, except where not possible, comply with the written or other established policies of the Department of Justice respecting enforcement of the criminal laws." . . . .

. . . .

III

The Appointments Clause of Article II reads as follows:

> [The President] shall nominate, and by and with the Advice and Consent of the Senate, shall appoint Ambassadors, other public Ministers and Consuls, Judges of the Supreme Court, and all other Officers of the United States, whose Appointments are not herein otherwise provided for, and which shall be established by Law: but the Congress may by Law vest the Appointment of such inferior Officers, as they think proper, in the President alone, in the Courts of Law, or in the Heads of Departments.

The parties do not dispute that "[t]he Constitution for purposes of appointment . . . divides all its officers into two classes." . . . . The initial question is, accordingly, whether appellant is an "inferior" or a "principal" officer. If she is the latter, as the Court of Appeals concluded, then the Act is in violation of the Appointments Clause. The line between "inferior" and "principal" officers is one that is far from clear, and the Framers provided little guidance into where it should be drawn. We need not attempt here to decide exactly where the line falls between the two types of officers, because in our view appellant clearly falls on the "inferior officer" side of that line. Several factors lead to this conclusion.

First, appellant is subject to removal by a higher Executive Branch official. Although appellant may not be "subordinate" to the Attorney General (and the President) insofar as she possesses a degree of independent discretion to exercise the powers delegated to her under the Act, the fact that she can be removed by the Attorney General indicates that she is to some degree "inferior" in rank and authority. Second, appellant is empowered by the Act to perform only certain, limited duties. An independent counsel's role is restricted primarily to investigation and, if appropriate, prosecution for certain federal crimes. Admittedly, the Act delegates to appellant "full power and independent authority to exercise all investigative and prosecutorial functions and powers of the Department of Justice," but this grant of authority does not include any authority to formulate policy for the Government or the Executive Branch, nor does it give appellant any administrative duties outside of those necessary to operate her office. . . .

Third, appellant's office is limited in jurisdiction. Not only is the Act itself restricted in applicability to certain federal officials suspected of certain serious federal crimes, but an independent counsel can only act within the scope of the jurisdiction that has been granted by the Special Division pursuant to a request by the Attorney General. Finally, appellant's office is limited in tenure. There is concededly no time limit on the appointment of a particular counsel. Nonetheless, the office of independent counsel is "temporary" in the sense that an independent counsel is appointed essentially to accomplish a single task, and when that task is over the office is terminated, either by the counsel herself or by action of the Special Division. Unlike other prosecutors, appellant has no ongoing responsibilities that extend beyond the accomplishment of the mission that she was appointed for and authorized by the Special Division to undertake. In our view, these factors relating to the "ideas of tenure, duration . . . and duties" of the independent counsel are sufficient to establish that appellant is an "inferior" officer in the constitutional sense.

. . . .

This does not, however, end our inquiry under the Appointments Clause. Appellees argue that even if appellant is an "inferior" officer, the Clause does not . . . contemplate congressional authorization of "interbranch appointments," in which an officer of one branch is appointed by officers of another branch. The relevant language of the Appointments Clause is worth repeating. It reads: ". . . but the Congress may by Law vest the Appointment of such inferior Officers, as they think proper, in the President alone, in the courts of Law, or in the Heads of Departments." On its face, the language of this "excepting clause" admits of no limitation on interbranch appointments. Indeed, the inclusion of "as they think proper" seems clearly to give Congress significant discretion to determine whether it is "proper" to vest the appointment of, for example, executive officials in the "courts of Law." . . . .

. . . .

We do not mean to say that Congress' power to provide for interbranch appointments of "inferior officers" is unlimited. In addition to separation-of-powers concerns, which would arise if such provisions for appointment had the potential to impair the constitutional functions assigned to one of the branches, . . . Congress' decision to vest the appointment power in the courts would be improper if there was some "incongruity" between the functions normally performed by the courts and the performance of their duty to appoint. In this case, however, we do not think it impermissible for Congress to vest the power to appoint independent counsel in a specially created federal court. . . .

. . . .

The decision of the Court of Appeals is therefore Reversed.

[JUSTICE SCALIA, dissenting.]

[T]he independent counsel is not an inferior officer because she is not *subordinate* to any officer in the Executive Branch (indeed, not even to the President). . . .

Underlying Case Documents

The case referenced:
The Ethics in Government Act of 1978

1. The debate regarding the power to remove a special prosecutor did not end with *Morrison v. Olsen*. During the Clinton administration the power of the independent counsel, then Kenneth Starr, was so substantial that when the time came to renew the Independent Counsel Act, Congress balked. The independent counsel system discussed in *Morrison* ceased to exist in 1999. In its place is an ad hoc special counsel connected to the Justice Department, though for the most part it is independent. *See* Evan J. Criddle, *Fiduciary Foundations of Administrative Law,* 54 UCLA L. REV. 117, 180 (2006).

Congressional concern regarding positions of this nature is not hard to understand. Without using too much imagination, one can envision a scenario in which a runaway special prosecutor uses the office to achieve political objectives. In fact, the legislation establishing the office of the special prosecutor contemplated the circumstance where the prosecutor "may try to remain as special prosecutor after his responsibilities under this chapter are completed . . . ." S. Rep. No. 170, 95th Congress, 1st sess. 75 (1977), *reprinted in* 1978 U.S. CODE CONG. & ADMIN. NEWS 4216, 4291.

2. Can you tell, after reading Morrison, who is an inferior officer? In *Edmond v. United States, 520 U.S. 651 (1997)*, the Court stressed that one key indicator would be whether the individual was supervised and directed by someone who is appointed by the President and approved with the advice and consent of the Senate.

3. The difficulty inherent in prosecuting senior members of the Executive branch by the Executive branch – whether they are genuinely "inferior officers" or not – should not be underestimated. In the last few years, the proceedings brought against I. Lewis (Scooter) Libby for allegedly disclosing the name of a CIA operative have produced a number of opinions in the U.S. Circuit Court of Appeals for the District of Columbia and in the U.S. District Court for the District of Columbia, including *In re Grand Jury Subpoena (Miller), 438 F.3d 1138 (D.C. Cir. 2006)*.

4. The *Morrison* Court upheld a system for investigation that intertwined the Judicial and Executive branches – and presumably the Legislative as well, at least in terms of funding. Strict separation of powers is hardly the hallmark of the case. For further reading on functionalism, see Paul R. Verkuil, *A Proposal to Resolve Interbranch Disputes on the Practice Field*, 40 Cath. U.L. Rev. 839, 841 (1991); Stephen L. Carter, *From Sick Chicken to Synar: The Evolution and Subsequent De-Evolution of the Separation of Powers*, 1987 BYU L. Rev. 719; Steven G. Calabresi & Saikrishna B. Prakash, *The President's Power to Execute the Laws*, 104 Yale L.J. 541 (1994); Harold J. Krent, *Separating the Strands in Separation of Powers Controversies*, 74 Va. L. Rev. 1253 (1988); Martin H. Redish & Elizabeth J. Cisar, *If Angels Were to Govern: The Need for Pragmatic Formalism in Separation of Powers Theory*, 41 Duke L.J. 449 (1991).

———————

Should agencies be permitted to hear claims when there is subject matter jurisdiction in a court of general jurisdiction? What is lost by having an agency decide a case that could be tried in an Article III court? *CFTC v. Schor*, below, may help you work through some of these issues.

Food for Thought

Half of the study of administrative law, and a substantial part of the Administrative Procedure Act, is devoted to adjudicatory determinations. Agencies act as adjudicators in an almost endless variety of settings. At what point does the adjudicatory function an agency undertakes usurp the activity of Article III courts?

COMMODITY FUTURES TRADING COMMISSION V. SCHOR

<u>478 U.S. 833 (1986)</u>

[JUSTICE O'CONNOR] The question presented is whether the Commodity Exchange Act (CEA or Act) empowers the Commodity Futures Trading Commission (CFTC or Commission) to entertain state law counterclaims in reparation proceedings and, if so, whether that grant of authority violates Article III of the Constitution.

I.

The CEA broadly prohibits fraudulent and manipulative conduct in connection with commodity futures transactions. . . . Congress . . . determined that the broad regulatory powers of the CEA were most appropriately vested in an agency which would be relatively immune from the "political winds that sweep Washington." It therefore created an independent agency, the CFTC . . . . Among the duties assigned to the CFTC was the administration of a reparations procedure through which disgruntled customers of professional commodity brokers could seek redress for the brokers' violations of the Act or CFTC regulations. . . . [These customers] may apply to the Commission for an order directing the offender to pay reparations to the complainant and may enforce that order in federal district court. Congress intended this administrative procedure to be an "inexpensive and expeditious" alternative to . . . the courts and arbitration. In conformance with the congressional goal of promoting efficient dispute resolution, the CFTC promulgated a regulation in 1976 which allows it to adjudicate counterclaims "[arising] out of the transaction or occurrence or series of transactions or occurrences set forth in the complaint." This permissive counterclaim rule leaves the respondent in a reparations proceeding free to seek relief against the reparations complainant in other fora.

The instant dispute arose in February 1980, when respondents Schor and Mortgage Services of America, Inc., invoked the CFTC's reparations jurisdiction by filing complaints against petitioner ContiCommodity Services, Inc. (Conti), a commodity futures broker, and Richard L. Sandor, a Conti employee. Schor had [a negative] account with Conti [due to] Schor's . . . futures trading losses and expenses, such as commissions . . . . Schor alleged that this debit balance was the result of Conti's numerous violations of the CEA.

Before receiving notice that Schor had commenced the reparations proceeding, Conti had filed a diversity action in Federal District Court to recover the debit balance. Schor counterclaimed . . . reiterating his charges that the debit balance was due to Conti's violations of the CEA. Schor also moved on two separate occasions to dismiss or stay the District Court action, arguing that the continuation of the federal action would be a waste of judicial resources . . . in view of the fact that "[the] reparations proceedings . . . will fully . . . resolve and adjudicate all the rights of the parties to this action with respect to the transactions which are the subject matter of this action." . . . . Conti voluntarily dismissed the federal court action and presented its debit balance claim by way of a counterclaim in the CFTC reparations proceeding. Conti denied violating the CEA and instead insisted that the debit balance resulted from Schor's trading, and was therefore a simple debt owed by Schor.

[T]he Administrative Law Judge (ALJ) . . . ruled in Conti's favor on both Schor's claims and Conti's counterclaims. After this ruling, Schor for the first time challenged the CFTC's statutory authority to adjudicate Conti's counterclaim. The ALJ rejected Schor's challenge, stating himself "bound by agency regulations and published agency policies." The Commission declined to review the decision and allowed it to become final, at which point Schor filed a petition for review with the Court of Appeals for the District of Columbia Circuit. Prior to oral argument, the Court of Appeals, sua sponte, raised the question whether CFTC could constitutionally adjudicate Conti's counterclaims in light of *Northern Pipeline Construction Co. v. Marathon Pipe Line Co.*, in which this Court held that "Congress may not vest in a non-Article III court the power to adjudicate, render final judgment, and issue binding orders in a traditional contract action arising under state law, without consent of the litigants, and subject only to ordinary appellate review." . . . . [T]he Court of Appeals . . . ordered the dismissal of Conti's counterclaims on the ground that "the CFTC lacks authority (subject matter competence) to adjudicate" common law counterclaims. . . . We . . . now reverse.

II.

. . . .

. . . Our examination of the CEA and its legislative history and purpose reveals that Congress plainly intended the CFTC to decide counterclaims . . . in reparations proceedings, and just as plainly delegated to the CFTC the authority to fashion its counterclaim jurisdiction in the manner the CFTC determined necessary to further the purposes of the reparations program. . . . We therefore are squarely faced with the question whether the CFTC's assumption of jurisdiction over common law counterclaims violates Article III of the Constitution.

III.

Article III, § 1, directs that the "judicial Power of the United States shall be vested in one supreme Court and in such inferior Courts as the Congress may from time to time ordain and establish," and provides that these federal courts shall be staffed by judges who hold office during good behavior, and whose compensation shall not be diminished during tenure in office. Schor claims that these provisions prohibit Congress from authorizing the initial adjudication of common law counterclaims by the CFTC, an administrative agency whose adjudicatory officers do not enjoy the tenure and salary protections embodied in Article III.

Although our precedents in this area do not admit of easy synthesis, they do establish that the resolution of claims such as Schor's cannot turn on conclusory reference to the language of Article III. Rather, the constitutionality of a given congressional delegation of adjudicative functions to a non-Article III body must be assessed by reference to the purposes underlying the requirements of Article III. . . .

A

Article III, § 1, serves both to protect "the role of the independent judiciary within the constitutional scheme of tripartite government," and to safeguard litigants' "right to have claims decided before judges who are free from potential domination by other branches of government." . . . . [O]ur prior discussions . . . intimated that this guarantee serves to protect primarily personal, rather than structural, interests. . . . [A]s a personal right, Article III's guarantee of an impartial and independent federal adjudication is subject to waiver, just as are other personal constitutional rights that dictate the procedures by which civil and criminal matters must be tried. . . .

In the instant cases, Schor indisputably waived any right he may have possessed to the full trial of Conti's counterclaim before an Article III court. Schor expressly demanded that Conti proceed on its counterclaim in the reparations proceeding rather than before the District Court, and was content to have the entire dispute settled in the forum he had selected until the ALJ ruled against him on all counts; it was [only then] that Schor raised any challenge to the CFTC's consideration of Conti's counterclaim.

Even were there no evidence of an express waiver here, Schor's . . . decision to seek relief . . . in a CFTC reparations proceeding constituted an effective waiver. . . . Schor had the option of having the common law counterclaim against him adjudicated in a federal Article III court, but, with full knowledge that the CFTC would exercise jurisdiction over that claim, chose to avail himself of the quicker and less expensive procedure Congress had provided him. In such circumstances, it is clear that Schor effectively agreed to an adjudication by the CFTC of the entire controversy by seeking relief in this alternative forum.

B

. . . Article III, § 1, [also] safeguards the role of the Judicial Branch in our tripartite system by barring congressional attempts "to transfer jurisdiction [to non-Article III tribunals] for the purpose of emasculating" constitutional courts and thereby preventing "the encroachment or aggrandizement of one branch at the expense of the other." To the extent that this structural principle is implicated in a given case, the parties cannot by consent cure the constitutional difficulty for the same reason that the parties by consent cannot confer on federal courts subject-matter jurisdiction beyond the limitations imposed by Article III, § 2. When these Article III limitations are at issue, notions of consent and waiver cannot be dispositive because the limitations serve institutional interests that the parties cannot be expected to protect.

In determining the extent to which . . . the adjudication of Article III business in a non-Article III tribunal impermissibly threatens the institutional integrity of the Judicial Branch, the Court has declined to adopt formalistic and unbending rules. Although such rules might lend a greater degree of coherence to this area of the law, they might also unduly constrict Congress' ability to take needed and innovative action pursuant to its Article I powers. Thus, in reviewing Article III challenges, we have weighed a number of factors, none of which has been deemed determinative, with an eye to the practical effect that the congressional action will have on the constitutionally assigned role of the federal judiciary. Among the factors upon which we have focused are the extent to which the "essential attributes of judicial power" are reserved to Article III courts, and, conversely, the extent to which the non-Article III forum exercises the range of jurisdiction and powers normally vested only in Article III courts, the origins and importance of the right to be adjudicated, and the concerns that drove Congress to depart from the requirements of Article III.

An examination of the relative allocation of powers between the CFTC and Article III courts . . . demonstrates that the congressional scheme does not impermissibly intrude on the province of the judiciary. The CFTC's adjudicatory powers depart from the traditional agency model in just one respect: the CFTC's jurisdiction over common law counterclaims. While wholesale importation of concepts of pendent or ancillary jurisdiction into the agency context may create greater constitutional difficulties, we decline to endorse an absolute prohibition on such jurisdiction out of fear of where some hypothetical "slippery slope" may deposit us. Indeed, the CFTC's exercise of this type of jurisdiction is not without precedent. . . .

. . . .

The CFTC, like the agency in *Crowell*, deals only with a "particularized area of law," whereas the jurisdiction of the bankruptcy courts found unconstitutional in *Northern Pipeline* extended to broadly "all civil proceedings arising under title

11 or arising in or *related to* cases under title 11." CFTC orders, like those of the agency in *Crowell*, but unlike those of the bankruptcy courts under the 1978 Act, are enforceable only by order of the district court. CFTC orders are also reviewed under the same "weight of the evidence" standard sustained in *Crowell*, rather than the more deferential standard found lacking in *Northern Pipeline*. The legal rulings of the CFTC, like the legal determinations of the agency in *Crowell*, are subject to de novo review. Finally, the CFTC, unlike the bankruptcy courts under the 1978 Act, does not exercise "all ordinary powers of district courts," and thus may not, for instance, preside over jury trials or issue writs of habeas corpus.

Of course, the nature of the claim has significance in our Article III analysis quite apart from the method prescribed for its adjudication. The counterclaim asserted in this litigation is a "private" right for which state law provides the rule of decision. It is therefore a claim of the kind assumed to be at the "core" of matters normally reserved to Article III courts. Yet this conclusion does not end our inquiry; just as this Court has rejected any attempt to make determinative for Article III purposes the distinction between public rights and private rights, there is no reason inherent in separation of powers principles to accord the state law character of a claim talismanic power in Article III inquiries. . . . [W]here private, common law rights are at stake, our examination of the congressional attempt to control the manner in which those rights are adjudicated has been searching. In this litigation, however, "[l]ooking beyond form to the substance of what" Congress has done, we are persuaded that the congressional authorization of limited CFTC jurisdiction over a narrow class of common law claims as an incident to the CFTC's primary, and unchallenged, adjudicative function does not create a substantial threat to the separation of powers.

It is clear that Congress has not attempted to "withdraw from judicial cognizance" the determination of Conti's right to the sum represented by the debit balance in Schor's account. Congress gave the CFTC the authority to adjudicate such matters, but the decision to invoke this forum is left entirely to the parties and the power of the federal judiciary to take jurisdiction of these matters is unaffected. In such circumstances, separation of powers concerns are diminished, for it seems self-evident that just as Congress may encourage parties to settle a dispute out of court or resort to arbitration without impermissible incursions on the separation of powers, Congress may make available a quasi-judicial mechanism through which willing parties may, at their option, elect to resolve their differences. This is not to say, of course, that if Congress created a phalanx of non-Article III tribunals equipped to handle the entire business of the Article III courts without any Article III supervision or control and without evidence of valid and specific legislative necessities, the fact that the parties had the election to proceed in their forum of choice would necessarily save the scheme from constitutional attack. But this case obviously bears no resemblance to such a scenario, given the degree of judicial control saved to the federal courts as well as the congressional purpose behind the jurisdictional delegation, the demonstrated need for the delegation, and the limited nature of the delegation.

When Congress authorized the CFTC to adjudicate counterclaims, its primary focus was on making effective a specific and limited federal regulatory scheme, not on allocating jurisdiction among federal tribunals. Congress intended to create an inexpensive and expeditious alternative forum through which customers could enforce the provisions of the CEA against professional brokers. Its decision to endow the CFTC with jurisdiction over such reparations claims is readily understandable given the perception that the CFTC was relatively immune from political pressures and the obvious expertise that the Commission possesses in applying the CEA and its own regulations. . . .

It also bears emphasis that the CFTC's assertion of counterclaim jurisdiction is limited to that which is necessary to make the reparations procedure workable. The CFTC adjudication of common law counterclaims is incidental to, and completely dependent upon, adjudication of reparations claims created by federal law, and in actual fact is limited to claims arising out of the same transaction or occurrence as the reparations claim. In such circumstances, the magnitude of any intrusion on the Judicial Branch can only be termed de minimis. . . .

Nor does our decision in *Bowsher v. Synar* require a contrary result. Unlike *Bowsher*, this case raises no question of the aggrandizement of congressional power at the expense of a coordinate branch. Instead, the separation of powers question presented in this litigation is whether Congress impermissibly undermined, without appreciable expansion of its own power, the role of the Judicial Branch. In any case, we have, consistent with *Bowsher*, looked to a number of factors in evaluating the extent to which the congressional scheme endangers separation of powers principles under the circumstances presented, but have found no genuine threat to those principles to be present in this litigation. . . .

C

. . . .

The judgment of the Court of Appeals for the District of Columbia Circuit is reversed, and the case is remanded for further proceedings consistent with this opinion. . . .

———————

Underlying Case Documents

The case referenced:
<u>The ALJ ruling</u>
<u>The denial of review by the Commission</u>

1. To what extent does *Schor* compromise the power of the courts? By affirming a process for resolution of claims ordinarily adjudicated in Article III tribunals, does *Schor*'s functionalism go too far? <u>Plaut v. Spendthrift Farm, 514 U.S. 211, 218-19 (1995)</u>, holds that "Congress cannot vest review of the decisions of Article III courts in officials of the Executive Branch . . . . [J]udicial decision[s are] the last word of the judicial department . . . ." Are these principles violated both in *Schor* and *Morrison*? See <u>United States v. Schooner Peggy, 5 U.S. 103 (1801)</u>, for the earliest assertion of the power of Article III courts.

2. Some time after *Schor* was decided the Court decided <u>Miller v. French, 530 U.S. 327 (2000)</u>, a case assessing legislation that temporarily stayed judicial review of complaints regarding unduly harsh prison conditions:

> The Constitution enumerates and separates the powers of the three branches of Government in Articles I, II, and III, and it is this "very structure" of the Constitution that exemplifies the concept of separation of powers. While the boundaries between the three branches are not "hermetically sealed," the Constitution prohibits one branch from encroaching on the central prerogatives of another. . . . The powers of the Judicial Branch are set forth in Article III, § 1, which states that the "judicial Power of the United States shall be vested in one supreme Court and in such inferior Courts as Congress may from time to time ordain and establish," and provides that these federal courts shall be staffed by judges who hold office during good behavior, and whose compensation shall not be diminished during tenure in office. As we explained in <u>Plaut v. Spendthrift Farm, Inc., 514 U.S. at 218-19</u>, Article III "gives the Federal Judiciary the power, not merely to rule on cases, but to decide them, subject to review only by superior courts in the Article III hierarchy. . . . [However,] separation of powers principles are primarily addressed to the structural concerns of protecting the role of the independent Judiciary within the constitutional design. In this action, we have no occasion to decide whether there could be a time constraint on judicial action that was so severe that it implicated these structural separation of powers concerns.

3. In <u>In re Kaiser Steel v. Frates, 95 B.R. 782 (Bankr. D. Colo. 1989)</u>, the court applied the "consent to jurisdiction" component of *Schor*. In that case, after the parties consented to the non-Article III tribunal, they sought a jury trial, a right unavailable in the bankruptcy process they elected. The court rejected the claim for a jury trial and found that *Schor* embodied a consent theory applicable to bankruptcy, with the defining caveat from *Schor*:

This is not to say, of course, that if Congress created a phalanx of non-Article III tribunals equipped to handle the entire business of the Article III courts without any Article III supervision or control and without evidence of valid and specific legislative necessities, the fact that the parties had the election to proceed in their forum of choice would necessarily save the scheme from constitutional attack.

What is a phalanx of non-Article III tribunals? When is a judicial remedy essential and when can the executive, via delegated authority from Congress, become the forum for resolution of claims? *See Northern Pipeline Constr. Co. v. Marathon Pipe Line Co., 458 U.S. 50, 73-74 (1982), Atlas Roofing Co. v. Occupational Safety and Health Review Comm'n, 430 U.S. 442, 450 (1977), and United States ex rel. Toth v. Quarles, 350 U.S. 11 (1955).*

4. In *Den ex dem. Murray v. Hoboken Land & Improvement Company, 59 U.S. 272, 18 How. 272, 284 (1856)*, the Court held: "Congress [may not] bring under the judicial power a matter which, from its nature, is not a subject for judicial determination. . . . [Congress also may not] withdraw from judicial cognizance any matter which, from its nature, is the subject of a suit at the common law, or in equity, or admiralty."

Does *Schor* undermine *Den ex dem. Murray*?

5. Does the holding in *Schor* permit a shift in the basic modalities of decision-making to administrative fora? After all, regulatory entities, generally speaking, are more open to public participation and scrutiny than courts – and, say some, more inherently democratic. Those who espouse this perspective are sometimes referred to as democratic experimentalists. Assuming one avoids the "phalanx of non-Article III tribunals" – the line in the sand the *Schor* Court drew and never defined – would agencies be a "better" forum for the resolution of disputes? See Jamison E. Colburn, *Democratic Experimentalism: A Separation of Powers For Our Time?, 37 Suffolk U. L. Rev. 287 (2004)*, for a compelling critique of democratic experimentalism.

6. Separation of powers and tort liability. In *McMellon v. United States, 387 F.3d 329 (4th Cir. 2004) (en banc)*, the court addressed the applicability of the discretionary function exception (DFE) barring governmental liability for claims brought against the federal government pursuant to the Suits in Admiralty Act, 46 U.S.C.A. § 30901. The court held that the DFE would apply based on separation of powers principles, finding that the Constitution prohibits "judicial" regulation that "prevents the Executive Branch from accomplishing its constitutionally assigned functions. . . . [T]he Judicial Branch [may] neither be assigned nor allowed tasks that are more properly accomplished by other branches."

Four years later, in *North Carolina ex rel. Cooper v. TVA, 515 F.3d 344, 347 (4th Cir. 2008)*, the court addressed a similar question.

As part of its mission, the TVA operates coal-fired power plants in Tennessee, Alabama, and Kentucky. The State of North Carolina brought this common-law nuisance action against the TVA, contending that these plants emit various pollutants which travel through the atmosphere into North Carolina, adversely impacting human health and environmental quality. . . .

The TVA "is a corporate entity, separate and distinct from the Federal Government itself." *Pierce v. United States, 314 U.S. 306 (1941)*. Thus, the TVA maintains a separate corporate identity, a separate legal staff, and a separate headquarters. . . . The Attorney General is prohibited from representing the TVA in a legal proceeding unless expressly requested by the TVA to do so. . . . TVA is removed from centralized control in Washington, enjoys discretionary ratemaking authority, and is exempt from at least 16 provisions of the Administrative Procedures Act. . . . Congress has, for example, exempted the TVA from suit in the Court of Federal Claims, 28 U.S.C. § 1491(c)[, from] civil service laws[, and from] purchasing requirements otherwise applicable to federal entities. . . . TVA funds its power-generating programs itself rather than with congressional appropriations.

Even more telling, Congress exempted the TVA from the FTCA, see 28 U.S.C. § 2680(l). . . . This degree of independence which the TVA possesses in large part alleviates the constitutional concerns which we recognized in *McMellon*. A lawsuit against the TVA is not a suit against the United States itself or one of its agencies subject to the direct executive control [b]ecause the TVA is so far removed from the control of the Executive Branch, operating as the functional equivalent of a private corporation, the judiciary does not run the same risk of overstepping its bounds and "prevent[ing] the Executive Branch from accomplishing its constitutionally assigned functions," *McMellon, 387 F.3d at 341*, that it did in *McMellon*.

> n.3 Although the President appoints the TVA's Board of Directors (with the advice and consent of the Senate), as with many independent government agencies and corporations, the President's power of appointment, standing alone, does not subject the agency to direct presidential control. *See Morrison v. Olson* . . . .

Even were the TVA more tightly linked with the Executive Branch, this case would not conflict with the principles recognized in McMellon. In this case, a judicial decision on the lawfulness of the TVA's plant emissions does not strip the TVA of its authority to execute its statutory duties. At most, it could require the TVA to take into account and to abide by certain air quality standards when operating its coal-fired power plants. . . . . Similarly, permitting this suit to go forward does not require the Judicial Branch to perform Executive Branch functions or decide issues it is not equipped to resolve. . . . This case, then, involves the "overlapping responsibility" between the three branches of government which the Constitution permits, *Mistretta v. United States*, 488 U.S. 361. . . .

Accordingly, we conclude that this suit does not implicate the separation-of-powers concerns. . . . We therefore hold that the broad waiver of sovereign immunity effected by the TVA's "sue-and-be-sued" clause is not restricted by a discretionary function exception in this case.

Do you agree that possible tort liability under the Federal Tort Claims Act,

28 U.S.C. § 1346 (assuming one sues an entity that is a governmental agency, unlike TVA, and further that one can get around the discretionary function exception) is a threat to the constitutionally compelled separation of powers?

Hypothetical – Separation of Powers Simulation

Inspired by the decision of the FCC to relax the rules on multi-entity ownership of media companies, the Secretary of Transportation decided, without consultation with any other agency of government, that all rules regarding airline ownership should be likewise relaxed. The Secretary issued the following statement announcing this goal:

> Most air carriers, and all U.S. Legacy Carriers (e.g., United, US Air, and American Airlines), are operating at or near a loss. Without a secure airline industry, the commerce of this country is in trouble. Ownership by non-airline entities, specifically, foreign banks, internationally owned insurance companies, and multinational corporations (who are cash flush and in search of investments in the U.S.), could provide the kind of financial support the airlines cannot secure on their own. Such a decision will require immunity from the antitrust laws (particularly the rules regarding mergers). However, this action would take pressure off of the President and Congress to bail out the industry.

Parties:
1. [in favor] The Secretary and the two trusted advisors from the **General Counsel's office at DOT**;
2. [opposed] Counsel for the **Traveling Consumer Association (TCA)**, a public interest group that advocates for travelers rights. The TCA issued a statement opposing the change on the premise that foreign owners would have no interest in continuing shorter or less profitable domestic U.S. routes;
3. [opposed] Counsel for the **Senate Judiciary Committee** (on behalf of the committee members) responded to the Secretary's press release, stating that the Secretary was not in the business of making public policy;
4. [opposed] A senior Department of Justice representative from the **Office of the Attorney General,** who has refused to issue a statement but who (according to unnamed sources) is furious with the Secretary for failing to consult with DOJ in advance of making this statement;
5. [in favor] A representative from the **World Bank** who praised the Secretary for having great vision and insight into the globalized future.

Role play:
A substantive round-table discussion with the above parties, convened by the Secretary and the trusted advisors, to explore the legal ramifications this proposal presents, focused on separation of powers.

CHAPTER 11

Administrative Hearings in Select Fields

While there are many ways of organizing the material that follows, we have chosen to break it into sections according to field.

The first group of cases examines administrative adjudicatory entitlements related to employment. Under what circumstances will the dismissal of a government employee require a full and fair adjudicatory hearing before the termination? What if the action the government takes damages an individual's reputation – does the individual have a right to a hearing to clear her or his name?

The second group of materials introduces you to some of the problems related to administrative adjudication as it pertains to immigration and detention of foreign nationals. This is a rapidly growing area and, in a basic course in administrative law, we attempt only to introduce you to the field.

The third area returns to the question of prosecutorial discretion, discussed earlier in the section on agency inaction. When can the government be compelled to act? What remedies, if any, does an individual have when the government's failure to act places that person in jeopardy or causes actual harm?

The next area looks at administrative law and schools. When does suspension or expulsion compel a hearing? To what type of hearing is one entitled? If a school disciplines a student, what right might that student have if the discipline causes injury?

The final area involves incarceration. What rights to a hearing remain after one has been convicted of a crime and incarcerated?

I. Administrative Hearings and Public Employment

PAUL V. DAVIS

424 U.S. 693 (1976)

[JUSTICE REHNQUIST] We granted certiorari in this case to consider whether respondent's charge that petitioners' defamation of him, standing alone and apart from any other governmental action with respect to him, stated a claim for relief under 42 U.S.C. § 1983 and the Fourteenth Amendment. For the reasons hereinafter stated, we conclude that it does not.

Petitioner Paul is the Chief of Police of the Louisville, Ky., Division of Police, while petitioner McDaniel occupies the same position in the Jefferson County, Ky., Division of Police. In late 1972 they agreed to combine their efforts for the purpose of alerting local area merchants to possible shoplifters who might be operating during the Christmas season. In early December petitioners distributed to approximately 800 merchants in the Louisville metropolitan area a "flyer," which began as follows:

TO: BUSINESS MEN IN THE METROPOLITAN AREA

The Chiefs of . . . Police . . . have approved the attached alphabetically arranged flyer of subjects known to be active in this criminal field.

This flyer is being distributed to you, the business man, so that you may inform your security personnel to watch for these subjects. These persons have been arrested during 1971 and 1972 or have been active in various criminal fields in high density shopping areas.

. . . .

The flyer consisted of five pages of "mug shot" photos, arranged alphabetically. Each page was headed "NOVEMBER 1972 CITY OF LOUISVILLE & JEFFERSON COUNTY POLICE DEPARTMENTS ACTIVE SHOPLIFTERS" In approximately the center of page 2 there appeared photos and the name of the respondent, Edward Charles Davis III.

Respondent appeared on the flyer because on June 14, 1971, he had been arrested in Louisville on a charge of shoplifting. . . . [U]pon his plea of not guilty, the charge had been "filed away with leave [to reinstate]," a disposition which left the charge outstanding. Thus, at the time petitioners caused the flyer to be prepared and circulated respondent had been charged with shoplifting but his guilt or innocence of that offense had never been resolved. Shortly after circulation of the flyer the charge against respondent was finally dismissed . . . .

At the time the flyer was circulated respondent was employed as a photographer by the Louisville Courier-Journal and Times. The flyer, and respondent's inclusion therein, soon came to the attention of respondent's supervisor, the executive director of photography for the two newspapers. This individual called respondent in to hear his version of the events leading to his appearing in the flyer. Following this discussion, the supervisor informed respondent that although he would not be fired, he "had best not find himself in a similar situation" in the future.

Respondent thereupon brought this § 1983 action . . . seeking redress for the alleged violation of rights guaranteed to him by the Constitution of the United States. . . . [R]espondent sought damages as well as declaratory and injunctive relief. . . . The District Court [dismissed the complaint], ruling that "[t]he facts alleged in this case do not establish that plaintiff has been deprived of any right secured to him by the Constitution of the United States." . . . . The Court of Appeals concluded that respondent had set forth a § 1983 claim "in that he has alleged facts that constitute a denial of due process of law." . . . .

I

Respondent's due process claim is grounded upon his assertion that the flyer, and in particular the phrase "Active Shoplifters" appearing at the head of the page upon which his name and photograph appear, "impermissibly deprived him of some 'liberty' protected by the Fourteenth Amendment." His complaint asserted that the "active shoplifter" designation would inhibit him from entering business establishments for fear of being suspected of shoplifting and possibly apprehended, and would seriously impair his future employment opportunities. Accepting that such consequences may flow from the flyer in question, respondent's complaint would appear to state a classical claim for defamation actionable in the courts of virtually every State. . . .

Respondent brought his action, however, not in the state courts of Kentucky, but in a United States District Court for that State. He asserted not a claim for defamation under the laws of Kentucky, but a claim that he had been deprived of rights secured to him by the Fourteenth Amendment of the United States Constitution. Concededly if the same allegations had been made about respondent by a private individual, he would have nothing more than a claim for defamation under state law. But, he contends, since petitioners are respectively an official of city and of county government, his action is thereby transmuted into one for deprivation by the State of rights secured under the Fourteenth Amendment. . . . We . . . pause to consider the result should respondent's interpretation of § 1983 and of the Fourteenth Amendment be accepted.

If respondent's view is to prevail, a person arrested by law enforcement officers who announce that they believe such person to be responsible for a particular crime in order to calm the fears of an aroused populace, presumably obtains a claim against such officers under § 1983. . . . It is hard to perceive any logical stopping place to such a line of reasoning. Respondent's construction would seem almost necessarily to result in every legally cognizable injury which may have been inflicted by a state official acting under "color of law" establishing a violation of the Fourteenth Amendment. We think it would come as a great surprise to those who drafted and shepherded the adoption of that Amendment to learn that it worked such a result, and a study of our decisions convinces us they do not support the construction urged by respondent.

II

The result reached by the Court of Appeals, which respondent seeks to sustain here, must be bottomed on one of two premises. The first is that the Due Process Clause of the Fourteenth Amendment and § 1983 make actionable many wrongs inflicted by government employees which had heretofore been thought to give rise only to state-law tort claims. The second premise is that the infliction by state officials of a "stigma" to one's reputation is somehow different in kind from the infliction by the same official of harm or injury to other interests protected by state law, so that an injury to reputation is actionable under § 1983 and the Fourteenth Amendment even if other such harms are not. We examine each of these premises in turn.

A

The first premise would be contrary to pronouncements in our cases on more than one occasion with respect to the scope of § 1983 and of the Fourteenth Amendment. In the leading case of *Screws v. United States*, the Court considered the proper application of the criminal counterpart of § 1983, likewise intended by Congress to enforce the guarantees of the Fourteenth Amendment. In his opinion for the Court plurality in that case, Justice Douglas observed:

> Violation of local law does not necessarily mean that federal rights have been invaded. The fact that a prisoner is assaulted, injured, or even murdered by state officials does not necessarily mean that he is deprived of any right protected or secured by the Constitution or laws of the United States.

. . . Respondent . . . apparently believes that the Fourteenth Amendment's Due Process Clause should ex proprio vigore extend to him a right to be free of injury wherever the State may be characterized as the tortfeasor. But such a reading would make of the Fourteenth Amendment a font of tort law to be superimposed upon whatever systems may already be administered by the States. We have noted the "constitutional shoals" that confront any attempt to derive from congressional civil rights statutes a body of general federal tort law; a fortiori, the procedural guarantees of the Due Process Clause cannot be the source for such law.

B

The second premise upon which the result reached by the Court of Appeals could be rested – that the infliction by state officials of a "stigma" to one's reputation is somehow different in kind from infliction . . . of harm to other interests protected by state law – is equally untenable. The words "liberty" and "property" as used in the Fourteenth Amendment do not in terms single out reputation . . . for special protection over and above other interests that may be protected by state law. . . . While not uniform in their treatment of the subject, we think that the weight of our decisions establishes no constitutional doctrine converting every defamation by a public official into a deprivation of liberty within the meaning of the Due Process Clause . . . .

[I]n *Joint Anti-Fascist Refugee Comm. v. McGrath*, the Court examined the validity of the Attorney General's designation of certain organizations as "Communist" on a list which he furnished to the Civil Service Commission. There was no majority opinion in the case . . . . JUSTICE DOUGLAS, who . . . concluded that petitioners had stated a claim, observed in his separate opinion:

> This is not an instance of name calling by public officials. This is a determination of status – a proceeding to ascertain whether the organization is or is not "subversive." This determination has consequences that are serious to the condemned organizations. Those consequences flow in part, . . . from actions of regulatory agencies that are moving in the wake of the Attorney General's determination to penalize or police these organizations.

[A]t least six of the eight Justices who participated in that case viewed any "stigma" imposed by official action of the Attorney General of the United States, divorced from its effect on the legal status of an organization or a person, such as loss of tax exemption or loss of government employment, as an insufficient basis for invoking the Due Process Clause of the Fifth Amendment. . . .

. . . .

Food for Thought

Why is stigmatization insufficient to demonstrate a loss of a constitutionally cognizable injury? Why require a loss of employment in addition to stigmatization? It is not hard to conceive of a situation where a person is stigmatized or "scarred for life" by inappropriate governmental action that results in emotional pain and psychological injuries disassociated from anything having to do with a job or a career.

It was against this backdrop that the Court in 1971 decided *Constantineau*. There the Court held that a Wisconsin statute authorizing the practice of "posting" was unconstitutional because it failed to provide procedural safeguards of notice and an opportunity to be heard, prior to an individual's being "posted." Under the statute "posting" consisted of forbidding in writing the sale or delivery of alcoholic beverages to certain persons who were determined to have become hazards to themselves, to their family, or to the community by reason of their "excessive drinking." The statute also made it a misdemeanor to sell or give liquor to any person so posted.

There is undoubtedly language in *Constantineau* which is sufficiently ambiguous to justify the reliance upon it by the Court of Appeals:

> Yet certainly where the state attaches "a badge of infamy" to the citizen, due process comes into play. . . . Where a person's good name, reputation, honor, or integrity is at stake because of what the government is doing to him, notice and an opportunity to be heard are essential.

[This] could be taken to mean that if a government official defames a person, without more, the procedural requirements of the Due Process Clause of the Fourteenth Amendment are brought into play. If read that way, it would represent a significant broadening of the holdings of *Wieman v. Updegraff*, and *Joint Anti-Fascist Refugee Comm. v. McGrath*, relied upon by the *Constantineau* Court in its analysis in the immediately preceding paragraph. We should not read this language as significantly broadening those holdings without in any way adverting to the fact if there is any other possible interpretation of *Constantineau's* language. We believe there is.

We think that the italicized language in the last sentence quoted, "because of what the government is doing to him," referred to the fact that the governmental action taken in that case deprived the individual of a right previously held under state law — the right to purchase or obtain liquor in common with the rest of the citizenry. "Posting," therefore, significantly altered her status as a matter of state law, and it was that alteration of legal status which, combined with the injury resulting from the defamation, justified the invocation of procedural safeguards. The "stigma" resulting from the defamatory character of the posting was doubtless an important factor in evaluating the extent of harm worked by that act, but we do not think that such defamation, standing alone, deprived Constantineau of any "liberty" protected by the procedural guarantees of the Fourteenth Amendment.

This conclusion is reinforced by our discussion of the subject a little over a year later in <u>Board of Regents v. Roth</u>. There we noted that "the range of interests protected by procedural due process is not infinite" . . . . While *Roth* recognized that governmental action defaming an individual in the course of declining to rehire him could entitle the person to notice and an opportunity to be heard as to the defamation, . . . the defamation had to occur in the course of the termination of employment. Certainly there is no suggestion in *Roth* to indicate that a hearing would be required each time the State in its capacity as employer might be considered responsible for a statement defaming an employee who continues to be an employee. . . .

III

It is apparent from our decisions that there exists a variety of interests which are difficult of definition but are nevertheless comprehended within the meaning of either "liberty" or "property" as meant in the Due Process Clause. These interests attain this constitutional status by virtue of the fact that they have been initially recognized and protected by state law, and we have repeatedly ruled that the procedural guarantees of the Fourteenth Amendment apply whenever the State seeks to remove or significantly alter that protected status. In *Bell v. Burson*, for example, the State by issuing drivers' licenses recognized in its citizens a right to operate a vehicle on the highways of the State. The Court held that the State could not withdraw this right without giving petitioner due process. In *Morrissey v. Brewer*, the State afforded parolees the right to remain at liberty as long as the conditions of their parole were not violated. Before the State could alter the status of a parolee because of alleged violations of these conditions, we held that the Fourteenth Amendment's guarantee of due process of law required certain procedural safeguards.

In each of these cases, as a result of the state action complained of, a right or status previously recognized by state law was distinctly altered or extinguished. It was this alteration, officially removing the interest from the recognition and protection previously afforded by the State, which we found sufficient to invoke the procedural guarantees contained in the Due Process Clause of the Fourteenth Amendment. But the interest in reputation alone which respondent seeks to vindicate in this action in federal court is quite different from the "liberty" or "property" recognized in those decisions. Kentucky law does not extend to respondent any legal guarantee of present enjoyment of reputation which has been altered as a result of petitioners' actions. Rather his interest in reputation is simply one of a number which the State may protect against injury by virtue of its tort law, providing a forum for vindication of those interests by means of damages actions. And any harm or injury to that interest, even where as here inflicted by an officer of the State, does not result in a deprivation of any "liberty" or "property" recognized by state or federal law, nor has it worked any change of respondent's status as theretofore recognized under the State's laws. For these reasons we hold that the interest in reputation asserted in this case is neither "liberty" nor "property" guaranteed against state deprivation without due process of law.

. . . .

None of respondent's theories of recovery were based upon rights secured to him by the Fourteenth Amendment. Petitioners therefore were not liable to him under § 1983. The judgment of the Court of Appeals holding otherwise is Reversed.

Underlying Case Documents

The case referenced:

The shoplifting flyer (image is the "best copy available")

1. In <u>Lambert v. Hartman, 517 F.3d 433, 445-46 (6th Cir. 2008)</u>, plaintiff Lambert "received a traffic citation for speeding. She later discovered that this citation, which contained personal identifying information (including her Social Security number), had been published on the Clerk's public website." Thereafter, Lambert was a victim of identity theft. Like the plaintiff in *Paul v. Davis*, Lambert brought suit, claiming the distribution of her name caused significant harm:

> Lambert has undoubtedly shown that, as a policy matter, the Clerk's decision to provide unfettered internet access to people's Social Security numbers was unwise. This much is evidenced by the fact that the Defendants have subsequently removed the citations in question from the website and changed the local rules to better protect sensitive personal information. But to constitutionalize a harm of the type Lambert has suffered would be to open a Pandora's box of claims under <u>42 U.S.C. § 1983</u>, a step that we are unwilling to take. *Paul v. Davis*. . . . Indeed, absent a showing of an infringement of a right that is "fundamental or implicit in the concept of ordered liberty," this court's precedents bar an action under <u>42 U.S.C. § 1983</u> from proceeding any further. Lambert has simply failed to make such a showing.

Lambert's credit was adversely affected – as well as her property. Why is this not "stigma plus?"

2. The right to a hearing to clear one's name, outside of a defamation action, is the topic of a very recent Eighth Circuit opinion. In <u>Stodghill v. Wellston School District, 512 F.3d 472 (8th Cir. 2008)</u>, a teacher was fired after it was alleged that a cheating incident had taken place involving students for whom the teacher was responsible. The teacher, Stodghill, sought a name-clearing hearing and the court found as follows:

> A procedural due process right to a name clearing hearing under certain circumstances is clearly established. <u>Putnam v. Keller, 332 F.3d 541, 546-47 (8th Cir. 2003)</u>. "A government employee is entitled to procedural due process in connection with being discharged from employment only when he has been deprived of a constitutionally protected property or liberty interest."

> In reviewing whether allegedly defamatory statements are sufficient to warrant a right to a name clearing hearing, "[t]he requisite stigma has generally been found when an employer has accused an employee of dishonesty, immorality, criminality, racism, and the like." . . . . [A]ccording to Stodghill's complaint, the [Board] members did not accuse Stodghill of cheating, but simply stated cheating occurred on his watch. Dishonesty, immorality, criminality, racism or other similar stigma relating to Stodghill

cannot be inferred from the general cheating charge. . . .

If Stodghill can show that this incident has effectively ended his career since he has been labeled "soft" on cheating, would the result differ?

3. Notice how the concept of a name-clearing hearing is separate from defamation in *Robinson v. County of Lancaster*, 2005 WL 3557825 (E.D. Pa. 2005):

> Robinson worked at Conestoga View for fifteen years providing recreational programs for the residents. On July 22, 2004, Robinson planned a . . . social at which pieces of summer fruit were served. . . . Without supervision, [untrained, teenage] volunteers served fruit to a resident who choked on the fruit and died. As a result of this death, Robinson was fired. Robinson appealed her termination as part of the grievance procedure at Conestoga View. After an informal hearing, a panel upheld the decision to terminate Robinson.

> Robinson alleges Lancaster County as owner of Conestoga View . . . violated her . . . liberty rights due to stigmatization of her reputation following her termination. Robinson claims the Defendants published false statements which destroyed her reputation and standing. *There is no constitutionally protected liberty or property interest in reputation. . . . Defamation in the course of dismissal from public employment, however, offends a liberty interest and demands procedural due process.* The Third Circuit held to allege a violation of a liberty interest under 42 U.S.C. § 1983, a plaintiff must demonstrate a valid "stigma-plus" claim. "Stigma" has been described as a governmental action that infringes upon a person's good game or reputation, and the "plus" is generally a termination of employment. If the government's stigmatizing comments violate a liberty interest, the plaintiff is entitled to a hearing to clear her name. . . . The Supreme Court has held that "where a person's good name, reputation, honor, or integrity is at stake because of what the government is doing to him, notice and opportunity to be heard are essential." *Wisconsin v. Constantineau*. If a plaintiff is "afforded . . . notice and the opportunity to respond to the allegations against [her]," her liberty rights were not violated.

> Accepting all allegations and inferences in a light most favorable to the non-moving party, this court concludes Robinson was provided with adequate notice and opportunity to be heard to overcome any liberty interest violation claim. In this case, Robinson was given an opportunity to appeal her termination through the established grievance procedures of Conestoga View. An informal hearing was held and her termination was upheld by the panel.

Do you agree – is there really no liberty or property interest implicated based on *Roth* and *Sindermann*? Alternatively, was this decision based on *Mathews v. Eldridge* – that while there was an interest, there was sufficient process provided, given the nature of the interests and the probability of accuracy in the reasoning underlying the dismissal?

4. *Chilingirian v. Boris, Jr.*, 882 F.2d 200 (6th Cir. 1989).

> [O]n December 8, 1983, the city council for Fraser, Michigan, appointed [Chilingirian's

law firm] as the city's legal counsel. . . . Chilingirian acted as the city attorney . . . . At a subsequent city council meeting . . . a resolution was passed dismissing Chilingirian from all city business effective August 1, 1987. Chilingirian was not present at that meeting. . . . In her motion to oust Chilingirian, defendant Councilwoman Wilson indicated, among other things, that Chilingirian elicited press publicity too often, . . . was not well respected by other attorneys or judges, . . . and was earning substantial sums at first class rates for less than first class legal services. Other council members present at the meeting ardently refuted each of Wilson's contentions . . . . Accounts of plaintiff's termination, including the previous remarks of council members, appeared in the newspaper, on the radio, and on television. . . .

[Upon request,] the City granted Chilingirian's request for a "name-clearing hearing." . . . . The city's response indicated that Chilingirian would be permitted to address the purportedly stigmatizing statements . . . and that, although council members could respond to those statements if they so chose, they would not be subjected to interrogation. . . . [T]he council did not respond to any questions [at the hearing]. Chilingirian [then] filed a . . . complaint [claiming] that he was denied due process in connection with the defendants' . . . refusal to conduct a name-clearing hearing consistent with due process requirements . . . .

[W]hen a "nontenured employee shows he has been stigmatized by the voluntary, public dissemination of false information in the course of a decision to terminate his employment, the employer is required to afford him an opportunity to clear his name." A name-clearing hearing is required only if an employer creates a false and defamatory impression about a particular employee in connection with his termination [and] need only provide an opportunity to clear one's name and need not comply with formal procedures to be valid. Chilingirian's failure to receive a hearing in the manner contemplated by him does not alter the fact that he did indeed receive a hearing at which he was extended ample opportunity to clear his name. No more process is required. Accordingly, summary judgment was properly granted . . . .

Why such limited process? What is actually at stake?

5. In *Hill v. Borough of Kutztown*, 455 F.3d 225, 239 (3d Cir. 2006), the mayor of Kutztown, Pennsylvania, allegedly cast severe dispersions on Hill, a public employee with no clear right to continue in his employment, i.e., with no *Roth*-like property interest. The case presented squarely the question of whether there is a right to a name-clearing hearing in a stigmatization case where the loss involves a liberty interest as opposed to a property interest.

We, too, have never clearly answered the question whether termination from a government job constitutes a sufficient "plus" under the "stigma-plus" test when, as a matter of state law, the plaintiff lacked a property interest in retaining the job. On at least one occasion we have suggested that it might. *See McKnight v. SEPTA*, 583 F.2d 1229, 1235-42 (3d Cir. 1978). . . .

We have in several cases used language that could be read broadly to require that the "plus" be loss of a job in which the plaintiff had a protectible property interest. . . . Here, however, Hill did lose his job. The "plus," consisting of Hill's constructive discharge was substantial – so substantial, in fact, that we can comfortably hold that Hill has met all requirements of "stigma-plus."

We therefore conclude today that a public employee who is defamed in the course of being terminated or constructively discharged satisfies the "stigma-plus" test even if, as a matter of state law, he lacks a property interest in the job he lost. We note that other courts have come to this conclusion, mostly based on Supreme Court language in *Paul v. Davis. See, e.g.*, <u>Doe v. United States Dep't of Justice, 753 F.2d 1092, 1104-12 (D.C. Cir. 1985)</u>. . . .

We believe that this conclusion makes good sense, and is logical. To hold otherwise – that a government employee must be deprived of a state law-created property interest in continued employment in order to satisfy the "plus" in a "stigma-plus" claim – would

> equate the interests protected by the property clause of the [Fourteenth A]mendment with those protected by the liberty clause . . . . [T]he liberty clause would be stripped of any independent meaning in the context of government defamation. Government employees who enjoy an independent property interest in continued employment, of course, must be afforded due process upon termination regardless of whether they are discharged in connection with stigmatizing allegations. That process will ordinarily afford those employees an opportunity to refute stigmatizing allegations. The liberty clause, by contrast, protects reputation, not job tenure, in the government employment context. Although *Paul* requires the alteration of some governmentally recognized status in addition to defamation, the *Paul* court plainly declined to equate that additional component with an independent, constitutionally protected property interest.

What is the specific liberty interest in play here? Is there a right not to be defamed? In <u>Bryant v. Gardner, 545 F. Supp. 2d 791 (N.D. Ill. 2008)</u>, the district court held that

> an individual can state an occupational liberty claim even if the adverse employment action involves a job in which the individual has no property interest. . . . [T]he issue for purposes of an occupational liberty claim is not whether the defendants have fired plaintiff from a particular position in which he possessed a property interest, but whether a discharge or other adverse employment action was carried out in such a manner that it will significantly impinge on the plaintiff's ability to pursue his chosen occupation.

6. On the question of the dismissal of public employees, particularly teachers, based on speech – a matter of consequence as you recall in <u>Roth</u> and <u>Sindermann</u> – JUSTICE MARSHALL defined the question to be posed in <u>Pickering v. Board of Education, 391 U.S. 563, 568 (1968)</u>:

> [I]t cannot be gainsaid that the State has interests as an employer in regulating the speech of its employees that differ significantly from those it possesses in connection with regulation of the speech of the citizenry in general. The problem in any case is

to arrive at a balance between the interests of the teacher, as a citizen, in commenting upon matters of public concern and the interest of the State, as an employer, in promoting the efficiency of the public services it performs through its employees.

In <u>Baranowski v. Waters, 2008 WL 728366 (W.D. Pa. 2008)</u>, plaintiff police officer was "constructively discharged" allegedly for comments he made regarding fellow officers who shot and killed a suspect. When plaintiff told officials that he believed the shooting was improper, he was warned not to discuss the matter and then sanctioned. The question for the court focused on the allegation that adverse action had been taken based allegedly on speech.

> Given the language in *Pickering* [above], it is clear that a public employee's right to be free from employer discipline in retaliation for speech must be grounded in the employee's interest as a citizen in speaking about matters of public concern. It is this interest which must be balanced against the employer's interest in promoting the efficiency of the public services it performs through its employees. Where a public employee does not speak as a citizen about matters of public concern, there is nothing to balance against the government's interest in the efficiency of the services that it performs through its employees. <u>Connick v. Myers, 461 U.S. 138, 147 (1983)</u> ("We hold only that when a public employee speaks not as a citizen upon matters of public concern, but instead as an employee upon matters only of personal interest, absent the most unusual circumstances, a federal court is not the appropriate forum in which to review the wisdom of a personnel decision taken by a public agency allegedly in reaction to the employee's behavior.").
>
> If it is determined that a public employee has spoken as a citizen about matters of public concern, and that his or her interest in doing so outweighed the government's interest in workplace efficiency, the employee must establish causation between his or her speech and the relevant retaliatory action in order to prevail in an action against his or her employer. . . .
>
> Since [Baranowski] did not speak "as a citizen" when he expressed his reservations about the . . . investigation . . . the Constitution did not protect him from retaliatory employer discipline. To hold otherwise would be to confuse "a public employee's right, as a citizen, to participate in discussions concerning public affairs" with Baranowski's "attempt to constitutionalize the employee grievance" in this case.

Why are comments relating to a shooting not of public concern?

ARNETT V. KENNEDY

<u>416 U.S. 134 (1974)</u>

[JUSTICE REHNQUIST] Prior to the events leading to his discharge, appellee Wayne Kennedy was a nonprobationary federal employee [in the] Office of Economic Opportunity (OEO). In March 1972, he was removed from the federal service pursuant to the provisions of the Lloyd-La Follette Act, 5 U.S.C. § 7501, after

. . . the Regional Director of the OEO, upheld written administrative charges . . . against appellee. The . . . most serious of the charges was that appellee "without any proof whatsoever and in reckless disregard of the actual facts" known to him . . . had publicly stated that Verduin and his administrative assistant had attempted to bribe a representative of a community action organization . . . . Appellee was advised of his right . . . to reply to the charges orally and in writing, and to submit affidavits to Verduin. . . . Appellee . . . instead asserted that the charges were unlawful because he had a right to a trial-type hearing before an impartial hearing officer before he could be removed from his employment . . . .

. . . .

The statutory provisions which the District Court held invalid are found in 5 U.S.C. § 7501. Subsection (a) of that section provides that "an individual in the competitive service may be removed or suspended without pay only for such cause as will promote the efficiency of the service." Subsection (b) establishes the administrative procedures by which an employee's rights under subsection (a) are to be determined, providing:

> (b) An individual in the competitive service whose removal or suspension without pay is sought is entitled to reasons in writing and to –
>
> > (1) notice of the action sought and of any charges preferred against him;
> >
> > (2) a copy of the charges;
> >
> > (3) a reasonable time for filing a written answer to the charges, with affidavits; and
> >
> > (4) a written decision on the answer at the earliest practicable date.
>
> Examination of witnesses, trial, or hearing is not required but may be provided in the discretion of the individual directing the removal or suspension without pay. . . .

. . . The only trial-type hearing available within the OEO is, by virtue of its regulations and practice, typically held after actual removal; but if the employee is reinstated on appeal, he receives full backpay, less any amounts earned by him through other employment during that period.

We must first decide whether these procedures established for the purpose of determining whether there is "cause" under the Lloyd-La Follette Act for the dismissal of a federal employee comport with procedural due process, and then decide whether that standard of "cause" for federal employee dismissals was within the constitutional power of Congress to adopt.

. . . .

[Based on *Roth* and *Perry*,] Appellee contends that he had a property interest or an expectancy of employment which could not be divested without first affording him a full adversary hearing. Here appellee did have a statutory expectancy that he not be removed other than for "such cause as will promote the efficiency of service." But the very section of the statute which granted him that right . . . expressly provided also for the procedure by which "cause" was to be determined, and expressly omitted the procedural guarantees which appellee insists are mandated by the Constitution. Only by bifurcating the very sentence of the Act of Congress which conferred upon appellee the right not to be removed save for cause could it be said that he had an expectancy of that substantive right without the procedural limitations which Congress attached to it. . . . Congress was obviously intent on according a measure of statutory job security to governmental employees which they had not previously enjoyed, but was likewise intent on excluding more elaborate procedural requirements which it felt would make the operation of the new scheme unnecessarily burdensome in practice.

Where the focus of legislation was thus strongly on the procedural mechanism for enforcing the substantive right which was simultaneously conferred, we decline to conclude that the substantive right may be viewed wholly apart from the procedure provided for its enforcement. The employee's statutorily defined right is not a guarantee against removal without cause in the abstract, but such a guarantee as enforced by the procedures which Congress has designated for the determination of cause. . . . To conclude otherwise would require us to hold that although Congress chose to enact what was essentially a legislative compromise, and with unmistakable clarity granted governmental employees security against being dismissed without "cause," but refused to accord them a full adversary hearing for the determination of "cause," it was constitutionally disabled from making such a choice. We would be holding that federal employees had been granted, as a result of the enactment of the Lloyd-La Follette Act, not merely that which Congress had given them in the first part of a sentence, but that which Congress had expressly withheld from them in the latter part of the same sentence. Neither the language of the Due Process Clause of the Fifth Amendment nor our cases construing it require any such hobbling restrictions on legislative authority in this area.

. . . .

Appellee also contends in this Court that because of the nature of the charges on which his dismissal was based, he was in effect accused of dishonesty, and that therefore a hearing was required before he could be deprived of this element of his "liberty" protected by the Fifth Amendment against deprivation without due process. . . . The liberty here implicated by appellants' action is . . . not offended by dismissal from employment itself, but instead by dismissal based upon an unsupported charge which could wrongfully injure the reputation of an employee. Since the purpose of the hearing in such a case is to provide the person "an opportunity to clear his name," a hearing afforded by administrative appeal procedures after the actual dismissal is a sufficient compliance with the requirements of the Due Process Clause. Here appellee chose not to rely on his administrative appeal, which, if his factual contentions are correct, might well have vindicated his reputation and removed any wrongful stigma from his reputation.

Appellee urges that the delays in processing agency and Civil Service Commission appeals, amounting to more than three months in over 50% of agency appeals, mean that the available administrative appeals do not suffice to protect his liberty interest recognized in *Roth*. . . . We assume that some delay attends vindication of an employee's reputation throughout the hearing procedures provided on appeal, and conclude that at least the delays cited here do not entail any separate deprivation of a liberty interest recognized in *Roth*.

. . . .

Underlying Case Documents

The case referenced:
The notice to Kennedy

---

1. *Arnett* raises fundamental First Amendment questions. To what extent are the speech interests of public sector employees protectable? In *Piscottano v. Murphy*, 511 F.3d 247 (2d Cir. 2007) (a remarkably thorough opinion and a great starting point for those interested in more information in this area), the plaintiffs were current and former employees of the Connecticut Department of Corrections. They were disciplined after it was learned that they were members of the Outlaws Motorcycle Club. Accordingly, both speech and associational interests – core First Amendment concerns – were in play:

> When acting as an employer, "the State has interests . . . in regulating the speech of its employees that differ significantly from those it possesses in connection with regulation of the speech of the citizenry in general." *Pickering v. Board of Education*, 391 U.S. 563 (1968). More than "[o]ne hundred years ago, the [Supreme] Court noted the government's legitimate purpose in 'promot[ing] efficiency and integrity in the discharge of official duties, and [in] maintain[ing] proper discipline in the public service.'" *Connick v. Myers*, 461 U.S. 138 (1983) (quoting *Ex parte Curtis*, 106 U.S. 371, 373 (1882)).

To this end, the Government, as an employer, must have wide discretion and control over the management of its personnel and internal affairs. This includes the prerogative to remove employees whose conduct hinders efficient operation and to do so with dispatch. Prolonged retention of a disruptive or otherwise unsatisfactory employee can adversely affect discipline and morale in the work place, foster disharmony, and ultimately impair the efficiency of an office or agency.

Connick. When someone who is paid a salary so that she will contribute to an agency's effective operation begins to do or say things that detract from the agency's effective operation, the government employer must have some power to restrain her. In sum, "the government as employer indeed has far broader powers than does the government as sovereign." . . . .

This does not mean that public employees, merely by accepting public employment, "relinquish the First Amendment rights they would otherwise enjoy as citizens to comment on matters of public interest in connection with the [government's] operation," *Pickering*. . . . [The task at hand is to] arrive at a balance between the interests of the [employee], as a citizen, in commenting upon matters of public concern and the interest of the State, as an employer, in promoting the efficiency of the public services it performs through its employees. *Pickering*. . . .

The *Pickering* test thus poses two questions . . . (1) whether the employee's speech as a citizen was on a matter of public concern, and if so (2) whether the employer has shown that the employee's interest in expressing himself on that matter is outweighed by injury that the speech could cause to the employer's operations. . . .

We have considered all of plaintiffs' arguments on this appeal and have found them to be without merit.

The case boils down to the government's argument that membership in the Outlaws, including clothing choices, was "conduct that could reflect negatively on DOC." Is this the type of harm that was used to balance interests in *Arnett*? See *Hartwell v. City of Montgomery*, 487 F. Supp. 2d 1313 (M.D. Ala. 2007), on tattooing, speech, and public employment.

2. In *Van Meter v. City of Lanett*, 504 F. Supp. 2d 1229 (M.D. Ala. 2007), Van Meter, a police officer, claimed he was fired because "he had expressed concern that Mayor Crawley had hired his girlfriend and other friends at unfairly high starting salaries. . . . The Van Meters also claim retaliation based on Van Meter's support for Crawley's opponent in the previous mayoral election." The City, defending its adverse action on the merits, claimed that plaintiff had taken some files without authorization. As you might guess, the issue soon focused on the speech interests of the plaintiffs. Based on what you have read thus far, how should this case have been decided? Does this speech relate to a public concern?

3. The question of disruption of the ongoing and smooth operation of a public office is central to *Arnett* — and continues to be a matter of some controversy. In

Curran v. Cousins, 509 F.3d 36 (1st Cir. 2007), an employee posted comments on a union website that attacked his supervisor (a sheriff). The comments asserted that the employer was harsh and disciplined his political rivals disproportionately. The government argued that these comments had the potential to "disrupt the sheriff's ability to discharge his duties." The court found that the speech was

Good Questions!

When would criticism of a supervisor not create the potential for disruption? Do the standards used by the court leave room for vigorous criticism? Are you convinced that the tone of speech plays a role in the extent to which the speech is protected by the First Amendment?

> defamatory of the Sheriff and put pejorative labels on those who did not engage in insubordination. Speech done in a vulgar, insulting, and defiant manner is entitled to less weight in the *Pickering* balance. . . .

> There is little question in this case that the Department's concerns about disruption were reasonable. The statements here directly went to impairing discipline by superiors, disrupting harmony and creating friction in working relationships, undermining confidence in the administration, invoking oppositional personal loyalties, and interfering with the regular operation of the enterprise.

4. In *Garcetti v. Ceballos*, 547 U.S. 410 (2006), a government lawyer wrote a memo highly critical of the actions of other public employees. The lawyer asserted that an affidavit that had been the basis for the issuance of a warrant was based on false and misleading information. Thereafter, the lawyer was allegedly, "subjected to a series of retaliatory employment actions . . . includ[ing] reassignment from his calendar deputy position to a trial deputy position, transfer to another courthouse, and denial of a promotion."

The Court held as follows: "We reject . . . the notion that the First Amendment shields from discipline the expressions employees make pursuant to their professional duties. Our precedents do not support the existence of a constitutional cause of action behind every statement a public employee makes in the course of doing his or her job."

Does this rule flow from *Arnett*? What remains of speech interests of public employees when the content of their discourse pertains to their employment?

See Press Release, American Federation of State, County and Municipal Employees *Supreme Court to Public Employees: Your Conscience or Your Job*, http://www.afscme. org/publications/6675.cfm (May 30, 2006): "The Supreme Court's recent ruling limiting the free-speech rights of public employees sends 'a chilling warning to potential government whistleblowers,' AFSCME Pres. Gerald W. McEntee says, adding that 'forcing public workers to either listen to their conscience or keep their job is just plain wrong.'"

II. Detention, Immigration, and Administrative Hearings

HAMDI V. RUMSFELD

542 U.S. 507 (2004)

[JUSTICE O'CONNOR] At this difficult time in our Nation's history, we are called upon to consider the legality of the Government's detention of a United States citizen on United States soil as an "enemy combatant" and to address the process that is constitutionally owed to one who seeks to challenge his classification as such. The United States Court of Appeals for the Fourth Circuit held that petitioner's detention was legally authorized and that he was entitled to no further opportunity to challenge his enemy-combatant label. We now vacate and remand. We hold that although Congress authorized the detention of combatants in the narrow circumstances alleged here, due process demands that a citizen held in the United States as an enemy combatant be given a meaningful opportunity to contest the factual basis for that detention before a neutral decisionmaker.

I

. . . One week [after September 11, 2001], Congress passed a resolution authorizing the President to "use all necessary and appropriate force against those nations, organizations, or persons he determines planned, authorized, committed, or aided the terrorist attacks" or "harbored such organizations or persons, in order to prevent any future acts of international terrorism against the United States by such nations, organizations or persons." Authorization for Use of Military Force ("the AUMF"). Soon thereafter, the President ordered United States Armed Forces to Afghanistan, with a mission to subdue al Qaeda and quell the Taliban regime that was known to support it.

This case arises out of the detention of . . . Yaser Esam Hamdi. Born an American citizen in Louisiana in 1980, Hamdi moved with his family to Saudi Arabia as a child. By 2001, the parties agree, he resided in Afghanistan. At some point that year, he was seized by members of the Northern Alliance . . . and eventually was turned over to the United States military. The Government . . . detained and interrogated Hamdi in Afghanistan before transferring him to . . . Guantanamo Bay . . . . In April 2002, upon learning that Hamdi is an American citizen, authorities transferred him to . . . Norfolk, Virginia, [and then to] Charleston, South Carolina. The Government contends that Hamdi is an "enemy combatant," and that this status justifies holding him in the United States indefinitely – without formal charges or proceedings – unless and until it makes the determination that access to counsel or further process is warranted.

In June 2002, Hamdi's father, Esam Fouad Hamdi, filed the present petition for a writ of habeas corpus under 28 U.S.C. § 2241 . . . . The elder Hamdi alleges in the petition that he has had no contact with his son since the Government took custody of him in 2001, and that the Government has held his son "without access to legal counsel or notice of any charges pending against him." The petition contends . . . that Hamdi's detention in the United States . . . "violated and continue to violate the Fifth and Fourteenth Amendments to the United States Constitution." The habeas petition asks that the court, among other things (1) appoint counsel for Hamdi; (2) order respondents to cease interrogating him; (3) declare that he is being held in violation of the Fifth and Fourteenth Amendments; (4) "[t]o the extent Respondents contest any material factual allegations in this Petition, schedule an evidentiary hearing, at which Petitioners may adduce proof in support of their allegations"; and (5) order that Hamdi be released from his "unlawful custody." . . . Hamdi's father has asserted . . . elsewhere in the record that his son went to Afghanistan to do "relief work," and that he had been in that country less than two months before September 11, 2001, and could not have received military training. The 20-year-old was traveling on his own for the first time, his father says, and "[b]ecause of his lack of experience, he was trapped in Afghanistan once that military campaign began."

The District Court . . . ordered that counsel be given access to Hamdi. The United States Court of Appeals for the Fourth Circuit reversed . . . holding that the District Court had failed to extend appropriate deference to the Government's security and intelligence interests. It directed the District Court to consider "the most cautious procedures first," and to conduct a deferential inquiry into Hamdi's status. It opined that "if Hamdi is indeed an 'enemy combatant' who was captured during hostilities in Afghanistan, the government's present detention of him is a lawful one."

On remand, the Government filed a response and a motion to dismiss the petition. It attached to its response a declaration from one Michael Mobbs (hereinafter "Mobbs Declaration"), who identified himself as Special Advisor to the Under Secretary of Defense for Policy. . . . Mobbs . . . set forth what remains the sole evidentiary support that the Government has provided to the courts for Hamdi's detention. The declaration states that Hamdi "traveled to Afghanistan" in July or August 2001, and that he thereafter "affiliated with a Taliban military unit and received weapons training." It asserts that Hamdi "remained with his Taliban unit following the attacks of September 11" and that, during the time when Northern Alliance forces were "engaged in battle with the Taliban," "Hamdi's Taliban unit surrendered" to those forces, after which he "surrender his Kalishnikov assault rifle" to them. . . . Mobbs states that Hamdi was labeled an enemy combatant "[b]ased upon his interviews and in light of his association with the Taliban." . . . .

. . . The District Court found that the Mobbs Declaration fell "far short" of supporting Hamdi's detention. It criticized the generic and hearsay nature of the affidavit, calling it "little more than the government's 'say-so.'" It ordered the Government to turn over numerous materials for in camera review, including copies of all of Hamdi's statements and the notes taken from interviews with him . . .; a list of all interrogators who had questioned Hamdi . . .; statements by members of the Northern Alliance regarding Hamdi's surrender and capture; . . . and the names and titles of the United States Government officials who made the determinations that Hamdi was an enemy combatant . . . . The court indicated that all of these materials were necessary for "meaningful judicial review" of whether Hamdi's detention was legally authorized and whether Hamdi had received sufficient process to satisfy the Due Process Clause of the Constitution and relevant treaties or military regulations.

The Government sought to appeal the production order, and the District Court certified the question of whether the Mobbs Declaration, "standing alone, is sufficient as a matter of law to allow meaningful judicial review of [Hamdi's] classification as an enemy combatant." The Fourth Circuit reversed, but did not squarely answer the certified question. It instead stressed that, because it was "undisputed that Hamdi was captured in a zone of active combat in a foreign theater of conflict," no factual inquiry or evidentiary hearing allowing Hamdi to be heard or to rebut the Government's assertions was necessary or proper. Concluding that the factual averments in the Mobbs Declaration, "if accurate," provided a sufficient basis upon which to conclude that the President had constitutionally detained Hamdi pursuant to the President's war powers, it ordered the habeas petition dismissed. . . .

II

The threshold question before us is whether the Executive has the authority to detain citizens who qualify as "enemy combatants." There is some debate as to the proper scope of this term, and the Government has never provided any court with the full criteria that it uses in classifying individuals as such. It has made clear, however, that, for purposes of this case, the "enemy combatant" that it is seeking to detain is an individual who, it alleges, was "part of or supporting forces hostile to the United States or coalition partners" in Afghanistan and who "engaged in an armed conflict against the United States" there. We therefore answer only the narrow question before us: whether the detention of citizens falling within that definition is authorized.

The Government maintains that no explicit congressional authorization is required, because the Executive possesses plenary authority to detain pursuant to Article II of the Constitution. We do not reach the question whether Article II provides such authority, however, because we agree with the Government's alternative position, that Congress has in fact authorized Hamdi's detention, through the AUMF. . . . The AUMF authorizes the President to use "all necessary and appropriate force" against "nations, organizations, or persons" associated with the September 11, 2001, terrorist attacks. There can be no doubt that individuals who fought against the United States in Afghanistan as part of the Taliban, an organization known to have supported the al Qaeda terrorist network responsible for those attacks, are individuals Congress sought to target in passing the AUMF. We conclude that detention of individuals falling into the limited category we are considering, for the duration of the particular conflict in which they were captured, is so fundamental and accepted an incident to war as to be an exercise of the "necessary and appropriate force" Congress has authorized the President to use.

III

Even in cases in which the detention of enemy combatants is legally authorized, there remains the question of what process is constitutionally due to a citizen who disputes his enemy-combatant status. . . . Our resolution of this dispute requires a careful examination both of the writ of habeas corpus, which Hamdi now seeks to employ as a mechanism of judicial review, and of the Due Process Clause, which informs the procedural contours of that mechanism in this instance.

A

Though they reach radically different conclusions on the process that ought to attend the present proceeding, the parties begin on common ground. All agree that, absent suspension, the writ of habeas corpus remains available to every individual detained within the United States. U.S. Const., Art. I, § 9, cl. 2. Only in the rarest of circumstances has Congress seen fit to suspend the writ. . . . All agree suspension of the writ has not occurred here. Thus, it is undisputed that Hamdi was properly before an Article III court to challenge his detention under 28 U.S.C. § 2241. Further, all agree that § 2241 and its companion provisions provide at least a skeletal outline of the procedures to be afforded a petitioner in federal habeas review. Most notably, § 2243 provides that "the person detained may, under oath, deny any of the facts set forth in the return or allege any other material facts," and § 2246 allows the taking of evidence in habeas proceedings by deposition, affidavit, or interrogatories. . . .

C

. . . .

[A] tension . . . often exists between the autonomy that the Government asserts is necessary in order to pursue effectively a particular goal and the process that a citizen contends he is due before he is deprived of a constitutional right. The ordinary mechanism that we use for balancing such serious competing interests . . . is the test that we articulated in *Mathews v. Eldridge*. . . .

1

It is beyond question that substantial interests lie on both sides of the scale in this case. Hamdi's "private interest . . . affected by the official action" is the most elemental of liberty interests – the interest in being free from physical detention by one's own government. "In our society liberty is the norm," and detention without trial "is the carefully limited exception." "We have always been careful not to 'minimize the importance and fundamental nature' of the individual's right to liberty," and we will not do so today.

Nor is the weight on this side of the *Mathews* scale offset by the circumstances of war or the accusation of treasonous behavior, for "[i]t is clear that commitment for *any* purpose constitutes a significant deprivation of liberty that requires due process protection" and at this stage in the *Mathews* calculus, we consider the interest of the *erroneously* detained individual. . . . Because we live in a society in which "[m]ere public intolerance or animosity cannot constitutionally justify the deprivation of a person's physical liberty," our starting point for the *Mathews v. Eldridge* analysis is unaltered by the allegations surrounding the particular detainee or the organizations with which he is alleged to have associated. We reaffirm today the fundamental nature of a citizen's right to be free from involuntary confinement by his own government without due process of law, and we weigh the opposing governmental interests against the curtailment of liberty that such confinement entails.

2

On the other side of the scale are the weighty and sensitive governmental interests in ensuring that those who have in fact fought with the enemy during a war do not return to battle against the United States. . . . Without doubt, our Constitution recognizes that core strategic matters of warmaking belong in the hands of those who are best positioned and most politically accountable for making them.

The Government also argues [that] military officers . . . would be unnecessarily and dangerously distracted by litigation half a world away, and discovery into military operations would both intrude on the sensitive secrets of national defense and result in a futile search for evidence buried under the rubble of war. To the extent that these burdens are triggered by heightened procedures, they are properly taken into account in our due process analysis.

3

Striking the proper constitutional balance here is of great importance to the Nation . . . . It is during our most challenging and uncertain moments that our Nation's commitment to due process is most severely tested; and it is in those times that we must preserve our commitment at home to the principles for which we fight abroad.

With due recognition of [this], we believe that neither the process proposed by the Government nor the process apparently envisioned by the District Court below strikes the proper constitutional balance when a United States citizen is detained in the United States as an enemy combatant. That is, "the risk of errone-ous deprivation" of a detainee's liberty interest is unacceptably high under the Government's proposed rule, while some of the "additional or substitute proce-dural safeguards" suggested by the District Court are unwarranted in light of their limited "probable value" and the burdens they may impose on the military in such cases.

We therefore hold that a citizen-detainee seeking to challenge his classifi-cation as an enemy combatant must receive notice of the factual basis for his classification, and a fair opportunity to rebut the Government's factual assertions before a neutral decisionmaker. ". . . . It is equally fundamental that the right to notice and an opportunity to be heard 'must be granted at a meaningful time and in a meaningful manner.'" These essential constitutional promises may not be eroded.

At the same time, the exigencies of the circumstances may demand that, aside from these core elements, enemy combatant proceedings . . . be tailored to alleviate their uncommon potential to burden the Executive at a time of ongo-ing military conflict. Hearsay, for example, may need to be accepted as the most reliable available evidence from the Government in such a proceeding. Likewise, the Constitution would not be offended by a presumption in favor of the Govern-ment's evidence, so long as that presumption remained a rebuttable one and fair opportunity for rebuttal were provided. Thus, once the Government puts forth credible evidence that the habeas petitioner meets the enemy-combatant criteria, the onus could shift to the petitioner to rebut that evidence with more persuasive evidence that he falls outside the criteria. A burden-shifting scheme of this sort would meet the goal of ensuring that the errant tourist, embedded journalist, or local aid worker has a chance to prove military error while giving due regard to the Executive once it has put forth meaningful support for its conclusion that the detainee is in fact an enemy combatant. In the words of *Mathews*, process of this sort would sufficiently address the "risk of erroneous deprivation" of a detainee's liberty interest while eliminating certain procedures that have questionable additional value in light of the burden on the Government.

We think it unlikely that this basic process will have the dire impact on the central functions of warmaking that the Government forecasts. The parties agree that initial captures on the battlefield need not receive the process we have discussed here; that process is due only when the determination is made to *continue* to hold those who have been seized. The Government has made clear in its briefing that documentation regarding battlefield detainees already is kept in the ordinary course of military affairs. Any factfinding imposition created by requiring a knowledgeable affiant to summarize these records to an independent tribunal is a minimal one. Likewise, arguments that military officers ought not have to wage war under the threat of litigation lose much of their steam when factual disputes at enemy-combatant hearings are limited to the alleged combatant's acts. This focus meddles little, if at all, in the strategy or conduct of war, inquiring only into the appropriateness of continuing to detain an individual claimed to have taken up arms against the United States. . . .

In sum, while the full protections that accompany challenges to detentions in other settings may prove unworkable and inappropriate in the enemy-combatant setting, the threats to military operations posed by a basic system of independent review are not so weighty as to trump a citizen's core rights to challenge meaningfully the Government's case and to be heard by an impartial adjudicator.

D

. . . .

. . . Plainly, the "process" Hamdi has received is not that to which he is entitled under the Due Process Clause. There remains the possibility that the standards we have articulated could be met by an appropriately authorized and properly constituted military tribunal. Indeed, it is notable that military regulations already provide for such process in related instances, dictating that tribunals be made available to determine the status of enemy detainees who assert prisoner-of-war status under the Geneva Convention. In the absence of such process, however, a court that receives a petition for a writ of habeas corpus from an alleged enemy combatant must itself ensure that the minimum requirements of due process are achieved. . . . As we have discussed, a habeas court in a case such as this may accept affidavit evidence like that contained in the Mobbs Declaration, so long as it also permits the alleged combatant to present his own factual case to rebut the

Government's return. . . . We have no reason to doubt that courts faced with these sensitive matters will pay proper heed both to the matters of national security that might arise in an individual case and to the constitutional limitations safeguarding essential liberties that remain vibrant even in times of security concerns.

IV

Hamdi asks us to hold that the Fourth Circuit also erred by denying him immediate access to counsel upon his detention and by disposing of the case without permitting him to meet with an attorney. Since our grant of certiorari in this case, Hamdi has been appointed counsel . . . with whom he is now being granted unmonitored meetings. He unquestionably has the right to access to counsel in connection with the proceedings on remand. No further consideration of this issue is necessary at this stage of the case.

The judgment of the United States Court of Appeals for the Fourth Circuit is vacated, and the case is remanded for further proceedings. . . .

[JUSTICE SCALIA, dissenting.]

President Lincoln, when he purported to suspend habeas corpus without congressional authorization during the Civil War, apparently did not doubt that suspension was required if the prisoner was to be held without criminal trial. . . . The proposition that the Executive lacks indefinite wartime detention authority over citizens is consistent with the Founders' general mistrust of military power permanently at the Executive's disposal. . . . Hamdi is entitled to a habeas decree requiring his release unless (1) criminal proceedings are promptly brought, or (2) Congress has suspended the writ of habeas corpus. . . . [Neither of which has occurred.]

[However, h]aving found a congressional authorization for detention of citizens where none clearly exists . . . the plurality then proceeds, under the guise of the Due Process Clause, to prescribe what procedural protections *it* thinks appropriate . . . and – just as though writing a new Constitution – comes up with an unheard-of system in which the citizen rather than the Government bears the burden of proof, testimony is by hearsay rather than live witnesses, and the presiding officer may well be a "neutral" military officer rather than judge and jury. It claims authority to engage in this sort of "judicious balancing" from *Mathews v. Eldridge*, a case involving . . . *the withdrawal of disability benefits!* Whatever the merits of this technique when newly recognized property rights are at issue (and even there they are questionable), it has no place where the Constitution and the common law already supply an answer. . . .

. . . If the situation demands it, the Executive can ask Congress to authorize suspension of the writ – which can be made subject to whatever conditions Congress deems appropriate, including even the procedural novelties invented by the plurality today. . . . If civil rights are to be curtailed during wartime, it must be done openly and democratically, as the Constitution requires, rather than by silent erosion through an opinion of this Court. . . .

[JUSTICE SOUTER, concurring in part.]

Because I find Hamdi's detention forbidden by § 4001(a) and unauthorized by the Force Resolution, I would not reach any questions of what process he may be due in litigating disputed issues . . . . Since this disposition does not command a majority of the Court, however, [I] join with the plurality in ordering remand on terms closest to those I would impose. . . .

[Therefore, theoretically, I could hardly disagree] that someone in Hamdi's position is entitled at a minimum to notice of the Government's claimed factual basis for holding him, and to a fair chance to rebut it before a neutral decision-maker; nor, of course, could I disagree with the plurality's affirmation of Hamdi's right to counsel. On the other hand, I do not mean to imply agreement that the Government could claim an evidentiary presumption casting the burden of rebuttal on Hamdi, or that an opportunity to litigate before a military tribunal might obviate or truncate enquiry by a court on habeas. . . .

Underlying Case Documents

The case referenced:
The Authorization for Use of Military Force
Geneva Convention

1. The topic of immigration and detention of both U.S. and foreign nationals has come up a number of different times in this casebook. Listed below are the cases and articles we have already addressed in this field. We recommend going to the online version of this text and clicking on each source to become re-acquainted with these materials.

Cases

Emokah v. Mukasey, 523 F.3d 110 (2d Cir. 2008)
Singh v. Gonzales, 468 F.3d 135, 138-39 (2d Cir. 2006)
Corovic v. Mukasey, 519 F.3d 90, 95 (2d Cir. 2008)

Ngure v. Ashcroft, 367 F.3d 975 (8th Cir. 2004)

Ekasinta v. Gonzales, 415 F.3d 1188, 1189 (10th Cir. 2005)

Lanza v. Ashcroft, 389 F.3d 917, 920 (9th Cir. 2004)

Chen v. Ashcroft, 378 F.3d 1081, 1088 (9th Cir. 2004)

Sayyadinejad v. Chertoff, 2007 WL 4410356 (S.D. Cal. 2007)

Tang v. Chertoff, 2007 WL 2462187 (E.D. Ky. 2007)

INS v. Enrico St. Cyr, 533 U.S. 289 (2001)

Jimenez-Angeles v. Ashcroft, 291 F.3d 594 (9th Cir. 2002)

Castello-Diaz v. United States, 174 Fed. Appx. 719 (3d Cir. 2006)

Campbell v. Ashcroft, 2004 WL 1563022 (E.D. Pa. 2004)

Falconi v. INS, 240 F. Supp. 2d 215 (E.D.N.Y. 2002)

Lopez v. Gonzales, 549 U.S. 47 (2006)

Ibrahim v. Chertoff, 529 F. Supp. 2d 611, 614 (E.D.N.C. 2007).

Zeru v. Gonzales, 503 F.3d 59 (1st Cir. 2007)

Lozada v. INS, 857 F.2d 10, 13 (1st Cir. 1988)

Saakian v. INS, 252 F.3d 21, 25 (1st Cir. 2001)

Hill v. Lockhart, 474 U.S. 52, 56 (1985)

Magallanes-Damian v. INS, 783 F.2d 931, 933 (9th Cir. 1986)

In re Cecilia Rivera-Claros, 21 I. & N. Dec. 232 (BIA 1996)

Lu v. Ashcroft, 259 F.3d 127, 131 (3d Cir. 2001)

Fadiga v. United States, 488 F.3d 142 (3d Cir. 2007)

Hernandez-Rodriguez v. Pasquarell, 118 F.3d 1034 (5th Cir. 1997)

Singh v. Gonzales, 451 F.3d 400 (6th Cir. 2006)

INS v. Cardoza-Fonseca, 480 U.S. 421 (1987)

Socop-Gonzalez v. INS, 272 F.3d 1176 (9th Cir. 2001)

Niam v. Ashcroft, 354 F.3d 652 (7th Cir. 2004)

Samirah v. Mukasey, 2008 WL 450823 (N.D. Ill. 2008)

The Japanese Immigrant Case, 189 U.S. 86, 100-01 (1903)

Johnson v. Gonzales, 478 F.3d 795, 798 (7th Cir. 2007)

Boumediene v. Bush, 128 S. Ct. 2229 (2008).

De la Llana-Castellon v. INS, 16 F.3d 1093 (10th Cir. 1994),

Yosd v. Mukasey, 514 F.3d 74, 77 (1st Cir. 2008)

Marincas v. Lewis, 92 F.3d 195, 203-04 (3d Cir. 1996)

Jian Yun Zheng v. DOJ, 409 F.3d 43, 46 (2d Cir. 2005)

Board of Immigration Appeals: Procedural Reforms to Improve Case Management, 67 Fed. Reg. 54,878, 54,893 (Aug. 26, 2002) (codified at 8 C.F.R. § 1003.1 (2002)

Zhong v. United States, 480 F.3d 104 (2d Cir. 2007)

Kambolli v. Gonzales, 449 F.3d 454, 459 (2d Cir. 2006)

Yu Sheng Zhang v. DOJ, 362 F.3d 155, 156-59 (2d Cir. 2004)

Articles

Jessica R. Hertz, Comment, <u>Appellate Jurisdiction over the Board of Immigration Appeals's Affirmance Without Opinion Procedure</u>, 73 U. Chi. L. Rev. 1019 (2006)

John R. B. Palmer, <u>Seeking Review: Immigration Law and Federal Court Jurisdiction: The Nature and Causes of the Immigration Surge in the Federal Courts of Appeals: A Preliminary Analysis</u>, 51 N.Y.L. Sch. L. Rev. 13 (2007)

Martin S. Krezalek, Note, <u>How to Minimize the Risk of Violating Due Process Rights While Preserving the BIA's Ability to Affirm Without Opinion</u>, 21 Geo. Immigr. L.J. 277 (2007)

John J. Francis, <u>Failure to Advise Non-Citizens of Immigration Consequences of Criminal Convictions: Should this Be Grounds to Withdraw a Guilty Plea?</u>, 36 U. Mich. J.L. Reform 691 (2003)

William Funk, <u>The Rise and Purported Demise of</u> Wong Yang Sung, 58 Admin. L. Rev. 881 (2006)

Bradley J. Wyatt, <u>Even Aliens Are Entitled to Due Process: Extending</u> Mathews v. Eldridge <u>Balancing to Board of Immigration Procedural Reforms</u>, 12 Wm. & Mary Bill of Rts. J. 605 (2004)

Ricardo J. Bascuas, <u>The Unconstitutionality of "Hold Until Cleared": Reexamining Material Witness Detentions in the Wake of the September 11th Dragnet</u>, 58 Vand. L. Rev. 677 (2005)

Jesselyn A. Radack, <u>You Say Defendant, I Say Combatant: Opportunistic Treatment of Terrorism Suspects Held in the United States and the Need for Due Process</u>, 29 NYU Rev. L. & Soc. Change 525 (2005)

Leti Volpp, <u>The Citizen and the Terrorist</u>, 49 UCLA L. Rev. 1575 (2002)

2. Does the Administrative Procedure Act apply to immigration proceedings? In <u>Marcello v. Bonds</u>, 349 U.S. 302 (1955), the Court held that the Immigration and Nationality Act of 1952 (INA), <u>8 U.S.C. § 1101</u> et. seq., "expressly supersedes" the APA, overruling that part of the holding in <u>Wong Yang Sung v. McGrath</u>, 339 U.S. 33 (1950). That means that independent claims based on the APA and <u>28 U.S.C. § 1331</u> are unavailable. <u>Ardestani v. INS</u>, 502 U.S. 129 (1991).

3. If not the APA, then what? What is the basis for a claim for a fair administrative hearing in the immigration area? In the last six months, the courts have addressed this question directly:

a. *Santosa v. Mukasey*, 528 F.3d 88 (1st Cir. 2008).

> We review de novo a claim that an immigration judge's conduct violated a petitioner's procedural due process rights. An alien in an immigration proceeding is entitled to "a reasonable opportunity to examine the evidence against the alien, to present evidence on the alien's own behalf, and to cross-examine witnesses presented by the Government . . . ." 8 U.S.C. § 1229a(b)(4)(B). . . . [This entitles] an alien . . . to a fair hearing, not necessarily a perfect one." *Pulisir v. Mukasey.* In the end, an alien must show prejudice in order to succeed on a due process claim. Prejudice is found where "an abridgment of due process is likely to have affected the outcome of the proceedings." *Pulsir.*

b. *Pulisir v. Mukasey*, 524 F.3d 302 (1st Cir. 2008), referred to above, provides the next piece of the puzzle:

> When a due process challenge is aimed at a trial-management ruling, a reviewing court must keep in mind the tension that exists between a trial judge's right to regulate the course of a hearing and an alien's right to present evidence to his own behoof. *Compare* 8 C.F.R. § 1240.1(c) *with* 8 U.S.C. § 1229a(b)(4)(B). . . .
>
> [E]videntiary standards are applied more loosely in administrative hearings than in court cases. See 8 C.F.R. § 1240.7; *see also Niam v. Ashcroft*, 354 F.3d 652, 659 (9th Cir. 2004) ("[A]dministrative agencies are not bound by the hearsay rule or any other of the conventional rules of evidence, but only by the looser standard of due process of law."). Still, the trial judge must be accorded some flexibility in his efforts to ensure that speculation and surmise do not become proxies for probative evidence.

c. The source of the entitlement to a fair hearing is the Fifth Amendment Due Process Clause. *Vasha v. Gonzales*, 410 F.3d 863 (6th Cir. 2005).

> We have stated that "Fifth Amendment guarantees of due process extend to aliens in [removal] proceedings, entitling them to a full and fair hearing. To constitute fundamental unfairness, however, a defect in the removal proceedings must have been such as might have led to a denial of justice." . . . . [R]eviewing an alleged due process violation is a two-step inquiry: first, whether there was a defect in the removal proceeding; and second, whether the alien was prejudiced because of it.

d. What about Sixth Amendment protections? In *Blanco v. Mukasey*, 518 F.3d 714 (9th Cir. 2008), the court held:

> Individuals in immigration proceedings do not have Sixth Amendment rights, so ineffective assistance of counsel claims are analyzed under the Fifth Amendment's due process clause. Ineffective assistance of counsel in a removal proceeding is a denial of due process if the proceeding "was so fundamentally unfair that the alien was prevented from reasonably presenting his case." . . . . [The alien] must also show that he was prejudiced by his counsel's ineffective performance.

4. The Supreme Court's most recent elaboration of *Hamdi*, and discussion of the legislation pertaining to fair hearings and detention, is in *Boumediene v. Bush*, 553

U.S. 723 (2008). Writing for the majority, JUSTICE KENNEDY explained:

> In *Hamdi* [we] recognized that detention of individuals who fought against the United States in Afghanistan "for the duration of the particular conflict in which they were captured, is so fundamental and accepted an incident to war as to be an exercise of the 'necessary and appropriate force' Congress has authorized the President to use."
> . . . . After *Hamdi*, the Deputy Secretary of Defense established Combatant Status Review Tribunals (CSRTs) to determine whether individuals detained at Guantanamo were "enemy combatants," as the Department defines that term. A later memorandum established procedures to implement the CSRTs. The Government maintains these procedures were designed to comply with the due process requirements identified by the plurality in *Hamdi*. . . .
>
> Congress passed the Detainee Treatment Act [Subsection (e) of § 1005,]- 28 U.S.C. § 2241 to provide that "no court, justice, or judge shall have jurisdiction to hear or consider . . . an application for a writ of habeas corpus filed by or on behalf of an alien detained by the Department of Defense at Guantanamo Bay, Cuba." 119 Stat. 2742. Section 1005 further provides that the Court of Appeals for the District of Columbia Circuit shall have "exclusive" jurisdiction to review decisions of the CSRTs.
>
> In *Hamdan v. Rumsfeld*, 548 U.S. 557, 576-577 (2006), the Court held this provision did not apply to cases (like petitioners') pending when the DTA was enacted. Congress responded by passing the MCA, 10 U.S.C. § 948a et seq. (Supp. 2007), which again amended § 2241. . . . (Four Members of the *Hamdan* majority noted that "[n]othing prevent[ed] the President from returning to Congress to seek the authority he believes necessary." . . . . The authority to which the concurring opinion referred was the authority to "create military commissions of the kind at issue" in the case. . . .
>
> The idea that the necessary scope of habeas review in part depends upon the rigor of any earlier proceedings accords with our test for procedural adequacy in the due process context. *See Mathews v. Eldridge* (noting that the Due Process Clause requires an assessment of, *inter alia*, "the risk of an erroneous deprivation of [a liberty interest;] and the probable value, if any, of additional or substitute procedural safeguards"). This principle has an established foundation in *habeas corpus* jurisprudence as well, as CHIEF JUSTICE MARSHALL's opinion in *Ex parte Watkins*, 28 U.S. 193 (1830). . . .
>
> Where a person is detained by executive order, rather than, say, after being tried and convicted in a court, the need for collateral review is most pressing. A criminal conviction in the usual course occurs after a judicial hearing before a tribunal disinterested in the outcome and committed to procedures designed to ensure its own independence. These dynamics are not inherent in executive detention orders or executive review procedures. In this context the need for habeas corpus is more urgent. The intended duration of the detention and the reasons for it bear upon the precise scope of the inquiry. Habeas corpus proceedings need not resemble a criminal trial, even when the detention is by executive order. But the writ must be effective. The habeas court must have sufficient authority to conduct a meaningful review of both the cause for detention and the Executive's power to detain. . . .
>
> [The Court found the bar to habeas corpus to be unconstitutional.]
>
> [CHIEF JUSTICE ROBERTS, dissenting.]

Today the Court strikes down as inadequate the most generous set of procedural protections ever afforded aliens detained by this country as enemy combatants. The political branches crafted these procedures amidst an ongoing military conflict, after much careful investigation and thorough debate. The Court rejects them today out of hand, without bothering to say what due process rights the detainees possess, without explaining how the statute fails to vindicate those rights, and before a single petitioner has even attempted to avail himself of the law's operation. And to what effect? The majority merely replaces a review system designed by the people's representatives with a set of shapeless procedures to be defined by federal courts at some future date.

a. For a general discussion of habeas corpus and fair hearings, see Mario L. Barnes & F. Greg Bowman, *The Uses and Abuses of Executive Power: Entering Unprecedented Terrain: Charting a Method To Reduce Madness in Post-9/11 Power and Rights Conflicts*, 62 U. MIAMI L. REV. 365 (2008) (setting out a balanced and scholarly perspective on detention, immigration and the use of executive power); and Emily Calhoun, *The Accounting: Habeas Corpus and Enemy Combatants*, 79 U. COLO. L. REV. 77 (2008), arguing that "[t]he judiciary should impose a heavy burden of justification on the executive when a habeas petitioner challenges the accuracy of facts on which an enemy combatant designation rests [because a] heavy burden of justification will ensure that the essential institutional purposes of the writ – and legitimate, separated-powers government – are preserved, even during times of national exigency."

b. *Munaf v. Geren*, 553 U.S. 674 (2008), a companion case to *Boumedeine*, involved the

availability of habeas corpus relief arising from [the] detention of American citizens who voluntarily traveled to Iraq and are alleged to have committed crimes there. We are confronted with two questions. First, do United States courts have jurisdiction over habeas corpus petitions filed on behalf of American citizens challenging their detention in Iraq by the Multi National Force-I (MNF-I)? Second, if such jurisdiction exists, may district courts exercise that jurisdiction to enjoin the MNF-I from transferring such individuals to Iraqi custody or allowing them to be tried before Iraqi courts?

We conclude that the habeas statute extends to American citizens held overseas by American forces operating subject to an American chain of command, even when those forces are acting as part of a multinational coalition. . . . [However, habeas corpus was deemed inappropriate in this case.]

[O]ur cases make clear that Iraq has a sovereign right to prosecute Omar and Munaf for crimes committed on its soil. As Chief Justice Marshall explained nearly two centuries ago, "[t]he jurisdiction of the nation within its own territory is necessarily exclusive and absolute." *The Schooner Exchange v. McFaddon*, 11 U.S. 116 (1812).

There appear to be limits on the doctrine announced above. In *Khouzam v. Hogan*, 529 F. Supp. 2d 543 (M.D. Pa. 2008), the complainant, Khouzam, was charged with a crime in Egypt. In a hearing involving his case in the United States, the court found that Khouzam had a right to a fair hearing and to be free from torture (which Khouzam claimed was prevalent in Egypt):

> [The] Due Process Clause mandates a fair process that includes review of the diplomatic assurance by an impartial adjudicator. . . . Accordingly, his habeas corpus petition will be granted. Because there is no probability that Khouzam will be removed from the United States in the reasonably foreseeable future, the Government will be ordered to release him subject to appropriate terms and conditions. . . ."

> Khouzam's "inalienable human right" to be free from torture is worthy of protection under the Due Process Clause. Ascertaining what process is required involves an assessment of the interests at stake, the risk of an erroneous determination resulting from the process employed, and the burden imposed on the Government by additional procedural safeguards. *See Mathews v. Eldridge.*

c. As this book goes to press, the question of the timing and nature of the hearing to which a detainee has an entitlement is still a matter of controversy. The Los Angeles Times reported that on July 9, 2008, United States District Court Senior Judge Thomas F. Hogan ordered the Department of Justice "to put other cases aside and give detainees their day in court. . . . The time has come to move these forward. . . . Set aside every other case that's pending in the division and address this case first."

> Attorneys, nearly all of them working without pay, have long asked for a judge to scrutinize the evidence, saying the detainees could not be held indefinitely simply on the government's say-so. . . . The government is asking for about eight weeks to . . . update and add to evidence that was originally used to justify holding the detainees. . . . Hogan was skeptical. If the evidence was enough to warrant holding the detainees for six years, he said, why must it be changed now?

Judge Orders Guantanamo Detainee Hearings, L.A. Times, July 9, 2008, http://www.latimes.com/news/nationworld/nation/la-na-gitmo9-2008jul09,0,3732280.story?track=rss (last visited July 12, 2008).

Based on *Hamdi*, how long can the federal government hold individuals designated enemy combatants without a hearing based on the "government's say-so?" Notice that in note 4.b (above), part of the calculus involves a *Mathews* assessment – how would you "fill in" the component parts of that assessment? Give it a try: What is the interest of the individual? The interest of the government? The risk of error? What issues of justice and fairness are in play? Read the note below carefully – does your answer change?

5. Along with *Hamdi*, if you have an interest in this field, we urge you to read in

full *Hamdan v. Rumsfeld, 548 U.S. 557 (2006)*. A short excerpt is set out below:

On September 11, 2001, agents of the al Qaeda terrorist organization hijacked commercial airplanes and attacked the World Trade Center in New York City and the national headquarters of the Department of Defense in Arlington, Virginia. Americans will never forget the devastation wrought by these acts. Nearly 3,000 civilians were killed.

Congress responded by adopting a Joint Resolution authorizing the President to "use all necessary and appropriate force against those nations, organizations, or persons he determines planned, authorized, committed, or aided the terrorist attacks . . . in order to prevent any future acts of international terrorism against the United States by such nations, organizations or persons." Authorization for Use of Military Force (AUMF), 115 Stat. 224, note following 50 U.S.C. § 1541 (2000 ed., Supp. III). Acting pursuant to the AUMF, and having determined that the Taliban regime had supported al Qaeda, the President ordered the Armed Forces of the United States to invade Afghanistan. In the ensuing hostilities, hundreds of individuals, Hamdan among them, were captured and eventually detained at Guantanamo Bay.

On November 13, 2001, while the United States was still engaged in active combat with the Taliban, the President issued a comprehensive military order intended to govern the "Detention, Treatment, and Trial of Certain Non-Citizens in the War Against Terrorism," 66 Fed. Reg. 57833 (hereinafter November 13 Order or Order). Those subject to the November 13 Order include any noncitizen for whom the President determines "there is reason to believe" that he or she (1) "is or was" a member of al Qaeda or (2) has engaged or participated in terrorist activities aimed at or harmful to the United States. Any such individual "shall, when tried, be tried by military commission for any and all offenses triable by military commission that such individual is alleged to have committed, and may be punished in accordance with the penalties provided under applicable law, including life imprisonment or death." The November 13 Order vested in the Secretary of Defense the power to appoint military commissions to try individuals subject to the Order, but that power has since been delegated to John D. Altenburg, Jr., a retired Army major general and longtime military lawyer who has been designated "Appointing Authority for Military Commissions."

On July 3, 2003, the President announced his determination that Hamdan and five other detainees at Guantanamo Bay were subject to the November 13 Order and thus triable by military commission. In December 2003, military counsel was appointed to represent Hamdan. Two months later, counsel filed demands for charges and for a speedy trial pursuant to Article 10 of the UCMJ, 10 U.S.C. § 810. On February 23, 2004, the legal adviser to the Appointing Authority denied the applications, ruling that Hamdan was not entitled to any of the protections of the UCMJ. Not until July 13, 2004, after Hamdan had commenced this action in the United States District Court for the Western District of Washington, did the Government finally charge him with the offense for which, a year earlier, he had been deemed eligible for trial by military commission. . . .

The military commission, a tribunal neither mentioned in the Constitution nor created by statute, was born of military necessity. . . . Though foreshadowed in some respects by earlier tribunals like the Board of General Officers that General Washington convened to try British Major John Andre for spying during the Revolutionary War, the commission "as such" was inaugurated in 1847. . . . As commander of occupied Mexican territory, and having available to him no other tribunal, General Winfield Scott that year ordered the establishment of both "military commissions" to try ordinary crimes committed in the occupied territory and a "council of war" to try offenses against the law of war. . . .

When the exigencies of war next gave rise to a need for use of military commissions, during the Civil War, the dual system favored by General Scott was not adopted. Instead, a single tribunal often took jurisdiction over ordinary crimes, war crimes, and breaches of military orders alike. . . .

Exigency alone, of course, will not justify the establishment and use of penal tribunals not contemplated by Article I, § 8, and Article III, § 1, of the Constitution unless some other part of that document authorizes a response to the felt need. . . .

The Constitution makes the President the "Commander in Chief" of the Armed Forces, Art. II, § 2, cl. 1, but vests in Congress the powers to "declare War . . . and make Rules concerning Captures on Land and Water," Art. I, § 8, cl. 11. . . .

[In *Ex parte Milligan* CHIEF JUSTICE CHASE held that]:

> The power to make the necessary laws is in Congress; the power to execute in the President. Both powers imply many subordinate and auxiliary powers. Each includes all authorities essential to its due exercise. But neither can the President, in war more than in peace, intrude upon the proper authority of Congress, nor Congress upon the proper authority of the President. . . . Congress cannot direct the conduct of campaigns, nor can the President, or any commander under him, without the sanction of Congress, institute tribunals for the trial and punishment of offences, either of soldiers or civilians, unless in cases of a controlling necessity, which justifies what it compels, or at least insures acts of indemnity from the justice of the legislature.

Contrary to the Government's assertion, [prior case law does] not view the authorization as a sweeping mandate for the President to "invoke military commissions when he deems them necessary. . . ."

Whether or not the President has independent power, absent congressional authorization, to convene military commissions, he may not disregard limitations that Congress has, in proper exercise of its own war powers, placed on his powers. . . .

Whether or not the Government has charged Hamdan with an offense against the law of war cognizable by military commission, the commission lacks power to proceed. The UCMJ [Uniform Code of Military Justice] conditions the President's use of military commissions on compliance not only with the American common law of war, but also with the rest of the UCMJ itself, insofar as applicable, and with the "rules and precepts of the law of nations," . . . including, *inter alia*, the four Geneva Conventions signed in 1949. The procedures that the Government has decreed will govern Hamdan's trial by commission violate these laws.

6. While *Hamdan* places some limits on executive power in the immigration and detention field, the power of Congress is another matter. Short of interfering with the enumerated power of the President in Article II, Congress has expansive power to establish norms and processes for detention and immigration. In *Chae Chan Ping (Chinese Exclusion Case) v. United States*, 130 U.S. 581 (1889), a foundational case regarding the treatment of foreign nationals, the Court recognized a plenary power regarding the capacity of Congress to define the parameters in the field and articulated a somewhat contorted contractarian theory to define the implicit obligations of non-U.S. persons and the federal government.

7. The magnitude of the challenge to fairly process immigration cases cannot be over-emphasized. *See* Migration Pol'y Inst., *Behind the Naturalization Backlog: Causes, Context, and Concerns*, IMMIGRATION FACTS (Jan. 2008), http://www.migrationpolicy.org/pubs/FS21_NaturalizationBacklog_022608.pdf. There are over one million pending cases – and applications have increased 82% in the last year. The complex political and ideological responses to immigration and detention are captured in MARK KRIKORIAN, THE NEW CASE AGAINST IMMIGRATION, BOTH LEGAL AND ILLEGAL (Sentinel, 2008). The economics of immigration also provokes debate. *See* Adam B. Cox & Eric A. Posner, *The Second-Order Structure of Immigration Law*, 59 STAN. L. REV. 809, 827-29 (2007) (assessing critically the treatment of immigrant workers as probationers).

8. Finally, you might give some thought to federalism issues raised in this field. Immigration enforcement, once thought exclusively a federal obligation, is now the subject of significant state and local government activity.

For More Information

See Cristina M. Rodriguez, *The Significance of the Local in Immigration Regulation*, 106 MICH. L. REV. 567 (2008); Michael A. Olivas, *Immigration-Related State and Local Ordinances: Preemption, Prejudice, and the Proper Role for Enforcement*, 2007 U. CHI. LEGAL F. 27; Peter H. Schuck, *Taking Immigration Federalism Seriously*, 2007 U. CHI. LEGAL F. 57; Matthew Parlow, *A Localist's Case for Decentralizing Immigration Policy*, 84 DENV. U.L. REV. 1061 (2007); Karla Mari McKanders, *Welcome to Hazleton! "Illegal" Immigrants Beware: Local Immigration Ordinances and What the Federal Government Must Do About It*, 39 LOY. U. CHI. L.J. 1 (2007); Nathan G. Cortez, *The Local Dilemma: Preemption and the Role of Federal Standards in State and Local Immigration Laws*, 61 SMU L. REV. 47 (2008).

III. Administrative Hearings and Prosecutorial Discretion

DeShaney v. Winnebago County Department of Social Services

489 U.S. 189 (1989)

[CHIEF JUSTICE REHNQUIST] The facts of this case are undeniably tragic. Petitioner Joshua DeShaney was born in 1979. In 1980, [a divorce court] awarded custody of Joshua to his father, Randy DeShaney. The father shortly thereafter moved to . . . Winnebago County, Wisconsin, taking the infant Joshua with him. . . .

The Winnebago County authorities first learned that Joshua DeShaney might be a victim of child abuse in January 1982, when his father's second wife complained to the police . . . . The Winnebago County Department of Social Services (DSS) interviewed the father, but he denied the accusations, and DSS did not pursue them further. In January 1983, Joshua was admitted to a local hospital with multiple bruises and abrasions. The examining physician suspected child abuse and notified DSS, which immediately obtained an order from a Wisconsin juvenile court placing Joshua in the temporary custody of the hospital. Three days later, the county convened an ad hoc "Child Protection Team" . . . to consider Joshua's situation. At this meeting, the Team decided that there was insufficient evidence of child abuse to retain Joshua in the custody of the court. The Team did, however, decide to recommend several measures to protect Joshua . . . . Randy DeShaney entered into a voluntary agreement with DSS in which he promised to cooperate with [these measures].

[The court] returned Joshua to the custody of his father. A month later, emergency room personnel called . . . to report that [Joshua] had once again been treated for suspicious injuries. The caseworker concluded that there was no basis for action. For the next six months, the caseworker made monthly visits to the DeShaney home, during which she observed a number of suspicious injuries on Joshua's head . . . . The caseworker dutifully recorded these incidents in her files, along with her continuing suspicions that someone in the DeShaney household was physically abusing Joshua, but she did nothing more. In November 1983, the emergency room notified DSS that Joshua had been treated once again for injuries that they believed to be caused by child abuse. On the caseworker's next two visits to the DeShaney home, she was told that Joshua was too ill to see her. Still DSS took no action.

In March 1984, Randy DeShaney beat 4-year-old Joshua so severely that he fell into a life-threatening coma. Emergency brain surgery revealed a series of hemorrhages caused by traumatic injuries to the head inflicted over a long period of time. Joshua did not die, but he suffered brain damage so severe that he is expected to spend the rest of his life confined to an institution for the profoundly retarded. Randy DeShaney was subsequently tried and convicted of child abuse.

Joshua and his mother brought this action under 42 U.S.C. § 1983 . . . against respondents Winnebago County, DSS, and various individual employees of DSS. The complaint alleged that respondents had deprived Joshua of his liberty without due process of law, in violation of his rights under the Fourteenth Amendment, by failing to intervene to protect him against a risk of violence at his father's hands of which they knew or should have known. The District Court granted summary judgment for respondents. The Court of Appeals for the Seventh Circuit affirmed, holding that petitioners had not made out an actionable § 1983 claim . . . . We now affirm.

II

The Due Process Clause of the Fourteenth Amendment provides that "[n]o State shall . . . deprive any person of life, liberty, or property, without due process of law." Petitioners contend that the State deprived Joshua of his liberty interest in "free[dom] from . . . unjustified intrusions on personal security," *see Ingraham v. Wright*, by failing to provide him with adequate protection against his father's violence. The claim is one invoking the substantive rather than the procedural component of the Due Process Clause; petitioners do not claim that the State denied Joshua protection without according him appropriate procedural safeguards, but that it was categorically obligated to protect him in these circumstances. n.2

> n.2 Petitioners also argue that the Wisconsin child protection statutes gave Joshua an "entitlement" to receive protective services in accordance with the terms of the statute, an entitlement which would enjoy due process protection against state deprivation under our decision in *Board of Regents of State Colleges v. Roth*. But this argument is made for the first time in petitioners' brief to this Court . . . . We therefore decline to consider it here.

But nothing in the language of the Due Process Clause itself requires the State to protect the life, liberty, and property of its citizens against invasion by private actors. The Clause is phrased as a limitation on the State's power to act, not as a guarantee of certain minimal levels of safety and security. It forbids the State itself to deprive individuals of life, liberty, or property without "due process of law," but its language cannot fairly be extended to impose an affirmative obligation on the State to ensure that those interests do not come to harm through other means. Nor does history support such an expansive reading of the constitutional text. Like its counterpart in the Fifth Amendment, the Due Process Clause of the Fourteenth Amendment was intended to prevent government "from abusing [its] power, or employing it as an instrument of oppression." Its purpose was to protect the people from the State, not to ensure that the State protected them from each other. The Framers were content to leave the extent of governmental obligation in the latter area to the democratic political processes.

Consistent with these principles, our cases have recognized that the Due Process Clauses generally confer no affirmative right to governmental aid, even where such aid may be necessary to secure life, liberty, or property interests of which the government itself may not deprive the individual. . . . "Although the liberty protected by the Due Process Clause affords protection against unwarranted *government* interference . . ., it does not confer an entitlement to such [governmental aid] as may be necessary to realize all the advantages of that freedom." If the Due Process Clause does not require the State to provide its citizens with particular protective services, it follows that the State cannot be held liable under the Clause for injuries that could have been averted had it chosen to provide them. As a general matter, then, we conclude that a State's failure to protect an individual against private violence simply does not constitute a violation of the Due Process Clause.

Petitioners contend, however, that even if the Due Process Clause imposes no affirmative obligation on the State to provide the general public with adequate protective services, such a duty may arise out of certain "special relationships" created or assumed by the State with respect to particular individuals. Petitioners argue that such a "special relationship" existed here because the State knew that Joshua faced a special danger of abuse at his father's hands, and specifically proclaimed, by word and by deed, its intention to protect him against that danger. Having actually undertaken to protect Joshua from this danger – which petitioners concede the State played no part in creating – the State acquired an affirmative "duty," enforceable through the Due Process Clause, to do so in a reasonably competent fashion. Its failure to discharge that duty, so the argument goes, was an abuse of governmental power that so "shocks the conscience" as to constitute a substantive due process violation.

We reject this argument. It is true that in certain limited circumstances the Constitution imposes upon the State affirmative duties of care and protection with respect to particular individuals. In *Estelle v. Gamble* we recognized that the Eighth Amendment's prohibition against cruel and unusual punishment, made applicable to the States through the Fourteenth Amendment's Due Process Clause, requires the State to provide adequate medical care to incarcerated prisoners. We reasoned that because the prisoner is unable "by reason of the deprivation of his liberty care for himself," it is only "just" that the State be required to care for him.

In *Youngberg v. Romeo* we extended this analysis beyond the Eighth Amendment setting, holding that the substantive component of the Fourteenth Amendment's Due Process Clause requires the State to provide involuntarily committed mental patients with such services as are necessary to ensure their "reasonable safety" from themselves and others. As we explained: "If it is cruel and unusual punishment to hold convicted criminals in unsafe conditions, it must be unconstitutional [under the Due Process Clause] to confine the involuntarily committed – who may not be punished at all – in unsafe conditions."

But these cases afford petitioners no help. Taken together, they stand only for the proposition that when the State takes a person into its custody and holds him there against his will, the Constitution imposes upon it a corresponding duty to assume some responsibility for his safety and general well-being. The rationale for this principle is simple enough: when the State by the affirmative exercise of its power so restrains an individual's liberty that it renders him unable to care for himself, and at the same time fails to provide for his basic human needs – e.g., food, clothing, shelter, medical care, and reasonable safety – it transgresses the substantive limits on state action set by the Eighth Amendment and the Due Process Clause. The affirmative duty to protect arises not from the State's knowledge of the individual's predicament or from its expressions of intent to help him, but from the limitation which it has imposed on his freedom to act on his own behalf. In the substantive due process analysis, it is the State's affirmative act of restraining the individual's freedom to act on his own behalf – through incarceration, institutionalization, or other similar restraint of personal liberty – which is the "deprivation of liberty" triggering the protections of the Due Process Clause, not its failure to act to protect his liberty interests against harms inflicted by other means.

The *Estelle-Youngberg* analysis simply has no applicability in the present case. Petitioners concede that the harms Joshua suffered occurred not while he was in the State's custody, but while he was in the custody of his natural father, who was in no sense a state actor. While the State may have been aware of the dangers that Joshua faced in the free world, it played no part in their creation, nor did it do anything to render him any more vulnerable to them. That the State once took temporary custody of Joshua does not alter the analysis, for when it returned him to his father's custody, it placed him in no worse position than that in which he would have been had it not acted at all; the State does not become the permanent guarantor of an individual's safety by having once offered him shelter. Under these circumstances, the State had no constitutional duty to protect Joshua.

It may well be that, by voluntarily undertaking to protect Joshua against a danger it concededly played no part in creating, the State acquired a duty under state tort law to provide him with adequate protection against that danger. *See* Restatement (Second) of Torts § 323 (1965) (one who undertakes to render services to another may in some circumstances be held liable for doing so in a negligent fashion). But the claim here is based on the Due Process Clause of the Fourteenth Amendment, which, as we have said many times, does not transform every tort committed by a state actor into a constitutional violation. A State may, through its courts and legislatures, impose such affirmative duties of care and protection upon its agents as it wishes. But not "all common-law duties owed by government actors were . . . constitutionalized by the Fourteenth Amendment." Because, as explained above, the State had no constitutional duty to protect Joshua against his father's violence, its failure to do so – though calamitous in hindsight – simply does not constitute a violation of the Due Process Clause.

Judges and lawyers, like other humans, are moved by natural sympathy in a case like this to find a way for Joshua and his mother to receive adequate compensation for the grievous harm inflicted upon them. But before yielding to that impulse, it is well to remember once again that the harm was inflicted not by the State of Wisconsin, but by Joshua's father. The most that can be said of the state functionaries in this case is that they stood by and did nothing when suspicious circumstances dictated a more active role for them. In defense of them it must also be said that had they moved too soon to take custody of the son away from the father, they would likely have been met with charges of improperly intruding into the parent-child relationship, charges based on the same Due Process Clause that forms the basis for the present charge of failure to provide adequate protection.

The people of Wisconsin may well prefer a system of liability which would place upon the State and its officials the responsibility for failure to act in situations such as the present one. They may create such a system, if they do not have it already, by changing the tort law of the State in accordance with the regular lawmaking process. But they should not have it thrust upon them by this Court's expansion of the Due Process Clause of the Fourteenth Amendment.

Affirmed.

[JUSTICE BLACKMUN, dissenting.]

Poor Joshua! . . . It is a sad commentary upon American life, and constitutional principles – so full of late of patriotic fervor and proud proclamations about "liberty and justice for all" – that this child, Joshua DeShaney, now is assigned to live out the remainder of his life profoundly retarded. Joshua and his mother . . . deserve . . . the opportunity to have the facts of their case considered in the light of the constitutional protection that 42 U.S.C. § 1983 is meant to provide.

Underlying Case Documents

For the current version of § 1983 click <u>HERE</u>.

1. <u>*Pappas v. City of Lebanon*, 331 F. Supp. 2d 311 (D. Pa. 2004)</u>.

After serving as an officer of the Lebanon Police Department for approximately eighteen years, Pappas submitted a letter of resignation to Robert A. Anspach ("Anspach"), the Mayor of Lebanon and chairperson of the Board. . . . The next day, Pappas notified the Board by letter that he wished to vest benefits that had accrued under a police pension plan . . . .

Upon receipt of the letter, Anspach recognized that the request was untimely under the governing statute and ordinance, which require notice of an intention to vest at least thirty days prior to the retiree's termination date. Had Pappas been informed of this problem before [his final day on the job], he could have deferred his termination date to render his notification timely. However, neither Anspach nor other members of the Board alerted Pappas to the issue. Instead, . . . the Board voted to deny the application to vest benefits. . . .

The crux of Pappas's argument is that the Board and its members had a legal obligation to alert him, before his resignation date, that a notice of intention to vest must be filed thirty days prior to termination of employment. He asserts that this failure precludes him from successfully prosecuting his claim for payments. Whatever the validity of this assertion, defendants' involvement was not so significant as to render the alleged deprivation attributable to them. . . .

As a matter of *federal* law, Pappas has presented insufficient evidence of a "special relationship" to establish a deprivation by defendants. Neither the Board nor its members exercised a form of custodial control over Pappas that restricted his ability to pursue his claim. Nothing in the record suggests that the Board or its members promised Pappas that they would provide assistance or otherwise induced him to refrain from taking necessary action. No special relationship existed, and Pappas suffered no deprivation attributable to defendants. . . .

2. <u>*Kallstrom v. City of Columbus*, 136 F.3d 1055 (6th Cir. 1998)</u>.

The three plaintiffs . . . are undercover officers employed by the Columbus Police Department. All three were actively involved in the drug conspiracy investigation of the Short North Posse, a violent gang in the Short North area of Columbus, Ohio. . . . During [a] criminal trial, defense counsel requested and obtained from the City [the personnel files of at least one of the plaintiffs], which defense counsel appears to have passed on to several of the . . . defendants. . . . The officers' personnel files include the officers' . . . phone numbers; the names, addresses, and phone numbers of immediate family members; . . . the officers' banking . . . account information, including account balances; their social security numbers; responses to questions regarding their personal life asked during the course of polygraph examinations; and copies of their drivers' licenses, including pictures and home addresses. . . .

Prior to accepting employment with the City, the plaintiffs were assured by the City that personal information contained in their files would be held in strict confidence. Despite its earlier promise of confidentiality, however, the City believed Ohio's Public Records Act required it to release the officers' files upon request from any member of the public. The officers brought suit under 42 U.S.C. §§ 1983 and 1988 against the City, claiming that the dissemination of personal information contained in their personnel files violates their right to privacy as guaranteed by the Due Process Clause of the Fourteenth Amendment. . . .

[Under *DeShaney*], before holding the City liable for violation of the officers' constitutional rights to privacy, we must address whether the actions or potential actions of private actors, namely the gang members of the Short North Posse, can be attributed to the City. . . . Liability under the state-created-danger theory is predicated upon affirmative acts by the state which either create or increase the risk that an individual will be exposed to private acts of violence. . . . However, because many state activities have the potential to increase an individual's risk of harm, we require plaintiffs alleging a constitutional tort under § 1983 to show "special danger" in the absence of a special relationship between the state and either the victim or the private tortfeasor. The victim faces "special danger" where the state's actions place the victim specifically at risk, as distinguished from a risk that affects the public at large. The state must have known or clearly should have known that its actions specifically endangered an individual.

Applying the state-created-danger theory to the facts of this case, we hold that the City's actions placed the officers and their family members in "special danger" by substantially increasing the likelihood that a private actor would deprive them of their liberty interest in personal security. Anonymity is essential to the safety of undercover officers investigating a gang-related drug conspiracy, especially where the gang has demonstrated a propensity for violence. In affirmatively releasing private information from the officers' personnel files to defense counsel . . . the City's actions placed the personal safety of the officers and their family members, as distinguished from the public at large, in serious jeopardy. The City either knew or clearly should have known that releasing the officers' addresses, phone numbers, and driver's licenses and the officers' families' names, addresses, and phone numbers to defense counsel . . . substantially increased the officers' and their families' vulnerability to private acts of vengeance. We therefore hold that the City's policy of freely releasing this information from the undercover officers' personnel files under these circumstances creates a constitutionally cognizable "special danger," giving rise to liability under § 1983. . . .

3. The limitation on claims after *DeShaney* involve "special relationships" and "state created" dangers. Those qualifiers alone, however, may be insufficient to hold accountable a governmental entity. In the following excerpt from the Second Circuit, the court finds that state created dangers must also "shock the conscience" in order to be a basis for liability.

Matican v. City of New York, 524 F.3d 151 (2d Cir. 2008).

Plaintiff-appellant Robert Matican participated in a sting to help officers of the New

York Police Department ("NYPD") arrest a suspected drug dealer: Matican set up a drug buy, and the police descended on the dealer in force when he arrived about an hour later. After the dealer was released on bail, he assaulted plaintiff Matican with a box cutter, injuring him severely. Matican sued the City of New York ("City") and three individual NYPD officers . . . arguing that the way they conducted the sting and their failure to alert Matican to the dealer's release gave away Matican's identity and left him in peril. . . .

Like the special relationship exception, the state-created danger exception arises from the Court's analysis in *DeShaney*. . . .

In applying the state-created danger principle, "we have sought to tread a fine line between conduct that is 'passive' (and therefore outside the exception) and that which is 'affirmative' (and therefore covered by the exception)" . . . . Thus, we have found state-created dangers (or denied summary judgment where state-created danger theories were alleged) where police officers told skinheads that they would not prevent them from beating up protesters in a park [and] where a prison guard told inmates that it was "open season" on a prisoner, and the inmates beat up the prisoner . . . . By contrast, we held that no state-created danger existed where a police officer failed to intervene to prevent a colleague from shooting someone during an altercation.

As the district court recognized, Matican's allegation that the officers failed to learn about, or inform him of, Delvalle's violent criminal history or his release on bail fall on the passive side of the line. . . . This is so notwithstanding Matican's assertion that the officers promised to protect him. . . . By contrast, Matican's allegation that the officers planned the sting in a manner that would lead Delvalle to learn about Matican's involvement is sufficiently affirmative to qualify as a state-created danger. . . . Until recently, Supreme Court and Second Circuit precedent gave little objective guidance as to whether a particular state action does or does not shock the contemporary conscience. . . .

[T]his court's decision last year in *Lombardi* provides sufficient guidance. . . . In that case, we considered the claims of rescue and cleanup workers at the World Trade Center site following the 9/11 attacks. The workers in that case alleged that the defendants, federal environmental and workplace-safety officials, issued intentionally false press releases stating that the air in Lower Manhattan was safe to breathe, and that in reliance on those statements, the workers did not use protective gear. We held that, regardless of whether the situation was a time-sensitive emergency, plaintiffs' allegations of deliberate indifference did not shock the conscience. "Hurried or unhurried, the defendants were subjected to the 'pull of competing obligations.'" . . . . We concluded that "[w]hen great harm is likely to befall someone no matter what a government official does, the allocation of risk may be a burden on the conscience of the one who must make such decisions, but does not shock the contemporary conscience."

The same considerations lead us to conclude that Matican's allegations of affirmative conduct by the officers, even if true, do not shock the contemporary conscience. In designing the sting, the officers here had two serious competing obligations: Matican's safety and their own. They could reasonably have concluded that the arrest of a potentially violent drug dealer demanded the use of overwhelming force, even if that show of force might jeopardize the informant's identity in the future. . . .

Because the officers were obliged to protect their own safety as well as Matican's, their design of the sting in this case does not shock the conscience. Matican therefore suffered no violation of his rights under the Due Process Clause.

Can you articulate the kinds of "affirmative" dangers that would "shock the conscience"?

4. What if the state failed to exercise due care and licensed a day care provider who caused the death of an eight-year-old child? Would that be sufficient to meet the requirements of "state-created danger" and "shock the conscience"? In *Robbins v. Oklahoma ex rel. Department of Human Services, 519 F.3d 1242 (10th Cir. 2008)*, the plaintiffs placed Renee, their infant daughter, in the care of Ms. McKinney. Renee was killed while in Ms. McKinney's care. The cause of death was "blunt force trauma." Plaintiffs unsuccessfully sued the state. The court found that

> the failure of [the state] and its employees to revoke Ms. McKinney's license . . . would be directed at the public in general rather than at Mr. Robbins, Ms. Gillum, and Renee specifically. . . . Given that the preponderance of imaginable circumstances encompassed by the complaint would be . . . a negligent licensing decision, this claim fails . . . absent specific factual allegations of additional affirmative acts by the individual defendants.

Can you articulate a circumstance where licensing would not be "directed to the general public"? Assume the Nuclear Regulatory Commission failed to exercise reasonable care in licensing a power plant. Assume further that throughout the licensing process, local residents, environmental groups, and anti-nuclear power interests all asserted the plant was unsafe. Finally, assume the worst – a core meltdown and massive release of plutonium into a populated area. Any chance of liability? Put aside the discretionary function exception and sovereign immunity – would this meet the standards in the above case or in *DeShaney*?

5. In *Burella v. City of Philadelphia, 501 F.3d 134 (3d Cir 2007)*, plaintiff complained to the police department that her spouse, a police officer, had abused her on numerous occasions. The city failed to act in response and soon after the last complaint the plaintiff was shot by and severely wounded by her husband who, thereafter, took his own life. Following *DeShaney*, the court held that the

> facts . . . if true, reveal a terrible deficiency on the part of the Philadelphia Police Department in responding to her complaints of domestic abuse. Binding precedent nevertheless compels our conclusion that the officers' failure to arrest her husband, or to handle her complaints more competently, did not violate her constitutional right to due process or equal protection of the law.

Can you articulate the factors needed to hold a governmental entity liable for failure to respond to reasonable requests for help?

6. What about medical malpractice? Can failure to provide competent care coupled with assurances regarding the patient's well-being suffice? In *Ye v. United States*, 484 F.3d 634 (3d Cir. 2007), the court faced this question, focused on the impact of an assurance that, allegedly, was predicated on diagnosis and treatment that failed to meet an appropriate standard of care. "The crux of the case before us is whether a mere assurance can be an affirmative act – a 'restraint of personal liberty' similar to incarceration or institutionalization. We hold that it cannot. Therefore, the plaintiff cannot proceed under the 'state-created danger' theory of liability derived from the Supreme Court's decision in *DeShaney*. . . ."

Under what circumstances would there be liability for malpractice by a government funded physician or lawyer? The *Ye* court left this glimmer of hope for victims of malpractice:

> Dr. Kim's assurances could, and almost certainly do, give rise to a state law medical malpractice claim. They cannot, however, constitute a deprivation of liberty within the meaning of *DeShaney*. . . . *DeShaney* [does] not totally foreclose the possibility that words could constitute an affirmative act and a deprivation of liberty (such as an assault).

For an interesting discussion of due care and governmental obligation, see Susan Bandes, *The Negative Constitution: A Critique*, 88 MICH. L. REV. 2271 (1990).

———————

TOWN OF CASTLE ROCK, COLORADO V. GONZALES

545 U.S. 748 (2005)

[JUSTICE SCALIA] We decide in this case whether an individual who has obtained a state-law restraining order has a constitutionally protected property interest in having the police enforce the restraining order when they have probable cause to believe it has been violated.

I

The horrible facts of this case are contained in the complaint that respondent Jessica Gonzales filed in Federal District Court. (Because the case comes to us on appeal from a dismissal of the complaint, we assume its allegations are true.) Respondent alleges that petitioner, the town of Castle Rock, Colorado, violated the Due Process Clause of the Fourteenth Amendment . . . when its police officers, acting pursuant to official policy or custom, failed to respond properly to her repeated reports that her estranged husband was violating the terms of a restraining order.

The restraining order had been issued by a state trial court several weeks earlier in conjunction with respondent's divorce proceedings. The original form order [was] issued on May 21, 1999, and served on respondent's husband on June 4, 1999 . . . . The preprinted text on the back of the form . . . included a "NOTICE TO LAW ENFORCEMENT OFFICIALS," which read in part:

> YOU SHALL USE EVERY REASONABLE MEANS TO ENFORCE THIS RESTRAINING ORDER. YOU SHALL ARREST, OR, IF AN ARREST WOULD BE IMPRACTICAL UNDER THE CIRCUMSTANCES, SEEK A WARRANT FOR THE ARREST OF THE RESTRAINED PERSON WHEN YOU HAVE INFORMATION AMOUNTING TO PROBABLE CAUSE THAT THE RESTRAINED PERSON HAS VIOLATED . . . ANY PROVISION OF THIS ORDER. . . .

On June 4, 1999, the state trial court modified the terms of the restraining order and made it permanent. The modified order gave respondent's husband the right to spend time with his three daughters (ages 10, 9, and 7) on alternate weekends, for two weeks during the summer, and, "upon reasonable notice," for a mid-week dinner visit "arranged by the parties"; the modified order also allowed him to visit the home to collect the children for such "parenting time."

According to the complaint, at about 5 or 5:30 p.m. on Tuesday, June 22, 1999, respondent's husband took the three daughters while they were playing outside the family home. No advance arrangements had been made for him to see the daughters that evening. When respondent noticed the children were missing, she suspected her husband had taken them. At about 7:30 p.m., she called the Castle Rock Police Department, which dispatched two officers. The complaint continues: "When [the officers] arrived . . ., she showed them a copy of the TRO and requested that it be enforced and the three children be returned to her immediately. . . . [The officers] stated that there was nothing they could do about the TRO and suggested that [respondent] call the Police Department again if the three children did not return home by 10:00 p.m."

At approximately 8:30 p.m., respondent talked to her husband on his cellular telephone. He told her "he had the three children [at an] amusement park in Denver." She called the police again and asked them to "have someone check for" her husband or his vehicle at the amusement park and "put out an [all points bulletin]" for her husband, but the officer with whom she spoke "refused to do so," again telling her to "wait until 10:00 p.m. and see if" her husband returned the girls.

At approximately 10:10 p.m., respondent called the police [again and] was now told to wait until midnight. She called at midnight and [then] went to her husband's apartment and, finding nobody there, called the police at 12:10 a.m.; she was told to wait for an officer to arrive. When none came, she went to the police station at 12:50 a.m. and submitted an incident report. The officer who took the report "made no reasonable effort to enforce the TRO or locate the three children. Instead, he went to dinner."

At approximately 3:20 a.m., respondent's husband arrived at the police station and opened fire with a semiautomatic handgun he had purchased earlier that evening. Police shot back, killing him. Inside the cab of his pickup truck, they found the bodies of all three daughters, whom he had already murdered.

On the basis of the foregoing factual allegations, respondent brought an action under Rev. Stat. § 1979, claiming that the town violated the Due Process Clause because its police department had "an official policy or custom of failing to respond properly to complaints of restraining order violations" and "tolerate[d] the non-enforcement of restraining orders by its police officers." The complaint also alleged that the town's actions "were taken either willfully, recklessly or with such gross negligence as to indicate wanton disregard and deliberate indifference to" respondent's civil rights.

[T]he defendants filed a motion to dismiss under Federal Rule of Civil Procedure 12(b)(6). The District Court granted the motion, concluding that, whether construed as making a substantive due process or procedural due process claim, respondent's complaint failed to state a claim upon which relief could be granted. A panel of the Court of Appeals affirmed the rejection of a substantive due process claim, but found that respondent had alleged a cognizable procedural due process claim. On rehearing en banc, a divided court [held] that respondent had a "protected property interest in the enforcement of the terms of her restraining order" and that the town had deprived her of due process because "the police never 'heard' nor seriously entertained her request to enforce and protect her interests in the restraining order." We granted certiorari.

II

The Fourteenth Amendment to the United States Constitution provides that a State shall not "deprive any person of life, liberty, or property, without due process of law." In 42 U.S.C. § 1983, Congress has created a federal cause of action for "the deprivation of any rights, privileges, or immunities secured by the Constitution and laws." Respondent claims the benefit of this provision on the ground that she had a property interest in police enforcement of the restraining order against her husband; and that the town deprived her of this property without due process by having a policy that tolerated nonenforcement of restraining orders.

As the Court of Appeals recognized, we left a similar question unanswered in *DeShaney*, another case with "undeniably tragic" facts: Local child-protection officials had failed to protect a young boy from beatings by his father that left him severely brain damaged. We held that the so-called "substantive" component of the Due Process Clause does not "requir[e] the State to protect the life, liberty, and property of its citizens against invasion by private actors." We noted, however, that the petitioner had not properly preserved the argument that – and we thus "decline to consider" whether – state "child protection statutes gave [him] an 'entitlement' to receive protective services in accordance with the terms of the statute, an entitlement which would enjoy due process protection."

The procedural component of the Due Process Clause does not protect everything that might be described as a "benefit": "To have a property interest in a benefit, a person clearly must have more than an abstract need or desire" and "more than a unilateral expectation of it. He must, instead, have a legitimate claim of entitlement to it." Such entitlements are "of course, . . . not created by the Constitution. Rather, they are created and their dimensions are defined by existing rules or understandings that stem from an independent source such as state law."

A

Our cases recognize that a benefit is not a protected entitlement if government officials may grant or deny it in their discretion. The Court of Appeals in this case determined that Colorado law created an entitlement to enforcement of the restraining order because the "court-issued restraining order . . . specifically dictated that its terms must be enforced" and a "state statute command[ed]" enforcement of the order when certain objective conditions were met (probable cause to believe that the order had been violated and that the object of the order had received notice of its existence). Respondent contends that we are obliged "to give deference to the Tenth Circuit's analysis of Colorado law on" whether she had an entitlement to enforcement of the restraining order. We will not, of course, defer to the Tenth Circuit on the ultimate issue: whether what Colorado law has given respondent constitutes a property interest for purposes of the Fourteenth Amendment. . . . We proceed, then, to our own analysis of whether Colorado law gave respondent a right to enforcement of the restraining order.

B

The critical language in the restraining order came not from any part of the order itself (which was signed by the state-court trial judge and directed to the restrained party, respondent's husband), but from the preprinted notice to law-enforcement personnel that appeared on the back of the order. That notice effectively restated the statutory provision describing "peace officers' duties" related to the crime of violation of a restraining order. At the time of the conduct at issue in this case, that provision read as follows:

(a) Whenever a restraining order is issued, the protected person shall be provided with a copy of such order. *A peace officer shall use every reasonable means to enforce a restraining order.*

(b) *A peace officer shall arrest, or, if an arrest would be impractical under the circumstances, seek a warrant for the arrest of a restrained person* when the peace officer has information amounting to probable cause that:

　　(I) The restrained person has violated or attempted to violate any provision of a restraining order; and

　　(II) The restrained person has been properly served with a copy of the restraining order or the restrained person has received actual notice of the existence and substance of such order.

(c) In making the probable cause determination described in paragraph (b) of this subsection (3), a peace officer shall assume that the information received from the registry is accurate. *A peace officer shall enforce a valid restraining order whether or not there is a record of the restraining order in the registry.*

The Court of Appeals concluded that this statutory provision – especially taken in conjunction with . . . another statute restricting criminal and civil liability for officers making arrests – established the Colorado Legislature's clear intent "to alter the fact that the police were not enforcing domestic abuse retraining orders," and thus its intent "that the recipient of a domestic abuse restraining order have an entitlement to its enforcement." Any other result, it said, "would render domestic abuse restraining orders utterly valueless."

This last statement is sheer hyperbole. Whether or not respondent had a right to enforce the restraining order, it rendered certain otherwise lawful conduct by her husband both criminal and in contempt of court. The creation of grounds on which he could be arrested, criminally prosecuted, and held in contempt was hardly "valueless" – even if the prospect of those sanctions ultimately failed to prevent him from committing three murders and a suicide.

We do not believe that these provisions of Colorado law truly made enforcement of restraining orders *mandatory.* A well established tradition of police discretion has long coexisted with apparently mandatory arrest statutes.

In each and every state there are long-standing statutes that, by their terms, seem to preclude nonenforcement by the police. . . . However, for a number of reasons, including their legislative history, insufficient resources, and sheer physical impossibility, it has been recognized that such statutes cannot be interpreted literally. . . . [T]hey clearly do not mean that a police officer may not lawfully decline to make an arrest. As to third parties in these states, the full-enforcement statutes simply have no effect, and their significance is further diminished.

The deep-rooted nature of law-enforcement discretion, even in the presence of seemingly mandatory legislative commands, is illustrated by *Chicago v. Morales*, which involved an ordinance that said a police officer "shall order" persons to disperse in certain circumstances. This Court rejected out of hand the possibility that "the mandatory language of the ordinance . . . afford the police *no* discretion." It is, the Court proclaimed, simply "common sense that *all* police officers must use some discretion in deciding when and where to enforce city ordinances."

Against that backdrop, a true mandate of police action would require some stronger indication from the Colorado Legislature than "shall use every reasonable means to enforce a restraining order" (or even "shall arrest . . . or . . . seek a warrant"). That language is not perceptibly more mandatory than the Colorado statute which has long told municipal chiefs of police that they "shall pursue and arrest any person fleeing from justice in any part of the state" and that they "shall apprehend any person in the act of committing any offense . . . . It is hard to imagine that a Colorado peace officer would not have some discretion to determine that – despite probable cause to believe a restraining order has been violated – the circumstances of the violation or the competing duties of that officer or his agency counsel decisively against enforcement in a particular instance. The practical necessity for discretion is particularly apparent in a case such as this one, where the suspected violator is not actually present and his whereabouts are unknown. . . .

Respondent does not specify the precise means of enforcement that the Colorado restraining-order statute assertedly mandated – whether her interest lay in having police arrest her husband, having them seek a warrant for his arrest, or having them "use every reasonable means, up to and including arrest, to enforce the order's terms." Such indeterminacy is not the hallmark of a duty that is mandatory. Nor can someone be safely deemed "entitled" to something when the identity of the alleged entitlement is vague. The dissent . . . ultimately contends that the obligations under the statute were quite precise: either make an arrest or (if that is impractical) seek an arrest warrant. The problem with this is that the seeking of an arrest warrant would be an entitlement to nothing but procedure – which we have held inadequate even to support standing, *see Lujan v. Defenders of Wildlife*; much less can it be the basis for a property interest. After the warrant is sought, it remains within the discretion of a judge whether to grant it, and after it is granted, it remains within the discretion of the police whether and when to execute it. Respondent would have been assured nothing but the seeking of a warrant. This is not the sort of "entitlement" out of which a property interest is created.

Even if the statute could be said to have made enforcement of restraining orders "mandatory" because of the domestic-violence context of the underlying statute, that would not necessarily mean that state law gave *respondent* an entitlement to *enforcement* of the mandate. Making the actions of government employees obligatory can serve various legitimate ends other than the conferral of a benefit on a specific class of people. *See, e.g.,* <u>*Sandin v. Conner*</u> (finding no constitutionally protected liberty interest in prison regulations phrased in mandatory terms, in part because "[s]uch guidelines are not set forth solely to benefit the prisoner"). . . .

Respondent's alleged interest stems only from a State's *statutory* scheme – from a restraining order that was authorized by and tracked precisely the statute on which the Court of Appeals relied. She does not assert that she has any common-law or contractual entitlement to enforcement. If she was given a statutory entitlement, we would expect to see some indication of that in the statute itself. Although Colorado's statute spoke of "protected person" such as respondent, it did so in connection with matters other than a right to enforcement. It said that a "protected person shall be provided with a copy of [a restraining] order" when it is issued, that a law enforcement agency "shall make all reasonable efforts to contact the protected party upon the arrest of the restrained person," and that the agency "shall give [to the protected person] a copy" of the report it submits to the court that issued the order. Perhaps most importantly, the statute spoke directly to the protected person's power to "initiate contempt proceedings against the restrained person if the order issued in a civil action or request the prosecuting attorney to initiate contempt proceedings if the order issued in a criminal action." The protected person's express power to "initiate" civil contempt proceedings contrasts tellingly with the mere ability to "request" initiation of criminal contempt proceedings – and even more dramatically with the complete silence about any power to "request" (much less demand) that an arrest be made. . . .

C

Even if we were to think otherwise concerning the creation of an entitlement by Colorado, it is by no means clear that an individual entitlement to enforcement of a restraining order could constitute a "property" interest for purposes of the Due Process Clause. Such a right would not, of course, resemble any traditional conception of property. Although that alone does not disqualify it from due process protection, as <u>*Roth*</u> and its progeny show, the right to have a restraining order enforced does not "have some ascertainable monetary value," as even our "*Roth*-type property-as-entitlement" cases have implicitly required. Perhaps most radically, the alleged property interest here arises *incidentally*, not out of some new species of government benefit or service, but out of a function that government actors have always performed – to wit, arresting people who they have probable cause to believe have committed a criminal offense.

The indirect nature of a benefit was fatal to the due process claim of the nursing-home residents in *O'Bannon v. Town Court Nursing Center*. We held that, while the withdrawal of "direct benefits" (financial payments under Medicaid for certain medical services) triggered due process protections, the same was not true for the "indirect benefit" conferred on Medicaid patients when the Government enforced "minimum standards of care" for nursing-home facilities. . . . In this case, as in *O'Bannon*, "[t]he simple distinction between government action that directly affects a citizen's legal rights . . . and action that is directed against a third party and affects the citizen only indirectly or incidentally, provides a sufficient answer to" respondent's reliance on cases that found government-provided services to be entitlements.

III

We conclude, therefore, that respondent did not, for purposes of the Due Process Clause, have a property interest in police enforcement of the restraining order against her husband. It is accordingly unnecessary to address the Court of Appeals' determination that the town's custom or policy prevented the police from giving her due process when they deprived her of that alleged interest.

In light of today's decision and that in <u>DeShaney</u>, the benefit that a third party may receive from having someone else arrested for a crime generally does not trigger protections under the Due Process Clause, neither in its procedural nor in its "substantive" manifestations. This result reflects our continuing reluctance to treat the Fourteenth Amendment as "a font of tort law," but it does not mean States are powerless to provide victims with personally enforceable remedies. Although the framers of the Fourteenth Amendment and the Civil Rights Act of 1871 (the original source of § 1983), did not create a system by which police departments are generally held financially accountable for crimes that better policing might have prevented, the people of Colorado are free to craft such a system under state law.

The judgment of the Court of Appeals is reversed.

Underlying Case Documents

The case referenced:
The restraining order

For the current version of § 1983 click HERE.

1. In <u>Howard v. Bayes, 457 F.3d 568 (6th Cir. 2006)</u>, the police were called to a home to investigate a possible drug overdose. When they arrived they spoke with a male, Williams and a female, Howard. There were signs of both drinking and drug use, but no overt signs of violence. The following morning, Howard was rushed to the hospital and died shortly thereafter. Williams was convicted of her murder. Howard's father brought suit both for wrongful death and violation of Howard's civil rights under the Fourth and Fourteenth Amendments pursuant to § 1983.

> Specifically, Plaintiff argues that [the police] breached [their] duty under Kentucky law to arrest Williams the night before Williams killed Howard, which violated Howard's procedural due process rights. . . .

> [L]ike the claim[] in *Castle Rock* . . . Plaintiff's claim here is based merely on an indirect benefit arising from a state enforcement scheme. The Kentucky statutes address law enforcement's response to domestic violence. They authorize police to take discretionary action against those suspected of physically abusing family members. Any resulting benefit to the victims, and society at large, is indirect. The incidental nature of this alleged property interest is fatal to Plaintiff's claim. *See Castle Rock.*

> In light of the Supreme Court's decision in *Castle Rock,* we conclude that . . . Plaintiff failed to demonstrate that a constitutional violation had occurred.

Good Question!

Assume there was a history of violence, the police were aware of that history, and that on the evening the police came to the home, Howard asked the police to arrest Williams, but no arrest occurred. Based on <u>De-Shaney</u> and *Castle Rock*, would these facts change the outcome?

2. <u>Hudson v. Hudson, 475 F.3d 741 (6th Cir. 2007)</u>.

> Jennifer Braddock was issued three protective orders against James Hudson, the father of her son, because Hudson repeatedly abused Braddock. In August 2001 . . . Hudson broke into Braddock's home and threatened her. She called the Memphis Police Department, but it made no attempt to find him. . . . Over the next two years, Braddock called the police several times to complain about various violations of the protective order, including acts of physical violence, but the Memphis Police took no action. Braddock's struggle against Hudson's violence ended when Hudson broke into her home, killed her and two of her friends, then turned the gun on himself and committed suicide.

> [Family members sued] the Memphis Police Department, and a number of Memphis Police Officers for violating the Fourteenth Amendment and various state-law rights. . . .

> As a general principle, state actors cannot be held liable for private acts of violence under a substantive due process theory. <u>DeShaney</u>, *Castle Rock*. We recognize two exceptions to this rule: (1) when the state has a special relationship to the victim, and (2) when the state creates the danger that led to the victim's harm. . . . [W]e hold that

> a protection order does not create a special relationship between police officers and the individual who petitioned for that order.
>
> Nor may the plaintiffs establish their claims under the state-created-danger theory. . . . These officers' alleged inaction fails to satisfy the "affirmative act" requirement necessary to establish a state-created-danger substantive due process claim. . . .
>
> While this loss of life was undeniably tragic, these officers simply did not violate the United States Constitution by failing to prevent James Hudson from murdering Jennifer Braddock.

The statute pertaining to the protective order in the above case directed the police to enforce the terms of the order. That said, the court found "seemingly mandatory statutes, such as this one, and police discretion coexist frequently." This somewhat odd phraseology is a recognition that all government agencies – including police departments – need considerable discretion in how and when to implement their statutory mandates. Assume the statute in this case stated that "protective orders shall be enforced." Would that change the outcome in the case?

3. In _Moore v. Board of County Commissioners, 470 F. Supp. 2d 1237 (D. Kan. 2007)_, Jared Moore, a volunteer firefighter, was heading to the scene of an accident when he collided with a police car, also on the way to the accident. The police officer was driving over 80 miles per hour, well in excess of the posted speed limit. Moore was killed in the accident and his family brought suit.

> [Plaintiffs argue that regulations for the] Department would support a deputy's decision to exceed the posted speed limit, but only up to ten miles per hour in excess, implying that deputies who violated the rule would be on their own to justify the violation. . . . [T]he Supreme Court has recognized that the "deep-rooted nature of law-enforcement discretion" may supplant even "seemingly mandatory" commands. *Town of Castle Rock v. Gonzales.*
>
> Department policy which limited deputies' driving speeds did not create a liberty interest under the Fourteenth Amendment for Jared Moore. Because a deputy could exercise discretion in proceeding at more than ten miles per hour in excess of the posted speed limit, the policy did not sufficiently limit official decision-making though specific criteria so as to create an expectation of protection.

What level of specificity would be required in the above case? High speed police chase rules are increasingly common – but do they create a constitutionally sufficient basis under *Castle Rock*? If the claim is constitutional in nature, the plaintiff will have to overcome _County of Sacramento v. Lewis, 523 U.S. 833, 835 (1998)_ ("[I]n a high-speed automobile chase aimed at apprehending a suspected offender . . . only a purpose to cause harm unrelated to the legitimate object of arrest will satisfy the element of arbitrary conduct shocking to the conscience. . . ."). If the claim is based on common law tort – and one can get around immunity defenses – the chances for a plaintiff are better. *See* _Rogers v. Detroit, 579 N.W.2d 840 (Mich. 1998)_ (applying common law tort standards to high speed police chases).

4. The principles underlying *DeShaney* and *Castle Rock* are the subject of some disagreement. *Compare* Kathryn E. Litchman, <u>Punishing the Protectors: The Illinois Domestic Violence Act Remedy for Victims of Domestic Violence Against Police Misconduct,</u> 38 Loy. U. Chi. L.J. 765 (2007), *with* Mackenzie Williams, Note, <u>When States Break Promises: Defining Property Interests in the Procedural Due Process Context,</u> Town of Castle Rock v. Gonzales, 6 Wyo. L. Rev. 657 (2006), *and* Laura Oren, <u>Some Thoughts on The State-Created Danger Doctrine:</u> DeShaney <u>Is Still Wrong and</u> Castle Rock <u>Is More of the Same,</u> 16 Temp. Pol. & Civ. Rts. L. Rev. 47 (2006).

IV. Administrative Hearings and Schools

Goss v. Lopez

419 U.S. 565 (1975)

[Justice White] This appeal by various administrators of the Columbus, Ohio, Public School System (CPSS) challenges the judgment of a three-judge federal court, declaring that appellees – various high school students in the CPSS – were denied due process of law contrary to the command of the Fourteenth Amendment in that they were temporarily suspended from their high schools without a hearing either prior to suspension or within a reasonable time thereafter, and enjoining the administrators to remove all references to such suspensions from the students' records.

I

Ohio law provides for free education to all children between the ages of six and 21. Section 3313.66 of the Code empowers the principal of an Ohio public school to suspend a pupil for misconduct for up to 10 days or to expel him. In either case, he must notify the student's parents within 24 hours and state the reasons for his action. A pupil who is expelled, or his parents, may appeal the decision to the Board of Education and in connection therewith shall be permitted to be heard at the board meeting. The Board may reinstate the pupil following the hearing. No similar procedure is provided . . . for a suspended student. . . . [A]t the time of the imposition of the suspensions in this case the CPSS itself had not issued any written procedure applicable to suspensions. Nor, so far as the record reflects, had any of the individual high schools involved in this case. Each, however, had formally or informally described the conduct for which suspension could be imposed.

The nine named appellees, each of whom alleged that he or she had been suspended from public . . . school in Columbus for up to 10 days without a hearing . . ., filed an action under 42 U.S.C. § 1983 against the Columbus Board of Education and various administrators of the CPSS. The complaint sought a declaration that § 3313.66 was unconstitutional in that it permitted public school administrators to deprive plaintiffs of their rights to an education without a hearing of any kind, in violation of the procedural due process component of the Fourteenth Amendment. . . .

The proof below established that the suspensions arose out of a period of widespread student unrest in the CPSS during February and March 1971. Six of the named plaintiffs . . . were students at the Marion-Franklin High School and were each suspended for 10 days on account of disruptive or disobedient conduct committed in the presence of the school administrator who ordered the suspension. . . . None was given a hearing to determine the operative facts underlying the suspension, but each, together with his or her parents, was offered the opportunity to attend a conference, subsequent to the effective date of the suspension, to discuss the student's future.

Two . . . plaintiffs, Dwight Lopez and Betty Crome, were students at the Central High School and McGuffey Junior High School, respectively. The former was suspended in connection with a disturbance in the lunchroom . . . . Lopez testified that at least 75 other students were suspended from his school on the same day. He also testified below that he was not a party to the destructive conduct but was instead an innocent bystander. Because no one from the school testified with regard to this incident, there is no evidence in the record indicating the official basis for concluding otherwise. Lopez never had a hearing. Betty Crome was present at a demonstration at a high school [that] she was [not] attending. There she was arrested together with others, taken to the police station, and released without being formally charged. Before she went to school on the following day, she was notified that she had been suspended for a 10-day period. Because no one from the school testified with respect to this incident, the record does not disclose . . . on what information the decision was based. . . . [N]o hearing was ever held.

. . . .

On the basis of this evidence, the three-judge court declared that plaintiffs were denied due process of law . . . . The defendant school administrators have appealed the three-judge court's decision. . . . We affirm.

II

At the outset, appellants contend that because there is no constitutional right to an education at public expense, the Due Process Clause does not protect against expulsions from the public school system. This position misconceives the nature of the issue and is refuted by prior decisions. . . . Protected interests in property are normally "not created by the Constitution. Rather, they are created and their dimensions are defined" by an independent source such as state statutes or rules entitling the citizen to certain benefits. <u>Board of Regents v. Roth</u>. . . . Although Ohio may not be constitutionally obligated to establish and maintain a public school system, it has nevertheless done so and has required its children to attend. Those young people do not "shed their constitutional rights" at the schoolhouse door. . . .

Appellants proceed to argue that even if there is a right to a public education protected by the Due Process Clause generally, the Clause comes into play only when the State subjects a student to a "severe detriment or grievous loss." The loss of 10 days, it is said, is neither severe nor grievous . . . . Appellants' argument is again refuted by our prior decisions; for in determining "whether due process requirements apply in the first place, we must look not to the 'weight' but to the *nature* of the interest at stake." <u>Board of Regents v. Roth</u>. . . . The Court's view has been that as long as a property deprivation is not de minimis, its gravity is irrelevant to the question whether account must be taken of the Due Process Clause. A 10-day suspension from school is not de minimis . . . . "[E]ducation is perhaps the most important function of state and local governments," *Brown v. Board of Education*, and the total exclusion from the educational process for more than a trivial period, and certainly if the suspension is for 10 days, is a serious event in the life of the suspended child. Neither the property interest in educational benefits temporarily denied nor the liberty interest in reputation, which is also implicated, is so insubstantial that suspensions may constitutionally be imposed by any procedure the school chooses, no matter how arbitrary.

III

"Once it is determined that due process applies, the question remains what process is due." . . . . The Due Process Clause will not shield [a student] from suspensions properly imposed, but it disserves both his interest and the interest of the State if his suspension is in fact unwarranted. The concern would be mostly academic if the disciplinary process were a totally accurate, unerring process, never mistaken and never unfair. Unfortunately, that is not the case . . . . Disciplinarians, although proceeding in utmost good faith, frequently act on the reports and advice of others; and the controlling facts and the nature of the conduct under challenge are often disputed. . . .

The difficulty is that our schools are vast and complex. Some modicum of discipline and order is essential if the educational function is to be performed. Events calling for discipline are frequent occurrences and sometimes require immediate, effective action. Suspension is considered not only to be a necessary tool to maintain order but a valuable educational device. . . . But it would be a strange disciplinary system in an educational institution if no communication was sought by the disciplinarian with the student in an effort to inform him of his dereliction and to let him tell his side of the story in order to make sure that an injustice is not done. . . . n.9

> n.9 The facts involved in this case illustrate the point. Betty Crome was suspended for conduct which did not occur on school grounds, and for which mass arrests were made – hardly guaranteeing careful individualized factfinding by the police or by the school principal. She claims to have been involved in no misconduct. . . . Similarly, Dwight Lopez was suspended, along with many others, in connection with a disturbance in the lunchroom. Lopez says he was not one of those in the lunchroom who was involved. . . . The school principals who suspended Crome and Lopez may have been correct on the merits, but it is inconsistent with the Due Process Clause to have made the decision that misconduct had occurred without at some meaningful time giving Crome or Lopez an opportunity to persuade the principals otherwise.

We recognize that both suspensions were imposed during a time of great difficulty for the school administrations involved. At least in Lopez' case there may have been an immediate need to send home everyone in the lunchroom in order to preserve school order and property; and the administrative burden of providing 75 "hearings" of any kind is considerable. However, neither factor justifies a disciplinary suspension without *at any time* gathering facts relating to Lopez specifically, confronting him with them, and giving him an opportunity to explain.

We do not believe that school authorities must be totally free from notice and hearing requirements if their schools are to operate with acceptable efficiency. . . . [D]ue process requires, in connection with a suspension of 10 days or less, that the student be given oral or written notice of the charges against him and, if he denies them, an explanation of the evidence the authorities have and an opportunity to present his side of the story. The Clause requires at least these rudimentary precautions against unfair or mistaken findings of misconduct and arbitrary exclusion from school.

There need be no delay between the time "notice" is given and the time of the hearing. In the great majority of cases the disciplinarian may informally discuss the alleged misconduct with the student minutes after it has occurred. We hold only that, in being given an opportunity to explain his version of the facts at this discussion, the student first be told what he is accused of doing and what the basis of the accusation is. . . . Since the hearing may occur almost immediately . . ., it follows that as a general rule notice and hearing should precede removal of the student from school. We agree with the District Court, however, that there are [certain] situations in which prior notice and hearing cannot be insisted upon. Students whose presence poses a continuing danger to persons or property or an ongoing threat of disrupting the academic process may be immediately removed from school. In such cases, the necessary notice and rudimentary hearing should follow as soon as practicable, as the District Court indicated.

In holding as we do, we do not believe that we have imposed procedures on school disciplinarians which are inappropriate in a classroom setting. Instead we have imposed requirements which are, if anything, less than a fair-minded school principal would impose upon himself in order to avoid unfair suspensions. . . . We stop short of construing the Due Process Clause to require, countrywide, that hearings in connection with short suspensions must afford the student the opportunity to secure counsel, to confront and cross-examine witnesses . . ., or to call his own witnesses . . . . Brief disciplinary suspensions are almost countless. To impose in each such case even truncated trial-type procedures might well overwhelm administrative facilities in many places . . . . Moreover, further formalizing the suspension process . . . may not only make it too costly as a regular disciplinary tool but also destroy its effectiveness as part of the teaching process.

On the other hand, . . . permitting the student to give his version of the events will provide a meaningful hedge against erroneous action. At least the disciplinarian will be alerted to the existence of disputes about facts and arguments about cause and effect. He may then determine himself to summon the accuser, permit cross-examination, and allow the student to present his own witnesses. In more difficult cases, he may permit counsel. In any event, his discretion will be more informed and we think the risk of error substantially reduced. . . . [This procedure] will add little to the factfinding function where the disciplinarian himself has witnessed the conduct forming the basis for the charge. But things are not always as they seem to be, and the student will at least have the opportunity to characterize his conduct and put it in what he deems the proper context.

We should also make it clear that we have addressed ourselves solely to the short suspension, not exceeding 10 days. Longer suspensions or expulsions . . . may require more formal procedures. Nor do we put aside the possibility that in unusual situations, although involving only a short suspension, something more than the rudimentary procedures will be required. . . . Affirmed.

————————

Underlying Case Documents

The case referenced:
Ohio Code Section 3313.66

For the current version of § 1983 click HERE.

For the letters sent home with the students click HERE.

1. The questions raised in *Goss* are of consequence. What was the precise constitutional interest the Court identified? Was this a property deprivation – it is not
hard to see the right to continue in a state-funded program as such – or was it a
liberty interest – the freedom to learn? What did the state guarantee before the
Goss decision in terms of process? After the decision, were students better off – or
were their rights so thoroughly marginalized by the minimalist hearing the Court
required that they were no better off than before?

When one is asked about "*Goss* hearings," there is almost an instinctual response:
Rudimentary due process. Rudimentary, in this instance, is not much, requiring
only "oral or written notice of the charges . . . an explanation of the basis for the
accusation, and an opportunity to present [the student's] side of the story." *Foo v.
Trs. of Ind. Univ.*, 88 F. Supp. 2d 937 (S.D. Ind. 1999).

2. From a student standpoint, *Goss* is the quintessential good news/bad news case.
The good news is that there is a constitutionally protectable interest in continued
enrollment in school that cannot be taken, for disciplinary reasons (as opposed to
academic reasons), without a hearing. The bad news is that a *Goss* hearing can be
a phone call. In *C.B. By and Through Breeding v. Driscoll*, 82 F.3d 383, 386-87 (11th
Cir. 1996), the court held:

> The dictates of Goss are clear and extremely limited: Briefly stated, once school
> administrators tell a student what they heard or saw, ask why they heard or saw
> it, and allow a brief response, a student has received all the process that the
> Fourteenth Amendment demands. The only other requirement arises from the Court's
> admonishment that the hearing come before removal from school "as a general rule,"
> unless a student's continued presence is dangerous or disruptive. In these instances,
> removal can be immediate.

3. There is another approach to *Goss*: It recognized the rights of students while
at the same time appreciating the need for great flexibility in assessing the processes schools provide. In this sense, it can be seen as one of many cases you may
have already studied (depending on how your course is organized) regarding the
need to defer to reasonable choices made by school systems – viewing schools as
administrative entities. There is also helpful commentary on *Goss. See* Emily Buss,
Constitutional Fidelity Through Children's Rights, 2004 SUP. CT. REV. 355; Jason J.
Bach, *Students Have Rights, Too: The Drafting of Student Conduct Codes*, 2003 BYU
EDUC. & L. J. 1; Paula Koellmann, Goss v. Lopez: *How Much Process Is Really Due?*,
14 J. CONTEMP. LEGAL ISSUES 459 (2004).

4. *Goss* is linked with case law pertaining to the rights of students and is easily
compared with *New Jersey v. T. L. O.*, 469 U.S. 325 (1985). In that case, the Court
found that a search of a student required "reasonable suspicion." Like *Goss*, this
seminal case left for another day important questions, not the least of which are
the quantum of information such reasonable suspicion requires and the question

of how the test should be applied when a search is undertaken in "conjunction with or at the behest of law enforcement agencies."

As Professor and State Senator JAMIN B. RASKIN noted in his wonderful text, WE THE STUDENTS: SUPREME COURT CASES FOR AND ABOUT STUDENTS 133 (2000), *T. L. O.* "did not directly deal with the question of when school officials can search the students themselves," a most fundamental problem. *See, e.g.,* <u>Phaneuf v. Cipriano, 330 F. Supp. 2d 74 (D. Conn. 2004)</u> (a strip search for marijuana was fully consistent with due process); <u>Williams v. Ellington, 936 F.2d 881 (6th Cir. 1991)</u> (strip searches are reasonable).

5. The best way to study *Goss* is to asses its many – and varied – applications:

a. <u>Paredes v. Curtis, 864 F.2d 426 (6th Cir. 1988).</u>

> Efren Paredes, an eighth grade student at Lakeshore Junior High School in Stevensville, Michigan, was suspended for ten days for possession of a drug look-alike substance. . . . Doe told Sanford that Paredes had some cocaine in his locker behind his books. Sanford stated that he opened the locker . . . and . . . found a plastic bag containing a powdery substance. . . . Sanford then returned to Paredes' locker twenty minutes later and found that the plastic bag was gone. . . . Sanford found Paredes and searched him. No powdery substance was found on Paredes' person. Paredes denied possessing any illegal drugs or ever having any powdery substance in his locker. Sanford contacted Paredes' mother and informed Paredes of a suspension hearing to be held the next day. . . . Despite objections by Paredes' counsel [at the hearing], Woods would not allow Doe to be cross-examined or divulge his name. . . . Woods decided to suspend Paredes. . . .

Food for Thought

Can a hearing be fair if there is no right to confront opposing evidence? *Goss* most assuredly did not guarantee cross-examination – in fact, we suggest you glance back at <u>Loudermill</u>. The *Goss* formula, notice and an opportunity to be heard, is not unique to schools.

As a preliminary matter, we have to determine whether this case is the type of "unusual situation" alluded to in *Goss* that would call for more formal procedures. Paredes argues that school suspensions involving drug charges such as this case are so stigmatizing and harmful to a student's reputation that they should be considered an "unusual situation." . . . . We do not agree . . . . In particular, we do not believe that an eighth grade student charged with possession of a drug look-alike substance and suspended for a relatively short period of ten days is forever faced with a tarnished reputation and restricted employment opportunities. Instead, we believe that this is precisely the type of situation the *Goss* standard was meant to address. . . .

Paredes . . . asserts that he had the right to cross-examine the anonymous student informant. . . . [*Goss* does] not require that the accused have a right to cross-examine his student accusers or know their identities. . . . [W]e believe that the *Goss* standard for procedural due process was met here. . . . Paredes was given the opportunity to present his side of the story and throughout the process received an adequate explanation of the evidence against him. . . .

As this text was going to press, the Supreme Court decided <u>Giles v. California, 128 S. Ct. 2678 (2008)</u>, a remarkable case – admittedly having nothing to do with student rights or *Goss* – that affirms a right to confront evidence in a criminal case under the most difficult of circumstances: The testimony that is unavailable (for confrontation) is from the victim of the violent crime for which the defendant is on trial.

b. <u>*Flaim v. Medical College of Ohio,* 418 F.3d 629 (6th Cir. 2005).</u>

Flaim was arrested . . . while at his off-campus apartment. At the time, Flaim was a third-year medical student. He was charged with Aggravated Possession of Drugs (Ecstasy) . . . in violation of state law. . . . [Flaim] ultimately pleaded guilty to one count of the lesser included offense of Attempted Possession of Drugs . . . and was sentenced to two years of unsupervised probation. Two days after his arrest, Medical College of Ohio notified Flaim by letter that he was suspended "until external investigations/hearings completed." . . . . On the advice of counsel and in an effort to avoid incriminating himself, Flaim declined to schedule a Medical College of Ohio internal investigation until the pending criminal charges were resolved. . . . At the hearing, the arresting officer testified and Committee members were able to ask the officer questions. Flaim's attorney was not allowed to ask questions or speak with Flaim. Flaim was not permitted to cross-examine the officer. . . . [After the hearing] Flaim . . . was expelled . . . .

Flaim argues that he was denied the right to counsel at his disciplinary hearing in violation of the Due Process Clause. . . . At the hearing, while Flaim's attorney was permitted to remain in the room, Flaim was not permitted to consult with his attorney nor was the attorney permitted to participate in the proceedings. . . . Flaim's complaint really boils down to the assertion that he was denied the opportunity to present his case as effectively as he would have wished – he could not reasonably claim that he was denied the opportunity to present his case at all due to the lack of legal counsel. Flaim's attorney may have been more articulate, but there is no indication that the hearing was so complex that only a trained attorney could have effectively presented his case. . . .

[As to cross examination], at the hearing, Flaim was not permitted to cross-examine the arresting officer. Flaim alleges that the officer's testimony was unreliable and contradictory. . . . Flaim was able to listen to and observe the officer's testimony. Flaim then had the opportunity to present his version of events, during which he had the opportunity to point out inconsistencies or contradictions in the officer's testimony. . . . Moreover, Flaim has been unable to identify any benefits that cross-examination would have provided at his hearing (not to mention the administrative burden and expense) other than the assertion that he could have identified discrepancies in the officer's testimony. . . .

c. *Nash v. Auburn University*, 812 F.2d 655 (11th Cir. 1987).

> Appellants were advised in writing . . . that they were charged with a violation of the Student Code of Professional Ethics (the code) of the Auburn University School of Veterinary Medicine [a state university] ". . . in that while taking examinations during 1984-1985 school year, information was allegedly obtained in an unethical manner." . . . . Counsel objected that [this] notice was . . . too general . . . . He requested a more specific notice . . . . The following day each appellant received a written memorandum . . . advising them that they were charged with a violation of the code in "giving or receiving assistance or communication between students during the anatomy examination given on or about May 16, 1985." Included in the memorandum was a list of students and anatomy faculty witnesses who were expected to testify at the hearing in support of the charge against appellants. . . .

> Both Nash and Perry attended [the hearing], in the company of their attorney. . . . The chancellor allowed appellants' counsel to advise his clients during the hearing, but he was not permitted to participate in the proceedings. . . . After the board completed its questioning, appellants were given the opportunity to question the opposing witnesses by submitting questions to the chancellor, who would then direct the questions to the witnesses. Appellants instead asked the board several questions. . . . [T]he board decided unanimously that appellants were guilty of the charge of academic dishonesty. . . .

> Although the [first] notice in their case was rudimentary, the [second] notice specified that appellants were accused of academic dishonesty on the May 16 neuroanatomy exam and it included a list of accusing witnesses. . . . [W]e find that appellants were afforded constitutionally adequate notice and were adequately prepared by the notice to defend the charge against them. . . .

> Although appellants were not allowed to ask questions directly of the adverse witnesses at the June 12 hearing, it is clear that they heard all of the testimony against them. Appellants were told they could pose questions of the accusing witnesses by directing their questions to the presiding board chancellor, who would then direct appellants' questions to the witnesses. . . . That they did not avail themselves of the opportunity to question the witnesses through the chancellor cannot be characterized as a denial of process. . . .

d. *Board of Curators of the University of Missouri v. Horowitz*, 435 U.S. 78 (1978).

> Respondent was admitted with advanced standing to the [University of Missouri-Kansas City] Medical School in the fall of 1971. . . . In the spring of respondent's first year of study, several faculty members . . . noted that respondent's "performance was below that of her peers in all clinical patient-oriented settings" . . . and that she lacked a critical concern for personal hygiene. Upon the recommendation of the Council on Evaluation, respondent was advanced to her . . . final year on a probationary basis. Faculty dissatisfaction with respondent's clinical performance continued during the following year. . . . In the middle of the year, the Council again reviewed respondent's academic progress and concluded that respondent should not be considered for graduation in June of that year; furthermore, the Council recommended that, absent "radical improvement," respondent be dropped from the school.

Respondent was permitted to take a set of oral and practical examinations as an "appeal" of the decision not to permit her to graduate [after which] the Council on Evaluation reaffirmed its prior position. The Council met again in mid-May to consider whether respondent should be allowed to remain in school beyond June of that year [and] unanimously recommended that "barring receipt of any reports that Miss Horowitz has improved radically, [she should] not be allowed to re-enroll . . . ."
. . . .

Academic evaluations of a student, in contrast to disciplinary determinations, bear little resemblance to the judicial and administrative factfinding proceedings to which we have traditionally attached a full-hearing requirement. . . . The decision to dismiss respondent . . . rested on the academic judgment of school officials that she did not have the necessary clinical ability to perform adequately as a medical doctor and was making insufficient progress toward that goal. Such a judgment is by its nature more subjective and evaluative than the typical factual questions presented in the average disciplinary decision. Like the decision of an individual professor as to the proper grade for a student in his course, the determination whether to dismiss a student for academic reasons requires an expert evaluation of cumulative information and is not readily adapted to the procedural tools of judicial or administrative decisionmaking. Under such circumstances, we decline to . . . formalize the academic dismissal process by requiring a hearing. . . .

The circumstances of the student in the above case is one to which law students should easily be able to relate: Imagine passing all your exams – and finding out that because of your attitude, commitment, or approach in an externship, you will not be given your degree nor will you be permitted to take the bar.

This is also a case of interest to professors and deans at law schools (as well as all other academic institutions). The proposition that academic judgments are entitled to substantial deference and are outside the probing reach of intermeddling courts is, as you might expect, fairly popular with faculty and administrators.

e. *State ex rel. Yarber v. McHenry*, 915 S.W.2d 325 (Mo. 1995).

Clint Yarber attends Mountain Grove High School . . . . Yarber was accused of violating the attendance policy during the fall 1993 semester. The school notified him that he would be required to make up three days over Christmas vacation and one day during the month of January. Yarber attended two of the scheduled make-up days, but when his mother allegedly saw students in the make-up classes eating pizza and watching a movie, she took him out of the classes and did not send him back for the remaining days. On January 12, 1994, Yarber, who had accrued credit for his class work, was notified by the school district that he had lost that credit for the semester because of the attendance policy violation. . . .

In Yarber's case, the penalty imposed – loss of a semester's worth of credit hours – is in no way de minimis; it is instead a considerable infringement on Yarber's property interest. For that reason, we hold that procedural due process requires a hearing with more formal and extensive procedures than that provided in *Goss*. . . . [However, the] Supreme Court, in *Horowitz*, qualified its decision in *Goss* by determining that procedural due process does not require a hearing when the deprivation is for academic reasons rather than disciplinary reasons. . . . The question then is squarely posed: Is the attendance policy of Mountain Grove High School academic or disciplinary in nature? If disciplinary in nature, then a hearing is required, and the underlying suit is a contested case. . . . On the other hand, if the nature of the attendance policy is academic, then a hearing is not required, and the underlying suit is not a contested case. . . .

We hold that the Mountain Grove attendance policy, as written and as applied to Yarber, is disciplinary in nature. The policy states that if the student fails to make up the absences, he or she will "lose credit for that semester." As conceded in the school district's pleading here, this provision takes away previously earned credit as punishment for unsatisfactory attendance. While an attendance policy might conceivably be structured to relate to academic performance, the policy in this case does not do so. . . .

Do you accept the disciplinary/academic distinction? Consider an honor code case for failure to provide sufficient documentation – academic or disciplinary?

INGRAHAM V. WRIGHT

430 U.S. 651 (1977)

[JUSTICE POWELL] This case presents questions concerning the use of corporal punishment in public schools: First, whether the paddling of students as a means of maintaining school discipline constitutes cruel and unusual punishment in violation of the Eighth Amendment; and, second, to the extent that paddling is constitutionally permissible, whether the Due Process Clause of the Fourteenth Amendment requires prior notice and an opportunity to be heard.

I

Petitioners James Ingraham and Roosevelt Andrews . . . were enrolled in . . . Drew Junior High School in Dade County, Fla., Ingraham in the eighth grade and Andrews in the ninth . . . . The [Florida] statute then in effect authorized limited corporal punishment by negative inference, proscribing punishment which was "degrading or unduly severe" or which was inflicted without prior consultation with the principal or the teacher in charge of the school. The regulation contained explicit directions and limitations. The authorized punishment consisted of paddling the recalcitrant student on the buttocks with a flat wooden paddle measuring less than two feet long, three to four inches wide, and about one-half inch thick. The normal punishment was limited to one to five "licks" or blows with the paddle and resulted in no apparent physical injury to the student. School authorities viewed corporal punishment as a less drastic means of discipline than suspension or expulsion. Contrary to the procedural requirements of the statute and regulation, teachers often paddled students on their own authority without first consulting the principal.

. . . The evidence, consisting mainly of the testimony of 16 students, suggests that the regime at Drew was exceptionally harsh. The testimony of Ingraham and Andrews, in support of their individual claims for damages, is illustrative. Because he was slow to respond to his teacher's instructions, Ingraham was subjected to more than 20 licks with a paddle while being held over a table in the principal's office. The paddling was so severe that he suffered a hematoma requiring medical attention and keeping him out of school for several days. Andrews was paddled several times . . . . On two occasions he was struck on his arms, once depriving him of the full use of his arm for a week.

The District Court made no findings on the credibility of the students' testimony. Rather, assuming their testimony to be credible, the court found no constitutional basis for relief. . . . A panel of the Court of Appeals voted to reverse. . . .

II

In addressing the scope of the Eighth Amendment's prohibition on cruel and unusual punishment, this Court has found it useful to refer to "[t]raditional common-law concepts," and to the "attitude(s) which our society has traditionally taken." . . . . The use of corporal punishment in this country as a means of disciplining schoolchildren dates back to the colonial period. . . . Despite the general abandonment of corporal punishment as a means of punishing criminal offenders, the practice continues to play a role in the public education of schoolchildren in most parts of the country. Professional and public opinion is sharply divided on the practice, and has been for more than a century. Yet we can discern no trend toward its elimination.

III

An examination of the history of the [Eighth] Amendment and the decisions of this Court construing the proscription against cruel and unusual punishment confirms that it was designed to protect those convicted of crimes. We adhere to this longstanding limitation and hold that the Eighth Amendment does not apply to the paddling of children as a means of maintaining discipline in public schools. . . .

IV

[Applying the _Mathews_ test] we find that corporal punishment in public schools implicates a constitutionally protected liberty interest, but we hold that the traditional common-law remedies are fully adequate to afford due process.

A

. . . .

While the contours of [the] historic liberty interest . . . have not been defined precisely, they always have been thought to encompass freedom from bodily restraint and punishment. . . . There is, of course, a de minimis level of imposition with which the Constitution is not concerned. But at least where school authorities, acting under color of state law, deliberately decide to punish a child for misconduct by restraining the child and inflicting appreciable physical pain, we hold that Fourteenth Amendment liberty interests are implicated. n.43

> n.43 Unlike *Goss v. Lopez*, this case does not involve the state-created property interest in public education. The purpose of corporal punishment is to correct a child's behavior without interrupting his education. That corporal punishment may, in a rare case, have the unintended effect of temporarily removing a child from school affords no basis for concluding that the practice itself deprives students of property protected by the Fourteenth Amendment. . . .

B

"[T]he question remains what process is due." Were it not for the common-law privilege permitting teachers to inflict reasonable corporal punishment on children in their care, and the availability of the traditional remedies for abuse, the case for requiring advance procedural safeguards would be strong indeed. But here we deal with a punishment – paddling – within that tradition, and the question is whether the common-law remedies are adequate to afford due process. . . . [This question] must turn on an analysis of the competing interests at stake, viewed against the background of "history, reason, [and] the past course of decisions . . . ." . . . .

1

[We do not] say that the child's interest in procedural safeguards is insubstantial. The school disciplinary process is not "a totally accurate, unerring process, never mistaken and never unfair. . . ." *Goss v. Lopez*. In any deliberate infliction of corporal punishment on a child who is restrained for that purpose, there is some risk that the intrusion on the child's liberty will be unjustified and therefore unlawful. In these circumstances the child has a strong interest in procedural safeguards that minimize the risk of wrongful punishment and provide for the resolution of disputed questions of justification. We turn now to a consideration of the safeguards that are available under applicable Florida law.

2

Florida has continued to recognize, and indeed has strengthened by statute, the common-law right of a child not to be subjected to excessive corporal punishment in school. Under Florida law the teacher and principal of the school decide in the first instance whether corporal punishment is reasonably necessary under the circumstances in order to discipline a child who has misbehaved. But they must exercise prudence and restraint. . . . If the punishment inflicted is later found to have been excessive – not reasonably believed at the time to be necessary for the child's discipline or training – the school authorities inflicting it may be held liable in damages to the child and, if malice is shown, they may be subject to criminal penalties. n.45

> n.45 . . . The dissent makes much of the fact that no Florida court has ever "recognized" a damages remedy for unreasonable corporal punishment. But the absence of reported Florida decisions hardly suggests that no remedy is available. Rather, it merely confirms the commonsense judgment that excessive corporal punishment is exceedingly rare in the public schools.

Although students have testified in this case to specific instances of abuse, there is every reason to believe that such mistreatment is an aberration. The uncontradicted evidence suggests that corporal punishment in the Dade County schools was, "[w]ith the exception of a few cases . . . unremarkable in physical severity." Moreover, because paddlings are usually inflicted in response to conduct directly observed by teachers in their presence, the risk that a child will be paddled without cause is typically insignificant. . . . In those cases where severe punishment is contemplated, the available civil and criminal sanctions for abuse – considered in light of the openness of the school environment – afford significant protection against unjustified corporal punishment. . . . n.46

> n.46 The low incidence of abuse, and the availability of established judicial remedies in the event of abuse, distinguish this case from *Goss v. Lopez*. . . . The subsequent civil and criminal proceedings available in this case may be viewed as affording substantially greater protection to the child than the informal conference mandated by *Goss*.

It still may be argued, of course, that the child's liberty interest would be better protected if the common-law remedies were supplemented by the administrative safeguards of prior notice and a hearing. . . . But where the State has preserved what "has always been the law of the land," the case for administrative safeguards is significantly less compelling. n.47

> n.47 "[P]rior hearings might well be dispensed with in many circumstances in which the state's conduct, if not adequately justified, would constitute a common-law tort. This would leave the injured plaintiff in precisely the same posture as a common-law plaintiff, and this procedural consequence would be quite harmonious with the

substantive view that the fourteenth amendment encompasses the same liberties as those protected by the common law."

We have no occasion in this case to decide whether or under what circumstances corporal punishment of a public school child may give rise to an independent federal cause of action to vindicate substantive rights under the Due Process Clause. . . .

3

. . . .

Such a universal constitutional requirement would significantly burden the use of corporal punishment as a disciplinary measure. Hearings – even informal hearings – require time, personnel, and a diversion of attention from normal school pursuits. . . . Teachers, properly concerned with maintaining authority in the classroom, may well prefer to rely on other disciplinary measures – which they may view as less effective – rather than confront the possible disruption that prior notice and a hearing may entail. Paradoxically, such an alteration of disciplinary policy is most likely to occur in the ordinary case where the contemplated punishment is well within the common-law privilege.

Elimination or curtailment of corporal punishment would be welcomed by many as a societal advance. But [w]e are reviewing here a legislative judgment, rooted in history and reaffirmed in the laws of many States, that corporal punishment serves important educational interests. . . . "[T]he Court has repeatedly emphasized the need for affirming the comprehensive authority of the States and of school officials, consistent with fundamental constitutional safeguards, to prescribe and control conduct in the schools."

"At some point the benefit of an additional safeguard to the individual . . . may be outweighed by the cost." *Mathews*. We think that point has been reached in this case. In view of the low incidence of abuse, the openness of our schools, and the common-law safeguards that already exist, the risk of error that may result in violation of a schoolchild's substantive rights can only be regarded as minimal. Imposing additional administrative safeguards as a constitutional requirement might reduce that risk marginally, but would also entail a significant intrusion into an area of primary educational responsibility. We conclude that the Due Process Clause does not require notice and a hearing prior to the imposition of corporal punishment in the public schools, as that practice is authorized and limited by the common law.

V

Petitioners cannot prevail on either of the theories before us in this case. The Eighth Amendment's prohibition against cruel and unusual punishment is inapplicable to school paddlings, and the Fourteenth Amendment's requirement of procedural due process is satisfied by Florida's preservation of common-law constraints and remedies. . . . Affirmed.

[JUSTICE WHITE, dissenting.]

The majority concedes that corporal punishment in the public schools implicates an interest protected by the Due Process Clause – the liberty interest . . . . To guard against this risk of punishing an innocent child, the Due Process Clause requires, not an "elaborate hearing" before a neutral party, but simply "an informal give-and-take between student and disciplinarian" . . . . The Court now holds that these "rudimentary precautions against unfair or mistaken findings of misconduct" are not required if the student is punished with "appreciable physical pain" rather than with a suspension, even though both punishments deprive the student of a constitutionally protected interest . . . because he can later sue . . . .

[A] tort action is utterly inadequate to protect against erroneous infliction of punishment for two reasons. First, under Florida law, a student punished for an act he did not commit cannot recover damages from a teacher proceeding in utmost good faith . . . . The "traditional common-law remedies" on which the majority relies thus do nothing to protect the student from the danger that concerned the Court in _Goss_ – the risk of reasonable, good-faith mistake in the school disciplinary process. Second, and more important, even if the student could sue for good-faith error in the infliction of punishment, the lawsuit occurs after the punishment has been finally imposed. The infliction of physical pain is final and irreparable . . . .

Underlying Case Documents

The case referenced:
The testimony of James Ingraham
The testimony of Roosevelt Andrews

For a picture of the paddles used in the case click HERE.

For the (relevant) medical records of the students click HERE.

1. While <u>Goss</u> provides students with rudimentary due process – and school systems with considerable discretion to run their program as they see fit – there are limits, and *Ingraham* is a foundational case establishing consequences when that discretion is abused. Like *Goss*, the case is best understood through its application.

a. <u>W.E.T. v. Mitchell, 2008 WL 151282 (M.D.N.C. 2008)</u>.

> On April 19, 2005, W.E.T. was talking with another student when Mitchell "sharply rebuked" him and "suddenly and without warning" ripped a piece of masking tape from a roll and "forcefully" placed it over W.E.T.'s mouth. . . . [B]ecause of W.E.T.'s severe asthma, a condition of which Mitchell was aware, he began to have problems breathing when the tape was placed over his mouth. Shortly thereafter, W.E.T. attempted to get Mitchell's attention by attempting to orally communicate through the tape without removing it. As a result, the tape began to fall off and W.E.T. informed Mitchell that the tape was no longer sticking. Mitchell responded that the tape was "not supposed to stick" and "forcefully" ripped it from his mouth. Plaintiffs allege that as a result of this incident, in addition to W.E.T.'s difficulty breathing, he has also suffered extensive mental and emotional damages. . . .

> [I]t is not necessary as Mitchell would suggest, that this specific conduct must have been the subject of some previous litigation. . . . [The] Supreme Court stated that students have a liberty interest in freedom from unreasonable restraint and mistreatment. See, *Ingraham v. Wright*. In *Hall v. Tawney*, the seminal case for addressing excessive force in public schools, the Fourth Circuit recognized a student's substantive due process right to be free from excessive force "inspired by malice or sadism," that is disproportionate to the need presented and inflicts severe injury. . . . Most recently, in *Meeker v. Edmundson*, the Fourth Circuit, rejecting a qualified immunity defense, held that "[i]n the Fourth Circuit, educators have been aware that arbitrary use of corporal punishment [has been] prohibited by the Fourteenth Amendment since at least' the issuance of *Hall* in 1980." The circuit court went on to state that, "[n]ot only has such conduct been unlawful in this circuit since our decision in *Hall*, but by November 2000, the Third, Sixth, Eighth, Ninth, and Tenth Circuits had adopted the *Hall* rationale and holding." See also, <u>Neal v. Fulton County Bd. of Educ., 229 F.3d 1069, 1075 (11th Cir. 2000)</u> (holding that excessive force may be actionable under the due process clause "when it is tantamount to arbitrary, egregious, and conscience-shocking behavior . . ."). More specifically, and similar to the conduct Plaintiff W.E.T. has alleged here, the Fifth Circuit has held that a student's right to bodily integrity also "applies to state-occasioned restraints which are not justified by the victim's conduct or other extenuating circumstances.". . . .

> Considering the abovementioned precedent, the Court finds that a constitutional violation is sufficiently alleged to the extent that a reasonable special needs educator would have known that forcefully and maliciously placing masking tape over a disabled student's mouth whom she knew to have severe asthma, and subsequently forcefully ripping it off, violates his constitutional right to bodily integrity.

This case suggests that corporal punishment is impermissible – do you agree? *See* <u>Williams v. Berney, 519 F.3d 1216 (10th Cir. 2008)</u> ("Police officers, prison officials, and even school authorities are cloaked with the state's imprimatur to use some level of force when necessary. . . . [O]rdinary corporal punishment violates no substantive due process rights of school children.").

2. *Neal v. Fulton County Board of Education, 229 F.3d 1069 (11th Cir. 2000).*

[P]laintiff was a 14-year-old freshman [when] Royonte Griffin, another [football] player, slapped Plaintiff in the face. Plaintiff reported this incident to Coach Ector, who told Plaintiff "you need to learn how to handle your own business." . . . . After practice was over, Griffin again approached Plaintiff. Plaintiff pulled [a] weight lock out of his bag [and] hit Griffin in the head with it . . . . The two students then began to fight. While the two were fighting . . . Ector came over and began dumping the contents of Plaintiff's bag on the ground, shouting repeatedly "what did you hit him with; if you hit him with it, I am going to hit you with it." Ector then . . . took the weight lock and struck Plaintiff in the left eye. As a result of the blow, Plaintiff's eye "was knocked completely out of its socket," leaving it "destroyed and dismembered." According to Plaintiff, even after this blow, as Plaintiff's eye "was hanging out of his head, and as he was in severe pain," neither Coach Ector nor Principal Robinson stopped the fight. . . . Plaintiff sued . . . . The district court granted Defendants' motion [to dismiss, holding] that under . . . *Ingraham v. Wright*, corporal punishment does not give rise to a substantive due process claim. . . .

Having determined that Ector's conduct was corporal punishment, we turn next to the question of whether . . . corporal punishment, regardless of its severity, may never give rise to a substantive due process claim. . . . *Ingraham* did not say that under no set of circumstances could corporal punishment rise to the level of a constitutional violation. . . . [W]e think for a number of reasons that a student-plaintiff alleging excessive corporal punishment can *in certain circumstances* assert a cause of action for a violation of his rights under the Fourteenth Amendment's Due Process Clause. . . .

We [also] join the vast majority of Circuits in confirming that excessive corporal punishment, at least where not administered in conformity with a valid school policy authorizing corporal punishment as in *Ingraham*, may be actionable under the Due Process Clause when it is tantamount to arbitrary, egregious, and conscience-shocking behavior. . . . We need not decide today how "serious" an injury must be to support a claim. The injury alleged by Plaintiff here – the utter destruction of an eye – clearly was serious. . . . On the facts of this case, and consistent with the logic of almost all courts considering the subject, we conclude that Plaintiff has stated a claim. . . .

Is the court correct? Is severity of injury not an issue in this field? *See* Scott Bloom, *Spare the Rod, Spoil the Child? A Legal Framework for Recent Corporal Punishment Proposals,* 25 GOLDEN GATE U.L. REV. 361 (1995).

3. *Hinson v. Holt, 776 So.2d 804 (Ala. Civ. App. 1998).*

On . . . the fifth day of the 1995-96 school term . . . 13-year-old Dustin reported to his first period eighth-grade physical education class . . . . As the students walked towards the gym, one student behind Dustin said to another "I will kick your ass." . . . . When another student asked Dustin what had been said, Dustin repeated the remark he had overheard . . . . Hinson turned around as Dustin uttered the remark, and upon hearing it directed him to . . . dress and to come to a stage inside the gymnasium. . . .

[Once on the state Hinson] struck Dustin three times. . . . The force of the third blow was sufficiently strong to cause the chair Dustin was grasping to slide several inches across the stage. . . . Dustin was in such pain that he was unable to sit through his remaining classes. . . . [Dustin developed] deep, eggplant-sized black bruises . . . .

"[A] state officer or employee is not protected under the doctrine of discretionary function immunity if he acts willfully, *maliciously*, fraudulently, or in bad faith." . . . . There was sufficient evidence from which the trial court could have concluded that Hinson acted maliciously . . . . First, according to the policy of the Tallassee City Board of Education, corporal punishment is not to be administered except "as a *last resort* in the *most unusual circumstances* and after *reasonable corrective measures have been used without success*" (emphasis added). In this case, Dustin was immediately subjected to the maximum corporal punishment for uttering the word "ass" . . . . There is no evidence that Dustin had a previous record of such offenses; further, Hinson made no attempt to consult with the principal before inflicting the punishment, and Hinson made no other attempt to correct Dustin before resorting to corporal punishment. . . .

Also, in determining the reasonableness of the punishment and the extent of malice, the trier of fact may consider the nature of the offense committed by the student, the age and physical condition of the student, and other attendant circumstances. Here, the evidence reveals that a physical education instructor inflicted three blows to the buttocks of a 13-year-old for using the word "ass," a word that amounts to, at most, a mildly profane reference to the human hindquarters. Taken together, the blows . . . were so severe that Dustin developed large, shocking bruises on his buttocks . . . .

Did *Ingraham* hold that the Eighth Amendment applied only in the event the harm the student experienced was criminal in nature? Was the Eighth Amendment "cruel and unusual" punishment clause written to apply to anything other than criminal sanctions? The excessive fines clause of the Eighth Amendment may well have been directed at both civil and criminal acts (it has been applied to civil forfeitures) – but did the founders have in mind the rights of school children when they adopted the cruel and unusual punishment clause of the Bill of Rights?

———————

V. Administrative Hearings and Prisoners

SANDIN V. CONNER

515 U.S. 472 (1995)

[CHIEF JUSTICE REHNQUIST] We granted certiorari to reexamine the circumstances under which state prison regulations afford inmates a liberty interest protected by the Due Process Clause.

I

DeMont Conner was convicted of numerous state crimes, including murder, kidnaping, robbery, and burglary, for which he is currently serving an indeterminate sentence of 30 years to life in . . . the Halawa Correctional Facility, a maximum security prison in central Oahu. In August 1987 [he was subjected] to a strip search, complete with an inspection of the rectal area. Conner retorted with angry and foul language directed at the officer [conducting the inspection]. Eleven days later he received notice that he had been charged with disciplinary *infrac*tions. The notice charged Conner with "high misconduct" for using physical interference to impair a correctional function, and "low moderate misconduct" for using abusive or obscene language and for harassing employees.

Conner appeared before an adjustment committee on August 28, 1987. The committee refused Conner's request to present witnesses at the hearing . . . . At the conclusion of proceedings, the committee determined that Conner was guilty of the alleged misconduct. It sentenced him to 30 days' disciplinary segregation in the Special Holding Unit for the physical obstruction charge, and four hours segregation for each of the other two charges to be served concurrent with the 30 days. . . .

II

Our due process analysis begins with *Wolff*. There, Nebraska inmates challenged the decision of prison officials to revoke good time credits without adequate procedures. Inmates earned good time credits under a state statute that bestowed mandatory sentence reductions for good behavior, revocable only for "flagrant or serious misconduct." We held that the . . . statutory provision created a liberty interest in a "shortened prison sentence" which resulted from good time credits, credits which were revocable only if the prisoner was guilty of serious misconduct. The Court characterized this liberty interest as one of "real substance" and articulated minimum procedures necessary to reach a "mutual accommodation between institutional needs and objectives and the provisions of the Constitution." . . . . Its short discussion of the definition of a liberty interest led to a more thorough treatment of the issue in *Meachum v. Fano*.

Inmates in *Meachum* sought injunctive relief, declaratory relief, and damages by reason of transfers from a . . . medium security prison to a maximum security facility with substantially less favorable conditions. The transfers . . . did not entail a loss of good time credits or any period of disciplinary confinement. The Court began with the proposition that the Due Process Clause does not protect every change in the conditions of confinement having a substantial adverse impact on the prisoner. It then held . . . that transfer to a maximum security facility, albeit one with more burdensome conditions, was "within the normal limits or range of custody which the conviction has authorized the State to impose." . . . .

. . . .

. . . In a series of cases since *Hewitt* [a case after *Meachum*], the Court has wrestled with the language of intricate, often rather routine prison guidelines to determine whether mandatory language and substantive predicates created an enforceable expectation . . . with respect to the prisoner's conditions of confinement. By shifting the focus of the liberty interest inquiry to one based on the language of a particular regulation, and not the nature of the deprivation, the Court encouraged prisoners to comb regulations in search of mandatory language on which to base entitlements to various state-conferred privileges. . . .

Hewitt has produced at least two undesirable effects. First, it creates disincentives for States to codify prison management procedures in the interest of uniform treatment. . . . [But] guidelines are not set forth solely to benefit the prisoner. They also . . . confine the authority of prison personnel in order to avoid widely different treatment of similar incidents. The approach embraced by *Hewitt* discourages this desirable development: States may avoid creation of "liberty" interests by having scarcely any regulations, or by conferring standardless discretion on correctional personnel. Second, the *Hewitt* approach has led to the involvement of federal courts in the day-to-day management of prisons, often squandering judicial resources with little offsetting benefit to anyone. In so doing, it has run counter to the view expressed in several of our cases that federal courts ought to afford appropriate deference and flexibility to state officials trying to manage a volatile environment.

In light of the above discussion, we believe that the [caselaw] has strayed from the real concerns undergirding the liberty protected by the Due Process Clause. The time has come to return to the due process principles we believe were correctly established and applied in *Wolff* and *Meachum.* Following *Wolff,* we recognize that States may under certain circumstances create liberty interests which are protected by the Due Process Clause. But these interests will be generally limited to freedom from restraint which, while not exceeding the sentence in such an unexpected manner as to give rise to protection by the Due Process Clause of its own force . . . nonetheless imposes atypical and significant hardship on the inmate in relation to the ordinary incidents of prison life. . . . Admittedly, prisoners do not shed all constitutional rights at the prison gate, but "lawful incarceration brings about the necessary withdrawal or limitation of many privileges and rights, a retraction justified by the considerations underlying our penal system." Discipline by prison officials in response to a wide range of misconduct falls within the expected parameters of the sentence imposed by a court of law.

. . . We hold that Conner's discipline in segregated confinement did not present the type of atypical, significant deprivation in which a State might conceivably create a liberty interest. The record shows that, at the time of Conner's punishment, disciplinary segregation, with insignificant exceptions, mirrored those conditions imposed upon inmates in administrative segregation and protective custody. We note also that the State expunged Conner's disciplinary record with respect to the "high misconduct" charge nine months after Conner served time in segregation. Thus, Conner's confinement did not exceed similar, but totally discretionary, confinement in either duration or degree of restriction. Indeed, the conditions at Halawa involve significant amounts of "lockdown time" even for inmates in the general population. Based on a comparison between inmates inside and outside disciplinary segregation, the State's actions in placing him there for 30 days did not work a major disruption in his environment.

Nor does Conner's situation present a case where the State's action will inevitably affect the duration of his sentence. Nothing in Hawaii's code requires the parole board to deny parole in the face of a misconduct record or to grant parole in its absence, even though misconduct is by regulation a relevant consideration. The decision to release a prisoner rests on a myriad of considerations. And, the prisoner is afforded procedural protection at his parole hearing in order to explain the circumstances behind his misconduct record. The chance that a finding of misconduct will alter the balance is simply too attenuated to invoke the procedural guarantees of the Due Process Clause. . . .

We hold, therefore, that neither the Hawaii prison regulation in question, nor the Due Process Clause itself, afforded Conner a protected liberty interest that would entitle him to the procedural protections set forth in *Wolff*. The regime to which he was subjected as a result of the misconduct hearing was within the range of confinement to be normally expected for one serving an indeterminate term of 30 years to life.

The judgment of the Court of Appeals is accordingly Reversed.

————

1. The topic of administrative hearings and prisons has come up several times in this casebook. Listed below are cases we have already mentioned in this field:

Dismas Charities v. United Federal Bureau of Prisons, 401 F.3d 666 (6th Cir. 2005)
Castellini v. Lappin, 365 F. Supp. 2d 197 (Mass. 2005)
McCarthy v. Madigan, 503 U.S. 140 (1992)
Booth v. Churner, 532 U.S. 731 (2001)
Jones v. Zenk, 495 F. Supp. 2d 1289 (N.D. Ga. 2007)

In addition, we have mentioned habeas corpus petitions several times:

Hamdi v. Rumsfeld, 542 U.S. 507 (2004)
Hamdan v. Rumsfeld, 548 U.S. 557 (2006)
Hernandez-Rodriguez v. Pasquarell, 118 F.3d 1034 (5th Cir. 1997)
Boumediene v. Bush, 128 S. Ct. 2229 (2008)
Zhong v. United States, 480 F.3d 104 (2d Cir. 2006)

Finally, we mentioned as additional habeas references:

Stephen Vladeck, Hirota: *Habeas Corpus, Citizenship, and Article III*, 95 GEO. L.J. 1497 (2007)

Anthony J. Colangelo, *Constitutional Limits on Extraterritorial Jurisdiction: Terrorism and the Intersection of National and International Law*, 48 HARV. INT'L L.J. 121 (2007)

Jared A. Goldstein, *Habeas Without Rights*, 2007 WIS. L. REV. 1165

2. *Sandin* is part of a substantial body of law regarding the constitutional entitlements – or lack thereof – of prisoners. Balanced against the prisoner's assertions of claims of mistreatment is the government agency's need to manage the complex and dangerous jails, prisons, and penitentiaries in the United States. Over the last quarter-century, this balance has been anything but easy.

In *Solem v. Helm*, 463 U.S. 277 (1983), the Court affirmed the importance of deferring to the discretionary judgments of the individuals and agencies involved in running the prison system. Much like *Skidmore*, *Goss*, *Vermont Yankee*, *Chevron*, and *Brand X*, *Solem* presents a solid and familiar principle in administrative law – deference is due reasonable agency judgments. There is, of course, a massive difference in these cases. In agency cases outside of prison decisions, those affected by the action of the agency come to the process with a full (or in the case of students, partial) set of constitutional rights. Asserting one's liberty or property interests requires thought – as *Roth* and *Sindermann* made clear – but the chances are that if the entitlements asserted are based on reasonable expectations, there is some level of protection either constitutionally or through the APA.

This is not the case with prisoners – by definition, they have compromised or in some instances lost entirely their liberty interests and have property interests at a most basic level. Thus *Sandin* and the cases that follow it often focus first on the limited or residual constitutional interests a prisoner might possess and only then, assuming some interest is present, move to the more basic administrative law problems of the range, nature, and process for a hearing.

3. Testing Prison Regulations. In *Turner v. Safley*, 482 U.S. 78 (1987), the Court set out four factors to determine whether regulations restricting the arguable entitle-

ments of prisoners were reasonable: (1) a "valid, rational connection" between the regulation and the state interest asserted; (2) the presence of "alternative means of exercising the right that remain open to prison inmates;" (3) the impact the asserted right would have on "guards and other inmates, and on the allocation of prison resources generally;" and (4) "alternatives to achieve the states goals."

This *Mathews*-like test was nominally applied in *Sandin* – and then, in 2006, the Court decided *Beard v. Banks*, 548 U.S. 521 (2006), in which the *Turner* factors seemed of limited consequence in the event the deprivation of an apparent right would create an incentive for better behavior in the prison system. To justify a regulation that denied prisoners newspapers and magazines (as well as certain visitation rights)

> [t]he Secretary . . . set forth several justifications for the prison's policy, including the need to motivate better behavior on the part of particularly difficult prisoners, the need to minimize the amount of property they control in their cells, and the need to ensure prison safety, by, for example, diminishing the amount of material a prisoner might use to start a cell fire. We need go no further than the first justification, that of providing increased incentives for better prison behavior. . . .

Compare this reasoning process with *Skidmore*. Do you see a meaningful difference?

4. Solitary? *Sandin* did not resolve the question of the extent to which disciplinary segregation or solitary confinement would constitute an atypical hardship and infringe on the fragments of rights a prisoner might possess. However, combined with other factors, solitary confinement has been the basis for recognizing a right to a fair hearing. In *Staples v. Casperson*, 6 Fed. Appx. 481 (7th Cir. 2001), the prisoner claimed (among eight other complaints all of which were set aside) his civil rights were transgressed, violating 42 U.S.C. § 1983, when he was denied the right to call the complainant, a prison guard, in a disciplinary hearing. As a result of the sanction he received, his sentenced was extended by 16 days.

> [A] prisoner is entitled to due process protections only when a prison employee's action imposes an "atypical and significant hardship on the inmate in relation to the ordinary incidents of prison life." *Sandin*. . . .

> [In this particular prison] whenever a prisoner is sentenced to segregation for violating a disciplinary rule, that inmate's mandatory release date is "extended by the number of days equal to 50% of the number of days spent in . . . segregation. . . ." [This] implicated a liberty interest for which he was entitled to due process protection. . . .

Would either the denial of the right to call the guard or the solitary confinement have been sufficient had there not been a concomitant increase in the time served?

5. It is not always the case that a sentence must be extended to fall within the rights *Sandin* preserved.

Sims v. Artuz, 230 F.3d 14 (2d Cir. 2000).

> [W]hile in a prison elevator, correction officer[s and others] punched [Sims] in the ribs, collar, upper right arm and skull . . . pulled on [his] handcuffs . . . punched Sims in the face four times . . . punched and kicked [Sims] in the rib cage, skull, knee cap, back bone, sacrum, base of spine, collar bone, [and] teeth, and pull[ed him] by his penis. . . .
>
> In an excessive-force case, whether conduct was "wanton" turns on "whether force was applied in a good-faith effort to maintain or restore discipline, or maliciously and sadistically to cause harm. . . . To prevail on a claim based on the conditions of his confinement, a prisoner must show "extreme deprivations," because routine discomfort is part of the penalty that criminal offenders pay for their offenses against society. . . .
>
> When prison officials maliciously and sadistically use force to cause harm, contemporary standards of decency always are violated. . . . The duration and the frequency of such deprivations are highly relevant to whether the conditions of a plaintiff's confinement should be considered atypical. . . . Sims [also] alleged, *inter alia*, that his punishments included his being placed in full restraints for nearly seven months; not being allowed even to exercise without those restraints; deprivation, for two 14-day periods, of his normal meals; and being forced to remain naked in his cell for a number of days. . . .
>
> [T]he complaint alleged that the . . . sentences imposed on Sims were of sufficient length to be atypical and significant. . . . Further, although the other sentences were shorter, it is possible that some or all of them should be aggregated for purposes of the *Sandin* inquiry. . . .
>
> Sims's complaint did not challenge the disciplinary proceedings on the basis that they affected the overall length of his confinement; he complained only of the conditions to which he was subjected without procedural due process. . . .
>
> [These circumstances] presented facially valid due process claims. . . .

6. *Austin v. Terhune*, 367 F.3d 1167 (9th Cir. 2004).

> At the time of the events in issue, Austin was incarcerated in the California State Prison at Solano. . . . James Williams, a correctional officer[,] announced from the control booth that all inmates were to return to their cells and that the cell doors would be locked. Austin requested that Williams allow the inmates to keep their cell doors open because of the heat. According to Austin, [w]hile still in the control booth, which had a large glass window, Williams allegedly unzipped his pants, exposed his penis to Austin, who is black, and said "come suck this white dick, boy," while shaking his exposed penis at Austin. . . .
>
> Austin attempted to report the incident, but the other officers on duty ignored his

complaints. Later that day, Williams apologized to Austin for his conduct and tried to persuade Austin not to report the incident. When Austin insisted that he would report it, Williams said he would cite Austin for misconduct. A supervisor, Lieutenant Roll, learned of the incident and questioned Williams about it. Williams allegedly lied about what had happened and accused Austin of misconduct. Austin was placed in administrative segregation for six weeks. . . .

Austin's second amended complaint alleges that Williams retaliated against him for reporting, or attempting to report, Williams' inappropriate behavior. The district court construed this claim to be a Fourteenth Amendment claim for deprivation of liberty without due process [and] granted summary judgment on the retaliation claim on the authority of *Sandin v. Conner*. . . . We have previously held, however, that a claim of retaliation for filing a prison grievance survives *Sandin* because it raises constitutional questions beyond the due process deprivation of liberty . . . rejected in *Sandin*. . . . It is understandable that the district court did not focus on the First Amendment aspects of the retaliation claim because the pleading of the claim was woefully inartful, . . . but it did allege facts that Austin was punished for filing a grievance. Under Federal Rule of Civil Procedure 8, that was enough. . . . We conclude that the complaint at least minimally informed the parties and the court of Austin's retaliation claim. . . . [T]hat claim is not foreclosed by *Sandin*. . . .

7. *Wilson v. Jones*, 430 F.3d 1113 (10th Cir. 2005).

Mr. Wilson's problem began with what seems an innocuous or even laudable action: he attempted to use his mandatory savings account to pay for the costs associated with copying the court documents he needed to pursue a post-conviction proceeding. Because of that attempt, he was charged with violating Oklahoma law [for attempting to obtain money by fraud], subjected to prison disciplinary proceedings, and convicted of a Class X misconduct. The Class X misconduct conviction triggered two automatic and mandatory consequences. First, Mr. Wilson was demoted from a class-level-four prisoner, earning 44 credits each month toward early release, to a class-level-one prisoner, ineligible to earn any credits. Second, the Class X misconduct made him ineligible for promotion beyond level two, where he could earn only 22 credits each month, for a period of two years. . . .

Prisoners in Oklahoma are required to keep a mandatory savings account, in which they must deposit twenty percent of the wages they earn from prison employment. They may only access the account to pay "fees or costs in filing a civil or criminal action" . . . . Mr. Wilson followed the usual procedures and requested, in writing from the proper prison authorities, the release of $ 170 from his mandatory savings account to pay for copies of proceedings in his criminal conviction for use in his post-conviction appeal . . . . The only evidence for the charge was the written form Mr. Wilson had submitted to prison officials. On the form, he requested payment from his account "to attain transcripts and court documents from Murray County Court Clerk." . . . .

Practice Pointer

If the government has secured consent from the person or entity to be searched, then there is no need for a warrant. Consent must be knowing (or informed) or voluntary.

We hold that the State's action here deprived Mr. Wilson of a liberty interest because the mandatory and automatic consequences of the Class X misconduct conviction inevitably affected the duration of his sentence. Therefore, Mr. Wilson's due process rights were violated when he was convicted of misconduct without any evidence. The misconduct conviction must be reversed and expunged from his record, and his former status in earning credits must be restored.

For More Information

For those interested in recent scholarship in the field we recommend: Jennifer N. Wimsatt, Note, *Rendering Turner Toothless: The Supreme Court's Decision in* Beard v. Banks, 57 DUKE L.J. 1209 (2008); Fred Cohen, *Prison Reform: Commission on Safety and Abuse in America's Prisons: Isolation in Penal Settings: The Isolation-Restraint Paradigm,* 22 WASH. U. J.L. & POL'Y 295 (2006); Donald F. Tibbs, *Peeking Behind the Iron Curtain: How Law "Works" Behind Prison Walls,* 16 S. CAL. INTERDIS. L.J. 137 (2006); Trevor N. McFadden Spring, Note, *When to Turn to* Turner? *The Supreme Court's Schizophrenic Prison Jurisprudence,* 22 J. L. & POLITICS 135 (2006); Laura I. Appleman, *Retributive Justice and Hidden Sentencing,* 68 OHIO ST. L.J. 1307 (2006).

VI. Search, Investigation, and Administrative Process

Government agencies are capable of acquiring information from parties through inspection, warrant, regular reports, and subpoena. So long as the agency has a reasonable basis to secure the information it seeks, the likelihood is that it will be allowed to obtain that information. Unlike a criminal case, a strict probable cause standard is not the activating factor to permit the government to secure data. There are similarities, however, to the criminal law area. For example, in order for there to be any legitimate claim to retain information the government seeks, there must be some "reasonable expectation of privacy" in the data or information the government wishes to access. Generally speaking, however, the power of the government to secure information in civil or administrative cases is more expansive than the power to secure information in criminal cases.

The starting point for understanding civil searches in administrative cases is the Fourth Amendment. The Fourth Amendment condemns unreasonable searches. It does not condemn all searches. In the civil search area (the terms civil and administrative are used interchangeably here) the government must secure a warrant if it will be searching an area in which an individual or entity has a reasonable expectation of privacy, outside a number of exceptions.

Civil searches without warrants are permitted in other settings, beyond consent. For example, for emergencies, e.g., the sale or distribution of poisoned food products, normal Fourth Amendment privacy protections may not apply, in order to protect the public safety.

For airport or border searches, or any search where a statute clearly delineates the limitation or elimination of privacy interests, a warrant may not be required.

In settings where the government has a specific trust interest, such as banking, public assistance, and even student loans (all settings where the government plays the role of a guarantor), strict Fourth Amendment privacy rights may be diluted.

As with criminal law, a search of an object or item that is in plain view is one in which there is no expectation of privacy. For that reason, warrants are not required.

The main exception associated with administrative law is for "pervasively regulated industries." In order for this exception to apply, obviating the need for a warrant, the expectation of privacy must have been eliminated by the presence of a statute. The industry must be genuinely regulated, not just broadly subject to general government requirements for safety or accounting procedures. The government must be able to show that its interest in the particular area necessitates warrantless searches. If these requirements are met, then the statute regulating the field, in effect, gives notice that the search will occur and thereafter an expectation of privacy is eliminated and no warrant is required. Suffice it to say that there is extensive litigation in this area.

In recent years, perhaps the greatest attention has been focused on the area of national security and the extent to which civil or administrative searches can be undertaken without satisfying conventional warrant requirements. One way to balance the need for secrecy in the area of national defense has been the use of the Foreign Intelligence Surveillance Act (FISA) court. FISA judges sit by special appointment and must grapple with balancing personal privacy against the need for effective intelligence gathering.

The use of special courts to handle the collection of highly sensitive intelligence data has considerable support. In addition to the FISA court, it has been suggested that a separate court be created, as a similarly highly secure and non-public forum, "to review complaints with national security ramifications." Editorial, *Keeping Secrets: How to Balance National Security with the People's Right to Have Their Day in Court*, WASH. POST, June 15, 2007, at B6.

The FISA court and other fora engaged in the process of reviewing requests for information make use of two highly conventional judicial processes, in camera review and ex parte process.

In camera review means that a judge will review in chambers information either for its value in a particular proceeding or for an assessment of the adverse consequences that would flow were that information to be disclosed. This simple mechanism entrusts any sitting judge with both the power to make sensitive security determinations and the responsibility of maintaining absolute silence and confidentiality regarding the data itself.

Ex parte means that the quest for a warrant or permission to search a particular area is done only in the presence of the governmental entity seeking that permission. For the most part, those who are the subject of a particular search are not present during the initial evaluation of whether there is a reasonable basis (in administrative or civil proceedings) for the warrant to issue. The protection of the privacy interests to which the individual or entity is justifiably entitled occurs exclusively from the evaluation by the magistrate, administrative law judge, or Article III judge who reviews the proposed search.

Most warrants issue ex parte. Thereafter, a person or entity served with a warrant may object to that search, file a motion to quash, and ultimately have his or her day in court. Resisting a search after a warrant has issued requires a client who is both well-counseled and willing to invest the considerable time and resources that will be needed to fight the warrant.

The elaboration of Fourth Amendment administrative search law is relatively modern. It was not until 1967 that the Supreme Court first articulated reliable standards to be applied for administrative searches in *Camara*.

1. Applicability of the Fourth Amendment to Civil Searches

CAMARA V. MUNICIPAL COURT OF THE CITY & COUNTY OF SAN FRANCISCO

387 U.S. 523 (1967)

[JUSTICE WHITE] On November 6, 1963, an inspector of the Division of Housing Inspection of the San Francisco Department of Public Health entered an apartment building to make a routine annual inspection for possible violations of the city's Housing Code. The building's manager informed the inspector that appellant, lessee of the ground floor, was using the rear of his leasehold as a personal residence. Claiming that the building's occupancy permit did not allow residential use of the ground floor, the inspector confronted appellant and demanded that he permit an inspection of the premises. Appellant refused to allow the inspection because the inspector lacked a search warrant.

The inspector returned on November 8, again without a warrant, and appellant again refused to allow an inspection. . . . [The statute in question read:]

> Authorized employees of the City departments or City agencies, so far as may be necessary for the performance of their duties, shall, upon presentation of proper credentials, have the right to enter, at reasonable times, any building, structure, or premises in the City to perform any duty imposed upon them by the Municipal Code.

. . . . Appellant was arrested on December 2 and released on bail. When his demurrer to the criminal complaint was denied, appellant filed this petition for a writ of prohibition. Appellant has argued throughout this litigation that § 503 is contrary to the Fourth and Fourteenth Amendments in that it authorizes municipal officials to enter a private dwelling without a search warrant and without probable cause to believe that a violation of the Housing Code exists therein. Consequently, appellant contends, he may not be prosecuted under § 507 for refusing to permit an inspection unconstitutionally authorized by § 503. Relying on *Frank v. Maryland* . . . the District Court of Appeal held that § 503 does not violate [the] Fourth Amendment . . . . Having concluded that *Frank v. Maryland*, to the extent that it sanctioned such warrantless inspections, must be overruled, we reverse.

I

The Fourth Amendment provides that, "The right of the people to be secure in their persons, houses, papers, and effects, against unreasonable searches and seizures, shall not be violated, and no Warrants shall issue, but upon probable cause, supported by Oath or affirmation, and particularly describing the place to be searched, and the persons or things to be seized." The basic purpose of this Amendment, as recognized in countless decisions of this Court, is to safeguard the privacy and security of individuals against arbitrary invasions by governmental officials. . . . As such, the Fourth Amendment is enforceable against the States through the Fourteenth Amendment.

Though there has been general agreement as to the fundamental purpose of the Fourth Amendment, translation of the abstract prohibition against "unreasonable searches and seizures" into workable guidelines for the decision of particular cases is a difficult task. . . . Nevertheless, one governing principle, justified by history and by current experience, has consistently been followed: except in certain carefully defined classes of cases, a search of private property without proper consent is "unreasonable" unless it has been authorized by a valid search warrant. . . .

In *Frank v. Maryland*, this Court upheld the conviction of one who refused to permit a warrantless inspection of private premises for the purposes of locating and abating a suspected public nuisance. . . . To the *Frank* majority, municipal fire, health, and housing inspection programs "touch at most upon the periphery of the important interests safeguarded by the Fourteenth Amendment's protection against official intrusion" because the inspections are . . . not . . . for "evidence of criminal action" . . . .

We may agree that a routine inspection of the physical condition of private property is a less hostile intrusion than the typical policeman's search for the fruits and instrumentalities of crime [b]ut we cannot agree that the Fourth Amendment interests at stake in these inspection cases are merely "peripheral." It is surely anomalous to say that the individual and his private property are fully protected by the Fourth Amendment only when the individual is suspected of criminal behavior. . . . And even accepting *Frank's* rather remarkable premise, inspections of the kind we are here considering do in fact jeopardize "self-protection" interests of the property owner. Like most regulatory laws, fire, health, and housing codes are enforced by criminal processes. In some cities, discovery of a violation by the inspector leads to a criminal complaint. Even in cities where discovery of a violation produces only an administrative compliance order, refusal to comply is a criminal offense, and the fact of compliance is verified by a second inspection, again without a warrant. Finally, as this case demonstrates, refusal to permit an inspection is itself a crime, punishable by fine or even by jail sentence.

The *Frank* majority suggested . . . two other justifications for permitting administrative health and safety inspections without a warrant. First, it is argued that these inspections are "designed to make the least possible demand on the individual occupant." The ordinances authorizing inspections are hedged with safeguards, and at any rate the inspector's particular decision to enter must comply with the constitutional standard of reasonableness even if he may enter without a warrant. . . . [Second] the argument proceeds, the warrant process could not function effectively in this field. The decision to inspect an entire municipal area is based upon legislative or administrative assessment of broad factors such as the area's age and condition. Unless the magistrate is to review such policy matters, he must issue a "rubber stamp" warrant which provides no protection at all to the property owner.

In our opinion, these arguments unduly discount the purposes behind the warrant machinery contemplated by the Fourth Amendment. Under the present system, when the inspector demands entry, the occupant has no way of knowing whether enforcement of the municipal code involved requires inspection of his premises, no way of knowing the lawful limits of the inspector's power to search, and no way of knowing whether the inspector himself is acting under proper authorization. These are questions which may be reviewed by a neutral magistrate without any reassessment of the basic agency decision to canvass an area. Yet, only by refusing entry and risking a criminal conviction can the occupant at present challenge the inspector's decision to search. And even if the occupant possesses sufficient fortitude to take this risk, as appellant did here, he may never learn any more about the reason for the inspection than that the law generally allows housing inspectors to gain entry. The practical effect of this system is to leave the occupant subject to the discretion of the official in the field. . . . We simply cannot say that the protections provided by the warrant procedure are not needed in this context; broad statutory safeguards are no substitute for individualized review, particularly when those safeguards may only be invoked at the risk of a criminal penalty.

The final justification suggested for warrantless administrative searches is that the public interest demands such a rule: it is vigorously argued that the health and safety of entire urban populations is dependent upon enforcement of minimum fire, housing, and sanitation standards, and that the only effective means of enforcing such codes is by routine systematized inspection of all physical structures. . . . But we think this argument misses the mark. The question is not, at this stage at least, whether these inspections may be made, but whether they may be made without a warrant. For example, to say that gambling raids may not be made at the discretion of the police without a warrant is not necessarily to say that gambling raids may never be made. . . . It has nowhere been urged that fire, health, and housing code inspection programs could not achieve their goals within the confines of a reasonable search warrant requirement. Thus, we do not find the public need argument dispositive.

In summary, we hold that administrative searches of the kind at issue here are significant intrusions upon the interests protected by the Fourth Amendment . . . . Because of the nature of the municipal programs under consideration, however, these conclusions must be the beginning, not the end, of our inquiry. . . .

II

[A]ppellant argues not only that code enforcement inspection programs must be circumscribed by a warrant procedure, but also that warrants should issue only when the inspector possesses probable cause to believe that a particular dwelling contains violations of the minimum standards prescribed by the code being enforced. We disagree. . . . To apply [probable cause], it is obviously necessary first to focus upon the governmental interest which allegedly justifies official intrusion upon the constitutionally protected interests of the private citizen. For example, in a criminal investigation, the police may undertake to recover specific stolen or contraband goods. But that public interest would hardly justify a sweeping search of an entire city conducted in the hope that these goods might be found. Consequently, a search for these goods, even with a warrant, is "reasonable" only when there is "probable cause" to believe that they will be uncovered in a particular dwelling.

Unlike the search pursuant to a criminal investigation, the inspection programs at issue here are aimed at securing city-wide compliance with minimum physical standards for private property. The primary governmental interest at stake is to prevent even the unintentional development of conditions which are hazardous to public health and safety. Because fires and epidemics may ravage large urban areas, because unsightly conditions adversely affect the economic values of neighboring structures, numerous courts have upheld the police power of municipalities to impose and enforce such minimum standards even upon existing structures. In determining whether a particular inspection is reasonable – and thus in determining whether there is probable cause to issue a warrant for that inspection – the need for the inspection must be weighed in terms of these reasonable goals of code enforcement.

There is unanimous agreement among those most familiar with this field that the only effective way to seek universal compliance with . . . municipal codes is through routine periodic inspections of all structures. It is here that the probable cause debate is focused, for the agency's decision to conduct an area inspection is unavoidably based on its appraisal of conditions in the area as a whole, not on its knowledge of conditions in each particular building. Appellee contends that, if the probable cause standard urged by appellant is adopted, the area inspection will be eliminated as a means of seeking compliance with code standards and the reasonable goals of code enforcement will be dealt a crushing blow.

In meeting this contention, appellant argues first, that his probable cause standard would not jeopardize area inspection programs because only a minute portion of the population will refuse to consent to such inspections, and second, that individual privacy in any event should be given preference to the public interest in conducting such inspections. The first argument, even if true, is irrelevant to the question whether the area inspection is reasonable within the meaning of the Fourth Amendment. The second argument is in effect an assertion that the area inspection is an unreasonable search. Unfortunately, there can be no ready test for determining reasonableness other than by balancing the need to search against the invasion which the search entails. But we think that a number of persuasive factors combine to support the reasonableness of area code-enforcement inspections. First, such programs have a long history of judicial and public acceptance. Second, the public interest demands that all dangerous conditions be prevented or abated, yet it is doubtful that any other canvassing technique would achieve acceptable results. Many such conditions – faulty wiring is an obvious example – are not observable from outside the building and indeed may not be apparent to the inexpert occupant himself. Finally, because the inspections are neither personal in nature nor aimed at the discovery of evidence of crime, they involve a relatively limited invasion of the urban citizen's privacy. Both the majority and the dissent in *Frank* emphatically supported this conclusion:

[From the majority]

[T]he power to inspect dwelling places . . . is of indispensable importance to the maintenance of community health; a power that would be greatly hobbled by the blanket requirement of the safeguards necessary for a search of evidence of criminal acts. . . . [T]hese inspections are apparently welcomed by all but an insignificant few. Certainly . . . society has not vitiated the need for inspections first thought necessary 158 years ago, nor has experience revealed any abuse or inroad on freedom in meeting this need . . . .

[From the dissent]

Experience may show the need for periodic inspections of certain facilities without a further showing of cause to believe that substandard conditions dangerous to the public are being maintained. The passage of a certain period without inspection might of itself be sufficient in a given situation to justify the issuance of a warrant. The test of "probable cause" required by the Fourth Amendment can take into account the nature of the search that is being sought. . . .

Having concluded that the area inspection is a "reasonable" search of private property within the meaning of the Fourth Amendment, it is obvious that "probable cause" to issue a warrant to inspect must exist if reasonable legislative or administrative standards for conducting an area inspection are satisfied with respect to a particular dwelling. Such standards, which will vary with the municipal program being enforced, may be based upon the passage of time, the nature of the building (e.g., a multi-family apartment house), or the condition of the entire area, but they will not necessarily depend upon specific knowledge of the condition of the particular dwelling. It has been suggested that so to vary the probable cause test from the standard applied in criminal cases would be to authorize a "synthetic search warrant" and thereby . . . lessen the overall protections of the Fourth Amendment. But we do not agree. The warrant procedure is designed to guarantee that a decision to search private property is justified by a reasonable governmental interest. But reasonableness is still the ultimate standard. If a valid public interest justifies the intrusion contemplated, then there is probable cause to issue a suitably restricted search warrant. . . .

III

[N]othing we say today is intended to foreclose prompt inspections, even without a warrant, that the law has traditionally upheld in emergency situations. . . . Moreover, most citizens allow inspections of their property without a warrant. Thus, as a practical matter and in light of the Fourth Amendment's requirement that a warrant specify the property to be searched, it seems likely that warrants should normally be sought only after entry is refused unless there has been a citizen complaint or there is other satisfactory reason for securing immediate entry. . . .

IV

. . . Assuming the facts to be as the parties have alleged, we therefore conclude that appellant had a constitutional right to insist that the inspectors obtain a warrant to search and that appellant may not constitutionally be convicted for refusing to consent to the inspection. . . . The judgment is vacated and the case is remanded for further proceedings not inconsistent with this opinion. . . .

Underlying Case Documents

The case referenced:
Sections 503 and 507
The complaint
The answer

Camara has been applied in literally thousands of cases. We provide below several excerpts, in part to reinforce the concepts and in part to give you a sense of the different applications and interpretations of the case.

1. Recently, the district court in Massachusetts provided a good overview of the civil search doctrine from *Camara* forward:

United States v. Stewart, 468 F. Supp. 2d 261 (D. Mass. 2007).

> [In] *Camara v. Municipal Court of San Francisco*, [t]he Supreme Court recognized that individualized suspicion would be impracticable and stated that "there can be no ready test for determining reasonableness other than by balancing the need to search against the invasion which the search entails." On one side of the balance the Court weighed the governmental interest in conducting the housing code inspections. On the other side, the Court looked to the intrusion that resulted from such a search. The Supreme Court weighed this balance in favor of the administrative search while stressing the importance of the administrative regulations that limited the discretion of the governmental official. In such cases, the administrative regulations stand in the place of probable cause.
>
> Over time, however, the Court began dispensing with the warrant requirement in situations where obtaining a warrant could inhibit the inspections, again relying on the existence of sufficiently defined regulations to provide an adequate substitute for the particularity requirements of a warrant. . . .
>
> In addition to the need for discretion-limiting regulations, the Supreme Court has

also required that the primary purpose of such searches to be something other than general crime control. See *City of Indianapolis v. Edmond*, 531 U.S. 32, 47-48 (2000) (holding a police checkpoint to interdict narcotic traffic invalid because the principal purpose of the checkpoint was to detect evidence of criminal wrongdoing). . . .

A subcategory has evolved from the administrative search rationale that is often denominated the "special needs" exception. JUSTICE BLACKMUN in a concurring opinion in a high school search case first used the term "special needs" when he spoke of an exception applying where "special needs, beyond the normal need for law enforcement, make the warrant and probable-cause requirement [sic] impracticable." *New Jersey v. T.L.O.*

In addition to this requirement, the "special needs" exception requires a governmental purpose narrowly tailored to the means used to effectuate that purpose. . . .

2. In *Dearmore v. City of Garland*, 400 F. Supp. 2d 894 (N.D. Tex. 2005):

Dearmore owns four properties . . . that he rents to various tenants. . . . [A recently enacted City Ordinance states that] as a condition of the permit [to rent the properties], the City will inspect the property a least once a year. Failure of an owner, who is not a resident at the property, to allow an inspection is an offense. When consent to inspect has been refused or cannot be obtained, the City is authorized to obtain a search warrant to conduct an inspection. . . .

Dearmore filed [a] request for . . . injunctive relief. . . . The court now considers the request for injunctive relief. . . . Dearmore contends that the Ordinance violates the Fourth Amendment by: (1) authorizing warrantless searches of private homes; (2) failing to advise the tenant or owner that he does not have to consent to a search; and (3) requiring private information in the application process. . . .

The leading case on the issue of warrantless administrative searches is *Camara*[, which] holds that an administrative search of a private residence, including a private residence owned by one person and rented by another, must include a warrant procedure. In this case the City ignores that the permitting process does not allow the owner to refuse consent when the property is unoccupied without being subject to criminal penalties, which can be quite substantial. The court finds the City's reasoning unpersuasive because the property owner is being penalized for his failure to consent in advance to a warrantless search of unoccupied property. . . .

While the City has shown a strong governmental need or interest to make such a requirement in most instances to protect the public health, safety and welfare, the court believes the Ordinance goes too far with respect to those situations in which the rental property is not occupied by a tenant. . . .

The court determines that in order to comply with the requirements of *Camara* and the protections of the Fourth Amendment, the Ordinance must give the landlord the opportunity to refuse to consent if the property is unoccupied and include a warrant procedure to be followed in the event the landlord refuses. . . . To hold otherwise would give the City carte blanche authority to conduct searches and inspections with impunity or without any type of safeguards on property in which the owner clearly has an expectation of privacy.

Take a look at the full version of this case. What would be required to make this ordinance acceptable?

3. <u>*The People of the State of Illinois v. Lewis*, 845 N.E.2d 39 (Ill. App. Ct. 2006)</u>, provides a good example of an "emergency assistance" civil search:

> In her 911 call, Constance Lewis said that defendant [Thomas Lewis] was unconscious and that she feared that he had overdosed on drugs . . . . "Almost instantly," [police officer] Clark arrived, went downstairs, and spoke briefly to John Lewis, who consented to a search of the room. Clark checked defendant's pulse, breathing, and color. . . . Clark made a "quick search of the room before the paramedics came." He saw . . . foil packets in plain view in the wastebasket. . . . Next, Clark opened the box on the desk and found [a] pacifier, leading him to believe that "this may be a situation involving Ecstasy." . . . .
>
> [W]e hold that scrutiny of an emergency-assistance search should be based on the objective circumstances of the situation, not on the subjective motives of the officers involved. Accordingly, we hold that an emergency-assistance search is valid where the following two factors are satisfied: (1) there are reasonable grounds to believe that there is an emergency that requires the intrusion; and (2) there is a reasonable basis, approximating probable cause, to associate the emergency with the area searched. . . .
>
> Although [many cases draw] a clear line between inventory and administrative searches (on one side) and criminal searches based on probable cause (on the other), a discerning reader might well hesitate to say on which side of the line emergency-assistance searches fall. As noted, emergency-assistance searches are exercises of the police's "community caretaking" function. Therefore, they do not require probable cause — at least in the criminal sense. However, unlike inventory and administrative searches, emergency-assistance searches are not "undertaken pursuant to a general scheme *without* individualized suspicion." Although the officer need not have probable cause to believe that a *crime* has been committed, he or she must have reasonable grounds to believe that there is an emergency requiring immediate assistance. Also, the need to respond to an emergency does not give the police a general warrant to search wherever they want. Rather, the intrusion "must be 'strictly circumscribed by the exigencies which justify its initiation.'" Thus, unlike an inventory or administrative search, an emergency-assistance search does require a type of individualized suspicion, albeit not one of criminal activity. . . . [The court found those requirements were met and the defendant's motions to suppress were denied.]

4. Among the more common warrantless civil searches are airport searches.

a. <u>*United States v. Hartwell*, 436 F.3d 174 (3rd Cir. 2006)</u>.

> [Christian] Hartwell arrived at the Philadelphia International Airport on Saturday, May 17, 2003, intending to catch a flight to Phoenix. He . . . set off the magnetometer when he walked through. He was told to remove all items from his pockets and try again. Hartwell removed several — including a large quantity of cash — from his pocket, and passed through again. . . . [He set it off again and was screened with a

wand, which reported a solid object.] What occurred next is the subject of some dispute. Hartwell claims that he was escorted to a private screening room near the checkpoint, where he refused Padua's repeated requests to reveal the contents of his pocket. Frustrated by Hartwell's unresponsiveness, Padua eventually reached into Hartwell's pocket and pulled out a package of drugs. . . .

Hartwell's search at the airport checkpoint was justified by the administrative search doctrine. . . . Suspicionless checkpoint searches are permissible under the Fourth Amendment when a court finds a favorable balance between "the gravity of the public concerns served by the seizure, the degree to which the seizure advances the public interest, and the severity of the interference with individual liberty." *Illinois v. Lidster*, 540 U.S. 419 (2004). . . . In this case, the airport checkpoint passes the [test since] there can be no doubt that preventing terrorist attacks on airplanes is of paramount importance [and] "absent a search, there is no effective means of detecting which airline passengers are reasonably likely to hijack an airplane." . . . . [Also] the procedures involved in Hartwell's search were minimally intrusive. . . . Hartwell [first] simply passed through a magnetometer . . . . Only after Hartwell set off the metal detector was he screened with a wand – yet another less intrusive substitute for a physical pat-down. And only after the wand detected something solid . . ., and after repeated requests that he produce the item, did the TSA agents (according to Hartwell) reach into his pocket.

In addition to being tailored to protect personal privacy, other factors make airport screening procedures minimally intrusive in comparison to other kinds of searches. Since every air passenger is subjected to a search, there is virtually no "stigma attached to being subjected to search at a known, designated airport search point." Moreover, the possibility for abuse is minimized by the public nature of the search. . . . Lastly, . . . air passengers are on notice that they will be searched. . . . The events of September 11, 2001, have only increased their prominence in the public's consciousness. It is inconceivable that Hartwell was unaware that he had to be searched before he could board a plane. Indeed, he admitted that he had previously been searched before flying. . . .

b. *United States v. Pulido-Baquerizo*, 800 F.2d 899 (9th Cir. 1986).

On September 30, 1985, at approximately 8:00 a.m., appellee [Jorge] Pulido attempted to board an airplane at . . . Los Angeles International Airport. Pulido . . . placed two briefcases onto the x-ray machine's conveyor belt. The security agent . . . noticed a "dark object with what looked to be lines in it" in one of the briefcases. Suspecting the object might be a bomb . . . a second agent [was] asked if she could determine what the object was. She could not. . . . [T]he agents' supervisor . . . was summoned to see if he could identify the object. He was also unable to identify the object, but . . . believed he saw wires which indicated a bomb . . . . At this point, Pulido was asked what was in the briefcase. He answered, "clothes." . . . . [The supervisor] removed the briefcase to a nearby inspection table and conducted a visual and hand search [that] disclosed 2138 grams of cocaine. . . .

At the pretrial suppression hearing, Pulido moved to suppress evidence obtained by the search . . . . [W]e hold that those passengers placing luggage on an x-ray machine's conveyor belt for airplane travel at a secured boarding area impliedly consent to a visual inspection and limited hand search of their luggage if the x-ray scan is inconclusive in determining whether the luggage contains weapons or other dangerous objects. . . . The scan and subsequent search involves only a slight privacy intrusion as long as the scope of the search is limited to the detection of weapons, explosives, or any other dangerous devices, and is conducted in a manner which produces negligible social stigma. Given these circumstances, a visual inspection and limited hand search of luggage which is used for the purpose of detecting weapons or explosives, and not in order to uncover other types of contraband, is a privacy intrusion we believe free society is willing to tolerate. . . .

c. *United States v. Marquez, 410 F.3d 612 (9th Cir. 2005)*.

On . . . October 3, 2002, [Sergio] Marquez attempted to board a domestic flight to Anchorage from Seattle. After checking in for his flight, he proceeded to the TSA security checkpoint where he was [randomly] diverted to Checkpoint B, the "selectee lane." A passenger chosen for the selectee lane is [automatically] subjected to more thorough search procedures . . . . The primary additional procedure involves a full-body wanding with a handheld magnetometer that uses technology similar to, but more sensitive than, the walkthrough magnetometer. . . .

[Marquez] walked through the magnetometer and was instructed to sit down in the screening area. . . . TSA screener Petersen . . . approached Marquez and began to scan his person . . . . [T]he wand "alarmed" when it passed over Marquez's right hip. Petersen testified that he understood TSA policy to require him to determine the cause of the alarm. . . . Marquez denied Petersen permission to touch his hip, and swatted Petersen's hand away when he tried to touch the area. Nonetheless, Petersen felt a "hard brick type of thing" and, on the basis of his experiences in the military and his TSA training, Petersen feared that the object might be C-4 explosives. . . . Petersen called for his supervisor. . . . Ultimately . . . Seattle Police were summoned . . . . The officers searched . . . Marquez and . . . retrieved four wrapped bricks of cocaine from his person.

Marquez was charged with one count of possession with intent to distribute over 500 grams of cocaine . . . . The issue here is whether the random selection of Marquez to go to the selectee lane, where he would automatically be subjected to the wanding of his person . . . was reasonable. We conclude that it was. . . . While it arguably constituted a "slight privacy intrusion," it was reasonably confined to procedures necessary to detect weapons and explosives . . . that may evade detection by the larger, less sensitive walkthrough magnetometer. . . . In their briefs and at oral argument, neither party suggested that there was any purpose or goal in the instant search other than to detect weapons or explosives. . . . The mere fact that a screening procedure ultimately reveals contraband other than weapons or explosives does not render it unreasonable, post facto. . . . The screening at issue here is not unreasonable simply because it revealed that Marquez was carrying cocaine rather than C-4 explosives. . . .

d. *United States v. Aukai, 440 F.3d 1168 (9th Cir. 2006)*.

On February 1, 2003 . . . Daniel Kuualoha Aukai arrived at the Honolulu International Airport intending to [fly] to Kona, Hawaii. He proceeded to check in at the ticket counter, but did not produce a government-issued picture identification. Accordingly, the ticket agent wrote the phrase "No ID" on Aukai's boarding pass. . . . Pursuant to

TSA procedures, a passenger who presents a boarding pass on which "No ID" has been written is subject to secondary screening even if he or she has passed through the initial screening without triggering an alarm or otherwise raising suspicion. . . .

Because Aukai's boarding pass had the "No ID" notation, Motonaga directed Aukai to a nearby, roped-off area for secondary screening. . . . Aukai . . . appealed to TSA Officer Andrew Misajon, who was to perform the secondary screening, explaining again that he was in a hurry to catch his flight. Misajon nonetheless had Aukai [screened]. At some point, . . . the wand [sounded]. Misajon then felt the outside of Aukai's pocket and concluded that something was inside the pocket. . . . Aukai then informed Misajon that he wanted to leave the airport. . . . TSA Supervisor Joseph Vizcarra [then] directed Aukai to empty his pocket. . . . Aukai finally removed . . . a glass pipe used to smoke methamphetamine. . . . Aukai was placed under arrest and was searched incident to his arrest. . . . [P]olice discovered . . . several transparent bags containing a white crystal substance. . . . Aukai [later pled] guilty pursuant to a written plea agreement that preserved his right to appeal the denial of his suppression motion. . . .

Aukai . . . argues that . . . he elected not to fly rather than undergo the secondary screening and, thereby, revoked his implied consent [to the search]. Although we [have previously] held . . . that "airport screening searches are valid only if they recognize the right of a person to avoid [the] search by electing not to board the aircraft," we did not address when such a choice must be made – that is, whether there is some stage during or after which a prospective passenger may not withdraw his implied consent to a search of his person or carry-on baggage by electing not to fly. . . . [W]e conclude that . . . Aukai impliedly consented to a secondary search of his person by walking through the magnetometer, and that he could not subsequently revoke his consent to the secondary screening. . . .

For More Information

For further development of this areas, we recommend the following: Steven R. Minert, Comment, *Square Pegs, Round Hole: The Fourth Amendment and Preflight Searches of Airline Passengers in a Post-9/11 World*, 2006 BYU L. Rev. 1631; Rasha Alzahabi, *Should You Leave Your Laptop at Home When Traveling Abroad?: The Fourth Amendment and Border Searches of Laptop Computers*, 41 Ind. L. Rev. 161 (2008); Kyle P. Hanson, *Suspicionless Terrorism Checkpoints Since 9/11: Searching for Uniformity*, 56 Drake L. Rev. 171 (2007); Timothy M. Ravich, *Is Airline Passenger Profiling Necessary?*, 62 U. Miami L. Rev. 1 (2007); Christine A. Colletta, Note, *Laptop Searches at the United States Borders and the Border Search Exception to the Fourth Amendment*, 48 B.C. L. Rev. 971 (2007); Charles J. Keeley III, Note, *Subway Searches: Which Exception to the Warrant and Probable Cause Requirements Applies to Suspicionless Searches of Mass Transit Passengers to Prevent Terrorism*, 74 Fordham L. Rev. 3231 (2007).

2. State Warrants

BLACK V. VILLAGE OF PARK FOREST

20 F. Supp. 2d 1218 (N.D. Ill. 1998)

[JUDGE GOTTSCHALL] Plaintiffs . . . brought this action under 42 U.S.C. § 1983 against the Village of Park Forest, challenging the constitutionality of the Village's annual inspections of rented single-family homes and of certain provisions of the Village's Housing Code. The Village is a home-rule municipality [and] is a "person" within the meaning of 42 U.S.C. § 1983. . . . The Village conducts routine annual inspections of the interior of rented, non-owner-occupied single-family homes. The Village does not conduct such inspections of occupied condominiums, duplexes, units in multi-family apartment complexes, or owner-occupied homes . . . . Plaintiffs are individuals who currently rent single-family homes in the Village. As such, they are subject to inspections under the Village's Housing Code. They do not want to have their homes searched by the Village without either their explicit consent or a valid search warrant issued upon probable cause.

The Village contacted Taylor's landlord to arrange an inspection. When the landlord objected, the Village obtained a warrant. . . . The warrant was based on the Village's allegation that an administrative inspection of Taylor's home had not occurred within the past year. Taylor was not present when the Village inspector went to her home. The inspection did not occur, and the inspector left a notice informing Taylor of the search warrant. The Village did not attempt to re-serve the warrant. Instead, the Village filed a petition for rule to show cause in the Cook County Circuit Court asking that Taylor, her landlord, and her 12-year old daughter, Afton Brown, be held in contempt and imprisoned for a minimum period of 24 hours. . . .

. . . .

Plaintiffs claim that the Housing Code unconstitutionally infringes the tenant's exclusive right to consent or withhold consent to an inspection. In *Camara*, the . . . Court held that if a tenant does not consent to a search of his or her home, government officials must obtain a search warrant before conducting an administrative search or inspection. Numerous cases have made clear that a landlord's consent is insufficient to authorize a search of a tenant's home; the right to consent or not consent to a search belongs to the tenant. . . . Although traditional probable cause is not necessarily required for administrative inspections of residences, *Camara* does provide some protection to ensure that residential inspections are conducted with respect for the residents' strong privacy interests in their homes. In *Camara*, the Supreme Court held that there is probable cause to issue a warrant to inspect a residential property if "reasonable legislative or administrative standards for conducting an area inspection are satisfied with respect to a particular dwelling." . . . . Although there are few cases discussing administrative inspections of residences, the requirement of "reasonable legislative or administrative standards" seems to offer two types of protection. First, the requirement may serve to protect against properties being unfairly targeted for searches. Thus, the requirement may be read to demand that, absent traditional probable cause, the decision to search a property must be based on some "neutral criteria." Second, the requirement may impose an obligation to limit the scope of the inspections to what is necessary to achieve the legitimate goals of the program.

. . . .

. . . The Village argues that its inspection program is constitutional because probable cause is based on reasonable legislative and administrative standards, including the passage of time between inspections. In the view of this court, however, *Camara* does not establish that the passage of time between inspections will invariably be sufficient to establish probable cause for an administrative inspection of a residence.

One factor that *Camara* indicates may constitute a reasonable legislative or administrative standard is "the nature of the building (e.g., a multifamily apartment house)." . . . . Here, however, the Village conducts annual inspections of the interiors of only rented single-family homes. . . . The Village notes that . . . non-owner-occupied properties have a higher incidence of building code violations than owner-occupied properties. This might provide justification for treating rental properties differently from owner-occupied properties, but it does not explain why rented single-family homes are treated differently from rented units in multi-unit dwellings, particularly when the Study indicates that the greatest number of Housing Code violations are found in rental apartment units.

The Village responds that it has decided to address the problem of code violations in multi-family properties through other methods, including routine inspections of the exteriors and common areas of such properties. This appears to be an important if unintentional concession – the Village acknowledges that for multi-unit dwellings, it uses a less intrusive method to ensure compliance with the Housing Code. . . . The differential treatment of tenants is significant . . . because it undermines the argument that the annual searches of rented single-family homes are necessary to ensure compliance with the Housing Code. This differential treatment indicates that there may be other, less intrusive methods for ensuring that rented single-family homes comply with the Housing Code.

. . . .

This court's conclusion that the inspection program is not based on reasonable legislative and administrative standards finds additional support in the Village's failure to place appropriate limits on the inspections. . . . [T]he Village's inspector is authorized by § 16-3(a) "to make inspections to determine the condition of dwellings, dwelling units, rooming units and premises located within the village in order that he may perform his duty of safeguarding the health and safety of the occupants of dwellings and of the general public." Nowhere in § 16-3(a) does it specify that the inspections are for the purpose of enforcing the specific minimum standards of the building code contained in §§ 16-22 et seq. of the Housing Code or any other specified standards.

Criteria for the frequency and scope of the inspections are an essential component of the legislative and administrative standards of which *Camara* speaks. Without such standards, an official issuing a warrant has no standards against which to assess the propriety of a warrant, an official conducting a search has no standards to guide his conduct, and a court reviewing the reasonableness of a search cannot determine if the search was properly limited. . . . This court views the "reasonable legislative and administrative standards" language in *Camara* as meaning, at a minimum, that the authorizing legislation, ordinance or regulation must contain a clear indication of the evils sought to be prevented by the inspection program (presumably supported by some legislative findings indicating that the evils in question exist) and some indication of appropriate parameters for the searches. The Village's program fails on both counts. This court can find nothing in the record to indicate why the Village undertook such an intrusive inspection program solely for rented single-family homes and can find nothing that limits in any way the scope of inspections. Because the Village's inspection of rented single-family homes is not governed by reasonable legislative and administrative standards, summary judgment . . . is granted to the plaintiffs.

. . . .

————————————

1. For civil searches, statutes can provide notice and can supplant a warrant requirement. Can a statute condition use or occupancy on a waiver of a warrant requirement thus compelling a homeowner to consent to warrantless searches? In *People v. Bifulco, 195 Misc. 2d 483 (D. Ct. Suffolk Ct. 2003)*, a homeowner was charged with leasing a garage as a residential unit without the proper permits. At issue was an ordinance that compelled a person leasing property to consent to warrantless searches as a condition of receiving the permits required to lease the property. The owner contended that the only purpose of the statute was to allow the state to develop a case against a homeowner – and the court agreed. The court began by noting that the ordinance was

a mere statute whose main purpose is to expedite discovery and jurisdictional challenges. . . . It is a fundamentally unchallengeable federal and New York State constitutional concept that searches of residential dwellings by governmental agents can only be conducted upon judicial warrant or consent of the homeowner. *Camara*. In the absence of a warrant, the Town subscribes to the theory that the defendant consented to the July 17, 2002 governmental inspection/search. The defendant asserts that the search was based upon "statutorily coerced consent" and offers an emerging body of case law in furtherance [of this argument].

The underlying premise in the New York Court of Appeals "statutorily coerced consent" rule is "an owner's ability to rent his premises may not be conditioned upon his consent to a warrantless inspection." Similarly "a property owner cannot . . . voluntarily give[] his consent to a search where the price he must pay to enjoy his rights . . . is the effective deprivation of any economic benefit from his rental property."

Accordingly, the court suppresses any evidence to be proffered by Inspector Parker which is related to, or arising out of, his inspection of the main house and will allow the Town to introduce evidence as to the inspection of the detached garage. . . .

2. As we noted at the outset of this section of the text, we understand you may not yet have taken Evidence. That said, the following case requires only a passing understanding of the exclusionary rule, which prohibits the introduction of evidence that was secured unlawfully. There is a "good faith" exception to that rule, i.e., if the search was conducted in good faith and thereafter is found to be inconsistent with the Fourth Amendment, the "fruits" of the search may, in certain instances, still be admitted as evidence.

In *People v. Bessler*, 548 N.E.2d 52 (Ill. App. 1989), the defendant was charged with unlawful possession of a firearm and unlawful possession of drugs. The evidence leading to his conviction came after housing inspectors, without a civil warrant, forced open a locked door and saw the alleged contraband.

Defendant appeals, contending that [the evidence was secured in an] unlawful warrantless administrative search of the premises.

[The] State has not contended that the village ordinance authorizing a village code enforcement official "to enter any structure or premises at any reasonable time for the purpose of making inspections and performing duties under this code . . . is constitutional. *Camara*. . . . Instead, the State maintains [that] *Illinois v. Krull*, 480 U.S. 340 (1987), [permits] the "good faith" exception to the exclusionary rule [to be] applicable here, where the initial search was based upon the officer's reasonable reliance upon a village ordinance which allowed warrantless administrative inspections on private residential property, even if the ordinance is later deemed unconstitutional.

In *Illinois v. Krull*, the question before the Supreme Court was whether a similar exception to the exclusionary rule . . . should be recognized when officers act in objectively reasonable reliance upon a statute authorizing warrantless administrative searches, but where the statute is ultimately found to violate the fourth amendment. . . . [The exception applies only if the unconstitutionality of the statute is] sufficiently obvious so as to render a police officer's reliance upon the statute objectively unreasonable. . . .

The warrantless administrative search undertaken here, as authorized under the municipal ordinance, was of a private residence [not] a heavily regulated business. The greater latitude to conduct warrantless inspections of commercial property reflects the fact that the expectation of privacy that the owner of commercial property enjoys in such property differs significantly from the sanctity accorded an individual's home. . . . The physical entry of the home is the chief evil against which the wording of the fourth amendment is directed. . . . In the absence of consent or exigent circumstances, the entry into a home to conduct a search or make an arrest is unreasonable under the fourth amendment unless done pursuant to a warrant. . . .

As this case does not come within the "good faith" exception to the exclusionary rule . . . we decline to create another exception to the exclusionary rule which would invade the long-protected sanctity of the home from warrantless searches. . . .

We, therefore, conclude that the officer's peering into the [home] without a warrant and not under some recognized exception to the warrant requirement was violative of defendant's Fourth Amendment rights.

3. In <u>*Kyllo v. United States*, 533 U.S. 27 (2001)</u>, the Court held that

any physical invasion of the structure of the home, "by even a fraction of an inch" was too much, and there is certainly no exception . . . for the officer who barely cracks open the front door and sees nothing but the non-intimate rug on the vestibule floor. In the home, our cases show, all details are intimate details, because the entire area is held safe from prying government eyes.

This strong statement of the sanctity of the home is not consistent with many cases in which civil warrantless searches conducted by uninvited government agency representatives invade the home – and are found thereafter to be consistent with the Fourth Amendment. Read the facts below from <u>*Taylor v. Michigan Department of Natural Resources*, 502 F.3d 452 (6th Cir. 2007)</u>:

On February 20, 2003, longtime conservation officer Paul Rose approached plaintiff's 240-acre fenced property, located in a rural area, Newaygo County, Michigan, to investigate a complaint regarding fencing. Under state law, it is a misdemeanor to unlawfully erect a barrier denying ingress or egress to an area where the lawful taking of animals may occur. Officer Rose found no violation but, after seeing tire tracks up to the open driveway and footprints continuing, proceeded onto the property, passing two "No Trespassing" signs, toward the log and stone house. His affidavit states that he called out to determine if anyone was home. Officer Rose peered into the windows of the home and garage, shielding his eyes from the daytime sun with cupped hands, and he rattled the doorknobs of the home and garage. At the end of his "rounds," Officer Rose came to the front door and left his business card in the door. The "property check" lasted approximately five minutes.

Based on *Kyllo*, what should have happened?

Here is the result:

> We accept that, informed by his twenty-plus years of experience as a conservation officer . . . Officer Rose felt that conditions consistent with a wintertime break in of a potentially-seasonal home warranted a brief protective check. Upon arriving on the property, Officer Rose announced his presence. In broad daylight, he spent approximately five minutes looking in open windows and jiggling door knobs to ensure the safety of the home. After engaging in minimally intrusive observations to quell his suspicions, he left his card in the front door. In this context, we cannot find such an inspection constitutionally infirm.

4. "Good faith" and "beneficial purpose" are at the heart of JUSTICE BRANDEIS' famous dissent in <u>Olmstead v. United States, 277 U.S. 438, 479 (1928)</u>:

> [I]t is . . . immaterial that the intrusion was in aid of law enforcement. Experience should teach us to be most on our guard to protect liberty when the Government's purposes are beneficent. Men born to freedom are naturally alert to repel invasion of their liberty by evil-minded rulers. The greatest dangers to liberty lurk in insidious encroachment by men of zeal, well-meaning but without understanding.

BLACKIE'S HOUSE OF BEEF, INC. V. CASTILLO

<u>659 F.2d 1211 (D.C. Cir. 1981)</u>

[JUDGE McGOWAN] Blackie's House of Beef . . . operates the Blackie's House of Beef Restaurant and Deja Vu Cocktail Lounge located in Washington, D.C. . . . In 1976, the INS began to receive information that illegal aliens were employed at Blackie's. One such indication was a sworn statement by an illegal alien who had been apprehended by the INS and was in the process of undergoing deportation hearings. This informant swore . . . he had personal knowledge that approximately 20 other illegal aliens were currently employed there. . . . Other information included three anonymous telephone calls in which informants notified the INS that Blackie's was employing illegal aliens. . . . INS officers apprehended two illegal aliens who were carrying wage statements from Blackie's. The latter of the two swore by affidavit that Blackie's was employing illegal aliens . . . .

On the basis of this information, INS Agent Foster twice asked the owner and manager of Blackie's for permission to enter the restaurant and question suspected illegal aliens. Ulysses "Blackie" Auger twice refused such consent. . . . [A search warrant was obtained.] On March 30, 1978, INS agents executed the warrant, entering Blackie's Restaurant during the dinner hour. . . . [Fifteen] employees were seized, at least 10 of whom proved to be illegal aliens subject to deportation. Blackie's subsequently filed suit in the District Court . . . alleging that the search warrant was not supported by probable cause and thus violated the Fourth Amendment. . . . [T]he court concluded that the warrant [was invalid].

. . . .

The INS continued to receive information that illegal aliens were being employed at Blackie's. The information that upwards of 30 illegal aliens were currently employed at Blackie's was supplied in an affidavit, dated October 27, 1978, by a previously reliable source. The affiant was . . . specific, revealing names, . . . explanations as to how he knew the suspects to be illegal aliens, and [other] details . . . . INS [also] surveyed Blackie's . . . and observed employees . . . whom Parry believed to be aliens of Hispanic descent, principally because of their attire and seeming inability to speak any language but Spanish. . . .

Armed with this information, the INS sought another warrant to search Blackie's. This time the INS claimed to derive its power . . . from its general powers to question aliens and to enforce the immigration laws. On November 16, 1978, the magistrate issued a warrant, concluding that the INS had established probable cause to believe illegal aliens were present on Blackie's premises. . . . [T]he warrant was entitled "Order For Entry on Premises to Search for Aliens in the United States Without Legal Authority." . . . . On November 17, 1978, INS agents conducted a search of the public area, kitchen, and second-floor offices of Blackie's [and] removed 14 suspected illegal aliens from Blackie's . . . .

Blackie's again filed suit for injunctive and declaratory relief, and for damages in the amount of $ 500,000, alleging that this second warrant violated the Fourth Amendment and that the search as executed was disruptive and exceeded all reasonable limits. Again the District Court . . . held the warrant invalid, ruling that this second warrant failed to satisfy the Fourth Amendment . . . because it failed to describe with particularity each alien sought. . . . The United States appealed the District Court's rulings in *Blackie's I* and *II*, arguing that both search warrants were valid under the Fourth Amendment . . . . We consolidated the cases for hearing and decision.

. . . .

Our task on appeal is to determine whether either or both of the warrants were sufficient to protect the Fourth Amendment rights of Blackie's. Neither party challenges the proposition that a warrant was necessary to support the INS searches of Blackie's premises. . . .

. . . .

We think that the District Court failed to recognize the unique aspects of an INS search, and thus erroneously concluded that Blackie's Fourth Amendment rights were violated by the second search warrant. Our decision rests on three determinations. First, we think that Congress, in passing the Immigration and Nationality Act, contemplated a vigorous enforcement program that might include INS entries onto private premises for the purpose of questioning "any alien or person believed to be an alien," and of detaining those aliens believed to be in this country illegally. Second, since an INS search is conducted pursuant to a civil administrative mandate, the warrant issued to permit such a search may therefore be evaluated under a standard of probable cause different from that applied to criminal warrants. *Marshall v. Barlow's, Inc.*, 436 U.S. 307 (1978). Last, we hold that the warrant in *Blackie's II* was properly tailored both to protect the Fourth Amendment rights of Blackie's and to aid the enforcement interests of the United States.

. . . .

The harder question is the showing of probable cause necessary to support an INS warrant to search for a suspected violation. The District Court held that the warrant in this case was invalid because it did not attain the level of "particularized description" necessary to justify a criminal search. It especially deplored the lack of detailed description of each individual alien, and the magistrate's failure to balance, on the face of the warrant, the public interest in law enforcement against Blackie's interest in privacy. The Government asserts in opposition that an INS search warrant need not and, moreover, cannot meet such a standard of probable cause, given the nature of the particular law enforcement activity. We agree that . . . *Marshall v. Barlow's, Inc.* calls for a more flexible definition of probable cause to comport with the multiplicity of "hybrid" administrative law enforcement activities in a non-criminal context.

. . . .

The second portion of *Marshall* is of primary importance to the resolution of this case. Having determined that the warrantless search provision of OSHA was unconstitutional, the Court then discussed the type of warrant sufficient to support a routine inspection conducted by OSHA in fulfillment of its regulatory responsibilities. To the argument that OSHA could only obtain a warrant on a showing that illegal working conditions existed on those very premises, the Court replied unequivocally:

> Probable cause in the criminal law sense is not required. For purposes of an administrative search such as this, probable cause justifying the issuance of a warrant may be based not only on specific evidence of an existing violation but also on a showing that "reasonable legislative or administrative standards for conducting an . . . inspection are satisfied with respect to a particular (establishment)."

. . . .

In the context of routine agency inspections, such as those involved in <u>Marshall</u> and <u>Camara</u>, the reasonableness of a search warrant obviously cannot depend on evidence of the condition of the particular building sought to be searched. In those cases, the Supreme Court held that the probable cause requirement would be satisfied if "reasonable legislative or administrative standards for conducting an area inspection are satisfied with respect to a particular dwelling." Such standards could be based upon "the passage of time, the nature of the building, or the condition of the entire area," in the case of the *Camara* fire inspection warrant, or upon the nature of the business being conducted, in the case of the *Marshall* OSHA warrant. Both the *Camara* and *Marshall* Courts turned deaf ears to the plea that a flexible probable cause requirement impermissibly lessens the protections of the Fourth Amendment. . . .

. . . .

In the present case, the District Court did not directly address the question of whether a flexible standard of probable cause would justify the type of warrant obtained in this case, but simply assumed that a formulation of probable cause differed from the traditional requirement of "particularized description" is appropriate only in the context of routine inspections. . . . We do not read <u>Marshall</u> so narrowly, however. . . . It is difficult to imagine any instance in which INS agents could satisfy the District Court's requirement and obtain the names of each illegal alien employed in the nonpublic areas of a restaurant, or even physical descriptions any more particularized than those proffered to the magistrate in this instance. Since an illegal alien is essentially a fugitive outside the law, it is unlikely that his vital statistics will be on file anywhere in the United States or even that he will customarily use his real name, either in his contacts with the Government or with anyone else. . . .

Furthermore, and most important to our way of thinking, is the fact that the stringent requirements laid down by the District Court would, in practical terms, have little effect on the activities of the law enforcement officers operating pursuant to the "stringent" warrant. If the INS agents in this case

For More Information

United States v. Wantuch, 525 F.3d 505 (7th Cir. 2008), is one of a number of cases involving the fraudulent sale of "green cards" to undocumented aliens. *Wantuch*, like many cases in the field, raises complex evidentiary issues since some of the evidence used against the defendant comes from confidential informants and undercover agents, frustrating basic confrontational rights. For a practical look at immigration law practice pertaining to green cards, see Heather L. Poole, *The Quickest Way to a Green Card Is Harder Than You Think*, 49 ORANGE COUNTY LAWYER 18 (July 2007).

had entered Blackie's with a more "particularized" warrant, perhaps one setting out the first names of certain aliens, the agents would still have been forced to pursue exactly the same course of conduct as was pursued here: the questioning of those employees appearing to be aliens and found in nonpublic areas of the restaurant. The INS could perhaps never have obtained in advance information specific enough to allow it to pick a dozen suspected illegal aliens out of a large crowd of employees without the need for further questioning. Thus, it is unlikely that the INS could meet the standard of probable cause applicable in criminal cases, at least as formulated by the District Court, except in the rare instance when an INS informer tips as to one specific violator and supplies the description and name of that person. . . .

. . . .

With the correct probable cause standard firmly in mind, we are forced to conclude that the District Court erred in striking down the warrant in *Blackie's II*. This warrant was as descriptive as was reasonably possible with respect to the persons sought, the place to be searched, and the time within which the search might take place. In our view, the warrant contained sufficient safeguards to assure that nothing impermissible would be left to the discretion of the INS agents. . . .

Underlying Case Documents

For a WASHINGTON POST story on the closing of Blackie's House of Beef click HERE.

---

1. Much has changed since *Blackie's House of Beef* was decided – though the issues are in some ways of more consequence today than in 1981. The questions raised regarding migrant workers and undocumented aliens are front and center in presidential campaigns, the press, and administrative law. When a government agency "checks" immigration status by a search, it is governed by the Fourth Amendment. One might think the standards for such activity are clear, but as *Blackie's* points out, there are most assuredly differing perspectives.

2. Professor Raquel Aldana notes that this is by no means a new set of issues:

> [T]he *Camara* legacy of balancing government regulatory powers against individual liberty interests has validated the use of indiscriminate warrants to conduct immigration raids for decades. The principle mischief of the Fourth Amendment balancing doctrine is that it has redefined the probable cause requirement as one of

a flexible inquiry of reasonableness, rather than requiring probable cause to fulfill the prerequisite of reasonableness. Judicial preapproval becomes a mere procedural formality when warrants do not require particularized suspicion based on probable cause.

Raquel Aldana, Symposium, *Rights and Remedies: Of Katz and "Aliens": Privacy Expectations and the Immigration Raids*, 41 U.C. Davis L. Rev. 1081, 1088-89 (2008).

3. There is both federal and state activity in this area raising basic federalism issues. *See* Hector O. Villagra, *Arizona's Proposition 200 and the Supremacy of Federal Law: Elements of Law, Politics, and Faith*, 2 Stan. J.C.R. & C.L. 295 (2006); Peter H. Schuck, *Taking Immigration Federalism Seriously*, 2007 U. Chi. Legal F. 57. In some instances, the local responses are extraordinarily harsh. *See, e.g.*, *Lozano v. City of Hazleton*, 496 F. Supp. 2d 477, 484-85 (M.D. Pa. 2007).

Moreover, when a workplace is "raided," consider the basis for the decision. Does it go beyond racial profiling? *See* Kevin R. Johnson, *The Case Against Race Profiling in Immigration Enforcement*, 78 Wash. U. L.Q. 675 (2000). If race is the sole or primary basis for a civil warrant, can it possibly pass constitutional scrutiny? A warrant to search a workplace will issue based on "reasonable belief" and without any specific identified subjects for the search. *Int'l Molders' & Allied Workers' Local Union No. 164 v. Nelson*, 799 F.2d 547, 553 (9th Cir. 1986). Does "reasonable" require more than a general profile of the workforce at a particular location?

Consider the above three notes from the perspective of a governmental agency obligated to enforce the immigration laws. How would you draft an affidavit in support of a civil warrant to search a workplace? What information would be needed?

4. Beyond the issues of race and immigration, there is the broader question in *Blackie's* of the general expectation of privacy one has in the workplace. In *United States v. Barrows*, 481 F.3d 1246 (10th Cir. 2007), the court assessed whether a person has a privacy interest in a personal computer, not owned by the employer, found in the workplace, on which child pornography was found. To answer that question, the court sought first to determine if there was a

> subjective expectation of privacy, and second whether that expectation [is] one society is prepared to recognize as reasonable. . . . The ultimate question is whether [the defendant's] claim to privacy from the government intrusion is reasonable in light of all the surrounding circumstances.

> Since this incident occurred in the workplace, those surrounding circumstances include (1) the employee's relationship to the item seized; (2) whether the item was in the immediate control of the employee when it was seized; and (3) whether the

employee took actions to maintain his privacy in the item. These factors are relevant to both the subjective and objective prongs of the reasonableness inquiry. . . .

To begin, Mr. Barrows makes much of the fact that he owned the computer. And he is right that private ownership is an important factor telling in favor of Fourth Amendment protection. . . . It is not, however, dispositive. . . . If it were, the Fourth Amendment would track neither tort law nor social expectations of privacy, for neither affords individuals an absolute veto over third-party access to an item by virtue of ownership alone. But the significance of personal ownership is particularly weakened when the item in question is being used for business purposes. . . . Mr. Barrows voluntarily transferred his personal computer to a public place for work-related use. In these circumstances, we cannot say that mere ownership is enough to demonstrate a subjective expectation of privacy or to make that expectation reasonable.

More weighty for determining privacy expectations in the workplace, which must be considered case-by-case[, is] Mr. Barrows's failure to password protect his computer, turn it off, or take any other steps to prevent third-party use [suggests that the defendant did not] harbor[] a subjective expectation of privacy. He certainly did not possess a reasonable one.

The above steps are standard in workplace privacy cases. *See, e.g.*, <u>United States v. Angevine, 281 F.3d 1130 (10th Cir. 2002)</u>. In <u>United States v. Bailey, 272 F. Supp. 2d 822 (D. Neb. 2003)</u>, the court found that:

Employees may have reasonable expectations of privacy within their workplaces which are constitutionally protected against intrusions by police. "As with the expectation of privacy in one's home, such an expectation in one's place of work is based upon societal expectations that have deep roots in the history of the [Fourth] Amendment." However, an employee's expectation of privacy in the content of offices, desks, and files may be reduced by an employer's practices, procedures, and legitimate regulation over the use of the employer's property. . . .

If an employer announces that workplace space, including computers, are subject to inspection, expectations of privacy diminish greatly. <u>Muick v. Glenayre Electronics, 280 F.3d 741 (7th Cir. 2002)</u>. On the other hand, if an employee has a private office and there are no routine inspections of workspace or computer content, one has a reasonable expectation of privacy. <u>Leventhal v. Knapek, 266 F.3d 64, 73-74 (2d Cir. 2001)</u>.

WIDGREN V. MAPLE GROVE TOWNSHIP

<u>429 F.3d 575 (6th Cir. 2005)</u>

[JUDGE MERRITT] Plaintiff Kenneth Widgren, Sr., solely owns twenty acres of largely undeveloped land in Maple Grove Township, Michigan. . . . In May or June of 2002, Mr. Widgren, Sr., began construction of a house in the middle of his . . . lot . . . . By the spring of 2003, the area immediately surrounding the house was cleared, routinely mowed and a clear line marked the perimeter of the mowed portion. The cleared area, which was not enclosed by a fence, contained a fire pit, pruned trees and a picnic table . . . . At the mouth of the driveway stands a metal gate [with] multiple "No Trespassing" signs, one of which warns "federal officers of the IRS . . . and other unconstitutional agencies" as well as "all local members of planning & zoning boards" of a $5,000 per person land use fee. The house . . . can be plainly seen only from two vantage points outside the property – from the adjoining parcel to the south and from the air.

The Widgrens did not obtain a building permit for the construction of the house. In the spring of 2003, defendants Louis Lenz, Jr., the zoning administrator of Maple Grove Township, and H. Wayne Beldo, the Township tax assessor, entered the property a total of three times to confirm the zoning violation, to post a civil *infraction* on the front door of the house, and to conduct a tax assessment through observation of the exterior of the house. Once the Widgrens learned of the three visits [they] brought suit . . . . Relying on the "open fields" doctrine, the District Court granted the defendants' motion and held that no Fourth Amendment violation occurred. . . .

. . . A search is defined in terms of a person's "reasonable expectation of privacy" and is analyzed under a two-part test first penned in *Katz v. United States*, 389 U.S. 347 (1967): (1) "has the individual manifested a subjective expectation of privacy in the object of the challenged search?" and (2) "is society willing to recognize that expectation as reasonable?"

. . . .

While driving [one day], Mr. Lenz, the Township's zoning administrator, apparently observed a reflection from the roof or window of the Widgrens' house. Unsure what he had seen but confident that no land use permit had been issued for a house there, Mr. Lenz parked on Puustinen Road and advanced up the Widgrens' driveway past the metal gate and "No Trespassing" signs until he came within 200 feet of the house, which, for the first time, was clearly visible. Not having entered the cleared area, Mr. Lenz returned to the Township offices to confirm that no land use permit had been issued for the Widgren property. He then promptly informed Mr. Widgren, Sr., by letter of the violation of the Township's zoning ordinance. Mr. Lenz' observations here, occurring in the open fields, did not constitute a Fourth Amendment search. . . . Mr. Lenz' conduct . . . while perhaps a trespass, was not a search under the Fourth Amendment.

Mr. Lenz revisited the Widgren property several weeks later, on April 17, 2003, to post a civil infraction on the front door of the house. This intrusion was not a Fourth Amendment search because, under any definition, no search of any kind occurred. . . . Mr. Lenz merely posted a citation in his capacity as the Township's zoning administrator and did not seek to discover incriminating evidence. . . .

The intrusion of Mr. Beldo, the Township's assessor, presents a more difficult question. . . . Upon reading the "No Trespassing" signs, he drove onto the neighboring property to the south and exited his truck. While still on the neighboring property, he observed the Widgren house. He then walked onto the Widgren property towards the plainly visible house where no one appeared to be home. He observed the house's exterior, measured it by counting the foundation cement blocks, and took a photograph of the house. . . . After conducting his assessment, he promptly left and sent Mr. Widgren, Sr., a letter informing him of the assessment.

. . . Mr. Beldo's naked-eye observations of the house's exterior from the neighboring property and from the open fields within the Widgren property for tax assessment purposes are not Fourth Amendment searches. A closer question, however, is whether Mr. Beldo's observation of the house that occurred within the cleared area constitute a Fourth Amendment search. . . . [A]s noted above, a Fourth Amendment search occurs only where a reasonable expectation of privacy exists under *Katz's* two part test. . . . "[T]he Fourth Amendment has drawn a firm line at the entrance to the house" so that, "absent exigent circumstances, that threshold may not reasonably be crossed without a warrant." This "distinction of constitutional magnitude" between a house's interior and exterior is firmly rooted in the text of the Fourth Amendment, "which guarantees the right of people 'to be secure *in* their . . . houses' against unreasonable searches and seizures." In the instant case, the Widgren house was plainly visible from a neighboring property and from the air. Accordingly, their expectation of privacy in "the plainly visible attributes and dimensions of the exterior of their home" is at the Fourth Amendment's periphery, not its core, when compared to the hidden features of the house's interior. . . . Mr. Beldo's actions were not unduly intrusive. . . . We also find it highly significant that the purpose of government intrusion here was an administrative, not criminal, inspection.

We, therefore, hold that, under the facts of this case, a property assessor does not conduct a Fourth Amendment search by entering the curtilage for the tax purpose of naked-eye observations of the house's plainly visible exterior attributes and dimensions – all without touching, entering or looking into the house.

. . . .

Underlying Case Documents

The case referenced:

<u>A metal gate with multiple "no trespassing" signs</u>
<u>A sign warning of a $ 5000 land use fee</u>
<u>A notice of the zoning violation posted on the door of the house</u>
<u>The tax assessment</u>
The <u>letter informing Mr. Widgren of the violation</u> of the Township's zoning ordinance

For the letter informing Mr. Widgren of the tax assessment click <u>HERE</u>.

For general pictures of the property click <u>HERE</u>.

For pictures of the house itself click <u>HERE</u> and <u>HERE</u>.

1. <u>*Palmieri v. Lynch*, 392 F.3d 73 (2d Cir. 2004)</u>.

Palmieri owns a parcel of residential waterfront property . . . on Long Island's Great South Bay [that] encompasses both New York State regulated tidal wetlands and a regulated adjacent area. . . . In March 1993, Palmieri submitted an application to the DEC for a tidal-wetland permit to extend his fifty-two-foot residential dock/pier (the "Dock") by an additional 110 feet into the Great South Bay, as well as to build two elevator boat lifts. This application was denied by the DEC in November 1993. After Palmieri filed an administrative appeal, the parties reached a settlement, pursuant to which the DEC issued a tidal-wetland permit to extend the Dock by forty feet and to build one additional boat lift. The permit contained a condition providing that the property . . . was "subject to inspection at reasonable hours and intervals by an authorized representative of the DEC to determine whether the permittee is complying with this permit" and the New York State Environmental Conservation Law ("ECL"). . . . Palmieri refused to grant the DEC physical access to his property to perform the inspections . . . . [T]he DEC complied with Palmieri's wishes, and its employees conducted inspections of the premises by boat without entering onto his property.

In May 1999, Palmieri submitted another application for a tidal-wetlands permit to extend his now ninety-two-foot-long Dock by an additional fifty feet . . . . Defendant . . . Lynch, a DEC Marine Resource Specialist was assigned to review Palmieri's application. . . . [O]n April 3, 2000, Specialist Lynch . . . visited the premises for the purpose of inspecting the Dock and the tidal wetlands in connection with the DEC's review of Palmieri's then-pending application . . . . to evaluate the possible impact of the proposed project . . . . Once Specialist Lynch arrived at Palmieri's property, she rang the front doorbell and knocked. Not hearing any response, Lynch walked around to the side of Palmieri's house to gain access to the Dock and the shorefront and adjoining areas of the premises. . . . As [Palmieri] was physically escorting her off his property, Specialist Lynch explained that, if she could not complete her inspection, she could not complete her review of Palmieri's permit application. . . .

In June 2000, Palmieri filed an action . . . against Lynch . . . alleging a violation of Palmieri's Fourth Amendment rights. . . .

"[I]n limited circumstances, a search unsupported by either warrant or probable cause can be constitutional," but only where "'special needs' other than the normal need for law enforcement provide sufficient justification. . . ." In applying the special needs doctrine, we must weigh the governmental conduct – in light of the purported special need and against the privacy interest advanced – by analyzing three principal factors: (1) the nature of the privacy interest allegedly compromised by the [challenged governmental conduct]; (2) the character of the intrusion imposed by the [challenged conduct]; and (3) the nature and immediacy of the concerns and the efficacy of the [challenged conduct] in meeting them.

Palmieri "clearly exhibited a legitimate . . . subjective expectation of privacy." . . . . [However,] Palmieri had a "privacy interest in his backyard" that was "severely diminished." . . . . [T]he "fence" along the bulkhead in the backyard is a single strand of heavy rope strung between upright posts several feet apart and provides virtually no obstruction to a view of the water from the backyard and, thus, no obstruction of the view of the backyard from the water. . . . Palmieri[] had [also] applied for a construction permit and was on notice that the application process would involve some form of site inspection. . . .

The second special-needs factor requires an analysis of the character of the intrusion imposed by the regulatory agency's attempted visual inspection of Palmieri's dock and backyard. Here, the District Court found that "the level of intrusion . . . was minimal." Specifically, Specialist Lynch sought to visually inspect Palmieri's Dock and adjoining wetlands to evaluate his permit application. Lynch did not seek to inspect the interior of his house, his personal property, his person, or any closed containers. As the District Court explained, Lynch "at worst, committed a trespass."

The third special-needs factor requires an examination of the nature of the governmental interest at issue. . . . It is axiomatic in this day and age that the state's interest in performing regulatory inspections associated with applications to permit construction on protected tidal wetlands is unquestionably of the highest order. . . .

In sum, we hold that the special needs exception applies here because (i) the Plaintiff had a diminished expectation of privacy in the publicly-viewable areas outside his home (ii) the character of the intrusion by Specialist Lynch was minimal and largely encompassed the same degree of observation that could be accomplished from the water by any member of the public; and (iii) the state's interest in regulating construction on tidal wetlands overrode any asserted expectation of privacy in the outside areas of Palmieri's home that were adjacent to the water. . . .

2. Was there no way the parties in *Widgren* or *Palmieri* could lay claim to a privacy interest? To Fourth Amendment protection? Both owned property in fee simple absolute – though, as you have probably learned in property, there isn't much simple or absolute about property ownership. *See* ANDREW POPPER ET AL., COMPAN-

ion to Bordering on Madness, An American Land Use Tale, Ch. 1, 4 (Carolina Academic Press 2008).

While the conventional vehicles to envision the intersection of public regulation and private rights are the Fifth and Fourteenth Amendments, consider the nature of land ownership and the Fourth Amendment a different – but nonetheless valuable – lens through which the field can be examined. For an interesting look at the nature of ownsership, see Patricia Salkin, *Intersection Between Environmental Justice and Land Use Planning,*

Take Note

Administrative law is very much a public law field – but the act of public regulation presupposes in most instances a private impact. When that impact is on one's perceived interest in ownership or use of land, historic and potent forces are at once in play. *Kelo v. City of New London,* 545 U.S. 469 (2005).

58 Plan. & Envt'l L. 5 (2006); Eric Freyfogle, *Commentary: Private Property – Correcting the Half-Truths*, 59 Plan. & Envt'l L. 10 (2007); Eric Freyfogle, *What Is Land? A Broad Look at Private Rights and Public Power*, 58 Plan. & Envt'l L. 6 (2006).

For those who are interested in the land use dimension of administrative law, take a look at Asimow & Sullivan, *Due Process in Local Land Use Decision Making: Is the Imperfect Way of Doing Business Good Enough or Should We Radically Reform It?, 29 Zoning & Plan. L. Rep. 1 (2006)*, two articles debating the long-term vitality of the conventional agency model in land use cases.

3. In *Taylor v. Michigan Department of Natural Resources, 502 F.3d 452 (6th Cir. 2007)*, an agency inspector with the state Department of Natural Resources approached private property, suspecting a violation of an ordinance. While no overt evidence was visible, there were tire tracks in the snow leading to the owner's home. The agent explained that out of a concern for the well-being of the owner (suggesting there might have been an intruder) the agent traveled across the private land, up a long driveway, peered in doors and windows, and then left. In subsequent litigation, the owner alleged, *inter alia*, that a government agency simply does not have the right to enter private land and explore the premises:

> "[T]he Fourth Amendment has drawn a firm line at the entrance to the house," requiring exigent circumstances to justify a warrantless search. There is . . . an exception to this rule based on suspicion of burglary. Past cases reveal an "established precedent that the police may enter a residence [if they] believe that there is a burglary in progress." . . . . While such cases have indicated that probable cause and exigency are both required to justify warrantless entry, it makes sense for the law to impose a greater burden on officers entering a home to ensure its safety than it demands to justify looking inside through open windows. Officer Rose did not enter plaintiff's home. He observed the interior of the house and its exterior from the outside only.

The Supreme Court has stated that even the fact "that [an] area is within the curtilage does not itself bar all police observation." Thus it becomes critical to examine the extent of the government intrusion, which *Widgren* has prescribed should include an inquiry into the methods used and purpose for the conduct at issue.

Considering Officer Rose's limited methods of observation and the purpose of his conduct, we conclude that this "property check" is not a Fourth Amendment search. In terms of methods, existing Fourth Amendment jurisprudence distinguishes between cases in which officers engaged in "ordinary visual surveillance" and those in which the officers employ "technological enhancement of ordinary perception." Like the officials in *Widgren*, Officer Rose "used naked-eye observations unaided by technological enhancements" to survey the property. Admittedly, the present case differs from *Widgren* in that Officer Rose quickly surveyed the interior of the house, visible through open drapes, while the officers in *Widgren* only examined exterior features of the home. Officer Rose, however, engaged in only a brief, minimally intrusive visual inspection. Appellant accurately cites cases from other courts that interpret observation of the interior of a home through windows to constitute a search. . . . However, all of these cases are distinguishable from the matter at hand because they involve the conduct of law enforcement officers attempting to investigate suspected wrongdoing by the home owner/occupier without any professed protective element. That is, the purpose of the officers' observations, a factor that we are to consider in such cases, differed from that of Officer Rose.

When considering whether the officials had conducted a search in *Widgren*, this court plainly stated that "[a] criminal investigation is generally more intrusive than an administrative or regulatory investigation." . . . . Of course, not all non-criminal investigations are permissible. As the Supreme Court stated in <u>*Camara*</u>, "it is surely anomalous to say that the individual and his private property are fully protected by the Fourth Amendment only when the individual is suspected of criminal behavior. . . ." Here, no evidence indicates that Officer Rose would have any purpose for looking inside plaintiff's property other than the protective one that he supplies. The record does not indicate that Officer Rose had reports of criminal activity occurring within the house, nor does it suggest that the officer harbored any personal ill-will for the plaintiff. There is no evidence that Officer Rose was engaged in the "dirty business" that often accompanies an unjustifiable government intrusion. *Widgren*.

4. In the search for agency efficiency and the passionate quest to fend off ossification, cases like *Widgren* seem compelling – after all, why burden a government inspector with the responsibility to secure a warrant – beyond the obvious constitutional arguments. There is, of course, the stark fact that *Widgren* upholds a completely warrantless search without fitting into any clear exception to the Fourth Amendment. For a discussion of similar issues, see Amy L. Peikoff, <u>*Beyond Reductionism: Reconsidering the Right to Privacy*</u>, 3 NYU J.L. & LIBERTY 1 (2008).

3. Regulated Industries

MARSHALL V. BARLOW'S, INC.

<u>436 U.S. 307 (1978)</u>

[JUSTICE WHITE] Section 8(a) of the Occupational Safety and Health Act of 1970 (OSHA or Act) empowers agents of the Secretary of Labor (Secretary) to search the work area of any employment facility within the Act's jurisdiction. The purpose of the search is to inspect for safety hazards and violations of OSHA regulations. No search warrant or other process is expressly required under the Act.

On the morning of September 11, 1975, an OSHA inspector entered the customer service area of Barlow's, Inc., an electrical and plumbing installation business located in Pocatello, Idaho. The president and general manager, Ferrol G. "Bill" Barlow, was on hand; and the OSHA inspector, after showing his credentials, informed Mr. Barlow that he wished to conduct a search of the working areas of the business. Mr. Barlow inquired whether any complaint had been received about his company. The inspector answered no, but that Barlow's, Inc., had simply turned up in the agency's selection process. The inspector again asked to enter the nonpublic area of the business; Mr. Barlow's response was to inquire whether the inspector had a search warrant. The inspector had none. Thereupon, Mr. Barlow refused the inspector admission to the employee area of his business. He said he was relying on his rights as guaranteed by the Fourth Amendment of the United States Constitution.

Three months later, the Secretary petitioned the United States District Court for the District of Idaho to issue an order compelling Mr. Barlow to admit the inspector. The requested order . . . was presented to Mr. Barlow on January 5, 1976. Mr. Barlow again refused admission, and he sought his own injunctive relief against the warrantless searches assertedly permitted by OSHA. A three-judge court . . . held that the Fourth Amendment required a warrant for the type of search involved here and that the statutory authorization for warrantless inspections was unconstitutional. An injunction against searches or inspections pursuant to § 8(a) was entered. The Secretary appealed . . . .

I

The Secretary urges that warrantless inspections to enforce OSHA are reasonable within the meaning of the Fourth Amendment. Among other things, he relies on § 8(a) of the Act, which authorizes inspection of business premises without a warrant and which the Secretary urges represents a congressional construction of the Fourth Amendment that the courts should not reject. Regrettably, we are unable to agree.

The Warrant Clause of the Fourth Amendment protects commercial buildings as well as private homes. . . . In <u>Camara</u> we held: "[Except] in certain carefully defined classes of cases, a search of private property without proper consent is 'unreasonable' unless it has been authorized by a valid search warrant." . . . . [This] prohibition against unreasonable searches protects against warrantless intrusions during civil as well as criminal investigations. The reason [is that] the "basic purpose of this Amendment . . . is to safeguard the privacy and security of individuals against arbitrary invasions by governmental officials." If the government intrudes on a person's property, the privacy interest suffers whether the government's motivation is to investigate violations of criminal laws or breaches of other statutory or regulatory standards. It therefore appears that unless some recognized exception to the warrant requirement applies, *See v. Seattle* would require a warrant to conduct the inspection sought in this case.

The Secretary urges that an exception from the search warrant requirement has been recognized for "pervasively regulated [industries.]" Liquor (*Colonnade*) and firearms (*Biswell*) are industries of this type; when an entrepreneur embarks upon such a business, he has voluntarily chosen to subject himself to a full arsenal of governmental regulation. . . . The element that distinguishes these enterprises from ordinary businesses is a long tradition of close government supervision . . . .

The . . . Secretary attempts to support a conclusion that all businesses involved in interstate commerce have long been subjected to close supervision of employee safety and health conditions. But the degree of federal involvement in employee working circumstances has never been of the order of specificity and pervasiveness that OSHA mandates. It is quite unconvincing to argue that the imposition of minimum wages and maximum hours on employers who contracted with the Government under the Walsh-Healey Act prepared the entirety of American interstate commerce for regulation of working conditions to the minutest detail. Nor can any but the most fictional sense of voluntary consent to later searches be found in the single fact that one conducts a business affecting interstate commerce; under current practice and law, few businesses can be conducted without having some effect on interstate commerce.

The Secretary [next argues that by] opening up his property to employees, the employer had yielded. . . . his private property rights. . . . [This is rejected as well.] The critical fact in this case is that entry over Mr. Barlow's objection is being sought by a Government agent. Employees are not being prohibited from reporting OSHA violations. What they observe in their daily functions is undoubtedly beyond the employer's reasonable expectation of privacy. The Government inspector, however, is not an employee. Without a warrant he stands in no better position than a member of the public. What is observable by the public is observable, without a warrant, by the Government inspector as well. The owner of a business has not, by the necessary utilization of employees in his operation, thrown open the areas where employees alone are permitted to the warrantless scrutiny of Government agents. That an employee is free to report, and the Government is free to use, any evidence of noncompliance with OSHA that the employee observes furnishes no justification for federal agents to enter a place of business from which the public is restricted and to conduct their own warrantless search.

II

The Secretary nevertheless stoutly argues that the enforcement scheme of the Act requires warrantless searches, and that the restrictions on search discretion contained in the Act and its regulations already protect as much privacy as a warrant would. The Secretary thereby asserts the actual reasonableness of OSHA searches, whatever the general rule against warrantless searches might be. . . .

The Secretary submits that warrantless inspections are essential to the proper enforcement of OSHA because they . . . preserve the advantages of surprise. While the dangerous conditions outlawed by the Act include structural defects that cannot be quickly hidden or remedied, the Act also regulates a myriad of safety details that may be amenable to speedy alteration or disguise. The risk is that during the interval between an inspector's initial request to search a plant and his procuring a warrant following the owner's refusal of permission, violations of this latter type could be corrected and thus escape the inspector's notice. To the suggestion that warrants may be issued ex parte and executed without delay and without prior notice, thereby preserving the element of surprise, the Secretary expresses concern for the administrative strain that would be experienced by the inspection system, and by the courts, should ex parte warrants issued in advance become standard practice.

We are unconvinced, however, that requiring warrants to inspect will impose serious burdens on the inspection system . . . . In the first place, the great majority of businessmen can be expected in normal course to consent to inspection without warrant; the Secretary has not brought to this Court's attention any widespread pattern of refusal. n.2 In those cases where an owner does insist on a warrant, the Secretary argues that inspection efficiency will be impeded by the advance notice and delay. . . . However, the Secretary has . . . promulgated a regulation providing that upon refusal to permit an inspector to enter the property or to complete his inspection, the inspector shall attempt to ascertain the reasons for the refusal and report to his superior, who shall "promptly take appropriate action, including compulsory process, if necessary." The regulation represents a choice to proceed by process where entry is refused; and on the basis of evidence available from present practice, the Act's effectiveness has not been crippled by providing those owners who wish to refuse an initial requested entry with a time lapse while the inspector obtains the necessary process. . . . If this safeguard endangers the efficient administration of OSHA, the Secretary should never have adopted it, particularly when the Act does not require it. . . .

> n.2 We recognize that today's holding itself might have an impact on whether owners choose to resist requested searches; we can only await the development of evidence not present on this record to determine how serious an impediment to effective enforcement this might be.

Whether the Secretary proceeds to secure a warrant or other process, with or without prior notice, his entitlement to inspect will not depend on his demonstrating probable cause to believe that conditions in violation of OSHA exist on the premises. Probable cause in the criminal law sense is not required. For purposes of an administrative search such as this, probable cause . . . may be based not only on specific evidence of an existing violation but also on a showing that "reasonable legislative or administrative standards for conducting an . . . inspection are satisfied with respect to a particular [establishment]." A warrant showing that a specific business has been chosen for an OSHA search on the basis of a general administrative plan for the enforcement of the Act derived from neutral sources such as, for example, dispersion of employees in various types of industries across a given area, and the desired frequency of searches in any of the lesser divisions of the area, would protect an employer's Fourth Amendment rights. We doubt that the consumption of enforcement energies in the obtaining of such warrants will exceed manageable proportions.

. . . .

. . . The authority to make warrantless searches devolves almost unbridled discretion upon executive and administrative officers, particularly those in the field, as to when to search and whom to search. A warrant, by contrast, would provide assurances from a neutral officer that the inspection is reasonable under the Constitution, is authorized by statute, and is pursuant to an administrative plan containing specific neutral criteria. Also, a warrant would then and there advise the owner of the scope and objects of the search, beyond which limits the inspector is not expected to proceed. . . . We conclude that the concerns expressed by the Secretary do not suffice to justify warrantless inspections under OSHA or vitiate the general constitutional requirement that for a search to be reasonable a warrant must be obtained.

III

We hold that Barlow's was entitled to a declaratory judgment that the Act is unconstitutional insofar as it purports to authorize inspections without warrant or its equivalent and to an injunction enjoining the Act's enforcement to that extent. The judgment of the District Court is therefore affirmed.

> ### Underlying Case Documents
>
> The case referenced:
> The Occupational Safety and Health Act of 1970
> The order compelling Mr. Barlow to admit the inspector

1. When regulation affects individuals and entities across sectors, and has a general and comprehensive impact on the economic or social order, will it fail inevitably to identify a specific governmental objective for which warrantless searches are justified? Will it fail to provide notice regarding the nature and probability of search or the orchestrated acquisition of otherwise private information? In *Marshall* the OSHA scheme was too general – but would it be possible to tighten the regulations to address the deficits the Court identified? What would OSHA need in order to avoid the obligation to secure warrants?

Having a hard time answering the above question? So is OSHA. *See Sturm, Ruger & Co. v. Chao*, 300 F.3d 867 (D.C. Cir. 2002) (holding that an OSHA inspector must secure a warrant after a consensual search request was turned down, notwithstanding 25 years of intervening regulations since *Marshall* was decided).

The starting point, as usual, is the statute. In *Bruce v. Beary*, 498 F.3d 1232 (11th Cir. 2007), a heavily armed swat team descended on a used car dealership allegedly looking for civil violations pertaining to vehicle registration violations. The statute, Fla. Stat. § 812.055 (2008), permitted "[p]hysical inspection of junkyards [and] licensed motor vehicle or vessel dealers . . . for the purpose of locating stolen vehicles [and] investigating the titling and registration of vehicles . . . or inspecting records." The court focused on the purpose of the search, discussed following the *Clifford* case, and the statute. The court announced the basic rules to be applied to determine if a statute supplants the warrant requirement:

> The authorizing statute must "carefully limit[and inspections] time, place, and scope."
> . . . . [The] authorizing statute [may not] commit the conduct of such an inspection

to the unbridled discretion of the inspector. The statute must "limit the discretion of the inspecting officers" and the inspection must have a "properly defined scope." There must be "reasonable legislative or administrative standards for conducting an . . . inspection." *Camara.* "Where a statute authorizes the inspection but makes no rules governing the procedures that inspectors must follow, the Fourth Amendment and its various restrictive rules apply." The fundamental function of these rules is to protect citizens from the "unbridled discretion [of] executive and administrative officers." *Marshall v. Barlow's, Inc.* . . .

Is the above statute sufficient based on *Marshall*? How is it different from the OSHA statute?

2. *Marshall* deals with a generalized regulatory scheme – what if the statute is directed to a specific industry – would that be sufficient? In *Wal Juice Bar, Inc. v. City of Oak Grove*, 2008 WL 1730293 (W.D. Ky. 2008), the court evaluated whether a statute could supplant a warrant in the field of sexually oriented businesses. The basic rules, the court announced, are straightforward:

> [T]here is a narrow exception to the warrant requirement for administrative searches conducted in closely regulated industries, but sexually oriented businesses do not qualify as highly regulated industries . . . like mining and firearms. . . . [B]ecause sexually oriented businesses are protected by the First Amendment, the government probably could not closely regulate them. . . .

Marshall requires a "pervasively regulated business" with a "a history of government oversight [such] that no reasonable expectation of privacy could exist . . . . [Pervasively regulated industries] represent the exception rather than the rule." That said, do you agree that a seller of sexually explicit materials is not pervasively regulated? See *Copar Pumice Co. v. Morris*, 2008 WL 2323488 (D.N.M. 2008) for a recent discussion of what is needed to establish pervasive regulation.

Take Note

The foundation cases for a pervasive regulatory scheme exception are *United States v. Biswell*, 406 U.S. 311 (1972) (firearms), and *Colonnade Catering Corp. v. United States*, 397 U.S. 72-77 (1970) (alcohol).

3. Assuming a warrant is sought, the reasonability test the court announced in *Marshall* does not require individualized suspicion or probable cause. Given that permissible lack of specificity (*Camara's* warrant requirements are similarly vague), are the requirements of the Fourth Amendment met or is this just paying lip-service to personal and commercial privacy? Keep in mind that warrants issue in ex parte proceedings. *See* Laura A. Matejik, *DNA Sampling: Privacy and Police Investigation in a Suspect Society*, 61 ARK. L. REV. 53 (2008); Tony LaCroix, Note, *Student Drug Testing: The Blinding Appeal of In Loco Parentis and the Importance of State Protection of Student Privacy*,

8 BYU Educ. & L.J. 251 (2008); Fabio Arcila, Jr., *In the Trenches: Searches and the Misunderstood Common-Law History of Suspicion and Probable Cause*, 10 U. Pa. J. Const. L. 1 (2007).

4. The politics of warrantless searches is a boundless topic. Should Congress be in the business of regularly supplanting the Fourth Amendment? *See* Amalia W. Jorns, Note, *Challenging Warrantless Inspections of Abortion Providers: A New Constitutional Strategy*, 105 Colum. L. Rev. 1563 (2005); Eric F. Citron, *Right and Responsibility in Fourth Amendment Jurisprudence: The Problem with Pretext*, 116 Yale L.J. 1072 (2007).

5. *Rush v. Obledo*, 756 F.2d 713 (9th Cir. 1985).

> [P]laintiffs, an operator of a licensed family day care home . . . brought suit seeking a declaratory judgment that a California state statute and its implementing regulation which permit warrantless inspections of family day care homes were unconstitutional. . . . California law authorize unannounced [and] warrantless inspections of family day care homes in four different situations: (1) prior to the initial licensing of a provider (2) for the renewal of a license (3) on the basis of a complaint and a follow-up visit to assure any violation has been corrected, and (4) for the mandatory annual inspection of ten percent of all licensed family day care homes. Under this statute, unannounced visits may be made at any time. . . .
>
> Family day care homes are private residences which operate as businesses [for part of the day]. The state contends that its policy of warrantless entry into family day care homes is justified under the "pervasively regulated business" exception to the warrant requirement. . . . [T]he Court [has] rejected the contention that the *Colonnade-Biswell* exception applied only to those heavily regulated industries which have a long history of government regulation. . . . Instead, the Court [has] held that "it is the pervasiveness and regularity of the federal regulation that ultimately determines whether a warrant is necessary to render an inspection program reasonable under the Fourth Amendment." Applying this analysis to the case before us, we conclude that warrantless inspections of family day care homes do not offend the Fourth Amendment. . . . If a warrant were required, a delay in inspecting a home, during which a violation can be corrected, is unavoidable. . . .
>
> Even though we have determined that the warrantless inspection of family day care homes does not necessarily violate the Fourth Amendment, we find that the current statutes authorizing such searches are overbroad – permitting general searches of any home providing care and supervision at any time of the day or night . . . . The state's warrantless inspection authority should not extend beyond the "closely regulated business" in which the provider engages. Warrantless inspections are permissible in those portions of the provider's home where day care activities take place only when the home is being operated as a family day care business. . . .

Given the strong and undeniably critical state interests in this case, why the hard line on search?

6. In *Shoemaker v. Handel*, 619 F. Supp. 1089 (D.N.J. 1985), a group of thoroughbred jockeys challenged a rule that permitted warrantless searches – in this instance breathalyzer and urine tests proximate to race time.

> [While the] Fourth Amendment generally requires [that] a warrant based on probable cause issue before a search occurs . . . exceptions exist to this requirement when a legitimate governmental purpose makes the intrusion into privacy reasonable. . . . The state may conduct administrative warrantless searches when necessary to further a regulatory scheme [provided] the . . . regulatory presence is sufficiently comprehensive and defined. . . . It is the pervasiveness and regularity of the regulatory scheme that ultimately determines whether a warrant is necessary to render an inspection program reasonable under the Fourth Amendment. . . . Certain industries have such a history of government oversight that no reasonable expectation of privacy . . . could exist for a proprietor over the stock of such an enterprise . . . . [W]hen an entrepreneur embarks upon such a business, he has voluntarily chosen to subject himself to a full arsenal of government regulation.
>
> The New Jersey courts have consistently considered horse racing and casino gambling as demonstrating the same pervasive regulatory factors as liquor and firearms. . . . A New Jersey court recently equated horse racing, casino gambling, and liquor as follows: "Liquor, with 'its inherent evils,' has been dealt with as a subject apart." The legislative power to regulate such a "nonessential and inherently dangerous commodity," as a wholly constitutional expression of concern for public health, safety, morals or general welfare, has been said to be almost without limit. . . .
>
> The public has a special interest in the strict regulation of horse racing. This industry has always been pervasively regulated, in order to minimize the criminal influence to which it is so prone. The danger of clandestine and dishonest activity inherent in the business of horse racing has been well recognized . . . . Corruption in horse racing activities is regarded as an affront to a publicly sponsored sport with the potential of far reaching consequences. . . .
>
> In this instant action, the court is asked to approve warrantless searches of persons on regulated property, not merely the regulated property itself. . . . However, the same considerations behind the exception to the warrant requirement are equally applicable to searches of licensed persons, such as jockeys while they are on the regulated premises, such as race tracks. . . .
>
> The court has applied the reasonableness test and has weighed the legitimate government interest in maintaining the integrity of the racing industry and the safety of the sport against the legitimate expectations of privacy retained by jockeys and finds that the breathalyzer tests, as administered under the regulations, are reasonable in the absence of a warrant.

Read the above closely – the court finds horseracing to be in the category of "inherent evil" and subject to "clandestine" actions and corruption. Are those appropriate considerations when determining whether a warrant is required? Couldn't the same be said of the vast majority of behavior subject to sanction in our civil and criminal justice system?

DONOVAN V. DEWEY

452 U.S. 594 (1981)

[JUSTICE MARSHALL] In this case we consider whether § 103(a) of the Federal Mine Safety and Health Act of 1977, which authorizes warrantless inspections of underground and surface mines, violates the Fourth Amendment.

I

[Under the] Federal Mine Safety and Health Act of 1977 [f]ederal mine inspectors are to inspect underground mines at least four times per year and surface mines at least twice a year to insure compliance with these standards, and to make follow-up inspections to determine whether previously discovered violations have been corrected. This section also . . . states that "no advance notice of an inspection shall be provided to any person." . . . .

In July 1978, a federal mine inspector attempted to inspect quarries owned by appellee Waukesha Lime and Stone Co. in order to determine whether all 25 safety and health violations uncovered during a prior inspection had been corrected. After the inspector had been on the site for about an hour, Waukesha's president, appellee Douglas Dewey, refused to allow the inspection to continue unless the inspector first obtain a search warrant. The inspector issued a citation to Waukesha for terminating the inspection, and the Secretary subsequently filed this civil action in the District Court for the Eastern District of Wisconsin seeking to enjoin appellees from refusing to permit warrantless searches of the Waukesha facility. The District Court granted summary judgment in favor of appellees on the ground that the Fourth Amendment prohibited the warrantless searches. . . . [The] Secretary appealed directly to this Court. . . .

II

[U]nlike searches of private homes, which generally must be conducted pursuant to a warrant in order to be reasonable under the Fourth Amendment, legislative schemes authorizing warrantless administrative searches of commercial property do not necessarily violate the Fourth Amendment. The greater latitude to conduct warrantless inspections of commercial property reflects the fact that the expectation of privacy that the owner of commercial property enjoys in such property differs significantly from the sanctity accorded an individual's home, and that this privacy interest may, in certain circumstances, be adequately protected by regulatory schemes authorizing warrantless inspections.

. . . Inspections of commercial property may be unreasonable if they are not authorized by law or are unnecessary for the furtherance of federal interests.

Similarly, warrantless inspections of commercial property may be constitutionally objectionable if their occurrence is so random, infrequent, or unpredictable that the owner, for all practical purposes, has no real expectation that his property will from time to time be inspected by government officials. . . . However, [*Colonnade Corp.* and *Biswell*] make clear that a warrant may not be constitutionally required when Congress has reasonably determined that warrantless searches are necessary to further a regulatory scheme and the federal regulatory presence is sufficiently comprehensive and defined that the owner of commercial property cannot help but be aware that his property will be subject to periodic inspections undertaken for specific purposes.

. . . .

Applying this analysis to the case before us, we conclude that the warrantless inspections required by the Mine Safety and Health Act do not offend the Fourth Amendment. As an initial matter, it is undisputed that there is a substantial federal interest in improving the health and safety conditions in the Nation's underground and surface mines. In enacting the statute, Congress was plainly aware that the mining industry is among the most hazardous in the country and that the poor health and safety record of this industry has significant deleterious effects on interstate commerce. . . . In designing an inspection program, Congress expressly recognized that a warrant requirement could significantly frustrate effective enforcement of the Act. Thus, it provided in § 103(a) of the Act that "no advance notice of an inspection shall be provided to any person." . . . .

These congressional findings were based on extensive evidence showing that the mining industry was among the most hazardous of the Nation's industries. Although Congress did not make explicit reference to stone quarries in these findings, stone quarries were deliberately included within the scope of the statute. Since the Mine Safety and Health Act, unlike the Occupational Safety and Health Act, is narrowly and explicitly directed at inherently dangerous industrial activity, the inclusion of stone quarries in the statute is presumptively equivalent to a finding that the stone quarrying industry is inherently dangerous. We see no reason not to defer to this legislative determination. Here, as in *Biswell*, Congress could properly conclude: "[I]f inspection is to be effective and serve as a credible deterrent, unannounced, even frequent, inspections are essential. In this context, the prerequisite of a warrant could easily frustrate inspection."

Because a warrant requirement clearly might impede the "specific enforcement needs" of the Act, the only real issue before us is whether the statute's inspection program, in terms of the certainty and regularity of its application, provides a constitutionally adequate substitute for a warrant. We believe that it does. Unlike the statute at issue in <u>*Barlow's*</u> the Mine Safety and Health Act applies to industrial activity with a notorious history of serious accidents and unhealthful working conditions. The Act is specifically tailored to address those concerns, and the regulation of mines it imposes is sufficiently pervasive and defined that the owner of such a facility cannot help but be aware that he "will be subject to effective inspection."

First, the Act requires inspection of all mines and specifically defines the frequency of inspection. Representatives of the Secretary must inspect all surface mines at least twice annually and all underground mines at least four times annually. Similarly, all mining operations that generate explosive gases must be inspected at irregular 5-, 10-, or 15-day intervals. Moreover, the Secretary must conduct follow-up inspections of mines where violations of the Act have previously been discovered and must inspect a mine immediately if notified by a miner or a miner's representative that a violation of the Act or an imminently dangerous condition exists. Second, the standards with which a mine operator is required to comply are all specifically set forth in the Act or in Title 30 of the Code of Federal Regulations. Indeed, the Act requires that the Secretary inform mine operators of all standards proposed pursuant to the Act. Thus, rather than leaving the frequency and purpose of inspections to the unchecked discretion of Government officers, the Act establishes a predictable and guided federal regulatory presence. . . .

Finally, the Act provides a specific mechanism for accommodating any special privacy concerns that a specific mine operator might have. The Act prohibits forcible entries, and instead requires the Secretary, when refused entry onto a mining facility, to file a civil action in federal court to obtain an injunction against future refusals. This proceeding provides an adequate forum for the mineowner to show that a specific search is outside the federal regulatory authority, or to seek from the district court an order accommodating any unusual privacy interests that the mineowner might have.

Under these circumstances, it is difficult to see what additional protection a warrant requirement would provide. The Act itself clearly notifies the operator that inspections will be performed on a regular basis. Moreover, the Act and the regulations issued pursuant to it inform the operator of what health and safety standards must be met in order to be in compliance with the statute. The discretion of Government officials to determine what facilities to search and what violations to search for is thus directly curtailed by the regulatory scheme. In addition, the statute itself embodies a means by which any special Fourth Amendment interests can be accommodated. Accordingly, we conclude that the general program of warrantless inspections authorized by § 103(a) of the Act does not violate the Fourth Amendment. . . .

———————

Underlying Case Documents

The case referenced:
The Federal Mine Safety and Health Act of 1977

1. *Pennsylvania Steel Foundry & Machine Company v. Secretary of Labor*, 831 F.2d 1211 (3d Cir. 1987).

[OSHA inspected Pennsylvania Steel and found several hundred safety violations. While some were remedied, others were not, leading to further inspections. When Pennsylvania Steel refused entry to OSHA inspectors, OSHA secured an ex parte warrant. Among many issues raised in the case is whether a history of prior violations can provide a reasonable basis for a warrant.]

[T]he Secretary argues that there was probable cause for the warrant on the facts set forth in the application particular to Penn Steel in light of its past violations and the letter of its counsel stating that at least some such violations had not been abated as Penn Steel had agreed to do. . . . Under the particular facts of this case in which the application referred to both Penn Steel's past violation and the NEP for foundries such as Penn Steel, we agree that the past violations of Penn Steel furnished an ample basis for its selection for early inspection. We therefore reject Penn Steel's contention that there was no probable cause to support the warrant.

2. *New York v. Burger*, 482 U.S. 691 (1987).

Joseph Burger is the owner of a junkyard in Brooklyn, N.Y. His business consists . . . of the dismantling of automobiles and the selling of their parts. . . . At approximately noon on November 17, 1982, Officer Joseph Vega and four other plainclothes officers . . . entered respondent's junkyard to conduct an inspection . . . . [T]he officers asked to see Burger's license and his "police book" – the record of the automobiles and vehicle parts in his possession. Burger replied that he had neither . . . . The officers then announced their intention to conduct a[n] inspection. Burger did not object. . . . [T]he officers copied down the Vehicle Identification Numbers of several vehicles . . . in the junkyard. After checking these numbers against a police computer, the officers determined that respondent was in possession of stolen vehicles . . . . Accordingly, Burger was arrested and charged with five counts of possession of stolen property . . . . Burger moved to suppress the evidence obtained as a result of the inspection, primarily on the ground that [the statute authorizing the search] was unconstitutional. . . .

[A] warrantless inspection, . . . even in the context of a pervasively regulated business, will be deemed to be reasonable only so long as three criteria are met. First, there must be a "substantial" government interest that informs the regulatory scheme pursuant to which the inspection is made. Second, the warrantless inspections must be "necessary to further a regulatory scheme." Finally, . . . the regulatory statute must perform the two basic functions of a warrant: it must advise the owner of the commercial premises that the search is being made pursuant to the law and has a properly defined scope, and it must limit the discretion of the inspecting officers. . . .

> The New York regulatory scheme satisfies the three criteria necessary to make reasonable warrantless inspections pursuant to § 415-a5. First, the State has a substantial interest in regulating the vehicle-dismantling and automobile-junkyard industry because motor vehicle theft has increased in the State and because the problem of theft is associated with this industry. . . . Second, regulation of the vehicle-dismantling industry reasonably serves the State's substantial interest in eradicating automobile theft. It is well established that the theft problem can be addressed effectively by controlling the receiver of, or market in, stolen property. . . . Moreover, the warrantless administrative inspections pursuant to § 415-a5 "are necessary to further the regulatory scheme." . . . . Because stolen cars and parts often pass quickly through an automobile junkyard, "frequent" and "unannounced" inspections are necessary in order to detect them. . . . Third, § 415-a5 provides a "constitutionally adequate substitute for a warrant." The statute informs the operator of a vehicle dismantling business that inspections will be made on a regular basis. . . . Finally, the "time, place, and scope" of the inspection is limited to place appropriate restraints upon the discretion of the inspecting officers. . . .

3. While *Burger* upholds warrantless searches so long as the regulatory scheme furthers a substantial government interest, the government must show that the warrantless search is required to achieve the regulatory objectives, and the inspection program provides constitutionally adequate notice as a substitute for a warrant. The application of the *Burger* factors has not always proven particularly easy.

In *Wisconsin v. Schwegler*, 490 N.W.2d 292 (Wisc. App. Ct. 1992), a government official responsible for the humane protection of animals went to Schwegler's horse barn and conducted a warrantless search of the facility. The inspector determined that the animals were in a deplorable condition with numerous health code violations apparent. The inspector explained that a warrant was not secured in advance because, in the past, the inspector had been granted consensual access to the property.

Applying *Burger*, the court found that the state's interest in the well-being of animals was high but that the statute was not clear in terms of the regularity of inspection. When the government argued that even if this was not a pervasively regulated industry where the statute provided notice, consent was presumptive based on prior practices. The court found that consent required a showing, "by clear and convincing evidence," that the party had agreed in advance to the search. Ultimately the search was deemed illegal and evidence regarding the condition of the animals inadmissible. . . .

4. *United States v. Delgado*, 2007 WL 173890 (S.D. Cal. 2007).

> Defendant Modesto Delgado, the owner of a tractortrailer truck, and his brother Cesar Delgado, were traveling [through] Missouri, when Missouri State Commercial Vehicle Enforcement Officer Jerrold Brooks asked the driver, Cesar Delgado, to stop for an administrative commercial vehicle inspection. Significantly, the driver of the truck did not have a valid driver's license. Additionally, the driver's log book failed

to contain all of the required information, and did not conform to the information in Defendant's log book. . . . Under the totality of the circumstances, Officer Brooks radioed Missouri Highway Patrol Sergeant Jack McMullin to assist him. Upon arriving, Sergeant McMullin asked Defendant for permission to search the truck. After Defendant consented . . . Sergeant McMullin found approximately 41.99 kilograms (92.57 pounds) of cocaine within the truck. . . .

Missouri Revised Statute section 304.230.4(2) authorizes Missouri commercial vehicle enforcement officers to "require the operator of any commercial vehicle to stop and submit to a vehicle and driver inspection to determine compliance with commercial vehicle laws, rules, and regulations . . . ." . . . . The circuits that have addressed the issue have indicated that commercial trucking is a closely regulated industry . . . . Furthermore, administrative searches performed under section 304.230.4 of the Missouri Revised Statutes do not violate the Fourth Amendment . . . . First, there is a substantial government interest that informs the regulatory scheme pursuant to which the inspection is made. . . . Second, [s]everal circuits have concluded that administrative searches of commercial carriers are necessary to further an effective regulatory scheme for commercial vehicles. . . . Finally, the [statute] limits the class of vehicles allowed to be administratively searched, and permits administrative searches to be performed in a pervasively regulated industry, such that commercial drivers may expect that they will be subject to administrative inspections from time to time. . . .

[Also,] Sergeant McMullin asked for and received the consent of Defendant to search the truck. . . . Such voluntary consent obviates the need for a warrant, and therefore the search of the truck, and the use at trial of the cocaine found during the search of the truck, did not violate Defendant's Fourth Amendment rights. . . .

5. *United States v. Herrera,* 444 F.3d 1238 (10th Cir. 2006).

On March 3, 2004, at 8:00 p.m., a Kansas state trooper encountered [Robert] Herrera driving a Ford F-350 pickup truck . . . on the Kansas turnpike. The trooper believed Herrera's truck to be a commercial vehicle under Kansas law because it had "dual wheels on the back and a utility bed with a heavy lift hydraulic lifter on the back, and also there was a sign on the back . . . for a paint company." . . . . [U]nder Kansas law, "commercial vehicles can be stopped at any time to check for compliance with . . . safety regulations." . . . . [However,] Herrera's vehicle did not in fact qualify as a commercial vehicle under Kansas law because it did not have a manufacturer's weight rating over 10,000 pounds [and therefore] could not have been [stopped under the statute]. After stopping Herrera, the state trooper arrested him because Herrera was unable to produce proof of insurance as required under Kansas law. The trooper then conducted an inventory search of the truck [and] discovered twenty-three kilograms of cocaine hidden amidst building materials in the truck's bed. . . .

The problem this case presents is that Herrera's truck did not fall within Kansas's definition of a commercial vehicle subject to . . . random regulatory seizures and searches. . . . It is clear, then, that the state trooper's stopping Herrera cannot be justified under the Kansas regulatory scheme. . . .

The Government further argues, however, that there can be no constitutional violation here because, even though Herrera's truck did not in fact qualify as a commercial vehicle under Kansas law, the state trooper had an objectively reasonable, yet mistaken, belief that it did. . . . The Government's argument . . . focuses on the wrong participant in the seizure at issue here. The validity of an administrative seizure and search does not turn on whether or not the trooper had an objectively reasonable belief that Herrera's truck qualified as a commercial vehicle subject to random inspections. Rather, it turns on Herrera's decision to engage in a pervasively regulated business, knowing that by doing so he would be subject to random warrantless inspections. . . .

The state trooper in this case testified that the only way to determine whether or not Herrera's truck weighed over 10,000 pounds and was thus a commercial vehicle subject to random seizures and searches under Kansas law was to stop the truck and check the VIN plate. But permitting a state trooper to stop any vehicle simply to ascertain whether or not the vehicle was subject to a random regulatory search would allow the officer the unbridled discretion that the Supreme Court sought to preclude . . . .

6. Mine safety inspection, the topic of *Donovan*, continues to be an issue. *See Copar Pumice Co. v. Morris*, 2008 WL 2323488 (D.N.M. 2008); R. Henry Moore, *The Doctrine of Judicial Deference and the Independence of the Federal Mine Safety and Health Review Commission*, 107 W. VA. L. REV. 187 (2004); Shari Ben Moussa, Note, *Mining for Morality at Sago: Big Business and Big Money Equal Modest Enforcement of Health and Safety Standards*, 18 U. FLA. J.L. & PUB. POL'Y 209 (2007) (concerning the 2006 Sago mine disaster).

7. *Donovan* gives Congress the opportunity to limit the applicability of the Fourth Amendment, subject to the factors discussed in the above materials. The notion that pervasive regulation is limited to firearm, alcohol, mine safety, or food inspection is far too limited. Consider the following two articles – and ask if the legislative powers they discuss and critique derive in part from *Donovan*: Marc Jonathan Blitz, *Video Surveillance and the Constitution of Public Space: Fitting the Fourth Amendment to a World that Tracks Image and Identity*, 82 TEX. L. REV. 1349 (2004); Robert Bloom & William J. Dunn, *The Constitutional Infirmity of Warrantless NSA Surveillance: The Abuse of Presidential Power and the Injury to the Fourth Amendment*, 15 WM. & MARY BILL OF RTS. J. 147 (2006).

————

4. Fire Searches

MICHIGAN V. CLIFFORD

464 U.S. 287 (1984)

[JUSTICE POWELL] In the early morning hours of October 18, 1980, a fire erupted at the Clifford home. The Cliffords were out of town on a camping trip at the time. . . . [F]ire units arrived on the scene about 5:40 a.m. The fire was extinguished and all fire officials and police left the premises at 7:04 a.m.

. . . Lieutenant Beyer, a fire investigator with the arson section of the Detroit Fire Department, received instructions to investigate the Clifford fire. . . . He and his partner . . . arrived at . . . about 1 p.m. on October 18. When they arrived, they found a work crew on the scene. The crew was boarding up the house and pumping some six inches of water out of the basement. . . . While the investigators waited for the water to be pumped out, they found a Coleman fuel can in the driveway that was seized and marked as evidence. n.1

> n.1 The can had been found in the basement by the fire officials who had fought the blaze. The firemen removed the can and put it by the side door where Lieutenant Beyer discovered it on his arrival.

By 1:30 p.m., the water had been pumped out of the basement and Lieutenant Beyer and his partner, without obtaining consent or an administrative warrant, entered the Clifford residence and began their investigation into the cause of the fire. Their search began in the basement and they quickly confirmed that the fire had originated there beneath the basement stairway. They detected a strong odor of fuel throughout the basement, and found two more Coleman fuel cans beneath the stairway. As they dug through the debris, the investigators also found a crock pot with attached wires leading to an electrical timer that was plugged into an outlet a few feet away. The timer was set to turn on at approximately 3:45 a.m. and to turn back off at approximately 9 a.m. It had stopped somewhere between 4 and 4:30 a.m. All of this evidence was seized and marked. After determining that the fire had originated in the basement, Lieutenant Beyer and his partner searched the remainder of the house. . . . They inspected the rooms and noted that there were nails on the walls but no pictures. They found wiring and cassettes for a video tape machine but no machine.

Respondents moved to exclude all exhibits and testimony based on the basement and upstairs searches on the ground that they were searches to gather evidence of arson, that they were conducted without a warrant, consent, or exigent circumstances, and that they therefore were per se unreasonable under the Fourth and Fourteenth Amendments. Petitioner, on the other hand, argues that the entire search was reasonable and should be exempt from the warrant requirement.

. . . .

. . . The constitutionality of warrantless and nonconsensual entries onto fire-damaged premises . . . normally turns on several factors: whether there are legitimate privacy interests in the fire-damaged property that are protected by the Fourth Amendment; whether exigent circumstances justify the government intrusion regardless of any reasonable expectations of privacy; and, whether the object of the search is to determine the cause of fire or to gather evidence of criminal activity. . . . Privacy expectations will vary with the type of property, the amount of fire damage, the prior and continued use of the premises, and in some cases the owner's efforts to secure it against intruders. Some fires may be so devastating that no reasonable privacy interests remain in the ash and ruins, regardless of the owner's subjective expectations. The test essentially is an objective one: whether "the expectation [is] one that society is prepared to recognize as 'reasonable.'" If reasonable privacy interests remain in the fire-damaged property, the warrant requirement applies, and any official entry must be made pursuant to a warrant in the absence of consent or exigent circumstances.

A burning building of course creates an exigency that justifies a warrantless entry by fire officials to fight the blaze. . . . Where, however, reasonable expectations of privacy remain in the fire-damaged property, additional investigations . . . generally must be made pursuant to a warrant or the identification of some new exigency. The aftermath of a fire often presents exigencies that will not tolerate the delay necessary to obtain a warrant or to secure the owner's consent to inspect fire-damaged premises. Because determining the cause and origin of a fire serves a compelling public interest, the warrant requirement does not apply in such cases.

If a warrant is necessary, the object of the search determines the type of warrant required. If the primary object is to determine the cause and origin of a recent fire, an administrative warrant will suffice. To obtain such a warrant, fire officials need show only that a fire of undetermined origin has occurred on the premises, that the scope of the proposed search is reasonable and will not intrude unnecessarily on the fire victim's privacy, and that the search will be executed at a reasonable and convenient time.

If the primary object of the search is to gather evidence of criminal activity, a criminal search warrant may be obtained only on a showing of probable cause to believe that relevant evidence will be found in the place to be searched. If evidence of criminal activity is discovered during the course of a valid administrative search, it may be seized under the "plain view" doctrine. This evidence then may be used to establish probable cause to obtain a criminal search warrant. Fire officials may not, however, rely on this evidence to expand the scope of their administrative search without first making a successful showing of probable cause to an independent judicial officer.

. . . .

The searches of the Clifford home, at least arguably, can be viewed as two separate ones: the delayed search of the basement area, followed by the extensive search of the residential portion of the house. . . . The Clifford home was a two-and-one-half story brick and frame residence. Although there was extensive damage to the lower interior structure, the exterior of the house and some of the upstairs rooms were largely undamaged . . . . At the time Lieutenant Beyer and his partner arrived, the home was uninhabitable. But personal belongings remained, and the Cliffords had arranged to have the house secured against intrusion in their absence. Under these circumstances, and in light of the strong expectations of privacy associated with a home, we hold that the Cliffords retained reasonable privacy interests in their fire-damaged residence and that the postfire investigations were subject to the warrant requirement. Thus, the warrantless and nonconsensual searches of both the basement and the upstairs areas of the house would have been valid only if exigent circumstances had justified the object and the scope of each.

. . . .

In *Tyler* we upheld a warrantless postfire search of a furniture store, despite the absence of exigent circumstances, on the ground that it was a continuation of a valid search begun immediately after the fire. The investigation was begun as the last flames were being doused, but could not be completed because of smoke and darkness. The search was resumed promptly after the smoke cleared and daylight dawned. Because the postfire search was interrupted for reasons that were evident, we held that the early morning search was "no more than an actual continuation of the first, and the lack of a warrant thus did not invalidate the resulting seizure of evidence."

As the State conceded at oral argument, this case is distinguishable for several reasons. First, the challenged search was not a continuation of an earlier search. Between the time the firefighters had extinguished the blaze and left the scene and the arson investigators first arrived about 1 p.m. to begin their investigation, the Cliffords had taken steps to secure the privacy interests that remained in their residence against further intrusion. These efforts separate the entry made to extinguish the blaze from that made later by different officers to investigate its origin. Second, the privacy interests in the residence – particularly after the Cliffords had acted – were significantly greater than those in the fire-damaged furniture store, making the delay between the fire and the midday search unreasonable absent a warrant, consent, or exigent circumstances. We frequently have noted that privacy interests are especially strong in a private residence. . . . At least where a home-owner has made a reasonable effort to secure his fire-damaged home after the blaze has been extinguished and the fire and police units have left the scene, we hold that a subsequent postfire search must be conducted pursuant to a warrant, consent, or the identification of some new exigency. So long as the primary purpose is to ascertain the cause of the fire, an administrative warrant will suffice.

Because the cause of the fire was then known, the search of the upper portions of the house, described above, could only have been a search to gather evidence of the crime of arson. Absent exigent circumstances, such a search requires a criminal warrant.

Even if the midday basement search had been a valid administrative search, it would not have justified the upstairs search. The scope of such a search is limited to that reasonably necessary to determine the cause and origin of a fire and to ensure against rekindling. As soon as the investigators determined that the fire had originated in the basement and had been caused by the crock pot and timer found beneath the basement stairs, the scope of their search was limited to the basement area. Although the investigators could have used whatever evidence they discovered in the basement to establish probable cause to search the remainder of the house, they could not lawfully undertake that search without a prior judicial determination that a successful showing of probable cause had been made. Because there were no exigent circumstances justifying the upstairs search, and it was undertaken without a prior showing of probable cause before an independent judicial officer, we hold that this search of a home was unreasonable under the Fourth and Fourteenth Amendments, regardless of the validity of the basement search.

. . . .

The only pieces of physical evidence that have been challenged on this interlocutory appeal are the three empty fuel cans, the electric crock pot, and the timer and attached cord. . . . The discovery of two of the fuel cans, the crock pot, the timer and cord – as well as the investigators' related testimony – were the product of the unconstitutional postfire search of the Cliffords' residence. . . . [That evidence is] excluded. One of the fuel cans was discovered in plain view in the Cliffords' driveway. This can was seen in plain view during the initial investigation by the firefighters. It would have been admissible whether it had been seized in the basement by the firefighters or in the driveway by the arson investigators. . . .

———————

1. *Michigan v. Clifford* was by no means the end of the discussion regarding the transition from a civil/administrative search to a criminal search. The following excerpt is fairly typical of recent cases posing the bottom-line questions in <u>Burger</u> and <u>Clifford</u>.

In <u>Bruce v. Beary, 498 F.3d 1232 (11th Cir. 2007)</u>, after a complaint to the state auto theft unit regarding allegedly false vehicle identification numbers (VINs) on cars at Wholesale Auto Advantage, a decision was made to conduct an administrative search of the premises.

[A]pproximately twenty officers . . . arrived in unmarked trucks and SUVs, and surrounded the entire Premises. . . . Some of the officers were dressed in SWAT uniforms – ballistic vests imprinted with SWAT in big letters, camouflage pants, and black boots. They entered the Premises with guns drawn – all were armed with Glock sidearms; some carried Bennelli automatic shotguns. . . . The officers patted down and searched the employees. Pockets and purses were searched. . . . [The] officers discovered two vans owned by Specialty Auto Rentals [and] other cars on the lot with suspicious identification. . . .

[The owner's] contention is that an administrative inspection, pursuant to an authorizing statute, must be a routine, random, suspicionless visit to a business to inspect books and records. He asserts that any time law enforcement has "particularized suspicion" of illegal activity at a business and seeks to investigate and gather evidence, it must arrive warrant in hand. . . .

[T]he Tenth Circuit's recent decision in _United States v. Johnson_, 408 F.3d at 1321 (10th Circuit 2005), supports [this] view. In _Johnson_, the Tenth Circuit stated that when the "evidence of criminal activity [is] so compelling that police have, in essence, probable cause to believe that specific criminal conduct has occurred," they must get a warrant. "[I]nspections of . . . business premises . . . conducted not as part of a pre-planned and dispassionate administrative procedure but instead pursuant to direct criminal suspicion . . . give[ ] cause for grave constitutional concern."

The Eighth Circuit has also recognized the danger of allowing administrative searches to become "pretexts for 'crime control.'" _United States v. Knight_, 306 F.3d 534, 537 (8th Cir. 2002) (holding unconstitutional the administrative search of personal belongings conducted in that case). . . .

[As to pervasive regulation as a basis for the search] _Donovan v. Dewey_ [holds that] pervasive regulation alone [is] insufficient to legitimize warrantless entry.

We need not, however, address [these] questions of where to draw that line, because we hold that under the circumstances of this case the officers did not cross it. The Supreme Court has made quite clear that an administrative search is not rendered invalid because it is accompanied by some suspicion of wrongdoing. In _United States v. Villamonte-Marquez_, 462 U.S. 579, 584 n.3 (1983), the Court approved an administrative search that was prompted by an informant's tip that a vessel was carrying marijuana, noting that there was "little logic in sanctioning . . . examinations of ordinary, unsuspect vessels but forbidding them in the case of suspected smugglers. . . ."

[I]n this case, the officers did not have "direct criminal suspicion" of wrongdoing. They received a criminal complaint regarding possible VIN violations at Bruce's auto body shop. This information alone did not rise to the level of probable cause. . . . In the absence of such direct criminal suspicion, the officers validly invoked their statutory authority to inspect Bruce's Premises to determine whether he was operating in accordance with Florida law governing use of VIN plates. Merely because the officers had "an objectively reasonable basis to suspect they might find stolen cars or car parts in their inspection does not invalidate that inspection." Therefore, we hold that defendants were permitted to conduct a warrantless administrative inspection of Bruce's Premises for the purpose of investigating VIN violations. . . .

[However, a separate question is] whether this administrative search was a pretext. . . . The wholesale seizure of virtually everything on Bruce's Premises (and the disinterest of the officers in proffered documentation of vehicle ownership) and the failure to return Bruce's property (especially after conclusion of the state court appeal) may be some evidence of illegal pretext. . . . [Furthermore, one of the investigators said] "[m]y intent was to shut down a chop shop."

More troubling . . . is the officers' execution of the administrative inspection of Bruce's Premises. Officer Root's own testimony raises doubt that the conduct of the inspection was either "routine" or "administrative." Root testified that [the vehicle registration statute did not authorize] use of a SWAT team, or the searching and prolonged detention of employees [and that there was] no reasonable suspicion to pat down the employees . . . .

[A]dministrative searches are an exception to the Fourth Amendment's warrant requirement, but they are not an exception to the Fourth Amendment's requirement for reasonableness. . . . This administrative inspection was conducted by 20 officers over a period of eight hours. . . . They entered the office with automatic shotguns and sidearms drawn. . . . This hardly seems to be what the Supreme Court had in mind in *Burger*, supra, when it held that the Constitution is not offended by statutes authorizing the regular, routine inspection of books and records required to be kept by auto salvagers. . . .

[T]he "massive show of force and excessive intrusion" evidenced in these raids was in marked contrast to other administrative inspections . . . and . . . "[n]o reasonable officer . . . could have believed that these were lawful, warrantless administrative searches. . . ."

The Third Circuit held that an administrative inspection that involved eight armed and uniformed officers who descended on a taxidermist's office and residence, and conducted an "exhaustive search of [the defendant's business] had "all the hallmarks of a purely criminal investigation." *Showers v. Spangler, 182 F.3d 165, 173 (3d Cir. 1999).* . . .

Because administrative searches require no warrant, however, they invest law enforcement with the power to invade the privacy of ordinary citizens. *United States v. Bulacan, 156 F.3d 963, 967 (9th Cir. 1998).* "This power carries with it a vast potential for abuse. . . ."

The facts in this case . . . are sufficient to raise genuine issues of material fact for trial as to whether defendants' conduct violated his Fourth Amendment right to be free from unreasonable administrative search and seizure.

Why do you suppose the government failed to secure criminal warrants in the above case? What is the benefit of proceeding with an administrative search under these circumstances?

2. *United States of America v. Parr, 716 F.2d 796 (11th Cir. 1983).*

[T]he Tampa Fire Department . . . responded to a fire at the residence of Richard Parr.

After the fire . . . was extinguished, the fire fighters [looked] for salvageable valuables in order to protect them from vandals. During this phase, Fire Fighter Stone went into the kitchen of the house, took down an opaque sugar bowl from a shelf above the sink, looked into the uncovered container and inside observed currency, namely sixteen ten dollar bills. He took the bowl and the currency, intending to salvage it as a valuable, and turned it over to Fire Inspector Burke. While counting the money for his own inventory, the inspector noticed all the bills had the same serial number and concluded the money was counterfeit. At that point he stopped counting and called the police. . . .

Appellant Parr . . . assert[s] that the Fourth Amendment does not condone investing in fire officials the unbridled discretion randomly to choose which parts of a burned dwelling should be searched pursuant to a general practice of salvaging valuables, ostensibly for the protection of the owner of the burned house. . . . The government . . . argues that the search for valuables after the fire has been extinguished . . . should fall within the same exigent circumstances that justified initial entry into Parr's home. . . .

This case, in which the fire had been extinguished and the search for and seizure of valuables was to protect those items from looters, is distinguishable from removal of valuables from a home to protect them from destruction by a raging fire. There the exigency created by the fire would make warrantless removal of goods totally reasonable. . . . Arguments can be made, of course, that the need to secure valuables against looters is an exigency . . . . The legitimacy of this interest, however, does not undercut the necessity for a warrant to safeguard the substantial privacy interests implicated by any entry into a person's home by a governmental official. . . . Prior to undertaking such searches, absent consent or the presence of other exceptions to the warrant requirement, warrants should be obtained pursuant to the procedures governing administrative searches.

As in *Clifford*, was this a question of timing? Is there any doubt that probable cause existed?

3. *United States of America v. Buckmaster*, 485 F.3d 873 (6th Cir. 2007).

On May 14, 2005, the Madison Township (Ohio) Fire Department responded to a fire at Buckmaster's home. . . . Firefighters safely evacuated all the residents . . . and extinguished the fire, which appeared to be confined to the headboard of Buckmaster's waterbed in an upstairs bedroom. . . . Byers [and] Perko . . . could not start their investigation . . . until the water was cleared . . . and thus they decided instead to check the residence for high carbon monoxide levels and for "other possible dangers to the structure from the fire." Byers and Perko used a hand-held meter [on] the second floor[,] the first floor, and then began checking the basement. . . . Upon entering the furnace room, Byers and Perko noticed in plain view . . . several boxes marked as containing 1.4G and 1.3G explosives. . . . Byers and Perko could plainly see the fireworks inside. The total amount of explosives was approximately 1,250 pounds. . . . Buckmaster was ultimately charged under 18 U.S.C. § 842(a)(3)(A). Buckmaster filed a motion to suppress the fireworks [claiming] that Sergeant Byers and Officer Perko violated his Fourth Amendment rights when they opened the door to, and subsequently entered, his basement furnace room. . . .

[F]ire officials may remain in a fire-damaged residence . . . to make sure that the residence is safe for its inhabitants to return to. . . . The first exigency arose from the fact that [a]lthough the fire in the bedroom had been put out, the water seeping throughout the house created a continued danger of electrical shorts. . . . It seems an unremarkable proposition that if firefighters are aware of lurking electrical dangers resulting from their efforts to put out a fire in a home . . . they should neither have to obtain a warrant nor the express permission of the homeowner in order to alleviate such dangers, especially when they do so, as here, *immediately* after the fire has been extinguished. . . .

The government [also] justifies its search on a second exigency, but this one we are less inclined to endorse on the instant facts. . . . [I]t seems almost beyond argument that before they allow residents to reenter a fire-damaged structure, firefighters should be allowed to check, immediately and without first obtaining a warrant, carbon monoxide levels in affected areas. After all, the firefighters would likely be deemed negligent if they were *not* to check . . . . [However, the] firefighters . . . had removed their breathing devices prior to the Byers/Perko sweep – in other words, it was obvious to most of those present that carbon monoxide levels were in the acceptable range. . . .

4. Checkpoint searches. In *United States v. Cortez-Rocha*, 394 F.3d 1115 (9th Cir. 2004), border agents stopped an individual and, without reasonable suspicion, slashed open a spare tire – and found unlawful drugs therein.

In this context, a vehicle's spare tire . . . is analogous to a closed suit-case or other container often found inside of a vehicle. The government's longstanding authority to search containers and concealed areas of vehicles crossing the border reflects the practical reality that "contraband goods rarely are strewn across the trunk or floor of a car; since by their very nature such goods must be withheld from public view, they rarely can be placed in an automobile unless they are enclosed within some form of container." *United States v. Ross*, 456 U.S. 798, 820 (1982); *see also Henderson v. United States*, 390 F.2d 805, 808 (9th Cir. 1967) ("Every person crossing our border may be required to disclose the contents of his baggage, and of his vehicle, if he has one."). In order for an inspector to search the inside of the tire, cutting the tire may be necessary. Were we to require reasonable suspicion to conduct similar searches of common vehicular compartments, we would seriously impair the ability of the government to deter, detect, and prevent . . . unlawful smuggling across the country's borders. Any locked container would be protected by the rule Cortez seeks. A reasonable suspicion requirement in this context would remove the significant deterrent effect of suspicionless searches and encourage the use of spare tires and other locked containers as a means of smuggling.

This is the common standard for checkpoints and border searches – but does it conform with the Fourth Amendment? As the cases below suggest, this is not a new policy.

a. *United States v. Martinez-Fuerte*, 428 U.S. 543 (1976).

Interdicting the flow of illegal entrants from Mexico poses formidable law enforcement problems. . . . Once within the country, . . . aliens seek to travel inland to areas where employment is believed to be available, frequently meeting by prearrangement with friends or professional smugglers who transport them in private vehicles. The Border Patrol conducts three kinds of inland traffic-checking operations in an effort to minimize illegal immigration. Permanent checkpoints, [t]emporary checkpoints, [and] roving patrols . . . .We are concerned here with permanent checkpoints . . . .

During an eight-day period in 1974 that included the arrests involved [here], roughly 146,000 vehicles passed through the checkpoint . . . . Of these, 820 vehicles were referred to the secondary inspection area, where Border Patrol agents found 725 deportable aliens in 171 vehicles. In all but two cases, the aliens were discovered without a conventional search of the vehicle. . . .

While the need to make routine checkpoint stops is great, the consequent intrusion on Fourth Amendment interests is quite limited. . . . First, the potential interference with legitimate traffic is minimal. Motorists using these highways are not taken by surprise as they know, or may obtain knowledge of, the location of the checkpoints . . . . Second, checkpoint operations both appear to and actually involve less discretionary enforcement activity. The regularized manner in which established checkpoints are operated is visible evidence, reassuring to law-abiding motorists, that the stops are duly authorized and believed to serve the public interest. . . . [Finally,] one's expectation of privacy in an automobile and of freedom in its operation are significantly different from the traditional expectation of privacy and freedom in one's residence. . . .

In summary, we hold that stops for brief questioning routinely conducted at permanent checkpoints are consistent with the Fourth Amendment and need not be authorized by warrant. . . .

b. *City of Indianapolis v. Edmond*, 531 U.S. 32 (2000).

In August 1998, the city of Indianapolis began to operate vehicle checkpoints on Indianapolis roads in an effort to interdict unlawful drugs. . . . The checkpoints are generally operated during daylight hours and are identified with lighted signs reading, "NARCOTICS CHECKPOINT __ MILE AHEAD, NARCOTICS K-9 IN USE, BE PREPARED TO STOP." Once a group of cars has been stopped, other traffic proceeds without interruption until all the stopped cars have been processed or diverted for further processing. . . . [T]he average stop for a vehicle not subject to further processing lasts two to three minutes or less. . . .

We have never approved a checkpoint program whose primary purpose was to detect evidence of ordinary criminal wrongdoing. Rather, our checkpoint cases have recognized only limited exceptions to the general rule that a seizure must be accompanied by some measure of individualized suspicion. . . . Because the primary purpose of the Indianapolis narcotics checkpoint program is to uncover evidence of ordinary criminal wrongdoing, the program contravenes the Fourth Amendment. . . . When law enforcement authorities pursue primarily general crime control purposes at checkpoints . . . stops can only be justified by some quantum of individualized suspicion.

Our holding also does not affect the validity of border searches or searches at places like airports and government buildings, where the need for such measures to ensure public safety can be particularly acute. . . . Our holding also does not impair the ability of police officers to act appropriately upon information that they properly learn during a checkpoint stop justified by a lawful primary purpose, even where such action may result in the arrest of a motorist for an offense unrelated to that purpose. . . .

c. *United States of America v. Portillo-Aguirre, 311 F.3d 647 (5th Cir. 2002)*.

On September 20, 2000, at about 10:15 p.m., an Americanos passenger bus arrived at the Sierra Blanca immigration checkpoint. . . . Once aboard the bus, Agent Woodruff announced . . . that he was performing an immigration inspection and asked non-United States citizens to have their documents ready. . . . After Agent Woodruff completed his immigration inspection, and while he was returning to the front of the bus to exit, he noticed a small carry-on bag underneath Portillo-Aguirre's seat. . . . Portillo-Aguirre appeared rigid and was looking straight ahead, which aroused Agent Woodruff's suspicion. Acting on this suspicion, he began to question Portillo-Aguirre . . . . Portillo-Aguirre began to fidget nervously and replied that the bag contained books and clothes. . . . Portillo-Aguirre attempted to show that the bag contained only books and clothes, but Agent Woodruff perceived that something was concealed in the bottom of the bag. . . . Agent Woodruff moved aside the top objects in the bag and discovered a brown tape-wrapped bundle that he recognized as being consistent with narcotics packaging. . . .

[T]he permissible duration of an immigration stop is the "time reasonably necessary to determine the citizenship status of the persons stopped." In this case, Agent Woodruff testified that he had determined the citizenship status of the bus passengers *before* he began to question Portillo-Aguirre about the bag underneath his seat. Consequently, the issue is whether Agent Woodruff unlawfully extended the stop beyond its permissible duration. . . . Of course, a Border Patrol agent may extend a stop based upon sufficient individualized suspicion. . . . Because Agent Woodruff did not develop reasonable suspicion during his initial, lawful encounter with Portillo-Aguirre, our final inquiry is whether he developed the requisite suspicion while returning to the front of the bus to exit. . . . [He did not.]

The government has an interest in intercepting illegal drugs, but the Supreme Court has held that this interest does not justify suspicionless detentions. . . . An individual's decision to travel by bus does not weaken this protection. . . . Our holding today reaffirms that those travelers are entitled to arrive at their destinations free from arbitrary government interference.

For further reading in this area, see John W. Nelson, *Border Confidential: Why Searches of Laptop Computers at the Border Should Require Reasonable Suspicion*, 31 Am. J. Trial Advoc. 137 (2007), and Larry Cunningham, *The Border Search Exception as Applied to Exit and Export Searches: A Global Conceptualization*, 26 Quinnipiac L. Rev. 1 (2007).

5. Consent Searches

WYMAN V. JAMES

400 U.S. 309 (1971)

[JUSTICE BLACKMUN] This appeal presents the issue whether a beneficiary of the program for Aid to Families with Dependent Children (AFDC) . . . may refuse a home visit by the caseworker without risking the termination of benefits.

[A] three-judge District Court [held] invalid and unconstitutional in application § 134 of the New York Social Services Law n.1, § 175 of the New York Policies Governing the Administration of Public Assistance n.2, and §§ 351.10 and 351.21 of Title 18 n.3 of the New York Code of Rules and Regulations [finding] that home visitation is a search and, when not consented to or when not supported by a warrant based on probable cause, violates the beneficiary's Fourth and Fourteenth Amendment rights. . . .

n.1 § 134. Supervision

[P]ersons [receiving public assistance] shall be visited as frequently as is provided by the rules . . . or required by the circumstances of the case . . . in order that assistance or care may be given only in such amount and as long as necessary. . . .

Section 134-a, effective April 1, 1967, provides:

[A]ny investigation or reinvestigation of eligibility . . . shall be limited to those factors reasonably necessary to insure that expenditures shall be in accord with applicable provisions of this chapter . . . and shall be conducted in such manner so as not to violate any civil right of the applicant or recipient. . . .

n.2 "Mandatory visits must be made . . . at least once every three months [for people] receiving . . . Aid to Dependent Children . . . ."

n.3 . . . Section 369.2 of Title 18 provides in part:

[T]he home shall be judged by the same standards as are applied to self-maintaining families in the community. When, at the time of application, a home does not meet the usual standards of health and decency but the welfare of the child is not endangered, ADC shall be granted . . . to improve the situation . . . .

. . . The pertinent facts . . . are not in dispute.

Plaintiff Barbara James is the mother of a son, Maurice, who was born in May

1967. They reside in New York City. Mrs. James first applied for AFDC assistance shortly before Maurice's birth. A caseworker made a visit to her apartment at that time without objection. The assistance was authorized. Two years later, on May 8, 1969, a caseworker wrote Mrs. James that she would visit her home on May 14. . . . Mrs. James telephoned the worker that, although she was willing to supply information "reasonable and relevant" to her need for public assistance, any discussion was not to take place at her home. The worker told Mrs. James that she was required by law to visit in her home and that refusal to permit the visit would result in the termination of assistance. Permission was still denied.

On May 13 the City Department of Social Services sent Mrs. James a notice of intent to discontinue assistance because of the visitation refusal. The notice advised the beneficiary of her right to a hearing before a review officer. . . . Mrs. James appeared with an attorney at that hearing. . . . The review officer ruled that the refusal was a proper ground for the termination of assistance. His written decision stated:

> The home visit which Mrs. James refuses to permit is for the purpose of determining if there are any changes in her situation that might affect her eligibility to continue to receive Public Assistance, or that might affect the amount of such assistance, and to see if there are any social services which the Department of Social Services can provide to the family.

A notice of termination issued on June 2.

Thereupon, without seeking a hearing at the state level, Mrs. James, individually and on behalf of Maurice, and purporting to act on behalf of all other persons similarly situated, instituted the present civil rights suit under 42 U.S.C. § 1983. She alleged the denial of rights guaranteed to her under the First, Third, Fourth, Fifth, Sixth, Ninth, Tenth, and Fourteenth Amendments, and under Subchapters IV and XVI of the Social Security Act and regulations issued thereunder. She further alleged that she and her son have no income, resources, or support other than the benefits received under the AFDC program. She asked for declaratory and injunctive relief. A temporary restraining order was issued on June 13 and the three-judge District Court was convened.

II

The federal aspects of the AFDC program deserve mention. . . . Section 402 provides that a state plan . . . must ". . . take into consideration any other income and resources of any child or relative claiming aid" . . . .

III

When a case involves a home and some type of official intrusion into that home, as this case appears to do, an immediate and natural reaction is one of concern about Fourth Amendment rights . . . .

IV

This natural and quite proper protective attitude, however, is not a factor in this case, for the seemingly obvious and simple reason that we are not concerned here with any search by the New York social service agency in the Fourth Amendment meaning of that term. . . . [T]he visitation in itself is not forced or compelled, and . . . the beneficiary's denial of permission is not a criminal act. If consent to the visitation is withheld, no visitation takes place. The aid then never begins or merely ceases, as the case may be. There is no entry of the home and there is no search.

V

If however, we were to assume that a caseworker's home visit . . . does possess some of the characteristics of a search in the traditional sense, we nevertheless conclude that the visit does not fall within the Fourth Amendment's proscription . . . because it does not descend to the level of unreasonableness. It is unreasonableness which is the Fourth Amendment's standard. . . . There are a number of factors that compel us to conclude that the home visit proposed for Mrs. James is not unreasonable:

1. . . . . The dependent child's needs are paramount, and only with hesitancy would we relegate those needs, in the scale of comparative values, to a position secondary to what the mother claims as her rights. . . .

. . . .

3. One who dispenses purely private charity naturally has an interest in and expects to know how his charitable funds are utilized and put to work. The public, when it is the provider, rightly expects the same. It might well expect more, because of the trust aspect of public funds . . . .

. . . .

5. The home visit, it is true, is not required by federal statute or regulation. n.4 But it has been noted that the visit is "the heart of welfare administration" [and] that it affords "a personal, rehabilitative orientation, unlike that of most federal programs" . . . . The home visit is an established routine in States besides New York.

n.4 The federal regulations require only periodic redeterminations of eligibility. But they also require verification of eligibility by making field investigations "including home visits" in a selected sample of cases.

6. . . . Mrs. James received written notice several days in advance of the intended home visit. n.5 The date was specified. . . . Forcible entry or entry under false pretenses or visitation outside working hours or snooping in the home are forbidden. . . . All this minimizes any "burden" upon the homeowner's right against unreasonable intrusion.

> n.5 It is true that the record contains 12 affidavits, all essentially identical, of aid recipients (other than Mrs. James) which recite that a caseworker "most often" comes without notice; . . . that the visit is "very embarrassing to me if the caseworker comes when I have company"; and that the caseworker "sometimes asks very personal questions" in front of children.

7. Mrs. James, in fact, on this record presents no specific complaint of any unreasonable intrusion of her home and nothing that supports an inference that the desired home visit had as its purpose the obtaining of information as to criminal activity. . . . She alleges only, in general and nonspecific terms, that on previous visits and, on information and belief, on visitation at the home of other aid recipients, "questions concerning personal relationships, beliefs and behavior are raised and pressed which are unnecessary for a determination of continuing eligibility." Paradoxically, this same complaint could be made of a conference held elsewhere than in the home, and yet this is what is sought by Mrs. James. . . . What Mrs. James appears to want from the agency that provides her and her infant son with the necessities for life is the right to receive those necessities upon her own informational terms, to utilize the Fourth Amendment as a wedge for imposing those terms, and to avoid questions of any kind. n.6

> n.6 We have examined Mrs. James' case record . . . . It discloses numerous interviews from the time of the initial one on April 27, 1967, until the attempted termination in June 1969. The record is revealing as to Mrs. James' failure ever really to satisfy the requirements for eligibility . . . . There are indications that all was not always well with the infant Maurice (skull fracture, a dent in the head, a possible rat bite). The picture is a sad and unhappy one.

8. We are not persuaded, as Mrs. James would have us be, that all information pertinent to the issue of eligibility can be obtained by the agency through an interview at a place other than the home, or . . . by examining a lease or a birth certificate, or by periodic medical examinations, or by interviews with school personnel. Although these secondary sources might be helpful, they would not always assure verification of actual residence or of actual physical presence in the home, which are requisites for AFDC benefits . . . . And, of course, little children, such as Maurice James, are not yet registered in school.

9. The visit is not one by police or uniformed authority. It is made by a case-worker of some training n.7 whose primary objective is, or should be, the welfare, not the prosecution, of the aid recipient . . . . The caseworker is not a sleuth but rather, we trust, is a friend to one in need.

> n.7 The amicus brief submitted on behalf of the [caseworker's union] recites that . . . "generally, a caseworker is not only poorly trained, but also young and inexperienced . . . ." Despite this astonishing description by the union of the lack of qualification of its own members for the work they are employed to do, we must assume that the caseworker possesses at least some qualifications and some dedication to duty.

10. The home visit is not a criminal investigation, does not equate with a criminal investigation, and despite the announced fears of Mrs. James and those who would join her, is not in aid of any criminal proceeding. If the . . . visit should, by chance, lead to the discovery of fraud and a criminal prosecution should follow, then, even assuming that the evidence discovered upon the home visitation is admissible, an issue upon which we express no opinion, that is a routine and expected fact of life and a consequence no greater than that which necessarily ensues upon any other discovery by a citizen of criminal conduct.

11. The warrant procedure . . . is not without its seriously objectionable features in the welfare context. If a warrant could be obtained . . . it presumably could be applied for ex parte, its execution would require no notice, it would justify entry by force, and its hours for execution would not be so limited as those prescribed for home visitation. The warrant necessarily would imply conduct either criminal or out of compliance with an asserted governing standard. . . . [The problem obtaining a warrant is that] probable cause in the welfare context, as Mrs. James concedes, requires more than the mere need of the caseworker to see the child in the home and to have assurance that the child is there and is receiving the benefit of the aid that has been authorized for it. In this setting the warrant argument is out of place.

It seems to us that the situation is akin to that where an Internal Revenue Service agent . . . asks that the taxpayer produce . . . some proof of a deduction the taxpayer has asserted to his benefit . . . . If the taxpayer refuses, there is, absent fraud, only a disallowance of the claimed deduction and a consequent additional tax. The taxpayer is fully within his "rights" in refusing to produce the proof, but in maintaining and asserting those rights a tax detriment results and it is a detriment of the taxpayer's own making. So here Mrs. James has the "right" to refuse the home visit, but a consequence in the form of cessation of aid, similar to the taxpayer's resultant additional tax, flows from that refusal. The choice is entirely hers, and nothing of constitutional magnitude is involved.

VI

Camara [is] not inconsistent with our result here. . . . Mrs. James is not being prosecuted for her refusal to permit the home visit and is not about to be so prosecuted. . . . The only consequence of her refusal is that the payment of benefits ceases. Important and serious as this is, the situation is no different than if she had exercised a similar negative choice initially and refrained from applying for AFDC benefits. . . .

VII

Our holding today does not mean, of course, that a termination of benefits upon refusal of a home visit is to be upheld against constitutional challenge under all conceivable circumstances. The early morning mass raid upon homes of welfare recipients is not unknown. But that is not this case. . . .

Food for Thought

Issues pertaining to "consent" are not unique to administrative law. Think back to your Torts course and the discussion of "informed consent." How do the standards for informed consent prior to medical treatment differ from the requirements for consent prior to an administrative search?

We therefore conclude that the home visitation as structured by the New York statutes and regulations is a reasonable administrative tool; that it serves a valid and proper administrative purpose for the dispensation of the AFDC program; that it is not an unwarranted invasion of personal privacy; and that it violates no right guaranteed by the Fourth Amendment. Reversed and remanded with directions to enter a judgment of dismissal. . . .

Underlying Case Documents

The case referenced:

The notice of intent to discontinue assistance

The review of the proposed case closing

Affidavits from other welfare recipients

The New York rules

1. <u>*Calabretta v. Floyd*, 189 F.3d 808 (9th Cir. 1999)</u>.

Some individual called the Department of Social Services [to say] that she was once awakened by a child screaming "No Daddy, no" at 1:30 A.M. at the Calabretta home. Then two days ago she . . . heard a child in the home scream "No, no, no" in the late afternoon. The caller said that the children "are school age and home studied" and that "this is an extremely religious family." . . . . On October 31, four days after the call, the social worker went to the Calabretta home to investigate. Mrs. Calabretta, the children's mother, refused to let her in. The children were standing at the door with their mother, and the social worker noted on her report that they "were easily seen and they did not appear to be abused/neglected." . . . . On November 10 . . . the social worker returned to the Calabretta house with a policeman. She did not tell the police dispatcher about the specific allegations, just that she needed police assistance to gain access so that she could interview the children. . . . Appellants concede that for purposes of appeal, the entry must be treated as made without consent. . . .

The social worker asked what kind of discipline the parents used, and understood the twelve year old to be saying that the parents used "a round, wooden dowel . . . ." The three year old came into the room at that point and said "I get hit with the stick too. . . ." The social worker wrote in her report "Minor is extremely religious – made continual references to the Lord and the Bible." . . . . The social worker [said to the mother] "The rod of correction" Mrs. Calabretta answered, "Oh, it's just a little . . . piece of Lincoln log roofing, nine inches long." . . . . The social worker repeated "It's against California law to hit your children with objects. This is breaking the law. And I insist on seeing her bottom." The . . . mother looked at the social worker to see whether she would relent, but she did not, and the mother pulled down the three year old's pants in obedience to the social worker's order. There were no bruises or marks on the three year old's bottom. . . . The social worker . . . "had a brief conversation with the mother in which we discussed her looking into alternative forms of discipline."

The Calabrettas sued the social worker and policeman and other defendants for damages, declaratory relief and an injunction under <u>42 U.S.C. § 1983</u>. . . .

The facts in this case are noteworthy for the absence of emergency. . . . A child screaming "no, Daddy, no" late at night could mean that the father was abusing the child. But . . . these words are often screamed at bedtime, and also in the middle of the night after a child has . . . enter[ed] his parents' room to say that he cannot sleep, when the father puts the child to bed the second time. The other scream, "no, no, no," likewise may mean abuse, or may mean that a child . . . perhaps does not care for her mother's choice of vegetable. . . . Had the information been more alarming, had the social worker or police officer been alarmed, had there been reason to fear imminent harm to a child, this would be a different case . . . .

The principle that government officials cannot coerce entry into people's houses without a search warrant or applicability of an established exception to the requirement of a search warrant is so well established that any reasonable officer would know it. . . . Appellants argue that *Wyman v. James*, establishes that where a social worker enters a house to investigate the welfare of a child, Fourth Amendment standards do not apply. It does not. *Wyman* holds that the state may terminate welfare where a mother refuses to allow a social worker to visit her home to see whether the welfare money is being used in the best interests of the child for whom it is being paid. It does not hold that the social worker may enter the home despite the absence of consent or exigency. . . . [I]n *Wyman*, "the visitation in itself is not forced or compelled." In the case at bar, by contrast, the entry into the home was forced and compelled. . . .

a. Ideally, consent must be informed and voluntary. Is it only valid in a civil case if the extent of the risk or obligation a party might confront is disclosed? In the criminal justice system *Miranda v. Arizona*, 384 U.S. 436 (1966), establishes not only a right to have counsel provided if the accused cannot afford a lawyer, it also requires disclosure of the risks of making statements and of the right to remain silent to limit self-incrimination. Why not provide a similar warning as part of securing consent?

b. In *United States v. New England Grocer Supply Co.*, 442 F. Supp. 47 (D. Mass. 1977), the court commented that "the prevailing law regarding administrative searches establishes that *Miranda* warnings were not required." The Supreme Court held that same year that "*Miranda* warnings are required only where there has been such a restriction on a person's freedom as to render him in custody." *Oregon v. Mathiason*, 429 U.S. 492 495 (1977). The "Supreme Court [has] refused to extend the safeguards of *Miranda* beyond cases where a suspect's freedom of action is curtailed to a 'degree associated with formal arrest.'" *Berkemer v. McCarty*, 468 U.S. 420, 440 (1984); *see also United States v. Macklin*, 900 F.2d 948, 951 (6th Cir. 1990).

2. *Smith v. Los Angeles County Board of Supervisors*, 128 Cal. Rptr. 2d 700 (Ct. App. 2002).

> In February 1999, following a television broadcast about welfare fraud in Los Angeles County, the board of supervisors instructed the Director of the Los Angeles County Department of Public Social Services to report on the feasibility of implementing a home call visitation program. . . . On September 15, 1999, DPSS implemented its home call visitation program . . . . The program called for home visits to all potentially eligible . . . applicants. The purpose of the home visits was "to complete the eligibility determination process by verifying information provided by all new applicants prior to granting . . . benefits, as well as to assess and discuss the family's need for supportive services, child care, training/education services, literacy training needs, and expedite the family's access to these services as appropriate." . . . .
>
> On September 14, 1999, Debra Smith, Alma Roe and Laura Bergantino filed a petition for [a] writ of mandate challenging the home call visitation pilot project. . . .
>
> The governmental interest in reducing welfare fraud is great. Given the limited resources available for public welfare programs, the government has a substantial interest in assuring that the aid goes to those truly eligible for the benefit. Nor does the home visit program impose a substantial intrusion into personal privacy. Eligibility workers must give notice that a home visit is planned within 10 days of the intake. The visit must take into account the applicant's work or education schedule, and may only be conducted during a weekday between 8:00 a.m. and 5:00 p.m. Eligibility

workers are prohibited from opening drawers or closets during their walk-through of the home. We conclude that whatever intrusion is involved is minimal, and is outweighed by the government's interest in preventing welfare fraud.

a. Why is the substantiality of the governmental interest relevant to the question of consent? In *Mathews v. Eldridge*, governmental interest is of obvious import – but that case does not address the overt deprivation of a clear and unequivocal existing right.

b. Is the consent discussed in *Wyman* truly voluntary? Is the Court holding that public assistance, then known as Aid to Families with Dependent Children (AFDC), is voluntary – but for one to accept public assistance, one must waive their Fourth Amendment right to the sanctity of one's home? (AFDC was codified originally at 42 U.S.C. § 601 (1935) then superseded by the Personal Responsibility and Work Opportunity Reconciliation Act of 1996, Pub. L. No. 104-193, 103(a)(1), 110 Stat. 2113 (1996), amended by, Pub. L. No. 105-33, 5514(c), 111 Stat. 620 (1997)).

c. Can the receipt of a benefit be conditioned on the waiver of a constitutional right? You might take a look at JUSTICE HOLMES' famous opinion in *McAuliffe v. Mayor, Etc., of City of New Bedford*, 29 N.E. 517 (Mass. 1892), and compare it with *Laird v. Tatum*, 408 U.S. 1, 11 (1972), and *Abood v. Detroit Board of Education*, 431 U.S. 209, 234 (1977).

3. *United States v. Moon*, 513 F.3d 527 (6th Cir. 2008). After reports that as part of a state funded chemotherapy program, the defendant doctor was administering "watered-down" or diluted doses of medications and billing the state for full doses, the doctor was visited by three agents of the government. They did not tell her the purpose of their visit and were permitted to review files and scan documents. The doctor later claimed the visit was a warrantless search governed by the Fourth Amendment to which she had not knowingly consented:

> The Fourth Amendment bars the government from conducting unreasonable searches and seizures. This prohibition extends to both private homes and commercial premises. Additionally, searches pursuant to criminal as well as administrative investigations must comport to the strictures of the Fourth Amendment. Under the Fourth Amendment, searches "conducted without a warrant issued upon probable cause [are] per se unreasonable . . . subject only to a few specifically established and well-delineated exceptions."
>
> The well-delineated exception at issue here is consent. . . . Such consent, however, must be voluntary and freely given. Consent is voluntary when it is "unequivocal, specific and intelligently given, uncontaminated by any duress or coercion." The burden of proving that a search was voluntary is on the government, and "must be proved by clear and positive testimony." . . . .

The only evidence on the question of verbal consent was provided in the form of testimony by Agent Andy Corbitt of TBI at the suppression hearing. Agent Corbitt testified that three members of the TBI investigative team entered Defendant's office dressed in "business professional" attire, with weapons concealed. Agents identified themselves to Defendant, explained that there was an ongoing investigation and requested access to particular patient files. Defendant inquired about the nature of the investigation but was not informed of the specific nature of the allegations. Following this conversation, Defendant stated it would be "fine" for agents to access requested files and that they "could scan whatever [they] needed to." Further, Defendant provided agents with a space where they could scan the requested files.

Defendant, however, claims that the verbal consent was not voluntary as she merely acquiesced to a claim of lawful authority. Indeed, while mere acquiescence does not suffice to establish free and voluntary consent, it does not appear from the record that Defendant's statement to government officials was "an expression of futility in resistence to authority or acquiescing in the officers' request." Defendant does not allege . . . she felt powerless to prohibit the search. Rather, in agreeing to allow officers to scan records and conduct an interview, Defendant made it clear that she would maintain her ability to see patients. Such conduct does not speak of mere acquiescence. Based on the totality of the circumstances, we find that Defendant voluntarily consented to the search of her office and therefore the motion to suppress was properly denied. . . .

The above case relies on the holding in *Wyman*. In the event you found some of the reasoning in *Wyman* strained, take a look at <u>*Sanchez v. County of San Diego*, 464 F.3d 916 (9th Cir. 2006)</u>, a direct reprise of *Wyman*, including the holding that welfare searches are not searches – but if they are, they are reasonable.

[The] County's welfare eligibility program ("Project 100%"), which requires all welfare applicants to consent to a warrantless home visit as a condition of eligibility, does not violate their rights under the United States Constitution, the California Constitution, or California welfare regulations prohibiting mass and indiscriminate home visits. . . . [H]ome visits are not Fourth Amendment searches under *Wyman*. Even assuming that they are searches, they are reasonable under *Wyman* and the Supreme Court's subsequent "special needs" cases. . . .

For More Information

For further reading on this topic, see Tracey Maclin, <u>*The Good and Bad News About Consent Searches in the Supreme Court*</u>, 39 MCGEORGE L. REV. 27 (2008).

CHAPTER 12

The Freedom of Information Act and the Government in the Sunshine Act

I. FOIA Overview

In 1966, Congress passed and the President signed the Freedom of Information Act (available in the supplement). Over the next four decades, the Act has been amended and interpreted countless times. In essence, the Freedom of Information Act (FOIA) requires the disclosure of information in the government's possession subject to a number of exceptions designed to protect national security, individual privacy, intellectual property, and matters traditionally deemed confidential.

There are many different ways to learn about the Freedom of Information Act. There are hundreds of law review articles, numerous treatises, and dozens of federal publications that will give you an idea of the basics of FOIA as well as the companion Privacy Act and related statutes. Most law schools have courses devoted to FOIA and, after one enters the practice of law, there are frequent continuing legal education programs designed to explain both in broad strokes and in detail the system for disclosure and protection of information underlying both FOIA and the Privacy Act. It is not the intention of this casebook to provide anything close to a comprehensive study on FOIA, but rather to allow for a basic exposure to some of the legal issues in the field.

The need for the government to disclose information in its possession has been recognized since the founding of the Republic. More than two centuries ago, James Madison wrote that "[a] popular Government, without popular information, or the means of acquiring it, is but a Prologue to a Farce or a Tragedy; or, perhaps both. Knowledge will forever govern ignorance: And a people who mean to be their own Governors, must arm themselves with the power which knowledge gives." 9 WRITINGS OF JAMES MADISON 103 (G. Hunt ed., 1910), *cited in Houchins v. KQED, Inc.*, 438 U.S. 1, 31-32 (1978) (JUSTICE STEPHENS, dissenting).

Notwithstanding the caution of Madison, the business of securing the information the government possesses remained complex and periodically impossible until FOIA was adopted. For much of the history of the United States, information could be secured only if an individual could demonstrate a "need to know" that information. After the passage of FOIA, the "need to know" limitation was substantially lessened.

FOIA is by no means a perfect piece of legislation. As a starting proposition, it does not require the government to find and secure documents. It relates only to documents and data within the government's possession. When it passed initially, it placed no temporal constraints on responding to a request for information. After the 1996 amendments to FOIA, referred to generally as FOIA, the government has 30 days to respond to a Freedom of Information request, a limitation that more often than not appears to be observed in the breach. An additional attempt was made to correct this in the latest amendment to FOIA, but the only penalty imposed on the agency for failing to observe the time limit is an inability to charge copying fees. Over the years, FOIA has been plagued by claims of executive privilege and by numerous "withholding statutes" that obligate agencies to limit or prohibit the release of certain types of information.

Food for Thought

Section 8 of a recent amendment to FOIA, 110 Pub. L. 175; 121 Stat. 2524; Dec. 31, 2007 (to be codified at 5 U.S.C. § 552(a)(4)(A)), provides: "An agency shall not assess search fees [or copying fees] if the agency fails to comply with any time limit under paragraph (6), if no unusual or exceptional circumstances . . . apply to the processing of the request." Does this strike you as the kind of penalty likely to inspire agencies to complete FOIA requests more efficiently?

One of the more important developments in FOIA practice came as a result of *Vaughn v. Rosen*, 484 F.2d 820 (D.C. Cir. 1973), *cert. denied*, 415 U.S. 977 (1974). *Vaughn* resulted in the requirement, under certain circumstances, that agencies produce an index of documents withheld after a FOIA request and an explanation for the nondisclosure. Prior to *Vaughn*, information requests were regularly turned down without an explanation for those denials.

Other improvements in FOIA came as the result of amendments that require agencies to establish electronic reading rooms and information guides on agency web sites to allow requestors to seek their information in a more precise and informed manner.

Not all amendments to FOIA have had the goal of facilitating the release of information. In 2003, the Intelligence Authorization Act was passed. Pub. L. No. 107-306, 116 Stat. 2383, § 312 (to be codified at 5 U.S.C. § 552(a)(3) (A), (E)). This legislation prohibits foreign governmental entities from making use of FOIA to secure information pertaining to the collection of intelligence. Two years earlier, the Justice Department issued a memorandum to all federal agencies, advising them that the potential for terrorism suggests great caution in the release of information to any person. This memo, dated October 12, 2001,

For More Information

The Ashcroft memo is available at: *Memorandum from John Ashcroft, Attorney General, to Heads of all Federal Departments and Agencies* (Oct. 12, 2001), http://www.usdoj.gov/oip/foiapost/2001foiapost19.htm. This memo was issued without notice and comment. Assume there was a well-drafted rationale appended to the memo. Based on your understanding of interpretative rules, to what level of deference is this memo entitled?

is available on the Justice Department web site, www.usdoj.gov. Written by then-Attorney General John Ashcroft, the memo was intended to update a Clinton administration memorandum, issued October 4, 1993, in which then-Attorney General Janet Reno advised the leadership of all government agencies that government favors disclosure in the absence of foreseeable harm to U.S. interests.

Before moving to the cases, it is worth noting the basic exceptions to the Freedom of Information Act. The government need not disclose:

1. National security, foreign and domestic intelligence, and classified foreign policy documents.

2. Internal agency matters that do not reflect general agency policy but instead are designed for use by those within an agency.

3. Other statutes that specifically withhold information.

4. Commercial information and trade secrets submitted by an individual with a reasonable expectation of confidentiality.

5. Inter-agency and intra-agency documents that reveal the strategic considerations the agency is making or involve information that would be protected under attorney-client, work product, or deliberative process privilege.

6. Information that is, by its very nature, personal and private, such as medical records.

7. Information compiled for law enforcement purposes.

8. Information maintained by banks and financial institutions that is reported to or in the possession of the federal government.

9. Geological information or data pertaining to mineral rights, mining operations or similar resources.

The case law that follows explores various issues in the Freedom of Information and Privacy Acts.

What is the current FOIA environment?

a. The testimony below provides both an overview and assessment of FOIA as currently applied. It also provides a succinct summary of how the Act functions. A more detailed summary of the Act is in the appendix to this text.

> Based on data reported by 21 major agencies in annual FOIA reports from 2002 to 2006, the numbers of FOIA requests received and processed continue to rise, but the rate of increase has flattened in recent years. The number of pending requests carried over from year to year has also increased, although the rate of increase has declined. . . .
>
> Requests received and processed continue to level off, showing only slight increases compared to previous years. Except for one agency – the Social Security Administration (SSA)8 – these increases were only about 1 and 2 percent, respectively, from 2005 to 2006 (compared to 23 percent from 2002 to 2006 both for requests received and for requests processed). . . .
>
> Median times to process requests varied greatly. These ranged from less than 10 days for some agency components to more than 100 days at others (sometimes much more than 100).
>
> Numbers of pending requests carried over from year to year have increased because of increases at the Department of Homeland Security (DHS). In particular, increases have occurred at DHS's Citizenship and Immigration Services, which accounted for about 89 percent of DHS's total pending requests. . . .
>
> [C]ases have remained open for long periods when requesters ask for information on ongoing investigations. In such cases, agencies may withhold material until the investigation is complete under various exemptions, but requesters have the option of asking that the request remain open until the investigation is complete. . . . [R]equests open for more than 6 years [are] given lower priority because the component believed they could no longer be pursued in litigation, in accordance with the general federal statute of limitations. . . .
>
> Following the emphasis on backlog reduction in the Executive Order [13,392, "Improving Agency Disclosure of Information" regarding "FOIA", 5 U.S.C. § 552 (2000 & Supp. IV 2004), which can be found at: 70 Fed. Reg. 75,373 (Dec. 14, 2005)] and agency improvement plans, many agencies have shown progress in decreasing their backlogs of overdue requests as of September 2007. Of 16 agencies providing statistics, 9 decreased overdue or pending requests, 5 experienced increases, and 2 had no material change. . . . However, the statistics provided by the 16 agencies varied widely, representing a mix of both overdue and total pending cases, as well as varying time frames. Further, 3 of the 21 agencies were unable to provide statistics supporting their backlog reduction efforts, and 1 provided statistics by component, which could not be aggregated to provide an agencywide result. . . .
>
> To avoid allowing cases open for more than 6 years to remain open indefinitely, we are recommending that Justice develop and implement a strategy for closing the oldest requests in its Criminal Division, including those over 6 years old. To help ensure that comparable statistics on overdue requests are available governmentwide, we are also recommending that Justice provide additional guidance to agencies on tracking and

reporting overdue requests and planning to meet the new backlog goals. . . .

Background.

FOIA establishes a legal right of access to government records and information on the basis of the principles of openness and accountability in government. Before the act (originally enacted in 1966), an individual seeking access to federal records had faced the burden of establishing a right to examine them. FOIA established a "right to know" standard for access, instead of a "need to know" standard, and shifted the burden of proof from the individual to the government agency seeking to deny access.

FOIA provides the public with access to government information either through "affirmative agency disclosure" – publishing information in the Federal Register or on the Internet or making it available in reading rooms – or in response to public requests for disclosure. Public requests for disclosure of records are the best known type of FOIA disclosure. Any member of the public may request access to information held by federal agencies without showing a need or reason for seeking the information.

Not all information held by the government is subject to FOIA. The act prescribes nine specific categories of information that are exempt from disclosure [and] requires agencies to notify requesters of the reasons for any adverse determination (that is, a determination not to provide records) and grants requesters the right to appeal agency decisions to deny access.

[Time limits.]

[A]gencies are required to meet certain time frames for making key determinations: whether to comply with requests (20 business days from receipt of the request); responses to appeals of adverse determinations (20 business days from filing of the appeal); and whether to provide expedited processing of requests (10 calendar days from receipt of the request). The Congress did not establish a statutory deadline for making releasable records available, but instead required agencies to make them available promptly.

Linda D. Koontz, *Agencies Are Making Progress in Reducing Backlog, But Additional Guidance Is Needed*, Gov't Acct. Office, GAO-08-344, March 14, 2008, *presented to* Subcomm. on Info. Pol'y, Census, and Nat'l Archives, Comm. on Oversight & Gov't Reform House of Representatives.

b. Not everyone agrees with the positive GAO assessment above. Since 2005, a dozen different bills have been be introduced to amend FOIA and thereby address various issues. Senator John Cornyn and Senator Patrick Leahy have introduced a bill that "updates the Freedom of Information Act (FOIA) to address undue delays and onerous burdens that often greet Americans looking for information from their government." The Bill, originally introduced in 2005 as S. 394, has not been adopted as this text goes to press. *See* John Cornyn, *Texas Times: More Texas Sunshine in Washington*, Southeast Tex. Rec. (Dec. 29, 2007).

For More Information

Senator John Cornyn's perspective on the need to amend FOIA is found at: http://www. setexasrecord.com/news/205681-texas-times-more-texas-sunshine-in-washington (last visited August 19, 2008). Cornyn's support of a change in FOIA is based on the following: "The OPEN Government Act bolsters the most fundamental requirement for an effective democracy – a free and informed citizenry. It reinforces Abraham Lincoln's notion of a government 'of the people, by the people, for the people' by facilitating the flow of information into the hands of Americans."

c. If you are interested in scholarly critiques, consider the following recent commentary on FOIA: Martin E. Halstuk, *When Secrecy Trumps Transparency: Why the Open Government Act of 2007 Falls Short*, 16 COMMLAW CONSPECTUS 427 (2008); Minjeong Kim, *Numbers Tell Part of the Story: A Comparison of FOIA Implementation Under the Clinton and Bush Administrations*, 12 COMM. L. & POL'Y 313 (2007); Robert Ratish, Note, *Democracy's Backlong: The Electronic Freedom of Information Act Ten Years Later*, 34 RUTGERS COMPUTER & TECH. L.J. 211 (2007).

d. The Department of Justice's current user guide to FOIA is available at http://www.usdoj.gov/oip/foi-act.htm (last visited July 4, 2008).

e. Within days of President Obama taking office, the following appeared in the Federal Register:

> *Government should be transparent.* Transparency promotes accountability and provides information for citizens about what their Government is doing. Information maintained by the Federal Governmetn is a national asset. My Administration will take appropriate action, consistent with law and policy, to disclose information rapidly in forms that the public can readily find and use. Executive departments and agencies should harness new technologies to put information about their operations and decisions online and readily available to the public. Executive departments and agencies should also solicit public feedback to identify information of greatest use to the public.

> *Government should be participatory.* Public engagement enhances the Government's effectiveness and improves the quality of its decisions. Knowledge is widely dispersed in society, and public officials benefit from having access to that dispersed knowledge. Executive departments and agencies should offer Americans increased opportunities to participate in policymaking and to provide their Government with the benefits of their collective expertise and information. Executive departments and agencies should also solicit public input on how we can increase and improve opportunities for public participation in Government.

> *Government should be collaborative.* Collaboration actively engages Americans in the work of their Government. Executive departments and agencies should use innovative tools, methods, and systems to cooperate among themselves, across all levels of Government, and with nonprofit organizations, businesses, and individuals in the

private sector. Executive departments and agencies should solicit public feedback to assess and improve their level of collaboration and to identify new opportunities for cooperation.

74 Fed. Reg. 4685 (January 26, 2009).

This policy varies considerably from the prior administration. Do you read the above text to apply only to the Freedom of Information Act? To what other areas of the administrative process does it apply? In particular, when an agency issues an "advanced notice of proposed rulemaking," is it obligated to solicit input or simply to make clear that input is welcomed? In response to some of these same questions, the Attorney General issued a memorandum in April 2009, explaining the Administration's FOIA policy. To access that memorandum, click HERE.

II. Public – But Unavailable

KISSINGER V. REPORTERS COMMITTEE FOR FREEDOM OF THE PRESS

445 U.S. 136 (1980)

[CHIEF JUSTICE REHNQUIST] Henry Kissinger served in the Nixon and Ford administrations for eight years. He assumed the position of Assistant to the President for National Security Affairs in January 1969. In September 1973, Kissinger was appointed to the office of Secretary of State, but retained his National Security Affairs advisory position until November 3, 1975. After his resignation from the latter position, Kissinger continued to serve as Secretary of State until January 20, 1977. Throughout this period of Government service, Kissinger's secretaries generally monitored his telephone conversations and recorded their contents either by shorthand or on tape. The stenographic notes or tapes were used to prepare detailed summaries, and sometimes verbatim transcripts, of Kissinger's conversations. Since Kissinger's secretaries generally monitored all of his conversations, the summaries discussed official business as well as personal matters. The summaries and transcripts prepared from the electronic or stenographic recording of his telephone conversations throughout his entire tenure in Government service were stored in his office at the State Department in personal files.

On October 29, 1976, . . . Kissinger arranged to move the telephone notes from his office in the State Department to the New York estate of Nelson Rockefeller. . . . Kissinger did not consult the State Department's Foreign Affairs Document and Reference Center (FADRC), the center responsible for implementing the State Department's record maintenance and disposal program. Nor did he consult the National Archives and Records Service (NARS), a branch of the General Services Administration (GSA) . . . responsible for records preservation throughout the Federal Government. Kissinger [instead] obtained an opinion from the Legal Adviser of the Department of State . . . advising him that the telephone summaries were not agency records but were his personal papers which he would be free to take when he left office.

After Kissinger effected this physical transfer of the notes, he entered into two agreements with the Library of Congress deeding his private papers. In the first agreement, dated November 12, 1976, Kissinger deeded to the United States, in care of the Library of Congress, one collection of papers. Kissinger's telephone notes were not included in this collection. . . . On December 24, 1976, by a second deed, Kissinger donated a second collection consisting of his telephone notes. This second agreement . . . provided . . . that public access to the transcripts would be permitted only with the consent, or upon the death, of the other parties to the telephone conversations in question.

On December 28, 1976, the transcripts were transported directly to the Library from the Rockefeller estate. Thus the transcripts were not reviewed by the Department of State Document and Reference Center . . . before they were delivered into the possession of the Library of Congress. Several weeks after they were moved to the Library, however, one of Kissinger's personal aides did extract portions of the transcripts for inclusion in the files of the State Department and the National Security Council. Pursuant to the instructions of the State Department Legal Adviser, the aide included in the extracts, "any significant policy decisions or actions not otherwise reflected in the Department's records."

B

Three separate FOIA requests form the basis of this litigation. All three requests were filed while Kissinger was Secretary of State, but only one request was filed prior to the removal of the telephone notes from the premises of the State Department. This first request was filed by William Safire, a New York Times columnist, on January 14, 1976. Safire requested the Department of State to produce any transcripts of Kissinger's telephone conversations between January 21, 1969, and February 12, 1971, in which (1) Safire's name appeared or (2) Kissinger discussed the subject of information "leaks" with certain named White House officials. The Department denied Safire's FOIA request by letter on February 11, 1976. The Department letter reasoned that the requested notes had been made while Kissinger was National Security Adviser and therefore were not agency records subject to FOIA disclosure.

The second FOIA request was filed on December 28 and 29, 1976, by the Military Audit Project (MAP) after Kissinger publicly announced the gift of his telephone notes to the United States and their placement in the Library of Congress. The MAP request, filed with the Department of State, sought records of all Kissinger's conversations made while Secretary of State and National Security Adviser. On January 18, 1977, the Legal Adviser of the Department of State denied the request on two grounds. First, he found that the notes were not agency records. Second, the deposit of the notes with the Library of Congress prior to the request terminated the Department's custody and control. The denial was affirmed on administrative appeal.

The third FOIA request was filed on January 13, 1977, by the Reporters Committee for Freedom of the Press (RCFP) . . . and a number of other journalists (collectively referred to as the RCFP requesters). This request also sought production of the telephone notes made by Kissinger both while he was National Security Adviser and Secretary of State. The request was denied for the same reasons given to the MAP requesters.

. . . .

We first address . . . whether the District Court possessed the authority to order the transfer of that portion of the deeded collection, including the transcripts of all conversations Kissinger made while Secretary of State, from the Library of Congress to the Department of State at the behest of the named plaintiffs. The lower courts premised this exercise of jurisdiction on their findings that the papers were "agency records" and that they had been wrongfully removed from State Department custody in violation of the Federal Records Disposal Act, 44 U.S.C. § 3303. We need not, and do not, decide whether the telephone notes are agency records, or were wrongfully removed, for even assuming an affirmative answer to each of these questions, the FOIA plaintiffs were not entitled to relief.

The question must be, of course, whether Congress has conferred jurisdiction on the federal courts to impose this remedy. . . . The FOIA represents a carefully balanced scheme of public rights and agency obligations designed to foster greater access to agency records than existed prior to its enactment. That statutory scheme authorizes federal courts to ensure private access to requested materials when three requirements have been met. Under 5 U.S.C. § 552(a)(4)(B) federal jurisdiction is dependent upon a showing that an agency has (1) "improperly"; (2) "withheld"; (3) "agency records." Judicial authority to devise remedies and enjoin agencies can only be invoked, under the jurisdictional grant conferred by § 552, if the agency has contravened all three components of this obligation. We find it unnecessary to decide whether the telephone notes were "agency records" since we conclude that a covered agency – here the State Department – has not "withheld" those documents from the plaintiffs. We also need not decide the full contours of a prohibited "withholding." We do decide, however, that Congress did not mean that an agency improperly withholds a document which has been removed from the possession of the agency prior to the filing of the FOIA request. In such a case, the agency has neither the custody nor control necessary to enable it to withhold.

In looking for congressional intent, we quite naturally start with the usual meaning of the word "withhold" itself. The requesters would have us read the "hold" out of "withhold." The act described by this word presupposes the actor's possession or control of the item withheld. A refusal to resort to legal remedies to obtain possession is simply not conduct subsumed by the verb "withhold."

The Act and its legislative history do not purport to define the word. An examination of the structure and purposes of the Act, however, indicates that Congress used the word in its usual sense. An agency's failure to sue a third party to obtain possession is not a withholding under the Act. . . . Following FOIA's enactment in 1966, the Attorney General issued guidelines for the use of all federal departments and agencies in complying with the new statute. The guidelines state that FOIA "refers, of course, only to records in being and in the possession or control of an agency. . . . [It] imposes no obligation to compile or *procure* a record in response to a request."

. . . .

The conclusion that possession or control is a prerequisite to FOIA disclosure duties is reinforced by an examination of the purposes of the Act. The Act does not obligate agencies to create or retain documents; it only obligates them to provide access to those which it in fact has created and retained. . . . If the agency is not required to create or to retain records under the FOIA, it is somewhat difficult to determine why the agency is nevertheless required to retrieve documents which have escaped its possession, but which it has not endeavored to recover. If the document is of so little interest to the agency that it does not believe the retrieval effort to be justified, the effect of this judgment on a FOIA request seems little different from the effect of an agency determination that a record should never be created, or should be discarded. n.8

> n.8 This is not to suggest that this discretionary determination by the agency relieves it of other obligations imposed by the records management Acts. The observation goes only to the nature of the public right of access provided by the FOIA.

[A]gencies normally must decide within 10 days whether to comply with a FOIA request unless they can establish "unusual circumstances" as defined in the Act. 5 U.S.C. §§ 552(a)(6)(A) (B). The "unusual circumstances" specified by the

Act include "the need to search for and collect the requested records from field facilities and other establishments that are separate from the office processing the request. "This exception for searching and collecting certainly does not suggest that Congress expected an agency to commence lawsuits in order to obtain possession of documents requested, particularly when it is seen that where an extension is allowable, the period of the extension is only for 10 days." . . . .

A similarly strong expression of congressional expectations emerges in 5 U.S.C. § 552(a)(4)(A) providing for recovery of certain costs incurred in complying with FOIA requests. This section was included in the Act in order to reduce the burdens imposed on the agencies. The agency is authorized to establish fees for the "direct costs" of "document search and duplication." The costs allowed reflect the congressional judgment as to the nature of the costs which would be incurred. Congress identified these costs, and thus the agency burdens, as consisting of "search" and "duplication." . . . . It is doubtful that Congress intended that a "search" include legal efforts to retrieve wrongfully removed documents . . . .

. . . .

C

This construction of "withholding" readily disposes of the RCFP and MAP requests. Both of these requests were filed after Kissinger's telephone notes had been deeded to the Library of Congress. The Government, through the Archivist, has requested return of the documents from Kissinger. The request has been refused. The facts make it apparent that Kissinger, and the Library of Congress as his donee, are holding the documents under a claim of right. Under these circumstances, the State Department cannot be said to have had possession or control of the documents at the time the requests were received. It did not, therefore, withhold any agency records, an indispensable prerequisite to liability in a suit under the FOIA.

III

The Safire request raises a separate question. At the time when Safire submitted his request for certain notes of Kissinger's telephone conversations, all the notes were still located in Kissinger's office at the State Department. For this reason, we do not rest our resolution of his claim on the grounds that there was no withholding by the State Department. As outlined above, the Act only prohibits the withholding of "agency records." We conclude that the Safire request sought disclosure of documents which were not "agency records" within the meaning of the FOIA.

Safire's request sought only a limited category of documents. He requested the Department to produce all transcripts of telephone conversations made by Kissinger from his White House office between January 21, 1969, and February 12, 1971, in which (1) Safire's name appeared; or (2) in which Kissinger discussed the subject of information "leaks" with General Alexander Haig, Attorney General John Mitchell, President Richard Nixon, J. Edgar Hoover, or any other official of the FBI.

The FOIA does render the "Executive Office of the President" an agency subject to the Act. 5 U.S.C. § 552(e). The legislative history is unambiguous, however, in explaining that the "Executive Office" does not include the Office of the President. . . . Safire's request was limited to a period of time in which Kissinger was serving as Assistant to the President. Thus these telephone notes were not "agency records" when they were made.

The RCFP requesters have argued that since some of the telephone notes made while Kissinger was adviser to the President may have related to the National Security Council they may have been National Security Council records and therefore subject to the Act. We need not decide when records which, in the words of the RCFP requesters, merely "relate to" the affairs of an FOIA agency become records of that agency. To the extent Safire sought discussions concerning information leaks which threatened the internal secrecy of White House policy-making, he sought conversations in which Kissinger had acted in his capacity as a Presidential adviser, only.

. . . .

The RCFP requesters nevertheless contend that if the transcripts of telephone conversations made while adviser to the President were not then "agency records," they acquired that status under the Act when they were removed from White House files and physically taken to Kissinger's office at the Department of State. We simply decline to hold that the physical location of the notes of telephone conversations renders them "agency records." The papers were not in the control of the State Department at any time. They were not generated in the State Department. They never entered the State Department's files, and they were not used by the Department for any purpose. If mere physical location of papers and materials could confer status as an "agency record" Kissinger's personal books, speeches, and all other memorabilia stored in his office would have been agency records subject to disclosure under the FOIA. It requires little discussion or analysis to conclude that the lower courts correctly resolved this question in favor of Kissinger.

Accordingly, we reverse the order of the Court of Appeals compelling production of the telephone manuscripts made by Kissinger while Secretary of State and affirm the order denying the requests for transcripts produced while Kissinger served as National Security Adviser.

Underlying Case Documents

The case referenced:

The Federal Records Disposal Act

The opinion from the legal advisor

The deed to move papers other than the telephone notes

The deed to move the telephone notes

The FOIA request of William Safire

The FOIA request of the Military Audit Project

The FOIA request of the Reporters Committee for Freedom of the Press

For sample phone transcripts click HERE, HERE and HERE.

1. In *Lechliter v. Rumsfeld*, 182 Fed. Appx. 113 (3d Cir. 2006), the appellant, Lechliter, sought review of a Department of Defense denial of a FOIA request. The lower court opinion outlined fully the details of the request. *Lechliter v. Dep't of Def.*, 371 F. Supp. 2d 589 (D. Del. 2005). Lechliter had been seeking "all [Department of Defense] documents related to the implementation of 10 U.S.C. § 1413." That section of the United States Code sets out the special compensation standards for various groups of profoundly disabled military services retirees. Lechliter claimed the Department both destroyed information and failed to generate information to which he was entitled:

> Furthermore, Lechliter alleges that the DoD improperly withheld documents by destroying responsive records. The FOIA "does not obligate agencies to create or retain documents, it only obligates them to provide access to those which it in fact has created and retained." *Kissinger v. Reporters Committee*. Here, the [DoD] employee's affidavit explained that "old papers/folders may be purged" when "program policy activity occurs," and that "[e]mail documents are regularly purged whenever time and attention allow." That affidavit, which is uncontradicted on this issue, also states that no documents "have ever been deliberately destroyed in response to, or in an effort to avoid release to Mr. Lechliter."
>
> Because the DoD is not required to produce documents "if [it] is no longer in possession of the documents for a reason that is not itself suspect," there has been no improper withholding.

a. Document retention programs – a term that actually refers to periodic document destruction – are a regular part of government agency activity. If a

Food for Thought

In recent years, varying standards have issued regarding document retention and it is unsafe to generalize about the period of time an agency (or a private practitioner, for that matter) must retain records. Given the obligations in FOIA, should there be a centralized electronic repository for all documents?

document is part of a "transaction of public business" it must be maintained. Under the Federal Records Act, 44 U.S.C. § 2101 et seq., an agency archivist must develop both retention programs and an enforcement scheme. If documents are destroyed, the archivist must report to the agency head and, in some instances, to Congress and the President. 44 U.S.C. § 2115(b). As *Kissinger* makes clear, however, this legislation does not create a private right of action.

b. The papers of the President, after leaving office, as opposed to those of his or her advisors, are handled through the Presidential Records Act (PRA), 44 U.S.C. §§ 2201-2207 (2000), rather than FOIA. The Act was passed in 1978 and makes records of a former President accessible through the Archivist of the United States. A President may restrict access if the content involves national defense and is classified though Executive Order for up to 12 years. Thereafter, the FOIA can be used to secure presidential records unless a legitimate claim of Executive privilege has been raised.

Take Note

In Fall, 2001, President George W. Bush issued Executive Order 13,233, a directive that purported to include work-product and attorney-client privilege claims within Executive privilege and required a showing of a "demonstrated, specific need," something not contemplated in the 1978 Act. Further, E.O. 13,233 gave the President the power to deny requests applicable to former holders of that office. For a thorough critique of this legislation and related fields, see Jane E. Kirtley, *Transparency and Accountability in a Time of Terror: The Bush Administration's Assault on Freedom of Information*, 11 COMM. L. & POL'Y 479 (2006). On January 21, 2009, President Barack Obama issued E.O. 13,489 repealling E.O. 13,233.

c. Does *Kissinger* cover message slips, appointment logs, appointment calendars? If these are created for personal reference, not relied on by agency staff, not part of agency files nor under the agency's control, they are outside FOIA. *Bloomberg, L.P. v. SEC*, 357 F. Supp. 2d 156 (D.D.C. 2004).

d. As to seemingly personal e-mail to and from government employees, take a look at the exceptions to FOIA, 5 U.S.C. § 552 et. seq., and FOIA, 5 U.S.C. § 552 (Supp. II 1996) – neither provide useful guidance on e-mail. Should they? Is it possible to generalize helpfully about this medium?

2. As you begin to work through FOIA, consider also the Federal Advisory Committee Act (FACA), 5 U.S.C. app. §§ 1-15 (2000) (enacted 1972). That legislation is designed to incorporate principles of open government and, while FACA disclosure requirements are subject to the FOIA exemptions, there are interesting differences and comparisons to be made. In *NRDC v. Johnson*, 488 F.3d 1002 (D.C. Cir. 2007), the court made clear that "the government's obligation to make documents available under FACA does not depend on whether someone has filed a

FOIA request for those documents. FACA incorporates the FOIA exemptions, see 5 U.S.C. App. 2, § 10(b), but the government's duty to disclose is otherwise independent of FOIA. We think it follows that a plaintiff does not have to file a formal FOIA request before bringing an action seeking a remedy for alleged FACA violations, including violations of the statute's disclosure requirements." This policy was first articulated in *Food Chemical News v. DHHS*, 980 F.2d 1468, 1472 (D.C. Cir. 1993).

3. *Forsham v. Harris, Secretary of Health, Education, and Welfare*, 445 U.S. 169 (1980), was the companion decision to *Kissinger*:

> **Make the Connection**
>
> FACA covers any "committee, board, commission, council, conference, panel, task force, or other similar group, or any subcommittee . . . established or utilized by the President," with at least one nongovernment member. 5 U.S.C. app. §§ 2-3 (2005). It does not include "various entities within the Executive Office of the President [such as] the Executive Residence of the President, the Council of Economic Advisers, the National Security Council, the Office of Counsel to the President, and the President's transition team." For an interesting article on FACA and the Office of the President, see Michael J. Mongan, *Fixing FACA: The Case for Exempting Presidential Advisory Committees from Judicial Review Under the Federal Advisory Committee Act,* 58 STAN. L. REV. 895 (2005).

> In 1959, a group of private physicians and scientists specializing in the treatment of diabetes formed the University Group Diabetes Program (UGDP). The UGDP conducted a long-term study of the effectiveness of five diabetes treatment regimens. . . . The study generated more than 55 million records documenting the treatment of over 1,000 diabetic patients who were monitored for a 5- to 8-year period. In 1970, the UGDP presented the initial results of its study indicating that the treatment of adult-onset diabetics with tolbutamide increased the risk of death from cardiovascular disease over that present when diabetes was treated by the other methods studied. The UGDP later expanded these findings to report a similarly increased incidence of heart disease when patients were treated with phenformin hydrochloride. These findings have in turn generated substantial professional debate.

> The Committee on the Care of the Diabetic (CCD), a national association of physicians involved in the treatment of diabetes mellitus patients, have been among those critical of the UGDP study. CCD requested the UGDP to grant it access to the raw data in order to facilitate its review of the UGDP findings, but UGDP has declined to comply with that request. CCD therefore sought to obtain the information under the Freedom of Information Act. . . . The UGDP study has been solely funded by federal grants in the neighborhood of $ 15 million . . . awarded . . . by the National Institute of Arthritis, Metabolism, and Digestive Diseases (NIAMDD), a federal agency [that is a sub, sub, sub brach of the Department of Health, Education and Welfare (HEW)]. The grantee [UGDP] retained control of its records . . . and neither the NIAMDD grants nor related regulations shift ownership of such data to the Federal Government. . . .

> An additional connection between the Federal Government and the UGDP study has

occurred through the activities of the Food and Drug Administration. After the FDA[, another agency within HEW,] was apprised of the UGDP results, the agency issued a statement recommending that physicians use tolbutamide in the treatment of diabetes only in limited circumstances. After the UGDP reported finding a similarly higher incidence of cardiovascular disease with the administration of phenformin, the FDA proposed changes in the labeling of these oral hypoglycemic drugs to warn patients of cardiovascular hazards. . . .

Petitioners . . . initiated a series of FOIA requests seeking access to the UGDP raw data. On August 7, 1975, HEW denied their request for the UGDP data on the grounds that no branch of HEW had ever reviewed or seen the raw data; that the FDA's proposed relabeling action relied on the UGDP published reports and not on an analysis of the underlying data; that the data were the property of the UGDP, a private group; and that the agencies were not required to acquire and produce those data under the FOIA. The following month petitioners filed this FOIA suit in the United States District Court for the District of Columbia . . . .

As we hold in the companion case of *Kissinger v. Reporters Committee for Freedom of the Press*, it must be established that an "agency" has "improperly withheld agency records" for an individual to obtain access to documents through a FOIA action. We hold here that HEW need not produce the requested data because they are *not* "agency records" within the meaning of FOIA. . . . Congress could have provided that the records generated by a federally funded grantee were federal property even though the grantee has not been adopted as a federal entity. But Congress has not done so, reflecting the same regard for the autonomy of the grantee's records as for the grantee itself. . . .

Congress contemplated that an agency must first either create or obtain a record as a prerequisite to its becoming an "agency record" within the meaning of FOIA. . . . [I]t would be stretching the ordinary meaning of the words to call the data in question here "agency records" . . . . [T]he Freedom of Information Act provides the following threshold requirement for agency records:

> "records" includes all books, papers, maps, photographs, machine readable materials, or other documentary materials, regardless of physical form or characteristics, *made or received* by an agency of the United States Government under Federal law or in connection with the transaction of public business. . . .

44 U.S.C. § 3301. (Emphasis added.) . . . . We think [this] conclusion is overborne neither by an agency's potential access to the grantee's information nor by its reliance on that information in carrying out the various duties entrusted to it by Congress. The Freedom of Information Act deals with "agency records," not information in the abstract. Petitioners place great reliance on the fact that HEW has a right of access to the data, and a right if it so chooses to obtain permanent custody of the UGDP records. But in this context FOIA applies to records which have been *in fact* obtained, and not to records which merely *could have been* obtained. To construe FOIA to embrace the latter class of documents would be to extend the reach of the Act beyond what we believe Congress intended. . . .

We . . . therefore conclude that the data petitioners seek are not "agency records" within the meaning of FOIA. UGDP is not a "federal agency" as that term is defined in FOIA, and the data petitioners seek have not been created or obtained by a federal agency. Having failed to establish this threshold requirement, petitioners' FOIA claim must fail, and the judgment of the Court of Appeals is accordingly affirmed.

Hypothetical

The newly appointed general counsel of a large manufacturer in Illinois, whose last general counsel was fired after 15 years of incompetent and negligent service, is concerned that she is not aware of significant pending fines, compliance warnings and other adverse actions issued by federal agencies with authority over the manufacturer. Because the manufacturer has had dealings with over 20 federal agencies over the years, the new general counsel would like to file a "blanket" FOIA request with the Federal government as a whole, requesting copies of all pending enforcement items involving the manufacturer. Will she be able to succeed in filing such a sweeping, all-inclusive FOIA request?

Hypothetical

Suppose that you are an employee of a federal agency and

a.   Your boss sends you to an inter-agency meeting. You take notes in long-hand to brief your boss when you get back. You do that and shove the notes into your desk and forget about them. Someone files a FOIA request for all agency records concerning the topic in question. Must you turn over your notes?

b.   You are daydreaming a bit. You sketch out an interesting project that you think would be helpful for the agency to undertake. You put your notes in your desk, thinking you will propose it to your boss, but somehow you never get around to it. Are your notes an agency record?

c.   You write a memo to your boss that makes four policy recommendations. She circles the third one and writes in the margin: "Let's do this one." A FOIA request is filed seeking all documents relevant to the decision. Must you turn over this document or only parts of it?

4. Interpretation of *Kissinger* and *Forsham* continued in *United States Department of Justice v. Tax Analysts*, 492 U.S. 136 (1989):

> The question presented is whether the Freedom of Information Act (FOIA or Act), 5 U.S.C. § 552, requires the United States Department of Justice (Department) to make available copies of district court decisions that it receives in the course of litigating tax cases on behalf of the Federal Government. We hold that it does.
>
> The Department's Tax Division represents the Federal Government in nearly all civil tax cases . . . . Because it represents a party in litigation, the Tax Division receives copies of all opinions and orders issued by these courts in such cases. Copies of these decisions are made for the Tax Division's staff attorneys. The original documents are sent to the official files kept by the Department. . . .
>
> Respondent Tax Analysts publishes a weekly magazine, Tax Notes, which reports on legislative, judicial, and regulatory developments in the field of federal taxation to a readership largely composed of tax attorneys, accountants, and economists. As one of its regular features, Tax Notes provides summaries of recent federal-court decisions on tax issues. To supplement the magazine, Tax Analysts provides full texts of these decisions in microfiche form. Tax Analysts also publishes Tax Notes Today, a daily electronic data base that includes summaries and full texts of recent federal-court tax decisions.
>
> In late July 1979, Tax Analysts filed a FOIA request in which it asked the Department to make available all district court tax opinions and final orders received by the Tax Division earlier that month. The Department denied the request on the ground that these decisions were not Tax Division records. Tax Analysts then appealed this denial administratively. While the appeal was pending, Tax Analysts agreed to withdraw its request in return for access to the Tax Division's weekly log of tax cases decided by the federal courts. These logs list the name and date of a case, the docket number, the names of counsel, the nature of the case, and its disposition.
>
> The FOIA confers jurisdiction on the district courts "to enjoin the agency from withholding agency records and to order the production of any agency records improperly withheld." § 552(a)(4)(B). Under this provision, "federal jurisdiction is dependent on a showing that an agency has (1) 'improperly' (2) 'withheld' (3) 'agency records.'" *Kissinger v. Reporters Committee for Freedom of Press*. Unless each of these criteria is met, a district court lacks jurisdiction to devise remedies to force an agency to comply with the FOIA's disclosure requirements.
>
> In this case, all three jurisdictional terms are at issue. Although these terms are defined neither in the Act nor in its legislative history, we do not write on a clean slate. Nine Terms ago we decided three cases that explicated the meanings of these partially overlapping terms. *Kissinger v. Reporters Committee for Freedom of Press*; *Forsham v. Harris*; [and] *GTE Sylvania, Inc. v. Consumers Union of United States, Inc.* These decisions form the basis of our analysis of Tax Analysts' requests.
>
> We consider first whether the district court decisions at issue are "agency records," a term elaborated upon both in *Kissinger* and in *Forsham*. . . . Two requirements emerge from *Kissinger* and *Forsham*, each of which must be satisfied for requested materials to qualify as "agency records." First, an agency must "either create or obtain" the

requested materials "as a prerequisite to its becoming an 'agency record' within the meaning of the FOIA." In performing their official duties, agencies routinely avail themselves of studies, trade journal reports, and other materials produced outside the agencies both by private and governmental organizations. To restrict the term "agency records" to materials generated internally would frustrate Congress' desire to put within public reach the information available to an agency in its decision-making processes. As we noted in *Forsham*, "The legislative history of the FOIA abounds with . . . references to records *acquired* by an agency."

Second, the agency must be in control of the requested materials at the time the FOIA request is made. By control we mean that the materials have come into the agency's possession in the legitimate conduct of its official duties. This requirement accords with *Kissinger's* teaching that the term "agency records" is not so broad as to include personal materials in an employee's possession, even though the materials may be physically located at the agency. This requirement is suggested by *Forsham* as well, where we looked to the definition of agency records in the Records Disposal Act, 44 U.S.C. § 3301. Under that definition, agency records include "all books, papers, maps, photographs, machine readable materials, or other documentary materials, regardless of physical form or characteristics, made or received by an agency of the United States Government *under Federal law or in connection with the transaction of public business* . . . ." Furthermore, the requirement that the materials be in the agency's control at the time the request is made accords with our statement in *Forsham* that the FOIA does not cover "information in the abstract."

Applying these requirements here, we conclude that the requested district court decisions constitute "agency records." First, it is undisputed that the Department has obtained these documents from the district courts. This is not a case like *Forsham*, where the materials never in fact had been received by the agency. The Department contends that a district court is not an "agency" under the FOIA, but this truism is beside the point. The relevant issue is whether an agency covered by the FOIA has "create[d] or obtaine[d]" the materials sought, *Forsham*, not whether the organization from which the documents originated is itself covered by the FOIA.

Second, the Department clearly controls the district court decisions that Tax Analysts seeks. Each of Tax Analysts' FOIA requests referred to district court decisions in the agency's possession at the time the requests were made. This is evident from the fact that Tax Analysts based its weekly requests on the Tax Division's logs, which compile information on decisions the Tax Division recently had received and placed in official case files. . . . The Department counters that it does not control these decisions because the district courts retain authority to modify the decisions even after they are released, but this argument, too, is beside the point. The control inquiry focuses on an agency's possession of the requested materials, not on its power to alter the content of the materials it receives. Agencies generally are not at liberty to alter the content of the materials that they receive from outside parties. An authorship-control requirement thus would sharply limit "agency records" essentially to documents generated by the agencies themselves. This result is incompatible with the FOIA's goal of giving the public access to all nonexempted information received by an agency as it carries out its mandate. Affirmed.

[JUSTICE BLACKMUN, dissenting.]

The Court's analysis, I suppose, could be regarded as a fairly routine one. I do not join the Court's opinion, however, because . . . the result the Court reaches cannot be one that was within the intent of Congress when the FOIA was enacted. Respondent Tax Analysts, although apparently a nonprofit organization for federal income tax purposes, is [a] business . . . . It sells summaries of these opinions . . . . There is no question that this material is available elsewhere. But it is quicker and more convenient, and less "frustrat[ing]," for respondent to have the Department do the work and search its files and produce the items than it is to apply to the respective court clerks. This, I feel, is almost a gross misuse of the FOIA.

What respondent demands, and what the Court permits, adds nothing whatsoever to public knowledge of Government operations[,] the real purpose of the FOIA . . . . If, as I surmise, the Court's decision today is outside the intent of Congress in enacting the statute, Congress perhaps will rectify the decision forthwith and will give everyone concerned needed guidelines for the administration and interpretation of this somewhat opaque statute.

———

1. Securing documents from the Office of Administration ("OA") of the President continues to present FOIA challenges. In Citizens for Responsibility & Ethics in Washington v. Office of Administration, 559 F. Supp. 2d 9 (D.D.C. 2008), the court found the OA is not an agency for purposes of the FOIA. Three weeks later, the court ordered the OA to preserve all records that may be subject to FOIA disclosure in the event the D.C. Circuit or the Supreme Court reverses the decision. Citizens for Responsibility & Ethics in Washington v. Office of Administration, 565 F. Supp. 2d 23 (D.D.C. 2008).

III. The Vaughn Index

Vaughn v. Rosen, 484 F.2d 820 (D.C. Cir. 1973), mentioned in the introduction to this chapter, can require agencies, in certain circumstances, to identify each document withheld and provide an explanation for that withholding. These indices can include a discussion of how a particular interest would be affected adversely, the FOIA exception on which the agency relies, and can be accompanied by other information – including sworn affidavits supporting the agency's position. That said, the D.C. Circuit noted that there is no requirement agencies produce "repetitive, detailed explanations" when "codes and categories may be sufficient[]." *Judicial Watch, Inc. v. Food & Drug Admin.*, 449 F.3d 141, 147 (D.C. Cir. 2006).

1. *Miccosukee Tribe of Indians of Florida v. United States*, 516 F.3d 1235 (11th Cir. 2008).

[The] Tribe contends that the district court erred by finding the EPA conducted an adequate search in response to the Tribe's two FOIA requests . . . for documents concerning the EPA's Clean Water Act review of Florida's amendments to the Everglades Forever Act ("EFA") and the Phosphorus Rule for the Everglades Protection Area. . . .

The D.C. Circuit observed in *Vaughn v. Rosen*, that because the nature of FOIA "seriously distorts the traditional adversary nature of our legal system's form of dispute resolution," the agency must give the requester of information "adequate specificity . . . to assur[e] proper justification by the governmental agency." The *Vaughn* decision marked the beginning of a tool (and in some Circuits, a requirement) . . . i.e., a list containing the information claimed as exempt and [in a later opinion, a] detailed justification, specifically identifying the reasons why a particular exemption is relevant and correlating those claims with the particular part of a withheld document to which they apply. . . .

This Circuit has held that in FOIA litigation, an agency has the burden of proving that it properly invoked any FOIA exemptions when it decided to withhold information. *Ely v. FBI*, 781 F.2d 1487, 1489-90 (11th Cir. 1986). In reviewing a district court's finding of privilege for exemptions, we have two duties: we must determine (1) whether the district court had an adequate factual basis for the decision rendered; and (2) whether, upon this basis, the decision reached was clearly erroneous. A trial court may utilize alternate methods by which to make the adequate factual basis determination: in camera review and the so-called *Vaughn* Index. . . . [An] agency may rely on affidavits (in lieu of a *Vaughn* Index) to meet its burden so long as they provide an adequate factual basis for the district court to render a decision.

Food for Thought

Even with the *Vaughn* index, this process still requires a modicum of good faith. How would a requester know if the agency is being forthright in its responses and explanations for nondisclosure – and how would one know if the list of documents the agency provides is complete? Faith in the process is helped somewhat by the fact that a nondisclosure is both a violation of the United States Code and results in a "dead" document, i.e., should it surface in the future, the agency staff responsible for the failure to reveal the existence of the document would be subject to personal sanction and the agency could end up with a "show cause order."

2. In *Campaign for Responsible Transplantation (CRT) v. FDA*, 511 F.3d 187 (D.C. Cir. 2007), the agency and CRT disagreed on the sufficiency of the agency's explanations for nondisclosure. To expedite resolution of the dispute, FDA produced and submitted to the court two sample *Vaughn* indices to demonstrate the adequacy of their procedure. The District Court found the indices insufficient and the case went to the D.C. Circuit:

A *Vaughn* index is created by an agency to assist courts and FOIA requesters when the agency claims that responsive documents are exempt from disclosure. The index is supposed to "describe with reasonable specificity the material withheld" and justify why each responsive document is exempt from disclosure under FOIA. . . .

FDA balked at CRT's request for a comprehensive *Vaughn* index. The agency argued

that it would take two years to compile the index sought by CRT and require review
of nearly a quarter of a million pages of documents. . . .

[In the *Vaughn* case] we were troubled by the fact that only the party opposing disclosure
had any knowledge about the documents sought. We also expressed concern over
the "distort[ing]" effects of this information asymmetry on "the traditional adversary
nature of our legal system's form of dispute resolution." We therefore held that the
District Court should "no longer accept conclusory and generalized allegations of
exemptions" from Government agencies in FOIA cases. . . .

c. In *Mead Data v. United States Air Force*, 566 F.2d 242, 251 (D.C. Cir. 1977),
the court held that the requirement for an explanation "cannot be satisfied by the
sweeping and conclusory citation of an exemption plus submission of disputed
material for *in camera* inspection. . . ." Does this mean the government should
spend two years and organize a quarter million pages of arguably exempt materials?

On one hand, there is the matter of cost, inefficiency, the dreaded ossification
phenomenon, flouting the goals of Paperwork Reduction Act, 44 U.S.C §§ 3501-
3520, and the balancing from *Mathews v. Eldridge* – in the end, even the right to
due process may be caught up in a cost/benefit calculus.

On the other (equally crowded) hand are James Madison and Thomas Jefferson: "A
popular Government, without popular information, or the means of acquiring it,
is but a Prologue to a Farce or a Tragedy; or, perhaps both. Knowledge will forever
govern ignorance; And a people who mean to be their own Governors, must arm
themselves with the power which knowledge gives." Letter from James Madison
to W.T. Barry (Aug. 4, 1822), *referenced in* THE COMPLETE MADISON 337, 337 (Saul
K. Padover ed., 1953). Jefferson wrote that, "an informed citizenry is vital to the
functioning of a democratic society." Attributed to Jefferson in Stephen Gidiere &
Jason Forrester, *Balancing Homeland Security and Freedom of Information*, 16 NAT.
RESOURCES & ENV'T 139 (2002). Prior to his presidency, Jefferson offered a Bill for
the More General Diffusion of Knowledge for the Commonwealth of Virginia "to
block the rise of tyranny, and [assert] that an informed citizenry was ultimately
the only effective barrier." Quite obviously, "[t]he idea that an informed citizenry
was critical to the success of the republic served as a guiding principle when [the
founders] designed American institutions." RICHARD D. BROWN, THE STRENGTH OF A
PEOPLE: THE IDEA OF AN INFORMED CITIZENRY IN AMERICA, 1650-1870 xv (1996). *See*
Ryan Blaine Bennett, *Safeguards of the Republic: The Responsibility of the American
Lawyer to Preserve the Republic Through Law-Related Education*, 14 N.D. J. L. ETHICS
& PUB. POL'Y 651 (2000).

JUDICIAL WATCH, INC. V. FOOD & DRUG ADMINISTRATION

449 F.3d 141 (D.C. Cir. 2006)

[JUDGE SENTELLE] In September 2000, the FDA approved the drug mifepristone, better known as RU-486, for "medical abortion" during the first 49 days of pregnancy. Shortly thereafter, Judicial Watch submitted a FOIA request seeking all mifepristone-related documents in the FDA's possession. A few months later, having not received any documents, Judicial Watch sought to enforce its request in the District Court. . . . The District Court ordered the FDA to produce all responsive documents by October 15, 2001.

After searching about 250,000 pages of information, the FDA disclosed over 9,000 relevant pages to Judicial Watch on a compact disc. It withheld over 4,000 other relevant documents in their entirety and parts of almost 2,000 more. The FDA compiled and produced a 1,500-page *Vaughn* index to summarize the withholdings. *See Vaughn v. Rosen*, 484 F.2d 820 (D.C. Cir. 1973). In addition to its *Vaughn* index, the FDA filed a supporting declaration by Andrea Masciale, who supervised the FDA's search and review of documents for Judicial Watch's FOIA request. The Masciale declaration described the types of withheld information and defended the application of [certain] FOIA Exemptions . . . to that information. . . .

The FDA moved for summary judgment. Judicial Watch opposed the motion claiming the FDA . . . filed an inadequately detailed *Vaughn* index . . . and invoked several FOIA exemptions improperly. The District Court granted summary judgment for the FDA as to all matters. Judicial Watch . . . appeals . . . . Although we find nothing structurally wrong with the FDA's submission, we find merit in the narrower part of Judicial Watch's adequacy argument, specifically that the FDA has vaguely described some individual documents. . . .

. . . .

. . . When a party submits a FOIA request, it faces an "asymmetrical distribution of knowledge" where the agency alone possesses, reviews, discloses, and withholds the subject matter of the request. The agency would therefore have a nearly impregnable defensive position save for the fact that the statute places the burden "on the agency to sustain its action." 5 U.S.C. § 552(a)(4)(B).

Possessing both the burden of proof and all the evidence, the agency has the difficult obligation to justify its actions without compromising its original withholdings by disclosing too much information. The *Vaughn* index provides a way for the defending agency to do just that. By allowing the agency to provide descriptions of withheld documents, the index gives the court and the challenging party a measure of access without exposing the withheld information. The *Vaughn* index . . . forces the government to analyze carefully any material withheld, it enables the trial court to fulfill its duty of ruling on the applicability of the exemption, and it enables the adversary system to operate by giving the requester as much information as possible, on the basis of which he can present his case to the trial court. . . . Among other things, the agency may [also] submit supporting affidavits or seek in camera review of some or all of the documents "so long as they give the reviewing court a reasonable basis to evaluate the claim of privilege." . . . .

In this case, the FDA took a combined approach. In response to Judicial Watch's FOIA request, it produced a 1,500-page *Vaughn* index and supplemented the index with the supporting declaration of Andrea Masciale. The index itself includes eleven categories, consisting of the following: (1) an index identification number; (2) the document's subject; (3) its date; (4) the author; (5) the recipient; (6) the total number of pages; (7) a category entitled "Attach Page"; (8) the disposition (that is, whether entirely or partially withheld); (9) the reason for being withheld; (10) the statutory authority for the withholding; and (11) the number of pages containing withheld information. Whereas the index takes a document-specific approach, the Masciale declaration steps through the claimed exemptions. It avoids discussion of individual documents, instead describing the kinds of information withheld and how they relate to the exemptions. . . .

Judicial Watch argues that the FDA's index/affidavit combination fails because it does not treat each document individually. Context dictates our approach to the particularity required of agencies. . . . Broad, sweeping claims of privilege without reference to the withheld documents would impede judicial review and undermine the functions served by the *Vaughn* index requirement. The agency must therefore explain why the exemption applies to the document or type of document withheld and may not ignore the contents of the withheld documents.

On the other hand, abstraction can aid court review when drawing from specific examples. We have never required repetitive, detailed explanations for each piece of withheld information – that is, codes and categories may be sufficiently particularized to carry the agency's burden of proof. Especially where the agency has disclosed and withheld a large number of documents, categorization and repetition provide efficient vehicles by which a court can review withholdings that implicate the same exemption for similar reasons. In such cases, particularity may actually impede court review and undermine the functions served by a *Vaughn* index.

. . . Judicial Watch asserts that the FDA claimed exemptions only in sweeping and conclusory generalities. We disagree. The FDA explained itself through *commonalities*, not *generalities*. Unsurprisingly, among thousands of withheld documents, certain topics and exemptions arose on multiple occasions. The index tied each individual document to one or more exemptions, and the Masciale declaration linked the substance of each exemption to the documents' common elements. No rule of law precludes the FDA from treating common documents commonly. The FDA's index/affidavit combination does not resemble the general assertions of privilege that we have rejected in the past.

And we do not fault the FDA for using the language of the statute as part of its explanation for withholding documents. As long as it links the statutory language to the withheld documents, the agency may even "parrot" the language of the statute. There are only so many ways the FDA could have claimed Exemptions 4, 5, and 6 for the thousands of documents generated during mifepristone's approval. Again, our focus is on the functions served by the *Vaughn* index: to organize the withheld documents in a way that facilitates litigant challenges and court review of the agency's withholdings. The FDA's decision to tie each document to one or more claimed exemptions in its index and then summarize the commonalities of the documents in a supporting affidavit is a legitimate way of serving those functions.

Our holding that the FDA produced a structurally sound *Vaughn* index[, however,] does not address the entirety of Judicial Watch's challenge to the adequacy of the index. Judicial Watch also argues that many of the index's document descriptions are indecipherable or lack information relevant to its merits claim. . . .

Exemption 4 allows agencies to withhold documents containing matters that are "trade secrets and commercial or financial information obtained from a person and privileged or confidential." 5 U.S.C. § 552(b)(4). Unlike many other types of information subject to an agency's control, materials implicating Exemption 4 are generally not developed within the agency. Instead, it must procure commercial information from third parties, either by requirement or by request. The agency thus has an incentive to be a good steward of that information: Disclosure could result in competitive disadvantages to the submitting entity, discouraging them from giving quality information in the future. The agency may therefore withhold involuntarily submitted information as confidential if disclosure would (1) impair the agency's ability to get information in the future or (2) cause substantial competitive harm to the entity that submitted the information. . . . [During the drug approval process the] FDA requires applying companies to submit volumes of information related to a drug's development, composition, safety, and manufacture. . . .

. . . .

The FDA asserts that its affidavit, along with those of the intervenors, makes up for any deficiency in its document descriptions. We agree that the three affidavits do a number of positive things. They show that the documents containing information from INDs or NDAs likely include either trade secrets or commercial information that would be valuable to competitors. They provide evidence, sufficient to satisfy the requirements of Exemption 4, of competitive harm in the medical abortion market that would result from the release of information in the IND. Finally, they also provide sufficient evidence to satisfy Exemption 4 of actual competition in markets for nonapproved uses of mifepristone, including cancer treatment. However persuasive, though, each of these points goes to the merits and does little to flesh out the vague document descriptions. Proving the merits of the exemption does no good if the court cannot tie the affidavits to the documents.

It is no surprise that the FDA labeled many index entries with scientific codes, lab jargon, or other identifications specific to the agency. But the FDA may not create its own cryptolect, unknown to the challenger and the court. Without a glossary or technical dictionary, any lay person would be hard pressed to understand the series of numbers and letters given as descriptions in this index. . . . By using this shorthand, the FDA missed sight of the *Vaughn* index's purpose – to enable the court and the opposing party to understand the withheld information in order to address the merits of the claimed exemptions. Scientific lingo and administrative slang, when unfamiliar, often baffle the brightest among us. To prevent confusion and aid resolution of this case, the FDA should have endeavored to make its technical world appear a little less foreign – and its shorthand a little less short – to Judicial Watch and the court. This is not to say that the FDA could not demonstrate that it properly claimed Exemption 4 as to these documents. Rather, the FDA "has failed to supply us with even the minimal information necessary to make a determination." We accordingly remand the case for further explanation of these technical descriptions.

. . . .

Underlying Case Documents

The case referenced:
Vaughn v. Rosen
The *Vaughn* index from the FDA

1. *Judicial Watch* is a complex FOIA case with many concepts in play beyond those in the edited opinion above. It is best appreciated in its full version.

In one commonly cited section of the case dealing with Exemption 6, the court permitted FDA to redact the names of agency staff in relation to the abortifacient drug RU-486 – to do otherwise the court found would be a "threat to privacy" and could create a "physical" danger to the well-being of government employees and others identified in a disclosure.

Should FOIA releases be limited based on a concern about a hypothetical unknown, unstable person lurking in the shadow of the imagination?

2. Another part of the *Judicial Watch* opinion allows the agency to protect documents if they are "both pre-decisional and deliberative." A document is pre-decisional if it is "generated before the adoption of an agency policy." The concern of the court was direct: "[T]he quality of administrative decisionmaking would be seriously undermined if agencies were forced to operate in a fishbowl because the full and frank exchange of ideas on legal or policy matters would be impossible."

Again, this is a rather vague basis for denial of information – and is of course inconsistent with the ideology and statutory mandate of "sunshined" decision-making. The Government in the Sunshine Act, 5 U.S.C. § 552b, directs that the decisional process of agencies be conducted publicly and that, *inter alia*, "[m]embers shall not jointly conduct or dispose of agency business other than in accordance with this." § 552b(b) 3(b).

Good Questions!

The idea that "business" cannot be conducted in a "fish bowl" is not difficult to understand – it is, however, in conflict with FOIA and the Sunshine legislation referenced above. What is the right balance? Are the faculty meetings that directly affect your interests conducted in the open? Assume a faculty member at your school is under consideration for tenure – would the tenure meeting be open? Should it be?

3. The concerns from *Judicial Watch* mentioned in notes 1 and 2 are balanced against what one court characterized as a "troubling history of dribbling disclosure," referring to the practice of releasing information pursuant to a FOIA request in less than a comprehensive and robust manner. *Nulankeyutmonen Nkihtaqmikon v. Bureau of Internal Affairs*, 493 F. Supp. 2d 91 (D. Me. 2007).

4. *Judicial Watch* is also used to help define when submissions to an agency are confidential, thus limiting the extent to which the agency should disclose the information through a FOIA request to a third person. In *New York City Apparel FZE v. United States Customs & Border Protection*, 484 F. Supp. 2d 77 (D.D.C.

2007), the court held as follows:

> The standard for determining whether the information is "confidential" depends on whether the information was submitted involuntarily or voluntarily. *See Judicial Watch.* Involuntarily submitted information is "confidential" if it either "(1) impair[s] the agency's ability to get information in the future; or (2) cause[s] substantial competitive harm to the entity that submitted the information." "[F]or the government to preclude disclosure based on a competitive injury claim, it must prove that the submitters [of the responsive information] (1) actually face competition, and [that] (2) substantial competitive injury would likely result from disclosure." Additionally, the agency must submit evidence showing that the submitters of the information themselves object to the disclosure of the information, as "[c]ourts have repeatedly rejected competitive harm claims when they are advanced solely by the defendant agencies."

It is not unusual to characterize FOIA requests as unfair "cheap" discovery – depositions and interrogatories are far more expensive than a FOIA request – or as a raid on the competitive secrets of one's competitors. Take a look at the "trade secret" exception to FOIA. For exemptions generally, see 5 U.S.C. § 552(a)(3) (E) (b), and for trade secrets see 5 U.S.C. § 552(b)(4), and see *Chrysler Corp. v. Brown, infra* Chapter 12, holding that there is no private right of action to protect disclosure that may be harmful to competitive interests. Consider the policies in conflict – disclosure and information on the one hand and maximizing competitive potential and supporting the copyright and patent process on the other.

IV. The Exemptions – and the Process

FOIA litigation is almost always focused on one or more of the nine exemptions to the Act 5 U.S.C. § 552(b). Below is a summary of the exemptions from the U.S. Department of Commerce web site:

> (b)(1) exemption – Protects Classified Matters of National Defense or Foreign Policy. This exemption protects from disclosure national security information concerning the national defense or foreign policy, provided that it has been properly classified in accordance with the substantive and procedural requirements of an executive order.
>
> (b)(2) exemption – Internal Personnel Rules and Practices. This exemption exempts from mandatory disclosure records "related solely to the internal personnel rules and practices of an agency." Courts have interpreted the exemption to encompass two distinct categories of information: (a) internal matters of a relatively trivial nature – sometimes referred to as "low 2" information; and (b) more substantial internal matters, the disclosure of which would risk circumvention of a legal requirement – sometimes referred to as "high 2" information.
>
> (b)(3) exemption – Information Specifically Exempted by Other Statutes. This exemption incorporates the disclosure prohibitions that are contained in various other federal statutes. As originally enacted in 1966, Exemption 3 was broadly phrased so

as to simply cover information "specifically exempted from disclosure by statute." The new Exemption 3 statute prohibits agencies from releasing under the FOIA any proposal "submitted by a contractor in response to the requirements of a solicitation for . . . competitive proposals," unless that proposal "is set forth or incorporated by reference in a contract entered into between the agency and the contractor that submitted the proposal."

(b)(4) exemption – Trade Secrets, Commercial or Financial Information. This exemption protects "trade secrets and commercial or financial information obtained from a person [that is] privileged or confidential." This exemption is intended to protect the interest of both the government and submitter of information.

(b)(5) exemption – Privileged Interagency or Intra-Agency Memoranda or Letters. This exemption protects "inter-agency or intra-agency memorandums of letters which would not be available by law to a party . . . in litigation with the agency." As such, it has been construed to "exempt those documents, and only those documents, normally privileged in the civil discovery context."

(b)(6) exemption – Personal Information Affecting an Individual's Privacy. This exemption permits the government to withhold all information about individuals in "personnel and medical files and similar files" when the disclosure of such information "would constitute a clearly unwarranted invasion of personal privacy." This exemption cannot be invoked to withhold from a requester information pertaining to the requester.

(b)(7) exemption – Investigatory Records Compiled for Law Enforcement Purposes. As amended, this exemption protects from disclosure "records or information compiled for law enforcement purposes.

> exemption 7(A) Records or information that could reasonably be expected to interfere with enforcement proceedings. This exemption authorizes the withholding of "records or information compiled for law enforcement purposes, but only to the extent that production of such law enforcement records or information . . . could reasonably be expected to interfere with enforcement proceedings."

> exemption 7(B) Disclosure which would deprive a person of a fair trial or an impartial adjudication. Records that would prevents prejudicial pretrial publicity that could impair a court proceeding, [this exemption also] protects "records or information compiled for law enforcement purposes [the disclosure of which] would deprive a person of the right to a fair trial or an impartial adjudication."

> exemption 7(C) Personal Information in Law Enforcement Records. This exemption provides protection for personal information in law enforcement records. This exemption is the law enforcement counterpart to Exemption 6, providing protection for law enforcement information the disclosure of which "could reasonably be expected to constitute an unwarranted invasion of personal privacy."

exemption 7(D) Identity of a Confidential Source. This exemption provides protection for "records or information compiled for law enforcement purposes [which] could reasonably be expected to disclose the identity of a confidential source – including a State, local, or foreign agency or authority or any private institution which furnished information on a confidential basis – and, in the case of a record or information compiled by a criminal law enforcement authority in the course of a criminal investigation, or by an agency conducting a lawful national security intelligence investigation, information furnished by a confidential source."

exemption 7(E) Circumvention of the Law. This exemption affords protection to all law enforcement information which "would disclose techniques and procedures for law enforcement investigations or prosecutions, or would disclose guidelines for law enforcement investigations or prosecutions if such disclosure could reasonably be expected to risk circumvention of the law."

exemption 7(F) Physical Safety to Protect a wide Range of Individuals. This exemption permits the withholding of information necessary to protect the physical safety of a wide range of individuals. Whereas Exemption 7(F) previously protected records that "would . . . endanger the life or physical safety of law enforcement personnel," the amended exemption provides protection to "any individual when disclosure of information about him or her "could reasonably be expected to endanger [his or her] life or physical safety."

(b)(8) exemption – Records of Financial Institutions. This exemption covers matters that are "contained in or related to examination, operating, or condition reports prepared by, on behalf of, or for the use of an agency responsible for the regulation or supervision of financial institutions."

(b)(9) exemption – Geographical and Geophysical Information Concerning Wells. This exemption covers "geological and geophysical information and data, including maps, concerning wells.

FOIA Exemptions, http://www.osec.doc.gov/omo/FOIA/exemptions.htm (last visited June 29, 2008).

The Department of Justice website lists the FOIA websites for most of the federal agencies: http://www.usdoj.gov/oip/referenceguidemay99.htm#initial (last visited June 29, 2008).

Each agency maintains a website and provides FOIA filing instructions. Just as an example, we have provided an excerpt from the Central Intelligence Agency website http://www.foia.ucia.gov/ (last visted June 29, 2008):

The CIA has established this site to provide the public with an overview of access to CIA information, including electronic access to previously released documents. Because of CIA's need to comply with the national security laws of the United

> States, some documents or parts of documents cannot be released to the public. In particular, the CIA, like other U.S. intelligence agencies, has the responsibility to protect intelligence sources and methods from disclosure. However, a substantial amount of CIA information has been and/or can be released following review. . . .

This site has links to: "What's New at FOIA?" identifying newly released or unclassified CIA documents, the 2007 CIA FOIA Annual Report, CIA FOIA backlog reduction goals for FY08, FY09, and FY10, as well as a guide on how to file a FOIA request with the CIA. The site notes that the process begins at the CIA, as at other agencies, with a simple letter providing a reasonable description of the record requested, the name and address of the requester, and a statement about the requester's fee category and willingness to pay applicable copying costs. The text recommended for the CIA is as follows:

> Under the Freedom of Information Act, 5 U.S.C. subsection 552, I am requesting information or records on [identify the subject(s) or record(s) as clearly and specifically as possible – for example, all previously released National Intelligence Estimates (NIEs) on the former Soviet Union's space program]. If there are any fees for searching for, reviewing, or copying the records, please let me know before you task my request. [or, please supply the records without informing me of the cost if the fees do not exceed a certain dollar amount, which I agree to pay.] If you deny all or any part of this request, please cite each specific exemption you think justifies your refusal to release the information and notify me of appeal procedures available under the law. Optional: If you have any questions about handling this request, you may telephone me at (home phone) or at my (office phone).

National security concerns have always affected the willingness of government to share information ("loose lips sink ships") and the first decade of the 21st Century is no exception. The FOIA exemptions begin with national security – and many requests end with an agency raising that exception. Here are several thoughtful pieces on the topic: Kam C. Wong, *The USA Patriot Act: A Policy of Alienation*, 12 MICH. J. RACE & L. 161 (2006); Paul Haridakas, *Citizen Access and Government Secrecy*, 25 ST. LOUIS U. PUB. L. REV. 3 (2006); Kathleen A. McKee, *Remarks on the Freedom of Information Act: The National Security Exemption in a Post 9/11 Era*, 4 REGENT J. INT'L L. 263 (2006); Kristen Elizabeth Uhl, Comment, *The Freedom of Information Act Post 9/11: Balancing the Public's Right to Know, Critical Infrastructure Protection, and Homeland Security*, 53 AM. U.L. REV. 261 (2003); Keith Anderson, *Is There Still a "Sound Legal Basis?": The Freedom of Information Act in the Post-9/11 World*, 64 OHIO ST. L.J. 1605 (2003).

"Loose Lips Might Sink Ships," (#6062). U.S. National Archives and Records Administration. This poster was published by the House of Seagram as part of its contribution to the national victory effort. (New York, Seagram-Distillers Corp. Artist: Essarge.) Accessed http://www.archives.gov/publications/posters/ww2.html and http://www.usmm.org/postertalk2b.html on September 15, 2008.

NATIONAL ARCHIVES & RECORDS ADMINISTRATION V. FAVISH

541 U.S. 157 (2004)

[JUSTICE KENNEDY] This case requires us to interpret the Freedom of Information Act (FOIA). FOIA does not apply if the requested data fall within one or more exemptions. Exemption 7(C) excuses from disclosure "records or information compiled for law enforcement purposes" if their production "could reasonably be expected to constitute an unwarranted invasion of personal privacy." § 552(b)(7)(C). . . . Here, the information pertains to an official investigation into the circumstances surrounding an apparent suicide. The initial question is whether the exemption extends to the decedent's family when the family objects to the release of photographs showing the condition of the body at the scene of death. If we find the decedent's family does have a personal privacy interest recognized by the statute, we must then consider whether that privacy claim is outweighed by the public interest in disclosure.

I

Vincent Foster, Jr., deputy counsel to President Clinton, was found dead in Fort Marcy Park, located just outside Washington, D.C. The United States Park Police conducted the initial investigation and took color photographs of the death scene, including 10 pictures of Foster's body. The investigation concluded that Foster committed suicide by shooting himself with a revolver. Subsequent investigations by the Federal Bureau of Investigation, committees of the Senate and the House of Representatives, and independent counsels Robert Fiske and Kenneth Starr reached the same conclusion. Despite the unanimous finding of these five investigations, a citizen interested in the matter, Allan Favish, remained skeptical. Favish . . . was the associate counsel for Accuracy in Media (AIM), which applied under FOIA for Foster's death-scene photographs. . . .

[T]he National Park Service, which then maintained custody of the pictures, resisted disclosure . . . . [C]onvinced that the Government's investigations were "grossly incomplete and untrustworthy," Favish filed the present FOIA request in his own name, seeking, among other things, 11 pictures . . . . Like the National Park Service, the Office of Independent Counsel (OIC) refused the request under Exemption 7(C). . . . [The case went through several appeals and remands after which] the District Court ordered release of the following five photographs:

> The photograph identified as "3 – VF's [Vincent Foster's] body looking down from top of berm" . . . .
>
> The photograph entitled "5 – VF's body – focusing on Rt. side of shoulder arm" . . . .
>
> The photograph entitled "1 – Right hand showing gun & thumb in guard" . . . .
>
> The photograph entitled "4 – VF's body focusing on right side and arm" . . . .
>
> The photograph entitled "5 – VF's body – focus on top of head thru heavy foliage" . . . .

On . . . appeal . . . the majority . . . affirmed in part. Without providing any explanation, it upheld the release of all the pictures, "except that photo 3 – VF's body looking down from top of berm is to be withheld." We granted OIC's petition for a writ of certiorari to resolve a conflict in the Courts of Appeals over the proper interpretation of Exemption 7(C). The only documents at issue in this case are the four photographs the Court of Appeals ordered released in its 2002 unpublished opinion. . . . It is common ground among the parties that the death-scene photographs in OIC's possession are "records or information compiled for law enforcement purposes" as that phrase is used in Exemption 7(C). This leads to the question whether disclosure of the four photographs "could reasonably be expected to constitute an unwarranted invasion of personal privacy."

Favish contends the family has no personal privacy interest covered by Exemption 7(C). His argument rests on the proposition that the information is only about the decedent, not his family. FOIA's right to personal privacy, in his view, means only "the right to control information about oneself." He quotes from our decision in *Reporters Committee*, where, in holding that a person has a privacy interest sufficient to prevent disclosure of his own rap sheet, we said "the common law and the literal understandings of privacy encompass the individual's control of information concerning his or her person." This means, Favish says, that the individual who is the subject of the information is the only one with a privacy interest.

We disagree. . . . Favish misreads the quoted sentence in *Reporters Committee* and adopts too narrow an interpretation of the case's holding. To say that the concept of personal privacy must "encompass" the individual's control of information about himself does not mean it cannot encompass other personal privacy interests as well. *Reporters Committee* had no occasion to consider whether individuals whose personal data are not contained in the requested materials also have a recognized privacy interest under Exemption 7(C).

. . . .

Certain amici in support of Favish rely on the modifier "personal" before the word "privacy" to bolster their view that the family has no privacy interest in the pictures of the decedent. This, too, misapprehends the family's position and the scope of protection the exemption provides. The family does not invoke Exemption 7(C) on behalf of Vincent Foster in its capacity as his next friend for fear that the pictures may reveal private information about Foster to the detriment of his own posthumous reputation or some other interest personal to him. If that were the case, a different set of considerations would control. Foster's relatives instead . . . seek to be shielded by the exemption to secure their own refuge from a sensation-seeking culture for their own peace of mind and tranquility, not for the sake of the deceased.

. . . Foster's sister, Sheila Foster Anthony, stated that . . . she was "horrified and devastated by [a] photograph [already] leaked to the press." "Every time I see it," Sheila Foster Anthony wrote, "I have nightmares and heart-pounding insomnia as I visualize how he must have spent his last few minutes and seconds of his life." She opposed the disclosure of the disputed pictures because "I fear that the release of photographs certainly would set off another round of intense scrutiny by the media. Undoubtedly, the photographs would be placed on the Internet for world consumption. Once again my family would be the focus of conceivably unsavory and distasteful media coverage." "[R]eleasing any photographs," Sheila Foster Anthony continued, "would constitute a painful unwarranted invasion of my privacy, my mother's privacy, my sister's privacy, and the privacy of Lisa Foster Moody (Vince's widow), her three children, and other members of the Foster family."

[W]e think it proper to conclude from Congress' use of the term "personal privacy" that it intended to permit family members to assert their own privacy rights against public intrusions long deemed impermissible under the common law and in our cultural traditions. . . . Burial rites or their counterparts have been respected in almost all civilizations from time immemorial. . . . The power of Sophocles' story in Antigone maintains its hold to this day because of the universal acceptance of the heroine's right to insist on respect for the body of her brother. The outrage at seeing the bodies of American soldiers mutilated and dragged through the streets is but a modern instance of the same understanding of the interests decent people have for those whom they have lost. . . .

[T]his well-established cultural tradition acknowledging a family's control over the body and death images of the deceased has long been recognized at common law. Indeed, this right to privacy has much deeper roots in the common law than the rap sheets held to be protected from disclosure in *Reporters Committee*. . . . We can assume Congress legislated against this background . . . when it enacted FOIA and when it amended Exemption 7(C) to extend its terms. Those enactments were also against the background of the Attorney General's consistent interpretation of the exemption to protect "members of the family of the person to whom the information pertains" . . . . We have observed that the statutory privacy right protected by Exemption 7(C) goes beyond the common law and the Constitution. It would be anomalous to hold in the instant case that the statute provides even less protection than does the common law.

. . . .

For these reasons . . . we hold that FOIA recognizes surviving family members' right to personal privacy with respect to their close relative's death-scene images. . . . Neither the deceased's former status as a public official, nor the fact that other pictures had been made public, detracts from the weighty privacy interests involved.

III

Our ruling that the personal privacy protected by Exemption 7(C) extends to family members who object to the disclosure of graphic details surrounding their relative's death does not end the case. Although this privacy interest is within the terms of the exemption, the statute directs nondisclosure only where the information "could reasonably be expected to constitute an unwarranted invasion" of the family's personal privacy. The term "unwarranted" requires us to balance the family's privacy interest against the public interest in disclosure.

FOIA is often explained as a means for citizens to know "what the Government is up to." This phrase should not be dismissed as a convenient formalism. It defines a structural necessity in a real democracy. The statement confirms that, as a general rule, when documents are within FOIA's disclosure provisions, citizens should not be required to explain why they seek the information. A person requesting the information needs no preconceived idea of the uses the data might serve. The information belongs to citizens to do with as they choose. Furthermore, as we have noted, the disclosure does not depend on the identity of the requester. As a general rule, if the information is subject to disclosure, it belongs to all.

When disclosure touches upon certain areas defined in the exemptions, however, the statute recognizes limitations that compete with the general interest in disclosure, and that, in appropriate cases, can overcome it. In the case of Exemption 7(C), the statute requires us to protect, in the proper degree, the personal privacy of citizens against the uncontrolled release of information compiled through the power of the state. . . . Where the privacy concerns addressed by Exemption 7(C) are present, the exemption requires the person requesting the information to establish a sufficient reason for the disclosure. . . . The Court of Appeals required no particular showing that any evidence points with credibility to some actual misfeasance or other impropriety. The court's holding . . . transformed Exemption 7(C) into nothing more than a rule of pleading. . . .

We hold that, where there is a privacy interest protected by Exemption 7(C) and the public interest being asserted is to show that responsible officials acted negligently or otherwise improperly in the performance of their duties, the requester must . . . produce evidence that would warrant a belief by a reasonable person that the alleged Government impropriety might have occurred. . . . [W]here the presumption is applicable, clear evidence is usually required to displace it. . . . Only when the FOIA requester has produced evidence sufficient to satisfy this standard[, however,] will there exist a counterweight on the FOIA scale for the court to balance against the cognizable privacy interests in the requested records. Allegations of government misconduct are "easy to allege and hard to disprove," so courts must insist on a meaningful evidentiary showing.

It would be quite extraordinary to say we must ignore the fact that five different inquiries into the Foster matter reached the same conclusion. . . . [T]he balancing exercise in some other case might require us to make a somewhat more precise determination regarding the significance of the public interest and the historical importance of the events in question. We might need to consider the nexus required between the requested documents and the purported public interest served by disclosure. We need not do so here, however. Favish has not produced any evidence that would warrant a belief by a reasonable person that the alleged Government impropriety might have occurred to put the balance into play.

. . . The judgment of the Court of Appeals is reversed, and the case is remanded with instructions to grant OIC's motion for summary judgment with respect to the four photographs in dispute.

————————

Underlying Case Documents

The case referenced:
The declaration of Vince Foster's sister
The district court order to release certain photographs
The affirmation by the appellate court of four of the five pictures

For information on the Fort Circle parks, of which Fort Marcy is one, click HERE or HERE.

1. A refusal to disclose information can provoke years of litigation and, at times, appear simply absurd. In *Bassiouni v. CIA*, 392 F.3d 244 (7th Cir. 2004), distinguished Professor of Law Mahmoud Cherif Bassiouni sought to have documents disclosed that the FBI had turned over to the CIA that identified – and discussed – Professor Bassiouni. After a prolonged struggle, the agency decided it was simply not inclined to turn them over. In a terse opinion upholding the government, JUDGE EASTERBROOK concluded that Professor Bassiouni – at best – could have asked for an in camera review of the documents the FBI "has clung to for 30 years." An in camera review vests in the court discretion to take action, including destruction of the materials, but does not disclose to the parties the documents in which they are identified. Unfortunately, Professor Bassiouni "want[ed] disclosure rather than erasure, and disclosure is the one thing that he cannot have."

2. The privacy interests inherent in 7(c) discussed in *Favish* produced a relatively complex balancing: First, the requester will have to show that a document that contains personal and private information should be disclosed because the "public interest sought to be advanced is a significant one, an interest more specific than having the information for its own sake." Second, the requester will have to prove the bona fides of his or her claim by "more than a bare suspicion. . . . Rather, the requester must produce evidence that would warrant a belief by a reasonable person that the alleged Government impropriety might have occurred." *Carpenter v. United States*, 470 F.3d 434 (1st Cir. 2006).

As with many FOIA doctrines, this one has a "cart before the horse" quality. How can one meet this burden in the absence of the information in the documents?

3. Among the many articles discussing *Favish*, two by Professor Clay Calvert are of particular note: Clay Calvert, *The Privacy of Death: An Emergent Jurisprudence and Legal Rebuke to Media Exploitation and a Voyeuristic Culture*, 26 LOY. L.A. ENT. L. REV. 133 (2005/2006) ("The bottom line is that we are a society . . . fixated on death. We also are a society . . . seemingly obsessively concerned with shielding

from minors' eyes images of sex on the Internet and representations of violence in video games. . . . [W]e should be similarly concerned about shielding our eyes – not just those of minors – from images of death when those images potentially exploit and degrade the personal privacy interests of relatives of the deceased."); and Clay Calvert, *Support Our [Dead] Troops: Sacrificing Political Expression Rights for Familial Control Over Names and Likenesses*, 16 Wm. & Mary Bill of Rts. J. 1169 (2008) (balancing a family's essential privacy concerns with the First Amendment and discussing, *inter alia*, the significant transformative elements test: "[W]hen a work contains significant transformative elements, it is not only especially worthy of First Amendment protection, but it is also less likely to interfere with the economic interest protected by the right of publicity. . . ." from *Comedy III Prods. v. Gary Saderup*, 21 P.3d 797 (Ca. 2001)).

4. *Favish* is, as you might guess, of great importance to the government, particularly given the desire to maintain control over information as suggested in the above notes. The Department of Justice published a summary of the main points on the case – just in case anyone missed them:

> "Survivor privacy." The concept of "survivor privacy" now is an entirely solid part of the FOIA landscape, with the Supreme Court's imprimatur, and it stands firmly available for use in appropriate (albeit by definition exceptional) cases. . . .

> "Public figure" status. The Court's decision in *Favish* also makes it clear that a person's status as a "public figure," including by virtue of being a high-level public official, should not be treated as a privacy-lessening factor under the FOIA. . . .

> "Public place." Likewise, the *Favish* decision illustrates that the occurrence of an event in a public place is no disqualifying factor for privacy protection under the FOIA either. . . .

> "Release to one is release to all." The well-known maxim under the FOIA that "release to one is release to all" was firmly reinforced in the *Favish* decision, where it was given specific application to the consequences of potential media "use" of any information disclosed. The Supreme Court in *Favish* took pains to articulate that "[a]s a general rule, if the information is subject to disclosure, it belongs to all" and . . . the potential consequences of FOIA disclosures must be viewed accordingly. . . .

> "Mere allegations." Because the *Favish* case was one in which the FOIA requester sought to justify disclosure based upon an asserted need to "show that responsible officials acted negligently or otherwise improperly in the performance of their duties," it stands first and foremost for the "public interest" proposition that requesters' mere allegations of such wrongdoing are simply "insufficient. . . ."

> "Specific public interest standard." The higher standard adopted by the Court in *Favish* for the evaluation of "agency wrongdoing" claims under the FOIA's privacy exemptions goes to both the existence and quality of the evidence that is to be required.

> "Required Nexus." Another closely related but distinct FOIA principle contained in the *Favish* decision is that especially in any case in which a FOIA requester seeks to override a privacy interest on an "agency wrongdoing" basis, neither agencies nor the courts should forget "the necessary nexus between the requested information and the asserted public interest that would be advanced by disclosure."

Supreme Court Rules for "Survivor Privacy" in *Favish*, http://www.usdoj.gov/oip/foiapost/2004foiapost12.htm (last visited June 29, 2008).

Does the Department have it right? Take a look at the opinion and run through the points raised above. Does your brief of the case match theirs?

SUN-SENTINEL COMPANY v. UNITED STATES DEPARTMENT OF HOMELAND SECURITY

431 F. Supp. 2d 1258 (D. Fla. 2006)

[JUDGE MARRA] In 2004, Florida was struck by four hurricanes in a single season. During the course of recovery from these hurricanes, FEMA . . . provide[d] Stafford Act assistance to approximately 600,000 disaster assistance applicants with damages and losses from these hurricanes. As of August 12, 2005, FEMA had disbursed . . . nearly $ 1.2 billion [to individuals nationally and] $ 31 million in individual assistance to Miami-Dade County, where the National Weather Service reported that the strongest sustained winds during Hurricane Frances were tropical storm strength, where the highest recorded accumulation of rainfall was 3.77 inches, and where there was no reported flooding. Over a dozen individuals were indicted by the United States Attorney's Office for making false claims of assistance in connection with Hurricane Frances.

The Department of Homeland Security Office of Inspector General conducted an Audit of FEMA's Individual Assistance Program in Miami-Dade County for Hurricane Frances. The Inspector General's Audit found that: (1) FEMA designated Miami-Dade County eligible for individual assistance without a proper preliminary damage assessment; (2) claims were not properly verified; (3) guidelines for making awards were generally lacking; (4) oversight of inspections was deficient and (5) funds disbursed in Miami-Dade County were not based on actual losses. Additionally, the Inspector General's Audit found that FEMA's inspectors were poorly trained and lacked oversight. That investigation, however, only examined three percent of the nearly $ 31 million awarded to Miami-Dade County residents.

[I]n January 2005, the United States Senate Committee on Governmental Affairs launched an investigation into "allegations of fraud and waste in the distribution of disaster aid by [FEMA]." The Committee . . . discovered that, in some instances, FEMA inspectors filled out forms without ever showing up at the houses to inspect the purportedly damaged property. Furthermore, as many as twenty-two percent of FEMA inspectors processing individual assistance claims in Florida had criminal records. . . . [T]he Sun-Sentinel, pursuant to the Federal Freedom of Information Act . . . requested a copy in electronic format of FEMA's National Emergency Management Information System ("NEMIS"), a database used to track FEMA assistance requests and awards associated with Hurricanes Charley, Frances, Ivan and Jeanne. In response, FEMA provided the Sun-Sentinel with 9,000 pages of eligibility and inspection spreadsheets, which provided a breakdown by zip codes of individual assistance applications and payouts for Hurricane Frances for Miami-Dade County from September 4, 2004 through October 18, 2004. FEMA withheld the names and addresses of individual aid claimants and the addresses of damaged properties. FEMA asserted FOIA Exemption 6 and the Privacy Act regulations, 6 C.F.R. § 5.21(f) as the bases for withholding that information.

By letter dated October 18, 2004, the Sun-Sentinel requested, among other things, the names of inspectors who conducted inspections in Miami-Dade County, certain e-mails to or from Michael Brown, the former Under Secretary of FEMA, and audits, inspector general reviews and quality control reviews of the FEMA Individual Assistance Programs. On January 6, 2005, FEMA provided the Sun-Sentinel with the names of the companies providing inspectors for Miami-Dade County. FEMA informed the Sun-Sentinel that it did not maintain records of the names of individual inspectors. FEMA withheld the inspectors' identification numbers under FOIA Exemption[] 6. Additionally, FEMA asserted that five e-mails were redacted and twenty pages of e-mails were withheld pursuant to FOIA Exemption 5.

By letter dated January 19, 2005, the Sun-Sentinel made a request, pursuant to FOIA, for the same information from the NEMIS database but expanded the new request to include several additional disasters. . . . In response to this request, FEMA provided . . . inspection information on each particular individual claimant which included: category of assistance[,] assistance status and type, eligibility date, eligible amount, ownership status, water level, cause of damage, insurance status for each item, description of each item, including personal property description, clothing, real property damage type, damage level as well as other information. . . . FEMA asserted FOIA Exemption 6 as its basis for withholding the names and addresses of individual aid claimants. . . . On March 8, 2005, the Sun-Sentinel filed the Complaint in this action. . . .

The following exemptions have been invoked by FEMA in the instant case:

. . . .

b. Exemption 5 which allows a government agency to withhold the "inter-agency or intra-agency memorandums or letters which would not be available by law to a party other than an agency in litigation with the agency." 5 U.S.C. § 552(b)(5). FEMA invoked this exemption with respect to the disclosure of the e-mails.

c. Exemption 6 which allows a government agency to withhold "personnel and medical files and similar files the disclosure of which would constitute a clearly unwarranted invasion of personal privacy." 5 U.S.C. § 552(b)(6). FEMA invoked this exemption with respect to the disclosure of the inspectors' names and identification numbers as well as the disaster claimants' names and addresses.

When Exemption 6 is claimed, the proper analysis begins with an examination of the Privacy Act. That act prohibits the disclosure of "any record which is contained in a system of records by any means of communication to any person . . . except pursuant to a written request by, or with the prior written consent of, the individual to whom the record pertains, unless disclosure of the record would be . . . required under [FOIA]." 5 U.S.C. § 552a(b)(2). The Privacy Act serves to "impose a standard of quality and diligence on the maintenance of government records." . . . . Although names and addresses meet the threshold requirement for protection under Exemption 6 [and therefore would not be protected by the Privacy Act], the Court must apply a balancing test to determine whether disclosure of the names and addresses would constitute a "clearly unwarranted" invasion of personal privacy within the meaning of Exemption 6. In conducting this test, the Court must balance . . . the "relevant public interest in disclosure" and the "extent to which disclosure would serve the core purpose of FOIA, which is contributing significantly to public understanding of the operations or activities of the government." . . . .

Applying these principles to the case at hand, the Court begins by examining the privacy interest in a home address. The Eleventh Circuit has stated, in examining this very question, that "individuals have an important privacy interest in their home address." Furthermore, the privacy interest in a home address is more substantial when personal information can be linked to a particular address. Clearly, here, the release of the home addresses of disaster claimants raises a substantial privacy interest. Indeed, by revealing the home addresses of disaster claimants, it would be possible to link the addresses to the already released personal information including the type of assistance received, eligibility date and amount of such assistance, whether the claimant owns the damaged property, the type and cause of damage sustained, descriptions of each item damaged and whether it was insured.

Finding a substantial privacy interest in a home address, however, does not end the Court's inquiry. The Court must also examine whether the invasion of privacy that would ensue from releasing the addresses of disaster claimants would be "clearly unwarranted." In undertaking such an examination, the Court must analyze how the disclosure of these addresses would serve to inform citizens as to "what their government is up to." A review of this record shows that there is a substantial and legitimate public interest in FEMA's handling of disaster assistance in the wake of recent hurricanes. . . . [I]nvestigations unearthed that FEMA's disbursement of assistance was rife with fraud and waste. . . .

Of course, a general public interest in FEMA's disaster response activities is not, standing alone, a sufficient basis on which to disclose the private and personal information of the disaster claimants' addresses. There must be a nexus between the information that is sought under FOIA and the ability of the public to gain an understanding about FEMA's disaster relief operations. The Court concludes that such a nexus exists and that the release of disaster claimants' addresses is not "clearly unwarranted."

The addresses sought are of the properties that were awarded disaster assistance based on claims of damage from the various hurricanes. . . . The record shows that the Inspector General of the Department of Homeland Security Office unearthed evidence that FEMA disbursed funds in Miami-Dade County without verifying the claims of property damage and without adequate oversight of the inspections of the properties in question. Despite the significance of the Inspector General's findings, that investigation only examined three percent of the nearly $ 31 million awarded to Miami-Dade County residents. The release of these addresses will shed light on the activities and operations of FEMA; namely, the extent to which ineffective quality controls and processing of aid applications may have resulted in wasteful spending of taxpayer dollars by FEMA. . . .

Turning to the release of names of disaster claimants, the Court finds that the privacy interest in names equals the privacy interest in home addresses [and therefore] constitutes a significant privacy interest. The next step in this analysis requires an examination as to whether this invasion of privacy would be "clearly unwarranted." . . . . After careful consideration, the Court concludes that the release of names would be "clearly unwarranted" and would not serve the purpose of informing the citizenry "what their government is up to."

Whereas the addresses goes to the heart of whether FEMA improperly disbursed funds to property that sustained no damage, the names of disaster claimants are not as probative. In cases where the name and addresses accurately reflect the property where the disaster claimant resides, the name of the disaster claimant would provide no further insight into the operations of FEMA. Once the addresses are released, the inquiry would concern whether the property sustained the damage claimed and the name of the disaster claimant would not shed additional light on this inquiry. In cases where a claimant provided an address that sustained property damage but that was not owned by that claimant, the name would not, in and of itself, show that fraud was perpetrated upon FEMA. Instead, the Sun-Sentinel would only reach that conclusion by researching who owns the property. Thus, the possibility of finding fraud through the release of the names is speculative. As such, the Court finds that the release of names would not serve the public interest of demonstrating the operations and activities of FEMA.

. . . .

B. Release of Names and Identification Numbers of FEMA Inspectors

FEMA argues that it is prohibited from releasing the names and identification of FEMA Inspectors under Exemption[] 6 of FOIA [because] the release of the inspectors' names and identification numbers would violate the privacy of the inspectors. . . . As previously discussed, the Court must balance "the public interest in disclosure against the interest Congress intended the exemption to protect." Typically, employment history, in and of itself, "is not normally regarded as highly personal." . . . . [T]he record demonstrates that there is a strong public interest in the disclosure of the identities of the FEMA inspectors. Indeed, the Sun-Sentinel points to record evidence that the Inspector General found that FEMA's inspectors were poorly trained and lacked oversight. Additionally, the Homeland Security and Government Affairs Committee discovered that inspectors filled out forms without examining the purported damaged property and that a significant number of inspectors had criminal records. Clearly, the release of the names and identification numbers of the FEMA inspectors will allow the public to examine fully whether the process of selecting FEMA inspectors should be improved and whether these inspectors violated the public's trust in awarding disaster assistance. . . .

. . . .

D. E-mail Correspondence

FEMA asserts that the withheld and redacted e-mails fall under Exemption 5 of FOIA. Exemption 5 protects government documents that are "inter-agency or intra-agency memorandums or letters which would not be available by law to a party other than an agency in litigation with the agency." 5 U.S.C. § 552(b)(5). FEMA argues that the withheld and the redacted e-mails fall under the "deliberative process privilege" and "attorney client privilege" of Exemption 5. . . . [T]he deliberative process privilege . . . allows government agencies to "freely explore possibilities, engage in internal debates, or play devil's advocate without the fear of public scrutiny." Additionally, this privilege protects against premature disclosure of policies before they are adopted as well as pub[l]ic confusion that might result from the disclosure of documents that were not the true reason for the agency's actions. To invoke the deliberative process privilege, the document must be predecisional and deliberative. "A document is deliberative if the disclosure of the materials would expose an agency's decision-making process in such a way as to discourage candid discussion within the agency and, thereby, undermine the agency's ability to perform its functions."

. . . .

The Court has conducted an in camera review of the e-mails that were redacted and/or withheld by FEMA. With respect to the invocation by FEMA of attorney-client privilege, the Court finds that these two e-mails were properly withheld in their entirety because the information contained in the e-mails falls within the scope of attorney-client privilege. These e-mails contain confidential legal advice from the General Counsel of FEMA to FEMA officials. As such, Exemption 5 applies to these e-mails.

FEMA asserts that the remaining e-mails that were either redacted and/or withheld qualify under Exemption 5 as deliberative process privilege. In making that argument, FEMA contends that these e-mails contained recommendations or advice from a subordinate to a superior official. After a careful in camera review, the Court concludes that these remaining e-mails do not contain information that is exempt from disclosure under FOIA. Although the e-mails contain advice and opinions for Brown to consider, these e-mails do not contain advice that relate[s to] the mission of FEMA, i.e., disaster recovery and assistance. Instead, the e-mails offer suggestions and comments regarding suitable responses to inquiries from the press that questioned the appropriateness of FEMA's decisions in the wake of the hurricane disasters. In other words, these e-mails have no relationship to a policy matter or a decision regarding the formulation of FEMA policy. Since these e-mails served to assist FEMA officials in answering questions and defending FEMA's disaster response, the Court finds that withholding these e-mails would be contrary to the primary objective of FOIA; namely, "to pierce the veil of administrative secrecy and to open agency action to the light of public scrutiny." Accordingly, the e-mails that were withheld or redacted pursuant to the deliberative process privilege do not fall within the scope of Exemption 5.

. . . .

———————

> ## Underlying Case Documents
>
> The case referenced:
> The Privacy Act
> *Hickman v. Taylor*
> The Inspector General's audit
>
> For more on the Sun-Sentinel's investigation click HERE.

1. The *Sun-Sentinel* case was one of a number of FOIA cases brought in various district courts by media entities seeking to get more specific information pertaining to FEMA's response to the horrific 2004 hurricane season. A number of those cases were consolidated on appeal, including *Sun-Sentinel*. In *News-Press v. DHS*, 489 F.3d 1173 (11th Cir. 2007), the court affirmed the *Sun-Sentinel* decision, concluding:

> The public interest in evaluating the appropriateness of FEMA's response to disasters is not only precisely the kind of public interest that meets the FOIA's core purpose of shedding light on what the government is up to; the magnitude of this public interest is potentially enormous. "The critical nature of [disaster] assistance makes reports of waste, mismanagement and outright fraud particularly disturbing. We cannot sweep such allegations under the rug; we must face them head-on to preserve public confidence in this critical program." Sen. Joseph I. Lieberman, *Senators Collins and Lieberman: Investigation Reveals Waste, Mismanagement and Fraud in FEMA's Disaster Aid Program in Miami-Dade* (May 18, 2005), available at http://lieberman.senate.gov/ newsroom/release.cfm?id=237837. "The tradition of Americans helping Americans in the aftermath of a disaster . . . . will be jeopardized if Americans come to feel their tax dollars are not being spent fairly, efficiently – and with accountability." Senate Hearings (written statement of Sen. Lieberman at 2). Nor is ensuring that FEMA properly spends taxpayer money only of concern to Floridians and residents of other hurricane-ravaged states. As Senator Bill Nelson of Florida told the Senate Committee, it is also of concern "to Californians, who live on fault lines, and Washingtonians, who live in the shadows of active volcanoes; rural Americans, who live near rivers that swell; and city-dwellers, who live in metropolitan areas that could be targeted by terrorists." Although we acknowledge the privacy interests at stake, given the enormous public interest involved, we cannot say that FEMA has come close to meeting its heavy burden of showing that the privacy interests are of such magnitude that disclosure of the . . . addresses would constitute a clearly unwarranted invasion of personal privacy under Exemption 6.

a. Is there really a value to the public in name and address information? There is certainly a value to a journalist looking to personalize a story – but is that the same phenomenon?

b. Does the importance of an event really determine the balancing Exemption 6 contemplates? Consider the possibility that the more "important" (notorious? scintillating?) an event, activity, or allegation of wrongdoing an agency considers, the greater the need for privacy. There is a saying regarding local television news – particularly the late-night or 11 p.m. news: "If it bleeds it leads" Take a look at your local late-night news one evening (when you are not reading administrative law) and see if this is an accurate statement.

2. The Nexus Requirement: Not every quest for names and addresses produces the desired information as it did in *Sun-Sentinel*. Consider *Seized Property Recovery v. United States Customs & Border Proection,* 502 F. Supp. 2d 50 (D.D.C. 2007):

> Plaintiff filed numerous Freedom of Information Act ("FOIA"), 5 U.S.C. §§ 552 et seq., requests with different Customs Ports in the United States. The requests sought names and addresses of certain individuals and commercial entities from whom Customs had seized property which it intended to forfeit. Plaintiff had learned of these seizures and planned forfeitures through notices published in local newspapers. (In accordance with agency regulations, the names and addresses of the interested parties had not been included in the published notices. (19 C.F.R. § 162.45(a)). Plaintiff wanted to obtain the names and addresses so that it could contact the interested parties and offer them its services in seeking remission of their property. . . .
>
> In order to serve the public interest contemplated by FOIA, disclosure must "shed light on an agency's performance of its statutory duties." . . . . Moreover, "[t]here must be a nexus between the information that is sought under FOIA and the ability of the public to gain an understanding" about the agency's operations. *Sun-Sentinel Co.* . . .
>
> The Court agrees with Plaintiff that there is an element of public interest in shedding light on how Customs performs its duties. However, there is no appropriate nexus between this public interest and the names and addresses of individuals whose property has been seized. . . .
>
> Given the privacy interest held by the individuals, balanced against the very limited or nonexistent public interest in disclosure, the Court concludes that Customs has overcome the presumption in favor of disclosure under Exemption 6.

3. *Sun-Sentinel* also discusses the question of "inter-agency or intra-agency memorandums or letters which would not be available by law to a party other than an agency in litigation with the agency." 5 U.S.C. § 552(b)(5). This is a frequently litigated area, and understandably so – access to agency thinking regarding future enforcement, for example, is of enormous value. What about simple notes taken by an agency official in the course of a phone call? In *Baker & Hostetler LLP v. United States Department of Commerce,* 473 F.3d 312 (D.C. Cir. 2006), the court agreed with the agency that most notes are unavailable, but ordered the agency to turn over a set of notes to the extent they "disclose . . . the identity of persons present or the date, time, or place of the meeting." The opinion affirms the notion that documents are not always unitary instruments. Certain documents are "rea-

sonably segregable" and "after deletion of the portions which are exempt," the remainder must be disclosed.

How might decisions like this affect the behavior of government officials? Would you advise colleagues in a government agency to maintain copious notes? No notes?

For a discussion on how this might affect lawyers in public service, take a look at: Kerri R. Blumenauer, Note, *Privileged or Not? How the Current Application of the Government Attorney-Client Privilege Leaves the Government Feeling Unprivileged*, 75 FORDHAM L. REV. 75 (2006).

NATIONAL LABOR RELATIONS BOARD V. SEARS, ROEBUCK & COMPANY

421 U.S. 132 (1975)

[JUSTICE WHITE] The National Labor Relations Board (the Board) and its General Counsel seek to set aside an order of the United States District Court directing disclosure to respondent, Sears, Roebuck & Co. (Sears), pursuant to the Freedom of Information Act, of certain memoranda, known as "Advice Memoranda" and "Appeals Memoranda," and related documents generated by the Office of the General Counsel in the course of deciding whether or not to permit the filing with the Board of unfair labor practice complaints.

. . . .

I

Crucial to the decision of this case is an understanding of the function of the documents in issue in the context of the administrative process which generated them. . . . Under . . . the National Labor Relations Act . . . the process of adjudicating unfair labor practice cases begins with the filing by a private party of a "charge." Although Congress has designated the Board as the principal body which adjudicates the unfair labor practice case based on such charge, the Board may adjudicate only upon the filing of a "complaint"; and Congress has delegated to the Office of General Counsel "on behalf of the Board" the unreviewable authority to determine whether a complaint shall be filed. In those cases in which he decides that a complaint shall issue, the General Counsel becomes an advocate before the Board in support of the complaint. In those cases in which he decides not to issue a complaint, no proceeding before the Board occurs at all. The practical effect of this administrative scheme is that a party believing himself the victim of an unfair labor practice can obtain neither adjudication nor remedy under the labor statute without first persuading the Office of General Counsel that his claim is sufficiently meritorious to warrant Board consideration.

. . . If the charge has no merit in the Regional Director's judgment, the charging party will be so informed by letter with a brief explanation of the reasons. In such a case, the charging party will also be informed of his right to appeal . . . to the Office of Appeals in the General Counsel's Office in Washington, D.C. . . . [After the appeal is heard by] the "Appeals Committee," which includes the Director and Associate Director of the Office of Appeals . . . the decision and the reasons for it are set forth in a memorandum called the "General Counsel's Minute" or the "Appeals Memorandum." . . . . [T]he Appeals Memorandum is then sent to the Regional Director who follows its instructions. . . . The Appeals Memoranda, whether sustaining or overruling the Regional Directors, constitute one class of documents at issue in this case.

The appeals process affords the General Counsel's Office in Washington some opportunity to formulate a coherent policy, and to achieve some measure of uniformity, in enforcing the labor laws. The appeals process alone, however, is not wholly adequate for this purpose: when the Regional Director initially decides to file a complaint, no appeal is available; and when the Regional Director decides not to file a complaint, the charging party may neglect to appeal. Accordingly, to further "fair and uniform administration of the Act," the General Counsel requires the Regional Directors, before reaching an initial decision in connection with charges raising certain issues specified by the General Counsel, to submit the matter to the General Counsel's "Advice Branch," also located in Washington, D.C. . . .

When a Regional Director seeks "advice" from the Advice Branch, he does so through a memorandum which sets forth the facts of the case, a statement of the issues on which advice is sought, and a recommendation. . . . Depending upon the conclusion reached in the memorandum, the Regional Director will either file a complaint or send a letter to the complaining party advising him of the Regional Director's decision not to proceed and informing him of his right to appeal. It is these Advice Memoranda which constitute the other class of documents of which Sears seeks disclosure in this case.

II

This case arose in the following context. By letter dated July 14, 1971, Sears requested that the General Counsel disclose to it pursuant to the Act all Advice and Appeals Memoranda issued within the previous five years on the subjects of "the propriety of withdrawals by employers or unions from multi-employer bargaining, disputes as to commencement date of negotiations, or conflicting interpretations in any other context of the Board's *Retail Associates* rule." The letter also sought the subject-matter index or digest of Advice and Appeals Memoranda. The letter urged disclosure on the theory that the Advice and Appeals Memoranda are the only source of agency "law" on some issues. By letter dated July 23, 1971, the General Counsel declined Sears' disclosure request in full. The letter stated that Advice Memoranda are simply "guides for a Regional Director" and are not final [and] that they are exempt from disclosure under 5 U.S.C. § 552(b)(5) as "intra-agency memoranda" which reflect the thought processes of the General Counsel's staff . . . . The letter said that Appeals Memoranda were not indexed by subject matter and, therefore, the General Counsel was "unable" to comply with Sears' request. . . .

. . . .

The District Court granted Sears' motion for summary judgment and denied that of the General Counsel. The court found that, although the General Counsel had delegated to the Regional Directors the power to file complaints, an Advice Memorandum constituted a pro tanto withdrawal of the delegation of that power. Accordingly, Advice Memoranda were held to constitute "instructions to staff that affect a member of the public," which are expressly disclosable pursuant to 5 U.S.C. § 552(a)(2)(C). Appeals Memoranda were held to be "final opinions." Both were held not to be "intra-agency memorandums" protected by 5 U.S.C. § 552(b)(5), since they were not expressions "of a point of view" but the "disposition of a charge." . . . .

The parties are in apparent agreement that Exemption 5 withholds from a member of the public documents which a private party could not discover in litigation with the agency. Since virtually any document not privileged may be discovered by the appropriate litigant, . . . and since the Act clearly intended to give any member of the public as much right to disclosure as one with a special interest therein, it is reasonable to construe Exemption 5 to exempt those documents, and only those documents, normally privileged in the civil discovery context. The privileges claimed by petitioners to be relevant to this case are (i) the "generally . . . recognized" privilege for "confidential intra-agency advisory opinions, . . ." disclosure of which "would be 'injurious to the consultative functions of government. . .'," . . . and (ii) the attorney-client and attorney work-product privileges generally available to all litigants.

. . . .

Manifestly, the ultimate purpose of this long-recognized privilege is to prevent injury to the quality of agency decisions. The quality of a particular agency decision will clearly be affected by the communications received by the decisionmaker on the subject of the decision prior to the time the decision is made. However, it is difficult to see how the quality of a decision will be affected by communications with respect to the decision occurring after the decision is finally reached; and therefore equally difficult to see how the quality of the decision will be affected by forced disclosure of such communications, as long as prior communications and the ingredients of the decisionmaking process are not disclosed. . . . The public is only marginally concerned with reasons supporting a policy which an agency has rejected, or with reasons which might have supplied, but did not supply, the basis for a policy which was actually adopted on a different ground. In contrast, the public is vitally concerned with the reasons which did supply the basis for an agency policy actually adopted. These reasons, if expressed within the agency, constitute the "working law" of the agency and have been held by the lower courts to be outside the protection of Exemption 5. . . .

This conclusion is powerfully supported by the other provisions of the Act. The affirmative portion of the Act, expressly requiring indexing of "final opinions," "statements of policy and interpretations which have been adopted by the agency," and "instructions to staff that affect a member of the public," 5 U.S.C. § 552(a)(2), represents a strong congressional aversion to "secret law," and . . . an affirmative congressional purpose to require disclosure of documents which have "the force and effect of law." We should be reluctant, therefore, to construe Exemption 5 to apply to the documents described in 5 U.S.C. § 552(a)(2); and with respect at least to "final opinions," which not only invariably explain agency action already taken or an agency decision already made, but also constitute "final dispositions" of matters by an agency, we hold that Exemption 5 can never apply.

(ii)

It is equally clear that Congress had the attorney's work-product privilege specifically in mind when it adopted Exemption 5 and . . . the case law clearly makes the attorney's work-product rule of *Hickman v. Taylor*, 329 U.S. 495 (1947), applicable to Government attorneys in litigation. Whatever the outer boundaries of the attorney's work-product rule are, the rule clearly applies to memoranda prepared by an attorney in contemplation of litigation which set forth the attorney's theory of the case and his litigation strategy.

B

Applying these principles to the memoranda sought by Sears, it becomes clear that Exemption 5 does not apply to those Appeals and Advice Memoranda which conclude that no complaint should be filed and which have the effect of finally denying relief to the charging party; but that Exemption 5 does protect from disclosure those Appeals and Advice Memoranda which direct the filing of a complaint and the commencement of litigation before the Board.

(i)

Under the procedures employed by the General Counsel, Advice and Appeals Memoranda are communicated to the Regional Director after the General Counsel, through his Advice and Appeals Branches, has decided whether or not to issue a complaint; and represent an explanation to the Regional Director of a legal or policy decision already adopted by the General Counsel. In the case of decisions not to file a complaint, the memoranda effect as "final" a "disposition," . . . representing, as it does, an unreviewable rejection of the charge filed by the private party. Disclosure of these memoranda would not intrude on predecisional processes, and protecting them would not improve the quality of agency decisions, since when the memoranda are communicated to the Regional Director, the General Counsel has already reached his decision and the Regional Director who receives them has no decision to make – he is bound to dismiss the charge. Moreover, the General Counsel's decisions not to file complaints together with the Advice and Appeals Memoranda explaining them, are precisely the kind of agency law in which the public is so vitally interested and which Congress sought to prevent the agency from keeping secret. . . .

. . . .

(ii)

Advice and Appeals Memoranda which direct the filing of a complaint, on the other hand, fall within the coverage of Exemption 5. The filing of a complaint does not finally dispose even of the General Counsel's responsibility with respect to the case. The case will be litigated before and decided by the Board; and the General Counsel will have the responsibility of advocating the position of the charging party before the Board. The Memoranda will inexorably contain the General Counsel's theory of the case and may communicate to the Regional Director some litigation strategy or settlement advice. Since the Memoranda will also have been prepared in contemplation of the upcoming litigation, they fall squarely within Exemption 5's protection of an attorney's work product. At the same time, the public's interest in disclosure is substantially reduced by the fact, as pointed out by the ABA Committee, that the basis for the General Counsel's legal decision will come out in the course of litigation before the Board; and that the "law" with respect to these cases will ultimately be made not by the General Counsel but by the Board or the courts.

We recognize that an Advice or Appeals Memorandum directing the filing of a complaint – although representing only a decision that a legal issue is sufficiently in doubt to warrant determination by another body – has many of the characteristics of the documents described in 5 U.S.C. § 552(a)(2). Although not a "final opinion" in the "adjudication" of a "case" because it does not effect a "final disposition," the memorandum does explain a decision already reached by the General Counsel which has real operative effect – it permits litigation before the Board; and we have indicated a reluctance to construe Exemption 5 to protect such documents. We do so in this case only because the decisionmaker – the General Counsel – must become a litigating party to the case with respect to which he has made his decision. The attorney's work-product policies which Congress clearly incorporated into Exemption 5 thus come into play and lead us to hold that the Advice and Appeals Memoranda directing the filing of a complaint are exempt whether or not they are, as the District Court held, "instructions to staff that affect a member of the public."

C

Petitioners assert that the District Court erred in holding that documents incorporated by reference in nonexempt Advice and Appeals Memoranda lose any exemption they might previously have held as "intra-agency" memoranda. We disagree. The probability that an agency employee will be inhibited from freely advising a decisionmaker for fear that his advice, if adopted, will become public is slight. First, when adopted, the reasoning becomes that of the agency and becomes its responsibility to defend. Second, agency employees will generally be encouraged rather than discouraged by public knowledge that their policy suggestions have been adopted by the agency. Moreover, the public interest in knowing the reasons for a policy actually adopted by an agency supports the District Court's decision below. Thus, we hold that, if an agency chooses expressly to adopt or incorporate by reference an intra-agency memorandum previously covered by Exemption 5 in what would otherwise be a final opinion, that memorandum may be withheld only on the ground that it falls within the coverage of some exemption other than Exemption 5.

. . . .

Underlying Case Documents

The case referenced:
The Board's Retail Associates rule
The July 14, 1971 letter from Sears
The July 23, 1971 letter from the General Counsel

1. Was *Sears* about more than FOIA? At least consider the possibility that this was a case about (1) the broad public goal of governmental transparency, (2) the frustrations of those in the private sector who are subject to what they perceive as secretive government actions, (3) the rights of government officials – including lawyers – to execute their legislative mandate without undue interference, and (4) the methodology to articulate informal – but highly consequential – standards.

2. Just how much must an agency disclose as it contemplates an enforcement action? The *Sears* holding is somewhat straightforward – advice memoranda reflecting discussions about the decision to initiate action is within Exemption 5 – but the determination not to pursue enforcement is outside of Exemption 5 and probably will have to be disclosed. This leaves open endless questions about timing – when is a document *deliberative and predecisional*? There is little question that the government can and does change positions – that flexibility is vital to agency decisionmaking. As facts unfold, different options emerge – that dynamism is not addressed at all in *Sears*.

3. *Sears* is very much a case about government lawyering, legal advice and consultation between and among lawyers and officials at various levels of an agency, agency professional staff, and agency political appointees. This was a major issue at the time the case was decided and is today as well.

Does the attorney-client privilege apply to government lawyers? That may be next to impossible if memos regarding enforcement actions – even those determining that no action will be taken – are available for the asking. *Sears* is hardly an explicit affirmation of attorney-client privilege – but it has provoked a good discussion about it. Nancy Leong, Note, *Attorney-Client Privilege in the Public Sector: A Survey of Government Attorneys*, 20 Geo. J. Legal Ethics 163 (2007); Melanie B. Leslie, *Government Officials as Attorneys and Clients: Why Privilege the Privileged?*, 11 Ind. L.J. 469, 480 (2002); Bryan S. Gowdy, Note, *Should the Federal Government Have an Attorney-Client Privilege?*, 51 Fla. L. Rev. 695, 710 (1999).

4. As to transparency, we already know that not every government action establishing a standard that may become the basis for liability must be subjected to some type of process allowing public input. Policy statements, interpretative rules, handbooks, manuals, guidelines, regulatory guides, and many other forms of policy formulation are, more often than not, produced without public participation. Furthermore, give some thought to whether Sears, Roebuck & Co. was interested in learning the state of law or of regulatory policy, or whether its goal was simply to maximize its options in the face of prospective enforcement. There is little doubt that FOIA requests are often made to secure opportunity or advantage. *See* Patricia M. Wald, *The Freedom of Information Act: A Short Case Study in the Perils and Paybacks of Legislating Democratic Values*, 33 Emory L.J. 649, 666-67, n.76 (1984).

5. At its core, *Sears* involves Exemption 5. The doctrinal parameters of that exemption were recently set forth in *Canaday v. United States Citizenship & Immigration Services*, 545 F. Supp. 2d 113 (D.D.C. 2008):

> Exemption 5 of FOIA provides for the withholding of "inter-agency or intra-agency memorandums or letters which would not be available by law to a party other than an agency in litigation with the agency." 5 U.S.C. § 552(b)(5). The deliberative process privilege exempts from disclosure documents "reflecting advisory opinions, recommendations and deliberations comprising part of a process by which governmental decisions and policies are formulated." *Sears*. Exemption 5 "covers recommendations, draft documents, proposals, suggestions, and other subjective documents which reflect the personal opinions of the writer rather than the policy of the agency." Such documents are protected in order to promote "the quality of agency decisions by protecting open and frank discussion among those who make them within the Government." *Tax Analysts v. IRS*, 117 F.3d 607, 617 (D.C. Cir. 1997) (the quality of decision-making would be seriously undermined if agencies were forced to operate in a "fish bowl" since open and frank discussion regarding legal or policy matters would be impossible). To qualify for withholding, material must be both predecisional and deliberative.
>
> A document is predecisional if it was prepared in order to assist an agency decisionmaker in arriving at his decision, rather than to support a decision already made. Material is deliberative if it reflects the give-and-take of the consultative process. . . . [The D.C. Circuit's] recent decisions on the deliberativeness inquiry have focused on whether disclosure of the requested material would tend to discourage candid discussion within an agency. *Petroleum Info. Corp. v. Dep't of Interior*, 976 F.2d 1429, 1434 (D.C. Cir. 1992) (citations and internal quotation marks omitted).

What about the "historic value" of predecisional documents? After a case is concluded, does a predecisional document become postdecisional – and if so, is it still subject to the restrictions in exemption 5? If a memo sets out the decision-making process of an agency in one case, it would be of value to know how the agency came to its decision for those subject to the jurisdiction of the agency in subsequent cases.

6. In *Mayer, Brown, Rowe & Maw LLP v. IRS*, 537 F. Supp. 2d 128 (D.D.C. 2008)

> a law firm sought information regarding two revenue rulings, settlement guidelines, and an IRS Notice. . . . [IRS claimed the documents were predecisional.]
>
> A document is predecisional if it is "'generated before the adoption of an agency policy. . . . The courts do not necessarily look to a specific, final agency decision, but emphasize that agencies engage in ongoing examinations and re-examinations of policies. Thus, "[a]gencies are, and properly should be, engaged in a continuing process of examining their policies; this process will generate memoranda containing recommendations which do not ripen into agency decisions; and lower courts should be wary of interfering with this process." *Sears*.

Predecisional documents are thought generally to reflect the agency "give and take" leading up to a decision that is characteristic of the deliberative process; whereas post-decisional documents often represent the agency's position on an issue. . . . The Court disagrees with [the IRS] when it asserts that "the deliberative process that is being protected by the non-disclosure of the withheld portions from these two pages is the process by which the agency deliberated and determined what information [the items] should and should not convey to a wider audience." This is too removed from an actual policy decision. Summary judgment on this point will be granted to Plaintiff.

Does this mean the working notes and teaching materials an agency (and particularly its government lawyers) uses to inform and educate professional staff and officials are outside exemption 5?

The following notes are current applications of various exemptions to FOIA.

1. Exemption 6 - Personal Information Affecting an Individual's Privacy.

Diemert, Jr. & Associates v. Federal Aviation Administration, 218 Fed. Appx. 479 (6th Cir. 2007).

Ms. Rebecca A. Nelson began receiving monthly payments of Five-Thousand One Hundred and xx/100 Dollars ($ 5,100.00) from the FAA after an "incident" that occurred while she was working as an air traffic controller . . . . According to Ms. Nelson, the "incident" caused her to experience an "adjustment reaction." Ms. Nelson was sent home by the FAA and has not returned to work. In 2002, Ms. Nelson allegedly confided these occurrences to Mr. Warren Anderson, stating that the payments had been arranged to essentially "buy her silence."

On December 21, 2004, plaintiff-appellant Joseph W. Diemert, Jr. & Associates Co., L.P.A. ("Diemert") sent a letter to the FAA's Acting FOIA Program Director requesting access to any agency records pertaining to a settlement between Ms. Nelson and the FAA. . . . [T]he FAA . . . sent Diemert a letter denying its request pursuant to Exemption 6 of FOIA, 5 U.S.C. § 552(b)(6), because such records may be in "personnel, medical files, and similar files the disclosures of which would constitute a clearly unwarranted invasion of person privacy." . . . .

The Court [concurs]. The documents requested in the instant matter are either workers' compensation files and/or documents similar in nature. Accordingly, the threshold requirement of Exemption 6 has been satisfied. In considering the rights of the private individual compared with the rights of the public, the Court finds that the release of the requested information is clearly an unwarranted invasion of personal privacy in that Diemert is seeking information and verification about a specific individual's income and/or medical information, which has no governmental public interest. The disclosure of such information would only serve the private interests of Diemert. The focus of FOIA is to ensure that the Government's actions are open for scrutiny, not to reveal private third party information, which happens to be in the warehouse of the Government.

Moreover, some courts have concluded that where personal privacy interests are implicated, only the individual who owns such interest may validly waive it. If Diemert wishes to pursue this matter, it is obvious that it can request that Ms. Nelson execute a release for the requested information. . . .

2. Exemption 7 – Investigatory Records Compiled for Law Enforcement Purposes.

Boyd v. United States Department of Justice, 475 F.3d 381 (D.C. Cir. 2007).

Boyd was arrested on a parole violation warrant at his girlfriend's house on February 1, 1997. Based on a gun and a black bag containing cocaine that were found in the master bedroom closet, Boyd was indicted and convicted of drugs and weapons charges, including being a felon in possession of a firearm and of possession with intent to distribute cocaine. His conviction was affirmed on appeal. Following his trial, Boyd learned that his girlfriend's brother, Bryant Troupe, had been a government informant for several years and had sold drugs in the past. This information was contained in the prosecutor's *Brady* disclosure letter in a case in which Troupe had testified at trial as a government informant. . . . [T]his information, which . . . could have been used to support Boyd's defense that the gun and drugs found in the closet belonged to Troupe . . . was withheld from Boyd during his criminal trial in violation of *Brady*.

In 1998 Boyd filed the first of several FOIA requests seeking information about himself and Troupe from several federal agencies involved in Boyd's prosecution, including the Executive Office for United States Attorneys ("Attorneys' Office"), the Bureau of Alcohol, Tobacco, Firearms, and Explosives ("BATF"), and the Bureau of Prisons ("BOP"). The agencies released some documents and withheld others pursuant to FOIA Exemptions 7(A), 7(C), and 7(D). In 1999, Boyd filed a complaint, and later an amended complaint, challenging the agencies' invocations of FOIA exemptions and the adequacy of their searches. . . .

Exemption 7(A) [of FOIA] authorizes the withholding of "records or information compiled for law enforcement purposes, but only to the extent that the production of such law enforcement records or information . . . could reasonably be expected to interfere with enforcement proceedings." 5 U.S.C. § 552(b)(7)(A) . The government meets its burden by demonstrating that release of the requested information would reveal "the size, scope and direction of investigation" and thereby "allow for the destruction or alteration of relevant evidence, and the fabrication of fraudulent alibis."

In Boyd's case, the government explained that disclosure would "promote the criminal activity of the targets of the investigation, "allow [the targets] to avoid arrest and prosecution," and "provide them information that would allow them to change their operations to avoid detection." Because the individuals under investigation are all "related [to], controlled [by], or influenced by" Boyd, disclosure of the information could reasonably be expected to reveal to the targets "the size, scope, and direction of investigation," and allow them to destroy or alter evidence, fabricate fraudulent alibis, and take other actions to frustrate the government's case. . . .

[T]he government's affidavit states that the investigation at issue involves the "ongoing collection of data" and that the withheld records relate to "potential criminal proceedings against individuals." The duration of the investigation was brief; the documents at issue are dated 1997, Boyd was convicted in April 1998, and the government invoked Exemption 7(A) in early 1999. . . .

Exemption 7(C) authorizes the government to withhold "records or information compiled for law enforcement purposes, but only to the extent that the production of such law enforcement records or information . . . could reasonably be expected to constitute an unwarranted invasion of personal privacy." 5 U.S.C. § 552(b)(7)(C). The government may nonetheless be required to disclose the documents if the individual seeking the information demonstrates a public interest in the information that is sufficient to overcome the privacy interest at issue. In order to trigger the balancing of public interests against private interests, a FOIA requester must (1) "show that the public interest sought to be advanced is a significant one, an interest more specific than having the information for its own sake," and (2) "show the information is likely to advance that interest." If the public interest is government wrongdoing, then the requester must "produce evidence that would warrant a belief by a reasonable person that the alleged Government impropriety might have occurred." . . . .

Even assuming Amicus has identified a sufficient public interest, we conclude that Exemption 7(C) was properly invoked because [appellant] has failed to "produce evidence that would warrant a belief by a reasonable person that the alleged Government impropriety might have occurred." Of the two evidentiary showings that [appellant] contends would warrant a belief of government misconduct, neither suffices. First, [appellant] suggests that Boyd's discovery of the disclosure letter in the *Miller* case containing potentially exculpatory information about Troupe suggests the government failed to comply with its *Brady* obligations. Even after discovery, however, [appellant] makes no showing that Boyd has identified anything withheld at his criminal trial but produced under FOIA that would suggest an actual *Brady* . . . violation. . . . [Appellant] also points to letters from Boyd's defense counsel indicating that he never received certain allegedly exculpatory documents and to the prosecutor's answer, when asked by defense counsel about his disclosures several years after the case . . . . However, letters the prosecutor wrote in 1998 suggest that the documents at issue were turned over and it is doubtful that a reasonable person would infer government misconduct from unsworn letters from defense counsel years after Boyd's 1998 conviction. . . .

Although in other circumstances a remand might be required for the district court to determine whether the government possesses the requested information and, if so, whether its withholding of the information is justified . . . none is required here. The government properly invoked Exemption 7(C) to protect information concerning Troupe. Because Boyd was not entitled to this information, he was not harmed by the government's refusal to confirm or deny whether it possessed responsive information. . . .

Exemption 7(D) authorizes the withholding of "records or information compiled for law enforcement purposes, but only to the extent that the production of such law enforcement records or information . . . could reasonably be expected to disclose the identity of a confidential source . . . and, in the case of a record or information compiled by criminal law enforcement authority in the course of a criminal investigation . . .

information furnished by a confidential source." 5 U.S.C. § 552(b)(7)(D). . . . "[A source] is confidential within the meaning of Exemption 7(D) if the source provided information under an express assurance of confidentiality or in circumstances from which such an assurance could be reasonably inferred."

Boyd's assertion that the government's declarations are inconsistent, because one refers to an express assurance while another refers to an implied assurance, ignores the possibility that more than one informant may have been involved in his case or that the informant may have received both assurances, albeit at different times; in any event, Boyd offers nothing that would call into question the evidence cited in the BATF affidavit to demonstrate the informant received an express grant of confidentiality. Hence, the government may properly invoke Exemption 7(D) to withhold the identity of the confidential informant in Boyd's case and the information furnished by the informant. . . .

3. Exemption 1 – Classified Matters of National Defense or Foreign Policy, and Exemption 3 – Information Specifically Exempted by Other Statutes.

Wolf v. CIA, 473 F.3d 370 (D.C. Cir. 2007).

On April 9, 1948, Gaitan, a former Colombian presidential candidate, was assassinated in Bogota, Colombia. In the wake of his assassination, riots erupted in Bogota which prompted a congressional investigation into the alleged failure of the CIA to predict such unrest. At the hearing, then-CIA Director Admiral R. K. Hillenkoetter (Hillenkoetter) testified that the Agency had in fact predicted the explosive situation brewing in Bogota in 1948. A half century later, Wolf, a historical researcher interested in the life and death of Gaitan, submitted a FOIA request to the CIA seeking "all records about Jorge Eliecer Gaitan." On September 22, 2000, the CIA issued a . . . response to Wolf's request, neither confirming nor denying the existence of records regarding Gaitan. Following an unsuccessful administrative appeal, Wolf filed suit in April 2001 seeking to compel the CIA to release responsive documents.

Before the district court, the CIA submitted the affidavit of Kathryn Dyer (Dyer Affidavit), the Agency's Information and Privacy Coordinator, in support of its . . . response. The Dyer Affidavit explained that official confirmation or denial of the existence of such records might damage both national security, through revelation of intelligence sources or methods, and foreign relations. [A]ccording to the Dyer Affidavit, acknowledgment of such records could disclose the identities of individuals, or categories of individuals, "in which the CIA is interested and upon which it focuses its methods and resources," [and] could upset diplomatic relations with foreign governments whose citizens had CIA files. As a consequence, the CIA claimed that the existence of records regarding a foreign national constitutes classified information . . . .

The CIA moved for summary judgment on the strength of the Dyer Affidavit. Wolf responded by filing a cross-motion for summary judgment, contending that the Agency waived the exemptions as a result of Hillenkoetter's 1948 congressional testimony. During [this testimony] Hillenkoetter read from official CIA dispatches referencing Gaitan, thereby acknowledging that the CIA had responsive records. . . . Because the district court found "no indication from the transcript [of the congressional hearing] that the CIA director was reading from anything more than a prepared statement for the hearing," the court held that the Agency did not waive FOIA exemptions through official acknowledgment of records regarding Gaitan. . . . Wolf now appeals.

FOIA mandates broad disclosure of government records to the public subject to nine enumerated exemptions. Given FOIA's broad disclosure policy, the United States Supreme Court has "consistently stated that FOIA exemptions are to be narrowly construed." Nevertheless, the CIA "may refuse to confirm or deny the existence of records where to answer FOIA inquiry would cause harm cognizable under an FOIA exception." Such an agency response is known as a *Glomar* response and is proper if the fact of the existence or nonexistence of agency records falls within a FOIA exemption.

Under FOIA, "the burden is on the agency to sustain its action," 5 U.S.C. § 552(a)(4)(B), and we review de novo the agency's use of a FOIA exemption to withhold documents. Yet in conducting de novo review in the context of national security concerns, courts "must 'accord *substantial weight* to an agency's affidavit concerning the details of the classified status of the disputed record.'" Indeed, "[s]ummary judgment is warranted on the basis of agency affidavits when the affidavits describe 'the justifications for nondisclosure with reasonably specific detail . . . and are not controverted by either contrary evidence in the record nor by evidence of agency bad faith.'" . . . .

The CIA submitted the Dyer Affidavit to support its refusal to either confirm or deny the existence of records pertaining to Jorge Gaitan. The question, then, is whether the existence of Agency records regarding an individual foreign national constitutes information itself protected by either FOIA Exemption 1 or Exemption 3. Proper invocation of, and affidavit support for, either Exemption, standing alone, may justify the CIA's *Glomar* response. . . . [*Glomar* refers to the Howard Hughes submersible vessel, the Glomar Explorer.]

The Agency justifies its *Glomar* response under Exemption 1 based on the classification criteria of Executive Order 12958. Executive Order 12958 permits an original classification authority to classify information only if "the original classification authority determines that the unauthorized disclosure of the information reasonably could be expected to result in damage to the national security . . . and . . . is able to identify or describe the damage." Such damage to national security may be claimed only with respect to certain categories of information, specifically information that "concerns . . . intelligence sources or methods" or the "foreign relations . . . of the United States." Further, the Supreme Court has recognized the broad sweep of "intelligence sources" warranting protection in the interest of national security. . . .

The Dyer Affidavit asserts that confirmation or denial of the existence of records regarding a foreign national could reasonably be expected to damage national security or foreign relations. Consequently, if the Dyer Affidavit plausibly explains the danger, the existence of records vel non is properly classified under Executive Order 12958 and justifies the Agency's invocation of Exemption 1. Initially, Dyer describes the CIA's interest in an individual foreign national as an intelligence source or method, an interest that could "be thwarted or made more difficult, reducing the CIA's effectiveness," upon disclosure that the Agency has such records. Dyer asserts that the Agency utilizes foreign nationals as sources in order to carry out its intelligence-gathering duties and also targets foreign nationals as subjects of surveillance. . . . Thus, the Dyer Affidavit explains, acknowledgment that the Agency maintains contact with a specific foreign national "would . . . seriously damage this nation's credibility with all other current intelligence sources and undermine CIA's ability to attract potential intelligence sources in the future." . . . .

In light of the substantial weight accorded agency assertions of potential harm made in order to invoke the protection of FOIA Exemption 1, the Dyer Affidavit both logically and plausibly suffices. It is plausible that either confirming or denying an Agency interest in a foreign national reasonably could damage sources and methods by revealing CIA priorities, thereby providing foreign intelligence sources with a starting point for applying countermeasures against the CIA and thus wasting Agency resources. . . .

Moreover, it is logical to conclude that the need to assure confidentiality to a foreign source includes neither confirming nor denying the existence of records even decades after the death of the foreign national. . . . Accordingly, we conclude that the existence or nonexistence of Agency records regarding Gaitan is properly classified information and therefore shielded from disclosure under Exemption 1.

The CIA invokes Exemption 3 as an alternative basis of its *Glomar* response. As noted earlier, Exemption 3 permits an agency to withhold information "specifically exempted from disclosure by statute." 5 U.S.C. § 552(b)(3). In this regard, the CIA maintains that the existence or nonexistence of records about a foreign national is protected from disclosure under the National Security Act. Specifically, the National Security Act makes the CIA Director responsible for "protecting intelligence sources and methods from unauthorized disclosure." n.6 Indeed, information is exempt under section 403-3(c)(6) if the Agency "demonstrates that an answer to the query can reasonably be expected to lead to unauthorized disclosure."

> n.6 The structure and responsibilities of the United States intelligence community have undergone reorganization in recent years. As a consequence, the duties of the CIA Director are described as they existed at the time of Wolf's FOIA request in 2000. Under the Intelligence Reform and Terrorism Prevention Act of 2004, Pub. L. No. 108-458, the new Director of National Intelligence is similarly required to "protect intelligence sources and methods from unauthorized disclosure." 50 U.S.C. § 403-1(i)(1).

The Supreme Court gives even greater deference to CIA assertions of harm to intelligence sources and methods under the National Security Act. *See Sims*, 471 U.S. at 168-69 ("The plain meaning . . . of the National Security Act . . . indicates that . . . Congress entrusted [the CIA] with sweeping power to protect its 'intelligence sources and methods.'"). Because "the purpose of national security exemptions to FOIA is to protect intelligence sources before they are compromised and harmed, not after" "the Director of Central Intelligence may protect all intelligence sources, regardless of their provenance". As with Exemption 1, the Agency relies on the Dyer Affidavit to establish that disclosure of information regarding whether or not CIA records of a foreign national exist would be unauthorized under Exemption 3 because it would be reasonably harmful to intelligence sources and methods. As discussed earlier, Dyer's detailing of harm satisfies the requirements of Exemption 1 and, coupled with the greater deference afforded the Agency under the National Security Act, we believe that the CIA also properly invoked Exemption 3 in support of its *Glomar* response.

Although the CIA properly invoked Exemptions 1 and 3, Wolf asserts that the Agency waived both of them by officially acknowledging the existence of records regarding Gaitan during the 1948 congressional testimony of then-CIA Director Hillenkoetter. . . .

While FOIA requesters often invoke agency waiver in order to overcome FOIA exemptions, the "official acknowledgment" standard has not yet been applied in the context of a *Glomar* response. In most waiver cases, the inquiry turns on the match between the information requested and the content of the prior disclosure. . . .

Wolf requested "[a] copy of all records about Jorge Eliecer Gaitan." The CIA's *Glomar* response pinpointed the "specific information at issue" as the existence of Agency "records about Jorge Eliecer Gaitan" vel non. In the *Glomar* context, then, if the prior disclosure establishes the *existence* (or not) of records responsive to FOIA request, the prior disclosure necessarily matches both the information at issue – the existence of records – and the specific request for that information.

We must now resolve the nature of the information to which Wolf is entitled. The CIA's official acknowledgment waiver relates only to the existence or nonexistence of the records about Gaitan disclosed by Hillenkoetter's testimony. As a result, Wolf is entitled to disclosure of that information, namely the existence of CIA records about Gaitan that have been previously disclosed (but not any others). To determine whether the *contents* – as distinguished from the *existence* – of the officially acknowledged records may be protected from disclosure by Exemptions 1 and 3 (or both), however, we remand the case to the district court where the CIA must either disclose any officially acknowledged records or establish both that their contents are exempt from disclosure and that such exemption has not also been waived by the 1948 congressional testimony. . . .

4. Exemption 7(C) Personal Information in Law Enforcement Records.

Davis v. Department of Justice, 460 F.3d 92 (D.C. Cir. 2006).

This case involves four audiotapes recorded more than twenty-five years ago during an FBI corruption investigation in Louisiana. The plaintiff, an author, seeks release of the tapes under the Freedom of Information Act (FOIA), 5 U.S.C. § 552. There are two speakers on the tapes, one a "prominent individual" who was a subject of the FBI's investigation, and the other an "undercover informant" in that investigation. The only question on this appeal is whether the FBI has undertaken reasonable steps to determine whether the speakers are now dead, in which event the privacy interests weighing against release would be diminished.

The FBI has not been able to determine whether either speaker is dead or alive. It says it cannot determine whether the speakers are over 100 years old (and thus presumed dead under FBI practice), because neither mentioned his birth date during the conversations that were surreptitiously recorded. It says it cannot determine whether the speakers are dead by referring to a Social Security database, because neither announced his social security number during the conversations. And it declines to search its own files for the speakers' birth dates or social security numbers, because that is not its practice. The Bureau does not appear to have contemplated other ways of determining whether the speakers are dead, such as Googling them.

[The question is whether] the FBI has . . . "made a reasonable effort to ascertain" whether the two speakers, on whose behalf it has invoked a privacy exemption from FOIA, are living or dead. . . .

FOIA Exemption 7(C) exempts law enforcement records from release "to the extent that" release "could reasonably be expected to constitute an unwarranted invasion of personal privacy." 5 U.S.C. § 552(b)(7)(C). In deciding whether the release of particular information constitutes an "unwarranted" invasion of privacy, an agency must balance the privacy interest at stake against the public interest in disclosure. *See United States Department of Justice v. Reporters Comm. for Freedom of the Press*, 489 U.S. 749, 777 (1989). We have recognized "that the privacy interest in nondisclosure of identifying information may be diminished where the individual is deceased." Indeed, the "fact of death, . . . while not requiring the release of information, is a relevant factor to be taken into account in the balancing decision whether to release information." Consequently, "without confirmation that the Government took certain basic steps to ascertain whether an individual was dead or alive, we are unable to say whether the Government reasonably balanced the interests in personal privacy against the public interest in release of the information at issue."

The government's obligation in this regard is to "ma[k]e a reasonable effort to ascertain life status." Its "efforts must be assessed in light of the accessibility of the relevant information." As we said in *Schrecker II*, there "would be a question whether the Bureau's invocation of the privacy interest represented a reasonable response to FOIA request . . . *if the Bureau has, or has ready access to, data bases that could resolve the issue.*" . . . . In short, "the proper inquiry is whether the Government has made reasonable use of the information readily available to it, and whether there exist reasonable alternative methods that the Government failed to employ."

A. The government's affidavits and pleadings declare that the FBI took three steps to determine whether the two speakers on the tapes were deceased. . . .

1. The government describes the first method it employed in the following paragraph from its principal affidavit:

> The FBI has institutional knowledge of the death of certain individuals from the processing of prior FOIA requests or internal records. The FBI relies on this institutional knowledge, as well as *Who Was Who*, a book of famous individuals [who have died].

From this description, it appears that the government's first step involved resort to two different sources: institutional knowledge and *Who Was Who*.

If the FBI truly used its "institutional knowledge" to determine whether the speakers were dead or alive, this first step might well be reasonable. But the Bureau's method of accessing that knowledge is so constrained as to render it effectively useless. Although the affidavit could be read as suggesting that the FBI uses its "internal records" to determine an individual's status, the same affidavit indicates that the Bureau did *not* search any records that were not themselves "responsive" to Davis' FOIA request – that is, it did not search any records other than the audiotapes themselves. Needless to say, the tapes themselves disclose nothing on this point, other than that the speakers were alive when they were speaking sometime during 1979-80.

If the FBI's reference to its institutional knowledge means anything more than what we have just described, we cannot determine that from the affidavit the Bureau filed. What we said of an earlier affidavit in this case, one that made a similar reference to the FBI's "institutional knowledge," remains equally true regarding this affidavit's treatment of that subject: "The FBI's affidavit is insufficient to determine the extent of the Bureau's efforts to ascertain whether putative beneficiaries of Exemption 7(C) are alive or dead." *Davis III v. Department of Justice*, 2001 WL 1488882 (D.C. Cir. 2001)

The other source mentioned in the FBI's affidavit is *Who Was Who*, a multi-volume set of books published periodically by Marquis Who's Who, LLC. Each new volume "includes the biographies of the most prominent and noteworthy people who have died since the publication of the previous edition." It is a select company: of the more than 7.2 million Americans who died during 2000-02, for example, no more than 4000 are portrayed in the *Who Was Who* volume covering that period. Marquis reports that most of the entries were originally listed with the subjects' permission in its sister *Who's Who in America* publication, and that many of the biographies "have been scrutinized and revised by relatives or legal representatives of the deceased Biographee." All of this suggests both considerable self-selection and considerable lag time. . . .

2. The government describes the second method it employed as follows:

> *When birth dates are provided in responsive records*, and these dates indicate the individual would be over 100 years of age, the name and/or any other identifiers will be released. Although the FBI is aware that many individuals live to be older than 100 years of age, . . . the FBI has consistently relied upon the 100-year rule in all of its FOIA processing.

The key to the utility of the FBI's 100-year rule is the clause that we have italicized. As explained above, when the FBI refers to "responsive records," it means those records – and only those records – actually sought in FOIA request. In this case, the only responsive records were the audiotapes, and "there were no birth dates on these tapes." Therefore, the affidavit concludes, since "no birth dates were provided in the responsive records, the FBI did not assume death of the individuals speaking on these tapes."

The reasonableness of this second method obviously depends upon the probability that the responsive records will contain the individual's birth date – as might well be the case if the records sought by FOIA requester were FBI investigative reports or personnel files. But unless the FBI has tape recorded a birthday party, it seems highly unlikely that the participants in an audiotaped conversation would have announced their ages or dates of birth. Accordingly, this second method was also destined to fail, as it did.

3. The third method the FBI used was the following:

> *If a social security number is revealed on the responsive records*, the FBI, in its administrative discretion, may check the Social Security Death Index (SSDI) – a database maintained by a third party on the Internet. This website is maintained by a private individual, and the FBI cannot verify or vouch for the accuracy of this index, which the website purchases from the Social Security Administration.

Once again, the rub is that the FBI will not even check the Social Security Death Index unless the speaker's social security number is revealed on responsive records. As expected, the FBI reports that, because "[t]his case concerns audio tapes," and "[a]s no social security numbers are on the tapes at issue, this website [the SSDI] was not checked." Needless to say, no one announces his or her social security number in ordinary conversation – not even at a birthday party. Accordingly, the Bureau again utilized a method that could not help but fail in the circumstances of this case.

It is plain, then, that the FBI could have searched its files by the names of the two speakers – one the subject of a criminal investigation, the other an informant – to determine whether records in those files disclose their dates of birth or social security numbers (or even their deaths). But the FBI did not do so. The Bureau gave no reason at all for not searching its records for the speakers' birth dates, and only one reason for not searching for their social security numbers . . . .

But if that is so, one has to ask why – in the age of the Internet – the FBI restricts itself to a dead-tree source with a considerable time lag between death and publication, with limited utility for the FBI's purpose, and with entries restricted to a small fraction of even the "prominent and noteworthy"? Why, in short, doesn't the FBI just Google the two names? Surely, in the Internet age, a "reasonable alternative" for finding out whether a prominent person is dead is to use Google (or any other search engine) to find a report of that person's death. n.10 Moreover, while finding a death notice for the second speaker – the informant – may be harder (assuming that he was not prominent), Googling also provides ready access to hundreds of websites collecting obituaries from all over the country, any one of which might resolve that speaker's status as well. *See, e.g.*, http://www.legacy.com (hosting the obituary sites of more than 275 newspapers, including three Louisiana papers); http://www.obituarycentral.com (containing a directory of links to online obituaries and death notices in every state).

> n.10 That is particularly so here, since an FBI affidavit declared that the Bureau knew the "prominent individual" at issue was alive as recently as 1994. (How the FBI knew the individual was living in 1994, but could not determine whether he was living or dead by 1998, remains a mystery.)

We do not suggest that the FBI must use one, or any, of the search methods outlined above. But when the only search methods the FBI did employ were plainly fated to reach a dead end (in a manner of speaking), and when there appear to be reasonable alternatives that the government failed to consider, there is a serious "question whether the Bureau's invocation of the privacy interest represented a reasonable response to FOIA request." This a question that has not yet been answered, and that the district court must address on remand.

For the foregoing reasons . . . we reverse its grant of summary judgment dismissing Davis' FOIA complaint. The case is remanded with directions that the FBI evaluate alternative methods for determining whether the speakers on the requested audiotapes are dead, and that thereafter the district court determine whether the FBI's chosen course is reasonable.

V. Reverse FOIA Actions

CHRYSLER CORPORATION V. BROWN

441 U.S. 281 (1979)

[JUSTICE REHNQUIST] The expanding range of federal regulatory activity and growth in the Government sector of the economy have increased federal agencies' demands for information about the activities of private individuals and corporations. These developments have paralleled a related concern about secrecy in Government and abuse of power. The Freedom of Information Act (hereinafter FOIA) was a response to this concern, but it has also had a largely unforeseen tendency to exacerbate the uneasiness of those who comply with governmental demands for information. For under FOIA third parties have been able to obtain Government files containing information submitted by corporations and individuals who thought that the information would be held in confidence.

This case belongs to a class that has been popularly denominated "reverse-FOIA" suits. The Chrysler Corp. (hereinafter Chrysler) seeks to enjoin agency disclosure on the grounds that it is inconsistent with FOIA and 18 U.S.C. § 1905, a criminal statute with origins in the 19th century that proscribes disclosure of certain classes of business and personal information. We agree with the Court of Appeals for the Third Circuit that FOIA is purely a disclosure statute and affords Chrysler no private right of action to enjoin agency disclosure. But we cannot agree with that court's conclusion that this disclosure is "authorized by law" within the meaning of § 1905. Therefore, we vacate the Court of Appeals' judgment and remand so that it can consider whether the documents at issue in this case fall within the terms of § 1905.

. . . .

II.

. . . .

In contending that FOIA bars disclosure of the requested equal employment opportunity information, Chrysler relies on . . . Exemption 4:

(b) [FOIA] does not apply to matters that are . . .

(4) trade secrets and commercial or financial information obtained from a person and privileged or confidential . . . .

5 U.S.C. § 552(b)(4). Chrysler contends that . . . Exemption 4 . . . reflect[s] a sensitivity to the privacy interests of private individuals and nongovernmental entities. That contention may be conceded without inexorably requiring the conclusion that the exemptions impose affirmative duties on an agency to withhold information sought. In fact, that conclusion is not supported by the language, logic, or history of the Act.

The organization of the Act is straightforward. Subsection (a), 5 U.S.C. § 552(a), places a general obligation on the agency to make information available to the public and sets out specific modes of disclosure for certain classes of information. Subsection (b), 5 U.S.C. § 552(b), which lists the exemptions, simply states that the specified material is not subject to the disclosure obligations set out in subsection (a). By its terms, subsection (b) demarcates the agency's obligation to disclose; it does not foreclose disclosure.

That FOIA is exclusively a disclosure statute is, perhaps, demonstrated most convincingly by examining its provision for judicial relief. Subsection (a)(4)(B) gives federal district courts "jurisdiction to enjoin the agency from withholding agency records and to order the production of any agency records improperly withheld from the complainant." 5 U.S.C. § 552(a)(4)(B). That provision does not give the authority to bar disclosure . . . . Congress appreciated that . . . much of the information within Government files has been submitted by private entities seeking Government contracts or responding to unconditional reporting obligations imposed by law [and that g]overnment agencies should have the latitude, in certain circumstances, to afford the confidentiality desired by these submitters. But the congressional concern was with the *agency's* need or preference for confidentiality; FOIA by itself protects the submitters' interest in confidentiality only to the extent that this interest is endorsed by the agency collecting the information. . . . Congress did not design FOIA exemptions to be mandatory bars to disclosure.

. . . .

III

Chrysler contends, however, that even if its suit for injunctive relief cannot be based on FOIA, such an action can be premised on the Trade Secrets Act. The Act provides:

> Whoever, being an officer or employee of the United States or of any department or agency thereof, publishes, divulges, discloses, or makes known in any manner or to any extent not authorized by law any information coming to him in the course of his employment or official duties or by reason of any examination or investigation made by, or return, report or record made to or filed with, such department or agency or officer or employee thereof, which information concerns or relates to the trade secrets, processes, operations, style of work, or apparatus, or to the identity, confidential statistical data, amount or source of any income, profits, losses, or expenditures of any person, firm, partnership, corporation, or association; or permits any income return or copy thereof or any book containing any abstract or particulars thereof to be seen or examined by any person except as provided by law; shall be fined not more than $ 1,000, or imprisoned not more than one year, or both; and shall be removed from office or employment.

There are necessarily two parts to Chrysler's argument: that § 1905 is applicable to the type of disclosure threatened in this case, and that it affords Chrysler a private right of action to obtain injunctive relief.

A

The Court of Appeals held that § 1905 was not applicable to the agency disclosure at issue here because such disclosure was "authorized by law" within the meaning of the Act. The court found the source of that authorization to be the OFCCP regulations that DLA relied on in deciding to disclose information . . . . Chrysler contends here that these agency regulations are not "law" within the meaning of § 1905.

It has been established in a variety of contexts that properly promulgated, substantive agency regulations have the "force and effect of law." This doctrine is so well established that agency regulations implementing federal statutes have been held to pre-empt state law under the Supremacy Clause. It would therefore take a clear showing of contrary legislative intent before the phrase "authorized by law" in § 1905 could be held to have a narrower ambit than the traditional understanding.

The origins of the Trade Secrets Act can be traced to Rev. Stat. § 3167, an Act which barred unauthorized disclosure of specified business information by Government revenue officers. There is very little legislative history concerning the original bill, which was passed in 1864. It was re-enacted numerous times . . . . Congressional statements made at the time of these re-enactments indicate that Congress was primarily concerned with unauthorized disclosure of business information by feckless or corrupt revenue agents, for in the early days of the Bureau of Internal Revenue, it was the field agents who had substantial contact with confidential financial information.

In 1948, Rev. Stat. § 3167 was consolidated with two other statutes . . . to form the Trade Secrets Act. . . . In its effort to [consolidate] the three statutes, Congress . . . essentially borrowed the form of Rev. Stat. § 3167 . . . . We find nothing in the legislative history of § 1905 and its predecessors which lends support to Chrysler's contention that Congress intended the phrase "authorized by law," as used in § 1905, to have a special, limited meaning. Nor do we find anything in the legislative history to support the respondents' suggestion that § 1905 does not address formal agency action – i.e., that it is essentially an "antileak" statute that does not bind the heads of governmental departments or agencies. That would require an expansive and unprecedented holding that any agency action directed or approved by an agency head is "authorized by law," regardless of the statutory authority for that action. . . .

In order for a regulation to have the "force and effect of law," it must have certain substantive characteristics and be the product of certain procedural requisites. . . . [H]owever, [these alone do not] give it the "force and effect of law." The legislative power of the United States is vested in the Congress, and the exercise of quasi-legislative authority by governmental departments and agencies must be rooted in a grant of such power by the Congress and subject to limitations which that body imposes. . . .

. . . .

The regulations relied on by the respondents in this case as providing "[authorization] by law" within the meaning of § 1905 certainly affect individual rights and obligations; they govern the public's right to information in records obtained under Executive Order 11246 and the confidentiality rights of those who submit information to OFCCP and its compliance agencies. It is a much closer question, however, whether they are the product of a congressional grant of legislative authority. . . . We think that it is clear that when it enacted these statutes, Congress was not concerned with public disclosure of trade secrets or confidential business information, and, unless we were to hold that any federal statute that implies some authority to collect information must grant *legislative* authority to disclose that information to the public, it is simply not possible to find in these statutes a delegation of the disclosure authority asserted by the respondents here.

. . . .

B

We reject, however, Chrysler's contention that the Trade Secrets Act affords a private right of action to enjoin disclosure in violation of the statute. In *Cort v. Ash*, we noted that this Court has rarely implied a private right of action under a criminal statute, and where it has done so "there was at least a statutory basis for inferring that a civil cause of action of some sort lay in favor of someone." Nothing in § 1905 prompts such an inference. Nor are other pertinent circumstances outlined in *Cort* present here. As our review of the legislative history of § 1905 – or lack of same – might suggest, there is no indication of legislative intent to create a private right of action. Most importantly, a private right of action under § 1905 is not "necessary to make effective the congressional purpose" for we find that review of DLA's decision to disclose Chrysler's employment data is available under the APA.

IV

While Chrysler may not avail itself of any violations of the provisions of § 1905 in a separate cause of action, any such violations may have a dispositive effect on the outcome of judicial review of agency action pursuant to § 10 of the APA. Section 10(a) of the APA provides that "[any] person suffering legal wrong because of agency action, or adversely affected or aggrieved by agency action . . . is entitled to judicial review thereof." 5 U.S.C. § 702. Two exceptions to this general rule of reviewability are set out in § 10. Review is not available where "statutes preclude judicial review" or where "agency action is committed to agency discretion by law." 5 U.S.C. § § 701(a)(1) (2). In *Citizens to Preserve Overton Park, Inc. v. Volpe* the Court held that the latter exception applies "where 'statutes are drawn in such broad terms that in a given case there is no law to apply.'" Were we simply confronted with the authorization in 5 U.S.C. § 301 to prescribe regulations regarding "the custody, use, and preservation of [agency] records, papers, and property," it would be difficult to derive any standards limiting agency conduct which might constitute "law to apply." But our discussion in Part III demonstrates that § 1905 and any "authoriz[ation] by law" contemplated by that section place substantive limits on agency action. Therefore, we conclude that DLA's decision to disclose the Chrysler reports is reviewable agency action and Chrysler is a person "adversely affected or aggrieved" within the meaning of § 10(a).

Both Chrysler and the respondents agree that there is APA review of DLA's decision. They disagree on the proper scope of review. Chrysler argues that there should be de novo review, while the respondents contend that such review is only available in extraordinary cases and this is not such a case. The pertinent provisions of § 10(e) of the APA, 5 U.S.C. § 706, state that a reviewing court shall

(2) hold unlawful and set aside agency action, findings, and conclusions found to be –

> (A) arbitrary, capricious, an abuse of discretion, or otherwise not in accordance with law;
>
> . . . .
>
> (F) unwarranted by the facts to the extent that the facts are subject to trial de novo by the reviewing court.

For the reasons previously stated, we believe any disclosure that violates § 1905 is "not in accordance with law" within the meaning of 5 U.S.C. § 706(2)(A). De novo review by the District Court is ordinarily not necessary to decide whether a contemplated disclosure runs afoul of § 1905. The District Court in this case concluded that disclosure of some of Chrysler's documents was barred by § 1905, but the Court of Appeals did not reach the issue. We shall therefore vacate the Court of Appeals' judgment and remand for further proceedings consistent with this opinion in order that the Court of Appeals may consider whether the contemplated disclosures would violate the prohibition of § 1905. Since the decision regarding this substantive issue – the scope of § 1905 – will necessarily have some effect on the proper form of judicial review pursuant to § 706(2), we think it unnecessary, and therefore unwise, at the present stage of this case for us to express any additional views on that issue.

> Vacated and remanded.

————————

1. The Basics of Reverse FOIA. Exemption 4 prohibits the release of trade secrets and commercial or financial information. When a company, usually a business, is required to submit information to an agency as part of its normal business of reporting or in response to a particular request from the agency, concerns often arise regarding the security of that information. In reverse FOIA cases, the party who has submitted information seeks to have the agency (and a court, if necessary) withhold that information from downstream FOIA requesters.

Given the broad policy compelling disclosure under FOIA, the initial burden lies with the individual or entity that first submitted the material to demonstrate how the subsequent FOIA disclosure would be injurious and, in the balance, a violation of the submitter's rights under exemption 4. When such claims end up in court, the review includes an assessment of the record to see if the agency adequately assessed the divergent interests (harm from the disclosure of sensitive information versus the obligation to provide access to information under FOIA). *See* Paul M. Nick, *De Novo Review in Reverse Freedom of Information Act Suits*, 50 Ohio St. L.J. 1307, 1308 (1989).

For a more comprehensive overview, see United States Department of Justice,

"Reverse" FOIA, http://www.usdoj.gov/oip/reverse.htm (last visited June 30, 2008), and National Archives and Records Administration Freedom of Information Act (FOIA) Reference Guide, http://www.archives.gov/foia/foia-guide.html (last visited June 30, 2008).

2. How would the initial submitter of information become aware that a FOIA request has been received – after all, there is nothing in FOIA that compels an agency to notify a party when requests are made?

OSHA Data/CIH, Inc. v. United States Department of Labor, 220 F.3d 153, 163-64 (2000).

> In 1987, President Ronald Reagan signed Executive Order 12,600 ("E.O. 12,600"), entitled "Predisclosure Notification Procedures for Confidential Commercial Information." E.O. 12,600's stated purpose is "to provide predisclosure notification procedures under the Freedom of Information Act concerning confidential commercial information, and to make existing agency notification provisions more uniform." The Executive Order directs agency heads to "establish procedures to notify submitters of records containing confidential commercial information." Section 3(b) of E.O. 12,600 provides that each agency head "shall . . . provide the submitter notice . . . whenever the department or agency determines that it may be required to disclose records . . . the disclosure of which the department or agency has reason to believe could reasonably be expected to cause substantial competitive harm." The Executive Order further states that the agency procedures should afford the submitter an opportunity to "object to the disclosure of any specified portion of the information and to state all grounds upon which disclosure is opposed," that the agency "shall give careful consideration to all such specified grounds for nondisclosure" prior to making a final determination whether the information is subject to disclosure, and that, in the event the agency shall decide to disclose information following a submitter's objection, the agency shall provide the submitter with a written statement explaining its decision to disclose. . . .

Compliance with this order, 20 years after its issuance, is the subject of some speculation, though a number of agencies do provide some type of notice. *See, e.g.*, 29 C.F.R. § 70.26(g)(2) (2006).

3. One of the more challenging questions that emerged from *Chrysler v. Brown* involves jurisdiction. Section § 552(a)(4)(B) provides a statutory basis for challenging disclosure of materials that would be injurious – but is it an independent jurisdictional base for a cause of action in federal court? *Chrysler* appears to hold that there is no "private right of action" for a reverse FOIA claim – however, if the disclosure violates the Trade Secrets Act, 18 U.S.C. § 1905 (2000), it (arguably) becomes agency action at odds with the judicial review provisions of the APA, 5 U.S.C. § 706(2)(A), that allows aggrieved parties judicial review when the acts of an agency are "not in accordance with law." *See* Evan Diamond, *Reverse-FOIA Limitations on Agency Actions to Disclose Human Gene Therapy Clinical Data*, 63

FOOD & DRUG L.J. 321 (2008). The Trade Secrets Act provides criminal sanctions for disclosure of "trade secrets, processes, operations, style of work, or apparatus. . . ." 18 U.S.C. § 1905 (2000).

4. *Canadian Commercial Corporation v. Deparment of the Air Force*, 514 F.3d 37 (D.C. Cir. 2008).

> Canadian Commercial Corporation and Orenda Aerospace Corporation (hereinafter collectively CCC) brought this "reverse" Freedom of Information Act case to prevent the Air Force from releasing line-item pricing information in CCC's contract to provide services to the Air Force. . . . [I]n 2002 CCC and the Air Force signed a three-year contract . . . for CCC to repair, overhaul, and modify J85 turbojet engines. In 2003 Sabreliner, which had bid unsuccessfully for the job, filed a FOIA request for a copy of the contract. CCC objected, contending the line-item prices as well as certain hourly labor rates listed in the contract constituted trade secrets. After the Air Force issued a Decision Letter in which it rejected CCC's contentions, CCC filed suit in the district court to enjoin disclosure of the information. . . . [The district] court entered a summary judgment holding the decision of the Air Force was arbitrary and capricious insofar as it concluded the line-item prices were not trade secrets; the court enjoined the Air Force from disclosing those prices . . . but not the hourly labor rates. . . .

> Exemption 4 of the Freedom of Information Act protects "matters that are . . . trade secrets and commercial or financial information obtained from a person and privileged or confidential." 5 U.S.C. § 552(b)(4). Commercial or financial information obtained from a person involuntarily "is 'confidential' for purposes of the exemption if disclosure [would either] impair the Government's ability to obtain necessary information in the future; or . . . cause substantial harm to the competitive position of the person from whom the information was obtained." *Nat'l Parks & Conservation Ass'n v. Morton*, 498 F.2d 765, 770 (D.C. Cir. 1974) . . . . We have long held [the] Trade Secrets Act . . . at least co-extensive with . . . Exemption 4 of FOIA . . . . The upshot is that, unless another statute or a regulation authorizes disclosure of the information, the Trade Secrets Act requires each agency to withhold any information it may withhold under Exemption 4 of the FOIA. . . .

> In its letter of objection, CCC claimed disclosure of its pricing information would cause it competitive harm by enabling rivals to undercut its prices in bidding. . . . [A]ccording to the Air Force, switching contractors would be so disruptive to its operations that it is almost certain to exercise the option [to extend the contract with CCC] even if CCC's competitors submit lower bids for the option years. . . .

> [W]e find [this argment] unconvincing. . . .

> In the Decision Letter, the Air Force faulted CCC for failing to present evidence that the Air Force has declined to exercise options in the past but surely the Air Force is the party best positioned to provide evidence of its own practice with respect to exercising or not exercising options and, once again, the burden of production properly falls upon the party with access to the information to be produced. . . . In sum, we will not defer to the Air Force's unsupported assertions.

> Because CCC has shown that release of the pricing information here at issue would

> cause it substantial competitive harm with respect to the option years in its contract with the Air Force, we need not address its alternative argument that release would cause it competitive harm when seeking future procurements. . . .

Is there really a harm in disclosing price lists for public contracts? Can you make the argument for and against such disclosure? Would disclosing a price list have a "ceiling" or a "floor" effect?

5. While FOIA protects highly personal information in the government's possession, state statutes requiring regular reporting by convicted sex offenders have been upheld even though the reported information is regularly disclosed to the public. *Doe v. Moore*, 410 F.3d 1337 (11th Cir. 2005).

VI. The Government in the Sunshine Act

1. Much like FOIA, the Government in the Sunshine Act of 1976, 5 U.S.C. § 552b, is a legislative mandate for transparency in the agency decisionmaking process. In those areas where it applies, the Act requires reasonable public notice (generally a week or more), often published in the Federal Register, of meetings to be held at which the agency is likely to take formal, dispositive, or official action. The Act applies to independent regulatory agencies (where there are two or more commissioners) as opposed to cabinet level single administrator executive agencies. Congress can and does have the option to exempt entire agencies from the mandates of the Act. *See, e.g.*, *Am. Postal Workers Union v. USPS*, 541 F. Supp. 2d 95 (D.D.C. 2008).

2. The Act has ten exemptions that parallel FOIA. 5 U.S.C. §§ 552b(c)(1)-(10). There is a broad exemption that allows a meeting to be closed if the agency determines that "sunshining" the meeting would unduly impede, prevent, or frustrate the likely agency action, and also an exemption for pending litigation. Failure to comply with the Act results in the obligation to disclose – frankly, not that weighty a sanction.

3. As you might guess, the Act has had a mixed reception. On the one hand, the Act insures accountability. Public scrutiny limits conscious ineptitude, laziness, arrogance, and, hopefully, most other forms of embarrassing misconduct. On the other hand, the Act can limit discussion, restrict the flow of information, and lead to a more secretive process within the agency. It is not hard to imagine special assistants to commissioners exchanging information and perspectives – "horse-trading" – before and after sunshined meetings, frustrating the goals of the Act. *See* Jennifer A. Bensch, *Seventeen Years Later: Has Government Let the Sun Shine In?*, 61 GEO. WASH. L. REV. 1475, 1476 (1993).

There are not that many major cases interpreting the Act. The ones in the notes that follow, however, are of consequence and fairly issue specific.

1. In *Common Cause v. Nuclear Regulatory Commission*, 674 F.2d 921 (D.C. Cir. 1982), the agency claimed that budget deliberations should not be sunshined, in part because of secrecy concerns and in part because of the need for efficiency in governmental action – and the court responded as follows:

> The Government in the Sunshine Act, 5 U.S.C. § 552b, requires that meetings of multi-member federal agencies shall be open to the public, with the exception of discussions in ten narrowly defined areas. In [this case] we must decide an important unresolved issue: whether any of the statutory exemptions from the Sunshine Act apply to agency budget deliberations. Interpreting the statutory language in light of the legislative history and underlying policies of the Act, we conclude that there is no blanket exemption for agency meetings at any stage of the budget preparation process. The availability of exemptions for specific portions of budgetary discussions must be determined upon the facts of each case. . . .
>
> Congress enacted the Sunshine Act to open the deliberations of multi-member federal agencies to public view. It believed that increased openness would enhance citizen confidence in government, encourage higher quality work by government officials, stimulate well-informed public debate about government programs and policies, and promote cooperation between citizens and government. In short, it sought to make government more fully accountable to the people. In keeping with the premise that "government should conduct the public's business in public," the Act established a general presumption that agency meetings should be held in the open. Once a person has challenged an agency's decision to close a meeting, the agency bears the burden of proof. Even if exempt subjects are discussed in one portion of a meeting, the remainder of the meeting must be held in open session.
>
> [T]he Commission contends that opening budget discussions to the public might affect political decisions by the President and OMB. . . . [T]he Commission fears that disclosure of its time-honored strategies of item-shifting, exaggeration, and fall-back positions would give it less leverage in its "arm's length" dealings with OMB and the President, who make the final budget decisions within the Executive Branch. The Commission argues that it would thereby be impaired in its competition with other government agencies . . . for its desired share of budgetary resources. . . .
>
> [However, we find] disclosure of budget deliberations would serve the affirmative purposes of the Sunshine Act: to open government deliberations to public scrutiny, to inform the public "what facts and policy considerations the agency found important in reaching its decision, and what alternatives it considered and rejected," and thereby to permit "wider and more informed public debate of the agency's policies. . . ." The budget deliberation process is of exceptional importance in agency policy making. The agency heads must review the entire range of agency programs and responsibilities in order to establish priorities. According to the Commission, a budget meeting "candidly consider(s) the merits and efficiencies of on-going or expected regulatory programs or projects" and then "decides upon the level of regulatory activities it proposes to pursue. . . ." These decisions, the government contends, have a significant impact on "the Commission's ability to marshal regulatory powers in a manner which insures

the greatest protection of the public health and safety with the most economical use of its limited resources."

If Congress had wished to exempt these deliberations from the Sunshine Act – to preserve the prior practice of budget confidentiality, to reduce the opportunities for lobbying before the President submits his budget to Congress, or for other reasons – it would have expressly so indicated. Absent any such statement of legislative intent, we will not construe Exemption 9(B) of the Sunshine Act to allow budget deliberations to be hidden from the public view.

Because the Commission has not carried its burden of proving that the July 27, 1981 and October 15, 1981 meetings were lawfully closed, the Commission shall release the transcripts of those meetings to the public forthwith. . . .

2. In one of the few Supreme Court cases focused directly on the Act, *Federal Communications Commission v. ITT World Communications, Inc.*, 466 U.S. 463 (1984), the agency claimed the Act did not apply since the agency was not likely to take formal, dispositive, or official action, and in part because the agency was engaged in a collaborative process and thus not acting solely on its own. The Court assessed these concerns as follows:

The Government in the Sunshine Act, 5 U.S.C. § 552b, mandates that federal agencies hold their meetings in public. This case requires us to consider whether the Act applies to informal international conferences attended by members of the Federal Communications Commission. . . .

Members of petitioner Federal Communications Commission (FCC) participate with their European and Canadian counterparts in what is referred to as the Consultative Process. This is a series of conferences intended to facilitate joint planning of telecommunications facilities through an exchange of information on regulatory policies. At the time of the conferences at issue in the present case, only three American corporations – respondents ITT World Communications, Inc. (ITT), and RCA Global Communications, Inc., and Western Union International – provided overseas record telecommunications services. Although the FCC had approved entry into the market by other competitors, European regulators had been reluctant to do so. The FCC therefore added the topic of new carriers and services to the agenda of the Consultative Process, in the hope that exchange of information might persuade the European nations to cooperate with the FCC's policy of encouraging competition in the provision of telecommunications services.

Respondents, opposing the entry of new competitors, initiated this litigation. First, respondents filed a rulemaking petition with the FCC concerning the Consultative Process meetings. The petition requested that the FCC disclaim any intent to negotiate with foreign governments or to bind it to agreements at the meetings, arguing that such negotiations were ultra vires the agency's authority. Further, the petition contended that the Sunshine Act required the Consultative Process sessions, as "meetings" of the FCC, to be held in public. The FCC denied the rulemaking petition, and respondents filed an appeal in the Court of Appeals for the District of Columbia Circuit.

The Sunshine Act, 5 U.S.C. § 552b(b), requires that "meetings of an agency" be open to the public. Section 552b(a)(2) defines "meetings" as "the deliberations of at least the number of individual agency members required to take action on behalf of the agency where such deliberations determine or result in the joint conduct or disposition of official agency business." Under these provisions, the Sunshine Act does not require that Consultative Process sessions be held in public, as the participation by FCC members in these sessions constitutes neither a "meeting" as defined by § 552b(a)(2) nor a meeting "of the agency" as provided by § 552b(b).

Congress in drafting the Act's definition of "meeting" recognized that the administrative process cannot be conducted entirely in the public eye. "[Informal] background discussions [that] clarify issues and expose varying views" are a necessary part of an agency's work. . . . [Opening these meetings] effectively would prevent such discussions and thereby impair normal agency operations without achieving significant public benefit. Section 552b(a)(2) therefore limits the Act's application to meetings "where at least a quorum of the agency's members . . . conduct or dispose of official agency business."

The evolution of the statutory language reflects the congressional intent precisely to define the limited scope of the statute's requirements. For example, the Senate substituted the term "deliberations" for the previously proposed terms – "assembly or simultaneous communication" or "gathering" – in order to "exclude many discussions which are informal in nature." Similarly, earlier versions of the Act had applied to any agency discussions that "[concern] the joint conduct or disposition of agency business". The Act now applies only to deliberations that "determine or result in" the conduct of "official agency business." . . . .

Three Commissioners, the number who attended the Consultative Process sessions, did not constitute a quorum of the seven-member Commission. The three members were, however, a quorum of the Telecommunications Committee. That Committee is a "subdivision . . . authorized to act on behalf of the agency." The Commission had delegated to the Committee, pursuant to § 5(d)(1) of the Communications Act of 1934, the power to approve applications for common carrier certification. The Sunshine Act applies to such a subdivision as well as to an entire agency. It does not appear, however, that the Telecommunications Committee engaged at these sessions in "deliberations [that] determine or result in the joint conduct or disposition of official agency business." . . . . As the Telecommunications Committee at the Consultative Process sessions did not consider or act upon applications for common carrier certification – its only formally delegated authority – we conclude that the sessions were not "meetings" within the meaning of the Sunshine Act. . . .

4. Finally, how does the Sunshine Act intersect with the ex parte communication prohibitions discussed earlier in this text? In *Electric Power Supply Association. FERC*, 391 F.3d 1255 (D.C. Cir. 2004), the Federal Energy Regulatory Commission issued an interpretation designed to exempt communications between private market monitors and FERC decisional employees from the Sunshine Act's ban on ex parte communications." The interpretation was challenged by the Electric Power Supply Association (ESPA) on the grounds that it violated the Sunshine Act, 5 U.S.C. §§ 552b, 557(d)(1)(A) (B), which

prohibits "ex parte communications relevant to the merits of [a prescribed] proceeding" between an "interested person outside the agency" and an agency decisionmaker. . . .

The Government in the Sunshine Act, 5 U.S.C. § 557(d) (2000), applies "when a hearing is required to be conducted in accordance with section 556 of [the APA]." § 557(a). . . . When such a hearing is required, the Government in the Sunshine Act provides:

No interested person outside the agency shall make or knowingly cause to be made to any member of the body comprising the agency, administrative law judge, or other employee who is or may reasonably be expected to be involved in the decisional process of the proceeding, an ex parte communication relevant to the merits of the proceeding[.] § 557(d)(1)(A).

An "ex parte communication" is defined as "an oral or written communication not on the public record with respect to which reasonable prior notice to all parties is not given. . . . When an ex parte communication occurs, the Sunshine Act requires disclosure of the communication and an opportunity for parties to file a response. § 557(d)(1)(C). There are no exceptions to the disclosure requirement.

The controlling provisions of the Sunshine Act were fully explored over two decades ago in *Professional Air Traffic Controllers Organization v. FLRA, supra* Chapter 9. . . .

PATCO also indicates that, while the communications subject to the Act are limited to those "relevant to the merits of the proceeding," the congressional reports underlying the Sunshine Act make it clear that the phrase should "be construed broadly and . . . include more than the phrase 'fact in issue' currently used in [§ 554(d)(1) of] the Administrative Procedure Act."

The key to exclusion under the Sunshine Act is not the label given the communication, but rather whether there is a possibility that the communication could affect the agency's decision in a contested on-the-record proceeding. . . .

On the merits, it is clear that the orders creating the market monitor exemption violate the explicit and sweeping proscription against ex parte communications contained in § 557(d). . . . The Commission is powerless to override Congress' directive banning ex parte communications relevant to pending on-the-record proceedings. . . .

Index

DEFINITIONS

IMMIGRATION MATTERS

JURISDICTION

†